NUTRITIONAL EVALUATION OF FOOD PROCESSING

Third Edition

Edited by
Endel Karmas
Department of Food Science
Rutgers University
New Brunwick, New Jersey

Robert S. Harris
Department of Nutritional Biochemistry
Massachusetts Institute of Technology
Cambridge, Massachusetts

An avi Book
Published by Van Nostrand Reinhold Company
New York

Dedicated to the memory of
Robert Samuel Harris

An AVI Book
(AVI is an imprint of Van Nostrand Reinhold Company Inc.)
Copyright © 1988 by Van Nostrand Reinhold Company Inc.

Library of Congress Catalog Card Number 87–29588

ISBN 0-442-24762-1

Printed in the United States of America

Van Nostrand Reinhold Company Inc.
115 Fifth Avenue
New York, New York 10003

Van Nostrand Reinhold Company Limited
Molly Millars Lane
Wokingham, Berkshire RG11 2PY, England

Van Nostrand Reinhold
480 La Trobe Street
Melbourne, Victoria 3000, Australia

Macmillan of Canada
Division of Canada Publishing Corporation
164 Commander Boulevard
Agincourt, Ontario M1S 3C7, Canada

16 15 14 13 12 11 10 9 8 7 6 5 4 3 2 1

Library of Congress Cataloging-in-Publication Data

Nutritional evaluation of food processing.

    "An AVI book."
    Includes bibliographies and index.
    1. Food—Analysis.   2. Food industry and trade.
I. Karmas, Endel.   II. Harris, Robert Samuel.
TP372.5.N873   1987   664   87–29588
ISBN 0-442-24762-1

Contents

iii

Contributors

Catherine E. Adams   International Life Sciences Institute/Nutrition Foundation, Washington, DC 20036

Lena Bergström   Nutrition Laboratory, The National Food Administration, S-75126 Uppsala, Sweden

H. C. Bittenbender   Department of Horticulture, University of Hawaii at Manoa, Honolulu, HI 96822

Peter M. Bluestein   Thomas J. Lipton, Inc., Englewood Cliffs, NJ 07632

M. Ann Bock   Nutrition Research Group, American Institute of Baking, Manhattan, KS 66502

Benjamin Borenstein   Roche Chemical Division, Hoffman-LaRoche, Inc., Nutley, NJ 07110

Ricardo Bressani   Division of Agricultural and Food Science, Institute of Nutrition of Central America and Panama, PO Box 1188, Guatemala City, Guatemala

Gus D. Coccodrilli, Jr.   Nutrition and Health Sciences Technical Center, General Foods Corporation, White Plains, NY 10625

Winifred M. Cort   4395 Brandywine Drive, Sarasota, FL 34241

B. B. Desai   Mahatma Phule Agricultural University, Maharashtra State, India

John W. Erdman, Jr.   Department of Food Science, University of Illinois, Urbana, IL 61801

Owen Fennema   Department of Food Science, University of Wisconsin, Madison, WI 53706

Michele C. Fisher   Department of Food Science, Rutgers University, New Brunswick, NJ 08903

Allan L. Forbes   Office of Nutrition and Food Sciences, Center for Food Safety and Applied Nutrition, Food and Drug Administration, Washington, DC 20204

Victor P. Frattali   Division of Nutrition, Food and Drug Administration, Washington, DC 20204

Glenn W. Froning   Department of Food Science and Technology, University of Nebraska, Lincoln, NE 68583

Seymour G. Gilbert   Department of Food Science, Cook College, Rutgers University, New Brunswick, NJ 08903

Howard T. Gordon   Roche Chemical Division, Hoffman LaRoche, Inc., Nutley, NJ 07110

Jesse F. Gregory III   Department of Food Science and Human Nutrition, University of Florida, Gainesville, FL 32611

Judson M. Harper   Vice President for Research, Colorado State University, Fort Collins, CO 80523

Robert S. Harris   Department of Nutritional Biochemistry, Massachusetts Institute of Technology, Cambridge, MA 02139

John P. Heybach   NutraSweet Group, Searle Food Resources, Inc., G.D. Searle & Co., Skokie, IL 60076

George E. Inglett   Northern Regional Research Center, ARS USDA, Peoria, IL 61604

Endel Karmas   Department of Food Science, Rutgers University, New Brunswick, NJ 08903

John F. Kelly   Department of Horticulture, Michigan State University, East Lansing, MI 48824–1325

Judith Krzynowek   Northeast Fisheries Center, Gloucester Laboratory, U.S. Department of Commerce, Gloucester, MA 01930

Theodore P. Labuza   Department of Food Science, University of Minnesota, St. Paul, MN 55108

Paul A. Lachance   Department of Food Science, Rutgers University, New Brunswick, NJ 08903

Gilbert A. Leveille   Nutrition and Health Science Technical Center, General Foods Corporation, White Plains, NY 10625

Daryl Lund   Department of Food Science, University of Wisconsin, Madison, WI 53706

Roger F. McFeeters   ARS USDA, North Carolina State University, Raleigh, NC 27695–7624

Steven Nagy   Scientific Research Department, Florida Department of Citrus, Lake Alfred, FL 33850

H. W. Ockerman   Department of Animal Science, Ohio State University, Columbus, OH 43210

Gur S. Ranhotra   Nutrition Research Group, American Institute of Baking, Manhattan, KS 66502

Edmund Renner   Department of Dairy Science, Justus-Liebig-Universität Giessen, D-6300 Giessen, West Germany

D. K. Salunkhe   Mahatma Phule Agricultural University, Maharashtra State, India

Miriam H. Thomas   57 Eaton Road, Framingham, MA 01701

John E. Vanderveen   Division of Nutrition, Food and Drug Administration, Washington, DC 20204

Wilfred F. Wardowski   Citrus Research and Education Center, University of Florida, Lake Alfred, FL 33850

Walter J. Wolf   Northern Regional Research Center, ARS USDA, Peoria, IL 61604

Y. Victor Wu   Northern Regional Research Center, ARS USDA, Peoria, IL 61604

Robert Samuel Harris
May 10, 1904–December 24, 1983

Preface

Dramatic changes in the attitudes toward human nutrition have taken place during the past decade. Food-related and medical professionals as well as consumers are now, more than ever before, aware of and concerned about diet, nutrition, and the beneficial and deleterious effects of food processing upon nutrients. The old saying "We are what we eat" is still relevant. Nutritious food will contribute greatly to consumers' good health and ultimately reduce medical bills.

Food processing is essential to maintaining our food reserves from one harvest to another, thus letting us serve our daily meals regularly. If food processing is defined as including all treatments of foodstuffs from harvest to consumption, then more than 95% of our food may be considered as processed. In most cases, food processing and storage cause some reduction in the nutritional value of foods. Advances in food science and food technology have resulted in an increase in nutrient retention after processing. In addition, today's consumer better understands how to avoid excessive nutrient losses during food preparation.

The information presented in this completely revised reference and textbook will help the reader to understand better the relationship between food processing and nutrient retention. The authors' scholarly contributions are greatly appreciated.

With the publication of the first edition of *Nutritional Evaluation of Food Processing*, Dr. Harris was the very first scientist in the world who compiled, systematized, and presented data on the effects of food processing on the nutrient composition of foods. I must state with deep sorrow that Dr. Harris passed away while the third edition was in preparation.

I remember the first time I met Dr. Harris. He invited me to collaborate on the second edition. At first I was reluctant to accept his invitation and suggested several names of renowned nutritionists, who, in my opinion, were much more qualified for the task. Dr. Harris replied, "I am a nutritionist! I need a food technologist, who already has experience in publishing books, to help me!" I accepted his invitation, and from that moment on, a close collaboration and friendship developed between us. The second edition and the present edition, the third, are the two last additions to Dr. Harris's nearly 300 scientific publications.

Perhaps one of the saddest moments in Dr. Harris's life occurred when he had to tell me that his illness prevented him from further helping me with this edition. At this tragic point, his battle with an incurable disease had already progressed too far. I will always remember, with great gratitude, my association with Dr. Harris who was a competent and distinguished scientist, a compassionate and generous man, and a committed and true friend!

ENDEL KARMAS

Part 1

Introduction

General Discussion on the Stability of Nutrients

Robert S. Harris

Nutrients are destroyed when foods are processed largely because they are sensitive to the pH of the solvent, to oxygen, light and heat, or combinations of these. Trace elements, especially copper and iron, and enzymes may catalyze these effects.

The relative stabilities of the vitamins and amino acids under these various conditions are tabulated in Table 1.1. Vitamin A is stable under an inert atmosphere, but rapidly loses activity when heated in the presence of oxygen, especially at higher temperatures. It is completely destroyed when oxidized or dehydrogenated. It is more sensitive to ultraviolet light than to other wavelengths of light.

Ascorbic acid is fairly stable in acid solution and decomposes in light. This decomposition is greatly accelerated by the presence of alkalies, oxygen, copper, and iron.

A 50% loss in biotin occurs when it is boiled for 6 hr in 30% hydrochloric acid or for 17 hr in 1 N potassium hydroxide, yet it is relatively stable in air and oxygen or when exposed to ultraviolet light. It is inactivated by agents which oxidize the sulfur atom, and by strong acids and alkalies.

Essential fatty acids isomerize when heated in alkali and are sensitive to light, temperature, and oxygen. When oxidized, they become inactive biologically and may even be toxic.

The stability of vitamin D is influenced by the solvent in which it is dissolved, but it is stable when crystals are stored in amber glass bottles. Generally, it is stable to heat, acids, and oxygen. It is slowly destroyed in foods and feeds which are slightly alkaline, especially in the presence of air and light.

The folic acid group is stable during boiling at pH 8 for 30 min, yet large losses occur during autoclaving in acids and alkalies. This destruction is accelerated by oxygen and light.

Inositol is stable during refluxing in strong hydrochloric acid or potassium hydroxide. It occurs in plants mainly in the form of phytic acid salts and as plant and animal phosphoinositides. These complexes are broken down by phosphatases and similar enzymes. The free inositol has the highest biological value.

Table 1.1. Stability of Nutrients[a]

Nutrient	Neutral pH 7	Acid <pH 7	Alkaline >pH 7	Air or oxygen	Light	Heat	Maximum cooking losses (%)
Vitamins							
Vitamin A	S	U	S	U	U	U	40
Ascorbic acid (C)	U	S	U	U	U	U	100
Biotin	S	S	S	S	S	U	60
Carotene (pro-A)	S	U	S	U	U	U	30
Choline	S	S	S	U	S	S	5
Cobalamin (B_{12})	S	S	S	U	U	S	10
Vitamin D	S		U	U	U	U	40
Folic acid	U	U	S	U	U	U	100
Inositol	S	S	S	S	S	U	95
Vitamin K	S	U	U	S	U	S	5
Niacin (PP)	S	S	S	S	S	S	75
Pantothenic acid	S	U	U	S	S	U	50
p-Aminobenzoic acid	S	S	S	U	S	S	5
Pyridoxine (B_6)	S	S	S	S	U	U	40
Riboflavin (B_2)	S	S	U	S	U	U	75
Thiamin (B_1)	U	S	U	U	S	U	80
Tocopheral (E)	S	S	S	U	U	U	55
Essential amino acids							
Isoleucine	S	S	S	S	S	S	10
Leucine	S	S	S	S	S	S	10
Lysine	S	S	S	S	S	U	40
Methionine	S	S	S	S	S	S	10
Phenylalanine	S	S	S	S	S	S	5
Threonine	S	U	U	S	S	U	20
Tryptophan	S	U	S	S	U	S	15
Valine	S	S	S	S	S	S	10
Essential fatty acids	S	S	U	U	U	S	10
Mineral salts	S	S	S	S	S	S	3

[a] S, stable (no important destruction); U, unstable (significant destruction).

Vitamin K is stable to heat and reducing agents and is labile to alcoholic alkali, oxidizing agents, strong acids, and light.

Niacin amide is partially hydrolyzed by acid and alkali, yet the resulting niacin has the same biological activity. Niacin is generally stable to air, light, heat, acids, and alkalies.

Pantothenic acid is most stable at pH 5.5–7.0, is rapidly hydrolyzed under stronger acid or alkaline conditions, and is labile to dry heat, hot acid, or hot alkalies.

p-Aminobenzoic acid is only slightly destroyed by autoclaving in 6 N sulfuric acid for 1 hr, is fairly stable in mild alkali, but is unstable in strong alkali.

Vitamin B_{12} (cobalamin) is stable to heat in neutral solution if pure, but is destroyed when heated in alkaline or acid media in crude preparations, as in foodstuffs. Choline is strongly alkaline and is slightly unstable in solutions in the presence of oxygen.

The vitamin B_6 group contains pyridoxine, pyridoxal, and pyridoxamine. Pyridoxine is stable to heat, strong alkali, or acid, but is sensitive to light, especially ultraviolet light, when in alkaline solutions. Pyridoxal and pyridoxamine are rapidly destroyed by exposure to air, heat, and light. All three are sensitive to ultraviolet light when in neutral or alkaline solution. Pyridoxamine in foods is sensitive to processing.

Riboflavin is very sensitive to light, and the rate of destruction increases as the pH and temperature increase. Thus, the riboflavin of milk is rapidly lost (50% in 2 hr) on exposure to sunlight, and the resulting derivative (lumiflavin) in turn destroys the ascorbic acid in milk. It is stable to heat if in dry form or in an acid medium.

Thiamin suffers no destruction when boiled in acid for several hours, yet the loss approaches 100% when boiled at pH 9 for 20 min. It is unstable in air, especially at higher pH values, and is destroyed by autoclaving, sulfites, and alkalies.

The tocopherols are stable to vigorous boiling in acid in the absence of oxygen and are stable to visible light. They are unstable at room temperature in the presence of oxygen, alkalies, ferric salts, and when exposed to ultraviolet light. Considerable loss of tocopherols occurs in the oxidation of fats and in deep-fat frying due primarily to destruction by chemically active fatty acid derivatives formed in the fats during heating and oxidation. The esters of tocopherols are more stable than the free phenols.

Amino acids racemize in alkaline solutions, and the biological value of some is reduced as a result. Arginine, cystine, threonine, and cysteine are partially destroyed, whereas glutamine and asparagine are deaminized by alkalies. In acid solution, tryptophan is rather readily destroyed, cysteine is partly converted to cystine, serine and threonine are partly destroyed. Phenylalanine and threonine are partially destroyed by ultraviolet light. All amino acids in foods, and especially lysine, threonine, and methionine, are sensitive to treatment with dry heat and radiations. Thus, in the roasting and toasting of cereals, legumes, and prepared dry mixtures of foodstuffs, a significant reduction of the biological values of their proteins may occur.

Mineral salts are not significantly affected by these chemical and physical treatments. Some may be oxidized to higher valences by exposure to oxygen, but there is no convincing evidence that their nutritional value is affected.

Table 1.1 also gives the limits of losses of these nutrients when the average food is cooked. More complete data on the losses of several of these nutrients in specific foods during processing are presented in the following chapters of this volume.

The Major Food Groups, Their Nutrient Content, and Principles of Food Processing

Endel Karmas

Nutrients are the building blocks of the human body. Nutrients are needed for growth, to maintain and repair the body tissues, to regulate body processes, and to furnish energy for the body's functions. The nutrients that must be supplied daily to keep man in good health are the macronutrients: proteins, fats, carbohydrates, and water; and the micronutrients: vitamins and minerals.

More than 50 essential nutrients have been identified, and the identification of other nutrients is not yet complete. All essential nutrients must be present in appropriate quantities to provide balanced nutrition. Thus, the nutrient composition of a food is described in terms of its content of all the macro- and micronutrients.

Man acquires his nutrients from foods of plant and animal origin. The biochemistry of plants, animals, and man have much in common; therefore, man requires essentially the same nutritional building blocks as do plants and animals.

THE MAJOR FOOD GROUPS AND THEIR NUTRIENT CONTENT

Both the growing and gathering of foods belong in the realm of the agricultural sciences and technology. Figure 2.1 illustrates the biochemical cycle of man's basic foods. The sun's energy combines carbon dioxide, water, and nutrients from the soil to produce the foods of plant origin: vegetables, fruits, grains, tubers, and others. Foods of animal origin are derived ultimately from herbivorous animals. Finally, animals produce foods, such as milk and eggs. It is noteworthy that proteins increase in nutritive value as the amino acids from the proteins of plant origin are converted to the various proteins of animal origin (National Academy of Sciences, National Research Council 1963).

Raw foods are biological systems that spoil rapidly. Since man needs food daily and food is harvested seasonally, foods must be preserved by

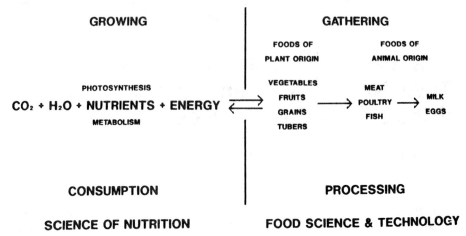

Fig. 2.1.   Biochemical cycle of man's basic foods.

various methods to provide food in off-seasons. This means that the bio-chemical cycle, pictured in Fig. 2.1, is temporarily arrested by food processing. During times of hunger, however, man consumes his pre-served food and starts the reverse of photosynthesis, the metabolism, to release free energy and obtain essential nutrients for his metabolic needs. According to Nobel laureate Albert Szent-Györgyi (1966), one of the basic principles of life is that free energy can be preserved and stored in food molecules and utilized when necessary.

Detailed data on food consumption in the United States are avail-able from government sources [U.S. Department of Agriculture (USDA) 1984A]. Table 2.1 summarizes the per capita consumption of major food commodities in 1983. Foods of animal origin and foods of plant origin share about equally in the American diet, totaling about 85% of all food consumed by weight. The total average per capita consumption of food in 1983 was 617 kg, which is equal to about nine times the weight of an average man.

Percentages of nutrients contributed by major food groups in the United States food supply in 1983 are presented in Table 2.2 (USDA 1984B). An essential part of the food energy, protein, vitamin A, niacin, vitamin B_6, vitamin B_{12}, iron, and zinc comes from the meat–poultry–fish group. Dairy products provide most of the riboflavin, calcium, phosphorus, and magnesium. Vegetables and fruits are rich in ascorbic acid, but also in vitamin A, folacin, and fiber. Flour and cereal products contain a plentiful supply of a wide variety of nutrients. Be-sides carbohydrates (food energy), they provide not only considerable amounts of the enrichment nutrients thiamin, riboflavin, niacin, and iron, but also plant protein, fiber, magnesium, phosphorus, and zinc.

Table 2.1. Per Capita Consumption of Major Food Commodities in the United States in 1983

Food groups	Consumption		
	kg		%
I. Foods of animal origin		257.4	41.7
Meats and meat products	65.6		10.6
Beef	35.8		
Veal	0.8		
Pork	28.3		
Lamb	0.7		
Poultry and poultry products	29.8		4.8
Chicken	24.5		
Turkey	5.3		
Eggs[a]	15.0		2.4
Fishery products	5.8		1.0
Fresh and frozen	3.6		
Canned and cured	2.2		
Dairy products	141.2		22.9
Whole milk	60.4		
Other milk beverages[b]	48.1		
Cheeses	11.3		
Frozen desserts	12.3		
Cream and canned milk	6.1		
Dry milk products	3.0		
II. Foods of plant origin		269.3	43.6
Vegetables	71.8		11.6
Fresh	45.4		
Canned	21.4		
Frozen	5.0		
Potatoes[c]	37.3		6.0
Fresh	25.0		
Processed	12.3		
Cereals	68.0		11.0
Wheat flour	52.7		
Rice	4.5		
Other cereals and products	10.8		
Fresh fruit	50.9		8.3
Citrus	14.0		
Noncitrus[d]	36.9		
Processed fruit	36.3		5.9
Canned fruit	7.3		
Canned juices	7.4		
Frozen fruit	1.4		
Frozen citrus juice	18.8		
Dried fruit	1.4		
Nuts	4.3		0.7
Spices and herbs	0.7		0.1

(continued)

Table 2.1.   *(Continued)*

Food groups		Consumption	
		kg	%
III. Other foods		90.6	14.7
Sweeteners		56.8	9.2
Sucrose	32.3		
Corn syrup sweeteners (dry wt)	23.7		
Honey and other syrups	0.8		
Fats and oils[e]		28.5	4.6
Butter[f]	2.3		
Margarine[f]	4.7		
Shortening	8.5		
Lard and tallow	1.7		
Other fats and oils	11.3		
Dry beverage products[g]		5.3	0.9
Coffee	3.5		
Tea	0.3		
Cocoa[h]	1.5		
Total food consumed		617.3	

Source: Data compiled from "Food Consumption, Prices, and Expenditures 1963–83," Statistical Bulletin No. 713, U.S. Dept. of Agriculture (1984A).
[a] An average of 253 eggs per capita per year.
[b] Skim, low-fat, buttermilk; flavored drinks and yoghurt.
[c] Includes sweet potatoes (5.5% of the total potatoes).
[d] Includes melons.
[e] Ratio of animal fats to vegetable oil consumption, 20:80.
[f] Fat content of butter and margarine, 80%.
[g] In addition, 151 liters of soft drinks and 92 liters of beer per capita per year were consumed.
[h] Mainly used for chocolate and candy manufacture.

Fats and oils, sucrose, and other sweeteners yield food energy, otherwise they are essentially devoid of the nutrients listed in Table 2.2. It should be mentioned that most cholesterol in the American diet comes from eggs (41%), followed by red meats (26%) and dairy products, excluding butter (15%).

Table 2.3 gives information about the quantities of nutrients available for consumption per capita per day in the United States in 1983 (USDA 1984A). These estimates include produce from home gardens. No deduction has been made for loss or waste of food, or for destruction and loss of nutrients during preparation of food. These data include nutrients added in fortification and enrichment to cereal products, margarine, milk, fruit juices and drinks, and breakfast cereals.

The nutrients available to the American population (Table 2.3) can be compared with the Recommended Daily Dietary Allowances (RDA) in Table 2.4, established, based on present knowledge of nutrition,

Table 2.2. Percentage of Nutrients Contributed by Major Food Groups in the United States Food Supply in 1983[a]

Food groups	Food energy	Protein	Fat	Cholesterol	Carbohydrate	Fiber	Vitamin A	Thiamin	Riboflavin	Niacin	Vitamin B6	Folacin	Vitamin B12	Ascorbic acid	Iron	Calcium	Phosphorus	Magnesium	Zinc
Meat	16.0	27.7	28.6	25.7	0.1	0.0	15.9	24.0	16.0	27.3	26.4	7.5	53.0	0.8	23.3	2.3	18.9	8.4	35.8
Poultry	3.4	10.6	4.8	10.4	0.0+	0.0	5.0	1.7	4.5	13.5	10.1	5.7	8.0	1.0	4.4	0.8	6.0	3.3	7.5
Fish	0.9	4.3	0.7	3.0	0.0+	0.0	0.3	0.6	1.0	4.9	3.7	1.1	10.3	0.1	1.4	1.1	3.1	1.8	3.2
Eggs	1.7	4.3	2.4	40.9	0.1	0.0	2.3	1.5	4.5	0.1	2.2	8.1	6.5	0.0	4.2	2.3	4.3	1.3	4.2
Dairy products, excluding butter	10.2	21.3	11.4	15.1	5.9	0.0	12.7	7.6	36.7	1.3	11.0	8.3	20.5	3.1	2.6	74.5	34.3	20.1	21.0
Fat and oils, including butter	19.1	0.1	44.7	4.9	0.0+	0.0	7.7	0.0+	0.1	0.0+	0.0+	0.1	0.0	0.0	0.1	0.2	0.1	0.0+	0.1
Citrus fruits	1.1	0.6	0.0+	0.0	2.3	1.3	1.8	3.3	0.5	0.9	1.6	11.9	0.0	29.8	0.9	1.2	0.9	2.7	0.5
Noncitrus fruits	2.3	0.7	0.4	0.0	4.9	12.9	5.8	1.9	1.8	1.9	7.3	4.3	0.0	11.9	3.8	1.3	1.3	4.4	0.9
Vegetables, dark green and deep yellow	0.2	0.4	0.0+	0.0	0.4	6.0	21.9	0.8	1.0	0.6	2.1	4.7	0.0	10.0	1.4	1.4	0.7	2.0	0.5
Other vegetables, including tomatoes	2.1	3.0	0.3	0.0	4.3	26.5	13.5	6.0	4.4	5.1	10.6	21.5	0.0	25.9	8.6	4.8	4.8	9.9	3.9
Potatoes and sweet potatoes	2.8	2.4	0.1	0.0	5.4	11.8	5.3	4.8	1.3	6.1	9.6	5.2	0.0	13.5	4.5	1.1	3.8	7.1	2.9
Dry beans, peas, nuts, and soya products	3.0	5.4	3.8	0.0	2.0	14.7	0.0+	5.1	1.9	6.6	4.8	10.5	0.0	0.0+	6.3	3.0	6.3	11.9	4.7
Flour and cereal products	19.7	18.5	1.3	0.0	36.2	17.2	0.4	42.3	22.4	28.2	10.5	11.0	1.7	0.0	33.2	3.7	13.1	18.3	12.3
Sucrose and other sweeteners	16.6	0.0+[a]	0.0	0.0	37.6	0.0	0.0	0.0+	0.0+	0.0+	0.0+	0.0+	0.0	0.0+	0.7	0.4	0.1	0.6	0.1
Miscellaneous foods[b]	0.9	0.7	1.5	0.0	0.8	9.6	7.4	0.4	3.9	3.5	0.1	0.1	0.0	3.9	4.6	1.9	2.3	8.2	2.4

Source: Unpublished data from Human Nutrition Information Service, U.S. Dept. of Agriculture (1984B).
[a] 0.0+ indicates amounts less than 0.05%.
[b] Coffee, tea, chocolate liquor, equivalent of cocoa beans, spices, and fortification not assigned to a specific food group.

Table 2.3.   Nutrients Available for Consumption Per Capita
Per Day in the United States in 1983

Nutrient	Unit	Quantity
Food energy	kcal[a]	3450
	MJ[b]	14.4
Protein	g	102
Carbohydrate	g	394
Fat	g	166
Vitamin A value	IU[c]	8100
Thiamin	mg	2.14
Riboflavin	mg	2.43
Niacin	mg	26.2
Vitamin B_6	mg	2.02
Vitamin B_{12}	μg	8.7
Ascorbic acid	mg	125
Iron	mg	18.1
Calcium	mg	880
Phosphorus	mg	1500
Magnesium	mg	347

Source: "Food Consumption, Prices, and Expenditures 1963–
83," Statistical Bulletin No. 713, U.S. Dept. of Agriculture
(1984A).
[a] 1 kcal = 4.184 kJ.
[b] 1 MJ = 239 kcal.
[c] 10 IU vitamin A activity from retinol = 3 μg retinol or 3
retinol equivalents.

by the Food and Nutrition Board of the National Academy of Sciences,
National Research Council (1980). These RDA requirements were designed to maintain good nutrition for practically all healthy people in
the United States.

Table 2.3 indicates that the average food energy available in the United
States in 1983 was 3450 kcal/capita/day, which is considerably higher
than the RDA for energy needs proposed for adult 23- to 50-year-old men
and women who require only 2700 and 2000 kcal/capita/day, respectively (National Academy of Sciences, National Research Council 1980).
The available quantities of protein, vitamin A, vitamin B_{12}, and ascorbic acid are about two to three times the RDA. However, vitamin B_6,
iron, calcium, and magnesium available are probably below the RDA
values for many people.

In addition, estimated safe and adequate daily dietary intakes of other
selected vitamins and minerals are given in Table 2.5 (National Academy
of Sciences, National Research Council 1980). For these nutrients, data
on their availability in the food supply have not yet been compiled.

Although good nutrition is important to keep the body in good health,
it should be emphasized that man eats food, composite macro- and micronutrients, and not single nutrients. Therefore, it is essential that foods

Table 2.4. Recommended Daily Dietary Allowances (RDA)[a]

	Weight		Height			Fat-soluble vitamins			Water-soluble vitamins							Minerals					
Age (yr)	(kg)	(lb)	(cm)	(in.)	Protein (g)	Vitamin A (µg R.E.)[b]	Vitamin D (µg)[c]	Vitamin E (mg α-T.E.)[d]	Vitamin C (mg)	Thiamin (mg)	Riboflavin (mg)	Niacin (mg N.E.)[e]	Vitamin B6 (mg)	Folacin (µg)[f]	Vitamin B12 (µg)	Calcium (mg)	Phosphorus (mg)	Magnesium (mg)	Iron (mg)	Zinc (mg)	Iodine (µg)
Infants																					
0.0–0.5	6	13	60	24	kg x 2.2	420	10	3	35	0.3	0.4	6	0.3	30	0.5[g]	360	240	50	10	3	40
0.5–1.0	9	20	71	28	kg x 2.0	400	10	4	35	0.5	0.6	8	0.6	45	1.5	540	360	70	15	5	50
Children																					
1–3	13	29	90	35	23	400	10	5	45	0.7	0.8	9	0.9	100	2.0	800	800	150	15	10	70
4–6	20	44	112	44	30	500	10	6	45	0.9	1.0	11	1.3	200	2.5	800	800	200	10	10	90
7–10	28	62	132	52	34	700	10	7	45	1.2	1.4	16	1.6	300	3.0	800	800	250	10	10	120
Males																					
11–14	45	99	157	62	45	1000	10	8	50	1.4	1.6	18	1.8	400	3.0	1200	1200	350	18	15	150
15–18	66	145	176	69	56	1000	10	10	60	1.4	1.7	18	2.0	400	3.0	1200	1200	400	18	15	150
19–22	70	154	177	70	56	1000	7.5	10	60	1.5	1.7	19	2.2	400	3.0	800	800	350	10	15	150
23–50	70	154	178	70	56	1000	5	10	60	1.4	1.6	18	2.2	400	3.0	800	800	350	10	15	150
≥51	70	154	178	70	56	1000	5	10	60	1.2	1.4	16	2.2	400	3.0	800	800	350	10	15	150
Females																					
11–14	46	101	157	62	46	800	10	8	50	1.1	1.3	15	1.8	400	3.0	1200	1200	300	18	15	150
15–18	55	120	163	64	46	800	10	8	60	1.1	1.3	14	2.0	400	3.0	1200	1200	300	18	15	150
19–22	55	120	163	64	44	800	7.5	8	60	1.1	1.3	14	2.0	400	3.0	800	800	300	18	15	150
23–50	55	120	163	64	44	800	5	8	60	1.0	1.2	13	2.0	400	3.0	800	800	300	18	15	150
≥51	55	120	163	64	44	800	5	8	60	1.0	1.2	13	2.0	400	3.0	800	800	300	10	15	150
Pregnant					+30	+200	+5	+2	+20	+0.4	+0.3	+2	+0.6	+400	+1.0	+400	+400	+150	h	+5	+25
Lactating					+20	+400	+5	+3	+40	+0.5	+0.5	+5	+0.5	+100	+1.0	+400	+400	+150	h	+10	+50

Source: National Academy of Sciences, National Research Council (1980).

[a] The allowances are intended to provide for individual variations among most normal persons as they live in the United States under usual environmental stresses. Diets should be based on a variety of common foods in order to provide other nutrients for which human requirements have been less well defined.

[b] Retinol equivalents: 1 R.E. = 1 µg retinol or 6 µg β-carotene.

[c] As cholecalciferol: 10 µg cholecalciferol = 400 IU vitamin D.

[d] α-tocopherol equivalents: 1 mg d-α-tocopherol = 1 α-T.E.

[e] 1 N.E. (niacin equivalent) = 1 mg of niacin or 60 mg of dietary tryptophan.

[f] The folacin allowances refer to dietary sources as determined by *Lactobacillus casei* assay after treatment with enzymes ("conjugases") to make polyglutamyl forms of the vitamin available to the test organism.

[g] The RDA for vitamin B12 in infants is based on average concentration of the vitamin in human milk. The allowances after weaning are based on energy intake (as recommended by the American Academy of Pediatrics) and consideration of other factors such as intestinal absorption.

[h] The increased requirement during pregnancy cannot be met by the iron content of habitual American diets nor by the existing iron stores of many women; therefore the use of 30–60 mg of supplemental iron is recommended. Iron needs during lactation are not substantially different from those of nonpregnant women, but continued supplementation of the mother for 2–3 months after parturition is advisable in order to replenish stores depleted by pregnancy.

Table 2.5. Estimated Safe and Adequate Daily Dietary Intakes of Additional Selected Vitamins and Minerals[a]

		Vitamins			Trace elements[b]						Electrolytes		
	Age (yr)	Vitamin K (µg)	Biotin (µg)	Pantothenic acid (mg)	Copper (mg)	Manganese (mg)	Fluoride (mg)	Chromium (mg)	Selenium (mg)	Molyb-denum (mg)	Sodium (mg)	Potassium (mg)	Chloride (mg)
Infants	0–0.5	12	35	2	0.5–0.7	0.5–0.7	0.1–0.5	0.01–0.04	0.01–0.04	0.03–0.06	115–350	350–925	275–700
	0.5–1	10–20	50	3	0.7–1.0	0.7–1.0	0.2–1.0	0.02–0.06	0.02–0.06	0.04–0.08	250–750	425–1275	400–1200
Children and	1–3	15–30	65	3	1.0–1.5	1.0–1.5	0.5–1.5	0.02–0.08	0.02–0.08	0.05–0.1	325–975	550–1650	500–1500
adolescents	4–6	20–40	85	3–4	1.5–2.0	1.5–2.0	1.0–2.5	0.03–0.12	0.03–0.12	0.06–0.15	450–1350	775–2325	700–2100
	7–10	30–60	120	4–5	2.0–2.5	2.0–3.0	1.5–2.5	0.05–0.2	0.05–0.2	0.1–0.3	600–1800	1000–3000	925–2775
	⩾11	50–100	100–200	4–7	2.0–3.0	2.5–5.0	1.5–2.5	0.05–0.2	0.05–0.2	0.15–0.5	900–2700	1525–4575	1400–4200
Adults		70–140	100–200	4–7	2.0–3.0	2.5–5.0	1.5–4.0	0.05–0.2	0.05–0.2	0.15–0.5	1100–3300	1875–5625	1700–5100

Source: National Academy of Sciences, National Research Council (1980).

[a] Because there is less information on which to base allowances, these figures are not given in the main table of the RDA and are provided here in the form of ranges of recommended intakes.

[b] Since the toxic levels for many trace elements may be only several times usual intakes, the upper levels for the trace elements given in this table should not be habitually exceeded.

Table 2.6.   USDA Agriculture Handbook No. 8 Series

Series no.	Food group	Year issued	Number of items
8–1	Dairy and egg products	1976	144
8–2	Spices and herbs	1977	43
8–3	Baby foods	1978	217
8–4	Fats and oils	1979	128
8–5	Poultry products	1979	304
8–6	Soups, sauces, and gravies	1980	214
8–7	Sausages and luncheon meats	1980	80
8–8	Breakfast cereals	1982	142
8–9	Fruits and fruit juices	1982	263
8–10	Pork products	1983	186
8–11	Vegetables and vegetable products	1984	470
8–12	Nut and seed products	1984	117

Source: USDA (1976–1984).

be as balanced in overall nutrient content as possible, but also palatable and safe.   The nutrient content of many raw and processed-prepared foods is listed in the Agriculture Handbook No. 8 Series (USDA 1976–1984) as shown in Table 2.6.

THE PRINCIPLES OF FOOD PROCESSING

Foods are processed for three reasons: (1) to preserve, package, and store foods (e.g., canning); (2) to manufacture desirable food products, including nutrification (e.g., baking); and (3) to prepare foods for serving.

All raw foods are perishable commodities. From the time of harvest or slaughter, the raw plant and animal tissues undergo gradual deterioration by various biochemical reactions. The rate of deterioration may be very fast or relatively slow. One of the primary factors of food spoilage is the content of biologically active water in the tissue. Raw foods with a high biologically active water content, such as leafy vegetables and meat, deteriorate in only a few days, whereas dry seeds, containing only structural water, can be stored for years under proper conditions.

The major causes of food spoilage are microbial growth and enzymatic and chemical changes, the first being by far the greatest cause of food loss. These actions and reactions take place rapidly at high water content as well as at favorable temperatures, pH, and other environmental conditions. The principles of food preservation are based on the manipulation of these environmental conditions. For instance, microorganisms require an optimum temperature for growth; higher temperatures are injurious, while lower temperatures greatly retard their metabolism.

There are only six basic principles of food processing for preservation:

1. Moisture removal — drying; dehydration; concentration; inter-
    mediate moisture processing
2. Heat treatment — blanching; pasteurization; sterilization; baking,
    cooking, frying, and so forth; extrusion cooking; microwaving
3. Low-temperature treatment — cold storage; refrigeration; freezing
4. Acidity control — fermentation; acidic additives
5. Chemical additive processing
6. Irradiation

Since all preserved foods have to be stored until they are consumed, proper food packaging is an important coprocessing factor to the basic food processing methods.

The metabolism of microorganisms requires plenty of free water. Removal of the biologically active water through drying or dehydration stops the growth of microorganisms. It also reduces the rate of enzymatic activity and chemical reactions. Rancidity of the lipid constituents of dehydrated foods is reduced if the protective structural water is left intact. The effect of water removal on nutrients is relatively small if the dehydration temperature is moderate and the food is subsequently adequately packaged. Freeze-dehydration offers decisive advantages in nutrient preservation over dehydration at elevated temperatures.

The principal effect of heat treatment is the denaturation of proteins, that is, the inactivation of the microbial and the native food enzymes. Pasteurization frees the food from human pathogens and most vegetative microorganisms, whereas sterilization, by definition, means the destruction of all viable microorganisms. Heat sterilization, the most effective process of food preservation, severely affects the labile vitamins and reduces, mainly through the Maillard reactions, the nutritional quality of proteins.

Low-temperature preservation, particularly freeze-preservation, is a relatively harmless method of food preservation. Low temperature inhibits microbial growth and slows down the rate of chemical and enzymatic reactions. The activity of meat enzymes is essentially stopped in commercial frozen storage, while many vegetables have to be blanched before freezing in order to avoid undesirable quality changes due to enzymatic activity at freezer temperatures. Vitamin losses are minimal compared to other methods of food preservation. Losses in overall quality occur mainly through unfavorable freezing, storage, and thawing conditions, but also through defective packaging.

Spoilage of low-acid foods is relatively rapid. The growth of food spoilage organisms is greatly inhibited in an acidic environment. Acidic fermentation lowers the pH of carbohydrate-containing foods by producing lactic acid. Acidity of some foods may also be increased by acidic additives, such as vinegar or citric acid, producing the same inhibitory effect on spoilage. Loss of nutrients through the acidic fermentation process is small. In some cases the nutrient level may even be increased, particularly through microbial vitamin and protein synthesis.

Chemical additives can substantially contribute to the preservation of foods by providing an inhibitory environment for microbial growth and for enzymatic and chemical reactions. The effect of these methods on nutrients is variable, but generally small.

Irradiation, the so-called cold-pasteurization and cold-sterilization processes, is the most recent method of food preservation. The Food and Drug Administration (FDA) categorizes it as "food additive," because ionizing radiation produces new unknown substances in irradiated foods. The free radical mechanism of irradiation destroys microorganisms, but is also detrimental to nutrients, particularly to vitamins. Another disadvantage of this method is the adverse flavor change, particularly in the sterilized dairy and meat products. Sterilization doses do not inactivate the enzymes, therefore the enzymes have to be heat-inactivated.

The title of this book, *Nutritional Evaluation of Food Processing*, refers to two sets of variables: changes in the initial level of nutrients that are dependent on the various methods of food processing, processing severity and duration. The initial level of a nutrient in a raw food is already a variable due to the environmental and genetic factors. The Agriculture Handbook No. 8 Series (USDA 1976–1984), the most voluminous reference source on the nutritional composition of foods, gives only the initial and the final levels for a particular nutrient in raw and processed prepared foods, respectively. However, relatively little is known about the rate of change in nutrient levels as a function of processing severity and duration. A better understanding of the nutrient destruction kinetics in the future will help reduce processing damage to nutrients by either eliminating or improving processing steps which cause most degradation.

Foods are composite macronutrient systems that serve as media for the micronutrients and influence their stability differently. This means that some labile vitamins, such as thiamin and ascorbic acid, may be protected by one food system more than by another. Figure 2.2, for instance, illustrates a study on thiamin stability in meat irradiated at various intensities (Karmas *et al.* 1962). The initial thiamin content of pork decreased to 12% of the initial level in fresh and freeze-dehydrated-rehydrated samples which contained 68.8% and 65.9% moisture, respectively. About one-third of the initial thiamin content was destroyed by the freeze-dehydration process. However, thiamin was stable in the medium of low water activity (moisture content 1.3%) of the freeze-dehydrated sample. These data strongly suggest that thiamin destruction resulted from the aqueous medium, present during both the freeze-dehydration and irradiation processes, whereas the dehydrated food was protective to thiamin.

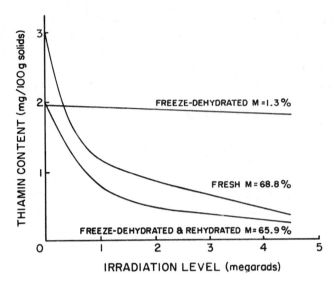

Fig. 2.2. Thiamin retention in irradiated pork. Source: Karmas *et al.* (1962).

In order to fully understand vitamin degradation resulting from food processing, a good knowledge of vitamin chemistry is prerequisite. Because there are numerous excellent monographs available on the nutritional, biochemical, chemical, and clinical aspects of vitamins (e.g., Machlin 1984), information on vitamin chemistry is not included in this volume.

In general, food processing techniques in greatest use today do not result in major losses in the nutritive value of foods (Institute of Food Technologists 1974). The more sophisticated food processing methods being developed by advanced technology should retain an even higher percentage of nutrients. Besides improvements in food processing technology, factors to be considered in efforts to increase the essential nutrients must include food storage and distribution, institutional food preparation, and an increasing awareness by the home consumer of the importance of proper food handling.

REFERENCES

Institute of Food Technologists 1974. The effects of food processing on nutritional values. A scientific status report by the IFT Expert Panel and the Committee on Public Information. Food Technol. 28(10), 77–80.

Karmas, E., Thompson, J. E., and Peryam, D. B. 1962. Thiamine retention in freeze-dehydrated irradiated pork. Food Technol. 16(3), 107.

Machlin, L. J. (Editor). 1984. Handbook of Vitamins. Marcel Dekker, New York.

National Academy of Sciences, National Research Council. 1963. Evaluation of Protein Quality. Food and Nutrition Board Pub. *1100*. National Academy of Sciences, National Research Council, Washington, DC.

National Academy of Sciences, National Research Council 1980. Recommended Dietary Allowances, 9th Edition. Food and Nutrition Board, National Academy of Sciences, National Research Council, Washington, DC.

Szent-Györgyi, A. 1966. The strategy of life. Intl. Sci. Technol. *6*, 48.

U.S. Department of Agriculture (USDA) 1976–1984. Composition of foods: Raw, processed, prepared. *In* Agriculture Handbook *8*, Vols. 8–1—8–12. USDA, Washington, DC.

U.S. Department of Agriculture (USDA) 1984A. Food consumption, prices, and expenditures, 1963–1983. Compiled by K. Bunch. Economic Research Service, USDA Statistical Bull. *713*. Washington, DC.

U.S. Department of Agriculture (USDA) 1984B. Unpublished data from Human Nutrition Information Service. Compiled by R. Marston and N. Raper. Washington, DC.

Part 2

Nutrients in Food—
Raw and Processed

Effects of Agricultural Practices, Handling, Processing, and Storage on Vegetables

D. K. Salunkhe
B. B. Desai

Today's world is faced with an acute need to provide enough nutritive food for all its people. Increased consciousness about nutrition, food, and health has significantly influenced our modern agriculture and food industry. About 90% of the world's food (measured in calories) is vegetable products, of which 80% constitutes starchy foods, such as grains and tubers. As pointed out by Salunkhe *et al.* (1974) in their account of assessment of nutritive value, quality, and stability of cruciferous vegetables during storage and subsequent processing, this is an appropriate time to assess food production, storage, and processing and to determine if vegetable crops with more nutrients can be produced and preserved for a longer time without much loss in quality and wholesomeness.

"Quality of vegetables" is an illusive concept which is difficult to define although it can be discussed in terms of four basic characteristics of food, namely, (1) color or eye appeal, (2) odor and flavor, (3) texture or feel, and (4) nutritive value. All of the above but the nutritional quality of food, a hidden characteristic, can be evaluated with human senses. Nutritive value and the presence of adulterants and toxic substances cannot.

MAJOR CHEMICAL COMPONENTS OF VEGETABLES AND THEIR NUTRITIONAL SIGNIFICANCE

Carbohydrates, proteins, fats, vitamins, minerals, and fiber are the major chemical components of fresh vegetables in addition to a large quantity of water. β-Carotene (provitamin A), thiamin (B_1), riboflavin (B_2), niacin, pyridoxine (B_6), pantothenic acid, folic acid (folacin), ascorbic acid, and vitamins E and K have been reported present in different vegetable products. Among the minerals present are calcium,

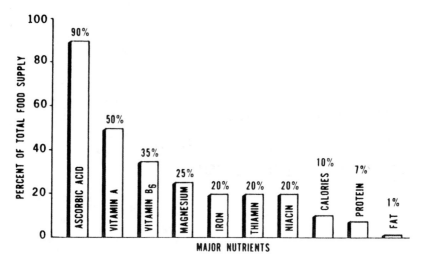

Fig. 3.1. The nutritional contribution of some important fruits and vegetables. Source: Salunkhe *et al.* (1974).

phosphorus, potassium, sodium, manganese, iron, magnesium, copper, cobalt, sulfur, zinc, and fluorine. Salunkhe *et al.* (1974) have described the major functions of these nutrients in the human body. The fruits and vegetables are generally bought and consumed for their characteristic flavor and taste rather than for their nutritive value. The nutritional contribution of 12 major fruits, 12 cruciferous vegetables, and 18 other important vegetables compared to the percentage of total food supply is depicted in Fig. 3.1.

Amount of Nutrients and Quantity of Food

Since the extent to which a food contributes nutrients to man's diet is governed both by the amount of nutrients present in the food and the quantity consumed, vegetables are generally not regarded as economic sources of energy, protein, fat, calcium, or riboflavin (Vittum 1963). A vegetable may be rich in vitamins and minerals, but the consumer will need another source of supply if only a small quantity of that vegetable is eaten. The concentration of ascorbic acid in green peppers is about seven times higher than that in potatoes, but the average consumer obtains more of this vitamin from potatoes than from peppers because of higher consumption of potatoes. The relative concentration of ten major vitamins and minerals in some fruits and vegetables and their importance in the typical U.S. diet (Table 3.1) shows that while tomatoes and oranges are relatively low in concentration of nutrients, they contribute greatly to the U.S. diet because they are consumed in large amounts (Rick 1978). Vegetables supply only negligible amounts of fat

Table 3.1. Relative Concentration of 10 Vitamins and Minerals in Some Fruits and Vegetables and Their Relative Contribution to the U.S. Diet

Crop	Nutrient concentration, rank	Crop	Contribution to diet, rank
Broccoli	1	Tomato	1
Spinach	2	Orange	2
Brussels sprout	3	Potato	3
Lima bean	4	Lettuce	4
Pea	5	Sweet corn	5
Asparagus	6	Banana	6
Artichoke	7	Carrot	7
Cauliflower	8	Cabbage	8
Sweet potato	9	Onion	9
Carrot	10	Sweet potato	10
Sweet corn	12	Pea	15
Potato	14	Spinach	18
Cabbage	15	Broccoli	21
Tomato	16	Lima bean	23
Banana	18	Asparagus	25
Lettuce	26	Cauliflower	30
Onion	31	Brussels sprout	34
Orange	33	Artichoke	36

Source: Rick (1978)

and protein (7 and 8% of the body's energy requirements and protein needs, respectively). Other foods such as cereals, meat, milk, and eggs are more efficient sources of these nutrients. Vegetables, however, contribute significantly to a well-balanced diet in that they are major sources of provitamin A (β-carotene) and vitamin C (ascorbic acid) and are good sources of thiamin, niacin, and iron (Table 3.2). They also furnish bulk (dietary fiber), which helps in the proper functioning of the human digestive system. Several diseases of man, such as appendicitis, colon cancer, constipation, deep vein thrombosis, diabetes, diverticulosis, gallstones, hemorrhoids, hiatus hernia, ischemic heart disease, obesity, tumors of the rectum, and varicose veins, have been claimed to be due to lack of fiber in the diet (Wills *et al.* 1981). Most vegetables, especially the leafy variety such as spinach, lettuce, celery, cabbage, and fenugreek, are characterized by high water content and a high percentage of cellulose. Owing to their succulence and large bulk (roughage), leafy greens and root vegetables aid in the digestion of concentrated foods.

Energy: Fats and Carbohydrates

The body requires food energy for basal metabolism, synthesis of body tissues, physical activity, excretory processes, and maintenance of thermal, physiological, and psychological balance. Caloric food allowances are established to provide energy and to maintain body

Table 3.2. Percentage of Total Money Value and of Total Nutritive Value of Vegetables in U.S. Diets

Nutrients	All vege-tables	Dark green and deep yellow	Tomato	Potato	Sweet potato	Dry beans and peas	Other green vege-tables	Other vege-tables
Cost	12.5	1.3	2.1	2.0	0.1	0.4	3.3	3.3
Calories	6.9	0.3	0.5	2.9	0.1	1.0	0.8	1.2
Protein	8.1	0.5	0.6	2.0	0.1	2.0	1.7	1.3
Fat	1.5	0.1	0.1	0.8	<0.1	0.1	0.1	0.3
Calcium	9.0	2.1	0.5	1.0	0.1	1.1	2.4	1.8
Iron	19.9	2.4	1.7	4.1	0.2	3.8	4.6	3.1
Vitamin A	43.6	26.8	7.2	<0.1	3.7	<0.1	4.3	1.6
Thiamin	15.8	1.0	1.9	5.3	0.2	1.9	3.4	2.1
Riboflavin	9.0	1.3	1.0	1.7	0.1	0.9	2.3	1.8
Niacin	14.2	0.9	2.4	5.8	0.1	1.1	2.1	1.9
Vitamin C	42.5	8.1	8.2	9.8	0.5	0.2	10.0	5.7

Source: Boswell (1961).

weight and health. Fats and carbohydrates are the most important sources of food energy. According to the Food and Nutrition Board of the National Academy of Sciences, National Research Council (1968), of the total calories consumed, the American diet consists of about 41% fats and 47% carbohydrates. The chemical (nutritional) composition of 12 cruciferous and 18 other vegetables in respect to proximate composition, minerals, and vitamins (Table 3.3) indicates that most vegetables are low in calories, fats, and carbohydrates (Salunkhe et al. 1974).

Proteins: Quantity, Quality, and Utility

The body's protein needs depend upon the individual's age, sex, metabolism, and other physiological factors. Protein quality is determined in terms of the pattern of essential amino acids in protein structures. Salunkhe et al. (1974) pointed out that to evaluate the status of vegetables with regard to their protein content, one must consider the protein quality in terms of balanced essential amino acids. The biological availablility of proteins is also an important consideration from a nutritional point of view and is determined by biological evaluation through human and animal feeding experiments. The biological value of proteins expresses the efficiency with which the body utilizes absorbed proteins as a dietary source of amino acids. This biological value may be altered if the body need for one amino acid or group of amino acids changes in relation to the requirements of other amino acids. According to Salunkhe et al. (1974), protein requirements are based on involvement of total nitrogen, pattern of essential amino acids, optimal ratio of essential to

Table 3.3. Nutritional Composition of Some Cruciferous and Other Vegetables (per 100 g edible portion)

Vegetable	Proximate composition					Minerals						Vitamins				
	Water (%)	Energy (Cal)	Protein (%)	Fat (%)	Carbohydrate (%)	Calcium (mg)	Phosphorus (mg)	Iron (mg)	Sodium (mg)	Potassium (mg)	Magnesium (mg)	Vitamin A (IU)	Thiamin (mg)	Riboflavin (mg)	Niacin (mg)	Vitamin C (mg)
Cabbage	92.2	24	1.3	0.2	5.4	49	29	0.4	20	233	13	130	0.05	0.05	0.3	47
Broccoli	89.1	32	3.6	0.3	5.9	103	78	1.1	15	382	24	2500	0.10	0.23	0.9	113
Brussels sprout	85.2	45	4.9	0.4	8.3	36	80	1.5	14	390	29	550	0.10	0.16	0.9	102
Cauliflower	91.0	27	2.7	0.2	5.2	25	56	1.1	13	295	24	60	0.11	0.10	0.7	78
Kale	82.7	53	6.0	0.8	9.0	249	93	2.7	75	238	37	10,000	0.16	0.26	2.1	186
Watercress	93.3	19	2.2	0.3	3.0	151	54	1.7	52	282	20	4900	0.08	0.16	0.9	79
Mustard green	89.5	31	3.0	0.5	5.6	183	50	3.0	32	377	27	7000	0.11	0.22	0.8	97
Turnip green	90.3	28	3.0	0.3	5.0	246	58	1.8	40[a]	250[a]	58	7600	0.21	0.39	0.8	139
Chinese cabbage	95.0	14	1.2	0.1	3.0	43	40	0.6	23	253	14	150	0.05	0.04	0.6	25
Rutabaga	87.0	46	1.1	0.1	11.0	66	39	0.4	5	239	15	580	0.07	0.07	1.1	43
Collard	85.3	45	4.8	0.8	7.5	250	82	1.5	40[a]	450	57	9300	0.16	0.31	1.7	152
Kohlrabi	90.3	29	2.0	0.1	6.6	41	51	0.5	8	372	37	20	0.06	0.04	0.3	66
Carrot	88.2	42	1.1	0.2	9.7	37	36	0.7	47	341	23	11,000	0.06	0.05	0.6	8
Sweet potato	70.6	114	1.7	0.4	26.3	32	47	0.7	10	243	31	8800	0.10	0.06	0.6	21
Tomato	93.5	22	1.1	0.2	4.7	13	27	0.5	3	244	14	900	0.06	0.04	0.7	23
Sweet corn	72.7	96	3.5	1.0	22.1	3	111	0.7	10[a]	280	48	400	0.15	0.12	1.7	12
Pepper	93.4	22	1.2	0.2	4.8	9	22	0.7	13	213	18	420	0.08	0.08	0.5	128
Lettuce	95.1	14	1.2	0.2	2.5	35	26	2.0	9	264	11	900	0.06	0.06	0.3	8
Potato	79.8	76	2.1	0.1	17.1	7	53	0.6	3	407	34	20[b]	0.10	0.04	1.5	20
Squash	94.0	19	1.1	0.1	4.2	28	29	0.4	1	202	17	410	0.05	0.09	1.0	22
Onion	89.1	38	1.5	0.1	8.7	27	36	0.5	10	157	12	40	0.03	0.04	0.2	10
Cucumber	95.1	15	0.9	0.1	3.4	25	27	1.1	6	160	11	250	0.03	0.04	0.2	11
Spinach	90.7	26	3.2	0.3	4.3	93	51	3.1	71	470	88	8100	0.10	0.20	0.6	51
Lima bean	67.5	123	8.4	0.5	22.1	52	142	2.8	2	650	67	290	0.24	0.12	1.4	29
Pea	78.0	84	6.3	0.4	14.4	26	116	1.9	2	316	35	640	0.35	0.14	2.9	27
Asparagus	91.7	26	2.5	0.2	5.0	22	62	1.0	2	278	20	900	0.18	0.20	1.5	33
Cantaloupe	91.2	30	0.7	0.1	7.5	14	16	0.4	12	251	17[a]	3400	0.04	0.03	0.6	33
Snap bean	90.1	32	1.9	0.2	7.1	56	44	0.8	7	243	32	600	0.08	0.11	0.5	19
Beet	87.3	43	1.6	0.1	9.3	16	33	0.7	60	335	25	20	0.03	0.05	0.4	10
Celery	94.1	17	0.9	0.1	3.9	39	28	0.3	126	341	22	240	0.03	0.03	0.3	9

Main Source: Agricultural Handbook No. 8, U.S. Dept. of Agriculture (1963).

[a] Nutritional composition of fresh California grown vegetables (1962), California Exp. Sta. Bull. No. 788, Davis.

[b] "The Heinz Handbook of Nutrition," McGraw-Hill, New York (1959), cited by Salunkhe, et al. (1974).

nonessential amino acids, and availability to body cells. Among the various fruits and vegetables surveyed, the cruciferous vegetables were found to be excellent sources of proteins and amino acids, especially the sulfur-containing amino acids. When compared with peas and beans, the crucifers were superior in terms of biological value, digestibility, and net protein utilization.

Vitamins and Minerals

Vitamins and minerals present in the diet are necessary for normal growth and metabolism and influence the utilization of other nutrients such as protein. The deficiency of essential vitamins or minerals leads to several physiological disorders and diseases, slowed growth, and lack of deposition of proteins in tissues. An adequate supply of B-complex vitamins is necessary for critical protein utilization. The deficiency of minerals such as potassium, phosphorus, sodium, calcium, and magnesium also influences the capacity of the body to utilize amino acids and proteins.

Vitamins

The vitamins are a group of organic compounds that are essential in relatively minute quantities for the metabolism of other nutrients in the body and for normal growth, maintenance of health, and reproduction. They prevent a number of systemic diseases and participate in the regulation of body processes. It has been recommended that a specific amount of the 13 known vitamins must be included in the adult diet each day (National Academy of Sciences, National Research Council 1968). These include the fat-soluble vitamins, provitamin A (β-carotene), vitamins D, E (α-tocopherol), and K, and water-soluble ascorbic acid (vitamin C), biotin, folacin, niacin, pantothenic acid, riboflavin, thiamin, pyridoxine (B_6), and cobalamine (B_{12}). Cruciferous and many other vegetables contain most of these vitamins in significant amounts (Table 3.3). Data presented in Table 3.3 show that vegetables contain substantial amounts of provitamin A (β-carotene), riboflavin, niacin, and thiamin. Information about folic acid, pantothenic acid, and pyridoxine is limited. According to Salunkhe et al. (1974), in general, the cruciferous vegetables are the most efficient plant products in synthesizing high concentrations of proteins, amino acids, minerals, and vitamins, and they are low in caloric content.

Gopala Rao et al. (1980) reported the contents of β-carotene, vitamins of the B group (B_1, B_2, B_6, niacin), reducing and nonreducing sugars, starch, protein, soluble protein, and total nitrogen, calcium, and iron in several leafy vegetables — amaranth (A. tricolor and A. spinosus), drumstick leaves (Moringa oleifera), coriander (Coriandrum sativum), mint (Menthasspicata), and garden sorrel (Rumex acetosa). They recommended a new leafy vegetable (Trianthema portulacastrum) as nutritionally rich. Celosia and drumstick leaves also could be used as leafy vegetables since they are rich in provitamin A and vitamin C.

Minerals

Minerals in the diet are required for proper growth and good health. Those needed in macro-, or major quantities are calcium, phosphorus, magnesium, potassium, sulfur, sodium, and chlorine, and those needed in micro- (trace) amounts are iron, iodine, copper, cobalt, chromium, manganese, selenium, zinc, fluorine, and molybdenum. Recent studies have shown that silica is essential for the normal growth of rats, but its essentiality in man is yet to be established. The cruciferous and many other vegetables are excellent sources of minerals, particularly of calcium, iron, magnesium, sodium, potassium, and phosphorus, and most of these minerals are present in the available form (Table 3.3). Tindall and Proctor (1980) summarized the nutritive values of some selected tropical vegetables (Table 3.4). They concluded that vegetables significantly contributed to man's dietary requirements of carbohydrates, proteins, vitamins, and essential minerals, especially in areas of low animal protein availability and where cereals form the major part of the human diet. Vegetables provide variety to an otherwise monotonous diet containing a limited number of items.

Flavor and Consumer Preferences

In addition to the above-mentioned nutritional attributes, flavor is one of the most important properties of vegetables. Aroma is constituted by the presence of volatiles and by sweetness (sugars), acidity, and the astringency contributed by the phenolics. Lindstrand (1979) stressed the value of eye appeal of vegetables, as well as their being a source of dietary fiber and minerals and their having physiological effects.

Water is the most abundant constituent of vegetables, with most containing over 80% moisture. Water is one of the most important nutrients, having vast significance for the utilization of all other nutrients. In addition to water, vegetables also supply lipids, organic acids, and volatile compounds.

Toxicological and Antinutrient Considerations

Vegetables have been known to contain certain toxic factors. Cruciferous vegetables in general, and those belonging to the genus *Brassica* in particular, contain goitrogens which are reported to be the antinutrients that cause enlargement of the thyroid glands. Natural thioglucosides (glycosinolate) are sources of goitrogens. The same thioglucosides, with their associated enzymes, impart the desirable culinary flavor of cabbage, broccoli, and cauliflower. A thioglucoside, allylthioglucoside (sinigrin), is present in cabbage, kale, brussels sprouts, broccoli, cauliflower, and

Table 3.4. Nutritive Values of Some Important Vegetables (per 100 g Edible Portion)[a]

Commodity	Proximate composition					Minerals					Vitamins				Source
	Water (g)	Calories	Protein (g)	Fat (g)	Carbohydrate (g)	Calcium (mg)	Phosphorus (mg)	Iron (mg)	Sodium (mg)	Potassium (mg)	Thiamin (mg)	Riboflavin (mg)	Nicotinic acid (mg)	Ascorbic acid (mg)	
Roots and tubers															
Cassava	60 ml	153	0.7	0.2	37.0	25	—	1.0	—	—	0.07	0.03	—	30	(1)
Yam	73.0	131	2.0	0.2	32.4	10	(40)	0.3	—	(500)	0.10	0.03	0.4	10	(2)
Sweet potato	70.0	91	1.2	0.6	21.5	(22)	(47)	(0.7)	(19)	(320)	0.10	0.16	0.8	25	(2)
Irish potato	75.8	87	2.1	0.1	20.8	8	40	0.5	7	520	0.11	0.04	1.2	8.20	(2)
Other vegetables and melons															
Onion	92.8	23	0.9	Tr	5.2	31	30	0.3	10	140	0.03	0.05	0.2	10	(2)
Tomato	93.4	14	0.9	Tr	2.8	13	21	0.4	3	290	0.06	0.04	0.7	20	(2)
Pumpkin melon	94.7	15	0.6	Tr	2.8	39	19	0.4	1	310	0.04	0.04	0.4	5	(2)
Cantaloupe	93.6	24	1.0	Tr	5.3	19	30	0.8	14	320	0.05	0.03	0.5	25	(2)
Watermelon	94.0	21	0.4	Tr	5.3	5	8	0.3	4	120	0.02	0.02	0.2	5	(2)
Low-carotene leaves (pale green, e.g., cabbage, kohlrabi, Chinese cabbage)	93 ml	23	1.5	0.2	4.0	40	—	0.5	—	—	0.05	0.05	—	40	(1)
Medium-carotene leaves (e.g., New Zealand spinach, cassava leaves, watercress, squash, pumpkin)	91 ml	28	2.0	0.3	4.0	80	—	2.5	—	—	0.08	0.20	—	50	(1)
High-carotene leaves (dark green, e.g., spinach, sweet potato, tops, kale)	85 ml	48	5.0	0.7	5.0	250	—	4.0	—	—	2.1	0.30	—	100	(1)

Sources: (1) Platt (1962), (2) Paul and Southgate (1978), (3) FAO (1972), and (4) Tindall and Proctor (1980).
[a] Tr, trace. Figures in parentheses are estimates from related foods or, more rarely, the tentative values based on limited number of published sources (Paul and Southgate, 1978).

mustard. When these vegetables are chopped, a specific enzyme, thio-glucosidase (myrosinase), hydrolyzes allylthioglucoside into glucose, potassium bisulfate, and allylthiocyanate, a goitrogenic compound. In another case, progoitrin or epiprogoitrin, which is responsible for the typical flavor of kale, rape, turnip, rutabaga, and kohlrabi, upon hydrolysis subsequent to chopping by thioglucosidase yields glucose, potassium bisulfate, and highly unstable intermediate compounds, namely thiocyanate, nitrile plus sulfur, and goitrin, which are goitrogenic. Goitrin (5-vinyloxazolidine-2-thione) is a potent thyrotoxin and is formed through cyclization of an unstable isothiocyanate containing the hydroxyl group. The thyroid-inhibiting effect of goitrins is due to the inhibition of organic binding of iodine. Such action is consistent with observations that this type of goiter is not alleviated by increasing iodine in thyroids. However, thiocyanate, isothiocyanate, and nitrile ions act as goitrogens only when the iodine content of the diet is low. In regions where the iodine content of the diet is low, benign goiter may be accentuated by eating excessive amounts of brassica vegetables (Salunkhe *et al.* 1974).

Ethyl acetate extracts from leaves of broccoli, cabbage, rutabaga, turnip, and radish inhibit human plasma choline esterase (Crosby 1966). Such extracts contain chemicals that may modify the functions of the nervous system. Salunkhe *et al.* (1974) stressed the need for identification and determination of the amount of each substance. Murphy (1973) reported that the flatulence-distress syndrome after eating cooked crucifers is not as chronic and offensive as that produced after the consumption of beans, sweet potatoes, and onions.

Most of the goitrogen properties of vegetable products are lost during cooking. Green (1962) estimated that iodine deficiency caused endemic nontoxic goiter in all but 4% of the cases. Of this 4%, it could not be demonstrated that goitrogens in brassica vegetables were the major causal agents. Cauliflower and kale, among the crucifers, have high concentrations of thiocyanate. However, a daily intake of about 10 kg of cauliflower or kale would be required to furnish a goitrogenic concentration of thiocyanate in the blood. Nevertheless, according to Salunkhe *et al.* (1974), these thyrotoxic substances could be a matter of concern to food technologists in developing new or improved processing methods for reasons of economy, convenience, nutrition, flavor, or aesthetic appeal. It is essential to ensure that processed cruciferous vegetable products are not concentrated with goitrogenic substances.

Other naturally occurring toxicants of vegetables include oxalates, salicylates, arsenic, nitrite, and alkaloids such as solanine. Potatoes have been known to contain alkaloid solanine, arsenic, and nitrite, and green leafy vegetables contain toxic oxalates. The anthraquinones of rhubarb are mainly in the root, but human poisoning generally occurs from eating rhubarb leaves. The petioles of rhubarb are a good food;

the leaf poison is commonly thought to be the oxalates, but other factors, possibly quinones, are also involved (Singleton and Kratzer 1973). In terms of human lives lost from phenols originating in plants, the salicylate aspirin is probably the most dangerous. The accidental and deliberate consumption of salicylates produces of the order of four deaths per million of the population every year. The salicylic acid content of vegetables has attracted the interest of food scientists, technologists, processors, and consumers since Feingold, in 1973, reported that low molecular-weight salicylates are associated with hyperactivity in man. Feingold (1975) further recommended a dietary treatment for hyperactivity based on an exclusion diet, omitting 21 fruits and vegetables containing natural salicylates. Robertson and Kermode (1981), using a sensitive spectrofluorometric technique, determined the concentration of salicylic acid in fresh vegetables which ranged from 0.01 mg/kg in cabbage to 0.10 mg/kg in whole-kernel sweet corn. Canned sweet corn and some tomato products contained higher levels of salicylic acid than fresh corn and tomatoes.

The distribution of oxalates varies with families and species of vegetables, but generally leaves are higher in oxalate content than are stalks. The ratio of oxalate:calcium content also varies widely. Based on this ratio, Fassett (1973) grouped vegetables into three classes: (1) those with an oxalate:calcium ratio of 2:7, e.g., spinach, beet leaves, and rhubarb; (2) those with a ratio of about 1 (unity), e.g., potatoes; and (3) those with a ratio of less than 1, lettuce, cabbage, and peas. Many kinds of mushrooms also contain oxalates and other toxic factors.

Wu and Salunkhe (1976) reported that mechanical injuries to potatoes such as brushing, cutting, dropping, and puncturing significantly increased glycoalkaloid synthesis in both the peel and flesh. The extent of its formation depended on cultivar, type of injury, temperature, and duration of storage. Ingestion of large amounts of green potatoes or sprouts can cause poisoning in man and animals. Solanine is one of the major alkaloids of potato.

EFFECTS OF AGRICULTURAL PRACTICES ON NUTRITIONAL COMPOSITION OF VEGETABLES

Climatic and environmental factors such as light, temperature, rainfall, season, location, altitude, soil fertility, irrigation, and plant protection measures have been known to influence the nutritional status of vegetable crops. The earlier work on effects of agricultural practices on foods of plant origin has been reviewed by Harris (1975) in the previous edition of this volume. The influence of environmental factors such as amount and intensity of light, temperature, season of the year, location, fertilization, and crop maturity on ascorbic acid, β-carotene, essential amino acids, and other nutrients has been discussed. According to Harris (1975), the nutrient content of freshly harvested edible plant parts, including vegetables, may vary as much as 20-fold. These wide variations result from the interplay of a number of factors, chiefly genetic, but soil and climatic factors such as sunlight, rainfall, topography, soil type, location, season, fertilization, and crop maturity significantly influence the nutritional quality of vegetables.

Fundamental studies carried out in the past have shown that a close relationship exists between genetics and plant biochemistry. Plant enzymes are required for the synthesis of growth substances which may later serve as vitamins for those who consume these products. Although ability to synthesize these compounds is controlled by genetic factors, the quantity of these principles present in vegetative tissue is influenced by environmental factors and soil composition (Harris, 1975).

Climate/Environment

Man has very little control over climate, but climate does indeed exert control over man through its influence on food production, nutritional status, and health. The unwise use of forests and grazing lands has contributed its share to droughts, floods, and drastic changes in weather adversely affecting agricultural production.

Some ecological, cultural, and physical factors significantly influence the nutritional composition and anatomical and morphological structure of vegetables. Light, temperature, and carbon dioxide, influence the plant's mechanism of conversion of sucrose and hexoses into ascorbic acid and the eventual accumulation of ascorbic acid. The precursors of ascorbic acid are produced during photosynthesis, which, in turn, is significantly influenced by environmental factors such as light, temperature, carbon dioxide, and location.

Light

Variations in amount and intensity of light influence the nutritional composition of leafy greens, especially their ascorbic acid. A precursor of ascorbic acid, produced by photosynthesis, is biologically converted into ascorbic acid within the plant. Owing to the instability of ascorbic acid in the detached leaves, its loss is caused more by metabolic activity of the plant than by oxidation. The rate of formation of precursors is influenced by changes in light intensity and does not affect the conversion of these precursors to ascorbic acid. The contrasting effects of light upon ascorbic acid are discussed in the literature.

Winsor (1979) described factors contributing to the overall quality of tomatoes, including appearance, firmness, and chemical composition. It was reported that shading of plants decreased both the dry matter content of the fruit and the sugar content of the expressed juices (Table 3.5). Mengel (1979), describing the influence of exogenous factors on

Table 3.5. Effects of Shading on the Dry-Matter Content of Tomato Fruit and on the Sugar Content of the Expressed Juices

Cultivar	Assessment	Unshaded	Shaded
'Potentate'	Dry matter (%)	6.4	5.7
	Sugars (g/100 ml)	3.8	3.0
'Ailsa Craig'	Dry matter (%)	7.0	5.6
	Sugars (g/100 ml)	3.7	2.7

Source: Winsor (1979).

the quality and composition of vegetables, stated that carbohydrates in vegetables are influenced by intensity of light and have an inverse relationship with each other. Warmth promotes growth processes and, thus, the consumption of photosynthates; light intensity promotes the production of photosynthates. Thus, low temperature and high light intensity favor the accumulation of carbohydrates in vegetables, whereas high temperature and low light intensity decrease the carbohydrate content (Warren-Wilson 1969). The latter environment often prevails under glasshouse conditions. Although carbohydrates per se are not generally regarded as nutritionally important constituents of vegetables, the synthesis of vitamin C (ascorbid acid) is closely associated with carbohydrate metabolism, which is influenced by variation in light intensity. The primary precursor is glucose, which is activated by UTP and then oxidized to the activated form of glucuronic acid, the direct precursor of vitamin C. Thus, all processes that promote the synthesis of UTP or ATP and glucose favorably influence the synthesis of ascorbic acid. The most important factors in this respect are light intensity and potassium supply. Light intensity is directly involved in photosynthetic ATP synthesis and, thus, in all synthetic processes of the plant.

Temperature

The optimum temperature for normal growth of vegetables does not always equate with the optimum for synthesizing and accumulating nutrients. Furthermore, the specific temperature promoting the greatest translocation, synthesis, and accumulation of one nutrient is often different for another. Mengel (1979) stated that temperature is inversely related to the synthesis of carbohydrates in vegetative plant material. High temperatures prevailing under glasshouse conditions often result in low carbohydrate content.

Rosenfeld (1979) reported the total ascorbic acid (TAA) content of eight kinds of vegetables, namely, broad bean (*Vicia faba*), chicory (*Cichorium intybus*), chive (*Allium schoenoprasum*), spinach beet (*Beta vulgaris, cicla*), parsley (*Petroselinum crispum* Nym), cress (*Lepidium sativum*), sorrel (*Rumex acetosa*), and turnip (*Brassica campestris*), grown at $12°$, $15°$, $18°$, $21°$, and $24°C$. The total ascorbic acid content was

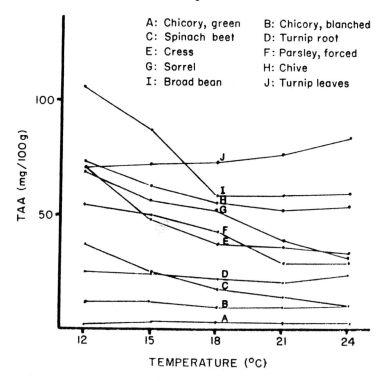

A: Chicory, green B: Chicory, blanched
C: Spinach beet D: Turnip root
E: Cress F: Parsley, forced
G: Sorrel H: Chive
I: Broad bean J: Turnip leaves

Fig. 3.2. The total ascorbic acid content of some vegetables at different temperatures. Source: Rosenfeld (1979).

highest at $12°$ and $15°C$, except for turnip leaves which gave increasing values with increasing temperatures. The lowest content of TAA was found at the highest temperatures, with the exception of turnip leaves (Fig. 3.2). Most of the vegetables studied seemed to obtain highest TAA content at low temperatures. Broad bean and cress showed unusually high content of TAA at low temperatures, which could be traced to the degree of development of the plants. Turnip leaves showed an opposite pattern of TAA content compared to its roots. The high TAA content of turnip leaves at $24°C$ was not due to high evaporation or lack of water, nor was the dry matter content significantly higher at high temperatures. Rosenfeld (1979) reasoned that an increased transport of carbohydrates from the root to the leaves at higher temperatures was probably responsible for the lower TAA content of dried leaves in some experiments. The rate of growth of vegetables was often highest at highest temperatures. This often coincided with the lowest TAA content, with the exception of turnips, in which the highest TAA content was obtained at the highest rate of growth. The correlation between TAA and dry matter content was positive for all kinds of vegetables. The higher TAA content at 24°C was attributed to higher respiration which probably encouraged TAA synthesis (Franke 1959).

Cantliffe (1972) demonstrated that under light conditions conducive to nitrate accumulation, nitrate accumulated at 5°C from 112 kg N/ha and at 10°C from 56 kg N/ha. Nitrate accumulation did not occur where nitrogen was not applied until the temperature reached 15°C, presumably because mineralization and nitrification were impeded at the lower temperatures (Maynard *et al.* 1976).

Bourne (1982) reported effects of temperature measured in the range 0°–45°C on the firmness of several raw fruits and vegetables. Most commodities showed decreasing firmness with increasing temperature, but there were several exceptions. For the majority of commodities tested, the firmness–temperature relationship was approximately linear.

Season

The season of the year has been known to influence the chemical composition of vegetables. Harris (1975) concluded that this was probably due to differences in temperature, length of day, light intensity, and light spectrum, as well as other minor factors.

Winsor and Adams (1976) reported the results of a study of the composition of tomatoes (cv. Grenadier) from a commercial nursery throughout the season (late March to early October). The sugar content

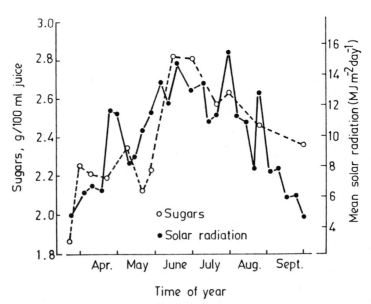

Fig. 3.3. Seasonal trends in the sugar content of the fruit juices of tomato (cv. Grenadier) together with integrated data for solar radiation. Source: Winsor and Adams (1976).

Table 3.6. Effects of Locality, Season (Year), and Planting Date on the Amino Acid Content of Dried Beans[a]

	Amino acids (mg/g)								
	Arginine	Histidine	Isoleucine	Leucine	Lysine	Methionine	Phenylalanine	Threonine	Valine
Locality									
Estancia	26.0 (8.4)	9.4 (3.0)	16.5 (5.3)	24.7 (8.0)	19.8 (6.4)	7.2 (2.3)	17.1 (5.5)	13.3 (4.3)	16.1 (5.2)
State College	14.8 (6.1)	7.8 (3.2)	14.6 (6.0)	20.8 (8.6)	17.2 (7.1)	6.4 (2.6)	14.3 (5.9)	12.2 (5.0)	13.8 (5.6)
Deming	12.1 (5.7)	6.8 (3.2)	13.6 (6.4)	18.4 (8.6)	15.4 (7.2)	5.5 (2.6)	13.0 (6.1)	11.3 (5.3)	12.5 (5.9)
Mean	17.6 (6.7)	8.0 (3.1)	14.9 (5.9)	21.3 (8.4)	17.5 (6.9)	6.4 (2.5)	14.8 (5.8)	12.3 (4.9)	14.1 (5.5)
LSD, $p = .01$	3.04 (0.66)	1.02 (N.S.)	0.75 (0.48)	1.38 (0.38)	0.93 (0.21)	0.48 (0.23)	9.0 (0.30)	0.66 (0.27)	2.26 (N.S.)
Season									
1948	9.5 (4.6)	4.8 (2.4)	12.2 (6.0)	16.6 (8.2)	13.9 (6.8)	5.9 (2.9)	11.2 (3.5)	9.2 (4.5)	10.9 (5.4)
1949	12.1 (5.7)	6.8 (3.2)	13.6 (6.4)	18.4 (8.6)	15.4 (7.2)	5.5 (2.6)	13.0 (6.1)	11.3 (5.3)	12.5 (5.9)
1950	12.7 (5.7)	6.6 (2.8)	14.4 (6.2)	19.8 (8.5)	16.5 (7.1)	6.6 (2.8)	12.8 (5.4)	11.2 (4.8)	13.0 (5.5)
Mean	12.5 (5.4)	7.3 (3.2)	14.4 (6.3)	19.4 (8.4)	16.5 (7.2)	6.3 (2.8)	12.8 (5.6)	10.9 (4.8)	13.1 (5.7)
Mean	11.4 (5.2)	6.1 (2.8)	13.4 (6.2)	18.3 (8.4)	15.3 (7.0)	6.0 (2.8)	12.3 (5.7)	10.6 (4.9)	12.1 (5.6)
LSD, $p = .01$	1.26 (0.13)	0.45 (0.30)	0.60 (N.S.)	1.23 (N.S.)	0.66 (N.S.)	0.33 (0.27)	0.075 (0.45)	0.63 (0.48)	1.17 (0.39)
LSD, $p = .05$	N.S. (N.S.)	N.S. (N.S.)	N.S. (N.S.)	N.S. (N.S.)	N.S. (N.S.)	N.S. (N.S.)	N.S. (N.S.)	N.S. (N.S.)	N.S. (N.S.)
Sowing									
Early	12.3 (5.4)	8.0 (3.6)	14.4 (6.4)	19.0 (8.4)	16.5 (7.2)	6.0 (2.7)	12.8 (5.7)	10.6 (4.7)	13.2 (5.8)
Late	12.7 (5.4)	6.6 (2.8)	14.4 (6.2)	19.8 (8.5)	16.5 (7.1)	6.6 (2.8)	12.8 (5.4)	11.2 (4.8)	13.0 (5.5)
Mean	12.5 (5.4)	7.3 (3.2)	14.4 (6.3)	19.4 (8.4)	16.5 (7.2)	6.3 (2.8)	12.8 (5.6)	10.9 (4.8)	13.1 (5.7)
LSD, $p = .01$	N.S. (N.S.)	1.19 (0.45)	N.S. (N.S.)	N.S. (N.S.)	N.S. (N.S.)	0.38 (0.12)	N.S. (N.S.)	0.68 (N.S.)	N.S. (N.S.)
LSD, $p = .05$	N.S. (N.S.)	N.S. (N.S.)	N.S. (N.S.)	N.S. (N.S.)	N.S. (N.S.)	N.S. (N.S.)	N.S. (N.S.)	N.S. (N.S.)	N.S. (N.S.)

Source: Lantz et al. (1958).

[a] Figures in parentheses are % protein content of respective samples. N.S., not scored.

Table 3.7. Effects of Cultivar and Location on Protein (N × 6.25) Content of Dried Beans (% protein)

| | Locations | | | |
Variety	Deming (4300 ft a.s.l.)[a]	Estancia (6000 ft a.s.l.)	State College (4000 ft a.s.l.)	Mean
295	20.0	30.8	22.8	24.53
641	20.9	32.1	24.8	25.93
'Michelite'	23.8	34.4	25.7	27.97
'Red Mexican'	19.9	29.0	22.5	23.90
2574	19.9	30.9	24.4	25.07
2534	20.0	29.9	26.2	25.37
'Calico'	19.8	30.1	23.9	24.40
Mean	20.44	30.91	24.33	25.23

Source: Lantz *et al.* (1958).
[a] a.s.l. = above sea level.

of the juices increased from a very low value (1.9 g/100 ml) in March to about 2.8 g/100 ml in June, declining to 2.4 g/100 ml early in October. The data, in general, followed the same pattern as solar radiation (Fig. 3.3). Lantz *et al.* (1958) studied the effects of seasons (year) on the protein and amino acid contents of beans. The contents of nine amino acids, arginine, histidine, isoleucine, leucine, lysine, methionine, phenylalanine, threonine, and valine, were studied (Tables 3.6 and 3.7).

Location/Area

Harris (1975) concluded that although the location or geographic area where vegetables were grown had an effect upon their nutritional status, this effect was generally very small. Salunkhe *et al.* (1974) reviewed the earlier research work. Klein and Perry (1982) recently reported the ascorbic acid and provitamin A activity of several selected vegetables from different geographic locations in the United States. They determined the reduced ascorbic acid (RAA) and provitamin A (carotenoid) contents of six vegetables obtained from six cities during two seasons of the year. The mean RAA content (mg/100 g) of cabbage was 45.2; carrots, 7.8; celery, 6.0; corn, 6.5; onion, 8.4; and tomato, 15.3. The vitamin C in cooked cabbage was 22.1, corn, 6.2, and onion, 5.7 mg/100 g. The mean vitamin A activity of carrot was 15,228; cabbage, 114; celery, 133; corn, 219; and tomato, 217 IU. Both the RAA and vitamin A content of vegetables from the six geographic areas varied significantly. The nutrient values of vegetables in the different areas were variable, but not predictable. Because plant foods are widely distributed from the point of growth, local growing and cultural conditions do not have an impact on the occurrence of specific nutrients in vegetables sold in supermarkets. The data obtained from this study (Figs. 3.4, 3.5, 3.6, and 3.7) indicated that the

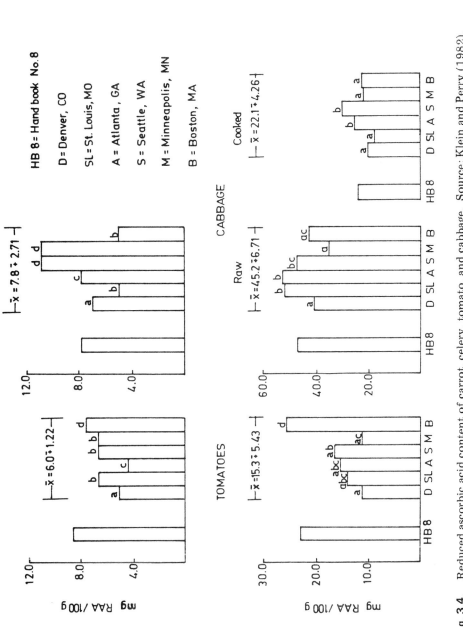

Fig. 3.4. Reduced ascorbic acid content of carrot, celery, tomato, and cabbage.   Source: Klein and Perry (1982).

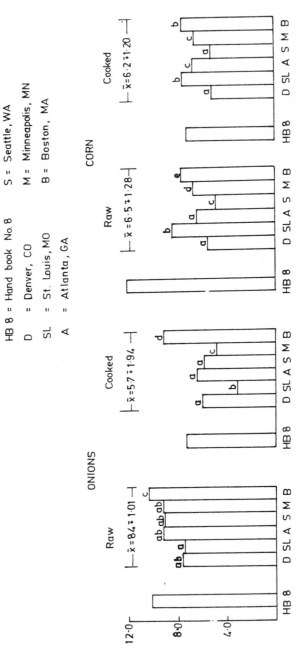

Fig. 3.5. Reduced ascorbic acid content of corn and onion. Source: Klein and Perry (1982).

HB 8 = Hand book No. 8   S = Seattle, WA

D   = Denver, CO   M = Minneapolis, MN

SL = St. Louis, MO   B = Boston, MA

A   = Atlanta, GA

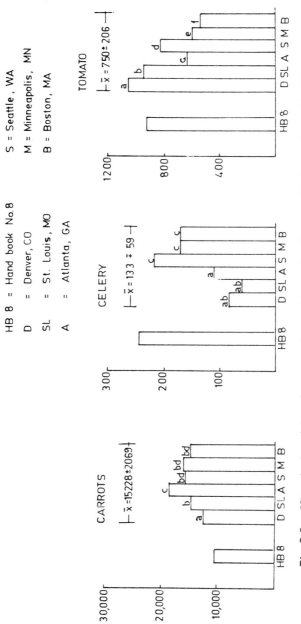

Fig. 3.6. Vitamin A activity of carrot, celery, and tomato. Source: Klein and Perry (1982).

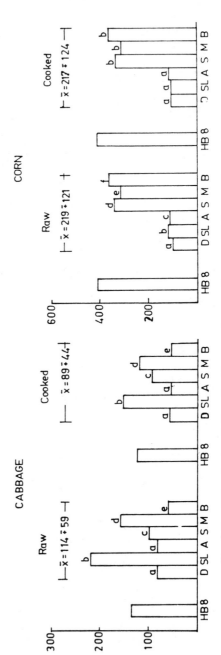

Fig. 3.7. Vitamin A activity of cabbage and corn. Source: Klein and Perry (1982).

ascorbic acid content and provitamin A activity of most of the vegetables examined were lower than the values reported in the USDA Handbook No. 8 (Table 3.3). Klein and Perry (1982) could not definitely state whether this was due to changes in cultivars being grown or to shipping and handling procedures. They further cautioned that if the dietary evaluation of these two important nutrients is based on the tabulated values without consideration of varietal differences or handling treatment, there may be an overestimation of their consumption.

The effects of locality, season (year), and planting data on amino acid content and of variety and location on the protein content of dried beans (Tables 3.6 and 3.7) indicated a very large influence of location on both the amino acid composition and protein content of dried beans. The differences due to variety and season were much less marked (Lantz *et al.* 1958; Smartt 1976).

Soil Fertility and Fertilization

Salunkhe *et al.* (1974) and Harris (1975) reviewed the voluminous literature concerning the early work on effects of soil fertility upon the nutrient contents of vegetables. The contradictory observations generally obtained with respect to effects of fertilization on nutritional quality of vegetables are probably due to variations in soil properties, water availability, and other environmental factors. Salunkhe *et al.* (1974) stated that adequate fertilization with nitrogen, phosphorus, potassium, calcium, magnesium, manganese, boron, and iron was essential for normal plant growth and adequate yields of high-quality nutritious crops. Harris (1975) summarized that the principal effects of improvement of soils was to increase the yield rather than to enhance the nutritional quality of crop plants. Endemic goiter caused by a deficiency of iodine was probably the only evidence of the direct relationship between soil deficiency and malnutrition. The complex interrelationships between nutrient elements of the soil, the effects of one element upon the availability of others to the crop, and their antagonistic and synergistic effects upon each other have created confusion in the literature relating to the effects of fertilizer elements upon nutrient content.

Vittum (1963) reviewed the effects of fertilizers on the quality of vegetables. Based on published reports, he concluded that although mineral fertilizers could increase the nutritional value of vegetables, their chief effect on quality was to correct defects caused by nutrient deficiencies. A well-fertilized crop is usually a high-quality crop.

Nitrogen

Nitrogen is usually deficient in most cultivated soils. The vegetable crops grown on such soils show delayed growth, yellow leaves, poor yields, and, occasionally, low protein content. The deficiency of nitrogen not only reduces yield but also quality of those vegetables in which dark green color is desired (e.g., leafy greens). Nitrogen is an important exogenous factor influencing the protein: carbohydrate ratio (Mengel 1979). The suboptimal nitrogen supply results in higher content of carbohydrates due to the fact that lack of nitrogen restricts protein synthesis so that more photosynthates are available for the accumulation of carbohydrates.

The generous application of nitrogen tends to decrease the vitamin C content of vegetables (Table 3.8). This effect probably results from the competition between carbohydrate and amino acid metabolism for photosynthesis. With high nitrogen supply, more photosynthates are used for the synthesis of amino acids and, thus, less photosynthates are available for the syntheses of hexoses, disaccharides, and polysaccharides (Mengel 1979). The content of carotene is directly linked with the supply of N to the plant. According to Mengel (1979), this relationship is associated with the formation of chloroplasts. Habben (1972) observed that carrot roots, which normally do not form chloroplasts, also showed a close relationship between N supply and carotene content (Table 3.9). Kansal *et al.* (1981) reported that the leaf proteins, β-carotene, and reducing sugars were maximum when spinach was grown on sandy loam soil with the highest level of N (90 kg/ha without FYM). However, the yield, uptake of P, Fe, Mn, Zn, and Cu, and ascorbic acid content were the greatest in response to the highest rates of both urea and FYM.

Geraldson *et al.* (1973) compiled an extensive list of deficient, intermediate, and sufficient NO_3–N concentrations for several vegetable crops at specific stages of maturity. Maynard *et al.* (1976) found that heavy N fertilization caused accumulation of potentially hazardous concentrations of NO_3–N, adversely affecting nutritional quality (Table 3.10). Nilsson (1979) reported that at normal fertilization, the nitrate content in cabbage and leek was highest in plots receiving organic fertilizers or organic nitrogen. Half the amount of fertilizer had a considerably

Table 3.8. Effects of N- and K-Fertilizer Application on the Content of Vitamin C in Various Vegetables

Species	Vitamin C (mg/100 g fresh matter)					
	N_1	N_2	N_3	K_1	K_2	K_3
Spinacia oleracea	27.8	30.3	32.0	28.8	30.8	34.8
Lactuca sativa	9.1	9.1	8.6	8.6	9.1	9.4
Beta vulgaris type *cicla*	67.8	56.1	47.6	49.9	56.1	59.3
Brassica oleracea type acephala	113.0	112.0	99.0	98.0	112.0	118.0
Cychorium endivia	14.0	13.8	13.1	13.1	13.8	14.2
Brassica oleracea type gemmifera	112.0	101.0	93.0	88.0	101.0	100.0

Source: Werner (1957), cited by Mengel (1979).

Table 3.9. Effects of N Supply and Degree of Maturation on the Carotene Content of Carrots

Treatment (g N/pot)	Carotene (mg/100 g dry matter)		
	First harvest	Second harvest	Third harvest
0.3	113	125	136
0.6	118	128	138
1.2	126	138	147
2.4	126	138	146

Source: Habben (1972).

lower nitrate content in the produce, regardless of the type of fertilizer applied. This effect was more pronounced in leeks where the nitrate content fell to about 20% of that present when the normal amount of fertilizer was applied. High doses of NH_4–N have been known to induce deficiency of potassium (Barker *et al.* 1967); specific symptoms of NH_4 excess appear as stem lesions on tomato. This can be controlled by maintaining the soil pH near neutrality or by supplying equivalent K concentrations to enhance incorporation of NH_4–N into nontoxic N compounds (Maynard *et al.* 1966, 1968).

Phosphorus

Kattan *et al.* (1957) reported that high rates of fertilizer phosphorus had a higher sugar content, as measured by soluble solids in the raw juice, than did tomatoes grown with low rates of phosphorus. However, the

Table 3.10. Nitrate–N Concentrations in the Edible Portion of Fresh Vegetables

Plant part	Vegetable	NO_3–N (ppm fresh wt)
Leaves	Cabbage	165
	Lettuce	170
	Spinach	534
Petiole	Celery	535
	Rhubarb	91
Roots	Beet	600
	Carrot	32
	Sweet potato	0
	Radish	402
Fruit	Peas	26
	Snap bean	35
	Tomato	20
Stem	Asparagus	25
Bulb	Onion	14
Tuber	Potato	42

Source: Maynard *et al.* (1976).

difference was barely significant, being detected only in the raw juice and not in the processed product. Phosphorus deficiency leads to poor fill of sweet corn ears, similar to that caused by imperfect pollination, and beets receiving high rates of phosphorus were observed to have better color than those grown at low rates (Blackmore *et al.* 1942). The direct effects of excess phosphorus on the mineralogical composition of vegetables are not known; some secondary effects include induced deficiency of copper and zinc (Maynard and Barker 1979).

Potassium

The differences in the ascorbic acid content of various vegetables by far outweigh the effects of nitrogen and potassium fertilizers (Table 3.8). Werner (1957) found that among those studied, cruciferous vegetables contained high vitamin C. Potassium enhances the efficiency of the conversion of radiant energy into chemical energy (Pfluger and Mengel 1972). Data presented in Table 3.8 show the favorable effects of potassium on vitamin C content of some vegetables. Winsor (1979) found that increasing levels of potassium significantly increased titratable and total acidity of tomato fruits. Under conditions of severe potassium deficiency, titratable acidity as low as 4.3 mEq/100 ml juice was recorded, in striking contrast to those for plants grown at high levels of potassium (8.3–10.9 mEq/100 ml). Winsor further reported that total acidity was highly correlated with potassium content of fruit juice (r = .96). Pushkarnath (1976) reported the effects of K fertilization on total solids and starch contents of several varieties of potato (Tables 3.11 and 3.12, respectively). Pushkarnath (1976) observed that potash fertilization brought about little improvement in total solids or starch content of potato. At low levels of potash fertilization (56 kg/ha), starch content could be increased only by about 1–2%. Vitamin C content of cabbage and leek and carotene content of carrots were not significantly influenced by organic or inorganic (mineral) fertilization (Table 3.13) (Nilsson 1979).

Table 3.11. Average Percentage of Total Solids in 'Kufri Red' and 'Up-to-Date' Potato Cultivars Treated with Potash

Potash (kg/ha)	Total solids (%)		
	'Kufri Red'	'Up-to-Date'	Mean
0	28.6	23.7	26.2
45	28.5	24.2	26.4
90	29.2	24.1	26.7
135	27.2	24.7	25.9
180	28.2	24.2	26.2

Source: Pushkarnath (1976).

Table 3.12. Average Percentage of Starch in Six Cultivars of Potato Treated with Potash

Cultivar	Average starch (%) with potash			
	No application	56 kg/ha	112 kg/ha	168 kg/ha
'Up-to-Date'	15.7	17.5	17.4	19.3
'Craig's Defiance'	18.1	18.6	19.3	19.1
Hybrid O.N. 1360	18.6	18.4	19.5	18.6
'Kufri Safed'	19.6	20.1	21.3	21.0
'Kufri Red'	19.7	19.2	18.5	20.1
'Kufri Kuber'	20.0	23.2	21.4	21.7
Average	18.5	19.4	19.6	20.7

Source: Pushkarnath (1976).

Table 3.13. Ascorbic Acid and Carotene Content of Vegetables (mg/100 g fresh wt) at Harvest (a) and after Storage (b) (mean of 1975 and 1976)[a]

Fertilization treatment	Ascorbic acid				Carotene			
	Cabbage		Leek (stems)		Leek (leaves)		Carrot	
	a	b	a	b	a	b	a	b
1/1 level								
NPK	54	54	13	25	29	29	17	20
Organic N	50	50	13	23	29	18	19	19
Organic N + PK	51	52	14	23	29	17	18	19
Average	52	52	14	24	29	17	18	19
1/2 level								
NPK	51	55	14	23	29	16	18	19
Organic N	49	50	14	23	29	16	19	20
Organic N + PK	42	55	14	23	30	15	18	18
Average	51	53	14	23	29	16	18	19
LSD (5%)	n.s.	1.9	n.s.	n.s.	n.s.	2.0	n.s.	n.s.
C.V. (%)	4.4	2.0	3.6	5.5	6.6	6.7	5.9	4.6
Fertilizers	—	***	—	—	—	—	—	—
Levels	—	—	—	—	—	*	—	—
Interaction	—	—	—	—	—	—	—	—

Source: Nilsson (1979).
[a] n.s., not scored.
*, ***: significant at 5, and 0.1% levels, respectively.

Calcium and Magnesium

The amounts of Ca and Mg in the soil have an important effect upon soil reaction (pH). The presence of adequate amounts of calcium in the soil is required to increase availability of other nutrient elements (e.g., N, Fe, P, and Mn). Adverse effects of high lime concentrations are usually the result of alkalinity rather than the direct effect of calcium. High alkaline conditions, in turn, decrease the availability of P, K, Mn, Fe, and

Table 3.14.   The Effects of Fertilization on Carotenoids of Carrot (mg/kg fresh wt)

Treatments[a]	β-Carotene	α-Carotene	β-+ α-Carotene	β-/α-Carotene	Xantho-phylls
0	105.7	44.0	149.7	2.4	10.1
NPKMg	134.3	51.9	186.2	2.6	17.2
–PKMg	143.5	47.8	191.3	3.0	14.1
N–KMg	122.7	55.2	177.9	2.2	11.9
NP–Mg	149.9	59.4	209.3	2.5	14.7
NPK–	137.3	59.4	196.7	2.3	12.7
Mean	132.2	53.0	184.9	2.5	13.5

Source: Vereecke *et al.* (1979).

[a] 0, without fertilization; NPKMG, complete fertilization; –PKMg, without N fertilization; N–KMg, without P fertilization; NP–Mg, without K fertilization; NPK–, without Mg fertilization.

B (Maynard 1979). Higher calcium content of vegetables grown in limed soil is reported to influence pectic components of the cell wall. Calcium salts have been used to enhance the firmness of canned tomatoes (Winsor 1979).

Vereecke *et al.* (1979) found that β-carotene and α-carotene contents of carrots from plots that were not fertilized with N, P, K, or Mg (controls) were markedly lower than those from plots receiving fertilization (Table 3.14). The ratios of β-carotene:α-carotene ranged from 3.0 (P, K, Mg treatment) to 2.2 (N, K, Mg treatment). These investigators observed that, in general, calcium content of carrot leaves increased, while magnesium content decreased with aging of leaves. The sum of K, Na, Mg, and Ca was almost constant, the lowest value being obtained with N, P, Mg treatment.

Micronutrients

During the growth period, iron content of carrot leaves decreased, and no relationship was observed between values of iron and N fertilization (Table 3.15). As noted in the experiments with onion, leek, and cauliflower (Van Maercke and Vereecke 1976, 1979; Vereecke and Van Maercke 1976), manganese content of leaves was lower for treatments without nitrogen, reflecting a higher ratio of Fe:Mn (Vereecke *et al.* 1979).

Salunkhe and Desai (1983) concluded that postharvest changes in the nutritional quality of vegetables in terms of their mineralogical composition with respect to both macro- and micronutrients are influenced by postharvest fertilization of these mineral elements and postharvest handling and storage procedures. Various physiological disorders of vegetable crops are related directly or indirectly to deficiencies or toxicities of micronutrients, which influence postharvest behavior and nutritional quality of the produce.

Table 3.15. Trace Element Content in the Leaves of Carrot (ppm or dry-matter basis)

Treatment[a]	29–8–1977				24–10–1977			
	Fe	Mn	Zn	Cu	Fe	Mn	Zn	Cu
0	400	85	63	7.3	194	56	33	8.1
NPKMg	472	126	61	6.9	234	136	45	9.0
–PKMg	425	59	47	7.6	214	55	27	7.4
N–KMg	447	98	64	8.0	220	137	48	8.3
NP–Mg	390	114	66	7.8	203	132	34	8.1
NPK–	420	99	59	6.8	158	120	44	7.3

Source: Vereecke *et al.* (1979).
[a] See Table 3.14 for key.

Bible *et al.* (1981) reported that boron-deficient radish plants showed reduced growth and an increased content of the ionic toxin thiocyanate both in foliage and roots. Copper is essential for normal photosynthesis, its deficiency being reflected in the disruption of this vital process. Molybdenum has an important role in nitrate reduction, and the nitrate ions may accumulate in Mo-deficient plants, leading to specific disorders, such as "whiptail" of cauliflower.

Irrigation/Soil Texture

Cevik *et al.* (1981) reported the effects of some irrigation systems on yield and quality of tomatoes grown in a plastic-covered greenhouse in southern Turkey. Tomato (cv. Linda F_1) was grown as a spring or autumn crop in a plastic structure on clay loam or fine sandy loam soil and irrigated by intermittent sprinkler, drip, or trickle irrigation. Intermittent irrigation on the fine sandy loam and drip irrigation on the clay loam soil increased yields of tomatoes in spring. Drip and trickle irrigation produced fruit with the highest vitamin C content in the spring. Dry matter content was higher on the clay loam than on the fine sandy loam soil, but was not affected by the irrigation method.

Species/Varieties

The nutritional composition of vegetables varies greatly with plant species and varieties and cultivars within the species. Watada (1982) determined the ascorbic acid content of fresh fruits and vegetables of several species. The vitamin C was extracted with 6% metaphosphoric acid and determined effectively using a C_{18} cartridge in a radial compression module and 0.5% $NH_4H_2PO_4$ mobile phase in a high-performance liquid chromatograph (HPLC). Watada (1982) tabulated data for snap bean, capsicum, kale, broccoli, cabbage, carrot, cauliflower, tomato, and other vegetables. Ter-Manuel' Yants (1980) estimated vitamin

Table 3.16. Cultivar Differences in Fruit Firmness of Tomato

Cultivar	Compression (mm)[a]	Walls and placentae (%)
'Potella'	3.35	73
J 168	4.13	65
ES 5	4.50	65
'Ailsa Craig'	5.60	63
'Harbinger'	6.07	56

Source: Winsor (1979.)
[a] Under a 2-kg load.

content in different *Brassica* species. Of the seven *Brassica* species studied, kale had the highest (134 mg/100 g) vitamin C content, red cabbage had the highest (11.2 mg/100 g) content of dehydroascorbic acid, broccoli had the highest (1.44 mg/100 g) content of nicotinic acid and choline (90.3 mg/100 g), and brussels sprout had the highest (2.73/100 g) content of vitamin K. Other species included in the study were head cabbage, savoy cabbage, cauliflower, and kohlrabi.

According to Winsor (1979), many aspects of vegetable quality are closely dependent on the choice of variety, including uniformity of color, shape, size, firmness, and hollowness. The varietal differences in fruit firmness and the inner-quality properties of certain varieties shown in Tables 3.16 and 3.17 substantiate these observations (Winsor 1979; Hardh *et al.* 1979). The inner quality varied significantly in tomato fruits of different varieties. The fruits of 'Virosa' and 'Sonato' had high dry matter and soluble dry matter content. 'Virosa,' in addition, had fairly high nitrogen and potassium content. The fruits of 'Sonato' showed the lowest potassium content. In the organoleptic tests, the flavor of 'Stella' was best (Table 3.17).

Table 3.17. Inner-Quality Properties of Tomato Cultivars in 1976

Cultivar	Soluble dry matter (%)	Dry matter (%)	Nitrogen (%)	Potassium (mg/100 g)	Acids (mEq/g)	Acids/ sugar	Flavor 0-5
'Stella'	4.0	5.7	0.13	264	1.72	0.43	3.5
'Sonato'	4.3	6.1	0.13	258	1.86	0.43	3.1
'Revermun'	4.0	5.3	0.10	268	1.53	0.38	1.7
'Virosa'	4.6	6.3	0.15	272	2.01	0.44	2.4

Source: Hardh *et al.* (1979).

Maturity/Harvesting Time

The correct harvest maturity of vegetables is of prime importance, since it is related directly to consumer preference. The purpose and method of utilization of vegetables markedly influence the stage of harvest maturity. Cabbage or cauliflower headed for local fresh markets, for example, is harvested at prime maturity. For shipping or processing, it should be harvested a week early. If harvested too early and stored for a length of time, the vegetable shrivels and loses characteristic aroma, and if harvested too late and then stored for a longer period, it may have higher than average concentrations of sulfur compounds and less ascorbic acid and other water-soluble vitamins (Salunkhe et al. 1974). Certain vegetables such as snap beans and leafy greens are preferred if eaten while semimature (e.g., lima beans, peas, and sweet corn) or fully mature (e.g., banana, potato, beans, and peas), and others if eaten while overmature or postmature (e.g., broccoli and cauliflower). Some vegetables reach their highest nutritive value while they are still immature, others when mature, and still others when overripe (Harris 1975).

Fritz and Weichmann (1979) harvested two early-maturing and two late-maturing carrot cultivars in a sequence of different dates (after one single sowing date for each of the two groups) (Table 3.18) and investigated the effects on quality and storage behavior. The carrots harvested earlier contained less carotene than the ones harvested later, all cultivars showing a similar trend (Table 3.19). The carotene concentration of fresh matter of carrots was higher after storage as well when the crop was harvested at later dates (Table 3.20). Fritz and Weichmann concluded that the carrots of a late harvesting date contained more carotene at harvesting as well as after storage. The ratio of sucrose:monosaccharides increased with harvesting dates and was preserved during storage. The later the harvesting date of early-maturing carrots, the smaller the storage losses, which, in turn, were related to weather conditions (rainfall intensity and relative humidity).

Table 3.18. Cultivation Data and Dates of Harvests of Late- and Early-Maturing Carrots

	Late-maturing carrots			Early-maturing carrots	
	1974	1975	1976	1975	1976
Sowing	2.4	8.4	6.4	24.4	21.4
First harvest	2.9	4.9	3.9	4.8	2.8
Second harvest	16.9	18.9	14.9	18.8	17.8
Third harvest	30.9	1.10	28.9	1.9	31.8
Fourth harvest	14.10	15.10	12.10	—	—
Fifth harvest	28.10	19.10	25.10	—	—

Source: Fritz and Weichmann (1979).

D. K. Salunkhe and B. B. Desai

Table 3.19. Influence of the Harvesting Date on the Carotene Concentration of Carrot[a]

Harvesting date	Late-maturing	Early-maturing
1	28.8	11.6
2	29.3	14.1
3	29.4	15.9
4	29.8	—
5	30.5	—

Source: Fritz and Weichmann (1979).
[a] Amount (mg/100 g) of fresh matter, mean of two cultivars and four replications.

Table 3.20. Carotene Concentration of Late-Maturing Carrots after Different Storage Periods and Different Harvesting Dates[a]

Harvesting date	Carotene (mg/100 g fresh matter) after storage			
	2 months	4 months	6 months	Mean
1	25.2	27.0	26.4	26.2
2	25.6	26.3	26.6	26.2
3	27.7	26.9	26.5	27.0
4	29.0	27.6	27.5	28.0
5	27.2	28.1	28.8	28.0

Source: Fritz and Weichmann (1979).
[a] Mean of two cultivars, three experiments, and four replications.

Table 3.21. Contents of Soluble Dry Matter, Dry Matter, Nitrogen, Potassium, and Acids of Tomato and the Relationship of Acids to Sugars for Different Harvest Dates in 1976

Harvest date	Soluble dry matter (%)	Dry matter (%)	Total nitrogen (%)	Potassium (mg/100 g)	Acids (mEq/g)	Acids/ sugars
May 19	4.0	5.0	0.13	299	1.93	0.48
July 21	4.3	6.2	0.14	272	1.77	0.41
Sept. 15	4.4	6.3	0.11	226	1.65	0.38
F	0.9	8.9*	3.3	40.6**	1.4	3.0
LSD at 1%	1.3	1.5	0.04	37	0.7	0.18

Source: Hardh *et al.* (1979).
*, **: significant at 5 and 0.1% levels, respectively.

from the first clusters (Table 3.21) (Hardh *et al.* 1979). Serdyukov and Emelin (1979) reported that it was necessary to harvest fruits of tomato, sweet pepper, and aubergine under 60–70% of maturity to increase marketability of the combine-harvested produce. The maturity of these vegetables was the reason for increased cracked, squashed, and rotten fruit in the gathered heap.

Days, Degree Days, and Heat Units

The number of days, degree days, and heat units required to grow vegetable crops depends on a number of factors such as species, variety, soil, climatic condition, and plant nutrition. The number of days and degree days required for maturation of three varieties of lima bean, namely, 'Clark's Bush,' 'Evergreen,' and 'Limagreen,' was almost identical, whereas 'Fordhook 242' and 'Concentrated Fordhook' required a greater length of time for maturity (Salunkhe *et al.* 1959). Total days and degree days for the maturity of each variety varied from year to year. Salunkhe *et al.* (1959) stated that both total days and degree days were too variable for the practical estimation of the harvest time of lima beans. These authors further reported that the amount of riboflavin and thiamin decreased progressively as the lima beans advanced in maturity. The Limagreen variety had significantly higher amounts of riboflavin and thiamin than the other varities studied. Regardless of variety, there was no striking effect of time of harvesting noticed on the physical tests (shear press, succulometer, refractometer, Hunter color and color difference meter, specific gravity, number of beans in 100 g, brine separation, and drained weight), chemical tests (contents total, alcohol-insoluble solids, and starch grain character), or taste tests (flavor, cotyledon texture, and color) of canned and frozen beans. Salunkhe *et al.* (1974) have described the influence of the heat units on the nutritional composition of several vegetables, including ascorbic acid and provitamin A (β-carotene). Ottosson (1979) reported the changes in ascorbic acid content of vegetables during the day and after harvest.

Size

Salunkhe *et al.* (1959) noted that regardless of varieties and harvest periods studied, the physical and chemical analyses were directly correlated with the size of the lima beans. As the size of beans increased from tiny to large, the shear press values, weight per bean, alcohol-insoluble solids, and ratio of amylose:amylopectin increased because of additional dry matter in limas.

EFFECTS OF HARVESTING, HANDLING, AND STORAGE ON NUTRITIONAL COMPOSITION OF VEGETABLES

The nutritional composition of vegetables is markedly influenced by various harvesting methods, handling procedures, and storage techniques.

Harvesting

Serdyukov and Emelin (1979) investigated conservation of quality of tomato, sweet potato, sweet pepper, and aubergines under mechanized harvesting, storage, and sale. Tomato fruits harvested by combine mechanized harvesters (SKT–2) were stored under natural conditions of storehouses for 2–3 weeks before sale or transported 1500 km with relatively small losses. Combine-harvested sweet pepper fruits were of high market quality and further sorting was not necessary. They were suitable for the natural conditions of storehouses or refrigerators. About 40–50% of the total yield was harvested at the first gathering, the rest at the second harvest, which was usually carried out by combines. Manual picking caused yield decreases of combine-harvested pepper of up to 25–36% and increased the number of red and rotten fruits. The biochemical analyses of sweet peppers carried out during the period from 25 to 30 days after the first harvest were characterized by intensive vitamin C accumulation in fruits. Peppers of the 'Mikhalev' variety showed the ability to increase vitamin C over 25% during these 5 days (Table 3.22). The combine harvesting of tomato fruits increased the content of insoluble dry substances and decreased the content of acids, while the content of cellulose was approximately doubled. These biochemical peculiarities increased content of dry substances (up to 4.6%). The biochemical composition of varieties and hybrids did not differ significantly (Table 3.23).

Handling, Transportation, and Distribution

Pantastico and Bautista (1976) described postharvest handling of tropical vegetable crops; the extent of their losses, handling procedures, transportation, packaging, and market preparation; and problems related to preservation of quality of vegetables during storage. According

Table 3.22. Dependence of Biochemical Content in Sweet Pepper Under Mechanized Harvesting (1977–1978)

		Mikhalev pepper			Padarok Moldovy		
Date of the first harvesting	Days between harvesting	Dry matter (%)	Total sugar (%)	Vitamin C (mg %)	Dry matter (%)	Total sugar (%)	Vitamin C (mg %)
August 5	20	6.2	3.4	104.4	5.0	2.6	122.2
	25	6.8	3.3	173.2	7.1	3.9	183.4
	30	7.2	3.6	220.8	6.5	3.2	200.3
August 10	20	6.1	3.2	76.8	5.5	2.6	53.9
	25	6.7	4.1	151.1	9.4	3.7	181.6
	30	7.3	3.0	198.6	6.4	9.4	190.4

Source: Serdyukov and Emelin (1979).

Table 3.23. Biochemical Analysis of Tomato Fruits Available for Mechanized Harvesting (1978)

Varieties	Dry matter (%)	Sugars (%)	Vitamin C (mg/g)	Acid (%)	Sugar–acid index
Novinka Pridnestrov'ya	5.9	3.2	18.7	0.6	5.0
Machinery 1	5.8	3.5	26.5	0.6	5.4
Cross 525	6.6	3.7	24.5	0.5	8.1
Ventura	5.4	3.9	18.5	0.6	6.3
Nistru	5.8	3.2	22.1	0.7	4.3
Fakel	5.2	2.8	20.7	0.7	4.2
Niagara 317	5.8	3.3	36.5	0.5	6.4
Florida MN–1	5.6	3.9	21.3	0.6	6.4
Florida 145	4.8	2.6	31.0	0.6	4.0
Ermak	6.4	3.7	20.8	0.5	6.8
Varieties of manual harvesting (average)	3.6	2.5	18.2	0.8	3.1

Source: Serdyukov and Emelin (1979).

to Schoorl and Holt (1982), distribution is an integral part of horticulture and, like production, it needs to be managed effectively. For fresh fruits and vegetables, the management of distribution must be based on the management of quality. This requires understanding of the nature of distribution of its components, namely, the produce, environment, transit time, and the interactions between these components. The management of quality relies on the ability to predict changes in quality (i.e., damage) to the produce. Physical deterioration leads to severe loss in nutritional quality of fresh vegetables during subsequent handling, distribution, storage, merchandising, and marketing.

Storage

Vegetables are living entities even after their harvest and carry out all their life processes until senescence and death. Significant changes in color, flavor, texture, and nutritional quality of vegetables occur during their storage. These changes are markedly influenced by temperature and storage environment (composition and relative humidity). Softening processes which occur during ripening continue throughout the subsequent shelf-life of the fruit. Significant biochemical changes occur during ripening and storage both in fruit walls and in locular contents. Salunkhe and Wu (1974) concluded that nutrient loss from vegetables during storage is largely controlled by storage temperature and the packaging medium. Vitamins, such as thiamin, are comparatively stable, but are noticeably degraded during normal storage. Ascorbic acid, being heat and oxygen sensitive, is easily lost from vegetable products stored under aerobic conditions. In general, niacin, vitamin B_{12} (cobalamine), and pyridoxine are stable during storage, especially in freeze-dried products (Hollingsworth 1970); therefore, none of these will be lost. However, riboflavin is degraded somewhat during storage.

Prestorage Treatments

Vacuum Cooling/Hydrocooling.   Leafy vegetables and salad crops are generally cooled by reducing the atmospheric pressure in hermetically sealed chambers until the reduced vaporizing point of water, created by low pressures in the cooling chambers, cools the produce. According to Ryall and Lipton (1979), the outstanding advantages of vacuum cooling are the speed and uniformity of cooling of adapted commodities. Leafy vegetables, such as lettuce, are difficult to cool with water or air, but they can be field packed and then cooled rapidly and uniformly by vacuum cooling. Other vegetables adapted to vacuum cooling are globe artichoke, asparagus, broccoli, brussels sprout, cabbage, celery, sweet corn, and peas. Rapid cooling methods such as vacuum cooling have been occasionally reported to cause damage to the produce from "shock." Ryall and Lipton (1979), however, stated that highly perishable leafy vegetables like head lettuce, asparagus, spinach, and sweet corn had better quality and longer shelf life when cooled as rapidly as the most efficient vacuum cooling or hydrocooling system permits.

Hydrocooling, or cooling with cold water, is a rapid and effective method of precooling, since water is an excellent material for transferring heat from the produce to the cooling medium (ice or refrigeration coils). Cooling is accomplished by flooding, spraying, or immersion. Sometimes a small amount of fungicide is dissolved in hydrocooling water in an attempt to control fungus growth during storage and transportation of vegetables.

Curing.   Sweet potato, Irish potato, taro, onion, and garlic are cured under the sun to heal injured or bruised surfaces. Curing extends the storage life of these vegetables by reducing their moisture content. It also decreases rotting by eliminating surface fungal growth and reducing internal necrosis of tissue.

Treatment with Ethylene.   Salunkhe and Wu (1974) reviewed the effects of ethylene and ethylene-releasing compounds on the storage behavior and nutritional composition of fruits and vegetables. An exogenous application as low as 1 ppm of ethylene stimulates the rate of respiration, hastens ripening, and inhibits seed germination and sprouting of potatoes. Ethylene responses of climacteric fruits have been noted only during the preclimacteric phase, whereas in nonclimacteric fruits, ripening and respiration can be accelerated at all stages of fruit maturity. This is probably due to the difference of climacteric and nonclimacteric fruits in their relative abilities to produce ethylene endogenously. If ethylene is produced in sufficient quantity, its external application would not produce a response. However, addition of ethylene to nonclimacteric fruit may be effective because of the low rates of ethylene production. Salunkhe and Wu (1974) concluded that foliar or postharvest applications of ethephon (2-chloroethylphosphonic acid) had the following advantages: (1) Sorting cost of tomatoes may be reduced due to uniformity of ripening; (2) fast ripening rates will reduce weight loss and may prolong shelf life; (3) ripening rooms are not necessary; (4) yield will increase from once-over harvest; and (5) maturity may be hastened early in the season to obtain marketable fruit with premium prices.

Significant differences in quality factors, such as color, acidity, and sweetness, between control and ethylene-treated tomatoes have been reported. Tomato fruits dipped in solutions of 2-(p-chloroethylthio)triethylamine hydrochloride (CPTA, at 1200, 2400, or 4800 ppm) developed red color in the exocarp, not because of ripening, but because of synthesis of lycopene and its accumulation in carotenogenic tissues (Rabinowitch and Rudich 1972).

Refrigerated Storage

Thorne and Segurajauregui Alvarez (1982) derived equations relating surface color and firmness of tomatoes to storage temperature. These equations were used to predict color and firmness after storage under various irregular temperature regimes. Changes in color and firmness could be used to predict the storage life of tomato fruit under fluctuating conditions between 12° and 27°C. Smittle and Hayes (1979) stored mechanically shelled southern peas (*Vigna unguiculata* L. Walp, cv. Purple Hull Pinkeye) at temperatures of 5°, 25°, and 45°C for 3, 6, and 12 hr. Changes in quality were minimal with 5°C storage and increased with prolonged storage at higher temperatures. These changes consisted of decreases in percentage of green seed, total chlorophyll, sugar, starch, and protopectin; increases in water-soluble pectin and Calgon®-soluble pectin; and discoloration (Table 3.24). The total solids, hemicellulose, and cellulose contents were not affected by storage treatments (Table 3.25). Smittle and Hayes (1979) developed a response curve relating the rate of loss of green seed to storage temperature that will assist in the coordination of harvesting, transport, and processing operations for the maintenance of high-quality product during storage.

Salunkhe et al. (1972) reported the effects of light and temperature on the formation of solanine in potato slices. At low temperatures (0° and 8°C) there was a slow but significant increase in solanine content during a 48-hr period in the dark while the storage temperatures of 15° and 24°C vigorously stimulated the formation of solanine. After 48 hr at

Table 3.24. Effects[a] of Storage Treatments on Percentage of Green Seed, Chlorophyll Content, and Seed Discoloration of 'Purple Hull Pinkeye' Southern Pea

Storage treatment		Green seed (%)		Total chlorophyll (mg/kg)[b]		Seed discoloration[c]
		1975	1976	1975	1976	1976
Initial		35a	59ab	3.0a	5.6a	1.0a
5°	3 hr	33a	59ab	3.0a	5.6a	1.0a
	6 hr	32a	62a	2.8ab	5.8a	1.0a
	12 hr	30ab	61a	2.6ab	5.6a	1.3ab
25°	3 hr	32a	57ab	2.7ab	4.6b	1.3ab
	6 hr	30ab	55bc	2.4bc	4.2b	1.3ab
	12 hr	27bc	53c	2.4bc	4.2b	2.0c
45°	3 hr	25bc	51cd	2.5abc	4.6b	1.3ab
	6 hr	24c	46d	2.3bc	4.0bc	2.0c
	12 hr	12d	29e	2.1c	3.4c	3.0d

Source: Smittle and Hayes (1979).
[a] Mean separation within columns, by Duncan's multiple-range test, 5% level.
[b] Chlorophyll concentration on a fresh-weight basis.
[c] Panel ratings for seed discoloration: 1, none; 2, marginal acceptability; 3, unacceptable.

24°C in the dark, the solanine content reached a concentration of 2.05 mg/100 g slices, which was seven times as much as that in the original (zero-time) sample (Fig. 3.8). The rate of solanine synthesis increased at the later stage. A considerable difference in solanine content between potato slices in cold (0° and 8°C) and warm (15° and 24°C) temperatures under light is illustrated in Fig. 3.9. In the 48-hr exposure

Table 3.25. Effects[a] of Storage Treatment on Carbohydrates of 'Purple Hull Pinkeye' Southern Pea[b]

Storage treatment		Sugar (%)	Starch (%)	Water-soluble pectin (%)	Calgon-soluble pectin (%)	Proto-pectin (%)	Hemicellulose (%)	Cellulose (%)
Initial		3.7a	22a	0.18b	0.19b	0.18ab	2.5a	4.2a
5°	3 hr	3.7a	22a	0.19b	0.19b	0.18ab	2.4a	4.0a
	6 hr	3.6ab	22a	0.18b	0.19b	0.18ab	2.6a	4.2a
	12 hr	3.4ab	22a	0.18b	0.19b	0.18ab	2.3a	3.9a
25°	3 hr	3.4ab	20ab	0.20ab	0.19b	0.18ab	2.8a	4.3a
	6 hr	3.2bc	20ab	0.20ab	0.20ab	0.19a	2.8a	4.3a
	12 hr	3.2bc	19ab	0.21a	0.20ab	0.18ab	2.6a	4.2a
45°	3 hr	2.9c	20b	0.19b	0.20ab	0.19a	2.5a	4.4a
	6 hr	2.4d	19b	0.20ab	0.21ab	0.17bc	2.5a	4.3a
	12 hr	2.0e	18b	0.21a	0.22a	0.16c	2.6a	3.9a

Source: Smittle and Hayes (1979).
[a] Mean separation within columns by Duncan's multiple-range test, 5% level.
[b] All carbohydrates are percentage of fresh weight.

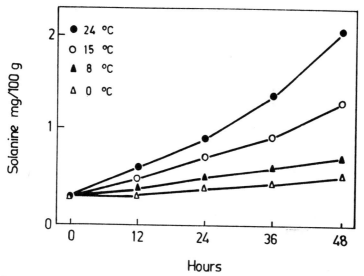

Fig. 3.8.   Effects of temperature on solanine formation in potato slices stored in the dark. Source: Salunkhe *et al.* (1972).

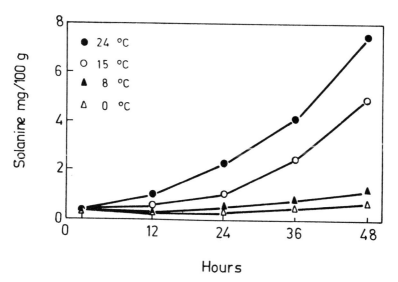

Fig. 3.9.   Effects of light exposure (200 fc) on solanine formation in potato slices at different temperatures. Source: Salunkhe *et al.* (1972).

to 200 fc light at 24°C, the solanine concentration increased up to 7.4 mg/100 g slices. In general, the light increased the rate of solanine synthesis three to four times more than in the dark.

Controlled Atmosphere (CA) Storage

Chang and Kays (1981) reported effects of low oxygen storage on sweet potato roots. Respiration of sweet potatoes was significantly depressed by low oxygen concentrations, from 5 to 15% compared to 20% O_2, but it was high at 2.5% O_2. The total sugar accumulated with low oxygen (2.5 and 5.0% O_2) storage. Protopectin was low in roots stored at low O_2 concentrations, but the water-soluble pectin was not significantly affected (Figs. 3.10 and 3.11). Kurki (1979) measured leek quality with reference to dry matter content, vitamin C and provitamin A, reducing sugars, chlorophyll, total N, and storage loss after 3, 4, 5, and 6 months in CA storage (1% O_2; 10% CO_2 at 0°C, and 100% RH) and in two normal air storages (−1°C, 75% RH and 0°C, 100% RH). In vegetables stored in the optimum CA conditions, provitamin A and the amount of chlorophyll were higher than in normal storage. The CA-stored leek had a strikingly higher amount of chlorophyll and carotene (Table 3.26).

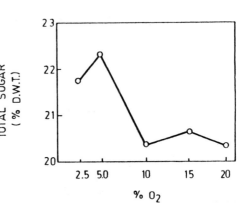

Fig. 3.10. Effects of storage gas oxygen concentration on the total sugar content (% dry weight) of stored sweet potato roots (mean separation by Duncan's multiple range test, 5% level). Source: Chang and Kays (1981).

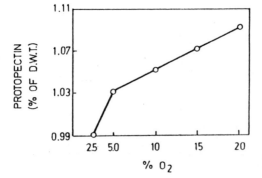

Fig. 3.11. Effects of storage gas oxygen concentration on protopectin (% dry weight) of potato roots (mean separation by Duncan's multiple range test, 5% level). Source: Chang and Kays (1981).

Table 3.26. Content of Dry Matter, Vitamin C, Reducing Sugars, Total N, Chlorophyll, and Carotene in Leek Stored in Different Conditions

Length of storage (months)	Dry matter (%)	Vitamin C (mg/g dry matter)	Reducing sugars (% of dry matter)	Total N (% of dry matter)	Chlorophyll (mg/g dry matter)	Carotene (mg/g dry matter)
1	2	3	4	5	6	7
CA storage: 0°C, R.H. > 95%, O_2 = 1%, CO_2 = 10%						
0	10.1	3.68	46.5	2.82	0.860	0.150
3	8.9	2.65	37.1	3.15	0.773	0.126
4	8.1	2.50	34.4	3.07	0.625	0.100
5	8.5	2.42	32.1	3.28	0.595	0.067
6	8.3	2.04	21.5	3.18	0.510	0.046
Cold storage: −1°C, R.H. = 75%, normal air						
0	10.5	3.68	46.5	2.82	0.860	0.150
3	12.0	2.24	40.9	3.01	0.467	0.044
4	12.5	1.98	36.2	3.21	0.285	0.024
5	12.9	1.12	22.0	3.28	0.165	0.012
6	13.6	1.01	14.0	3.29	0.090	0.009
Cold storage: 0°C, R.H. > 95%, normal air						
0	10.1	3.68	46.5	2.82	0.860	0.150
3	9.1	2.65	41.0	3.46	0.638	0.038
4	9.3	2.59	33.1	3.30	0.190	0.004

Source: Kurki (1979).

Singh *et al*, (1972A) observed that CA (2.5% CO_2 and 2.5% O_2 at 2°C) with or without prestorage treatment with Phaltan® (1000 ppm) or polyethylene packaging inhibited chlorophyll degradation in lettuce (*Lactuca sativa* L. cv. Great Lakes) throughout a 75-day storage period. A further study by these authors indicated that lettuce heads could be stored for up to 75 days in CA (2.4% O_2 at 1.7°C and 90–95% RH). The prestorage treatments with microbe- or senescence-inhibiting chemicals (Captan®, 1000 ppm; Phaltan, 1000 ppm; Mycostatin®, 400 ppm; and N^6 -benzyladenine, 20 ppm) had detrimental effects on lettuce in CA storage. Neither dry weight nor moisture content of the lettuce, however, was affected by the CA storage. Singh *et al.* (1972B) reported the effects of controlled atmospheric storage on the biochemical composition of lettuce leaves.

Modified Atmospheric Storage/Packaging

In a test of packaging treatments, it was found that polyethylene bags retarded respiration and transpiration and increased shelf life of several fruits and vegetables (Salunkhe and Wu 1974). The use of plastic containers usually resulted in less spoilage of vegetables. Cellulose acetate was the most promising film for wrapping fruits and vegetables. The

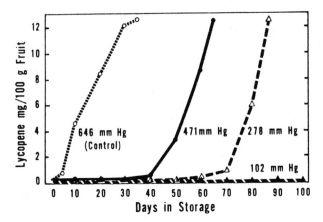

Fig. 3.12. Effects of subatmospheric pressure storage on the formation of lycopene in tomatoes at 12.8°C and 90–95% RH. Source: Wu *et al.* (1972).

modified atmosphere developed (increase in CO_2 or N_2 and decrease in O_2) in the individual packages has been reported to enhance the quality of the produce. Patil *et al.* (1971) exposed Russet Burbank potatoes to a light intensity of 100 fc for 5 days at 21.1°C after irradiation with gamma rays in CO_2-enriched (15%) clear polyethylene packaging. The polyethylene packaging with CO_2 inhibited 33% of the chlorophyll synthesis, but irradiation and the CO_2 environment, alone or in combination, did not affect solanine synthesis.

Subatmospheric Pressure (Hypobaric) Storage

Hypobaric storage has been shown to increase the storage life of several fruits and vegetables (Burg and Burg 1966; Dilley 1977). The main effects

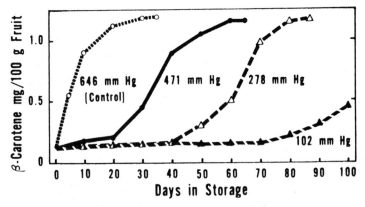

Fig. 3.13. Effects of subatmospheric pressure storage on the β-carotene content of tomatoes at 12.8°C and 90–95% RH. Source: Wu *et al.* (1972).

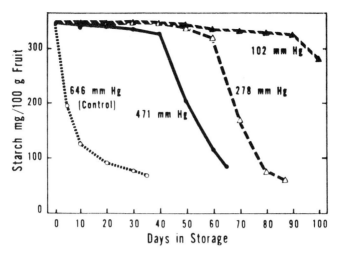

Fig. 3.14.   Effects of subatmospheric pressure storage on the starch content of tomatoes at 12.8°C and 90–95% RH.   Source: Wu *et al.* (1972).

of subatmospheric storage are retardation of ripening, lowering of respiration rate, and removal of volatiles. Salunkhe and Wu (1975) reported the effects of subatmospheric storage on the biochemical composition of several fruits and vegetables such as tomatoes, potatoes, and others. The effects of hypobaric storage on the contents of lycopene, β-carotene, starch, and sugar of tomatoes are depicted in Figs. 3.12, 3.13, 3.14, and 3.15, respectively (Wu *et al.* 1972). The synthesis of lycopene and β-carotene of tomato fruits was strongly inhibited by subatmospheric pressures (Figs. 3.12 and 3.13); the lower the pressure, the longer the inhibition, especially for the lycopene content. With storage at 102 mm Hg,

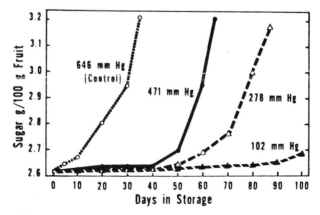

Fig. 3.15.   Effects of subatmospheric pressure storage on the sugar content of tomatoes at 12.8°C and 90–95% RH.   Source: Wu *et al.* (1972).

lycopene formation was completely inhibited for 100 days. After transfer to 646 mm Hg, lycopene formation was stimulated. The formation of β-carotene was less inhibited by subatmospheric pressure storage when compared with that of lycopene. In tomatoes, decreases in chlorophyll and starch and increases in lycopene, β-carotene, sugar, and flavor accompanied the ripening process. The inhibition of these changes under subatmospheric pressure was attributed to the inhibition of the ripening of tomato fruits.

Radurization

Radurization is preservation with ionizing radiation. In recent years, it has mainly been used to inhibit sprouting of potatoes and onions and to retard microbial growth and ripening in some fresh fruits and vegetables. Salunkhe (1961) reviewed the effects of gamma radiation on the storage behavior and nutritional quality of several fruits and vegetables. Ascorbic acid is the most radiosensitive vitamin. According to Salunkhe (1961), at the pasteurization and sprout inhibition dose, negligible losses of nutrients take place in the irradiated fruits and vegetables. The radiation dose effects were determined on several nutritional components of fruits and vegetables such as vitamins, carbohydrates, proteins, pigments (β-carotene), and minerals. In general, the degradation of the complex components of fruits and vegetables such as cellulose, hemicellulose, and protopectin was noticed when these were irradiated at high (over 5×10^5 rad) doses. The softening effects of radiation showed some promising possibilities. Slightly older corn, asparagus, or peas could be irradiated (the pericarp of corn, the fiber of asparagus, and the cellulose of peas could be "softened") and the product could be made more "edible." Subsequent to irradiation, storage life of strawberries, sweet cherries, and mushrooms can be increased by inhibiting microbial growth.

Chemicals Used to Preserve Vegetable Quality

Chemicals protect the quality of fruits and vegetables during their growth, development, and postharvest storage. Various types of chemicals are used to protect food, including insecticides, herbicides, fungicides, nematocides, growth regulators, desiccants, antioxidants, ethylene absorbents, senescence retardants, and wax emulsions. Chemical preservation of food brings full flavor and nourishment to the consumer. Several physiological disorders have been controlled by the direct postharvest application of calcium to fruit and vegetable products. The ripening of green tomatoes (cv. Daydream), as expressed by change of color, increased ethylene evolution, and respiration was inhibited when the calcium content of the fruit was raised to greater than 40 mg Ca/100 g fresh weight (Wills and Tirmazi 1979). The inhibition of ripening was not specific to calcium; other divalent ions such as Mn, Co, and Mg were as effective as calcium. The monovalent metal ions such as Na and K were comparatively less effective than calcium, but did give some retardation of ripening. It is thus possible that the nutritional quality of certain fruits and vegetables can be preserved by treating them with more effective chemicals, especially to protect the loss of valuable mineral nutrients such as calcium, phosphorus, and iron.

Wu and Salunkhe (1974) described the use of several chemicals to increase the nutritional value and quality of economic plants, including vegetables. Growth regulators such as auxins (2,4-D, s-triazines, and other herbicides) have been used to increase protein content and to favorably alter the amino acid composition. Increases in carbohydrate, vitamin, mineral, and pigment contents due to chemical treatments have been noticed. Salunkhe et al. (1962) reported that treatment of N^6-benzyladenine (BA, at 5, 10, and 20 ppm) increased the shelf-life of cauliflower, endive, parsley, snap bean, lettuce, radish, bunching onion, and cabbage. General degradation sets in soon after the crop is harvested, resulting in destruction of soluble ribonucleic acid (s-RNA). Thus, protein synthesis slows down and, as the mechanism of protein formation is hindered, the pigments and other biochemical constituents disintegrate. Salunkhe et al. (1962) reasoned that the primary step in the degradation of s-RNA probably involves the loss of the end group, adenine. The treatment of crops with BA, therefore, provides the necessary adenine to restore s-RNA molecules. Due to this, protein synthesis will be maintained and the treated produce will stay fresh for a longer time.

El-Mansy et al. (1967) reported that pre- or postharvest treatments of lettuce with 6-furfurylamino purine (kinetin) or BA, followed by storage at 4.4°C and 85% RH, resulted in higher values of moisture content, total chlorophyll, and total insoluble nitrogen. Inhibition of respiration (CO_2 evolution) during storage was directly related to the concentrations of both kinetin and BA. On the other hand, the stimulation of O_2 consumption under the action of both chemicals was conversely related to their concentrations. The postharvest application of the hormones yielded the most promising results. Kinetin was more effective than BA, and both maintained higher quality ratings than untreated (control) lettuce.

Salunkhe et al. (1971A) reported that the treatment of peas and sweet corn with s-triazine compounds (Simazine®, Atrazine®, Igran®, or 2-methylthio-4-ethyl amino-6-isopropylamino-s-triazine, Ametryne®) at the rate of 2 lb/acre decreased the total nitrogen and soluble-protein contents in the seeds of peas. However, Simazine or Igran at 0.5 and 0.125 lb/acre, Propazine® at 2 and 0.5 lb/acre, Prometone® at all three rates, and Ametryne at 0.125 lb/acre significantly increased the total nitrogen and soluble-protein contents, while decreasing the starch and soluble sugars of pea seeds. The contents of total and individual amino acids in most

Table 3.27. Effects of Soil Treatment of Telone and Nemagon on the Content of Total and Reducing Sugars, Total Nitrogen, Total Carotenes, and β-Carotene, and the Rate of Respiration of Carrots under Field Conditions

Chemical	Dosage (gal./acre)	Total sugars (%)	Reducing sugars (%)	Total N (%)	Total carotenes (μg/100 g)	β-Carotene (μg/100 g)	Respiration (μl O$_2$/hr/g)
Control		4.70	2.27	0.14	5359	4927	108.8
Telone	10	5.95**	1.89ns	0.13ns	6361**	5881**	94.9*
	20	5.42**	2.04ns	0.14ns	6746**	6270**	88.5*
	30	5.72**	2.18ns	0.16ns	7790**	7315**	79.1**
Nemagon	1	5.00*	2.28ns	0.15ns	6216**	5668**	82.8*
	2	6.10**	1.98ns	0.14ns	6734**	6182**	82.8*
	3	5.95**	2.10ns	0.15ns	7724**	6650**	75.3*

Source: Salunkhe *et al.* (1971B).
*, **, Significantly different from control at 0.05 and 0.01 levels, respectively. ns, Not significantly different from control at 0.05 level.

cases were in higher amounts when the plants were treated with s-triazine compounds. In almost every treatment, isoleucine, histidine, and cystine were lower in amount than the controls in pea seeds. In sweet corn, only glutamic acid was lower in both years.

In an extensive study, Wu *et al.* (1970) demonstrated that soil fumigation with Telone® (1,3-dichloropropane) and Nemagon® (1,2-dichloro-3-chloropropane) brought about significant increases in the content of total carotenes and β-carotene of carrot and sweet corn. The amounts of total carotenes were 10–46% and that of β-carotene 11–48% above control values. Further study by Salunkhe *et al.* (1971B) indicated that soil fumigation with Telone and Nemagon brought about a considerable increase in the contents of total carotenes (16–45%) and β-carotene (15–48%) in carrot roots grown under field conditions (Table 3.27). Soil fumigation with these chemicals also influenced the composition of sweet corn seeds. The total carotenoids of sweet corn seeds increased up to 33% in 1969 and 26% in 1970. The beneficial effects of these chemicals on increase in β-carotene were attributed to the probable increase in the rate of degradation of carotenoids in the plant or the absorption of Telone or one of its metabolites and further metabolization taking part directly in carotenoid biosynthesis.

REFERENCES

Barker, A. V., Maynard, D. N., and Lachman, W. H. 1967. Induction of tomato stem and leaf lesions and potassium deficiency by excessive ammonium nutrition. Soil Sci. *103*, 319–327.

Bible, B. B., Ju, H. Y., and Chong, C. 1981. Boron deficiency in relation to growth and thiocyanate toxin content of radish. Sci. Hortic. *15*, 201–205.

Blackmore, R., Neuman, F., Brown, H. D., and Burrell, R. C. 1942. Relation of fertility levels and temperature of the colour and quality of garden beets. Proc. Am. Soc. Hortic. Sci. *40*, 545–548.

Boswell, V. R. 1961. What we need in quality of vegetables. Proc. 23rd Eastern States Agron. Conf. (mimeo), 7–16.

Bourne, M. C. 1982. Effect of temperature on firmness of raw fruits and vegetables. J. Food Sci. *47*, 440–444.

Burg, S. P., and Burg, E. A. 1966. Fruit storage at subatomospheric pressure. Science *153*, 314–315.

Cantliffe, D. J. 1972. Nitrate accumulation in spinach grown at different temperatures. J. Am. Soc. Hortic. Sci. *97*, 674–676.

Cevik, B., Kirda, C., and Ding, G. 1981. Effect of some irrigation systems on yield and quality of tomato grown in a plastic covered greenhouse in the south of Turkey. Acta Hortic. *119*, 333–342.

Chang, L. A., and Kays, S. J. 1981. Effect of low oxygen storage on sweet potato roots. J. Am. Soc. Hortic. Sci. *106*(4), 481–483.

Crosby, D. G. 1966. Natural cholinesterase inhibitors in food. *In* Toxicants Occurring Naturally in Foods, Publ. *1354*, 112. National Academy of Sciences, National Research Council, Washington, DC.

Dilley, D. R. 1977. Hypobaric storage of perishable commodities, fruits, vegetables, flowers, and seedlings. Acta Hortic. *62*, 61–70.

El-Mansy, H. I., Salunkhe, D. K., Hurst, R. L., and Walker, D. R. 1967. Effects of pre- and postharvest applications of 6-furfuralaminopurine and N^6-benzyladenine on physicochemical changes in lettuce (*Lactuca sativa* L.). Int. J. Hortic. Res. *7*, 81–83.

Fassett, D. W. 1973. Oxalates. *In* Toxicants Occurring Naturally in Foods. Second edition. Report of the Committee on Food Protection, Food and Nutrition Board, National Academy of Sciences, National Research Council, Washington, DC.

FAO. 1972. Food Composition Table for Use in East Asia. FAO and U.S. Department of Health, Education and Welfare, Washington, DC.

Feingold, B. F. 1973. Food additives and child development. Hosp. Prac. *8*, 10–21.

Feingold, B. F. 1975. Why Your Child Is Hyperactive? Random House, New York.

Franke, W. 1959. Ueber die Biosynthese des Vitamins C. 2. Mitteilung. Planta *45*, 166–197. Cited by Rosenfeld (1979).

Fritz, D., and Weichmann, J. 1979. Influence of the harvesting date of carrots on quality and quality preservation. Acta Hortic. *93*, 91–100.

Geraldson, C. M., Klacan, G. R., and Lorenz, O. A. 1973. Plant analysis as an aid in fertilizing vegetable crops. *In* Soil Testing and Plant Analysis. L. M. Walsh and J. D. Beaton, (Editors). Soil Science Society of America, Madison, WI.

Gopala Rao, P., Mallikarjuna, K., and Gururaja Rao, G. 1980. Nutritional evaluation of some green leafy vegetables. Indian J. Nutr. Diet. *17*, 9–12.

Green, M. A. 1962. The natural occurrence of goitrogenic agents. Rec. Progr. Horm. Res. *18*, 187.

Habben, J. 1972. Einfluss von Dungung und Standort auf die buildung Wertgebender Inhaltsstoffe in Mohren (*Daucus carota* L.). Dissertation der Fakultat fur Landwirtschaft und Gartenbau der Technischen Universitat, Munchen. Cited by Mengel (1979).

Hardh, K., Murmann, T., and Seppala, J. 1979. Effect of chemical constituents of tomato on its keeping quality. Acta Hortic. *93*, 387–393.

Harris, R. S. 1975. Effects of agricultural practices on the composition of foods. 1. Effects of agricultural practices on foods of plant origin. *In* Nutritional

Evaluation of Food Processing. 2nd Edition, pp. 33–57. R. S. Harris and E. Karmas (Editors). AVI Publishing Co., Westport, CT.

Hollingsworth, D. F. 1970. Effects of some new production and processing methods on nutritive values. J. Am. Diet. Assoc. 57(3), 247.

Kansal, B. D., Singh, B., Bajaj, K. L., and Kaul, G. 1981. Effect of different levels of nitrogen and FYM on yield and quality of spinach (Spinacia oleracea L.). Qualitas Plant. Foods Hum. Nutr. 31(2), 163–170.

Kattan, A. A., Stark, F. C., and Kramer, A. 1957. Effect of certain preharvest factors on yield and quality of raw and processed tomatoes. Proc. Am. Soc. Hortic. Sci. 69, 327–342.

Klein, B. P., and Perry, A. K. 1982. Ascorbic acid and vitamin A activity in selected vegetables from different geographical areas of the United States. J. Food Sci. 47, 941–945.

Kurki, L. 1979. Leek quality changes in CA storage. Acta Hortic. 93, 85–90.

Lantz, E. M., Gough, H. W., and Cambell, A. M. 1958. Nutrients in beans, effects of variety, location and years on the protein and amino acid content of dried beans. J. Agric. Food Chem. 6, 58–60.

Lindstrand, K. 1979. Food value of vegetables (abstract). Acta Hortic. 93, 19.

Maynard, D. N. 1979. Nutritional disorders of vegetables: A review. J. Plant Nutr. 1, 1.

Maynard, D. N., and Barker, A. V. 1979. Regulation of nitrate accumulation in vegetables. Acta Hortic. 93, 153–162.

Maynard, D. N., Barker, A. V., and Lachman, W. H. 1966. Ammonium-induced stem and leaf lesions of tomato plants. Proc. Am. Soc. Hortic. Sci. 88, 516–520.

Maynard, D. N., Barker, A. V., and Lachman, W. H. 1968. Influence of potassium on the utilization of ammonium by tomato plants. Proc. Am. Soc. Hortic. Sci. 92, 537–542.

Maynard, D. N., Barker, A. V., Minotti, P. L., and Peck, N. H. 1976. Nitrate accumulation in vegetables. Adv. Agron, 28, 71–118.

Mengel, K. 1979. Influence of exogenous factors on the quality and chemical composition of vegetables. Acta Hortic. 93, 133–151.

Murphy, E. L. 1973. Personal communication. Cited by D. K. Salunkhe et al. Assessment of nutritive value, quality and stability of cruciferous vegetables during storage and subsequent processing. In Storage, Processing and Nutritional Quality of Fruits and Vegetables. D. K. Salunkhe (Editor). CRC Press, Boca Raton, FL.

National Academy of Sciences, National Research Council. 1968. Food and Nutrition Board Recommended Dietary Allowances. 7th Edition. National Academy of Sciences, National Research Council, Washington, DC.

Nicholls, L., Sinclair, H. M., and Jelliffe, D. B. 1961. Tropical Nutrition and Dietetics. 4th Edition. Bailliere, Tindall and Cox, London.

Nilsson, T. 1979. Yield, storage ability, quality and chemical composition of carrot, cabbage and leek at conventional and organic fertilizing. Acta Hortic. 93, 209–223.

Ottosson, L. 1979. Changes in ascorbic acid in vegetables during the day and after harvest. Acta Hortic. 93, 435–442.

Pantastico, E. B., and Bautista, O. K. 1976. Postharvest handling of tropical vegetable crops. HortSci. 11, 122–124.

Patil, B. C., Singh, B., and Salunkhe, D. K. 1971. Formation of chlorophyll and solanine in Irish potato (Solanum tuberosum L.) tubers and their control by gamma radiation and CO_2 enriched packaging. Lebensm. Wiss. Technol. 4(4), 123–125.

Paul, A. A., and Southgate, D. A. T. 1978. In The Composition of Foods. 4th Edition. R. A. McCance and E. M. Widdowson (Editors). HMSO, London.

Pfluger, R., and Mengel, K. 1972. The photochemical activity of chloroplasts from various plants with different potassium nutrition. Plant and Soil *36*, 417–425.

Platt, B. S. 1962. Table of Representative Values of Foods Commonly Used in Tropical Countries. Medical Research Council, Special Report Series *302*.

Pushkarnath, 1976. Potato in Subtropics. Orient Longman, New Delhi.

Rabinowitch, H. D., and Rudich, J. 1972. Effects of Ethephon and CPTA on colour development of tomato fruits at night temperatures. HortSci. *22*, 315–322.

Rick, C. M. 1978. The tomato. Scient. Am. *239*(2), 66–76.

Robertson, G. L., and Kermode, W. J. 1981. Salicylic acid in fresh and canned fruits and vegetables. J. Sci. Food Agric. *32*, 833–836.

Rosenfeld, H. J. 1979. Ascorbic acid in vegetables grown at different temperatures. Acta Hortic. *93*, 425–433.

Ryall, A. L., and Lipton, W. J. 1979. Handling, Transportation and Storage of Fruits and Vegetables. 2nd Edition, Vol. 1: Vegetables and Melons. AVI Publishing Co., Westport, CT.

Salunkhe, D. K. 1961. Gamma radiation effects on fruits and vegetables. Econ. Bot. *15*(1), 28–56.

Salunkhe, D. K., and Desai, B. B. 1983. Postharvest quality changes: Nutritional quality: Minerals. *In* Postharvest Physiology of Vegetables. J. Weichmunn (Editor). Marcel Dekker, NY.

Salunkhe, D. K., and Wu, M. T. 1974. Developments in technology of storage and handling of fresh fruits and vegetables. *In* Storage, Processing and Nutritional Quality of Fruits and Vegetables, 121–160. D. K. Salunkhe (Editor). CRC Press, Boca Raton, FL.

Salunkhe, D. K., and Wu, M. T. 1975. Subatmospheric storage of fruits and vegetables. *In* Postharvest Biology and Handling of Fruits and Vegetables, pp. 153–171. N. F. Haard and D. K. Salunkhe (Editors). AVI Publishing Co., Westport, CT.

Salunkhe, D. K., Pollard, L. H., Wilcox, E. B., and Burr, H. K. 1959. Evaluation of yield and quality in relation to harvest time of lima beans grown for processing in Utah. Utah State Agric. Exp. Sta. Bull. *407*, 1–30.

Salunkhe, D. K., Dhaliwal, A. S., and Boe, A. A. 1962. N^6-benzyladenine as a senescence inhibitor for selected horticultural crops. Nature (London) *195*, 724–725.

Salunkhe, D. K, Wu, M. T., and Singh, B. 1971A. The nutritive composition of pea and sweet corn seeds as influenced by *s*-triazine compounds. J. Am. Soc. Hortic. Sci. *96*(4), 489–492.

Salunkhe, D. K., Wu, M. T., and Singh, B. 1971B. Effects of Telone and Nemagon on essential nutritive components and the respiratory rates of carrot (*Daucus carota* L.) roots and sweet corn (*Zea mays* L.) seeds. J. Am. Soc. Hortic. Sci. *96*(3), 357–359.

Salunkhe, D. K., Wu, M. T., and Jadhav, S. J. 1972. Effects of light and temperature on the formation of solanine in potato slices. J. Food Sci. *37*, 969–970.

Salunkhe, D. K., Pao, S. K., and Dull, G. G. 1974. Assessment of nutritive value, quality and stability of cruciferous vegetables during storage and subsequent to processing. *In* Storage, Processing and Nutritional Quality of Fruits and Vegetables, pp. 1–38. D. K. Salunkhe (Editor). CRC Press, Boca Raton, FL.

Schoorl, D., and Holt, J. E. 1982. Fresh fruit and vegetable distribution — Management of quality. Sci. Hortic. *17*, 1–8.

Serdyukov, A. E., and Emelin, V. G. 1979. Conservation of tomato, sweet pepper, and aubergines quality under mechanized harvesting, storage and sale. Acta Hortic. *93*, 125–132.

Singh, B., Yang, C. C., Salunkhe, D. K., and Rahman, A. R. 1972A. Controlled atmosphere storage of lettuce. I. Effects on quality and the respiration rate of lettuce heads. J. Food Sci. *37*(1), 48–51.

Singh, B., Wang, D. J., Salunkhe, D. K., and Rahman, A. R. 1972B. Controlled atmosphere storage of lettuce. II. Effects on biochemical composition of the leaves. J. Food Sci. *37*(1), 52–55.

Singleton, V. L., and Kratzer, F. H. 1973. Plant phenolics. *In* Toxicants Occurring Naturally in Foods. 2nd Edition, pp. 309–345. Report of the Committee on Food Protection, Food and Nutrition Board, National Academy of Sciences, National Research Council, Washington, DC.

Smartt, J. 1976. Tropical Pulses, Tropical Agriculture Series. Longman Group, London.

Smittle, D. A., and Hayes, M. J. 1979. Influence of short-term storage conditions on quality of shelled southern pea. J. Am. Soc. Hortic. Sci. *104*(6), 783–786.

Ter-Manuel' Yants, E. E. 1980. Vitamin content in different *Brassica* species. Tr. Prikl. Bot. Genet. Sel. *66*(2) 99–102; Hort. Abstr. *57*(2), 783 (1982).

Thorne, S., and Segurajauregui Alvarez, J. S. 1982. The effect of irregular storage temperatures on firmness and surface colour in tomatoes. J. Sci. Food Agric. *33*, 671–676.

Tindall, H. D., and Proctor, F. J. 1980. Loss prevention of horticultural crops in the tropics. Progr. Food Nutr. Sci. *4* (3–4), 25–39.

U.S. Department of Agriculture. 1963. Agriculture Handbook No. 8. Washington, DC.

Van Maercke, D., and Vereecke, M. 1976. Substractive fertilization experiment on leek (*Allium porrum* L.) in relation to soil and leaf analysis, yield and quality. Proc. Fourth Int. Colloquium, "Control of Plant Nutrition" *II*, 217–227. Cited by Vereecke, *et al.* (1979).

Van Maercke, D., and Vereecke, M. 1979. Substractive fertilization experiment on leek (*Allium porrum* L.) in relation to soil and leaf analysis, yield and quality. Cited by Vereecke *et al.* (1979).

Vereecke, M., and Van Maercke, D. 1976. Influence of mineral nutrition on cauliflower in relation with leaf analysis and curd quality. Proc. Fourth Int. Colloquium, "Control of Plant Nutrition" *I*, 228–236. Cited by Vereecke *et al.* (1979).

Vereecke, M., Van Maercke, D., Bosman, Ir. G., and Cottenie, Ir. A. 1979. Substractive fertilization experiment on carrots (*Daucus carota* L.) in relation to soil and leaf analysis, yield and quality. Acta Hortic. *93*, 197–203.

Vittum, M. T. 1963. Effect of fertilizers on the quality of vegetables. Agron. J. *55*, 425–429.

Warren-Wilson, J. 1969. Maximum yield potential. *In* Transition from Extensive to Intensive Agriculture with Fertilizers. Proc. Seventh Colloquium, pp. 34–56. Intl. Potash Inst., Berne.

Watada, A. E. 1982. An HPLC method for determining ascorbic acid content of fresh fruits and vegetables. HortSci. *17*(3), 334–335.

Werner, W. 1957. Über die quantitative Bestimmung and das Vorkommen der Ascorbinäure (Vitamin C) in der Pflanze sowie die Abhängigkeit ihrer Bildung von der Ernährung. Diss. Landw. Fakultat der Justus Liebig Hochschule, Giessen. Cited by Mengel (1979).

Wills, R. B. H., and Tirmazi, S. I. H. 1979. Effects of calcium and other minerals on ripening of tomatoes. Aust. J. Plant Physiol. *6*, 221–227.

Wills, R. B. H., Lee, T. H., Graham, D., McGlasson, W. B., and Hall, E. G. 1981. Postharvest: An Introduction to the Physiology and Handling of Fruits and Vegetables. Granada, London/NY.

Winsor, G. W. 1979. Some factors affecting the quality and composition of tomatoes. Acta Hortic. *93*, 335–346.

Winsor, G. W., and Adams, P. 1976. Changes in the composition and quality of tomato fruit throughout the season. Rep. Glasshouse Crops Res. Inst. 1975, 134–142. Cited by Winsor (1979).

Wu, M. T., and Salunkhe, D. K. (1974). The use of certain chemicals to increase nutritional value and to extend quality in economic plants. *In* Storage, Processing, and Nutritional Quality of Fruits and Vegetables, pp. 79–120. D. K. Salunkhe, ed. CRC Press, Cleveland, OH.

Wu, M. T., and Salunkhe, D. K. 1976. Changes in glycoalkaloid content following mechanical injuries to potato tubers. J. Am. Soc. Hortic. Sci. *101*(3), 329–331.

Wu, M., Singh, B., Wu, M. T., Salunkhe, D. K., and Dull, G. G. 1970. Effects of certain soil fumigants on essential nutritive components and the respiratory rate of carrot (*Daucus carota* L.) roots. HortSci. *5*(4), 604–609.

Wu, M. T., Jadhav, S. J., and Salunkhe, D. K. 1972. Effects of subatmospheric pressure storage on ripening of tomato fruits. J. Food Sci. *37*, 952–956.

Effects of Agricultural Practices, Handling, Processing, and Storage on Fruits

Steven Nagy
Wilfred F. Wardowski

Fruits are held in high public regard as sources of wholesome food and are valued for flavor, aroma, and texture. Fresh fruits appeal to virtually all the senses: smell, taste, touch, sight, and even sound, as when one bites into a crunchy apple. Vitamins and minerals are the major contributions of fruits to the human diet; although some fruits are also considered good energy sources and some may contribute notable amounts of fat (e.g., avocados and nuts), sugar (e.g., dates and figs), and protein (e.g., tucuma) (Hall *et al.* 1980; Nagy and Shaw 1980). Fruits may play an important role in the diet by supplying fiber (White 1979). In the United States, there has been a decrease in consumption of fiber from whole grain cereals with a concomitant increase in consumption of fiber from fruits and vegetables. Studies on the dietary fiber contents of apples (Reiser 1979), citrus (Ferguson and Fox 1978; Braddock and Crandall 1981), bananas (Forsyth 1980), and dates (Vandercook *et al.* 1980) have recently appeared. Apples and oranges are reported to produce higher plasma glucose levels and to be more satiating than their respective fiber-free juices (Theander and Aman 1979). Fruits play an especially important role in low-sodium diets for certain disease conditions, including hypertension and kidney disorders (Goddard and Matthews 1971).

One of the greatest health problems in the Western world is obesity (White 1979), and fresh fruits can supply a large portion of a diet while contributing very few calories (Goddard and Matthews 1979). Fruits show favorable nutrient density ratios for some vitamins, that is, a normal serving will supply the recommended daily dietary allowance without concomitantly supplying excess calories (Hansen *et al.* 1979).

Human nutrient deficiencies are most commonly found in developing countries and in specific subsections of industrialized nations

(Munger 1979). Munger concluded that a breeding program to increase nutrients would not change the nutrition of consumers in any important way, but he and White (1979) agreed that the difficult task of changing the eating habits of those with unbalanced diets would be the most logical approach to improving nutrition. In fact, White (1979) judged "increased consumption by those people who need more variety in their diets for nutritional reasons" as the major challenge to the fruit and vegetable interests.

AGRICULTURAL PRACTICES

Through the ages man has learned which crops grow best in his environment. With time, he has developed an appreciation of the interplay of complex variables associated with plant growth and the ability to manipulate those variables. The external environment of plants may be divided into three major divisions: soils, physiography, and climate. These primary factors essentially control where a crop may be grown; if one or more of these factors is limiting, the chances for high productivity are greatly diminished.

Soils

One of the first requirements for the successful growing of a fruit crop is the selection of soil which allows good water drainage, aeration, and extensive root development. Soil, loose surface material of the earth, has been defined in terms of the proportions of particles of different sizes that it contains. The particle-size composition of a soil may be separated into three major size classes, sand, silt, and clay, which, in turn, determine what is called the soil class, textural class, textural grade, or texture (Black 1968). With certain exceptions, the texture of the soil determines whether a fruit crop can be successfully cultivated. Fruit trees differ in their requirements of rooting depth. Citrus and apple trees grow well on well-drained, sandy loam soils which permit deep root penetration, whereas the annonas are shallow rooted and do not require deep soils (Ochse *et al.* 1961). Fruit trees show a wide tolerance to soil pH, but most fruit trees thrive best under slightly acidic conditions.

The attainment of a productive level for any given fruit crop depends upon the supply to the tree of adequate levels of available essential plant nutrients. Many fruit-growing soils around the world are supplied with the necessary elements for tree growth. Sandy soils, however, as found in Florida's citrus growing region, provide a paucity of these necessary elements, and these soils are regarded as infertile. Citrus trees that grew on the sandy loam soils of Florida during the nineteenth and early twentieth century produced low yields of fruit. As research generated information on the nutrient requirements for effective tree growth, fruit productivity increased as the result of judicious fertilization.

Nutrients required for fruit tree growth are customarily divided into three groups on the basis of normal requirements (Ochse *et al.* 1961; Black 1968; Childers 1975): major elements, nitrogen, phosphorus and potassium; secondary elements, calcium, magnesium, sulfur and chlorine; and minor or trace elements, iron, manganese, copper, zinc, boron, and molybdenum. Knowledge of the total amount of individual nutrients in soils is only of limited value in predicting the adequacy of supply of nutrients for tree and fruit growth. Availability, or the effective amount of a nutrient for plant growth, is decidedly the more important factor.

Fertilization

When a fruit crop is unable to obtain sufficient supplies of essential nutrients, either because of insufficient quantity or availability, the plant manifests a number of deficiency symptoms: defects of leaves, flowers, roots, stems, twigs, branches, and trunks; reduced fruit yields; and inferior quality fruit (Ochse *et al.* 1961). Replacement of soil nutrients by fertilization is principally directed to restoring the health of the plant's vegetative parts and to improving the fruit yield. Effects on the nutritive quality of the fruit are seldom considered (Beeson 1949; Maynard 1950, 1956). Nevertheless, direct as well as indirect evidence show that fertilization does affect the nutrient content of tree fruits.

Nitrogen

Nitrogen deficiency unquestionably is the most common nutrient deficiency of soils (Childers 1975). Although soils vary considerably in their content of organic matter and hence, nitrogen, even the richest soil soon becomes impoverished if not supplemented with this important element. The concentration of nitrogen in citrus fruit is usually increased by the application of nitrogen fertilizers (Sinclair 1961). In addition, high nitrogen fertilization tends to increase total titratable acidity (Jones and Parker 1949) and total soluble solids (mostly sugars; Koo 1979) in oranges. Smith and Rasmussen (1961) and Smith (1969) reported an inverse relationship between the quantity of nitrogen applied to grapefruit trees and the amount of vitamin C found in juices of those grapefruit. Reduced levels of vitamin C in juices of oranges (Jones and Parker 1947), lemons (Jones *et al.* 1970), and mandarins (Marsanija 1970), and in cantaloupe (Finch *et al.* 1945) and apple fruits (Murneek and Wittwer 1948) have also resulted from the application of elevated levels of nitrogen fertilizer to these fruit crops. This effect may be caused by increased acid metabolism (Harris 1975).

Phosphorus

Phosphorus plays a direct role as a carrier of energy, takes part in photosynthesis and is a component of both storage and structural compounds, for example, phytin, phospholipids, and nucleic acids. Citrus fruits show variable responses to increasing phosphorus fertilization. Increasing the phosphorus content of fertilizers from deficient to adequate levels markedly affects fruit quality, but increasing the phosphorus content above those adequate levels results in debatable benefits (Embleton *et al.* 1973A). The most consistent effect of phosphorus when applied in amounts beyond those necessary for normal crop yield is to cause the reduction of the juice's citric acid and vitamin C contents (Sinclair 1961).

Potassium

Deficiency of potassium in plants causes dysfunctions in many metabolic processes. Potassium is essential for several enzymatically catalyzed reactions and is involved in protein synthesis and carbohydrate metabolism (Black 1968). Dalldorf (1979) showed, in trials on the effects of potassium manuring of 'Smooth Cayenne' pineapples, that fruits from soil deficient in K had an average sugar content of 11.5%, whereas those fruits that received K_2O at 200 kg/ha showed a sugar content of 14%. Potassium fertilization influences citrus fruit quality more than crop yield. High potassium fertilization is correlated with a greater concentration of vitamin C and total acid in the juice and lower total soluble solids, juice percentage, and ratio of total soluble solids to acid (Embleton *et al.* 1973B).

Secondary and Trace Elements

Nutritional enhancement of fruit by soil or foliar application of secondary (Ca, Mg, S, and Cl) or trace (Fe, Mn, Cu, Zn, B, and Mo) elements is not as apparent when compared to supplementation with the major elements (N, P, and K). In Florida, most citrus trees are grown on sandy soils which are naturally deficient in Zn, Mg, Mn, and Cu. Stearns and Sites (1943) showed that Mg deficiency of oranges and grapefruit in Florida resulted in lower total soluble solids and total acids in the juice. Sites (1944) reported that correction of Zn, Mg, Mn, and Cu deficiency in Florida soils resulted in citrus fruit with enhanced vitamin C levels. Sites (1947) later concluded that no improvement in fruit quality or vitamin C levels would result from the addition of Zn, Mg, Mn, and Cu in amounts exceeding those needed for normal maintenance.

Climate and Geographical Growing Area

Temperature is the most important climatic factor affecting the geographical distribution of fruits. Many studies have demonstrated that the location where a fruit is grown has a definite bearing on the nutrient content of that fruit.

Rathore (1979) showed that guavas harvested in the winter season had a higher ascorbic acid content than fruits harvested in the spring or in the summer. As the ascorbic acid content of the fruits harvested in spring and summer did not differ much, Rathore concluded that the low temperatures in the winter was the factor responsible for the difference, rather than day length or humidity.

Bloom delay of 'Bartlett' and 'Bosc' pears by evaporative cooling caused a reduction in the soluble solids of these fruits (Collins *et al.* 1978).

Growth and maturation of citrus fruits are influenced by the climate of the region in which the fruits are grown. Total available heat is probably the single most important factor in determining the growth rate and time of ripening of citrus fruit (Jones 1961). Scora and Newman (1967) followed seasonal changes in the ratios of total soluble solids to titratable acidity (Brix:acid ratio) for 'Valencia' oranges in six major citrus-producing regions of the United States (Weslaco, Texas; Orlando, Florida; Tempe, Arizona; and Riverside, Indigo, and Santa Paula, California). From November to March, the highest Brix:acid ratios were found in fruit from Weslaco (climate classified as warm, semiarid, subtropical, steppe) and the lowest ratios in fruit from Santa Paula (subtropical climate; cool, dry summers; limited rainfall occurring in late fall, winter, and early spring). 'Valencia' oranges require about 17 months after the mean blooming period to attain commercial maturity in the coastal areas of California (e.g., Santa Paula), whereas they require only 8 months to attain the same marketable maturity in Weslaco. In controlled-environment studies in Japan with fruiting satsuma trees, Kurihara (1969) showed that a programmed day–night temperature regimen of $28°–23°C$ applied during the 3-month preharvest period produced lower total soluble solids concentration in juice than did $18°–13°C$ or $13°–18°C$.

Comparison of grapefruit grown in desert areas of Arizona (summer conditions of hot days and warm nights) to fruit of coastal areas of California (cooler climate) shows that coastal fruit generally contains more vitamin C than desert fruit when harvested on the same date (Rygg and Getty 1955). In a controlled study, Reuther and Nauer (1972) showed that 'Frost Satsuma' fruit contained more vitamin C when grown under cool temperatures ($20°–22°C$ day, $11°–13°C$ night) than under hot temperatures ($30°–35°C$ day, $20°–25°C$ night). Tropical temperatures might have been responsible for the low vitamin C values reported for Nigerian sweet oranges by Mudambi and Rajajopal (1977).

Sunlight Exposure and Location of Fruit

The role of the microclimate within a tree in determining fruit quality has long been recognized. Many investigations (Smock 1953; Heinicke

1966; Jackson *et al.* 1971) have shown that the shading of individual apples and entire apple-bearing trees during fruit development adversely affects the fruit's red color development, size, and storage quality. Seeley and co-workers (1980) showed that when 'Delicious' apples were grown under differing radiant flux densities, red fruit color, soluble solids, starch content, and size were positively correlated with high flux densities.

Wolpert and co-workers (1980) showed that the quality of 'Concord' grapes was affected by sunlight exposure. Exterior cluster grapes exposed to sunlight had a higher sugar content and weighed more when compared to interior cluster grapes.

Sites and Reitz (1949, 1950) studied the effects of light exposure on the rates of chemical changes in 'Valencia' oranges and correlated various chemical constituents with the position of the fruit on the tree. Total soluble solids content was highest in the outside fruit, intermediate in concentration in fruit located in the canopy of the tree, and lowest in fruit located on the inside. Fruit increased in soluble solids with increased height on the tree. In an elaborate experiment, Sites and Reitz (1951) determined the vitamin C content of each orange from a single 'Valencia' tree. Each fruit was removed from the tree and classified as to the direction of exposure to light and the amount of light or shade that it received. Figure 4.1 shows that outside fruit grown on the north and northeast side contained lower amounts of vitamin C than outside fruit from the south side. Canopy fruit, that is, fruit that are partially shaded at all times, were lower in vitamin C than outside fruit from their respective sector. Canopy fruit from the north side were generally lower than canopy fruit from the other sides. Inside fruit, that is, the fruit which hung inside the main body of the leaf canopy, contained the lowest amounts of vitamin C for their respective sectors.

Maturation

Biochemical changes occur throughout a fruit's growth and maturation periods with the result that its composition varies considerably, depending upon its degree of ripeness. Some fruits reach their highest nutritive value while still immature, others when mature, and some when overmature. Furthermore, even within a species, some cultivars will differ significantly from other cultivars in their nutrient contents.

Vitamin C

Kiwi fruit (Okuse and Ryugo 1981) shows an increase in vitamin C with maturation. Quinic acid, the main organic acid in young kiwi fruit, disappears concurrently with the appearance of vitamin C. Papaya (Arriola *et al.* 1980) also shows an increase in vitamin C with maturation, but mangoes (Askar *et al.* 1971), bananas (Thornton 1943), maracuya passion fruit (Arriola *et al.* 1976), and acerola (Asenjo and Moscoso 1950) show a decrease.

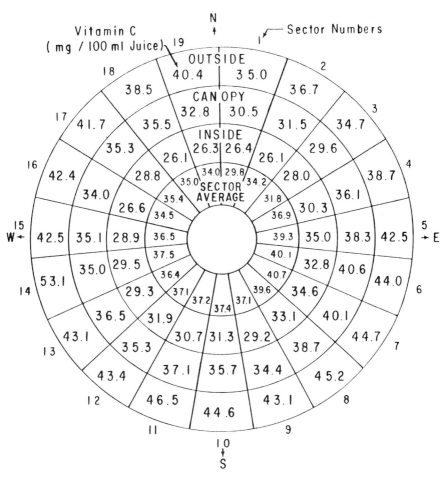

Fig. 4.1. Effect of direction of exposure and amount of shading on vitamin C (mg/100 ml) of juice from 'Valencia' oranges. Source: Sites and Reitz (1951).

Figure 4.2 shows the relationship between stage of maturity and the vitamin C contents of oranges, grapefruit, and tangerines (Harding *et al.* 1940; Harding and Fisher 1945; Harding and Sunday 1949). Immature fruit contained the highest concentration of vitamin C, whereas ripe fruit contained the least. Although there was a lowering of vitamin C concentration (mg/100 g juice) during ripening, the total vitamin C content per fruit tended to increase because the volume of juice and size of fruit also increased with advancing maturity.

Carotenoids and Vitamin A Precursors

It is well known that fruits do not synthesize vitamin A; however, they do synthesize vitamin A precursors, which can be converted by humans into vitamin A. Some provitamin A compounds which can be

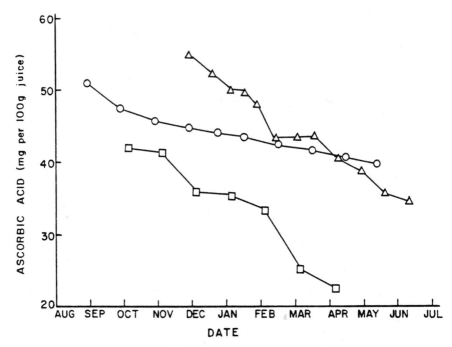

Fig. 4.2. Effect of maturation on the vitamin C contents of 'Valencia' orange (△), 'Duncan' grapefruit (○), and 'Dancy' tangerine (□). Source: Harding *et al.* (1940, 1945, 1949).

transformed into vitamin A are α-carotene, β-carotene, β-cryptoxanthin, and β-apo-8'-carotenal. During the maturation of mangoes, a significant increase in total carotenoids and β-carotenoids (provitamin A compounds) occur both in the peel and in the pulp (John *et al.* 1970). At maturity, β-carotene (= 1.667 vitamin A/μg) constitutes about 50–60% of the total carotenoids in Alphonso mangoes (Jungalwala and Cama 1963). Fair quantities of provitamin A carotenoid compounds have been reported in cantaloupe (Howard *et al.* 1962), papaya (Arriola *et al.* 1975), citrus (Stewart 1980), acerola (Asenjo 1980), and plantains; all of these fruits show an increase in the quantity of carotenoids with maturation.

Thiamin (Vitamin B_1)

Hsu (1974) reported that the thiamin content of citrus fruit increased with maturity. When compared at similar maturity levels, the early season orange, 'Hamlin,' had the lowest vitamin B_1 content, whereas 'Valencia,' a late season orange, had the highest. Compared with many other fruits, grapes and blackcurrants show the highest content of thiamin; the thiamin content of grapes increases during ripening (Peynaud and Ribereau-Gayon 1971). Other fruits showing modest amounts of thiamin (μg/100 g flesh) are pineapples (69–125), raspberries (20–30), mangoes (35–60), melons (60–80), acerola (28–30), dates (80–150), figs (61–79), and tamarinds (44–154) (Hulme 1971; Nagy and Shaw 1980).

Folic Acid

Folic acid, generically described as folacin, is chemically known as pteroylmonoglutamic acid. There are several compounds that exhibit folic acid activity and they differ only in the number of glutamic acid residues they contain. Folic acid is generally found in minimal quantities in fruits; however, it was recently shown that citrus fruits are a rich source of folacin (Ting *et al.* 1974). Amounts in the range of 20–50 μg/100 ml citrus juice have been reported by Ting *et al.* (1974) and Varsel (1980). Ting (1977) reported that wide variation in the folic acid content occurs throughout the growing season and that the concentration increases with the maturation of the fruit. Of other fruits, figs (39 μg/100 g dried; Hall *et al.* 1953), mangoes (36 μg/100 g flesh; Gosh 1960), and avocados (10–60 μg/100 g flesh; Hall *et al.* 1955) contain modest amounts of folic acid, whereas grapes contain the least (1–2 μg/liter juice; Peynaud and Ribereau-Gayon 1971).

Other Vitamins

Pantothenic acid, riboflavin, niacin, vitamin B_6 (pyridoxine, pyridoxamine, pyridoxal), vitamin B_{12}, and tocopherols are found in many fruits at levels below 10% of the U.S. RDA (Hulme 1971). Studies relating fruit maturation to changes in concentration of these minor vitamins are limited. Mapson (1971) states that apricots, gooseberries, blackcurrants, figs, and citrus fruits contain moderate amounts of pantothenic acid. Mango, pineapple, papaya, ascerola, and passion fruit are good sources of riboflavin, whereas tamarind, guava, and passion fruit are good sources of niacin (Nagy and Shaw 1980). Among 26 fruits tested by Polansky and Murphy (1966), bananas (5.4 μg/g) and avocados (4.5 μg/g) contained the highest and the second highest content of vitamin B_6, respectively.

Rootstocks

Many tree fruit crops are scions budded to rootstocks. The selection of a rootstock is based on many factors such as resistance to specific diseases, compatibility with the scion, drought resistance, and tolerance to soil conditions (e.g., salinity effect on scion fruit size, quality, and other desirable features).

The chemical composition of citrus fruit is often influenced by the type of rootstock to which the scion is attached. There are numerous examples that show the effects of the rootstock on the scion fruit's soluble solids (Sinclair 1961; Castle and Phillips 1980), acids (Hearn and Hutchison 1977), lipids (Nordby *et al.* 1979), β-carotene (Issa and Mielke 1980), and vitamin C (Nagy 1980).

Chemical Agents Affecting Fruit Composition

There is an extensive literature on the effects of phytohormones and growth regulators on fruit development and composition; the reader is referred to those comprehensive works (Boysen Jensen 1936; Avery *et al.* 1974; Audus 1953; Evans 1963; Coggins and Hield 1968; Nitsch 1971; Childers 1975) for a better understanding of this subject. In addition, there are a multitude of sprays applied to fruit crops which improve the marketability of the fruit; some of these sprays also cause changes in the nutrient composition of the fruit. It is not our intent to comprehensively cover this vast subject area. There are five main categories of plant hormones that take part in fruit growth regulation and composition: gibberellins, auxins, cytokinins, abscissic acid, and ethylene. In sweet cherry production, growth regulators are extensively used. Maturity of sweet cherries is delayed by gibberellic acid (GA) and advanced by daminozide (succinic 1,1-dimethylhydrazide). GA applied 4 to 6 weeks before harvest increased the ascorbic acid content and decreased the anthocyanin content, but showed no effect on soluble solids, malic acid, or fruit weight (Drake *et al.* 1978). Daminozide application, on the other hand, increased the anthocyanin content of Rainer cherries (Drake *et al.* 1980) and increased the soluble solids of Bing cherries (Proebsting and Mills 1976). In nectarine fruit, application of daminozide and/or fenoprop (2,4,5-TP) at the initiation of pit hardening enhanced fruit ripening and decreased the content of malic acid (Ben-Arie and Guelfat-Reich 1979). Figaron (ethyl 5-chloro-1*H*-3-indazolyl acetate), initially developed as a chemical thinning agent for satsuma mandarins, was shown when sprayed at a later stage in fruit growth to decrease acids, increase sugars, and enhance peel color of the fruit (Iwahori 1978).

Ethylene is an important ripening hormone whose mode of action is not understood. Preharvest spraying of fruit with ethylene precursors (e.g., ethephon) or compounds which stimulate the production of ethylene with the tissues of the fruit (e.g., auxins) causes noticeable changes in the fruit's composition (McGlasson 1971). In contrast, compounds that inhibit production of ethylene cause a slowing of the ripening process and therefore alter the fruit's nutrient content. Aminoethoxyvinylglycine (AVG) reduced ethylene production in apples (Bangerth 1978; Bramlage *et al.* 1980) and blueberries (Dekazos 1980); these AVG-treated fruit showed higher acid levels than their controls.

Soil Fumigation

Soil fumigants are used to control nematodes that attack the roots of plants. Wilting, decreased growth, decreased yields, or total loss of the fruit crop can result if these pests are left unchecked. Brominated and/or chlorinated hydrocarbons are the usual fumigants used. Inorganic bromine is commonly found as a residue in the harvested crop. Masui *et al.* (1978) found that bromine in muskmelon (grown in fumigated soil) was most concentrated in the pericarp, less so in the outer flesh, and least concentrated in the inner flesh. The concentration of bromide in tomatoes grown in fumigated soil is related to the concentration of inorganic bromide present in the soil (Kempton and Maw 1973). There is no relationship between bromide concentration found in fruit and the state of ripeness or the position of the fruit on the plant (Kempton and Maw 1973).

Working with different tomato cultivars, Wambeke *et al.* (1979) observed proportional increases in bromide residue with the rate of methyl bromide used, but this effect was no longer apparent in the second crop. The bromide content was lower in the higher trusses of the second crop. The K content was higher in fruits from fumigated plots and the pH was lower in fruit from plots fumigated with 25 and 50 g/m^2 methyl bromide. The titratable acid content was higher, but these changes did not remain in the second crop. Fumigation reduced the soluble sugars content of the first crop (Wambeke *et al.* 1979).

The uptake of nutrients (N, P, K, S, Ca, and Mg) by tomato plants was increased when they were grown in soil treated with 75 and 150 ppm 1,2-dibromo-3-chloropropane (DBCP) and decreased in plants treated with 300 ppm DBCP (Elliott and Edmunds 1977). No adverse effects on any nutritional components were found in carrots and citrus grown on EDB-, DBCP-, or 1,3-dichloropropene-treated soil (Thomason *et al.* 1971); however, these crops had higher β-carotene contents than ones grown on untreated soil (Thomason *et al.* 1971).

Sass (1975) found that treating soil, 2 months before planting Senga strawberries, with Shell-DD® (a mixture of 1,3-dichloropropene, 1,2-dichloropropane, and traces of higher chlorides) raised the protein content of the fruit. For the most part, there are no detrimental effects from soil fumigation and, indeed, some nutrients actually increase.

HARVESTING AND HANDLING

The care exercised in harvesting and handling fruit often has an important bearing on the quality and nutrient content of that fruit. Chemical and biochemical changes continue throughout a fruit's preharvest and postharvest life. The interruption of water supply to the fruit after removal from the parent plant must be a trauma of the first magnitude. Environmental conditions of temperature, humidity, and atmospheric composition are important to the quality and indeed the very life of fruits after harvest. Quality will decline concurrently with transpiration, respiration, and a number of other biochemical and physical changes. Fruit ultimately reaches a point at which it is not acceptable to the consumer or processor, as, for example, the excessive softening of apples caused by pectic enzymes and/or the spoilage of citrus fruits by microorganisms. The principles and information for fresh fruit generally apply whether they are to be consumed as fresh fruit or utilized for processing (see Part III).

Time of Harvest

Most fruits are harvested before they reach optimum flavor, color, and nutrient content. Fruits picked before the onset of ripening tend to be firmer and less susceptible to bruising during harvesting and subsequent premarket handling. Harvest times for fruit differ considerably and depend, in large measure, on the fruit's ripening pattern. A large number of fruits show a sudden sharp rise in respiratory activity, termed the climacteric rise, during their life cycle; whereas others, which do not show this rise, are classified as nonclimacteric. The time of harvest for climacteric fruit is critical for maximum storage and market life (Fig. 4.3). With the exception of the avocado, climacteric fruits normally ripen on the tree; however, they are usually harvested prior to the onset of the climacteric and stored under carefully controlled conditions to suppress the ripening process (Krochta and Feinberg 1975). Nonclimacteric fruits, such as citrus, are normally allowed to ripen on the parent plant prior to harvesting (Sinclair 1961; Eskin *et al.* 1971). Harvesting of citrus fruits in Florida, for example, is strictly

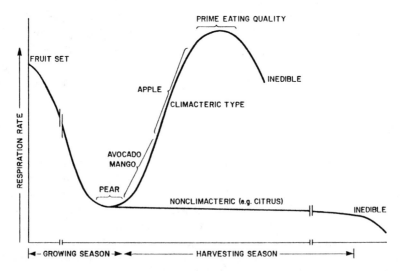

Fig. 4.3. Life cycles of typical fruits. The respiration rate of a typical "climacteric-type" fruit may increase 10-fold after harvest. This is not true of "nonclimacteric" fruit such as citrus. Source: Grierson (1973).

regulated (Florida Department of Citrus 1975). Maturity tests covering color break, juice content, Brix, total (titratable) acid, and ratio of Brix:total acid are conducted on citrus fruit to ascertain whether they can be legally sold (Wardowski *et al.* 1979).

Effects of Harvest Methods on Nutrients

The trend in harvesting fruit is toward more mechanization, although hand picking is still an established practice for some fruits. Advantages of hand picking over mechanical harvesting are as follows (Woodroof 1975): (1) The fruit is bruised less and can be held longer before processing; (2) the fruit may be allowed to become more mature before harvesting; (3) picking is more complete and the total yield is greater; and (4) the plants are bruised less and continue to produce over a longer period of time. Ever-bearing varieties are hand picked to avoid damaging both the mature and immature fruit. Some fruits, especially berries, require multiple pickings because they ripen over several weeks.

Limited studies are available on the effects of rough-handled, hand-picked fruit on nutrient contents. Rough handling generally causes structural and physiological disorganization of fruit tissue with a concomitant increase in the activities of degradative enzymes. As a result of cellular disorganization, oxidative destruction of vitamin C in fruits by ascorbic acid oxidase, phenolase, cytochrome oxidase, and peroxidase is enhanced. Dropping grapefruit from heights of up to 1.52 m onto a hard surface increased respiration and ethylene production in relation to the height of the drop (Vines *et al.* 1968). With grapefruit, ethylene evolution contributes to the overall ripening phase by causing membrane changes, increasing the activity of certain membrane-oriented enzymes, and accelerating the activity of proteolytic enzymes associated with color development (Sinclair 1972). Bruising of tomatoes had little effect on ascorbic acid content (Krochta *et al.* 1975), whereas dropping mangoes to the ground caused a decided decrease of this vitamin during storage (Yagi *et al.* 1978).

Mechanical harvesting of fruits may affect the composition of the fruit and/or juice product. In mechanically harvested Montmorency cherries, Arnold and Mitchell (1970) observed a greater movement of tannins into the outer cortical cells during a 24-hr soak. Wounding of mechanically harvested Engishofer apples stimulated acid breakdown and increased glycerol production (Schumacher *et al.* 1974).

With the use of abscission chemicals to aid in mechanical harvesting, an accompanying change in the physiological development of a fruit can take place. The growth regulator ethephon (2-chloroethylphosphonic acid) was found to reduce the ascorbic acid content in papaya and increase the total and reducing sugars and pectin content (Shanmugavelu *et al.* 1973A). Conversely, the effect of ethephon on pumpkin was to increase the ascorbic acid and decrease the reducing sugars contents (Shanmugavelu *et al.* 1973B).

Warren *et al.* (1973) showed that ethephon's effect on fruit acidity of blueberries varies with time of application. Early applications of 2000–8000 ppm lowered acidity and late applications raised acidity. Ethephon at 50 to 200 ppm had no effect on the titratable acidity of 4 peach cultivars regardless of application date (Sims *et al.* 1974). Sweet orange fruits dipped in ethephon at 200 and 400 ppm or in GA (gibberellic acid) at 50 and 100 ppm 1 month before harvest showed a reduction in acidity and an increase in total soluble solids (TSS) and total sugars (Mazumdar and Bhatt 1976). Shaybany and Sharifi (1973), working with 'Rabbab' pomegranate, found that with increased ethephon concentrations the percent TSS and TSS:acid ratio of the juice decreased appreciably.

Pigment content can also be affected by ethephon use. Kvale (1974) found that ethephon at 400 ppm increased the anthocyanin content of 'Raud Prins' apples when applied in July. Applications in June or August had no effect unless combined with daminozide. Anthocyanin levels in peaches were raised as a result of ethephon treatment (Morini *et al.* 1974). Tomatoes treated with ethephon synthesized more lycopene than untreated fruit (Russo *et al.* 1975).

Mechanical harvesting of citrus fruit has necessitated a need for abscission chemicals that reduce the force for separating the fruit from the stem. However, many of these abscission chemicals have been shown to affect the chemical composition of cold-pressed orange oil (Moshonas *et al.* 1976; Moshonas and Shaw 1977). Abscission agents that caused injury to the peel also caused the formation of six phenolic ethers not reported earlier as citrus constituents, namely, eugenol, *cis*-methylisoeugenol, *trans*-methylisoeugenol, methyleugenol, elemicin, and isoelemicin (Moshonas and Shaw 1978). Moshonas and co-workers speculated that abscission chemicals enhance the aging process of fruit and thereby cause adverse effects on the flavor quality of the juice extracted from these fruit.

HOLDING AND STORAGE CONDITIONS

The separation of fruits from vegetables is an arbitrary division not used in Tables 4.1 and 4.2, wherein the length of holding after harvest and the usual cause of the end of produce storage life are listed. Horticultural fruits are included in all length holding categories (Table 4.1), but are included in only 3 of the 5 groups for termination of storage and marketing life (Table 4.2). The economic loss of fruit to overwhelming hazards, such as overmaturity and decay, results in virtually the complete loss of the nutrient content of the fruit. Control of wilting

Table 4.1. Most Common Relative Length of Postharvest Life Required for Selected Produce

Time	Produce
Immediate marketing	Asparagus, usually citrus (except lemons), radishes, parsley, green onions, mushrooms, celery, watermelons, endive, lettuce, eggplant, rhubarb, spinach, globe artichokes, berries
Immediate marketing after ripening	Tomatoes, bananas, apricots, mangoes, cantaloupes, papayas
Short-term storage (or equivalent long distance transportation)	Peaches, kohlrabi, citrus exports
Long-term storage	Most apples and pears, parsnips, rutabagas, potatoes, onions, sweet potatoes

Source: Grierson and Wardowski (1978).

Table 4.2. Major Hazards Responsible for the End of Effective Storage and Marketing Life of Produce

Limitation	Produce
Wilting	Lettuce, endive, celery, asparagus, spinach, broccoli
Overmaturity	Apples, pears, cucumbers, bananas, corn on the cob
Decay	Citrus, berries, tomatoes, sweet potatoes
Regrowth and sprouting	Onions, Irish potatoes
Chilling injury in cold storage	Grapefruit, limes, most purely tropical fruits and most vegetables that are botanically fruits

Source: Grierson and Wardowski (1978).

decay, and fruit ripening after harvest has been attempted by adjustment of humidity, temperature, manipulation of the concentration of gases in the surrounding atmosphere, and use of fungicides.

Humidity Control

Relative humidity (RH) is deceptive in that vapor pressure deficit more accurately predicts the weight loss and shrinkage of fruits (Grierson and Wardowski 1978). At constant temperatures, variations in high (over 75 to 85%) RH are proportional to weight loss (Christopher *et al.* 1948; Smith 1933); with the exception of grapes for which transpiration increases down to 40% RH (Allen and Pentzer 1935). Constant RH with increasing temperatures can cause large increases in moisture loss because of increasing vapor pressure deficit. For example, apples lose twice as much weight at constant RH with an increase from $15°$ to $16°C$ than with an increase from $2°$ to $3°C$ (Smith 1933). A more recent constant temperature study of apples, peaches, lemons, oranges, grapefruit, and avocados showed that the increase in weight loss was about 50% for each doubling of vapor-pressure deficit (Wells 1962).

The market tolerance for weight loss for apples (Pieniazek 1942) and oranges (Kaufman *et al.* 1956) is about 5%, and although this value varies with type of produce, visible shriveling is apparent at about half the weight loss tolerated in markets (Hruschka 1977; Kaufman *et al.* 1956; Smock and Neubert 1950). The optimum storage RH for individual fruits has generally been recognized to be higher as research has revealed that high RH does not necessarily result in increased decay and that excessive weight loss frequently means total loss of the commodity (Grierson and Wardowski 1978). A discussion of humidity and storage necessarily must include consideration of temperature. Even slight variations in temperature as the refrigeration cycles on and off can cause wide fluctuations in relative humidity and result in the dehydration of produce (Grierson and Wardowski 1975). With the recognition that very high relative humidities result in less rather than more decay for many crops, jacketed storages were developed to provide constant high humidities under refrigerated conditions (van den Berg and Lentz 1978).

Temperature Control

The factor of colder temperatures (above freezing) to extend the marketing life of fruits seems simple until some of the exceptions, difficulties, and costs are considered. Specific storage temperatures are recommended for individual fruits and vegetables (Lipton and Harvey 1977), and these can be followed, even to specific temperatures for certain cultivars of apples [e.g., $30°-32°F$ except for $35°-38°F$ for 'Yellow Newton,' 'McIntosh,' and 'Rhode Island Greensy' and $34°-36°F$ for 'Grimes Golden' (Patchen 1971)] as long as each storage room has only one commodity. Specific ideal temperatures are not economically feasible when refrigerated trucks carry mixed loads, and grocery warehouses and stores handle all produce, ornamental plants, and dairy products at one or two temperatures. Also, refrigerated shelf space is so limited in supermarkets that only the most perishable commodities are provided that luxury.

Rapid precooling (by hydrocooling) before storage or transit has been widely adopted for peaches, but not for apples (Schomer and Patchen 1968). Peaches that are ripened to softness become firm when cooled and resoften when warmed (Werner and Frenkel 1978). Citrus in California and Arizona is frequently precooled with air, but Florida and

Texas citrus is rarely precooled (Grierson 1976). Vacuum cooling is very efficient for leafy vegetables, but due to the low surface:weight ratio is not practical for fruits.

Most storage studies with fruits have reported changes in keeping quality, decay, weight loss, and in the case of citrus, sugar and acid. Stahl and Camp (1936) confirmed earlier reports that for grapefruit and, to a greater extent, for oranges, citric acid decreased and sugars increased to an even greater extent than by weight loss concentration during storage for several months at various temperatures. Reports of changes in vitamin content of fruits during storage are rare. One report by Bratley (1939) indicated that during 8 weeks of storage at 0°C, tangerines nearly maintained their vitamin C levels, but at 7°–9°C nearly one-fourth of the vitamin C was lost. Only slight loss of vitamin C was observed for oranges held 10 to 16 days under simulated marketing conditions (Harding 1954). The latter case is much more representative of the time and conditions for citrus marketed in the United States.

Chilling injury occurs at temperatures above freezing. Bananas and grapefruit are fruits well known to be injured by chilling. This injury sometimes results in decay as pathogens can enter the weakened tissue. Chilling injury of grapefruit is reduced by high (over 90%) relative humidity and hypobaric (low pressure) storage (Grierson 1976), by thiabendazole and benomyl fungicides (Schiffman-Nadel *et al.* 1975), and even by benomyl applied several months before harvest (Wardowski *et al.* 1975). Grierson (1976) observed that there is a generalization with peel color for the sensitivity of citrus to chilling injury, wherein green fruit are most susceptible, yellow fruit are somewhat less susceptible, and orange fruit are the most resistant.

Gas-Concentration Manipulation

Controlled Atmosphere (CA) Storage

The basis of CA storage is that the storage atmosphere differs mainly in the proportions of oxygen and carbon dioxide from normal air; the proportion of O_2 is usually lowered and that of CO_2 increased. The best mixture of gases, however, varies with commodity, temperature, and length of storage (Ryall and Lipton 1979). Lipton (1975) lists the main reasons for using CA as (1) retardation of ripening, (2) reduction of decay, (3) prevention of specific disorders and retardation of aging, and (4) alteration of the texture of the commodity.

Long-term CA storage is largely confined to apples because the climacteric rise can be effectively delayed by temperature and CA control. Anderson *et al.* (1967) indicated the feasibility of extending the storage life of various stone fruits, namely 'Redhaven,' 'Sunhigh,' and 'Loring' peaches and 'Late Le Grand' nectarines, by CA storage.

Organoleptic tests favored storage of these fruits in 1% O_2 and 5% CO_2. Covey (1960) found the best CA storage for Eldorado plums to be 7% O_2, 7% CO_2, and 86% N_2; these conditions delayed ripening and reduced the loss of soluble solids.

The storage of avocado in CA has been studied by various workers (Biale 1946; Biale and Young 1962; Spalding and Reeder 1972, 1975). The optimum temperature for CA storage will vary with the cultivar, and maximum storage time for any cultivar CA has been 60 days (Spalding and Reeder 1972). Early studies with Fuerte avocados showed that within the range of 2.5 to 21% O_2 concentration, the time to reach the respiratory climacteric peak was extended in proportion to the decrease in O_2 concentration (Biale 1946). The presence of low O_2 and high CO_2 (5 to 10%) tends to suppress the intensity of respiration. Studies by Hatton and Reeder (1965) and Spalding and Reeder (1972) have shown that the use of 2% O_2 and 10% CO_2 at 7.2°C doubled the normal storage life over refrigeration alone of 'Lula,' 'Booth 8,' 'Fuchs,' and 'Waldin' avocados. Maximum storage time for these cultivars was 6–8 weeks (results of 'Booth 8' and 'Lula' shown in Table 4.3).

Initiation of banana ripening can be delayed by holding the green fruit in an atmosphere of 1–10% O_2 and 5–10% CO_2 or a combination of low O_2 and high CO_2 (Young et al. 1962; Mapson and Robinson 1966). Studies on pineapples (Dull 1971) and mangoes (Hatton and

Table 4.3. Fruit Quality of 'Booth 8' and 'Lula' Avocados after Storage for 20 and 40 Days in Controlled Atmosphere (CA) of 2% O_2 and 10% CO_2 or in Air at 2.5°C followed by Ripening at 21°C

Storage time and temperature (°C)	Acceptable fruits (%)		Softening time (days)	
	Air	CA	Air	CA
	'Booth 8'			
No storage	100	—	6.5	—
20 days				
4.5	80	93	4.8	5.8
10.0	33	60	1.6	5.2
40 days				
4.5	17	73	—	6.4
10.0	0	43	—	3.8
	'Lula'			
No storage	100	—	6.4	—
20 days				
4.5	80	100	3.3	6.0
10.0	47	100	3.1	6.0
40 days				
4.5	0	100	—	5.1
10.0	0	100	—	5.4

Source: Spalding and Reeder (1972).

Reeder 1966; Lakshminarayana 1980) showed no obvious benefits from CA storage. Storage of citrus fruits under CA conditions has also not been successful because, as shown in Fig. 4.3, with these fruits there is no climacteric to delay (Grierson 1970).

Ethylene

Ethylene gas is used in several commercial fruit ripening or degreening processes (Mitchell *et al.* 1972). Degreening of citrus fruit grown in humid subtropical conditions is standard practice; 1–5 ppm ethylene is used in Florida (McCornack and Wardowski 1977). Controlled ripening of bananas with ethylene is a precise science (Smock 1967) and this technology has been adopted for plantains (Hernadez 1972). At times, ethylene removal is desirable for bananas and plantains to delay the time of ripening. For limes (Spalding and Reeder 1976), lemons (Wild and Rippon 1973), and other citrus fruits, ethylene functions by delaying senescence rather than preventing ripening. Ethylene gas can be used commercially to reduce the ripening time of mangoes. Conditions recommended by Barmore and Mitchell (1975) for treating mangoes are 10–30 ppm ethylene for 24–48 hr at 21°C with high humidity (95% RH).

Fruit Fumigation

The use of fumigation techniques for both fruit and soil disinfestation has been a major success. The Mediterranean fruit fly can destroy more than 200 varieties of fruits and vegetables. Disinfestation treatments do not vary much among fruit, and the focus here will be on citrus fumigation.

Japanese importation requirements call for the fumigation of fresh Florida citrus with ethylene dibromide (EDB). In Florida, citrus is fumigated in cardboard cartons palletized in trailers. Fumigation at a dosage of 8 to 16 g/m^3 for 2 hr is followed by a 1-hr ventilation period (Miller and Ismail 1977). Citrus fruit, especially, may be severely injured if placed in refrigeration before desorption of the fumigant is essentially complete (USDA 1976). Singh *et al.* (1979), working with navel and 'Valencia' orange fruit found EDB residue concentrations (after fumigation at 24–42 g/m^3) exceeded 0.5 $\mu g/g$ after storage for less than or equal to 14 days but none was detectable after 28 days. Inorganic bromine concentrations were well below the Australian and Codex Alimentarius legal limit (30 $\mu g/g$).

Respiration changes in papayas subjected to fumigation and hot water treatments were studied (Akamine 1966). These treatments accelerated the rate of ripening if the fruits were not promptly stored at 7°–13°C for 7 days.

Ethylene dibromide fumigation of tomato fruits reduced red color development in the outer pericarp, although the inner tissues remained unaffected at EDB doses as high as 35 g/m^3 (Rigney *et al.* 1978). Carotene accumulation was enhanced by EDB at 4 g/m^3, but at higher doses the carotene content of the tomato pericarp was reduced.

Sulfur dioxide, trichloroamine, and ethylene oxide gases are used to reduce or control decay in grapes and citrus. Fumigation with SO$_2$ reduces the rate of respiration in grapes. Emperor grapes receiving 22 ppm of sulfur dioxide had their rate of respiration reduced 82% while in storage at 28°C (Winkler 1962). Increasing the amount of free sulfur dioxide caused a proportional increase in the destruction of thiamin (Winkler 1962).

REFERENCES

Akamine, E. K. 1966. Respiration of fruits of papaya (*Carica papaya* L. var. 'Solo') with reference to the effect of quarantine disinfestation treatments. Proc. Am. Soc. Hortic. Sci. *89*, 231–236.

Allen, F. W., and Pentzer, W. T. 1935. Studies on the effect of humidity in the cold storage of fruits. Proc. Am. Soc. Hortic. Sci. *33*, 215–223.

Anderson, R. E., Parsons, C. S., and Smith, W. L. 1967. For peaches, nectarines, oxygen–carbon dioxide storage. Agric. Res. *15*(11), 7.

Arnold, C. E., and Mitchell, A. E. 1970. Histology of blemishes of cherry fruits (*Prunus cerasus* L. cv. Montmorency), resulting from mechanical harvesting. J. Am. Soc. Hortic. Sci. *95*, 723–725.

Arriola, M. C. de, Madrid, M. D. de, and Rolz, C. 1975. Some physical and chemical changes in papaya during its storage. Proc. Trop. Reg. Am. Soc. Hortic. Sci. *19*, 97.

Arriola, M. C. de, Menchu, J. F., and Rolz, C. 1976. Characterization, handling and storage of some tropical fruits. Ctrl. Am. Res. Inst. Ind. (ICAITI), Guatemala. (Spanish.)

Arriola, M. C. de, *et al.* 1980. Papaya. *In* Tropical and Subtropical Fruits. S. Nagy and P. E. Shaw (Editors). AVI Publishing Co., Westport, CT.

Asenjo, C. F. 1980. Acerola. *In* Tropical and Subtropical Fruits. S. Nagy and P. E. Shaw (Editors). AVI Publishing Co., Westport, CT.

Asenjo, C. F., and Moscoso, C. G. 1950. Ascorbic acid content and other characteristics of the West Indian cherry. Food Res. *15*, 103–106.

Askar, A., El-Tamini, A., and Raouf, M. 1972. Constituents of mango fruit and their behavior during growth and ripening. Mitt. Rebe Wein, Obstanu Fruchteverwert. *22*, 120–125.

Audus, L. J. 1953. Plant Growth Substances. Leonard Hill, London.

Avery, G. S., Johnson, E. B., Addams, R. M., and Thomson, B. F. 1947. Hormones and Horticulture. McGraw-Hill, New York.

Bangerth, F. 1978. The effect of a substituted amino acid on ethylene biosynthesis, respiration, ripening and preharvest drop of apple fruits. J. Am. Soc. Hortic. Sci. *103*, 401–404.

Barmore, C. R., and Mitchell, E. F. 1975. Ethylene peripening of mangos prior to shipment. Proc. Fla. State Hortic. Soc. *88*, 469–471.

Beeson, K. C. 1949. The soil factor in human nutrition problems. Nutr. Rev. *7*, 353–355.

Ben-Arie, R., and Guelfat-Reich, S. 1979. Advancement of nectarine fruit ripening with daminozide and fenoprop. J. Am. Soc. Hortic. Sci. *104*, 14–17.

Biale, J. B. 1946. Effect of oxygen concentration on respiration of the Fuerte avocado fruit. Am. J. Bot. *33*, 363–373.

Biale, J. B., and Young, R. E. 1971. The avocado-pear. *In* The Biochemistry of Fruits and Their Products. A. C. Hulme (Editor). Academic Press, New York.

Black, C. A. 1968. Soil–Plant Relationships. 2nd Edition. John Wiley, New York.

Boysen Jensen, P. 1936. Growth Hormones in Plants. McGraw-Hill, New York.

Braddock, R. J., and Crandall, P. G. 1981. Carbohydrate fiber from orange albedo. J. Food Sci. *46*, 650–651.

Bramlage, W. J., Greene, D. W., Autio, W. R., and McLaughlin, J. M. 1980. Effects of aminoethoxyvinylglycine on internal ethylene concentrations and storage of apples. J. Am. Soc. Hortic. Sci. *105*, 847–851.

Bratley, C. O. 1939. Loss of ascorbic acid (vitamin C) from tangerines during storage on the market. Proc. Am. Soc. Hortic. Sci. *37*, 526–528.

Castle, W. S., and Phillips, R. L. 1980. Performance of Marsh grapefruit and Valencia orange trees on eighteen rootstocks in a closely spaced planting. J. Am. Soc. Hortic. Sci. *105*, 496–499.

Childers, N. F. 1975. Modern Fruit Science. Horticultural Publications, Rutgers Univ., New Brunswick, NJ.

Christopher, E. P., Pieniazek, S. A., Shutak, V., and McElroy, L. 1948. Transpiration of apples in cold storage. Proc. Am. Soc. Hortic. Sci. *51*, 114–119.

Coggins, C. W., and Hield, H. Z. 1968. Plant-growth regulators. *In* The Citrus Industry, Vol. 2. W. Reuther, L. D. Batchelor, and H. J. Webber (Editors). Univ. of Calif. Press, Riverside.

Collins, M. D., Lombard, P. B., and Wolfe, J. W. 1978. The effects of evaporative cooling for bloom delay in 'Barlett' and 'Bosc' pear fruit maturity and quality. J. Am. Soc. Hortic. Sci. *103*, 187–189.

Convey, H. M. 1960. Effects of temperature and modified atmosphere on the storage life, ripening behavior, and dessert quality of Eldorado plums. Proc. Am. Soc. Hortic. Sci. *75*, 207–215.

Dalldorf, R. 1979. Factors influencing the sugar content of Smooth Cayenne pineapples. Inf. Bull. Citr. Subtrop. Fruit Res. Inst. *83*, 5–6.

Dekazos, E. D. 1980. Effect of aminoethoxyvinylglycine, carboxymethylcellulose and growth regulators on longevity of fresh rabbiteye blueberries. Proc. Fla. State Hortic. Soc. *93*, 145–149.

Drake, S. R., Proebsting, E. L., Carter, G. H., and Nelson, J. W. 1978. Effect of growth regulators on ascorbic acid content, drained weight and color of fresh and processed Rainer cherries. J. Am. Soc. Hortic. Sci. *105*, 162–164.

Drake, S. R., Proebsting, E. L., Thompson, J. B., and Nelson, J. W. 1980. Effects of daminozide, maturity and cultivar on the color grade and character of sweet cherries. J. Am. Soc. Hortic. Sci. *105*, 668–670.

Dull, G. G. 1971. The pineapple. *In* The Biochemistry of Fruits and Their Products, Vol. 2. A. C. Hulme (Editor). Academic Press, New York.

Elliott, A. P., and Edmunds, J. E. 1977. Effect of 1,2-dibromo-3-chloropropane on soil nutrients and nutrient uptake by tomatoes. Soil Sci. *124*, 343–346.

Embleton, T. W., Jones, W. W., Labanauskas, C. K., and Reuther, W. 1973A. Leaf analysis as a diagnostic tool and guide to fertilization. *In* The Citrus Industry, Vol. 3. W. Reuther (Editor). Univ. of Calif. Press, Riverside.

Embleton, T. W., Reitz, H. J., and Jones, W. W. 1973B. Citrus fertilization. *In* The Citrus Industry, Vol. 3. W. Reuther (Editor). Univ. of Calif. Press, Riverside.

Eskin, N. A. M., Henderson, H. N., and Townsend, R. J. 1971. Biochemistry of Foods. Academic Press, New York.

Evans, L. T. (Editor). 1963. Environmental Control of Plant Growth. Academic Press, New York.

Ferguson, R. R., and Fox, K. I. 1978. Dietary citrus fibers. Trans. Citrus Eng. Conf. A.S.M.E., Fla. Sect. *24*, 23–33.

Finch, A. H., Jones W. W., and Van Horn, C. W. 1945. The influence of nitrogen nutrition upon the ascorbic acid content of several vegetable crops. Proc. Am. Soc. Hortic. Sci. *46*, 314–318.

Florida Department of Citrus. 1975. Official rules affecting the Florida citrus industry pursuant to Chapter 601, Florida Statutes. State of Fla., Dept. of Citrus, Lakeland.

Forsyth, W. G. C. 1980. Banana and plantain. *In* Tropical and Subtropical Fruits. S. Nagy and P. E. Shaw (Editors). AVI Publishing Co., Westport, CT.

Ghosh, S. 1960. The content of folic acid and its conjugates in some common Indian fruits. Sci. Cult. *26*, 287–288.

Goddard, M. S., and Mathews, R. H. 1979. Contribution of fruits and vegetables to human nutrition. HortScience *14*, 245–247.

Green, A. 1971. Soft fruits. *In* Biochemistry of Fruits and Their Products. A. C. Hulme (Editor). Academic Press, New York.

Grierson, W. 1970. Prospects for controlled atmosphere storage in Florida. Univ. Fla. Sunshine State Agric. Res. Rep. *15*, 8–10.

Grierson, W. 1973. Quality of produce as affected by prestorage treatments and packaging. Int. Inst. Refrig. Comm. *C-2*, 51–65.

Grierson, W. 1976. Preservation of citrus fruits. Refrig. Serv. Eng. Soc. Sect. 7, 1–11.

Grierson, W., and Wardowski, W. F. 1975. Humidity in horticulture. HortScience *10*, 356–360.

Grierson, W., and Wardowski, W. F. 1978. Relative humidity effects on the postharvest life of fruits and vegetables. HortScience *13*, 570–574.

Hall, A. P., Morgan, A. F., and Wheeler, P. 1953. The amount of six B-vitamins in fresh and dried figs. Food Res. *18*, 206–216.

Hall, A. P., More, J. F., and Morgan, A. F. 1955. B-vitamin content of California-grown avocados. J. Agric. Food Chem. *3*, 250–252.

Hall, N. T., Smoot, J. M., Knight, R. J., and Nagy, S. 1980. Protein and amino acid compositions of ten tropical fruits by gas-liquid chromatography. J. Agric. Food Chem. *28*, 1217–1221.

Hansen, R. G., Wyse, B. W., and Sorenson, A. W. 1979. Nutritional Quality Index of Foods. AVI Publishing Co., Westport, CT.

Harding, P. L. 1954. Effects of simulated transit and marketing periods on quality of Florida oranges. Food Technol. *8*, 311–312.

Harding, P. L., and Fisher, D. F. 1945. Seasonal changes in Florida grapefruit. USDA Tech. Bull. *886*, Washington, DC.

Harding, P. L., and Sunday, M. B. 1949. Seasonal changes in Florida tangerines. USDA Tech. Bull, *988*, Washington, DC.

Harding, P. L., Winston, J. R., and Fisher, D. F. 1940. Seasonal changes in Florida oranges. USDA Tech. Bull. *753*, Washington, DC.

Harris, R. S. 1975. Effects of agricultural practices on the composition of foods. *In* Nutritional Evaluation of Food Processing, 2nd Edition. R. S. Harris and E. Karmas (Editors). AVI Publishing Co., Westport, CT.

Hatton, T. T., Jr., and Reeder, W. F. 1965. Controlled atmosphere storage of Lula avocados—1965 test. Proc. Caribbean Reg. Am. Soc. Hortic. Sci. *9*, 152–159.

Hatton, T. T., and Reeder, W. F. 1966. Controlled atmosphere storage of Keitt mangos. Proc. Carib. Reg. Am. Soc. Hortic. Sci. *10*, 114–119.

Hearn, C. J., and Hutchison, D. J. 1977. The performance of Robinson and Page citrus hybrids on 10 rootstocks. Proc. Fla. State Hortic. Soc. *90*, 47–49.

Heinicke, D. R. 1966. Characteristics of McIntosh and Red Delicious apples as influenced by exposure to sunlight during the growing season. Proc. Am. Soc. Hort. Sci. *89*, 10–13.

Hernandez, I. 1972. Storage of green plantains. J. Agric. Univ. P. R. *56*, 100–106.

Howard, F. D., MacGillivray, J. H., and Yamaguchi, M. 1962. Nutrient composition of fresh California grown vegetables. Calif. Agric. Exp. Stn. Bull. *778*.

Hruschka, H. W. 1977. Postharvest weight loss and shrivel in five fruits and five vegetables. USDA Mkt. Res. Rpt. *1059*, Washington, DC.

Hulme, A. C. (Editor). 1971. The Biochemistry of Fruits and Their Products, Vol. 2. Academic Press, New York.

Hsu, J. W. 1974. Seasonal variations of thiamin in citrus juices. Florida Dep. of Citrus. Unpublished.

Issa, J., and Mielke, E. A. 1980. Influence of certain citrus interstocks on β-carotene and lycopene levels in 10-year-old 'Redblush' grapefruit. J. Am. Soc. Hortic. Sci. *105*, 807–809.

Iwahori, S. 1978. Use of growth regulators in the control of cropping of mandarin varieties. Proc. Int. Soc. Citriculture, 263–270.

Jackson, J. E., Sharples, R. O., and Palmer, J. W. 1971. The influence of shade and within-tree position on apple fruit size, color and storage quality. J. Hortic. Sci. *46*, 277–287.

John, J., Subbarayan, C., and Cama, H. R. 1963. Carotenoids in mango (*Mangifera indica*) fruit. Indian J. Chem. *1*, 36–40.

Jones, W. W. 1961. Environmental and cultural factors influencing the chemical composition and physical characters. *In* The Orange: Its Biochemistry and Physiology. W. B. Sinclair (Editor). Univ. of Calif. Press, Riverside.

Jones, W. W., and Parker, E. R. 1947. Ascorbic acid–nitrogen relations in Navel orange juice, as affected by fertilizer applications. Proc. Am. Soc. Hortic. Sci. *50*, 195–198.

Jones, W. W., and Parker, E. R. 1949. Effects of nitrogen, phosphorus, and potassium fertilizers and of organic materials on the composition of Washington Navel orange juice. Proc. Am. Soc. Hortic. Sci. *53*, 91–102.

Jones, W. W., Embleton, T. W., Boswell, S. B., Goodall, G. E., and Barnhart, E. L. 1970. Nitrogen rate effects on lemon production, quality and leaf nitrogen. Proc. Am. Soc. Hortic. Sci. *95*, 46–49.

Jungalwala, F. B., and Cama, H. R. 1963. Carotenoids in mango (*Mangifera indica*) fruit. Indian J. Chem. *1*, 36–40.

Kaufman, J., Hardenburg, R. E., and Lutz, J. M. 1956. Weight losses and decay of Florida and California oranges in mesh and perforated polyethylene consumer bags. Proc. Am. Soc. Hortic. Sci. *67*, 244–250.

Kempton, R. J., and Maw, G. A. 1973. Soil fumigation with methyl bromide: The uptake and distribution of inorganic bromide in tomato plants. Ann. Appl. Biol. *74*, 91–98.

Koo, R. C. J. 1979. The influence of N, K, and irrigation on tree size and fruit production of 'Valencia' orange. Proc. Fla. State. Hortic. Soc. *92*, 10–13.

Krochta, J. M., and Feinberg, B. 1975. Effects of harvesting and handling fruits and vegetables. *In* Nutritional Evaluation of Food Processing, 2nd Edition. R. S. Harris and E. Karmas (Editors). AVI Publishing Co., Westport, CT.

Krochta, J. M., Tillin, S. J., and Whitehand, L. C. 1975. Ascorbic acid content of tomatoes damaged by mechanical harvesting. Food Technol. *29*, 28–30.

Kurihara, A. 1969. Fruit growth of satsuma orange under controlled conditions. I. Effects of preharvest temperature on fruit growth, color development, and fruit quality in satsuma orange. Bull. Hortic. Res. Stn. Jpn. *A*, (8), 15–30.

Kvale, A. 1974. The effect of ethylene alone or in combination with daminozide on fruit maturation, yield and quality of Raud Prins apples. Forsk, Fors. Landbruket *25*, 339–346.

Lakshminarayana, S. 1980. Mango. *In* Tropical and Subtropical Fruits. S. Nagy and P. E. Shaw (Editors). AVI Publishing Co., Westport, CT.

Lipton, W. J. 1975. Controlled atmospheres for fresh vegetables and fruits—why and when. *In* Postharvest Biology and Handling of Fruits and Vegetables. N. F. Haard and D. K. Salunkhe (Editors). AVI Publishing Co., Westport, CT.

Lipton, W., and Harvey, J. M. 1977. Compatibility of fruits and vegetables during transport of mixed loads. USDA Mkt. Res. Rep. *1070*, Washington, DC.

Mapson, L. W. 1971. Vitamins in fruits. *In* The Biochemistry of Fruits and Their Products, Vol. 1. A. C. Hulme (Editor). Academic Press, New York.

Mapson, L. W., and Robinson, J. E. 1966. Relation between oxygen tension, biosynthesis of ethylene, respiration and ripening changes in banana fruit. J. Food Technol. *1*, 212–225.

Marsanija, I. I. 1970. The effect of long-term application of fertilizers on the vitamin C content in mandarin and lemon fruit. Trudy suhum. opyt. Stan efirno-mas. Kul'tur 9, 49–56; Hortic. Abstr. *41*, 1165 (1971).

Masui, M., Nukaya, A., Ogura, T., and Ishida, A. 1978. Bromine uptake of muskmelon and cucumber plants following soil fumigation with methyl bromide. J. Jpn. Soc. Hortic. Sci. *47*, 343–350.

Maynard, L. A. 1950. Soils and health. Council on Food and Nutrition. J. Am. Med. Assoc. *143*, 807.

Maynard, L. A. 1956. Effect of fertilizers on the nutritional value of foods. J. Am. Med. Assoc. *161*, 1478–1480.

Mazumdar, B. C., and Bhatt, D. N. V. 1976. Effect of preharvest application of GA and Ethrel on sweet orange (*Citrus sinensis* Osb.) fruits. Prog. Hortic. *8*, 89–91.

McCornack, A. A., and Wardowski, W. 1977. Degreening Florida citrus fruit: Procedures and physiology. Proc. Int. Soc. Citriculture *1*, 211–215.

McGlasson, W. B. 1971. The ethylene factor. *In* The Biochemistry of Fruits and Their Products, Vol. 1. A. C. Hulme (Editor). Academic Press, New York.

Miller, W. M., and Ismail, M. A. 1977. Removal of ethylene dibromide from citrus fumigation chambers. Trans. ASAE *20*, 1138–1141, 1150.

Mitchell, F. G., Guillou, R., and Parsons, R. A. 1972. Commercial cooling of fruits and vegetables. Univ. Calif. Agr. Exp. Stn. Serv. Manual *43*.

Morini, S., Vitagliano, C., and Xiloyannis, C. 1974. The effect of ethephon and 2,4,5-TP on fruit drop, size and ripening of peaches. Riv. Ortoflorofruittie. Ital. *58*, 235–243.

Moshonas, M. G., and Shaw, P. E. 1977. Effects of abscission agents on composition and flavor of cold-pressed orange peel oil. J. Agric. Food Chem. *25*, 1151–1153.

Moshonas, M. G., and Shaw, P. E. 1978. Compounds new to essential orange oil from fruit treated with abscission chemicals. J. Agric. Food Chem. *26*, 1288–1290.

Moshonas, M. G., Shaw, P. E., and Sims, D. A. 1976. Abscission agent effects on orange juice flavor. J. Food Sci. *41*, 809–811.

Mudambi, S. R., and Rajagopal, M. V. 1977. Vitamin C content of some fruits grown in Nigeria. J. Food Technol. *12*, 189–191.

Munger, H. M. 1979. The potential of breeding fruits and vegetables for human nutrition. HortScience *14*, 247–250.

Murneek, A. E., and Wittwer, S. H. 1948. Some factors affecting ascorbic acid content of apples. Proc. Am. Soc. Hortic. Sci. *51*, 97–102.

Nagy, S. 1980. Vitamin C contents of citrus fruit and their products: A review. J. Agric. Food Chem. *28*, 8–18.

Nagy, S., and Shaw, P. E. (Editors). 1980. Tropical and Subtropical Fruits. AVI Publishing Co., Westport, CT.

Nitsch, J. P. 1971. Hormonal factors in growth and development. *In* The Biochemistry of Fruits and Their Products, Vol. 1. A. C. Hulme (Editor). Academic Press, New York.

Nordby, H. E., Nagy, S., and Smoot, J. M. 1979. Relationship of rootstock to leaf and juice lipids in citrus. J. Am. Soc. Hortic. Sci. *104*, 280–282.

Ochse, J. J., Soule, M. J., Dijkman, M. J., and Wehlburg, C. 1961. Tropical and Subtropical Agriculture, Vol. 1. Macmillan, New York.

Okuse, I., and Ryugo, K. 1981. Compositional changes in the developing Hayward kiwi fruit in California. J. Am. Soc. Hortic. Sci. *106*, 73–76.

Patchen, G. O. 1971. Storage for apples and pears. USDA Mktg. Res. Rep. *924*, Washington, DC.

Peynaud, E., and Ribereau-Gayon, P. 1971. The grape. *In* The Biochemistry of Fruits and Their Products, Vol. 2. A. C. Hulme (Editor). Academic Press, New York.

Pieniazek, S. A. 1942. External factors affecting water loss from apples in cold storage. Refrig. Eng. *44*, 171–173.

Polansky, M. M., and Murphy, E. W. 1966. Vitamin B_6 components in fruits and nuts. J. Am. Diet. Assoc. *48*, 109–111.

Proebsting, E. L., and Mills, H. H. 1976. Effect of daminozide on growth, maturity, quality and yield of sweet cherries. J. Am. Soc. Hortic. Sci. *101*, 175–179.

Rathore, D. S. 1979. A possibility of inverse relationship between the ascorbic acid content of guava fruits and ripening temperatures. Indian J. Hortic. *36*, 128–130.

Reiser, S. 1979. Effect of dietary fiber on parameters of glucose tolerance in humans. *In* Dietary Fibers: Chemistry and Nutrition. G. E. Inglett and S. I. Falkehag (Editors). Academic Press, New York.

Reuther, W., and Nauer, E. M. 1972. The influence of climatic factors on the growth and fruiting of citrus and other subtropical fruits. Univ. Calif. Agric. Exp. Stn. Proj. *2120*.

Rigney, C. J., Graham, D., and Lee, T. H. 1978. Changes in tomato fruit ripening caused by ethylene dibromide fumigation. J. Am. Soc. Hortic. Sci. *103*, 420–423.

Russo, L., Jr., Dougherty, R. H., Dostal, H. C., Wilcox, G. E., and Nelson, P. E. 1975. Quality of processed tomato products from ethephon-ripened fruit. HortScience *10*, 138–139.

Ryall, A. L., and Lipton, W. J. 1979. Handling, Transportation and Storage of Fruits and Vegetables, Vol. 1, 2nd Edition. AVI Publishing Co., Westport, CT.

Rygg, G. L., and Getty, M. R. 1955. Seasonal changes in Arizona and California grapefruit. USDA Tech. Bull. *1130*, Washington, DC.

Sass, B. 1975. Experiences with soil disinfection in strawberries. Kert. Kut. Int. Kozl. *5*, 73–86.

Schiffmann-Nadel, M., Chalutz, E., Waks, J., and Dagan, M. 1975. Reduction of chilling injury in grapefruit by thiabendazole and benomyl during long-term storage. J. Am. Soc. Hortic. Sci. *100*, 270–272.

Schomer, H. A., and Patchen, G. O. 1968. Effects of hydrocooling on the desert quality and storage of apples in the Pacific Northwest. USDA ARS *51–24*, Washington, DC.

Schumacher, R., Tanner, H., Fankhauser, F., and Stadlers, W. 1974. The effect on the constituents of apple juice of harvesting method, length of storage and Ethrel treatment. Schweiz. Z. Obst. Weinbau *110*, 676, 681.

Scora, R. W., and Newman, J. E. 1967. A phenological study of the essential oils of the peel of Valencia oranges. Agric. Meteorol. *4*, 11–26.

Seeley, E. J., Micke, W. C., and Kammereck, R. 1980. 'Delicious' apple fruit size and quality as influenced by radiant flux density in the immediate growing environment. J. Am. Soc. Hortic. Sci. *105*, 645–647.

Shanmugavelu, K. G., Rao, V. N. M., and Srinivasan, C. 1973A. Studies on the effect of certain plant regulators and boron on papaya (*Carica papaya* L.). South Indian Hortic. *21*, 19, 26.

Shanumgavelu, K. G., Srinivasan, C., and Thamburaj, S. 1973B. Effect of Ethrel (ethephon, 2-chloroethylphosphonic acid) on pumpkin (*Cucurbita moschata* Poir). South Indian Hortic. *21*, 94–99.

Shaybany, B., and Sharifi, H. 1973. Effect of preharvest applications of ethephon on leaf abscission, fruit drop and constitutents of fruit juice in pomegranates. J. Hortic. Sci. *48*, 293–296.

Sims, E. T., Jr., Gambrell, C. E., Jr., and Stembridge, G. E. 1974. The influence of (2-chloroethyl) phosphonic acid on peach quality and maturation. J. Am. Soc. Hortic. Sci. *99*, 152–155.

Sinclair, W. B. 1961. The Orange: Its Biochemistry and Physiology. Univ. of Calif. Press, Berkeley.

Sinclair, W. B. 1972. The Grapefruit. Univ. of Calif. Press, Riverside.

Singh, G., Rigney, C. J., and Gilbert, W. S. 1979. Ethylene dibromide and inorganic bromide residues in oranges after fumigation and storage. Aust. J. Exp. Agric. Anim. Husb. *19*, 377–381.

Sites, J. W. 1944. Sourness in grapefruit in relation to seasonal variation and nutritional programs. Proc. Fla. State Hortic. Soc. *57*, 122–132.

Sites, J. W. 1947. Internal fruit quality as related to production practices. Proc. Fla. State Hortic. Soc. *60*, 55–62.

Sites, J. W., and Reitz, H. J. 1949. The variation in individual Valencia oranges from different locations on the tree as a guide to sampling methods and spot-picking for quality. I. Soluble solids in the juice. Proc. Am. Soc. Hortic. Sci. *54*, 1–10.

Sites, J. W., and Reitz, H. J. 1950. The variation in individual Valencia oranges from different locations on the tree as a guide to sampling methods and spot-picking for quality. II. Titratable acid and the soluble solids: Titratable and ratio of the juice. Proc. Am. Soc. Hortic. Sci. *55*, 73–80.

Sites, J. W., and Reitz, H. J. 1951. The variation in individual Valencia oranges from different locations on the tree as a guide to sampling methods and spot-picking for quality. III. Vitamin C and juice content of the fruit. Proc. Am. Soc. Hortic. Sci. *56*, 103–110.

Smith, P. F. 1969. Effects of nitrogen rates and timing of application on Marsh grapefruit in Florida. *In* Proceedings of the First International Citrus Symposium. Vol. 3, pp. 1559–1567. H. D. Chapman (Editor). Univ. of Calif. Press, Riverside.

Smith, P. F., and Rasmussen, G. K. 1961. Effect of nitrogen source, rate, and pH on the production and quality of Marsh grapefruit. Proc. Fla. State Hortic. Soc. *74*, 32–38.

Smith, W. H. 1933. Evaporation of water from apples in relation to temperature and atmospheric humidity. Ann. Appl. Biol. *20*, 220–235.

Smock, R. M. 1953. Some effects of climate during the growing season on keeping quality of apples. Proc. Am. Soc. Hortic. Sci. *62*, 272–278.

Smock, R. M. 1967. Methods of storing bananas. Philipp. Agric. *51*, 501–517.

Smock, R. M., and Neubert, A. M. 1950. Chemical changes and physiology of apple fruit after harvest: A. Transpiration (water loss). *In* Apples and Apple Products. Interscience, New York.

Spalding, D. H., and Reeder, W. F. 1972. Quality of Booth 8 and Lula avocados stored in a controlled atmosphere. Proc. Fla. State Hortic. Soc. *85*, 337–341.

Spalding, D. H., and Reeder, W. F. 1975. Low oxygen and high-carbon dioxide controlled atmosphere storage for control of anthracnose and chilling injury of avocados. Phytopathology *65*, 458–460.

Spalding, D. H., and Reeder, W. F. 1976. Low pressure (hypobaric) storage of limes. J. Am. Soc. Hortic. Sci. *101*, 367–370.

Stahl, A. L., and Camp, A. F. 1936. Cold storage studies of Florida citrus fruits. Univ. Fla. Bull. *303*.

Stearns, C. R., and Sites, J. W. 1943. Fruit quality studies. Fla. Agric. Exp. Stn. Ann. Rep. *1943*, 203–213.

Stewart, I. 1980. Color as related to quality in citrus. *In* Citrus Nutrition and Quality. S. Nagy and J. A. Attaway (Editors). ACS Symposium Series *143*. Am. Chem. Soc., Washington, DC.

Theander, O., and Aman, P. 1979. The chemistry, morphology and analysis of dietary fiber components. *In* Dietary Fibers: Chemistry and Nutrition. G. E. Inglett and S. I. Falkehag (Editors). Academic Press, New York.

Thomason, I. J., Castro, C. E., Baines, R. C., and Mankau, R. 1971. What happens to soil fumigants after nematode control? Calif. Agric. *25*, 10–12.

Thornton, N. C. 1943. CO_2 storage. XIV. Influence of CO_2, O and ethylene on the vitamin C content of ripening bananas. Contrib. Boyce Thompson Inst. *13*, 201–220.

Ting, S. V. 1977. Nutritional labeling of citrus products. *In* Citrus Science and Technology, Vol. 2. S. Nagy, P. E. Shaw, and M. K. Veldhuis (Editors). AVI Publishing Co., Westport, CT.

Ting, S. V. 1980. Nutrients and nutrition of citrus fruits. *In* Citrus Nutrition and Quality. S. Nagy and J. A. Attaway (Editors). Am. Chem. Soc. Symposium Series *143*.

Ting, S. V., *et al.* 1974. Nutrient assay of Florida frozen concentrated orange juice for nutrition labeling. Proc. Fla. State Hortic. Soc. *87*, 206–209.

U.S. Department of Agriculture (USDA) 1976. Plant Protection and Quarantine Treatment Manual. Animal and Plant Health Inspection Service, USDA, Washington, DC.

van den Berg, L., and Lentz, C. P. 1978. High humidity storage of vegetables and fruits. HortScience *13*, 565–569.

Vandercook, C. E., Hasegawa, S., and Maier, V. P. 1980. Dates. *In* Tropical and Subtropical Fruits. S. Nagy and P. E. Shaw (Editors). AVI Publishing Co., Westport, CT.

Varsel, C. 1980. Citrus juice processing as related to quality and nutrition. *In* Citrus Nutrition and Quality. Am. Chem. Soc. Symposium Series *143*.

Vines, H. M., Grierson, W., and Edwards, G. J. 1968. Respiration, internal atmosphere, and ethylene evolution of citrus fruit. Proc. Am. Soc. Hortic. Sci. *92*, 227–234.

Wambeke, E. Van, Achter, A. Van, and Assche, C. Van 1979. Influences of repeated soil disinfection with methyl bromide on bromide content in different tomato cultivars and some quality criteria of these tomato fruit. Meded, Fac. Landbouwwet., Rijksuniv. Gent *44*, 895–900.

Wardowski, W. F., Albrigo, L. G., Grierson, W., Barmore, C. R., and Wheaton, T. A. 1975. Chilling injury and decay of grapefruit as affected by thiabendazole, benomyl and CO_2. HortScience *10*, 381–383.

Warren, J. M., Ballinger, W. E., and Mainland, C. M. 1973. Effects of ethephon upon fruit development and ripening of highbush blueberries in the greenhouse. HortScience *8*, 504–507.

Wells, A. E. 1962. Effects of storage temperature and humidity on loss of weight by fruit. USDA Mktg. Res. Rpt. *539*, Washington, DC.

Werner, R. A., and Frenkel, C. 1978. Rapid changes in the firmness of peaches as influenced by temperature. HortScience *13*, 470–471.

White, P. L. 1979. Challenge for the future: Nutritional quality of fruits and vegetables. HortScience *14*, 257–258.

Wild, B. L., and Rippon, L. E. 1973. Quality control in lemon storage. Agric. Gaz. N.S.W. *84*, 142–144.

Winkler, A. J. 1962. General Viticulture. Univ. of Calif. Press, Berkeley.

Wolpert, J. A., Howell, G. S., and Cress, C. E. 1980. Sampling strategies for estimates of cluster weight, soluble solids and acidity of Concord grapes. J. Am. Soc. Hortic. Sci. *105*, 434–438.

Woodroof, J. G. 1975. Fruit harvesting, handling and storing. *In* Commercial Fruit Processing. J. G. Woodroof and B. S. Luh (Editors). AVI Publishing Co., Westport, CT.

Yagi, M. I., Habish, H. A., and Agab, M. A. 1978. Effect of the method of harvest on the development of microorganisms and quality of mango fruit. Sudan J. Food Sci. Technol. *10*, 83–89.

Young, R. E., Romani, R. J., and Biale, J. B. 1962. Carbon dioxide effects on fruit respiration. II. Response of avocados, bananas, and lemons. Plant Physiol. Lancaster *37*, 416–422.

Effects of Agricultural Practices, Handling, Processing, and Storage on Cereals

Y. Victor Wu
George E. Inglett

Cereals are seed grains grown worldwide, principally as food sources. The major cereals are wheat, corn (maize), rice, oats, barley, rye, grain sorghum, and millet. Civilization could not exist today without early man's careful cultivation of these plants.

CEREAL COMPOSITION

The average chemical composition of wheat, corn, rice, oats, barley, rye, grain sorghum, triticale, and millet is given in Table 5.1. All cereal grains contain starch as the principal component, which is indicated by the high nitrogen-free extract values in Table 5.1. The second highest component of cereal grains is protein. Both content and nutritive value of cereal protein vary widely and depend particularly on seed heredity and environment during cultivation and harvest. An indication of protein composition differences can be seen by the amino acid patterns of the different cereal proteins (Table 5.2). Improvement in cereal protein quality and quantity has been a major thrust in plant breeding since the discovery by Mertz *et al.* (1964) that *opaque-2* corn (high lysine) has a protein composition that provides considerably better nutrition than ordinary corn.

WHEAT

Milling

Milling of good clean wheat (*Triticum aestivum*) is controlled by modern processes to give as much quality flour, farina, and germ as

Table 5.1. Average Composition of Cereal Grains

Property	Wheat[a]	Corn[b]	Rice[c]	Oats[d]	Barley[e]	Rye	Sorghum	Millet	Triticale
Moisture, %	12.5	13.8	12.0	8.3	11.1	11.0	11.0	11.8	12.0
Calories/100 g	330	348	360	390	349	334	332	327	—
Protein, %	12.3	8.9	7.5	14.2	8.2	12.1	11.0	9.9	13.9
Fat, %	1.8	3.9	1.9	7.4	1.0	1.7	3.3	2.9	1.5
N-free extract, %	71.7	72.2	77.4	68.2	78.8	73.4	73.0	72.9	66.9
Fiber, %	2.3	2.0	0.9	1.2	0.5	2.0	1.7	3.2	1.2
Ash, %	1.7	1.2	1.2	1.9	0.9	1.8	1.7	2.5	1.9
Thiamin, mg/100 g	0.52	0.37	0.34	0.60	0.12	0.43	0.38	0.73	0.65
Riboflavin, mg/100 g	0.12	0.12	0.05	0.14	0.05	0.22	0.15	0.38	0.25
Niacin, mg/100 g	4.3	2.2	4.7	1.0	3.1	1.6	3.9	2.3	3.5

Sources: USDA (1963), Moolani and Wagle (1977), Anderson et al. (1972), Anonymous (1975).
[a] Whole grain, hard red winter.
[b] Field, whole grain, raw.
[c] Raw, brown.
[d] Oatmeal, dry.
[e] Pearled, light.

Table 5.2. Amino Acid Content of Cereals (Percentage of Amino Acid in the Protein)

Amino acid	Wheat	Corn (field)	Rice (brown)	Barley	Oats	Rye	Sorghum	Millet	Triticale
Tryptophan	1.2	0.6	1.1	1.2	1.3	1.1	1.1	2.2	1.2
Threonine	2.9	4.0	3.9	3.4	3.3	3.7	3.6	4.0	3.4
Isoleucine	4.3	4.6	4.7	4.3	5.2	4.3	5.4	5.6	3.5
Leucine	6.7	13.0	8.6	7.0	7.5	6.7	16.1	15.3	7.8
Lysine	2.8	2.9	4.0	3.4	3.7	4.1	2.7	3.4	3.7
Methionine	1.3	1.9	1.8	1.4	1.5	1.6	1.7	2.4	1.3
Cystine	2.2	1.3	1.4	2.0	2.2	2.0	1.7	1.3	1.9
Phenylalanine	4.9	4.5	5.0	5.2	5.3	4.7	5.0	4.4	5.8
Tyrosine	3.7	6.1	4.6	3.6	3.7	3.2	2.7	—	4.0
Valine	4.6	5.1	7.0	5.0	5.9	5.2	5.7	6.0	4.7
Arginine	4.8	3.5	5.8	5.2	6.6	4.9	3.8	4.6	9.0
Histidine	2.0	2.1	1.7	1.9	1.8	2.3	1.9	2.1	2.4
Alanine	3.5	9.9	3.6	4.6	6.1	—	—	—	4.8
Aspartic acid	5.5	12.4	4.7	5.6	4.1	—	—	—	7.2
Glutamic acid	31.2	17.6	13.7	22.4	20.1	21.3	21.9	—	30.3
Glycine	6.1	3.4	6.8	4.6	4.6	—	—	—	5.5
Proline	10.4	8.4	4.8	9.0	5.7	—	—	—	10.6
Serine	4.6	5.6	5.1	4.6	4.0	4.1	5.1	—	5.2
Total protein, %	14.0	10.0	7.5	12.8	14.2	12.1	11.0	11.4	13.8

Sources: Orr and Watt (1968), Juliano *et al.* (1964), Villegas and Bauer (1974).

practical. Products from hard wheat are farina, patent flour, first clear flour, second clear flour, germ, shorts, and bran. Since flour products from milling are primarily for food applications, the wheat is cleaned before conditioning (or tempering) and grinding. Modern flour milling requires an intricate process involving many grinding and sifting steps. Similar flour milling processes for soft and durum wheats provide products for many foods that differ from those incorporating hard wheat products. Additives, such as maturing agents, bleaching agents, and self-rising ingredients are frequently blended into wheat flours at the mill. Flour being shipped to the baker is not enriched at the mill, but at the bakery. Family flour, packaged at the mill, is enriched at the mill (Anderson and Inglett 1974).

A small amount of the wheat in the world is processed to starch and gluten by wet milling, and the total production of wheat gluten was about 120,000 tons a year (Sarkki 1980). The baking industry is the largest user of gluten. Alkaline extraction procedures were used to yield protein and starch from whole wheat (Wu and Sexson 1975A) and mill feeds (Saunders *et al.* 1975). Protein concentrates from whole wheat and mill feeds had higher lysine content (first limiting amino acid in wheat) than wheat gluten (Wu and Sexson 1975B; Saunders and Betschart 1977).

Nutrient Composition of Wheat Flour

Wheat flour, the principal refined product of wheat milling, is the major ingredient in almost all breads, rolls, chapaties, crackers, cookies, biscuits, cakes, doughnuts, muffins, pancakes, waffles, noodles, macaroni, and spaghetti. Flour composition and functionality vary greatly, depending upon the milled wheat's heredity and the environmental conditions of its culture and harvest (Inglett 1974). The nutritional value of wheat foods depends largely on the chemical composition of the refined flour used in their preparation. The average percentage composition of hard wheat milled products is given for illustrative purposes in Table 5.3.

Table 5.3. Average Percentage Composition of Hard-Wheat Products

Constituent	Wheat	Farina	Patent flour	First clear flour	Second clear flour	Germ	Shorts	Bran
Moisture	12.0	14.2	13.9	13.4	12.4	10.5	13.5	14.1
Ash	1.8	0.4	0.4	0.7	1.2	4.0	4.1	6.0
Protein	12.0	10.3	11.0	12.7	13.5	30.0	16.0	14.5
Crude fiber	2.5	—	—	—	—	2.0	5.5	10.0
Fat	2.1	0.8	0.9	1.3	1.3	10.0	4.5	3.3

Source: Inglett (1974).

Vitamin and mineral compositions vary directly with the degree of flour extraction. These relationships have been extensively reviewed by Dimler (1960). Vitamin concentrations in wheat and wheat food products from later data are recorded in Table 5.4 (Toepfer *et al.* 1972).

The protein content of wheat is usually around 12%, but heredity and environment exert a strong influence on that level. Since the discovery of high-lysine corn (Mertz *et al.* 1964), some research emphasis has been placed on increasing the protein quality and quantity of wheat (Johnson *et al.* 1972). In the World Wheat Collection, maintained by the Agricultural Research Service, U.S. Department of Agriculture, 15,000 hexaploid and tetraploid wheats have been screened for protein and lysine contents. Mean protein value was nearly 13%, ranging between 7 and 22%. The lysine content of wheat protein varied between 2.2 and 4.2%, with a mean value of approximately 3%. Successful breeding of wheat for better protein quality and quantity can have an important impact on the nutrient content of wheat food products.

CORN

Milling

Corn (*Zea mays* L.) is processed to give food ingredients, industrial products, feeds, and alcoholic beverages. Approximately 1,100 million bushels were used by wet-corn processors, corn dry millers, and fermentation processors in 1985. Wet millers produce starch; modified starch products, including dextrose and syrups; feed products; and oil (Anderson 1970). The corn dry-milling process and the effects of dry milling on nutrient composition have been reviewed by Inglett (1975). In modern corn dry-milling plants a degerming system is the principal process employed. In this system the corn kernel is separated into hull, germ, and endosperm fractions that vary in particle size and fat content. Endosperm products (grits, meal, and flour) are the primary products used by the food processors and in consumer markets (Brekke 1970; Inglett 1970).

Nutrient Composition of Corn Dry-Milled Products

A modern corn dry miller, using a conventional degerming system, can produce a wide variety of products. Typical yields and analyses of products are reported for illustrative purposes in Table 5.5 (Brekke 1970). Human diets are improved by fortifying corn dry-milled products with vitamins and minerals. Enriched corn grits contain thiamin, riboflavin, niacin, and iron according to Federal Standards of Identity from Code of Federal Regulations, U.S. Food and Drug Administration. Calcium and vitamin D may be added as optional ingredients. These nutrients may be blended with such carriers as wheat or corn starches containing anticaking agents. The nutrients are added in powder form to the milled products (Brockington 1970).

Table 5.4. Vitamin Concentration in Wheat and Wheat Products

| Nutrient | Hard red wheat (dry wt) (μg/g) | Flour (%) | Bread | | Durum wheat (dry wt) (μg/g) | Semolina (%) | Macaroni (%) |
			Conventional dough mix (%)	Continuous dough mix (%)			
Thiamin	5.7	23	30	30	6.7	48	48
Riboflavin	1.2	34	161	122	1.1	88	86
Niacin							
Total	74	28	39	36	111	35	40
Free	36	44	64	61	47	47	45
Vitamin B₆	3.5	15	15	12	4.3	28	25
Pyridoxine	2.6	11	5	6	3.3	24	20
Pyridoxal	0.5	28	41	26	0.6	31	31
Pyridoxamine	0.4	22	55	35	0.4	53	58
Tocopherols	58	11	2	11	58	43	5
α-T	13	2	1	2	10	30	2
β-T	7	7	3	4	5	31	4
γ-T	—	—	—	1.9	—	—	—
δ-T	—	—	—	3.6	—	—	—
α-T-3	5	30	50	0	7	37	3
β-T-3	33	17	3	3	36	48	6

Source: Toepfer *et al.* (1972).

Table 5.5. Typical Yields and Analyses for Products That a Degerming-type Corn Dry Mill Might Produce

Product	Yield (%)	Typical particle size range[a]	Moisture (% wet basis)	Fat (% dry basis)	Crude fiber (% dry basis)	Ash (% dry basis)	Crude protein (% dry basis)
Corn	100		15.5	4.5	2.5	1.3	9.0
		Primary products					
Cereal flaking (hominy) grits	12	−3.5 + 6	14.0	0.7	0.4	0.4	8.4
Coarse grits	15	−10 + 14	13.0	0.7	0.5	0.4	8.4
Regular grits	23	−14 + 28	13.0	0.8	0.5	0.5	8.0
Coarse meal	3	−28 + 50	12.0	1.2	0.5	0.6	7.6
Dusted meal	3	−50 + 75	12.0	1.0	0.5	0.6	7.5
Flour[b]	4	−75 + pan	12.0	2.0	0.7	0.7	6.6
Oil	1						
Hominy feed	35		13.0	6.3	5.4	3.3	12.5
Shrinkage	4						
		Alternative products					
Brewers' grits	30	−12 + 30	13.0	0.7	0.5	0.5	8.3
100% Meal	10	−28 + Pan	12.0	1.5	0.6	0.6	7.2
Fine meal	7	−50 + Pan	12.0	1.6	0.6	0.7	7.0
Germ fraction[c]	10	−3.5 + 20	15.0	18.0	4.6	4.7	14.9

Source: Brekke (1970).
[a] U.S. standard sieve.
[b] Break flour.
[c] Yield is distributed between corn oil and hominy feed.

The discovery of the superior protein quality of *opaque-2* corn (Mertz *et al.* 1964) makes possible the production of dry-milled products with improved nutritional value. Conventional dry milling of *opaque-2* corn (high-lysine) gave products of acceptable fat content using ordinary dry-milling equipment (Brekke *et al.* 1971). However, the prime product spectrum of the high-lysine corn produced no flaking grits, but a considerable amount of table grits, meal, and flour resulted. *Opaque-2* corn is a floury variety, so the lack of large grit particles after milling is not surprising. Corn breeding programs are underway to develop high-lysine corn varieties with a greater horny (flinty) character.

A review of compositional and nutritional values of corn germ, a product of current degerming dry-milling operations, indicated that this fraction would provide a good quality protein source when properly handled (Inglett 1972). Corn germ flour prepared from a commercial dry-milled fraction appears to be a promising fortifying ingredient for the food industry (Blessin *et al.* 1973, 1979; Tsen 1975, 1976).

Protein concentrates from normal and high-lysine corns (Wu and Sexson 1976A) and from defatted dry-milled corn germ (Nielsen *et al.* 1973) were obtained by alkaline extraction of corn or corn germ and by precipitating the extracted proteins by acid. The protein concentrates had higher lysine content than the corns from which they were derived (Wu and Sexson 1976B).

RICE

Milling

Rice (*Oryza sativa* L.) is one of the leading food crops of the world. Rice-milling processes have been reported by Witte (1970, 1972). Four basic operations are performed by all rice mills: (1) removal of foreign matter from rough rice, (2) removal of hulls, (3) removal of bran, and (4) sizing of milled rice. A primary objective of rice milling is to obtain the maximum yield of unbroken grain. Broken kernels have about half the commercial value of unbroken kernels.

Solvent extractive rice milling is a relatively new process with reported higher yields of rice, fewer broken kernels, and two by-products—an edible defatted bran and a crude dewaxed oil (Hunnel and Nowlin 1972). The basic steps involved in this process are (1) pretreatment of brown rice before milling, (2) milling the pretreated brown rice in the presence of rice oil/hexane miscella, and (3) separation and recovery of the defatted bran, crude oil, and hexane.

The major constituent of milled rice is starch, and it is most concentrated in the endosperm portion of the kernel. Protein is the second most abundant constituent of rice grain and is unique among the cereal proteins because it contains at least 80% glutelin (alkali-soluble protein).

Table 5.6. Levels of Essential Amino Acids of Protein Fractions and Protein of Milled Rice (g/16.8 g N)

Amino acid	Protein fraction				Milled rice protein (%)
	Albumin	Globulin	Prolamin	Glutelin	
Isoleucine	4.05	3.03	4.68	5.27	4.13
Leucine	7.89	6.56	11.3	8.19	8.24
Lysine	4.92	2.56	0.51	3.47	3.80
Methionine	2.54	2.27	0.50	2.61	3.37
Methionine + cystine	5.40	2.27	0.80	4.09	4.97
Phenylalanine	2.97	3.32	6.26	5.42	6.02
Threonine	4.65	4.55	2.86	3.92	4.34
Tryptophan	1.88	1.34	0.94	1.16	1.21
Valine	8.72	6.18	6.97	7.31	7.21

Source: Juliano (1972).

Glutelin has the closest amino acid composition to milled rice protein, probably because it is the major protein fraction (Table 5.6). The protein content of rice of any variety can vary considerably even when grown at the same location (Cagampang *et al.* 1966; Tecson *et al.* 1971). For example, protein content of the high-protein variety BPI-76-1 may range from 8 to 14% and the low-protein variety, Intan, from 5 to 11% protein (at 12% moisture). Although protein quality tended to decrease as protein contents increased, the decrease in quality was less than proportional to the increase in protein content (Juliano 1972).

Nutrient Composition of Milled Rice

The composition of milled rice will vary depending on the variety, its agronomic conditions during growth, and the extent of milling. The

Table 5.7. Chemical Composition of Outer Layer, Endosperm, and Entire Kernel of Milled Rice[a]

Constituent	Unit	Outer layer[b]	Endosperm	Entire kernel[c]
Starch[d]	%	61.86	92.00	90.68
Amylose[d]	%	16.12	29.85	29.46
Reducing sugars	g maltose/100 g rice	0.50	0.07	0.12
Nonreducing sugars	g sucrose/100 g rice	2.42	0.11	0.26
Total sugars	%	2.92	0.18	0.38
Fiber	%	1.47	0.22	0.28
Total N	g N/100 g rice	2.53	1.27	1.39
Nonprotein N	g N/100 g rice	0.04	0.02	0.02
Protein N	g N/100 g rice	2.49	1.25	1.37
Albumin	g (N × 5.95)/100 g rice	1.75	0.29	0.30
Globulin	g (N × 5.95)/100 g rice	1.12	0.60	0.67
Prolamin	g (N × 5.95)/100 g rice	0.72	0.22	0.25
Glutelin	g (N × 5.95)/100 g rice	7.93	5.05	5.25
Insoluble fraction	g (N × 5.95)/100 g rice	3.28	1.48	1.69
Free amino N	mg/100 g	25.11	2.55	3.40
Total lipids[e]	%	4.44	0.45	0.66
Free fatty acids	%	1.34	0.15	0.21
Neutral fats	%	2.53	0.26	0.38
Phospholipids	%	0.57	0.04	0.07
Ash	%	6.10	0.45	0.72
Calcium[d]	%	0.36	0.05	0.02
Iron[f]	%	0.03	—	0.00
Phosphorus[d]	%	1.02	0.10	0.14

[a] Dry-basis data adopted from Barber (1972).
[b] Unless otherwise specified, 5% by weight of entire kernel.
[c] Unless otherwise specified, approximately 10% milling.
[d] Commercially milled rice; outer layer 4.4%.
[e] Chloroform:methanol (2:1) extractable lipids.
[f] Commercially milled rice; outer layer 4.27%.

Table 5.8.   Vitamin Content of Rice and Its By-Products (mg/100 g)

Vitamin	Brown rice	Milled rice	Rice bran	Rice polish	Rice germ
Thiamin	0.34	0.07	2.26	1.84	6.5
Riboflavin	0.05	0.03	0.25	0.18	0.5
Niacin	4.7	1.6	29.8	28.2	3.3
Pyridoxine	1.03	0.45	2.5	2.0	1.6
Pantothenic acid	1.5	0.75	2.8	3.3	3.0
Folic acid	0.02	0.02	0.15	0.19	0.43
Inositol	119	10	463	454	373
Choline	112	59	170	102	300
Biotin	0.01	0.01	0.06	0.06	0.06

Source: Houston and Kohler (1970).

milled rice kernel is not homogeneous in composition, but will vary by layers. The outer layer and the amount removed during milling are most important in determining the nutrient composition of the rice. The compositional differences of rice are illustrated by data given in Table 5.7. The chemical composition of the outer layer and the endosperm of milled rice is compared with the parent milled kernel. These data are based mainly on short-grain 'Balilla' rice originally milled to 10% (bran removed by weight of brown rice). The outer layer, accounting for 5% by weight of the milled kernel, was obtained by tangential-abrasive milling that left mainly the endosperm portion.

Vitamin contents of rice and its by-products are summarized in Table 5.8 (Houston and Kohler 1970). The refining of rice to give the milled product causes significant losses of essential vitamins. The enrichment of breakfast cereals based on milled rice appears justified.

OATS

Milling

The groat, or oat fruit, represents about 75% of the kernel weight and is tightly held within the chaff or hull. The fat content of oat groats will average about 7%, which is distributed throughout the kernel with a slight concentration in the germ and outer layers. The protein content will average 16–17%, with only a slight concentration in the germ and outer layers (Salisbury and Wichser 1971).

The initial step in oat milling is cleaning to remove foreign materials, such as sticks, corn, seeds, soybeans, barley, wheat, and dust. The cleaned oats are dried on pan driers normally 10–12 ft in diameter and placed one above the other in stacks of 7 to 14. As the oats gradually pass down the stack, normally 3–4% moisture is removed. The temperature of the oats seldom exceeds 93°C, but it is sufficient to cause a slight roasted flavor considered desirable. Rotary steam-tube driers are sometimes used by smaller millers, and many European plants use charcoal-fired kilns.

In some mills that dehull oats without drying or conditioning, the groats are heated separately to develop the desired toasted flavor. Besides flavor development, heating inactivates the lipolytic or fat-splitting enzymes sufficiently to prevent the development of undesirable flavors during processing.

Oats after drying and cooling are ready for the huller, which separates the hulls from the groats. An impact huller produces the best yields and requires less horsepower than earlier stone hullers did. Sizing the grain before hulling assists oat and groat separation in the United States.

In a large system, the final step is the separation of free groats used for producing old-fashioned flakes. Cutting converts the groats into uniform pieces with a minimum of fine granules or flour. Cutting is done with rotary granulators giving 2–4 pieces per groat. Cut groats are separated from the uncut groats, oats, and long hulls by a cylinder separator or disc machine. The cut material is heated with live steam at atmospheric pressure just before flaking. The steam-heated groats or cut groats are flaked on rolls that are adjusted to produce flakes of uniform thickness or density measurement. Oat flour is made by grinding steam-heated groats. For a white, lower-fiber flour, high-fiber fractions must be removed from the groats.

Nutrient Composition of Oat Products

The composition of oats, like other cereal grains, is greatly influenced by variety (heredity) and agronomic conditions during culture and harvest. Milled products will vary some between processors because of differences in milling operations. Typical compositions for groats, rolled oats, and oat flour are listed in Table 5.9.

The nutritional quality of oat protein is good; rolled oats have a protein efficiency ratio (PER) of 2.2 compared to casein with a PER of 2.5. Feeding studies of 7 pure oat varieties (Garland, Clintland, Bonkee, Newton, Beedee, Lodi, and Newaha) which had PER values between 2.25 and 2.38, indicated that the small variations in amino acids observed in these oat samples were not great enough to influence growth response (Clark and Potter 1972; Hischke et al. 1968). The protein content of oat groats being used for food has a value between 11 and 15%. However, some oats found in the Near East have protein contents varying between 14 and 25% in the groats.

Practically no research had been done on individual oat protein fractions until the pioneering work by Wu et al. (1972) at the USDA Northern Regional Research Center. Protein concentrates have been

Table 5.9. Composition of Groats, Rolled Oats, and Oat Flour (%, As-is Basis)

Fraction	Moisture	Protein (N × 6.25)	Crude fat	Crude fiber	Ash	Nitrogen-free extract	Calcium	Phosphorus	Iron
Whole groats									
Groats to rolls	7.0	15.6	8.0	1.5	1.8	66.1	0.0625	0.4456	0.0054
Fines from flaking	10.0	18.6	10.0	2.0	3.0	56.4	0.0748	0.7078	0.0065
Package-grade regular rolled oats	10.0	15.7	7.8	1.5	1.8	63.2	0.0576	0.4362	0.0053
Cut groats									
Groats to rolls	7.0	15.5	7.8	1.5	1.8	66.4	0.0613	0.4522	0.0046
Fines from flaking	10.0	11.0	7.5	1.2	1.1	69.2	0.0380	0.2687	0.0030
Package-grade quick-cooking rolled oats	10.0	15.4	7.7	1.5	1.8	63.4	0.0638	0.4544	0.0047
Whole oat flour	6.4	16.7	6.0	1.1	1.7	68.1	—	—	—

Source: Salisbury and Wichser (1971).

Table 5.10. Selected B-vitamin Contents of Oats and Oat Products from Same Milling (mg/100 g)

Product	Thiamin	Riboflavin	Niacin	Pyridoxine
Dry-milled oats	0.65	0.14	1.15	0.20
Finished groats	0.77	0.14	0.97	0.12
Hulls	0.15	0.16	1.04	—
Oat shorts	0.44	0.35	1.62	—
Oat flour, chips, and meal	0.78	0.17	1.25	—

Source: Geddes (1960).

prepared from oat flours of ordinary and high-protein varieties by air classification (Wu and Stringfellow 1973) and by wet-milling procedures (Wu *et al.* 1973; Cluskey *et al.* 1973). These protein products appear to have some promise for food applications.

Studies on selected B-vitamin contents of oats and oat products have been reviewed by Geddes (1960) and are summarized in Table 5.10.

BARLEY

Barley is used for human food in the form of parched grain, pearled grain for soups, flour for flat bread, and ground grain for porridge. Barley flour is milled generally by conventional roller milling (Pomeranz *et al.* 1971). Air classification can be used to separate barley flours into high-protein and low-protein fractions.

Conventional roller milling of barley gives four major products: flour, tailings flour, shorts, and bran. The flour contains primarily the starchy endosperm; the shorts and tailings flour, a mixture of aleurone and pericarp with some germ and endosperm; and the bran, hulls, and pericarp. On a dry-matter basis, barley contains 63–65% starch, 1–2% sucrose, 1% other sugars, 1–1.5% soluble gums, 8–10% hemicellulose, 4–5% cellulose, 2–3% lipids, 8–11% protein (N × 6.25), 2–2.5% ash, and 5–6% other substances. The protein content of milled products can vary widely. The yield, protein contents, and amino acid composition of roller-milled barley to 65% extraction barley flour are shown in Table 5.11 (Robbins and Pomeranz 1972).

A screening program of the World Barley Collection for genetic varieties having high lysine and high protein was successful, and the most promising variety, CI 3947 (Hagberg and Karlsson 1969) was later called Hiproly. The opportunities offered by this improved barley variety and its properties have been reviewed by Munck (1972).

Barley protein concentrate from normal and high-protein, high-lysine varieties was prepared by an alkaline extraction procedure (Wu *et al.* 1979). The essential amino acid composition of protein concentrate

Table 5.11.   Yield, Protein Contents, and Amino Acid Composition of Roller-Milled Barley Products

Assay	Whole kernel	Flour, 65% extraction	Tailings flour	Shorts	Bran
Yield, %	100.0	65.0	17.7	11.9	5.4
Protein, N × 6.25, %	9.3	9.8	11.3	8.8	3.1
Amino acids[a]					
Lysine	4.2	4.1	4.1	4.8	5.0
Histidine	2.4	2.4	2.4	2.1	1.4
Ammonia	3.1	3.1	3.0	2.9	3.5
Arginine	5.3	5.5	5.7	5.9	4.6
Aspartic acid	7.4	7.1	7.5	8.2	8.6
Threonine	3.6	3.6	3.6	3.8	4.2
Serine	4.1	4.0	4.1	4.2	4.7
Glutamic acid	22.6	23.3	22.9	21.2	20.6
Proline	11.4	10.1	9.6	9.2	9.9
Cystine/2	1.1	1.4	1.3	1.1	0.3
Glycine	4.5	4.3	4.7	5.1	5.0
Alanine	4.6	4.4	4.7	5.1	5.0
Valine	5.3	5.2	5.3	5.5	6.1
Methionine	2.5	2.7	2.5	2.5	2.3
Isoleucine	3.6	3.7	3.6	3.7	3.7
Leucine	6.8	7.0	6.8	6.9	7.5
Tyrosine	2.7	3.2	3.0	2.9	2.5
Phenylalanine	4.9	5.0	5.2	5.0	5.1

Source: Robbins and Pomeranz (1972).
[a] Grams of amino acid per 100 g recovered.

from high-protein, high-lysine varieties was greatly improved compared with normal barley. Fractionation of barley and malted barley flours by air classification to yield high-protein flour and starch fractions was reported by Vose and Youngs (1978).

SORGHUM

Dry milling of sorghum grain ranges from cracking, to produce a crude product, to debranning and degermination that yield refined fractions of bran, germ, meal, and grits. The composition of typical commercial sorghum dry-milled products is shown in Table 5.12. Wall and Ross (1970) and Rooney *et al.* (1980) provided information on sorghum production and utilization.

Normal sorghum has the lowest lysine content among the cereal grains. However, two floury lines of Ethiopian origin were exceptionally high in lysine at relatively high levels of protein (Singh and Axtell 1973). Another high-lysine sorghum, P721 opaque, was produced by chemical mutagen treatment of normal grain (Mohan and Axtell 1975).

Table 5.12.   Composition of Dry-Milled Commercial Sorghum Products (%)

Product	Protein	Oil	Fiber	Ash
Whole	9.6	3.4	2.2	1.5
Pearled	9.5	3.0	1.3	1.2
Flour				
Crude	9.5	2.5	1.2	1.0
Refined	9.5	1.0	1.0	0.8
Brewers' grits	9.5	0.7	0.8	0.4
Bran	8.9	5.5	8.6	2.4
Germ	15.1	20.0	2.6	8.2
Hominy feed	11.2	6.5	3.8	2.7

Source: Hahn (1969).

An alkaline extraction process gives protein concentrate and starch from ground sorghum of normal and high-lysine contents (Wu 1978). The protein concentrate from normal sorghum has a lysine content that exceeded that of sorghum by 50%, whereas the concentrates from high-lysine varieties showed an even larger increase in lysine content over the already elevated lysine levels of the high-lysine grains. Air classification of flour and horny endosperm from high-lysine sorghum yielded fractions with enriched protein content compared with the starting flour or horny endosperm (Wu and Stringfellow 1981). In addition, the high-protein fraction from horny endosperm also had considerably higher lysine content than the starting material.

TRITICALE

Triticale is a cross between wheat and rye. Now, triticales are competitive in yield with wheat [Centro Internacional de Merjoramiento de Maiz y Trigo (CIMMYT) 1982]. In acid soils, semitropical highlands, and some specific disease areas, triticale usually shows better yield performance than wheat. Most of the food products made from wheat flour can be made successfully from pure triticale flour, including fermented and nonfermented dough products. Good-quality bread can be made in mixtures of up to 75% triticale flour and 25% wheat flour. The loaf volume of bread made with triticale–wheat flour mixtures is higher than the loaf with 100% wheat flour in some cases.

Commercial dry milling of triticale is limited to 100% triticale flour in the United States. Wu *et al.* (1976) prepared protein concentrates and starch from ground triticale by an alkaline extraction process. Lorenz (1974) reviewed the history, development, and utilization of triticale; Hulse and Laing (1974) reported the nutritive value of triticale protein; Wu *et al.* (1978) summarized some food uses of triticale; and Bushuk and Larter (1980) reviewed the production, chemistry, and technology of triticale.

REFERENCES

Anderson, R. A. 1970. Corn wet milling industry. *In* Corn: Culture, Processing, Products. G. E. Inglett (Editor). AVI Publishing Co., Westport, CT.

Anderson, R. A., and Inglett, G. E. 1974. Flour milling. *In* Wheat: Production and Utilization. G. E. Inglett (Editor). AVI Publishing Co., Westport, CT.

Anderson, R. A., Stringfellow, A. C., and Griffin, E. L., Jr. 1972. Preliminary processing studies reveal triticale properties. Northwest. Miller *279*(2), 10–13.

Anonymous 1975. Genetic breakthrough unblocks commercial application for nutritious meal concentrate from triticale. Food Prod. Dev. *9*(2), 65.

Barber, S. 1972. Milled rice and changes during aging. *In* Rice Chemistry and Technology. D. F. Houston (Editor). Am. Assoc. Cereal Chem., St. Paul, MN.

Blessin, C. W., Garcia, W. J., Deatherage, W. L., Cavins, J. F., and Inglett, G. E. 1973. Composition of three food products containing defatted corn germ flour. J. Food Sci. *38*, 602–606.

Blessin, C. W., Deatherage, W. L., Cavins, J. F., Garcia, W. J., and Inglett, G. E. 1979. Preparation and properties of defatted flours from dry-milled yellow, white, and high-lysine corn germ. Cereal Chem. *56*, 105–109.

Brekke, O. L. 1970. Corn dry milling industry. *In* Corn: Culture, Processing, Products. G. E. Inglett (Editor). AVI Publishing Co., Westport, CT.

Brekke, O. L., Griffin, E. L., Jr., and Brooks, P. 1971. Dry-milling of *opaque-2* (high-lysine) corn. Cereal Chem. *48*, 499–511.

Brockington, S. F. 1970. Corn dry milled products. *In* Corn: Culture, Processing, Products. G. E. Inglett (Editor). AVI Publishing Co., Westport, CT.

Bushuk, W., and Larter, E. N. 1980. Triticale: Production, chemistry, and technology. Adv. Cereal Sci. Technol. *3*, 115–157.

Cagampang, G. B., Cruz, L. J., Espiritu, S. G., Santiago, R. G., and Juliano, B. O. 1966. Studies on the extraction and composition of rice proteins. Cereal Chem. *43*, 145–155.

Centro Internacional de Mejoramiento de Maiz y Trigo (CIMMYT) 1982. CIMMYT Review, El Baton, Mexico.

Clark, W. L., and Potter, G. C. 1972. The compositional and nutritional properties of protein in selected oat varieties. *In* Symposium: Seed Proteins. G. E. Inglett (Editor). AVI Publishing Co., Westport, CT.

Cluskey, J. E., Wu, Y. V., Wall, J. S., and Inglett, G. E. 1973. Oat protein concentrates from a wet-milling process: Preparation. Cereal Chem. *50*, 475–481.

Dimler, R. J. 1960. Effects of commercial processing on nutrient content. A. Milling. 1. Wheat. *In* Nutritional Evaluation of Food Processing. R. S. Harris and H. von Loesecke (Editors). John Wiley, New York. Revised in 1971 by AVI Publishing Co., Westport, CT.

Geddes, W. F. 1960. Oats and oat products. *In* Nutritional Evaluation of Food Processing. R. S. Harris and H. von Loesecke (Editors). John Wiley, New York. Revised in 1971 by AVI Publishing Company, Westport, CT.

Hagberg, A., and Karlsson, K. E. 1969. Breeding for high protein content and quality in barley. Symposium: New Approaches to Breeding for Improved Plant Protein, 1968. Int. Atomic Energy Agency, Vienna.

Hahn, R. R. 1969. Dry milling of grain sorghum. Cereal Sci. Today *14*, 234–237.

Hischke, H. H., Jr., Potter, G. C., and Graham, W. R. 1968. The nutritive value of oat protein. I. Varietal differences as measured by amino acid analysis and rat growth response. Cereal Chem. *45*, 374–378.

Houston, D. F., and Kohler, G. O. 1970. Nutritional properties of rice. Food and Nutrition Board, Natl. Res. Council–Natl. Acad. Sci., Washington, DC.

Hulse, J. H., and Laing, E. M. 1974. Nutritive Value of Triticale Protein. International Development Research Center, Ottawa, Canada.

Hunnell, J. W., and Nowlin, J. F. 1972. Solvent extractive rice milling. In Rice Chemistry and Technology. D. F. Houston (Editor). Am. Assoc. Cereal Chem., St. Paul, MN.

Inglett, G. E. 1970. Food uses of corn around the world. In Corn: Culture, Processing, Products. G. E. Inglett (Editor). AVI Publishing Co., Westport, CT.

Inglett, G. E. 1972. Corn proteins related to grain processing and nutritional value of products. In Symposium: Seed Proteins. G. E. Inglett (Editor). AVI Publishing Co., Westport, CT.

Inglett, G. E. 1974. Wheat in perspective. In Wheat: Production and Utilization. G. E. Inglett (Editor). AVI Publishing Co., Westport, CT.

Inglett, G. E. 1975. Effects of refining operations on cereals. In Nutritional Evaluation of Food Processing. 2nd Edition. R. S. Harris and E. Karmas (Editors), AVI Publishing Co., Westport, CT.

Johnson, V. A., Mattern, P. J., and Schmidt, J. W. 1972. Genetic studies of wheat proteins. In Symposium: Seed Proteins. G. E. Inglett (Editor). AVI Publishing Co., Westport, CT.

Juliano, B. O. 1972. Studies on protein quality and quantity of rice. In Symposium: Seed Proteins. G. E. Inglett (Editor). AVI Publishing Co., Westport, CT.

Juliano, B. O., Bautista, G. M., Lugay, J. C., and Reyes, A. C. 1964. Studies on physiochemical properties of rice. J. Agric. Food Chem. 12, 131–138.

Lorenz, K. 1974. The history, development, and utilization of triticale. CRC Crit. Rev. Food Technol. 5(2), 175–280.

Mertz, E. T., Bates, L. S., and Nelson, O. E. 1964. Mutant gene that changes protein composition and increases lysine content of maize endosperm. Science 145, 279–280.

Mohan, D. P., and Axtell, J. D. 1975. Proc. Ninth Biennial Grain Sorghum Research and Utilization Conference, Lubbock, TX.

Moolani, M., and Wagle, D. S. 1977. Chemical composition and protein quality of some high yielding varieties of triticale. J. Food Sci. Technol. 14, 53–55.

Munck, L. 1972. Barley seed proteins. In Symposium: Seed Proteins. G. E. Inglett (Editor). AVI Publishing Co., Westport, CT.

Nielsen, H. C., Inglett, G. E., Wall, J. S., and Donaldson, G. L. 1973. Corn germ protein isolate—Preliminary studies on preparation and properties. Cereal Chem. 50, 435–443.

Orr, M. L., and Watt, B. K. 1968. Amino acid contents of foods. USDA Home Econ. Res. Rept. 4.

Pomeranz, Y., Ke, H., and Ward, A. B. 1971. Composition and utilization of milled barley products. I. Gross composition of roller-milled and air-separated fractions. Cereal Chem. 48, 47–58.

Robbins, G. S., and Pomeranz, Y. 1972. Composition and utilization of milled barley products. III. Amino acid composition. Cereal Chem. 49, 240–246.

Rooney, L. W., Khan, M. N., and Earp, C. F. 1980. The technology of sorghum products. In Cereals for Food and Beverages. G. E. Inglett and L. Munck (Editors). Academic Press, New York.

Salisbury, D. K., and Wichser, W. R. 1971. Oat milling—Systems and products. Assoc. Operative Millers Bull., 3242–3247.

Sarkki, M–L. 1980. Wheat gluten. In Cereals for Food and Beverages. Recent Progress in Cereal Chemistry and Technology, p. 156. G. E. Inglett and L. Munck (Editors). Academic Press, New York.

Saunders, R. M., and Betschart, A. A. 1977. Nutritional quality of wheat millfeed protein concentrates. J. Food Sci. 42, 974, 975, 981.

Saunders, R. M., Conner, M. A., Edwards, R. H., and Kohler, G. O. 1975. Preparation of protein concentrates from wheat shorts and wheat mill run by wet alkaline process. Cereal Chem. *52*, 93–101.

Singh, R., and Axtell, J. D. 1973. High lysine mutant gene HL that improves protein quality and biological value of grain sorghum. Crop Sci. *13*, 535–539.

Tecson, E. M. S., Esmama, B. V., Lontok, L. P., and Juliano, B. O. 1971. Studies on the extraction and composition of rice endosperm glutelin and prolamin. Cereal Chem. *48*, 168–181.

Toepfer, E. W., Polansky, M. M., Eheart, J. F., Slover, H. T., and Morris, E. R. 1972. Nutrient composition of selected wheats and wheat products. XI. Summary. Cereal Chem. *49*, 173–186.

Tsen, C. C. 1975. Defatted corn germ flour: A nutritive ingredient for breadmaking. Baker's Dig. *49*, 42–44, 55.

Tsen, C. C. 1976. Regular and protein fortified cookies from composite flours. Cereal Foods World *21*, 633, 634, 637, 638, 640.

U.S. Department of Agriculture (USDA) 1963. Composition of foods. Agricultural Handbook 8. USDA, Washington, DC.

Villegas, E., and Bauer, R. 1974. Protein and lysine content of improved triticale. *In* Triticale: First Man-made Cereal. C. C. Tsen (Editor). Am. Assoc. Cereal Chem., St. Paul, MN.

Vose, J. R., and Youngs, C. G. 1978. Fractionation of barley and malted barley flours by air classification. Cereal Chem. *55*, 280–286.

Wall, J. S., and Ross, W. M. 1970. Sorghum Production and Utilization. AVI Publishing Co., Westport, CT.

Witte, G. C., Jr. 1970. Rice milling in the United States. Assoc. Operative Millers Bull., 3147–3159.

Witte, G. C., Jr. 1972. Conventional rice milling in the United States. *In* Rice Chemistry and Technology. D. F. Houston (Editor). Am. Assoc. Cereal Chem., St. Paul, MN.

Wu, Y. V. 1978. Protein concentrate from normal and high-lysine sorghums: Preparation, composition, and properties. J. Agric. Food Chem. *26*, 305–309.

Wu, Y. V., and Sexson, K. R. 1975A. Preparation of protein concentrate from normal and high-protein wheats. J. Agric. Food Chem. *23*, 903–905.

Wu, Y. V., and Sexson, K. R. 1975B. Composition and properties of protein concentrate from normal and high-protein wheats. J. Agric. Food Chem. *23*, 906–909.

Wu, Y. V., and Sexson, K. R. 1976A. Protein concentrates from normal and high-lysine corns by alkaline extraction: Preparation. J. Food Sci. *41*, 509–511.

Wu, Y. V., and Sexson, K. R. 1976B. Protein concentrates from normal and high-lysine corns by alkaline extraction: Composition and properties. J. Food Sci. *41*, 512–515.

Wu, Y. V., and Stringfellow, A. C. 1973. Protein concentrates from oat flours by air classifications of normal and high-protein varieties. Cereal Chem. *50*, 489–496.

Wu, Y. V., and Stringfellow, A. C. 1981. Protein concentrate from air classification of flour and horny endosperm from high-lysine sorghum. J. Food Sci. *46*, 304–305.

Wu, Y. V., Sexson, K. R., Cavins, J. F., and Inglett, G. E. 1972. Oats and their dry-milled fractions: Protein isolation and properties of four varieties. J. Agric. Food Chem. *20*, 757–761.

Wu, Y. V., Cluskey, J. E., Wall, J. S., and Inglett, G. E. 1973. Oat protein concentrates from a wet-milling process: Composition and properties. Cereal Chem. *50*, 481–488.

Wu, Y. V., Sexson, K. R., and Wall, J. S. 1976. Triticale protein concentrate: Preparation, composition, and properties. J. Agric. Food Chem. *24*, 511–517.

Wu, Y. V., Stringfellow, A. C., Anderson, R. A., Sexson, K. R., and Wall, J. S. 1978. Triticale for food uses. J. Agric. Food Chem. *26*, 1039–1048.

Wu, Y. V., Sexson, K. R., and Sanderson, J. E. 1979. Barley protein concentrate from high-protein, high-lysine varieties. J. Food Sci. *44*, 1580–1583.

6

Effects of
Agricultural Practices,
Handling, Processing, and
Storage on Legumes and Oilseeds[1]

Walter J. Wolf

Legumes and oilseeds are important sources of protein and oil for the human diet. Major legumes used as foods include peas, beans, lentils, peanuts, and soybeans. In some countries legumes are the main source of dietary protein, but in the United States, where animal protein consumption is high, legumes provide only a minor portion of the daily protein intake. Although they are legumes, peanuts and soybeans are high in oil content and are also classified as oilseeds. Other oilseeds of economic importance in the United States are cottonseed and sunflower seed.

EDIBLE LEGUMES

There are more than 13,000 species of legumes, but only about 20 are eaten by man (Aykroyd and Doughty 1964). In the United States, annual per capita consumption of peas and beans in 1983 was only 227 and 2815 g, respectively (USDA 1984), or a total of about 8 g/capita/day. This quantity supplies about 2 g of protein/day or 2% of the protein intake. In contrast, in many tropical and subtropical regions of the world, legumes provide the major supply of dietary protein and calories. For example, in India the per capita consumption of legumes is about 40 g/day (Udayasekhara Rao and Belavady 1978), and in Latin America, the common bean, *Phaseolus vulgaris*, is a staple, along with corn, in the traditional diet (Bressani and Elias 1974). Many legumes are rich in lysine, whereas cereals are low in this essential amino acid; consequently, legumes and cereals complement each other, with cereals providing

---

[1] Contribution from the Northern Regional Research Center, Agricultural Research Service, U.S. Department of Agriculture, Peoria, IL 61604.

119

methionine and cystine, which tend to be low in legumes. Legumes also provide several B-complex vitamins plus minerals and dietary fiber.

For purposes of discussion here, the term edible legumes is restricted to mature seeds of peas and beans; peanuts and soybeans are covered in the section on oilseeds. Five groups of peas and beans important as foods include chick-peas (*Cicer arietinum*, also called garbanzo, Bengal gram, chenata, or chana); peas (*Pisum sativum* var. *arvense* Poir., field or smooth pea, and *P. sativum* L., or wrinkled pea); broad beans (*Vicia faba*, also called horse or field bean); lentils (*Lens esculenta*); and beans (*P. vulgaris, P. lunatus, P. aureus,* and *P. mungo*). More detailed information on these legumes (often referred to as pulses) can be found elsewhere (Pattee *et al.* 1982; Reddy *et al.* 1982A,B; Sgarbieri and Whitaker 1982). Other legumes, such as certain *Lathyrus* species that contain toxic compounds, have been excluded; they have been reviewed recently (Padmanaban 1980).

Seed Structure

Pea and bean seeds consist of a seed coat (hull), hypocotyl-radicle axis, plummule, and two cotyledons. In chick-peas (*C. arietinum*), for example, the distribution is seed coat, 15%, cotyledons, 84%, and the remaining portion of the embryo, 1% (Lal *et al.* 1963). The seed coat is a protective barrier during storage and handling, and generally legume seeds with thin seed coats absorb water more rapidly than seeds with thick seed coats (Sefa-Dedeh and Stanley 1979). The cotyledons make up 80–90% of the seed and are sites of the energy stores, which in peas and beans is starch. Typically, cotyledon cells contain ovoid starch granules 10–40 μm long and 8–25 μm wide embedded in a matrix of protein bodies that contain the storage proteins (Fig. 6.1).

Composition

Representative proximate analyses of various peas and beans (Table 6.1) indicate that protein contents range from 22 to 31%, whereas fat contents vary from 1 to 6%. Ash (2–4%) and fiber (4–7%) constitute the remaining minor fractions. The major constituents are the carbohydrates that make up from 58 to 68% of the legumes. Composition of some legumes may vary considerably; in peas, for example, protein content varied from 14.5 to 28.5 (dry, dehulled basis) in one crop year (Reichert and MacKenzie 1982).

Proteins

The proteins of legumes include metabolic, structural, and storage types. Storage proteins are laid down during seed development and are mobilized as nitrogen and carbon sources during germination; they make up as much as 80% of the total protein (Sgarbieri and Whitaker 1982).

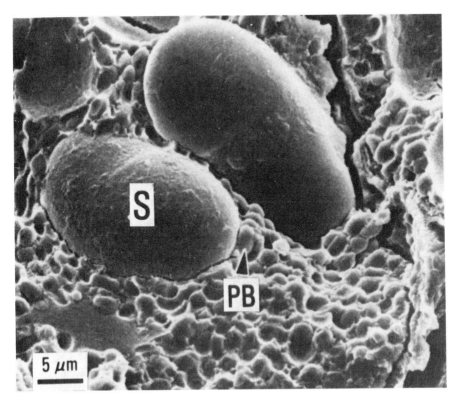

Fig. 6.1. Scanning electron micrograph of a cross section of a white bean (*P. vulgaris*) cotyledon showing starch granules (S) and protein bodies (PB). Source: Sefa-Dedeh and Stanley (1979).

Table 6.1. Composition of (g/100 g, dry basis) Peas and Beans

Legume	Protein	Fat	Ash	Crude fiber	Carbohydrate[a]
Chick pea (*Cicer arietinum*)	21.9	6.1	2.3	4.9	64.8
Pea (*Pisum sativum*)	24.6	1.2	2.8	3.9	67.5
Lentil (*Lens culinaris*)[b]	30.8	0.9	3.0	7.1	58.2
Navy bean (*Phaseolus vulgaris*)	25.8	1.8	3.6	6.6	62.2
Baby lima bean (*Phaseolus limensis*)	23.5	0.9	3.9	6.9	64.8
Cowpeas (*Vigna unguiculata*)	25.3	1.3	3.7	7.1	62.6
Broad bean (*Vicia faba*)[c]	30.3	1.1	3.5	6.8	58.3

Source: Meiners *et al.* (1976B), except as indicated otherwise.
[a] Nitrogen-free extract, by difference.
[b] Without seed coat.
[c] From Al-Nouri and Siddigi (1982).

The storage proteins consist mainly of two fractions, legumin and vicillin (Derbyshire *et al.* 1976). Legumins from various legumes have sedimentation coefficients of about 11 S and molecular weights in the range of 300,000 to 400,000. They are globulins with quarternary structures consisting of six subunits. Each subunit is comprised of an acidic polypeptide (MW 27,000–37,000) and a basic polypeptide (MW 20,000–24,000). Nielsen (1985) has reviewed the structures of the polypeptides of soybean 11 S globulin. Legumins have a high content of glutamic and aspartic acids that occur largely as amides. Vicillin-type proteins have sedimentation coefficients of approximately 7 S, molecular weights of 140,000 to 200,000, and subunits with molecular weights falling in the range of 23,000 to 56,000 (Derbyshire *et al.* 1976). Several vicillins are glycoproteins (containing covalently linked carbohydrate), in contrast to the legumins, which generally are low in carbohydrate content. In addition to the storage proteins, legumes contain phytohemagglutinins ($\sim$2–10% of total protein), protease inhibitors (0.2–2% of total soluble protein), and α-amylase inhibitors (Sgarbieri and Whitaker 1982).

Essential amino acid contents of selected peas and beans (Table 6.2) show that these legumes are good sources of lysine, but are low in methionine.

Lipids

Total lipids found in legumes vary with variety, origin, location of growth, climate, seasonal and environmental factors, and soil type in which the legumes are grown (Worthington *et al.* 1972). The lipids found in peas and beans consist of neutral lipids (primarily triacylglycerols plus di- and monoacylglycerols, free fatty acids, sterols, and sterol esters), phospholipids, and glycolipids (Pattee *et al.* 1982). The relative amounts of the three lipid classes vary with species. In peas, for example, distribution is as follows: neutral lipids, 46%; glycolipids, 10%; and phospholipids, 44% (Miyazawa *et al.* 1974). Representative values for fatty acids found in pea and bean lipids (Table 6.3) show that unsaturated fatty acids predominate, but that composition varies considerably from species to species. Noteworthy is a content of 48% linolenic acid in lipids of common beans; the other legumes contain only from 3 to 19% of this highly unsaturated fatty acid.

Carbohydrates

The major carbohydrate in peas and beans is starch, but numerous other sugar constituents are also present; there are the cell wall polysaccharides plus the oligosaccharides, sucrose, raffinose, stachyose, and verbascose. Table 6.4 shows the distribution of carbohydrates in six species of peas and beans. Sugars range from 6 to 12%, whereas starch varies from 24 to 41%. Contents of raffinose and stachyose are of practical interest because of the propensity of these sugars to form flatus on ingestion; the pentosans also appear to promote flatulence (Fleming 1981).

Table 6.2. Essential Amino Acid Content of Peas and Beans

	Pea[a] (Pisum sativum)	Chick pea[b] (Cicer arietinum)	Broad bean[c] (Vicia faba)	Lentil[d] (Lens esculenta)	Lima bean[c] (Phaseolus lunatus)	Kidney bean[c] (Phaseolus vulgaris)	Mung bean[d] (Phaseolus aureus)
Protein content, %, moisture-free basis	19.3	22.1	31.3	24.1	22.2	22.6	26.0
Amino acids, g/16 g N							
Arginine	9.2	—	7.6	8.5	6.8	5.6	5.2
Histidine	2.4	—	1.8	3.8	2.5	2.0	3.3
Isoleucine	4.0	4.9	4.2	6.3	4.0	3.7	5.8
Leucine	7.2	8.3	9.0	10.9	8.8	8.3	10.5
Lysine	7.4	7.4	6.2	8.0	8.1	6.6	6.8
Methionine	0.9	1.5	0.6	0.7	0.8	0.7	1.1
Phenylalanine	4.6	6.9	3.8	6.3	4.8	4.4	6.3
Threonine	3.8	4.0	3.6	4.5	4.3	3.4	3.9
Tryptophan	1.1	—	1.0	1.2	1.3	0.6	1.4
Valine	4.5	5.2	4.4	5.4	5.1	4.7	5.6

[a] Mean for 16 samples of 'Century' cultivar; protein, N × 5.25. Holt and Sosulski (1979).
[b] Shehata and Fryer (1970).
[c] Kanamori et al. (1982).
[d] Kahn and Baker (1957).

Table 6.3. Fatty Acid Composition (%) of Pea and Bean Lipids

	Chick pea (Cicer arietinum)	Pea (Pisum sativum)	Broad bean (Vicia faba)	Lentil (Lens esculenta)	Lima bean (Phaseolus lunatus)	Common bean (Phaseolus vulgaris)
Total lipid	4.99	2.40	1.60	1.17	1.41	1.48
Total fatty acids	3.86	1.78	1.24	0.90	1.09	1.15
Acid[a]						
Myristic	—	0.6	—	—	—	—
Palmitic	11.9	17.4	14.5	16.7	25.7	13.9
Stearic	1.6	2.8	2.4	1.1	2.8	1.7
Oleic	28.2	20.8	25.8	21.1	11.9	9.6
Linoleic	56.0	48.9	52.4	47.8	40.4	27.0
Linolenic	2.6	9.0	4.0	11.1	19.3	47.8
Arachidic	—	—	0.8	1.1	—	—
Eicosenic	—	—	—	1.1	—	—

Source: Calculated from data compiled by Exler *et al.* (1977).
[a] As percentage of total fatty acids. Values may not total 100% because of rounding off.

Table 6.4. Distribution of Sugars and Polysaccharides in Peas and Beans

	Chick pea (Cicer arietinum)	Wrinkled field pea (Pisum sativum)	Green lentil (Lens culinaris)	Mung bean (Vigna radiata)	Navy bean (Phaseolus vulgaris)	Kidney bean (Phaseolus vulgaris)
			Sugars[a]			
Total[b]	9.00	12.39	7.88	7.24	6.19	7.98
Sucrose	1.5–3.0	5.0	1.5–3.0	0.81	1.5–3.0	1.5–3.0
Raffinose	0.67	1.47	0.60	0.37	0.67	0.37
Unknown I	2.76	—	1.67	0.17	—	—
Stachyose	2.16	4.50	1.70	1.67	3.53	4.00
Unknown II	0.44	—	0.22	0.25	—	—
Verbascose	0.43	2.70	0.70	1.73	0.50	0.40
			Polysaccharides[a]			
Starch	37.2	24.0	41.0	40.4	30.4	32.8
Glucans	0.72	0.41	0.45	0.45	0.62	0.66
Pentosans	1.60	1.90	0.91	0.85	1.76	2.22
Cellulose	2.19	4.15	3.20	2.49	3.18	2.52
Hemicellulose	0.35	0.91	0.66	0.63	0.54	0.31
Lignin	7.08	0.74	11.35	7.33	0.13	2.69

Source: Fleming (1981).
[a] Content expressed as percentage of whole seed, dry basis.
[b] Total sugars extracted by 80% aqueous methanol.

Table 6.5. Vitamin Content of Peas and Beans[a]

Vitamin	Chick pea[b] (Cicer arietinum)	Pea[c,d] (Pisum sativum)	Red kidney bean[d] (Phaseolus vulgaris)	Mung bean[d] (Phaseolus aureus)	Lentils[e] (Lens esculenta)	Broad bean[b] (Vicia faba)
Ascorbic acid	0.72	9.6	5.0	6.0	8	5.38
Tocopherol	N.D.	0.76	0.79	2.20	N.D.	N.D.
Carotene	0.07	39.82	3.35	4.53	N.D.	0.09
Thiamin	0.81	0.95	1.53	0.48	0.80	1.00
Riboflavin	0.19	0.26	0.19	0.25	0.32	0.34
Niacin	1.68	2.32	3.46	2.57	3.5	2.52

[a] In mg/100 g whole seed (dry basis), N.D., not determined.
[b] Craviotto et al. (1951).
[c] Early Alaska variety.
[d] Fordham et al. (1975).
[e] Kylen and McCready (1975).

Vitamins and Minerals

Vitamin contents of several peas and beans are summarized in Table 6.5. Peas and beans are poor sources of fat-soluble vitamins but contain moderate amounts of the water-soluble vitamins.

Mineral analyses (Table 6.6) indicate that peas and beans are high in potassium and very low in sodium. Phosphorus is the second highest mineral and exists in several forms. In Bengal gram or chick-pea (C. arietinum), phosphorus is distributed as follows: acid-soluble, 74%; inorganic, 11%; phytate, 45%; phosphatide, 16%; and unaccounted (mainly nucleic acid?), 10% (Verma and Lal 1966). Analyses of 50 varieties and lines of mature dry beans (P. vulgaris) revealed ranges of 0.26–0.57% total phosphorus, 0.54–1.58% phytic acid, 0.02–0.04% inorganic phosphorus, and 0.05–0.14% organic, nonphytic acid phosphorus (Lolas and Markakis 1975).

Minor Constituents

Legumes also contain minor components, including phytates and tannins, that are important from a nutritional standpoint. In P. vulgaris, 54–82%, or an average of 69% of the total phosphorus, is phytic acid (Lolas and Markakis 1975). A survey of 11 legumes revealed a range of 0.4% (faba bean) to 1.2% (soybean) in phytic acid content (Elkowicz and Sosulski 1982). Reviews are available of phytates in legumes (Reddy et al. 1982C) and their interactions in food systems (Cheryan 1980).

Tannins are found in several legumes, including broad bean (V. faba) and chick-pea (C. arietinum). Testa (seed coat) of broad beans with colored flowers contain 4–8% tannins, whereas the testa from white-flowered broad beans contain less than 0.6% tannins (Griffiths and

Table 6.6. Mineral Content of Peas and Beans[a]

Legume	Calcium	Copper	Iron	Magnesium	Manganese	Phosphorus	Potassium	Sodium	Iron
Chick pea (*Cicer arietinum*)	103.1	0.86	5.82	91.7	1.71	354	692	12.69	2.86
Pea (*Pisum sativum*)[b]	34.9	0.63	2.22	87.2	1.08	348	1075	2.95	2.04
Lentil (*Lens culinaris*)[b]	47.2	0.89	9.56	90.7	1.42	522	862	2.49	3.15
Navy bean (*Phaseolus vulgaris*)	135.5	0.80	5.34	162.8	1.02	453	821	1.66	2.17
Baby lima bean (*Phaseolus limensis*)	76.1	0.64	6.79	163.6	1.64	397	1158	3.76	2.42
Cowpea (*Vigna unguiculata*)	69.0	0.91	7.97	206.3	1.25	518	838	8.39	2.89

Source: Meiners *et al.* (1976A).

[a] In mg/100 g edible portion. Moisture contents 13–19% (Meiners *et al.* 1976B).
[b] Without seed coat.

Jones 1977). Tannin contents of other legumes are cowpea (*Vigna unguiculata*), 0.0–0.6%; pigeon pea (*Cajanus cajan*), 0.0–0.1%; black gram (*P. mungo*), 0.3%; and adzuki bean (*V. angularis*), 0.3% (Price *et al.* 1980). Dehulling reduces the tannin content of dry beans (*P. vulgaris*) by 68–95% because the pigments are concentrated in the seed coat (Deshpande *et al.* 1982).

Nutritional Properties

The proteins of a number of legumes are deficient in sulfur-containing amino acids (methionine, cysteine, and cystine); methionine, the first limiting amino acid, is often less than 1% of the protein, whereas lysine may range from 6 to 8% (Table 6.2). The biological value of legume proteins is generally lower than that of other food proteins, partly because of the low methionine content. Part of the poor biological value is also attributed to heat-stable antinutritional factors such as cyanogenic glycosides, phytic acid, phenolic compounds, saponins, and estrogens. Other antinutritional factors such as protease inhibitors, amylase inhibitors, and hemagglutinins are heat-labile proteins and can be, thus, inactivated by cooking (Sgarbieri and Whitaker 1982). The low nutritive value of legume proteins has also been ascribed to their poor digestibility in the raw state, which can be markedly improved by cooking (Liener and Thompson 1980). Tobin and Carpenter (1978) and Sgarbieri and Whitaker (1982) have reviewed the nutritional properties of dry beans (*P. vulgaris*).

Processing

Soaking, cooking, and canning are the major processes used in the United States in preparing peas and beans for edible consumption, but other processes such as sprouting and roasting are being studied and applied. Fractionation of peas and beans into starch and proteins is not practiced in the United States, but extensive research and development in this area has occurred in Canada.

Sprouting

Consumption of sprouted legume seeds in the United States has increased since the mid-1970s because of consumer interest in nutrition and health foods. Changes in proximate analysis and vitamin and mineral content have received attention because of claims by health food proponents for sprouted seeds. Generally, legume sprouts are good sources of protein, minerals, and some vitamins (Augustin *et al.* 1983; Fordham *et al.* 1975; Kylen and McCready 1975; Vanderstoep 1981). Some vitamins, such as ascorbic acid, increase in concentration in some seeds upon sprouting (Fordham *et al.* 1975).

Quick-Cooking Process

A major deterrent to greater home use of peas and beans in the United States is the long time required for soaking and cooking. Soaking shortens the cooking time; salts such as sodium bicarbonate are often added to the soaking and cooking waters to further reduce the cooking time. Rockland *et al.* (1979) developed a procedure for quick cooking of various legumes using a mixture of sodium chloride, sodium tripolyphosphate, sodium carbonate, and sodium bicarbonate for soaking. After draining, such soaked beans cook very quickly (6–20 min) as compared to beans soaked only in water (40–220 min). The quick-cooking salt mixture apparently facilitates solubilization of intercellular pectic substances, thereby permitting cellular separation and softening of the beans (Varriano-Marston and de Omana 1979). Kinetics of cooking for salt-soaked beans have been reported (Silva *et al.* 1981).

Canning

Consumer interest in nutritional information has prompted studies on cooked legumes and canned products. Dry matter and nutrient loss during processing may be significant. For example, with cowpea (*V. unguiculata*) dehulling, soaking, and boiling result in losses of 19% in dry matter and 16% in crude proteins (Walker and Kochhar 1982). Generally, protein and fat are well retained during cooking, but losses may occur in minerals and vitamins because of leaching into the cook water and thermal destruction (Augustin *et al.* 1981; Meiners *et al.* 1976A).

Nutrient data for canned beans (*P. vulgaris*) and lima beans (*P. lunatus*) have been reported and are being used to provide nutritional information on product labels (Halaby *et al.* 1981).

Roasting

Dry roasting also has been explored for preparing bean products that are more convenient to use than conventional dry legumes (Aguilera *et al.* 1982A). Roasted navy beans (*P. vulgaris*) can be ground into a whole-bean flour or fractionated to yield a hull flour, a high-starch fraction, and a high-protein product (Aguilera *et al.* 1982B). The latter two fractions are obtained by pin milling and air classification.

Flours, Concentrates, and Isolates

In the United States, commercial conversion of peas and beans into products analogous to those of soybeans (e.g., flours, protein concentrates, and protein isolates) is limited to flours made from peas, Great Northern beans, lentils, or pinto beans.

Fractionation of legumes has been studied extensively in Canada. For example, fine grinding and air classifying have been applied to a variety of legumes, including field peas (*P. sativum*), navy beans (*P. lunatus*), mung beans (*V. radiata*), lentils (*L. culinaris*), and horse beans

(*V. faba*) (Reichert 1982; Sosulski and Youngs 1979; Vose *et al.* 1976). Pilot plant preparations of isolates from faba beans (*V. faba*), mung beans (*P. aureus*), and peas (*P. sativum*) have been described (Bramsnaes and Sejr Olsen 1979; Sumner *et al.* 1981; Thompson 1977). In 1987 production in Canada consisted of flours, starches, high cell wall-containing fractions, and hulls made from peas by pin milling and air classifying. Pea protein isolates were also being produced.

Food Uses

Consumption of peas and beans is widespread, especially in countries where animal proteins are scarce and expensive. In Mexico, for example, the black variety of kidney bean (*P. vulgaris*) is a staple of the diet. The legumes can be prepared by soaking in water, removing the seed coat, and then cooking for 1 hr or more to soften them. In India, the beans are mashed, cooked, and dried to form "grams." Grinding into powders or "dhals" is another popular method of preparation in India. Most of these legume products are consumed directly in the home.

In the United States, where consumption is lower than in other countries, peas and beans are both prepared in the home and processed commercially. In home use, the dried peas and beans are utilized in soups and the latter are also baked. Home preparation of dried legumes is low, however, because of the long time required for soaking and cooking. The major bean produced in the United States in 1981 was the pinto bean, followed by navy and 'Great Northern' beans. Pinto beans are prepared in canned forms such as chili with beans and related products, whereas navy beans are processed into canned pork and beans, baked beans, and beans in tomato sauce.

OILSEEDS

Soybean, cottonseed, peanut, and sunflower are the major oilseeds grown in the United States. Soybeans and peanuts are legumes, but are atypical because of their high oil contents and little or no starch. Soybeans, sunflowers, and particularly peanuts are consumed directly as foods, but the four oilseeds primarily serve as sources of edible oils and high-protein meals that are the mainstay of the animal feed industry. Of the four oilseeds, the soybean is the largest supplier of edible oil and edible protein products.

Seed Structure

Soybeans, peanuts, and cottonseed are dicotyledons consisting of a seed coat (hull), two cotyledons, and the axial organs, hypocotyl and

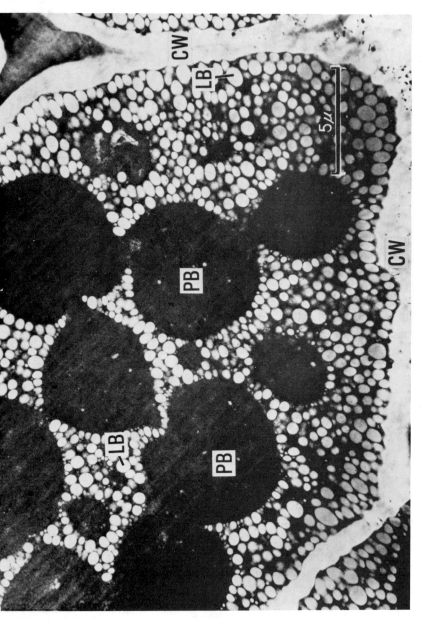

Fig. 6.2. Transmission electron micrograph of a mature, hydrated cotyledonary cell. Cell wall (CW), protein bodies (PB), and lipid bodies (LB) are identified. Source: Saio and Watanabe (1968).

radicle. Sunflower seeds consist of a pericarp or hull plus a single kernel. The oil and the bulk of the protein are stored in membrane-bound lipid bodies and protein bodies, respectively, as illustrated for soybeans in Fig. 6.2. In soybeans, the lipid bodies are from 0.2 to 0.5 μm and the protein bodies range from 2 to 20 μm in diameter. Cotyledons of most cottonseed varieites also contain pigment glands (storage sites for gossypurpurin and gossypol) 100–400 μm long (Berardi and Goldblatt 1980). Glandless cottonseed varieties are available but are not grown on a large scale. In contrast to peas and beans (Fig. 6.1), the oilseeds contain only an occasional starch granule (not shown in Fig. 6.2).

Composition

Compositions for the oilseeds are given in Table 6.7. Except for soybeans all have a high seed-coat or hull content. The high hull content of the other seeds results in high crude fiber levels; some confectionary varieties of sunflowers have as much as 28% crude fiber (Wan et al. 1979). Because of their high fiber content, the hulls are usually removed when oilseeds are processed into food products; dehulling has a significant effect on protein content of defatted meals (Table 6.7), because the hulls are high in cellulose and other polysaccharides.

Proteins

The proteins in the four oilseeds are complex mixtures consisting of storage, metabolic, and structural proteins that fall into four major groups with molecular weights of 8,000 to 700,000, exemplified by the

Table 6.7. Approximate Compositions of Oilseeds[a]

Oilseed	Hulls (%)	Oil (%)	Protein (N × 6.25)(%)	Ash (%)	Protein in dehulled, defatted meal[b] (%)
Cottonseed[c]	36	21.6	21.5	4.2	—
Cottonseed kernels	—	36.4	32.5	4.7	63
Peanuts	20–30	—	—	—	—
Peanut kernels	2–3.5[d]	50.0	30.3	3.0	57
Soybean	8	20	43	5.0	52
Sunflower[e]	47	29.8	18.1	—	67
Sunflower[f]	31	48.0	16.9	—	60
Sunflower kernels[f]	—	64.7	21.2	—	—

[a] Moisture-free basis. Taken from Smith (1958), except as noted otherwise.
[b] Data vary with efficiency of dehulling and oil extraction, variety of seed, and climatic conditions during growth.
[c] Acid delinted.
[d] Red skins or testa.
[e] Arrowhead variety low-oil type (Earle et al. 1968).
[f] Armavirec variety high-oil type (Earle et al. 1968).

2   7   11   15

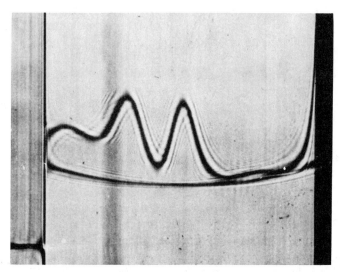

Fig. 6.3. Ultracentrifuge patterns for the proteins extracted with water from de-fatted soybean flakes in pH 7.6, 0.5 ionic strength buffer. Sedimentation coefficients in Svedberg units (S) are given above peaks. Approximate molecular weights for the fractions are 2 S: 8,000–50,000; 7 S: 100,000–180,000; 11 S: 300,000–350,000; 15 S: 700,000. Source: Wolf (1970).

ultracentrifuge pattern for soybean proteins (Fig. 6.3). The 7 S and 11 S fractions are the major proteins, except in sunflowers where the 2 S and 11 S fractions predominate (Rahma and Narasinga Rao 1979). Considered to be storage proteins, the 7 S and 11 S fractions are of the legumin and vicillin types and are located in the protein bodies (Fig. 6.2, Derbyshire *et al.* 1976).

Amino acid compositions for the proteins in the defatted oilseed meals are given in Table 6.8. Also shown is the essential amino acid pattern for a high-quality protein to meet human dietary requirements as established by the Food and Nutrition Board (FNB) of the National Research Council. Soybean proteins meet or exceed the reference pattern requirements, except for valine and the sulfur amino acids, which are only slightly low. The other proteins, however, are deficient in four or five amino acids, including lysine, threonine, valine, isoleucine, and leucine.

Lipids

Fatty acid compositions for the crude oils obtained from the four oilseeds indicate that the oils contain 70–85% unsaturated fatty acids, with sunflower being the highest (Table 6.9). Soybean oil differs from

Table 6.8. Amino Acid Composition (g/16 g N) of Defatted Oilseed Meals

Amino acid	Cottonseed[a]	Peanut[b]	Soybean[c]	Sunflower[d]	FNB pattern[e]
Lysine	4.4	3.4	6.4	3.8	5.1
Histidine	2.7	2.4	2.6	2.5	1.7
Ammonia	2.1	1.7	1.9	2.2	1.7
Arginine	11.6	12.0	7.3	8.9	—
Aspartic acid	9.2	13.0	11.8	8.7	—
Threonine	3.0	2.5	3.9	3.2	3.5
Serine	4.2	5.2	5.5	3.9	—
Glutamic acid	21.7	20.6	18.6	21.0	—
Proline	3.6	5.1	5.5	5.0	—
Glycine	4.1	6.6	4.3	5.1	—
Alanine	3.9	3.8	4.3	4.1	—
Valine	4.5	3.1	4.6	4.8	4.8
Cystine	2.6	2.5	1.4	1.8	⎫ 2.6
Methionine	1.5	1.1	1.1	1.9	⎭
Isoleucine	3.1	2.3	4.6	4.0	4.2
Leucine	5.8	6.2	7.8	6.1	7.0
Tyrosine	3.1	3.6	3.8	2.7	⎫ 7.3
Phenylalanine	5.4	5.0	5.0	4.7	⎭
Tryptophan	1.2	1.0	1.4	1.1	1.1

[a] Means for eight glanded seed varieties (Lawhon et al. 1977).
[b] Means for 16 varieties (Young et al. 1973), except for tryptophan (Lusas 1979).
[c] Means based on 32 hydrolyzates except for proline, cystine, and tryptophan (Cavins et al. 1972).
[d] Means for seven varieties (Earle et al. 1968).
[e] Food and Nutrition Board pattern for high-quality protein for human (NAS 1980).

Table 6.9. Fatty-Acid Composition (%) of Unprocessed Oils from Four Oilseeds

Fatty acids	Cottonseed[a]	Peanut[b]	Soybean[a]	Sunflower[a]
Saturated				
10:0	0.48	—	—	—
12:0	0.38	—	0.10	—
14:0	0.79	—	0.16	0.1
16:0	22.0	10.5	10.7	5.81
18:0	2.24	3.2	3.87	4.11
20:0	0.19	1.4	0.22	0.29
22:0	—	2.1	—	0.61
24:0	—	0.7	—	—
Unsaturated				
16:1	0.78	—	0.29	0.10
18:1	18.1	50.3	22.8	20.7
18:2	50.3	30.6	50.8	63.5
18:3	0.40	—	6.76	0.32
20:1	—	1.0	—	0.10

[a] From Brignoli et al. (1976).
[b] Mean values for 1968 crop of 82 peanut genotypes (Worthington et al. 1972).

the others because it contains 4–10% linolenic acid, which is especially sensitive to oxidative deterioration.

Carbohydrates

Oilseeds contain soluble mono- and oligosaccharides plus insoluble polysaccharides. Data for the soluble sugars and total carbohydrates of defatted oilseed flours are listed in Table 6.10. Sucrose, raffinose, and stachyose are the main sugars present. Total carbohydrates minus the total soluble sugars range from 11 to 19% of the flours and estimate the amount of polysaccharides. Raffinose and stachyose are of practical significance because of their contribution to flatulence when defatted flour products are ingested (Rackis 1981).

Vitamins, Minerals, and Minor Constituents

Mineral and vitamin contents for the four oilseeds are compiled in Table 6.11. Noteworthy are the low sodium and high potassium contents of oilseeds.

Among minor constituents of the oilseeds is phytic acid, which occurs at the following levels:

Seed	Phytic acid (%)	Reference
Cottonseed kernels	2.2–3.8	Pons *et al.* (1953)
Peanuts	0.8	Pons *et al.* (1953)
Soybeans	1.0–1.5	Lolas *et al.* (1976)

Cottonseed kernels contain 1.1–1.3% gossypol (Lawhon *et al.* 1977) plus related pigments that affect color and nutritional properties of the oil and meal. In addition, cottonseed contains the cyclopropenoid fatty acids, malvalic and sterculic acids in the form of glycerides that are extractable with hexane. Crude cottonseed oils contain 0.6–1.0% of these fatty acids (Bailey *et al.* 1966), whereas in refined oils the values are lower, 0.04–0.42% (Harris *et al.* 1964).

Phenolic acids occur at low levels in soybeans, but are important constituents of sunflower seeds. Chlorogenic acid (2.7%), quinic acid (0.38%), and caffeic acid (0.2%) are found in defatted sunflower meal (Cater *et al.* 1972). Chlorogenic acid is sensitive to pH and turns from yellow to green and finally to brown as the pH is elevated from 7 to 11. These chromophoric properties give rise to undesirable colors in sunflower protein preparations, thereby limiting their use in foods (Robertson 1975).

Soybeans contain the isoflavone glucosides, genistin, daidzin, and glycetein-7-β-glucoside plus small amounts of the corresponding aglycones. Isoflavone contents range from 0.047 to 0.36% (Eldridge and Kwolek 1983).

Other minor constituents are saponins found in soybeans and peanuts. Soybeans are reported to contain 5.6% and defatted flours 2.2–2.5%

Table 6.10. Carbohydrate Contents (%) of Defatted Oilseed Flours

Constituent	Cottonseed Deglanded[a]	Glandless	Peanut	Soybean	Sunflower
Soluble sugars					
Glucose	Trace	Trace	2.12	Trace	0.60
Sucrose	2.41	2.62	7.70	7.80	2.29
Trehalose	—	—	—	—	0.79
Raffinose	7.93	11.95	Trace	1.25	3.22
Stachyose	0.95	0.68	—	6.30	—
Total	11.29	15.25	9.82	15.35	6.90
Total carbohydrate[b]	22.5	26.8	22.4	34.0	24.2

Source: Data from Cegla and Bell (1977).
[a] Prepared by liquid cyclone process.
[b] Obtained by difference: 100 − (protein + oil + ash + crude fiber) = nitrogen-free extract.

Table 6.11. Mineral and Vitamin Contents of Oilseeds

Constituent	Cottonseed[a]	Peanut[b]	Soybean[c]	Sunflower[d]
Calcium, %	0.18	0.02–0.09	0.22[e]	0.13
Phosphorus, %	0.55	0.25–0.66	0.71[e]	0.88
Sodium, %	0.14	0.001–0.05	0.0004[e]	—
Potassium,%	0.97	0.54–0.89	2.52[e]	0.97
Magnesium, %	0.33	0.09–0.34	0.31[e]	—
β-Carotene, $\mu g/g$	0.22	0.26	0.2–2.4	—
Thiamin, $\mu g/g$	17–22[f]	2.5–14.0	11.0–17.5	21
Riboflavin, $\mu g/g$	2.3	1.05–1.57	2.3	2.4
Niacin, $\mu g/g$	16	—	20.0–25.9	57
Pantothenic acid, $\mu g/g$	11	25–35	12	—
Pyrodoxine, $\mu g/g$	9.8	3.0	6.4	—
Biotin, $\mu g/g$	0.29	0.34–1.1	0.6	—
Folic acid, $\mu g/g$	3.8	2.8	2.3	—
Inositol, $\mu g/g$	3400	1800	1.9–2.6	—
Choline, $\mu g/g$	3.0	1650–1740	3400	—
Ascorbic acid, $\mu g/g$	—	58	5.8	—

[a] From Altschul et al. (1958).
[b] From Rosen (1958). Data for kernels.
[c] From Liener (1972), Fordham et al. (1975), and Osborn (1977).
[d] From Adams and Richardson (1977). Data for kernels.
[e] Values for defatted, undehulled meal; values for seeds are about 20% lower.
[f] Values for dehulled meats.

saponins (Fenwick and Oakenfull 1981), but these values are about 10 times higher than those of earlier workers.

Nutritional Properties

Oil

Unhydrogenated and partially hydrogenated oils from cottonseed, peanuts, soybeans, and sunflowers are good sources of linoleic acid, an essential fatty acid. Hydrogenation of soybean oil is used extensively to impart high-temperature stability to cooking oil, extend shelf life, and to give better flavor stability and physical and plastic properties. Such processing lowers the content of linoleic and linolenic acid but also causes migration of double bonds up and down the chain and converts cis to trans isomers (positional and geometrical isomerization). Long-term tests with rats and short-term studies with humans have not shown toxic effects on ingesting partially hydrogenated soybean oil, but the problem is being studied further (Erickson *et al.* 1980). Hydrocarbons, cyclic hydrocarbons, alcohols, cyclic dimeric acids, and polymeric fatty acids form during heating and oxidation of fats. Although some of these compounds are toxic, an oil such as soybean oil is considered safe and nontoxic under normal cooking conditions (Erickson *et al.* 1980).

Cyclopropenoid fatty acids occurring in cottonseed oil affect several species. The laying hen deposits these fatty acids in the egg yolks; on storage the yolks become rubbery and the whites turn pink (Phelps *et al.* 1965). Cyclopropenoid fatty acids act synergistically with aflatoxins and as liver carcinogens (Hendricks *et al.* 1980). Adverse effects have not been noted in humans; it is presumed that humans are not affected at normal levels of ingestion (Mattson 1973). Processing lowers the content of cyclopropenoid acids in crude cottonseed oil, especially during deodorization (Harris *et al.* 1964).

Proteins and Meals

Nutritional properties of the oilseed meals and derived protein products depend on their amino acid compositions plus the presence of biologically active proteins and a variety of nonprotein compounds that occur in the defatted meals. For example, phytic acid found in all four oilseeds has been implicated in preventing absorption of dietary zinc, calcium, magnesium, and iron (Reddy *et al.* 1982C).

Cottonseed. Cottonseed proteins are low in lysine, threonine, isoleucine, and leucine when compared with the FNB ideal amino acid pattern (Table 6.8). On moist heating of cottonseed, the ϵ-amino group of lysine reacts with the aldehyde groups of gossypol to form a derivative that makes the lysine unavailable during digestion, thus creating an even greater imbalance with respect to lysine (Berardi and Goldblatt 1980).

Gossypol has other undesirable properties. It is toxic to monogastric animals and, when fed to laying hens, it causes discoloration of the yolks (Berardi and Goldblatt 1980; Phelps *et al.* 1965). Gossypol toxicity is not a problem with ruminants unless large amounts are fed (Lindsey *et al.* 1980). No toxicity has been observed when cottonseed flour containing gossypol was fed to humans, and cottonseed flour was used commercially for many years (Berardi and Goldblatt 1980). The Food and Drug Administration (FDA) limits free gossypol [the fraction extractable with acetone:water, 70:30 (v/v)] in edible cottonseed flour to 450 ppm.

The cyclopropenoid acids, sterculic and malvalic acids, occur as glycerides in the seed, but extraction with hexane lowers their concentration from about 0.05–0.2% in the seed to 0.002–0.008% in defatted meal (Levi *et al.* 1967).

Peanuts.   Low levels of lysine, threonine, isoleucine, and leucine (Table 6.8) make peanut proteins lower in nutritional value than soybean proteins, but peanut proteins generally are better than wheat or corn proteins (Rosen 1958). Raw peanuts have a trypsin inhibitor level that is about one-fifth that found in raw soybeans, yet it is high enough in concentration to induce pancreatic hypertrophy (enlargement) in rats. The inhibitor is inactivated by moist heat, but such processing does not improve the nutritive value of peanut flour (Anantharaman and Carpenter 1969).

Soybeans.   Methionine is the first limiting amino acid in soybean proteins, and synthetic methionine is commonly added to broiler rations to correct this deficiency. Methionine supplementation, however, appears unnecessary for human consumption of soybean proteins except possibly for infants (Wilcke *et al.* 1979). It has been known for many years that raw soybeans have poor nutritive value, but on cooking, the nutritional quality is greatly increased. Trypsin inhibitors are believed responsible for part of the low nutritive value of raw soybeans. Trypsin inhibitor activity in raw soybeans is high, and when fed to rats, it causes poor growth and pancreatic hypertrophy. Moist heat, however, destroys most of the inhibitor activity, and there is no evidence that residual activity is of any consequence when soybean proteins are ingested by humans (Liener 1981). Ingestion by rats of commercial soy flour, concentrate, or isolate for about 300 days failed to demonstrate pancreatic hypertrophy (Rackis *et al.* 1979). Different species respond in dissimilar ways to ingestion of raw soy flour that is high in trypsin inhibitor activity.

Rats, mice, and chicks exhibit pancreatic enlargement when they are fed raw soy flour, whereas pigs and monkeys do not (Struthers *et al.* 1983).

Poor digestibility has also been suggested as a factor responsible for the poor nutritional properties of unheated soybean proteins (Liener 1981).

Sunflower Seed.   Sunflower proteins are deficient in lysine and leucine and borderline in threonine and isoleucine content as compared to the ideal protein for humans (Table 6.8). Heating the seed before extracting the oil improves the nutritional value of the defatted meal (Amos *et al.* 1975). Although this result suggests the presence of heat-labile antinutritional factors, none has been clearly identified at present (Robertson 1975).

Processing

Oil and Meal

Depending on the oil content of the seed, processing may consist of screw pressing, prepress solvent extraction, or direct solvent extraction. Pressing is usually used only with seeds having a high oil content. All three techniques are used in processing cottonseed (Fig. 6.4). The seed is cleaned (removal of sticks, stones, leaves, and other foreign materials), delinted (mechanical removal of cotton fibers remaining after ginning), dehulled, and flaked (passage between smooth rolls). Some processors extract the flakes directly; others cook the flakes and then screw press them or use a combination of screw pressing followed by solvent

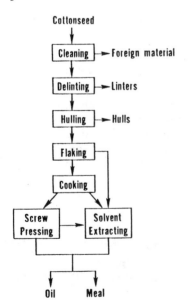

Fig. 6.4.   Outline for processing cottonseed into oil and meal.

extraction. Peanuts are processed by screw pressing or by screw pressing followed by solvent extraction, whereas sunflower seeds are screw pressed, direct solvent extracted, or prepress solvent extracted.

Because soybeans contain only about 20% oil, virtually all are processed by direct solvent extraction (Fig. 6.5). Soybeans are cleaned and dried, if necessary, and then stored. After storage, they are cleaned further, cracked to loosen the hulls, dehulled, and conditioned to 10–11% moisture for flaking. After conditioning, the meats are flaked and extracted with hexane. Hexane and crude oil in the miscella (oil-rich hexane extract) are separated by evaporation to recover the hexane. Residual hexane in the flakes is recovered by evaporation in the desolventizer-toaster, and the defatted flakes are cooked with moist heat (toasting) to inactivate antinutritional factors and increase protein digestibility (Liener 1981).

Edible Oil Products

Crude oils obtained from oilseeds are processed further into salad and cooking oils, shortenings, and margarines as exemplified by soybean oil (Fig. 6.6).

Phosphatides and gums are removed first by degumming to yield crude lecithin, which is further refined or added back to the defatted flakes just before the desolventizing-toasting step. Free fatty acids, color bodies, and metallic prooxidants are removed by the alkali refining. Activated earth in the bleaching step removes additional color bodies, and soaps. The deodorization process decomposes peroxides and removes odors and residual free fatty acids. Partial hydrogenation, under conditions for selective hydrogenation of linolenate, yields an oil more stable at elevated temperatures to oxidation and flavor deterioration. Winterization (cooling and removing solids that crystallize in the cold) yields salad and cooking oils. Hardened fats are obtained by partial hydrogenation and may be utilized directly or blended with other vegetable oils or animal fats for use as shortening and margarine. Blends of oils of varying melting points are used to obtain desired mouth feel and plastic melting ranges plus the most economical formulation.

Polyunsaturated fatty acids, especially linolenic esters in vegetable oils, undergo oxidative deterioration resulting in undesirable flavors such as beany, grassy, painty, or fishy. Exclusion of metal contaminants (iron and copper), addition of metal chelators (citric acid), minimum exposure to air, protection from light, and selective hydrogenation to reduce the linolenate to about 3% are measures employed to control oxidation (Erickson *et al.* 1980).

Edible Protein Products

At present, only defatted soybean flakes are processed into edible protein products. Until about 1986, peanut flour and grits were prepared from prepress hexane-extracted flakes and used as food ingredients (Ayres

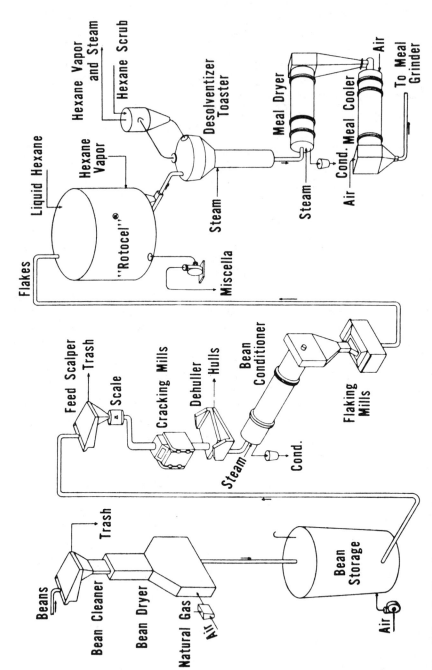

Fig. 6.5. Outline for processing soybeans into oil and meal by hexane extraction. Courtesy of Dravo Corporation.

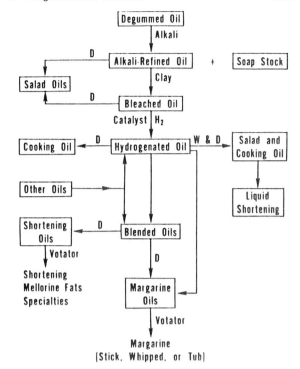

Fig. 6.6 Outline for manufacture of edible soybean oil products. D, deodorization; W, winterization; Votator, heat exchange equipment for solidification of fats. Source: Erickson *et al.* (1980), courtesy of the American Soybean Association and the American Oil Chemists' Society.

et al. 1974); however, production has since been discontinued. Partially defatted peanut flours made by hydraulic pressing are still available commercially. Soybeans, on the other hand, are converted into defatted flours and grits, concentrates, and isolates; their preparation is described below.

Defatted Soybean Flours and Grits

Edible-grade, defatted soybean flakes are manufactured basically as shown in Fig. 6.5, but under more sanitary conditions than are needed to produce feeds, and the hexane is removed in a vapor desolventizer-deodorizer or flash desolventizer (Becker 1978) rather than with the desolventizer-toaster. After desolventizing, the defatted flakes are ground and classified by screening. Grits have particle sizes larger than 100 mesh, whereas flours are 100 mesh or finer in particle size. Varying degrees of heat treatment are given to grits and flours to inactivate enzymes and to improve flavor and nutritional quality. Extent of heat treatment is measured by determining the Nitrogen Solubility Index (NSI) or the Protein Dispersibility Index (PDI), which estimate the amounts of undenatured protein that remains dispersible in water under conditions of the tests (American Oil Chemists' Society 1976). Raw, uncooked flours or grits have a PDI or NSI of about 90, and a fully cooked product has values of 5–15. Defatted flours and grits have a minimum protein content of 50% on a dry basis but will often analyze higher, as illustrated by the compositional data for commercial products (Table 6.12). Essential amino acid contents are summarized in Table 6.13.

Table 6.12.   Typical Compositions of Soybean Protein Products[a]

Constituent	Defatted flours and grits	Protein	
		Concentrates	Isolates
Protein (N × 6.25)	56.0	72.0	96.0
Fat	1.0	1.0	0.1
Fiber	3.5	4.5	0.1
Ash	6.0	5.0	3.5
Soluble carbohydrates	14.0	2.5	0
Insoluble carbohydrates	19.5	15.0	0.3

[a] Analytical values on a moisture-free basis (Horan 1974).

Table 6.13.   Essential Amino Acid Composition (g/16 g N) of Soybean Flour, Concentrate and Isolate

Amino acid	Defatted flour	Concentrate	Isolate
Lysine	6.3	6.3	5.7
Methionine	1.3	1.3	0.9
Cystine	1.6	1.5	1.2
Tryptophan	1.4	1.5	1.1
Isoleucine	4.4	4.6	4.6
Leucine	7.7	7.9	7.8
Phenylalanine	5.1	5.1	5.2
Valine	4.8	4.8	4.5

Source: Technical Service Manuals, Central Soya Co., Fort Wayne, IN.

Soybean Protein Concentrates

These products are made from defatted soybean flakes or flours by removing the soluble sugars and other low-molecular-weight constituents. Three basic processes have been used to prepare protein concentrates (Fig. 6.7). The first method employs aqueous ethanol to dissolve the sugars; the proteins and polysaccharides are insoluble in alcohol and make up the concentrate after the solvent is removed (Mustakas *et al.* 1962). In the second process, defatted flakes (or flour) are extracted with dilute acid at pH 4.5. At this pH, the isoelectric region, the bulk of the proteins are insoluble; after neutralizing and drying, the proteins and insoluble polysaccharides constitute the second type of protein concentrate (Sair 1959). In the third process, the flakes or flour are first toasted to heat-denature and insolubilize the proteins. Water washing then removes the sugars, leaving the denatured proteins plus the polysaccharides (McAnelly 1964). A variation of the first process consists of adding alcohol to hexane–wet flakes after they leave the extractor. The hexane-alcohol mixture is separated to remove lipids not

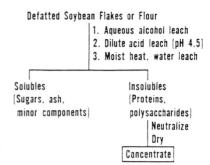

Defatted Soybean Flakes or Flour
1. Aqueous alcohol leach
2. Dilute acid leach (pH 4.5)
3. Moist heat, water leach

Solubles
(Sugars, ash, minor components)

Insolubles
(Proteins, polysaccharides)
Neutralize
Dry
Concentrate

Fig. 6.7. Outline of processes for preparing soybean protein concentrates. Initial extraction is made by one of the three solvents, as described in the text.

extracted by hexane alone. Washing the flakes with aqueous alcohols then removes the sugars and yields a protein concentrate (Hayes and Simms 1973).

Protein concentrates by definition contain a minimum protein content of 70% on a dry basis. A typical composition is given in Table 6.12. Essential amino acid content for a concentrate prepared by alcohol washing is shown in Table 6.13.

Soybean Protein Isolates

Isolates are the most refined form of soybean proteins available. They are processed one step beyond the protein concentrates by removing both the water-insoluble polysaccharides and the water-soluble sugars (Fig. 6.8). Defatted flakes with a high protein solubility (high NSI or PDI) are extracted with dilute alkali (pH 7–9) at 50°–55°C. The spent flake residue (insoluble polysaccharides) is removed by centrifuging to yield an extract containing the dissolved proteins plus the soluble sugars. The extract is then adjusted to pH 4.5, the isoelectric point where the bulk of the proteins are insoluble and precipitate as a curd. The curd is recovered by centrifuging to remove the whey (soluble sugars, some proteins, salts, and other minor constituents). The curd is then washed and may be spray-dried to obtain the isoelectric (water-insoluble) form of the protein. More commonly, however, the washed curd is resolubilized by neutralizing to pH 7 and then is spray-dried. This latter process yields the sodium, potassium, or calcium proteinates, depending on the alkali used for neutralization. The proteinates are water-dispersible and thus easier to incorporate into wet food systems.

An isolate contains a minimum of 90% protein on a dry basis, and a typical composition is given in Table 6.12. Essential amino acid content for an isolate is listed in Table 6.13.

Oriental Soybean Foods

Since the mid-1970s, several Oriental soybean products, including tofu, miso, and tempeh, have become popular in the United States. A

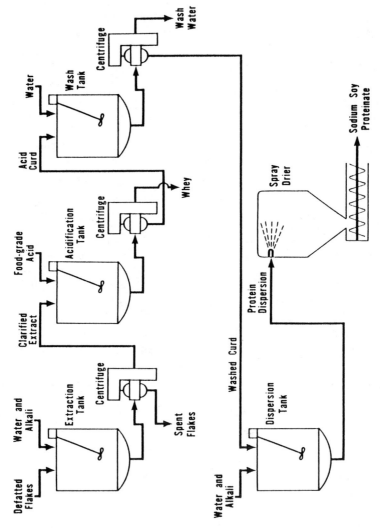

Fig. 6.8. Outline of process for commercial production of soy protein isolates.

brief description for their preparation, as well as that for soy milk and soy sauce, follows.

Soy Milk.   This product traditionally is made by soaking soybeans in water, grinding with water to form a slurry, cooking, and filtering to remove the insoluble materials, cell wall polysaccharides and hulls (Shurtleff and Aoyagi 1979A). The process has been modified over the past 20 years to include heat treatment before or during grinding to inactivate the enzyme lipoxygenase, and thus prevent formation of grassy/beany flavors that are objectionable to many Caucasians. Additional innovations include use of vacuum pans to remove volatile flavors and aseptic packaging by companies in Japan and the United States. Some of the soy milks are sweetened and flavored; fermented (yogurt-like) variations are also available.

Tofu.   This product is made by adding a coagulant such as calcium sulfate to soy milk to precipitate the protein and oil as a gelatinous curd. The curd is then separated from the soluble fraction (whey), pressed, and soaked in water to yield a traditional food staple of Japan (Shurtleff and Aoyagi 1975).

Miso.   Cooked soybeans are fermented with *Aspergillus oryzae* in the presence of salt with or without a cereal such as rice or barley to form this paste-like product (Shurtleff and Aoyagi 1976). It is used as a soup base and is consumed in Japan, China, Indochina, and the East Indies and is produced on a small scale in the United States.

Tempeh.   Cooked beans are inoculated with *Rhizopus oligosporus* and fermented for 25 hr, resulting in an extensive mold mycellium that binds the soybeans together (Shurtleff and Aoyagi 1979B). It is sliced and deep-fat fried to a crisp golden brown. It is a traditional food of Indonesia and is produced on a limited scale in the United States.

Soy sauce.   This well-known soybean condiment is made by fermentation or acid hydrolysis. The fermented type is made by mixing cooked soybeans or defatted soybean grits with roasted wheat, and the mixture is blended with a pure culture of *A. oryzae*. Brine is added and fermentation proceeds for 6 to 8 months. The product is then filtered and pasteurized (Fukushima 1981).

Food Uses

Cottonseed

Glandless (lacking the pigment glands containing gossypol) cottonseed is produced on a commercial scale near Lubbock, Texas, and the roasted kernels are used in breads and confectionary items. A defatted flour made from glandless seed became available commercially in 1986. Glanded cottonseed is processed into oil and meal. The oil is refined and used for salad and cooking oils, shortenings, and margarines. The meal is utilized for animal feeds, primarily for beef and dairy cattle because of its low lysine, gossypol, and crude fiber content. Some cottonseed meal is also used for poultry feeds. Edible defatted cottonseed flour prepared by screw pressing became available commercially in the United States in the 1930s (Altschul *et al.* 1958), but manufacture was discontinued in about 1977. It formerly was used in doughnuts, biscuits, crackers, and prepared food mixes. A prepressed-hexane extracted cottonseed flour has been used since the 1960s in Latin America in the form of a blend with corn flour, sorghum flour, and torula yeast; the blend is known as Incaparina.

Peanuts

About one-half of the U.S. crop is processed into edible products; peanut butter is the main edible form and others include peanut candy, salted nuts, and roasted in-the-shell items. Peanut butter is made by shelling the peanuts, dry-roasting the kernels, removing the skins, and then grinding finely. The ground peanuts are then mixed with salt and other ingredients that may include hydrogenated fat, dextrose, corn syrup solids, lecithin, and antioxidants. Peanut butter is made and consumed mainly in the United States.

About 20–30% of the peanut crop is exported and the rest is processed into edible oil and defatted meal (see this chapter, Oilseed Processing). The defatted meal goes into animal feeds.

Soybeans

About 35–45% of the United States soybean crop is exported and the rest is mainly processed into edible oil and defatted meal. Small portions of the defatted soybean material are converted into edible flours, concentrates, and isolates (see this chapter, Oilseed Processing) that are used as ingredients for processed foods (Wolf and Cowan 1975).

Soybean flours are used in breads and other baked goods, breakfast cereals, infant foods, and dietary foods. Soy flours are also texturized by thermoplastic extrusion to impart fibrous and chewy properties resembling meat. Such texturized flours are used as extenders for ground meats (especially beef) and as meat analogs (e.g., fried bacon analogs). Soybean protein concentrates are used in meat products, infant foods, instant breakfast bars, and meat analogs. They are also texturized by extrusion to form extenders for ground beef. Isolates are added to meat products and are used to make meat analogs, dairy analogs (coffee creamers, milk replacers, and infant formulas), infant foods, and confections.

Small amounts of soybeans are roasted and sold as snacks, canned in tomato sauce, and converted into soy milk-based infant formulas. Larger amounts of soybeans are converted into Oriental foods that have become popular in the United States since the mid-1970s. These include tofu, miso, and tempeh. Soy sauce is a well-known condiment whose consumption has been increasing in the last two decades. In Japan, soy milk markets expanded rapidly in the early 1980s with the introduction of improved processing, but then leveled off. A new soy milk plant with modern Japanese technology opened in the United States in 1986.

Sunflower Seeds

The bulk of the sunflower seed crop is exported (about 75% in 1980–1981), although the domestic crushing industry is growing. Processing yields a high-quality edible oil and a high-protein meal that is used for animal feeds. Direct food use of sunflower consists of roasting both in the shell and in the dehulled form. Roasted nutmeats are utilized in candies, cookies, snack items, spreads, and cakes. Small amounts are sold through health food stores, and one variety of seed is grown and sold solely as bird feed (Robertson 1975).

REFERENCES

Adams, C. F., and Richardson, M. 1977. Nutritive value of foods. USDA Home and Garden Bull. 72. Washington, DC.

Aguilera, J. M., Lusas, E. W., Uebersax, M. A., and Zabrik, M. E. 1982A. Roasting of navy beans (*Phaseolus vulgaris*) by particle-to-particle heat transfer. J. Food Sci. 47, 996–1000, 1005.

Aguilera, J. M., Lusas, E. W., Uebersax, M. A., and Zabrik, M. E. 1982B. Development of food ingredients from navy beans (*Phaseolus vulgaris*) by roasting, pin milling, and air classification. J. Food Sci. 47, 1151–1154.

Al-Nouri, F. F., and Siddigi, A. M. 1982. Biochemical evaluation of twelve broad bean cultivars. Can. Inst. Food Sci. Technol. J. 15, 37–40.

Altschul, A. M., Lyman, C. M., and Thurber, F. H. 1958. Cottonseed meal. *In* Processed Plant Protein Foodstuffs, pp. 469–534. A. M. Altschul (Editor). Academic Press, New York.

American Oil Chemists' Society. 1976. Methods *Ba 10–65* and *Ba 11–65*. Official and Tentative Methods. 3rd Edition. Champaign, IL.

Amos, H. E., Burdick, D., and Seerley, R. W. 1975. Effect of processing temperature and L-lysine supplementation on utilization of sunflower meal by the growing rat. J. Anim. Sci. 40, 90–95.

Anantharaman, K., and Carpenter, K. J. 1969. Effects of heat processing on the nutritional value of groundnut products. I. Protein quality of groundnut cotyledons for rats. J. Sci. Food Agric. 20, 703–708.

Augustin, J., Beck, C. B., Kalbfleish, G., Kagel, L. C., and Matthews, R. H. 1981. Variation in the vitamin and mineral content of raw and cooked commercial *Phaseolus vulgaris* classes. J. Food Sci. 46, 1701–1706.

Augustin, J., Cole, C. L., Fellman, J. K., Matthews, R. H., Tassinari, P. D., and Woo, H. 1983. Nutrient content of sprouted wheat and selected legumes. Cereal Foods World 28, 358–361.

Aykroyd, W. R., and Doughty, J. 1964. Legumes in human nutrition. FAO Nutr. Stud. 19, 1–138.

Ayres, J. L., Branscomb, L. L., and Rogers, G. M. 1974. Processing of edible peanut flour and grits. J. Am. Oil Chem. Soc. 51, 133–36.

Bailey, A. V., Harris, J. A., Skau, E. L., and Kerr, T. 1966. Cyclopropenoid fatty acid content and fatty acid composition of crude oils from twenty-five varieties of cottonseed. J. Am. Oil Chem. Soc. 43, 107–110.

Becker, K. W. 1978. Solvent extraction of soybeans. J. Am. Oil Chem. Soc. 55, 754–761.

Berardi, L. C., and Goldblatt, L. A. 1980. Gossypol. In Toxic Constituents of Plant Foodstuffs. 2nd Edition, pp. 183–237. I. E. Liener (Editor). Academic Press, New York.

Bramsnaes, F., and Sejr Olsen, H. 1979. Development of field pea and faba bean proteins. J. Am. Oil Chem. Soc. 56, 450–454.

Bressani, R., and Elias, L. G. 1974. Legume foods. In New Protein Foods. Vol. 1A, Technology, pp. 230-297. A. M. Altschul (Editor). Academic Press, New York.

Brignoli, C. A., Kinsella, J. E., and Weihrauch, J. L. 1976. Comprehensive evaluation of fatty acids in foods. V. Unhydrogenated fats and oils. J. Am. Diet. Assoc. 68, 224–229.

Cater, C. M., Gheyasuddin, S., and Mattil, K. F. 1972. The effect of cholorgenic, quinic, and caffeic acids on the solubility and color of protein isolates, especially from sunflower seed. Cereal Chem. 49, 508–514.

Cavins, J. F., Kwolek, W. F., Inglett, G. E., and Cowan, J. C. 1972. Amino acid analysis of soybean meal: Interlaboratory study. J. Assoc. Off. Anal. Chem. 55, 686–691.

Cegla, G. F., and Bell, K. R. 1977. High pressure liquid chromatography for the analysis of soluble carbohydrates in defatted oilseed flours. J. Am. Oil Chem. Soc. 54, 150–152.

Cheryan, M. 1980. Phytic acid interactions in food systems. CRC Crit. Rev. Food Sci. Nutr. 13, 297–335.

Craviotto, R. O., Massieu, H. G., and Guzman G., J. 1951. Composition of Mexican foods. Ciencia (Mexico) 11(5–6), 129–155.

Derbyshire, E., Wright, D. J., and Boulter, D. 1976. Legumin and vicillin, storage proteins of legume seeds. Phytochemistry 15, 3–24.

Deshpande, S. S., Sathe, S. K., Salunkhe, D. K., and Cornforth, D. P. 1982. Effects of dehulling on phytic acid, polyphenols, and enzyme inhibitors of dry beans (Phaseolus vulgaris L.). J. Food Sci. 47, 1846–1850.

Earle, F. R., Van Etten, C. H., Clark, T. F., and Wolff, I. A. 1968. Compositional data on sunflower seed. J. Am. Oil Chem. Soc. 45, 876–879.

Eldridge, A. C., and Kwolek, W. F. 1983. Soybean isoflavones: Effect of environment and variety on composition. J. Agric. Food Chem. 31, 394–396.

Elkowicz, K., and Sosulski, F. W. 1982. Antinutritive factors in eleven legumes and their air-classified protein and starch fractions. J. Food Sci. 47, 1301–1304.

Erickson, D. R., Pryde, E. H., Brekke, O. L., Mounts, T. L., and Falb, R. A. (Editors) 1980. Handbook of Soy Oil Processing and Utilization. American Soybean Association, St. Louis, MO and American Oil Chemists' Society, Champaign, IL.

Exler, J., Avena, R. M., and Weihrauch, J. L. 1977. Comprehensive evaluation of fatty acids in foods. J. Am. Diet. Assoc. 71, 412–415.

Fenwick, D. E., and Oakenfull, D. 1981. Saponin content of soya beans and some commercial soya bean products. J. Sci. Food Agric. 32, 273–278.

Fleming, S. E. 1981. A study of relationships between flatus potential and carbohydrate distribution in legume seeds. J. Food Sci. 46, 794–798, 803.

Fordham, J. R., Wells, C. E., and Chen, L. H. 1975. Sprouting of seeds and nutrient content of seeds and sprouts. J. Food Sci. 40, 552–556.

Fukushima, D. 1981. Soy proteins for foods centering around soy sauce and tofu. J. Am. Oil Chem. Soc. 58, 346–354.

Griffiths, D. W., and Jones, D. I. H. 1977. Cellulase inhibition by tannins in the testa of field beans (Vicia faba). J. Sci. Food Agric. 28, 983–989.

Halaby, G. A., Lewis, R. W., and Rey, C. R. 1981. Variations in nutrient content of commercially canned legumes. J. Food Sci. 47, 263–266.

Harris, J. A., Magne, F. C., and Skau, E. L. 1964. Methods for the determination of cyclopropenoid fatty acids. IV. Application of the step-wise HBr titration method to the analysis of refined and crude cottonseed oils. J. Am. Oil Chem. Soc. 41, 309-311.

Hayes, L. P., and Simms, R. P. 1973. Defatted soybean fractionation by solvent extraction. U.S. Patent 3,734,901. May 22.

Hendricks, J. D., Sinnhuber, R. O., Loveland, P. M., Pawlowski, N. E., and Nixon, J. E. 1980. Hepatocarcinogenicity of glandless cottonseeds and cottonseed oil to rainbow trout (Salmo gairdnerii). Science 208, 309-311.

Holt, N. W., and Sosulski, F. W. 1979. Amino acid composition and protein quality of field peas. Can. J. Plant Sci. 59, 653-660.

Horan, F. E. 1974. Soy protein products and their production. J. Am. Oil Chem. Soc. 51, 67A-73A.

Kahn, N. A., and Baker, B. E. 1957. The amino-acid composition of some Pakastani pulses. J. Sci. Food. Agric. 8, 301-305.

Kanamori, M., Ikeuchi, T., Ibuki, F., Kotaru, M., and Kan, K. K. 1982. Amino acid composition of protein fractions extracted from Phaseolus beans and the field bean (Vicia faba L.). J. Food Sci. 47, 1991-1994.

Kylen, A. M., and McCready, R. M. 1975. Nutrients in seeds and sprouts of alfalfa, lentils, mung beans and soybeans. J. Food Sci. 40, 1008-1009.

Lal, B. M., Prakash, V., and Verma, S. C. 1963. The distribution of nutrients in the seed parts of Bengal gram. Eperientia 19, 154-155.

Lawhon, J. T., Cater, C. M., and Mattil, K. F. 1977. Evaluation of the food use potential of sixteen varieties of cottonseed. J. Am. Oil Chem. Soc. 54, 75-80.

Levi, R. S., Reilich, H. G., O'Neill, H. J., Cucullu, A. F., and Skau, E. L. 1967. Quantitative determination of cyclopropenoid fatty acids in cottonseed meal. J. Am. Oil Chem. Soc. 44, 249-252.

Liener, I. E. 1972. Nutritional value of food protein products. In Soybeans: Chemistry and Technology. Vol. 1, Proteins, pp. 203-277. A. K. Smith and S. J. Circle (Editors). AVI Publishing Co., Westport, CT.

Liener, I. E. 1981. Factors affecting the nutritional quality of soya products. J. Am. Oil Chem. Soc. 58, 406-415.

Liener, I. E., and Thompson, R. M. 1980. In vitro and in vivo studies on the digestibility of the major storage protein of the navy bean (Phaseolus vulgaris). Qual. Plant.-Plant Foods Hum. Nutr. 30, 13-25.

Lindsey, T. O., Hawkins, G. E., and Guthrie, L. D. 1980. Physiological responses of lactating cows to gossypol from cottonseed meal rations. J. Dairy Sci. 63, 562-573.

Lolas, G. M., and Markakis, P. 1975. Phytic acid and other phosphorus compounds of beans (Phaseolus vulgaris L.). J. Agric. Food Chem. 23, 13-15.

Lolas, G. M., Palamidis, N., and Markakis, P. 1976. The phytic acid-total phosphorus relationship in barley, oats, soybeans, and wheat. Cereal Chem. 53, 867-871.

Lusas, E. W. 1979. Food uses of peanut protein. J. Am. Oil Chem. Soc. 56, 425-430.

Mattson, F. H. 1973. Potential toxicity of food lipids. In Toxicants Occurring Naturally in Foods, 2nd Edition, pp. 189-209. National Academy of Sciences, Washington, DC.

McAnelly, J. K. 1964. Method for producing a soybean protein product and the resulting product. U.S. Patent 3,142,571. July 28.

Meiners, C. R., Derise, N. L., Lau, H. C., Crews, M. G., Ritchey, S. J., and Murphy, E. W. 1976A. The content of nine mineral elements in raw and cooked mature dry legumes. J. Agric. Food Chem. 24, 1126-1130.

Meiners, C. R., Derise, N. L., Lau, H. C., Ritchey, S. J., and Murphy, E. W. 1976B. Proximate composition and yield of raw and cooked mature dry legumes. J. Agric. Food Chem. 24, 1122-1126.

Miyazawa, T., Ito, S., and Fujino, Y. 1974. Sterol lipid isolated from pea seeds (*Pisum sativum*). Cereal Chem. *51*, 623–629.

Mustakas, G. C., Kirk, L. D., and Griffin, E. L., Jr. 1962. Flash desolventizing defatted soybean meals washed with aqueous alcohols to yield a high-protein product. J. Am. Oil Chem. Soc. *39*, 222–226.

National Academy of Sciences (NAS) 1980. Recommended Dietary Allowances, pp. 39–54. Committee on Dietary Allowances, Food and Nutrition Board, Washington, DC.

Nielsen, N. C. 1985. The structure and complexity of the 11 S polypeptides in soybeans. J. Am. Oil Chem. Soc. *62*, 1680–1686.

Osborn, T. W. 1977. Elemental composition of soybean meal and interlaboratory performance. J. Agric. Food Chem. *25*, 229–232.

Padmanaban, G. 1980. Lathyrogens. *In* Toxic Constituents of Plant Foodstuffs. 2nd Edition, pp. 239–266. I. E. Liener (Editor). Academic Press, New York.

Pattee, H. E., Salunkhe, D. K., Sathe, S. K., and Reddy, N. R. 1982. Legume lipids. CRC Crit. Rev. Food Sci. Nutr. *17*, 97–139.

Phelps, R. A., Shenstone, F. S., Kemmerer, A. R., and Evans, R. J. 1965. A review of cyclopropenoid compounds: Biological effects of some derivatives. Poult. Sci. *44*, 358–394.

Pons, W. A., Jr., Stansbury, M. F., and Hoffpauir, C. L. 1953. An analytical system for determining phosphorus compounds in plant materials. J. Assoc. Off. Agric. Chem. *36*, 492–504.

Price, M. L., Hagerman, A. E., and Butler, L. G. 1980. Tannin content of cowpeas, chickpeas, pigeon peas, and mung beans. J. Agric. Food Chem. *28*, 459–461.

Rackis, J. J. 1981. Flatulence caused by soya and its control through processing. J. Am. Oil Chem. Soc. *58*, 503–509.

Rackis, J. J., McGee, J. E., Gumbmann, M. R., and Booth, A. N. 1979. Effects of soy proteins containing trypsin inhibitors in long term feeding studies in rats. J. Am. Oil Chem. Soc. *56*, 162–168.

Rahma, E. H., and Narasinga Rao, M. S. 1979. Characterization of sunflower proteins. J. Food Sci. *44*, 579–582.

Reddy, N. R., Pierson, M. D., Sathe, S. K., and Salunkhe, D. K. 1982A. Legume-based fermented foods: Their preparation and nutritional quality. CRC Crit. Rev. Food Sci. Nutr. *17*, 335–370.

Reddy, N. R., Salunkhe, D. K., and Sathe, S. K. 1982B. Biochemistry of black gram (*Phaseolus mungo* L.): A review. CRC Crit Rev. Food Sci. Nutr. *16*, 49–114.

Reddy, N. R., Sathe, S. K., and Salunkhe, D. K. 1982C. Phytates in legumes and cereals. Adv. Food Res. *28*, 1–92.

Reichert, R. D. 1982. Air classification of peas (*Pisum sativum*) varying widely in protein content. J. Food Sci. *47*, 1263–1267, 1271.

Reichert, R. D., and MacKenzie, S. L. 1982. Composition of peas (*Pisum sativum*) varying widely in protein content. J. Agric. Food Chem. *30*, 312–317.

Robertson, J. A. 1975. Use of sunflower seed in food products. CRC Crit. Rev. Food Sci. Nutr. *6*, 201–240.

Rockland, L. B., Zaragosa, E. M., and Oracca-Tetteh, R. 1979. Quick-cooking wing beans (*Psophocarpus tetragonolobus*). J. Food Sci. *44*, 1004–1007.

Rosen, G. D. 1958. Groundnuts (peanuts) and groundnut meal. *In* Processed Plant Protein Foodstuffs, pp. 419–468. A. M. Altschul (Editor). Academic Press, New York.

Saio, K., and Watanabe, T. 1968. Observation of soybean foods under electron microscope. Nippon Shokuhin Kogyo Gakkai-Shi *15*, 290–296.

Sair, L. 1959. Proteinaceous soy composition and method of preparing. U.S. Patent 2,881,076. April 7.

Sefa-Dedeh, S., and Stanley, D. W. 1979. Textural implications of the microstructure of legumes. Food Technol. 33 (10), 77–83.

Sgarbieri, V. C., and Whitaker, J. R. 1982. Physical, chemical, and nutritional properties of common bean (Phaseolus) proteins. Adv. Food Res. 28, 93–166.

Shehata, N. A., and Fryer, B. A. 1970. Effect on protein quality of supplementing wheat flour with chickpea flour. Cereal Chem. 47, 663–670.

Shurtleff, W., and Aoyagi, A. 1975. The Book of Tofu. Food for Mankind. Vol. 1. Autumn Press, Hayama-shi, Kanagawa-ken, Japan.

Shurtleff, W., and Aoyagi, A. 1976. The Book of Miso. Autumn Press, Brookline, MA.

Shurtleff, W., and Aoyagi, A. 1979A. Tofu and Soymilk Production (Vol. 2 of The Book of Tofu). New-Age Foods Study Center, Lafayette, CA.

Shurtleff, W., and Aoyagi, A. 1979B. The Book of Tempeh—A Superfood from Indonesia. Harper & Row, New York.

Silva, C. A. B., Bates, R. P., and Deng, J. C. 1981. Influence of pre-soaking on black bean cooking kinetics. J. Food Sci. 46, 1721–1725.

Smith, A. K. 1958. Vegetable protein isolates. In Processed Plant Protein Foodstuffs, pp. 249–276. A. M. Altschul (Editor). Academic Press, New York.

Sosulski, F., and Youngs, C. G. 1979. Yield and functional properties of air-classified protein and starch fractions from eight legume flours. J. Am. Oil Chem. Soc. 56, 292–295.

Struthers, B. J., MacDonald, J. R., Dahlgren, R. R., and Hopkins, D. T. 1983. Effects on the monkey, pig and rat pancreas of soy products with varying levels of trypsin inhibitor and comparison with the administration of cholecystokinin. J. Nutr. 113, 86–97.

Sumner, A. K., Nielsen, M. A., and Youngs, C. G. 1981. Production and evaluation of pea protein isolate. J. Food Sci. 46, 364–366, 372.

Thompson, L. U. 1977. Preparation and evaluation of mung bean protein isolates. J. Food Sci. 42, 202–206.

Tobin, G., and Carpenter, K. J. 1978. The nutritional value of the dry bean (Phaseolus vulgaris): A literature review. Nutr. Abstr. Rev. Ser. A 48, 919–936.

Udayasekhara Rao, P., and Belavady, B. 1978. Oligosaccharides in pulses: Varietal differences and effects of cooking and germination. J. Agric. Food Chem. 26, 316–319.

U.S. Department of Agriculture (USDA) 1984. Agricultural Statistics. USDA, Washington, DC.

Vanderstoep, J. 1981. Effect of germination on the nutritive value of legumes. Food Technol. 35(3), 83–85.

Varriano-Marston, E., and de Omana, E. 1979. Effects of sodium salt solutions on the chemical composition and morphology of black beans (Phaseolus vulgaris). J. Food Sci. 44, 531–536.

Verma, S. C., and Lal, B. M. 1966. Physiology of Bengal gram seed. II. Changes in phosphorus compounds during ripening of the seed. J. Sci. Food Agric. 17, 43–46.

Vose, J. R., Basterrechea, M. J., Gorin, P. A. J., Finlayson, A. J., and Youngs, C. G. 1976. Air classification of field peas and horsebean flours: Chemical studies of starch and protein fractions. Cereal Chem. 53, 928–936.

Walker, A. F., and Kochhar, N. 1982. Effect of processing including domestic cooking on nutritional quality of legumes. Proc. Nutr. Soc. 41, 41–51.

Wan, P. J., Baker, G. W., Clark, S. P., and Matlock, S. W. 1979. Characteristics of sunflower seed and meal. Cereal Chem. 56, 352–355.

Wilcke, H. L., Hopkins, D. T., and Waggle, D. H. 1979. Soy Protein and Human Nutrition, Academic Press, New York.

Wolf, W. J. 1970. Soybean proteins: Their functional, chemical, and physical properties. J. Agric. Food Chem. 18, 969–976.

Wolf, W. J., and Cowan, J. C. 1975. Soybeans as a Food Source. Revised edition. CRC Press, Cleveland, OH.

Worthington, R. E., Hammons, R. O., and Allison, J. R. 1972. Varietal differences and seasonal effects of fatty acid composition and stability of oil from 82 peanut genotypes. J. Agric. Food Chem. 20, 727–730.

Young, C. T., Waller, G. R., and Hammons, R. O. 1973. Variations in total amino acid content of peanut meal. J. Am. Oil Chem. Soc. 50, 521–523.

Effects of Agricultural Practices, Handling, Processing, and Storage on Meat

H. W. Ockerman

WORLD MEAT DIETARY PATTERNS

A total production of 137 million tons of meat was produced in 1979, and pork, beef, poultry, sheep, and goat meat accounted for 97% of this total (Jensen 1980). A great percentage of the meat is consumed in the country in which it is produced, with only 5% being exported [excluding trade between European Economic Community (EEC) countries], and the developing countries, if considered as a block, import approximately the same amount as they export (FAO 1980).

World meat production and consumption is extremely varied by area and economic level (consumption is shown in Table 7.1). Two-thirds of the world meat supply is produced and consumed in the developed countries where one-fourth of the people live, and, three-fourths of the world meat supply is consumed in the United States, USSR, EEC, Eastern Europe, and China (Jensen 1980). Table 7.2 shows the production of the world's four main types of meat (beef, sheep and goats, pork, and poultry) for developing and developed countries. On a world scale, pork and beef are almost equally important, with poultry also being very significant and sheep and goat meat contributing only in minor proportions. Not only are the totals of the developed and developing areas different, but a greater subdivision indicates considerably more variability in total consumption and types of meat consumed by the different areas, as may be seen in Table 7.3. This table indicates differences in areas of the world, but does not take into account socio-economic, ethnic, or religious groups within a country.

Consumption of meat in the United States in 1981 averaged 145.5 pounds of red meat at the retail level and this represents 3.3% ($291.25) of total disposable income (NLSMB 1983A). These figures compare with 135.9 lb and 4.2% of income in 1965. The average consumer in

Table 7.1. Contribution (%) of Vegetable and Animal Products to Calorie and Protein Levels

	Developed market economics	45 Poorest countries	World
	Energy		
Vegetables	67	94	83
Total animal products	33	6	17
Meat and offals (variety meat)	15	1	8
	Protein		
Vegetables	41	85	65
Total animal products	59	15	35
Meat and offals (variety meat)	29	4	19

Source: FAO (1977).

Table 7.2. World Meat Production, 1979

	Millions of tons	Percentage
World	133	100
Beef	47	35
Sheep and goat meat	7	5
Pork	51	39
Poultry	28	21
Developed countries	87	66
Beef	32	24
Sheep and goat meat	3	2
Pork	32	25
Poultry	20	15
Developing countries	46	34
Beef	15	11
Sheep and goat meat	4	3
Pork	19	14
Poultry	8	6

Source: FAO (1980).

the United States spends approximately one-fifth of his/her food and beverage money on red meat.

Meat animals are often criticized as being in competition with the human population for the scarce resources of the world. When viewed from a cropland standpoint, economics dictates how much of the product will be fed to animals. Animals are fed cropland products only when there is no higher economic demand for the products for human food, export, or manufacture. A great deal of the plant material fed to animals is not desirable for human food and, of the products grown for

Table 7.3. Consumption Patterns in Different Parts of the World

| Area | Percentage of total meat consumption | | | | Total meat consumption (kg/person/year) |
	Beef and veal	Mutton and lamb	Pork	Poultry	
Oceania	47	36	10	7	134
North America	46	1	26	27	113
Western Europe	37	6	42	15	57
Eastern Europe	29	4	57	10	55
USSR	47	10	35	8	43
South America	69	5	18	8	39
Central America	46	5	37	12	18
China	15	4	61	19	16
Eastern Africa	68	17	5	11	13
Near East	42	47	0	11	12
Northwestern Africa	39	43	1	17	11
East and Southeast Asia	23	2	57	18	9
Western Africa	46	31	8	15	7
Central Africa	63	13	16	8	6
South Africa	56	33	0	11	2

Source: FAO (1971).

human food, many of the plant by-products are also utilized as feed for animals. Cellulose, the most abundant constituent of plants, cannot be digested by humans but can be utilized by ruminants as an energy source to manufacture protein for human consumption. Much of the world's land (44% in the United States) is not suitable for crops, and the only way it can be harvested is through grazing livestock.

The world has and will continue to have approximately 30 tons per person of unutilizable organic biomass that is suitable for feeding ruminants, but unsuitable for human consumption. This biomass can be utilized through animals to produce highly nutritious human food (Briggs 1980). Pasture, grass, and forage are traditional foods for ruminants but research is currently being conducted, and in some cases product utilized, for animal diets that would include stalks, stover, straw, paper by-products, animal manure and litter, aquaplants, corncobs, municipal wastes, and wood and tree by-products (Briggs 1980).

Animals, in most cases, do not compete with humans (since humans make the choice) for resources but convert products that cannot be utilized or would not be utilized economically into products for human consumption.

OVERVIEW OF NUTRIENTS IN MEAT PRODUCTS

Nutritional composition of meat products is extremely variable due to species, genetic background, nutritional level of the animal, animal age, animal sex, parts of carcass utilized, mixture of ingredients used, and processing techniques involved. Some of this variability can be observed in Tables 7.4–7.9 for beef, lamb, pork, veal, sausage, and miscellaneous meat items, respectively. In spite of this variability, some generalities (Ockerman 1981) can be drawn for the nutritional value of meat products (Ockerman 1981). Lean meat tissue (including pork) contains approximately 18.5–20.0% of extremely well-balanced protein. As the fat level increases, the protein level decreases, and as the moisture level decreases (as would happen during cooking), the protein percentage increases. Most variety meat is also high in protein level. Most bologna-type products would contain 11–18% protein, with the protein level of dried sausage being much higher. Fat level in meat varies with the nutritional level of the animal and even more with the location in the carcasses. Lean meat will usually contain 5–10% fat. Fresh pork sausage in the United States is usually less than 50% fat, and bologna products are usually less than 30% fat; the maximum level is controlled by the USDA. Variety meat, like lean meat, is usually low in fat level. The mineral level in lean meat and variety meat is normally in the 1% range and decreases as the fat level increases. Most of the minerals in meat are readily available to the digestive processes of the human. Mechanically deboned meat can vary in mineral level, depending on machine adjustment, but the current maximum Ca level is 0.75% [equivalent to a maximum bone content of 3% (CAST 1980)]. Cured products vary in mineral level with the quantity of salt added. Generally, the mineral level is equivalent to the salt level plus 1%. Muscle and organ tissues are considered excellent sources of most of the B vitamins and, in addition, organ tissue contains significant amounts of vitamins A and C. Liver, in particular, is considered a source of vitamins A, C, B_6, B_{12}, nicotinic acid, pantothenic acid, and biotin. Pork is very high in thiamin (Ockerman 1980).

Fat and cholesterol compositions for animal fats are shown in Table 7.10 and the quantity of saturated, oleic, and linoleic acids for individual meat items can be located in Tables 7.4–7.9. In general, animal fats, like all fats and oils, are extremely concentrated forms of energy and yield 9 kcal/g. Fat, in general, is low in ash and consequently is not a particularly good source of minerals. Fatty acid composition varies with digestive systems, with the ruminant animals (beef and lamb) depositing a more saturated fat in their body than nonruminant (pork) animals; but even with ruminant animals, the ratio of saturated to unsaturated fat is approximately 1:1. In pork carcasses, the saturated fat is only approximately 40% of the total fat. Another difference in digestive systems is that the depot fat of ruminant animals cannot be easily varied with the type of feed consumed, whereas the depot fat of nonruminant animals can be influenced by varying the diet.

Table 7.4. Nutritive Values of the Edible Parts of Beef[a]

Food, approximate measure[b]	Unit	Total weight (g)	Water (%)	Food energy (cal)	Protein (g)	Fat (g)	Fatty Acids Saturated (total, g)	Unsaturated Oleic (g)	Linoleic (g)	Carbohydrate (g)	Calcium (mg)	Phosphorus (mg)	Iron (mg)	Potassium (mg)	Vitamin A value (IU)	Thiamin (mg)	Riboflavin (mg)	Niacin (mg)	Ascorbic acid (mg)
Beef, cooked[c]																			
Cuts braised, simmered, or pot roasted:																			
Lean and fat (piece, 2-1/2 × 2-1/2 × 3/4 in.)	3 oz	85	53	245	23	16	6.8	6.5	0.4	0	10	114	2.9	184	30	0.04	0.18	3.6	—
Lean only	2.5 oz	72	62	140	22	5	2.1	1.8	0.2	0	10	108	2.7	176	10	0.04	0.17	3.3	—
Ground beef, broiled																			
Lean, 10% fat	3 oz or patty 3 × 5/8 in.	85	60	185	23	10	4.0	3.9	0.3	0	10	196	3.0	261	20	0.08	0.20	5.1	—
Lean, 21% fat	2.9 oz or patty 3 × 5/8 in.	82	54	235	20	17	7.0	6.7	0.4	0	9	159	2.6	221	30	0.07	0.17	4.4	—
Roast, oven cooked, no liquid added																			
Relatively fat, such as rib																			
Lean and fat (2 pieces, 4-1/8 × 2-1/4 × 1/4 in.)	3 oz	85	40	375	17	33	14.0	13.6	0.8	0	8	158	2.2	189	70	0.05	0.13	3.1	—
Lean only	1.8 oz	51	57	125	14	7	3.0	2.5	0.3	0	6	131	1.8	161	10	0.04	0.11	2.6	—
Relatively lean, such as heel of round																			
Lean and fat (2 pieces, 4-1/8 × 2-1/4 × 1/4 in.)	3 oz	85	62	165	25	7	2.8	2.7	0.2	0	11	208	3.2	279	10	0.06	0.19	4.5	—
Lean only	2.8 oz	78	65	125	24	3	1.2	1.0	0.1	0	10	199	3.0	268	Trace	0.06	0.18	4.3	—
Steak																			
Relatively fat–sirloin, broiled																			
Lean and fat (piece, 2-1/2 × 2-1/2 × 3/4 in.)	3 oz	85	44	330	20	27	11.3	11.1	0.6	0	9	162	2.5	220	50	0.05	0.15	4.0	—
Lean only	2.0 oz	56	59	115	18	4	1.8	1.6	0.2	0	7	146	2.2	202	10	0.05	0.14	3.6	—
Relatively lean-round, braised																			
Lean and fat (piece, 4-1/8 × 2-1/4 × 1/2 in.)	3 oz	85	55	220	24	13	5.5	5.2	0.4	0	10	213	3.0	272	20	0.07	0.19	4.8	—
Lean only	2.4 oz	68	61	130	21	4	1.7	1.5	0.2	0	9	182	2.5	238	10	0.05	0.16	4.1	—

(Continued)

Table 7.4. (Continued)

Food, approximate measure[b]	Unit	Total weight (g)	Water (%)	Food energy (cal)	Protein (g)	Fat (g)	Fatty Acids Saturated (total, g)	Unsaturated Oleic (g)	Linoleic (g)	Carbohydrate (g)	Calcium (mg)	Phosphorus (mg)	Iron (mg)	Potassium (mg)	Vitamin A value (IU)	Thiamin (mg)	Riboflavin (mg)	Niacin (mg)	Ascorbic acid (mg)
Beef, canned																			
Corned beef	3 oz	85	59	185	22	10	4.9	4.5	0.2	0	17	90	3.7	—	—	0.01	0.20	2.9	—
Corned beef hash	1 cup	220	67	400	19	25	11.9	10.9	0.5	24	29	147	4.4	440	—	0.02	0.20	4.6	—
Beef, dried, chipped	2-1/2 oz jar	71	48	145	24	4	2.1	2.0	0.1	0	14	287	3.6	142	—	0.05	0.23	2.7	0
Beef and vegetable stew	1 cup	245	82	220	16	11	4.9	4.5	0.2	15	29	184	2.9	613	2400	0.15	0.17	4.7	17
Beef potpie (home recipe), baked (piece, 1/3 of 9-in. diam pie)[d]	1 piece	210	55	515	21	30	7.9	12.8	6.7	39	29	149	3.8	334	1720	0.30	0.30	5.5	6
Chili con carne with beans, canned	1 cup	255	72	340	19	16	7.5	6.8	0.3	31	82	321	4.3	594	150	0.08	0.18	3.3	—
Chop suey with beef and pork (home recipe)	1 cup	250	75	300	26	17	8.5	6.2	0.7	13	60	248	4.8	425	600	0.28	0.38	5.0	33
Heart, beef, lean, braised	3 oz	85	61	160	27	5	1.5	1.1	0.6	1	5	154	5.0	197	20	0.21	1.04	6.5	1
Liver, beef, fried[e] (slice, 6-1/2 X 2-3/8 X 3/8 in.)	3 oz	85	56	195	22	9	2.5	3.5	0.9	5	9	405	7.5	323	45,390[f]	0.22	3.56	14.0	23

Source: Nutritive value of foods, Home and Garden Bull. 72, Science and Education Administration, USDA (1978).
[a] Dashes denote lack of reliable data for a constituent believed to be present in measurable amount.
[b] Edible part only unless indicated otherwise.
[c] Outer layer of fat on the cut was removed to within approximately 1/2 in. of the lean. Deposits of fat within the cut were not removed.
[d] Crust made with vegetable shortening and enriched flour.
[e] Regular-type margarine used.
[f] Value varies widely.

Table 7.5. Nutritive Values of the Edible Parts of Lamb[a]

Food, approximate measure[b]	Unit	Total weight (g)	Water (%)	Food energy (cal)	Protein (g)	Fat (g)	Fatty Acids Saturated (total, g)	Unsaturated Oleic (g)	Unsaturated Linoleic (g)	Carbohydrate (g)	Calcium (mg)	Phosphorus (mg)	Iron (mg)	Potassium (mg)	Vitamin A value (IU)	Thiamin (mg)	Riboflavin (mg)	Niacin (mg)	Ascorbic acid (mg)
Chop, rib (cut 3/lb with bone), broiled																			
Lean and fat	3.1 oz	89	43	360	18	32	14.8	12.1	1.2	0	8	139	1.0	200	—	0.11	0.19	4.1	—
Lean only	2 oz	57	60	120	16	6	2.5	2.1	0.2	0	6	121	1.1	174	—	0.09	0.15	3.4	—
Leg, roasted																			
Lean and fat (2 pieces, 4-1/8 × 2-1/4 × 1/4 in.)	3 oz	85	54	235	22	16	7.3	6.0	0.6	0	9	177	1.4	241	—	0.13	0.23	4.7	—
Lean only	2.5 oz	71	62	130	20	5	2.1	1.8	0.2	0	9	169	1.4	227	—	0.12	0.21	4.4	—
Shoulder, roasted																			
Lean and fat (3 pieces, 2-1/2 × 2-1/2 × 1/4 in.)	3 oz	85	50	285	18	23	10.8	8.8	0.9	0	9	146	1.0	206	—	0.11	0.20	4.0	—
Lean only	2.3 oz	64	61	130	17	6	3.6	2.3	0.2	0	8	140	1.0	193	—	0.10	0.18	3.7	—

Source: Nutritive value of foods, Home and Garden Bull. 72, Science and Education Administration, USDA (1978).
[a] Dashes denote lack of reliable data for a constituent believed to be present in measurable amount.
[b] Edible part only unless indicated otherwise.

Table 7.6. Nutritive Values of the Edible Parts of Pork[a]

Food, approximate measure[b]	Unit	Total weight (g)	Water (%)	Food energy (cal)	Protein (g)	Fat (g)	Saturated (total, g)	Unsaturated Oleic (g)	Lino-leic (g)	Carbo-hydrate (g)	Cal-cium (mg)	Phos-phorus (mg)	Iron (mg)	Potas-sium (mg)	Vitamin A value (IU)	Thia-min (mg)	Ribo-flavin (mg)	Niacin (mg)	Ascorbic acid (mg)
Pork, cured																			
Bacon (20 slices/lb, raw), broiled or fried, crisp	2 slices	15	8	85	4	8	2.5	3.7	0.7	Trace	2	34	0.5	35	0	0.08	0.05	0.8	—
Pork, cured, cooked																			
Ham, light cure, lean and fat, roasted (2 pieces, 4-1/8 X 2-1/4 X 1/4 in.)[c]	3 oz	85	54	245	18	19	6.8	7.9	1.7	0	8	146	2.2	199	0	0.40	0.15	3.1	—
Luncheon meat																			
Boiled ham, slice (8 per 8-oz pkg)	1 oz	28	59	65	5	5	1.7	2.0	0.4	0	3	47	0.8	—	0	0.12	0.04	0.7	—
Canned, spiced or unspiced,																			
Slice, approx. 3 X 2 X 1/2 in.	1 slice	60	55	175	9	15	5.4	6.7	1.0	1	5	65	1.3	133	0	0.19	0.13	1.8	—
Pork, fresh, cooked[d]																			
Chop, loin (cut 3/lb with bone), broiled																			
Lean and fat	2.7 oz	78	42	305	19	25	8.9	10.4	2.2	0	9	209	2.7	216	0	0.75	0.22	4.5	—
Lean only	2 oz	56	53	150	17	9	3.1	3.6	0.8	0	7	181	2.2	192	0	0.63	0.18	3.8	—
Roast, oven cooked, no liquid added																			
Lean and fat (piece, 2-1/2 X 2-1/2 X 3/4 in.)	3 oz	85	46	310	21	24	8.7	10.2	2.2	0	9	218	2.7	233	0	0.78	0.22	4.8	—
Lean only	2.4 oz	68	55	175	20	10	3.5	4.1	0.8	0	9	211	2.6	224	0	0.73	0.21	4.4	—
Shoulder cut, simmered																			
Lean and fat (3 pieces, 2-1/2 X 2-1/2 X 1/4 in.)	3 oz	85	46	320	20	26	9.3	10.9	2.3	0	9	118	2.6	158	0	0.46	0.21	4.1	—
Lean only	2.2 oz	63	60	135	18	6	2.2	2.6	0.6	0	8	111	2.3	146	0	0.42	0.19	3.7	—

Source: Nutritive value of foods, Home and Garden Bull. 72, Science and Education Administration, USDA (1978).
[a] Dashes denote lack of reliable data for a constituent believed to be present in measurable amount.
[b] Edible part only unless indicated otherwise.
[c] About one-fourth of the outer layer of fat on the cut was removed. Deposits of fat within the cut were not removed.
[d] Outer layer of fat on the cut was removed to within approximately 1/2 in. of the lean. Deposits of fat within the cut were not removed.

Table 7.7. Nutritive Values of the Edible Parts of Veal[a]

Food, approximate measure[b]	Unit	Total weight (g)	Water (%)	Food energy (cal)	Protein (g)	Fat (g)	Fatty Acids Saturated (total, g)	Unsaturated Oleic (g)	Unsaturated Linoleic (g)	Carbohydrate (g)	Calcium (mg)	Phosphorus (mg)	Iron (mg)	Potassium (mg)	Vitamin A value (IU)	Thiamin (mg)	Riboflavin (mg)	Niacin (mg)	Ascorbic acid (mg)
Veal, medium fat, cooked, bone removed																			
Cutlet (4-1/8 × 2-1/4 × 1/2 in.), braised or broiled	3 oz	85	60	185	23	9	4.0	3.4	0.4	0	9	196	2.7	258	—	0.06	0.21	4.6	—
Rib (2 pieces, 4-1/8 × 2-1/4 × 1/4 in.) roasted	3 oz	85	55	230	23	14	6.1	5.1	0.6	0	10	211	2.9	259	—	0.11	0.26	6.6	—

Source: Nutritive value of foods, Home and Garden Bull. 72, Science and Education Administration, USDA (1978).
[a] Dashes denote lack of reliable data for a constituent believed to be present in measurable amount.
[b] Edible part only unless indicated otherwise.

161

Table 7.8. Nutritive Values of the Edible Parts of Sausage[a]

Food, approximate measure[b]	Unit	Total weight (g)	Water (%)	Food energy (cal)	Protein (g)	Fat (g)	Fatty Acids Saturated (total, g)	Unsaturated Oleic (g)	Unsaturated Linoleic (g)	Carbohydrate (g)	Calcium (mg)	Phosphorus (mg)	Iron (mg)	Potassium (mg)	Vitamin A value (IU)	Thiamin (mg)	Riboflavin (mg)	Niacin (mg)	Ascorbic acid (mg)
Bologna, slice (8 per 8-oz pkg)	1 slice	28	56	85	3	8	3.0	3.4	0.5	Trace	2	36	0.5	65	—	0.05	0.06	0.7	—
Braunschweiger, slice (6 per 6-oz pkg)	1 slice	28	53	90	4	8	2.6	3.4	0.8	1	3	69	1.7	—	1850	0.05	0.41	2.3	—
Brown and serve (10–11 per 8-oz pkg), browned	1 link	17	40	70	3	6	2.3	2.8	0.7	Trace	—	—	—	—	—	—	—	—	—
Deviled ham, canned	1 tbsp	13	51	45	2	4	1.5	1.8	0.4	0	1	12	0.3	—	0	0.02	0.01	0.2	—
Frankfurter (8 per 1-lb pkg), cooked (reheated)	1 frankfurter	56	57	170	7	15	5.6	6.5	1.2	1	3	57	0.8	—	—	0.08	0.11	1.4	—
Meat, potted (beef, chicken, turkey), canned	1 tbsp	13	61	30	2	2	—	—	—	0	—	—	—	—	—	Trace	0.03	0.2	—
Pork link (16 per 1-lb pkg), cooked	1 link	13	35	60	2	6	2.1	2.4	0.5	Trace	1	21	0.3	35	0	0.10	0.04	0.5	—
Salami																			
Dry type, slice (12 per 4-oz pkg)	1 slice	10	30	45	2	4	1.6	1.6	0.1	Trace	1	28	0.4	—	—	0.04	0.03	0.5	—
Cooked type, slice (8 per 8-oz pkg)	1 slice	28	51	90	5	7	3.1	3.0	0.2	Trace	3	57	0.7	—	—	0.07	0.07	1.2	—
Vienna sausage (7 per 4-oz can)	1 sausage	16	63	40	2	3	1.2	1.4	0.2	Trace	1	24	0.3	—	—	0.01	0.02	0.4	—

Source: Nutritive value of foods, Home and Garden Bull. 72, Science and Education Administration, USDA (1978).
[a] Dashes denote lack of reliable data for a constituent believed to be present in measurable amount.
[b] Edible part only unless indicated otherwise.

Table 7.9. Nutritive Values of the Edible Parts of Miscellaneous Meat Items[a]

Food, approximate measure[b]	Unit	Total weight (g)	Water (%)	Food energy (cal)	Protein (g)	Fat (g)	Saturated (total, g)	Unsaturated Oleic (g)	Unsaturated Linoleic (g)	Carbohydrate (g)	Calcium (mg)	Phosphorus (mg)	Iron (mg)	Potassium (mg)	Vitamin A value (IU)	Thiamin (mg)	Riboflavin (mg)	Niacin (mg)	Ascorbic acid (mg)
									Fatty Acids										
Gelatin, dry	7-g envelope	7	13	25	6	Trace	0	0	0	0	—	—	—	—	—	—	—	—	—
Gelatin dessert prepared with gelatin dessert powder and water	1 cup	240	84	140	4	0	0	0	0	34	—	—	—	—	—	—	—	—	—
Soups																			
Canned, condensed, prepared with equal volume of water																			
Bean with pork	1 cup	250	84	170	8	6	1.2	1.8	2.4	22	63	128	2.3	395	650	0.13	0.08	1.0	3
Beef broth, bouillon, consomme	1 cup	240	96	30	5	0	0	0	0	3	Trace	31	0.5	130	Trace	Trace	0.02	1.2	—
Beef noodle	1 cup	240	93	65	4	3	0.6	0.7	0.8	7	7	48	1.0	77	50	0.05	0.07	1.0	Trace
Vegetable beef	1 cup	245	92	80	5	2	—	—	—	10	12	49	0.7	162	2700	0.05	0.05	1.0	—
Dehydrated,																			
Bouillon cube, 1/2 in.	1 cube	4	4	5	1	Trace	—	—	—	Trace	—	—	—	4	—	—	—	—	—

Source: Nutritive value of foods, Home and Garden Bull. 72, Science and Education Administration, USDA (1978).
[a] Dashes denote lack of reliable data for a constituent believed to be present in measurable amount.
[b] Edible part only unless indicated otherwise.

Table 7.10. Composition of Animal Fat[a]

Nutrients	Unit	Lard (pork) 100 g	1 cup = 205 g	1 tbsp = 12.8 g	1 lb	Beef tallow 100 g	1 cup = 205 g	1 tbsp = 12.8 g	1 lb	Mutton tallow 100 g	1 cup = 205 g	1 tbsp = 12.8 g	1 lb
Proximate													
Water	g	0.0	0.0	0.0	0.0	0.0	0.0	0.0	0.0	0.0	0.0	0.0	0.0
Food energy	kcal	902.0	1849.1	115.5	4,091.5	902.0	1849.1	115.5	4,091.5	902.0	1849.1	115.5	4,091.5
	kJ	3774.0	7736.6	483.1	17,118.7	3774.0	7736.6	483.1	17,118.7	3774.0	7736.6	483.1	17,118.7
Protein	g	0.0	0.0	0.0	0.0	0.0	0.0	0.0	0.0	0.0	0.0	0.0	0.0
Total lipid (fat)	g	100.0	205.0	12.8	453.6	100.0	205.0	12.8	453.6	100.0	205.0	12.8	453.6
Carbohydrate, total	g	0.0	0.0	0.0	0.0	0.0	0.0	0.0	0.0	0.0	0.0	0.0	0.0
Fiber	g	0.0	0.0	0.0	0.0	0.0	0.0	0.0	0.0	0.0	0.0	0.0	0.0
Ash	g	0.0	0.0	0.0	0.0	0.0	0.0	0.0	0.0	0.0	0.0	0.0	0.0
Minerals													
Calcium	mg	0.07	0.13	0.01	0.29	—	—	—	—	—	—	—	—
Magnesium	mg	0.02	0.03	0.00	0.08	—	—	—	—	—	—	—	—
Potassium	mg	0.02	0.04	0.00	0.08	0.01	0.02	0.00	0.04	—	—	—	—
Sodium	mg	0.01	0.03	0.00	0.06	0.01	0.02	0.00	0.05	—	—	—	—
Zinc	mg	0.11	0.23	0.01	0.50	—	—	—	—	—	—	—	—
Vitamins													
Total tocopherol	mg	1.3	2.7	0.2	6.1	2.7	5.4	0.3	12.0	—	—	—	—
α-Tocopherol	mg	1.2	2.5	0.2	5.4	—	—	—	—	—	—	—	—
Lipids													
Fatty acids:													
Saturated, total	g	39.2	80.4	5.0	178.0	49.8	102.1	6.4	226.0	47.3	96.9	6.1	214.4
10:0	g	0.1	0.1	0.0	0.2	—	—	—	—	—	—	—	—
12:0	g	0.2	0.4	0.0	0.8	0.9	1.9	0.1	4.1	—	—	—	—
14:0	g	1.3	2.6	0.2	5.8	3.7	7.5	0.5	16.6	3.8	7.8	0.5	17.3
16:0	g	23.8	48.7	3.0	107.8	24.9	51.1	3.2	113.1	21.5	44.2	2.8	97.7
18:0	g	13.5	27.6	1.7	61.1	18.9	38.8	2.4	85.8	19.5	39.9	2.5	88.3
Monounsaturated, total	g	45.1	92.5	5.8	204.7	41.8	85.6	5.3	189.5	40.6	83.2	5.2	184.0
16:1	g	2.7	5.6	0.3	12.3	4.2	8.6	0.5	19.1	2.3	4.7	0.3	10.5
18:1	g	41.2	84.5	5.3	187.1	36.0	73.8	4.6	163.3	37.6	77.1	4.8	170.6
20:1	g	1.0	2.1	0.1	4.6	0.3	0.5	0.0	1.2	—	—	—	—
Polyunsaturated, total	g	11.2	23.0	1.4	51.0	4.0	8.2	0.5	18.2	7.8	15.9	1.0	35.2
18:2	g	10.2	20.9	1.3	46.1	3.1	6.3	0.4	14.0	5.5	11.2	0.7	24.9
18:3	g	1.0	2.1	0.1	4.7	0.6	1.3	0.1	2.9	2.3	4.7	0.3	10.4
Cholesterol	mg	95	195	12	431	109	223	14	494	102	209	13	463

Source: Agriculture Handbook No. 8–4; U.S. Dept. of Agriculture, Science and Education Administration (1979).
[a] Dashes denote lack of reliable data for a nutrient believed to be present in measurable amount.

For example, if a more unsaturated pork fat is desired, it can be obtained by feeding the animal more unsaturated fats. A few of the fatty acids (linoleic, linolenic, and arachidonic) are essential for good health and fats are a solvent for fat-soluble vitamins, so some fats are essential for good human nutrition. Animal fats do contain some cholesterol, and the quantity per unit of fat for the three species is shown in Table 7.10.

The chemical composition, including proximate analysis, minerals, vitamins, fatty acids, cholesterol, and amino acids, of baby food items containing meat is shown in Table 7.11.

GENETICS

Animal muscle composition varies not only by type of digestive system and species, but also there are large amounts of variability within the species types. For example, most beef cattle have a heavier, thicker muscular conformation than dairy cattle, which are usually much more angular in shape. Also, wool and mutton types of sheep are very different in body styles. Even within a body type and breed, various strains of animals perform differently and this variability is considered by animal geneticists when they are designing a breeding program. Heritability estimates for many of the carcass characteristics can be found in Table 7.12. Most of these values are sufficiently large so that there appears to be a high degree of genetic control and, therefore, animal structure can be altered within a few generations. A word of caution should be added, however, since the correlation between conformation and productive characteristics has been consistently poor (e.g., dairy beef gives as much lean beef as beef breeds at the same degree of fatness).

INFLUENCE OF AGE, SEASON, SEX, TYPE, AND GRADE

Beef

As cattle increase in age, within a practical range, moisture level decreases, fat normally increases, muscle becomes darker (increased myoglobin level), flavor increases, and tenderness decreases (increased branching of collagen). Mature bulls increase in forequarter muscling, particularly in the neck area. Grass-fed cattle are normally sold in late summer or early fall and usually grade no higher than U.S. Good. Often their fat is somewhat yellow due to carotenoid pigments contained in the grass they consume. Most feedlot cattle do not change drastically with the season, are normally 10–20 months of age, and usually qualify for the U.S. Good or Choice grade. Young bulls are normally castrated and used as feeder animals in the United States, but bulls are used in Europe as meat animals and are attracting increased attention as such in this country.

Table 7.11. Chemical Composition of Baby Foods Containing Meat

Nutrient	Unit	Beef, strained 1 jar = 99 g	Beef, junior 1 jar = 99 g	Beef with beef heart, strained 1 jar = 99 g	Ham, strained 1 jar = 99 g	Ham, junior 1 jar = 99 g
Proximate						
Water	g	79.8	79.1	81.7	78.6	77.8
Food energy	kcal	106	105	93	110	123
	kJ	443	441	389	462	516
Protein (N X 6.25)	g	13.5	14.3	12.6	13.7	14.9
Total lipid (fat)	g	5.3	4.9	4.4	5.7	6.6
Carbohydrate, total	g	0.0	0.0	0.0	0.0	0.0
Fiber	g	0.00	0.00	0.1	0.00	0.00
Ash	g	0.8	0.8	0.9	1.0	1.0
Minerals						
Calcium	mg	7	8	4	6	5
Iron	mg	1.46	1.63	1.97	1.02	1.00
Magnesium	mg	17	9	12	13	11
Phosphorus	mg	83	71	93	80	88
Potassium	mg	218	189	198	202	208
Sodium	mg	80	65	62	40	66
Zinc	mg	2.430	1.980	1.817	2.224	1.683
Copper	mg	0.043	0.091	0.128	0.064	
Vitamins						
Ascorbic acid	mg	2.1	1.8	2.1	2.1	2.1
Thiamin	mg	0.010	0.010	0.022	0.138	0.141
Riboflavin	mg	0.141	0.157	0.353	0.152	0.192
Niacin	mg	2.821	3.250	3.846	2.607	2.812
Pantothenic acid	mg	0.337	0.349	0.000	0.505	0.526
Vitamin B_6	mg	0.139	0.119	0.117	0.249	0.198
Folacin	μg	5.5	5.7	5.0	1.9	2.0
Vitamin B_{12}	μg	1.406	1.459	0.00	0.00	0.00
Vitamin A	RE	55	31	37	11	9
	IU	183	102	124	38	31
Lipids						
Fatty acids:						
Saturated, total	g	2.55	2.57	2.06	1.92	2.21
10:0	g	0.00	0.00	0.00	0.00	0.00
12:0	g	0.00	0.00	0.00	0.00	0.00
14:0	g	0.16	0.14	0.13	0.07	0.08
16:0	g	1.00	1.23	1.06		
18:0	g	0.88	1.00	0.75	0.59	0.68
Monounsaturated, total	g	2.18	1.83	1.83	2.73	3.15
16:1	g	0.20	0.13	0.16	0.16	0.18
18:1	g	1.89	1.64	1.61	2.49	2.88
20:1	g	0.05	0.00	0.01	0.06	0.07
Polyunsaturated, total	g	0.20	0.16	0.21	0.78	0.90
18:2	g	0.09	0.11	0.15	0.70	0.81
18:3	g	0.05	0.03	0.02	0.03	0.03
20:4	g	0.05	0.02	0.03	0.04	0.05
Cholesterol	mg					
Amino acids						
Tryptophan	g	0.136	0.145	0.125	0.137	0.148
Threonine	g	0.591	0.629	0.506	0.597	0.649
Isoleucine	g	0.613	0.652	0.613	0.654	0.711
Leucine	g	1.080	1.150	1.000	1.100	1.196
Lysine	g	1.122	1.194	1.040	1.168	1.270
Methionine	g	0.414	0.441	0.326	0.351	0.382
Cystine	g	0.157	0.167	0.129	0.169	0.184
Phenylalanine	g	0.522	0.555	0.518	0.525	0.570
Tyrosine	g	0.448	0.477	0.361	0.461	0.501
Valine	g	0.681	0.726	0.683	0.709	0.771
Arginine	g	0.919	0.978	0.824	0.931	1.012
Histidine	g	0.457	0.487	0.336	0.467	0.509
Alanine	g	0.849	0.905	0.857	0.830	0.902
Aspartic acid	g	1.186	1.262	1.161	1.313	1.428
Glutamic acid	g	2.048	2.181	1.997	2.068	2.248
Glycine	g	0.860	0.916	0.814	0.788	0.857
Proline	g	0.675	0.719	0.650	0.639	0.695
Serine	g	0.494	0.526	0.438	0.498	0.542

Lamb, strained 1 jar = 99 g	Liver, strained 1 jar = 99 g	Meat sticks, junior 1 jar = 71 g	Pork, strained 1 jar = 99 g	Veal, strained 1 jar = 99 g	Veal, junior 1 jar = 99 g
79.5	78.5	49.3	77.6	80.0	79.0
102	100	130	123	100	109
426	417	545	514	418	455
13.9	14.2	9.5	13.8	13.4	15.1
4.7	3.7	10.4	7.1	4.7	4.9
0.1	1.4	0.8	0.0	0.0	0.0
0.00	0.00	0.1	0.00	0.1	0.2
0.8	1.2	1.0	1.1	0.9	0.9
7	3	24	5	7	6
1.48	5.23	0.98	0.99	1.26	1.24
13	13	0.00	10	12	11
96	201	73	93	97	97
203	224	81	221	214	234
62	73	388	42	64	68
2.728	2.947		2.247	1.980	2.493
0.054	1.965		0.071	0.040	0.074
1.2	19.1	1.7	1.8	2.3	2.1
0.019	0.049	0.042	0.145	0.016	0.018
0.198	1.796	0.122	0.201	0.157	0.181
2.896	8.245	1.052	2.246	3.516	3.770
0.406	0.00	0.00	0.00	0.426	0.449
0.150	0.340	0.057	0.203	0.148	0.117
2.3	334.0		1.9	5.9	6.6
2.168	2.138		0.980	0.00	0.00
25	11,337	15	11	14	15
85	37,754	49	38	45	50
2.29	1.36	4.13	2.37	2.27	2.37
0.00		0.01	0.00	0.00	0.00
0.00	0.00	0.02	0.00	0.01	0.01
0.11	0.04	0.18	0.08	0.24	0.18
1.02	0.06	2.53		1.17	1.21
0.98	0.60	1.26	0.71	0.66	0.81
1.85	0.77	4.60	3.55	2.03	2.10
0.06	0.07	0.33	0.22	0.19	0.17
1.76	0.68	4.18	3.24	1.77	1.86
0.00	0.00	0.05	0.07	0.00	0.00
0.19	0.06	1.13	0.77	0.16	0.16
0.13	0.22	1.04	0.69	0.10	0.10
0.05	0.05	0.05	0.03	0.03	0.03
0.01	0.14	0.04		0.02	0.03
	181.50				
0.139	0.220	0.065	0.135	0.154	0.174
0.636	0.676	0.413	0.611	0.558	0.632
0.655	0.694	0.474	0.673	0.604	0.682
1.101	1.307	0.740	1.116	1.034	1.168
1.237	0.926	0.734	1.146	1.074	1.215
0.437	0.372	0.219	0.394	0.295	0.334
0.192	0.213	0.052	0.152	0.173	0.196
0.548	0.678	0.431	0.564	0.518	0.585
0.488	0.569	0.370	0.505	0.428	0.484
0.707	0.898	0.491	0.695	0.650	0.736
0.914	0.831	0.618	0.939	0.888	1.004
0.352	0.363	0.327	0.443	0.411	0.464
0.873	0.875	0.557	0.870	0.837	0.946
1.311	1.342	0.799	1.297	1.181	1.336
2.134	1.808	1.436	2.112	1.920	2.170
0.811	0.803	0.484	0.752	0.918	1.038
0.780	0.766	0.539	0.740	0.739	0.835
0.535	0.633	0.351	0.536	0.475	0.538

(Continued)

Table 7.11. *(Continued)*

Nutrient	Unit	Vegetables and bacon, junior 1 jar = 213 g	Vegetables and bacon, strained 1 jar = 128 g	Vegetables and beef, strained 1 jar = 128 g	Vegetables and beef, junior 1 jar = 213 g	Vegetables and ham, strained 1 jar = 128 g
Proximate						
Water	g	183.5	110.0	113.3	187.3	114.2
Food energy	kcal	150	88	67	113	62
	kJ	629	367	282	472	258
Protein (N X 6.25)	g	3.9	2.0	2.5	5.0	2.2
Total lipid (fat)	g	8.2	4.2	2.6	3.6	2.2
Carbohydrate, total	g	16.1	11.0	9.0	15.8	8.8
Fiber	g	0.4	0.5	0.3	0.4	0.2
Ash	g	1.3	0.8	0.6	1.2	0.6
Minerals						
Calcium	mg	23	17	16	22	11
Iron	mg	0.88	0.45	0.49	1.01	0.38
Magnesium	mg	0.00	0.00	7	13	6
Phosphorus	mg	81	40	52	91	29
Potassium	mg	184	115	129	224	109
Sodium	mg	96	55	27	52	15
Zinc	mg			0.422	0.882	0.246
Copper	mg			0.013	0.083	0.037
Vitamins						
Ascorbic acid	mg	2.4	1.7	1.5	3.1	2.1
Thiamin	mg	0.109	0.042	0.027	0.066	0.041
Riboflavin	mg	0.064	0.042	0.036	0.066	0.037
Niacin	mg	1.163	0.678	0.646	1.397	0.517
Pantothenic acid	mg	0.00	0.00	0.154	0.266	0.00
Vitamin B_6	mg	0.136	0.102	0.069	0.136	0.042
Folacin	μg	19.2	11.7	6.0	10.4	6.3
Vitamin B_{12}	μg	0.00	0.128	0.320	0.556	0.00
Vitamin A	RE	463	382	219	410	122
	IU	3356	3409	1520	3011	872
Lipids						
Fatty acids:						
Saturated, total	g	2.98	1.52			
10:0	g	0.01	0.00			
12:0	g	0.00	0.00			
14:0	g	0.10	0.05			
16:0	g					
18:0	g	0.90	0.46			
Monounsaturated, total	g	3.97	2.03			
16:1	g	0.22	0.11			
18:1	g	3.67	1.88			
20:1	g	0.07	0.03			
Polyunsaturated, total	g	0.10	0.05			
18:2	g	0.82	0.42			
18:3	g	0.05	0.03			
20:4	g	0.01	0.01			
Cholesterol	mg		4.10			
Amino acids						
Tryptophan	g	0.036	0.019	0.026	0.049	0.023
Threonine	g	0.130	0.069	0.091	0.181	0.084
Isoleucine	g	0.175	0.084	0.106	0.213	0.100
Leucine	g	0.273	0.133	0.173	0.345	0.165
Lysine	g	0.232	0.109	0.179	0.358	0.152
Methionine	g	0.079	0.041	0.041	0.081	0.047
Cystine	g	0.055	0.029	0.024	0.049	0.023
Phenylalanine	g	0.164	0.079	0.087	0.175	0.084
Tyrosine	g	0.121	0.070	0.065	0.130	0.068
Valine	g	0.207	0.109	0.128	0.256	0.118
Arginine	g	0.258	0.142	0.151	0.302	0.148
Histidine	g	0.085	0.044	0.056	0.113	0.060
Alanine	g	0.185	0.111	0.173	0.345	0.133
Aspartic acid	g	0.432	0.261	0.250	0.498	0.202
Glutamic acid	g	0.763	0.402	0.460	0.920	0.443
Glycine	g	0.173	0.091	0.197	0.396	0.111
Proline	g	0.181	0.088	0.157	0.315	0.119
Serine	g	0.147	0.077	0.092	0.183	0.086

Vegetables and ham, junior 1 jar = 213 g	Vegetables and ham, toddler 1 jar = 177 g	Vegetables and lamb, strained 1 jar = 128 g	Vegetables and lamb, junior 1 jar = 213 g	Vegetables and liver, strained 1 jar = 128 g	Vegetables and liver, junior 1 jar = 213 g	Vegetables, dumplings, and beef, strained 1 jar = 128 g	Vegetables, dumplings, and beef, junior 1 jar = 213 g
188.2	148.0	113.4	188.8	115.2	189.4	113.8	188.7
110	128	67	108	50	93	61	103
459	537	279	453	208	390	257	432
5.2	7.4	2.5	4.4	2.8	3.9	2.6	4.4
3.6	5.2	2.6	3.7	0.6	1.2	1.2	1.7
14.9	13.9	8.9	15.1	8.8	17.5	9.8	17.0
0.4	0.00	0.4	0.4	0.2	0.6	0.00	0.00
1.0	2.4	0.6	1.0	0.6	1.0	0.6	1.2
16	41	15	27	9	20	18	30
0.47	1.23	0.44	0.72	2.83	3.86	0.49	1.00
15	30	9	16	0.00	0.00	8	14
55	71	63	104	51	81	0.00	0.00
197	271	120	202	120	189	0.00	0.00
37	531	26	28	24	27	62	110
0.475	0.832	0.276	0.471			0.512	0.697
0.066	0.071	0.037	0.062				
2.7	6.6	1.5	3.7	2.3	3.8	1.0	1.7
0.079	0.076	0.023	0.045	0.023	0.047	0.063	0.083
0.047	0.097	0.044	0.068	0.339	0.479	0.051	0.077
0.748	1.237	0.677	1.180	1.536	2.460	0.735	1.044
0.00	0.00	0.205	0.339	0.00	0.00	0.00	0.00
0.068	0.152	0.059	0.094	0.105	0.211	0.00	0.00
11.3		4.7	7.7	36.8	68.1	9.2	15.7
0.00		0.204	0.339	0.00	0.00		
173		363	423	940	1524		
1310	629	2554	3158	3981	8368	533	1407
	1.85						
	0.00						
	0.00						
	0.07						
	0.54						
	2.52						
	0.15						
	2.32						
	0.05						
	0.30						
	0.27						
	0.04						
	0.02						
	13.63						
0.055	0.101	0.029	0.051	0.041	0.058		
0.194	0.301	0.093	0.164	0.114	0.158		
0.232	0.370	0.115	0.202	0.133	0.183		
0.381	0.575	0.188	0.330	0.244	0.339		
0.354	0.540	0.187	0.328	0.209	0.290		
0.109	0.143	0.038	0.066	0.064	0.089		
0.055	0.083	0.022	0.038	0.037	0.051		
0.194	0.320	0.101	0.177	0.133	0.183		
0.158	0.251	0.079	0.141	0.097	0.134		
0.271	0.405	0.124	0.217	0.175	0.243		
0.343	0.471	0.170	0.300	0.168	0.232		
0.141	0.202	0.059	0.102	0.068	0.094		
0.307	0.384	0.145	0.256	0.168	0.232		
0.469	0.837	0.253	0.445	0.284	0.394		
1.022	1.243	0.508	0.890	0.415	0.575		
0.256	0.354	0.128	0.224	0.148	0.207		
0.275	0.395	0.140	0.245	0.150	0.207		
0.198	0.313	0.093	0.164	0.110	0.151		

(Continued)

Table 7.11. *(Continued)*

Nutrient	Unit	Beef and egg noodles, strained 1 jar = 128 g	Beef and egg noodles junior 1 jar = 213 g	Beef and rice, toddler 1 jar = 177 g	Beef lasagna, toddler 1 jar = 177 g	Beef stew, toddler 1 jar = 177 g
Proximate						
Water	g	113.4	186.9	144.9	145.7	153.8
Food energy	kcal	68	122	146	137	90
	kJ	286	511	610	572	375
Protein (N × 5.98)	g	2.9	5.4	8.9	7.4	9.1
Total lipid (fat)	g	2.2	4.0	5.1	3.8	2.1
Carbohydrate, total	g	9.0	15.7	15.5	17.7	9.6
Fiber	g	0.4	0.4	0.5	0.4	0.5
Ash	g	0.5	1.0	2.6	2.4	2.4
Minerals						
Calcium	mg	12	18	20	32	16
Iron	mg	0.53	0.92	1.23	1.55	1.27
Magnesium	mg	9	16	15	20	20
Phosphorus	mg	37	64	62	70	78
Potassium	mg	61	99	212	216	251
Sodium	mg	37	37	632	804	611
Zinc	mg	0.480	0.854	1.623	1.239	1.540
Copper	mg	0.038	0.068	0.096	0.00	0.00
Vitamins						
Ascorbic acid	mg	1.5	2.9	6.8	3.4	5.3
Thiamin	mg	0.045	0.060	0.028	0.127	0.025
Riboflavin	mg	0.054	0.077	0.122	0.158	0.115
Niacin	mg	0.925	1.240	2.377	2.395	2.324
Pantothenic acid	mg	0.274	0.490	0.00	0.00	0.00
Vitamin B_6	mg	0.061	0.066	0.246	0.126	0.131
Folacin	μg	6.5	11.7			
Vitamin B_{12}	μg	0.115	0.204			
Vitamin A	RE	141	187			
	IU	1053	1397	889	2058	2918
Lipids						
Fatty acids:						
Saturated, total	g					1.03
10:0	g					0.00
12:0	g					0.00
14:0	g					0.05
16:0	g					0.14
18:0	g					0.39
Monounsaturated, total	g					0.77
16:1	g					0.06
18:1	g					0.71
20:1	g					0.00
Polyunsaturated, total	g					0.05
18:2	g					0.15
18:3	g					0.02
20:4	g					0.01
Cholesterol	mg					22.18
Amino acids						
Tryptophan	g	0.032	0.058	0.081	0.083	0.094
Threonine	g	0.114	0.211	0.354	0.289	0.372
Isoleucine	g	0.159	0.294	0.434	0.365	0.435
Leucine	g	0.238	0.443	0.694	0.573	0.687
Lysine	g	0.212	0.394	0.666	0.526	0.697
Methionine	g	0.060	0.113	0.218	0.145	0.251
Cystine	g	0.033	0.062	0.096	0.085	0.094
Phenylalanine	g	0.134	0.249	0.349	0.322	0.356
Tyrosine	g	0.106	0.198	0.285	0.234	0.281
Valine	g	0.151	0.281	0.487	0.409	0.481
Arginine	g	0.180	0.334	0.598	0.448	0.625
Histidine	g	0.084	0.158	0.227	0.181	0.227
Alanine	g	0.172	0.317	0.600	0.469	0.588
Aspartic acid	g	0.252	0.469	0.821	0.625	0.858
Glutamic acid	g	0.594	1.101	1.540	1.574	1.457
Glycine	g	0.175	0.326	0.644	0.494	0.621
Proline	g	0.214	0.396	0.542	0.577	0.568
Serine	g	0.113	0.209	0.317	0.212	0.340

Lamb and noodles, junior 1 jar = 213 g	Macaroni and bacon, junior 1 jar = 213 g	Beef with vegetables, strained 1 jar = 128 g	Beef with vegetables, junior 1 jar = 28.35 g	Ham with vegetables, strained 1 jar = 128 g	Ham with vegetables, junior 1 jar = 128 g	Veal with vegetables, strained 1 jar = 128 g	Veal with vegetables, junior 1 jar = 128 g
184.3	181.2	109.3	23.6	107.6	107.0	108.2	107.9
138	160	96	24	97	98	89	93
579	669	400	100	406	412	372	391
4.8	5.4	7.3	1.8	8.0	8.2	7.6	7.8
4.7	7.1	5.3	1.3	4.4	4.2	3.4	4.0
18.6	18.2	5.3	1.5	7.1	7.9	7.8	7.4
0.00	0.00	0.4	0.1	0.3	0.2	0.4	0.2
0.6	1.1	0.7	0.2	0.8	0.8	0.9	0.9
39	152	15	3	14	12	12	14
0.78	0.80	0.93	0.22	0.75	0.76	0.76	1.13
0.00	0.00	10	2	11	12	10	12
0.00	0.00	62	15	72	71	69	69
165	180	179	42	198	208	196	201
39	166	46	9	29	28	30	32
0.00	0.00	1.664	0.397	1.280	1.385	1.280	1.408
0.00	0.00	0.102	0.026	0.00	0.00	0.128	0.131
4.1	4.5	2.5	0.5	2.3	2.4	2.4	2.1
0.077	0.098	0.044	0.010	0.129	0.138	0.028	0.029
0.138	0.179	0.084	0.023	0.106	0.110	0.095	0.105
1.427	1.342	1.702	0.404	1.800	1.482	2.065	1.974
		0.307	0.078	0.499	0.515	0.320	0.324
		0.113	0.024	0.136	0.122	0.106	0.090
		7.3	1.8	8.1	8.3	0.00	0.00
		0.653	0.165	0.344	0.355	0.577	0.585
		141	28	52	85	96	101
1667	2471	1003	225	214	332	349	545
				1.51	1.44		
				0.00	0.00		
				0.00	0.00		
				0.05	0.05		
				0.44	0.41		
				2.05	1.94		
				0.13	0.12		
				1.87	1.78		
				0.04	0.04		
				0.32	0.30		
				0.57	0.54		
				0.03	0.03		
				0.04	0.04		
					22.59		
		0.059	0.014	0.078	0.079	0.078	0.079
		0.279	0.068	0.312	0.317	0.307	0.312
		0.307	0.075	0.353	0.360	0.343	0.351
		0.544	0.133	0.599	0.608	0.596	0.608
		0.539	0.132	0.626	0.636	0.608	0.620
		0.204	0.050	0.198	0.201	0.174	0.178
		0.078	0.019	0.092	0.093	0.091	0.093
		0.275	0.067	0.284	0.288	0.294	0.301
		0.209	0.051	0.224	0.227	0.221	0.227
		0.361	0.088	0.371	0.378	0.378	0.385
		0.449	0.110	0.494	0.502	0.520	0.529
		0.219	0.054	0.287	0.291	0.244	0.250
		0.460	0.112	0.421	0.429	0.468	0.476
		0.663	0.162	0.742	0.755	0.735	0.749
		1.073	0.262	1.211	1.230	1.272	1.297
		0.598	0.146	0.434	0.442	0.563	0.573
		0.431	0.105	0.407	0.413	0.415	0.422
		0.243	0.060	0.262	0.266	0.273	0.278

Source: Composition of Foods: Baby Food, Agricultural Handbook 8–3, U.S. Dept. of Agriculture, Science and Education Administration (1978).

Table 7.12. Heritability Factors for Meat Animals

Species	Trait	Breed	Heritability (%)	Reference[a]
Beef	Weaning conformation score	All breeds	25–30	1
	Carcass grade	All breeds	30–40	1
	Ribeye area	All breeds	30–40	1
	Fat thickness over ribeye	All breeds	25–45	1
	Tenderness	All breeds	40–70	1
	Mature cow weight	All breeds	50–70	1
	Carcass yield	Hereford, Angus, Shorthorn	43 ± 19	2
	Primal cuts	Hereford, Angus, Shorthorn	34	2
	Color–firmness–structure	General	30	3
	Tenderness	General	60	3
Sheep	Average daily gain	Rambouillet, Columbia		
		Corriedale	24 ± 9	4
	Loin eye area	Rambouillet, Columbia		
		Corriedale	34 ± 11	4
	Retail cuts	Rambouillet, Columbia		
		Corriedale	40 ± 12	4
	Fat percentage	Rambouillet, Columbia		
		Corriedale	54 ± 13	4
Pork	Body type and condition	Rambouillet	13–16	5
	Loin area	Composite	72	6
	Percentage lean cuts	Composite	43	6
	Backfat	Durocs	49	6
	Conformation	Poland China	20	6
	Color–firmness–structure	General	30	3
	Marbling	General	25	3
	Tenderness	General	30	3

[a] References: 1, Warwick (1968); 2, Cundiff *et al.* (1969); 3, Forrest *et al.* (1975); 4, Botkin *et al.* (1969); 5, Hazel and Terrill (1946); 6, Altman and Dittmer (1962).

They are leaner and more efficient than steers, but are slightly less tender. If bulls are slaughtered at the appropriate age, however, their palatability traits are very acceptable. Steers are slightly more efficient and acceptable than heifers for feedlot usage. Beef cattle are generally preferred for carcass beef but the feeding of dairy cattle is attracting attention due to feed conversion efficiency and the Holstein is probably the most popular breed among the dairy cattle for feedlot usage. U.S. Department of Agriculture (USDA) grades of Prime, Choice, Good, Standard, and Utility are reserved for cattle less than 48 months of age, and Choice is the most popular grade found in the supermarkets; however, Good, or equivalent (ungraded), and Prime beef can be located in certain markets. Prime beef is often preferred by fine restaurants. Canner and Cutter grades usually are used for sausage products.

Sheep

Sheep usually give birth in late winter and lambs are normally slaughtered before reaching 1 year of age. Therefore, there is normally a good correlation between age and season. The first lambs normally reach market around Easter at approximately 20 kg of weight and contain no more than 30% fat. Similar, but older lambs are slaughtered during summer and early fall. Thin lambs usually go to feedlots and are fed for a winter supply of market lambs (Byerly 1975). These feedlot lambs are normally older, heavier, and fatter. The lean tissue is lower in moisture and higher in fat with more marbling, greater juiciness, darker color, and less tender lean. Older lambs are referred to as yearlings and still older ones as sheep or mutton. Mutton flavor may be pronounced in some of the carcasses from older sheep, but its intensity has often been exaggerated. Ram lambs are often superior in rate of gain and cutability to ewe and weather lambs and even heavy ram carcasses are acceptable in palatability and tenderness. Sheep breeds are normally divided into wool and mutton types. As the name would suggest, the mutton breeds have more thickness in conformation, are heavier muscled, and are normally considered superior for meat production. Most of the supermarket lamb cuts would qualify for the Prime and Choice grades, with a great percentage of the Good and lower grades of lamb, and most of the mutton, being diverted into processed products.

Pork

Pork carcasses have changed tremendously in the past 30 years, with a great deal of emphasis being placed on the production of lean meat tissue. Swine have also become more efficient and, therefore, hogs are reaching market weight at a younger age (in general, from 5 to 6 months). Since hogs also tend to become fatter as they increase in weight, the normal slaughter weight of 220–260 lb tends to also encourage production of lean. As pigs mature, they tend to increase the percentage of total saturated fatty acids in their fat, with a decrease in linoleic and oleic acids (Ellis and Hankins 1925). With farrowing taking place throughout the year, there is not much seasonal difference in swine production except for the fact that heavy hogs tend to be marketed in greater numbers in the summer months. In the United States, boars are generally not used to produce pork because of an off-odor that is produced as these animals mature, which is objected to by a fairly large percentage (Plimpton 1971; 10% in young 70-kg boars and 30% in 100-kg boars) of the population. Interest is growing in Europe in utilizing the young boar as a producer of pork, and research is continuing in the United States on methods of utilizing this leaner, more efficient sex. Historically, hog breeds were classified into bacon and fat types, but with the emphasis on lean production, these types today are very similar. Market weight hogs are graded into U.S. 1, 2, 3, 4, and Utility (thin belly thickness) based on carcass weight or degree of muscling, length, and backfat thickness. A much larger percentage of desirable-quality pork is cured than in the case of the ruminant animals. Boars are inspected for odor and young boars, if acceptable, are utilized with market-weight barrow and gilts in fresh and cured products. Mature boars and stags are either condemned for odor or used in manufactured products. Heavyweight sows are utilized in fresh pork sausage or for comminuted product manufacturing.

LEVEL OF NUTRITION

Quantitative differences in animal diets are a major source of the variability in chemical components of muscle for all species. In many areas of the world, feed is restricted due to unfavorable environmental conditions. If young ruminant animals follow this period of restriction with full feeding, the carcasses are usually acceptable (Dockerty *et al.* 1973). Moderate restriction of feed results in approximately the same quantity of protein, but less fat deposited in a ruminant carcass (Hiner and Bond, 1971). Increased level of nutrition often results in improved flavor and tenderness in ruminants (Barbella *et al.* 1936), and this is the reason why feedlot practices are so popular.

Mild limited feeding of pork is often practiced in Europe to produce a leaner carcass. This can be accomplished by reducing feed availability or by the use of fibrous feeds to reduce the energy level. Because of labor costs, restricted feeding of pork is usually not practiced in the United States. If excess fat is removed by trimming, a satisfactory carcass can be produced by either limited or full feeding of the animal.

FAT IN THE DIET

Ruminant animals usually hydrogenate dietary fat to manufacture a more saturated depot fat, but feeding unsaturated fat can increase slightly the linoleic acid content of body fat (Dryden and Marchello 1973) and feeding a high-roughage diet can slightly increase the oleic acid of the depot fat (Rumsey *et al.* 1972). Major changes in depot fat are possible by a new experimental technique of feeding unsaturated fat treated with formaldehyde-casein, which encapsulates the fat and allows it to pass through the ruman without being hydrogenated.

As they get older and heavier, swine produce firmer carcasses due to the conversion of more carbohydrate to saturated fat (Ellis and Hankins 1925), but, in general, both young and old pigs tend to store fat similar to the type they are fed. Therefore, feed containing soybeans, peanuts, or garbage tends to produce a soft pork fat.

VITAMINS

Vitamin A is stored in beef and lamb liver and the quantity fluctuates a great deal, depending on the diet of the animal. For example, feedlot cattle that consume little roughage would have livers lower in vitamin A than grass-fed cattle. Vitamin A from beef liver is lost on heating and follows first-order kinetics with activation energy ranging from 36 to 122 kJ/mol (Wilkinson *et al.* 1981, 1982).

Swine are particularly dependent on vitamins in their feed to meet metabolic and tissue storage requirements. Pork is much higher in thiamin than beef or lamb and tocopherol storage is reported to be related to tocopherol level in the feed. Increased tocopherol level in pork tissue also extends the stability of pork during refrigerated and frozen storage (Buckley and Connolly 1980).

MINERALS

Soils in substantial areas of the United States are deficient in essential minerals; therefore, forages grown in these areas are deficient in essential minerals needed for animal nutrition. For example, ruminants grown in areas deficient in phosphorus or cobalt are thin and poorly fleshed (Beeson 1941). Copper, molybdenum, sulfate, and possibly manganese metabolism and retention in the muscle and liver tissue seem to be interrelated.

Copper is often used as a growth promoter in swine diets (Braude and Ryder 1973; Braude 1976; Lima *et al.* 1981). Zinc is an essential nutrient and zinc, copper, and calcium contents of the diet are interrelated and influence zinc storage in the tissue. Zinc levels in the muscle have been postulated to be related to the type of energy metabolism occurring in these muscles (Schricker *et al.* 1982) and most of the endogenous zinc in beef tissue has been proven to be water insoluble (Rosenbloom and Potter 1981).

Iodine is deficient in many areas, but is generally supplemented in animal diets by the use of iodized salt and organic iodine additives in the feed. Iodine content of meat does increase with the iodine level of the diet but the percentage transfer of iodine to the tissue is relatively small (Hemken 1980).

Selenium is deficient in many soils and forages and is also a necessary constituent for proper animal nutrition. The supplementation of selenium increased its level in the muscle and liver tissue (Ammerman *et al.* 1980), but selenium naturally occurring in plants has a greater influence on animal tissue selenium than equal quantities added to the diet in the form of an inorganic supplement. However, high levels of selenium in forage can be toxic to animals, and this is a problem in some western areas of the United States.

Tonic levels of arsenic are used as growth promoters for swine. At these levels, arsenic accumulation in the animal tissue is not considered hazardous to human health. Liver residues are likely to be higher than those found in muscle samples (Frost and Spruth 1956); however, in a USDA sampling (second quarter of 1973) of pork liver, no samples were found that exceeded 2 ppm, the established tolerance level for arsenic in liver. Arsenic is seldom found in measurable amounts of beef tissue.

Lead is normally an accidental contaminant, usually originating on painted objects and, of course, in seafood from contaminated water. Lead in the diet of animals has been shown to elevate the level of lead in the liver and kidney tissues (Dinius *et al.* 1973). Spalding (1972) reported average levels of lead in USDA-inspected animals to be liver, 0.536; muscle, 0.361; and kidney, 0.625 ppm.

Spalding (1972), in the same report, listed the average level of cadmium as liver, 0.207; muscle, 0.082; and kidney, 0.546 ppm.

Mercury is present in insignificant amounts in the tissue of animals used for foods, with the exception of large marine fish. Another exception might be animals fed seeds treated with mercurial fungicides that were intended for planting. These treated seeds would be toxic to animals or to man if consumed (Nelson 1971). Animals intentionally fed mercury had accumulation in the liver and kidney much higher than that found in the brain or muscle tissue (Wright *et al.* 1973A,B). Spalding (1972) reported 18% of beef livers, 26% of beef muscles, and 53% of beef kidneys were positive for mercury but averaged only 26 ng/g of tissue. Selenium has been shown to protect against mercury toxicity.

Fluorine is found in feed components such as bone meal, rock phosphate, phosphatic limestone, and smelter effluents and may also contaminate water supplies (Byerly 1975). It may be transferred in small amounts to soft tissue, but is found in higher concentrations in bone.

HORMONES

Diethylstilbestrol (DES), a synthetic female hormone, was used for a number of years to increase feed efficiency in beef animals (approximately 12%). Owing to small residues sometimes appearing in the fed animal's liver, this hormone was removed from animal feed, and its use as an implant was prohibited in 1973 (FDA 1972, 1973A,B), even though this product was used for two decades without a single known instance of harm to humans (FDA 1973B).

Several growth promoters are still available, including melengestrol acetate (MGA), which suppresses estros and increases rate of gain in heifers (Ray *et al.* 1969; Hawkins *et al.* 1972); Zeranol® (resorcyclic acid lactate), which is used as an implant in steers and lambs; Synovex S® (progesterone and estradiol benzoate), which is used as an implant for steers; Synovex H® (testosterone proprionate and estradiol benzoate), which is used as an implant for heifers (Byerly 1975); and Compudase® (estradiol benzoate), which improves growth rate and feed efficiency in steers (Eli Lilly 1982). Androgens have been reported to increase the percentage of round and lower the percentage of loin in calves (Burris *et al.* 1953). Hormones have generally not been used in swine because most reports do not indicate a rate of gain increase or a change in composition. Pseudopregnancy and mammary development are undesirable effects. DES has been proved experimentally to be effective in controlling boar odor when used on intact males, but was never approved or used commercially.

ANTIBIOTICS

Antibiotics are often used by veterinarians for therapeutic treatment of animals and are sometimes used in dairy calves, particularly those raised on milk replacers, to promote growth and for prophylactic purposes. With antibiotics, there is always a concern that selecting for resistant bacterial strains may result in the antibiotics being less effective for therapeutic use with humans and in veterinary medicine. For these reasons, carcasses are periodically examined by the USDA for antibiotic residues; USDA (1973) reported that 11% of the cow carcasses had levels above the tolerances and that 9% of the calf carcasses exceeded the tolerance level for streptomycin, penicillin, and other antibiotics.

Antibiotics are also used as growth promoters in swine and again, tissue is monitored (Swann 1969; FDA 1972) to ensure compliance with therapeutic use of the antibiotics. Clausen (1956) reported that fatter swine carcasses would be produced with ad lib feeding of low-protein diets containing antibiotics, and Ashton *et al.* (1955) found little evidence of an effect of antibiotics on carcass composition with ad lib feeding and with protein levels of 10–20%. Broquist and Kohler (1953) could detect no antibiotic activity in carcasses of pigs fed chlortetracycline at 200 mg/kg of body weight, but did find 0.3 g/kg in tissue of pigs fed 2 g/kg of body weight. This agrees with Jukes (1955), who could find no activity in the flesh of animals fed 200 mg/kg of body weight, but found 0.3 g/kg in tissue of swine fed 2 g/kg of body weight.

INSECTICIDES

Insecticide residue in animal tissue may result directly from application to the animal, or indirectly through treated feed or treated facilities or from naturally occurring chlorinated hydrocarbons. Chlorinated hydrocarbon insecticides accumulate in animal tissue (Rubin *et al.* 1947; Stadelman *et al.* 1965; Stadelman 1973), but these insecticides are regulated to prevent residues which might be hazardous to human health. Marsden and Bird (1947) reported 6235 ppm of 1,1-bis(*p*-chlorophenyl)-2,2,2-trichloroethane (DDT) in turkey fat for birds that were fed 1500 ppm of DDT in their diet, and Draper *et al.* (1952) found 2000 ppm in fat from hens fed 56 ppm in their diet. Stadelman *et al.* (1965) and Stadelman (1973) reported on lindane, heptachlor epoxide, dieldrin, and DDT residues in poultry fat and also reported on the disappearance of residues after treatment ceased. Hens were fed 10–15 ppm lindane for 5 days; the lindane level in the fat 1 week after treatment was 0.7 ppm and was zero at 26 weeks after treatment. Heptachlor epoxide fat levels were 10.2 ppm 1 week after treatment and had decreased to 0.3 ppm after 26 weeks; dieldrin was 3.6 ppm 1 week after treatment and 1.0 ppm after 26 weeks; and DDT and DDE were 9.6 ppm after 1 week and 0.7 ppm after 26 weeks. Spalding (1972) reported on poultry slaughtered at USDA-inspected plants and found the following: DDT and metabolites were not detected in 23% of the carcasses, less than 0.5 ppm in 67% of the carcasses, and greater than 0.5 ppm in 10% of the carcasses; dieldrin was not detected in 64% of the carcasses, and less than 0.5 ppm in 0.1% of the carcasses. DeCampos *et al.* (1979) reported that extensive and heavily pesticide-sprayed cotton fields in the Pacific coastal plains of Guatemala are interspersed with pasture used for cattle. Residues are a problem resulting in decreased use of DDT; a new pesticide law resulted in a legal limit in beef fat of 7 ppm and, for meat shipped to the United States, of less than 5 ppm.

SLAUGHTER AND PROCESSING

Several operations during the slaughtering process can influence the chemical and physical characteristics and, consequently, the nutritional properties of the carcass.

Some hogs are very stress susceptible and, if subjected to moderate stress, may die prior to slaughter; under these conditions, the animals are condemned and are not used for human food. If the stress is less severe or if the animal is more tolerant, the preslaughter stress can still influence the biochemical reactions that follow slaughter (Ockerman 1980). Under these preslaughter stress conditions, the glycolysis reactions are accelerated and the pH drops faster than normal. The combination of a low pH and a high temperature will denature some of the tissue proteins, making them less efficient in binding water. The resulting condition is called PSE, which means pale-soft and exudative, and the term is fairly descriptive of the muscle appearance. The muscle is light in color, soft in consistency, and will release some of its natural juices. This muscle, though not detrimental from a nutritional stand-point, is discriminated against in the fresh state by the consumer because of appearance. Due to the denatured properties of the protein, it also does not work as well, although still satisfactorily for cured meat and sausage production.

Electrical stimulation is a process of applying electrical current to a carcass after slaughter (Ockerman 1980). It causes the carcass muscles to contract, which accelerates glycolysis and causes a faster decline in pH. It is primarily used on ruminant animals to speed up the post-mortem aging process and, normally, make the tissue more tender. It also slightly reduces the microbiological population on the tissue. Its influence on carcass nutritional value at the present time appears to be limited in nature.

Hot boning is also gaining in popularity for meat tissue destined for sausage manufacturing. This allows curing ingredients such as salt to be added to the product while the tissue is still warm. This extracts the protein and makes the tissue much more acceptable for processing and also decreases the water activity prior to the time that microorganisms have multiplied to any great extent, thus dramatically increasing the shelf life of the manufactured product. This technique does not work as well for nonground tissue since the technique also allows the muscle to contract during rigor without restraint by the bone and, consequently the solid tissue is less tender than would be produced by normal chilling. The primary influence of hot boning on nutrition of meat would appear to be a reduction in bacterial numbers and a slight retardation of glycolysis.

SALTING AND CURING

Salting is one of the primary methods of food preservation and has been used with meat tissue since recorded history. Its function is to reduce microbial growth, improve flavor, tenderize, bind water, and extract proteins (Ockerman 1980). Salting also accelerates oxidation, dilutes other meat constituents, and adds sodium and chloride ions to the consumable product.

Curing adds nitrite, and sometimes nitrate, to the muscle tissue. The purpose of these additions is to retard bacterial growth, including *Clostridium botulinum*, develop cured color, produce cured flavor, act as a potent antioxidant, and react as a wholesomeness indicater (Ockerman 1980). Nitrites and nitrates were first added as an impurity in salt, and the early meat processors soon realized that this salt was superior for curing; therefore, the history of its use also goes back to the same area as salting. Nitrite is toxic in high levels, but the author could find no documented case of human poisoning by consuming cured meat.

Tumbling and massaging is a newer system being used in the curing areas and uses rotating or stirring energy to manipulate the muscle and extract the salt-soluble proteins. These proteins, in turn, act as a binding agent to hold small pieces together and give the appearance of a solid meat tissue. This technique also more evenly distributes the curing ingredients.

Mechanical deboning is a new process that removes soft tissue from hard tissue and allows the processor to salvage nutrients that were previously wasted due to inaccessibility or economics of removal. The soft and bone tissues are ground or mashed and then placed under pressure, at which time the soft tissue is pressed out through extremely small holes. By machine adjustment, different ratios of soft and hard tissues are obtained. The soft tissue is extremely fine in texture and will contain higher than normal calcium, which is normally deficient in the U.S. diet.

Sausage making, in addition to chopping and emulsifying, uses salt and nitrite as well as other additives such as water (to distribute cure), sweeteners (several types of sugars), reducing compounds (to protect color), phosphates (to increase binding properties, water-holding capacity, and, in some cases, to accelerate cured color development), binders (usually of cereal or milk origin), spices (usually a mixture to give characteristic flavor), and smoke (natural or artificial smoke collected from natural smoke). The quantity of water is regulated by the inspection service and depends on label designators but seldom exceeds 10% and often is zero. Binders are the only other ingredients added in sufficient quantities to have even a minor influence on diluting nutritional properties of the meat and normally (type of labeling regulates quantity) the levels do not exceed 3½% and, again, this is regulated by meat inspection regulations.

Fermented meat products contain microorganisms (either added or occurring naturally) that ferment carbohydrates into acids, which lower the pH and give the product a "tangy flavor." This lowered pH also retards the growth of spoilage bacteria and, consequently, these products have an extended shelf life. They are often dried, which also decreases their perishability.

The chemical composition of sausage products can be studied in Table 7.13.

Smoking and cooking are usually accomplished at the same time and, normally, dehydration occurs during this process. In addition to depositing smoke, which reduces the microbial load, improves flavor, and acts as an antioxidant, smoking also tends to case harden the external surface, which results in some product protection. The loss of moisture and, in some cases, fat during the heating process concentrates the remaining nutrients, except those that are volatilized or denatured by the heat. Cooking temperatures normally denature some of the more sensitive vitamins, oxidize some of the fat and flavor components, and denature some of the proteins, which lowers their functionality (water binding and emulsifying capacity).

STORAGE

Since meat is a perishable product, it has a somewhat limited refrigerated shelf life, which is normally shortened by microbiological growth. If strict sanitation is practiced in the slaughter and processing areas, this shelf life can be extended; and, if salt and nitrite are added, the cured meat tissue has a greatly extended refrigerated shelf life. Fresh meat freezes at 28.5°F (salted meat at lower temperatures) and keeping it as cold as possible will retard the bacterial growth and extend the useful refrigerated shelf life of the product. Packaging can also help extend the shelf life by protecting the product from contamination. Vacuum packaging can dramatically alter the type of microorganisms that can grow and also can extend the shelf life. Under ideal conditions, however, refrigerated storage life of ground meat (microorganisms mixed and more surface area) should be limited to approximately 2 days and solid refrigerated tissue for approximately twice that long. Vacuum-packaged cured product can have refrigerated shelf life of several weeks under ideal conditions.

Table 7.13. Chemical Composition of Sausage Products[a]

Nutrient	Unit	Berliner, pork, beef	Blood sausage	Bologna Beef	Bologna Beef and pork	Bologna Pork	Bratwurst, cooked, pork	Braunschweiger, Pork	Brotwurst, pork, beef	Chorizo pork, beef
Proximate										
Water	g	60.97	47.33	54.84	54.30	60.60	56.13	48.01	51.30	31.85
Food energy	kcal	230	378	313	316	247	301	359	323	—
	kJ	962	1583	1311	1320	1035	1261	1503	1352	—
Protein (N × 6.25)	g	15.27	14.61	11.69	11.69	15.30	14.08	13.50	14.27	24.10
Total lipid (fat)	g	17.20	34.48	28.36	28.26	19.87	25.87	32.09	27.80	38.27
Carbohydrate, total	g	2.60	1.28	1.95	2.79	0.73	2.07	0.00	2.97	—
Fiber	g	0.00	0.00	0.00	0.00	0.00	0.00	0.00	0.00	—
Ash	g	3.97	2.31	3.16	2.97	3.50	1.85	3.27	3.67	—
Minerals										
Calcium	mg	12	—	12	12	11	44	9	48	—
Iron	mg	1.15	—	1.40	1.51	0.77	1.29	9.36	1.03	—
Magnesium	mg	15	—	10	11	14	15	11	16	—
Phosphorus	mg	130	—	82	91	139	149	168	134	—
Potassium	mg	283	—	155	180	281	212	199	281	—
Sodium	mg	1297	—	1001	1019	1184	557	1143	1112	—
Zinc	mg	2.47	—	2.00	1.94	2.03	2.30	2.81	2.10	—
Copper	mg	0.08	—	0.03	0.08	0.08	0.09	0.24	0.08	—
Manganese	mg	0.041	—	0.028	0.039	0.036	0.046	0.155	0.038	—
Vitamins										
Ascorbic acid[b]	mg	7	—	19	21	35	1	10	28	—
Thiamin	mg	0.380	—	0.056	0.172	0.523	0.505	0.249	0.250	—
Riboflavin	mg	0.213	—	0.128	0.137	0.157	0.183	1.525	0.227	—
Niacin	mg	3.110	—	2.631	2.580	3.900	3.200	8.368	3.300	—
Pantothenic acid	mg	—	—	0.28	0.28	0.72	0.32	3.38	0.06	—
Vitamin B_6	mg	0.20	—	0.18	0.18	0.27	0.21	0.33	0.13	—
Folacin	µg	—	—	5	5	5	—	—	—	—
Vitamin B_{12}	µg	2.67	—	1.41	1.33	0.93	0.95	20.09	2.05	—
Vitamin A	RE	—	—	—	—	—	—	4220	—	—
	IU	—	—	—	—	—	—	14,051	—	—

Lipids

Fatty acids:									
Saturated, total	g	6.08	13.37	11.66	10.70	6.88	9.32	10.90	9.93	14.38
10:0	g	0.02	0.00	0.07	0.06	0.02	0.03	0.06	0.04	0.00
12:0	g	0.01	0.03	0.04	0.04	0.02	0.01	0.13	0.02	0.00
14:0	g	0.22	0.62	0.82	0.62	0.24	0.30	0.39	0.35	0.87
16:0	g	3.69	8.30	6.55	6.27	4.33	5.85	6.75	6.11	9.15
18:0	g	2.14	4.41	4.19	3.70	2.27	3.13	3.57	3.40	4.12
Monounsaturated, total	g	8.00	15.85	13.28	13.39	9.78	12.19	14.91	13.29	18.40
16:1	g	0.66	0.88	1.56	1.38	0.72	0.82	1.20	1.04	1.65
18:1	g	7.34	14.97	11.72	12.01	9.07	11.37	13.71	12.26	16.31
Polyunsaturated, total	g	1.58	3.46	1.05	2.40	2.12	2.74	3.74	2.83	3.46
18:2	g	1.40	3.20	0.81	1.99	1.84	2.48	3.34	2.54	2.93
18:3	g	0.18	0.26	0.24	0.41	0.28	0.26	0.40	0.29	0.38
20:4	g	—	—	—	—	—	—	—	—	0.09
Cholesterol	mg	46	120	56	55	59	60	156	63	—
Amino acids										
Tryptophan	g	0.175	—	0.107	0.105	0.149	0.113	0.145	0.131	0.278
Threonine	g	0.654	—	0.442	0.511	0.641	0.556	0.534	0.598	1.473
Isoleucine	g	0.682	—	0.505	0.507	0.663	0.514	0.484	0.606	2.206
Leucine	g	1.201	—	0.859	0.898	1.168	0.944	1.032	1.080	1.708
Lysine	g	1.319	—	0.896	0.883	1.204	1.070	0.909	1.139	2.414
Methionine	g	0.391	—	0.271	0.277	0.412	0.342	0.311	0.369	0.470
Cystine	g	0.221	—	0.149	0.136	0.171	0.142	0.248	0.163	—
Phenylalanine	g	0.600	—	0.421	0.462	0.585	0.471	0.553	0.541	1.149
Tyrosine	g	0.480	—	0.381	0.359	0.482	0.406	0.430	0.443	—
Valine	g	0.703	—	0.514	0.621	0.737	0.566	0.616	0.675	0.914
Arginine	g	1.041	—	0.722	0.699	1.004	0.831	0.767	0.946	1.693
Histidine	g	0.588	—	0.372	0.318	0.482	0.406	0.320	0.436	0.721
Alanine	g	0.940	—	0.841	0.729	0.979	0.789	0.762	0.925	—
Aspartic acid	g	1.484	—	1.144	1.028	1.403	1.172	1.125	1.292	—
Glutamic acid	g	2.355	—	1.904	1.874	2.296	1.947	1.631	2.109	—
Glycine	g	0.867	—	0.976	0.864	1.077	0.854	0.886	1.025	—
Proline	g	0.736	—	0.841	0.748	0.773	0.656	0.767	0.742	—
Serine	g	0.605	—	0.472	0.509	0.634	0.545	0.588	0.588	—

(Continued)

Table 7.13. (Continued)

Nutrient	Unit	Corned Beef Loaf, jellied	Dutch Brand Loaf pork, beef	Frankfurter, beef	Frankfurter, beef and pork	Ham Sliced, extra lean	Ham Sliced, regular	Headcheese, pork	Kielbasa, Kolbassy, pork, beef	Knackwurst, Knockwurst, pork, beef	Liver Sausage, Liverwurst, pork
Proximate											
Water	g	67.32	59.41	54.00	53.87	70.52	64.64	64.75	53.95	55.50	52.08
Food energy	kcal	163	240	322	320	131	182	212	310	308	326
	kJ	680	1002	1349	1341	548	763	887	1296	1288	1365
Protein (N × 6.25)	g	23.70	13.42	11.29	11.28	19.35	17.56	16.00	13.26	11.88	14.13
Total lipid (fat)	g	6.80	17.82	29.42	29.15	4.96	10.57	15.78	27.15	27.76	28.53
Carbohydrate, total	g	0.00	5.57	2.39	2.55	0.96	3.11	0.35	2.14	1.76	2.23
Fiber	g	0.00	0.00	0.00	0.00	0.00	0.00	0.00	0.00	0.00	0.00
Ash	g	2.80	3.78	2.90	3.15	4.21	4.11	3.13	3.50	3.10	3.06
Minerals											
Calcium	mg	11	84	12	11	7	7	16	44	11	26
Iron	mg	2.03	1.24	1.33	1.15	0.76	0.99	1.17	1.45	0.91	6.4
Magnesium	mg	10	21	10	10	17	19	9	16	11	—
Phosphorus	mg	64	162	82	86	218	247	59	148	98	230
Potassium	mg	89	376	159	167	350	332	31	271	199	—
Sodium	mg	1037	1250	1024	1120	1429	1317	1257	1076	1010	—
Zinc	mg	3.83	1.72	2.12	1.84	1.93	2.14	1.30	2.02	1.66	—
Copper	mg	0.06	0.07	0.06	0.08	0.07	0.10	0.12	0.10	0.06	—
Manganese	mg	0.031	0.032	0.033	0.032	0.033	0.031	0.019	0.040	—	—
Vitamins											
Ascorbic acid[b]	mg	8	18	25	26	26	28	22	21	27	—
Thiamin	mg	0.010	0.303	0.051	0.199	0.932	0.863	0.037	0.228	0.342	0.272
Riboflavin	mg	0.117	0.269	0.102	0.120	0.223	0.252	0.182	0.214	0.140	1.030
Niacin	mg	1.637	2.387	2.527	2.634	4.838	5.251	1.127	2.879	2.734	—
Pantothenic acid	mg	0.19	0.60	0.29	0.35	0.47	0.45	0.22	0.82	0.32	2.95
Vitamin B_6	mg	0.14	0.23	0.11	0.13	0.46	0.34	0.19	0.18	0.17	—
Folacin	μg	—	—	4	4	4	3	2	—	—	30
Vitamin B_{12}	μg	1.18	1.32	1.64	1.30	0.75	0.83	1.05	1.61	1.18	85.60
Vitamin A	RE										
	IU										

Lipids

Fatty acids:											
Saturated, total	g	2.68	6.35	11.96	10.76	1.62	3.39	4.94	9.91	10.20	10.59
10:0	g	0.02	0.06	0.03	0.08	0.02	0.02	0.03	0.03	0.11	0.00
12:0	g	0.02	0.05	0.03	0.06	0.01	0.02	0.02	0.02	0.09	0.00
14:0	g	0.18	0.31	0.89	0.53	0.08	0.15	0.27	0.36	0.58	0.43
16:0	g	1.39	3.82	6.91	6.45	1.01	2.13	3.08	6.13	5.97	6.85
18:0	g	1.08	2.11	4.09	3.65	0.51	1.08	1.52	3.36	3.46	3.31
Monounsaturated, total	g	3.03	8.33	14.35	13.67	2.35	4.95	8.10	12.94	12.81	13.33
16:1	g	0.47	0.79	1.79	1.31	0.22	0.43	0.83	0.97	1.28	1.06
18:1	g	2.56	7.54	12.56	12.36	2.13	4.52	7.27	11.97	11.53	12.04
Polyunsaturated, total	g	0.38	1.91	1.16	2.73	0.48	1.21	1.65	3.08	2.92	2.60
18:2	g	0.29	1.66	0.86	2.34	0.43	1.04	1.45	2.68	2.48	2.45
18:3	g	0.09	0.25	0.30	0.39	0.05	0.17	0.19	0.40	0.44	0.14
20:4	g	—	—	—	—	—	—	—	—	—	—
Cholesterol	mg	43	47	48	50	47	57	81	67	58	158
Amino acids											
Tryptophan	g	0.169	0.148	0.103	0.082	0.236	0.214	0.084	0.138	0.108	0.153
Threonine	g	0.927	0.619	0.426	0.406	0.861	0.781	0.445	0.432	0.479	0.678
Isoleucine	g	0.890	0.558	0.487	0.485	0.873	0.792	0.543	0.639	0.466	0.660
Leucine	g	1.638	1.076	0.829	0.819	1.554	1.411	1.008	0.874	0.821	1.150
Lysine	g	1.820	1.076	0.865	0.904	1.730	1.571	0.967	1.010	0.933	1.166
Methionine	g	0.525	0.322	0.262	0.228	0.510	0.464	0.266	0.276	0.287	0.287
Cystine	g	0.248	0.107	0.145	0.130	0.291	0.264	0.223	0.225	0.147	0.152
Phenylalanine	g	0.838	0.511	0.407	0.359	0.780	0.708	0.606	0.501	0.407	0.624
Tyrosine	g	0.638	0.446	0.368	0.314	0.601	0.545	0.466	0.490	0.361	0.366
Valine	g	1.026	0.619	0.496	0.471	0.904	0.821	0.658	0.639	0.515	0.866
Arginine	g	1.642	0.801	0.697	0.849	1.359	1.233	1.146	0.942	0.709	0.818
Histidine	g	0.623	0.412	0.359	0.350	0.786	0.714	0.297	0.314	0.361	0.452
Alanine	g	1.631	0.784	0.812	0.769	1.126	1.022	1.024	0.848	0.675	0.836
Aspartic acid	g	2.016	1.209	1.105	1.115	1.875	1.703	1.423	1.218	1.011	1.175
Glutamic acid	g	3.278	2.248	1.838	1.852	2.931	2.661	1.689	1.618	1.619	2.215
Glycine	g	2.244	0.841	0.942	0.824	0.935	0.849	1.922	1.039	0.703	1.108
Proline	g	1.554	0.888	0.812	0.542	0.786	0.714	1.295	0.687	0.539	0.859
Serine	g	0.947	0.635	0.455	0.462	0.761	0.692	0.627	0.530	0.477	0.701

(Continued)

185

Table 7.13. *(Continued)*

| Nutrient | Unit | Luncheon meat | | Mortadella, beef, pork | Pepperoni pork, beef | Pork sausage | | Salami | | | Summer sausage, beef, pork |
		Beef, loaved	Pork, beef			Fresh, raw	Fresh, cooked	Cooked, beef	Cooked, beef and pork	Dry or hard, pork, beef	
Proximate											
Water	g	52.53	49.28	52.30	27.06	44.52	44.57	59.34	60.40	34.70	48.00
Food energy	kcal	308	353	311	497	417	369	254	250	418	347
	kJ	1290	1476	1300	2080	1746	1543	1061	1044	1748	1453
Protein (N × 6.25)	g	14.37	12.59	16.37	20.97	11.69	19.65	14.70	13.92	22.86	16.04
Total lipid (fat)	g	26.20	32.16	25.39	43.97	40.29	31.16	20.10	20.11	34.39	29.93
Carbohydrate, total	g	2.90	2.33	3.05	2.84	1.02	1.03	2.49	2.25	2.59	2.29
Fiber	g	0.00	0.00	0.00	0.00	0.00	0.00	0.00	0.00	0.00	0.00
Ash	g	4.00	3.64	2.89	5.17	2.49	3.60	3.38	3.32	5.47	3.74
Minerals											
Calcium	mg	11	9	18	10	18	32	9	13	8	7
Iron	mg	2.32	0.86	1.40	1.40	0.91	1.25	2.00	2.67	1.51	2.04
Magnesium	mg	14	14	11	16	11	17	13	15	17	12
Phosphorus	mg	119	86	97	119	118	184	101	115	142	100
Potassium	mg	208	202	163	347	205	361	225	198	378	231
Sodium	mg	1329	1293	1246	2040	804	1294	1158	1065	1860	1453
Zinc	mg	2.53	1.66	2.10	2.50	1.59	2.50	2.14	2.14	3.23	2.02
Copper	mg	0.12	0.04	0.06	0.07	0.07	0.14	0.09	0.23	0.08	0.09
Manganese	mg	0.045	0.029	0.030	—	—	0.071	0.047	0.057	0.038	0.031
Vitamins											
Ascorbic acid[b]	mg	13	13	26		2	2	15	12	26	23
Thiamin	mg	0.110	0.314	0.119	0.320	0.545	0.741	0.127	0.239	0.600	0.169
Riboflavin	mg	0.220	0.152	0.153	0.250	0.164	0.254	0.257	0.376	0.285	0.299
Niacin	mg	3.660	2.830	2.673	4.960	2.835	4.518	3.412	3.553	4.867	4.088
Pantothenic acid	mg	0.52	0.63	—	1.87	0.40	0.72	0.96	0.85	1.06	0.55
Vitamin B6	mg	0.19	0.20	0.12	0.25	0.25	0.33	0.22	0.21	0.50	0.30
Folacin	μg	—	6	—	—	4	—	2	2	—	—
Vitamin B12	μg	3.89	1.28	1.48	2.51	1.13	1.73	4.85	3.65	1.90	4.61
Vitamin A	RE										
Vitamin A	IU										

Lipids

Fatty acids:											
Saturated, total	g	11.18	11.59	9.51	16.13	14.47	10.81	8.43	8.09	12.20	12.03
10:0	g	0.03	0.08	0.12	0.00	0.11	0.12	0.06	0.10	0.06	0.05
12:0	g	0.01	0.05	0.07	0.00	0.08	0.09	0.05	0.07	0.04	0.05
14:0	g	0.75	0.48	0.51	0.86	0.57	0.45	0.58	0.47	0.51	0.72
16:0	g	6.32	7.09	5.43	10.29	8.87	6.53	4.71	4.53	7.60	6.83
18:0	g	4.08	3.89	3.22	4.69	4.85	3.62	3.04	2.93	4.00	4.38
Monounsaturated, total	g	12.25	15.09	11.38	21.11	18.53	13.90	9.30	9.19	17.10	13.93
16:1	g	1.54	1.35	1.14	1.77	1.45	1.09	1.20	0.89	1.69	1.79
18:1	g	10.71	13.74	10.24	18.92	17.09	12.81	8.10	8.30	15.40	12.14
Polyunsaturated, total	g	0.87	3.16	3.12	4.37	5.24	3.81	0.88	2.02	3.21	1.89
18:2	g	0.65	2.91	2.91	3.74	4.39	3.28	0.67	1.61	2.87	1.56
18:3	g	0.21	0.58	0.22	0.41	0.85	0.54	0.21	0.41	0.33	0.33
20:4	g	—	—	—	0.14	—	—	—	—	—	—
Cholesterol	mg	64	55	56	—	68	83	60	65	79	68
Amino acids											
Tryptophan	g	—	0.133	0.152	0.200	0.094	0.157	0.134	0.114	0.210	0.154
Threonine	g	—	0.544	0.633	0.848	0.462	0.777	0.555	0.521	0.959	0.688
Isoleucine	g	—	0.643	0.708	0.908	0.427	0.717	0.635	0.675	0.971	0.768
Leucine	g	—	1.048	1.213	1.578	0.784	1.317	1.080	0.929	1.732	1.048
Lysine	g	—	1.185	1.262	1.635	0.889	1.494	1.107	1.107	1.824	1.383
Methionine	g	—	0.288	0.394	0.536	0.284	0.478	0.341	0.301	0.593	0.352
Cystine	g	—	0.230	0.204	0.247	0.118	0.198	0.188	0.196	0.262	0.197
Phenylalanine	g	—	0.510	0.598	0.669	0.391	0.657	0.529	0.481	0.868	0.577
Tyrosine	g	—	0.502	0.530	0.785	0.337	0.566	0.480	0.552	0.710	0.542
Valine	g	—	0.713	0.735	0.669	0.469	0.789	0.647	0.668	1.083	0.804
Arginine	g	—	0.925	1.025	0.978	0.691	1.160	0.908	0.855	1.516	0.993
Histidine	g	—	0.405	0.520	1.346	0.337	0.566	0.468	0.359	0.699	0.469
Alanine	g	—	0.806	1.149	0.664	0.655	1.101	1.058	0.880	1.480	1.014
Aspartic acid	g	—	1.312	1.580	1.403	0.973	1.635	1.439	1.285	2.073	1.438
Glutamic acid	g	—	1.769	2.619	1.970	1.617	2.716	2.394	1.929	3.383	2.205
Glycine	g	—	0.985	1.318	3.245	0.709	1.192	1.228	1.189	1.641	1.103
Proline	g	—	0.729	1.099	1.577	0.544	0.914	1.058	0.831	1.188	0.860
Serine	g	—	0.528	0.664	1.225	0.452	0.761	0.593	0.537	0.942	0.678

Source: Composition of Foods: Sausages and Luncheon Meats, Agriculture Handbook 8–7, U.S. Dept. of Agriculture, Science and Education Administration (1980).

a Amount in 100 g, edible portion.

b Values based on data from products containing added sodium ascorbate. Some products may not contain sodium ascorbate and their ascorbic acid content would be negligible; refer to listing of ingredients on label.

Freezing stops most microbial growth but a few molds can continue to grow at the higher freezer temperatures. Oxidation, though retarded, is not stopped and salted products can only be stored a few months without flavor deterioration. Tissue with unsaturated fat (pork, poultry, and fish) also has a shorter frozen shelf life than more saturated tissue such as beef, which can be stored up to 1 year under appropriate temperature and packaging conditions.

Dried products have reduced water activity and often can be stored without refrigeration. Mold growth is still encountered and some additional denaturation takes place due to the drying. Usually these products are very nutritionally dense due to the low water level.

MEETING NUTRITIONAL NEEDS

Setting recommended nutritional standards for humans is very difficult because of the tremendous range in variation for individual requirements. This task is usually accomplished by setting the requirements high enough to satisfy the highest end of the requirement spectrum. Also, compositional variation in food complicates the use of any standards that might be developed. Varying composition is found naturally in fresh food, and this variability may be increased or decreased by processing and is usually increased in cooked foods. Meat can vary considerably in even its major constituents (Table 7.4), depending primarily on areas of the carcass, species, and animal nutritional level, and vitamins and minerals can be influenced by animal diet and by the animal husbandry practices followed. In developed countries, more nutritional attention is also being placed on "diseases of affluence," under the assumption that most people are adequately nourished and that overnutrition is a major problem. Overconsumption in many countries is a major problem, but even in the best nutritional environment many people, because of financial considerations, education, or lack of discipline, do not receive the appropriate balance of foods even if the calorie content is adequate (in a few cases, the calorie level is not even met).

Meat is a major supplier of nutritional ingredients and is a very desirable food source for a variety of reasons. In most developed countries it is a major portion of the diet and supplies a large percentage of the nutrients. The quantity of meat needed under different economic conditions may be estimated from Table 7.14. Even some people who are vegetarian by choice prepare foods with meat-like flavors when possible, and people who are vegetarians by necessity increase their consumption of meat when it becomes available (Bender 1981). Meat makes a unique contribution to the nutritional well-being of the human population by supplying an extremely well-balanced source of protein, almost

Table 7.14. Family Food Budgeting for Good Meals and Good Nutrition (Other Food Categories Not Shown Are Adjusted as the Meat Category Is Adjusted)

Family member	Amount of food (lb) for a week as purchased (raw)[a]								Food (oz) to serve each day (cooked)[b]			
	Thrifty plan		Low-cost plan		Moderate-cost plan		Liberal plan		Thrifty plan	Low-cost plan	Moderate-cost plan	Liberal plan
	Meat, poultry, fish[c]	Fats, oils	Meat, poultry, fish[c]	Fats, oils	Meat, poultry, fish[c]	Fats, oils	Meat, poultry, fish[c]	Fats, oils	Cooked lean meat or alternate[d]	Cooked lean meat or alternate[d]	Cooked lean meat or alternate[d]	Cooked lean meat or alternate[d]
Child												
7 months–1 year	0.39	0.04	0.56	0.05	0.80	0.05	0.97	0.05	1.5–2	2–3	2.5–3	3–3.5
1–2 years	0.83	0.11	1.26	0.12	1.69	0.12	2.07	0.13	1.5–2	2–3	2.5–3	3–3.5
3–5 years	0.95	0.38	1.52	0.38	1.88	0.41	2.35	0.45	1.5–2	2–3	2.5–3	3–3.5
6–8 years	1.27	0.51	2.03	0.52	2.60	0.56	3.18	0.60	2.5–3	3–4	4–5	5–6
9–11 years	1.61	0.60	2.57	0.61	3.31	0.66	4.04	0.71	2.5–3	3–4	4–5	5–6
Male												
12–14 years	1.79	0.77	2.98	0.77	3.77	0.85	4.57	0.92	3–4	5–6	5–7	6–8
15–19 years	2.35	1.00	3.74	1.05	4.65	1.05	5.59	1.07	3–4	5–6	5–7	6–8
20–54 years	3.03	0.95	4.56	0.91	5.73	0.95	6.83	0.95	4–5	6–7	7–8	9
55 years and over	2.45	0.79	3.63	0.77	4.64	0.87	5.54	0.94	4	5	6–7	7–8
Female												
12–19 years	1.80	0.51	2.55	0.53	3.32	0.56	3.97	0.54	3	4	4–5	5–6
20–54 years	2.41	0.57	3.21	0.59	4.12	0.65	4.86	0.66	4	4–5	5–6	6–7
55 years and over	1.84	0.37	2.45	0.38	3.21	0.45	3.79	0.48	3	3–4	4–5	5–6
Pregnant	2.69	0.59	3.68	0.55	4.57	0.46	5.43	0.46				
Nursing	3.00	0.80	4.16	0.76	5.01	0.69	5.97	0.68				

Source: Home and Garden Bulletin 94; Prepared by Human Nutrition Information Service; U.S. Dept. of Agriculture (1981).

[a] Amounts allow for a discard of about 5% of the edible food as plate waste, spoilage, etc.

[b] Amounts shown allow for some plate waste.

[c] Bacon and salt pork should not exceed 1/3 lb for each 5 lb of this group.

[d] As alternates: 1 oz of cooked poultry or fish, one egg, 1/2 cup of cooked dry beans or peas, or 2 tbsp of peanut butter may replace 1 oz of cooked lean meat.

the only source of vitamin B_{12}, one of the most valuable forms of iron, a major source of zinc, and an important source of many of the B vitamins. In fact, the British Committee on Medical Aspects of Food Policy (Department of Health and Social Security 1980) suggested that replacements or substitutes for meat should be nutritionally equivalent to meat in certain aspects such as vitamins B_1 and B_{12}, iron, and zinc. Also, it was recommended that these substitutes should contain 45–50% protein on a dry-weight basis, which should have a protein efficiency of 1.6 or net protein utilization of 60; not less than 2 mg thiamin, 1.6 mg riboflavin, and 10 μg vitamin B_{12}/100 g of protein; and a minimum of 20 mg iron and 20 mg zinc/100 g of protein.

BIOAVAILABILITY

Bioavailability is the movement of a nutrient across the intestinal mucosa in a form that can be utilized by the body. When bioavailability and composition are combined with appetite appeal and satiety value, meat is almost all encompassing when compared with the nutrients required by humans (Davis 1981).

For efficient use of amino acids in body protein synthesis, the essential amino acids must be present in the bloodstream at the same time and this suggests that the correct balance must be present in a meal. This places a special value on items such as meat that contain the quantity and distribution of amino acids required by humans. The biological value and availability of amino acids in meat protein have consistently been demonstrated to be effective in supplying the amino acids needed to build body protein. The bioavailability of meat protein compares favorably with the acknowledged leaders in protein bioavailability such as milk and eggs. The first step in bioavailability is digestibility; the protein of meat is 97% digestible and meat fat is 96% digestible, so composition of these items in a consumable form is almost equivalent to the bioavailability of these two components (Davis 1981).

The value of meat, especially liver, as a supplier of trace minerals, especially iron, has long been recognized. Iron has normally been considered to be approximately 30% available in meat and has an added benefit in that meat increases the absorption of nonheme iron present in other proteins of a meal.

Meat and meat products also are an excellent source of zinc and copper in a highly bioavailable form, while these two elements are often chelated and made unavailable by high-fiber, high-carbohydrate components of foods.

Phosphorus and magnesium in meat are also readily bioavailable sources of these two essential elements.

THE RELATIONSHIP OF MEAT TO HEALTH PROBLEMS

Heart Problems

Atherosclerosis, or arteriosclerosis, is a blockage of the arteries caused by fatty material which is involved in most coronary heart diseases. The blockage consists in large part of cholesterol, a substance found in meat (Rogowski 1981). Cholesterol is an essential part of the body's chemistry and is manufactured in the body at the rate of 800 to 1500 mg/day even if no cholesterol is consumed (NLSMB 1983B). Three ounces of cooked beef, pork, or lamb contain 75, 75, and 85 mg of cholesterol, respectively (USDA 1974). Numerous research projects and disagreement among heart specialists have failed to resolve the question as to whether there is a relationship between dietary cholesterol and heart disease. In the United States, deaths from heart and circulatory diseases have declined by 20% from 1960 to 1980, and, at the same time, the per capita consumption of meat has increased by 10%. This, like other epidemiology data, particularly since it is related to time, could be misleading. The "facts" seem to be clouded with varying degrees of uncertainty. It is possible, but not certain, there is an association between serum cholesterol content in the blood and the probability of developing atherosclerosis (NLSMB 1983B). Even more hypothetical is the possibility that dietary cholesterol and unsaturated fats (less than 50% in most meat fat) have some significant influence on serum cholesterol levels (Glueck 1979, Nichols *et al.* 1976, Porter *et al.* 1977; Flynn *et al.* 1979; Hill *et al.* 1979A,B; NLSMB 1983B). Other dietary components such as carbohydrates, minerals, proteins, and vitamins also have been reported to have an influence on the blood triglycerides and cholesterol level (Ross *et al.* 1978; Dayton 1975; Yudkin 1972; Masironi 1975; Classen 1977; Voors and Johnson 1979). Of even greater uncertainty is the assumption that lowering the intake of cholesterol and saturated fats will have any influence on a person's chances of having a heart disease problem (NLSMB 1983B; Rogowski 1981).

A publication from the National Academy of Science (FNB 1980) on "healthy" nutrition made no explicit recommendations with regard to the consumption of cholesterol and polyunsaturated fatty acids (PUFA) for healthy persons. The Surgeon General's report on health and disease prevention (Richmond 1979) stated that a good case could be made for the role of high intake of cholesterol and saturated fat (usually of animal origin) in producing high blood cholesterol levels, which are associated with atherosclerosis and cardiovascular diseases and that Americans consuming high fat diets should attempt to reduce serum cholesterol by changing eating patterns.

These two references indicate the contradictory nature of advice in the literature that could be best summarized by stating that current knowledge suggests that the best route in preventing coronary heart disease is to avoid the temptation to suggest that simple dietary change alone can solve a problem of such complexity (Department of Health and Social Security 1974).

One area where there seems to be little disagreement is that people who are overweight are at greater risk not only of circulatory problems, but of a great number of other health problems. Since, on the average, the U.S. population is overweight and since fat is the most condensed form of calories, most scientists agree that overweight people should probably reduce fat (animal or vegetable) or calorie intake.

Cancer

In the area of meat's relationship to cancer, there seem to be three current areas of concern: colon carcinogenesis, nitrosamines, and smoking meat.

Fiber in food decreases the intestinal transit time and increases fecal bulk, and Burkitt (1971) suggested that the incidence of colon cancer is inversely related to the intake of dietary fiber. Hypotheses (Kritchevsky 1981) on the influence of fiber take many routes and some of them are as follows: Reduce transit time of intestinal contents containing a carcinogen to reduce contact time with intestinal mucosa, dilute concentration of a carcinogen, and dilute bacterial contamination that might modify a precursor into a carcinogen. Since meat is devoid of fiber, these theories suggest that obtaining calories from meat and not from high fiber foods would aggravate the problem. Other researchers (Berg 1975) have suggested that calorie intake may play a role, and Enig *et al.* (1978) implicated vegetable fat, but these, too, remain to be proved.

Meat is presently cured with sodium or potassium nitrite and, in some cases, with nitrate, which is converted to nitrite in a reducing environment. These curing ingredients are used to produce the characteristic flavor and color of cured meat, retard rancidity development and "warmed-over flavors," and inhibit the growth of microorganisms, particularly *Clostridium botulinum*, which is the most deadly type of food poisoning. Nitrite can react, under specific environmental conditions, with certain nitrogen-containing substances (naturally present in meat) to produce nitrosamines. Certain nitrosamines have been found to be carcinogenic when given in large doses to laboratory animals. Nitrosamines are sometimes found in extremely small quantities in meat cured with nitrite (Krol and Tinbergen 1974). High-temperature cooking of bacon seems to provide the best environment for this reaction, but still results only occasionally in extremely small amounts being formed. There is no evidence that human cancer has resulted from exposure to nitrosamines from any source (Smith 1980). Also, there is no evidence of increase of tumors or cancer in laboratory animals fed diets high in cured meats even when some of the meats were cured with a sizable excess of nitrite (Olsen and Meyer 1977; Van Logten *et al.* 1972).

Smoke is known (Pearson 1983) to contain a number of polycyclic aromatic hydrocarbons (PAHs) that are carcinogens. In the production of smoke condensates and liquid smoke, steps are taken to eliminate these PAHs. The phenols, which give smoke its desirable properties, do not appear to be either mutagenic or carcinogenic (Pearson 1983).

Mycotoxin Residues Originating from Animal Feed

Animals must be considered as an active metabolic relay that can modify items consumed as food. These modifications may be good or bad. They may detoxify material or they may accumulate by binding (especially with proteins) undesirable items. With the discovery of aflatoxins, the possible transfer from animal feed to meat and the bioavailability of these products or their metabolites became a concern. The presence of aflatoxins in muscle and organs of animals having ingested mycotoxins in their feed have been summarized by Ferrando (1981) and, in general, quantities are in the parts per billion (ppb) range, with Germany having established a tolerance of 10 ppb maximum for aflatoxin B_1. There is no current evidence to suggest the accumulation of mycotoxin or its metabolites in muscle products (Ferrando 1981).

Pesticides

The possibility of agricultural pesticides reaching meat products by way of the alimentary chain have been studied in fairly extensive detail.

Table 7.15.   Pesticide Limits in Meat Items

Pesticides	Products	Maximal limits of residue (mg/kg)	Indicative percentages
Chlordimeform	Meat of cattle, sheep, pigs and poultry		No residue at the actual threshold of detection (0.05 mg/kg)
Cyhexatin	Meat	0.2	
DDT	Carcass	5 on the base of the lipids	
Phosmet	Beef fat	1	
Pirimicarb	Meats	0.05	
Trichlorfon	Mutton	0.01	
Carbendazine	Beef and poultry meat	0.01	
	Mutton	0.01	

Source: OMS–FAO Committee (1979).

Table 7.16.   Pesticide Residues (ppm) Found in Italy in 1975

	BHC	Lindane	Epoxyde of heptachlor	DDT + metabolites	PCB	Dieldrine
Meats	0.026	0.017	0.012	0.041	0.02	0.013
Perirenal fat						
1-year-old calf	0.084	0.030	0.072	0.133	0.17	0.163
6-year-old ox	0.113	0.098	0.102	0.856	0.07	0.237

Source: Crisetig *et al.* (1975).

Daily allowable tolerances for certain pesticides have often been established, but they frequently refer to fruit and vegetables, sometimes to fat and milk, and rarely to meat products. A few references to meat were published by a joint OMS-FAO committee (1979) and are shown in Table 7.15.

Quantities of pesticide residues reported in Italy by Crisetig *et al.* (1975) for animal tissue are shown in Table 7.16.

Reports by Campanini *et al.* (1980) suggest that contamination of animal products by organochlorinated compounds in Italy is not a human health hazard and that the highest contamination is in the least consumed products.

As pesticides are currently being utilized in a more controlled and rational manner, it is expected that residue levels will decrease. The negative publicity response to pesticide residues in animal products must be counterbalanced with the alternative of consuming mycotoxins and microbial pollution due to insects if these products were not utilized and a tremendous reduction in the quantity of nutrients available due to insect damage. Also, there have been several reports (Ferrando 1981) of pesticide residues being beneficial to biological systems.

Minerals

Minerals in meat and variety meats such as liver are usually biologically available and contribute to the human body's requirements for these essential elements. Meat is a particularly good source of iron, which is normally deficient in the U.S. diet. The quantities of calcium, phosphorus, iron, and potassium in meat and meat items can be found in Tables 7.4–7.9; the calcium, magnesium, potassium, sodium, and zinc in animal fat is reported in Table 7.10, and the same minerals, plus iron, in baby food items can be found in Table 7.11.

Public concern over the mineral content of meat can be categorized into three primary areas: heavy metals, sodium or salt, and minerals contributed by the animal's bone in mechanically deboned meat.

Table 7.17. Mercury (ppm) in Carcass Products

| Part of carcass | Added to feed[a] | | | Control[a] | Control[b] |
	50 ppm mineral mercury	5 ppm organic mercury	5 ppm mineral mercury		
Pork					
Long dorsal muscle	0.36	0.12–1.43	0.12–0.73	0.10	
Semitendinosus muscle	0.41	0.41–0.46	0.14–0.94	0.10	
Myocardium	0.69	0.28–0.60	0.13–0.29	0.13	
Liver	2.88	3.74	1.78	0.11	
Kidney					0.001–0.013 for certain samples
Beef liver					0.007

[a] Ferrando (1981).   [b] Prior (1976).

Mercury poisoning of animals fed cereal treated with mercurial derivatives and people who consumed tissue from these animals have been reported by Curley et al. (1971) and Haselein et al. (1973). The normal level of mercury in the carcass parts of animals fed mercury derivatives are shown in Table 7.17.

Lead concentrates in an animal's liver and kidney more so than in the muscle tissue (FAO/OMS 1972), as presented in Table 7.18.

Cadmium levels reported in swine tissue are shown in Table 7.19. Holm (1976A,B) and Durury and Hammons (1979) suggested that cadmium levels are below the tolerance amounts suggested for consumers of 400–500 µg/person/week.

Copper is added as a growth stimulant in feed for swine and sometimes for chickens. This mineral is also concentrated in the liver, as shown in Table 7.19.

Table 7.18. Lead (ppm) in the Meat and Organs of Various Animal Species

Species	Meat	Organs	Reference
Pigs (raised in an industrial area)	4.08 of the wet tissue		Nagy et al. (1975)
Pig		0.85 (liver and kidney)	Prior (1976)
Ox		1.02 (liver) 0.73 (kidney)	Prior (1976)
Pig		0.003–0.098 (liver) 0.003–0.75 (kidney)	Hecht (1977)
Ox	0.05	0.15 (liver) 0.33 (kidney)	Kreuzer et al. (1978)

Table 7.19. Cadmium and Copper Found in Animal Products

Species	Mineral	Level fed	Tissue	Level/tissue	Reference
Swine	Cadmium	0.20 mg/kg dry matter	Muscle Liver Cortical zone of kidney	0.0032 mg 0.085 mg 0.55 mg	Vemmer and Petersen (1977)
Swine	Copper	Normal diet	Bacon	Not detectable	NRC (1977)
Beef	Copper	Normal diet	Kidney	0.35 mg/100 g	NRC (1977)
Beef	Copper	Normal diet	Liver	2.1 mg/100 g	NRC (1977)
Swine	Copper	Normal diet	Muscle	0.09 mg/100 g	NRC (1977)
Swine	Copper	250 ppm		18 ppm	Price et al. (1979)

Ferrando (1981) suggests that mercury, lead, cadmium, and copper residues in meat are not significant except for the exceptional reference to misuse of mercury. Marketbasket sampling has also suggested (Duggan 1968; Duggan et al. 1966, Manske and Johnson 1977) that the average intake of potentially toxic metals is below the dietary intake levels established by FAO-WHO and, therefore, the normal intake does not present a known hazard.

Salt (sodium chloride) is added to processed meats to retard bacterial growth, improve flavor, tenderize, and also to extract protein and promote cohesion in a comminuted product (Ockerman 1980). Salt levels normally range from 2.25 to 2.75% for most cured products. The average U.S. citizen consumes 10–12 g of salt (3900–4700 mg sodium)/day (Terrell and Olson 1981). Sodium chloride has been associated with problems related to human health including hypertension, and a number of reports have suggested a lowering of salt intake [Senate Select Committee on Nutrition and Human Needs 1977A,B; Kolari 1980; American Medical Association (AMA) 1978] might be desirable. The major problem with lowering the salt levels in processed meat is "reduction in shelf life" due to bacterial growth and a greater dependence on other types of preservation which would reduce the safety factor these meats have so long enjoyed.

Mechanically processed (species) product or mechanically deboned meat is meat with a very finely ground appearance because the meat is forced through very small openings to separate it from the bone. The product contains some bone powder (smaller than 0.5 mm) and bone marrow. This separation system allows the processor to salvage great quantities of protein that would otherwise be wasted. The maximum amount of mechanically deboned meat permitted in processed meat is 20% of the meat block (CAST 1980).

The additional nutritional properties of mechanically deboned meat include easily available quantities of calcium and iron (CAST 1980).

Trace elements are not present in sufficient quantities to be a health hazard (Kolbye and Nelson 1977), but the fluorine level has been a concern to a few (CAST 1980). The protein quality is high (2.5 protein efficiency ratio) and the cholesterol level is similar to that of hand deboned meat.

PROCESSING OF MEAT

Meat is processed in order to preserve it and to provide variety and convenience. The influence of processing on nutritional value is fairly slight but if high temperatures are used some vitamins may be reduced and the physiological availability of some proteins may also be lowered. Curing has normally been reported (Hendricks *et al.* 1947; Hoagland *et al.* 1947) to have no significant effect on the nutritional value.

The USDA and/or FDA examine the justification for and the prescribed use of all extenders and additives used in processed meats. There is also continuous surveillance sampling of food products for additives.

SUMMARY

Muscle tissue as a source of human food receives excellent marks when evaluated from almost any direction. It allows conversion of unusable crop residue into a high-density, highly nutritious, and well-balanced source of protein. The flavor is very desirable and meat has a great deal of satiety value. Although a few problems are possible for special high-risk patients, there seem to be no major health problems associated with its consumption, except perhaps excess calorie consumption, which could be said of all foods and particularly those with less nutritional benefits. Processing procedures do not seem to drastically alter quality, currently approved additives have a very favorable risk-benefit value, and surveillance monitoring for unapproved and/or unintentional adulterants is in place. Nothing is perfect, but meat as a food source seems to come relatively close.

REFERENCES

Altman, P. L., and Dittmer, D. S. 1962. Growth Federation. Am. Soc. Exp. Biol., Washington, DC.

AMA 1978. Sodium and Potassium in American Foods. Conference Proceeding. Am. Med. Assoc., Chicago.

Ammerman, C. B., Chapman, H. L., Bowman, G. W., Fontenot, J. P., Bagley, C. P., and Moxon, A. L. 1980. Effect of supplemental selenium for beef cows on the performance and tissue selenium concentration of cows and suckling calves. J. Anim. Sci. *51*, 1381–1386.

Ashton, G. C., Kastelic, J., Acker, D. C., Jensen, A. H., Maddock, H. M., Kline, E. A., and Catron, D. V. 1955. Protein levels and carcass leanness. J. Anim. Sci. *14*, 82–93.

Barbella, N. G., Hankins, O. G., and Alexander, L. M. 1936. The influence of retarded growth in lambs on flavor and other characteristics of the meat. Proc. Am. Soc. Anim. Prod., 29th Ann. Mtg., 289–294.

Beeson, K. C. 1941. The mineral composition of crops with particular reference to the soils in which they were grown. USDA Misc. Publ. *369*. Washington, DC.

Bender, A. E. 1981. Meeting nutritional needs in meat. *In* Nutrition and Health. National Live Stock and Meat Board, Chicago.

Berg, J. W. 1975. Can nutrition explain the pattern of international epidemiology of hormone-dependent cancers. Cancer Res. *35*, 33–45.

Botkin, M. P., Field, R. A., Riley, M. L., Nolan, J. C., Jr., and Roehrkasse, G. P. 1969. Heritability of carcass traits in lamb. J. Anim. Sci. *29*, 251–255.

Braude, R. 1975. Copper as a performance promoter in pigs. Copper in Farming Symposium, Copper Devel. Assoc., London.

Braude, R., and Ryder, K. 1973. Copper levels in diets of growing pigs. J. Agric. Sci. *80*, 489–493.

Briggs, G. M. 1980. Meat in nutrition and health—An overview. *In* Meat in Nutrition and Health. National Live Stock and Meat Board, Chicago.

Broquist, H. P., and Kohler, A. R. 1953. Studies of the antibiotic potency in meat animals fed chlortetracycline. *In* Antibiotics Annual. Medical Enclyclopdia, New York.

Buckley J., and Connolly, J. F. 1980. Influence of alpha-tocopherol (vitamin E) on storage stability of raw pork and bacon. J. Food Prot. *34*, 265–267.

Burkitt, D. P. 1971. Epidemiology of cancer of the colon and rectum. Cancer *28*, 3.

Burris, M. J., Bogast, R., and Oliver, A. W. 1953. Effect of male hormones on beef cattle. J. Anim. Sci. *12*, 740–746.

Byerly, T. C. 1975. Effects of agricultural practices on foods of animal origin. *In* Nutritional Evaluation of Food Processing. 2nd Edition. AVI Publishing Co., Westport, CT.

Campanini, G., Maggi, E. and Artioli, D. 1980. Present situation of organochlorine pesticide residues in food of animal origin in Italy. World Rev. Nutr. Diet. *35*, 129–171.

CAST 1980. Foods from Animals: Quantity, Quality and Safety. Report *82*. Council for Agric. Sci. and Technol., Ames, IA.

Classen, H. G. 1977. Erfolgreiche Tierversuche mit vorbeugendem Medikament gegen Herzinfarkt. AID—Info. 24/9, 54.

Clausen, H. J. 1956. Influence of antibiotics on carcass quality of pigs. *In* Antibiotics in Agriculture. Publ. *397*. National Academy of Sciences, National Research Council, Washington, DC.

Crisetig, G., Mora, A., and Viviani, R. 1975. Residus des composes organochlores dans les tissue des bovins. Folia Vet. Latina *5*, 1–26.

Cundiff, L. V., Gregory, K. E., Koch, R. M., and Dickerson, G. E. 1969. Genetic variation in total and differential growth of carcass components in beef cattle. J. Anim. Sci. *29*, 233–244.

Curley, A., Sedlak, V. A., Girling, E. F., Hawk, A. E., Barthel, W. F., Price, P. E., and Likoky, W. H. 1971. Organic Hg identified as the cause of poisoning in humans and hogs. Science *172*, 65.

Davis, G. K. 1981. Bioavailability of nutrients. *In* Meat in Nutrition and Health. National Live Stock and Meat Board, Chicago.

Dayton, S. 1975. Nutrition and atherosclerosis. Prog. Food Nutr. Sci. *1*, 191.

DeCampos, M., Gutierney, B., and Olszyna-Marzys, A. E. 1979. Correlation between total DDT residues in blood and fat of beef cattle. J. Food Prot. *42*, 948–949, 953.

Department of Health and Social Security 1974. Report on Health and Social Subjects, 7: Diet and Coronary Heart Disease. Her Majesty's Stationery Office, London.

Department of Health and Social Security 1980. Foods which simulate meat. Report on Health and Social Subjects 17. Her Majesty's Stationery Office, London.

Dinius, D. A., Bimsfield, T. A., and Williams, E. E. 1973. Effect of subclinical lead intake on calves. J. Anim. Sci. *37*, 169–173.

Dockerty, T. R., Cahill, V. R., Ockerman, H. W., Fox, D. G., and Johnson, R. R. 1973. Carcass development in beef cattle subsequent to interrupted growth. J. Anim. Sci. *36*, 1057–1062.

Draper, C. I., Harris, J. R., Greenwood, D. A., Biddulph, C., Harris, L. E., Mangelson, F., Binnus, W., and Miner, M. L. 1952. The transfer of DDT from feed to eggs and body tissue of White Leghorn hens. Poult. Sci. *31*, 388–393.

Dryden, F. B., and Marchello, J. A. 1973. Influence of dietary fats on carcass lipid composition in the bovine. J. Anim. Sci. *37*, 33–37.

Duggan, R. E. 1968. Pesticide residue levels in foods in the United States from July 1, 1963 to June 30, 1967. Pest. Monit. J. *2*, 2.

Duggan, R. E., Barry, H. C., and Johnson, L. Y. 1966. Pesticide residues in total diet samples. Science *151*, 101.

Durury, J. S., and Hammons, A. S. 1979. Cadmium in foods: A review of the world's literature. Report 1979. EPA/560/2-708/007.

Eli Lilly 1982. Compudose. Technical Manual. Elanco Products Co., Indianapolis, IN.

Ellis, N. R., and Hankins, O. G. 1925. Soft pork studies. J. Biol. Chem. *66*, 101–122.

Enig, M. G., Munn, R. J., and Keeney, M. 1978. Dietary fat and cancer trends. A critique. Fed. Proc. *37*, 2215.

FAO 1971. Agricultural Commodity Projections, 1970–1980. FAO, Rome.

FAO 1977. The Fourth World Food Survey. FAO Statistics Series 11. FAO, Rome.

FAO 1980. World Meat Situation and Outlook. CCP:ME 80/Misc. Commodities and Trade Division. FAO, Rome.

FAO/OMS 1972. Evaluation de certains additifs alimentaires et des contaminants: Mercure, plomb et cadmium. *16*. Geneva.

FDA 1972. Diethylstilbestrol: Revocation of all provisions for use in animal feed. Fed. Regist. *37*, No. 236, 26307.

FDA 1973A. Diethylstilbestrol: Order denying a hearing and withdrawing approval of new drug applications for diethylstilbestrol implants. Fed. Regist. *38*, No. 81, 10185.

FDA 1973B. Diethylstilbestrol. Health, Education, Welfare New Release 73–17, April 25.

Ferrando, R. 1981. Residue of meats and additives studies and perspective. *In* Meat in Nutrition and Health. National Live Stock and Meat Board, Chicago.

Flynn, M. A., Nolph, G. B., Flynn, T. C., Kahrs, R., and Krause, G. 1979. Effect of dietary egg on human serum cholesterol and triglycerides. Am. J. Clin. Nutr. *32*:1051.

Food and Nutrition Board (FNB) 1980. Toward Healthful Diets. National Academy of Science, Washington, DC.

Forrest, J. C., Aberle, E. D., Hedrick, H. B., Judge, M. D., and Merkel, R. A. 1975. Principles of Meat Science. Freeman, San Francisco.

Frost, D. V., and Spruth, H. C. 1956. Arsenicals in feeds. *In* Symposium on Medicated Foods. Medical Encyclopedia, New York.

Glueck, C. J. 1979. Appraisal of dietary fat as a causative factor in atherogenesis. Am. J. Clin. Nutr. *32*, 2637.

Haselein, I., Grubmann, H. D., and Schulz, W. 1973. Intoxications par le mercure et residus dams les aliments chez des porcs ayant consomme des cereales traitees per des composes mercuriels. Monatsh. Veterinaermed. *28*, 54.

Hawkins, D. R., Handirson, E. H., and Newland, H. W. 1972. Melengesterol acetate and feedlot performance. J. Anim. Sci. *35*, 1257–1262.

Hazel, L. N., and Terrill, C. E. 1946. Heritability of weanling traits in range sheep. J. Anim. Sci. *5*, 371–377.

Hecht, H. 1977. Teneurs en elements toxiques de la viande. Ber. Landwirtsch. *55*, 828.

Hemken, R. W. 1980. Milk and meat iodine content: Relation to human health. J. Vet. Med. *176*, 1119–1121.

Hendricks, D. G., Mahoney, A. W., and Gillett, T. 1947. Influence of removing connective tissue, cooking and nitrite curing on the protein quality of beef shank muscle. J. Food Sci. *42*, 186.

Hill, J. E., Flaim, E., Thye, F. W., and Ritchey, S. J. 1979A. Effects of whole egg consumption on serum cholesterol HDL cholesterol, and triglycerides in exercising and nonexercising males. Fed. Proc. *38*(1), 550.

Hill, P., Reddy, B. S., and Wynder, E. L. 1979B. Effect of unsaturated fats and cholesterol on serum and fecal lipids. J. Am. Diet. Assoc. *75*, 414.

Hiner, R. L., and Bond, J. 1971. Growth of muscle and fat in beef steers from 6 to 36 months of age. J. Anim. Sci. *32*, 225–232.

Hoagland, R., Hankins, O. G., Nellis, N. R., Hiner, R. L., and Snider, G. G. 1947. Composition and nutritive value of hams as affected by method of curing. Food Technol. *1*, 540.

Holm, J. 1976A. Recherches sur les teneurs en plomb et cadmium d' echantillons d' organes ou de viandes de volailles. Fleischwirtschaft *56*, 1649.

Holm, J. 1976B. Studies on lead and cadmium levels in meat and organ samples from slaughter animals. Fleischwirtschaft *56*, 413.

Jensen, J. H. 1980. Meat in international dietary patterns. *In* Meat in Nutrition and Health. National Live Stock and Meat Board, Chicago.

Jukes, T. H. 1955. Antibiotics in Nutrition. Medical Encyclopedia, New York.

Kolari, E. 1980. Salt dietary concerns. Proc. Meat Ind. Res. Conf. American Meat Institute, Washington, DC.

Kolbye, A., and Nelson, M. A. 1977. Health and safety aspects of the use of mechanically deboned meat. Final report and recommendations. Select Panel, Meat and Poultry Inspection Program, Food Safety and Quality Service. USDA, Washington, DC.

Kreuzer, W., Kracke, W., Sansoni, B., and Wissmath, P. 1978. Lead and cadmium contents in the meat and organs of slaughter cattle. 1. Cattle from an area where there is little contamination of the environment. Fleischwirtschaft *58*, 1022.

Kritchevsky, D. 1981. Current concepts in colon carcinogenesis. *In* Meat in Nutrition and Health. National Live Stock and Meat Board, Chicago.

Krol, B., and Tinbergen, B. J. (Editors) 1974. Proceedings of the International Symposium on Nitrite in Meat Products. Center for Agricultural Publishing and Documentation (Pudoc), Wageningen, The Netherlands.

Lima, F. R., Stahly, T. S., and Cromwell, G. L. 1981. Effect of copper, with and without ferrous sulfide and antibiotics on the performance of pigs. J. Anim. Sci. *52*, 241–247.

Manske, D. D., and Johnson, R. D. 1977. Pesticides and other chemical residues in total diet samples. Pest. Monit. J. *10*, 134.

Marsden, S. J., and Bird, H. R. 1947. Effects of DDT on growing turkeys. Poult. Sci. *26*, 3–6.

Masironi, R. 1975. International studies on trace elements in the etiology of cardio-vascular diseases. Proc. Ninth Int. Congr. Nutr., Mexico, 1972. Vol 1, p. 123.

Nagy, S., Tartia, G., Muresan, C., and Iancut, A. 1975. Le plomb dans quelques types d' aliments d' origine animale provenant de regions polluees. Rev. Ig. Bacteriol. Virusol. Parazitol. Epidemiol. Pneumoftizol Ig., 24, 25.

National Research Council (NRC) 1977. Copper. National Academy of Science, Washington, DC.

Nelson, N. 1971. Hazards of mercury. Environ. Res. *4*, 1–69.

Nichols, A. B., Ravenscroft, C., Lamphire, D. E., and Ostrander, L. D. 1976. Independence of serum lipid levels and dietary habits. The Tucumseh Study. JAMA *236*, 1548.

NLSMB 1983A. Meat Board Reports, January. National Live Stock and Meat Board, Chicago.

NLSMB 1983B. Meat Board Reports, March, National Live Stock and Meat Board, Chicago.

Ockerman, H. W. 1980. Chemistry of Meat Tissue. Department of Animal Science, Ohio State Univ., Columbus.

Ockerman, H. W. 1981. Quality Control of Post-Mortem Tissues. Vol. 1. Department of Animal Science, Ohio State Univ. Columbus.

Olsen, P., and Meyer, O. 1977. Carcinogenicity study on rats fed on canned heated nitrite treated meat: Preliminary communication P. 275. *In* Proceedings of the Second International Symposium on Nitrite in Meat Products. B. Krol and B. J. Tinbergen (Editors) Center for Agricultural Publishing and Documentation (Puboc), Wageningen, The Netherlands.

OMS-FAO Committee 1979. OMS (WHO) et Comites mixtes FAO-OMS. Serie de rapports techniques sur les residus de pesticides dans les produits alimentaires. *15.* FAO, Rome.

Pearson, A. M. 1983. What's new in research. Nat. Provisioner *188*(20), 29.

Plimpton, R. F., Ockerman, H. W., Teague, H. S., Grifo, A. P., and Cahill, V. R. 1971. Palatability, composition and quality of boar pork. J. Anim. Sci. *32*, 51–56.

Porter, M. W., and Flynn, M. H. 1977. Effect of dietary egg on serum cholesterol and triglyceride of human males. Am. J. Clin. Nutr. *30*, 490.

Price, T. J., Hays, V. W., and Cromwell, G. L. 1979. Effects of copper sulfate and ferrous sulfide on performance and liver copper and iron stores of pigs. J. Anim. Sci. *49*, 507.

Prior, M. G. 1976. Lead and mercury residues in kidney and liver of Canadian slaughter animals. Can. J. Comp. Med. *40*, 9.

Ray, D. E., Hale, W. H., and Marchello, J. A. 1969. Influence of season, sex and hormonal growth stimulant on feed-lot performance of beef cattle. J. Anim. Sci. *29*, 490–495.

Richmond, J. B. 1979. Healthy People. The Surgeon General's report on health promotion and disease prevention. U.S. Department of Health, Education and Welfare, Public Health Service. Washington, DC.

Rogowski, B. 1981. Inquiries into cardiovascular disease. *In* Meat in Nutrition and Health. National Live Stock and Meat Board, Chicago.

Rosenbloom, N. J., and Potter, N. N. 1981. Effects of processing on zinc levels in spinach, beef and potatoes. J. Food Sci. *46*, 1707–1709.

Ross, A. C., Minick, C. R., and Zilversmith, D. B. 1978. Equal artherosclerosis in rabbits fed cholesterol-free, low fat diet or cholesterol-supplemented diets. Atherosclerosis *29*, 301.

Rubin, M., Bird, H. R., Green, N., and Carter, R. H. 1947. Toxicity of DDT to laying hens. Poult. Sci. *26*, 410–413.

Rumsey, T. S., Oltjen, R. R., Bovard, K. P., and Priode, B. M. 1972. Depot fat composition in beef cattle. J. Anim. Sci. *35*, 1069–1075.

Schricker, B. R., Miller, D. D., and Stouffer, J. R. 1982. Content of zinc in selected muscles from beef, pork and lamb. J. Food Sci. *47*, 1020, 1022.

Senate Select Committee on Nutrition and Human Needs. 1977A. Dietary Goals for the United States. U.S. Gov't. Printing Office, Washington, DC.

Senate Select Committee on Nutrition and Human Needs. 1977B. Dietary Goals for the United States. Revised Edition. U.S. Gov't. Printing Office, Washington, DC.

Smith, G. C. (Task Force Chairman) 1980. Foods from Animals: Quantity, Quality and Safety. Report 82. CAST, Ames, IA.

Spalding J. F. 1972. Pesticide and heavy metal residues. *In* Proc. Meat Inst. Res. Conf., American Meat Institute Foundation, Chicago.

Stadelman, W. J. 1973. Record of some chemical residues in poultry products. Bioscience *23*, 424–428.

Stadelman, W. J., 1965. Persistence of chlorinated hydrocarbon insecticide residues in chicken tissue and eggs. Poult. Sci. *44*, 435–437.

Swann, M. 1969. Report. Joint Committee on Use of Antibiotics in Animal Husbandry and Veterinary Medicine. Her Majesty's Stationery Office, London.

Terrell, R. N., and Olson, D. G. 1981. Shelf-Stability and Safety of Reduced Sodium Products. Proceedings of the Meat Research Conference. American Meat Institute, Washington, DC.

U.S. Department of Agriculture (USDA) 1973. Reports on residues found in meat and poultry. USDA Press Rel. *2475*, Aug. 10, Washington, DC.

U.S. Department of Agriculture (USDA) 1974. Fats in Food and Diet. Bull. *361*. USDA, Washington, DC.

U.S. Department of Agriculture (USDA) 1975. Nutritive Value of American Foods. USDA Handbook *456*. Washington, DC.

U.S. Department of Agriculture (USDA) 1978. Composition of food. *In* Agriculture Handbook *8–3*. USDA, Washington, DC.

U.S. Department of Agriculture (USDA) 1978. Nutritive Value of Foods. Home and Garden Bull. *72*. USDA, Washington, DC.

U.S. Department of Agriculture (USDA) 1979. Agriculture Handbook *8–4*. USDA, Washington, DC.

U.S. Department of Agriculture (USDA) 1980. Composition of foods: Sausage and luncheon meats. *In* Agriculture Handbook *8–7*. USDA, Washington, DC.

U.S. Department of Agriculture (USDA) 1981. Home and Garden Bull. *94*. Human Nutrition Service, USDA, Washington, DC.

Van Logten, M. J., den Tonkelaac, E. M., Kroes, R., Berkvens, J. M., and Van Esch, G. J. 1972. Long-term experiment with canned meat treated with sodium nitrite and glucono delta lactone in rats. Food Cosmet. Toxicol. *10*, 475.

Vemmer, H., and Petersen, U. 1977. Lead and cadmium contents of various tissues in normal fed feeder pigs. Landwirtsch. Forsch. Sonderh. *34*, 62.

Voors, A. W., and Johnson, W. D. 1979. Altitude and arteriosclerotic heart disease mortality in white residents of 99 of the 100 largest cities in the United States. J. Chron. Dis. *32*, 157.

Warwick, E. J. 1968. Effective performance recording in beef cattle. *In* Proceedings Second World Congress on Animal Production. Bruce Publishing Co., St. Paul, MN.

Wilkinson, S. A., Earle, M. D., and Cleland, A. C. 1981. Kinetics of vitamin A degradation in beef liver puree on heat processing. J. Food Sci. *46*, 32–33, 40.

Wilkinson, S. A., Earle, M. D., and Cleland, A. C. 1982. Effects of food composition, pH and copper on the degradation of vitamin A in beef liver puree during heat processing. J. Food Sci. *47*, 844–848.

Wright, F. C., Palmer, J. S., and Riner, J. C. 1973A. Accumulation of mercury in tissues of cattle, sheep and chickens given the mercurial fungicide Panogen 150, orally, J. Agric. Food Chem. *21*, 414–416.

Wright, F. C., Palmer, J. S., and Riner, J. C. 1973B. Retention of mercury in tissue of cattle and sheep given oral doses of a mercurial fungicide. Ceresan M. J. Agr. Food Chem. *21*, 614–618.

Yudkin, J. 1972. Sucrose and cardiovascular disease. Proc. Nutr. Soc. *31*, 331.

Effects of
Agricultural Practices
on Milk and Dairy Products

Edmund Renner

MILK FAT COMPOSITION

Milk fat consists of more than 200 different fatty acids, many of them, however, occurring only in trace amounts. The fatty acids include saturated, unsaturated, and branched-chain fatty acids as well as hydroxy acids and cyclic compounds. Milk fat has, therefore, the most diverse composition of the natural fats. Only 15 fatty acids occur in proportions greater than 1% of the milk fat (Table 8.1). The fatty acid composition of milk fat is quite variable.

With regard to feeding, there is a positive correlation between the content of unsaturated fatty acids in the fat of the feed and that in the milk fat. However, the content of polyunsaturated fatty acids in the milk fat is considerably reduced as a large part of these fatty acids is hydrogenated by the rumen bacteria. Certain constituents of concentrate, for example, coconut oil, soya bean oil, linseed oil, cottonseed oil, and safflower oil, influence the fatty acid composition of milk fat (Banks *et al.* 1976; Renner *et al.* 1971).

The content of polyunsaturated fatty acids in milk fat can be considerably increased by feeding if the animals are given highly unsaturated oils (safflower, soya bean, or sunflower oil) encapsulated in casein hardened by formaldehyde. This casein is resistant to degradation in the rumen so that the encapsulated polyunsaturated acids are protected from hydrogenation there. The casein is hydrolyzed later in the acidic part of the alimentary tract so that the fatty acids are absorbed in the small intestine. In this way the proportion of the polyunsaturated fatty acids, particularly that of linoleic acid, can be increased to 20–30%, in some cases even to 35%. At the same time, the fraction of myristic, palmitic, stearic, and oleic acid is reduced (Fig. 8.1). However, the milk fat shows an increased sensitivity to oxidation (Aicken 1974; Renner and Hahn 1978, 1979).

Table 8.1. Seasonal Variations in the Fatty Acid Composition of Milk Fat

Fatty acid		Proportion (%) in milk fat during	
		Winter	Summer
Butyric acid	C_4	3.9	3.6
Caproic acid	C_6	2.5	2.1
Caprylic acid	C_8	1.5	1.2
Capric acid	C_{10}	3.2	2.5
Lauric acid	C_{12}	3.9	2.9
Myristic acid	C_{14}	11.7	9.7
Myristoleic acid	$C_{14:1}$	2.1	1.8
Pentadecanoic acid	C_{15}	1.5	1.3
Palmitic acid	C_{16}	30.6	24.0
Palmitoleic acid	$C_{16:1}$	2.2	1.8
Margaric acid	C_{17}	1.4	0.9
Stearic acid	C_{18}	8.8	12.2
Oleic acid	$C_{18:1}$	22.2	29.5
Linoleic acid	$C_{18:2}$	2.0	2.1
Linolenic acid	$C_{18:3}$	1.2	2.4

Source: Renner (1983).

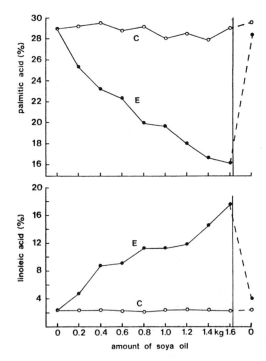

Fig. 8.1. Effect of feeding encapsulated soya bean oil on the content of linoleic and palmitic acid in milk fat (E, experimental animals; C, control animals). Source: Kreuder and Renner (1975).

There are clear seasonal variations in the composition of milk fat because it is affected by the composition of the feed. Table 8.1 shows that during the summer months all C_{18}- fatty acids, but particularly oleic acid, are found in greater concentrations in milk fat than in the winter months, while, on the other hand, the fraction of palmitic acid is much reduced.

Only the cis- forms of unsaturated fatty acids occur in vegetable fats and oils. However, in the production of hardened fats catalytic hydrogenation takes place and, during the passage of the feed through the rumen, bacterial hydrogenation occurs, producing trans- isomers of the unsaturated fatty acids. It has been reported that 70–90% of the linoleic acid in the fat of the feeding stuff is biologically hydrogenated. This would account for the relatively low linoleic acid concentration in milk fat. Such hydrogenation processes explain why trans- fatty acids are found in milk fat as well as in margarine and vegetable frying fats. Milk fat contains on average 2.5% (0–5%) of elaidic acid (*trans*-octadecenoic acid). The concentration of trans- fatty acids is higher in summer than in winter (Akesson *et al.* 1981; Renner and Yoon 1982).

MILK PROTEIN

Table 8.2 shows the average values of the amino acid composition of milk protein and its main fractions, casein and whey protein. The data show that milk proteins are relatively rich in essential amino acids and that there are considerable differences between the individual protein fractions, whey proteins containing more threonine, lysine, isoleucine, and tryptophan than casein. Because the proportions of the individual protein fractions in the total milk protein are subject to seasonal variations, the amino acid composition of the total protein varies with the season. It has been noted that it is related to the outside temperature: In the warmer months the animal produces less protein, but this protein has a higher essential amino acid content (Kirchmeier 1973).

Table 8.3 compares the biological value of the milk proteins as well as the protein efficiency ratio (PER) and net protein utilization (NPU) values with those of other dietary proteins. The figures show that the nutritional value of milk proteins is only a little lower than that of whole egg protein. There is a clear difference between casein and lactalbumin. The latter has the highest biological value of all the milk proteins, higher even than that of whole egg protein.

Because milk proteins contain a surplus of some essential amino acids, they can raise the biological value of a diet when added to other dietary proteins, particularly vegetable proteins. It has been suggested that milk proteins be added to bread and other cereal products to increase the lysine content of the diet. A mixture consisting of 76% milk

Table 8.2. Amino Acid Composition of Milk Protein, Casein, and Whey Protein

| | Content (g/100 g protein) | | |
Amino acid	Total protein	Total casein	Total whey protein
Tryptophan	1.4	1.4	2.1
Phenylalanine	5.2	5.1	3.8
Leucine	10.4	10.4	11.1
Isoleucine	6.4	5.7	6.8
Threonine	5.1	4.6	8.0
Methionine	2.7	2.8	2.4
Lysine	8.3	8.3	9.9
Valine	6.8	6.8	6.8
Histidine	2.8	2.9	2.2
Arginine	3.7	4.0	3.0
Cystine	0.9	0.3	2.4
Proline	10.1	11.2	5.2
Alanine	3.5	3.1	5.0
Aspartic acid	7.9	7.3	11.3
Serine	5.6	5.8	5.2
Glutamic acid	21.8	23.0	19.2
Glycine	2.1	2.1	2.2
Tyrosine	5.3	6.0	3.5

Source: Renner (1983).

Table 8.3. Nutritional Value of Milk Proteins and of a Number of Other Dietary Proteins

Food protein	Biological value	PER value	NPU value
Whole egg	100	3.8	94
Cows' milk	91	3.1	82
Casein	77	2.9	76
Lactalbumin	104	3.6	92
Beef	80	2.9	73
Potato	71	—	—
Soya protein	74	2.1	61
Rice	59	2.0	57
Wheat	54	1.5	41
Beans	49	1.4	39

Source: Renner (1983).

protein and 24% cereal protein is said to be ideal, as its biological value is higher even than that of milk protein alone. As a general rule, the biological value of such a mixture is higher than that calculated from the individual values of the components (den Hartog 1980; Porter 1978).

MINERALS AND TRACE ELEMENTS IN MILK

Cow's milk contains, on average, 7.3 g of minerals per liter. Table 8.4 shows the average content of minerals and trace elements. Of the calcium and phosphorus, 20% is bound to casein in the form of a calcium caseinate complex. These elements are, thus, important for the stability of that complex. Trace elements in milk occur largely as organic compounds. Some, such as copper, zinc, manganese, and iron, are found in the fat globule membrane. Of the iron, 60–70% is bound to the casein micelles, 80% of the zinc is bound to casein, and 20% to immunoglobulins. Most of the copper and iodine are associated with milk proteins (Basch *et al.* 1974; Mendy *et al.* 1981).

The concentration of minerals in milk cannot easily be influenced by feeding. The content of some of the minerals, namely, Ca, P, Na, and Cl, is increased at the end of the lactation period. Being insensitive to feeding the mineral content varies little with seasons (Renner and Kosmack 1977).

The large range in the content of some trace elements in milk can, in part, be explained by the influence of such factors as feeding, season, and the stage of lactation. An increased uptake of the elements Co, B, Al, Mo, Mn, F, Br, Ti, and Se from the feed may increase their content in milk, but feeding can only very slightly influence the content of Fe, Ni, As, and Si (Conrad and Moxon 1979; Schwarz and Kirchgessner 1978, 1979).

Udder disinfectants in the form of iodophores are often used as prophylactic measures against udder disease. In such cases, iodine can

Table 8.4. Minerals and Trace Elements in Milk

Minerals	Unit	Mean value
Ca	g/liter	1.21
P		0.95
K		1.50
Na		0.47
Cl		1.03
Mg	mg/liter	120
S		320
Zn		3.6
Fe		0.53
Cu	μg/liter	120
F		125
I		75
Mo		55
Mn		50
Co		0.8

Source: Renner (1983).

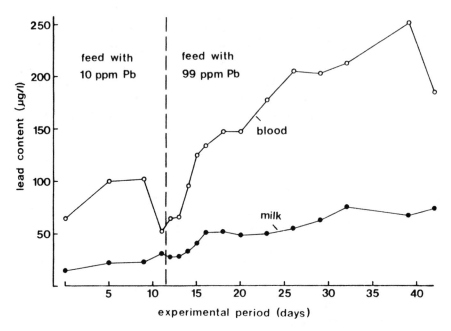

Fig. 8.2. Lead content of milk and blood of cows fed contaminated feeds. Source: Blanc *et al.* (1971).

be transferred into the milk. Investigations have revealed that the iodine content of milk rose after such an application from a normal value of 30–90 μg/liter to 120–150 μg/liter, in some cases even to 350 μg/liter (Hemken 1979).

With regard to the heavy metals lead, mercury, and cadmium, their concentrations in milk are hardly changed by an increased uptake from the feed. Analysis of hay from the side of the road or from the middle of a motorway in Switzerland showed a lead content of 99 mg/kg of dry matter. When this was fed to cows, the lead content of the milk was 40–70 μg/liter compared to 20 μg/liter in the milk of cows fed hay from a traffic-free area (Fig. 8.2).

VITAMINS IN MILK

Milk contains all the known vitamins. Table 8.5 shows the average vitamin content and the contribution by 1 liter of milk to the recommended daily vitamin intake. Some of the vitamin requirements, such as those for some of the B-group vitamins (B_2 and B_{12}), are completely met by the consumption of 1 liter of milk, while milk and milk products can make a significant contribution to the supply of the vitamins A, B_1, B_6, D, and pantothenic acid.

Table 8.5. Vitamin Content of Milk and the Contribution to the Recommended Vitamin Intake

Vitamin	Content of milk (mg/1liter)	Supply by 1 liter of milk (%)
A + Carotene	0.58	46
B_1 (thiamin)	0.42	32
B_2 (riboflavin)	1.72	104
B_6 (pyridoxine)	0.48	25
B_{12} (cobalamin)	0.0045	113
Nicotinic acid	0.92	6
Folic acid	0.053	15
Pantothenic acid	3.6	43
C (ascorbic acid)	18	30
D (cholecalciferol)	0.0008	32
E (tocopherol)	1.1	11

Source: Renner (1983).

The vitamin A and carotene content of milk can be influenced by the type of feed because there is a close relationship between the carotene content of the feedstuff and that of the milk. The same applies to vitamin E. The ascorbic acid content of milk, on the other hand, is not affected by the feed. Similarly, the vitamin B content can be influenced to only a very small extent by feeding. An exception is vitamin B_{12}, whose concentration in milk can be increased by adding cobalt to the feed. The vitamin D content of milk is not influenced by the amount taken in orally by the animal because the body produces this vitamin from dehydrocholesterol under the influence of ultraviolet (UV) light. This is why increased concentrations of vitamin D (maximum values of 2.8 μg/liter) have been found in the milk of cows on summer pasture, especially in mountainous regions where the UV content of the sunlight is high. The effect of season is shown by the fact that milk contains more carotene and vitamins A, D, and E in the summer months (or during the period of grazing) than in winter (Fig. 8.3) (Antila *et al.* 1979; Gregory 1975; Olson *et al.* 1974).

EFFECT OF PROCESSING AND STORAGE

Effect of Heat

The heating of milk at the time/temperature conditions used in the dairy technology is not expected to produce any adverse effects on the nutritional properties of the milk fat because the photochemical oxidation of lipids is affected only slightly by temperature. Pasteurization of milk does not affect the content of polyunsaturated and essential fatty

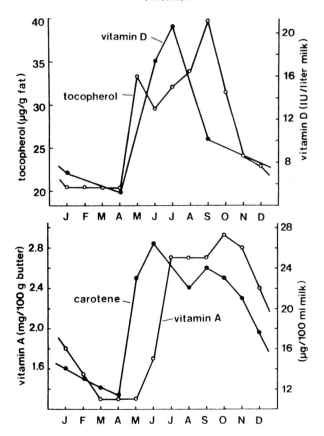

Fig. 8.3. Seasonal variations in the concentration of carotene and vitamins A, D, and E. Source: Renner (1983).

acids in the milk fat since, for example, linoleic acid is stable at high temperatures. There are only a few reports of a slight reduction in essential fatty acid concentration in sterilized and ultrahigh temperature (UHT) -treated milk (Henderson *et al.* 1980; Reimerdes and Diekmann 1979).

The casein in milk is relatively stable to heat, since proline prevents the formation of hydrogen bonds, which are necessary for aggregation. The whey proteins, on the other hand, are denatured by the various types of heat treatment to differing extents, the degree of denaturation being a function of temperature and time: 10–20% of the whey proteins are denatured in pasteurized milk, 70–80% in UHT milk made by the indirect heating process, and 40–60% in UHT milk produced by the direct process; the whey proteins are not completely denatured even in traditional sterilized milk (Deissmann 1977; Snoeren and Both 1981).

The denaturation of milk proteins is not detrimental from the point of view of nutrition. Heating produces changes in the specific spatial configuration, that is, in the secondary and tertiary structure of the proteins. Since the loosened structure of the protein makes it more accessible to the enzymes, heat-denatured milk proteins are more easily digested than native ones. It has therefore, been often found that the protein of pasteurized and UHT-treated milk was better utilized than that of raw milk. Digestion experiments with trypsin, pepsin, and pancreatin confirmed that the enzymes attacked such proteins more easily. Moreover, heated milk proteins are precipitated by the acid in the stomach in the form of more finely dispersed particles, and this also makes enzyme attack easier. Fewer problems with digestion were encountered when UHT-treated milk was given to babies and small children (Belikov et al. 1981; Roy 1981).

The changes in the milk proteins taking place during UHT treatment are so small that their biological value is not affected. The PER and NPU values of the proteins of pasteurized and UHT-treated milk also showed no appreciable differences (Sieber et al. 1980).

When proteins are heated under alkaline conditions, chemical reactions occur that lead to the formation of lysinoalanine (LAL). When LAL was included in the diet of rats, they developed kidney damage in the form of nephromegalocytosis. LAL was much less toxic for mice, and for other animals it does not appear to be toxic at all. Therefore, it has been concluded that LAL is also nontoxic for humans. Milk, milk products, and baby foods do not contain any LAL at all or only very small amounts of it (Fritsch and Klostermeyer 1981).

At high temperatures or during long periods of storage, aidehydes, ketones, and reducing sugars react with amino acids, amines, peptides, and proteins (Maillard reaction). One of the first reaction products detected in milk is often hydroxymethylfurfural (HMF), the concentration of which increases with an increasing intensity of heat treatment. With regard to the nutritional aspects of the reaction products of the Maillard reaction, animal experiments have shown that HMF can hardly be considered harmful to health. Since mankind has taken in considerable amounts of these reaction products ever since fire was used for the preparation of food, it can be concluded that these products are harmless (Askar and Treptow 1982; Renner and Dorguth 1980).

In the Maillard reaction, aldehydes combine preferentially with the ε amino groups of lysine. However, normal heating processes cause only very small losses of available lysine: 1–2% in pasteurized milk, 1–4% in UHT milk, 5% in briefly boiled milk, 6–10% in sterilized milk, and about 20% in evaporated milk. Because the original lysine content of milk is high, these small losses of available lysine in pasteurized and UHT milk can be ignored (Blanc 1981).

Table 8.6.   Effect of Different Methods of Heat Treatment on the Vitamin Losses in Milk

	Losses (%) of				
Procedure	Vitamin B_1	Vitamin B_6	Vitamin B_{12}	Folic acid	Vitamin C
Pasteurization	<10	0–8	<10	<10	10–25
UHT treatment	0–20	<10	5–20	5–20	5–30
Boiling	10–20	10	20	15	15–30
Sterilization	20–50	20–50	20–100	30–50	30–100

Source: Renner (1983).

The fat-soluble vitamins A, D, and E and the vitamins B_2, pantothenic acid, biotin, and nicotinic acid are relatively insensitive to heat, and there are generally no losses of these vitamins when milk is heated. The vitamins B_1, B_6, B_{12}, folic acid, and C, on the other hand, are less stable to heat. Table 8.6 gives values of the average losses of these vitamins due to different heating processes. It can be concluded that the vitamin losses in pasteurized milk are so small that there is practically no reduction in the nutritional value of the milk. The same applies to UHT milk where the vitamin losses are of the order of 10–20%. It is possible to optimize the UHT process conditions so that the required destruction of spores is achieved while, for example, thiamin losses are kept at less than 3%. The reduction in the vitamin potency of sterilized milk is more serious (Kessler and Horak 1981; Zadow 1980).

Homogenization of Milk

The object of homogenizing milk is to reduce the size of the fat globules in order to prevent creaming in the longer-keeping types of milk. It also has nutritional advantages because fat absorption is easier the smaller the fat globules are. In rat experiments, homogenized milk also produced a better utilization of protein (Lembke 1971).

Effect of Storage

On its way to the consumer, milk can be affected and its nutritional value impaired, particularly by light and oxygen. Riboflavin and ascorbic acid are very sensitive to light, while vitamin C and folic acid are very sensitive to oxygen. When milk is exposed to direct sunlight, up to 90% of the vitamin B_2 is destroyed within a few hours. Milk packages should therefore provide sufficient protection from light. This is the case for cartons with an additional inner layer of aluminum foil, but clear glass or plastic bottles and plastic films offer hardly any protection from light. Figure 8.4 shows that the ascorbic acid content

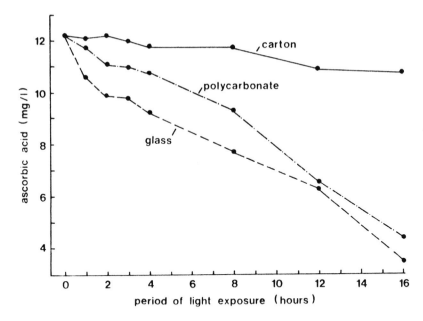

Fig. 8.4. Effect of light on the ascorbic acid content of milk in different types of packages stored in illuminated display cabinets. Source: Renner (1981).

of milk kept in glass or in polycarbonate bottles in display cabinets already begins to fall during the first few hours of storage, and after 16 hours only very little remains. Cartons, on the other hand, give sufficient protection. In addition, the exposure of milk to sunlight causes considerable flavor defects in the form of sunlight flavor (Kiermeier and Waiblinger 1969).

Pasteurized milk loses some of its ascorbic acid after 2 days due to the oxygen present. UHT milk made by the indirect process contains approximately 8 ppm of dissolved oxygen, and its ascorbic acid content is considerably reduced after 2 weeks of storage, whereas the vitamin C content of UHT milk made by the direct process, during which oxygen is almost completely eliminated, is practically unchanged. Folic acid is also inactivated in an oxygen-rich milk, but in the absence of oxygen, it remains at its original value over the whole of the storage period (Ford et al. 1978; Renner 1979).

Cultured Milk Products

The composition of the starting milk is not changed significantly by its conversion into cultured milk products. In protein-enriched yogurt, the protein content is increased to 4–5% and the protein and mineral content of yogurt is also higher when concentrated milk is used in its manufacture, as is often the case (O'Neil *et al.* 1979).

During the manufacture of yogurt, the lactic acid bacteria make use of the vitamins in the milk, particularly during the phase of rapid growth, but it seems that they are able to synthesize some of these vitamins again at a later stage. Some authors have reported higher values for folic acid, nicotinic acid, biotin, pantothenic acid, B_6, and B_{12} in ripened yogurt compared to the original milk (Ayebo and Shahni 1980).

Cultured milk products are more digestible than unfermented ones. This is thought to have two reasons: (1) The slow acid formation by the lactic acid bacteria causes the milk to curdle in the form of small particles; which present a large surface to the digestive enzymes, and (2) during the ripening, the microorganisms break down a part of the protein into peptides and free amino acids, causing what might be called a predigestion of the protein. Raw milk needs twice as much time as yogurt to reach the same degree of digestion (Alm 1981).

Fermented milk products improve the utilization of calcium even more than lactose because lactic acid is additionally involved in the utilization of calcium (Figure 8.5).

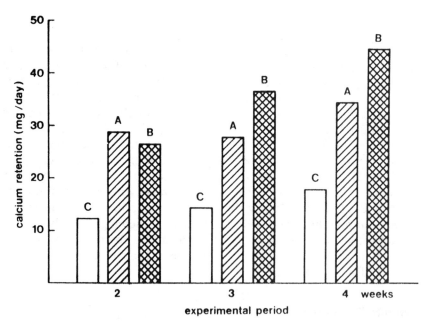

Fig. 8.5. Effect of the consumption of yogurt on the calcium retention of rats [C, control group (usual balanced diet); A and B, experimental groups receiving 20.25 or 40.50% of the dry matter in the ration in the form of yogurt]. Source: Dupuis (1964).

The two optical isomers of lactic acid, L-(+) and D-(−), have different physiological properties because the human organism has only a limited capacity for metabolizing D-(−)-lactic acid. Cultured milk products contain both lactic acid isomers in different proportions: soured milk, kefir, buttermilk, and fresh cheese contain very little D-lactic acid (2–14%), while yogurt contains more (25–60%). The World Health Organization (WHO) has suggested that the maximum daily intake of D-(−)-lactic acid should not be more than 100 mg/kg of body weight. This shows that only an extremely unbalanced diet could bring about an accumulation of this compound in the body (Krusch 1978; Renner and Müller 1981).

It was thought that the consumption of cultured milk products and the microorganisms contained in them would help to establish a natural intestinal flora. Therefore, yogurt was additionally inoculated with *Lactobacillus acidophilus* and *L. bifidus*, which are organisms originally derived from the gut. But it is generally not possible to colonize the intestinal tract with microorganisms from food because of the strongly acid gastric juices (pH value of 0.9–1.6) and because of the bactericidal substances in the upper part of the small intestine, particularly the desoxycholic acid in the bile. Therefore, it comes as a surprise to read quite frequently that organisms taken in with food can colonize the gut (Auclair and Mocquot 1974; Lembke 1976). These results may be explained as follows:

1. It cannot be concluded from the presence of certain bacteria in the intestinal flora that they originate in the food because a number of constituents of the diet (in the case of cultured milk products, mainly lactose and lactic acid) can change the composition of the intestinal flora.
2. Such changes have been observed mainly in persons suffering from intestinal disorders, but not in healthy people. It might also be possible to influence the composition of the intestinal flora of children by diet (Bianchi-Salvadori *et al.* 1978).

Cheese

The ripening of cheese is accompanied by a partial protein degradation. The products of proteolysis are proteoses, peptones, polypeptides, peptides, and free amino acids. Thereby a part of the water-insoluble casein is converted into water-soluble nitrogenous compounds. The nutritional importance of cheese arises from its high content of biologically valuable proteins. Cheese can contribute significantly to the required supply of essential amino acids. Table 8.7 shows that the protein content varies between 20 and 30%. In the manufacture of cheese, it is mainly the casein of the milk that forms the cheese while most of

Table 8.7. Average Content of Fat, Protein, Calcium, Vitamin A, and Riboflavin of a Number of Cheese Varieties

Cheese variety	Content of				
	Fat (%)	Protein (%)	Ca (g/kg)	Vitamin A (mg/kg)	Riboflavin (mg/kg)
Emmental	29.0	27.9	10.8	3.3	3.5
Cheddar	32.4	25.4	8.0	3.6	4.7
Edam	26.0	25.5	7.5	2.5	3.5
Blue cheese	29.0	22.4	7.0	3.6	2.9
Camembert	22.3	22.0	4.0	3.0	5.8
Cottage cheese	4.6	14.7	0.8	0.4	2.9
Fresh cheese	0–12	12–16	0.8	0–1	2.8

Source: Renner (1983).

the biologically valuable whey proteins pass into the whey. This is why the biological value of the proteins in cheese is somewhat lower than that of the total milk protein but still higher than that of casein alone. If the essential amino acid index of milk protein is given a value of 100, then the corresponding values of the proteins in a number of cheese varieties range from 91 to 97. Cheese ripening can be looked upon as a sort of predigestion whereby the digestibility of the proteins is increased (Blanc 1982).

The decarboxylation of free amino acids during cheese ripening produces amines. The concentration of individual amines in cheese shows great variation. The tyramine content of Cheddar cheese can vary between 0 and 155 μg/kg and the histamine content between 0 and 1300 μg/kg. Physiologically active amines can affect the blood pressure, with tyramine and phenylethylamine having a hypertensive and histamine a hypotensive effect. However, mono- and diamine oxidases break down the biogenous amines relatively quickly and therefore the amines contained in cheese and in other foods do not constitute a health hazard for the consumer (Edwards and Sandine 1981; de Vuyst *et al.* 1976).

The average Ca concentration in a number of cheese varieties is shown in Table 8.7. For example, 100 g of hard cheese will completely meet the daily Ca requirement and contribute 40–50% to the protein requirement. Cheeses produced by rennet coagulation usually have higher calcium contents than those made from acid-coagulated milk. The minerals calcium, phosphorus, and magnesium in cheese are as well utilized by the body as those in milk (Kansal and Chaudhary 1982).

Only 10–60% of the water-soluble B vitamins pass from the milk into the cheese, the rest remain in the whey. However, milk contains such high concentrations of some vitamins of the B complex that cheese is still able to contribute significantly to the supply of these vitamins.

This is especially true of vitamin B_{12}. Some mold-ripened cheeses contain more of the B vitamins than other types of cheese. An example is the high content of vitamins B_2, B_6, and nicotinic acid in Camembert (Reif *et al.* 1976).

Because molds, particularly strains of *Penicillium*, are used in the manufacture of blue cheese as well as of cheeses with a surface mold, the question arises whether mycotoxins could be formed. The following substances are degradation products formed by the action of *Penicillium roqueforti:*

1. From 0.05 to 6.8 ppm of the alkaloid roquefortin have been detected in blue cheese. According to the currently available toxicity data, these concentrations are too low to be toxic.
2. The so-called PR toxin is formed only by a few *P. roqueforti* strains and then only on artificial nutrient media. This toxin has therefore never been found in cheese.
3. The toxic mold product patulin, which is carcinogenic for mice, is not produced by those strains of *P. roqueforti* that are used in cheese making (Bullerman 1981; Moreau 1980).

In the case of cheese varieties that undergo a long ripening period, there is the danger that anaerobic spore-forming clostridia, particularly *Clostridium tyrobutyricum*, which cannot be destroyed by pasteurization, may produce considerable butyric acid fermentation, resulting in bloating of the cheese, which would make it unfit for consumption. The addition of a maximum of 20 g of sodium or potassium nitrate per 100 liters of cheese milk is therefore permitted in the manufacture of some types of cheese. During the ripening period the nitrates are reduced to nitrites, which inhibit the growth of clostridia. As nitrite is a toxic compound, cheese should not contain any harmful amounts of it at the end of its ripening period. This is actually the case, because the nitrite is rapidly destroyed again so that the finished product contains only traces of nitrite (Monzani *et al.* 1981; Zerfiridis and Manolkidis 1981).

There is the possibility that nitrosamines might be formed by a reaction between secondary amines and nitrite. Sixty different nitrosamines are known and the majority of them have been found strongly carcinogenic in rats. Histamine and tyramine, which are the chief amines occurring in cheese, are not among those that can be converted to nitrosamines. The reaction is taking place preferentially in a pH range of 2 to 4.5, but cheese has a higher pH value, and this prevents the reaction leading to the formation of nitrosamines. This is the reason why nitrosamines are found only rarely, and then in very small concentrations, in cheeses that have been made with the addition of the permitted amounts of nitrates. The average daily intake of nitrosamines in the United Kingdom is said to be about 1 μg, of which cheese contributes only 4% (Gray and Morton 1981; Klein *et al.* 1980).

In the production of processed cheese, the casein is hydrated and peptized by the action of the emulsifying salts, and the proportion of water-soluble protein therefore increases considerably. Polyphosphates have the widest range of application. These salts taken in with food are unable to exert a physiological effect because they are quickly broken down by enzymes to monophosphates, which are then absorbed. In this way, the phosphate contained in processed cheese might even contribute to meeting the protein requirement (Brieskorn 1972).

Processed cheese contains roughly the same proportion of nutrients as the cheese from which it has been made. The digestibility of the proteins is increased. No change in the availability of lysine could be detected. Some losses of vitamins B_1, B_2, B_{12}, nicotinic acid, and pantothenic acid occur during the manufacture of processed cheese (Deodhar and Duggal 1981; Lee and Alais 1981).

Whey

During cheese making, a large proportion of a number of milk constituents passes into the whey, which therefore has a relatively high content of whey protein, lactose, minerals, and vitamins. The total global whey production is estimated to be about 80 million tonnes per year, containing more than 500,000 tonnes of high-quality protein. Because of its high nutritional value, various attempts are currently being made to increase its use in human nutrition. As the lactose content of whey is very high, modern technology is used to separate the whey proteins in as concentrated a form as possible. The same methods are used to obtain the proteins from milk. The following milk protein products can be obtained: rennet and acid casein, caseinates, coprecipitates, heat-precipitated whey proteins, and whey protein or milk protein concentrates obtained by ultrafiltration (van der Merwe and Downes 1981; Müller and Kabus 1979).

Depending on the degree of ultrafiltration, the protein in dry-matter content can be increased from 12% in the whey to 70% in the whey protein concentrate. The concentration of lactose in dry matter is reduced from 70 to about 20% and that of the ash from 10 to 4% (Fig. 8.6). The biological value of the proteins in a whey protein concentrate is as high as that of the whey proteins themselves. Therefore, they are particularly suitable for incorporation into special diets, which are thereby enriched with high-quality protein, for example, to baby foods as well as to the diets of sportsmen, children, and elderly people. It should be pointed out again that whey proteins can increase the biological value of vegetable proteins, such as those from wheat, maize, and rice. Whey protein concentrates are especially suitable for the

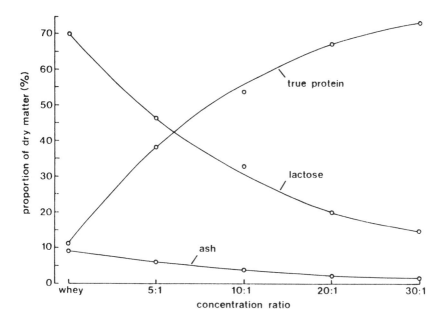

Fig. 8.6. Changes in the concentration of protein, lactose, and minerals of whey during ultrafiltration. Source: Delaney (1976).

protein enrichment of milk products and other foods such as low-fat liquid milk, cultured milk products, quark, processed cheese, baked goods, meat products, noodles, drinks, and confectionaries (Forsum 1979; Renner *et al.* 1981).

Evaporated Milk

Evaporated milk is manufactured by removing water from milk, thereby increasing the proportion of dry matter two- to threefold. Evaporation under low pressure and at the relatively low temperature of about 55°–65°C causes only slight changes in the constituents of milk. Greater changes occur during the subsequent sterilization of the concentrated product. Therefore, in evaporated milk, as in sterilized milk, the whey proteins are almost completely denatured. But the amino acid composition of the proteins in evaporated milk is hardly different from that of the proteins in the starting milk. Lysine losses produced by the whole manufacturing process are about 20%, but there is no significant change in the biological protein value. Losses of vitamins in evaporated milk are very similar to those found in sterilized milk, but vitamin losses in sweetened condensed milk are lower because the sucrose in this milk type acts as a preservative so that a sterilization procedure is not used (Graham 1974; Vitali 1974).

The extent of the changes in the constituents of evaporated milk during storage is mainly influenced by the storage temperature. Losses of vitamins are small, even after several years, if the milk is cold stored. There is no appreciable change in the amino acid composition or the PER value of the proteins after a 12-month storage period. The lead-tin used for soldering the seams of cans does not cause an appreciable rise in the lead content of evaporated milk during storage (Loney and Bassette 1971).

Milk Powder

Since the degree of whey protein denaturation is related to temperature, the mild treatment of spray drying causes little denaturation, whereas roller drying affects the whey proteins much more. The grading of skim milk powders according to heat treatment (low, medium, and high heat) is based on the proportion of undenatured whey protein nitrogen. Normal drying conditions produce only small losses of lysine, that is, up to 5% in spray drying and 3–15% in roller drying. Determinations of PER and NPU have shown that the biological value of the proteins of dried milk is very similar to that of the proteins of the starting milk. Milk powder, especially skim milk powder, has a high protein content of about 36%. The mineral content, particularly that of calcium, is also high, as is that of the vitamins of the B group. Spray drying produces relatively small losses of vitamins B_1, B_{12}, and C, but in roller-dried powders they are considerably higher (Marschke and Houlihan 1980; Renner and Maier 1981).

The quality of the protein is changed only very little when milk powder is properly stored at not too high a temperature and a low relative humidity. Some investigations have revealed a slight reduction in PER values. Lysine losses of only 2% were found after 6 months of storage. Also, the vitamin losses of milk powder during storage are relatively low. In one case, losses of vitamins B_1 and C were 10% after 2 years of storage (Kramer *et al.* 1977; Womack and Holsinger 1979).

REFERENCES

Aicken, K. A. 1974. Polyunsaturated ruminant products. CSIRO Food Res. Quart. *34*, 84–88.

Akesson, B., Johansson, B-M., Svensson, M., and Oeckerman, P-A. 1981. Content of trans-octadecenoic acid in vegetarian and normal diets in Sweden, analyzed by the duplicate portion technique. Am. J. Clin. Nutr. *34*, 2517–2520.

Alm, L. 1981. The effect of fermentation on the biological value of milk proteins evaluated using rats. A study on Swedish fermented milk products. J. Sci. Food Agr. *32*, 1247–1253.

Antila, P., Antila, V., and Kuujo, S. 1979. The determination of vitamin D from the aqueous phase of cows' and human milk. Meijerit. Aikakausk. *37*, 1–22.

Askar, A., and Treptow, H. 1982. Food poisoning. II. Toxic contaminants in raw materials and in processed foods (in German). Alimenta *21*, 3–9.

Auclair, J., and Mocquot, G. 1974. Cultured Milks. Proc. Symp. Milk Prod. Future, 33–36.

Ayebo, A. D., and Shahani, K. M. 1980. Role of cultured dairy products in the diet. Cultured Dairy Prod. J. *15*(4), 21–29.

Banks, W., Clapperton, J. L., and Ferrie, M. E. 1976. Effect of feeding fat to dairy cows receiving a fat-deficient basal diet. II. Fatty acid composition of the milk fat. J. Dairy Res. *43*, 219–227.

Basch, J. J., Jones, S. B., Kalan, E. B., and Wondolowski, M. V. 1974. Distribution of added iron and polyphosphate phosphorus in cows' milk. J. Dairy Sci. *57*, 545–550.

Belikov, V. M., Antonova, T. V., and Bezrikov, M. G. 1981. Effect of heating various proteins on their hydrolysis by proteolytic enzymes (in German). Nahrung *25*, 91–97.

Bianchi-Salvadori, B., Gotti, M., Brughera, F., and Polinelli, U. 1978. Variations in the lactic and bifidus flora in the intestine after administration of yoghurt lactic cultures (in French). Lait *58*, 17–42.

Blanc, B. 1981. Influence of heat treatment on the physiological properties of milk (in German). Kieler Milchw. Forsch. Ber. *33*, 39–58.

Blanc, B. 1982. Biosynthesis of cheese: Basis of its nutritional value (in German). Alimenta *21*, 125–134.

Blanc, B., Hofmann, W., Bosset, J., Graber, H., Liechti, D., and Bovay, E. 1971. Trials with dairy cows fed hay contaminated with Pb from motor car exchaust gases. II. Pb accumulation in blood and udder and its effect on milk secretion (in German). Schweiz. Landw. Forsch. *10*, 206–215.

Brieskorn, C. H. 1972. The effect of preparation and processing on the protein substances in food (in German). Ernaehr. Umschau *19*, 198–202.

Bullerman, L. B. 1981. Public health significance of molds and mycotoxins in fermented dairy products. J. Dairy Sci. *64*, 2439–2452.

Conrad, H. R., and Moxon, A. L. 1979. Transfer of dietary selenium to milk. J. Dairy Sci. *62*, 404–411.

Deissman, R. 1977. Changes in protein fractions of milk during technological processes (in German). Dr. agr. Thesis Univ. Giessen.

Delaney, R. A. M. 1979. Composition, properties and uses of whey protein concentrates. J. Soc. Dairy Technol. *29*, 91–101.

den Hartog, C. 1980. Thinking about the correct nutrition (in German). Ernaehrungsforschung *25*, 65–71.

Deodhar, A. D., and Duggal, K. 1981. Nutritional evaluation of cheese spread powder. J. Food Sci. *46*, 925–929.

de Vuyst, A. Vervack, W., and Foulon, M. 1976. Nonvolatile amines in cheeses (in French). Lait *56*, 414–422.

Dupuis, Y. 1964. Fermented milk and utilization of inorganic constituents. IDF Ann. Bull. *3*, 36–43.

Edwards, S. T., and Sandine, W. E. 1981. Public health significance of amines in cheese. J. Dairy Sci. *64*, 2431–2438.

Ford, J. E., Scott, K. J., and Blair, J. A. 1978. The biological availability of folate in stored ultra-heat-treated milk. Int. Dairy Congr. *E*, 1069–1070.

Forsum, E. 1979. Biological evaluation of wheat supplemented by a whey protein concentrate of whey cheese on growing rats. J. Dairy Sci. *62*, 1207–1210.

Fritsch, R. J., and Klostermeyer, H. 1981. The occurrence of lysinoalanine in foods containing milk protein (in German). Z. Lebensm. Unters. Forsch. *172*, 440–445.

Graham, D. M. 1974. Alteration of nutritive value resulting from processing and fortification of milk and milk products. J. Dairy Sci. 57, 738–745.

Gray, J. I., and Morton, I. D. 1981. Some toxic compounds produced in food by cooking and processing. J. Hum. Nutr. 35, 5–23.

Gregory, M. E. 1975. Water-soluble vitamins in milk and milk products, J. Dairy Res. 42, 197–216.

Hemken, R. W. 1979. Factors that influence the iodine content of milk and meat: A review. J. Anim. Sci. 48, 981–985.

Henderson, S. K., Witchwoot, A., and Nawar, W. W. 1980. The autoxidation of linoleates at elevated temperatures. J. Am. Oil Chem. Soc. 57, 409–413.

Kansal, V. K., and Chaudhary, S. 1982. Biological availability of calcium, phosphorus and magnesium from dairy products. Milchwissenschaft 37, 261–263.

Kessler, H. G., and Horak, P. 1981. Objective evaluation of UHT-milk-heating by standardization of bacteriological and chemical effects (in German). Milchwissenschaft 36, 129–133.

Kiermeier, F., and Waiblinger, W. 1969. Effect of fluorescent lighting on ascorbic acid and riboflavin contents of milk in polyethylene packs (in German). Z. Lebensm. Unters. Forsch. 141, 320–331.

Kirchmeier, O. 1973. Influence of climatic factors on the protein quality of milk (in German). Milchwissenschaft 28, 440–443.

Klein, D., Girard, A-M., Cabarrou, C., and Derby, G. 1980. Presence of volatile nitrosamines in foods (in French). Ann. Nutr. Aliment. 34, 915–928.

Kramer, A., King, R. L., Westhoff, D. C., Olowofoyeku, A. D., and Farquhar, J. W. 1977. Extended storage study of prepared frozen foods containing protein concentrates. J. Food Qual. 1, 305–326.

Kreuder, K., and Renner, E. 1975. Use of encapsulated oil for feeding dairy cows (in German). Ergeb. Landw. Forsch. Univ. Giessen 13, 126–135.

Krusch, U. 1978. Nutritional and physiological aspects of L(+) and D(-)-lactic acid (in German). Kieler Milchw. Forsch. Ber. 30, 341–346.

Lee, B. O., and Alais, C. 1981. Biochemical study of the processing of cheese. III. Changes in free amino acid contents and in digestibility of the proteins in vitro (in French). Lait 61, 140–148.

Lembke, A. 1971. Nutritional evaluation of homogenized milk (in German). Schriftenr. Verb. Grossstaedt. Milchversorg. Betr. 28, 57–59.

Lembke, A. 1976. Stool or intestinal flora — Contribution to the microbiology of the intestinal organs (in German). Milchwissenschaft 31, 199–203.

Loney, B. E., and Bassette, R. 1971. Changes in free fatty acids and lactones in sterile concentrated milk during storage. J. Dairy Sci. 54, 343–348.

Marschke, R. J., and Houlihan, D. B. 1980. Rapid estimation of undenatured whey protein nitrogen in the manufacture of skim milk powder. Aust. J. Dairy Technol. 35, 13–15.

Mendy, F., Brachfogel, N., and Spielman, D. 1981. Use of milk proteins in human nutrition (in French). Rev. Lait. Fr. 400, 37–58.

Monzani, A., Parenti, C., Plessi, M., and Coppini, D. 1981. Nitrates and nitrites in Parmesan cheese (in Italian). Sci. Tec. Latt.-Casear. 32, 1–14.

Moreau, C. 1980. Penicillium roqueforti, its morphology, physiology, use in cheese-making, and mycotoxins (in French). Lait 60, 254–271.

Müller, W., and Kabus, M. 1979. Milk protein for food. I. Some aspects of the use of milk proteins for the protein supply to the population in the German Democratic Republic (in German). Nahrung 23, 263–273.

Olson, W. G., Jorgensen, N. A., Bringe, A. N., Schultz, L. H., and Deluca, H. F. 1974. 25-Hydroxycholecalciferol (25-OH-D₃). III. Effect of dosage on soft tissue integrity and vitamin D activity of tissue and milk from dairy cows. J. Dairy Sci. 57, 677–682.

O'Neil, J. M., Kleyn, D. H., and Hare, L. B. 1979. Consistency and compositional characteristics of commercial yogurts. J. Dairy Sci. 62, 1032–1036.

Porter, J. W. G. 1978. The present nutritional status of milk proteins. J. Soc. Dairy Technol. 31, 199–202.

Reif, G. D., Shahani, K. M., Vakil, J. R., and Crowe, L. K. 1976. Factors affecting B-complex vitamin content of cottage cheese. J. Dairy Sci. 59, 410–415.

Reimerdes, E. H., and Diekmann, F. W. 1979. Chemical, technological and biochemical aspects of UHT milk production (in German). Molkereitechnik 43, 5–14.

Renner, E. 1979. Nutritional and biochemical characteristics of UHT milk, Proc. Int. Conf. UHT Processing, Raleigh, NC, 21–52.

Renner, E. 1981. Nutritive value of differently packaged pasteurized milk (in German). Deut. Milchwirtsch. 32, 853–854.

Renner, E. 1983. Milk and Dairy Products in Human Nutrition. Volkswirtsch. Verlag, Munich.

Renner, E., and Dorguth, H. 1980. Study of protein quality of UHT milk (in German). Deut. Milchwirtsch. 31, 505–508.

Renner, E., and Hahn, C. 1978. Influence of feeding protected fodder oil on the quality of milk fat. I. Consistency of milk fat (in German). Milchwissenschaft 33, 422–424.

Renner, E., and Hahn, C. 1979. Influence of feeding protected fodder oil on the quality of milk fat. II. Oxidation stability and sensory quality (in German). Milchwissenschaft 34, 11–13.

Renner, E., and Kosmack, U. 1977. Genetic aspects of the minerals content of milk (in German). Zuechtungskunde 49, 99–109.

Renner, E., and Maier, I. 1981. Study of protein value of dried skim milk (in German). Deut. Molkerei-Ztg. 102, 588–589.

Renner, E., and Müller, U. 1981. Study of buttermilk quality (in German). Deut. Milchwirtsch. 32, 1179–1182.

Renner, E., and Yoon, Y. C. 1982. Investigations on isomeric unsaturated fatty acids in edible fats (in German). Milchwissenschaft 37, 264–266, 408–411.

Renner, E., Huth, F. W., and Klobasa, F. 1971. Effect of changeover from stall feeding to pasturing of dairy cows on fat content and fatty acid composition of milk (in German). Wirtschaftseigene Futter 17, 218–233.

Renner, E., Bressanello, M. C. B. De, Bacchetta, R., Castelao, E., Gonzalez, R., and Sanchez, H. 1982. Fortification of vegetable foods with whey protein concentrates (in French). Lait 62, 615–623.

Roy, D. D. 1981. Proteolysis of milk from different species by trypsin in vitro. Milchwissenschaft 36, 360–362.

Schwarz, F. J., and Kirchgessner, M. 1978. Copper and zinc in milk and plasma of cows on rations highly supplemented with copper (in German). Z. Lebensm. Unters. Forsch. 166, 5–8.

Schwarz, F. J., and Kirchgessner, M. 1979. Trace elements contents of cows' milk and their changes through feeding (in German). Deut. Molkerei-Ztg. 100, 959–960.

Sieber, R., Ruest, P., and Blanc, B. 1980. Comparison of the long-term physiological effects of raw, pasteurized and UHT milks in rat diets (in German). Alimenta 19, Spec. Issue, 49–56.

Snoeren, T. H. M., and Both, P. 1981. Proteolysis during the storage of UHT-sterilized whole milk. 2. Experiments with milk heated by the indirect system for 4 s at 142°C. Neth. Milk Dairy J. 35, 113–119.

van der Merwe, N. L., and Downes, T. E. H. 1981. Denaturization and recovery of protein from cheese whey. S. Afr. J. Dairy Technol. 13, 17–20.

Vitali, G. 1974. Nutritive value of dried milk (in Italian). Riv. Ind. Aliment. 13, 82–86.

Womack, M., and Holsinger, V. H. 1979. Protein quality of stored dry skim milk with standard and lysin-limiting diets. J. Dairy Sci. *62*, 855–860.

Zadow, J. G. 1980. UHT milk — Standards and quality assurance. Aust. J. Dairy Technol. *35*, 140–144.

Zerfiridis, G. K., and Manolkidis, K. S. 1981. Contents of nitrates and nitrites in some Greek and imported cheeses. J. Food Pro. *44*, 576–579.

Effects of
Agricultural Practices
on Poultry and Eggs

Glenn W. Froning

POULTRY MEAT

General Composition

Poultry meat is an excellent source of many of the nutrients needed in our diets. It has high-quality protein, is low in fat, and is easily digested (Mountney 1976).

Recently, Posati (1979) updated the data on nutritive properties of poultry meat. Table 9.1 presents the proximate composition of chicken and turkey skin and meat without skin. Both chicken and turkey meat are low in fat content. Skin is high in fat content and low in protein content. The predominant protein found in skin is collagen, which is a low-quality protein. White meat is generally highest in protein content and lowest in fat content as compared to dark meat and skin. Since poultry today is bred to have more breast (white) meat, the birds today are likely more nutritious than their counterparts many years ago. Scott (1956) reported that poultry meat contains high-quality protein with all of the essential amino acids needed in our diets.

Poultry meat is high in unsaturated fatty acids and low in cholesterol content (Table 9.2). Generally, turkey white meat contains the lowest level of cholesterol.

Poultry meat is a good source of niacin and a moderately good source of riboflavin and thiamin (Mountney 1976). Poultry livers are also an excellent source of vitamin A. With respect to minerals, poultry meat contains many of the minerals needed in our diets, including potassium, magnesium, calcium, iron, and phosphorus. Poultry also is excellent for those individuals on low-sodium diets.

EFFECT OF PRODUCTION FACTORS

Poultry Diet

Summers *et al.* (1965) reviewed previous work and indicated that dietary changes could alter the ratio of moisture:fat in chicken carcasses.

Table 9.1. Proximate Composition (%) of Edible Portion of Roasted Poultry Meat

	Water	Protein	Total lipid	Ash	Caloric value (Kcal)
Chicken broiler					
Skin	40.29	20.36	40.68	0.50	454
White meat without skin	64.76	30.91	4.51	1.02	173
Dark meat without skin	63.06	27.37	9.73	1.02	205
Turkey, young hens					
Skin	35.53	19.03	44.45	0.63	482
White meat without skin	65.74	29.89	3.74	1.10	161
Dark meat without skin	62.74	28.42	7.79	1.02	192
Turkey, young toms					
Skin	41.54	20.14	37.25	0.67	422
White meat without skin	66.56	29.88	2.92	1.05	154
Dark meat without skin	63.07	28.68	6.98	1.01	185

Source: Posati (1979).

Table 9.2. Lipid Composition (%) of Edible Portion of Roasted Poultry Meat

	Chicken white meat, no skin	Broiler meat		Turkey, white meat	Young hens	
		Dark meat	Skin		Dark meat	Skin
Total fatty acids						
Saturated	1.27	2.66	11.42	1.19	2.61	11.59
Monounsaturated	1.54	3.56	17.03	0.66	1.77	18.94
Polyunsaturated	0.98	2.26	8.57	1.00	2.33	10.18
Cholesterol, mg/100 g	85	93	83	68	80	106

Source: Posati (1979).

Their work further showed that protein content was not affected by diet. Past work has shown that increased dietary fat is generally deposited in skin and adipose tissue, with muscle tissue being little affected (Dansky and Hill 1952; Essary and Dawson 1965).

Several workers have shown that dietary fat affects fatty acid composition of whole carcass lipid, neutral lipid, and phospholipid in chicken muscle (Marion and Woodroof 1963, Marion 1965; Marion et al. 1967; Jen et al. 1971; Schuler and Essary 1971; Salmon 1969). They observed that fatty acid composition of turkey meat was similar to that of the dietary fat. Salmon and O'Neil (1971) further noted that dietary fat influenced turkey carcass fat score, carcass composition, and cooking losses.

Marion et al. (1967) observed typical changes in fatty acid composition due to diet, with the neutral lipid fraction of chicken meat showing the most pronounced changes in the C_{16} and C_{18} fatty acids (Table 9.3). Dietary soybean oil greatly increased the level of 18:2 fatty acids in the neutral lipid fraction as compared to the other dietary treatments.

Table 9.3. Effect of Diet on Neutral Lipid Fatty Acids in Chicken Meat

Fatty acid[a]	Added fat (%), 16% protein[b]					Added fat (%), 24% protein[b]				
	None	CO	BT	SO	MO	None	CO	BT	SO	MO
10:0	0.0	2.9	0.0	0.0	0.0	0.0	2.0	0.0	0.0	0.0
12:0	0.0	9.7	0.0	0.0	0.0	0.0	13.9	0.0	0.0	0.0
14:0	0.7	6.2	1.8	0.6	2.7	0.9	9.2	2.4	0.6	2.6
16:0	25.7	20.7	23.4	17.8	25.6	26 0	20.3	25.2	18.1	25.7
16:1	6.8	4.5	5.3	2.8	6.8	4.4	3.3	4.8	2.4	5.7
18:0	7.4	6.3	9.1	6.8	7.8	9.4	7.2	11.5	7.8	10.9
18:1	38.5	30.9	39.3	26.0	33.1	34.4	23.8	35.1	22.2	27.4
18:2	19.4	17.1	19.4	44.1	18.3	22.8	17.2	18.3	45.9	18.4
18:3	0.5	0.4	0.6	0.4	1.0	0.8	0.7	0.9	0.7	1.3
18:4	0.0	0.0	0.0	0.0	0.5	0.0	0.0	0.0	0.0	1.5
20:4	1.1	1.9	0.8	1.4	0.4	1.5	1.2	1.6	2.0	2.4
20:5	0.0	0.0	0.1	0.0	1.1	0.0	0.0	0.2	0.0	1.5
24:1	0.0	0.0	0.2	0.0	1.3	0.0	0.0	0.0	0.0	1.7
22:5	0.0	0.0	0.0	0.0	0.5	0.0	0.0	0.0	0.0	0.3
22:6	0.0	0.0	0.0	0.0	0.7	0.0	0.0	0.0	0.0	0.5

Source: Marion et al. (1967).

[a] Fatty acid denoted by carbon chain length and number of double bonds. Each fatty acid expressed as a percentage of total fatty acids.

[b] CO, coconut oil; BT, beef tallow; SO, safflower oil; MO, menhaden oil.

Menhaden oil in the diet increased the levels of 20:5, 24:1, 22:5, and 22:6 in the neutral lipid fraction. Within the phospholipid fraction of chicken meat, Marion et al. (1967) further observed that the most marked difference due to diet was indicated in the substitution of 20:5 and 22:6 for 20:4 fatty acids when menhaden oil was fed. Thus, these studies indicate that the amount of saturated or unsaturated fatty acids in the meat may be markedly influenced by dietary fat.

Abdominal fat in chicken broilers has received major emphasis. There have been increased consumer complaints related to the high amount of abdominal fat in broilers. Both nutritional and genetic factors have been found to be involved in fat deposition (Cherry et al. 1978). Deaton et al. (1981) reported that higher abdominal fat was noted in birds on diets with increased dietary animal fat. Coon et al. (1981) and Kubena et al. (1974A) also observed that as dietary energy increases the quantity of abdominal fat increases. Thus, these studies generally indicate that abdominal fat could be decreased by reducing dietary energy intake, although body weights were somewhat lower in the birds receiving less dietary energy.

Wilson et al. (1983) determined the effectiveness of thyroactive iodinated casein (protamine) in preventing fat deposition in broilers. A protamine level of 100 mg/kg in the feed decreased fat deposition without decreasing body weight. Higher levels of protamine in the diet progressively reduced fat deposition but also induced some loss of body weight. Protamine feeding also resulted in poorer feed conversion, greater shrink and dressing losses, and, at the highest levels, increased mortality, lower carcass grade, and lower conformation scores. Nevertheless, these authors felt that protamine has potential as a tool in reducing excess fat in broilers.

In another study, Maurice and Deodato (1982) observed that 50–100 mM sodium chloride solutions provided in the drinking water, are effective in reducing abdominal fat. This aspect may warrant further study to ascertain its effectiveness.

Sheldon (1983) noted that dietary dl-tocopherol increased tissue tocopherol levels in turkey meat. As dietary levels of tocopherol increased, there were corresponding increases in tocopherol deposition for breast and thigh meat, but not for skin and fat. Dietary tocopherol also decreased fat oxidation in stored meat, as measured by thiobarbituric acid (TBA) values.

Age

Scott (1956) reported that fat content of turkey meat increases and moisture content decreases with advancing age of the bird, especially between the period marking the first stage of maturity and the completely mature stage.

Kubena et al. (1972) reported that protein and fat content of chicken broiler meat increased and moisture content decreased with age of the birds. In another study by Kubena et al. (1974B), there was no significant difference in the quantity of abdominal fat in broilers slaughtered at 7, 8, or 9 weeks of age when expressed as a percentage of body weight. In general, females had a larger percentage of abdominal fat. Posati (1979) updated the USDA handbook and reported that fat content of both chicken and turkey meat increased with advancing age of the bird. Sonaiya and Benyi (1983), analyzed 12- to 16-week-old chicken broilers and reported that the proportion of fat in the body is heavily influenced by body weight and not age. They indicated that fat estimation can be accomplished by perintestinal fat thickness.

Breed and Strain

The poultry industry has made significant improvements in increased efficiency through genetic selection. Today we are marketing turkeys and chickens at a much younger age than we did 25 years ago. Also, the birds today are bred to have more breast meat. Breast meat is preferred by most consumers and is also lower in fat than dark meat.

Several workers have investigated the effect of breed and strain on body composition. Edwards and Denman (1975) studied carcass composition of various breeds. Significant differences in the quantity of moisture, protein, total lipid, and ash present in the total carcass were found among certain breeds. The light Brahma contained the largest amounts of total lipid, 10.4%, followed by White Plymouth Rock, 10.2; Black Jersey Giant, 9.5; Single Comb White Leghorn, 8.8; and Dark Cornish, 8.6. Significant differences in fatty acid composition were noted among breeds, but these differences were not considered to be of major importance.

Genetists have studied the possibility of reducing abdominal fat in chicken broilers through genetic selection (Aman and Becker 1981; Ren-Yu Tzeng and Becker 1981). These studies generally indicate that significant progress in reducing abdominal fat in chicken broilers is feasible through genetic selection. Becker and Spencer (cited in Tzeng and Becker 1981) have estimated that the poultry industry sustained a loss of $92 million in 1978 while consumers lost $158 million in the same year due to abdominal fat. The industry now is endeavoring to lower abdominal fat through a two-pronged approach, using genetic selection and modifying diets fed to birds.

EFFECT OF PROCESSING AND STORAGE

Poultry consumption has dramatically increased during the past 20 years. Much of this increased consumption may be attributed to the further processing of poultry products. Today more than 50% of the turkey products marketed are in the form of further processed items such as turkey roasts, turkey hams, turkey frankfurters, and numerous other products. The same trend has occurred in the marketing of chicken meat. The consumer can now purchase breaded chicken breast patties, chicken nuggets, precooked and battered chicken, canned chicken, and chicken frankfurters as examples of the many products available.

Posati (1979) has presented data on the composition of these processed products (Table 9.4). Composition of these products varies, depending on ingredients and processing procedures. For example, a battered and fried turkey pattie picks up considerable fat from the deep-fat frying process. Further, the added carbohydrate (flour, etc.) further dilutes the other components in the meat. Salt also raises the ash content. Sodium intake has been a concern of many consumers and processors. There have been attempts to replace sodium chloride with other salts such as potassium. However, consumers generally object to these alternative salts because of their adverse influence on the flavor and functional properties of processed meat products.

Since deep-fat fried poultry products have become of increased importance, their composition has received emphasis by some workers. Heath et al. (1971) reviewed some of the recent work in this area and

Table 9.4.   Proximate Composition (%) of Various Processed Poultry Products

	Moisture	Protein	Total lipid	Carbohydrate	Ash
Boned canned chicken with broth	68.65	21.77	7.95	0.0	1.81
Chicken frankfurter	57.53	12.93	19.48	6.79	3.28
Chicken roll	68.60	19.53	7.38	2.45	2.05
Turkey ham	71.38	18.93	5.08	0.37	4.23
Turkey pastrami	70.64	18.36	6.21	1.66	3.13
Turkey roll, light	71.55	18.70	7.22	0.53	2.00
Turkey pattie, breaded, battered, fried	49.70	14.00	18.00	15.70	2.60

Source: Posati (1979).

studied the effect of cooking oil, batter recipe, and cooking time on the fatty acid composition of batter-coated chicken parts. Cooking oils were absorbed into and/or through the batter and into the tissue during deep-fat frying, as evidenced by changes in fatty acid composition. The tissue content of both linoleic and linolenic acids were found to be affected by the cooking oil. Cottonseed and mixed oils contributed more saturated fatty acids than did corn and peanut oils. Corn oil contributed less stearic and oleic acids than peanut but more linoleic and linolenic acids. The increase of cooking time resulted in an increased content of myristic, palmitic, oleic, and linoleic acids in the tissue.

Sheldon *et al.* (1983) studied the effect of tumbling turkey meat in brine on the retention of thiamin, riboflavin, and niacin. Niacin concentration in the muscle tissue was significantly lowered by tumbling. Although their results indicated a loss of niacin from the muscle tissue to the exudate, there was no indication of destruction of the vitamin in the exudate.

With respect to storage, Wladyka and Dawson (1968) reported larger quantities of essential amino acids in the drip from frozen light meat than that observed from dark meat after storage for 30 or 90 days. The concentration of each amino acid, as a percentage of total amino acids, was similar in meat and drip.

EFFECT OF MANAGEMENT SYSTEMS

Management systems have been changing through the years and there has been increasing interest relative to their influence on carcass composition. Deaton *et al.* (1974) compared broilers raised in cages versus those reared in litter-floor pens. Results indicated that more abdominal fat and ether extract percentage of body weight were obtained from broilers reared in cages as compared to birds reared in litter-floor pens. Jeffrey and Britt (1941) also found that chickens maintained for egg production in cages have more fat than those maintained on the floor.

Kubena *et al.* (1974B) and Kubena *et al.* (1972) studied the effect of environmental rearing temperature on carcass composition. Their studies indicated that higher rearing temperatures increased the percentage of abdominal fat and total carcass fat content. Thus, broilers produced in the cool months would likely be more lean than those produced during the hot summer months.

COMPOSITION OF MECHANICALLY DEBONED POULTRY MEAT

Mechanical deboning of poultry meat results in a finely ground paste-like product (Froning 1981). The process affects the proximate composition of the final product. Considerable quantities of lipid and heme components are released from the bone marrow and thereby accumulate in the mechanically separated meat product. Components from the bone marrow dilute the protein fraction and increase the lipid fraction in the resultant mechanically deboned meat product.

Froning (1981) reviewed the proximate composition data of mechanically deboned poultry meat (Table 9.5). He indicated considerable variability in the composition of mechanically deboned poultry meat, which may be attributed to age of the bird, bone:meat ratio, cutting methods, skin content, and possible protein denaturation during the deboning process.

Protein quality, as measured by protein efficiency ratio (PER) using the rat method and computed technique (C-PER), of mechanically deboned poultry meat has been reported to be comparable to hand deboned sources (Babji *et al.* 1980; Mott *et al.* 1982). Babji *et al.* (1980) reported that mechanically deboned turkey meat has a higher PER and C-PER than did mechanically deboned chicken meat or cooked mechanically deboned fowl meat.

Table 9.5. Composition (%) of Mechanically Deboned Poultry Meat from Different Sources

Source	Protein	Moisture	Fat
Chicken backs and necks	14.5	66.6	17.6
Backs	13.2	62.4	21.2
Skinless backs	15.3	76.7	7.9
Turkey frame	12.8	70.7	14.4
Spent layers	13.9	65.1	18.3

Source: Froning (1981).

Ang and Hamm (1982) studied the vitamin, mineral, and cholesterol contents of mechanically deboned broiler meat. Cholesterol content was about 14% higher in mechanically deboned broiler meat as compared to the hand deboned counterpart. Calcium content of mechanically deboned broiler meat was higher than the hand deboned counterpart. Froning (1981) reported that the increased calcium found in mechanically deboned poultry meat would likely be beneficial to many individuals. Essary (1979) and Murphy *et al.* (1979) analyzed several minerals from various types of mechanically deboned poultry. They concluded that none of the minerals present in mechanically deboned poultry meat presented any health hazard.

Fluorine content of mechanically deboned poultry meat has been a concern of some consumers. Froning (1981) and Klose (1979) reported that the fluorine content of mechanically deboned young chicken or turkey meat was quite similar to that noted in hand deboned sources. Mechanically deboned fowl meat, however, may have a higher quantity of fluorine, which is due to the cumulative effect of the increased age of the bird.

Overall, mechanically deboned poultry meat is quite comparable to the hand deboned poultry meat sources in many aspects of nutritional quality. It is an economical source of high-quality protein that can be obtained from underutilized poultry parts.

EFFECT OF COOKING

Composition of food products as affected by cooking is important to the consumer: raw poultry meat is an excellent source of many nutrients, but are these nutrients lost during the cooking process? This aspect has received the attention of several researchers.

Singh and Essary (1971) indicated that cooked chicken broiler meat showed lower niacin and thiamin content than that found in uncooked muscles. Riboflavin was not affected by cooking. Lee *et al.* (1981) also noted that the thiamin content of oven-baked chicken was significantly lower than that observed from the raw meat. Hall and Lin (1981) reported that broilers cooked in a microwave oven retained more thiamin than broilers cooked in an electric oven. There was no difference in thiamin retention between broilers cooked in the microwave oven at 800 and 1600 W. Broilers cooked in an electric oven at 204°C retained more thiamin than broilers cooked at 121°C. In another study, Gilbert *et al.* (1981) observed that spent hen meat, which was boiled, contained less thiamin than meat that was pressure cooked or roasted.

Unklesbay *et al.* (1983) compared nutrient retention in turkey breast roasts which were heat-processed by infrared and convection ovens.

The analyses included proximate analyses, thiamin, riboflavin, 7 fatty acids, 18 amino acids, ammonia, sodium, phosphorus, and iron. There were few significant differences in nutrient retention when comparing these cooking methods. After convection heating of turkey breasts, arachidonic acid was significantly higher than that obtained after infrared heating.

Sheldon *et al.* (1980) studied the effect of various end-point cooking temperatures (74°, 79°, 85°, and 91°C) for turkey meat on protein quality. The cooked meat was fed to mice and growth rates determined. Average weights of mice were greatest when fed turkey meat roasted to an internal temperature of 79° and 85°C. Amino acid levels were highest in turkey meat roasted to an end-point temperature of 79°C.

Thus, with the exception of possibly thiamin, there is very little loss of any essential nutrients from cooking of poultry meat.

EGGS

General Composition

Nutrient composition of eggs has been studied by several workers and the composition of eggs has been well defined. Everson and Souders (1957) reviewed and summarized much of the earlier work on egg composition and factors influencing the nutrient makeup of the egg. More recently, Cotterill *et al.* (1977) reevaluated nutrient composition of shell eggs (Table 9.6).

Eggs are an excellent source of high-quality protein. Eggs are used as a standard for measuring the protein quality of other foods. The protein efficiency ratio for whole egg is approximately 3.2, as compared to whole corn at 1.4 or nonfat dry milk at 2.7 (Hsu *et al.* 1978).

Lipids are concentrated in the yolk. Eggs are high in unsaturated fatty acids. Cotterill *et al.* (1977) reported that 62% of the total fatty acids are unsaturated with 15% of the total being polyunsaturated. Linoleic accounted for 87% of the polyunsaturated fatty acid. Everson and Souders (1957) reported a 2:1 ratio of unsaturated to saturated fatty acids in whole eggs.

The egg is known to be high in cholesterol (Everson and Souders 1957; Cotterill *et al.* 1977). The dietary cholesterol issue and its relationship to heart disease has been discussed for years and has become quite controversial.

Eggs contain all of the vitamins needed in our diets, with the exception of vitamin C. The protein avidin, found in egg white, binds biotin in raw eggs, thereby rendering the biotin unavailable nutritionally (Everson and Souders 1957). Test animals that have eaten raw egg white have developed a biotin deficiency. Cooking eggs releases biotin from the avidin–biotin complex, thereby making biotin available

Table 9.6. Nutrient Composition of Fresh Shell Eggs per 100 g

	Whole	White	Yolk
Gross composition			
Solids (g)	25.28	10.72	50.78
Protein	12.03	9.41	16.16
Total lipids (g)	12.30	—	34.10
Saturated	4.50	—	11.73
Monosaturated	5.36	—	14.51
Polyunsaturated	1.69	—	4.48
Cholesterol	0.49	—	1.37
Calories (C)	183	56	401
Ash	0.98	0.69	1.65
Vitamins			
A (IU)	221	—	796
D (IU)	36.2	—	169.8
E (mg)	1.01	—	3.92
B_{12} (μg)	1.08	.02	3.16
Biotin (μg)	18.30	5.05	40.78
Choline (mg)	824	1.25	1109
Folic acid (mg)	0.029	0.001	0.067
Inositol (mg)	15.47	3.73	33.97
Niacin (mg)	0.089	0.095	0.059
Pantothenic acid (mg)	1.376	0.127	4.904
Pyridoxine (mg)	0.137	0.005	0.349
Riboflavin (mg)	0.320	0.253	0.457
Thiamin (mg)	0.089	0.003	0.253
Minerals (mg)			
Calcium	58.5	8.6	136.4
Chlorine	172.1	175.5	161.8
Copper	0.062	0.023	0.132
Iodine	0.072	0.007	0.167
Iron	2.25	0.011	5.92
Magnesium	12.41	12.44	12.35
Manganese	0.041	0.006	0.113
Phosphorus	237.9	14.26	607.3
Potassium	138.0	147.2	110.1
Sodium	139.1	183.4	60.7
Sulfur	165.3	158.4	165.5
Zinc	1.50	0.009	3.76

Source: Cotterill *et al.* (1977).

nutritionally. Most diets contain an abundance of biotin. Thus, it is quite unlikely that an individual would develop a biotin deficiency from consuming raw eggs.

Therefore, eggs are one of nature's most perfect foods, containing most of the nutrients needed in our diets. Further, they are low in calories and are highly digestible.

Erroneous Information on Egg Composition

Occasionally, promotors will make invalid claims concerning the nutritional attributes of eggs.

Eggs from Araucana (a South American breed of chicken) hens have been sometimes advertised as having little or no cholesterol. Cunningham (1977) collected eggs from Araucana hens at several different places throughout the midwest and compared their composition to eggs from commercial strains commonly used in the United States. There were no differences observed in proximate composition. The cholesterol content of Araucana egg yolks was observed to be similar to that found from egg yolks of White Leghorn hens.

Another common fallacy perpetuated by some food stores and the popular press is that fertile eggs are more nutritious than infertile eggs. There is no research to substantiate this claim according to Walczak (1974). It has been stated that fertile eggs are lower in cholesterol. Spencer *et al.* (1978) found that fertile eggs were not lower in cholesterol content than infertile eggs. Furthermore, fertile eggs deteriorate much more rapidly than infertile eggs in the marketplace.

Some consumers wrongly feel that brown shell eggs are more nutritious than white shell eggs, or vice versa. Again, there are no reported differences in the composition of white and brown shell eggs.

So-called organic eggs are often merchandized as being more nutritious than commercially produced eggs. Organic eggs are produced from hens which are allowed to range outside. In actuality, eggs from hens raised outdoors may be exposed to more pesticides and herbicides than those birds under environmentally controlled housing. Further, birds on range will have a varied diet, likely not as well balanced as that of hens in confined housing. Thus, organic eggs could possibly not be as uniform in composition as eggs produced from commercial hens and definitely would not be superior to commercially produced eggs.

EFFECT OF PRODUCTION FACTORS

Diet of Hen

Diet of the hen has been observed to markedly affect several nutrients in the egg, as reviewed by Everson and Souders (1957). Total water, calories, protein, fat, and carbohydrates in the egg are not affected by the diet of the hen. However, virtually all of the vitamins may be increased substantially in the egg by feeding a higher level of vitamins in the hen's diet. Tuite and Austic (1974) found that high levels of dietary vitamin B_{12} exerted a striking negative effect on riboflavin concentrations in egg yolk. Also, certain minerals in the egg, including iodine, fluorine, and manganese may be influenced by the diet of the hen.

Latshaw and Osman (1975) observed dietary selenium will increase the selenium content in eggs. Selenium content of feedstuffs may vary from different areas of the country.

Numerous studies have endeavored to reduce the cholesterol content of the egg through dietary means. Clarenburg *et al.* (1971) reduced egg yolk cholesterol by feeding the hen 2–4% sitosterol. Their work indicated that cholesterol was replaced by sitosterol in the egg. They postulated that the simultaneous presence of sitosterol may depress intestinal absorption of cholesterol in human diets. Singh *et al.* (1972) fed two azaterol compounds, 20,25-diazacholesterol and U-22,593 A (Upjohn Company). These drugs induced accumulation of desmosterol in the blood and egg yolk at the expense of cholesterol. Egg production and egg size were reduced for birds receiving these two drugs, suggesting that they interfered with the estrogen synthesis of cholesterol. These data indicate that sterol composition of eggs can be altered. Further research is needed to ascertain whether this approach is economically feasible. Turk and Barnett (1972) found that feeding oat hulls and pectin in wheat diets reduced egg yolk cholesterol, but there was also a decrease in feed efficiency and egg size. Alfalfa in corn–soy rations was also effective in reducing egg yolk cholesterol. Apparently, increased fiber in the diet of the hen reduces absorption of cholesterol.

Fatty acid content of egg yolk has been observed by several workers to be influenced by the dietary fat (Cruickshank *et al.* 1939; Reiser 1950; Fisher *et al.* 1957). Chung *et al.* (1964) reported that corn oil or soybean oil in the diet of laying hens increased linoleic acid and decreased oleic acid in egg yolk. In contrast, dietary hydrogenated coconut oil increased short-chain fatty acids (lauric, myristic, and myristoleic acids) in egg yolk.

Pankey and Stadelman (1969) studied fatty acid composition of eggs from laying pullets that were fed a low-fat semipurified diet or a low-fat diet supplemented with 10% vegetable oil (corn, soybean, olive, safflower, or hydrogenated coconut oil) (Table 9.7). Corn, soybean, and safflower oil increased linoleic acid at the expense of oleic acid. Olive oil increased the oleic acid content of egg yolk, while hydrogenated coconut oil increased lauric, myristic, and myristoleic acids. The fatty acid composition of the fractions of the lipoprotein was influenced by the dietary fats and varied between fractions.

Sim and Bragg (1978) fed basal diets containing either hydrogenated coconut oil (HCO) or safflower oil (SFO), with or without supplemental cholesterol (CH), soysterols (ST), or a combination of both (Table 9.8). They noted that both dietary cholesterol and soysterols altered the fatty acid composition of egg yolk lipids by increasing oleic acid and decreasing palmitic and/or stearic acids. These changes were observed to be significantly greater upon feeding cholesterol than soysterols. However, the simultaneous feeding of cholesterol with soysterols exerted

Table 9.7. Average Fatty Acid Composition of Total Yolk Lipid of Chicken Fed for Days on Experimental Rations[a]

Ration	Fatty acid[b] (%)								
	12:0	14:0	14:1	16:0	16:1	18:0	18:1	18:2	20:4
LF	—	0.95	—	25.05	4.73	8.48	55.26	4.84	1.04
SO	—	0.38–	—	22.33	3.02–	7.98	40.64–	22.29+	2.34
HCO	1.04	5.93+	1.66	25.76	5.84	8.37	45.92–	4.95	0.77
CO	—	0.32–	—	23.51	2.79–	6.77	42.70–	21.13+	2.03
OO	—	0.24–	—	22.16–	3.94	4.86	58.13+	9.74	0.92
SFO	—	0.20–	—	23.55	2.38	8.60	37.15–	27.03+	1.10

Source: Pankey and Stadelman (1969).
[a] LF, low fat; SO, soybean oil; HCO, hydrogenated coconut oil; CO, corn oil; OO, olive oil; SFO, safflower oil ration; (+), significant increase, (–), significant decrease in this value as compared to the low fat ration ($p < .05$).
[b] Chain length:double bonds.

the least effect on fatty acid composition. These authors postulated that laying hens were stimulated to increase fatty acid synthesis, mainly from palmitic or stearic acid, when large amounts of exogenous cholesterol was fed.

Age of the Hen

Nutritive properties of the egg do change with the age of the hen. These changes are generally related to the increasing egg size as the hen becomes older. Cunningham et al. (1960) reported that egg weight varied markedly, tending to be larger in the spring and smaller in the summer. The relative amount of albumen to yolk per egg was not

Table 9.8. Effect of Dietary Oil, Cholesterol, and Soysterols on Fatty-Acid Composition of Egg Yolk Lipids[a]

Treatments	Fatty acids[b] (%)						
	12:0	14:0	16:0	16:1	18:0	18:1	18:2
HCO	0.9	4.2	22.8ab	3.9c	9.6bc	49.5c	7.9a
HCO + CH	0.8	3.6	22.9ab	4.2cd	8.0ab	50.1c	9.3b
HCO + ST	1.1	4.0	22.5ab	5.0e	9.6a	49.7c	9.0b
HCO + CH + ST	1.4	4.0	24.3b	4.8de	7.2a	42.0b	11.2c
SFO	—	0.3	33.0c	2.1a	9.9a	32.8a	20.8d
SFO + CH	—	0.6	19.9a	2.8b	9.5bc	42.5b	24.1e
SFO + ST	—	0.5	24.5b	2.6a	9.9c	35.0a	27.9g
SFO + CH + ST	—	0.5	21.3ab	3.0b	9.2bc	39.2b	26.3f

Source: Sim and Bragg (1978).
[a] Means within column followed by same letters are not significant at the 1% level of probability.
[b] Carbon chain length:number of double bonds.

influenced by the seasons of the year, but as the birds advanced in age the percentage of yolk increased. The percentage of total solids in albumen declined steadily with advancing age of the bird. The yield of albumen solids tended to be higher during March and April and was greater in eggs produced by older hens.

Fletcher *et al.* (1981) observed that as a layer flock increases in age, egg weight, dry shell weight, deformation, and percentage of yolk increases while the percentages of shell, albumen, and albumen solids decreases. Their work indicated that these differences would result in an approximately 2% increase in dry yolk solids by using eggs from older hens.

Marion *et al.* (1966) studied changes in egg lipids with advancing age of the hen and observed that all fatty acids were significantly influenced by age of the hen. Generally, saturated fatty acids (14:0, 16:0, and 18:0) and arachidonic acid (20:4) decreased with age while unsaturated fatty acids (oleic acid and linoleic) increased with advancing age of the hen. Bair and Marion (1978) further noted a lower cholesterol content of eggs from older hens.

Tolan *et al.* (1974) observed an upward trend in riboflavin content of eggs from older hens. Trends in folic acid and vitamin B_{12} content varied throughout the year. It was postulated that the intake of these vitamins over the year may vary because of the large number of factors involved in feed intake.

Breed, Strain, and Specie

Several researchers have reported differences in composition of eggs attributed to breed, strain, or specie. Cotterill and Winter (1954) indicated strain variation with respect to total solids and total protein in eggs. May and Stadelman (1960) also showed that strain of the hen significantly influenced moisture percentage, protein of fresh egg, and protein of dry egg (Table 9.9). Lipid and fatty acid composition has been shown to be influenced by both breed and strain of the bird (Edwards 1964; Marion *et al.* 1965, 1966).

Table 9.9. Means of Egg Components for Five Strains

Variable	Strain				
	A	11	21	22	23
Egg weight	62.2	61.1	60.1	59.6	60.8
Contents weight	54.8	53.5	53.1	52.9	53.6
Percentage water	72.9	73.0	72.7	73.5	74.4
Percentage protein (fresh)	13.2	12.8	12.9	13.2	12.7
Percentage protein (dry)	48.8	47.6	47.3	50.1	49.8

Source: May and Stadelman (1960).

Since cholesterol content of eggs has been an important concern, the relationship to strain and breed has received emphasis. Turk and Barnett (1971) observed that egg production strains had a lower yolk cholesterol content than broiler strains. Washburn and Nix (1974) observed a similar relationship when studying the genetic basis of yolk cholesterol in two randomly bred populations. These studies generally indicate a negative relationship between egg production and yolk cholesterol level.

Bair and Marion (1978) studied yolk cholesterol of various avian species. Species listed in increasing concentrations of cholesterol per gram of yolk were guinea fowl, chicken, pheasant, quail, turkey, duck, goose, and dove, with an overall range of 12.77–21.99 mg/g. Significant differences in cholesterol concentrations also were found between domestic and wild genetic groups for turkeys and ducks. They also compared eggs from 7 inbred lines of chickens and observed significant differences in yolk cholesterol.

These studies generally indicate that some progress could be made in lowering yolk cholesterol through genetic selection. The effort, however, would likely be expensive (Bair and Marion 1978).

Management Systems

Tolan *et al.* (1974) investigated the nutrient content of eggs from hens in battery, deep-litter, and range management systems used in commercial operations. Free range eggs contained significantly more vitamin B_{12} than eggs from deep-litter or battery systems and significantly more folic acid than eggs from battery systems. Eggs from battery management systems were observed to have a higher calcium content than eggs from either deep-litter or free range birds. Eggs from deep-litter management systems were noted to be significantly higher in iron than eggs from the other two systems. Although these differences in nutrients among management systems were significant, they are not likely to be important to the average consumer.

EFFECT OF PROCESSING AND STORAGE

Everson and Souders (1957) reviewed the effect of processing and storage on egg composition (Table 9.10). Drying essentially has no affect on nutrient content of eggs. Nevertheless, storage of dried eggs may affect several nutrients, depending on the conditions of storage. Maintenance of low moisture content, good packaging, and low temperature will largely eliminate the loss of nutrients. There are some nutrients lost in cold storage of shell eggs for storage times of 6 months or more. However, shell eggs today are moved through market channels within a few days. Thus, there should be essentially no loss of nutrients in the

Table 9.10. Effect of Storage on Nutrient Composition of Eggs

Type of egg	Effect
Dehydrated eggs	
Protein	Generally no loss of protein
Vitamin A	Significant losses due to oxidation particularly at high storage temperatures; 9 months storage at $-9.4°C$ resulted in 60% loss; 75% loss at $21.1°C$, and 80% loss at $370°C$
Vitamin D	Little effect
Thiamin	Little loss at $-9.4°C$; 46% loss at $21.1°C$; less loss if packed under nitinger
Riboflavin	Stable
Niacin	Stable
Shell eggs in cold storage	
Moisture	Loss of moisture through shell and transfer of moisture from white to yolk
Vitamin A	No loss
Vitamin D	No loss
Thiamin	No loss
Riboflavin	14% loss in 6 months at $0°C$
Niacin	17% loss in 7 months
Folic acid	16% loss in 12 months at $0°C$
Pantothenic acid	8% loss in 12 months at $0°C$

Source: Everson and Souders (1957).

cartoned eggs bought by the consumer under the present marketing systems used in the United States.

Recently, Cotterill *et al.* (1978) analyzed the nutrient composition of spray-dried egg products to update the data base. Nutrient composition of dried eggs was found to be comparable to shell eggs.

Protein quality is an important consideration in processed foods. Hopkins *et al.* (1976) reported that spray-dried eggs had a protein efficiency ratio comparable to lyphilized eggs. If glucose is not removed from eggs prior to drying, the Maillard reaction may take place, causing loss of protein quality during storage (Fennema 1976). The removal of glucose from eggs today, prior to drying, has greatly improved the quality of dried egg products presently produced in the United States and has essentially eliminated any loss of protein quality during drying.

EFFECT OF COOKING

Everson and Souders (1957) reviewed the previous research on the effect of cooking on the nutrient content of eggs. Previous work reported by these authors indicated loss of B vitamins depending on the cooking methods used. Loss of thiamin was about 15% regardless of the cooking method used. Riboflavin loss was increased when eggs were cooked in an uncovered pan and exposed to light. Folic acid was the most susceptible to loss, exhibiting a 65% loss during baking of eggs. Research reported by Hanning (1957) indicated that approximately 20% of the riboflavin was lost during scrambling, whereas little or no riboflavin was lost during hard-boiling of eggs. Thiamin content was affected minimally by all the cooking methods used.

With respect to protein quality, Hopkins et al. (1976) reported that the adjusted PER value of hard-boiled eggs was slightly lower than that found from lyophilized eggs. They offered no explanation for these results.

REFERENCES

Aman, N., and Becker, W. A. 1981. Relationship between six and seven week old male broilers using live, carcass and abdominal fat weights. Poult. Sci. 60, 1615.

Ang, C. Y. W., and Hamm, D. 1982. Proximate analyses, selected vitamins and minerals and cholesterol content of mechanically deboned and hand-deboned broiler parts. J. Food Sci. 47, 885–888.

Babji, A. S., Froning, G. W., and Satterlee, L. D. 1980. Protein nutritional quality of mechanically deboned poultry meat as predicted by the C-PER assay. J. Food Sci., 441–443.

Bair, C. W., and Marion, W. W. 1978. Yolk cholesterol in eggs from various avain species. Poult. Sci. 57, 1260.

Cherry, J. A., Siegel, P. B., and Beane, W. L. 1978. Genetic–nutritional relationships in growth and carcass characteristics of broiler chickens. Poult. Sci. 57, 1482–1487.

Chung, R. A., Rogler, J. C., and Stadelman, W. J. 1964. Fatty acid changes in the egg and tissues of hens fed different fats and cholesterol. Poult. Sci. 43, 1308.

Clarenburg, R., Chung, I. A. K., and Wakefield, L. M. 1971. Reducing the egg cholesterol level of including emulsified sitosterol in standard chicken diet. J. Nutr. 101, 289–298.

Coon, C. N., Becker, W. A., and Spencer, J. V. 1981. The effect of feeding high energy diets containing supplement fat on broiler weight gain, feed efficiency and carcass composition. Poult. Sci. 60, 1264–1271.

Cotterill, O. J., and Winter, A. R. 1954. Egg white lysozyme. 1. Relative lysozyme activity in fresh eggs having low and high interior quality. Poult. Sci. 33, 607–611.

Cotterill, O. J., Marion, W. W., and Naber, E. C. 1977. A nutrient re-evaluation of shell eggs. Poult. Sci. 56, 1927–1934.

Cotterill, O. J., Glavert, J., and Froning, G. W. 1978. Nutrient composition of commercially spray-dried egg products. Poult. Sci. 57, 439–442.

Cruickshank, E. M., Houston, J., and Moore, T. 1939. Spectroscopic changes in fatty acids. V. The effect of the dietary fat on the body fat and egg fat of the hen. Biochem. J. 33, 1630.

Cunningham, F. E. 1977. Composition of Araucana eggs. Poult. Sci. 56, 463–467.

Cunningham, F. E., Cotterill, O. J., and Funk, E. M. 1960. The effect of season and age of bird. 1. On egg size, quality and yield. Poult. Sci. 39, 289–299.

Dansky, L. M., and Hill, F. W. 1952. The influence of dietary energy on the distribution of fats in various tissues of the growing chicken. Poult. Sci. 31, 912.

Deaton, J. W., Kubena, L. F., Chen, T. C., and Reece, F. N. 1974. Factors influencing the quantity of abdominal fat in broilers. 2. Cage versus floor rearing. Poult. Sci. 53, 574–576.

Deaton, J. W., McNaughton, J. L., Reece, F. N., and Lott, B. D. 1981. Abdominal fat of broilers as influenced by dietary level of animal fat. Poult. Sci. 60, 1250–1253.

Edwards, H. M., Jr. 1964. The influence of breed and/or strain on the fatty acid composition of egg lipids. Poult. Sci. 43, 751–754.

Edwards, H. M., and Denman, F. 1975. Carcass Composition Studies. 2. Influences of breed, sex and diet on gross composition of the carcass and fatty acid composition of the adipose tissue. Poult. Sci. 54, 1230–1238.

Essary, E. O. 1979. Moisture, fat, protein and mineral content of mechanically deboned poultry meat. J. Food Sci. 44, 1070–1073.

Essary, E. O., and Dawson, L. E. 1965. Quality of fryer carcasses as related to protein and fat levels in diet. 1. Fat deposition and moisture pick-up during chilling. Poult. Sci. 44, 7.

Everson, G. J., and Souders, H. J. 1957. Composition and nutritive importance of eggs. J. Am. Diet. Assoc. 33(12), 1244–1254.

Fennema, O. R. 1976. Principles of Food Science. In Food Chemistry. Vol. 1. Marcel Dekker, New York.

Fisher, H., and Leveille, G. A. 1957. Observation on the cholesterol linoleic and linolenic acid content of eggs as influenced by dietary fats. J. Nutr. 63, 119–129.

Fletcher, D. L., Britton, W. M., Rahn, A. P., and Savage, S. I. 1981. The influence of layer flock age on egg component yields and solids content. Poult. Sci. 60, 983–987.

Froning, G. W. 1981. Mechanical deboning of poultry and fish. Advances in Food Res. 27, 110–113.

Gilbert, L., Bowers, J. A., Craig, J., and Cunningham, F. E. 1981. Sensory characteristics and thiamin and vitamin B_6 content.

Hall, K. N., and Lin, C. S. 1981. Effect of cooking rates in electric or microwave oven on cooking losses and retention of thiamin in broilers. J. Food Sci. 46, 1292–1293.

Hanning, F. 1957. The effect of a plastic coating of shell eggs on changes which occur during storage and cooking. Poult. Sci. 36, 1365–1369.

Heath, J. L., Teekell, R. A., and Watts, A. B. 1971. Fatty acid composition of batter coated chicken parts. Poult. Sci. 50, 219–226.

Hopkins, D. T., Steinke, F. H., and Kolar, C. W. 1976. The effect of cooking and water content of ground beef and eggs on the determination of the protein efficiency ratio. J. Food Sci. 41, 1426–1427.

Hsu, H. W., Sutton, N. E., Banjo, M. O., Satterlee, L. D., and Kendrick, J. G. 1978. The C-PER and T-PER assays for protein quality. Food Technol. 38(12), 69–73.

Jeffrey, F. P., and Britt, R. E. 1941. Effect of confinement in laying cages on the physical composition of hens. Poult. Sci. 20, 302–303.

Jen, J. J., Williams, W. P., Acton, J. C., and Paynter, V. A. 1971. Effect of dietary fats on the fatty acid contents of chicken adipose tissue. J. Food Sci. 36, 925–929.

Klose, A. A. 1979. Fluoride content of commercial samples of mechanically deboned poultry meat and fluoride distribution in the deboning process. Poult. Sci. 58, 1074.

Kubena, L. F., Lott, B. D., Deaton, J. W., Reece, F. N., and May, J. D. 1972. Body composition of chicks as influenced by environmental temperature and selected dietary factors. Poult. Sci. 51, 517–522.

Kubena, L. F., Chen, T. C., Deaton, J. W., and Reece, F. N. 1974A. Factors influencing the quantity of abdominal fat in broilers. 3. Dietary energy level. Poult. Sci. 53, 974–978.

Kubena, L. F., Deaton, J. W., Chen, T. C., and Reece, F. N. 1974B. Factors influencing the quantity of abdominal fat in broilers. 1. Rearing temperature, sex, age or weight and dietary choline chloride and inositol supplementation. Poult. Sci. 53, 211–214.

Latshaw, J. D., and Osman, M. 1975. Distribution of selenium in egg white and yolk after feeding natural and synthetic selenium compounds. Poult. Sci. 54, 1244–1252.

Lee, F. V., Khan, M. A., and Klein, B. P. 1981. Effect of preparation and service on the thiamin content of oven-baked chicken. J. Food Sci. 46, 1560–1562.

Marion, J. E. 1965. Effect of age and dietary fat on lipids of chicken muscle. J. Nutr. 85, 38.

Marion, J. E., and Woodroof, J. G. 1963. The fatty acid composition of breast, thigh and skin tissues of chicken broilers as influenced by dietary fats. Poult. Sci. 42, 1202–1207.

Marion, J. E., Woodroof, J. G., and Cook, R. E. 1965. Some physical and chemical properties of eggs from hens of five different stocks. Poult. Sci. 44, 529–534.

Marion, J. E., Woodroof, J. G., and Tindell, D. 1966. Physical and chemical properties of eggs as affected by breeding and age of hens. Poult. Sci. 45, 1189–1195.

Marion, J. E., Boggess, T. S., Jr., and Woodroof, J. G. 1967. Effect of dietary fat and protein on lipid composition and oxidation on chicken muscle. J. Food Sci. 32, 426–429.

Maurice, D. V., and Deodato, A. P. 1982. Sodium chloride-induced reduction of abdominal fat in broilers. Poult. Sci. 61, 1508.

May, K. N., and Stadelman, W. J. 1960. Some factors affecting components of eggs from adult hens. Poult. Sci. 31, 560–565.

Mott, E. L., MacNeil, J. H., Mast, M. G., and Leach, R. M. 1982. Protein efficiency ratio and amounts of selected nutrients in mechanically deboned spent layer meat. J. Food Sci. 47, 655–663.

Mountney, G. J. 1976. Poultry Products Technology. 2nd Edition. AVI Publishing Co., Westport, CT.

Murphy, E. W., Brewington, C. R., Willis, B. W., and Nelson, M. A. 1979. Health and safety aspects of the use of mechanically deboned poultry. Food Safety and Quality Service, USDA, Washington, DC.

Pankey, R. D., and Stadelman, W. J. 1969. Effect of dietary fats on chemical and functional properties of eggs. J. Food Sci. 34, 312–317.

Posati, L. P. 1979. Composition of foods: Poultry products: Raw processed, prepared. In Agriculture Handbook 8-5. USDA, Washington, DC.

Reiser, R. 1950. Fatty acid changes in egg yolks of hens on a fat free and cottonseed oil ration. J. Nutr. 40, 429.

Salmon, R. E. 1969. Soybean versus rapeseed oil in turkey starter diets. Poult. Sci. 48, 87–93.

Salmon, R. E., and O'Neil, J. B. 1971. The effect of the level and source of dietary fat on growth, feed efficiency, grade and carcass composition of turkeys. Poult. Sci. 50, 1456–1467.

Schuler, G. A., and Essary, E. O. 1971. Fatty acid composition of lipids from broilers fed saturated and unsaturated fats. J. Food Sci. 36, 431–434.

Scott, M. L. 1956. Composition of turkey meat. J. Am Diet. Assoc. 32(10), 941.

Sheldon, B. W. 1983. Dietary tocopherol as an antioxidant in turkey meat. Poult. Sci. 62, 1500.

Sheldon, B. W., Essary, E. O., Bovard, K. P., and Young, R. W. 1980. Effect of endpoint cooking temperature upon nutritive value and composition of turkey meat. Poult. Sci. 29, 2725–2732.

Sheldon, B. W., Ball, H. R., and Kimsey, H. R., Jr. 1983. Influence of tumbling turkey meat on vitamin retention. Poult. Sci. 62, 1806–1809.

Sim, J. S., and Bragg, D. B. 1978. Effect of dietary oil, cholesterol and soysterols on the lipid concentration and fatty acid composition of egg yolk, liver and serum of laying hens. Poult. Sci. 57, 466–472.

Singh, S. P., and Essary, E. O. 1971. Vitamin content of broiler meat as affected by age, sex, thawing and cooking. Poult. Sci. 50, 1150–1155.

Singh, R. A., Weiss, J. F., and Naber, E. C. 1972. Effect of azasterols on sterol metabolism in the laying hen. Poult. Sci. 51, 449–457.

Sonaiya, E. B., and Benyi, K. 1983. Abdominal fat in 12 to 16 week old broiler birds as influenced by age, sex and strain. Poult. Sci. 62, 1793–1799.

Spencer, J. V., Becker, W. A., Mirosh, L. W., and Verstrate, J. A. 1978. Effect of fertilization and age of hen on the cholesterol content of chicken egg yolk. Poult. Sci. 57, 261–264.

Summers, J. D., Slinger, S. J., and Ashton, G. C. 1965. The effect of dietary energy and protein on carcass composition with a note on a method for estimating body composition. Poult. Sci. 44, 501.

Tolan, A., Robertson, J., Orton, C. R., Head, M. J., Christie, A. A., and Millburn, B. A. 1974. Studies on the composition of food. 5. The chemical composition of eggs produced under battery deep litter and free range conditions. Brit. J. Nutr. 31, 185–200.

Tuite, P. J., and Austic, R. E. 1974. Studies on a possible interaction between riboflavin and vitamin B-12 as it affects hatchability of the hen's egg. Poult. Sci. 50, 1303–1306.

Turk, D. E., and Barnett, B. D. 1971. Cholesterol content of market eggs. Poult. Sci. 50, 1303–1306.

Turk, D. E., and Barnett, B. D. 1972. Diet and egg cholesterol content. Poult. Sci. 51, 1881.

Tzeng, R.-Y., and Becker, W. A. 1981. Growth patterns of body and abdominal fat weights in male broiler chickens. Poult. Sci. 60, 1101–1106.

Unklesbay, N., Davis, M. E., and Krause, G. 1983. Nutrient retention in pork, turkey breast and corned beef roasts after infrared and convective heat processing. J. Food Sci. 48, 865–868.

Walczak, M. 1974. The bad egg. J. Appl. Nutr. 26, 2–3.

Washburn, K. W., and Nix, D. F. 1974. Genetics basis of yolk cholesterol content. Poult. Sci. 53, 109–115.

Whiteford, C., Pickering, C., Summers, K., Weis, A., and Bisbey, B. 1951. The vitamin content of eggs as affected by dehydration and storage. Mont. Agric. Exp. Stn. Bull. 433.

Wilson, H. R., Boone, M. A., Arafa, A. S., and Janky, D. M. 1983. Abdominal fat pad reduction in broilers with throactive iodinated casein. Poult. Sci. 62, 811–818.

Wladyka, E. J., and Dawson, L. E. 1968. Essential amino acid composition of chicken meat and drip after 30 and 90 days of frozen storage. J. Food Sci. 33, 453–455.

Effects of Handling, Processing, and Storage on Fish and Shellfish

Judith Krzynowek

BASELINE INFORMATION

Proximate Composition

It would be very convenient if a simple table of proximate composition for a variety of seafoods, such as Table 10.1, could give baseline information. Table 10.1 can only supply approximate values for many different reasons. Finfish are mobile and are exposed to a variety of nutrients, contaminants, and water temperatures before they are caught. Fish harvested year-round will exhibit compositional differences due to physiological changes and reproductive cycles. Bivalves are usually sedentary, and they must rely on the available food that drifts over them. Season of harvest, therefore, becomes a very significant variable in terms of the food supply.

Baseline fat data for any one species vary more than any of the other proximate compositional components. Most natural flavors, the essential fatty acids, and the fat-soluble vitamins are just a few of the components contained in the fat portion of the fish. The sex and body part (Table 10.2) of the fish contribute to its proximate composition, yet these parameters are rarely defined when reporting compositional data. The body part becomes important because fat is not distributed evenly throughout the fish muscle. The portion of the muscle in contact with the skin, called the flank muscle or dark muscle, the belly flap, and the nape of the head tend to be about four to five times higher in fat than other portions of the fish. Fat content ranged from 1.2 to 2.0% for muscle meat without orange-colored tissue in Atlantic sturgeon (*Acipenser oxyrhynchus*) to 7.2% for whole steaks marbled with orange tissue (Ackman *et al.* 1975). The bulk of the lipids of the dark muscle or the fattier portions are usually neutral lipids, generally triglycerides. The leaner muscles, containing little depot fat, will contain a larger percentage of cellular lipids, about 90% of which are polar lipids.

Table 10.1. Proximate Composition of Raw Edible Portions of Selected Seafoods[a]

	Number of samples	Water (%)	Ash (%)	Protein (%)	Fat (%)	Na (mg%)	Thiamin (mg%)	Riboflavin (mg%)	Niacin (mg%)	Calories (%)	Reference
Red sockeye salmon *Oncorhynchus nerka*	6	71.9	1.2	22.8	6.3	63	0.190	0.141	5.90	154	Dudek et al. (1981)
Yellowtail flounder *Limanda ferruginea*	3	79.4	1.1	19.6	1.5	176	0.043	0.088	1.43	97	Dudek et al. (1981)
Shrimp *Pandalus jordani*	6	80.0	1.2	17.6	1.4	N.D.	0.034	0.034	1.58	N.D.	Gordon et al. (1979)
Pacific cod *Gadus macrocephalus*	?	82.1	1.0	16.7	0.7	73	0.098	0.158	N.D.	70	Sidwell (1981)
Eastern oyster *Ostrea virginica*	?	84.0	1.6	7.9	1.7	N.D.	0.147	0.191	1.96	72	Sidwell (1981)
Rainbow trout *Salmo gairdneri*	6	76.9	1.3	18.8	3.1	N.D.	N.D.	N.D.	N.D.	N.D.	Kinsella et al. (1978)
Rock bass *Ambloplites rupestris*	3	80.5	1.0	17.8	0.7	N.D.	N.D.	N.D.	N.D.	N.D.	Kinsella et al. (1978)

[a] N.D., no data.

Table 10.2. Concentration (%) of Lipids in Various Edible Portions

Portion sampled	Atlantic mackerel *Scomber scombrus*[a]	White sucker *Catostomus commersoni*[b]	Atlantic mackerel *Scomber scombrus*[c]		Pink salmon *Oncorhynchus gorbuscha*[d]	
			Male	Female	Male	Female
Dark muscle	14.1	6.2	12.84	8.94	11.3	13.7
White muscle	9.1	1.4	3.32	2.21	1.7	2.3
Belly portion	18.6	No data	27.84	22.20	8.8	11.3

[a] Leu *et al.* (1981) (seasonal means).
[b] Mai and Kinsella (1979).
[c] Ackman and Eaton (1971) (June sampling).
[d] Stansby and Hall (1967).

Fat is also distributed unevenly throughout the edible body parts of crustacea. However, there appears to be no hard and fast rule as to which body part has the largest concentration of lipids. Krzeczkowski and Stone (1974) reported values of 1.0 and 1.6% for claws and body, respectively, in the snow crab, *Chionoecetes bairdi*. The reverse was found for legs and claws (1.14%) and for body meat (0.86%) in the queen crab, *Chionoecetes opilio*. Equal amounts of fat were found in legs and claws (0.99%) and body meat (0.88%) in the red crab, *Geryon quinquedens* (Lauer *et al.* 1974) and in the Alaskan king crab, *Paralithodes camtschatica*, with about 1.5% in both body and claws (Krzeczkowski *et al.* 1971).

Season of catch can be a major factor affecting the fat content of seafood, with some species fluctuating between summer maximums of 12–20% fat to winter lows of 3–5% (Stansby 1973). There are two major reasons for this fluctuation. The quantity and type of food available to fish and shellfish is seasonally dependent. This is particularly true in colder climates. As the supply of food is depleted through the winter months, the animals draw on their fat reserves for energy. This is usually reflected in a lowered fat content. The season of year, for many species, also dictates the spawning cycles. Sexually ripe blue mussels, *Mytilus edulis*, have a moisture content of 76% in the spring, in contrast to a high of 86% for postspawned mussels in the fall (Krzynowek and Wiggin 1979). Fat content was maximum at 2.6% in the fall, to a low of 1.7% in the spring, probably reflecting availability of food. Postspawned mussels have low yields and suffer flavor and texture deterioration within 4 months of frozen storage. Slabyj *et al.* (1978) noted similar seasonal changes in mussels. Oyster lipid content (Sidwell *et al.* 1979) fluctuates seasonally from 1.4 to 3.0%.

The fat content of seafood deserves further scrutiny because of its unique contribution to the human diet and the special problems it

Table 10.3. Fatty-Acid Composition from Total Lipids in Finfish and Shellfish

Fatty acid[a]	Prawn *Macrobrachium rosenbergii*[b]		Rainbow trout *Salmo gairdneri*[c]	Red crab *Geryon quinquedens*[d]	Blue mussels *Mytilus edulis*[e]		Yellowtail flounder *Limanda ferruginea*[f]
	a	b			a	b	
14:0	1.5	1.1	3.5	0.4	3.1	2.0	7.6
16:0	14.9	15.2	13.3	11.4	13.1	13.2	14.3
18:0	8.0	8.3	3.8	4.1	1.7	3.8	4.3
16:1	1.0	1.3	4.8	3.4	12.9	7.5	4.3
18:1	19.7	17.3	18.7	18.9	3.7	1.7	11.9
20:1	—	—	—	4.5	.5	6.0	7.7
22:1	—	—	—	1.7	2.0	3.6	8.5
18:2ω6	29.8	24.2	5.5	0.9	1.00	—	1.6
18:3ω3	2.5	2.0	5.9	—	—	—	1.5
20:4ω6	2.4	3.2	2.8	4.8	1.3	3.2	3.9
20:5ω3	7.0	12.1	5.1	23.7	26.5	20.5	2.0
22:6ω3	3.2	5.0	21.0	15.9	7.0	12.2	8.2

[a] Weight percent composition.
[b] Sandifer and Joseph (1976): (a) commercial diet, (b) commercial diet plus "ω3" fatty acids.
[c] Kinsella *et al.* (1978).
[d] Krzynowek *et al.* (1982).
[e] Krzynowek, unpublished data: (a) March harvest, (b) August harvest.
[f] Dudek *et al.* (1981).

brings to the seafood industry. The American Heart Association has advised substituting foods high in polyunsaturated fatty acids in place of saturated fatty acids for the prevention of artherosclerosis. Most of the polyunsaturates of land animals and vegetables are dienes, which means they have two double bonds per fatty acid molecule. We can see from Table 10.3 that fish and shellfish contain fatty acids with five and six double bonds. The predominant polyunsaturated fatty acids for fish and shellfish are eicosapentaenoic acid (20:5ω3) and docosahexaenoic acid (22:6ω3). The common usage notation for fatty acids is as follows —carbon chain length (:) number of double bonds (ω) placement of the first double bond relative to the terminal methyl group. All other double bonds are separated by one methylene group, unless otherwise specified. The nutritional significance of these two fatty acids is still subject for debate, but it appears that they are more effective in lowering serum cholesterol levels than the dienes. The absence of the 22:6ω3 fatty acid in the human central nervous system has been associated with multiple sclerosis (Alter 1972; Crawford and Sinclair 1972; Stansby 1973). These multiple sites of unsaturation, however, make fishery products especially susceptible to oxidative rancidity which creates unique problems for the seafood industry.

The fatty acid values in Table 10.3 are also subject to fluctuations, depending on size, sexual maturity, and season of catch (Ackman 1976; Stansby 1981). The practice of fish farming and aquaculture and the use of artificial food and growing conditions has altered the "norm" of fatty acid profiles. Cultivated fish and shellfish fed commercial diets containing plant materials tend to have higher levels of 20:4ω6 and its precursor acid, 18:2ω6, than "wild" fish and shellfish. Both acids are commonly associated with plant materials. Surf clams, *Spisula solidissima*, raised in two different environs, but from the same parent stock, had differing amounts of 22:1 (all isomers) and 20:5ω3. The clams raised artificially with estuary water had twice the amount of fat, about six times less 22:1, and about three times more 20:5ω3 than the clams raised in tidal waters (Krzynowek *et al.* 1983).

Stressful situations can also cause changes in fatty acid composition. Increases in total phospholipids and unsaturated fatty acids in response to extreme temperature fluctuations have been reported in crayfish, *Procambarus clarkii* (Farkas and Nevenzel 1981); in crustaceans (Chapelle *et al.* 1979; Farkas and Kariko 1981; Brichon *et al.* 1980); in carp, *Cyprinus carpio* L. (Wodtke 1981); and in rainbow trout, *Salmo gairdneri* (Hazel 1979A,B; Leger *et al.* 1977). It is speculated that species unable to metabolize the long-chain polyunsaturated fatty acids, which have low melting points, would not be able to survive reduced temperatures. It is the polyunsaturated fatty acids which appear to be preferentially utilized by fish under the stress of starvation. Cell membranes begin to disrupt during periods of acute starvation, with mobilization of phospholipids.

Cholesterol is another component of the lipid fraction. Its content in seafood has been the subject for much debate. One myth about shellfish is that they contain large quantities of cholesterol. Bivalves, which are filter feeders, contain many sterols, roughly 50% of which are plant sterols obtained through their diet of algae. Before gas chromatographic (GC) instrumentation was available for separating sterols, all sterols were mistakenly labeled as cholesterol, thus accounting for the overestimation of cholesterol in clams, oysters, and so forth. Cholesterol is the major sterol (greater than 90%) in crustaceans that feed primarily on other animals, and pre-GC data are probably reliable for crustaceans such as lobsters and crabs. Table 10.4 shows cholesterol values for selected shellfish. An ordinary serving of many of the species can be consumed under the recommended low-cholesterol dietary allowance of 300 mg/day. Fish usually contain less than 75 mg cholesterol/100 g raw muscle, and some species have as little as 10 mg/100 g (Sidwell 1981). The roe in fish is considerably higher in cholesterol than the muscle, sometimes as much as 100 times greater.

Fish is comparable to other animal sources as a supply of high-quality, highly digestible protein. Protein constitutes about 16–20%

Table 10.4.   Cholesterol Content in Cooked Shellfish

Species	mg/100 g	Reference[a]
Softshell clam	40	1
Mya arenaria		
Quahog	65	1
Mercenaria mercenaria		
Blue mussel	60	1
Mytilus edulis		
Rock shrimp	90	1
Surf clam	50	1
Spisula solidissima		
White shrimp	150	1
Penaeus setiferus		
Blue crab	120	2
Callinectes sapidus		
Jonah crab	78	2
Cancer borealis		
Rock crab	71	2
Cancer irroratus		
Red crab	78	2
Geryon quinquedens		

[a] Key to references: 1, Krzynowek, unpublished data; 2, Krzynowek *et al.* (1982).

of the raw fish weight. Fish contain the essential amino acids in amounts
equal to that of land animals (Table 10.5).   As a generalization, fish
protein supplies more lysine and isoleucine and less tryptophan and
arginine than meat.   Methionine is the limiting amino acid in fish.

Raw fish and shellfish are low in carbohydrates (0–5%) and ash
(0–3%).   They contain roughly 80% moisture, accounting for the bulk
of the compositional constituents.

Many studies have dealt with seasonal variation in proximate composition: Leu *et al.* (1979); de Andrade and de Almeida Lima (1980); and
Whyte and Englar (1982), to name some of the more recent findings.
Stansby's proposed system (Stansby 1982) for generalizing the categories
of fish according to their oil and protein content probably classifies fish
as well as can be done with such widely fluctuating variables.   Five
categories are suggested, ranging from Category A with low oil (under
5%) and high protein (15–20%), as in Pacific cod, *Gadus macrocephalus*,
to Category E with low oil (under 5%) and low protein (under 15%),
as in butter clams, *Saxidomus nuttalli*.

Vitamins and Minerals

Table 10.1 lists some of the water-soluble vitamins in raw seafood.
Fish supply about 10–15% of the recommended daily allowance of
niacin and 5–10% of riboflavin.   Fish contain a little less thiamin, riboflavin, and pantothenic acid than beef and lamb, but are a good source

Table 10.5. Amino Acid Composition (g amino acid/100 g protein)

Amino acid	Grey mullet *Mugil cephalus*[a]	Milkfish FPC *Chanos chanos*[b]	Oyster *Crassostrea* spp.[c]		Snow crab *Chionoecetes bairdi*[d]	Atlantic mackerel *Scomber scombrus*[e]	
			K	E		D	W
Alanine	—	6.8	5.1	3.1	5.5	7.3	7.3
Aspartic	7.0	10.3	3.0	1.1	10.3	12.2	11.4
Glutamic	23.2	15.8	4.6	3.4	15.9	18.0	15.6
Glycine	0.6	7.4	3.2	0.8	5.7	6.2	4.6
Proline	4.5	5.1	0.5	0.2	3.9	4.6	1.5
Serine	3.7	4.3	1.6	0.9	4.2	5.2	4.1
Arginine	4.1	6.8	5.7	3.3	9.8	5.9	7.1
Histidine	4.5	2.1	0.5	0.1	2.2	3.8	5.2
Isoleucine	9.3	4.5	0.5	0.5	4.8	6.0	5.6
Leucine	5.1	7.8	1.0	0.7	8.2	10.0	8.8
Lysine	10.0	8.2	1.0	0.8	8.5	8.0	7.6
Methionine	4.0	3.0	0.9	1.0	3.2	4.6	2.8
Cystine	0.7	0.8	N.D.	N.D.	N.D.	N.D.	N.D.
Phenylalanine	6.0	3.8	0.7	0.4	4.4	4.0	3.1
Tyrosine	3.9	3.6	0.9	0.4	3.9	3.9	3.4
Threonine	4.6	4.9	1.3	0.3	4.6	5.5	5.5
Valine	5.4	5.4	0.9	0.4	4.6	6.8	8.5
Tryptophan	1.6	1.3	—	—	1.1	—	—

[a] Mukundan *et al.* (1978) (raw sample).
[b] Sikka *et al.* (1979) (raw sample).
[c] Burnette *et al.* (1979) (freeze-dried); K, Korean—*C. gigas;* E, Eastern—*C. virginica.*
[d] Krzeczkowski *et al.* (1974) (canned sample).
[e] Leu *et al.* (1981) (raw sample): D, dark muscle; W, white muscle.

of niacin and vitamin B_{12}, the latter being especially rich in the fatty species. Vitamin B is concentrated in the fish dark muscle, as much as ten times higher than in the light muscle.

The fat-soluble vitamins A, D, E, and K, like the fat which transports them, are not distributed evenly throughout the body. Vitamin A is present in lean fish muscle at about 50–200 IU/100 g. Fatty fish, such as herring, and pigmented fish, such as salmon, have substantially greater amounts of vitamin A (about 500 IU/100 g). Vitamin D is present at 0–40 IU/100 g for lean fish and 300–1500 IU/100 g for fatty fish. Fish livers are a good source of these vitamins, but some fish livers (e.g., northern puffer) are toxic.

Seafood can make a significant contribution to man's daily need for essential minerals. Saltwater fish are an almost unique, natural source of iodine and fluorine, containing nearly 10–50 times more iodine than freshwater fish. Calcium is generally higher in crustaceans than in finfish. Nutritionists are beginning to view selenium as an essential trace element for humans, and seafood is the richest source of selenium.

Selenium values in parts per million (ppm) for salmon (.35), shrimp (.41), flounder (.50), mackerel (.46), whiting (.33), and pollock (.28) have been reported by Dudek *et al.* (1980). Oysters have 100 times more zinc than any other food.

Contaminants

Occasionally, fish from a specified area of a particular species will be considered unsafe for human consumption because of heavy metal accumulation, elevated pesticide concentrations, or harmful levels of similar pollution-related compounds. Table 10.6 shows current Food and Drug Administration (FDA) action levels for several deleterious substances in fishery products. Polycyclic aromatic hydrocarbons (PAH) find their way into the water from air and petroleum pollution, creosoted docks, and land runoff. They are known carcinogens with, as yet, no FDA health/safety limit. Marine fish have a slightly lower level than do freshwater species primarily because of a dilution effect. Lobsters held in tidal impoundments formed by creosoted pilings had higher values than freshly caught lobsters (Dunn and Fee 1979). PAH are soluble in the fat portion of animals, and, therefore, a greater accumulation should be expected in the hepatopancreas (tomalley) of the lobster than in the meat, because the tomalley is higher in fat content.

Polychlorinated biphenyls (PCB) are ubiquitous in the environment due to the uncontrolled industrial practices of the past decades. The acute toxic effects of PCB were first reported in Japan from studies on humans exposed to high dosages of PCB. The current allowable tolerance in seafoods is 5.0 ppm. The proposed reduction to 2.0 ppm has not been finalized by the FDA.

Some metals in foods, such as mercury, cadmium, arsenic, and lead, are toxic. Mercury is cumulative. The older, longer-living, and larger fish and those higher in the food chain will have an increased bioaccumulation

Table 10.6. FDA Legal Action Levels for Various Substances in Fish

Substance	Product	Action level (ppm)
Aldrin, dieldrin	Fish and shellfish: raw, smoked, frozen, canned	0.3
DDT, DDE	Fish: raw, smoked, frozen, canned	5.0
Endrin	Fish and shellfish: raw, smoked, frozen, canned	0.3
Mercury	Fish and shellfish: edible portion only, fresh, frozen, or processed	1.0
Mirex	Fish	0.1
Toxaphene	Fish: raw, smoked, frozen, canned	5.0

of mercury. Thus, swordfish and tuna, both large apex predators, must be closely monitored for mercury content. The current action level for mercury in fish is 1 ppm. Lead and cadmium block the absorption of iron in the body. The digestive glands of shellfish contain the highest naturally occurring levels of cadmium. These organs are consumed by people who enjoy eating oysters, whole clams, and the tomalley of lobsters. While lobster digestive gland is also high in arsenic, it does not constitute a health/safety hazard. The bioavailability of these elements in seafood needs to be considered when determining human tolerance. Fishery products containing bone and viscera contain higher levels of lead than fillets. Values for lead, cadmium, and arsenic in fishery products have been determined by Uthe *et al.* (1982).

Raw Seafood

Mention should be made when discussing baseline data of the nutritional significance of consuming raw fish. Some freshwater fish, a few saltwater species, and some shellfish (e.g., clams, shrimp, and mussels) contain an enzyme, thiaminase, which splits any thiamin present, making it unavailable for metabolic purposes. This enzyme is heat labile and is destroyed by cooking. Regular consumption of raw seafood products could result in eventual thiamin deficiency and poor nutritional health. Also, fish may contain parasites such as tapeworms and nematodes. Under crowded, live pen-held conditions with inadequate water and circulation, some fish may become heavily infested (Hoffman and Sindermann 1962; Sindermann 1970). A few of the parasites can continue to live in humans if the fish is eaten raw. They are rendered harmless when the fish is thoroughly cooked. Cooking of seafood is highly recommended for health and safety reasons.

HARVESTING AND HANDLING OF FRESH SEAFOOD

Now that baseline seafood nutritional information has been established, what becomes of the product as it makes its way to the consumer? A simple formula will highlight those practices that could alter the nutritional composition of seafood:

$$\text{Nutritional value to consumer} = \text{Original content} - \text{Harvesting, fresh handling, preservation, storage losses}$$

This formula addresses nutritional quality and should not be confused with what is commonly called seafood quality. Quality changes such as textural toughening, the development of off-odors and flavors, and browning are beyond the scope of this chapter. The formula does seem to imply that there are only losses encountered along the route to the consumer. For other foods, some of the processing practices could be put in the formula with a plus (+) sign. Moderate heating improves the digestibility and, therefore, the protein utilization of some foods, but not necessarily fish. Additional nutrients are added to bakery products, but generally not to fish and shellfish. A great many of the practices employed by seafood processors have been imposed by the fragile nature of the raw material in an attempt to retain the organoleptic quality of fish and are used to deliver a product that closely resembles a freshly caught product, possibly at the expense of nutritional quality.

Shipboard Practices

Before seafood reaches the processing plants, it is subjected to fairly rough handling on board the fishing vessel. The catch is towed through the water, brought aboard, possibly handled by hand (i.e., headed and gutted), stowed, unloaded, and transferred. Fish destined for the retail market as whole fish or fillets will not realize a good price if it is battered, bruised, or torn. The end use of the fish, therefore, whether as a whole fish or as a minced product, determines, to some extent, the type of harvesting gear and method of transport and storage.

Spoilage of fish begins the minute the fish are hauled from the water (Licciardello 1980), at a rate dependent on many factors. Some factors are inherent to the fish, such as species and sexual maturity. The salinity of the harvesting water, for example, influences the development of yeast in oysters (Hood 1983). Other spoilage factors are the consequence of human handling.

Deterioration is a result of three processes: (1) bacterial decomposition, (2) endogenous enzymatic activity, and (3) lipid oxidation. Lowering the storage temperature and eliminating slime and overcrowding can reduce bacterial growth. Heading and gutting the fish can reduce the enzymatic activity by removing blood and digestive organs. Bleeding can reduce the heme content which in turn can depress the rate of oxidation. Dragging huge nets and entrapping many thousands of pounds of fish leads to great physical damage and the reduction of glycogen and a decrease in pH in the fish through struggling. Many different kinds of parasites can be found on the surface of fish. In the natural environment, the parasites are kept to a level that does not harm the fish. This is probably due to the fact that the parasites are continually being washed from the fish with the swimming motion or eaten from the surface of the fish. Poorly penned or boxed fish which are crowded together with inadequate ventilation and poor water circulation can become heavily infested with parasites and bacteria with a resulting reduction in the original weight of the fish.

The use of chilled (CSW) and/or refrigerated (RSW) seawater for storage at sea offers a few advantages over iced storage (Licciardello

1980). First, there is no loss of soluble protein, as occurs with iced fish, and second, there is a slight reduction in the formation of enzymatically produced formaldehyde. There is, however, a slight increase in salt content for those fish held in CSW and RSW, and the soaking brine provides a good medium for psychrophilic bacteria.

Sodium tripolyphosphate dips have been tried on fillets prior to freezing for use at sea in an attempt to reduce the drip loss. In an experiment using filleted cod, *Gadus morhua*, Sutton and Ogilvie (1968) found sodium levels increased in muscle at all concentrations, but phosphorus content decreased in fish muscle that had been dipped in dilute solutions. They attributed the reduction to diffusion of phosphorus from the fish into the more dilute dip solution. V. G. Ampola (unpublished, 1982) found phosphorus levels doubled in clams after 30 min using a solution of 7% sodium tripolyphosphate and 2.5% salt. The ideal phosphorus:calcium ratio should be 1:1 in the human diet. This ratio is already greater than 1 whenever meat is included in the diet, and the phosphorus added by this practice may be nutritionally undesirable.

Mechanical Processing

Discards of fish and shellfish at sea can account for 70–90% of the total catch, a substantial waste! Many of the fish are discarded because they have storage instability, are not marketable, or are difficult to process. Mechanical deboners have been developed in response to a need to utilize the fish that are difficult to process by traditional methods and have, therefore, previously been discarded. The finished product, called minced fish, is usually darker in color than fillets because of the inclusion of more blood during the deboning. The dark minced product, which has been reformed into sausages or cakes or patties, has met with considerable consumer resistance in the United States. Bleaching comminuted flesh with hydrogen peroxide in buffered solutions of varying pH has been tried experimentally (Young *et al.* 1980). While the product is lightened with no appreciable lipid oxidation, there is a reduction in total amino acid concentration with an almost complete disappearance of the sulfur amino acids such as methionine and cystine, and almost total destruction of the fat-soluble vitamins. Washing of the minced fish also washes away the water-soluble vitamins as well as some flavor (Higashi 1962). Surimi is water-washed, minced flesh with added sucrose, sorbitol, or glucose, and sodium tripolyphosphate. Kamaboko, a traditional food consumed in Japan, is made by steaming or boiling surimi. If the mince is bleached in acidic cystein solution while making kamaboko, mercury is removed (Suzuki 1974).

PRESERVATION TECHNIQUES

Curing

As stated previously, preservation techniques have been primarily directed toward organoleptic quality. Nutritional losses, prior to spoilage, are small. The use of marinades as a preservative extends the shelf life of fish. Acid, generally acetic acid, is used to retard bacterial activity by lowering the pH to a point where food poisoning bacteria and most spoilage bacteria cannot grow. Salt is also added to the marinade to slow down the enzymatic textural softening process. Both bacterial and enzymatic activities will proceed steadily, however, and the product will have a limited shelf life, dependent upon the storage temperature. The end result nutritionally is a product with elevated salt content.

Smoking used to be considered a primary preservation technique. Today, smoked fish is usually frozen shortly after smoking for storage, and the smoking itself is a means of adding flavor to the fish. Freezing, therefore, is the primary preservation technique, and the literature does address quality changes of frozen smoked fish. Little has been written on the nutritional changes in smoked seafood.

Fish is usually salted prior to smoking. There is an initial loss of water-soluble proteins across the fish–salt interface and a denaturation of the protein as the salt penetrates into the flesh. The latter effect has little nutritional significance. Water losses during light salting result in an unavoidable, but insignificant, loss of water-soluble vitamins. Heavy salting has resulted in the reduction of 50% of the B vitamins in salted herring. Clifford *et al.* (1980) reported a destruction of about 12–24% lysine after a 5 hr smoke. The phenolic substances associated with smoking appear to be antioxidative and protect against nutritional losses due to fat oxidation.

Total lipids and cholesterol decreased over storage after smoking and preserving in tomato sauce (de Andrade and de Almeida Lima 1980), but it is difficult from the data to discern which of the processes actually caused the decrease. Smoked salmon had higher fat content than raw salmon due to the loss of moisture from the smoked product, and cholesterol decreased from 62 to 50 mg/100 g after dry salting and smoking (Krzynowek, unpublished, 1982). There was no significant difference in relative percentages of fatty acids for the salmon. Mullet (Koburger and Mendenhall 1973) showed increases in fat and protein content with a subsequent decrease in moisture after soaking in a 20% brine for 30 min and smoking over Red Oak sawdust at 180°F for 6 hr. The salt content in the mullet tripled after this treatment. There were losses of 6–33% in available lysine in five species of smoked African fish (Hoffman *et al.* 1977).

Many PAH have been identified in wood smoke. The fish absorbs these compounds during the smoking process. Smoked fish containing the highest levels of PAH were smoked in the traditional kilns, which use smouldering wood or sawdust. Newer smoking facilities, utilizing external smoke generators that can scrub the smoke prior to entering the smoking chamber, offer a possibility of reducing PAH concentrations in fish. Larsson (1982), in reporting on practices in Sweden, has found that the skin contains the greatest level of PAH and seems to preferentially barricade against the absorption of the higher molecular weight PAH. Larsson reports mean total PAH values in parts per billion (ppb) for smoked herring of 235 for alderwood smoke, 220 for for spruce or juniper twig smoke, 77–123 for a home smoking cabinet held at $60°–80°C$ for 1.5–3 hr, 10–17 for a home smoke box using sawdust smoke for 8–15 min, 879–1100 for a homemade kiln using spruce twigs, and 28–46 for canned smoked herring in tomato sauce. The use of liquid smoke will reduce the hazards from PAH in natural smoking.

Nitrites have traditionally been added to smoked fish to inhibit bacterial growth and for the production of a "cured" flavor. The addition of nitrites to fish is being reassessed because of the ability of nitrites to react with amines to form nitrosamines which are potent carcinogens. The amines can be formed during cooking or through bacterial or endogenous enzymatic action. The amines may also be initially present in fish in the form of free amino acids, such as histidine or tryptophan, or, in many marine species, in the form of trimethylamine oxide, trimethylamine, and dimethylamine. The latter two compounds are formed in the degradation of trimethylamine oxide during storage.

Prevention of Oxidation

Many techniques are employed to retard oxidation of the fish oils. Oxidation in dark muscle may proceed 100 times faster than in light muscle due to the presence of prooxidants such as heme compounds. Oxidation results in the characteristic rancid odor and flavor, but, more important nutritionally, is the loss of the fat-soluble vitamin activity and the formation of potentially toxic oxidized fatty acids. Oxidized fish oil may not be absorbed across the intestinal wall and may cause membrane irritation. Oxidized lipids form covalent bonds with proteins, thereby damaging some proteins before the fish is considered unfit for human consumption. Severely oxidized marine products would probably not be consumed, however, because of the rancid taste and smell. Butylated hydroxytoluene (BHT), butylated hydroxyanisole (BHA), propyl gallate, and *tert*-butylhydroquinone (TBHQ) are used in the fish industry to delay oxidation of the fish lipids, but their use in fishery products is not as effective as for other foods. Caldironi and

Bazan (1982), Zama *et al.* (1979), Mai and Kinsella (1981), and Hale *et al.* (1982) have reported on the efficacy of using these various antioxidants for the extension of shelf life, but nutritional data is missing. The first three have been shown to inhibit chemical carcinogenesis in laboratory animals (Anonymous 1982). Flexible packaging materials of varying oxygen permeability have been tried to reduce the inclusion of oxygen into the packaged fish product. No data are available on detrimental effects to the nutrition of the packaged product.

Packaging of fish in modified atmospheres (MA) for the extension of storage life has received considerable attention. Wang and Brown (1983) investigated modified atmospheres with crayfish, *Pacifastacus leniusculus;* Fey and Regenstein (1982), MA and potassium sorbate ice with red hake and salmon; Lannelongue *et al.* (1982A,B), swordfish, *Xiphias gladius*, and sheepshead, *Archosargus probatocephalus;* Brown *et al.* (1980), rockfish, *Sebastes miniatus*, and silver salmon, *Oncorhychus kisutch;* Mitsuda *et al.* (1980), sodium chloride dip prior to sealing with CO_2 of *Seriola aurevittata;* and Varga *et al.* (1980), hypobaric storage of cod, herring, and mackerel. A review of the methods has been written by Wilhelm (1982). This literature, however, deals primarily with organoleptic changes, the reduction of bacteria, and the reduction in the formation of trimethylamine. Morey *et al.* (1982) determined from protein efficiency ratio (PER) calculations that rockfish, *Sebastes* spp., suffered no loss of nutritional quality from storage in an atmosphere of 80:20%, $CO_2:O_2$.

Irradiation

Although there is a recognized potential for the use of high-energy radiation for the preservation of seafood (Brooke *et al.* 1964, 1966; Dubravcic and Nawar, 1969; Ronsivalli *et al.* 1971), the method does not currently have the approval of the FDA. Some of the nutritional research will be mentioned in this chapter, because the issue of irradiation continues to recur. Net increases in free amino acids, as much as a 40% increase in clams, have been reported by Brooke *et al.* (1964) and decreases of up to 10% have been reported by Proctor and Bhatia (1950). There was a loss of riboflavin equivalent to the losses encountered in normal cooking, a 47% loss of thiamin and no loss of nicotinic acid upon irradiation of cod fillets (Kennedy and Ley 1971). Warrier and Ninjoor (1981) used gamma irradiation (200 Krad) and heat ($60°C$ for 10 min) to prepare food protein concentrate (FPC) from Bombay Duck, *Harpodon nehereus*, and the resulting FPC maintained normal growth in rats when fed at 11% protein level. Irradiated Kamaboko with added 5'-inosinic acid and hypoxanthine (Uchiyama and Uchiyama 1979) showed no mutagenecity using *Salmonella typhimurium*. There was a 10% reduction in thiamin, riboflavin, and pyridoxine in scallops which had been sterilized with high-voltage cathode rays (Licciardello *et al.* 1959). Exposure to either ultraviolet or to gamma irradiation significantly reduced levels of a chlorinated hydrocarbon insecticide, mirex, in environmentally contaminated brown trout, *Salmo trutto* (Cin and Kroger, 1982). Ultraviolet irradiation is low-energy radiation. Bacterial counts were reduced when using ultraviolet irradiation prior to packaging for mackerel (Huang and Toledo 1982). An overview of food irradiation has been written by Josephson *et al.* (1976).

Canning

Preservation by canning is frequently used in the seafood industry. Vitamins B_1 and C are substantially destroyed during canning if heated in air. Vitamin C can be retained if heated with the exclusion of oxygen. If the product is canned with brine, the water-soluble vitamins will diffuse into the brine with a subsequent loss of about 30% of these vitamins from the product if the brine is discarded. Table 10.7 shows losses of about 70% for the B vitamins after canning for all but the albacore tuna and small losses of riboflavin and niacin. If the product is packed in oil, the fat-soluble vitamins will diffuse into the oil and be discarded if the product is washed free of oil. Fat-soluble vitamins A and E suffer the greatest destruction by canning. However, because a ¼ lb serving of fish supplies only a very small percentage of the daily recommended allowance for vitamins, the vitamin losses due to canning and freezing are probably insignificant. Fish is consumed because it is a good source of high-quality protein, and it is the protein fraction that should concern us nutritionally during canning. There is destruction of cystine–cysteine, a decrease in the availability of many amino acids (about 50% decrease), and a diminution of digestibility when foods such as fish, which are low in carbohydrates and high in moisture, are severely heated, as occurs in the canning process.

Table 10.7. Effect of Canning on B Vitamins

	Thiamin (μg/100 g)		Riboflavin (μg/100 g)		Niacin (mg/100 g)	
	Raw	Canned	Raw	Canned	Raw	Canned
Albacore tuna[a]	44	43	45	60	15.75	13.43
Chinook salmon[a]	37	12	114	130	8.42	7.25
Pacific shrimp[a]	34	11	34	15	1.58	0.78
Albacore tuna[b]	189	9	305	150	28.00	20.00
Red sockeye salmon[c]	190	34	141	184	5.90	5.29
Atlantic mackerel[c]	140	45	320	310	6.71	6.40

[a] Gordon and Martin (1982).
[b] Seet and Brown (1983).
[c] Dudek *et al.* (1981).

Freezing

Freezing and thawing must be mentioned together, because thawing is a natural consequence of the freezing process. If oxidative rancidity can be prevented, the fat-soluble vitamins will remain stable during frozen storage. Several water-soluble vitamins may be discarded with the water expelled from the fish (drip) during the thawing cycle, but little nutritional work has been done on the drip. The amount of drip from saltwater fish varies between 5 and 15% and is slightly higher than the drip from freshwater fish. Drip can also vary depending on the freezing process. Fish held several days before freezing have a greater drip loss than freshly frozen fish. Fish held for long storage have greater drip loss than fish held for short-term storage. Fish stored at high temperatures have greater drip loss than those stored at low temperatures, and slow-frozen fish have greater drip loss than quick-frozen fish. The proteins do become denatured with freezing, but the biological value appears to remain intact. Values for proximate composition, sodium, potassium, and phosphate have been reported by Dyer et al. (1977) for over 200 frozen retail fishery products.

Convenience Foods

To conclude, we will look at available data on novelty fishery products. Sims (1978) reported values of about 11% protein and 14% carbohydrates for products called cod sticks, crab snacks, and smokies. Fish cakes and fish and chips had slightly lower protein and higher carbohydrate contents. Ahamad et al. (1983) compared fresh white shrimp, Penaeus setiferus, with three commercially available breaded frozen shrimp from different areas of the United States. Fat, niacin, iron, and calories were equivalent among the products, and protein,

Table 10.8. Composition of Fast Foods per 100 g

	Burger Chef Skipper's Treat	Burger King Whaler	McDonald Filet-O-Fish
Weight (g)	121.7	170.4	129.3
Fat (%)	12.6	14.0	18.7
Moisture (%)	42.5	48.6	36.5
Fatty acids (g)			
14:0	0.64	0.12	0.36
16:0	2.73	1.84	2.81
16:1ω7	0.26	0.11	0.20
18:0	1.49	1.01	1.55
18:1ω9	3.22	3.18	4.03
Other	1.79	1.15	1.13
Cholesterol (mg)	47.2	53.3	47.5

Source: Slover et al. (1980).

carbohydrates, and calcium variability was attributed to geographical variations of the samples. Thiamin values were considerably lower in the commercial samples (18.3, 11.6, and 12.9 μg/100 g) compared to the fresh and fresh breaded shrimp (29.6 and 24.5 μg/100 g, respectively). This is probably due to the presence of the enzyme thiaminase, which still actively cleaves thiamin in the muscle tissue post mortem. Table 10.8 is reprinted in part from Slover *et al.* (1980) and shows the fatty acid profiles for some of the favorite fast fish foods in the United States. Dyer *et al.* (1977) have also reported values for many convenience foods and have found high salt levels (about 500 mg sodium/100 g) in some fish sticks and cakes.

Conclusion

There are numerous fishery products and relatively little nutritional data. However, as has been pointed out, fish is a very perishable commodity and quality deterioration would probably occur before there would be any significant loss of nutrients. Fishery products seem to be able to maintain their integrity as a source of high-quality protein through multiple processes.

REFERENCES

Ackman, R. G. 1976. Fish oil composition. *In* Objective Methods for Food Evaluation. National Academy of Sciences, Washington, DC.

Ackman, R. G., and Eaton, C. A. 1971. Mackerel lipids and fatty acids. Can. Inst. Food Technol. *4*(4), 169–174.

Ackman, R. G., Eaton, C. A., and Linke, B. A. 1975. Differentiation of freshwater characteristics of fatty acids in marine specimens of the Atlantic sturgeon, *Acipenser oxyrhynchu.* Fish. Bull. *73*(4), 838–845.

Ahamad, I. H., Rao, R. M., Liuzzo, J. A., and Khan, M. A. 1983. Comparison of nutrients in raw, commercially breaded and hand-breaded shrimp, J. Food Sci. *48*, 307–308.

Alter, M. 1972. Progress in Multiple Sclerosis, Proceedings Int. Symposium 1970, pp. 99–131. V. Leibowitz (Editor). Academic Press, New York.

Anonymous 1982. Effects of dietary fat, butylated hydroxytoluene and propyl gallate on microsomal drug metabolism in rats. Nutr. Rev. *40*(6), 189–190.

Brichon, G., Chapelle, S., and Zwingelstein, G. 1980. Phospholipids composition and metabolism in the hemolymph of *Carcinus maenas* (Crustacea, Decapoda)— Effect of temperature. Comp. Biochem. Physiol. *67B*, 647–652.

Brooke, R. O., and Steinberg, M. A. 1964. Preservation of fresh unfrozen fishery products by low-level radiation. I. Introduction. Food Technol. *18*(7), 112–113.

Brooke, R. O., Ravesi, E. M., Gadbois, D. F., and Steinberg, M. A. 1966. Preservation of fresh unfrozen fishery products by low-level radiation. V. The effects of radiation pasteurization on amino acids and vitamins in haddock fillets. Food Technol. *20*(11), 99–102.

Brown, W. D., Albright, M., Watts, D. A., Heyer, B., Spruce, B., and Price, R. J. silver salmon (*Oncorhynchus kisutch*). J. Food Sci. *45*, 93–95.

Burnette, J. A., Flick, G. J., Ward, D. R., and Young, R. W. 1979. Comparison of composition and selected enzyme activities in *Crassostrea virginica* and *Crassostrea gigas*, Eastern and Korean oysters. J. Food Prot. 42(3), 251–255.

Caldironi, H. A., and Bazan, N. G. 1982. Effect of antioxidants on malonaldehyde production and fatty acid composition in pieces of bovine muscle and adipose tissue stored fresh and frozen. J. Food Sci. 47, 1329–1332.

Chapelle, S., Zwingelstein, G., Meister, R., and Brichon, G. 1979. The influence of acclimation temperature on the phospholipid metabolism of an aquatic crustacea (*Carcinus maenas*). J. Exp. Zool. 210, 371–380.

Cin, D. A., and Kroger, M. 1982. Effects of various kitchen heat treatments, ultraviolet light, and gamma irradiation on mirex insecticide residues in fish. J. Food Sci. 47(2), 350–354.

Clifford, M. N., Tang, S. L., and Eyo, A. A. 1980. The development of analytical methods for investigating chemical changes during fish smoking. *In* Advances in Fish Science and Technology, pp. 286–290. J. J. Connell (Editor). Fishing News Books, Farnham, Surrey, England.

Crawford, M. A., and Sinclair, A. J. 1972. The limitations of whole tissue analysis to define linolenic-acid deficiency. J. Nutr. 102, 1315–1322.

de Andrade, M. O., and de Almeida Lima, U. 1980. The effects on season and processing on the lipids of mandi (*Pimelodus clarias*, Bloch), a Brazilian freshwater fish. *In* Advances in Fish Science and Technology, pp. 387–393. J. J. Connell (Editor). Fishing News Books, Farnham, Surrey, England.

Dubravcic, M. F., and Nawar, W. W. 1969. Effects of high-energy radiation on the lipids of fish. Agric. Food Chem. 17(3), 639–644.

Dudek, J. A., Behl, B. A., Elkins, E. R., Jr., Hagen, R. E., and Chin, H. B. 1981. Determination of effects of processing and cooking on the nutrient composition of selected seafoods. Final Report of the National Food Processors Assoc., prepared for NOAA. NMFS, Washington, DC.

Dunn, B. P., and Fee, J. 1979. Polycyclic aromatic hydrocarbon carcinogens in commercial seafoods. J. Fish. Res. Bd. Can. 36, 1469–1476.

Dyer, W. J., Fraser Hiltz, D., Hayes, E. R., and Munro, V. G. 1977. Retail frozen fishery products—Proximate and mineral composition of the edible portion. Can. Inst. Food Sci. Technol. J. 10(3), 185–190.

Farkas, T., and Kariko, K. 1981. Incorporation of [1–14C] acetate into fatty acids of the crustaceans *Daphnia magna* and *Cyclops strenus* in relation to temperature. Lipids 16(6), 418–422.

Farkas, T., and Nevenzel, J. C. 1981. Temperature effects on crayfish fatty acids. Lipids 16(5), 341–346.

Fey, M.S., and Regenstein, J. M. 1982. Extending shelf-life of fresh wet red hake and salmon using CO_2–O_2 modified atmosphere and potassium sorbate ice at 1°C. J. Food Sci. 47, 1048–1049.

Gordon, D. T., and Martin, R. E., 1982. Vitamins and minerals in seafoods of the Pacific Northwest. *In* Chemistry and Biochemistry of Marine Food Products, pp. 429–445. AVI Publishing Co., Westport, CT.

Gordon, D.T., Roberts, G. L., and Heintz, D. M. 1979. Thiamin, riboflavin, and niacin content and stability in Pacific coast seafoods. J. Agric. Food Chem. 27(3), 483–489.

Hale, M. B., Joseph, J. D., and Seaborn, G. T. 1982. Lipid oxidation in blueback herring, *Alosa aestivalis*, during frozen and superchilled (−2°C) storage; effect of TBHQ antioxidant. NOAA Tech. Memo. NMFS, *SEFC-75*, February. Washington, DC.

Hazel, J. R. 1979A. Influence of thermal acclimation on membrane lipid composition of rainbow trout liver. Am. J. Physiol. 236(1), R91–R101.

Hazel, J.R. 1979B. The influence of temperature adaptation on the composition of the neutral lipid fraction of rainbow trout (*Salmo gairdneri*) liver. J. Exp. Zool. 209, 33–42.

Higashi, H. 1962. Relationship between processing techniques and the amount of vitamins and minerals in processed fish. *In* Fish in Nutrition, pp. 125–131. Fishing News Books, London, England.

Hoffman, A., Barranco, A., Francis, B. J., and Disney, J. G. 1977. The effect of processing and storage upon the nutritive value of smoked fish from Africa. Trop. Sci. *19*(1), 41–53.

Hoffman, G., and Sindermann, C. J. 1962. Common Parasites of Fishes. Fish Wildlife Serv. Circ. *144*. USDI, Washington, DC.

Hood, M. A. 1983. Effects of harvesting waters and storage conditions on yeast populations in shellfish. J. Food Prot. *46*, 105–107.

Huang, Y., and Toledo, R. 1982. Effect of high doses of high and low intensity UV irradiation on surface microbiological counts and storage-life of fish. J. Food Sci. *47*, 1667–1731.

Josephson, E. S., Thomas, M. H., and Calhoun, W. K. 1976. Nutritional aspects of food irradiation: An overview. Presented at the First Int. Cong. Eng. Food, Boston, MA.

Kennedy, T. S., and Ley, F. J. 1971. Studies on the combined effect of gamma radiation and cooking on the nutritional value of fish. J. Sci. Food Agric. *22*(3), 146–148.

Kinsella, J. E., Shimp, J. L., and Mai, J. 1978. The proximate and lipid composition of several species of freshwater fishes. NY Food Life Sci. Bull. *69* (March), 1–20.

Koburger, J. A., and Mendenhall, V. T. 1973. Smoked mullet quality: An assessment. J. Milk Food Technol. *36*(4), 194–195.

Krzeczkowski, R. A., and Stone, F. E. 1974. Amino acid, fatty acid and proximate composition of snow crab (*Chionoecetes bairdi*). J. Food Sci. *39*, 386–388.

Krzeczkowski, R. A., Tenney, R. D., and Kelley, C. 1971. Alaska king crab: Fatty acid composition, carotenoid index and proximate analysis. J. Food Sci. *36*, 604–606.

Krzynowek, J., and Wiggin, K. 1979. Seasonal variation and frozen storage stability of blue mussels (*Mytilus edulis*). J. Food Sci. *44*(6), 1644–1648.

Krzynowek, J., Wiggin, K., and Donahue, P. 1982. Cholesterol and fatty acid content in three species of crab found in the northwest Atlantic. J. Food Sci. *47*, 1025–1026.

Krzynowek, J., Wiggin, K., and Donahue, P. 1983. Sterol and fatty acid content in three groups of surf clams (*Spisula solidissima*): Wild clams (60 and 120 mm size) and cultured clams (60 mm size). Comp. Biochem. Physiol. *74B*(2), 289–293.

Lannelongue, M., Finne, G., Hanna, M. O., Nickelson, R., II, and Vanderzant, C. 1982A. Storage characteristics of finfish filets (*Archosargus probatocephalus*) packaged in modified gas atmospheres containing carbon dioxide. J. Food Prot. *45*(5), 440–444.

Lannelongue, M., Finne, G., Hanna, M. O., Nickelson, R., II, and Vanderzant, C. 1982B. Microbiological and chemical changes during storage of swordfish (*Xiphias gladius*) steaks in retail packages containing CO_2-enriched atmospheres. J. Food Prot. *45*(13), 1197–1203.

Larsson, B. K. 1982. Polycyclic aromatic hydrocarbons in smoked fish. Z. Lebensm Unters. Forsch. *174*, 101–107.

Lauer, B. H., Murray, M. C., Anderson, W. E., and Guptill, E. B. 1974. Atlantic queen crab (*Chionoecetes opilio*), Jonah crab (*Cancer borealis*), and red crab (*Geryon quinquedens*). Proximate composition of crabmeat from edible tissues and concentrations of some major mineral constituents in the ash. J. Food Sci. *39*, 383–385.

Leger, C., Bergot, P., Luquet, P., Flanzy, J., and Meurot, J. 1977. Specific distribution of fatty acids in the triglycerides of rainbow trout adipose tissue. Influence of temperature, Lipids *12*(7), 538–543.

Leu, S., Jhaveri, S. N., Karakoltsidis, P. A., and Constantinides, S. M. 1981. Atlantic mackerel (*Scomber scombrus*, L.): Seasonal variation in proximate composition and distribution of chemical nutrients. J. Food Sci. 46, 1636–1638.

Licciardello, J. J. 1980. Handling whiting aboard fishing vessels. Mar. Fish. Rev., Jan., 21–25.

Licciardello, J. J., Nickerson, J. T. R., Proctor, B. E., and Campbell, C. L. 1959. Storage characteristics of some irradiated foods held at various temperatures above freezing. Food Technol. 13, 405–409.

Mai, J., and Kinsella, J. E. 1979. Lipid composition of dark and white muscle from white sucker (Catostomus commersoni). J. Food Sci. 44, 1101–1105.

Mai, J., and Kinsella, J. E. 1981. Changes in the lipid components of minced carp (Cyprinus carpio) following cooking. J. Sci. Food Agric. 32, 293–299.

Mitsuda, H., Nakajima, K., Mizuno, H., and Kawai, F. 1980. Use of sodium chloride and carbon dioxide for extending shelf-life of fish fillets. J. Food Sci. 45, 661–666.

Morey, K. S., Satterlee, L. D., and Brown, W. D. 1982. Protein quality of fish in modified atmospheres as predicted by the C-PER assay. J. Food Sci. 47, 1399–1409.

Mukundan, M. K., and James, M. A. 1978. Nutritional quality of some food fish. Fish. Technol. 15, 85–87.

Proctor, B. E., and Bhatia, D. S. 1950. Effects of high voltage cathode rays on amino acids in fish muscle. Food Technol. 4, 357–361.

Ronsivalli, L. J., King, F. J., Ampola, V. G., and Holston, J. A. 1971. Study of irradiated-pasteurized fishery products. Isotopes and Radiation Technol. 8(3), 321–340.

Sandifer, P. A., and Joseph, J. D. 1976. Growth responses and fatty acid composition of juvenile prawns (Macrobrachium rosenbergii) fed a prepared ration augmented with shrinp head oil. Aquaculture 8, 129–138.

Seet, S. T., and Brown, W. D. 1983. Nutritional quality of raw, precooked and canned albacore tuna (Thunnus alalunga). J. Food Sci. 48, 288–289.

Sidwell, V. D. 1981. Chemical and Nutritional Composition of Finfishes, Whales, Crustaceans, Mollusks, and their Products. NOAA Tech. Memo NMFS F/SEC-11. Washington, DC.

Sidwell, V. D., Loomis, A. L., Grodner, R. M. 1979. Geographic and monthly variation in composition of oysters, Crassostrea virginica. Mar. Fish. Rev. 41(3), 13–17.

Sikka, K. C., Singh, R., Gupta, D. P., and Duggal, S. K. 1979. Comparison nutritive value of fish protein concentrate (FPC) from different species of fishes. J. Agric. Food Chem. 23(24), 946–949.

Sims, G. G. 1978. Rapid estimation of carbohydrates in formulated fishery products—Protein by difference. J. Sci. Food and Agric. 29, 281–284.

Sindermann, C. J. 1970. Principal Diseases of Marine Fish and Shellfish. Academic Press. New York.

Slabyj, B. M., Creamer, D. L., and True, R. H. 1978. Seasonal effect on yield, proximate composition, and quality of blue mussel, Mytilus edulis, meats obtained from cultivated and natural stock. Mar. Fish. Rev. 40(8), 18–23.

Slover, H. T., Lanza, E., and Thompson, R. H., Jr. 1980. Lipids in fast foods. J. Food Sci. 45, 1583–1591.

Stansby, M. E. 1973. Polyunsaturates and fat in fish flesh. J. Am. Diet. Assoc. 63(6), 625–630.

Stansby, M. E. 1981. Reliability of fatty acid values purporting to represent composition of oil from different species of fish. J. Am. Oil Chem. Soc. 58(1), 13–16.

Stansby, M. E. 1982. Properties of fish oils and their application to handling of fish and to nutritional and industrial use. In Chemistry and Biochemistry of Marine Food Products, pp. 75–90. R. E. Martin, G. J. Flick, C. E. Hebard, and D. R. Ward (Editors). AVI Publishing Co., Westport, CT.

Sutton, A. H., and Ogilvie, J. M. 1968. Uptake of sodium and phosphorus, and weight changes in prerigor cod muscle dipped in sodium tripolyphosphate solutions. J. Fish. Res. Bd. Can. 25(7), 1475–1484.

Suzuki, T. 1974. Developing a new food material from fish flesh. 3. Removal of mercury from fish flesh. Bull. Tokai Reg. Res. Lab. 78, 67–72.

Uchiyama, S., and Uchiyama, M. 1979. Gamma-irradiation of 5'-inosinic acid in fish meat cake. J. Food Sci. 44, 681–683.

Uthe, J. F., Freeman, H. C., Sirota, G. R., and Chou, C. L. 1982. Studies on the chemical nature of bioavailability of arsenic, cadmium, and lead in selected marine fishery products. In Chemistry and Biochemistry of Marine Food Products, pp. 105–112. R. E. Martin, G. J. Flick, C. E. Hebard, and D. R. Ward (Editors). AVI Publishing Co., Westport, CT.

Varga, S., Keith, R. A., Michalik, P., Sims, G. G., and Regier, L. W. 1980. Stability of lean and fatty fish fillets in hypobaric storage. J. Food Sci. 45, 1487–1491.

Wang, M. Y. and Brown, W. D. 1983. Effects of elevated CO_2 atmosphere on storage of freshwater crayfish (Pacifastacus leniusculus). J. Food Sci. 48, 158–162.

Warrier, S. B., and Ninjoor, V. 1981. Fish protein concentrate (FPC) from Bombay Duck isolated by radiation-heat combination procedure: Functional and nutritional properties. J. Food Sci. 46, 234–238.

Whyte, J. N. C., and Englar, J. R. 1982. Seasonal variation in the chemical composition and condition indices of Pacific oyster, Crassostrea gigas, grown in trays or on the sea bed. Can. J. Fish. Aquat. Sci. 39, 1084–1094.

Wilhelm, K. A. 1982. Extended fresh storage of fishery products with modified atmospheres: A survey. Mar. Fish. Rev. 44(2), 17–20.

Wodtke, E. 1981. Temperature adaptation of biological membranes. The effects of acclimation temperature on the unsaturation of the main neutral and charged phopholipids in mitochondrial membranes of the carp (Cyprinus carpio L.). Biochim. Biophys. Acta. 640, 698–709.

Young, K. W., Neumann, S. L., McGill, A. S., and Hardy, R. 1980. The use of dilute solutions of hydrogen peroside to whiten fish flesh. In Advances in Fish Science and Technology, pp. 242–250. J. J. Connell (Editor). Fishing News Books, Farnham, Surrey, England.

Zama, K., Takama, K., and Mizushima, Y. 1979. Effect of metal salts and antioxidants on the oxidation of fish lipids during storage under the conditions of low and intermediate moistures. J. Food Proc. Preserv. 3, 249–257.

Part **3**

Effects of
Commercial Processing and
Storage on Nutrients

Effects of
Freeze Preservation
on Nutrients

Owen Fennema

The handling, storage, and preservation of food often involves changes in nutritive value, most of which are undesirable. The freezing process (prefreezing treatments, freezing, frozen storage, and thawing), if properly conducted, is generally regarded as the best method of long-term food preservation when judged on the basis of retention of sensory attributes and nutrients. The freezing process is, however, not perfect, as is apparent from the fact that substantial amounts of the more labile nutrients can be lost. Vitamin losses during freezing preservation vary greatly depending on the food, the package, and the conditions of processing and storage. Losses of nutrients can result from physical separation (e.g., peeling and trimming during the prefreezing period, or exudate loss during thawing), leaching (especially during blanching), or chemical degradation. The seriousness of these losses depends on the nutrient (whether it is abundant or meager in the average diet), and on the particular food item (whether it generally supplies a major or a minor amount of the nutrient in question).

The approach taken in this chapter is to summarize nutrient losses that occur in important classes of foods during various stages of the freezing process. Although most of the important English literature has been reviewed, no claim is made as to total coverage Because of the emphasis in the literature, attention is given mainly to vitamins, especially vitamin C in fruits and vegetables and the B vitamins in animal products. Values of vitamin C reported in this chapter refer to reduced L-ascorbic acid unless otherwise stated. Vitamin C and thiamin have been studied most extensively, since they are water soluble (cannot be stored in the body and are subject to leaching during processing), highly susceptible to chemical degradation, present in many foods, and sometimes deficient in the diet. If these vitamins are well retained during processing, it generally can be assumed that all other nutrients also are well retained.

When considering the various data presented in this chapter, it is important to note that the reference value used for calculating nutrient losses differs depending on the phase of the freezing process that is under consideration. For example, blanching losses are based on the difference in nutrient content between blanched and fresh products, freezing losses in vegetables are based on the difference in nutrient content between blanched–frozen–unstored products and blanched–unfrozen products, and storage losses are based on the difference in nutrient content between frozen–stored and frozen–unstored products. This is mentioned so that improper conclusions will be avoided. For example, if a given product loses 20% of its vitamin C content during blanching and another 20% of its vitamin C content during frozen storage, the absolute amounts of vitamin C lost during these two phases will not be the same, since the vitamin C content of the fresh product (large value) is used as the reference value for computing blanching losses, and the vitamin C content of the blanched–frozen–unstored product (a lower value) is used as the reference value for computing storage losses.

It will be seen that nutrient losses reported for a given product differ greatly from one investigator to another and in some instances the results are contradictory. This should not be regarded as unusual, since nutrient losses depend on many factors (product, handling, processing, and packaging) and when any two studies are compared, it is rare to find that all factors have been controlled in a similar fashion.

The reader will soon note, especially with animal tissues, that apparent increases in the amounts of some vitamins occasionally occur during the freezing process [indicated by plus signs (+) in the tables]. In some instances this can be attributed to analytical errors or to biological variability, but there are instances where the increase is too large to be accounted for in this manner. In such instances, it has been suggested that the freezing process releases bound, biologically inactive forms of the vitamin, or converts inactive precursors to the active vitamin.

Since this is a new edition of this volume, it is appropriate to briefly indicate what changes have been made. Important new references have been added, but for the most part, these new data have not been incorporated in the previously existing summary figures and tables. Exceptions occur when the new data are extensive and/or they differ substantially from the previously summarized data. Usually, new data are discussed in the text and/or are presented in the form of new tables. This approach is taken since the summary figures and tables from the earlier edition accurately represent numerous studies that were carefully selected for reliability and comparability of conditions, and the addition of a few new data would not have a significant effect on the means and ranges presented. A point to keep in mind, however is that handling, processing, and storage conditions for frozen foods have improved over the years, so new data will often indicate somewhat smaller losses of nutrients than the older data. Specific examples are the greater use of steam blanching rather than water blanching (less loss of water-soluble nutrients) and improved conditions encountered during product distribution in retail channels.

VEGETABLES

Loss of Nutrients during Blanching and Cooling

Shown in Table 11.1 are mean losses of vitamins C and B_1 that occur during water blanching and water cooling of vegetables. Losses of vitamin C often amount to about 10–50% and losses of vitamin B_1 are often about 9–60%, depending on the product and the conditions. Water blanching also causes approximately a 30% (14–53) loss of niacin from lima beans (Cook et al. 1961; Guerrant et al. 1947; Guerrant and O'Hara 1953), a 19% (14–24) loss of riboflavin from green peas (Guerrant and O'Hara 1953; Guerrant et al. 1947; Lee and Whitcombe 1945; Van Duyne et al. 1950), a 14% (11–17) loss of riboflavin from green beans (Guerrant and Dutcher 1948; Lee and Whitcombe 1945; Phillips and Fenton 1945; Van Duyne et al. 1950), and no significant loss of carotene from broccoli, green peas, green beans, corn, brussels sprouts, spinach, squash, collards, kale, beet greens, endive, carrots, and sweet potatoes (Guerrant and O'Hara 1953; Guerrant et al. 1947; Stimson and Tressler 1939; Sweeney and Marsh 1971; Zimmerman et al. 1940).

Losses of water-soluble vitamins during blanching occur primarily by leaching rather than by chemical degradation. This is borne out by the behavior of broccoli and spinach. Both of these products have large surface:mass ratios that favor leaching, and both exhibit very large losses of vitamin C during water blanching.

Several investigators have compared water and steam blanching with respect to losses of nutrients in vegetables (Batchelder et al. 1947; Dietrich and Neumann 1965; Dietrich et al. 1959; Guerrant et al. 1947; Holmquist et al. 1954; Moyer and Stotz 1945; Nobel and Gordon 1964; Odland and Eheart 1975; Pala 1983, Proctor and Goldblith 1948; Retzer et al. 1945; Wedler 1971). Substantially smaller losses of water-soluble vitamins and most minerals generally occur during steam blanching than during water blanching. This is particularly true when products with large surface:volume ratios are being blanched, and when steam blanching is followed by a method of cooling that does not involve liquid water (e.g., air cooling). Furthermore, microwave blanching reportedly results in substantially smaller losses of nutrients than steam blanching (Moyer and Stotz 1945; Proctor and Goldblith 1948; Samuels and Weigand 1948).

Table 11.1. Loss of Vitamins C and B_1 from Vegetables during Blanching and Cooling[a]

Product	C	B_1	References
Asparagus	10 (6–15)		b
Beans, green	23 (12–42)	9 (0–14)	c
Beans, lima	24 (19–40)	36 (20–67)	d
Broccoli	36 (12–50)		e
Brussels sprouts	21 (9–45)		f
Cauliflower	20 (18–25)		g
Peas, green	21 (1–35)	11 (1–36)	h
Spinach	50 (40–76)	60 (41–80)	i

[a] Vitamin content after cooling or after freezing, as compared to vitamin content of the fresh product. The effect of freezing has been shown to be negligible. Almost all of the data relate to water blanching and water cooling. Expressed as mean % and range.

[b] Gordon and Noble (1959), Noble and Gordon (1964).

[c] Bedford and Hard (1950), Dawson et al. (1949), Farrell and Fellers (1942), Fisher and Van Duyne (1952), Gordon and Noble (1959), Guerrant and Dutcher (1948), Guerrant et al. (1947), Hartzler and Guerrant (1952), Lee and Whitcombe (1945), Melnick et al. (1944), Morrison (1975), Noble and Gordon (1964), Phillips and Fenton (1945), Proctor and Goldblith (1948), Retzer et al. (1945).

[d] Cook et al. (1961), Guerrant and O'Hara (1953), Guerrant et al. (1947, 1953), Gustafson and Cooke (1952), Tressler et al. (1937).

[e] Batchelder et al. (1947), Eheart (1967), Fisher and Van Duyne (1952), Gordon and Noble (1959), Hartzler and Guerrant (1952), Noble and Gordon (1964), Proctor and Goldblith (1948).

[f] Adams (1975), Dietrich and Neumann (1965), Gordon and Noble (1959), Noble and Gordon (1964).

[g] Gordon and Noble (1959), Noble and Gordon (1964), Retzer et al. (1945).

[h] Barnes and Tressler (1943), Batchelder et al. (1947), Bedford and Hard (1950), Feaster et al. (1949), Guerrant and O'Hara (1953), Guerrant et al. (1947, 1953), Hartzler and Guerrant (1952), Holmquist et al. (1954), Jenkins and Tressler (1938), Lamb et al. (1948), Lee and Whitcombe (1945), Morrison (1974), Moyer and Tressler (1943), Proctor and Goldblith (1948), Tressler et al. (1936), Van Duyne et al. (1950).

[i] Bedford and Hard (1950), Fisher and Van Duyne (1952), Guerrant et al. (1947), Hartzler and Guerrant (1952), Proctor and Goldblith (1948), Sweeney and Marsh (1971), Tressler et al. (1936), von Kamienski (1972).

One purpose of blanching is to render the product more resistant to vitamin losses during frozen storage (the major effect, apparently, is to inactivate enzymes that otherwise would catalyze degradation of vitamins). The advantage of blanching with respect to retarding losses of vitamin C, B_1, B_2, and carotene from vegetables during frozen storage is clearly shown in Table 11.2.

One final point should be considered with respect to blanching. If nutritional differences result from different blanching techniques, do these differences persist during subsequent phases of the freezing process?

Table 11.2. Effect of Blanching on Loss (%) of Vitamins from Vegetables during Frozen Storage[a]

Product	Storage conditions	C	B₁	B₂	Caro-tene	References
Beans, green						
Unblanched	9 months at	35			A	Bedford and Hard
Blanched	–19°C	10			≪A	(1950)
Unblanched	1 yr at	91	74	39		Farrell and Fellers
Blanched	–20°C	47	22	3		(1942)
Beans, lima						
Unblanched	6–24 months				B	Zscheile *et al.* (1943)
Blanched	at –20°C				B-10	
Peas, green						
Unblanched	6–24 months				C	Batchelder *et al.* (1947)
Blanched	at –20°C				C-50	Zscheile *et al.* (1943)
Unblanched	9 months at				40	Batchelder *et al.* (1947)
Blanched	–19°C				14	
Unblanched	6 months at	D				Jenkins and Tressler
Blanched	–18°C	≪D				(1938)
Spinach						
Unblanched	9 months at	54			E	Bedford and Hard
Blanched	–19°C	24			E	(1950)
Unblanched	6–24 months				F	Zscheile *et al.* (1943)
Blanched	at –20°C				F-28	

[a] When absolute loss values were unavailable, it was necessary to express losses between blanched and unblanched products on a comparative basis. For example, if the loss of vitamin C in a given unblanched product is set equal to A, then the loss in the comparable blanched product can be expressed in terms of A.

Unfortunately, only a few studies have dealt with this question and the results are contradictory (Fisher and Van Duyne 1952; Retzer *et al.* 1945). Additional information on blanching is available elsewhere in this volume.

Although blanching can decrease significantly the amount of water-soluble vitamins in vegetables, it is not the only prefreezing treatment of concern. Substantial losses of vitamins can occur if vegetables are not promptly frozen following harvest. This important matter is discussed in another chapter in this volume.

Loss of Nutrients during Freezing

The losses of vitamins that occur in vegetables during freezing (effect of freezing alone) are shown in Table 11.3. The values reported are percentage losses based on comparable unfrozen products. In addition to the data in Table 11.3, freezing was reported to cause no loss of certain nutrients in the following products: B_6 in potatoes (Secomska *et al.* 1973), pantothenic acid in kale (Holmes *et al.* 1945), and carotene in

Table 11.3.   Loss (mean %) of Vitamins from Vegetables during Freezing

Product	C	B_1	B_2	Niacin	Carotene	References
Asparagus	6 (ns)[a]					b
Beans, green	3 (0–10)	3 (0–7)	~0		8	c
Beans, lima	14 (0–28)	5 (0–9)	6		~0	d
Broccoli	6 (5–7)				~0	e
Brussels sprouts	5 (ns)				~0	f
Cauliflower	3 (0–6)					g
Kale	~0			~0	~0	h
Peas, green	9 (0–18)	8 (1–15)	2 (0–4)	16	~0	i
Potatoes		~0	~0	~0		j
Spinach	4 (0–8)		~0		~0	k
Grand means	6	4	2	4	1	

[a] Not significant.

[b] Gordon and Noble (1959).

[c] Fisher and Van Duyne (1952), Gordon and Noble (1959), Lee et al. (1946), Phillips and Fenton (1945), Retzer et al. (1945), Van Duyne et al. (1950).

[d] Cook et al. (1961), Guerrant and O'Hara (1953), Guerrant et al. (1953).

[e] Fisher and Van Duyne (1952), Gordon and Noble (1959), Sweeney and Marsh (1971).

[f] Gordon and Noble (1959), Sweeney and Marsh (1971).

[g] Gordon and Noble (1959), Retzer et al. (1945).

[h] Holmes et al. (1945), Sweeney and Marsh (1971).

[i] Guerrant and O'Hara (1953), Guerrant et al. (1953), Lee et al. (1946), Van Duyne et al. (1950).

[j] Secomska et al. (1973).

[k] Fisher and Van Duyne (1952), Noble and Gordon (1964), Sweeney and Marsh (1971), Tinklin and Filinger (1956), Van Duyne et al. (1950).

collards, beet greens, endive, carrots, squash, and sweet potatoes (Sweeney and Marsh 1971). In judging these data, it should be noted that (1) loss values of less than 5% probably are not significant, and (2) in many instances, the period studied was somewhat longer than that needed to complete freezing; for example, some data were collected 24 hr after the conclusion of freezing, while other data relate to the period beginning after blanching and cooling and ending when the final storage temperature had been attained. In the latter instance, this could, particularly in commercial situations, involve a significant holding period between postblanch cooling and the start of freezing (grading, packaging, handling). With these factors in mind, it must be concluded from the data presented that losses of vitamins during freezing generally are negligible.

Loss of Nutrients during Frozen Storage

Shown in Fig. 11.1 and Tables 11.4 and 11.5 are losses of various vitamins and minerals that occur from vegetables during frozen storage.

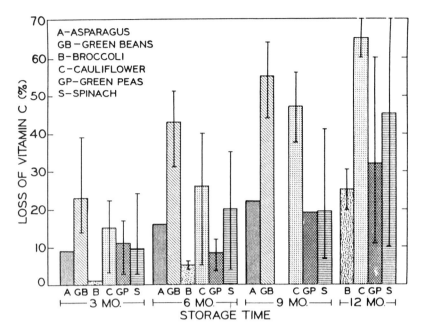

Fig. 11.1. Cumulative losses (after completion of freezing) of vitamin C from vegetables during storage at –18°C (means plus ranges). References: Asparagus [Gordon and Noble 1959; Guerrant 1957; Jenkins *et al.* 1940 (reduced ascorbic acid plus dehydroascorbic acid)]; green beans (Derse and Teply 1958; Dietrich *et al.* 1959; Pierce *et al.* 1955; Retzer *et al.* 1945); broccoli (Fisher and Van Duyne 1952; Gordon and Noble 1959; Guerrant 1957); cauliflower [Gordon and Noble 1959; Guerrant 1957; Jenkins *et al.* 1940 (reduced ascorbic acid plus dehydro-ascorbic acid); Retzer *et al.* 1945]; green peas (Bedford and Hard 1950; Derse and Teply 1958; Guerrant and O'Hara 1953; Guerrant *et al.* 1953; Volz *et al.* 1949; Weits *et al.* 1970); spinach (Bedford and Hard 1950; Dietrich *et al.* 1960; Fisher and Van Duyne 1952; Guerrant 1957; Jurics 1970; Tinklin and Filinger 1956; Volz *et al.* 1949; Weits *et al.* 1970).

Percentage loss values are based on the difference in nutrient content between blanched–frozen–stored products and blanched–frozen–unstored products. Cumulative losses of vitamin C during storage of frozen vegetables (Fig. 11.1) vary with the product and increase with time at –18°C. Percentage losses of vitamin C are large in green beans and cauliflower and small in broccoli and peas. The fact that losses of vitamin C from broccoli are very large during blanching and relatively small during frozen storage, again indicates that losses during blanching occur primarily by the mechanism of leaching rather than by chemical degradation.

Loss of minerals and vitamins (other than vitamin C) from six vegetables during storage for 12 months at –18°C are listed in Table 11.4.

Table 11.4. Approximate Losses (%) of Vitamins and Minerals from Vegetables during Frozen Storage, 12 Months at −18°C

Product	B$_1$	B$_2$	Niacin	B$_6$	K	Folic acid	Panothenic acid	Carotene	Fe	Other minerals[a]	References
Beans, green	0–32	0	0	0–21	0	6	53	0–23	18	0	b
Beans, lima		45	26	0				0			c
Broccoli					6						d
Cabbage				0	0						e
Peas, green	0–16	0–8	0–8	7		0	29	0–4	20	0	f
Spinach		0				42					g

[a] P, Mg, Ca, K, Na.
[b] Barnes and Tressler (1943), Dawson et al. (1949), Derse and Teply (1958), Lee et al. (1946), Richardson et al. (1961A,B), Tinklin and Filinger (1956).
[c] Guerrant and O'Hara (1953), Richardson et al. (1961A).
[d] Martin et al. (1960), Richardson et al. (1961B).
[e] Richardson et al. (1961A,B).
[f] Barnes and Tressler (1943), Derse and Teply (1958), Guerrant and O'Hara (1953), Lee et al. (1946), Stimson and Tressler (1939), Van Duyne et al. (1950).
[g] Richardson et al. (1961B), Van Duyne et al. (1950).

Table 11.5. Comparative Losses of Vitamins in Vegetables Held at $-18°$ and $-7°C$[a]

Product	Storage time, months (x)	C	β-carotene	Folic acid	Niacin	Pantothenic acid	B_2	B_1	B_6
Beans, green, French style									
	3	39:66	20:37	0:0	0:0	51:68	0:0	0:0	0:0
	6	44:69	53:57	0:61	0:0	16:16	9:0	0:12	12:22
	12	52:76	23:27	6:0	0:0	53:57	0:9	0:0	21:21
Peas, green									
	3	17:48	15:15	12:37	0:0	27:53	0:8	0:0	0:0
	6	12:52	15:17	50:75	0:0	0:4	8:17	0:0	9:0
	12	11:64	4:10	0:6	0:1	29:40	0:0	3:0	7:9

Source: Derse and Teply (1958).
[a] Ratio of % loss at constant $-18°C$ for x months to % loss at $-18°C$ for x-1 months + 1 month at $-7°C$.

Iron is the only mineral that appears to undergo a significant loss, and this is probably an analytical inaccuracy rather than a real loss. Vitamin losses vary greatly depending on the product. Losses of vitamins from green beans generally are greater than from peas, and losses of B_2 and niacin from lima beans are quite large compared to losses of these vitamins from other vegetables. Vitamins B_1 and pantothenic acid appear to be the least stable of the vitamins listed in Table 11.4, and losses of these vitamins are similar to the losses of vitamin C reported in Fig. 11.1.

In Table 11.5, losses of nutrients in green beans and peas during storage at a constant temperature of $-18°C$ are compared to losses during storage at the same time–temperature condition except that temperature during the last month of storage was $-7°C$. Exposure to the $-7°C$ condition almost invariably resulted in greater losses of vitamin C, β-carotene, folic acid, and pantothenic acid, but had no significant effect on losses of niacin, riboflavin (B_2), thiamin (B_1), B_6 and minerals (not shown). It is also evident that losses of vitamin C, β-carotene, pantothenic acid, and B_6 are greater in green beans at any given time than in peas. Vitamin C and pantothenic acid are by far the most labile vitamins in both green beans and peas.

The effect of storage temperature on loss of vitamin C from four frozen vegetables is shown in Fig. 11.2. Supplementary information for the products in Fig. 11.2 is given in Table 11.6. Each line in Fig. 11.2 is a mean of at least three studies and most of the studies involve at least three temperatures. Below $-18°C$ the data sometimes departed from a linear relationship and, when this occurred, loss values generally were larger than would be expected from extrapolation of the lines presented. Considerable variability is associated with each mean in Fig. 11.2, so little significance should be attached to the relative positions of the products. The lines, however, fit the mean values quite well, indicating that the slopes probably are reasonably accurate. If this is true, then it is apparent that changes in temperature affect the rate of vitamin C degradation to a similar degree in all products, that is, a $10°C$ rise in temperature within the range $-18°$ to $-7°C$ causes the rate of vitamin C degradation to accelerate in all products by a factor of $6-20\times$ (Q_{10} = $6-20$). This is an uncommonly large dependence on temperature. Thus, low storage temperatures ($-18°C$ or lower) will preserve vitamin C content of vegetables far better than higher subfreezing temperatures. Comparable information is not available for nutrients other than vitamin C.

A few studies have dealt with nutrient losses during storage of products at fluctuating storage temperatures as compared to comparable constant temperatures. With respect to frozen green peas (Boggs *et al.* 1960; Gortner *et al.* 1948), frozen cauliflower (Dietrich *et al.* 1962), and green beans (Gortner *et al.* 1948), losses of vitamin C do not differ significantly between the two conditions.

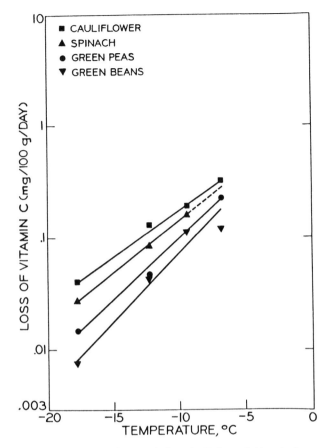

Fig. 11.2.   Temperature dependence of vitamin C degradation in frozen vegetables. (See Table 11.6 for conditions and references.)

Table 11.6.   Approximate Maximum Storage Period over Which Rates of Vitamin C Degradation Are Valid for the Products in Fig. 11.2[a]

Product	Months at:				References
	$-7°C$	$-9°C$	$-12°C$	$-18°C$	
Beans, green	1.5	3	4	6	b
Cauliflower	2	3	4	6	c
Peas, green	2	—	12	12+	d
Spinach	4	6	6	8	e

[a] Periods vary greatly, depending on the conditions.
[b] Bennett *et al.* (1954), Dietrich *et al.* (1957, 1959), Jenkins *et al.* (1940 data include both reduced ascorbic acid and dehydroascorbic acid), Jurics (1970).
[c] Bennett *et al.* (1954), Dietrich *et al.* (1957, 1962), Jenkins *et al.* (1940, data include both reduced ascorbic acid and dehydroascorbic acid).
[d] Dietrich *et al.* (1957), Guerrant *et al.* (1953), Lindquist *et al.* (1950).
[e] Bennett *et al.* (1954), Dietrich *et al.* (1960), Jurics (1970).

In some instances, the method of packaging can influence the degree to which labile nutrients are retained during frozen storage. For example, in one study involving green beans and carrots stored for 24–40 weeks at –21°C, retention of vitamin C was greater in the unblanched, vacuum–packaged products than it was in products that were blanched and vacuum packaged (Pala 1983). This leads one to suspect that methods of excluding oxygen from frozen foods deserve greater attention than they have received.

Loss of Nutrients during Thawing

Only a few studies of frozen vegetables have been conducted in a manner so that the effect of thawing on nutrient value can be determined (Fenton and Tressler 1938; Jenkins and Tressler 1938; Holmes *et al.* 1945; Phillips and Fenton 1945). Results of these studies indicate that proper thawing, as such, has a very small and probably insignificant effect on the nutrient contents of foods.

Loss of Nutrients during the Entire Freezing Process

Shown in Table 11.7 are losses of vitamin C from seven important vegetables during the entire freezing process (based on differences of vitamin C contents of fresh products and products that were blanched,

Table 11.7. Loss of Vitamin C from Various Vegetables during the Entire Freezing Process

Product	Typical amount of vitamin C in fresh product (mg/100 g)[a]	Loss of vitamin C during 6–12 months at –18°C (mean % and range)	References
Asparagus	33	10 (12–13)	b
Beans, green	19	45 (30–68)	c
Beans, lima	29	51 (39–64)	d
Broccoli	113	49 (35–68)	e
Cauliflower	78	50 (40–60)	f
Peas, green	27	43 (32–67)	g
Spinach	51	65 (54–80)	h

[a] From USDA Handbook 456 (Adams 1975).
[b] Batchelder *et al.* (1947), Gordon and Noble (1959).
[c] Bedford and Hard (1950), Dawson *et al.* (1949), Fisher and Van Duyne (1952), Gordon and Noble (1959), Jurica (1970), Retzer *et al.* (1945).
[d] Guerrant and O'Hara (1953), Guerrant *et al.* (1953).
[e] Batchelder *et al.* (1947), Fisher and Van Duyne (1952), Gordon and Noble (1959).
[f] Gordon and Noble (1959), Retzer *et al.* (1945).
[g] Batchelder *et al.* (1947), Bedford and Hard (1950), Guerrant and O'Hara (1953), Guerrant *et al.* (1953).
[h] Bedford and Hard (1950), Fisher and Van Duyne (1952), von Kamienski (1969).

frozen, and stored for 6–12 months at –18°C). Losses differ among products, among different lots, and among cultivars of the same type of product. With the exception of asparagus and spinach, losses of vitamin C average about 50% during the freezing process. This is unfortunate since all of the vegetables, with the exception of green beans, contain substantial amounts of vitamin C in the fresh state.

The losses in Table 11.7 can be directly compared to those in Table 11.1 (for blanching), since losses in both instances are calculated on the basis of the fresh product. This comparison shows that blanching is responsible for a major share of the loss of water-soluble nutrients that occurs in vegetables during the entire freezing process.

Absolute values for a broad range of nutrients in frozen vegetables "as purchased" are available in the USDA Agriculture Handbook 456 (Adams 1975) and in reports by Burger et al. (1956) and by the National Food Processors Association (Dudek et al. 1982A).

Loss of Nutrients during Cooking of Previously Frozen Vegetables

This topic is appropriate for coverage since there is no assurance that cooking will cause the same loss of nutrients from frozen and fresh vegetables. Shown in Table 11.8 are losses of vitamin C that occur in various frozen vegetables during cooking. These losses are calculated on the basis of comparable uncooked products. Since large differences are apparent with respect to conditions of frozen storage and cooking, it is not proper to condense the data any further than has been done. It is evident that vegetables usually lose substantial amounts of vitamin C during cooking, and that time of frozen storage prior to cooking usually is unimportant; but when it is, storage usually is detrimental (green beans, grean peas). It is also evident from the amounts of vitamin C that are recoverable in the cooking water, that leaching is a major mechanism of loss. The independent effects of cooking time and amount of cooking water cannot be determined from these data.

Losses of minerals and vitamins (other than vitamin C) from various frozen vegetables during cooking are listed in Tables 11.9 and 11.10. When losses of minerals are averaged over all vegetables, it can be seen that losses of iron are greatest and losses of phosphorus and manganese are least. Losses of many of the minerals can be accounted for in the cooking water. One would expect 100% recovery of lost minerals in the cooking water. According to Teply and Derse (1958), "These exceptions may have been due in part to package-to-package variation, but were probably due mainly to large errors, percentage wise, in determining some of the components present at low levels."

When the vitamin losses shown in Table 11.10 are averaged over all vegetables, losses of B_6 (24%), pantothenic acid (17%), and folic acid (16%) are the greatest; losses of niacin (12%) and riboflavin (9%) are intermediate; and loss of β-carotene is least (5%). Mean loss of vitamin C from frozen vegetables (31%, Table 11.8) during cooking exceeds any of the mean values in Table 11.10.

Table 11.8. Loss of Vitamin C from Previously Frozen Vegetables during Cooking[a]

Product	Conditions of frozen storage prior to cooking	Total cooking time in boiling water (min)	Cooking water ÷ product (by wt)	Loss of vitamin C (%)	Amount of lost vitamin C recoverable in cooking water (%)	References
Asparagus	No storage	10–15	2.33	49		Gordon and Noble (1959)
	6 months, −18°C	10–15	2.33	51		Gordon and Noble (1959)
	APP	8	0.2	9[b]	100[b]	Teply and Derse (1958)
Beans, green	No storage	15	?	13		Dawson et al. (1949)
	10 months, −18°C	15	?	47		Dawson et al. (1949)
	No storage	10–15	3.7	36		Gordon and Noble (1959)
	6 months, −18°C	10–15	3.7	25		Gordon and Noble (1959)
	3 weeks, −18°C	25	0.17	27		Phillips and Fenton (1945)
	3 weeks, −18°C	25	0.8	48		Phillips and Fenton (1945)
	No storage	10	2.0	32		Lee et al. (1946)
	6 months, −21°C	10	2.0	31		Lee et al. (1946)
	APR	11–22	0.46	33		Sweeney et al. (1961)
	APP			49[b]	10[b]	Teply and Derse (1958)
	APR	10	0.31	40		Dudek et al. (1982A)
Beans, lima, baby	APP	9	0.4	35[b]	49[b]	Teply and Derse (1958)
Beans, lima, Fordhook	APP	9	0.4	25[b]	60[b]	Teply and Derse (1958)
	APR	13–14	0.3	28		Sweeney et al. (1961)
Beans, lima, Elite or Bridgeton	PF	25	0.22	44		Dudek et al. (1982A)
Broccoli	?	11	0.5	34[b]		Guerrant et al. (1953)
	No storage	8–10	5.5	35		Gordon and Noble (1959)
	6 months, −18°C	8–10	5.5	33		Gordon and Noble (1959)
	APR	5–10	0.4–0.8	23–34	75–80	Martin et al. (1960)
	APR	12	0.3	25		Sweeney et al. (1961)
	PF	11	0.53	27		Eheart (1970)

Broccoli, chopped	APR	3	0.28	39		Dudek et al. (1982A)
Broccoli, spears	APR	8	0.47	19		Dudek et al. (1982A)
Brussels sprouts	No storage	9–10	5	31	ns	Gordon and Noble (1959)
	6 months, –18°C	9–10	5	22		Gordon and Noble (1959)
	APR	13–16	0.3	26		Sweeney et al. (1961)
	APP	10	0.2	7[b]	70[b]	Teply and Derse (1958)
Cauliflower	APR	10	0.31	18		Dudek et al. (1982A)
	No storage	8–10	3.7	24		Gordon and Noble (1959)
	6 months, –18°C	8–10	3.7	22		Gordon and Noble (1959)
	APP	7	0.2	27[b]	37[b]	Teply and Derse (1958)
Carrots	PF	14	0.11	0		Dudek et al. (1982A)
Corn, cut	?	7	0.3	25	100	Barnes and Tressler (1943)
	APP	6	0.2	55[b]	13[b]	Teply and Derse (1958)
	APR	1	0.21	23		Dudek et al. (1982A)
Corn, on cob	3–12 weeks –34°C	?	?	Slight		Payne (1967)
Peas, green	No storage	9	1.64	17		Lee et al. (1946)
	6 months, –18°C	9	1.64	52		Lee et al. (1946)
	APR	10–12	0.2	32		Sweeney et al. (1961)
	APP	8	0.2	17[b]	53[b]	Teply and Derse (1958)
	PF	4	0.05	28		Dudek et al. (1982A)
Potatoes, sweet	PF	35	0.78	34		Dudek et al. (1982A)
Spinach, chopped	APR	9–10	0.3	42		Sweeney et al. (1961)
	APP	11	0.17	34[b]	21[b]	Dudek et al. (1982A)
	APP	5	?	52		Dudek et al. (1982A)
Squash	PF	7	0.02	55		Dudek et al. (1982A)
Mean				31		

[a] APP, as purchased frozen from processor; APR, as purchased frozen in retail market; PF, obtained fresh, then frozen and stored until used.

[b] Total ascorbic acid (reduced ascorbic acid plus dehydroascorbic acid).

Table 11.9. Loss (%) of Minerals from Frozen Vegetables during Cooking[a]

Product	Sample history[b]	Total cooking time (min)[c]	Cooking water ÷ product (by wt)	Ca Loss	Ca RCW	Fe Loss	Fe RCW	P Loss	P RCW	Mg Loss	Mg RCW	K Loss	K RCW	Na Loss	Na RCW	Cu Loss	Mn Loss	Zn Loss	Reference
Asparagus spears	APR	8	0.2	10	60	13	70	5	60	17	53	8	100	0	—	—	—	2	d
Beans, green, cut	APR	11	0.2	6	67	+	—	2	100	10	70	3	100	11	100	—	—	—	d
Beans, lima, baby	APR	10	0.31	0	—	0	0	3	—	0	—	—	—	—	—	0	0	0	e
Beans, lima, Fordhook	APR	9	0.4	5	100	12	50	10	40	8	62	13	77	10	100	—	—	—	d
Beans, lima, Elite or Bridgeton	APR	9	0.4	10	100	1	100	0	—	13	100	7	100	3	100	—	—	—	d
Broccoli, chopped	PF	25	0.22	0	—	0	—	0	—	0	—	0	—	0	—	0	0	—	e
Broccoli, chopped	APR	10	0.2	4	100	31	13	0	—	6	100	7	100	17	76	—	—	25	d
Broccoli, spears	APR	3	0.28	10	—	1	—	7	—	17	—	13	—	17	—	0	0	25	e
Broccoli, spears	APR	8	0.2	4	100	38	11	8	50	9	100	14	71	25	36	—	—	24	d
Brussels sprouts	APR	8	0.47	3	—	13	—	2	100	14	—	20	—	15	—	27	19	24	e
Brussels sprouts	APR	10	0.2	9	100	+	—	10	—	4	100	4	100	11	55	6	9	0	d
Carrots	PF	10	0.31	0	—	5	—	10	—	5	—	0	—	2	—	5	0	0	e
Cauliflower	APR	14	0.11	8	87	1	45	0	—	0	—	15	—	0	—	—	—	—	d
Corn, cut	APR	7	0.2	12	42	11	11	+	—	9	100	1	100	0	—	—	—	—	d
Corn, cut	APR	6	0.2	5	—	37	—	9	67	9	100	10	90	12	100	0	4	0	e
Peas, green	PF	2	0.21	6	83	21	19	0	—	2	—	0	—	—	—	—	—	—	d
Peas, green	APR	8	0.2	0	—	3	—	3	—	8	87	10	100	13	85	0	0	4	e
Potatoes, sweet	PF	4	0.05	13	—	0	—	5	—	15	—	0	—	0	—	0	2	7	e
Spinach, chopped	PF	35	0.78	+	—	9	11	+	—	8	—	3	67	5	100	3	—	—	e
Spinach, leaf	APR	11	0.17	0	—	12	?	0	—	14	21	4	?	6	?	—	—	—	d
Spinach, leaf	APR	11	0.17	0	—	27	—	8	—	5	80	3	—	24	—	10	10	10	d
Squash	APP	5	?	17	—	19	—	13	—	8	—	7	—	0	—	10	10	32	e
Squash	PF	7	0.02	17	—	19	—	13	—	12	—	10	—	0	—	37	0	32	e
Mean				6		11		4		8		7		7		7	3	9	

[a] Losses based on comparable frozen uncooked samples. —, No data; RCW, approximate amount of lost nutrient recoverable in cooking water; +, apparent increase.
[b] APR, as purchased frozen from retail market; APP, as purchased frozen from processor; PF, purchased fresh, then frozen and stored for a short period before use.
[c] Boiling or near-boiling water.
[d] Teply and Derse (1958).
[e] Dudek et al. (1982A).

Table 11.10. Loss (%) of Vitamins (Other Than Vitamin C) from Frozen Vegetables during Cooking[a]

Product	Sample history[b]	Total cooking time (min)[c]	Cooking water ÷ product (by wt)	β-carotene Loss	β-carotene RCW	Folic acid Loss	Folic acid RCW	Niacin Loss	Niacin RCW	Pantothenic acid Loss	Pantothenic acid RCW	Riboflavin, B_2 Loss	Riboflavin, B_2 RCW	Thiamin, B_1 Loss	Thiamin, B_1 RCW	B_6 Loss	B_6 RCW	Reference
Asparagus spears	APR	8	0.2	+	—	26	62	19	53	21	38	15	60	10	70	42	14	d
Beans, green, cut	APR	11	0.2	+	—	19	84	26	35	35	20	14	50	0	—	27	26	d
Beans, lima, baby	APR	10	0.31	0	—	0	—	0	—	13	—	2	—	0	0	3	—	e
Beans, lima, Fordhook	APR	9	0.4	1	0	23	70	23	26	11	100	17	59	15	100	26	23	d
Beans, lima, Elite or Bridgeton	APR	9	0.4	+	—	15	100	23	50	11	100	19	74	27	37	30	23	d
Broccoli, chopped	PF	25	0.22	13	—	21	—	8	—	7	—	0	—	0	—	40	—	e
Broccoli, chopped	APR	10	0.2	+	—	26	42	9	100	14	100	11	91	+	—	6	100	d
Broccoli, spears	APR	3	0.28	0	—	29	100	26	100	13	34	20	54	13	—	20	—	e
Broccoli, spears	APR	8	0.2	1	0	25	—	14	—	32	—	22	—	14	79	26	38	d
Brussels sprouts	APR	8	0.47	0	—	18	—	39	—	7	19	26	50	13	—	24	—	e
Brussels sprouts	APR	10	0.2	+	—	12	67	8	62	28	—	8	—	16	50	19	26	d
Carrots	APR	10	0.31	9	—	0	—	13	—	0	—	0	—	3	—	42	—	e
Carrots	PF	14	0.11	4	—	0	—	0	—	12	—	5	—	21	—	26	—	e
Cauliflower	APR	7	0.2	0	—	50	28	15	87	31	32	16	69	26	35	36	22	d
Corn, cut	APR	6	0.2	11	—	56	12	0	—	40	15	7	100	20	35	39	15	d
Corn, cut	APR	2	0.21	0	0	0	—	0	—	—	—	0	—	0	—	9	—	e
Peas, green	APR	8	0.2	15	7	+	—	0	—	34	29	+	—	12	67	33	52	d
Peas, green	PF	4	0.05	0	—	10	—	0	—	0	—	1	—	0	—	0	—	e
Potatoes, sweet	PF	35	0.78	13	—	0	—	12	—	0	—	0	—	3	—	39	10	e
Spinach, chopped	APR	11	0.17	+	—	3	100	4	100	26	23	+	—	22	36	26	46	d
Spinach, leaf	APR	11	0.17	0	—	11	55	+	—	36	14	0	—	18	28	13	—	d
Spinach, leaf	APP	5	?	3	—	0	—	16	—	—	—	0	—	16	—	16	—	e
Squash	PF	7	0.02	48	—	19	—	18	—	13	—	27	—	31	—	—	—	e
Mean				5		16		12		17		9		12		24		

[a] Losses based on comparable frozen uncooked samples. —, No data; RCW, approximate amount of lost nutrient recoverable in cooking water; +, apparent increase.
[b] APR, as purchased frozen from retail market; APP, as purchased frozen from processor; PF, purchased fresh, then frozen and stored for a short period before use.
[c] Boiling or near-boiling water.
[d] Teply and Derse (1958).
[e] Dudek et al. (1982A).

Large but variable amounts of the water-soluble vitamins are recoverable in the cooking water, again indicating that leaching is a major mechanism by which water-soluble vitamins are lost.

Vitamin losses during cooking generally vary greatly from product to product, and no doubt depend on factors such as product pH, surface: mass ratio, and, perhaps, on the amount of the original vitamin content that was lost during earlier stages of processing (von Kamienski 1972).

The vitamin data in Table 11.10 are in reasonably good agreement with other comparable studies dealing with cooking losses of β-carotene in peas and green beans (Lee *et al.* 1946), thiamin in green peas (Barnes and Tressler 1943; Lee *et al.* 1946; Martin *et al.* 1960), and riboflavin in green beans (Lee *et al.* 1946; Phillips and Fenton 1945; Van Duyne *et al.* 1950).

Lee *et al.* (1946) reported that riboflavin losses during cooking of frozen green peas range from 0 to 39%, which is contrary to the results in Table 11.10. Studies by Dawson *et al.* (1949), Lee *et al.* (1946), and Phillips and Fenton (1945) indicate that thiamin losses during cooking of frozen green beans range from 10 to 35%, which also is contrary to the result in Table 11.10. Divergent results, such as these, are to be expected for reasons already discussed.

The adverse effects of increased cooking time and increased cooking water on losses of vitamin C from frozen spinach are clearly indicated in Table 11.11.

The results of a study by Sweeney *et al.* (1961) indicate that average losses of vitamin C during cooking of six commonly frozen vegetables

Table 11.11. Loss (%) of Vitamin C (Reduced Ascorbic Acid Plus Dehydroascorbic Acid) during Cooking of Previously Frozen Leaf Spinach

Cooking water ÷ Product (wt)	Loss	Percentage recoverable in cooking water[a]
Underdone		
0.17	30	40
0.33	42	31
0.67	49	49
Done		
0.17	35	17
0.33	55	24
0.67	65	28
Overdone		
0.17	45	4
0.33	60	12
0.67	66	20

[a] Percentage of the amount represented in column to the left. From Teply and Derse (1958).

do not differ between products obtained directly from the processor and products obtained from the retail market.

According to van der Meer *et al.* (1973), loss of vitamin C in packaged potatoes, spinach, green peas, and brussels sprouts is the same, regardless of whether they are cooked in a microwave oven, in a convection oven, or in hot water.

FRUITS

Loss of Nutrients during Prefreezing Treatments

Prefreezing treatments that have adverse effects on the nutrient content of fruits usually involve storage for excessive periods or storage at a temperature that is too high. For example, Loeffler (1946) found that raspberries, when allowed to stand at ambient temperatures for 24 or 48 hr prior to freezing, lost, respectively, 17 and 30% of their vitamin C content. On the other hand, storage of strawberries for 2–4 days at 0°–11°C prior to freezing apparently has only a slight effect on vitamin C content (Scott and Schrader 1947). Additional information on this subject is available elsewhere in this book.

Loss of Nutrients during Freezing

Unfortunately, data on this subject are almost nonexistent. Two studies on raspberries and black currants indicate that losses of vitamin C during freezing are insignificant (Loeffler 1946; Sulc 1973).

Loss of Nutrients during Frozen Storage

Losses of vitamin C from several fruits during storage at –18°C are indicated in Fig. 11.3. Losses of vitamin C from muskmelon can be large, particularly if the melons are not packed in syrup. The variety of muskmelon also has a large influence on loss of vitamin C during frozen storage (Wolfe *et al.* 1949). According to Guadagni *et al.* (1957C), raspberries packed in syrup lose only small amounts of vitamin C during frozen storage. Based on several studies, losses of vitamin C from frozen peaches (Bennett *et al.* 1954; DuBois and Colvin 1945; Guadagni *et al.* 1957A; Guerrant 1957) and strawberries (Bennett *et al.* 1954; Crivelli *et al.* 1969; Derse and Teply 1958; Guadagni *et al.* 1961; Guerrant 1957; Pierce *et al.* 1955) generally are moderate during frozen storage. The oxygen-barrier properties of the package have a profound influence on losses of vitamin C during frozen storage, as is clearly indicated in Figs. 11.4 and 11.5.

Losses of vitamin C from citrus juice concentrates during storage for 9–12 months at –18°C usually are less than 5% (Derse and Teply 1958; Huggart *et al.* 1954; McColloch *et al.* 1957; Wolfe *et al.* 1949). Plain or

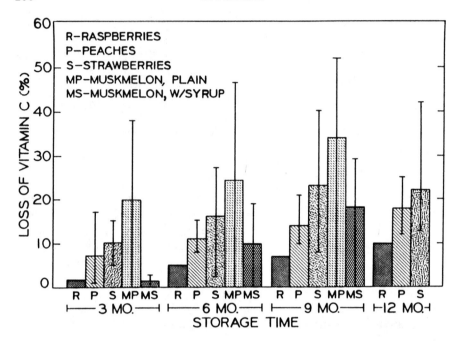

Fig. 11.3. Cumulative losses (after completion of freezing) of vitamin C from fruits during storage at −18°C (means plus ranges). References and conditions: Raspberries, whole, 3 + 1 part 50% sucrose syrup, retail composite cartons (Guadagni *et al.* 1957C); peaches, sliced, in syrup, various packages (Bennett *et al.* 1954; DuBois and Colvin 1945; Guadagni *et al.* 1957A; Guerrant 1957); strawberries, whole or sliced, sugared or plain, various packages (Bennett *et al.* 1954; Crivelli *et al.* 1969; Derse and Teply 1958; Guadagni *et al.* 1961; Guerrant 1957; Pierce *et al.* 1955); muskmelon, two varieties, sliced, packaged in cellophane-lined pint containers (Wolfe *et al.* 1949).

syruped boysenberries, regardless of the kind of container, apparently lose less than 1% vitamin C during storage for 3 months at −18°C (Guadagni *et al.* 1960).

Few data are available concerning losses of minerals and vitamins other than vitamin C from fruits during frozen storage.

The effect of storage temperature on losses of vitamin C from four frozen fruits and fruit juices is shown in Fig. 11.6. Supplementary information for the products in Fig. 11.6 is given in Table 11.12. Separation of the strawberry data into two groups (I and II) was done simply because the two groups behaved differently. The cultivars used could account for the differences observed (Crivelli *et al.* 1969).

With the exception of the data for boysenberries, each line in Fig. 11.6 represents at least two studies, and most of the studies involved at least three temperatures. All data points have been plotted for peaches and strawberries II, whereas points for strawberries I, boysenberries

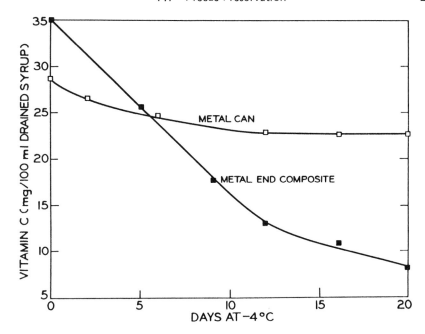

Fig. 11.4.   Effect of container type on losses of vitamin C from frozen peaches. (Sliced peaches, 50% sucrose syrup containing 0.1% ascorbic acid, enameled metal cans or 12-oz composite-type containers.)   Source: Adapted from Guadagni and Nimmo (1957), courtesy of Institute of Food Technologists.

(plain and syruped products), and citrus juices are means.   The ranges of values for strawberries I are indicated on Fig. 11.6.   The data ranges for boysenberries and citrus juices are much smaller than those for strawberries I.

Rates of vitamin C loss in peaches, strawberries I, and boysenberries are affected similarly by temperature.   For these products, a 10°C rise in temperature in the range from –18°C to –7°C causes the rate of vitamin C degradation to accelerate by a factor of 30–70X (Q_{10} = 30–70). This is an uncommonly large dependence on temperature.   For strawberries II the factor is 10X and for citrus juice concentrates 1.5X. Thus, low storage temperatures (–18°C or lower) will preserve vitamin C contents of fruits (not applicable to citrus juice concentrates) much better than high subfreezing temperatures.   Comparable information is unavailable for nutrients other than vitamin C.

A few studies have dealt with the effect of fluctuating storage temperatures versus comparable constant temperatures on nutrient losses from fruits.   With respect to strawberries and raspberries, losses of vitamin C do not differ significantly between the two conditions (Gortner *et al.* 1948; Guadagni and Nimmo 1958).

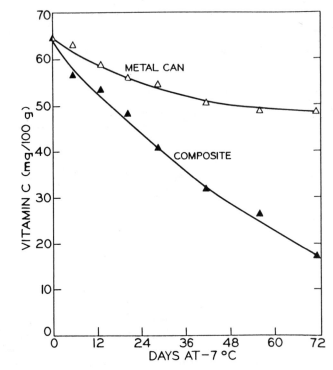

Fig. 11.5.   Effect of container type on losses of vitamin C from frozen strawberries. (Sliced strawberries, 4 + 1 sugar, enameled metal cans or composite-type containers.) Source: Adapted from Guadagni *et al.* (1957B), courtesy of Institute of Food Technologists.

Loss of Nutrients during and following Thawing

Information concerning losses of nutrients from fruits during thawing is almost nonexistent and what little there is deals only with vitamin C.   As would be expected, losses of vitamin C from citrus juice concentrates during thawing are insignificant (Huggart *et al.* 1954). According to Bauernfeind *et al.* (1946), the vitamin C contents of packaged peaches, apricots, nectarines, and fruit salad (all in syrup), are not affected significantly by the method of thawing (thawing times ranged from 20 min to 19 hr).   Thus, it is probably reasonable to assume that properly conducted thawing has almost no detrimental effect on the nutrient contents of fruits provided the syrup and thaw-exudate are consumed.

Holding periods following thawing can result in significant losses of vitamin C.   For example, thawed raspberries in syrup can lose 15% vitamin C when held 1 day at 20°C (Loeffler 1946), and thawed peaches in syrup can lose 13% vitamin C when held 2 hr at room temperature (Strachan and Moyls 1949).

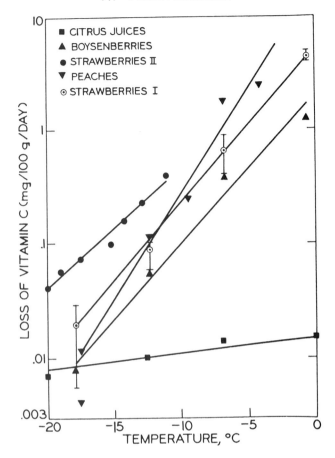

Fig. 11.6. Temperature dependence of vitamin C degradation in frozen fruits. (See Table 11.12 for conditions and references.)

Loss of Nutrients during the Entire Freezing Process

Shown in Table 11.13 are losses of vitamin C from several fruits and fruit juices during the entire freezing process (based on differences in the vitamin C contents of fresh products and products that were frozen and stored for various times at $-18°C$). Losses vary greatly depending on the type of product, the cultivar (Crivelli *et al.* 1969), whether or not syrup is present, the solids content of the juices, and the type of package. Most of the conventional fruits, when processed in a recommended manner, lose less than 30% of their origianl vitamin C content during the entire freezing process, and concentrated citrus juices lose less than 5%. Most of these losses occur during frozen storage. The small losses of vitamin C from citrus juice concentrates are probably

Table 11.12.   Approximate Maximum Storage Period over Which Rates of Vitamin C Degradation Are Valid for the Products in Fig. 11.6

Product	Conditions	Months at: –18°C	–12°C	–7°C	–1°C	References
Strawberries I	Sliced or whole, 4 + 1 sugar, 30-lb tins or composite retail cartons	12	6	1	1 week	b
Strawberries II	Sliced or whole, sugared or plain, plastic packages	10	2	–[a]	—	c
Peaches	Sliced, in syrup, composite or plastic cartons	12	6	2 week	—	d
Boysenberries	Whole, plain or in syrup, packaged in cardboard cartons, or composite retail containers	4	4	1 week	1 week	e
Citrus juices	Grapefruit, orange, tangerine, 42° Brix; type of package unknown	>12	>12	>12	>12	f

[a] —, No data.
[b] Bennett et al. (1954), Guadagni et al. (1957B, 1961).
[c] Crivelli et al. (1969), Pierce et al. (1955).
[d] Bennett et al. (1954), Guadagni et al. (1957A).
[e] Guadagni et al. (1960).
[f] Huggart et al. (1954).

attributable to the low pH values and low oxygen content of these products (Thompson and Fennema 1971).

Some fruits are fortified with vitamin C (150–350 mg/lb of finished pack; Bauernfeind and Pinkert 1970) prior to freezing so that enzyme-catalyzed oxidative browning will be restricted. It has been shown that about 80% of the vitamin C added to peaches, apricots, nectarines, and cantaloupes is retained after 8 months at –18°C (Bauernfeind et al. 1946; Crow and Scoular 1955).

Information on the absolute nutritive composition of frozen fruits "as purchased" can be obtained from USDA Agriculture Handbook 8–9 (Gebhardt et al. 1982), from a report by the National Food Processors Association (Dudek et al. 1982A) and in papers by Burger et al. (1956) and Lowenberg and Wilson (1959).

Table 11.13. Loss of Vitamin C from Fruits During the Entire Freezing Process[a]

Product	Storage time at −18°C (months)	Loss of vitamin C (%), range	References
Strawberries			
44 brands "as purchased"	?	45 (9–85)	Fagerson et al. (1954)
17 cultivars, sliced, sugared, in metal cans	5	17 (0–44)	Scott and Schrader (1947)
Puree, 5 + 1 or 3 + 1 sugar	6	16	Wolfe et al. (1949)
Whole, no syrup or sugar, in polyethylene bags	10	34	Crivelli et al. (1969)
Partially sliced, 6 + 1 sugar, polyethylene boxes	10	42	Pierce et al. (1955)
Citrus products			
Orange juice, concentrate, 42° Brix	9	1	Marshall et al. (1955)
Orange juice, unconcentrated	6	32	Tingleff and Miller (1960)
Orange segments	6	31	Tingleff and Miller (1960)
Grapefruit juice concentrate, 42° Brix	9	5	Marshall et al. (1955)
Grapefruit sections			
Plain	9	4	Wolfe et al. (1949)
With syrup	9	4	Wolfe et al. (1949)
Apricots, in syrup	5	19	Crow and Scoular (1955)
Apricots, in syrup + added vitamin C	5	22	Crow and Scoular (1955)
Acerola juice, natural or diluted, + added sugar, pH 3.3	8	16	Fitting and Miller (1960)
Cantaloupes			
In syrup	5–9	9–44	Crow and Scoular (1955), Wolfe et al. (1949)
In syrup + added vitamin C	5	23	Crow and Scoular (1955)
Plain	9	65–85	Wolfe et al. (1949)
Cherries, sweet, pitted, in syrup, with or without added vitamin C and citric acid	10	19 (11–28)	Strachan and Moyls (1949)
Peaches			
Sliced, in syrup, with added vitamin C, 12 cultivars	8	23 (12–40)	Crow and Scoular (1955), Strachan and Moyls (1949)
Sliced, in syrup, 12 cultivars, moisture-proof containers	8	69 (38–82)	Strachan and Moyls (1949)
Sliced, in syrup, in glass jars	5	29	Crow and Scoular (1955)

[a] Based on estimated initial concentration of 60 mg vitamin C per 100 g of product.

ANIMAL TISSUES

Loss of Nutrients during Prefreezing Treatments

A major prefreezing treatment for some animal tissues is aging. In one study, 0.5-lb samples of longissimus dorsi and semimembranosus muscles from beef were aged 21 days at 1°C (Meyer *et al.* 1963). This resulted in no loss of thiamin and riboflavin, but a 35% loss of niacin. The same types of muscles were aged up to 42 days prior to freezing and storage, and this treatment did not significantly decrease the amounts of vitamin B_6 or pantothenic acid (Meyer *et al.* 1966). In another study, pork roasts were aged 7 days at –1°C and this had no consistent effect on the amounts of thiamin, riboflavin, pantothenic acid, and nicotinic acid (Westerman *et al.* 1955). If these data are typical, it is likely that short-term aging at low nonfreezing temperatures has little adverse effect on the nutritive value of animal tissue.

Treatment of fish with phosphates is a common practice and the effects of this treatment on retention of vitamins and minerals were studied by the National Food Processors Association (Dudek *et al.* 1981, 1982B). Fillets of Pacific whiting and Alaskan pollack were immersed for 2 min in a solution containing 8% sodium tripolyphosphate and 2% sodium chloride, frozen and stored for 2 weeks, thawed, and broiled. When these samples were compared to samples treated identically except for omission of the phosphate treatment, no important differences were observed with respect to retention of vitamins B_1, B_2, B_{12}, and niacin or the minerals Fe, K, Na, Zn, Se, and Ar. However, the samples treated with sodium tripolyphosphate did contain levels of sodium three to seven times greater than that of untreated samples and this will be of concern to persons on low-sodium diets.

Loss of Nutrients during Freezing

Losses of B vitamins in various animal tissues during freezing are listed in Table 11.14. With the exception of pork, losses of the five B vitamins are insignificant. Since freezing, as such, causes no significant alteration in the nutrient contents of vegetables, fruits, and most animal tissues, the losses encountered during freezing pork are indeed puzzling. The losses for pork may be inflated somewhat, since both freezing and thawing are involved, but even after compensating for the approximate effects of thawing, the values are still substantial. Furthermore, these values represent the work of two groups, so it is not possible to simply disregard the findings. Thus, more detailed consideration of these results is justified. Lee *et al.* (1954) reported that pork, during freezing, lost sizable amounts of thiamin, riboflavin, pantothenic acid, and pyridoxine and a small amount of niacin, whereas, after storage for 6 months at –18°C, they reported increases in the amounts of thiamin and niacin, no change in the amounts of riboflavin and pantothenic acid, and a further decrease in pyridoxine. Lehrer *et al.* (1951) reported that pork, during freezing, lost sizable amounts of thiamin and niacin, whereas, during storage for 6 months at –18°C, the amount of thiamin did not change and niacin decreased further. Although it is

Table 11.14.   Loss (%) of B Vitamins from Various Animal Tissues during Freezing[a]

Vitamin	Product	Loss (%)	References
Thiamin	Beef steak	ns	Lee *et al.* (1950)
	Beef liver slices	ns	Kotschevar (1955)
	Beef stew	ns	Kahn and Livingston (1970)
	Chicken à la king	ns	Kahn and Livingston (1970)
	Shrimp Newburg	ns	Kahn and Livingston (1970)
	Oysters	ns	Fieger (1956)
	Pork chops	17–20[b]	Lee *et al.* (1954), Lehrer *et al.* (1951)
Riboflavin	Beef steak	ns	Lee *et al.* (1950)
	Beef liver slices	ns	Kotschevar (1955)
	Oysters	ns	Fieger (1956)
	Pork chops	+16–25[b]	Lee *et al.* (1954), Lehrer *et al.* (1951)
Niacin	Beef steak	ns	Lee *et al.* (1950)
	Beef liver slices	ns	Kotschevar (1955)
	Pork chops	6–18[b]	Lee *et al.* (1954) Lehrer *et al.* (1951)
Pantothenic acid	Beef steak	ns	Lee *et al.* (1950)
	Oysters	ns	Fieger (1956)
	Pork chops	18[b]	Lee *et al.* (1954)
Pyridoxine	Beef steak	ns	Lee *et al.* (1950)
	Oysters	ns	Fieger (1956)
	Pork chops	22[b]	Lee *et al.* (1954)

[a] Effect of freezing alone, unless stated otherwise; ns, not significant.
[b] Includes effect of thawing, but no frozen storage.

possible that large losses of vitamins could occur during freezing (acceleration of reaction rates by freeze concentration, Fennema *et al.* 1973) and be followed by no further losses, or even apparent increases in some vitamins during extended frozen storage, this pattern is not normal in frozen foods.   These results with pork, therefore, should be viewed with skepticism until they are verified by other workers.

Loss of B vitamins during freezing muscles of bovine (Lee *et al.* 1950), ovine (Lehrer *et al.* 1952), and porcine (Lee *et al.* 1954; Lehrer *et al.* 1951) animals is not affected significantly by freezing rate. However, freezing rate can influence the amounts of exudate during thawing and cooking (discussed later) and the extent of structural damage in poultry (damage assessed by the amount of thaw-exudate) and cod (damage assessed by the concentration of DNA–phosphorus in the expressible juice from thawed cod). Furthermore, structural damage in poultry and cod is not linearly related to freezing rate (Crigler and Dawson 1968; Love 1958).

One final point, with respect to freezing rate, is that oxidative changes in beef and pork apparently occur more slowly following slow freezing than following rapid freezing (Nestorov *et al.* 1969). If this result is verified, it will have nutritional significance, since several vitamins can be inactivated by oxidation.

Fluctuating temperatures apparently are not detrimental to vitamin stability in meats. Gortner *et al.* (1948) stored pork loin roasts at constant and comparable conditions of fluctuating subfreezing temperatures and found that thiamin stability did not differ between these two conditions. Moleeratanond *et al.* (1981) stored seven types of beef products for 1 year at three different temperature conditions: (1) constant $-23°C$, (2) fluctuating $-23°$ to $-21°C$ with 12 hr at each temperature, and (3) fluctuating $-21°$ to $-18°C$ with 12 hr at each temperature. These three conditions did not significantly differ in their influence on the stability of thiamin, riboflavin, or niacin.

A study by Lane (1966) is also worth mentioning. He found that frozen fish, once it leaves the warehouse for distribution to retail outlets, is generally exposed to temperatures that average well above $-18°C$. This situation probably applies to most frozen foods and is highly undesirable from the standpoint of vitamin retention.

Loss of Nutrients during Frozen Storage

Shown in Table 11.15 are limited data with respect to losses of B vitamins in several animal tissues during storage for 6 months at $-18°C$. Losses of pyridoxine appear to be the greatest and losses of niacin and pantothenic acid the least. B vitamins are apparently more unstable in pork and oysters than in beef and lamb. Unavailability of data prevents this subject from being covered as thoroughly as was done for fruits and vegetables.

Table 11.15. Loss (%) of B Vitamins from Animal Tissues during Frozen Storage, 6 Months at $-18°C$[a]

Product	B_1	B_2	Niacin	Pantothenic acid	Pyridoxine	References
Beef steaks[b]	0	1	+	10	22	c
Pork, chops and roasts	+ to 18	0–37	+ to 5	0–8	18[b]	d
Lamb chops	+		+			e
Oysters[b]	33	19	3	17	59	f

[a] Independent effect of storage, except some values include effect of thawing. +, Indicates an apparent increase in vitamin content.

[b] Data are of limited value, since only one study is involved.

[c] Kotschevar (1955).

[d] Lee *et al.* (1954), Lehrer *et al.* (1951), Westerman *et al.* (1955).

[e] Lehrer *et al.* (1952).

[f] Fieger (1956).

Table 11.16. Loss (%) of Thiamin from Animal Tissue during Various Methods of Thawing

Product	Loss	References
Beef liver, sliced[a]	22[b]	Kotschevar (1955)
Beef stew	1–11	Kahn and Livingston (1970)
Chicken à la king	2–9	Kahn and Livingston (1970)
Shrimp Newburg	4–10	Kahn and Livingston (1970)

[a] Apparent values for riboflavin and niacin increased during thawing.
[b] Probably mostly thaw-exudate.

Loss of Nutrients during Thawing

Shown in Table 11.16 are thiamin losses that occur during thawing of a few animal tissues. Loss of thiamin from beef liver is substantial, but much of this loss is probably accountable for in the thaw-exudate. Losses of thiamin in the other products are relatively small and probably border on being within the range of experimental error. If these limited results are typical of all vitamins and all animal products, then nutrient losses during thawing (aside from losses in the thaw-exudate) are small.

Several studies have been conducted to determine the effect of thawing method on nutrient losses. Losses of B vitamins from unpackaged beef steak are generally greater when thawing is conducted in water rather than in air at various temperatures (Westerman et al. 1949). Leaching is undoubtedly an important mechanism of loss when meat is thawed directly in water. When heat-transfer methods of thawing (air or water) are applied to beef steak or poultry, the slowest method of thawing (in refrigerator) generally results in losses of B vitamins that are less, or no greater than, those which occur during more rapid thawing (Westerman et al. 1949; Singh and Essary 1971B).

With respect to beef stew, chicken à la king, and shrimp Newburg, thiamin losses are least during microwave thawing, slightly greater during infrared thawing, and greatest during thawing in boiling water (packaged, Kahn and Livingston 1970). Except when unpackaged products are thawed in water (undesirable), the method of thawing appears to have a small influence on losses of B vitamins from animal tissues.

Loss of Nutrients in the Thaw-Exudate

This topic is appropriate for discussion since thaw-exudate contains a substantial amount of nutrients, as is indicated in Table 11.17. It is apparent that the concentrations of thiamin, riboflavin, and niacin present in thaw-exudate from the products listed are roughly equal to those existing in the parent products.

Table 11.17. Composition of Thaw-exudate from Mammalian Meat

Component	Calves liver[a]	Beef[b] (% wt/wt)	Beef[c] (mg/100 g)	Pork[d] (mg/100 g)	Lamb[e] (mg/100 g)
Total solids	20% wt/wt (66%)[f]	13.8	—	—	—
Soluble nitrogen	—	2.24	—	—	—
Ash	—	1.16	—	—	—
Chloride	—	0.032	—	—	—
Thiamin	73 mg/100 g (116%)[f]	—	0.14 (233%)[g]	0.2 (100%)[g]	7 (150%)[g]
Riboflavin	5 mg/100 g (50%)[f]	—	1.0 (98%)[g]	0.2 (100%)[g]	4 (68%)[g]
Niacin	46 mg/100 g (116%)[f]	—	0.16 (94%)[g]	0.2 (66%)[g]	8.6 (166%)[g]

[a] Sliced fresh, frozen slowly, and stored 60 days at −20°C (Kotschevar 1955).

[b] Pieces of psoas and longissimus dorsi muscles measuring 6 × 3 × 1 cm (the shortest dimension being along the fibers) were cut from frozen sirloin immediately after removal from storage, placed on glass grids inside air-tight dishes, and thawed for 48 hr at 10°C. Thaw-exudate was collected under the samples (Howard et al. 1960).

[c] Means for blade roasts, rib roasts, short ribs, and rib steaks. Samples were slowly frozen and stored 60 days at −20°C (Kotschevar 1955).

[d] Means for tenderloin, loin roast, chops. Samples were slowly frozen and stored 60 days at −20°C (Kotschevar 1955).

[e] Means for leg roasts and stew meat. Samples were slowly frozen and stored for 60 days at −20°C (Kotschevar 1955).

[f] Expressed as percentage of the concentration in the product (after exudate was lost).

[g] Expressed as percentage of the concentration in the fresh product.

Table 11.18. Nutrients Lost (%) from Beef and Pork in Thaw-exudate

Nutrient	Beef steak[a]	Pork chops[b]
Thiamin	12	9
Riboflavin	10	4
Niacin	15	10.7
B_6 (pyrimidine)	9	8.7
Pantothenic acid	33	6.9
Folic acid	8	—
B_{12}	—	5.1
Isoleucine	—	11.1
Leucine	—	9.7
Lysine	—	8.6
Methionine	—	7.6
Tryptophan	—	7.1

[a] Frozen at −18°C, stored at this temperature until needed for analysis, then thawed 14–15 hr in air at 26°C (Pearson *et al.* 1951).
[b] Frozen at −18°C, stored at this temperature until needed for analysis, then thawed 18–20 hr in air at 2°C (Pearson *et al.* 1959).

Actual percentage losses of vitamins and amino acids that can occur in beef and pork via the mechanism of thaw-exudate are illustrated in Table 11.18. Although losses of most nutrients generally are not large, an awareness should be created about them so that thaw-exudate will be utilized by the consumer and so that the processor will exercise whatever control is feasible to minimize the amount of thaw-exudate.

The amount of thaw-exudate from animal tissue can range from less than 1% to more than 30%. Factors that influence the amount of thaw-exudate can be categorized as follows: (1) type of product, (2) natural variations within a given product, and (3) processing variables.

Type of Product

Differences in the amount of thaw-exudate can occur depending on the type of product being frozen. Amounts of thaw-exudate obtained from beef (Bennett *et al.* 1954; Cook *et al.* 1926; Kotschevar 1955; Ramsbottom and Koonz 1939, 1940, 1941; Pearson and Miller 1950; Westerman *et al.* 1949) and pork muscle (Kotschevar 1955; Pearson *et al.* 1959) often range from about 1 to 10%, amounts from poultry (Crigler and Dawson 1968; Engler and Bowers 1975; Kahn and Lentz 1965; Kahn and van den Berg 1967) are generally less than 5%, and amounts from fish are highly variable, but values of 5–10% are common for salmon, halibut, and freshwater species (Botta *et al.* 1973; Manohar *et al.* 1973). Other product characteristics also have a bearing on the amount of thaw-exudate. For example, thaw-exudate from saltwater fish is greater then that from freshwater fish (Botta *et al.* 1973; Manohar *et al.* 1973), and glandular meats generally exhibit greater thaw-exudate than muscle meats (Kotschevar 1955).

Properties of a Given Product

The pH of meat has a profound influence on the amount of thaw-exudate. A high ultimate pH of 6.4 will minimize thaw-exudate in pork, mutton, and beef, and thaw-exudate will increase as the pH is lowered to 5–5.2 (Ramsbottom and Koonz 1940; Sair and Cook 1938).

State of rigor at the time of freezing also can have a profound effect on the amount of thaw-exudate. For tissues which are sensitive to this effect (some fish, whale muscle, poultry, mammalian muscle), an undesirable processing sequence involving rapid freezing prerigor, storage at low temperature, and rapid thawing can result in very large amounts of thaw-exudate (Bendall 1972; Kahn and Lentz 1965; Manohar *et al.* 1973; Tanaka and Tanaka 1956A, 1957).

Processing Variables

Aging of beef prior to freezing has been found to decrease the amount of thaw-exudate (Ramsbottom and Koonz 1940).

Thaw-exudate is usually greater from small cuts of animal tissue (large surface:volume ratio) than it is from large cuts of animal tissue (Larson, 1956; Ramsbottom and Koonz 1939, 1941).

Rapid freezing often results in less thaw-exudate than slow freezing, particularly with small cuts of animal tissue (Ramsbottom and Koonz 1939, 1941; Cook *et al.* 1926; Kahn and van den Berg 1967). With large cuts of beef, freezing rate generally has no influence on the amount of thaw-exudate (Ramsbottom and Koonz 1941). With poultry, freezing rate and the amount of thaw-exudate are not linearly related (Fig. 11.7), and this behavior may well extend to small cuts of other kinds of animal tissue (Love 1958). When animal tissues are frozen prerigor, slow freezing generally results in less thaw-exudate than rapid freezing (Tanaka and Tanaka 1957). Slow freezing causes the product to remain at high subfreezing temperatures for a relatively long period, thus allowing glycolysis to continue, and, thereby lessening the possibility of thaw-rigor (a large amount of thaw-exudate is often associated with thaw-rigor).

The effect of storage temperature on the amount of thaw-exudate apparently varies with the product and with other processing variables. In two studies, large and small cuts of beef were stored for 4–12 months at temperatures ranging from $-12°$ to $-29°C$ and no difference was noted in the amount of thaw-exudate as a function of storage temperature (Bennett *et al.* 1954; Ramsbottom and Koonz 1941). However, with cod the amount of thaw-exudate apparently increases as the storage temperature is increased over the range $-29°$ to $-7°C$ (Miyauchi 1962).

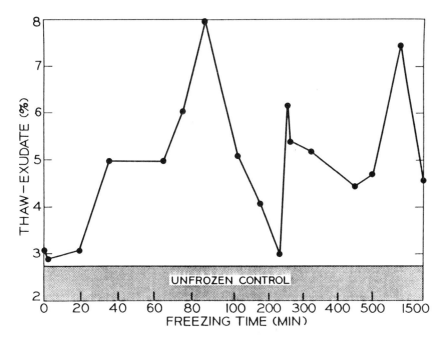

Fig. 11.7. Effect of freezing time (rate) on the percentage of thaw-exudate from poultry. Source: Adapted from Crigler and Dawson (1968), courtesy of Institute of Food Technologists.

The amount of thaw-exudate generally increases with increased storage time, especially with small cuts of animal tissue (Ramsbottom and Koonz 1941; Pearson and Miller 1950). The opposite effect can sometimes occur when animal muscles are frozen prerigor (Tanaka and Tanaka 1956B). When this occurs, prolonged storage apparently allows glycolysis to proceed sufficiently so that thaw-rigor is less likely.

Thawing rate may or may not influence the amount of thaw-exudate. In two studies involving pork and beef steaks, thawing rate was shown to have little or no affect on the amount of thaw-exudate (Vail *et al.* 1943; Westerman *et al.* 1949). However, the amount of thaw-exudate from animal tissues frozen prerigor often will be less if thawing is slow rather than rapid (Tanaka and Tanaka 1957). The reason for this was mentioned earlier when freezing rates and storage times were discussed. With chicken broilers, very slow thawing has been reported to result in a greater amount of exudate than rapid thawing (Singh and Essary, 1971A).

In a study involving thawing of relatively large blocks of postrigor whale meat, very rapid dielectric thawing was shown to result in much less thaw-exudate than very rapid thawing by resistance heating or by slow thawing in air (Tanaka and Tanaka 1956A).

Table 11.19. Loss (%) of Vitamins from Animal Tissues during the Entire Freezing Process[a]

Product	Storage conditions	B_1	B_2	Niacin	Pantothenic acid	Pyridoxine	References
Beef liver, sliced	60 days, −20°C	32	35	+			Kotschevar (1955)
Beef steak, l. dorsi	6 months, −18°C	8	9	0	8	24	Lee et al. (1950)
	10–12 months, −18°C	2	43	4			
Beef (l. dorsi and semimembranosus)	3 years, −18°C, unaged	+34	+9	20			Meyer et al. (1963)
	3 years, −18°C, aged	3	+8	+1			
Pork loins[b]	1 year, −18°C	11	+44	+14	+6		Westerman et al. (1952)
Poultry, fowls, whole	8 months, −18°C						Millares and Fellers (1949)
light meat		12	3	+10			
dark meat		42	11	0			
Poultry, less than 84 days old	8–12 months, −18°C						Morgan et al. (1949)
breast		16	0	9			
leg		5	33	22			
Turkeys, 27–36 weeks old	3 months, −23°C						Cook et al. (1949)
breast		0	8	0			
leg		18	0	0			
Oysters[b]	6 months, −18°C	22	0	35	+	46	Fieger (1956)

[a] May or may not include thawing.
[b] Data are highly variable.

Chemical treatments also can influence the amount of thaw-exudate. For example, if fish, prior to freezing, are dipped in a solution of trisodium polyphosphate, the amount of thaw-exudate will be reduced (Manohar *et al.* 1973).

Loss of Nutrients during the Entire Freezing Process

Losses of B vitamins from animal tissues during the entire freezing process are shown in Table 11.19. It is evident that losses are quite variable. Changes in thiamin content during the freezing process range from +34 to −42%, changes in riboflavin content range from +44 to −43%, changes in niacin content range from +14 to −35%, and, based on limited data, changes in pantothenic acid content range from +6 to −8% and changes in pyridoxine content range from −24 to −46%.

Variability of vitamin losses within a given type of product (e.g., beef) appears to be fully as large as variability among different types of products.

The phases of the freezing process that cause the greatest losses of B vitamins appear to be frozen storage and thawing (thaw-exudate). With pork, it is also possible that substantial amounts of B vitamins are lost during freezing, but further work is needed to confirm or reject this notion.

Loss of Nutrients during Cooking of Previously Frozen Animal Tissues

Shown in Table 11.20 are the results of two studies dealing with losses of B vitamins during cooking of previously frozen beef and pork. The losses indicated presumably are total losses; that is, they include both cook-exudate and chemical degradation of vitamins within the meat. Losses of most B vitamins, with the exception of thiamin, are relatively small.

Shown in Table 11.21 are results of a study dealing with losses of various nutrients during broiling of previously frozen seafoods. In most instances, losses of vitamins and minerals are insignificant to moderate. The only nutrient lost in excess of 25% is riboflavin in shrimp.

With turkeys, retention of vitamin B_6 following cooking is not influenced in a consistent manner by the physical state (frozen, partially frozen, thawed) of the bird at the onset of cooking (Engler and Bowers 1975).

Comparative Losses of B Vitamins from Fresh-Cooked and Frozen–Stored–Cooked Animal Tissues

The results of two studies pertinent to this topic are summarized in Table 11.22. Frozen–stored–cooked lamb chops, in one study, contained

Table 11.20. Loss (%) of B Vitamins during Cooking of Previously Frozen Beef and Pork[a]

Product	Conditions of frozen storage prior to cooking	B_1	B_2	Niacin	Pantothenic acid	Pyridoxine	References
Beef steak (l. dorsi)	No storage	40	5	6	+2	14	Lee *et al.* (1950)
	6–10 months, −18°C	35	3	15	15	+16	
Pork chops (l. dorsi)	No storage	15	0	+	+	8	Lee *et al.* (1954)
	6 months, −18°C	19	0	14			

[a] Losses based on thawed, uncooked product that had been stored for the same time and temperature.

Table 11.21. Loss (%) of Nutrients during Cooking of Previously Frozen Seafoods[a]

Product	B_1	B_2	Niacin	B_{12}	Fe	K	Na	Zn	Se	Ar
Flounder	2	0	2	17	12	4	6	4	0	0
Salmon	8	6	0	24	0	0	5	3	0	0
Atlantic mackerel	0	0	0	0	0	5	8	0	0	0
Shrimp[b,c]	0	41	0	6	13	17	21	0	0	5
Alaskan pollack[b]	14	0	11	0	8	19	24	12	0	8
Pacific whiting[b]	0	1	0	0	1	2	6	0	0	0
~ S.D.	±15	±15	±15	±30	±20	±12	±10	±15	±15	±25

Source: Dudek *et al.* (1982B).
[a] Frozen–cooked compared to frozen.
[b] No microwave, just baked or broiled.
[c] Less loss baked than broiled.

Table 11.22. Comparative Nutritive Values of Fresh-Cooked and Frozen–Stored–Cooked Meats[a]

Product	Fresh-cooked			Cooked from frozen state after 6 months at $-22°C$[b]			References
	B_1	B_2	Niacin	B_1	B_2	Niacin	
Lamb chops	4		82	4 (0)[b]		134 (+63)[b]	Lehrer *et al.* (1952)
Pork chops	15	3.5	207	14 (−7)[b]	3.1 (−11)[b]	113 (−45)[b]	Lehrer *et al.* (1951)

[a] Vitamin content, $\mu g/g$.
[b] Percentage change as compared to cooked, unfrozen product.

as much thiamin and more niacin than the fresh-cooked product. Frozen–stored–cooked pork chops contained slightly less thiamin and riboflavin and considerably less niacin than the fresh-cooked product.

DAIRY PRODUCTS AND MARGARINE

During freezing and storage for 24 months at $-10°C$, butter loses only a small amount of its original vitamin D content, and butter and margarine lose about 17% of their vitamin A contents (Chick and Roscoe 1926; Deuel and Greenberg 1953). According to Holmes *et al.* (1946), ice cream frozen and stored for 7 months at $-23°C$ loses 5% of its original riboflavin, 16% of its original carotene, and 100% of its vitamin C (actually, freshly made ice cream contains little or no vitamin C). According to Lawrence *et al.* (1946), frozen milk stored for 19 weeks at $-14°C$ loses no biotin or nicotinic acid.

MISCELLANEOUS OBSERVATIONS

The stabilities of various antibiotic residues in frozen bovine muscle have been studied by O'Brien *et al.* (1981). Residues of chloramphenicol, oxytetracycline, and sulfadimidine lost little or no activity during storage for at least 50 weeks at $-20°C$, whereas ampicillin lost 20–40% of its activity during 80 weeks storage at $-20°C$.

Information on the stability of pesticide residues in frozen foods has been reviewed by Kawar *et al.* (1973). All of the organochlorine insecticides studied (DDT, dieldrin, endrin, heptachlor, and lindane) were stable in butter and ice cream stored for 4 months at $-26°C$. Among the organophosphorus insecticides studied (Bidrin®, chlorfenvinphos, dichlorvos, dioxanthion, malathion, mevinphos, parathion, and tetrachlorvinphos), the only ones exhibiting instability at subfreezing temperatures were dichlorvos (2–62% loss in wheat stored for 2–11 months at $-15°C$), malathion, (40–47% loss in apples and plums stored for 1–8 months at $-18°C$, but stable in black currants and spinach stored for 6 months at $-10°$ to $-15°C$), and perhaps parathion (conflicting results). Also, Kilgore and Windham (1970) reported that 45–77% of the malathion residue on broccoli is lost during blanching, freezing, and storage for 6 months at $-9°C$. Among the fungicides studied by Kawar *et al.* (1973) (captan, maneb, zineb) only captan was unstable (22–56% loss in apples, plums, and strawberries stored for 1 month at $-18°C$). Among the herbicides studied (chlorthiamid, cyanazine, dalapon, and dichlobenil), all were stable during periods of storage normally encountered for frozen foods.

Only limited information is available on the subject of protein bioavailability as influenced by freeze preservation. Russian investigators studied the effects of frozen storage on the nutritive value of semitendinosus muscles from beef (Golovkin and Meluzova 1974; Meluzova 1977). Nutritive value, as estimated by the in vitro susceptibility of muscle extracts to trypsin, or trypsin and chymotrypsin, was studied in samples that were raw or cooked, prerigor or postrigor, then stored for 12 months at $-10°$, $-18°$, or $-28°C$.

When raw samples were frozen prerigor and then stored for 12 months at any of the three temperatures, susceptibility to enzyme attack generally decreased significantly. When similar samples were cooked prior to frozen storage, changes in susceptibility to enzymes after 12 months storage were inconsistent.

When postrigor samples, either cooked or raw, were frozen for 12 months at any of the three temperatures, susceptibility to enzyme attack decreased, usually by amounts that appear to be of practical significance.

During the course of the 12-month storage period, cooking prior to freezing influenced the behavior of the prerigor samples but not the postrigor samples. For prerigor samples, cooking resulted in decreased susceptibility to enzyme attack during the first 3 months of storage at all temperatures, but for the remainder of the 12-month storage period, differences between cooked and raw prerigor samples were insignificant.

It was also observed that susceptibility to enzyme attack changed, sometimes dramatically, during the course of the 12-month storage period. The authors correlated these changes with changes in the amount of mucopolysaccharides (from the connective tissue) that bound to the myofibrillar proteins. When binding of mucopolysaccharides was substantial, susceptibility of myofibrillar proteins to enzyme attack was minimal and this condition was consistently observed after 5 months storage at all temperatures.

Kramer and associates (Kramer 1977; Kramer *et al.* 1979) used a conventional method (protein efficiency ratio, PER) to evaluate changes in protein bioavailability during storage of frozen foods, and their results differ from those of the Russian investigators. The products studied by Kramer's group were texturized vegetable protein (TVP) that had been rehydrated and canned, and beef patties supplemented with either TVP (8.5% dry powder by weight) or with TVP (8.5%) and single-cell protein (2.5%). Samples were stored for periods up to 18 months at temperatures ranging from $-10°$ to $-30°C$. PER values did not change significantly during storage at any given temperature, and it is therefore not surprising that storage for 18 months at $-30°C$ resulted in only marginally better retention of original PER values than storage for the same time at $-10°C$. Since the PER approach to evaluating bioavailability of proteins is well accepted, it appears justifiable to conclude that the freezing process, as typically conducted commercially, is unlikely to have a significant detrimental effect of the bioavailability of food proteins.

DISCUSSION

Several points of interest are apparent when losses of vitamins during freeze processing of vegetables, fruits, and animal tissues are compared (Table 11.23). During the freezing process, vitamin losses in vegetables are caused primarily by blanching and prolonged (6–12 months) frozen storage, in fruits by prolonged frozen storage and thawing (if the syrup and thaw-exudate are not consumed), and in animal tissues by prolonged frozen storage and by thawing (thaw-exudate).

Moderate to large amounts of water-soluble vitamins are lost from vegetables during blanching, from animal tissues during thawing (thaw-exudate), and presumably from fruits by leaching into the syrup and during thawing (thaw-exudate). Almost all of these losses could be avoided if (1) vegetables were blanched and cooled by means that do not involve liquid water, and (2) the thaw-exudate from animal tissues and the syrup and thaw-exudate from fruits were consumed.

With vegetables and animal tissues, significant losses of water-soluble nutrients can occur during cooking (Table 11.23). With vegetables, these losses can be minimized by using minimal cooking times and minimal amounts of cooking water, and with animal tissues by consuming the cooking-exudate, for example, in the form of gravy.

Table 11.23. Summary of Vitamin Losses from Various Classes of Foods during Freezing–Processing and Cooking

Processing step	Vegetables	Fruits	Animal tissues
Prefreezing treatments	10–44% loss of vitamin C during blanching; substantial losses can occur during storage if time–temperature conditions are abusive	Slight if properly handled prior to freezing	Slight if properly handled prior to freezing
Freezing	Slight	Slight (two studies)	Insignificant, except perhaps for B vitamins in pork
Frozen storage	Substantial losses of vitamin C and pantothenic acid; moderate losses of vitamins B_1 and B_2; losses of vitamin C are highly temperature dependent ($Q_{10} = 6$–20)	Substantial losses of vitamin C except in citrus juice concentrate; losses of vitamin C are highly temperature dependent ($Q_{10} = 30$–70)	Data limited; substantial losses of pyridoxine from beef, pork, oysters; moderate losses of vitamins B_1 and B_2 in pork; substantial losses of B vitamins in oysters
Thawing	Slight	Little data; probably slight, except perhaps for loss of vitamins in the syrup and thaw-exudate	Moderate losses of B vitamins and amino acids in thaw-exudate
Total freezing process	Many common vegetables lose ~50% of their original vitamin C contents	Losses of vitamin C are usually less than 30%, except in citrus juice concentrate, where losses of vitamin C are less than 5%	Losses of B vitamins are highly variable; losses of B_1 usually 25%, B_2 often 15%, niacin often 10%, pyridoxine about 25–50% (few data)
Cooking of frozen food	Mean values (variability large): vitamin C, 30%; β-carotene, 5%; folic acid, 15%; niacin, 12%; B_1, 12%; B_6, 25%; B_2, 10%; pantothenic acid, 17%; leaching is an important factor	Not applicable for most fruits	B_1, 15–40%; B_2, 0–40%; niacin, 0–15%; pantothenic acid, 0–15%; pyridoxine, 0–15%; B_{12}, 0–25%; substantial losses in cooking exudate

The temperature dependence of vitamin C degradation in frozen fruits and vegetables is also worthy of comment. The rates of vitamin C degradation in several fruits and vegetables at $-18°C$ are similar (Figs. 11.2 and 11.6). Furthermore, a rise in temperature causes uncommonly large increases in the rates of vitamin C degradation in several vegetables (Q_{10} = 6–20 for green beans, cauliflower, green peas, and spinach) and in several fruits (Q_{10} = 30–70 for peaches, boysenberries, and some strawberries). This large temperature dependence is no doubt caused by the fact that a high concentration of solutes exists in the unfrozen phases of frozen foods and that this concentration (and accordingly, oxygen solubility, viscosity, and molecular mobility) changes markedly with a change in temperature (Fennema *et al.* 1973; Pincock and Kiovsky 1966; Thompson and Fennema 1971). From the standpoint of retention of vitamin C, the desirability of storing fruits and vegetables at temperatures of $-18°C$ or lower should be abundantly clear.

It would be useful as well as interesting to accurately compare the nutrient losses incurred in foods during the primary methods of long-term preservation (freezing, canning, and drying). Unfortunately, this is not possible to do with reasonable accuracy, even though two major sources of nutrient data have recently appeared in print: the USDA handbooks on "Composition of Foods" (USDA 1976–1982) and the reports of the National Food Processors Association on the nutrient contents of raw, frozen, and cooked fruits, vegetables, and seafoods (Dudek *et al.* 1981, 1982A,B).

The USDA source of data is unsuitable for comparing nutrient losses in foods preserved by various methods because data pertaining to the three major methods of food preservation are not presented for all major food products, and even when they are, users of the data are warned, for valid reasons, not to make this kind of comparison. For example, in the section (Gebhardt *et al.* 1982) dealing with fruits, the following statement is presented.

> Nutrient data for different forms of a fruit were not derived from the same sample. That is, a sample of peaches was not subdivided and analyzed raw, canned, dried, and frozen. The data on the various forms were obtained from many sources and represent different growing years, growing areas, cultivars, laboratories, and possibly different methods of analysis. Therefore, differences in values for various forms of a fruit do not necessarily show the effect of processing.

With regard to the studies conducted by the National Food Processors Association, attention was directed primarily to the effects of various methods of heating on nutrient retention. Drying was not studied and freezing (storage conditions usually not indicated) was used as a common preservative technique for samples that were ultimately cooked by various means. Thus, comparative losses of nutrients during freezing, canning, and drying can not be assessed from these data.

Probably the most that can be appropriately said at this time is that properly conducted freezing (no frozen storage) of foods that are not normally blanched (fruits and animal tissues) results in better retention of most of the labile nutrients than does canning or dehydration. However, if the frozen foods are blanched prior to freezing (as are most vegetables), especially if water-blanched, and the frozen products are exposed to conditions of frozen storage as normally encountered during retail marketing, then thawed and typically prepared for consumption, the nutrient content of these foods will differ in few, if any, important respects from the nutrient contents of canned or dehydrated foods as typically marketed and prepared for consumption.

Furthermore, fresh-cooked vegetables will generally contain greater amounts of chemically labile or leachable nutrients than will canned, frozen, or dehydrated vegetables that have been normally marketed and normally prepared for consumption; provided the fresh vegetables are truly fresh, that is, they are utilized soon after harvest (within 2 days) and are kept cool during the interval between harvest and consumption. Foods purchased as "fresh" in the grocery stores often do not conform to these stipulations.

Finally, vitamins in fresh fruits and animal tissues are generally less labile than vitamins in vegetables.

REFERENCES

Abrams, C. I. 1975. The ascorbic acid content of quick frozen brussels sprouts. J. Food Technol. *10*, 203–213.

Adams, C. F. 1975. Nutritive value of American foods in common units. *In* Agriculture Handbook *456*. USDA, Washington, DC.

Barnes, B., and Tressler, D. K. 1943. Thiamin content of fresh and frozen peas and corn before and after cooking. Food Res. *8*, 420–427.

Batchelder, E. L., Kirkpatrick, M. E., Stein, K. E., and Marron, I. M. 1947. Effect of scalding method on the quality of three home-frozen vegetables. J. Home Econ. *39*, 282–286.

Bauernfeind, J. C., and Pinkert, D. M. 1970. Food processing with added ascorbic acid. Advan. Food Res. *18*, 219–315.

Bauernfeind, J. C., Jahns, F. W., Smith, E. G., and Siemers, G. F. 1946. Vitamin C stability in frozen fruit processed with crystalline L-ascorbic acid. Fruit Prod. J. *25*, 324–330, 347.

Bedford, C. L., and Hard, M. M. 1950. The effect of cooling method on the ascorbic acid and carotene content of spinach, peas, and snap beans preserved by freezing. Proc. Am. Soc. Hort. Sci. *55*, 403–409.

Bendall, J. R. 1972. Postmortem changes in muscle. *In* The Structure and Function of Muscle. Vol. 2, Part 2. G. H. Bourne (Editor). Academic Press, New York.

Bennett, G., *et al.* 1954. Some factors affecting the quality of frozen foods. II. Penn State Coll. Agric. Exp. Stn. Bull. *580*.

Boggs, M. M., *et al.* 1960. Time–temperature tolerance of frozen foods. XXI. Frozen peas. Food Technol. *14*, 181–185.

Botta, J. R., Richards, J. F., and Tomlinson, N. 1973. Flesh pH, color; thaw drip, and mineral concentration of Pacific halibut (*Hippoglossus stenolepis*) and

Chinook salmon (*Oncorhynchus tshawytscha*) frozen at sea. J. Fish. Res. Bd. Can. *30*, 71–77.

Burger, M., *et al.* 1956. Vitamin, mineral, and proximate composition of frozen fruits, juices, and vegetables. J. Agric. Food Chem. *4*, 418–425.

Chick, H., and Roscoe, M. H. 1926. LXXXIV. Influence of diet and sunlight upon the amount of vitamin A and vitamin D in the milk afforded by a cow. Biochem. J. *20*, 632–649.

Cook, B. B., Morgan, A. F., and Smith, M. B. 1949. Thiamin, riboflavin, and niacin content of turkey tissues as affected by storage and cooking. Food Res. *14*, 449–458.

Cook, B. B., Gunning, B., and Uchimoto, D. 1961. Variations in nutritive value of frozen green baby lima beans as a result of methods of processing and cooking. J. Agric. Food Chem. *9*, 316–321.

Cook, G. A., Love, E. F. J., Vickery, J. R., and Young, W. J. 1926. Studies on the refrigeration of meat. I. Investigations into the refrigeration of beef. Australian J. Exp. Biol. Med. Sci. *3*, 15–31.

Crigler, J. C., and Dawson, L. E. 1968. Cell disruption in broiler breast muscle related to freezing time. J. Food Sci. *33*, 248–250.

Crivelli, G., Rosati, P., and Monzini, A. 1969. Chemical stability of frozen strawberries during storage. *In* Frozen Foods. International Institute of Refrigeration, Paris, France.

Crow, L. S., and Scoular, F. I. 1955. Effects of antioxidant ascorbic acid upon the ascorbic acid content of certain frozen fruits. J. Home Econ. *47*, 259–260.

Dawson, E. H., Reynolds, H., and Toepfer, E. W. 1949. Home-canned versus home-frozen snap beans. J. Home Econ. *41*, 572–574.

De Groot, A. P. 1963. The influence of dehydration of foods on the digestibility and the biological value of the proteins. Food Technol. *17*, 339–343.

Derse, P. H., and Teply, L. J. 1958. Effect of storage conditions on nutrients in frozen green beans, peas, orange juice, and strawberries. J. Agric. Food Chem. *6*, 309–312.

Deuel, H. J., Jr., and Greenberg, S. M. 1953. A comparison of the retention of vitamin A in margarines and in butters based upon bioassays. Food Res. *18*, 497–503.

Dietrich, W. C., and Neumann, H. J. 1965. Blanching brussels sprouts. Food Technol. *19*, 1174–1177.

Dietrich, W. C., *et al.* 1957. The time–temperature tolerance of frozen foods. IV. Objective tests to measure adverse changes in frozen vegetables. Food Technol. *11*, 109–113.

Dietrich, W. C., *et al.* 1959. Time–temperature tolerance of frozen foods. XIV. Quality retention of frozen green snap beans in retail packages. Food Technol. *13*, 136–145.

Dietrich, W. C., Boggs, M. M., Nutting, M-D. F., and Weinstein, N. E. 1960. Time–temperature tolerance of frozen foods. XXIII. Quality changes in frozen spinach. Food Technol. *14*, 522–527.

Dietrich, W. C., Nutting, M-D. F., Boggs, M. M., and Weinstein, N. E. 1962. Time–temperature tolerance of frozen foods. XXIV. Quality changes in cauliflower. Food Technol. *16*, 123–128.

DuBois, C. W., and Colvin, D. L. 1945. Loss of added vitamin C in the storage of peaches. Fruit Prod. J. Am. Food Mfgr. *25*, 101–103.

Dudek, J. A., Behl, B. A., Elkins, E. R., Hagen, R. E., and Chin, H. B. 1981. Determination of effects of processing and cooking on the nutrient composition of selected seafoods. National Food Processors Assoc., Washington, DC.

Dudek, J. A., Elkins, E. R., Chin, H. B., and Hagen, R. 1982A. Investigations to determine nutrient content of selected fruits and vegetables—raw, processed and prepared. National Food Processors Assoc., Washington, DC.

Dudek, J. A., Berman, S. C., Behl, B. A., Elkins, E. R., Chin, H. B., and Farrow, R. P. 1982B. Determination of effects of processing and cooking on the nutrient composition of selected seafoods. National Food Processors Assoc., Washington, DC.

Eheart, M. S. 1967. Effect of microwave vs. water-blanching on nutrients in broccoli. J. Am. Diet. Assoc. *50*, 207–211.

Eheart, M. S. 1970. Effect of storage and other variables on composition of frozen broccoli. Food Technol. *24*, 1009–1011.

Engler, P. P., and Bowers, J. A. 1975. Vitamin B_6 content of turkey cooked from frozen, partially frozen and thawed states. J. Food Sci. *40*, 615–617.

Fagerson, I. S., Anderson, E. E., Hayes, K. M., and Fellers, C. R. 1954. Vitamin C and frozen strawberries. Quick Frozen Foods *16*(9), 84–85.

Farrell, K. T., and Fellers, C. R. 1942. Vitamin content of green snap beans. Influence of freezing, canning and dehydration on the content of thiamin, riboflavin and ascorbic acid. Food Res. *7*, 171–177.

Feaster, J. F., Mudra, A. E., Ives, M., and Tompkins, M. D. 1949. Effect of blanching time on vitamin retention in canned peas. Canner *108*(1), 27–30.

Fennema, O., Powrie, W. D., and Marth, E. H. 1973. Low-Temperature Preservation of Foods and Living Matter. Marcel Dekker, New York.

Fenton, F., and Tressler, D. K. 1938. Losses of vitamin C during commercial freezing, defrosting and cooking of frosted peas. Food Res. *3*, 409–416.

Fieger, E. A. 1956. Vitamin content of fresh, frozen oysters. Quick Frozen Foods *19*(4), 152, 155.

Fisher, W. B., and Van Duyne, F. O. 1952. Effect of variations in blanching on quality of frozen broccoli, snap beans, and spinach. Food Res. *17*, 315–325.

Fitting, K. O., and Miller, C. D. 1960. The stability of ascorbic acid in frozen and bottled acerola juice alone and combined with other fruit juices. Food Res. *25*, 203–210.

Gebhardt, S. E., Cutrufelli, R., and Matthews, R. H. 1982. Composition of foods: fruits and fruit juices. Agriculture Handbook *8–9*. USDA, Washington, DC.

Golovkin, N. A., and Meluzova, L. A. 1974. Effect of temperature conditions on the enzymatic degradation of myofibrillar proteins at long-time meat storage. Proc. Fourth Int. Cong. Food Sci. Technol. *1*, 641–647.

Gordon, J., and Noble, I. 1959. Effects of blanching, freezing, freezing-storage and cooking on ascorbic acid retention in vegetables. J. Home Econ. *51*, 867–870.

Gortner, W. A., Fenton, F., Volz, F. E., and Gleim, E. 1948. Effect of fluctuating storage temperatures on quality of frozen foods. Ind. Eng. Chem. *40*, 1423–1426.

Guadagni, D. G., and Nimmo, C. C. 1957. The time–temperature tolerance of frozen foods. III. Effectiveness of vacuum, oxygen removal, and mild heat in controlling browning in frozen peaches. Food Technol. *11*, 43–47.

Guadagni, D. G., and Nimmo, C. C. 1958. Time–temperature tolerance of frozen foods. XIII. Effect of regularly fluctuating temperatures in retail packages of frozen strawberries and raspberries. Food Technol. *12*, 306–310.

Guadagni, D. G., Nimmo, C. C., and Jansen, E. F. 1957A. The time–temperature tolerance of frozen foods. II. Retail packages of frozen peaches. Food Technol. *11*, 33–42.

Guadagni, D. G., Nimmo, C. C., and Jansen, E. F. 1957B. Time–temperature tolerance of frozen foods. VI. Retail packages of frozen strawberries. Food Technol. *11*, 389–397.

Guadagni, D. G., Nimmo, C. C., and Jansen, E. F. 1957C. Time–temperature tolerance of frozen foods. X. Retail packs of frozen red raspberries. Food Technol. *11*, 633–637.

Guadagni, D. G., Eremia, K. M., Kelly, S. H., and Harris, J. 1960. Time–temperature tolerance of frozen foods. XX. Boysenberries. Food Technol. *14*, 148–150.

Guadagni, D. G., Downes, N. J., Sanshuck, D. W., and Shinoda, S. 1961. Effect of temperature on stability of commercially frozen bulk pack fruits—strawberries, raspberries and blackberries. Food Technol. *15*, 207–209.

Guerrant, N. B. 1957. Changes in light reflectance and ascorbic acid content of foods during frozen storage. J. Agric. Food Chem. 5, 207–212.

Guerrant, N. B., and Dutcher, R. A. 1948. Further observations concerning the relationship of temperature of blanching to ascorbic acid retention in green beans. Arch. Biochem. 18, 353–359.

Guerrant, N. B., and O'Hara, M. B. 1953. Vitamin retention in peas and lima beans after blanching, freezing, processing in tin and in glass, after storage and after cooking. Food Technol. 7, 473–477.

Guerrant, N. B., et al. 1947. Effect of duration and temperature of blanch on vitamin retention by certain vegetables. Ind. Eng. Chem. 39, 1000–1007.

Guerrant, N. B., et al. 1953. Some factors affecting the quality of frozen foods. Penn State Coll. Agric. Exp. Stn. Bull. 565.

Gustafson, F. G., and Cooke, A. R. 1952. Oxidation of ascorbic acid to dehydroascorbic acid at low temperatures. Science 116, 234.

Hartzler, E. R., and Guerrant, N. B. 1952. Effect of blanching and of frozen storage of vegetables on ascorbic acid retention and on the concomitant activity of certain enzymes. Food Res. 17, 15–23.

Holmes, A. D., et al. 1945. Vitamin content of field-frozen kale. Am. J. Diseases Children 70, 298–300.

Holmes, A. D., Kuzmeski, J. W., and Canavan, F. T. 1946. Stability of vitamins in stored ice cream. J. Am. Diet. Assoc. 22, 670–672.

Holmquist, J. W., Clifcorn, L. E., Heberlein, D. G., and Schmidt, C. F. 1954. Steam blanching of peas. Food Technol. 8, 437–445.

Howard, A., Lawrie, R. A., and Lee, C. A. 1960. Studies on beef quality. VIII. Some observations on the nature of drip. CSIRO, Melbourne, Australia.

Huggart, R. L., Harman, D. A., and Moore, E. L. 1954. Ascorbic acid retention in frozen concentrated citrus juices. J. Am. Diet. Assoc. 30, 682–684.

Jenkins, R. R., and Tressler, D. K. 1938. Vitamin C content of vegetables. VIII. Frozen peas. Food Res. 3, 133–140.

Jenkins, R. R., Tressler, D. K., Moyer, J., and McIntosh, J. 1940. Storage of frozen vegetables. Vitamin C experiments. Refrig. Eng. 39, 381–382.

Jurics, E. W. 1970. Comparative investigations of the vitamin C contents of frozen and fresh vegetables in the raw and cooked states. (German). Nahrung 14, 107–114.

Kahn, L. N., and Livingston, G. E. 1970. Effect of heating methods on thiamin retention in fresh or frozen prepared food. J. Food Sci. 35, 349–351.

Kawar, N. S., DeBatista, G. C., and Guther, F. A. 1973. Pesticide stability in cold-stored plant parts, soils and dairy products, and in cold-stored extractive solutions. Residue Rev. 48, 54–77.

Khan, A. W., and Lentz, C. P. 1965. Influence of prerigor, rigor and postrigor freezing on drip losses and protein changes in chicken meat. J. Food Sci. 30, 787–790.

Khan, A. W., and van den Berg, L. 1967. Biochemical and quality changes occurring during freezing of poultry meat. J. Food Sci. 32, 148–150.

Kilgore, L., and Windham, F. 1970. Disappearance of Malathion residue in broccoli during cooking and freezing. J. Agric. Food Chem. 18, 162–163.

Kotschevar, L. H. 1955. B-vitamin retention in frozen meat. J. Am. Diet. Assoc. 31, 589–596.

Kramer, A. 1977. Effect of storage on nutritive value of food. J. Food Quality 1, 23–55.

Kramer, A., King, R. L., Westhoff, D. C., Olowofoyeku, A. K., and Farquhar, J. W. 1979. 18-Month storage study of prepared frozen foods containing protein concentrates. ASHRAE Trans. 85, 31–55.

Lamb, F. C., Lewis, L. D., and Lee, S. K. 1948. Effect of blanching on retention of ascorbic acid and thiamin in peas. West. Canner Packer 5, 60–62.

Lane, J. P. 1966. Time–temperature tolerance of frozen seafoods. Food Technol. *20*, 549–553.

Larson, E. R. 1956. Vitamin losses in the drip from thawed, frozen poultry. J. Am. Diet. Assoc. *32*, 716–718.

Lawrence, J. M., Herrington, B. L., and Maynard, L. A. 1946. The nicotinic acid, biotin and pantothenic acid content of cows' milk. J. Nutr. *32*, 73–91.

Lee, F. A., and Whitcombe, J. 1945. Blanching of vegetables for freezing. Effect of different types of potable water on nutrients of peas and snap beans. Food Res. *10*, 465–468.

Lee, F. A., Gortner, W. A., and Whitcombe, J. 1946. Effect of freezing rate on vegetables. Ind. Eng. Chem. *38*, 341–346.

Lee, F. A., et al. 1950. Effect of freezing rate on meat. Appearance, palatability and vitamin content of beef. Food Res. *15*, 8–15.

Lee, F. A., et al. 1954. Effect of rate of freezing on pork quality. J. Am. Diet. Assoc. *30*, 351–354.

Lehrer, W. P., Jr., Wiese, A. C., Harvey, W. R., and Moore, P. R. 1951. Effect of frozen storage and subsequent cooking on the thiamin, riboflavin, and nicotinic acid content of pork chops. Food Res. *16*, 485–491.

Lehrer, W. P., Jr., Wiese, A. C., Harvey, W. R., and Moore, P. R. 1952. The stability of thiamin, riboflavin and nicotinic acid of lamb chops during frozen storage and subsequent cooking. Food Res. *17*, 24–30.

Lindquist, F. E., Dietrich, W. C., and Boggs, M. M. 1950. Effect of storage temperature on quality of frozen peas. Food Technol. *4*, 5–9.

Loeffler, H. J. 1946. Retention of ascorbic acid in raspberries during freezing, frozen storage, pureeing and manufacture into velva fruit. Food Res. 11, 507–515.

Love, R. M. 1958. Expressible fluid of fish fillets. VIII. Cell damage in slow freezing. J. Sci. Food Agric. *9*, 257–262.

Lowenberg, M. E., and Wilson, E. D. 1959. Nutrients in frozen foods. Natl. Assoc. Frozen Food Packers, Washington DC.

Manohar, S. V., Rigby, D. L., and Dugal, L. C. 1973. Effect of sodium tripolyphosphate on thaw drip and taste of fillets of some freshwater fish. J. Fish. Res. Bd. Can. *30*, 685–688.

Marshall, J. R., Hayes, K. M., Fellers, C. R., and DuBois, C. W. 1955. Stability of ascorbic acid in citrus concentrates during storage. Quick Frozen Foods *17*(12), 50–52, 129.

Martin, M. E., Sweeney, J. P., Gilpin, G. L., and Chapman, V. J. 1960. Factors affecting the ascorbic acid and carotene content of broccoli. J. Agric. Food Chem. *8*, 387–390.

McColloch, R. J., Rice, R. G., Bandurski, M. B., and Gentili, B. 1957. Time-temperature tolerance of frozen foods. VII. Frozen concentrated orange juice. Food Technol. *11*, 444–449.

Melnick, D., Hochberg, M., and Oser, B. L. 1944. Comparative study of steam and hot water blanching. Food Res. *9*, 148–153.

Meluzova, L. A. 1977. Effect of mucopolysaccharide contents in intramuscular connective tissues on nutritive value of myofibrillar proteins during meat storage at low temperatures. *In* Freezing, Frozen Storage and Freeze-Drying of Biological Materials and Foodstuffs, pp. 145–152. International Institute of Refrigeration, Paris.

Meyer, B., Mysinger, M., and Buckley, R. 1963. The effect of three years of freezer storage on the thiamin, riboflavin and niacin content of ripened and unripened beef. J. Agric. Food Chem. *11*, 525–527.

Meyer, B. H., Mysinger, M. A., and Cole, J.W. 1966. Effect of finishing and ripening on vitamin B_6 and pantothenic acid content of beef. J. Agric. Food Chem. *14*, 485–486.

Millares, R., and Fellers, C. R. 1949. Vitamin and amino acid content of processed chicken meat products. Food Res. *14*, 131–143.

Miyauchi, D. 1962. Application of centrifugal method for measuring shrinkage during the thawing and heating of frozen cod fillets. Food Technol. *16*(1), 70–72.

Moleeratanond, W., Ashby, B. H., Kramer, A., Berry, B. W., and Lee, W. 1981. Effect of a di-thermal storage regime on quality and nutritional changes and energy consumption of frozen boxed beef. J. Food Sci. *46*, 829–833, 837.

Morgan, A. F., *et al.* 1949. Thiamin, riboflavin and niacin content of chicken tissues, as affected by cooking and frozen storage. Food Res. *14*, 439–448.

Morrison, M. H. 1974. The vitamin C contents of quick frozen peas. J. Food Technol. *9*, 491–500.

Morrison, M. H. 1975. The vitamin C content of quick frozen green beans. J. Food Technol. *10*, 19–28.

Moyer, J. C., and Stotz, E. 1945. Electronic blanching of vegetables. Science *102*, 68–69.

Moyer, J. C., and Tressler, D. K. 1943. Thiamin content of fresh and frozen vegetables, Food Res. *8*, 58–61.

Nestorov, N., *et al.* 1969. Proc. Eur. Mktg. Meat Res. Workers *15*, 110. Cited by Burger, I. H., and Walters, C. L. 1973. The effect of processing on the nutritive value of flesh foods. Proc. Nutr. Soc. *32*, 1–8.

Noble, I., and Gordon, J. 1964. Effect of blanching method on ascorbic acid and color of frozen vegetables. J. Am. Diet. Assoc. *44*, 120–123.

O'Brien, J. J., Campbell, N., and Conaghan, T. 1981. Effect of cooking and cold storage on biologically active antibiotic residues in meat. J. Hyg. (Cambridge) *87*, 511–523.

Odland, D., and Eheart, M. S. 1975. Ascorbic acid, mineral and quality retention in frozen broccoli blanched in water, steam and ammonia–steam. J. Food Sci. *40*, 1004–1007.

Pala, M. 1983. Effect of different pretreatments on the quality of deep frozen green beans and carrots. Int. J. Refrig. *6*(4), 238–246.

Payne, I. R. 1967. Ascorbic acid retention in frozen corn. J. Am. Diet. Assoc. *51*, 344–348.

Pearson, A.M., and Miller, J. I. 1950. The influence of rate of freezing and length of freezer-storage upon the quality of beef of unknown origin. J. Anim. Sci. *9*, 13–19.

Pearson, A. M., *et al.* 1951. Vitamin losses in drip obtained upon defrosting frozen meat. Food Res. *16*, 85–87.

Pearson, A. M., West, R. G., and Luecke, R. W. 1959. The vitamin and amino acid content of drip obtained upon defrosting frozen pork. Food Res. *24*, 515–519.

Phillips, M. G., and Fenton, F. 1945. Effects of home freezing and cooking on snap beans: Thiamin, riboflavin, ascorbic acid. J. Home Econ. *37*, 164–170.

Pierce, R. T., Shaw, M. D., Heck, J. G., and Bennett, G. 1955. Small storage temperature differences can affect the quality of frozen strawberries and green beans. Refrig. Engr. *63*(11), 52–57.

Pincock, R. E., and Kiovsky, T. E. 1966. Kinetics of reactions in frozen solutions. J. Chem. Educ. *43*, 358–362.

Proctor, B. E., and Goldblith, S. A. 1948. Radar energy for rapid food cooking and blanching, and its effect on vitamin content. Food Technol. *2*, 95–104.

Ramsbottom, J. M., and Koonz, C. H. 1939. Freezing temperature as related to drip of frozen–defrosted beef. Food Res. *4*, 425–431.

Ramsbottom, J. M., and Koonz, C. H. 1940. Relationship between time of freezing beef after slaughter and amount of drip. Food Res. *5*, 423–429.

Ramsbottom, J. M., and Koonz, C. H. 1941. Freezer storage temperature as related to drip and color in frozen–defrosted beef. Food Res. *6*, 571–580.

Retzer, J. L., Van Duyne, F. O., Chase, J. T., and Simpson, J. I. 1945. Effect of steam and hot-water blanching on ascorbic acid content of snap beans and cauliflower. Food Res. *10*, 518–524.

Richardson, L. R., Wilkes, S., and Ritchey, S. J. 1961A. Comparative vitamin B_6 activity of frozen, irradiated and heat-processed foods. J. Nutr. *73*, 363–368.

Richardson, L. R., Wilkes, S., and Ritchey, S. J. 1961B. Comparative vitamin K activity of frozen, irradiated and heat-processed foods. J. Nutr. *73*, 369–373.

Sair, L., and Cook, W. H. 1938. Relation of pH to drip formation in meat. Can. J. Res. *16D*, 255–267.

Samuels, C. E., and Wiegand, E. H. 1948. Radiofrequency blanching of cut corn and freestone peaches. Fruit Prod. J. Am. Food Mfgr. *28*, 43–44, 61.

Scott, L. E., and Schrader, A. L. 1947. Ascorbic acid content of strawberry varieties before and after processing by freezing. Proc. Am. Soc. Hort. Sci. *50*, 251–253.

Secomska, B., Iwanska, W., and Nadolna, I. 1973. Retention of some vitamins in cooked potatoes stored in the frozen state. Thirteenth Int. Cong. Refrig. *3*, 311–316.

Singh, S. P., and Essary, E. O. 1971A. Influence of thawing methods on the composition of drip from broiler carcasses. Poult. Sci. *50*, 364–369.

Singh, S. P., and Essary, E. O. 1971B. Vitamin content of broiler meat as affected by age, sex, thawing and cooking. Poult. Sci. *50*, 1150–1155.

Stimson, C. R., and Tressler, D. K. 1939. Carotene (vitamin A) content of fresh and frozen peas. Food Res. *4*, 475–483.

Strachan, C. C., and Moyls, A. W. 1949. Ascorbic, citric and dihydroxymaleic acids as antioxidants in frozen pack fruits. Food Technol. *3*, 327–332.

Sulc, S. 1973. Influence of different freezing methods, temperature and time, on the preservation of important factors. Thirteenth Int. Cong. Refrig. *3*, 447–454.

Sweeney, J. P., and Marsh, A. C. 1971. Effect of processing on provitamin A in vegetables. J. Am. Diet. Assoc. *59*, 238–243.

Sweeney, J. P., Chapman, V. J., Martin, M. E., and Dawson, E. H. 1961. Quality of frozen vegetables purchased in selected retail markets. Food Technol. *15*, 341–345.

Tanaka, K., and Tanaka, T. 1956A. Defrosting of frozen whale meat. J. Tokyo Coll. Fish. *42*, 80–82.

Tanaka, K., and Tanaka, T. 1956B. Biochemical condition of whalemeat before or after freezing and cold storage of frozen meat. J. Tokyo Coll. Fish. *42*, 83–88.

Tanaka, K., and Tanaka, T. 1957. Drip from frozen whalemeat affected by freezing rate and air temperature in air defrosting. J. Tokyo Coll. Fish. *43*, 19–23.

Teply, L. J., and Derse, P. H. 1958. Nutrients in cooked frozen vegetables. J. Am. Diet. Assoc. *34*, 836–840.

Thompson, L. U., and Fennema, O. 1971. Effect of freezing on oxidation of L-ascorbic acid. J. Agric. Food Chem. *19*, 121–124.

Tingleff, A. J., and Miller, E. V. 1960. Studies on ascorbic acid retention in frozen juice, segments, and whole oranges. Food Res. *25*, 145–147.

Tinklin, G. L. and Filinger, G. A. 1956. Effects of different methods of blanching on the quality of home frozen spinach. Food Technol. *10*, 198–201.

Tressler, D. K., Mack, G. L., and King, C. G. 1936. Factors influencing the vitamin C content of vegetables. Am. J. Public Health *26*, 905–909.

Tressler, D. K., Mack, G. L., and Jenkins, R. R. 1937. Vitamin C in vegetables. VII. Lima beans. Food Res. *2*, 175–181.

U.S. Department of Agriculture (USDA). 1976–1982. Composition of Foods. *In* Agricultural Handbook 8-1 through 8-9. USDA, Washington, DC.

Vail, G. E., Jeffrey, M., Forney, H., and Wiley, C. 1943. Effect of method of thawing upon losses, shear, and press fluid of frozen beefsteaks and pork roast. Food Res. 8, 337–342.

van der Meer, M. A., Lassche, M. J. B., and Pashcha, C. N. 1973. Nutritive value and sensory qualities of deep-frozen components of meals and the effect of three reheating methods on these properties. (Dutch). Voeding 34, 2–15.

Van Duyne, F. O., Wolfe, J. C., and Owen, R. F. 1950. Retention of riboflavin in vegetables preserved by freezing. Food Res. 15, 53–61.

Volz, F. E., Gortner, W. A., and Delwiche, C. V. 1949. The effect of desiccation on frozen vegetables. Food Technol. 3, 307–313.

von Kamienski, E. S. 1969. Retention of vitamin C during the processing of frozen spinach. In Frozen Foods. International Institute of Refrigeration, Paris.

von Kamienski, E. S. 1972. Retention of vitamin C during the processing of frozen spinach. Sci. Aliment. 18(7), 243–244.

Wedler, A. 1971. Results of experiments on the change in contents of nutritional compounds through processing and preparation of vegetables. Qual. Plant. Mater. Veg. 21(1–2), 79–95.

Weits, J., van der Meer, M. A., and Lassche, J. B. 1970. Nutritive value and organoleptic properties of three vegetables fresh and preserved in six different ways. Int. Z. Vitaminforsch. 40, 648–658.

Westerman, B. D., Vail, G. E., Tinklin, G. L., and Smith, J. 1949. B-complex vitamins in meat. II. The influence of different methods of thawing frozen steaks upon their palatability and vitamin content. Food Technol. 3, 184–187.

Westerman, B. D., et al. 1952. B-complex vitamins in meat. III. Influence of storage temperature and time on the vitamins in pork muscle. J. Am. Diet. Assoc. 28, 49–52.

Westerman, B. D., Oliver, B., and MacKintosh, D. L. 1955. Influence of chilling rate and frozen storage on B-complex vitamin content of pork. J. Agric. Food Chem. 3, 603–605.

Wolfe, J. C., Owen, R. F., Charles, V. R., and Van Duyne, F. O. 1949. Effect of freezing and freezer storage on the ascorbic acid content of muskmelon, grapefruit sections, and strawberry puree. Food Res. 14, 243–252.

Zimmerman, W. I., Tressler, D. K., and Maynard, L. A. 1940. Determination of carotene in fresh and frozen vegetables. 1. Carotene content of green snap beans and sweet corn. Food Res. 5, 93–101.

Zscheile, F. P., Beadle, B. W., and Kraybill, H. R. 1943. Carotene content of fresh and frozen green vegetables. Food Res. 8, 299–313.

Effects of
Heat Processing
on Nutrients

Daryl Lund

Heat processing is one of the most important methods for extending the storage life of foodstuffs. Because of this extended storage life, foods which are abundantly available only during relatively short harvesting periods are made available throughout the year. There is no doubt that this has increased the availability of nutrients to the consumer. However, heat processing also has a detrimental effect on nutrients since thermal degradation of nutrients can and does occur. Therefore, thermal processing makes it possible to extend and increase availability of a foodstuff to the consumer, but the foodstuff may have a lower nutrient content (compared to the fresh foodstuff). The challenge to the food processing industry is to minimize the loss of nutrients during thermal processing while providing an adequate process to ensure an extended storage life.

Several processes involving the use of heat are currently applied to foodstuffs. For some, the primary objective is to increase the palatability of the food. An example is cooking which includes baking, broiling, roasting, boiling, frying, and stewing. For other thermal processes, the objectives are to increase storage life of the foodstuff and to minimize food-borne diseases. Blanching, pasteurization, and sterilization are examples of these processes.

Reduction in nutrient content of the foodstuff as a result of a thermal process depends on the severity of the process. In this chapter effects of blanching, pasteurization, and sterilization on nutrients will be discussed. The approach will be to define each of these heat processes, mention general reviews currently available, discuss the effects of heat on nutrients in general, examine the interaction between current technology for accomplishing the objectives of each process and nutrient retention, and review the effect of storage on nutrients in foodstuffs that have received these heat processes.

DEFINITION OF BLANCHING, PASTEURIZATION, AND STERILIZATION

Blanching is a heat process frequently applied to tissue systems prior to freezing, drying, or canning. The objectives of the blanching process depend on the subsequent treatment of the foodstuffs. For example, blanching prior to freezing or drying is used primarily to inactivate enzymes which would contribute to undesirable changes in color, flavor, or nutritive value during storage. Blanching prior to canning serves several different functions including wilting the tissue to facilitate packing, removing tissue gases prior to container filling, increasing the temperature of the tissue prior to container closing, and inactivating or activating enzymes. Although the objectives of the blanching process are dependent on the subsequent treatment, a criterion frequently used for evaluating the adequacy of the blanching operation, regardless of subsequent treatment, is enzyme inactivation. Generally, if enzymes are inactivated, the heat treatment was sufficient to accomplish the objectives of blanching prior to canning. In the special case of blanching to activate the enzyme pectin methylesterase, van Buren *et al.* (1960) and Kaczmarzyk *et al.* (1963) showed that blanching water temperature must be greater than $150°F$, but less than $180°F$. An important concept about blanching is that microbial destruction is not a primary objective of the process.

Pasteurization is a heat process designed to inactivate part, but not all, of the vegetative microorganisms present in the food. Since the food is not sterile, pasteurization, like blanching, must also be used in conjunction with other preservation techniques such as fermentation (e.g., pickles), refrigeration (e.g., milk), maintenance of anaerobic conditions (e.g., beer), or must be used on products such as high acid fruit juices where the environment is not particularly suited for growth of spoilage and health hazard microorganisms. The basis of the process may be a spoilage microorganism (e.g., yeast in beer, yeast and molds in high acid fruit juices) or a health hazard organism (e.g., *Coxiella burnetti*, the *Rickettsia* organism responsible for Q fever in milk).

Sterile is a term that refers to a condition in which no viable microorganisms are present, a viable organism being one that is able to reproduce under conditions optimum for its growth. Sterilization, then, is a term applied to any process that produces a sterile condition in food. Some microorganisms and their spores are extremely heat resistant and generally it is not practical to render a food sterile by heat processing. To do so would alter the organoleptic and nutritive value of the food to the point that it would be unacceptable. Therefore, the "sterilization" process used in heat processing foods is also used in conjunction with other preservation techniques, namely, packaging and control of storage temperature. The requirement for these techniques is that the remaining dormant microorganisms or their spores will not grow in the environment of the food under the conditions of storage. Foods that have been thermally processed and meet this requirement are said to be "commercially sterile."

GENERAL REVIEWS ON THE EFFECTS OF PROCESSING ON NUTRIENTS

Several review articles which discuss the effect of heat processing on nutrients have been published, and their contents are summarized in Table 12.1. With the consumer demand for more nutrition information, particularly as it applies to processed foods, it is understandable that there is great interest and increased publication on this subject. Several of these reviews treat only one particular product, process, or nutrient while others are quite general. Most, however, point out that thermal processing can in some instances enhance the nutritive value of food. Examples of this are given elsewhere in this book.

EFFECT OF HEAT ON NUTRIENTS

Although several review articles have been published on the effects of heat processing on nutrients, few authors have attempted to summarize the kinetic data which can be used to describe the time–temperature effect on nutrients. Labuza (1972) took this approach in an excellent review article on the effects of dehydration and subsequent storage on nutrient content of dehydrated foods. But as Labuza pointed out, not much data exist. The same situation is true for the thermal destruction of nutrients under conditions normally found in blanching, pasteurization, and commercial sterilization processes. Many authors have reported the percentage loss of a nutrient in a food product that was given a particular treatment. But these data usually have not been complete enough to allow estimation of the kinetic parameters that can be used to predict or calculate the response of the nutrient to the heat treatment. For example, after analyzing the data compiled by Orr (1969), Schroeder (1971) concluded that vitamin B_6 and pantothenic acid losses could be as high as 91% in canned foods and that the recommended daily allowance (RDA) for these two nutrients probably could not be obtained from a menu of refined, processed, and canned foods. Yet the parameters which are needed to predict the susceptibility of these two nutrients to thermal processing were not known. The necessary parameters cannot be obtained from the data presented by Schroeder or Orr due to the wide variation in processing conditions used in the canning industry. Therefore, optimization of the process for retention of these two nutrients could not be determined.

Table 12.1. General Reviews on the Effect of Processing on Nutrients

References	Products[a] V	F	M	D	Ce	Fi	E	C	Processes[b] P	B	C	D	Fr	F	R	Pa	Nutrients[c] V	M	P	C	L	Other	Number of references cited
Ashton (1972)				X							X	X				X	X	X	X	X	X		42
Barratt (1973)	X	X	X	X													X	X	X				0
Bender (1966)	X	X	X	X	X	X						X			X		X	X	X				132
Bender (1972)		X	X	X	X	X					X								X				76
Bender (1978)	X	X	X	X	X	X	X	X	X	X	X	X	X	X	X	X	X	X	X	X	X	Heat, fractionation	937
Berk (1970)			X	X	X				X	X	X	X	X	X	X		X	X	X				13
Burger and Walters (1973)	X	X				X											X	X	X				55
Burton et al. (1970)	X	X	X	X												X	X					Ultra-high temperature	9
Cain (1967)	X	X							X	X	X	X		X			X						45
Cameron et al. (1955)	X	X				X	X		X	X	X	X					X	X	X				88
Chichester (1973)	X	X	X		X				X	X	X	X					X	X	X	X	X		30
Clifcorn (1948)	X	X						X	X	X	X	X					X						90
Dugan (1968)			X			X		X													X	Heat, oxidation	68
Ford et al. (1969)				X			X									X	X					Ultra-high temperature	24
Goldblith (1971)								X	X	X	X	X	X	X	X	X	X	X					21
Gortner (1972)									X								X	X					0
Harris and Von Loesecke (1960)	X	X	X	X	X	X	X	X	X	X	X	X	X	X	X	X	X	X	X	X	X		
Harris and Karmas (1975)	X	X	X	X	X	X	X	X	X	X	X	X	X	X	X	X	X	X	X	X	X		
Hartman and Dryden (1965)				X											X	X	X						1212
Hein and Hutchings (1971)																							
Henshall (1973)	X	X							X	X	X	X					X						27
Hollingsworth (1970)											X			X			X						19

Reference	Comment	No.
Hollingsworth and Martin (1972)		175
Holmquist et al. (1954)		5
Klein (1982)	Cooking included	14
Klein (1984)	Foodservice	22
Labuza (1972)		79
Lang (1970)	Cooking	408
Lawrie (1968)		90
Lee (1958)		63
Lillard (1983)		67
Lund et al. (1973)		23
Lund (1982)		21
Mapson (1956)		51
Orr (1969)	Composition Table for B_6, B_{12}, pantothenic acid	107
Osner and Johnson (1968)	Protein degradation	62
Rolls and Porter (1973)		29
Sabry (1968)		5
Schroeder (1971)	Heat, extraction	26
Tannenbaum (1979)		
Thompson (1969)	Ultra-high temperature	60
Thompson (1982)		85
Villota and Hawkes (1983)	Composition tables	205
Watt and Murphy (1970)		27
Woodham (1973)	Texturizing	46
Zadow (1984)	Membrane processing included	13

[a] V, vegetable; F, fruit; M, meat; D, dairy; Ce, cereal; Fi, fish; E, eggs; C, canned products.
[b] P, preparation; B, blanching; C, canning; D, dehydration; Fr, freezing; F, fermentation; R, radiation; Pa, pasteurization.
[c] V, vitamins; M, minerals; P, protein; C, carbohydrate; L, lipid.

Several kinetic parameters have been used to describe the effect of time–temperature treatments on the rate and extent of nutrient destruction. Basically two parameters are needed: (1) the rate of nutrient destruction at a reference temperature and (2) the dependence of the rate of destruction on temperature. In most chemical and engineering applications these two parameters have been the reference reaction rate constant (k_r) at temperature T_r and the Arrhenius activation energy (E_a).

The general rate expression for concentration dependence on time is

$$\frac{dc}{dt} = -k_R c^n$$

where c is concentration of component c, t is time, k_R is the rate constant at temperature T_R, and n is the order of the reaction for component c. For thermal destruction of nutrients in foods, the order of the reaction (n) is often one (i.e., first-order reaction), or at least the disappearance of the nutrient can be described by a first-order model (i.e., pseudo-first order). For the canning industry, the time constant base 10 has been used to characterize the time dependence of concentration as follows:

$$dc/dt = (-2.03/D_R)\, c$$

where D_R is the decimal reduction time (time constant base 10) at temperature T_R. The decimal reduction time (D_R) is the time at temperature T_R for the concentration of the nutrient (or microorganism, spore, or enzyme) to decrease by 90% (become one-tenth the initial value).

For temperature dependence of the reaction rate constant (k or D), the Arrhenius activation energy is used.

$$\ln (k/k_R) = 2.303 \log (D_R/D) = (-E_a/R)[(1/T) - (1/T_R)]$$

where k is the first-order rate constant at temperature T, k_R is the first-order rate constant at temperature T_R, E_a is the Arrhenius activation energy, and R is the gas law constant. For the food processing industry, an empirical equation has been used extensively to describe temperature dependence.

$$\log (D/D_R) = (T_R - T)/z$$

where z is the temperature change necessary to change D by a factor of 10.

For biological scientists, the Q_{10} is used to express temperature dependence.

$$Q_{10} = k_{T+10}/k_T$$

where k_{T+10} is the first-order rate constant at $(T + 10)°C$, and k_T is the first-order rate constant at $T°C$.

Determination and use of these values and concepts are covered elsewhere (e.g., Aiba $et\ al.$ 1965; Blakeborough 1968; Pflug and Schmidt 1968; Stumbo 1973) and will not be reviewed here.

Table 12.2 is a compilation of data from existing literature where the authors have determined E_a and D_R (or their corresponding values in other terms) or have provided sufficient data to allow calculation of these parameters. The parameters E_a and D_R for a particular nutrient or component are dependent on several variables: (1) pH, (2) oxidation–reduction potential, and (3) medium composition (including presence of catalytic factors such as heavy metals). For each study, information is given on the component that was evaluated, the medium, pH, and temperature range over which the parameters were determined. In addition to presenting data on nutrients, some parameters for factors such as color (pigments and nonenzymatic browning), texture, flavor precursors, enzymes, microbial toxins, and microbial vegetative and spore cells are given. These values are included in order to examine how each of the three processes (blanching, pasteurization, and commercial sterilization) may be optimized with respect to nutrient retention. It should be pointed out that for each of the studies reported in Table 12.2, the component under study obeyed first-order reaction kinetics.

Several conclusions can be drawn from Table 12.2. Most important, perhaps, is the observation that the table contains many more entries than a similar table in the previous edition of this book. This attests to the fact that investigators are more conscientious of producing quantitative data on effects of processing on nutrients. Furthermore, more nutrients that have demonstrated some sensitivity to high temperatures have been investigated. This contrasts sharply to data available in 1975 in which only thiamin (vitamin B_1) and ascorbic acid (vitamin C) were widely used in kinetic studies.

Data on thiamin degradation in a variety of media can be used to illustrate two important points. First, the destruction rate (D_{121}) is highly dependent on pH and medium composition. However, the Arrhenius activation energy (E_a) is relatively insensitive to those parameters.

Another important observation is that rate of destruction of many nutrients under a variety of conditions exhibits similar temperature dependence (20–30 kcal/mol). These Arrhenius activation energies are in the range for chemical reactions. This would be expected for many nutrients, since loss of biological activity is through hydrolysis or oxidation of the nutrient. Observations on temperature dependence of other constituents in foods has led to the generalizations shown in Table 12.3.

Table 12.2. Kinetic Parameters for the Thermal Destruction of Food Components

Reference	Component	Medium	pH	Temperature range (°F)	E_a (kcal-mole)	$D_{121}{}^a$	Other
Lathrop and Leung (1980)	Vitamin C	Peas	Nat	110–132	39	1003	
Saguy et al. (1978)	Vitamin C	Grapefruit juice	Nat	60–95	5.0	577	11.2° Brix
					5.3	495	31.2° Brix
					6.7	348	47.1° Brix
					8.6	198	55.0° Brix
					11.3	82	62.5° Brix
Bendix et al. (1951)	Thiamin	Whole peas	Nat	220–270	21	164	
Feliciotti and Esselen (1951)	Thiamin	Carrot puree	5.9	228–300	27	158	
		Green bean puree	5.8	228–300	27	145	
		Pea puree	6.6	228–300	27	163	
		Spinach puree	6.5	228–300	27	134	
		Beef heart puree	6.1	228–300	27	115	
		Beef liver puree	6.1	228–300	27	124	
		Lamb puree	6.2	228–300	27	120	
		Pork puree	6.2	228–300	27	157	
Mulley et al. (1975)	Thiamin	Phosphate buffer	6.0	250–280	29	157	
		Pea puree	Nat	250–280	28	247	
		Beef puree	Nat	250–280	27	254	
		Peas-in-brine puree	Nat	250–280	27	227	
Lenz and Lund (1980)	Thiamin	Pea puree	Nat	115–138	23	174	
		Pork puree	Nat	115–138	26	101	
Skjöldebrand et al. (1983)	Thiamin	Meatloaf	Nat	71–98	27	87	
Navankasuttusas and Lund (1982)	Vitamin B₆	Cauliflower puree	Nat	106–138	?	413	
Gregory and Hiner (1983)	Vitamin B₆	Casein-based liquid	Nat	105–133	29	775	
	Pyridoxine		Nat	105–133	24	297	
	Pyridoxamine		Nat	105–133	21	194	

Hamm and Lund (1983)	Pantothenic acid free	Beef puree	5.4	118–143	20	2304	
	Pantothenic acid total		5.4	118–143	25	2388	
	Pantothenic acid free	Pea puree	7.0	118–143	38	2262	
	Pantothenic acid total		7.0	118–143	36	2406	
	Pantothenic acid total	Buffer	4.0	118–143	20	246	
			5.0	118–143	22	1602	
			6.0	118–143	27	1950	
Mnkeni and Beveridge (1982)	Folic acid	Apple juice	3.4	100–140	20	524	
		Tomato juice	4.3	100–140	20	636	
		Citrate buffer	3.0	100–140	22	191	
			4.0	100–140	19	499	
			5.0	100–140	18	2123	
Wilkinson et al. (1981)	Vitamin A	Beef liver puree	Nat	103–127	27	42	
Stefanovich and Karel (1982)	Vitamin A	Butternut squash	Nat	60–80	12	358	trans-Retinol
		Sweet potato	Nat	60–80	11	448	
		Yellow corn	Nat	60–80	21	112	
Garrett (1956)	Thiamin	Liquid multi-vitamin preparation	3.2	39–158	26	1.35 days	
	Pantothenic acid		3.2	39–158	21	4.46 days	
	Vitamin C		3.2	39–158	23	1.12 days	
	Vitamin B_{12}		3.2	39–158	23	1.94 days	
	Folic acid		3.2	39–158	17	1.95 days	
	Vitamin A		3.2	39–158	15	12.4 days	
Davidek et al. (1972)	Inosinic acid (IMP)	Buffer solution	3	140–208	34	—	
	(IMP)		4	140–208	30	—	
	(IMP)		5	140–208	28	—	
Gupte et al. (1964)	Chlorophyll a	Spinach	6.5	260–300	15.5	13.0 min	
	Chlorophyll b	do[c]	5.5	260–300	7.5	14.7 do	

(Continued)

Table 12.2. *(Continued)*

Reference	Component	Medium	pH	Temperature range (°F)	E_a (kcal-mole)	D_{121}[a]	Other
Gold and Weckel (1959)	Chlorophyll	Pea puree	Nat	240–280	16.1	14.0 min	Blanched
	do	do	do	do	12.6	13.9 do	Unblanched
Lenz and Lund (1980)	Chlorophyll	Pea puree	6.5	175–280	22	113 min	
	do	Spinach puree	6.5	do	19	166 do	
Mackinney and Joslyn (1941)	Chlorophyll a	Buffered solution	—	32–122	7.5	—	
	Chlorophyll b	do	—	do	9.0	—	
Dietrich et al. (1959)	Chlorophyll	Green beans	Nat	190–212	12.0	10.1 min	
Timbers (1971)	Color	Peas	Nat	175–300	15.0	25.0 min	
		Asparagus	do	do	14.0	17.0 do	
		Green beans	do	do	15.0	21.0 do	
	Quality by taste panel	Whole kernel corn	do	do	19.5	6.0 do	Time for taste panel to judge 4.0/9.0 compared to frozen control.
		Whole peas	do	do	22.5	2.3 do	
		Whole green beans	do	do	22.0	4.0 do	
Herrmann (1970)	Chlorophyll a	Spinach	Nat	212–266	12.5	34.1 min	
	Chlorophyll b	do	do	do	10.0	48.3 do	
	Maillard reaction	Apple juice	do	100–266	27.0	4.52 hr	
	Nonenzymic browning	do	do	do	20.7	4.75 hr	
	B_1	Pork	do	?–250	19.5	6.03 hr	
Ponting et al. (1960)	Anthocyanin	Grape juice	Nat	68–250	28.0	17.8 min	
		Boysenberry juice	do	do	20.0	102.5 do	
		Strawberry juice	do	do	19.0	110.3 do	
Tanchev and Joncheva (1973)	Cyanidin-3-rutinoside	Citrate buffer	4.5	170–225	23.7	28.5 min	
		Plum juice	4.5	do	23.1	41.6 do	
	Peonidin-3-rutinoside	Citrate buffer	4.5	do	26.2	21.6 do	
		Plum juice	4.5	do	22.1	27.7 do	
Ramakrishnan and Francis (1973)	Carotenoids	Paprika	Nat	125–150	34.0	0.038 min	

Reference	Compound/Attribute	Food/Medium	pH[b]	Range	Value	Time	Notes
von Elbe et al. (1974)	Bentanin	Buffer	5.0	122–212	12.5	19.5 min	Homogenized
	do	Beet juice	do	do	10.0	46.6 do	Unhomogenized
Burton (1963)	Browning	Goat's milk	6.5–6.6	200–250	27.0	1.08 min	
	do	do	do	do	do	0.91 do	
Williams and Nelson (1974)	Methylmethionine sulfonium bromide, DMS	Sodium-citrate buffer	6.0	178–212	34.8	8.4 min	
		Sweet corn	6.9	do	31.6	4.5 do	
		Tomato	4.4	do	27.2	23.2 do	
Taira et al. (1966)	Lysine	Soybean meal	—	212–260	30.0	13.1 hr	Time to acceptable product.
Mansfield (1974)	Texture	Peas	Nat	170–200	19.5	1.4 min	
	Overall cook quality	Peas		210–240	19.5	2.5 do	
	do	Beets		180–210	34.0	2.0 do	
	do	Whole kernel corn		212–250	16.0	2.4 do	
	do	Broccoli		212–250	13.0	4.4 do	
	do	Squash		182–240	25.0	1.5 do	
	do	Carrots		176–240	38.0	1.4 do	
	do	Green beans		182–240	41.0	1.0 do	
	do	Potato		161–240	27.5	1.2 do	
Hackler et al. (1965)	Trypsin inhibitor	Soybean milk	—	200–250	18.5	13.3 min	
Adams and Yawger (1961)	Peroxidase	Whole peas	Nat	230–280	16.0	3.0 min	
Licciardello et al. (1967)	C. botulinum toxin-type E	Growth Media	6.2	125–135	26.4	3.8 min	Temp.-dependent activation energy
		do	do	135–140	57.4	@ 60°C	
		do	do	140–145	153.5		
Read and Bradshaw (1966)	Staphylococcus enterotoxin B	Milk	6.4–6.6	210–260	25.9	9.4 min	
Stumbo (1973)	C. botulinum spores (types A and B)	Variety	4.5	220–?	64–82	0.1–0.2 min	
	B. stearothermophilus	do	do	do	53–82	4.0–5.0 min	

[a] Value at 121°C.
[b] Nat, natural pH of the system.
[c] do, ditto.

329

Table 12.3. Effect of Temperature on Rate of Destruction of Various Food Components

Component	D_{121} (min)^a	E_a(kcal/mol)
Vitamins	100–1000	20–30
Quality factors (texture, color, flavor)	5–500	10–30
Enzyme inactivation	1–10	10–100
Vegetative cell inactivation	0.001–0.01	80–200
Spore inactivation	0.1–5	50–200

^{a} D_{121} is the time (min) at 121°C to decrease the component by 90%.

Vitamins and quality factors (e.g., texture and flavor) exhibit similar temperature dependence, whereas inactivation of vegetative cells and spores is much more temperature dependent. For enzymes, the range of activation energies is very large due to the presence of heat-resistant and heat-labile isozymes. For example, Ling and Lund (1978) reported an activation energy of 22 kcal/mol for the heat-resistant fraction of horseradish peroxidase and 36 kcal/mol for the heat-labile isozyme. The fact that the thermal destruction rate for the basis of a thermal process (enzymes, vegetative cells, or spores) is more temperature dependent than thermal destruction of nutrients, means that for a given increase in processing temperature, the rate of destruction for the basis will increase more than the rate of destruction of nutrients. This has been used to optimize thermal processes for nutrient retention.

OPTIMIZATION OF THERMAL PROCESSES FOR NUTRIENT RETENTION

More recently, there has been an attempt to optimize the thermal process for nutrient retention. This has resulted primarily from the use of computers and the increasing public concern over the nutrient content of processed foods. To determine optimum conditions for nutrient retention, equations describing the time–temperature history of a product must be coupled with the parameters describing the reaction kinetics for destruction of nutrients and other factors. This allows the process to be optimized with respect to nutrient retention, while assuring that the objective of the process has been accomplished.

Optimization of the blanching process with respect to nutrient retention involves consideration of losses of nutrients in addition to losses by thermal degradation. For example, blanching in hot water can result in a considerable loss of nutrients due to leaching (Lee 1958). Similarly, losses due to oxidation can result during blanching in hot air.

However, even if one only considers thermal degradation of nutrients for blanching optimization, it is difficult to predict an optimum process. This is true because the basis for the process (heat-resistant enzymes) and nutrient factors exhibit nearly the same temperature dependence. Therefore, blanching for a long time at a low temperature has no real advantage over blanching for a short time at a high temperature. If, however, significant leaching or oxidative losses could occur, then high-temperature–short-time (HTST) blanching would result in a greater retention of nutrients.

For pasteurization and commercial sterilization, there is an opportunity to optimize the process for nutrient retention. For foods or food fluids which are pasteurized, the HTST process results in maximum nutrient retention (Hartman and Dryden 1965). This can be predicted by comparing the activation energies of microorganisms to those of nutrients. An increase in process temperature (with an appropriate decrease in process time) will have a greater effect on increasing the rate of microbial destruction than it will on the rate of nutrient destruction. Consequently, HTST results in greater nutrient retention.

For commercial sterilization, optimization of the thermal process is not as straightforward. For commercial sterilization either out of container (aseptic thermal processing) or in container by convection heating, HTST processes will result in maximum retention of nutrients and quality factors (Anonymous 1969; Clifcorn et al. 1950; Everson et al. 1964A,B; Feaster et al. 1949; Jackson and Benjamin 1948). As in pasteurization treatments, this is caused by the difference in temperature response of the rate of microbial destruction compared to the rate of destruction of nutrients and quality factors. This is used to advantage in aseptic canning units where temperatures up to 350°F can be employed. In food systems where natural enzymes may be present, however, there are limitations on the maximum temperature that may be used. That maximum occurs when the thermal process may impart sufficient lethality for microorganisms but insufficient lethality for enzymes. This is a consequence of the difference in the response of microbial and enzymic rates of degradation to temperature (Farkas et al. 1956).

At relatively low thermal processing temperatures, the destruction rate for enzymes is greater than that for microorganisms, but as process temperature is increased the destruction rate for microorganisms increases faster than that for enzymes. Hence, there exists some temperature at which the destruction rate for the heat-resistant enzyme is equal to the destruction rate for the microorganism used as the basis of the process. Above that temperature, inactivation of the enzyme must be used as the basis of the process, since the destruction rate of the enzyme is less than that of the microorganism. If this is not considered in processing products containing natural heat-resistant enzymes, product quality can deteriorate during storage because of residual enzymic activity (Anonymous 1969). The temperature range where the destruction rate of enzymes equals that for microorganisms is generally $270°-290°F$. Therefore, for products containing heat-resistant enzymes, processes above this crossover temperature must be based on enzyme inactivation. Under these circumstances, process optimization for nutrient retention is difficult to predict, since the rate of destruction for nutrients and quality factors exhibit a temperature dependence similar in magnitude to that of heat-resistant enzymes.

In addition to considering enzyme activity as a basis of the process, Mansfield (1962) suggested that HTST processes over approximately $260°F$ may have to be based on product quality considerations. In particular, the desired degree of cooking may not be attained under these processing conditions. From Table 12.2 it can be seen that the texture (degree of cook) for many vegetable products exhibits a dependence on temperature similar to that for heat-resistant enzymes. Therefore, HTST processes may result in adequate microbial lethality, but poor consumer preference because of a too firm texture. This is particularly important to the consumer, since "heat and serve" items appear more desirable than "cook and serve."

For products that heat primarily by convection and contain particulates, two important assumptions are made: (1) Surfaces of pieces in the brine or fluid are at the temperature of the surrounding fluid, and (2) particulates are sterile in the interior. Thus, if the thermal process is based on the slowest heating point in the container, the lethality at all points in the container and at the surface of the particulates will be adequate for commercial sterilization. However, in foods containing particulates that may not be sterile in the center (e.g., foods containing fabricated pieces such as meatballs or stuffed noodles), the basis of the process should be the temperature at the center of a particulate (the slowest heating point). Under these conditions, and provided it can be assumed that the nutrients are located in the particulates, designing the process for optimizing nutrient retention is basically the same as that for conduction-heating foods.

Optimization of thermal processes for conduction-heating foods is much more difficult than for the previously discussed situations. The difficulty in optimizing the process lies in the fact that each point in the cross section of the container or particulate receives a different thermal process and these thermal histories may or may not be equivalent in microbial and nutrient destruction. It had previously been thought that the center point received the least lethality. However, it has been shown that the location of the least lethal point (critical lethal point) is dependent on the geometry of the container and the boundary conditions of the process (Teixeira *et al.* 1969A). Although this will not be discussed here, suffice it to say that the overall lethality is the mass-average (or volume-average) lethality obtained by integrating the effect of the heat treatment at every point in the container over the volume of the container.

Several investigators have developed methods for calculating the average destruction of nutrients and microorganisms in foods which heat by conduction (Ball and Olson 1957; Cohen and Wall 1971; Hayakawa 1969; Jen et al. 1971; Lenz and Lund 1977; Manson et al. 1970; Stumbo 1973; Teixeira et al. 1969B). Most of these mehtods require major computational effort and some require a computer. However, for conduction-heating foods, the general considerations for optimizing a thermal process for nutrient retention can be illustrated by considering calculations presented in the study by Teixeira et al. (1969B).

Figure 12.1 shows the percentage of retention of a component (with the D_R and z value indicated on the curves) as a function of processes

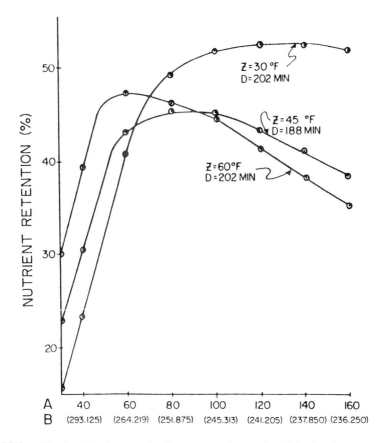

Fig. 12.1. Multinutrient optimization, percentage of nutrient retention versus process time (min) (A) with corresponding retort temperature ($^\circ$F) (B).

of equivalent microbial lethality. It can be seen that the optimum retention of a low z value nutrient is obtained at a low-temperature– long-time process, whereas a high-temperature–short-time process is optimum for a nutrient with a high z value. The curve for $z = 45°F$, $D = 188$ min is that for thiamin destruction in green bean puree (Feliciotti and Esselen 1957). It can be seen that the optimum process for thiamin retention is 90 min at 248°F, very close to existing processes for green bean puree. More significantly, as the temperature of the process is increased, thiamin retention decreases sharply. Thus in- container HTST is not the best thermal process for nutrient retention in conduction-heating foods, and, moreover, each process must be individually optimized.

Teixeira et al. (1975) also studied the effect of container geometry on nutrient retention, and showed that by minimizing the critical dimension for heat transfer (the smallest dimension of the container) nutrient retention was maximized. These studies and the results presented in Fig. 12.1 were simulated using a constant retort tempera- ture. Teixeira et al. (1975) also examined the effect of selected variable retort temperature profiles on nutrient retention. Retort policies considered included constant functions, ramp functions, single- and multiple-step functions and sine functions. Unfortunately, the max- imum nutrient retention for the best temperature profile for each of the process control functions was not significantly different than that for the constant retort temperature process (current practice). Others have used more rigorous search techniques to determine the best retort temperature policy and have also shown that nutrient and quality fac- tor retention are not significantly improved over constant retort tempera- ture process (current practice). Others have used more rigorous search techniques to determine the best retort temperature policy and have also shown that nutrient and quality factor retention are not signifi- cantly improved over constant retort temperature policies (Saguy and Karel 1979; Hildenbrand 1980; Martens 1980).

In conclusion, optimization of a thermal process for nutrient reten- tion is dependent on the relative temperature dependence of the rate of destruction of nutrients. In Table 12.4 the methods by which blanching, pasteurization, and commercial sterilization can be opti- mized with respect to nutrient retention are summarized.

EFFECT OF BLANCHING METHODS ON NUTRIENTS

For the blanching process, the effect of various methods of accomplish- ing the objectives of blanching on nutrients can be assessed by con- sidering thermal, leaching, and oxidative losses. For data published prior to 1958, Lee (1958) presented an excellent review of the blanching

Table 12.4. Optimization of Thermal Processes for Nutrient Retention

Process	Method of Optimization
Blanching	Based on considerations other than thermal losses (e.g., leaching losses, oxidative degradation, damage to product)
Pasteurization	HTST if heat-resistant enzymes are not present
Commercial sterilization	Convection-heating foods and aseptic processing: HTST until heat-resistant enzymes become important
	Conduction-heating foods: not necessarily HTST; difficult but not impossible calculation

process. Feaster (1960B) also considered nutrient losses in the blanching operation. Table 12.5 is a supplement to those reviews, and illustrates the effect of various methods of blanching on nutrient losses.

The two traditional methods of blanching use either hot water or steam as the heat transfer medium. Many systems have been designed to contact product with the heating medium for the time required to achieve a "blanched" condition. Since a process designed with either of these heating mediums would accomplish the desired objectives of the blanching operation, and since there would not appear to be an advantage for an HTST process from the standpoint of thermal degradation of nutrients (see previous discussion on blanching optimization), the primary difference between these two processes with respect to nutrient retention is the extent of leaching. As expected, for water blanching the loss of water-soluble vitamins increases with contact time, and fat-soluble vitamins are relatively unaffected (Table 12.5) (Guerrant et al. 1947). Factors expected to affect losses during water blanching would be those factors affecting mass transfer: (1) surface area, (2) concentration of solutes in the hot water, and (3) agitation of the water.

Steam blanching results in greater retention of water-soluble nutrients than water blanching (Table 12.5) (Raab et al. 1973; Dietrich and Neumann 1965; Holmquist et al. 1954; Korobkina et al. 1969; Schwerdtfeger 1971). A steam-blanching method called individual quick blanch (IQB) was designed to reduce blanching effluent (Lazar et al. 1971). Bomben et al. (1973) (Table 12.5) indicate that there may be a slight improvement in ascorbic acid retention with IQB as compared to conventional steam blanching. The slight improvement may be the result of the fact that in IQB each individual particle receives nearly the same heat treatment. With conventional steam blanching, the particles on the periphery of the bed are generally overblanched while particles in the center of the bed are just adequately blanched.

Table 12.5. Effects of Blanching on Nutrients

References	Product	Nutrient	Process[a]	Loss (%)	Comment
Bomben et al. (1973)	Green beans	Vitamin C	S, 2.5 min	8 mg/100 g	No initial content available; content after blanching
			IQB	11 mg/100 g	
			IQB predry	7 mg/100 g	
	Lima beans		S, 3.0 min	16 mg/100 g	
			IQB	24 mg/100 g	
			IQB predry	22 mg/100 g	
	Brussels sprouts		S	47 mg/100 g	
			IQB	46 mg/100 g	
			IQB predry	43 mg/100 g	
	Peas		S	21 mg/100 g	
			IQB	18 mg/100 g	
			IQB predry	20 mg/100 g	
Dietrich and Neumann (1965)	Brussels sprouts	Vitamin C	W, 9 min/190°F	24	
			S, 11 min/190°F	16	
			W, 6 min/200°F	16	
			S, 7 min/200°F	16	
			W, 5 min/212°F	19	
			W, 6 min/212°F	20	
Dietrich et al. (1970)	Brussels sprouts	Vitamin C	W, 6 min/212°F	43	
			M, 1 min + W 4 min/212°F	29	
			M, 3 min + W 2 min/212°F	35	
Guerrant et al. (1947)	Peas	Ascorbid acid	W, 3 min/200°F	33	Other temperature/ time combinations were done on other vegetables: green beans, lima beans, spinach
			W, 6 min/200°F	46	
			W, 9 min/200°F	58	
		Riboflavin	W, 3 min/200°F	30	
			W, 6 min/200°F	30	
			W, 9 min/200°F	50	
		Thiamin	W, 3 min/200°F	16	
			W, 6 min/200°F	16	
			W, 9 min/200°F	34	
		Carotene	W, 3 min/200°F	2	
			W, 6 min/200°F	0	
			W, 9 min/200°F	0	

Reference	Material	Nutrient	Treatment	Value	Comments
Holmquist et al. (1954)	Lima beans	Niacin	W, 2 min/200°F	32	
			W, 4 min/200°F	32	
			W, 6 min/200°F	37	
	Peas	Vitamin C	S	12.3	
			W	25.8	
Korobkina et al. (1969)	Mussels	Niacin	S	57.6	
			W	71.8	
		B_6	S	42.4	
			W	67.5	
		Co	S	50.6	
			W	49.8	
		Mn	S	17.7	
			W	36.5	
Raab et al. (1973)	Lima beans	B_6	W, 10 min/212°F	21	
			S, 10 min/212°F	14	
Ralls et al. (1973)	Spinach	Carotene	W	5.4 mg/100 g	Evaluation after canning and processing; initial level not reported
			Hot gas	3.9 mg/100 g	
		Riboflavin	W	0.12 mg/100 g	
			Hot gas	0.10 mg/100 g	
		Vitamin C	W	20.8 mg/100 g	
			Hot gas	34.2 mg/100 g	
		Ca, Mg, P	W	No differences	
			Hot gas		
Schwerdtfeger (1971)	Peas	Amino acid	W, 212°F	25	
			S	13	
	Spinach	Protein	W, 212°F	None	
	Peas	Protein	S	None	
	Spinach	Amino acid	W, 212°F	80	
			S	60	

[a] Process to blanch adequately. Generally determined by peroxidase inactivation. W, water; S, steam; IQB, individual quick blanch; hot gas, hot gas blanching; M, microwave.

Microwave heating has also been applied for blanching food products. Since it can be assumed that microwave energy has no direct enhancing effect on degradation of food components, other than through temperature elevation (Lopez and Baganis 1971), microwave blanching should result in nutrient retentions at least equal to that achieved during steam blanching and better than that achieved during water blanching. Dietrich et al. (1970) compared microwave, steam, and water blanching and verified that microwave blanching resulted in better ascorbic acid retention in brussels sprouts; however, the best product was achieved with combination processes involving microwave and water-blanching procedures. The microwave treatment gave rapid heat input into the product, and a holding period in hot water following microwave treatment allowed thermal equilibration in the brussels sprouts. Although microwave blanching is inviting from a nutrient retention consideration, the cost per unit of product is generally exorbitant (Huxsoll et al. 1970). Other efforts have been reported with respect to combination blanching processes involving microwave heating and hot gas treatments (Jeppson 1968, 1969); however, no data are available on the retention of nutrients.

Hot gas blanching also has been developed primarily to reduce effluent generated during the blanching operation (Ralls et al. 1972). Although temperatures up to 250°F are used, product temperature would not be expected to exceed 212°F because of evaporation of surface moisture. Ralls et al. (1973) (Table 12.5) reported the content of selected nutrients in spinach after water or hot gas blanching. The authors concluded that there was no significant difference between the two blanching methods. Although no studies have been reported on the effect of hot air blanching on nutrients, one of the factors which would contribute significantly to nutrient loss is oxidation.

Superheated steam also has been used to blanch and partially dry vegetables (Lazar 1972). Although no data were reported on the effect of this process on nutrients, based on the fact that an enzyme was used to assess blanching efficacy, it is likely that this treatment would have no more effect on nutrients than hot gas blanching.

In conclusion, it appears that the blanching operation can significantly reduce the nutrient content of foods, the extent being dependent on the blanching method and the product. Variation of nutrient losses between blanching methods can be rationalized on the basis of losses by leaching and oxidative degradation.

STORAGE OF BLANCHED FOODS

As previously pointed out, blanching is a thermal operation applied to foods which will subsequently receive an additional treatment. For those foods that are frozen or dehydrated, see the appropriate sections in this book (Chapters 10 and 11, respectively) on the effect of subsequent storage on nutrients. Those foods receiving an additional thermal process will be covered later.

EFFECT OF PASTEURIZATION METHODS ON NUTRIENTS

Some foods which receive pasteurization treatments are listed in Table 12.6 (Shapton et al. 1971). Examination of Table 12.6 reveals that most of the products which are pasteurized have a low pH either because the natural pH of the system is low or because the product has been fermented to produce an acid environment. Since most of the heat-labile nutrients are relatively stable in acid conditions, nutrient losses in those products are relatively minor.

Although thermal losses during pasteurization may be small, oxidative losses can be high. Thus, pasteurization of food fluids such as fruit juices, beer, and wine is generally accomplished in indirect heat exchangers (such as the plate or double-tube heat exchanger) rather than open film-type pasteurizers (Heid 1960). Often, fluids are de-aerated prior to pasteurization.

Table 12.6. Examples of Pasteurization Treatments Used for Food Products

Temperature range (°C)	Product pasteurized
60–65	Milk (holding process), milk for butter manufacture, egg, ice cream mix, smoked hams (meat temperature), carbonated beverages
65–70	Ready to eat smoked meats (meat temperature), pickled sausages ([U.S.] meat temperature), canned hams (U.S.), wine (low-temperature pasteurization), nonalcoholic fruit drinks
70–75	Dill pickles, piccalilli, milk (flash process), carbonated fruit juices, mortadella sausage (pork and tongue)
75–80	Apple juice (holding process), grape juice, bread and butter pickles, cream for butter manufacture, raspberries, strawberries, bilberries, in syrup in cans or jars
80–85	Jamaica pickle, wine (U.S.), preserved and pickled vegetables, vegetables in oil, ice cream mix (flash process), dessicated coconut (other temperatures have been suggested)
85–90	Apple juice (flash process), canned olives, citrus juices, peeled tomatoes (pH 4.1)
90–95	Marroni sciroppati (chestnuts in syrup), tomato puree, citrus juices (flash process), prosciutti salati inscatolati (packaged hams), tomato juice, peeled tomatoes (pH 4.5), jam
95–100	Wine (flash process), fruit puree, fruit juices, canned fruits (internal can temperature), canned mortadella sausage (pork and tongue)

Source: Shapton et al. (1971).

Table 12.7.   Loss (%) of Nutrients in Milk during Processing

Nutrient	Pasteurized		Sterilized	
	HTST	Holder	UHT	In bottle
Protein	0	0	Whey proteins denatured	
Fat	0	0	Some loss of polyunsaturated fatty acids	
Sugar	0	0	0	Slight loss of nutritive value
Minerals	0	0	0	0
Vitamin A				
Vitamin D				
Riboflavin				
Vitamin B_6	0	0	0	0
Pantothenic acid				
Biotin				
Nicotinic acid				
Thiamin	10	10	10	35
Vitamin C	10	20	10	50
Folic acid	0	0	10	50
Vitamin B_{12}	0	10	20	30

Source: Thompson (1969).

The most important nonacid food fluid is milk. The effect of pasteurization treatments on nutrients in milk has received considerable attention. Vitamins in milk and milk products were extensively reviewed by Hartman and Dryden (1965) in one of the best reviews published on the effects of processing on nutrients in milk. Zadow (1984) reviewed the effect of new technology on the nutritional value of dairy products. Table 12.7 summarizes the effect of pasteurization and sterilization on nutrients in milk.

As indicated in our earlier discussion, the HTST process results in greater nutrient retention for those nutrients affected by the pasteurization treatment (primarily thiamin, vitamin C, and vitamin B_{12}). Milk and milk products can be considered as primary sources for these nutrients, especially for the younger age groups (Hartman and Dryden 1965), and, therefore, these losses are very important nutritionally. However, this is a perfect example of the need to provide a heat treatment even though there are adverse nutritional consequences. The data in Table 12.7 indicate that ultra-high-temperature (UHT) processing results in significantly greater retention of the heat-labile nutrients when compared to in-bottle sterilization. In UHT processing, temperatures up to 300°F are used for very short periods (on the order of seconds).

STORAGE OF PASTEURIZED FOODS

Little information has been published on the storage stability of nutrients in high acid, pasteurized products. However, those nutrients that are more sensitive to high temperature are generally the same ones that are of concern during storage. It would be reasonable that the lower the storage temperature, the slower the rate of nutrient degradation. Usually in these kinds of products, proper packaging is paramount for extending the storage life, since oxidative losses and light-catalyzed (both visible and ultraviolet) losses can be the major mechanism of loss.

In contrast to other pasteurized products, storage of pasteurized milk has received extensive consideration (Hartman and Dryden 1965). Low storage temperature and the relatively short storage time minimize the loss of nutrients in milk. However, some nutrient destruction does occur and is catalyzed primarily by visible and ultraviolet light. Therefore, packaging considerations are of primary importance (Karel 1960; Singh *et al.* 1975). Packaging as a means of maintaining nutrients in foods is covered in another section of this book.

EFFECT OF COMMERCIAL STERILIZATION METHODS ON NUTRIENTS

The various methods available for commercial sterilization of food have been reviewed by Brody (1971). Since the destruction of nutrients during the thermal process is dependent on (1) time–temperature treatment used as the basis of the process and (2) rate of heat transfer into the product, commercial developments have focused primarily on increasing the rate of heat transfer into the product (Gutterson 1972). Hence, agitated retorts such as the orbitort, steritort, flame sterilizer, and hydrostatic cooker have been developed.

In addition to increasing the rate of heat transfer, however, there also has been a gradual shift to higher processing temperatures. As pointed out in the discussion on optimizing nutrient retention in commercial sterilization, a HTST process results in greater nutrient retention in those products heating primarily by convection. Ammerman (1957) presented an excellent study on the effects of heat treatments of equal microbial lethality on selected food constituents including nutrients, color, proteins, and flavor compounds. Figure 12.2 from Ammerman (1957) illustrates that retention of vitamin C in tomato juice is improved when processing is conducted at a HTST condition. For natural products containing enzymes the limitation of the benefits of HTST processing, as pointed out earlier, occurs when the basis of the process shifts from microbes to enzymes (about $270°-290°F$).

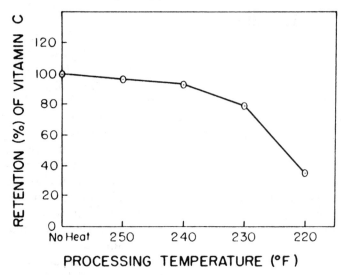

Fig. 12.2.   The effect of equivalent lethal heat treatments at the indicated temperature on the retention of vitamin C in tomato juice.

The use of HTST processes is particularly adaptable to aseptic processing.   In this system, processing temperatures in excess of $300°F$ are used for very short periods (order of seconds).   Under these conditions nutrient retention may be greatly enhanced.   In an evaluation of HTST aseptic processing, Everson et al. (1964A,B) found that thiamin retention was significantly greater in HTST products than in conventionally canned and retorted products (Table 12.8).   For pyridoxine, the benefit of HTST was not as evident, probably indicating that thermal destruction of pyridoxine is not as temperature dependent as that of thiamin.   HTST aseptic canning also results in a significant improvement in organoleptic qualities (Anonymous 1970).   Currently, there is activity in developing aseptic processing equipment for handling food particulates.

As pointed out earlier, most of the reports on the effect of thermal processing on nutrients only contain information on the content of a specific nutrient after the thermal process and give the percentage retention or loss of the nutrient.   In light of the fact that there are numerous processing methods and time–temperature possibilities for accomplishing commercial sterilization, it is not appropriate to assume that the nutrient losses reported in the literature represent the average or norm for the industry.   For this reason, data of this type are of limited value.   However, these reports can be used, as Schroeder (1971) used them, to point out a critical lack of particular nutrients in our processed food supply.

Table 12.8. Effect of Aseptic and Conventional Thermal Processing Methods on Nutrient Losses

Product	Thiamin loss (%)		Pyridoxine loss (%)	
	HTST	Conventional	HTST	Conventional
Strained lima beans	15.8	40.3	9.5	10.1
Strained beef	9.2	21.6	4.1	2.9
Tomato juice concentrate	0	2.8	0	0

Source: Everson *et al.* (1964A,B).

USDA Agriculture Handbook 8 (Watt and Merrill 1963), Orr (1969), and Mitchell *et al.* (1968) report nutrient content of processed foods. Some of the data that they assembled were used to calculate percentage loss of nutrients in selected vegetables during canning and are presented in Table 12.9. Nutrient losses range from 0 to 91%, depending on the nutrient and product. These losses represent the sum of the losses during the entire canning process and, as pointed out in Table 12.5, blanching losses can be quite large. However, the important observation is that nutrient losses appear to be quite significant in the canning process.

STORAGE OF COMMERCIALLY STERILE FOODS

A common misconception among consumers and many foods industry personnel is that commercially sterile products remain unchanged during storage. This is not the case. Organoleptic and nutrient changes do occur during storage, the extent of the changes being dependent on the time and temperature of storage, the packaging system, and the product characteristics. Several extensive studies have been conducted on the storage stability of nutrients in canned foods (Cameron *et al.* 1949; Goresline *et al.* 1955; Cecil and Woodroof 1962; Ball *et al.* 1963).

Cameron *et al.* (1955) reviewed thermal processing and storage of foods and compiled Table 12.10 from existing literature. It can be seen that low temperature storage results in an improvement in nutrient retention. The 50° and 65°F storage temperatures would require refrigerated warehousing and would be economically feasible only if the consumer is willing to pay for the increased cost.

With the increased consumer awareness of nutrition, and with the advent of nutritional labeling requirements, it may become economically and legally advantageous to select storage temperatures that will result in a stated shelf life with a specified level of nutrient.

Kramer (1974) adapted data from Feaster (1960A) and Cecil and Woodroof (1962) to predict the maximum storage temperatures that could be used for a variety of canned foods to assure that no more than

Table 12.9. Losses (%) of Nutrients in the Canning Process

Product	Biotin[a]	Folacin[a]	B$_6$[b]	Pantothenic acid[b]	A[c]	Thiamin[c]	Riboflavin[c]	Niacin[c]	C[c]
Asparagus	0	75.2	64.0	—	43.3	66.7	55.0	46.6	54.5
Lima beans	—	61.8	47.1	72.3	55.2	83.3	66.7	64.2	75.9
Green beans	—	57.1	50.0	60.5	51.7	62.5	63.6	40.0	78.9
Beets	—	80.0	9.1	33.3	50.0	66.7	60.0	75.0	70.0
Carrots	40.0	58.8	80.0	53.6	9.1	66.7	60.0	33.3	75.0
Corn	63.3	72.5	0	59.2	32.5	80.0	58.3	47.1	58.3
Coropeas	—	36.6	90.6	84.8	83.8	79.1	61.5	68.8	89.7
Mushrooms	54.4	83.8	—	54.5	—	80.0	45.6	52.3	33.3
Green peas	77.7	58.8	68.8	80.0	29.7	74.2	64.3	69.0	66.77
Spinach	66.7	34.7	75.0	78.3	32.1	80.0	50.0	50.0	72.5
Tomatoes	55.0	53.75	—	30.3	0	16.7	25.0	0	26.1

[a] Mitchell et al. (1968).
[b] Orr (1969).
[c] Watt and Merrill (1963).

Table 12.10. Retention (%) of Vitamins in Canned Foods during Storage

Product	°F	Months	Ascorbic acid	Carotene	Niacin	Riboflavin	Thiamin
Apricots	50	12	96	94	—	—	—
	65	12	93	85	—	—	—
	80	12	85	83	—	—	—
	50	24	94	91	—	—	—
	65	24	90	84	—	—	—
	80	24	56	76	—	—	—
Asparagus, green	50	12	97	97	89	92	89
	65	12	94	88	85	87	79
	80	12	89	85	84	83	66
	50	24	93	88	93	81	85
	65	24	91	84	91	77	72
	80	24	86	76	87	72	54
Asparagus, white	50	12	96	—	96	—	82
	65	12	94	—	94	—	74
	80	12	87	—	97	—	62
	50	24	90	—	96	—	72
	65	24	87	—	98	—	65
	80	24	82	—	97	—	52
Beans, green	50	12	92	—	83	72	92
	65	12	90	—	81	69	86
	80	12	85	—	80	62	78
	50	24	88	—	86	62	82
	65	24	81	—	86	57	80
	80	24	74	—	86	42	67
Beans, lima	50	12	100	—	101	95	88
	65	12	98	—	100	91	82
	80	12	95	—	99	88	74
	50	24	86	—	99	75	87
	65	24	83	—	97	75	76
	80	24	78	—	100	70	66
Carrots	50	12	—	94	—	—	—
	65	12	—	97	—	—	—
	80	12	—	93	—	—	—
	50	24	—	90	—	—	—
	65	24	—	95	—	—	—
	80	24	—	91	—	—	—
Corn, white	50	12	98	—	82	—	97
	65	12	92	—	85	—	85
	80	12	86	—	88	—	78
	50	24	90	—	84	—	94
	65	24	88	—	86	—	89
	80	24	78	—	88	—	71
Corn, yellow	50	12	98	85	89	84	90
	65	12	94	87	89	80	86
	80	12	89	84	91	78	74
	50	24	92	69	91	71	89
	65	24	89	72	90	68	76
	80	24	81	87	96	61	60

(Continued)

Table 12.10. *(Continued)*

Product	Storage conditions °F	Months	Ascorbic acid	Carotene	Niacin	Riboflavin	Thiamin
Grapefruit	50	12	95	—	—	—	99
juice	65	12	91	—	—	—	100
	80	12	75	—	—	—	93
	50	24	94	—	—	—	99
	65	24	82	—	—	—	94
	80	24	57	—	—	—	84
Grapefruit	50	12	94	—	—	—	—
segments	65	12	91	—	—	—	—
	80	12	73	—	—	—	—
	50	24	87	—	—	—	—
	65	24	77	—	—	—	—
	80	24	46	—	—	—	—
Orange juice	50	12	97	—	—	—	100
	65	12	92	—	—	—	98
	80	12	77	—	—	—	89
	50	24	95	—	—	—	101
	65	24	80	—	—	—	94
	80	24	50	—	—	—	83
Peaches	50	12	98	95	101	—	92
	65	12	85	90	102	—	90
	80	12	72	86	101	—	81
	50	24	98	75	100	—	88
	65	24	80	64	98	—	100
	80	24	53	63	99	—	86
Peas, Alaska	50	12	91	97	82	91	91
	65	12	89	95	77	84	86
	80	12	84	91	82	82	75
	50	24	90	95	99	80	89
	65	24	88	93	87	73	85
	80	24	81	89	85	68	68
Peas, sweet	50	12	94	98	95	93	93
	65	12	92	92	87	89	88
	80	12	88	91	90	84	73
	50	24	92	94	96	88	91
	65	24	89	90	95	84	85
	80	24	81	90	95	81	72
Pineapple	50	12	110	—	—	—	93
juice	65	12	108	—	—	—	93
	80	12	93	—	—	—	87
	50	24	108	—	—	—	100
	65	24	100	—	—	—	100
	80	24	79	—	—	—	93
Pineapple,	50	12	100	—	—	—	97
sliced	65	12	95	—	—	—	96
	80	12	74	—	—	—	89
	50	24	83	—	—	—	102
	65	24	78	—	—	—	103
	80	24	53	—	—	—	89

Table 12.10. *(Continued)*

Product	Storage conditions °F	Months	Ascorbic acid	Carotene	Niacin	Riboflavin	Thiamin
Plums, purple	50	12	—	102	95	84	—
(prunes)	65	12	—	100	93	82	—
	80	12	—	97	103	78	—
	50	24	—	90	86	84	—
	65	24	—	98	91	82	—
	80	24	—	86	95	76	—
Spinach	50	12	93	91	100	92	96
	65	12	91	90	103	89	89
	80	12	86	84	99	85	76
	50	24	90	80	96	82	90
	65	24	88	80	100	80	82
	80	24	81	81	101	69	71
Tomatoes	50	12	95	94	91	94	94
	65	12	94	98	93	95	93
	80	12	82	95	93	91	82
	50	24	89	75	88	96	91
	65	24	87	75	88	98	87
	80	24	70	74	85	97	70
Tomato juice	50	12	100	98	99	88	95
	65	12	97	100	99	84	93
	80	12	86	99	99	83	85
	50	24	102	94	92	92	103
	65	24	92	97	91	94	94
	80	24	74	98	90	94	77

Source: Cameron *et al.* (1955).

10% of a specified nutrient was lost during a stated storage period (Table 12.11). It can be seen that the maximum storage temperature is dependent upon the nutrient under consideration, since each nutrient has a characteristic activation energy. It is also evident that most of the temperatures are below ambient temperature and, therefore, the products would require refrigerated storage.

In conclusion, it is evident that there is a significant loss of nutrients during canning and that these losses increase during storage. Altering processing and storage conditions to maximize nutrient retention is an important and necessary direction for the food processing industry.

SUMMARY

The fact that application of thermal energy to foods reduces the nutritive value of some components cannot be contested. However,

Table 12.11. Maximum Storage Temperatures (°F) for Canned Foods to Assure Not More Than 10% Loss of a Selected Vitamin for 12, 18, and 24 Months' Storage

Canned product	Ascorbic acid (vitamin C)			Thiamin (vitamin B$_1$)			Carotene (vitamin A precursor)			Niacin			Riboflavin (vitamin B$_2$)		
	12	18	24	12	18	24	12	18	24	12	18	24	12	18	24
Apricots	76	68	60	32	—	—	70	62	54	[b]	[b]	[b]	—	—	—
Asparagus	74	65	58	45	38	32	72	58	45	[b]	[b]	[b]	57	50	45
Beans, green	60	45	32	57	45	32	—	—	—	[c]	[c]	[c]	57	50	45
Beans, lima	74	60	45	32	—	—	—	—	—	[c]	[c]	[c]	65	40	32
Carrots	—	—	—	—	—	—	≥80	≥80	≥80	[d]	[d]	[d]	—	—	—
Corn, sweet	71	60	50	64	58	53	58	66	75	[d]	[d]	[d]	70	55	48
Frankfurters and beans	—	—	—	56	47	41	—	—	—	—	—	—	—	—	—
Grapefruit segments	60	45	32	—	—	—	—	—	—	[c]	[c]	[c]	—	—	—
Peaches	65	50	40	76	80	84	70	40	32	[b]	[b]	[b]	—	—	—
Peas	74	66	52	62	56	50	72	58	45	[d]	[d]	[d]	55	50	45
Plums	—	—	—	—	—	—	≥80	≥80	≥80	—	—	—	[f]	[f]	[f]
Pineapple slices	68	54	32	80	80	80	—	—	—	[c]	[c]	[c]	—	—	—
Spinach	68	60	52	63	57	49	46	41	38	[e]	[e]	[e]	63	46	32
Tomatoes	68	60	45	70	60	45	[a]	[a]	[a]	[e]	[e]	[e]	[d]	[d]	[d]

Source: Kramer (1974).

[a] 10% loss in 17 months, no temperature effect.
[b] 20% loss in 12 months, 15% in 24 months, no temperature effect.
[c] No loss.
[d] 10% loss, no time or temperature effect.
[e] 8% loss in 12 months, 13% in 24 months, no temperature effect.
[f] 20% loss, no time or temperature effect.

it is necessary to evaluate that consequence in view of the fact that application of thermal processes results in decreased food wastage through spoilage and decreased food-borne diseases. It is the responsibility of the preserved food industry to produce the most nutritious food supply possible.

REFERENCES

Adams, H. W., and Yawger, E. S. 1961. Enzyme inactivation and color of processed peas. Food Technol. *15*, 314–317.

Aiba, S., Humphrey, A. E., and Millis, N. F. 1965. Biochemical Engineering. Academic Press, New York.

Ammerman, G. R. 1957. The effect of equal lethal heat treatments at various times and temperatures upon selected food components. Ph.D. Thesis. Purdue Univ., W. Lafayette, IN.

Anonymous 1969. Aseptic Processing. 2nd Edition. Tech. Dig. *Cb–201*. Cherry-Burrell Corp.

Anonymous 1970. Physiocochemical differences of pureed vegetables packed by the aseptic and retort processes. United States Steel ADUSS 33–4406–01.

Ashton, W. M. 1972. The components of milk, their nutritive value and the effects of processing. I; II. Dairy Ind. *37*, 535–536, 538; *37*, 602–606, 611.

Ball, C. O., and Olson, F. C. W. 1957. Sterilization in Food Technology. McGraw-Hill Book Co., New York.

Ball, C. O., Joffe, F. M., Stier, E. F., and Hayakawa, K. 1963. The role of temperature in retaining quality in canned foods. ASHRAE J *5*(6), 93–108, 144, 146.

Barratt, B. 1973. Nutrition 1: The building blocks. Nutrition 2: Effects of processing. Food Can. *33*(1), 13–16; *33* (2), 28–31.

Bender, A. E. 1966. Nutritional effects of food processing. J. Food Technol. *1*, 261.

Bender, A. E. 1972. Processing damage to protein food. J. Food Technol. *7*, 239–250.

Bender, A. E. 1978. Food Processing and Nutrition. Academic Press, New York.

Bendix, G. H., Heberlein, D. G., Ptak, L. R., and Clifcorn, L. E. 1951. Thiamine destruction in peas, corn, lima beans, and tomato juice from 104.5° to 132°C (220°–270°F). J. Food Sci. *16*, 494–503.

Berk, Z. 1970. Processing and storage damage to nutritional value of foods. Proc. Third Int. Cong. Food Sci. Technol. 189–191.

Blakeborough, N. 1968. Preservation of biological materials especially by heat treatment. *In* Biochemical and Biological Engineering Science, Vol. 2. N. Blakeborough (Editor). Academic Press, New York.

Bomben, J. L., *et al.* 1973. Pilot plant evaluation of individual quick blanching (IQB) for vegetables. J. Food Sci. *38*, 590–594.

Brody, A. L. 1971. Food canning in rigid and flexible packages. Crit. Rev. Food Technol. *2*, 187–244.

Burger, I. H., and Walters, C. L. 1973. The effect of processing on the nutritive value of flesh foods. Proc. Nutr. Soc. *32*, 1–8.

Burton, H. 1963. A note on the effect of heat on the colour of goat's milk. J. Dairy Res. *30*, 217–222.

Burton, H., *et al.* 1970. Comparison of milks processed by the direct and indirect methods of ultra-high temperature sterilization. IV. The vitamin composition of milks processed by different processes. J. Dairy Res. *37*, 529–533.

Cain, R. F. 1967. Water-soluble vitamins: Changes during processing and storage of fruits and vegetables. Food Technol. *21*, 998–1007.

Cameron, E. J., Pilcher, R. W., and Clifcorn, L. E. 1949. Nutrient retention during canned food production. Am. J. Public Health *39*, 756–763.

Cameron, E. J., *et al.* 1955. Retention of nutrients during canning. National Canners Association, Washington, DC.

Cecil, S. R., and Woodroof, J. G. 1962. Long-term storage of military rations. Quartermaster Food and Container Institute for the Armed Forces, Chicago.

Chichester, C. O. 1973. Nutrition in food processing. World Rev. Nutr. Diet. *16*, 318–333.

Clifcorn, L. E. 1948. Factors influencing the vitamin content of canned foods. Food Res. *1*, 39–104.

Clifcorn, L. E., Peterson, G. T., Boyd, J. M., and O'Neil, J. H. 1950. A new principle for agitating in processing of canned foods. Food Technol. *4*, 450–457.

Cohen, J. S., and Wall, M. A. 1971. A method of calculating average sterilizing value in cylindrical containers. Trans. ASAE *3*, 329–333.

Davidek, J., Velisek, J., and Janicek, G. 1972. Stability of inosinic acid, inosine and hypoxanthine in aqueous solutions. J. Food Sci. *37*, 789–790.

Dietrich, W. C., and Neumann, H. J. 1965. Blanching brussels sprouts. Food Technol. *19*, 1174–1177.

Dietrich, W. C., *et al.* 1959. Time–temperature tolerance of frozen foods. XVIII. Effect of blanching conditions on color stability of frozen beans. Food Technol. *13*, 258–261.

Dietrich, W. C., Huxsol, C. C., and Guadagni, D. G. 1970. Comparison of microwave, conventional and combination blanching of brussels sprouts for frozen storage. Food Technol. *24*, 613–617.

Dugan, L. R., Jr. 1968. Processing and other stress effects on the nutritive value of lipids. World Rev. Nutr. Diet. *9*, 181–205.

Everson, G. J., *et al.* 1964A. Aseptic canning of foods. II. Thiamine retention as influenced by processing method, storage time and temperature and type of container. Food Technol. *18*, 84–86.

Everson, G. J., *et al.* 1964B. Aseptic canning of foods. III. Pyridoxine retention as influenced by processing method, storage time and temperature and type of container. Food Technol. *18*, 87–88.

Farkas, D. F., Goldblith, S. A., and Proctor, B. E. 1956. Stopping storage off-flavor by curbing peroxidase. Food Eng. *28*(1), 52–53.

Feaster, J. F. 1960A. Effects of commercial storage on the nutrient content of processed foods. A. Foods of plant origin. 1. Fruits and vegetables. *In* Nutritional Evaluation of Food Processing. R. S. Harris and H. von Loesecke (Editors). John Wiley, New York. Reprinted in 1971 by AVI Publishing Co., Westport, CT.

Feaster, J. F. 1960B. A. Washing, trimming, and blanching. *In* Nutritional Evaluation of Food Processing. R. S. Harris and H. von Loesecke (Editors). John Wiley, New York. Reprinted in 1971 by AVI Publishing Co., Westport, CT.

Feaster, J. F., Tompkins, M. D., and Ives, M. 1949. Retention of vitamins in low acid canned foods. Food Ind. *20*, 14–17, 150, 152, 154.

Feliciotti, E., and Esselen, W. B. 1957. Thermal destruction rates of thiamine in pureed meats and vegetables. Food Technol. *11*, 77–84.

Ford, J. E., *et al.* 1969. Effects of ultra-high temperature (UHT) processing and of subsequent storage on the vitamin content of milk. J. Dairy Res. *36*, 447–454.

Garrett, E. R. 1956. Prediction of stability in pharmaceutical preparations. J. Am. Pharm. Assoc. *45*, 171–178.

Gold, H. J., and Weckel, K. G. 1959. Degradation of chlorophyll to pheophytin during sterilization of canned green peas by heat. Food Technol. *13*, 281–286.

Goldblith, S. A. 1971. Thermal processing of foods: A review. World Rev. Nutr. Diet. *13*, 165–193.

Goresline, H. E., Leinen, N. J., and Mrak, E. M. (Editors) 1955. Establishing optimum conditions for storage and handling of semiperishable subsistence items. Office of the Quartermaster General, Washington, DC.

Gortner, W. A. 1972. The impact of food technology on nutrient supplies. Food Technol. Australia 24, 504–517.

Gregory, J. F., II, and Hiner, M. E. 1983. Thermal stability of vitamin B₆ compounds in liquid model food systems. J. Food Sci. 48, 1323–1327, 1339.

Guerrant, N. B., et al. 1947. Effect of duration and temperature of blanch on vitamin retention by certain vegetables. Ind. Eng. Chem. 39, 1000–1007.

Gupte, S. M., El-Bisi, H. M., and Francis, F. J. 1964. Kinetics of thermal degradation of chlorophyll in spinach puree. J. Food Sci. 29, 379–382.

Gutterson, M. 1972. Food Canning Techniques. Noyes Data Corp., Park Ridge, NJ.

Hackler, L. R. et. al. 1965. Effect of heat treatment on nutritive value of soymilk protein fed to weanling rats. J. Food Sci. 31, 723–728.

Hamm, D. J., and Lund, D. B. 1978. Kinetic parameters for thermal inactivation of pantothenic acid. J. Food Sci. 43, 631–633.

Harris, R. S., and Karmas, E. (Editors) 1975. Nutritional Evaluation of Food Processing, 2nd Edition. AVI Publishing Co., Westport, CT.

Harris, R. S., and von Loesecke, H. (Editors) 1960. Nutritional Evaluation of Food Processing. John Wiley, New York. Reprinted in 1971 by AVI Publishing Co., Westport, CT.

Hartman, A. M., and Dryden, L. P. 1965. Vitamins in milk and milk products. American Dairy Science Association, Champaign, IL.

Hayakawa, K. 1969. New parameters for calculating mass average sterilizing value to estimate nutrients in thermally conductive foods. Can. Inst. Food Technol. 2, 165–172.

Heid, J. L. 1960. C. Pasteurization, sterilization and storage. In Nutritional Evaluation of Food Processing. R. S. Harris and H. von Loesecke (Editors). John Wiley, New York. Reprinted in 1971 by AVI Publishing Co., Westport, CT.

Hein, R. E., and Hutchings, I. J. 1971. Influence of processing on vitamin mineral content and biological availability in processed foods. Council Foods Nutrition, AMA and AMA–Food Liaison Comm., New Orleans.

Henshall, J. D. 1973. Fruit and vegetable products. Proc. Nutr. Soc. 32, 17–22.

Herrmann, J. 1970. Calculation of the chemical and sensory alterations in food during heating and storage processes. Ernaehrungsforschung 15, 279–299.

Hildenbrand, P. 1980. An approach to solve the optimal temperature control problem for sterilization of conduction-heating foods. J. Food Proc. Eng. 3, 123–142.

Hollingsworth, D. F. 1970. Effects of some new production and processing methods on nutritive values. J. Am. Diet. Assoc. 57, 246–249.

Hollingsworth, D. F., and Martin, P. E. 1972. Some aspects of the effects of different methods of production and of processing on the nutritive value of foods. World Rev. Nutr. Diet. 15, 1–34.

Holmquist, J. W., et al. 1954. Steam blanching of peas. Food Technol. 8, 437–445.

Huxsoll, C. C., Dietrich, W. C., and Morgan, A. I., Jr. 1970. Comparison of microwave with steam or water blanching of corn-on-the-cob. 1. Characteristics of equipment and heat penetration. Food Technol. 24, 290–292.

Jackson, J. M., and Benjamin, A. A. 1948. Sterilization of foods. Ind. Eng. Chem. 40, 2241–2246.

Jen, Y., Manson, J. E., Stumbo, C. R., and Zahradnik, J. W. 1971. A procedure for estimating sterilization of and quality factor degradation in thermally processed foods. J. Food Sci. 36, 692–698.

Jeppson, M. R. 1968. Treating food products with microwave energy and hot gas of decreasing humidity. U.S. Pat. 3,409,447, Nov. 5.

Jeppson, M. R. 1969. Apparatus for treating food products and the like with microwave energy. U.S. Pat. 3,478,900, Nov. 18.

Kaczmarzyk, L. M., Fennema, O., and Powrie, W. D. 1963. Changes produced in Wisconsin green snap beans by blanching. Food Technol. *17*, 943–946.

Karel, M. 1960. Effects of packaging on maintenance of nutrients in food products. *In* Nutritional Evaluation of Food Processing. R. S. Harris and H. von Loesecke (Editors). John Wiley, New York. Reprinted in 1971 by AVI Publishing Co., Westport, CT.

Klein, B. P. 1982. Losses of nutrients during processing of foods. Am. Soc. Agric. Eng. Paper *82–6503*. St. Joseph, MI.

Klein, B. P., Matthews, M. E., and Setser, C. S. 1984. Foodservice systems: Time and temperature effects on food quality. North Central Res. Publ. *293*, Ill. Bull. *779*. Agr. Exp. Stn., Univ. of Illinois.

Korobkina, G. S., Danilova, E. N., and Kalinina, N. N. 1969. Effect of processing on the food value of mussels. (Russian). Vopr. Pitaniya *28*(5), *85–86*. From Nutr. Abstr. *40*, 2, 2384.

Kramer, A. 1974. Storage retention of nutrients. Food Technol. *28*, 50–58.

Labuza, T. P. 1972. Nutrient losses during drying and storage of dehydrated foods. Crit. Rev. Food Technol. *3*, 217–240.

Lang, K. 1970. Influence of cooking on foodstuffs. World Rev. Nutr. Diet. *12*, 266–317.

Lathrop, P. J., and Leung, H. K. 1980. Rates of ascorbic acid degradation during thermal processing of canned peas. J. Food Sci. *45*, 152–153.

Lawrie, R. A. 1968. Chemical changes in meat due to processing. A review. J. Sci. Food Agric. *19*, 233–240.

Lazar, M. E. 1972. Blanching and partial drying of foods with super-heated steam. J. Food Sci. *37*, 163–166.

Lazar, M. E., Lund, D. B., and Dietrich, W. C. 1971. IQB — A new concept in blanching. Food Technol. *25*, 684–686.

Lee, F. A. 1958. The blanching process. Advan. Food Res. *8*, 63–109.

Lenz, M. K., and Lund, D. B. 1977. The lethality–Fourier number method: Experimental verification of a model for calculating temperature profiles and lethality in conduction-heating canned foods. J. Food Sci. *42*, 989–996, 1001.

Lenz, M. K., and Lund, D. B. 1980. Experimental procedures for determining kinetics of food components. Food Technol. *32*(2), 51–55.

Licciardello, J. J., Ribich, C. A., Nickerson, J. T. R., and Goldblith, S. A. 1967. Kinetics of thermal inactivations of type E *Clostridium botulinum* toxin. Appl. Microbiol. *15*, 344–349.

Lillard, D. A. 1983. Effect of processing on chemical and nutritional changes in food lipids. J. Food Prot. *46*, 61–67.

Ling, A. C., and Lund, D. B. 1978. Determining kinetic parameters of heat resistant and heat labile isozymes from thermal destruction curves. J. Food Sci. *43*, 1307–1310.

Lopez, A., and Baganis, N. A. 1971. Effect of radio-frequency energy at 60 MHz on food enzyme activity. J. Food Sci. *36*, 911–914.

Lund, D. B. 1982. Influence of processing on nutrients in foods. J. Food Prot. *45*, 367–373.

Lund, D. B., *et al.* 1973. Symposium. Effects of processing storage and handling on nutrient retention in foods. Food Technol. *27*(1), 16–38, 51.

MacKinney, G., and Joslyn, M. A. 1941. Chlorophyll-pheophytin: Temperature coefficients of the rate of pheophytin formation. J. Am. Chem. Soc. *63*, 2530–2531.

Mansfield, T. 1962. High temperature short time sterilization. Proc. First Int. Cong. Food Sci. Technol., London.

Mansfield, T. 1974. A brief study of cooking. FMC Corp., San Jose, CA. (Pers. commun.)

Manson, J. E., Zahradnik, J. W., and Stumbo, C. R. 1970. Evaluation of lethality and nutrient retention of conduction-heating foods in rectangular containers. Food Technol. *24*, 1297–1301.

Mapson, L. W. 1956. Effect of processing on the vitamin content of foods. Brit. Med. Bull. *12*, 73–77.

Martens, T. 1980. Mathematical model of heat processing in flat containers. Ph.D. Thesis. Catholic Univ., Leuven, Belgium.

Mitchell, A. S., Rynbergen, H. J., Anderson, L., and Dibble, M. V. 1968. Cooper's Nutrition in Health and Disease. 15th Edition. J. B. Lippincott, Philadelphia.

Mnkeni, A. P., and Beveridge, T. 1982. Thermal destruction of pteroylglutamic acid in buffer and model systems. J. Food Sci. *47*, 2038–2041, 2063.

Mulley, E. A., Stumbo, C. R., and Hunting, W. M. 1975. Kinetics of thiamine degradation by heat: A new method for studying reaction rates in model systems and food products. J. Food Sci. *40*, 985–988.

Navankasattusas, S., and Lund, D. B. 1982. Thermal destruction of vitamin B_6 vitamers in buffer solution and cauliflower puree. J. Food Sci. *47*, 1512–1518.

Orr, M. 1969. Pantothenic acid, vitamin B_6 and vitamin B_{12} in foods. Home Econ. Res. Rept. *36*. Agric. Res. Serv, USDA, Washington, DC.

Osner, R. C., and Johnson, R. M. 1968. Nutritional changes in protein during heat processing. J. Food Technol. *3*, 81–86.

Pflug, I. J., and Schmidt, C. F. 1968. Thermal destruction of microorganisms. *In* Disinfection, Sterilization, and Preservation. C. A. Lawrence and S. S. Block (Editors). Lea & Febiger, Philadelphia.

Ponting, J. D., Sanshuck, D. W., and Brekke, J. E. 1960. Color measurement and deterioration in grape and berry juices and concentrates. J. Food Sci. *25*, 471–478.

Raab, C. A., Luh, B. S., and Schweigert, B. S. 1973. Effects of heat processing on the retention of vitamin B_6 in lima beans. J. Food Sci. *38*, 544–545.

Ralls, J. W., Maagdenberg, H. J., Yacoub, N. L. and Mercer, W. A. 1972. Reduced waste generation by alternate vegetable blanching system. Proc. 3rd Nat. Symp. Food Proc. Wastes, New Orleans.

Ralls, J. W., *et al.* 1973. In-plant, continuous hot-gas blanching of spinach. J. Food Sci. *38*, 192–194.

Ramakrishnan, T. V., and Francis, F. J. 1973. Color degradation in paprika. J. Food Sci. *38*, 25–28.

Read, R. B., Jr., and Bradshaw, J. G. 1966. Staphylococcal enterotoxin by thermal inactivation in milk. J. Dairy Sci. *49*, 202–203.

Rolls, B. A., and Porter, J. W. G. 1973. Some effects of processing and storage on the nutritive value of milk and milk products. Proc. Nutr. Soc. *32*, 9–15.

Sabry, Z. I. 1968. The nutritional consequences of developments in food processing. Can. J. Public Health *59*, 471–474.

Saguy, I., and Karel, M. 1979. Optimal retort temperature profile in optimizing thiamin retention in conduction-type heating of canned foods. J. Food Sci. *44*, 1485–1490.

Saguy, I., Kopelman, I. J., and Mizraki, S. 1978. Simulation of ascorbic acid stability during heat processing and concentration of grapefruit juice. J. Food Proc. Eng. *2*, 213–225.

Schroeder, H. A. 1971. Losses of vitamins and trace minerals resulting from processing and preservation of foods. Am. J. Clin. Nutr. *24*, 562–573.

Schwerdtfeger, E. 1971. Changes in the content of nutritive components during preparation and processing of vegetables. 3. Protein and amino acids. Qual. Plant. Mater. Veg. *21*, 97–110. From Nutr. Abstr. *42*, 3, 5190.

Shapton, D. A., Lovelock, D. W., and Laurita-Longo, R. 1971. The evaluation of sterilization and pasteurization processes from measurements in degrees Celsius (°C). J. Appl. Bacteriol. *34*, 491–500.

Singh, R. P., Heldman, D. R., and Kirk, J. R. 1974. Kinetic analysis and light-induced vitamin loss in liquid foods. Presented at the 34th Ann. Meeting Inst. Food Technol., New Orleans.

Skjöldebrand, C., Anas, A., Ö, R., and Sjödin, P. 1983, Prediction of thiamin content in convective heated meat products. J. Food Technol. *18*, 61–73.

Stefanovich, A. F., and Karel, M. 1982. Kinetics of β-carotene degradation at temperatures typical of air drying of foods. J. Food Proc. Preser. *6*, 227–242.

Stumbo, C. R. 1973. Thermobacteriology in Food Processing. 2nd Edition. Academic Press, New York.

Taira, H., Taira, H., and Sukural, Y. 1966. Studies on amino acid contents of processed soybeans. 8. Effect of heating on total lysine and available lysine in defatted soybean flour. Jpn. J. Nutr. Food *18*, 359.

Tanchev, S. S., and Joncheva, N. 1973. Kinetics of the thermal degradation of cyanidin-3-rutinoside and peonidin-3-rutinoside. Z. Lebensm. Unters. Forsch. *153*, 37–41.

Tannenbaum, S. R. (Editor) 1979. Nutritional and Safety Aspects of Food Processing. Marcel Dekker, New York.

Teixeira, A. A., Dixon, J. R., Zahradnik, J. W., and Zinsmeister, G. E. 1969A. Comptuer determination of spore survival distributions in thermally-processed conduction-heated foods. Food Technol. *23*, 352–354.

Teixeira, A. A., Dixon, J. R., Zahradnik, J. W., and Zinsmeister, G. E. 1969B. Computer optimization of nutrient retention in the thermal processing of conduction-heating foods. Food Technol. *23*, 845–850.

Teixeira, A. A., Zinsmeister, G. E., and Zahradnik, J. W. 1975. Computer simulation of variable retort control and container geometry as a possible means of improving thiamine retention in thermal processed foods. J. Food Sci. *40*, 656–659.

Thompson, S. Y. 1969. Nutritional aspects of UHT products. *In* Ultra-high Temperature Processing of Dairy Products. Soc. of Dairy Technol., London.

Thompson, D. R. 1982. The challenge in predicting nutrient changes during food processing. Food Technol. *36*(2), 97–108, 115.

Timbers, G. E. 1971. Some aspects of quality degradation during the processing and storage of canned foods. Ph.D. Thesis. Rutgers University, New Brunswick, NJ.

Van Buren, J. P., *et al.* 1960. Influence of blanching conditions on sloughing splitting, and firmness of canned snap beans. Food Technol. *14*(5), 233–236.

Villota, R., and Hawkes, J. G. 1983. Effect of processing on kinetics of nutrients and organoleptic changes in foods. Am. Soc. Agric. Eng. Paper. St. Joseph, MI.

von Elbe, J. H., Maing, I. Y., and Amundson, C. H. 1974. Color stability of betanin. J. Food Sci. *39*, 334–337.

Watt, B. K., and Merrill, A. L., 1963. Composition of foods. *In* Agriculture Handbook 8. USDA, Washington, DC.

Watt, B. K., and Murphy, E. W. 1970. Tables of food composition—Scope and needed research. Food Technol. *24*, 674–684.

Wilkinson, S. A., Earle, M. D., and Cleland, A. C. 1981. Kinetics of vitamin A degradation in beef liver puree on heat processing. J. Food Sci. *46*, 32–33, 40.

Williams, M. P., and Nelson, P. E. 1974. Kinetics of the thermal degradation of methyl methionine sulfonium ions in citrate buffers and in sweet corn and tomato serum. J. Food Sci. *39*, 457–460.

Woodham, A. A. 1973. The effect of processing on the nutritive value of vegetable-protein concentrates. Proc. Nutr. Soc. *32*, 23–29.

Zadow, J. G. 1984. The effect of new technology on the nutritional value of dairy products. Aust. J. Dairy Technol.

Effects of
Baking on Nutrients

Gur S. Ranhotra
M. Ann Bock

Various heat-utilizing techniques are employed in the commercial processing of foods. Of these, baking is the major one. Destruction of one or more nutrients often occurs during the baking process. This adverse effect on nutrients is more intense in the crust portions since the interior (crumb) of most baked foods rarely approaches the oven temperature. Temperature aside, other factors that influence nutrient stability include time, pH, moisture (water activity), light, oxygen, metals, oxidants, enzymes, and possibly certain additives.

Nutrient losses, or the possible formation of antinutritional substances, are not the only consequence of baking. Baking may also improve the nutritional profile of food products, although this aspect of baking is often not considered. Improvement results from inactivation/ destruction of undesirable microorganisms, certain antinutrients, for example, amylase and protease inhibitors, and breakup of complexes that otherwise render some nutrients poorly absorbable. In some cases, content of some of the nutrients, B vitamins in particular, may actually increase, for example, during fermentation because of synthesis by yeast cells. These various effects on nutrients are briefly discussed here under group headings of (1) protein and amino acids, (2) vitamins, (3) minerals, and (4) fats and carbohydrates.

PROTEIN AND AMINO ACIDS

While the heat of baking denatures protein and this enhances protein digestibility, in the presence of reducing sugars, for example, maltose, fructose, and lactose, the quality of protein may be adversely affected by nonenzymatic (chemical type) browning—the Maillard reaction. Maillard reaction primarily affects the basic amino acids of which lysine is particularly significant.

Maillard reactions are complex and, as yet, incompletely understood. The initial step involves a reaction between the carbonyl group of the reducing sugar and the free amino group of an amino acid. The Amadori rearrangement converts this reaction product to deoxyketosyl compound, and the browning reaction then proceeds along complex pathways (Dworschak and Carpenter 1980). These reactions are responsible, in part, for the odors and flavors of freshly baked products.

A variety of factors influence the Maillard reaction, such as the amount and type (pentoses react more intensely than hexoses) of reducing sugar present, the time and temperature of baking, and the moisture and pH of the foodstuffs. Milk solids or milk replacers (whey–soy blends) added to bread intensify the Maillard reaction (from the high concentration of lactose), as does the excessive addition of sweeteners. A rise in pH enhances the Maillard reaction, whereas reduction of pH, as results from increased dough fermentation, lessens this reaction.

Maillard reaction products appear to have no nutritional value for the mammalian system (Anonymous 1978). In fact, they may be of toxicological concern, although a few studies have also shown them to possess hypocholesterolemic properties (O'Brien and Reiser 1982).

Lysine, the most limiting amino acid in grain products, is not the only amino acid destroyed during the Maillard reaction; almost all amino acids are adversely affected. In one study (Ranhotra et al. 1971) where breads were made with flour increasingly replaced with wheat protein concentrate (a product prepared by the grinding and sifting of wheat bran and shorts), significant losses in the contents of all essential amino acids except tryptophan occurred (Table 13.1); lysine loss, in particular, increased as the level of replacement, and hence the lysine content, increased.

Assays (chemical/biological/microbiological) readily detect amino acid losses during Maillard reaction, but they are time-consuming methods, especially the bioassays. Jokinen and Reineccius (1976) proposed mathematical models to predict lysine losses during thermal processing of soy protein. However, practical significance of this approach remains to be tested.

While lysine losses invariably occur during breadmaking, bread products (and other baked foods) may yet show improved protein quality if ingredients are included that increase the lysine content of the bread mix substantially. This is often observed in products made with whole grain flours as compared to those made with refined flours. Results in Table 13.2 exemplify this; in these studies, Iranian flat breads were prepared with wheat flour of increasing extraction and thus increasing lysine content (Faridi et al. 1982).

VITAMINS

In addition to amino acids, the effect of baking on vitamins has also been widely investigated. Vitamins are quite heat-labile nutrients, with thiamin and vitamin C being the most susceptible to baking losses.

Table 13.1. Losses of Essential Amino Acids in Breadmaking

Amino acid	Flour, 100%; WPC[a], 0%		Flour, 85%; WPC, 15%		Flour, 70%; WPC, 30%		Flour, 55%; WPC, 45%	
	Amino acid in bread mix[b] (mg/100 g)	Loss in breadmaking (%)	Amino acid in bread mix (mg/100 g)	Loss in breadmaking (%)	Amino acid in bread mix (mg/100 g)	Loss in breadmaking (%)	Amino acid in bread mix (mg/100 g)	Loss in breadmaking (%)
Lysine	0.272	2.6	0.343	11.7	0.414	11.9	0.458	18.8
Histidine	0.276	4.0	0.297	3.1	0.334	7.2	0.348	6.7
Arginine	0.474	0.2	0.560	3.6	0.637	4.6	0.695	8.7
Threonine	0.376	9.1	0.390	5.4	0.426	13.0	0.458	11.4
Cystine	0.216	6.5	0.191	8.4	0.175	5.8	0.172	—
Valine	0.649	1.6	0.673	5.0	0.706	4.6	0.741	6.8
Methionine	0.206	—	0.217	7.0	0.217	5.1	0.225	11.6
Isoleucine	0.536	4.0	0.551	3.9	0.574	0.9	0.589	7.0
Leucine	1.043	6.9	1.049	4.3	1.079	4.8	1.129	5.9
Tyrosine	0.336	4.5	0.341	7.4	0.342	2.7	0.349	2.3
Phenylalanine	0.679	6.4	0.692	2.7	0.697	4.8	0.701	7.5
Tryptophan	0.147	2.0	0.146	—	0.151	—	0.174	—

Source: Ranhotra *et al.* (1971).
[a] WPC, wheat protein concentrate.
[b] Moisture-free basis.

Table 13.2.   Protein Efficiency Ratio (PER) of Iranian Flat Breads

Product name	Extraction rate of flour used (%)	Lysine in bread (g/100 g protein)	PER value[a]
Barbari	78	2.0	1.13 ± 0.19
Lavash	82	2.2	1.14 ± 0.09
Taftoon	84	2.2	1.29 ± 0.12
Sangak	87	2.6	1.29 ± 0.09
Village	97	2.7	1.39 ± 0.14

Source: Faridi *et al.* (1982).
[a] Corrected to PER value for casein diet of 2.50 ± 0.09.

Table 13.3.   Vitamin Losses (%) in Fortified Graham Crackers

Vitamin	Loss	
	Average	Maximum
A	18.0	24.8
E	27.2	50.2
C	59.8	61.6
Thiamin	20.3	25.8
B_{12}	10.3	23.6
Folic Acid	7.2	15.3

Source: Bednarcyk (1978).

Vitamin C is often added to bread systems for functional reasons. However, this addition confers no nutritional value on the product since the vitamin rarely survives the baking temperatures. Losses are quite substantial even when the exposure to baking temperatures is only brief, as in the making of graham crackers (Table 13.3). Prolonged warming of foods at low temperatures seems to be equally detrimental. Hallberg *et al.* (1982) reported vitamin C losses of 76% and 87% in two hamburger-based meals which were warmed for 4 hours at 75°C (Table 13.4).

Thiamin is relatively stable at acidic pH. During the fermentation process in breadmaking, the environment is mildly acidic (pH 4.5 to 5.5) and, thus, thiamin losses are rather small. Thiamin losses during the baking of bread normally do not exceed 25%. Maleki and Daghir (1967) examined the loss of thiamin (also riboflavin and niacin) in enriched white Arabic bread (pita-type bread) and reported thiamin losses in the range of 7–24% (Table 13.5).

When pH of the baked product rises above 6, nearly all of the thiamin is destroyed. Such conditions exist in a variety of chemically leavened

Table 13.4. Effect of Prolonged Warming of Meals on Vitamin C Content

Meal[a]	Content (mg)	Loss (%)
A	112 ± 4	76
B	48 ± 3	87

Source: Hallberg *et al.* (1982).
[a] Meals contained hamburger, potatoes, and onion sauce; meal A also contained brussels sprouts. Warming was done at 75°C for 4 hr.

Table 13.5. Effect of Baking on Losses of Niacin, Riboflavin, and Thiamin in Enriched White Arabic Bread

Vitamin	Level of enrichment (mg/100 g flour)	Vitamin content (mg/100 g)	Loss (%)
Niacin	0.00	3.07	2
	1.00	4.19	0
	4.00	7.03	1
	6.00	8.56	0
Riboflavin	0.00	0.05	19
	0.10	0.14	15
	0.30	0.29	13
	0.60	0.65	9
Thiamin	0.00	0.16	24
	0.20	0.41	18
	0.50	0.88	8
	1.00	1.34	7

Source: Maleki and Daghir (1967).

baked goods, including cookies and crackers. In a recent study on high-protein cookies (Ranhotra *et al.* 1980), calculations based on ingredient contributions revealed thiamin losses in these products to exceed 90%. In contrast, losses of riboflavin and niacin were only modest. Products baked at lower temperatures may show lower thiamin losses. For example, Bednarcyk (1978) reported average thiamin loss of no more than 20.3% in graham crackers made with fortified flour (Table 13.3). It must be emphasized that thiamin loss, as well as the loss of any other vitamin, in baked products differs from product to product and no universal loss factor can be used. However, some vitamins, such as vitamin C, thiamin, pantothenic acid, and folic acid, are, no doubt, less stable than others.

Keagy and Stokstad (1973) studied folic acid losses during bread-making and reported nearly doubling of the content during fermentation, but about half this amount was destroyed during breadmaking. In graham crackers, Bednarcyk (1978) reported an average folic acid loss of 7.2% (Table 13.3).

In baked products, as studies with cookies revealed (Ranhotra *et al.* 1980), riboflavin and niacin appear to be relatively stable, with niacin being more so than riboflavin (Table 13.5). A good portion of the niacin in grain products, especially those made with less refined flours, is present as bound niacin. This form of niacin is mostly unavailable to man and animals. Carter and Carpenter (1982) demonstrated that steam cooking does not free isolated bound niacin. The effect of baking on bound niacin may be somewhat different, however, since it has been shown by Hepburn (1971) that the proportion of the free niacin (available niacin) was higher in bread, cakes, and crackers than in the flours from which they were made. Alkali treatment of bound niacin, as occurs in the processing of tortillas, improves niacin absorption probably through hydrolysis of bound niacin at the baking stage of tortilla production.

In the United States, most of the white pan bread and a number of variety breads are made with enriched flour (thiamin, riboflavin, niacin, iron, and possibly calcium added). No significant losses of these vitamins occur in bread products. In addition, baking probably exerts minimal adverse effect on fat-soluble vitamins, although at extreme conditions of baking, fat breakdown products are known to cause oxidation of tocopherols. Bednarcyk (1978) reported some loss of vitamin A in graham crackers (Table 13.3), but in general, information on fat-soluble vitamins in baked products is quite limited.

MINERALS

Unless some discarding of the baking medium occurs, which is an unlikely situation with most baked products, baking is not likely to affect the content of minerals in foods. On the other hand, heat treatment may profoundly affect the absorption/utilization of certain minerals, primarily through cleavage of complexes, which otherwise render these minerals less absorbable even in the face of physiological needs. Phytate, fiber, proteins, and certain minerals are particularly suspect as components of these complexes.

Phytate can undergo hydrolysis during the breadmaking process (Ranhotra *et al.* 1974). This most likely improves the absorption of both the phosphorus as resultant inorganic phosphorus (Table 13.6) and the mineral(s) phytate is suspected to complex. This was observed in a study on zinc present in soy-fortified breads (Ranhotra *et al.* 1978). Increasing yeast and fermentation periods appears to increase (Harland and Harland 1980) phytate hydrolysis during breadmaking (Table 13.7);

Table 13.6.   Phytate Hydrolysis during Breadmaking[a]

Protein supplement	Phytate		Inorganic phosphorus	
	In bread mix (mg/loaf)	Hydrolyzed (%)	In bread mix (mg/loaf)	Increase (mg/loaf)
Soy protein isolate	318	80	44	195
Soy concentrate	337	89	45	251
Full-fat soy flour	261	84	54	157
High-fat soy flour	290	78	46	172
Defatted soy flour	320	84	45	220

Source: Ranhotra *et al.* (1974).
[a] Breads were made using a mix of 90% wheat flour and 10% soy protein supplement.

Table 13.7.   Effect of Yeast on Phytate Hydrolysis during Breadmaking[a]

Bread type	Rising time (hr)	Yeast added		
		None	One package	Two packages
Rye	0	0.78	0.80	0.43
	2	0.77	0.41	0.28
	4	0.76	0.34	0.23
	8	0.76	0.37	0.21
White	0	0.03	0.04	0.03
	2	0.03	0.03	0.02
	4	0.03	0.02	0.02
	8	0.03	0.01	0.02
Whole wheat	0	0.64	0.64	0.60
	2	0.59	0.56	0.57
	4	0.59	0.48	0.47
	8	0.59	0.42	0.43

Source: Harland and Harland (1980).
[a] Amount of phytate in bread (%).

greater reduction in rye breads is postulated to be a function of more phytase in rye flour. Phytate hydrolysis may also be closely related to the pH of the medium (influenced, or not, by yeast activity), becoming intense as it approaches the pH optimum of phytase activity.

Where chemical leavening instead of yeast leavening is used in baked products, phytate hydrolysis may not be significant. Under this condition, phytate is likely to continue to adversely affect mineral absorption. Using rat as the test model, this was found to be the case (Table 13.8) for zinc in soy-fortified cookies (Ranhotra *et al.* 1979).

During the baking process, some fiber components, for example, hemicelluloses, may undergo transformation. In fact, some fiber components may be formed, for example, Maillard reaction products. How these transformations may affect mineral absorption is not known. Also,

Table 13.8.   Bioavailability of Zinc in Protein-fortified Cookies

	Added protein source				
	Egg albumin	Egg albumin	Soy flour	Soy concentrate	Soy isolate
Phytate[a] (mg)	0	1107	1107	1107	1107
Phytate hydrolyzed (%)	—	20	7	10	18
Zinc intake (μg)	3197 ± 162	2995 ± 296	3188 ± 182	3204 ± 258	3132 ± 296
Femur zinc (μg)	46 ± 3	34 ± 3	34 ± 3	33 ± 3	32 ± 4
Zinc absorbed (%)	89	85	83	83	81
Relative BV of zinc in bread[b]	100	76	77	77	73

Source: Ranhotra *et al.* (1979).

[a] Total amount in the formula contributed by wheat flour (100 g), soy protein source used, and added sodium phytate.

[b] Relative (diet in first column = 100%) biological value (BV) of zinc in cookies, as based on femur zinc content.

little is known of the effect of baking on protein–mineral and mineral–mineral complexes and how these might affect mineral absorption.

Some minerals, such as iron, may undergo oxidation (or reduction) during the baking process, and this might affect their absorbability or biological value (BV). However, in a study done by Ranhotra *et al.* (1973) where two iron compounds of widely different BVs were used to make soda crackers, differences in BV persisted (Table 13.9), as measured using the hemoglobin depletion–repletion technique in rats. Also, iron in crackers made without soda or with soda or iron added to the ground baked product showed the same BV.

Table 13.9.   Biological Value (BV) of Iron in Soda Crackers

	Iron source						
	Ferrous sulfate		Reduced iron				
				Crackers			
					Soda		Iron added after baking
					Not added	Added after baking	
	Bread	Crackers	Bread	Crackers			
Hemoglobin gain (mg/mg iron consumed)	206 ± 26	214 ± 28	99 ± 26	94 ± 15	90 ± 18	96 ± 9	86 ± 24
Relative BV of iron[a]	100	104	48	46	44	47	42

Source: Ranhotra *et al.* (1973).

[a] Relative (diet in first column = 100%) BV of iron in baked products.

FATS AND CARBOHYDRATES

The effect of baking on fats and carbohydrates is generally related to their hydrolysis. For example, baking that gelatinizes starch increases its digestibility. Participation of simple and hydrolyzed complex carbohydrates in the Maillard reaction, on the other hand, adversely affects the available carbohydrate content of baked products. At extremes of baking conditions, linoleic acid and possibly other fatty acids may be converted (due to lipoxygenase activity) to unstable hydroperoxides which may affect both the lipid and vitamin (oxidation of fat-soluble vitamins) nutriture of the product.

CONCLUSIONS

Baking, while it may cause destruction of some nutrients, especially the basic amino acids and water-soluble vitamins, may also improve the absorption/utilization of other nutrients through inactivation/destruction of antinutrients and undesirable microorganisms and complexes.

REFERENCES

Anonymous 1978. Nutritional implications of the Maillard reaction. Nutr. Rev. 36, 28–30.

Bednarcyk, N. E. 1978. Nutritional value of biscuits and crackers. 53rd Ann. Tech. Conf. Biscuit and Crackers Manuf. Assoc., San Francisco. Feb. 5–9.

Carter, E. G. A., and Carpenter, K. J. 1982. The bioavailability for humans of bound niacin from wheat bran. Am. J. Clin. Nutr. 36, 855–861.

Dworschak, E., and Carpenter, K. J. 1980. Nonenzyme browning and its effect on protein nutrition. CRC Crit. Rev. Food Sci. Nutr. 15, 1–33.

Faridi, H. A., Ranhotra, G. S., Finney, P. L., and Rubenthaler, G. L. 1982. Protein quality characteristics of Iranian flat breads. J. Food Sci. 47, 676–679.

Hallberg, L., Rossander, L., Persson, H., and Svahn, E. 1982. Deleterious effects of prolonged warming of meals on ascorbic acid content and iron absorption. Am. J. Clin. Nutr. 36, 846–850.

Harland, B. F., and Harland, J. 1980. Fermentative reduction of phytate in rye, white and wholewheat breads. Cereal Chem. 57, 226–229.

Hepburn, F. N. 1971. Nutrient composition of selected wheats and wheat products. VII. Total and free niacin. Cereal Chem. 48, 369–372.

Jokinen, J. E., and Reineccius, G. A. 1976. Losses in available lysine during thermal processing of soy protein model systems. J. Food Sci. 41, 816–819.

Keagy, P. M., and Stokstad, E. L. R. 1973. Folacin stability during flour storage and bread processing. 58th Ann. Meeting, AACC, St. Louis, Nov. 4–8.

Maleki, M. and Daghir, S. 1967. Effect of baking on retention of thiamine, riboflavin, and niacin in Arabic bread. Cereal Chem. 44, 483–487.

O'Brien, B. C. and Reiser, R. 1982. Cholesterolemic responses of rats to human-type diet ingredients. J. Nutr. 112, 1490–1497.

Ranhotra, G. S., Hepburn, F. N., and Bradley, W. B. 1971. Supplemental effect of wheat protein concentrate on the protein quality of white wheat flour. Cereal Chem. *48*, 699–706.

Ranhotra, G. S., Loewe, R. J., and Puyat, L. V. 1973. Availability of iron in enriched soda crackers. Cereal Chem. *50*, 745–749.

Ranhotra, G. S., Loewe, R. J., and Puyat, L. V. 1974. Phytic acid in soy and its hydrolysis during breadmaking. J. Food Sci. *39*, 1023–1025.

Ranhotra, G. S., Lee, C., and Gelroth, J. A. 1978. Bioavailability of zinc in soy-fortified wheat breads. Nutr. Rep. Int. *18*, 487–494.

Ranhotra, G. S., Lee, C., and Gelroth, J. A. 1979. Bioavailability of zinc in cookies fortified with soy and zinc. Cereal Chem. *56*, 552–554.

Ranhotra, G. S., Lee, C., and Gelroth, J. A. 1980. Nutritional characteristics of high-protein cookies. J. Agric. Food Chem. *28*, 507–509.

Effects of Extrusion Processing on Nutrients

Judson M. Harper

INTRODUCTION

The use of food extrusion as a commercial technology dates back to the mid-1930s. Since that time, the range of extrusion equipment has expanded considerably along with the types of products manufactured. Today, extrusion-processed foods consist of a variety of snack foods, ready-to-eat (RTE) breakfast cereals, textured vegetable proteins used as meat analogs or extenders, infant food formulations, beverage and soup bases, and precooked starches. Details of the development of extruded food products have been given by Harper (1981A,B). To manufacture this array of products, extruders must process a wide range of food ingredients. The most common ingredients are cereal flours or grits, used as a source of carbohydrate and the base of most products, defatted oilseed meals, which are high in protein and, to a much lesser degree, lipids, starches, and mono- and disaccharides.

EXTRUSION PROCESSING

Complete descriptions of the extrusion process have been given by Harper (1979) and Linko *et al.* (1981). In brief, an extruder consists of a shallow flighted screw which turns within a tightly fitting stationary barrel as shown in Fig. 14.1. The feed ingredients enter the initial flights of the screw through a feed hopper. Here, they are conveyed forward by the action of the flights into the constricted channels between the flights, which become completely filled with the food material being processed. In the process, the food is worked and heated by a combination of heat sources, including fluid friction dissipating the mechanical energy required to turn the screw, direct steam injection through the barrel wall into the product, and heat transfer from steam or water in jackets surrounding the extruder barrel. The temperature

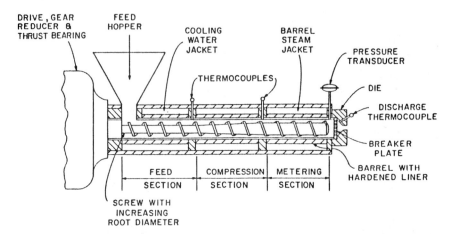

Fig. 14.1.   Cross section showing principal parts of a food extruder. Source: Harper (1978).

of the product can rise far above normal boiling temperature in the later turns of the screw, but flashing of moisture does not occur because of the elevated pressure which exists there.

During the passage of the food ingredients down the length of the extrusion screw, they are transformed from a raw granular state into a continuous mass having viscous properties, called a dough. This transformation, described as cooking, involves the disruption and melting of starch granules, the denaturation and reorientation of protein molecules, and a number of other reactions which can change the nutritional, textural, and organoleptic properties of the finished product. These transformations occur at relatively low water contents in the range of 15–35% on a wet basis.

At the discharge of the extruder, the high-temperature pressurized cooked dough mass is forced through a small restrictive opening called a die. The die maintains the elevated pressure within the extruder and shapes the manufactured product as it emerges from the machine. Pieces of varying length are cut with a rotating knife at the face of the die.

Puffing of pieces emerging from the die, to form a rigid open cellular structure, often occurs because of the expansion of the superheated moisture within the extruded product once the pressure is released. Immediate cooling occurs upon puffing, since the heat necessary to convert about 5% of the product's water into steam comes from the sensible heat content of the product. The cooling process occurs nearly instantaneously at the die face, bringing the product temperature to approximately 100°C.

In addition to the single-screw extruder shown, there are now twin-screw extruders which are becoming increasingly popular. The two types of machines look quite similar but the twin-screw extruder has intermeshing screws which lie side by side. Their normal corotating action conveys and works the product in a manner that can increase the uniformity and controllability of the finished product, as compared to the single-screw extruder.

PROCESSING CONDITIONS

The processing environment controlled within the extruder can vary widely, depending upon the type of product being produced. For example, many expanded crisp snacks are extruded at low moisture conditions (i.e., less than 18%) and high temperatures (140°–190°C), with high elevated discharge pressures (60–80 bar). The total residence time for the cereal grit ingredients varies between 15 and 60 sec. Smith (1976) termed this type of process HTST (high temperature–short time). Much of the heat energy necessary to raise the product temperature in this short time comes from the conversion of the mechanical shaft energy, used to turn the screw, into heat, through fluid friction arising within the high shear environment that exists within the flow channels of the screw.

The severe thermal and mechanical shear environment within the extruder can cause both beneficial and detrimental effects on the nutritional value of the extruded food (Björck and Asp 1983). The short exposure of the food ingredients to temperatures above 150°C in the absence of oxygen at relatively low moistures prevents extensive destruction of vitamins while promoting desirable cooking reactions, such as the disorganization of starch granules and denaturation of protein, thus aiding in their digestibility. The inactivation of enzymes and antinutritional agents, such as trypsin inhibitors in soy, can be achieved with the short residence times at the high temperatures within the extruder because of the kinetics of these reactions.

At the other extreme of the extrusion processing spectrum is the forming extruder, which is used for shaping macaroni or making pellets as part of an RTE process. These extruders can take a moistened cereal flour and work and force it through a die to give the precise macaroni shape. Forming extruders are also used to form cooled precooked cereal doughs into precise shapes under conditions where high-temperature puffing is not desired. In forming extruders, temperatures are kept below 60°C and residence times may exceed 120 sec. With these types of processing conditions, relatively little change in the food's nutritional quality occurs.

This description of extrusion shows it to be a process that can be applied over a wide range of conditions. Unfortunately, this essential point has not been grasped by all researchers in the field, so that much of the literature on the effects of extrusion on product characteristics or the nutritional value of foods does not contain sufficient information about the exact extrusion conditions used to make specific comparisons between the various pieces of work possible. Instead, the resulting body of literature allows only relatively vague generalization and in some cases contains unexplainable differences in findings.

Given the above background on the extrusion process, the remainder of the chapter focuses on its impact on the nutritional quality of extruded foods. Since the extruder is capable of accomplishing HTST processing of low-moisture food systems under conditions of flow-induced shear, a number of unique observations have been made by researchers in the field.

STARCH DIGESTIBILITY

HTST extrusion processes are known to alter the organized physical structure of raw starch granules, making them less crystalline, more water soluble, and susceptible to hydrolysis by saccharifing enzymes. This process has been termed cooking or gelatinization. Because of low moisture conditions found in the extruder, traditional gelatinization involving swelling and hydration of the starch granule and the loss of birefringence in polarized light does not occur. Rather, the combination of high-temperature hydration in a shear environment within the extruder leads to the disruption and melting of the starch granule and, to some extent, the breaking of the starch biopolymeric chain. These extrusion-induced transformations also lead to a loss in birefringence.

The extent of physical changes in starch have been related to changes in the viscosity of hydrated samples, iodine binding, X-ray defraction and water solubility. New techniques to measure the extent to which the extrusion process affects the starchy components of cereals have been proposed. For example, Paton and Spratt (1981) used the area between the heating and cooling curves produced on the Ottawa Starch Viscometer as a measure of degree of cook. Chiang and Johnson (1977A) and Shetty *et al.* (1974) related the susceptibility of extruded starch to glucoamylose as a measure of starch gelatinized by extrusion. However, the specific correlation between the values measured by these tests and starch digestibility has not been made.

The effects of extrusion on cereals and pure starches containing varying amounts of amylose and amylopectin were studied by Mercier and Feillet (1975). Data on corn starch extruded on a Creusot-Loire BC45 twin-screw extruder at 22% initial moisture are shown in Fig. 14.2. As extrusion temperature increased, the puffing or expansion also increased to a maximum at about $170°C$ discharge temperature. Water-soluble carbohydrate, which is a high-molecular-weight polysaccharide

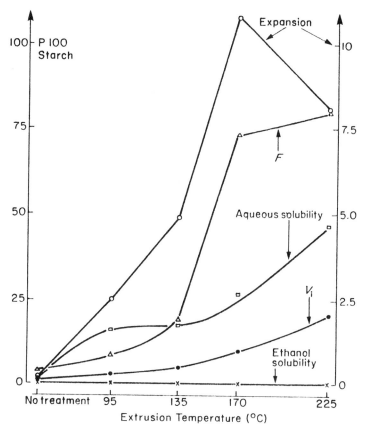

Fig. 14.2. Effect of temperature on corn starch extruded at 22% moisture. Source: Mercier and Feillet (1975).

similar to swollen starch, rather than an oligosaccharide such as maltodextrin, also increased with increasing temperature. The initial rate of α-amylolysis (V_i) increased along with the fraction (F) of starch easily degradable by amylases as extrusion temperature increased. These latter factors also showed increases with highly expanded samples indicating the importance of product form on digestibility.

The effects of moisture content, temperature, screw speed, and die size on the gelatinization of wheat flour were studied by Chiang and Johnson (1977B). Increasing moistures of feed ingredients from 18 to 27% along with elevated extrusion discharge temperatures increased the extent of starch disorganization following extrusion as measured by its susceptibility to hydrolysis by glucoamylose. Higher extrusion temperatures were required when lower moisture samples were extruded to achieve the same amount of enzyme susceptibility in the final sample. Increased screw speeds cause higher shear within the screw channel, which should enhance disruption of the native starch granule. The opposite was found in the study indicating that the reduced residence time within the extruder, also caused by the increased screw speed, can overcome the effect of the higher shear environment. Smaller die sizes did cause increased susceptibility of the extruded starch to glucoamylose hydrolysis, because of the increased shear exposure it causes within the extruder.

Björck et al. (1984) extruded wheat flour and starch and measured hydrolysis in vitro with salivary α-amylase and in vivo as plasma levels of glucose and insulin in rats. They concluded extrusion rendered the starch more susceptible to α-amylase than boiling. Severe extrusion conditions increased the plasma levels of glucose and insulin response more quickly than boiled samples, indicating extrusion can affect both the glycaemic and cariogenic properties of extruded starch.

Both Chiang and Johnson (1977B) and Mercier (1977) reported that some hydrolysis of starches occurs during the extrusion process. The presence of mono- and oligosaccharides, such as glucose, fructose, melibiose, maltose, and maltotriose, suggested that polysaccharides were degraded during extrusion to give a more digestible product. Similarly, Davidson et al. (1984) reported the size reduction of the amylopectin fraction of wheat starch, which they attributed to mechanical rupture.

The effects of extrusion on the amylose and amylopectin fractions of wheat (Colonna et al. 1984) and manioc (Colonna and Mercier 1983) were determined. Their results showed random macromolecular chain splitting of both molecules, as indicated by intrinsic viscosity, gel-permeation chromatography, and average molecular weight determinations. The effect of these changes on digestibility was not specifically measured, but it is expected that both starch fractions would become more digestible.

The formation of amylose–lipid complexes during extrusion has been demonstrated by Mercier et al. (1980). Manioc starch was extruded in a twin-screw extruder with varying amounts and types of fatty acids (C_2 through C_{18}), monoglycerides, an emulsifier (calcium stearyl lactylate), and purified fats. Initial moisture contents of ingredients were 22%, and extrusion temperatures were varied between 200° and 225°C. Samples extruded with 2% of C_{12} or longer fatty acids, monoglycerides, and emulsifiers, formed a complex between the amylose fraction of the starch and these materials. The resulting water solubility of the complexed starch decreased with the increased chain length of the fatty material to which it was complexed. The complexed amylose fraction is resistant to α-amylolysis, which could lower in vitro digestibility of starch samples high in amylose; similar impacts on the digestibility of normal or waxy starches which have higher amylopectin contents would not be expected (Mercier 1980).

A unique effect of twin-screw extrusion on potato starch was observed by Mercier (1977). Unlike extruded cereal starch, the 80% aqueous ethanol-soluble fraction of extruded potato starch increased indicating oligosaccharides of molecular weight less than 2000 were greatly increased at elevated extrusion temperatures. It was suggested that this technology would have particular application potential to infant foods where the child may be deficient in debranching enzymes.

BLENDED FOODS

The extrusion cooker has been applied to the production of pre-cooked blended foods which are specifically designed to meet the nutritional needs of pregnant and lactating mothers and the weaning-aged child 6 months of age or older. Such foods often are blends of precooked cereal, a vegetable protein source, such as soy, and fat, supplemented with a vitamin and mineral mixture. Their production dates back to 1966, when the USDA developed Title II foods (Senti 1974) described as WSB (wheat–soy blend), ICSM (instant corn–soy-milk), and so forth, for distribution internationally in addition to milk powder. In these initial products, the extruder was used to precook the cereal flour portion which was blended with the defatted soy flour, the principal remaining ingredient, which was already precooked.

Recent work in the area of blended foods has focused on their production in developing countries, using locally grown ingredients (Jansen and Harper 1980A,B). Special emphasis has been placed on the use of low-cost extruder cookers (LEC) such as the Brady® or Insta-Pro® extruders, which are capable of heating blends of ground cereal grains and whole dehulled soybeans to temperatures in excess of 150°C. These machines process the ingredients under low moisture conditions (less than 18% moisture), so that normal moisture loss during the cooling process will bring the finished product down to a safe storage moisture. A process flow chart is shown in Fig. 14.3 that adequately describes the simplicity of the process and accounts for its ready acceptance as an appropriate food process in the developing country setting.

Protein Quality

Of significant importance to the production of blended foods, consisting of mixtures of cereal grains and vegetable protein sources, is the requirement that the finished product contain sufficient food energy and generous amounts of protein of high quality to support the needs of the pregnant or lactating mother and child (Jansen 1980). A com-

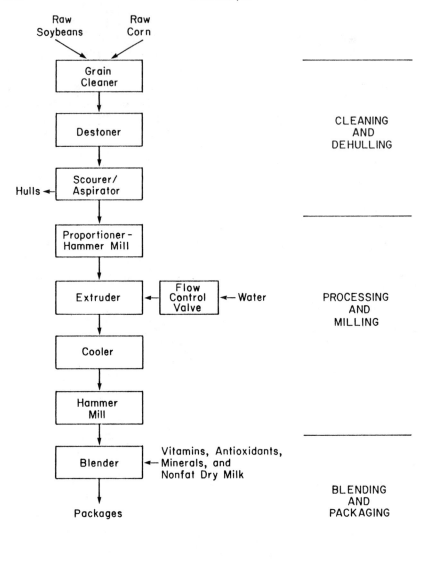

Fig. 14.3. Equipment used in low-cost extrusion cooking (LEC) of nutritious food blends. Source: Jansen and Harper (1980B).

monly used measure of protein quality has been the PER (protein efficiency ratio), with casein being the standard at 2.5.

Numerous studies have shown that an extrusion-cooked mixture of about 70 parts grain and 30 parts whole soy will lead to a product having a PER approximately equal to that of casein. Work by Jansen *et al.*

(1978) and Jansen (1976) showed that extrusion cooking a blend of soy and corn at 172°C produced products having PERs at least as high as when the two ingredients were extruded separately (Table 14.1). It was concluded that no major loss in the availability of the essential amino acid lysine occurred when the soybean protein, rich in lysine, was heated in the extruder with lysine-deficient corn, which can supply small amounts of reducing sugars necessary for Maillard browning reactions, either through a partial hydrolysis of the starch or as a minor constituent in the raw materials.

Bressani (1976) and Bressani *et al.* (1978) reported that improved PERs were measured in extruded products made using LECs when the raw corn and soy ingredients were ground to a particle size essentially less than 45 mesh and water was added to achieve 21.4% moisture content in the mixture prior to extrusion. In an HTST process, the extent of heat penetration into the particles, necessary for their cooking and melting, is inversely proportional to their diameter squared. Molina *et al.* (1978) found that trypsin inhibitor inactivation was enhanced under conditions of lowest feed rate and greatest restriction of the die opening of the LEC tested. Both of these conditions would lead to increased product temperature, enhancing the thermal inactivation of trypsin and other inhibitors with correspondingly improved protein quality.

An infant formula produced from a combination of oats–soy, 1:1.25 extruded at 160°C, was described by Del Valle *et al.* (1981). The finished product required the addition of 0.2% DL-methionine to achieve a PER of 2.4, compared to casein at 2.5, because the relatively low level of cereal in the formulation supplied insufficient methionine to compensate for the deficiency of the soy. These extruded products also had net protein utilization (NPU) values of around 52, compared to 59 for casein. Molina *et al.* (1977) also showed that extruded snacks made from mistures of corn or cassava in combination with black-eyed peas required 0.3% addition of DL-methionine to reach optimum PER. Similar results were supported by Joao *et al.* (1980) for combinations of cowpea–corn and cowpea–cassava.

In addition to the use of soy as the high-protein source for the production of blended foods, other products have been used. Aguilera and Kosikowski (1978) used a partially demineralized, delactosed whey product to supplement corn meal and soy flour which were roll-cooked or extruded at 90°C to make a precooked food blend. Using a variety of formulations, they concluded that the PER of all mixes was essentially equivalent to casein and that roll-cooking was less deleterious than extrusion.

Potato protein powder enrichment of extrusion-cooked corn grits was evaluated by Meuser *et al.* (1980). They found the potato protein

Table 14.1. Nutritional Evaluation of Corn–Soy Blends

Sample	Weight gain (g)	PER[b]	Corrected PER[c]	PRE[d]
Whole corn–dehulled soy (70/30)				
Extruded together (172°C)	146.3 ± 5.2[a]	3.20 ± 0.07	2.53 ± 0.06	66.7 ± 0.8
Extruded separately (172°/139°C)	113.6 ± 4.4	2.93 ± 0.06	2.31 ± 0.05	63.4 ± 1.2
Degermed corn–dehulled soy (70/30)				
Extruded together (172°C)	121.0 ± 6.4	3.13 ± 0.06	2.47 ± 0.05	65.7 ± 1.2
Extruded separately (172°/139°C)	117.0 ± 5.0	2.98 ± 0.05	2.35 ± 0.04	63.4 ± 0.7
Extruded together (172°C) – Vitamins and minerals added before extrusion	126.9 ± 7.2	3.09 ± 0.07	2.44 ± 0.06	64.6 ± 1.1
ANRC Casein	119.0 ± 4.8	3.16 ± 0.09	2.50	71.7 ± 1.7

Source: Jansen et al. (1978).

[a] Mean ± standard error.

[b] Protein efficiency ratio PER = $\dfrac{\text{Weight gain (g)}}{\text{Protein consumed (g)}}$.

[c] Corrected relative to an assigned value for ANRC casein of 2.50.

[d] Protein retention efficiency (PRE) = $\dfrac{16\,[\text{weight gain (g)} + \text{weight loss protein-free group (g)}]}{\text{protein consumed (g)}}$, 2-week growth data used.

powder to contain higher levels of essential amino acids, so less was required to correct the deficiencies in the corn used in the blend. Protein digestibility and NPU for potato- and soy-enriched extruded products were essentially identical.

The extrusion of food blends where rice was the cereal constituent has been conducted by Cilindro (1980). A product consisted of rice and dry milk powder extruded together. It was found that extrusion slightly reduced the PER, while the digestibility and NPU remained constant. Since the milk was already a dry powder, there appeared to be no benefit in its being part of the mixture prior to extrusion.

Protein Utilization in Humans

The ultimate value in extruded, nutritious blended foods requires that they be highly digestible and contain protein which can be utilized by human populations, especially children. The evaluation of many samples has depended heavily on animal studies. Actual clinical evaluations have been relatively few, but point to the potential for the extrusion production of nutritious foods from vegetable sources.

Title II blended food samples containing extrusion-processed cornmeal along with soy and 5% nonfat dry milk have been clinically evaluated. In comparing the results for samples containing partially gelatinized cornmeal (Graham et al. 1971) with another containing fully gelatinized cornmeal (Graham et al. 1973), it appears that both the nitrogen absorbed and retained as a percentage of the casein control was higher for the sample containing fully gelatinized cornmeal, indicating a benefit for increased extrusion processing of the cereal component of these products.

In another evaluation of protein utilization, corn–soy blends (CSB) (70:30) containing 17 to 18.6% protein were precooked in a Brady extruder and evaluated by Graham and MacLean (1979) using previously malnourished infants aged 5–20 months. The results are summarized in Table 14.2. In one evaluation, apparent nitrogen absorption and retention of extruded products were compared with diets containing casein. The nitrogen absorption for infants fed the CSB diet was significantly lower than those fed the casein diet; however, the percentage of nitrogen intake retained was not significantly lower. These findings are similar to feeding trial results performed on comparable Title II foods.

Protein utilization studies were made by Del Valle et al. (1981) on an extruded oats–soy blend (OSB), with similar results. In a nitrogen balance determination with six children between the ages of 3 and 28 months, their oats–soy formula showed that 31% of the nitrogen absorbed was retained and digestibility was 71%. These values were reported to be essentially equivalent to a commercial cow's milk formula.

Table 14.2.   Nitrogen Utilization of Infants Fed CSB Compared with Casein[a]

	Casein	CSB (70/30) Degermed corn/dehulled soy
N intake, mg/day	1991 ± 356	1982 ± 376
N absorption, % of intake	84.1 ± 4.0	76.6 ± 9.0
N retention, % of intake	34.5 ± 7.3	28.9 ± 12.5
Weight gain, g/kg/day	4.9 ± 2.9	5.0 ± 2.0

Source: Graham and McLean (1979).
[a] Study carried out with nine infants, ages 5–20 months. Protein fed at 6.4% of calories. Mean ± S.D.

Fatty Acids

It is known that hydrogenation of fats results in some isomerization of the naturally occurring cis form of linoleic to the trans form of linoleic and oleic acids to the extent of 8% of the double bonds. Maga (1978) evaluated the impact of extrusion on the cis to trans isomerization of the unsaturated fats in blends of whole corn and whole soy (70:30). All extrusion was done at 155° or 171°C at approximately 15% moisture. A relatively small 1–1.5% conversion of double bonds from cis to trans occurred, with the higher values associated with the highest extrusion temperatures.

Inactivation of Gossypol

Cottonseed flour represents a vegetable protein source which has been used in the production of blended foods such as Incaparina® in Guatemala. For glanded cottonseed to be suitable for this purpose, it is essential that proper heat treatment be applied to inactivate the pigment gossypol occurring within the cottonseed. Thermal inactivation involves the binding of gossypol to the free amino group of lysine. For heat-treated cottonseed flours, the Protein Advisory Group (1975) of the United Nations recommends free gossypol levels of less than 0.06%. Jansen *et al.* (1978) reported LEC processing of the whole cottonseed kernel reduced gossypol only to 0.21%, and the products produced rat growth and PERs which were only fair.

The LEC processing of cottonseed–cereal blends performed by Jansen *et al.* (1978) is described in Table 14.3. These data show the extrusion process reduced the free gossypol significantly at the expense of the availability of lysine in the finished product. To correct this deficiency, samples supplemented with 0.5% L-lysine monohydrochloride resulted in a product with a corrected PER of 2.2, which showed the potential importance of lysine supplementation of products containing heat-treated glanded cottonseed.

Table 14.3. Nutritional Evaluation of Cereal–Cottonseed Blends

Sample	Total gossypol (%)	Free gossypol (%)	Weight gain (g)	PER	Corrected PER	PRE
Whole corn/glanded cottonseed 70/30 extruded together (170°C) +0.5% L-lysine monohydrochloride[b]	0.26	0.03	50.4 ± 3.8[a]	1.73 ± 0.09[a]	1.51 ± 0.08[a]	46.6 ± 2.4[a]
	0.26	0.03	94.9 ± 4.8	2.54 ± 0.07	2.21 ± 0.06	57.1 ± 1.1
ANRC casein	—	—	111.4 ± 4.2	2.88 ± 0.09	2.50	60.3 ± 1.7

Source: Jansen et al. (1978).
[a] Mean ± standard error. See Table 14.1 for definitions.
[b] Lysine monohydrochloride added after extrusion.

Calorie Density

The volume of food a young infant can consume limits food intake, suggesting that weaning foods should have a high calorie and nutrient density. The concentration of ingredients in a prepared gruel is a function of the consistency or viscosity of the product that can be fed, which, in turn, is related to the functionality of the product ingredients, particularly starch. Products having their starch gelatinized and intact will produce thick gruels at relatively low solids concentrations and, as a consequence, have low calorie density.

The effects of LEC processing on the calorie densities of blended foods were investigated by Jansen *et al.* (1981). An LEC was used to cook blends of corn–soy (70:30) at varying temperatures. These samples, along with Food for Peace Title II foods, were prepared at different total solids concentrations and the resulting viscosity of the gruel was measured. Some results, shown in Fig. 14.4, indicate that the LEC–CSB had a similar calorie density to Title II ICSM. The addition of 15% nonfat dry milk gave the LEC–CSM a further increase in calorie density. Title II CSM contains only partially gelatinized starch, thus requiring a higher concentration of solids to yield a gruel that has the same consistency as one made with more thoroughly cooked starch ingredients if no further cooking is applied.

The extrusion temperature of LEC–CSB samples also affected their calorie density when made up as gruels. Extrusion discharge temperatures

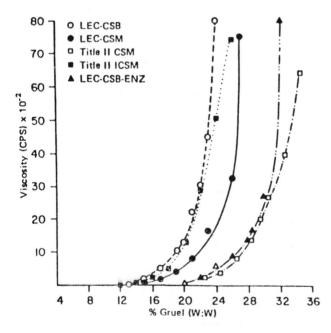

Fig. 14.4. Viscosity of different concentrations of gruels made from various blended foods. Source: Jansen *et al.* (1981).

of 171°C produced more starch damage in the products than extrusion at 149°C and their resulting calorie density was correspondingly about 10% higher. These data suggest that the dry extrusion processes, which subjects the product to a combination of high temperature and shear, disrupts the ordered structure of the starch granules and cleaves the starch chains to give a readily hydratable product whose degree of functionality is reduced by these severe conditions. The addition of a very small amount of an amylase to the LEC–CSB, as allowed by the Codex Alimentarius Commission (1976), had the effect of further increasing calorie density, since the partially hydrolyzed starch molecule is unable to produce viscous gels at low concentrations. Similar results occurred through the addition of sugar, oil, or dry milk.

DIETARY FIBER

There has been renewed interest in dietary fiber as a constituent in the human diet (Heaton 1979; Owen and Cotton 1982). It is known that fiber binds large amounts of water to increase stool volume and reduce transit time through the intestine. In addition, fiber binds essential minerals such as calcium, iron, and zinc, and specific lipids, while also reducing vitamin availability. High-fiber diets help prevent constipation and diverticulosis along with increased glucose tolerance. There is also evidence that high intakes of some fibers may lower plasma cholesterol and decrease the incidence of colon cancer.

Dietary fiber is a complex material consisting of hemicellulose, cellulose, lignin, pectin, and a number of gums and mucilages (Baker *et al.* 1979). A variety of tests are used to measure fiber, including the classical crude fiber determination, which grossly underestimates the quantity of enzyme-undigestible material in the human gut. The neutral detergent fiber (NDF) method and Southgate procedure use enzymes as a pretreatment to remove starches from food samples in order to give a better indication of indigestible carbohydrate in food products.

Cereals and their bran are considered good sources of fiber and, since many of these are extruded, it is appropriate to consider the effects of extrusion on these components. In actuality, relatively little has been published on the subject.

The effect of extrusion on the levels of fiber in products measured by the crude and NDF analyses was undertaken by Al-Hooti (1979). Three samples of a CSB (corn–soy, 70:30) were extruded with the Brady extruder at a discharge temperature of 163° using ingredients with approximately 15% moisture. Each sample differed in the degree to which the raw ingredients were dehulled by an impact mill, which cracked the grain, followed by air aspiration to remove the hulls. Their crude fiber levels varied from 1.4 to 2.0%. Crude fiber and NDF were measured on all samples before and after extrusion, and it was found that the extrusion process made very little difference in the quantities measured.

To evaluate the role of fiber levels on the nutritional value of extruded blended foods, Jansen (1981) first reviewed the data on allowable fiber levels in weaning foods. His summary of nitrogen-balance studies on infants fed extruded foods with varying fiber levels is given in Table 14.4. The data for Title II CSB and ICSM were done on single samples tested with relatively few subjects, making it difficult to draw any conclusions about the effects of the extrusion process. The LEC–CSB samples containing the highest fiber levels showed significantly lower N absorption and retention. Apparently the extrusion processing did nothing to ameliorate the effect of the higher fiber in these foods. Consequently, Jansen (1980) recommended that all soy used to manufacture blended foods should be dehulled prior to extrusion.

The effects of extrusion of a high-fiber crispbread product were studied by Andersson et al. (1981). The product had formulations of varying quantities of wheat bran up to 50%, 10% gluten, with the remainder wheat starch. Extrusion was done on the Creusot-Loire BC45 twin-screw extruder using feed moistures of 11–17% and discharge temperatures from 142° to 150°C. The higher fiber products were denser and harder, as is typical of these types of products. The levels of phytate, which is partially responsible for the mineral binding properties of bran, showed reductions of 15–35% as the result of extrusion. From this study, it was not clear whether the loss of phytate was due to the heat treatment provided by the extruder or the denaturation of protein components reducing the extractability of phytate following extrusion. Regardless, these authors concluded that extrusion was not suitable as a phytate-reducing process.

Similar observations were made about high-fiber products extruded by Seiler and Seibel (1978) using wheat bran and a wheat starch mixture at 20–28% moisture.

EXTRUDED WHOLE BEAN FLOUR

Interest has continued in the use of the extruder to heat treat a variety of legume grains to produce a nutritious food source with relatively high protein content. The initial work on the extrusion processing of whole soybeans to produce stable full-fat soy flour (FFSF) was done by Mustakas et al. (1964, 1970). The principal focus of that work was on the destruction of antitrypsin agents, lipoxydase enzymes, and urease, which occur in the raw beans, and the impact of extrusion processing on product characteristics and nutritional value. They concluded that extrusion processes, carried out on Wenger equipment at

Table 14.4. Summary of Nitrogen-Balance Studies in Infants

Sample	Crude fiber (%)	Protein fed (% kcal)	Casein N absorbed (%)	Casein N retained (%)	Test Sample N absorbed (%)	Test Sample N retained (%)	Test Sample N absorbed (% of casein)	Test Sample N retained (% of casein)	Number of children fed the experimental blend
CSM[b]	0.8	6.5	83.8 ± 1.3[a]	36.3 ± 2.0[a]	73.1 ± 1.8[a]	27.5 ± 2.0[a]	83.8	75.8	6
ICSM[c]	0.8	6.7	86.5 ± 1.6	33.8 ± 2.4	78.8 ± 0.5	34.2 ± 2.3	91.1	>100	3
OSB[d]	1.1	15.0	82.6 ± 6.9	24.7 ± 3.7	74.3 ± 1.5	23.2 ± 4.2	89.9	93.9	6
CSB-1[e]	0.8	6.4	84.1 ± 0.8	34.5 ± 2.4	76.7 ± 3.0	28.9 ± 4.2	91.2	84.8	9
CSB-1[e]	0.8	8.5	—	—	81.1 ± 1.6	35.3 ± 2.2	—	—	9
CSB-2[f]	1.9	8.5	—	—	74.7 ± 2.6	25.3 ± 2.6	—	—	9
CSB-3[g]	2.3	8.5	—	—	77.1 ± 2.7	27.9 ± 1.6	—	—	8

Source: Jansen (1981).

[a] Mean ± standard error.
[b] 68% partially gelatinized cornmeal, 25% toasted defatted soy flour, 5% nonfat dry milk (Graham et al. 1971).
[c] 40% completely gelatinized cornmeal, 38% full-fat soy flour, 5% nonfat dry milk, 15% sugar (Graham et al. 1973).
[d] 25.6% pearled oats, 32.1% dehulled soy, 34.1% sucrose, 5.8% vegetable oil — extruded at 160°C (Del Valle et al. 1981).
[e] 70% degerminated corn grits, 30% dehulled soy — extruded at 163°C (Graham and McLean 1979).
[f] 70% whole corn, 30% dehulled soy — extruded at 163°C (Graham and McLean 1979).
[g] 70% whole corn, 30% whole soy — extruded at 163°C (Graham and McLean 1979).

moistures of approximately 25%, could yield useful products for the fortification of bread, beverages, and the like.

The more recent interest in using LECs to process nutritious foods in developing countries has led to work to determine if low-moisture extrusion would be an effective process for the production of FFSF. Rackis (1974) provides a complete summary of the biological and physiological factors in soybeans which affect their use as a nitrogen source for animals and man and concludes that more knowledge is needed on the conditions associated with new technologies to inactivate antinutritional factors.

The suitability of LEC-processed FFSF for the fortification of bread was studied by Tsen et al. (1975). These researchers found that increasing extrusion temperature from 115° to 140°C increased trypsin inhibitor destruction from 50 to 100% while reducing urease activity 10-fold and reduced the nitrogen solubility of the samples from 59 to 15%. These products were found suitable for fortification of baked goods, such as bread, if the surface-active agent sodium stearoyl-2-lactylate (SSL) was added at the 0.5% level.

Lorenz et al. (1980) extended the work on LEC-produced FFSF. Increasing extrusion temperature caused increased destruction of the trypsin inhibitor and urease along with reductions in nitrogen solubility, as shown in Table 14.5. When these samples were fed to rats, the optimum PER occurred with product extruded at 143°C, which had only 57% of its trypsin inhibitor destroyed. Since increased protein functionality is desirable for the use of these products as cereal food fortificants, it is interesting to note that optimal PER came at an intermediate extrusion temperature where trypsin inhibitor activity was not completely absent. The addition of 3% water to the ground beans prior to

Table 14.5.   Effects of Temperature on Soybeans Processed with a Brady Extruder

Temperature (°C)	Nitrogen solubility index	Trypsin inhibitor			
		Urease pH units	TIU/mg	Destroyed (%)	Corrected PER[a]
Unextruded	55.6	2.07	64.5	—	1.01 ± 0.08
121	41.9	1.96	64.8	0.0	1.35 ± 0.04
127	56.1	1.82	57.2	11.2	1.42 ± 0.05
132	44.3	1.46	45.5	29.5	1.41 ± 0.04
138	47.1	0.34	47.2	26.7	1.55 ± 0.04
143	21.6	0.02	28.0	56.7	1.94 ± 0.05
149	16.6	0.01	16.8	74.0	1.78 ± 0.08

Source: Lorenz et al. (1980).
[a] Protein efficiency ratios corrected relative to casein at 2.50. Composition of dehulled soybeans: 39.2 ± 0.03 protein, 21.0 ± 0.02 fat, 5.9 ± 0.1 ash, 2.4 ± 0.1 fiber, and 5.9 ± 0.5 carbohydrates.

extrusion also increased trypsin inhibitor inactivation by about 20% at a constant extrusion temperature.

These studies all point to the potentially important role extrusion can play in the heat processing of oilseeds, legumes, and possibly lentils to make them suitable for human food. Since more conventional cooking techniques require long times and high moistures to heat-inactivate enzyme systems and antinutritional factors in beans, the relatively dry short-time processing in extrusion serves as an ideal technique to bring the nutritional benefits of these products to larger population segments.

VITAMIN STABILITY

Cereals have been a traditional source of B vitamins. Many are lost during milling, but are added back to the milled products as part of a fortification step. Moreover, it is becoming increasingly popular to fortify cereal-based products with a wide spectrum of vitamins to enhance their nutritional value, such as in RTE breakfast cereals.

The impact of high-temperature extrusion of cereal-based food products on vitamin retention has been studied to a limited degree. Beetner *et al.* (1974) evaluated the effect of extrusion discharge temperature and screw speed on the retention of thiamin (B_1) and riboflavin (B_2) added to corn grit ingredients moistened to 13 and 16% moisture. They found that thiamin was lost in the extrusion process to a much greater extent than riboflavin, as would be expected because of the known thermal lability of thiamin. Specifically, thiamin retention was 21% lower for each 22°C increase in extrusion discharge temperature between 150° and 190°C, and 15% lower for each 25 rpm increase in screw speed. Riboflavin retention was not affected specifically by temperature, but showed reductions with increases in moisture and screw speed. These data would imply that higher shear rates in the extruder, resulting from increased screw speeds, were detrimental to vitamin retention. Higher screw speeds would also shorten product residence time in the extruder, which would normally be associated with greater retention of the vitamins, but in this particular case the effect of shear seemed to predominate.

In the extrusion process, the temperature, pressure, and shear increase as the product moves down the barrel. To separate these effects, Beetner (1978) studied the effects of temperature and static pressure on thiamin and riboflavin loss and concluded that elevated pressure had little impact on vitamin loss. In these tests, temperature–time regions tested were similar to those in the extrusion tests.

In another study, Beetner *et al.* (1976) again examined the retention of thiamin and riboflavin added to the raw flour during the extrusion of triticale. Over the range of conditions studied, increased extrusion temperatures reduced thiamin retention, while riboflavin retention showed a slight increase. It is hard to explain the increase in riboflavin retention, and the result is likely to be an artifact of the microbiological assay used in its determination. The thiamin degradation was of the same magnitude found in the Beetner *et al.* (1974) study. Also, these authors found that reducing the size of the die opening caused a reduction in thiamin, which is consistent with the increased residence times resulting from this change.

Lorenz *et al.* (1980) reported that added thiamin, riboflavin, vitamin B_6, and folic acid were quite stable during the extrusion of CBS (corn–soy, 70:30) at 171°C discharge temperature. However, there was an indication that vitamins A and C were the least stable through the extrusion process. In addition to adding the vitamins before extrusion, the study also added vitamins to unfortified samples after their extrusion and compared the vitamin retention during storage at –18°, 31°, and 49°C to determine the impact of extrusion on their stability. They found that thiamin retention was not affected by whether it was added before or after extrusion, but vitamin C activity was nearly completely lost after 1 month of storage in samples where it was added before extrusion, while that which was added afterward to the product surface was lost at a much slower pace. The accelerated loss of the extruded vitamin C during storage was attributed to the loss of antioxidants.

Because of vitamin loss occurring during RTE cereal processing, Anderson *et al.* (1976) recommended that vitamins A, D, and C added as vitamin A palmitate, calciferol, and ascorbic acid be added to these products as a surface coating following processing. The other alternative is adding an excess to account for processing losses (Williams 1977). The shelf life of added vitamins in RTE cereals was quite good as long as the moisture content of these products remained below 6%. In addition, the shelf life of vitamins A and C, which are subject to loss through oxidation, appeared to be enhanced when both were present in the product.

The stability of vitamin A and provitamin A (carotenoids) during extrusion was reported by Lee *et al.* (1978). The carotenoids added before extrusion were found to be relatively unstable and were deemed unsuitable as a vitamin A source or coloring agent. Vitamin A alcohol (retinol) and vitamin A acetate were found to be retained better during extrusion of a white corn flour than was vitamin A palmitate, suggesting these as better forms for addition prior to extrusion.

The retention of thiamin and ascorbic acid during the extrusion of potato flakes was studied by Maga and Sizer (1978). The loss of each was greatest at the highest extrusion temperature of 160°C, with ascorbic acid generally being the most labile. Thiamin, however, showed losses of 50–80% under low-moisture (22%)–high-temperature (160°C) extrusion, which was attributed to a reaction with sulfite present in the potato flakes.

The heat-stable B vitamins and pantothenic acid appear to be relatively resistant to loss during the extrusion process as measured by recoveries following extrusion. Vitamins subject to oxidative loss, such as ascorbic acid and vitamin A, may be lost to a limited degree during extrusion, but lose activity rapidly during storage because of an extensive exposure to oxygen due to their expanded surface area once puffed.

AMINO ACID LOSS

The loss of essential amino acids such as lysine and methionine during extrusion processes is of interest because of potential impact on protein quality. Nonenzymatic browning of the Maillard type involves the reaction of free amino groups, a good example being the reaction of the ε-amino group of lysine with reducing sugars. The Strecker degradation of methionine can lead to methional, an important flavor compound.

The loss of available lysine in model systems containing ingredients and water activities typical of extrusion processes has been studied. In these types of studies, Warmbier et al. (1976) and Warren and Labuza (1977) have shown that extensive lysine loss occurs before much visual brown color is noticed. Thompson et al. (1976) modeled the initial available lysine loss in these unstirred systems by zero-order kinetics. The reaction rates determined were temperature dependent and followed the Arrhenius equation.

Jokinen (1976) found the fraction of available lysine retained in heated samples to be increased by higher pHs and diminished by increased glucose concentrations, extrusion temperatures, and heating times. The effect of water activity was quadratic, so that maximum loss of available lysine occurred at water activities between 0.65 and 0.7. Browning of the samples occurred at water activities above 0.2 or that associated with the monolayer of bound water. At water activities above 0.7, browning was also reduced because of a dilution of reactants. Tsao et al. (1978) did not find a similar relationship between lysine loss and moisture, probably because they used a relatively narrow range of moistures which would translate to a small change in water activity.

A study of Maillard reactions on the loss of reactive lysine during extrusion was conducted by Cheftel et al. (1981) and Noguchi et al. (1982), using a soy protein enriched wheat flour as a model product. All samples were extruded on the Creusot-Loire BC45 twin-screw extruder at temperatures from $170°$ to $210°C$ and moisture contents from 13 to 18%. These authors found lysine loss increasing rapidly with increasing temperatures, similar to the findings with the static studies reported previously. They also reported that increased moisture reduced lysine availability to a lesser extent because of less product heating from the mechanical work used to turn the screws, which can bring the dough above the barrel temperature.

Similar effects have been reported by Beaufrand *et al.* (1978). The addition of reducing sugars to the extrusion blend was five times more detrimental to the loss of lysine than was the same amount of sucrose. Sucrose hydrolyzes slowly in the extruder, with the reaction rate varying with the water content and pH of the extrusion mixture. Andersson *et al.* (1981) also found a reduction in sucrose and reducing sugars during extrusion, but felt that the level of reduction was more than could be accounted for by hydrolysis and reaction with amino acids and was, therefore, probably due to some carmelization. The loss of lysine availability in extruded wheat flour studied by Björck *et al.* (1984) was related to the formation of reducing carbohydrates through the hydrolysis of starch. They found that biological value reduction was directly related to loss of lysine. Lysine unavailability, however, was not related to total digestibility.

Extrusion cooking was found by Björck *et al.* (1983) to affect the loss in available lysine in a manner similar to baking for a protein-enriched biscuit. As the temperature of extrusion increased and/or the moisture content decreased, a biological assay for lysine showed increasing unavailability, while chemical methods were less sensitive. In addition to lysine loss, they also found a decrease in sulfur-containing amino acids, arginine, and tryptophane with increasing severity of extrusion conditions. The loss of available lysine in fortified cereal foods was also studied by Li Sui Fong (1980). A low-calorie high-protein food and a protein-enriched product were extruded on a twin-screw extruder at 190° to 230°C. They also concluded that elevated extrusion temperatures caused increasing losses in available lysine, with values ranging from 4 to 12%.

Free amino acid loss has also been reported in the extrusion of dried potato flakes (Maga and Sizer 1979). The potato flakes were moistened to 48% moisture and extruded at temperatures ranging from 70° to 160°C in a Brabender laboratory extruder. At 160°C, all amino acids measured were reduced extensively, with the average destruction rate being 89%. At extrusion temperatures less than 130°C, isoleucine, leucine, phenylalanine, tyrosine, and serine were lost to a surprisingly high degree. Since free amino acids in these products exist at less than 5% of total amino acid content, this loss has little nutritional significance.

Clearly, the elevated temperatures, processing conditions, water activities, and combination of reactive ingredients in extruded foods lead to a substantial loss of availability of amino acids during the extrusion process. Extrusion under conditions of reduced temperature and shear that will tend to provide reactive reducing sugars will minimize these losses. The complexity of the extrusion environment and the influence of many ingredients, such as protein, salt, moisture, and oil, on the loss of free amino acids has made it difficult to develop predictive equations which adequately explain all the effects.

TEXTURED PROTEIN

Textured Soy Protein

The extrusion texturization of soy protein is accomplished by moistening defatted soy flour to a moisture content between 20 and 40%, followed by cooking and heating to temperatures in excess of 150°C within the extruder before expansion through a die and cooling. In the extruder, the protein molecules denature and form new cross-links to create a layered and fibrous structure that, when rehydrated with water, provides a meat-like structure. The process has been thoroughly described by Harper (1981B), Kinsella (1978), and Horan (1974). The products have become increasingly important as meat replacers or extenders for a variety of convenience foods.

The heating of moistened soy flour can produce several effects. These include loss of essential amino acids such as lysine, denaturation of the protein, which improves its digestibility, and the destruction of antinutritional factors, such as trypsin inhibitors, phytohemagglutinins, phytic acid, goitrogens, saponins, and phenolic compounds (Kinsella 1978).

Most of the literature on textured soy proteins reports the effects of the extrusion process on the physical and functional properties of the product rather than their nutritional value. A number of studies have been reported which indicate textured soy protein consumed, either separately or as a meat product extender, results in products having very satisfactory PER values. Kies and Fox (1973A) performed nitrogen-balance studies on adult humans under conditions of controlled protein intake and observed no difference between a meat or a textured soy diet when sufficient quantities of protein were fed. Nearly identical results were reported by Korslund et al. (1973) on a study with 12- to 16-year-old boys, with the added fact that supplementation with methionine improves the nutritional value of textured soy under conditions of insufficient nitrogen intake. The importance of niacin in improving nitrogen retention of textured soy has also been reported (Kies and Fox 1973B). Wilding (1974) specifically evaluated the nutritional value of mixtures of ground beef and textured soy and concluded that blends containing up to 30% rehydrated textured soy had an amino acid balance comparable to beef, although supplementation with 1% methionine will improve it. Further, PERs on these same blends showed values exceeding those for ANRC casein.

PERs for textured soy are about 95% of the values for casein (Wilding 1974), indicating low residual values of trypsin inhibitor activity in these products. Aguilera and Kosikowski (1976) showed that increasing discharge temperature and extrusion screw speed decreased trypsin inhibitor activity, while increasing moisture content increased these values. In well-textured samples, 80–90% of the trypsin inhibitor was inactivated.

Other Textured Proteins

The effects of extrusion texturization of defatted peanut flour were reported by Alid *et al.* (1981). Extrusion at 140°C and 25.1% moisture in a Wenger X-25 extruder had no significant effect on the amino acid pattern or the PER of the texturized product compared to the defatted flour. Supplementation of the textured products with 0.3% DL-threonine, 0.2% L-lysine, and 0.2% DL-methionine improved the PER by 40%, to 2.2.

REFERENCES

Aguilera, J. M., and Kosikowski, F. V. 1976. Soybean extruded product: A response surface analysis. J. Food Sci. *41*, 647–651.

Aguilera, J. M., and Kosikowski, F. V. 1978. Extrusion and roll-cooking of corn–soy–whey mixtures. J. Food Sci. *43*, 225–227.

Al-Hooti, S. 1979. Effect of extrusion on digestibility and mineral availability in cereal blends. M.S. Thesis. Colorado State University, Fort Collins.

Alid, G., Uanez, E., Aguilera, J. M., Monckeberg, F., and Chichester, C. O. 1981. Nutritive value of an extrusion-texturized peanut protein. J. Food Sci. *46*, 948–949.

Anderson, R. H., Maxwell, D. L., Mulley, A. E., and Fritsch, C. W. 1976. Effects of processing and storage on micronutrients in breakfast cereals. Food Technol. *30*(5), 110–114.

Andersson, Y., Hedlund, B., Jonsson, L., and Svensson, S. 1981. Extrusion cooking of a high-fiber cereal product with crispbread character. Cereal Chem. *58*, 370–374.

Baker, D., Norris, K. H., and Li, B. W. 1979. Food Fiber Analysis: Advances in Methodology in Dietary Fibers: Chemistry and Nutrition. G. W. Inglett and S. L. Falkehog (Editors). Academic Press, New York.

Beaufrand, M. J., de la Gueriviere, J. F., Monnier, C., and Poullain, B. 1978. Effect of extrusion cooking on protein. (French). Ann. Nutr. Alim. *32*, 353–357.

Beetner, G. 1978. Processing effects on vitamin retention. Ph.D. Thesis. Colorado State University, Fort Collins.

Beetner, G., Tsao, T., Frey, A., and Harper, J. 1974. Degradation of thiamine and riboflavin during extrusion processing. J. Food Sci. *39*, 207–208.

Beetner, G., Tsao, T., Frey, A., and Lorenz, K. 1976. Stability of thiamine and riboflavin during extrusion processing of triticale. J. Milk Food Technol. *39*(4), 244–245.

Björck, I., and Asp, N–G. 1983. The effects of extrusion cooking on nutritional value — A literature review. J. Food Engr. *2*, 281–308.

Björck, I., Noguchi, A., Asp, N–G., Cheftel, J. C., and Dahlqvist, A. 1983. Protein nutritional value of a biscuit processed by extrusion cooking: Effects on available lysine. J. Agric. Food Chem. *31*, 488–492.

Björck, I., Asp, N–G., Birkhed, D., and Lunquist, I. 1984. Effects of processing on starch availability *in vitro* and *in vivo*. I. Extrusion cooking of wheat flours and starch. J. Cereal Sci. *2*, 91–103.

Björck, I., Asp, N–G., and Dahlqvist, A. 1984. Protein nutritional value of extrusion-cooked wheat flours. Food Chem. *15*, 165–178.

Bressani, R. 1976. Exploration of the potential for low-cost extrusion cookers in Latin America. *In* Low-Cost Extrusion Cookers — International Workshop Proceedings LEC–1, pp. 75–80. J. M. Harper and G. R. Jansen (Editors). Colorado State University, Fort Collins.

Bressani, R., Braham, J. E., Elias, L. G., Cuevas, R., and Molina, M. R. 1978. Protein quality of a whole corn/whole soybean mixture processed by a simple extruder. J. Food Sci. *43*, 1563–1565.

Cheftel, J. C., Li Sui Fong, J. C., Mosso, K., and Arnauld, J. 1981. Maillard reactions during extrusion-cooking of protein-enriched biscuits. Prog. Food Nutr. *5*, 487–489.

Chiang, B. Y., and Johnson, J. A. 1977A. A measurement of total and gelatinized starch by glucoamylase and *o*-toluidine reagent. Cereal Chem. *54*, 429–435.

Chiang, B. Y., and Johnson, J. A. 1977B. Gelatinization of starch in extruded products. Cereal Chem. *53*, 436–443.

Cilindro, A. G. 1980. Adaptation of extrusion technology in the preparation of infant food. *In* Extruder Technology — Proceedings Eighth ASEAN Workshop, pp. 193–196. A. Bhumiratana (Editor). Institute of Food Research and Product Development, Kasetsart University, Bangkok, Thailand.

Codex Alimentarius Commission. 1976. Recommended International Standards for Foods for Infants and Children. CAC/RS 72/74–1976, Food and Agriculture Organization, Rome.

Colonna, P., and Mercier, C. 1983. Macromolecular modifications of manioc starch components by extrusion-cooking with and without lipids. Carbohydr. Polym. *3*, 87–108.

Colonna, P., Doublier, J. L., Melcion, J. P., de Monredon, F., and Mercier, C. 1984. Extrusion cooking and drum drying of wheat starch. I. Physical and macromolecular modifications. Cereal Chem. *61*, 538–543.

Davidson, V. J., Paton, D., Diosady, L. L., and Larocque, G. 1984. Degradation of wheat starch in a single-screw extruder: Characteristics of extruded starch polymers. J. Food Sci. *49*, 453–458.

Del Valle, F. R., Villanueva, H., Reyes-Govea, J., Escobedo, M., Bourges, H., Ponce, J., and Munoz, M. J. 1981. Development, evaluation and industrial production of a powdered soy–oats infant formula using a low-cost extruder. J. Food Sci. *46*, 192–197.

Graham, G. G., and Mc Lean, W. L. 1979. Digestibility and utilization of extrusion-cooked corn–soy blends. Report submitted to Office of Nutrition, Agency for International Development, Washington, DC. January 29.

Graham, G. G., Morales, E., Acevedo, G., Placko, R. P., and Cardano, A. 1971. Dietary protein quality in infants and children. IV. A corn–soy–milk blend. Am. J. Clin. Nutr. *24*, 416–422.

Graham, G. G., Baertl, J. M., Placko, R. P., and Morales, E. 1973. Dietary protein quality in infants and children. IX. Instant sweetened corn–soy–milk blend. Am. J. Clin. Nutr. *26*, 491–496.

Harper, J. M. 1978. Extrusion processing of food. Food Technol. *32*(7), 67–72.

Harper, J. M. 1979. Food extrusion. CRC Crit. Rev. Food Sci. Nutr. *11*(2), 155–175.

Harper, J. M. 1981A. Extrusion of Foods, Vol. 1. CRC Press, Boca Raton, FL.

Harper, J. M. 1981B. Extrusion of Foods, Vol. 2. CRC Press, Boca Raton, FL.

Heaton, K. W. 1979. Dietary Fiber: Current Developments of Importance to Health. Technomic Publishing Co., Westport, CT.

Horan, F. E. 1974. Meat analogs. *In* New Protein Foods, Vol. 1A. A. M. Atschul (Editor). Academic Press, New York.

Jansen, G. R. 1976. Nutritional evaluation of extruded products. *In* Low-cost Extrusion Cookers — International Workshop Proceedings LEC-1, pp. 57–65. J. M. Harper and G. R. Jansen (Editors). Colorado State University, Fort Collins.

Jansen, G. R. 1980. The nutritional advantages of extruded foods. *In* Extruder Technology — Proceedings Eighth ASEAN Workshop, pp. 35–60. A. Bhumiratana (Editor). Institute of Food Research and Product Development, Kasetsart University, Bangkok, Thailand.

Jansen, G. R. 1981. A consideration of allowable fibre levels in weaning foods. Food Nutr. Bull. — U.N. Univ. 2(4), 38–47.

Jansen, G. R., and Harper, J. M. 1980A. Application of low-cost extrusion cooking to weaning foods in feeding programmes. Part 1. FAO Food Nutr. Quart. 6(1), 2–9.

Jansen, G. R., and Harper, J. M. 1980B. Application of low-cost extrusion cooking to weaning foods in feeding programmes. Part 2. FAO Food Nutr. Quart. 6(2), 15–19.

Jansen, G. R., Harper, J. M., and O'Deen, L. 1978. Nutritional evaluation of blended foods made with a low-cost extruder cooker. J. Food Sci. 43, 912–915.

Jansen, G. R., O'Deen, L., Tribelhorn, R. E., and Harper, J. M. 1981. The calorie densities of gruels made from extruded corn–soy blends. Food Nutr. Bull. — U.N. Univ. 3(1), 39–44.

Joao, W. S. J., Elias, L. G., and Bressani, R. 1980. Effect of the cooking-extrusion process (Brady Crop Cooker) on the nutritive value of cowpea–maize and cowpea–cassava blends. (Spanish). Arch. Latinoam. Nutr. 30(4), 539–550.

Jokinen, J. E., Reineccius, G. A., and Thompson, D. R. 1976. Losses in available lysine during thermal processing of soy protein model systems. J. Food Sci. 41, 816–819.

Kies, C., and Fox, H. M. 1973A. Effect of varying the ratio of beef and textured vegetable protein on protein nutritive value for humans. J. Food Sci. 38, 1211–1216.

Kies, C., and Fox, H. M. 1973B. Vitamin/protein interrelationships influencing the nutritive value of a soy TVP product for humans. (Abstr.). Cereal Sci. Today 18, 298.

Kinsella, J. E. 1978. Texturized proteins: Fabrication, flavoring and nutrition. CRC Crit. Rev. Food Sci. Nutr. 10(2), 147–207.

Korslund, M., Kies, C., and Fox, H. M. 1973. Comparison of the protein nutritional value of TVP, methionine-enriched TVP and beef for adolescent boys. J. Food Sci. 38, 637–641.

Lee, T–C., Chen, T., Alid, G., and Chichester, C. O. 1978. Stability of vitamin A and provitamin A (carotenoids) in extrusion cooking. AICHE Symp. Ser. 74(172), 192–195.

Li Sui Fong, J. C. 1980. Effects of extrusion cooking on the availability of lysine. (French). Rev. Agric. Suer. Ile Maurice 59(2), 63–75.

Linko, P., Colonna, P., and Mercier, C. 1981. High-temperature, short-time extrusion cooking. In Advances in Cereal Sciences and Technology, pp. 145–235. Y. Pomarang (Editor). Am. Assoc. Cereal Chemists, St. Paul, MN.

Lorenz, K., Jansen, G. R., and Harper, J. M. 1980. Nutrient stability of full-fat soy flour and corn–soy blends produced by low-cost extrusion. Cereal Foods World 25, 161–162, 171–172.

Maga, J. A. 1978. Cis–trans fatty acid ratios as influenced by product and temperature of extrusion cooking. Lebensm. Wiss. Technol. 11, 183–184.

Maga, J. A., and Sizer, C. E. 1978. Ascorbic acid and thiamin retention during extrusion of potato flakes. Lebensm. Wiss. Technol. 11, 192–194.

Maga, J. A., and Sizer, C. E. 1979. The fate of free amino acids during the extrusion of potato flakes. Lebensm. Wiss. Technol. 12, 13–14.

Mercier, C. 1977. Effect of extrusion-cooking on potato starch using a twin-screw French extruder. Staerke 29, 48–52.

Mercier, C. 1980. Structure and digestibility alterations of cereal starches by twin-screw extrusion-cooking. In Food Process Engineering Food Processing Systems, Vol. 1, pp. 795–807. P. Linko, Y. Malkki, J. Olkku, and J. Larinkari (Editors). Applied Science Publishers, London.

Mercier, C., and Feillet, P. 1975. Modification of carbohydrate components by extrusion-cooking of cereal products. Cereal Chem. 52, 283–297.

Mercier, C., Charbonniere, R., Grebaut, J., de la Gueriviere, J. F. 1980. Formation of amylose–lipid complexes by twin-screw extrusion cooking of manioc starch. Cereal Chem. *57*, 4–9.

Meuser, F., Kohler, F., Mohr, G., and Steyrer, W. 1980. Improvement of nutritional value of corn extrusions with the application of potato proteins. (German). Staerke *32*, 238–243.

Molina, M. R., Bressani, R., and Elias, L. G. 1977. Nonconventional legume grains as protein sources. Food Technol. *31*(5), 188–190.

Molina, M. R., Bressani, R., Cuevas, R., Gudiel, H., and Chauvin, V. 1978. Effects of processing variables on some physiochemical characteristics and nutritive quality of high protein food. AICHE Symp. Ser. *74*(172), 153–157.

Mustakas, G. C., Griffin, E. L., Jr., Allen, L. E., and Smith, O. B. 1964. Production and nutritional evaluation of extrusion-cooked full-fat soybean flour. J. Am. Oil Chem. Soc. *41*, 607–614.

Mustakas, G. C., Albrecht, W. J., Bookwalter, G. N., McGee, J. E., Kwolek, W. F., and Griffin, E. L., Jr. 1970. Extruder-processing to improve nutritional quality, flavor, and keeping quality of full-fat soy flour. Food Technol. *24*, 1290–1295.

Noguchi, A., Mosso, K., Aymard, C., Jeunink, J., and Cheftel, J. C. 1982. Maillard reactions during extrusion-cooking of protein-enriched biscuits. Lebensm. Wiss. Technol. *15*, 105–110.

Owen, D. F. and Cotton, R. H. 1982. Dietary fiber. Cereal Foods World *27*, 519–521.

Paton, D., and Spratt, W. A. 1981. Simulated approach to the estimation of degree of cooking of an extruded cereal product. Cereal Chem. *58*, 216–220.

Protein Advisory Group 1975. Tentative Quality and Processing Guide for Human Grade Cottonseed Protein Concentrate. The PAG Compendium, Vol. C. Worldmark Press, John Wiley, New York.

Rackis, J. J. 1974. Biological and physiological factors in soybeans. J. Am. Oil Chem. Soc. *51*, 161A–174A.

Seiler, K., and Seibel, W. 1978. The production of enriched fiber extrusion upon the base of wheat. (German). Gordian *78*, 284–289.

Senti, F. R. 1974. Soy protein foods in U.S. assistance programs. J. Am. Oil Chem. Soc. *51*, 138A–140A.

Shetty, R. M., Lineback, D. R., and Sieb, P. A. 1974. Determining the degree of starch gelatinization. Cereal Chem. *54*, 364–369.

Smith, O. B. 1976. Extrusion cooking. *In* New Protein Foods, Vol. 2B, pp. 86–121. A. M. Altschul (Editor). Am. Assoc. of Cereal Chemists, St. Paul, MN.

Thompson, D. R., Wolf, J. C., and Reineccius, G. A. 1976. Lysine retention in food during extrusion-like processing. Trans. ASAE *19*, 989–992.

Tsao, T. F., Frey, A. L., and Harper, J. M. 1978. Available lysine in heated fortified rice meal. J. Food Sci. *43*, 1106–1108.

Tsen, C. C., Farrell, E. P., Hoover, W. J., and Crowley, P. R. 1975. Extruded soy products from whole and dehulled soybeans cooked at various temperatures for bread and cookie fortification. Cereal Foods World *20*, 413–418.

Warmbier, H. C., Schnickels, R. A., and Labuza, T. P. 1976. Non-enzymatic browning kinetics in an intermediate moisture model system: Effect of glucose to lysine ratio. J. Food Sci. *41*, 981–983.

Warren, R. M., and Labuza, T. P. 1977. Comparison of chemically measured available lysine with relative nutritive value measured by a tetrahymena bioassay during early stages of non-enzymatic browning. J. Food Sci. *42*, 429–431.

Wilding, M. D. 1974. Textured proteins in meats and meat-like products. J. Am. Oil Chem. Soc. *51*, 128A–130A.

Williams, M. A. 1977. Direct extrusion of convenience foods. Cereal Foods World *22*, 152–153.

Effects of Moisture Removal on Nutrients

Peter M. Bluestein
Theodore P. Labuza

Dehydrated foods and concentrated foods, both as ingredients for further processing and as consumer products, are major industrial products. Milk, eggs, fruits, fruit juices, vegetables, meat, and other items of nutritional importance can be found in the dehydrated form. Fruit juices and milk are the major products of nutritional significance that can be found in concentrated form. Products produced by both of these processing operations have a wide variety of preliminary processes, such as washing, peeling, blanching, and cooking, which can affect nutritional value, these have been reviewed by Bender (1966). Dehydrated foods, if stored under proper conditions, will not spoil from microbial attack. Concentrated products are usually not stable to microbial attack and, therefore, concentration is often used with a further preservative process.

Evaporation and most drying processes involve the addition of heat to the food and the removal of moisture as water vapor. In many cases, the temperature of processing is above room temperature, but below the temperatures used for sterilization. There are a wide variety of processes available for producing dried and concentrated products. Each process has its own advantages when compared to other methods of production. For any single process, there is a range of processing conditions that will affect the nutrient retention of the processed product. It would simplify this discussion greatly if a simple rule could be devised for all drying operations to predict the best processing conditions for drying and concentration. This is not possible because of the complexity of the changes in foods which occur during these processes. Some of these changes will be considered here. However, for more detailed discussions, reference works on drying and concentration should be consulted (Van Arsdel 1963; Van Arsdel and Copley 1964).

CHEMICAL KINETICS AND MOISTURE REMOVAL

Chemical Kinetics

It is worthwhile to review some aspects of chemical kinetics, with emphasis on the phenomena that occur during processing and storage of dried and concentrated foods. Since the loss of nutritive value is usually the destruction of a single chemical compound, this loss can be described by a simple monomolecular reaction, as in Eq. 1:

$$A \xrightarrow{\ k\ } B \tag{1}$$

where compound A reacts to form compound B with a reaction rate constant, k. If Eq. 1 applies to the loss of nutrient A, then the rate of that loss can be described by Eq. 2:

$$-(d[A]/dt) = k[A] \tag{2}$$

where $d[A]/dt$ is the rate of loss of nutrient A, k is the reaction rate constant, and $[A]$ is the concentration of A. The reaction rate constant is related to temperature by Eq. 3:

$$k = k_0 e^{[E_a/RT]} \tag{3}$$

where k_0 is a constant, E_a is the activation energy of the reaction, R is the gas constant and equal to 1.986 cal/g-mol K, and T is the absolute temperature, K.

If the reaction rate constant is a true constant and the only change in the concentration of A is due to chemical reaction, the extent of the loss of A can be found by integrating Eq. 2 and substituting the appropriate boundary conditions to obtain Eq. 4:

$$-\ln ([A]/[A]_0) = kt \tag{4}$$

where $[A]_0 = [A]$ initially. Many food reactions can be described by Eq. 4 when the limitations above are observed. This may be the case during storage when the temperature and moisture content of the product are held constant. However, during drying and most concentration processes neither temperature nor moisture content are held constant. To include the effects of variation in moisture content and temperature rigorously would complicate the discussion in this section and limit the usefulness of the equations derived.

Temperature

The temperature of a food during drying or concentrating varies over a wide range during the process and with different processing techniques.

Temperatures usually found can range from $-30°$ to above $100°C$, depending on the process and product. This range is much smaller when considering the processing alternatives for a single product. In considering a product dried or concentrated by one process, it is clear that higher temperatures experienced by the food result in increased rates of chemical reactions. This effect is a result of the change in the reaction rate constant with a change in temperature. Since nonenzymatic chemical reactions have activation energies between 10 and 40 kcal/g-mol, the reaction rate constant can be expected to increase from 2-fold to 15-fold for a $10°C$ increase (Labuza 1972). The activation energy for moisture removal is approximately 10 kcal/g/mol (King 1970). Because of this difference to activation energies for chemical deterioration and moisture removal, low-temperature processing should produce products with the least amount of chemical deterioration. However, low-temperature processing is usually more expensive because of the longer processing time. In addition, there is also the possibility of microbial growth during processing, at least between $4°$ and $40°C$. Therefore, methods which reduce the processing time without going much above the upper temperature for microbial growth in the food will result in maximum nutrient retention. These methods would include better airflow patterns and increased surface:volume ratio.

Water

Water is distributed throughout dried and concentrated foods in many forms. Water may be found as a liquid containing solutes when the food is "wet" and associated with other constituents. The thermodynamic parameter that describes the state of water is the water activity, which, as a working definition, can be defined as the relative humidity in equilibrium with a food divided by 100. Water activity is related to the moisture content of a product by the moisture sorption isotherm,

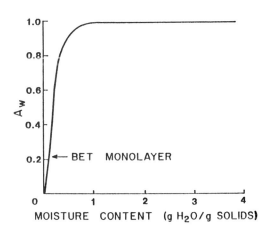

Fig. 15.1.   A typical water sorption isotherm.

as shown in Fig. 15.1. As the water activity of a product decreases, as it does during drying and concentration, the state of water changes. Over most of the range of the water activity scale, water behaves as a solvent even though some literature classifies it as bound. In concentrated products, this aqueous solution is a liquid, but in dried and "semimoist" foods this solution may be found in capillaries or held by swollen protein or polysaccharide gels. As the water activity decreases, the predominating form of water shifts to water-hydrating hydrophilic constituents. However, water in this region still acts as an aqueous phase down to the BET (Brunauer-Emmett-Tetler) monolayer (Brunauer *et al.* 1938). Above this point water acts to dissolve solutes, mobilizes them, and allows them to react within the aqueous environment. The BET monolayer thus describes the moisture content below which most reactions cease (Labuza 1970). Below this point (see Fig. 15.1), water is thought to be nonliquid and to be tightly bound or absorbed to specific sites on various constituents in foods. Additional discussions of the states of water can be found in the literature on water activity and sorption (Bone 1969; Karel 1973; Labuza 1968; Rockland 1969).

The state of water has a significant effect on the loss of nutrients. As noted, above the monolayer value, the water acts as a solvent for reactants and catalysts. Water may also be a product of some reversible reactions and, therefore, could slow the forward rate of reaction (Eichner and Karel 1972). Some of the reactants, such as water-soluble vitamins are present in low concentrations. As the moisture content and water activity decrease from the natural value, as would happen in drying, several important effects occur. The aqueous solutions become more concentrated. Some components of the food may form supersaturated solutions and ultimately precipitate. According to Eq. 2, as the concentration in solution increases, the reaction rate increases. This leads to increased rates of losses of the nutrient as the moisture content or water activity is lowered. Some metal catalysts may lose part of the water of hydration. This can increase their catalytic effect toward unsaturated lipids. Diffusion of components in the aqueous phase may become more difficult since the observed viscosity increases. This would also decrease reaction rates. Finally, when all liquid water has been removed, reactions which proceed in water cease. This usually occurs at the BET monolayer.

It is important to distinguish between reaction of water-soluble nutrients and reactions of oil-soluble nutrients when discussing the effects of water on chemical reactions. Some of the water-soluble vitamins are highly soluble. It is unlikely that these highly soluble vitamins become supersaturated until the moisture content is greatly reduced. For example, ascorbic acid, which is easily oxidized to dehydroascorbic acid, is present at approximately 0.05 wt% in orange juice. Since the solubility of ascorbic acid is approximately 25 wt%, ascorbic acid will not become supersaturated until the moisture content has decreased from the natural >50% to 1.3% db (dry basis) (data from Watt and Merrill 1963). Until this low moisture content is reached, ascorbic acid becomes more concentrated as water is removed. This increase in concentration causes an increased reaction rate as shown in Eq. 1. However, although the reaction rate is greater, the percentage lost during processing is independent of the concentration as shown by Eq. 4. This conclusion holds when the nutrient degrades by a first-order chemical reaction. Nonenzymatic unimolecular reactions are likely to be first order. Bimolecular reactions are not likely to be first order. The Maillard reaction between reducing sugars and amines, which make lysine unavailable, and the degradation of unsaturated lipids are not first-order kinetics and the loss of these nutrients during processing should be dependent on the concentration. Unfortunately, kinetic data are not available to predict the effect of concentration on the loss of most water-soluble nutrients.

Some "water-soluble" nutrients, such as riboflavin, are not very soluble in water. These compounds would form saturated and supersaturated solutions during drying and concentration. Should these nutrients actually precipitate, the losses would be reduced.

The concentration of oil-soluble nutrients, such as the essential fatty acids and vitamins A, D, E, and K, is extremely low in the aqueous phase of foods. Since a large part of these nutrients is found in the dispersed phase, their concentration does not change as water is removed. Other phenomena that occur during water removal are more important. Water is the solvent for heavy metals, which catalyze the free-radical oxidation of some unsaturated nutrients. As the moisture is decreased, catalyst mobility is decreased. At very low moisture contents in dried food, diffusion of catalysts decreases (Duckworth 1962); however, they are no longer hydrated and their effectiveness may increase (Labuza 1971). Finally, water may act as a free-radical quencher to reduce the rate of reaction (Labuza 1971). These effects are not the result of direct water-nutrient interaction and remain complicated in terms of reaction rate predictions.

The overall effects of water on chemical and enzymatic reactions are shown in Fig. 15.2. The reaction rate for destruction of water-soluble nutrients may go through a maximum at a water activity of approximately 0.7. The maximum is due to dilution of the reactant concentration and possible product (water) inhibition. Below a water activity of 0.7, the reaction rate decreases because solutes which are reactants either precipitate out or the viscosity of the aqueous phase becomes high enough to slow diffusion. As seen, these reactions all cease at the BET monolayer, which is the point where an aqueous phase ceases to exist.

For the lipid-soluble nutrients there is a minimum in the reaction rate at a_w = 0.3–0.4. This minimum is caused by the balance between

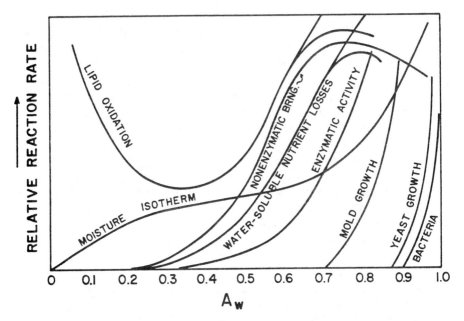

Fig. 15.2.   General scheme of reaction rates as a function of water activity.

catalyst hydration, mobility of catalysts, hydration of intermediates in the sequence, and free radical quenching. Considering the general picture of reactions during concentration and dehydration, the conditions to be avoided are high temperature at intermediate-moisture contents.

This brief theoretical discussion of some of the factors which contribute to nutrient retention during drying and concentration provides some insight into the mechanisms of changes. These mechanisms are not completely understood at this time and the relative importance of one mechanism versus another cannot be predicted. Further research is needed to establish the important mechanisms which lead to significant loss of nutrients. Once the mechanisms are understood, process development work can proceed on a rational basis.

CONCENTRATION

Fruit juices, purees, jams, soups, condensed milk, and dried dairy product ingredients are among the products that are concentrated as part of production. Evaporation of water is by far the most commonly used method of reducing moisture content. Membrane processes and freeze concentration are relatively new processes, which are likely to find increasing use in the future. The obvious advantage of concentrated products is the reduction of weight and volume by processing. In addition, if the product is to be dried after concentration, the total cost of processing will be substantially lower when part of the moisture has been removed by concentration before drying. Recent work has shown that concentration before drying can lead to better volatile flavor retention during the drying operation (Thijssen 1971). Few concentrated products are produced without some additional processing.

Evaporation

Evaporation is by far the most common method of concentrating liquid food products. This process can be viewed as the simple boiling off of water at temperatures that vary depending on the product and process. Because water requires approximately 540 kcal/kg for vaporization from the liquid, heat must be supplied to the liquid during the evaporation. The equipment used to transfer heat into the food is varied and has undergone considerable technical development, with the objective of producing products with minimal amounts of change due to processing. Single evaporators are rarely used in industry for economic reasons. The important aspects of evaporators and processing schemes will be considered here, with the purpose of understanding the cause of the nutritional changes occurring during evaporation. Additional processing technology can be found in several other texts (Armerding 1966; Brennan et al. 1969; Charm 1971; Perry et al. 1964).

It is useful to consider a simple batch evaporation in a steam-jacketed kettle to illustrate the principles of evaporation. The steam-jacketed kettle is a simple piece of equipment which finds uses in the production of candy, jam, jelly, and some condensed milk products, but is not widely used for other products. Once the original liquid has filled the kettle, the steam is fed into the jacket surrounding the bottom. The steam transfers heat into the liquid and boiling begins. If the kettle is open to the atmosphere, then the boiling temperature at the beginning of evaporation is near $100°C$. After boiling begins, heat is continuously fed to the kettle to supply the heat required to evaporate water. As the water boils off and the solution becomes more concentrated, several important changes occur which affect the ease of evaporation and, therefore, the nutrient retention. First, reactive solutes are more concentrated and the rate of chemical deterioration can increase. Second, the boiling point of the liquid rises slightly as predicted by Raoult's law. The boiling point of a 60 wt% solution of sucrose is $3°C$ above the boiling point of water at atmospheric pressure. Third, the viscosity of the solution can increase dramatically. The viscosity of a 50 wt% solution of grape juice is 40 cp (centipose), 40 times more viscous than water (Saravacos 1970). The viscosity is important because it affects the ease of heat transfer to the boiling liquid. As the viscosity increases, it is more difficult to heat the liquid. This difficulty results in a nonuniform temperature distribution in the liquid food. Hot spots and burning on the wall of the kettle can result. This has a large effect on the nutrient retention, resulting in large decreases in quality.

The steam-jacketed kettle can be used to perform an evaporation under vacuum. When a liquid is boiled under a partial vacuum, the boiling point is lowered considerably. Water boils at 65°C when the vacuum is 187 mm Hg. This has the effect of lowering the temperature of processing but does not affect the rate of evaporation greatly. Lower temperatures in evaporation result in higher nutrient retentions. Other reasons for performing the evaporation under a partial vacuum will be considered later.

The steam-jacketed kettle is the simplest piece of equipment to be used to perform an evaporation. Other types of evaporators are considered by Brennan *et al.* (1969) and Perry *et al.* (1964). For the purpose of this discussion, it is useful to separate all evaporators into two classes: (1) evaporators with a considerable amount of liquid holdup and (2) evaporators with minimal holdup. The holdup of an evaporator refers to the amount of liquid in the piece of equipment. If the holdup of an evaporator is large, relative to the net liquid flow rate through the evaporator, the boiling liquid is in contact with the hot heat-transfer surface of the equipment for a long period of time. Evaporators with long residence times are the short-tube evaporators, the Wurling® evaporator (Carlson *et al.* 1967), and evaporators with recirculating fluid. The ideal type of evaporator for maximum nutrient retention has a minimum retention time of the liquid in the equipment. Such evaporators, like the plate, rising film, and falling film evaporators, pass the liquid through the equipment only once with little or no recirculation. The design of these evaporators ensures that heat transfer is efficient and the evaporation rate is high. High evaporation rates are required for single-pass processing. Evaporation with single-pass equipment can result in a reduction by a factor of 10 in the time of processing at elevated temperatures (Moore and Hesler 1963).

Evaporations are usually not performed in a single evaporator. The economics of steam usage requires that the steam produced in one evaporator be used in another evaporator to boil off more water from the product of the first evaporator. The second evaporator is operated at a lower pressure, which results in boiling at a lower temperature. This usage of the steam from one evaporator to heat the liquid in another evaporator is called "multieffect evaporation." Chemical processing generally uses large numbers of effects. However, the food industry, because of its concern for the quality of the final concentrate, uses no more than three or four effects. Wiegrand (1971) reports on a triple-effect evaporation of milk with boiling temperatures of 70°, 60°, and 42°C in the three effects. A larger number of effects in this case would require a longer residence time in the equipment and a higher temperature of evaporation.

Evaporation provides a rapid, cheap method of producing concentrated products. Reverse osmosis and freeze-concentration are more expensive (Bomben *et al.* 1973). The temperature is high but the time of processing can be very short. The short time of processing can result in products with close to 100% nutrient retention.

Freeze Concentration

Although useful reports on the nutrient retention of freeze-concentrated products have not appeared in the literature, it is appropriate to consider this process here as a competitor of evaporation. The process involves the freezing of liquids, with carefully controlled conditions, to produce large ice crystals and the separation of the ice from the remaining concentrate. Thijssen (1970) has reviewed the equipment available. This process is performed at low temperatures, below the freezing point of feed liquid. As a low-temperature process, it is expected that the nutrient retention of freeze-concentrated products would be close to 100%. The only loss would be in any solute loss that remained with the ice or fluid adhering to the ice.

Membrane Processes

The membrane processes of reverse osmosis and ultrafiltration are finding increasing uses for final product production and ingredient manufacture. Reverse osmosis is a concentration process with the objective of removing only the water (Leightell 1972). Ultrafiltration is a concentration and purification process. Applications of ultrafiltration have been reviewed by Porter and Michaels (1970). Both processes pass the liquid to be concentrated (and purified) through equipment holding a membrane. The membrane allows the selective passage of water and perhaps other compounds. In reverse osmosis, compounds which are soluble in the membrane can be lost. Most nutrients would not be soluble in a reverse-osmosis membrane. In most applications of ultrafiltration, all low-molecular-weight material is allowed to pass through the membrane.

DEHYDRATION

A large number of techniques are available for the production of dehydrated foods. Only the concepts of drying and a limited number of the processes used can be discussed here. Further discussions are available in the literature (Van Arsdel 1963; Van Arsdel and Copley 1964; Charm 1971; Holdsworth 1971; Masters 1972; Williams-Gardner 1971).

Before considering the individual properties of different drying procedures, a short discussion of the concepts of dehydration is required.

In most types of drying, heat is supplied to the food and moisture in the vapor state is removed. The methods of supplying heat and transporting the moisture and the product are the basic variations between the different techniques of drying. As heat is supplied to a food, either the temperature of the food is raised or water is evaporated. During the initial stages of most drying operations the rates of heat transfer to the food and moisture transfer from the food are balanced and the temperature of the drying food remains at the wet-bulb temperature of the air. The wet-bulb temperature of the air does not vary over a wide range in relation to the normally measured or dry-bulb temperatures for fairly dry air. The temperature of the food during the first period of drying is relatively independent of air dry-bulb temperature and is much lower than the air temperature. During this first period, which is usually called the constant rate period, the moisture content of the piece of food decreases uniformly to a level which is still above the maximum in the chemical reaction rate curve (Fig. 15.2). The absolute moisture is still high enough that it does not affect the rate. The rate of drying remains at this constant and high level until the surface of the food begins to lose water at a high water activity. It would be desirable to increase the length of time a food dries in the constant rate period if nutrient retention is critically important. During this period, the temperature is low. However, the constant rate period is also the time when the greatest amount of shrinkage and other undesirable changes occur, and for these quality reasons this period should be short for most products.

Once the constant rate period is over, the drying rate decreases. This occurs because the surface of the piece is not completely saturated with water. The interface between water and air recedes into the piece and moisture content and water activity vary with the location in the piece. The temperature of the piece rises from the wet-bulb temperature and ultimately approaches the dry-bulb temperature of the air. It is during this time that the conditions of moderate-moisture content and high temperature are present and these conditions promote chemical reactions. Actual drier designs recognize this and the effects of chemical reactions on product organoleptic quality. Most driers designed to produce high-quality products should also produce products with reasonably high nutrient retention.

The conditions during all drying operations are changing. The time, temperature, and moisture content of the food during drying have the greatest effects on the rate of reactions. The presence of dissolved oxygen and sulfur compounds, which can have an effect on nutrient retention, is controlled by the operations preceding drying. It would be useful to have a sufficiently accurate description (model) of the phenomena that occur during drying and the influence of the dynamic conditions on the rates of nutrient degradation. Unfortunately, these descriptions do not exist at this time, and further research is needed in this area to be able to predict and explain the effects of processing variables on the nutritional quality of dehydrated foods (Labuza 1972).

Sun Drying

Sun drying is still of importance throughout the world. Fruit, fish, meat, and grain are spread out in the sun. The radiant energy of the sun provides the heat to evaporate the water. Drying proceeds well in warm and dry weather. At night and during the rainy seasons drying will not take place. The temperatures of the food during sun drying are usually $5°-15°C$ above ambient temperature. The time of drying is 3–4 days or longer, depending on the product and conditions.

Tunnel Drying

Tunnel driers of various types are an extremely important class of driers. Fruits and vegetables can be dried by this method. There are several types of tunnel driers. All types follow the same basic operations. The food is spread onto trays or a conveyor and passed into a high-velocity air stream. The basic discussion of drying presented earlier can be applied to tunnel drying. The rate of drying is related to the air velocity, the loading of the product, the wet-bulb and dry-bulb temperatures of the air, and the thickness and other properties of the food. During the constant rate period, the properties of the air are most important in determining the rate of drying. The properties of the food materials are more important during the other periods of drying. Tunnel dryers are usually designed to take advantage of these characteristics.

Tunnel driers are classified based on the food moving mechanisms and the direction of airflow. Trays or conveyors are used to move the food through the tunnel. The directions of airflow are either parallel to the food movement, countercurrent to the food movement, through, or across the food bed. If air is introduced parallel to the food movement, the initial conditions for drying are optimal but, as the air picks up moisture from the drying food, the ability of the air for further drying is decreased. If counterflow drying is used exclusively, the conditions for drying are optimal near the product end of the drier, but not at the feed end. Usually, these two methods of air flow are combined into a two-stage drier. Parallel flow is used in the first stage and countercurrent flow in the second stage of the drier. This provides the best compromise for efficient drying and good product quality. The temperatures of the air used depend on the product and are in the range of $70°-90°C$ in the first stage and $55°-70°C$ in the second stage, which results in a drying time of 8–16 hr. In many cases, the product is removed from the tunnel before drying is completed, and the final moisture content is lowered in bins operated at $40°-55°C$ for 7 hr or more (Van Arsdel and Copley 1964).

Flow of air through a bed of food provides better contact between the heated air and the product. Higher drying rates are obtained and the times of drying are decreased to a few hours. The temperatures of drying are in the range of two-stage drying. Fluid-bed drying is conceptually similar to flow-through drying. In the fluid bed, high-velocity air is forced upward through the food and suspends the particles in warm air. Drying is usually faster. Fluid-bed drying, foam-mat drying, and drying of puffed foods have been reviewed by Holdsworth (1971).

Spray Drying

Spray drying is an important process for milk, other dairy products, coffee, eggs, and juices. In spray drying, a liquid feed is sprayed into a stream of hot air. The small size of the drops, which average approximately 100 μm in diameter, results in a very large surface which dries quickly. Although the air dry-bulb temperature is approximately 200°C, the air wet-bulb temperature rarely exceeds 55°C and the time in the drier is very short. Drying takes place over the first few seconds and the dried particles are removed from the drier, usually within 30 sec. The temperatures of the particles during drying can range from the wet-bulb temperature of the inlet air to above 100°C as they exit in the dry state. Particles are usually at a temperature of 60°–80°C when removed from the drier. Although these temperatures are high in comparison to tunnel-drying operations, the moisture near the end is usually near the BET monolayer and the time of exposure is very short. Thus, deterioration during processing is minimal. It is extremely difficult to predict the time–temperature–moisture content history of a particle and to use this to predict the nutrient retention during spray drying.

Masters (1972) has discussed many modifications of spray driers which are likely to result in better nutrient retentions. Cooling the walls of the drier and injecting dehumidified cool air into the drier to lower the temperature of the product offers advantages for certain products. Multiple zones of air temperatures will allow the engineer to obtain optimum drying and a product of maximum nutrient retention. The combination of spray drying with other methods of drying, such as flow-through bed drying, offers new opportunities for the future (Meade 1973).

Drum Drying

Viscous slurries, such as mashed potatoes and sweet potatoes, are dried by drum driers. The slurry is fed into the trough between two steel drums heated from the inside with steam. The drums are rotating and spread a thin film of the slurry over the surface. As the drums turn, the product dries. Drum temperatures are in the range of 120°–170°C and drying time is 20 sec to 3 min. Although drum drying is one of the cheapest methods of drying (Greig 1971), the product is in contact with the hot drums and ultimately leaves the drums at a high temperature. This should result in deterioration greater than that resulting from spray drying or tunnel drying. Usually, drum-dried products cannot be dried by spray driers and tunnel driers.

Freeze Drying

Freeze drying should result in the highest nutritional quality of all the drying processes (Calloway 1962). The food, which has been previously frozen, is placed into a chamber which is evacuated. When the pressure has been reduced to below the triple point pressure of water (4.6 mm Hg), heat is supplied to the frozen food. Because of the low pressure, ice does not melt and the water vapor sublimes without going through the liquid phase. The heating-plate temperature varies during processing from above 100° to about 55°C. The heating-plate temperature is highest when the food is at the lowest temperature. As drying proceeds, the temperatures of the food and the plate approach each other at an intermediate temperature The warmest parts of the food, the outside surfaces, have already achieved a low moisture content. Therefore, the problem of nutritional deterioration is minimized. The time, temperature, and moisture content relationships during freeze drying have received considerable attention and are reviewed by King (1971). Because freeze drying results in minimal damage, these relationships are of little interest here.

Other Drying Processes

New drying processes and important modifications of current techniques are continually being developed. One interesting new technique is the use of a solvent to extract all or part of the moisture in foods. The use of a concentrated sugar solution to extract water from fruits has been called osmotic dehydration. Peaches produced by the method are soaked in 75° Brix for 4–6 hr to remove part of the water and then dried further (Farkas and Lazar 1969; Anonymous 1973). Fish protein concentrate is produced by the extraction of water with isopropyl alcohol (Finch 1970). Hieu and Schwartzberg (1973) have proposed the use of various water-soluble solvents for the dehydration of shrimp. Most of these processes do not decrease the moisture content to a suitable level for storage and require further processing to remove the solvent and the remaining water.

Many other drying processes are used in the food industry. Many of these are reviewed by Williams-Gardner (1971) and others. Foam-spray drying (Brennan and Priestly 1972), foam-mat drying (Hertzendorf and Moshy 1970), pneumatic drying, and other processes could be considered, but are not used to any degree by the food industry because of cost and their special nature. Many new drying processes are likely to be developed in the future. If nutrient retention data is lacking, as it usually is, the only possible statement is that nutrient retention is likely to be higher in a high-quality product than in a low-quality product.

NUTRIENT LOSSES

Although there has been some new work, little of it can be used to predict the effects of processing variables on nutrient retention. Work that has been performed has been concerned with the retention of nutrients in an established product and process and not with the effects of a wide range of conditions available for the process. It would be useful to examine the approach required to provide this information. This approach integrates the kinetics of deterioration with the time–temperature–moisture content history of the sample. This has been applied successfully to packaging studies by Mizrahi *et al.* (1970A) and Quast and Karel (1972). First, the reaction rate is determined as a function of temperature and moisture content using constant conditions. Some ingenuity will have to be used to overcome some of the problems of holding foods at high temperatures or high humidities for extended periods of time. Once those data have been collected, a suitable model of drying behavior that is sensitive to the variables of air wet- and dry-bulb temperature, air velocity, food properties, and drier characteristics can be integrated with the deterioration data. The drying model must be suitably refined to be able to account for the variation in moisture content and temperature throughout a single piece of food. The model required for the nutrient retention of concentrated products is simpler because the liquid is well mixed and the moisture and temperature gradients are small.

Hendel *et al.* (1955) and Kluge and Heiss (1967) applied data on the browning reaction obtained during storage to the drying of potato to predict the extent of browning after drying. The reaction rate as a function of moisture content and temperature is shown in Fig. 15.3. The reaction rate of browning shows the typical response to temperature and moisture content (Labuza 1970; Lonein *et al.* 1968; Mizrahi *et al.* 1970B). There is a peak in the reaction rate at a moisture content near a_w = 0.7 and the rate increases as temperature increases. The rate is zero order, which means the rate of brown pigment production is linear with time. This indicates that pigment may be formed without significant decreases in the concentrations of reducing sugar and lysine in the potato. Hendel *et al.* (1955) used the average moisture content and temperature measured at a point to represent the conditions in a piece of potato. Because the reaction rate does not vary linearly with

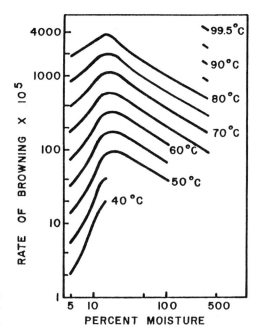

Fig. 15.3. Browning rate of potato dice as a function of moisture content (dry basis) and temperature.

respect to moisture content, and the center temperature of a piece underestimates the temperature elsewhere in the piece, the predicted values for the extent of browning deviate from the measured values. The moisutre distribution and temperature gradients depend on the air, food, and drier properties. If these properties had been measured and a suitable model of moisture and temperature distributions had been used, the calculated results would have been in better agreement with the experimental results. This approach can be applied to predict nutrient retention. The results of this work would contribute to knowledge in the areas of drying behavior and chemical deteriorations during drying. Similar work on browning of applesauce was done by Escher and Neukom (1970, 1971).

As will be shown, the losses of nutritive values during most drying and concentration processes are small in relation to losses during cooking. Many factors preceding the drying or concentration operation have an influence on the nutrient retention measured. For example, the presence of sulfur dioxide is known to protect ascorbic acid but decreases thiamin retention. The presence of copper or iron affects ascorbic acid retention. Heavy metals are likely to catalyze the oxidation of carotenes. Each of these factors will be considered in the appropriate sections.

Proteins

Damage to proteins in the processing of foods has been reviewed by Bender (1972). He suggests that many diets are limited by the sulfur-containing amino acids and that reactions of lysine, which is in surplus, is not critical. However, the reaction of lysine, more particularly the ∈-amino group, with reducing sugars is one of the most studied reactions in foods and is heat sensitive. This provides a ready index for the extent of other deteriorations. Woodham (1973), in addition, has reviewed the area of vegetable protein concentrates and notes that destruction of naturally present antinutritional factors is just as important.

The reaction of lysine and reducing sugars is also important because it is involved in the reaction mechanism for one scheme of nonenzymatic browning. Browning reactions can be desirable, as in the case of bread crust, syrups, and coffee, but are considered undesirable in products not expected to have a brown color such as dried milk products.

Work in the area of protein deterioration during drying can be divided into two broad areas: (1) work on animal feeds and protein sources at temperatures not usually encountered in drying operations, and (2) work with foods under normal processing conditions. Not very many studies exist which relate the deterioration taking place to changes in processing conditions over a wide range of variables and which can be used as a model.

Studies with soy-product drying must consider the inactivation of naturally occurring toxicants, such as the trypsin inhibitor. It would be useful to design a process which accomplishes this destruction with minimal heat damage to other proteins. Drying after inactivation of the trypsin inhibitor is required because of the usual addition of water to the dry meal to increase heat transfer and effect the rate of inhibitor destruction. The data of Taira $et\ al.$ (1966) for lysine loss indicate that the reaction rate constant, assuming a first order reaction is 0.166 hr^{-1} with an activation energy of 30 kcal/g-mol in the wet state. The destruction of trypsin inhibitor occurs at a rate approximately 100 times faster with an activation energy of 18.5 kcal/g-mol (Hackler $et\ al.$ 1965). Because lysine is more sensitive to the ultimate temperature reached (higher activation energy), trypsin inhibitor destruction should be performed at the lowest temperature possible. Hackler $et\ al.$ (1965) present data to substantiate this and this is shown in Table 15.1. The protein efficiency ratio (PER) measured reflects the destruction of sulfur-containing amino acids, which are limiting but it can be used as an index for lysine loss in dried soy milk. During spray-drying experiments, trypsin inhibitor destruction increases as the air inlet temperature increases. The PER shows only small changes until the temperature of 277°C and decreases dramatically as the temperature is increased. In this case, the air inlet temperature of 277°C is optimum when

Table 15.1. Effect of Drying on Soy Meal[a]

	Trypsin inhibitor retained (%)	PER
Spray drying with air inlet at (°C)		
166	10	2.22
182	8	2.10
227	4	1.99
277	5	1.63
316	3	0.16
Drum drying		
Air drum, 150°C	5	2.19
Vacuum drum, 29 in. Hg, 108°C	10	2.22
Freeze drying, 1000 μHg	10	2.14

Source: Hackler *et al.* (1965).
[a] Initial value 14% inhibitor retention after cooking.

considering the balance between trypsin inhibitor destruction and PER decrease. It is difficult to explain the quantitative change in PER without further engineering data on the spray-drying technique used. It appears that when the air inlet temperature is increased to 277°C, the drops are drying very fast. These drying conditions lead to an increase in droplet temperature before the inner portions of the drop is dry. These are the conditions which favor reactions of the water-soluble nutrients.

The data of Hackler *et al.* (1965) can also be used to compare spray drying to drum drying and freeze drying. Drum drying in air with a drum temperature of 150°C results in a significant reduction in trypsin inhibitor without affecting the PER. Drying in this case occurs at a lower temperature during the intermediate water-activity range than in the high-temperature spray-drying runs. The time of drying would be longer. A high-temperature–short-time (HTST) drying process favors the lowering of PER over trypsin inhibitor destruction. Drum drying in

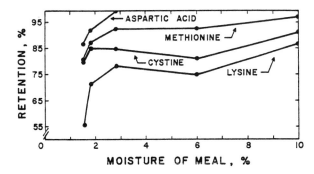

Fig. 15.4. Retention of amino acids during drying of alfalfa.

Table 15.2. Effect of Heat and Moisture on Fish Meal

Conditions of treatment			Freeze-dried control (%)			
					NPU	
Temp (°C)	Moisture (%)	Time (min)	Available lysine	Pepsin digestibility	Rats	Chicks
96	7.7	80	94	88	—	98.6
	8.8	60	96	84	—	102.0
	10.8	120	87	76	—	98.1
	36.0	60	87	71	97.7	98.6
116	6.4	120	94	78.1	95.3	96.8
	7.5	60	100	78.2	97.0	98.8
	8.4	30	96.0	80.0	97.4	99.7
132	2.5	120	97	58.4	91.8	97.1

Source: Myklestad *et al.* (1972).

a vacuum of 29 mm Hg and freeze drying are low-temperature processes which do not show marked changes in PER or trypsin inhibitor.

Livingston *et al.* (1971) dried alfalfa in a rotary drier at temperatures above the normal range for drying foods. These results are shown in Fig. 15.4 and are useful to establish the upper limits of loss in this product. Again, sufficient data are not available for a complete quantitative description of the losses of amino acids. However, a simplified analysis is possible. Air dry-bulb temperatures to the drier ranged from 650° to 950°C and outlet temperatures were 100°–170°C. These conditions are typical of high-efficiency drying without concern for product quality. Estimated air wet-bulb temperatures are in the range from 70° to 120°C. Drying begins at the wet-bulb temperature and the temperature of the pieces quickly increases. As the air temperature at the inlet is increased, the temperature of the piece throughout drying is increased, the outlet temperature is increased, and the final moisture content is decreased. Because the heat treatment is more severe as the final moisture content is lowered, the destruction of amino acids is increased as the final moisture content is lowered. The data are shown in Fig. 15.4.

Myklestad *et al.* (1972) heated fish meal prepared from herring at different temperatures, times, and moisture contents. Table 15.2 shows the available lysine loss, protein digestibility by an in vitro test, and two in vivo tests on the processed fish meal. As noted, there seems to be substantial decreases in available lysine and chemical digestibility with pepsin when moisture content of the meal during heating was high or heating time was long. However, because of the scattered conditions used, no real pattern can be established. What is more interesting is that the in vivo studies show only a 4–5% nutritional loss of the meal. This makes suspect many of the considerations presented in the literature based solely on chemical tests. It also indicates that even high-temperature, high-moisture contents during drying do not affect protein nutritional values significantly, although available lysine decreases.

Aitken *et al.* (1967) also showed that, based on rat NPU (net protein utilization) studies, there was no significant difference between freeze-dried cod meal versus that which was rapidly dried at either 110°, 115°, or by slow drying with salt and pressing, at 27°C.

The biological quality of the protein in 12 different foods, both before and after drying, was measured by de Groot (1963). The effects of the drying methods were small and in most cases insignificant. The products used were meats, egg, legumes, leafy vegetables, and sweet corn. The drying methods included hot-air drying, vacuum drying, spray drying, and freeze drying. The vegetables were sulfited and the conditions were in the range of commercial practice. A slightly larger decrease in NPU was found for green beans dried at 71°C for 0.5 hr compared to 60°C for 1.0 hr or 49°C for 20 hr when compared to the undehydrated sample. However, when the experiment was repeated, the results were not significant and the NPU difference between the experiments was 8%, approximately five times the standard error. This indicates the importance of good controls and use of the same lot of sample. For the above reasons, experiments which just report the chemical protein quality or vitamin content after a certain process do not always represent the true effect of processing.

Milk is particularly susceptible to the loss of lysine by reaction with lactose. This is especially true in whey processing (Rolls and Porter 1973). Considerable work has been done in this area because of the industrial importance of dried milk. MacDonald (1966) took samples of milk from commercial spray-drying and drum-drying installations. Spray drying resulted in losses of lysine of 0–4.1%. Drum-drying losses of lysine from five drum-drying installations ranged from 3 to 16%. The larger losses due to drum drying can be explained based on the time–temperature–moisture content relationships for the two drying methods. Drum drying creates a sheet of material in contact with the hot drum during the time when the milk is in the intermediate moisture-content range and has the greatest reaction rate. Spray drying has much faster drying rates, which indicates that the milk passes through this maximum in the reaction rate curve (Figs. 15.2 and 15.3) while still at a low temperature. What is also interesting about the work is the variability in available lysine from different production plants, although this may be due to analytical technique. Rolls and Porter (1973) report that in efficient spray drying, available lysine only decreases by 3–10% whereas with roller-dried milk the loss was 5–40%. Methionine loss in severely heated samples was about 10%. The biological value (animal tests) was higher for the spray-dried product.

If milk is to be used as the sole source of food, which would only be the case for a limited number of infants, the losses in the limiting sulfur amino acids are of greater concern than lysine loss, since lysine is at high concentration. Bickel and Mauron (1959) showed that severely roller-dried milk was satisfactory for infant feeding. However, when the dry milk was incorporated into a diet, which makes lysine limiting, as was shown by Van den Beuel et al. (1972), the NPU for rats was decreased. They fed them gluten with diets in which the available lysine of the milk was 64 and 86%. This shows the problem with man versus animal studies.

Mauron (1960) reported data on the availability of lysine for spray-dried and three grades of drum-dried milk. The tests were conducted by chemical methods and rat feeding studies with a diet supplemented with methionine, the limiting amino acid in milk. The addition of methionine makes lysine the limiting amino acid. Spray-dried powder showed negligible reduction in the availability of lysine. Commercial drum-dried milk showed a reduction of available lysine of approximately 30%. A slightly scorched sample had reductions in available lysine of approximately 75%. Tryptophan and tyrosine were not affected by any of the drying methods used. Methionine was inactivated to the extent of 20% in the most severely heat-processed drum-dried sample. The dried milk available to the consumer has been processed further by rewetting and drying, to produce an instant powder. Posati et al. (1974) reported reductions in lysine, methionine, and cystine, due to instantizing, for commercial samples of instantized dried milk in the range of 0 to 4%. Since spray drying with instantizing is the major industrial production method today, nonfat dry milk can be expected to have amino acid retentions of over 90%.

Milk and dairy products are the major products concentrated with significant protein contents. Because of the presence of reducing sugar, the major deterioration of any consequence is the reduction in lysine availability. Mauron (1960) reports that approximately 80% of the lysine is available in evaporated milk that has been retorted at 113°C for 15 min. The lysine availability of sweetened condensed milk that is not retorted is 97%. The evaporations were performed at 50°–55°C. At this low temperature the loss of lysine is minimal. Further processing, such as retorting, results in additional losses. The temperatures that can be used for evaporation cover a wide range, depending on the design of the evaporators. The process described by Wiegrand (1971) uses temperatures above those used by Mauron (1960). Nutritional data and retention times were not given by Wiegrand. It is not possible to predict the lysine availability of evaporated milk from this multi-effect installation; however, Shields (1973) reports that the work of Mitchell at the University of Illinois in the 1930s and 1940s showed no loss of biological value or vitamins during proper evaporation or commercial drying operations.

Water-Soluble Vitamins

Water-soluble vitamins are considered separately from the oil-soluble vitamins because of the difference in deteriorative mechanisms. The most unstable water-soluble vitamin is ascorbic acid. Retention of ascorbic acid is very sensitive to the presence and type of heavy metals, such as copper and iron, light, and dissolved oxygen. Because of the high sensitivity to variables which are not well controlled, the losses of ascorbic acid vary widely. In the early work reviewed in Harris and von Loesecke (1960), the losses of ascorbic acid on drying ranged from 10 to 50%. Washing, blanching, and other pretreatments covered elsewhere account for part of these losses. Although sulfite protects ascorbic acid, it reacts with and reduces the availability of thiamin. Since dried products which are sulfited are not major sources of thiamin, the overall nutritional effect is positive since sulfite prevents browning reactions and, thus, protein loss.

Considerable data have been collected on the loss of ascorbic acid in dried foods. These data can be used to explain the losses during drying. The loss of ascorbic acid is very sensitive to water activity. The reaction rate constant varies over three orders of magnitude for the whole water activity range. This relationship is shown in Fig. 15.5 for several

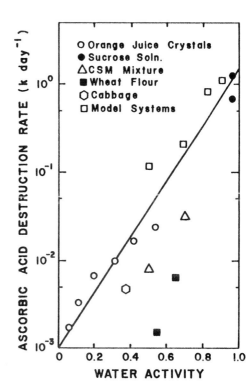

Fig. 15.5. Ascorbic acid destruction rate as a function of water activity.

works. At low water activity, ascorbic acid is relatively stable. At high water activity it is rapidly destroyed. The differences in the reaction rate constant between different foods and model systems is considerable; however, at intermediate a_w the half-life is less than 2 months even in foods. It is interesting to note that the systems that contain high soluble sugar or glycol concentrations [such as the orange juice crystals used by Karel and Nickerson (1964), the glycerol model system of Lee and Labuza (1975), and the sucrose solutions of Kyzlink and Curda (1970)] have higher destruction rate constants than cereals or cereal–soy mixes [such as used by Vojnovich and Pfeifer (1970) or the dehydrated cabbage of Gooding (1962)]. The difference may be explained by water sorption phenomena. Sorption of water with high-sugar foods is likely to contain more liquid water at lower water activities, since the BET monolayer is very low ($a_w < 0.1$). If more liquid water is present, the volume available for reaction is greater and the aqueous phase has a lower viscosity. In studies with a model system, Lee and Labuza (1975) have shown that by using the sorption hysteresis phenomena and nuclear magnetic resonance (NMR) data, the viscosity of the aqueous environment is, indeed, one of the most important factors in controlling the destruction of vitamin C. The higher the viscosity, the lower is the rate. If this is the mechanism responsible for the difference, the addition of soluble proteins or some other viscosity agent before drying high-sugar products (Mizrahi et al. 1967; Brennan et al. 1971) may have a nutritional as well as a process aid justification. The additive should, however, not be a glycol, such as glycerol, which has a high water retention.

The reaction is also very sensitive to the temperature of processing. The activation energy depends on the product and the moisture content. Data for other products have been reported by Labuza (1972). In general, the activation energy is greatest at high water activities. The activation energy may change from 10 to 30 kcal/g-mol over the water activity range although it is usually about 20 kcal/g-mol. This high sensitivity to temperature at high water activity suggests that ascorbic acid retention is very dependent on the wet-bulb temperature at the beginning of drying and the temperature of evaporation.

Fruits are major sources of ascorbic acid. The drying of fruits, which are high in sugar, is a difficult problem. The temperature of the product must be kept low. However, the losses in drying are usually a small part of the total loss occurring. Escher and Neukom (1970) showed that for apple flakes there was 8% loss of vitamin C in slicing, 62% loss in blanching, 10% loss during puree preparation and only 5% loss in drum drying. Many new drying methods have been reported for the drying of fruits and purees, but ascorbic acid retention data are not usually included, probably because, as shown, the other steps are the major problems. Low-temperature drying processes, such as the vacuum drying method of Kaufman et al. (1955), report no loss of ascorbic acid for tomato concentrates. The ultimate temperatures of 65° and 89°C were reached when the product was dried and ascorbic acid was most stable. More attention should be given to rapid blanching processes.

The evaporation of fruit juices can result in ascorbic acid losses if not performed properly. Usually, the pressed juice is deaerated and evaporated at low temperatures. Henshall (1973) reports that concentrated products after freezing have ascorbic acid retentions of 92–97%. The same range should apply to freeze-concentration processes.

Of all the B vitamins, the one most studied and probably most sensitive to temperature is thiamin, vitamin B_1. Farrer (1955) analyzed the data available up to that time. Labuza (1972) corrected the activation energies reported by Farrer. The activation energies for the destruction of thiamin are approximately 20 kcal/g-mol. Rice *et al.* (1944) report data that can be used to calculate the rate of thiamin degradation. At 63°C, the highest temperature reported, 20 hr are required for a 50% loss of thiamin in dried pork. For samples held at 49°C at moisture contents of 0, 2, 4, 6, and 9%, the losses of thiamin were 9, 40, 80, 90, and 89% respectively. These losses are on the order for losses of ascorbic acid. However, the activation energies for thiamin loss are slightly less than those for ascorbic acid loss at high moisture contents and the losses of thiamin in drying are less than the losses of ascorbic acid.

Most data in the literature report low loss levels of thiamin. Many of the reports are summarized in Table 15.3. Hein and Hutchings (1971) report average losses of thiamin after blanching for air-dried vegetables. These values range from a low of approximately 5% for snap beans, beets, corn, peas, and rutabagas to high values of 29% for carrots and 25% for potato. Thiamin losses are sensitive to the presence of sulfite, which may account for some of the high losses found.

Data for the other water-soluble vitamins are sparse. Schroeder (1971) lists losses that vary over a wide range. Vitamin B_6 losses of

Table 15.3. Thiamin Loss in Drying

Product	Conditions	Loss (%)	Reference
Freeze-dried pork	?	30	Karmas *et al.* (1962)
Freeze-dried chicken	?	5–6	Rowe *et al.* (1963)
Freeze-dried pork	−40°C	5	Thomas and Calloway (1961)
Freeze-dried chicken	1000 μHg	5	Thomas and Calloway (1961)
Freeze-dried beef		5	Thomas and Calloway (1961)
Vegetables[a]			
Beans	Air-dried	5	Harris and von Loesecke (1960)
Cabbage	?	9	Harris and von Loesecke (1960)
Corn		4	Harris and von Loesecke (1960)
Peas		3	Harris and von Loesecke (1960)
Air-dried pork	?	50–70	Calloway (1962)

[a] Does not include blanching losses.

0–30% and pantothenic acid losses of 20–30% were reported for freeze-dried fish. These losses seem somewhat high when compared to other data and are suspect. Hein and Hutchings (1971) reported loss of riboflavin, niacin, and pantothenic acid for nine vegetables; in only two cases did the losses of any of these vitamins exceed 10% when the blanched product is considered as 100%. Including blanching losses, the average losses for the three vitamins were approximately 10%. Rowe *et al.* (1963) report losses of riboflavin in freeze-dried chicken of 4–8%. In general, the losses of thiamin and other water-soluble vitamins, excluding ascorbic acid, are less than 10% in conventional drying. However, Miller *et al.* (1973) reported on vitamin losses in drum drying of bean powders (double drum 127°C for 30 sec) and found about a 20% loss for thiamin, pyridoxine, niacin, and folacin. This suggests that the other B vitamins have a stability similar to that of thiamin, at least during drying. It is interesting to note that when the beans were acid treated to pH 3.5, niacin loss was only 1%, thiamin loss increased to 35%, folacin loss to 60%, and pyridoxine remained at 20%.

Mossman *et al.* (1973) reported on the loss of thiamin during the hot-air toasting of wheat for rolled wheat flakes. Various initial moisture contents and toasting times from 10 to 40 sec were used with an air temperature of 325°C. Because of the low air humidity, the product dried as it was toasted. The results are shown in Fig. 15.6. It is obvious that less thiamin is lost at higher initial moisture contents. This is

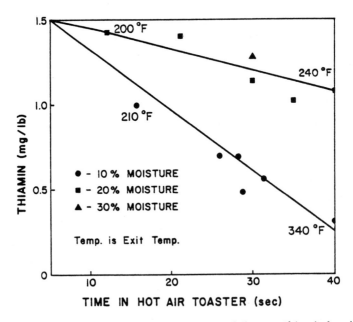

Fig. 15.6.   Effect of toasting, moisture content, and time on thiamin loss in wheat.

opposite to the effect expected from chemical kinetics because the rate of thiamin loss should increase with moisture content. However, as the moisture content of the feed increases, two changes occur that modify the prediction based on chemical kinetic considerations. First, more drying occurs at the lower wet-bulb temperature. Second, as more moisture is evaporated into the air, the air dry-bulb temperature decreases further and the product temperature during and after drying is lower. This is confirmed by the exit temperature shown in Fig. 15.6. In fact, higher moisture contents of the feed in these experiments result in a lower temperature toasting or drying operation. The lower temperatures of processing result in better thiamin retentions. The same concepts and reasoning apply to protein quality losses during toasting. However, the changes in quality as measured biologically are nonlinear with respect to chemical changes. This accounts for the fact that only the sample toasted at the most detrimental conditions, 40 sec and 10% initial moisture content, showed a significant drop in PER from 1.25 for the original to 0.88 for the toasted product.

Loss of water-soluble vitamins during concentration processes has not received much attention. Most of the B vitamins in milk are not affected by evaporation (Harris and von Loesecke 1960). Thiamin is the single exception, and these losses range from 14 to 27%. Glover (1971) reports the losses of ascorbic acid, pantothenic acid, nicotinic acid, riboflavin, biotin, B_{12}, B_6, thiamin, and folic acid after the ultrafiltration and reverse-osmosis processing of skim milk, whole milk, and whey. Ultrafiltration was performed with a membrane with a nominal-molecular-weight cutoff of 12,000. Ascorbic acid retention was only 13%, probably due to oxidation. Folic acid and B_{12}, which are associated with proteins, were retained 100%. Oil-soluble vitamins in whole milk were not measured, but losses would be small. All other vitamins were lost to a significant extent. The losses appear to vary with the amount of concentration. The average of all vitamins lost, excluding ascorbic acid, are shown in Table 15.4. The results indicate that the low-molecular-weight vitamins pass through the membrane in proportion

Table 15.4. Retention of Vitamins in Ultrafiltration

Product	Solution retained (%)	Average water-soluble vitamins retained[a] (%)
Whole milk	50	63
Skim milk	64	77
Whey	34	39

[a] Pantothenic acid, nicotinic acid, riboflavin, biotin, thiamin, and B_6 (Glover 1971).

to the amount of water recorded. Reverse osmosis, which is performed at moderate temperatures, appears to be a good process for vitamin retention.

Fat-Soluble Vitamins

The fat-soluble vitamins have been separated from the water-soluble vitamins because of a difference between the deteriorative mechanisms. The fat-soluble vitamins would be expected to degrade by a free-radical oxidation mechanism. The free-radical oxidation of lipids has been reviewed by Labuza (1971). The reaction is characterized by a low activation energy (10–15 kcal/mol) and a long induction time.

Della Monica and McDowell (1965) dried carrots by the procedures shown in Table 15.5. They measured total β-carotene and the trans-isomer, which is the form with 100% provitamin A activity. The losses of total β-carotene are higher than would be expected if the loss rate was due solely to a free-radical oxidation mechanism. Thus, some direct thermal reaction must be taking place, as evidenced by the loss in freeze drying. Sweeney and Marsh (1971) report a loss of 13% for freeze-dried carrots. Foda et al. (1970) report losses of β-carotene of approximately 4% for freeze-dried orange juice of various concentrations.

Reports of other oil-soluble vitamin retentions are limited to milk. There is little or no loss of vitamin A or D during the spray drying, drum drying, or evaporation of milk (Hartman and Dryden 1965; Harris and von Loesecke 1960).

There are also no reports in the literature of vitamin E loss during drying. Considering that it is also involved in the lipid oxidation scheme it would be expected to be low. In oilseed processing, for example, where very high temperatures are used, it is assumed that only 5% of the vitamin is lost.

Table 15.5. Retention of Carotene in Drying Carrots to 3% H_2O

Drying process	Temperature, time, conditions	Average retention (%)	
		Total β-carotene	trans-β-carotene
Tray air drying[a]	93°C, 2 hr 66°C, 6 hr	74	60
Explosion puff[a]	93°C, 2 hr in tray; exploded at 1800 mm Hg; finished at 66°C; total time 5.5 hr.	81	60
Freeze dried[a]	71°C, 1 mm Hg, 4–5 hr	85	80
Freeze dried[b]	?	90	80

[a] Della Monica and McDowell (1965).
[b] Sweeney and Marsh (1971).

CONCLUSION

Drying processes appear to offer good nutrient retentions with the exceptions of ascorbic acid and β-carotene losses. Of the concentration procedures, ultrafiltration shows the highest losses. Protein, quality deteriorations due to drying or evaporation are minimal in products currently in production (Mauron 1960; de Groot 1963). The losses of water-soluble vitamins other than ascorbic acid during drying average approximately 5% (Hein and Hutchings 1971). Oil-soluble vitamins in milk are not lost in either drying or evaporation (Hartman and Dryden 1965; Harris and von Loesecke 1960). Losses of β-carotene in dried carrots are significant (Della Monica and McDowell 1965), but small in freeze-dried orange juice (Foda *et al.* 1970). Ultrafiltration results in highly significant losses of most water-soluble vitamins (Glover 1971). Ascorbic acid losses are high in drying, but concentration offers minimal losses (Henshall 1973). No experimental reports of nutrient retentions after freeze concentration could be found but this process should offer excellent nutrition retention.

The real problem with the current literature is that little work has been done on the kinetics of nutrient losses at constant temperatures and humidities. With this knowledge and the time–temperature–moisture content distribution in the product during drying, process optimization procedures could be calculated where necessary.

REFERENCES

Aitken, A., Jason, A. C., Dilley, J., and Payne, P. R. 1967. Effects of drying, salting and high temperatures on the nutritive value of dried cod. Fish News Int. Sept., 42–43.

Anonymous 1973. Superior, natural fruit ingredient produced by new drying process. Food Prod. Dev. 7, 40.

Armerding, G. D. 1966. Evaporation methods as applied to the food industry. Adv. Food Res. 15, 303–358.

Bender, A. E. 1966. Nutritional effects of food processing. J. Food Technol. 1, 261–289.

Bender, A. E. 1972. Processing damage to protein food: A review. J. Food Technol. 7, 239–250.

Bickel, H., and Mauron, J. 1959. Investigation of the lysine requirements of young infants: Feeding studies with a milk product of low lysine content. Ann. Pediat. 193, 55.

Bomben, J. L., Bruin, S., and Thijssen, H. A. C. 1973. Aroma recovery and retention in concentration and drying of foods. Adv. Food Res. 20, 1–111.

Bone, D. 1969. Water activity: Its chemistry and applications. Food Prod. Dev. 3, 81, 84–85, 88, 90, 92, 94.

Brennan, J. G., and Priestly, R. J. 1972. Foam-spray drying using a centrifugal atomizer. Proc. Biochem. 7(3), 25–26.

Brennan, J. G., Butters, J. R., Cowell, N. D., and Lilly, A. E. V. 1969. Food Engineering Operations. Elsevier, Amsterdam.

Brennan, J. G., Herrera, J., and Jowitt, R. 1971. A study of some of the factors affecting the spray drying of concentrated orange juice, on a laboratory scale. J. Food Technol. 6, 295–307.

Brunauer, S., Emmett, H. P., and Tetler, E. 1938. Adsorption of gases in multimolecular layers. J. Am. Chem. Soc. 60, 309.

Calloway, D. H. 1962. Dehydrated foods. Nutr. Rev. 20, 257–260.

Carlson, R. A., Randall, J. M., Graham, R. P., and Morgan, A. I. 1967. The rotary steam-coil vacuum evaporator. Food Technol. 21, 194–196.

Charm, S. E. 1971. Fundamentals of Food Engineering, 2nd Edition. AVI Publishing Co., Westport, CT.

de Groot, A. P. 1963. The influence of dehydration of foods on digestibility and the biological value of protein. Food Technol. 17, 339–343.

Della Monica, E. S., and McDowell, P. E. 1965. Comparison of β-carotene content of dried carrots prepared by three dehydration processes. Food Technol. 19, 141–143.

Duckworth, R. B. 1962. Diffusion of solutes in dehydrated vegetables. In Recent Advances in Food Science, Vol. 2. J. Hawthorn and J. M. Leitch (Editors). Butterworths, London.

Eichner, K., and Karel, M. 1972. The influence of water content and water activity on the sugar-amino browning reaction in model systems under various conditions. J. Agric. Food Chem. 20, 218–223.

Escher, F., and Neukom, H. 1970. Studies on drum-drying apple flakes. (German). Trav. Chim. Aliment. Hyg. 61, 339–348.

Escher, F., and Neukom, H. 1971. Non-enzymatic browning and the optimization of the drying conditions for the drum drying of apple sauce. Lebensm. Wiss. Technol. 4, 145–151.

Farkas, D. F., and Lazar, M. E. 1969. Osmotic dehydration of apple pieces: Effect of temperature and syrup concentration on rates. Food Technol. 23, 688–690.

Farrer, K. T. H. 1955. The thermal destruction of vitamin B_1 in foods. Adv. Food Res. 6, 257–311.

Finch, R. 1970. Fish protein for human foods. CRC Crit. Rev. Food Technol. 1, 519–580.

Foda, Y. H., Hamed, M. G., and Abd-Allah, M. A. 1970. Preservation of orange juice and guava juices by freeze drying. Food Technol. 24, 74–80.

Glover, F. A. 1971. Concentration of milk by ultrafiltration and reverse osmosis. J. Dairy Res. 38, 373–379.

Gooding, E. G. B. 1962. The storage behavior of dehydrated foods. In Recent Advances in Food Science, Vol. 2. J. Hawthorn and J. M. Leitch (Editors). Butterworths, London.

Greig, N. 1971. Economics of Food Processing. AVI Publishing Co., Westport, CT.

Hackler, L. R. et al. 1965. Effect of heat treatment on nutritive value of soymilk protein fed to weanling rats. J. Food Sci. 30, 723–728.

Harris, R. S., and von Loesecke, H. 1960. Nutritional Evaluation of Food Processing. John Wiley, New York. Reprinted in 1971 by AVI Publishing Co., Westport CT.

Hartman, A. M., and Dryden, L. P. 1965. Vitamins in milk and milk products. ADSA, USDA, Washington, DC.

Hein, R. E., and Hutchings, I. J. 1971. Influence of processing on vitamin–mineral content and biological availability in processed foods. Symp. Vitamins, Minerals, Processed Foods, Am. Med. Assoc. Council Foods Nutr. Food Ind. Liaison Comm, New Orleans.

Hendel, C. E., Silveira, V., and Harrington, W. O. 1955. Rates of non-enzymatic browning of white potato during dehydration. Food Technol. 9, 433–438.

Henshall, J. D. 1973. Fruit and vegetable products. Proc. Nutr. Soc. 32, 17–22.

Hertzendorf, M. S., and Moshy, H. J. 1970. Foam drying in the food industry. CRC Crit. Rev. Food Technol. *1*, 25–70.

Hieu, T. C. and Schwartzberg, H. G. 1973. Dehydration of shrimp by distillation. AIChE Symp. Ser. *69*(132), 70–80.

Holdsworth, S. D. 1971. Dehydration of food products. J. Food Technol. *6*, 331–370.

Karel, M. 1973. Recent research and development in the field of low moisture and intermediate moisture foods. CRC Crit. Rev. Food Technol. *4*, 329–373.

Karel, M., and Nickerson, J. T. R. 1964. Effect of relative humidity, air, and vacuum on browning of dehydrated orange juice. Food Technol. *18*, 1214–1218.

Karmas, E., Thompson, J. E., and Peryam, D. B. 1962. Thiamin retention in freeze-dehydrated irradiated pork. Food Technol. *16*, 107–108.

Kaufman, V. F., Wong, F., Taylor, D. H., and Talburt, W. F. 1955. Problems in production of tomato juice powder in vacuum. Food Technol. *9*, 120–123.

King, C. J. 1970. Recent developments in food dehydration technology. Proc. Third Int. Cong. Food Sci. Technol., pp. 565–574.

King, C. J. 1971. Freeze-drying of Foods. CRC Press, Cleveland.

Kluge, G., and Heiss, R. 1967. Studies to improve the quality of dried foods during various conditions of freeze-drying. (German). Verfahrenstechnik. (Mainz) *1*, 251–258.

Kyzlink, V., and Curda, D. 1970. Influence of sucrose concentration and oxygen access on the course of L-ascorbic acid oxidation in liquid medium. Z. Lebensm Untersuch. Forsch. *143*, 263–273.

Labuza, T. P. 1968. Sorption phenomena in foods. Food Technol. *22*, 263–265, 268, 270, 272.

Labuza, T. P. 1970. Properties of water as related to the keeping quality of foods. Proc. Third Int. Cong. Food Sci. Technol., pp. 618–635.

Labuza, T. P. 1971. Kinetics of lipid oxidation in foods. CRC Crit. Rev. Food Technol. *2*, 355–405.

Labuza, T. P. 1972. Nutrient losses during drying and storage of dehydrated foods. CRC Crit. Rev. Food Technol. *3*, 217–240.

Lee, S. H., and Labuza, T. P. 1975. Destruction of ascorbic acid as a function of water activity. J. Food Sci. *40*, 370–373.

Leightell, B. 1972. Reverse osmosis in the concentration of food. Proc. Biochem. *7*, 40–42.

Livingston, A. L., Allis, M. E., and Kobler, G. O. 1971. Amino acid stability during alfalfa dehydration. J. Agric. Food Chem. *19*, 947–950.

Loncin, M., Bimbenet, J. J., and Lenges, J. 1968. Influence of the activity of water on spoilage of foodstuffs. J. Food Technol. *3*, 131–142.

MacDonald, F. J. 1966. Available lysine content of dried milk. Nature (London) *209*, 1134.

Masters, K. 1972. Spray Drying. CRC Press, Cleveland.

Mauron, J. 1960. The concept of amino acid availability and its bearing on protein evaluation. Int. Conf. Protein Needs, Washington, DC., Aug. 21–22.

Meade, R. E, 1973. Combination process dries crystallizable materials. Food Technol. *27*, 18, 20, 24–26.

Miller, C. F., Guadagni, D., and Kow, S. 1973. Vitamin retention in bean powders: Cooked, canned and instant. J. Food Sci. *38*, 493–495.

Mizrahi, S., Berk, Z., and Cogan, U. 1967. Isolated soybean protein as a banana spray drying aid. Cereal Sci. Today *12*, 322, 324–325.

Mizrahi, S., Labuza, T. P., and Karel, M. 1970A. Computer-aided predictions of extent of browning in dehydrated cabbage. J. Food Sci. *35*, 799–803.

Mizrahi, S., Labuza, T. P., and Karel, M. 1970B. Feasibility of accelerated tests for browning in dehydrated cabbage. J. Food Sci. *35*, 804–807.

Moore, J. G., and Hesler, W. E. 1963. Evaporation of heat sensitive materials. Chem. Eng. Progr. *59*, 87–92.

Mossman, A. P., Rockwell, W. C., and Fellers, D. A. 1973. Hot air toasting and rolling whole wheat. J. Food Sci. *38*, 879–884.

Myklestad, O., Bjornstad, J., and Njaa, L. 1972. Effects of heat treatment on composition and nutritive value of herring meal. Fiskerdinetoratets Skrifter Ser. Technol. Undersok. *5*, No. 10, 1–15.

Perry, R. H., Chilton, C. H., and Kirkpatrick, S. D. (Editors) 1964. Chemical Engineer's Handbook. McGraw-Hill Book Co., New York.

Porter, M. C., and Michaels, A. S. 1970. Applications of membrane ultrafiltration. Proc. Third Int. Cong. Food Sci. Technol., pp. 462–473.

Posati, L. P., Holsinger, V. H., DeVilbiss, E. D., and Pallansch, M. J. 1974. Effect of instantizing an amino acid content of non-fat dry milk. J. Dairy Sci. *57*, 258–260.

Quast, D. G., and Karel, M. 1972. Computer simulation of storage life of foods undergoing spoilage by two interacting mechanisms. J. Food Sci. *37*, 679–683.

Rice, E. E. *et al.* 1944. Preliminary studies on stabilization of thiamin in dehydrated foods. Food Res. *9*, 491–499.

Rockland, L. B. 1969. Water activity and storage stability. Food Technol. *23*, 1241–1246, 1248, 1251.

Rolls, B. A., and Porter, J. G. 1973. Some effects of processing and storage of milk and milk products. Proc. Nutr. Soc. *32*, 9–15.

Rowe, D. M., Mountrey, G. J., and Prudent, I. 1963. Effect of freeze-drying on the thiamin, riboflavin and niacin content of chicken muscle. Food Technol. *17*, 1449–1450.

Saravacos, G. D. 1970. Effect of temperature on viscosity of fruit juices and purees. J. Food Sci. *35*, 122–125.

Schroeder, H. A. 1971. Losses of vitamins and trace minerals resulting from processing and preservation of foods. Am. J. Clin. Nutr. *24*, 562–572.

Shields, J. B. 1973. Personal communication. American Potato Co., Blackfoot, ID.

Sweeney, J. P., and Marsh, A. C. 1971. Effect of processing on provitamin A in vegetables. J. Am Diet. Assoc. *59*, 238–243.

Taira, H., Taira, H., and Sukarai, Y. 1966. Studies on amino acid contents of processed soybeans. 8. Effect of beating on total lysine and available lysine in defatted soybean flour. Jpn. J. Nutr. Food, *18*, 359–362.

Thijssen, H. A. C. 1970. Freeze concentration of food liquids. Proc. Third Int. Cong. Food Sci. Technol., pp. 491–498.

Thijssen, H. A. C. 1971. Flavour retention in drying preconcentrated food liquids. J. Appl. Chem. Biotechnol. *21*, 372–377.

Thomas, M., and Calloway, D. 1961. Nutritional value of dehydrated food. J. Am. Diet Assoc. *39*, 105–116.

Van Arsdel, W. B. 1963. Food Dehydration, Vol. 1. Principles. AVI Publishing Co., Westport, CT.

Van Arsdel, W. B., and Copley, M. J. 1964. Food Dehydration. Vol. 2. Products and Technology. AVI Publishing Co., Westport, CT.

van den Beuel, A., Jamnskens, P., and Mol, J. 1972. Availability of lysine in skim milk powders processed under various conditions. Neth. Milk Dairy J. *26*, 19.

Vojnovich, C., and Pfeifer, V. F. 1970. Stability of ascorbic acid in blends with wheat flour, CSM and infant cereals. Cereal Sci. Today *15*, 317–322.

Watt, B. K., and Merrill, A. L. 1963. Composition of Foods. Agriculture Handbook *8*, USDA, Washington, DC.

Wiegrand, J. 1971. Falling-film evaporators and their applications in the food industry. J. Appl. Chem. Biotechnol. *21*, 351–358.

Williams-Gardner, A. 1971. Industrial Drying. Leonard Hill, London.

Woodham, J. A. 1973. The effects of processing on the nutritive value of vegetable-protein concentrates. Proc. Nutr. Soc. *32*, 23–29.

Zimmerman, O. T., and Lavine, I. 1964. Psychrometric Tables and Charts. Industrial Research Service, Dover, NH.

Effects of Fermentation on the Nutritional Properties of Food[1]

Roger F. McFeeters

Fermented foods, such as breads, cheeses, various soybean products, cassava, vegetables, and sausages, have made important contributions to human diets for thousands of years and continue to do so. Certainly the most significant role of fermentation in human nutrition has been to help make the nutrients naturally present in the starting food materials more palatable and more widely available than would be possible without fermentation. Thus, even if fermentations had no direct effect upon the nutrient content and quality of foods, these processes would be very important to the food supply. However, it is clear that fermentation processes can have significant direct effects on the nutritive qualities of foods. It is the purpose of this chapter to review these direct nutritional consequences of fermentation and to consider some of the uncertainties and limitations of current data.

CHARACTERIZATION OF NUTRIENT CHANGES IN FERMENTED FOODS

Food fermentations are very complex processes because they normally involve the interaction of plant or animal tissues with a group of microorganisms. This means that changes depend upon the available nutrients and nutrient precursors in the starting materials, the metabolic capabilities of the starting materials, the metabolic abilities of

[1] Paper 9729 of the Journal Series of the North Carolina Agricultural Research Service, Raleigh, NC 27695–7601. Mention of a trademark or proprietary product does not constitute a guarantee or warranty of the product by the U.S. Department of Agriculture or North Carolina Agricultural Research Service, nor does it imply approval to the exclusion of other products that may be suitable.

the fermentative microorganisms, and possible interactions among all of these elements. To complicate matters further, many fermentations occur in solid or semisolid states so that particle sizes, diffusion rates of oxygen and nutrients, and distribution of fermentative organisms may be important factors in both the organoleptic quality and nutrient content of the product. Considering these complexities and the many types of food fermentations that are employed around the world, it is not surprising that our understanding of nutrient changes in most fermented foods is very incomplete. Particularly notable is the fact that examples are lacking in which the biochemical mechanisms underlying nutrient changes in fermented foods are understood well enough to allow control of final nutrient concentrations.

Since many groups of microorganisms participate in food fermentations, there should be opportunities to use advances in genetic modification and biochemical engineering techniques to increase critical nutrients in fermented foods. One example might be the increased production of a limiting amino acid, such as lysine, by fermentative organisms (Sands and Hankin 1974, 1976; Haidaris and Bhattacharjee 1978). However, the mechanisms by which nutrients are formed or degraded during food fermentations must be better defined before we can expect to produce consistent, useful changes in fermented foods.

Table 16.1 is a list of important questions that can be asked about almost any nutrient change in any food fermentation. With limited and scattered research efforts to characterize nutrient changes in fermented foods, undoubtedly it will be a number of years before all of the questions can be answered for any particular fermentation. Considering the variety and complexity of fermentation processes, it is not reasonable to expect research workers to address all of these questions, except in cases that are judged to be of special importance.

EFFECT OF FERMENTATION ON THE ENERGY CONTENT OF FOOD

Data have not been published on changes in the caloric content of food as a result of fermentation processes. Generally only small changes would be expected. In processes such as tempeh production, which are aerobic, the fermentation period is too short to allow large decreases in the total lipids, carbohydrate, or protein components of the food. During alcoholic or lactic acid fermentations, a large proportion of the sugars are metabolized. However, the energy produced by fermentation of sugars to either ethanol or lactic acid is only 2 mol ATP/mol hexose. This compares with the potential production of 38 mol ATP/mol of hexose when the sugar is completely oxidized. Therefore, approximately 95% of the energy available in the sugars remains after the fermentation.

Table 16.1. Questions for Characterization of Nutrient Changes in Fermented Foods

1. What are the most important nutrients in the fermented food?
2. What is the initial concentration and variability of a nutrient in the starting materials used in a fermentation?
3. What is the final concentration of a nutrient at the end of a defined process that results in a fermented product with acceptable chemical and organoleptic characteristics?
4. What is the final concentration of a nutrient after storage of a fermented product under a defined set of conditions of time, temperature, pH, humidity, microbiological flora, etc.?
5. If an increase in a nutrient occurs during a fermentation, is the increase a result of:
   (a) moisture loss or other physical concentration effects during processing?
   (b) synthesis of the nutrient by a fermentative microorganism?
   (c) synthesis of the nutrient by the material which is undergoing fermentation?
   (d) release of the nutrient from some bound, unavailable condition?
6. Which microorganism is responsible for synthesis of a nutrient?
7. What are the precursors used for the synthesis of a nutrient during fermentation?
8. What is the pathway used for synthesis of a nutrient during fermentation?
9. If a nutrient declines during fermentation, is the decrease a result of:
   (a) removal of a nutrient due to washing, draining, or addition of water to the fermentation?
   (b) degradation due to enzymes in the material being fermented?
   (c) exposure of the nutrient to oxygen or light?
   (d) change in pH, which results in decreased stability of the nutrient?
   (e) metabolism of the nutrient by a microorganism in the fermentation?
   (f) binding of the nutrient into a nonavailable form?
   (g) uptake of the nutrient by microbial cells, which are removed after fermentation?
10. Which microorganism is responsible for degradation of a nutrient?
11. What is the pathway of nutrient degradation?
12. If a nutrient does not change during fermentation, is this a result of:
    (a) stabilization of the nutrient due to a favorable pH change, exclusion of oxygen, exclusion of light, or another environmental factor?
    (b) a balance between synthesis and degradation of the nutrient?
    (c) a lack of any enzymatic or nonenzymatic mechanisms to cause a change?

Zimmer (1980) has estimated that the unavoidable energy loss due to microbial fermentation of silage is only 2–4%.

Fermentation processes will not be discussed in detail in this chapter. Descriptions for most of the fermentations considered in this review can be found in the literature references and in several recent books (Pederson 1979; Rose 1982; Steinkraus 1983). Unless otherwise indicated in the text, changes in nutrient content are stated relative to the nonfermented ingredients which were used in the experiments.

LACTIC ACID ISOMERS IN FOOD FERMENTATIONS

Lactic acid is the major product formed from sugars in vegetable, dairy and meat fermentations. Lactic acid bacteria produce two stereoisomers of lactic acid (Stetter and Kandler 1973), which have been designated D(-) and L(+). Since animals, including human beings, normally produce only the L(+) isomer of lactic acid when muscles are in oxygen deficit, the question of the fate of the D(-) isomer, when it is consumed, has been investigated.

Cori and Cori (1929) were the first to observe that the D(-) form of lactic acid is metabolized more slowly than the L(+) isomer. This basic observation has been confirmed in rabbits (Drury and Wick 1965), ducks (Brin 1964), cattle (Dunlop *et al.* 1964; Giesecke and Stangassinger 1980), and sheep (Giesecke and Stangassinger 1980). Even though the D(-) isomer is not produced in muscle tissue, it has been found that animals, whether ruminant or monogastric, normally absorb this isomer because it is formed by bacteria in the rumen or intestinal tract (Giesecke *et al.* 1980; Giesecke and Stangassinger 1980). Recent research has emphasized that mammals have normal mechanisms to metabolize the D(-) isomer. Giesecke *et al.* (1981) found that both the rabbit and the rat excreted only about 6% of an injected sample of the D(-) isomer, even though these animals metabolize the isomer differently. Thus, present data indicate that the energy yield from lactic acid will be similar regardless of the isomer consumed.

The differences between the rates of metabolism of lactic acid isomers and indications that infants have difficulty metabolizing DL-lactic acid (Droese and Stolley 1962, 1965) resulted in a recommendation by the Food and Agriculture Organization/World Health Organization Expert Committee on Food Additives that infants not be given foods containing D(-) lactic acid and that adults limit their intake of the D(-) isomer to not more than 100 mg/kg/day (World Health Organization 1966). Subsequently, the recommendation regarding limits on adult intake was dropped (World Health Organization 1974).

There are only limited data on the distribution of lactic acid isomers in foods. Kunath and Kandler (1980) found a mixture of isomers in both commercial and laboratory prepared yogurts. The proportions of the isomers varied with the fermentation and storage temperatures and the lactic acid bacteria present. Though an excess of L(+)-lactic acid was common, it usually did not exceed 70% of the total lactic acid. Alm (1982B) found 42% D(-)-lactic acid in yogurt which contained 1.2% total lactic acid. The D(-) isomer was not found in kefir, ropy milk fermented with *Streptococcus lactis* var. *longi* and *Leuconostoc cremoris*, low-fat acidophilus milk, and bifidus milk. Lactic acid isomers have not been analyzed in fermented cucumbers or sauerkraut. However, *Lactobacillus plantarum*, *Pediococcus pentosaceus*, and

Lactobacillus brevis are known to produce DL-lactic acid and *Leuconostoc mesenteroides* D(−)-lactic acid (Garvie 1967; Stetter and Kandler 1973), so it would be expected that fermented vegetables would contain both isomers.

EFFECTS OF FERMENTATION ON PROTEIN CONTENT, QUALITY, AND AVAILABILITY

Many fermentations are done on foods such as cereals, legumes, dairy products, and meats, which are important protein sources. Changes in the nutritive value of proteins as a result of fermentation are particularly important for cereals and legumes. These sources of protein often are of lower nutritional quality than animal products, and they tend to be major dietary sources of protein for people with marginal or submarginal protein intake. Therefore, fermentation processes that consistently improve protein quality or availability of cereals or legumes could have a positive impact on the diets of many people. Conversely, any fermentation that resulted in unnecessary loss of protein content or quality could have a particularly negative impact.

Protein Content

The primary objectives for most fermentations of high-protein foods are to modify the flavor or texture characteristics of the starting-food ingredients. These changes generally are produced by fermentations that are limited both in the time and extent to which microorganisms are allowed to grow. Therefore, large changes in total protein content would not normally be expected. Available data tend to support this expectation. Fermentations have not been found to significantly affect the protein content of idli (Reddy *et al.* 1981; van Veen *et al.* 1967; Rajalakshmi and Vanaja 1967) or khaman (Rajalakshmi and Vanaja 1967). Small increases in protein were found after fermentation in the production of tempeh (Murata *et al.* 1967; Wang *et al.* 1968). Wang *et al.* (1968) attributed the increase in protein to the loss of other components during fermentation. Alm (1982C) observed an increase in protein content during the fermentation of several types of fermented milk, while Rao *et al.* (1982) found small, but statistically significant decreases. In both instances, the changes were attributed to the loss of volatile components from the samples. One exception to the general result that fermentations will not cause large changes in the amount of protein is the growth of *Candida tropicalis* on cassava flour to produce yeast biomass (Azoulay *et al.* 1980). The protein content of the flour increased from 3.1 to 18% as a result of the fermentation.

Table **16.2.**   Changes in PER of Proteins as a Result of Food Fermentations

Product	PER		ΔPER	Reference
	Before	After		
Chickpea tempeh	1.95	2.11	0.16	Kao and Robinson (1978)
Horsebean tempeh	0.89	1.51	0.62	Kao and Robinson (1978)
Horsebean tempeh + met + try	2.22	2.60	0.32	Kao and Robinson (1978)
Soybean tempeh	1.77	2.03	0.26	Kao and Robinson (1978)
Oncom	1.51	1.41	−0.10	Fardiaz and Markakis (1981B)
Idli				
4:1 black gram/rice	2.28	2.55	0.27	Rao (1961)
1:1 black gram/rice	1.99	1.84	−0.15	van Veen et al. (1967)
1:2 black gram/rice	1.50	2.00	0.50	Rajalakshmi and Vanaja (1967)
Wheat tempeh	1.28	1.71	0.43	Wang et al. (1968)
Soybean tempeh	2.17	2.27	0.10	Wang et al. (1968)
1:1 Wheat/soybean tempeh	2.49	2.79	0.30	Wang et al. (1968)
Wheat tempeh				
0 hr	1.25	—	—	Wang et al. (1968)
12 hr	—	1.28	0.03	Wang et al. (1968)
24 hr	—	1.78	0.50	Wang et al. (1968)
48 hr	—	1.84	0.56	Wang et al. (1968)
72 hr	—	1.73	0.45	Wang et al. (1968)
Soybean tempeh				
0 hr	2.63	—	—	Hackler et al. (1964)
12 hr	2.47	—	−0.16	Hackler et al. (1964)
24 hr	2.56	—	−0.07	Hackler et al. (1964)
36 hr	2.49	—	−0.14	Hackler et al. (1964)
72 hr	2.44	—	−0.19	Hackler et al. (1964)
Ontjom	2.17	2.17	0.00	van Veen and Steinkraus, (1970)
Ecuadorian rice	1.90	1.63	−0.27	van Veen and Steinkraus, (1970)
Fish paste	3.12	2.96	−0.16	van Veen and Steinkraus, (1970)
Dry sausage	3.24	3.92	0.68	Eskeland and Nordal (1980)

Nutritional Quality of Proteins in Fermented Foods

Even though changes in the quantity of protein as a result of food fermentation appear to be small or nonexistent, considerable effort has been made to investigate changes in the nutritional quality of the protein. Table 16.2 is a compilation of reported changes in the protein efficiency ratio (PER) of various foods as a result of fermentation. The results of these studies suggest that protein quality can be improved by fermentation in some instances. A number of studies showed no significant change in protein quality. None of the PER evaluations showed a significant decline in protein quality as a result of fermentation. The data in Table 16.2 may be somewhat complicated by the fact that during fermentation other nutrients may change so that variations in growth response of rats may not be exclusively a result of changes in amino acids or proteins (Kao and Robinson 1978).

Evaluations of protein quality changes also have been made by techniques other than PER measurements. Hargrove and Alford (1978) found that the growth rate and feed efficiency of yogurt prepared with *Lactobacillus bulgaricus* and *Saccharomyces thermophilus* were improved, compared to nonfermented milk, when fed to rats. There was no improvement when other fermented milks were tested, including cultured buttermilk, acidophilus milk, kefir, and Bulgarian buttermilk. The effect of natural fermentations on the protein quality of corn, chickpea, and cowpea flours has been investigated by Fields and co-workers (Hamad and Fields 1979; Zamora and Fields 1979), using the growth response of *Tetrahymena pyriformis* relative to casein. They found significant increases in nutritive value as a result of fermenting each type of flour.

The results of protein quality studies suggest that fermentations can improve protein quality, but also that there is no improvement in many instances. Therefore, if fermentation is to be used for this purpose, the ingredients, conditions, and fermentative organisms that can give improvement need to be defined for each case.

Amount and Availability of Limiting Amino Acids

The nutritive value of proteins will depend primarily upon the amount and availability of the limiting essential amino acid in a food. There is the possibility that during fermentation the total amount of any particular amino acid may increase or decrease or that the availability may change significantly. For most foods, including those that are fermented, the limiting amino acids are lysine or the sulfur amino acids.

In an investigation of several types of fermented milks, Rao *et al.* (1982) found that both lysine and the sulfur amino acids tended to decline as a result of fermentation. Lysine decreased by nearly 40% when skim milk was fermented by *Lactobacillus acidophilus.* Buttermilk was the only product to show an increase in lysine during fermentation. The largest methionine loss, 30%, occurred when whole milk was fermented by *L. acidophilus.* Several studies of tempeh fermentations generally showed little change in either lysine or methionine (Wang *et al.* 1968; Stillings and Hackler 1965; Kao and Robinson 1978; Murata *et al.* 1967). Lactic acid fermentation of dry sausages also showed no change in these amino acids.

An instance in which fermentation increased the level of the most limiting amino acid was a 60% increase in methionine during the preparation of idli from black gram (Padhye and Salunkhe 1978).

Table 16.3. Modified Essential Amino Acid (MEAA) Indexes and Percentage Digestible Crude Protein of Single-Cell Protein (SCP) from Certain Lactobacilli

SCP Source	MEAA index	Digestible crude protein (%)
Casein	91	98.5 ± 0.2
L. acidophilus 3532	73	79.3 ± 0.5
L. acidophilus 3205	86	83.7 ± 0.5
L. bulgaricus 2217	76	89.2 ± 0.1
L. bulgaricus 3533	69	81.3 ± 0.4
L. casei 14435	80	82.3 ± 0.2
L. delbrueckii B-443	80	82.5 ± 0.2
L. fermenti 3954	85	86.5 ± 0.5
L. fermenti 3957	69	81.6 ± 0.5
L. plantarum 14431	59	79.9 ± 0.8
L. plantarum 8014	62	80.6 ± 0.3
L. thermophilus 3863	69	88.0 ± 0.3

Source: Erdman *et al.* (1977).

However, van Veen *et al.* (1967) did not find any change in methionine when idli was fermented to give optimum product quality. Padhye and Salunkhe (1978) attributed the differences between the results of the two studies to variations in preparation techniques and different microflora in a natural fermentation. This points up the need to control the organisms and conditions of fermentation if a positive nutritional effect is to be consistently attained.

There are limited data on the amino acid profiles and content of the organisms that carry out fermentations. Stillings and Hackler (1965) reported that a strain of *Rhizopus oligosporus* was low in most essential amino acids. *Saccharomyces cerevisiae* has an excellent amino acid profile with the exception of a low methionine content (Kihlberg 1972). Erdman *et al.* (1977) found that lactobacilli have good amino acid profiles and good digestibilities (Table 16.3). They are relatively high in lysine and low in methionine, though the methionine content is generally higher than *S. cerevisiae* cells, soy protein, or wheat flour. There were quite large differences in amino acids, both among species and among strains within a single species, indicating a potential for selecting favorable organisms from the standpoint of amino acid profile. Unfortunately, the strains of *L. plantarum* evaluated had both the lowest essential amino acid index and lowest digestibility. This species dominates the later stages of most natural lactic acid fermentations (Pederson 1979).

Information is needed on the amount of protein that is provided by microbial cells in food fermentations and the quality of protein in other organisms to determine whether there may be opportunities to improve overall protein quality of fermented foods with the proteins from the cells of the fermentation microorganisms.

In addition to the amino acid content, the nutritional quality of a food may be improved if, in the process of fermentation, the amino acids become more available. This can occur as a result of proteolytic activity by the fermentation microorganisms. Molds used in food fermentations have active proteolytic enzymes (Ko 1982). Most lactic acid bacteria used in dairy fermentations have limited proteolytic activity, though the species that participate in other lactic acid fermentations appear to have almost no proteolytic activity (Law and Kolstad 1983).

Increases in soluble amino acids during fermentation have been observed in milk products (Alm 1982A; Rao *et al.* 1982), peanuts (Cherry and Beuchat 1976), tempeh (Murata *et al.* 1967; Robinson and Kao 1977), and natural fermentations of corn (Tongnual *et al.* 1982), chickpeas, and cowpeas (Zamora and Fields 1979). Whether increases in free amino acids contribute to the improvement of protein quality remains to be clarified.

EFFECTS OF FERMENTATION ON CHANGES IN VITAMINS

As indicated from the questions in Table 16.1, fermentations may result in changes in vitamin content by several mechanisms, including (1) synthesis of vitamins by the fermentation organisms, (2) loss of vitamins by metabolism of the fermentation organism or the food which undergoes fermentation, (3) loss of vitamins by chemical reactions not directly related to fermentation, (4) increase or decrease in the stability of vitamins as a result of pH changes, and (5) soaking or cooking losses associated with preparation of a product before or after fermentation. We will review the limited information available for the vitamins that have been investigated in fermented foods. Shahani and Chandan (1979) have previously reviewed vitamin changes in cultured dairy products. Smith and Palumbo (1981) have reviewed vitamin changes in a variety of fermented foods.

Riboflavin

Riboflavin changes have been investigated primarily in cereal and legume fermentations. No increase was found in a natural fermentation of chickpeas (Zamora and Fields 1979), in the fermentation of coconut press cake to produce oncom (Reddy *et al.* 1982), and in one study of idli fermentation (van Veen *et al.* 1967). Riboflavin concentration was also unchanged after fermentation of milk with several lactic acid bacteria (Alm 1982B). However, increases in riboflavin have been the most often observed result of fermentation. Products in which increases have been observed are (1) tempeh prepared from soybean (Roelofsen and Talens 1964; Murata *et al.* 1967; van Veen and Steinkraus 1970;

Robinson and Kao 1977), chickpea, and horsebean (Robinson and Kao 1977), (2) miso prepared from soybeans, chickpeas, or horsebeans (Robinson and Kao 1977), (3) idli (Rajalakshmi and Vanja 1967; Ramakrishnan *et al.* 1976), (4) khaman (Rajalakshmi and Vanaja 1967), (5) ogi (Akinrele 1970), (6) dhokla (Aliya and Geervani 1981), and (7) ambali (Aliya and Geervani 1981). Aliya and Geervani (1981) observed decreases in riboflavin when products were steamed after fermentation.

There have been few data which indicate the specific organisms or reactions leading to increases in riboflavin concentration. Akinrele (1970) sterilized ogi batter and inoculated it with either *Aerobacter cloacae* or *L. plantarum* and compared the vitamin content with a natural fermentation and a nonfermented control. *Aerobacter cloacae* caused a doubling of riboflavin compared to the controls, while the vitamin concentration decreased in the *L. plantarum*-inoculated sample. This result suggested that *A. cloacae* was the microorganism responsible for the fact that, after a natural fermentation, the riboflavin content was slightly higher than the nonfermented batter.

Extensive studies have been carried out to investigate the characteristics of idli prepared with soybeans replacing the traditional blackgram (Ramakrishnan *et al.* 1976). Changes in thiamin, niacin, and riboflavin were measured after pure culture fermentations of idli batter with microorganisms isolated from natural fermentations, including lactobacilli, *Streptococcus faecalis*, and *Aerobacter aerogenes*. A 2.5-fold increase in riboflavin occurred during natural fermentation. Fermentation with *Lactobacillus delbrueckii* resulted in a riboflavin concentration equal to the natural fermentation. Fermentations with other lactobacilli resulted in riboflavin levels intermediate between the sterilized batter and the idli made with *L. delbrueckii*.

Niacin

Niacin, like riboflavin, generally has been found to increase as a result of fermentation, increases up to fivefold have been observed in soy tempeh (Roelofsen and Talens 1964; van Veen and Steinkraus 1970; Robinson and Kao 1977). A time course study by Murata *et al.* (1967) indicated that nicotinic acid concentration continued to increase throughout a 72-hr fermentation (Fig. 16.1). Organoleptically, a 24-hr fermentation tends to give the best quality product.

Increases in niacin have also been observed in natural idli and khaman fermentations (Rajalakshmi and Vanaja 1967; Ramakrishnan *et al.* 1976). Ramakrishnan *et al.* (1976) measured niacin changes in batters fermented with several lactobacilli, *A. aerogenes*, and *S. faecalis*. The niacin content increased significantly above the sterilized control in every case. An unidentified lactobacillus and a *Lactobacillus fermenti*

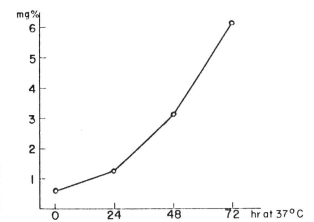

Fig. 16.1. Changes in nicotinic acid content of tempeh during fermentation. Source: Murata *et al.* (1967).

strain caused increases which were similar to the 40% increase found in a natural fermentation.

In ogi fermentations, Akinrele (1970) obtained a 25% increase in niacin concentration with a traditional fermentation. Inoculation of a sterile batter with *L. plantarum* isolated from ogi caused no change, but inoculation with *A. cloacae*, which is also found in the natural fermentation, resulted in an 84% increase in niacin.

Shahani and co-workers have studied changes in several B vitamins during the manufacture of cottage cheese (Reif *et al.* 1976) and Cheddar cheese (Nilson *et al.* 1965). In both studies, the vitamin retention in the cheese relative to the starting milk was evaluated. The effect of draining and washing cheese curd on the retention of niacin in the curd was evaluated. Only 22% of the total niacin in the milk was retained in Cheddar curd. However, the niacin concentration in the curd was doubled relative to the concentration in the milk due to the loss of whey. In cottage cheese, 63% of the niacin from the skim milk was retained in the curd, and the concentration of the niacin in the curd was 3.6-fold greater than in the milk.

During fermentation and aging of Cheddar cheese (Nilson *et al.* 1965), niacin increased about 25% in the first month, remained nearly constant from 1 to 6 months, and then increased slowly from 6 to 12 months if the storage temperature was $10°C$ or higher (Fig. 16.2). More than a doubling of niacin in the cheese could be induced if lactose was added early in the ripening period (Fig. 16.3). Vitamin B_6 also increased after lactose addition. This was attributed to increased microbial activity as a result of extra substrate availability. Only a slight increase in niacin content was observed as a result of the activity of the cottage cheese starter culture. However, almost a doubling of the niacin content of the curd was obtained by the addition of rennet. No explanation of this effect was given.

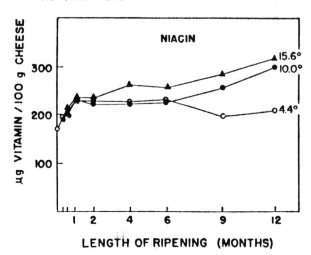

Fig. 16.2. Effect of temperature and length of ripening upon niacin content of Cheddar cheese. Source: Nilson *et al.* (1965).

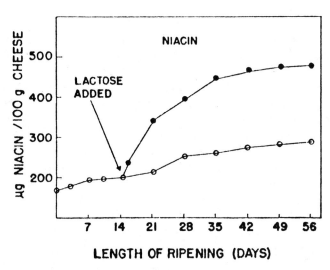

Fig. 16.3. Relationship between lactose metabolism and the biosynthesis of niacin in Cheddar cheese. Source: Nilson *et al.* (1965).

Alm (1982A) found almost no change in the niacin content of fermented milks prepared with the usual cultures of lactic acid bacteria. Costilow and Fabian (1953) found no substantial changes in the niacin content of cucumber brine after pure culture fermentations with *L. plantarum* and four yeasts, which had been isolated from cucumber fermentations. Zamora and Fields (1979) observed an unusual case in which a significant decrease of niacin occurred during a natural fermentation of cowpeas and chickpeas.

Folic Acid

Studies of folic acid changes have been limited, probably due to the difficulties in the assay of the different forms of this vitamin. Rao (1961) reported a 59% increase of folate in fermented steamed idli compared to the nonfermented starting material. Akinrele (1970) observed no change in folic acid in ogi fermentations.

In their studies of cheese fermentations, Shahani and co-workers found an increase in folic acid from 1 to 14 μg/100 g during a 16-hr fermentation of cottage cheese (Reif *et al.* 1976; Fig. 16.4). As a result of this synthesis, there was over 10 times more folic acid in the cottage cheese than in the skim milk used in the manufacture of the cheese. Folic acid concentration also tripled during the first week of Cheddar cheese ripening (Nilson *et al.* 1965; Fig. 16.5). However, after the initial increase, it decreased until after 2 months of aging, the folate level was the same as at the beginning of aging. Alm (1982A) found large increases in folic acid in all of the fermented milks she prepared,

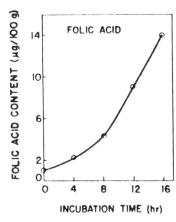

Fig. 16.4. Biosynthesis of folic acid by cottage cheese starter culture. Source: Reif *et al.* (1976).

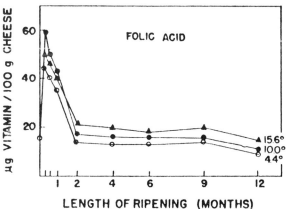

Fig. 16.5. Effect of temperature and length of ripening upon folic acid of Cheddar cheese. Source: Nilson *et al.* (1965).

except acidophilus milk, which showed over a 30% decline. It appears that folic acid can be synthesized by a number of the organisms used in the fermentation of dairy products.

Thiamin

Increases of thiamin from 30 to 150% were observed in dhokla and ambali fermentations (Aliya and Geervani 1981). Thiamin decreased when the fermented batter was steamed, but fermentation after steaming resulted in the thiamin content returning to levels equal to or greater than before steaming. Rajalakshmi and Vanja (1967) found a 176% increase of thiamin in the fermentation of idli and a 49% increase in khaman. Thiamin content also increased in soy idli with either a natural fermentation or fermentation of sterilized batters inoculated with lactobacilli or *S. faecalis. Lactobacillus delbrueckii* caused the largest increase, just as it did for riboflavin. *Aerobacter aerogenes* caused a decrease of thiamin. Akinrele (1970) found a doubling of thiamin in a natural ogi fermentation. However, he was unable to show an increase in inoculated fermentations. Thiamin decreased when sterilized batters were inoculated with *L. plantarum, A. cloacae*, or a combination of these organisms.

Consistent decreases of thiamin have been found as a result of fermentation of soybeans to tempeh (Roelofsen and Talens 1964; Murata *et al.* 1967; van Veen and Steinkraus 1970; Robinson and Kao 1977). No change in thiamin concentration was found as a result of fermentation of chickpeas and horsebeans to tempeh (Robinson and Kao 1977). Zamora and Fields (1979) saw no change in thiamin during a natural fermentation of cowpeas and a 25% decrease during chickpea fermentation. Little or no change in the thiamin occurred as a result of fermentation of milk with different lactobacilli (Alm 1982A).

Vitamin B_{12}

Vitamin B_{12} is absent or present in extremely low concentrations in foods from plant sources. For people on a vegetarian diet, formation of B_{12} in a fermented food can be very important. Robinson and Kao (1977) found small increases in B_{12} in tempeh prepared from soybeans, chickpeas, and horsebeans. Van Veen and Steinkraus (1970) reported an increase of over 30-fold from 0.15 to 5 $\mu g/kg$ in the B_{12} concentration of tempeh compared to the starting soybeans. Liem *et al.* (1977) found that tempeh prepared with a pure culture of *R. oligosporus* had very low levels of B_{12} compared to tempeh prepared by a traditional method. They concluded that the B_{12} was formed by contaminating bacteria normally present in the traditional procedure. Subsequently, Ro *et al.* (1979) increased the B_{12} content of kimchi by addition of *Propionibacterium freudenreichii* subsp. *shermanii* to the natural fermentation (Fig. 16.6).

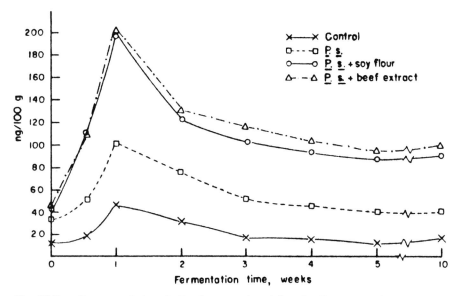

Fig. 16.6.   Content of vitamin B_{12} in control and *Propionibacterium freudenreichii* subsp. *shermanii*-inoculated (*P. s.*) kimchi, with or without soy flour or beef extract, fermented at 4°C. Source: Ro *et al.* (1979).

Milk contains substantial amounts of B_{12}. Alm (1982A) found decreases of up to 50% in yogurt and other fermented milk products inoculated with lactic acid bacteria. In Cheddar cheese, there was little change in the B_{12} content during 9 months of aging (Nilson *et al.* 1965). However, from 9 to 12 months the vitamin concentration increased. Vitamin B_{12} increased approximately fourfold during the production of cottage cheese with starter culture.

Vitamin B_6

Murata *et al.* (1967) observed increases in vitamin B_6 concentrations of 4.4- and 14-fold in two batches of soybean tempeh. Figure 16.9 shows the time course of vitamin B_6 changes. Increases of pyridoxine were also found in tempeh and miso prepared from chickpeas, horsepeas, and soybeans (Robinson and Kao 1977).

In dairy fermentations, Alm (1982A) found only slight changes in pyridoxine in milks fermented with lactic acid bacteria. Almost no change occurred in the preparation of cottage cheese (Reif *et al.* 1976). In Cheddar cheese ripening (Fig. 16.7), B_6 concentration increased initially and then declined until, after 2 months, the vitamin level was the same as in the initial curd (Nilson *et al.* 1965). Over the next 10 months, the B_6 concentration gradually increased until the final concentration was two to three times the initial level. When lactose was

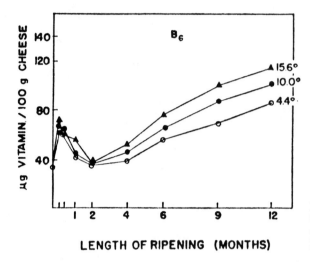

Fig. 16.7. Effect of temperature and length of ripening upon vitamin B_6 of Cheddar cheese. Source: Nilson *et al.* (1965).

added to the cheese during ripening, B_6 increased rapidly and then declined until it was similar to the concentration in the nonsupplemented cheese.

Biotin

Very limited data concerning changes in biotin in food fermentations are available. Only small changes were observed in fermented milks (Alm 1982A). Generally, the biotin concentration declined by less than 20%. During Cheddar cheese ripening (Fig. 16.8), the biotin level increased during the first 2 months by 60%, but then declined such that after 6 months the concentration was less than the initial concentration (Nilson *et al.* 1965).

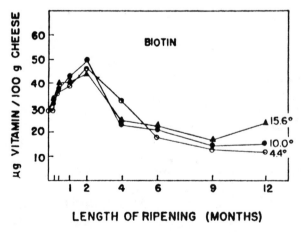

Fig. 16.8. Effect of temperature and length of ripening upon biotin content of Cheddar cheese. Source: Nilson *et al.* (1965).

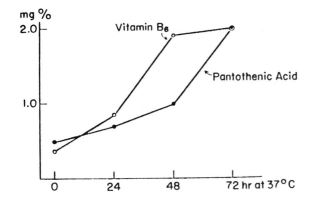

Fig. 16.9. Changes in pantothenic acid and vitamin B_6 content of tempeh during fermentation. Source: Murata *et al.* (1967).

Fermentation of cucumber brine with *L. plantarum* resulted in a 25% decline in biotin, while fermentation with four salt-tolerant yeasts caused decreases of 10–25% (Costilow and Fabian 1953).

Pantothenic Acid

Pantothenic acid did not change in fermented milks, except for a 20–30% decline during the fermentation of yogurt (Alm 1982A). During Cheddar cheese aging, there was a decline for the first 2 months, then a gradual increase. Storage at 15.6°C resulted in almost no net change in the pantothenate content, but there was an overall decline at lower temperatures (Nilson *et al.* 1965).

Van Veen and Steinkraus (1970) found a 28% decrease in pantothenic acid during tempeh fermentation, but Murata *et al.* (1967; Fig. 16.9) and Robinson and Kao (1977) observed substantial increases in tempeh compared to the starting materials. Increases in pantothenate were also found for the production of miso from chickpeas, horsebeans, and soybeans (Robinson and Kao 1977). Pantothenate declined during ogi fermentation whether a traditional fermentation or fermentations with inoculated *A. cloacae* or *L. plantarum* were tried (Akinrele 1970).

Cucumber brine fermented with *L. plantarum* showed a 26% decline in pantothenic acid concentration, while yeast fermentations resulted in 3–17% increases (Costilow and Fabian 1953).

Ascorbic Acid

Ascorbic acid is stabilized by acid conditions and the exclusion of oxygen (Kahn and Martell 1967; Kurata and Såkurai 1967; Huelin *et al.* 1971). Since it is desirable to ferment and store vegetables under these conditions, good retention of ascorbic acid might be expected. However, little is known about the ability of either fermenting vegetable tissue or lactic acid bacteria to metabolize ascorbic acid. Vegetable materials are often exposed to oxygen during preparation for fermentation and during tank-emptying operations. Also, vegetables may be drained or desalted after fermentation (Jones and Etchells 1944), which may result in large losses of the water-soluble vitamins.

Jones (1975) reported nearly complete loss of ascorbic acid when salt-stock cucumbers were desalted from 8–16% NaCl to 2–4% NaCl for use in finished products. Fellers (1960) found an 86% loss of vitamin C in desalted cucumbers. A range of 1–35 mg ascorbic acid/100 g of sauerkraut was found in commercially canned sauerkraut in the 1950s (Pederson *et al.* 1956). This wide range of concentrations was attributed to variations in handling and processing procedures and to variations in the fresh product. Kimchi, which consists of a fermented mixture of Chinese cabbage, radishes, onions, spices, and sometimes shrimp, decreased 50% in ascorbic acid concentration during the first 5 weeks of fermentation, then remained constant for the next 5 weeks (Ro *et al.* 1979; Fig. 16.10). Lee *et al.* (1960) observed a transient increase of

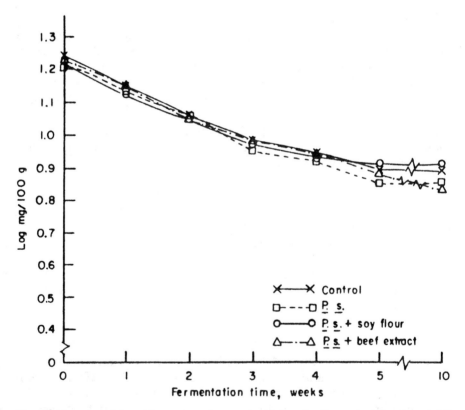

Fig. 16.10. Ascorbic acid content of control and *Propionibacterium freudenreichii* subsp. *shermanii*-inoculated (*P. s.*) kimchi, with or without soy flour or beef extract, and fermented at 4°C. Source: Ro *et al.* (1979).

ascorbic acid in kimchi during the second week of fermentation. Kimchi held at 0°C increased in vitamin C over a 60-day period by about 150% and then gradually declined (Rhie and Chun 1982). Lee and Lee (1981) studied vitamin C changes in radish kimchi fermented at 22°–23°C in a nitrogen atmosphere. Vitamin C initially decreased, then increased and reached a maximum when the kimchi was most acceptable organoleptically, and declined. The increase in vitamin C was attributed to synthesis by the radish enzymes. Addition of galacturonic acid to either kimchi or radish juice fermentation increased the amount of vitamin C formed. Large percentage increases of ascorbic acid were observed in both tempeh and miso prepared from chickpeas, horsebeans, and soybeans (Robinson and Kao 1977).

REMOVAL OF PHYTIC ACID BY FERMENTATION

The presence of high concentrations of phytic acid in cereals and legumes is of nutritional concern because of its apparent ability to reduce the bioavailability of minerals, particularly divalent cations including calcium, zinc, iron, and magnesium (Reddy et al. 1982). It has been found in a number of cases that phytates are significantly reduced

Table 16.4. Losses of Phytic Acid Phosphorus during Fermentation and Cooking of Foods

Nature of flour used	Nature of product	Phytic acid phosphorus present originally in flour (mg/100 g)	Amount of phytic acid phosphorus hydrolyzed (mg/100 g)	Phytic acid phosphorus hydrolyzed (%)
White flour (70% extraction)	Bread made with yeast	51	43.4	85.0
National wheat meal (85% extraction)	Bread made with yeast	127	87.6	69.0
Wheat meal (92% extraction)	Bread made with yeast	214	66.3	31.0
	Baking powder bread	214	10.7	5.0
	Steamed pudding	214	34.2	16.0
	Pastry	214	0.0	0.0
White flour with added sodium phytate	Baking powder bread	214	32.1	15.0
	Steamed pudding	214	128.4	60.0
	Pastry	214	32.1	15.0

Source: Calculated from the data of Widdowson (1941). From Reddy et al. (1982).

during fermentation processes, as a result of the presence of phytase in the grain itself or production of the enzyme by the fermentation organisms. Thus, in wheat bread, phytic acid was hydrolyzed to a greater extent when yeast rather than baking powder was used to raise the dough (Table 16.4; Widdowson 1941, as calculated by Reddy *et al.* 1982). Ranhotra *et al.* (1974) found complete hydrolysis of phytic acid in wheat bread and over 75% removal in bread prepared from soy-fortified wheat flour. Addition of yeast to Iranian whole wheat meal (Reinhold 1975) or to traditionally unleavened Indian chapaties prepared from whole wheat meal (Swaranjeet *et al.* 1982) also resulted in larger decreases in phytic acid concentration than occurred without yeast addition.

Fermentation of rice–black gram blends to make idli has been found to reduce the phytate content by 30% (Rajalakshmi and Vanaja 1967) and 41% (Reddy and Salunkhe 1980). A 45% decrease in phytate was observed by Ramakrishnan *et al.* (1976) in soy idli in which black gram dal was replaced by soy dal. They fermented sterilized idli batter with a number of bacteria found in natural idli fermentations. Only those bacteria which produced measurable levels of phytase activity caused significant reductions in phytate. *Lactobacillus buchneri*, an unidentified *Bacillus*, and *Microbacterium flavum* reduced the phytate by 16, 39, and 57%, respectively, during a 14-hr fermentation. *Aerobacter aerogenes* and several lactic acid bacteria produced no measurable phytase.

Markakis and co-workers have analyzed phytic acid changes during fermentation of tempeh (Sudarmadji and Markakis 1977) and oncom (Fardiaz and Markakis 1981A). In both studies reduction of phytic acid was attirbuted to phytase production by the inoculated mold, since the soybeans and peanut press cake were boiled prior to fermentation. A 33% reduction of phytic acid occurred in the tempeh fermentation. *Rhizopus oligosporus* caused almost complete destruction of phytic acid, while fermentation with *Neurospora sitophila* resulted in about a 50% decline.

OUTLOOK

Given the many examples cited in which substantial increases in nutrients have been observed, it seems that there must exist many opportunities to improve the nutritional consequences of food fermentations. The development of genetic transfer and modification technologies for microorganisms would appear to expand these opportunities. Newman *et al.* (1984) have recently described efforts to introduce mutant cultures of *L. plantarum*, which produce high levels of lysine in traditional cereal fermentations, in areas where protein availability is limited.

Morishita *et al.* (1981) have shown that it is possible to mutate lacto-bacilli to recover their ability to synthesize amino acids. These pathways were apparently inactivated, but not completely lost, during the course of evolution of this group of organisms.

Before the potential for consistent nutritional improvements can be translated into practical manufacturing technologies, much more must be done to establish mechanisms of nutrient synthesis and degradation during fermentations. At its most basic, this must include identification of the microorganisms and substrates responsible for nutrient improvements in important food fermentations.

REFERENCES

Akinrele, I. A. 1970. Fermentation studies on maize during the preparation of a traditional African starch-cake food. J. Sci. Food Agric. *21*, 619–625.

Aliya, S., and Geervani, P. 1981. An assessment of the protein quality and vitamin B content of commonly used fermented products of legumes and millets. J. Sci. Food Agric. *32*, 837–842.

Alm, L. 1982A. Effect of fermentation on B vitamin content of milk in Sweden. J. Dairy Sci. *65*, 353–359.

Alm, L. 1982B. Effect of fermentation on L(+) and D(−) lactic acid in milk. J. Dairy Sci. *65*, 515–520.

Alm, L. 1982C. Effect of fermentation on proteins of Swedish fermented milk products. J. Dairy Sci. *65*, 1696–1704.

Azoulay, E., Jouanneau, F., Bertrand, J. C., Raphael, A., Janssens, J., and Lebeault, J. M. 1980. Fermentation methods for protein enrichment of cassava and corn with *Candida tropicalis*. Appl. Environ. Microbiol. *39*, 41–47.

Brin, M. 1964. Chemistry and metabolism of D- and L-lactic acids. J. Assoc. Food Drug Offic. *1964*, 178–188.

Cherry, J. P., and Beuchat, L. R. 1976. Comparative studies of protein and amino acid changes in peanuts infected with *Neurospora sitophila* and *Rhizopus oligosporus*. Cereal Chem. *53*, 750–761.

Cori, C. F., and Cori, G. T. 1929. Glycogen formation in the liver from D- and L-lactic acid. J. Biol. Chem. *81*, 389–403.

Costilow, R. N., and Fabian, F. W. 1953. Effect of various microorganisms on the vitamin and amino acid content of cucumber brines. Appl. Microbiol. *1*, 327–329.

Droese, W., and Stolley, H. 1962. Functional investigations on infant nutrition: Effect of fermented milk on the nutrition of young infants. (German) Deut. Med. J. *13*, 107–112.

Droese, W., and Stolley, H. 1965. The effect of D/L lactic acid, citric acid and protein on the organic acids in the urine of healthy infants during their first 3 months. (German) Symp. ueber die Ernahrung der Fruhgeborenen, Bad Schachen, May 1964, pp. 63–72.

Drury, D. R., and Wick, A. N. 1965. Chemistry and metabolism of L(+) and D(−) lactic acids. Ann. N.Y. Acad. Sci. *119*, 1061–1069.

Dunlop, R. H., Hammond, P. B., and Stevens, C. E. 1964. D-Lactate in bovine blood following carbohydrate engorgement. Fed. Proc., Fed. Am. Soc. Exp. Biol. *23*, 262.

Erdman, M. D., Bergen, W. G., and Reddy, C. A. 1977. Amino acid profiles and presumptive nutritional assessment of single cell protein from certain lactobacilli. Appl. Environ. Microbiol. *33*, 901–905.

Eskeland, B., and Nordal, J. 1980. Nutritional evaluation of protein in dry sausages during the fermentation process with special emphasis on amino acid availability. J. Food Sci. *45*, 1158–1161.

Fardiaz, D., and Markakis, P. 1981A. Degradation of phytic acid in oncom (fermented peanut press cake). J. Food Sci. *46*, 523–525.

Fardiaz, D., and Markakis, P. 1981B. Oligosaccharides and protein efficiency ratio of oncom (fermented peanut press cake). J. Food Sci. *46*, 1970–1971.

Fellers, C. R. 1960. Effects of fermentation on food nutrients. *In* Nutritional Evaluation of Food Processing, p. 161. R. S. Harris and H. von Loesecke (Editors). AVI Publishing Co., Westport, CT.

Garvie, E. L. 1967. The production of L(+) and D(−) lactic acid in cultures of some lactic acid bacteria, with a special study of *Lactobacillus acidophilus* NCDO 2. J. Dairy Res. *34*, 31–38.

Giesecke, D., and Stangassinger, M. 1980. Lactic acid metabolism. *In* Digestive Physiology and Metabolism in Ruminants, pp. 523–539. AVI Publishing Co., Westport, CT.

Giesecke, D., Wallenberg, P., and Fabritius, A. 1980. D(−) Lactic acid—A physiological isomer in the rat. Experientia *36*, 571–572.

Giesecke, D., Fabritius, A., and Wallenberg, P. V. 1981. A quantitative study on the metabolism of D(−) lactic acid in the rat and the rabbit. Comp. Biochem. Physiol. *69B*, 85–89.

Hackler, L. R., Steinkraus, K. H., Van Buren, J. P., and Hand, D. B. 1964. Studies on the utilization of tempeh protein by weanling rats. J. Nutr. *82*, 452–456.

Haidaris, C. G., and Bhattacharjee, J. K. 1978. Lysine production by thialysine-resistant mutants of *Saccharomyces cerevisiae*. J. Ferm. Technol. *56*, 189–192.

Hamad, A. M., and Fields, M. L. 1979. Nutritional and sensory evaluation of bread made from fermented wheat meal and corn chips made from fermented corn meal. J. Food Sci. *44*, 1514–1516.

Hargrove, R. E., and Alford, J. A. 1978. Growth rate and feed efficiency of rats fed yogurt and other fermented milks. J. Dairy Sci. *61*, 11–19.

Huelin, F. E., Coggiola, I. M., Sidhu, G. S., and Kennett, B. H. 1971. The anaerobic decomposition of ascorbic acid in the pH range of foods and in more acid solutions. J. Sci. Food Agric. *22*, 540–542.

Jones, I. D. 1975. Effects of processing by fermentation on nutrients. *In* Nutritional Evaluation of Food Processing. 2nd Edition, p. 324. R. S. Harris and E. Karmas (Editors). AVI Publishing Co., Westport, CT.

Jones, I. D., and Etchells, J. L. 1944. Nutritive value of brined and fermented vegetables. Am. J. Public Health *34*, 711–718.

Kahn, M. M. T., and Martel, A. E. 1967. Metal ion and metal chelate catalyzed oxidation of ascorbic acid by molecular oxygen. I. Cupric and ferric ion catalyzed oxidation. J. Am. Chem. Soc. *89*, 4176–4185.

Kao, C., and Robinson, R. J. 1978. Nutritional aspects of fermented foods from chickpea, horsebean, and soybean. Cereal Chem. *55*, 512–517.

Kihlberg, R. 1972. The microbe as a source of food. Ann. Rev. Microbiol. *26*, 427–466.

Ko, S. D. 1982. Indigenous fermented foods. *In* Fermented Foods, Vol. 7, pp. 15–38. A. H. Rose (Editor). Academic Press, New York.

Kunath, V. P., and Kandler, O. 1980. Der Gehalt an L(+) and D(−)-Milchsaure in Joghurtprodukten. Milchwissenschaft *35*, 470–473.

Kurata, T., and Sakurai, Y. 1967. Degradation of L-ascorbic acid and mechanism of nonenzymic browning reaction. II. Nonoxidative degradation of L-ascorbic acid including formation of 3-deoxy-L-pentosone. Agric. Biol. Chem. *31*, 170–176.

Law, B. A., and Kolstad, J. 1983. Proteolytic systems in lactic acid bacteria. Antonie van Leeuwenhoek J. Microbiol. Serol. *49*, 225–245.

Lee, T. Y., and Lee, J. W. 1981. The change of vitamin C content and the effect of galacturonic acid addition during kimchi fermentation. Hanguk Nonghwa Hakhoe Chi *24*, 139–144.

Lee, T. Y., Kim, J. S., Chung, D. H., and Kim, H. S. 1960. Studies on the composition of kimchi. 2. Variations of vitamins during kimchi fermentation. Bull. Sci. Res. Inst., Korea *5*, 43–50.

Liem, I. T. H., Steinkraus, K. H., and Cronk, T. C. 1977. Production of vitamin B_{12} in tempeh, a fermented soybean food. Appl. Environ. Microbiol. *34*, 773–776.

Morishita, T., Deguchi, Y., Yajima, M., Sakurai, T., and Yura, T. 1981. Multiple nutritional requirements of lactobacilli: Genetic lesions affecting amino acid biosynthetic pathways. J. Bacteriol. *148*, 64–71.

Murata, K., Ikehata, H., and Miyamoto, T. 1967. Studies on the nutritional value of tempeh. J. Food Sci. *32*, 580–585.

Newman, R. K., Sands, D. C., and Scott, K. 1984. A microbiological approach to nutrition. J. Am. Diet. Assoc. *84*, 820–821.

Nilson, K. M., Vakil, J. R., and Shahani, K. M. 1965. B complex vitamin content of cheddar cheese. J. Nutr. *86*, 362–368.

Padhye, V. W., and Salunkhe, D. K. 1978. Biochemical studies on black gram (*Phaseolus mungo* L.). III. Fermentation of the black gram and rice blend and its influence on the in vitro digestibility of the proteins. J. Food Biochem. *2*, 327–347.

Pederson, C. S. 1979. Microbiology of Food Fermentations. 2nd Edition. AVI Publishing Co., Westport, CT.

Pederson, C. S., Whitcomb, J., and Robinson, W. B. 1956. The ascorbic acid content of sauerkraut. Food Technol. *10*, 365–367.

Rajalakshmi, R., and Vanaja, K. 1967. Chemical and biological evaluation of the effects of fermentation on the nutritive value of foods prepared from rice and grams. Br. J. Nutr. *21*, 467–473.

Ramakrishnan, C. V., Parekh, L. J., Akolkar, P. N., Rao, G. S., and Bhandari, S. D. 1976. Studies on soy idli fermentation. Plant Foods Man *2*, 15–33.

Ranhotra, G. S., Loewe, R. J., and Puyat, L. V. 1974. Phytic acid in soy and its hydrolysis during breadmaking. J. Food Sci. *39*, 1023–1025.

Rao, M. V. R. 1961. Some observations on fermented foods. *In* Progress in Meeting Protein Needs of Infants and Pre-school Children. Publ. *843*. National Academy of Sciences, National Research Council, Washington, DC.

Rao, D. R., Pulvsani, S. R., and Rao, T. K. 1982. Amino acid composition and nutritional implications of milk fermented by various lactic cultures. J. Food Qual. *5*, 235–243.

Reddy, N. R., and Salunkhe, D. K. 1980. Effects of fermentation on phytate phosphorus and minerals of black gram, rice and black gram blends. J. Food Sci. *45*, 1708–1712.

Reddy, N. R., Sathe, S. K., Pierson, M. D., and Salunkhe, D. K. 1981. Idli, an Indian fermented food: A review. J. Food Qual. *5*, 89–101.

Reddy, N. R., Pierson, M. D., Sathe, S. K., and Salunkhe, D. K. 1982. Legume-based fermented foods: Their preparation and nutritional quality. CRC Crit. Rev. Food Sci. Nutr. *17*, 335–370.

Reddy, N. R., Sathe, S. K., and Salunkhe, D. K. 1982. Phytates in legumes and cereals. Adv. Food Res. *28*, 1–92.

Reif, G. D., Shahani, K. M., Vakil, J. R., and Crowe, L. K. 1976. Factors affecting B-complex vitamin content of cottage cheese. J. Dairy Sci. *59*, 410–415.

Reinhold, J. G. 1975. Phytate destruction by yeast fermentation in whole wheat meals. J. Am. Diet. Assoc. *66*, 38–41.

Rhie, S. G., and Chun, S. K. 1982. The influence of temperature on fermentation of kimchi. Hanguk Yongyang Siklyong Hakhoechi *11*, 63–66.

Ro, S. L., Woodburn, M., and Sandine, W. E. 1979. Vitamin B_{12} and ascorbic acid in kimchi inoculated with *Propionibacterium freudenreichii* ss. *shermanii*. J. Food Sci. *44*, 873–877.

Robinson, R. J., and Kao, C. 1977. Tempeh and miso from chickpea, horsebean and soybean. Cereal Chem. *54*, 1192–1197.

Roelofsen, P. A., and Talens, A. 1964. Changes in some B vitamins during molding of soybeans by *Rhizopus oryzae* in the production of tempeh kedelee. J. Food Sci. *29*, 224–226.

Rose, A. H. 1982. Economic Microbiology. Fermented Foods, Vol. 7. Academic Press, New York.

Sands, D. C., and Hankin, L. 1974. Selecting lysine-excreting mutants of lactobacilli for use in food and feed enrichment. Appl. Microbiol. *28*, 523–524.

Sands, D. C., and Hankin, L. 1976. Fortification of foods by fermentation with lysine-excreting mutants of lactobacilli. J. Agric. Food Chem. *24*, 1104–1106.

Shahani, K. M., and Chandan, R. C. 1979. Nutritional and healthful aspects of cultured and culture-containing dairy foods. J. Dairy Sci. *62*, 1685–1694.

Smith, J. L., and Palumbo, S. A. 1981. Microorganisms as food additives. J. Food Protec. *44*, 936–955.

Steinkraus, K. H. 1983. Handbook of Indigenous Fermented Foods. Marcel Dekker, New York.

Stetter, K. O., and Kandler, O. 1973. Formation of DL-lactic acid by lactobacilli and characterization of lactic acid racemase from several streptobacteria. (German). Arch. Mikrobiol. *94*, 221–247.

Stillings, B. R., and Hackler, L. R. 1965. Amino acid studies on the effect of fermentation time and heat-processing of tempeh. J. Food Sci. *30*, 1043–1048.

Sudarmadji, S., and Markakis, P. 1977. The phytate and phytase of soybean tempeh. J. Sci. Food Agric. *28*, 381–383.

Swaranjeet, K., Maninder, K., and Bains, G. S. 1982. Chapaties with leavening and supplements: Changes in texture, residual sugars, and phytic phosphorus. Cer. Chem. *59*, 367–372.

Tongnual, P., Nanson, N. J., and Fields, M. L. 1982. Effect of proteolytic bacteria in the natural fermentation of corn to increase its nutritive value. J. Food Sci. *46*, 100–104, 109.

van Veen, A. G., and Steinkraus, K. H. 1970. Nutritive value and wholesomeness of fermented foods. J. Agric. Food Chem. *18*, 576–578.

van Veen, A. G., Hackler, L. R., Steinkraus, K. H., and Mukherjee, S. K. 1967. Nutritive quality of idli, a fermented food of India. J. Food Sci. *32*, 339–341.

Wang, H. L., Ruttle, D. I., and Hesseltine, C. W. 1968. Protein quality of wheat and soybeans after *Rhizopus oligosporus* fermentation. J. Nutr. *96*, 109–114.

Widdowson, E. M. 1941. Phytic acid and the preparation of food. Nature *148*, 219–220.

World Health Organization. 1966. Specifications for the Identity and Purity of Food Additives and Their Toxicological Evaluation: Some Antimicrobials, Antioxidants, Emulsifiers, Stabilizers, Flour-treatment Agents, Acids, and Bases. Ninth Report of the Joint FAO/WHO Expert Committee on Food Additives. Rome.

World Health Organization. 1974. Toxicological evaluation of some food additives including anticaking agents, antimicrobials, antioxidants, emulsifiers, and thickening agents. WHO Food Additive Series 5. Rome.

Zamora, A. F., and Fields, M. L. 1979. Nutritive quality of fermented cowpeas (*Vigna sinensis*) and chickpeas (*Cicer arietinum*). J. Food Sci. *44*, 234–236.

Zimmer, E. 1980. Efficient siliage systems. British Grassland Society Occasional Symp. *11*, Brighton, 1979. pp. 186–197.

Effects of Treatment with Food Additives on Nutrients

Winifred M. Cort

Food additives[1] are substances other than basic foodstuffs which are put into foods during production, processing, and packaging. Additives are used in commercial processing not only to reduce microbial hazards, but also to reduce chemical and physical spoilage and to aid processing. Processing additives may be used as anticaking agents, chemical preservatives, emulsifiers, and stabilizers, to modify or improve flavor, texture, or colors, and they also may include nutrients added to enhance nutritional value. The number of food additives greatly exceeds the number of nutrients. Since the function of food additives is so varied, the total effect on nutrients often is not known. If one makes a list of all the food additives (e.g., the list in Title 21, 121.101 U.S. Code of Federal Regulations, published in 1973, CFR, and Sections 172, 173, 181, 182, 184, and 186, published in 1981, CFR) and a list of all the nutrients, it becomes evident that potential interactions have hardly been explored.

The effects of food additives will be divided into two sections, namely, additives which decrease the nutrient content of foods and additives which are beneficial to nutrients. Unfortunately, as can be seen, at times this type of division will be ambiguous, since some additives will be deleterious to one nutrient and beneficial to another.

ADDITIVES DETRIMENTAL TO NUTRIENTS

Sulfites

The deleterious effect of sodium bisulfite and sulfur dioxide on thiamin has been known for many years. In fact, sodium bisulfite is not allowed in meats, or in foods recognized as a source of thiamin in the CFR 121.101. Sulfites cause a nucleophilic displacement on the methylene bridge of thiamin and it is cleaved into free thiazole and

---

[1] This is a deviation from the broad definition used by the Food Protection Committee, National Academy of Science, National Research Council (see Anonymous 1973).

pyrimidylmethane-sulfuric acid. The reaction occurs faster at a neutral pH. One might expect sulfites to react with some of the other less stable vitamins. In model systems, DeRitter (1969) reports that sulfur dioxide and acid will cleave folic acid to pteridine and p-aminobenzoyl glutamic moieties and the latter undergoes further destruction of the free amino group. Other than the beneficial effect of sulfur dioxide on ascorbic acid, which will be discussed later, reactions with other vitamins in food systems have not been explored.

Alkalies

Thiamin also is destroyed in alkaline foods such as chocolate cake containing sodium bicarbonate and carbonate and lime-treated corn used for tortillas. In fact, aluminum sodium sulfate and the di- and trisodium potassium phosphates also aid in the destruction of thiamin. Dwivedi and Arnold (1973) have identified a number of breakdown products from alkaline oxidation of thiamin. These include thiamin disulfide, which has thiamin activity, and thiochrome and thiothiazalone, which do not have any thiamin bioactivity. In addition, thiamin is cleaved to the pyrimidine and thiazole moieties and the thiazole may degrade further to a number of compounds including 3-mercaptopropanol, hydrogen sulfide, 2-methylfuran, 2-methylthiophene, 2-methyl-4,5-dihydrothiophene, and 2-methylthio-5-methylfuran. The thiophenes are associated with the odor from the decomposition of thiamin.

In tortilla studies, Massieu *et al.* (1949) also noted 30% loss of tryptophan, threonine, histidine, and arginine. Many of the basic amino acids are prepared as the hydrochloride because the free bases are alkali labile. The addition of alkali to lysine hydrochloride forms the free base which decomposes and produces an odor. We would expect lysine to decompose in chocolate cake and tortillas. Amino acids also will racemize in alkaline solution and thus reduce their biological activity.

Although it has not been demonstrated in alkaline foods, from information in the pharmaceutical literature, one would expect losses of pantothenic acid, vitamin K_1, cysteine, cystine, and vitamin D by slow degradation; riboflavin by conversion to lumiflavin; and the essential fatty acids by isomerization. In a food publication, Sistrunk and Cash (1970) showed a loss of ascorbic acid in squash as the pH was adjusted from 5 to 7.5.

Acids

Citric, phosphoric, lactic, malic, tartaric, fumaric, adipic, acetic, hydrochloric, and sulfuric acids have been added to foods. In liquid or semiliquid foods adjusted to pH 4 or below, vitamin A will de-esterify and isomerize to the less bioactive cis forms. Folic acid, pantothenic acid, and threonine would be expected to decompose under acidic conditions.

Moore and Folkers (1968) showed that dilute acids cleaved vitamin B_{12} to the inactive corrin nucleus. Proteins with acid isoelectric points can be denatured and thus are not available for enzymatic hydrolysis and subsequent utilization. Miller *et al.* (1973) studied vitamin loss in bean products and slurries adjusted with hydrochloric acid to pH 3.5. They showed a loss of folacin although there was no loss of pyridoxine, and thiamin or decrease in protein efficiency ratio (PER).

Curing and Smoking

The modern, mild curing methods employ small amounts of sodium chloride, sugar, nitrite, ascorbates, phosphates, and liquid smoke concentrates in processed meat, poultry, and fish products to improve their flavor and color characteristics. Losses of specific nutrients due to curing appear to be very small. Thiamin is the only vitamin lost, up to about 20% as a result of heat treatment in curing processing, whereas riboflavin and niacin are very stable (Schweigert and Lushbough 1960). Light salting and phosphate addition significantly decrease the exudation of meats and thus reduce the loss of water-soluble vitamins, minerals, and proteins.

Nitrite can react with susceptible amines to form carcinogenic nitrosamines. However, ascorbic acid can block this reaction by reacting directly with nitrogen oxide to form nitric oxide gas and dehydroascorbic acid. For this reason it is particularly important to add ascorbic acid or ascorbates to bacon. Newmark *et al.* (1974) reported losses of 30% ascorbic acid in bacon after processing and an additional 30% loss after 6 months of storage and frying.

Polycyclic aromatic hydrocarbons, especially benz[a]pyrene, a strong carcinogen, are present in the smoke. Benz[a]pyrene can be found in much lesser amounts in smoked foods than in barbecued meats. The use of liquid smoke preparations in cured meat products nearly eliminates the presence of polycyclic aromatic hydrocarbons.

Copper and Iron

Copper is generally not added, but it is present in many foods. Only within the broad definition of a food additive can the presence of copper be considered. On the other hand, iron is added to many foods. Because their interactions are somewhat similar and more detrimental to other nutrients than generally recognized, these reactions will be discussed together.

Ascorbic acid is known to be destroyed by copper. The ascorbic acid first is converted to dehydroascorbic acid, which has antiscorbutic activity but is unstable and degrades to diketogulonic acid, which is inactive. Simultaneously, the Cu^{2+} is converted by ascorbic acid to the lower oxidation state(s) and Fe^{3+} to Fe^{2+} as shown by Laurence and Ellis (1972).

Fe^{3+} and Cu^{2+} oxidation and destruction of organic free radicals have been reviewed by Jukes (1974). The interactions of Fe^{3+} and Cu^{2+} with all the phenolic antioxidants were shown (Cort 1974; Cort et al. 1974).

Furthermore, Cu^{2+} reacts with tocopherol to form the p-tocopherol-quinone, which has no vitamin E or antioxidant activity. Reduction of Fe^{3+} to Fe^{2+} and the subsequent measurement of Fe^{2+} has been the basis of the colorimetric assay for tocopherol for many years. The tocopherol will go to the inactive p-tocopherolquinone under most conditions. However, if EDTA is present, the dimeric keto-ether is formed (Cort et al. 1974).

Less than 3% loss has been found when 95% tocopherol is kept in thin layers for 4 years and alcoholic solutions have been stable for 1 year when metals are not present. If Cu^{2+} or Fe^{3+} are added to the latter, 40–50% of the tocopherol is decomposed within 15 days. However, the lower oxidation states, Fe^{2+} and Cu^{1+} and ground state copper, do not react with tocopherol.

Destruction of the tocopherols and phenolic antioxidants would lead to the loss of natural and added vitamin A. Furthermore, the Fe^{3+}- and Cu^{2+}-caused breakdown of tocopherols in vegetable oils, especially γ-tocopherol, which is a better antioxidant than the α homologue, decreases the oxidative stability of vegetable oils. The loss of antioxidants leads to oxidation of fatty acids in the naturally occurring glycerides. The unsaturated fatty acids oxidize to peroxides which decompose to acids, aldehydes, ketones, alkanes, and so forth, and represent a loss of essential fatty acid. Also, oxidized fats have been shown to react with essential amino acids and make them nonavailable. Aylward and Haisman (1969) have shown that oxidized oils will oxidize vitamin A and β-carotene.

Thiamin is also destroyed by Cu^{2+} as shown by Dwivedi and Arnold (1973). Borenstein (1971), in a review article, has reported that copper catalyzes folic acid destruction. Methionine and linolenic acid, as well as a number of other substrates, have been degraded to ethylene by ascorbic acid and copper as shown by Lieberman and Kunishi (1967).

Other Detrimental Interactions

Feller and Macek (1955) have shown that thiazole produced by decomposed thiamin promotes the breakdown of vitamin B_{12}. This is a problem in pharmaceuticals; and, in fact, most of our information (DeRitter 1969) on vitamin interactions is found in pharmaceutical research and publications. Fortunately in most foods, the thiamin level is sufficiently low that this is not a major pathway for vitamin B_{12} decomposition. Gambier and Rahn (1957) have shown that riboflavin aids the oxidation of thiamin to thiochrome in concentrated solutions.

Niacinamide and ascorbic acid react to form a yellow nicotin-amide-ascorbic acid complex listed as a source of niacin and vitamin C in CFR 121.1095. However, in some food systems, the bright yellow color is not acceptable.

Amen (1973) reports that phosphates, phytates, and oxalates in spinach complex iron and make it unavailable. He also claims that calcium acts as a zinc antagonist by competing for absorption sites when phytates or phosphates are present. Furthermore, low-protein diets result in decreased apoferritin production and ultimately cause iron deficiency. Carbonyls present in flavor adjuncts can react with pyridoxamine to form inactive Schiff bases and pyridoxal could react with amines similarly. Schroeder (1971) reports losses of natural pyridoxal and pyridoxamine as well as pantothenic acid, biotin, folacin, choline, and inositol in food processing, and some of the B_6 losses may be due to interactions.

Morrison and McLaughlin (1972) reviewed the availability of amino acids in foods. Casein and glucose combination when heated together markedly reduced the biological value of the casein; this could be corrected by the addition of supplemental lysine. Propanal formed from oxidized lipids inactivated lysine. Bressani *et al.* (1972) reported that amino acids react with proteins to form enzyme-resistant bonds, and that proteins heated with carbohydrates resulted in loss not only of lysine, but also methionine, arginine, histidine, and tryptophan. Hydrogen peroxide used in milk for cheese manufacture causes a 30% loss in bioavailable methionine. Cuq *et al.* (1973) demonstrated oxidation of methionine to the sulfoxide in casein decreases the enzymatic digestion of casein, which further explains the previous workers' results.

Studies on vitamin A fortification of rice in our laboratory revealed a vitamin A and talc interaction which turned green and destroyed the vitamin A. As a result, in rice premix containing talc, the vitamin A had to be added separately and coated.

ADDITIVES BENEFICIAL TO NUTRIENTS

Sulfites

As stated in the introduction, compounds which are detrimental to some nutrients can be beneficial to others. Sulfites react in solution to scavenge oxygen. Ascorbic acid reacts by the same mechanism and decomposes in the process. Thus, sodium metabisulfite, sodium sulfite, and cysteine increase the stability of ascorbic acid in solution. Very recently Bolin and Stafford (1974) revealed sulfur dioxide protection of ascorbic acid and β-carotene. In addition, sodium metabisulfite is used to extract and stabilize cobalamines present in nature.

Ascorbic Acid

Ascorbic acid converts Fe^{3+} to Fe^{2+} and Cu^{2+} to lower oxidation state(s) and as a result protects against Fe^{3+}- and Cu^{2+}-promoted reactions (Cort *et al.* 1975). It will, therefore, protect essential fatty acids, essential amino acids, vitamin A, vitamin E, thiamin, folic acid, and make iron more available. In addition to its protective effect, Schudel *et al.* (1972) have shown that it will convert the keto-ether dimer of tocopherol to "bi-α-tocopheryl" and tocopheroxide to α-tocopherol.

Antioxidants

Vitamin A with 5 conjugated double bonds, β-carotene with 11, and apocarotenal with 9 are susceptible to oxidation. Apparently the double bonds in the β-ionone ring oxidize first to the epoxides in the carotenoids and probably in vitamin A, and the epoxides have reduced vitamin A activity. Classically BHT, BHA, and α-tocopherol are used to stabilize food-grade vitamin A. In general, the antioxidants are added to the vitamin A palmitate, which is homogenized into gelatin and made into beadlets. The gelatin acts as an impermeable barrier to oxygen. Unstabilized vitamin A in thin films will lose potency in 1 day, which fully explains the necessity of antioxidants. Vitamins D_2 and D_3 also contain oxidizable double bonds and should be protected similarly.

Water-solubilizers and Mechanisms to Solubilize

The vitamin manufacturers have made a number of water-soluble, stabilized market forms of the water-insoluble vitamins. Homogenization into thick matrixes such as acacia, dextrins, and gelatin results in reduction of the particle size of the vitamin A to 1–3 μm. The emulsions are made into beadlets or used as is. In addition to vitamin A and antioxidants, these emulsions also contain preservatives such as the parabens or sodium benzoate and sorbic acid.

More recently, acacia emulsions have been spray dried in order to have a particle size below 100 μm to facilitate adding to flour because it will not rebolt out. Spray-dried vitamin A is useful also in premixes made with other fine particulate vitamins. The dried forms contain other additives such as sucrose and lactose to increase stability, and sometimes coconut oil to increase flavor stability. Often "slip" agents such as silicic acid are added to increase flow and prevent caking of dried products.

Water-dispersible solutions of water-insoluble vitamins are made in Polysorb 80. Other additives, such as ethanol, and propylene glycol are added to make the Polysorb soluble in cold water. Antifoam agents sometimes are added. These dispersible solutions also are stabilized with antioxidants and are used to fortify foods. A description of the commercial vitamin A application forms available and related stability have been published (Bauernfeind and Cort 1973).

Tocopheryl acetate, on the other hand, does not require additives to prevent oxidation, since it is an extremely stable, water-insoluble, viscous liquid. In order to make it into dry products, it has been homogenized to 1- to 3-μm particle size into gelatin or dextrins, and made into beadlets or spray dried for water-soluble applications. Free tocopherol is not as stable as the acetate. On standing in air it will form tocored, which is the quinone on the 5- and 6-position. However, as has been shown, this never exceeds 0.7% tocored and is not a major breakdown product. As previously described, it is susceptible to Cu^{2+}- and Fe^{3+}-caused breakdown and protected by ascorbic acid and chelating agents.

In skimmed milk, the fat-soluble vitamins are removed with the cream. Stabilized water-soluble vitamin A is added to nonfat milk products, but not tocopherol. Experimentally, water-soluble forms of vitamin E have been added to skim milk, nonfat dry skim milk, filled milk, the imitation milk at 1.5, 15, and 150 IU per quart, with 100% stability for 4 weeks in the liquid products and 1 year in the dry products.

Special Additives for B Vitamins

Since thiamin breakdown products cause off-odors and riboflavin and niacin can be bitter, special coatings have been applied. These usually are mixtures of mono- and diglycerides and, in fact, are water insoluble. The vitamins are usually 33% concentration. They are useful in dry products; although in some foods, Borenstein (1968) reports that the coated thiamin still causes off-flavor. Coated B vitamins are used in chewable vitamin tablets.

Other Additives

Ascorbic acid has been lightly coated with ethocel (97% ascorbic acid) and fat coated (30% ascorbic) to increase stability, since at 3% moisture and above ascorbic acid becomes tan. The speculation has been that free radicals on the 2- and 3-positions are formed. Levandoski et al. (1971) isolated monodehydroascorbic acid–ascorbic acid complex, which is yellow and may also be involved in color formation by ascorbic acid.

Cysteine has also been proposed as a protectant to thiamin, although levels which protect have caused an off-odor from cysteine in the Hoffmann-LaRoche laboratories.

In pharmaceuticals, iron salts and chelating agents (disodium EDTA or citrates) are used to stabilize vitamin B_{12} in solution (Newmark 1958; Federal Register 1962). Natural materials such as liver contain sufficient iron to stabilize vitamin B_{12} as shown by Shenoy and Ramasarma (1955). The stability of B_{12} in foods during processing will depend on the content of iron and chelates.

REFERENCES

Anonymous 1973. The use of chemicals in food production, processing, storage and distribution. Nutr. Rev. *31*, 191–198.

Amen, R. J. 1973. Trace minerals as nutrients. Food Prod. Develop. *7*(8), 74–78.

Ames, S. R. 1972. Tocopherols occurrence in foods. *In* The Vitamins, Vol. 5. W. H. Sebrell, Jr. and R. S. Harris (Editors). Academic Press, New York.

Aylward, F., and Haisman, D. R. 1969. Oxidation systems. Adv. Food Res. *17*, 1–76.

Bauernfeind, J. C. 1970. Vitamin fortification and nutrification foods. Third Intern. Cong. Food Sci. Technol., Washington, DC.

Bauernfeind, J. C., and Cort, W. M. 1973. Nutrification of foods with added vitamin A. CRC Crit. Rev. Food Technol. *4*(3), 337–375.

Bauernfeind, J. C., and Cort, W. M. 1974. Tocopherols. *In* Encyclopedia of Food Technology. A. H. Johnson and M. S. Peterson (Editors). AVI Publishing Co., Westport, CT.

Bauernfeind, J. C., and Pinkert, D. M. 1970. Food processing with added ascorbic acid. Advan. Food Res. *18*, 219.

Bielski, B. H. J., Comstock, D. A., and Bowen, R. A. 1971. Ascorbic acid free radicals. 1. Pulse radiolysis study of optical absorption and kinetic properties. J. Am. Chem. Soc. *93*, 5624–5629.

Bolin, H. R., and Stafford, A. E. 1974. Effect of processing and storage on provitamin A and vitamin C in apricots. Food Sci. *37*, 1034–1036.

Borenstein, B. 1968. Vitamins and amino acids. *In* Handbook of Food Additives. T. E. Furia (Editor). CRC Press, Cleveland.

Borenstein, B. 1969. Vitamin A for flour and corn meal. Northwest Miller *276*, 18.

Borenstein, B. 1971. Rationale and technology of food fortification. CRC Crit. Rev. Food Technol. *2*(2), 171–186.

Borenstein, B., and Cort, W. M. 1970. Vitamin A for flour. French Pat. 2,011,564, Mar. 6.

Bressani, R., Elias, L. G., and Gomez Brenes, R. A. 1972. Improvement of protein quality by amino acid and protein supplementation. *In* International Encyclopedia of Food and Nutrition, Vol. 11. E. J. Bigwood (Editor). Pergamon Press, Elmsford, N.Y.

Bunnell, R. H., *et al.* 1968. Vitamin E stability in milk products. Unpublished data.

Butterfield, S., and Calloway, D. H. 1972. Folacin in wheat and selected foods. J. Am. Diet Assoc. *60*, 310–314.

Cort, W. M. 1973. Vitamin A and talc in rice. Unpublished data.

Cort, W. M. 1974. Antioxidant activity of tocopherols, ascorbyl palmitate and ascorbic acid and their mode of action. J. Am. Oil Chem. Soc. *51*, 321–325.

Cort, W. M. 1982. Antioxidant properties of ascorbic acid in foods. Adv. Chem. Ser. *200*, 533–550.

Cort, W. M., *et al.* 1974. Antioxidant Activity and Stability of a Number of Chromans. Presented at 65th Ann. Spring Meeting, Am. Oil Chem., Mexico, Apr. 27. Abstr. J. Am. Oil Chem. Soc. *51*, 279A.

Cort, W. M., *et al.* 1975. Antioxidant activity and stability of 6-hydroxy-2,5,7,8-tetramethylchroman-2-carboxylic acid. J. Am. Oil Chem. Soc. *52*, 174–178.

Cort, W. M., Mergens, W., and Greene, A. 1978. Stability of alpha- and gamma-tocopherol: Fe^{3+} and Cu^{2+} interactions. J. Food Sci. *43*, 797–798.

Cuq, J. L., Provansal, M., Guilleux, F., and Cheftel, C. 1973. Oxidation of methionine residues of casein by hydrogen peroxide. J. Food Sci. *38*, 11–13.

DeRitter, E. 1969. Vitamin liquid formulation. Unpublished data presented at Meeting of Soc. of Pharmacists, St. Louis.

Dwivedi, B. K., and Arnold, R. G. 1973. Chemistry of thiamin degradation in food products and model systems: A review. J. Agric. Food Chem. 21, 54–60.

Federal Register. 1962. Disodium EDTA for use with iron salts to stabilize vitamin B_{12}. Fed. Regist. 27, 883, Jan. 31.

Feller, B. A., and Macek, T. J. 1955. Effect of thiamin hydrochloride on the stability of solutions of crystalline vitamin B_{12}. J. Am. Pharm. Assoc. 44(11), 662–665.

Gambier, A. S., and Rahn, E. P. G. 1957. The combination of B-complex vitamins and ascorbic acid in aqueous solutions. J. Am. Pharm. Assoc., Sci. Ed. 46, 134–140.

Jukes, A. E. 1974. The organic chemistry of copper. In Advances in Organometallic Chemistry, Vol. 12. F. G. A. Stone and R. West (Editors). Academic Press, New York.

Laurence, G. S., and Ellis, K. J. 1972. The detection of a complex intermediate in the oxidation of ascorbic acid by ferric ion. J. Chem. Soc., Dalton Trans., 1667–1670.

Levandoski, N. G., Baker, E. M., and Canham, J. E. 1971. A monodehydro form of ascorbic acid in the autoxidation of ascorbic acid to dehydro-ascorbic acid. Biochemistry 3, 1465–1469.

Lieberman, M., and Kunishi, A. T. 1967. Propanal may be a precursor of ethylene in metabolism. Science 158, 938.

Markakis, P., and Embs, R. J. 1966. Effect of sulfite and ascorbic acid on mushroom phenol oxidase. J. Food Sci. 31, 807–811.

Massieu, G. H., Guzman, J., Craviota, R. O., and Calvo, J. 1949. Determination of some essential amino acids in several uncooked and cooked Mexican foodstuffs. J. Nutr. 38, 293–304.

Mauron, J. 1974. Influence of industrial and household handling of food protein quality. In International Encyclopedia of Food and Nutrition, Vol. 2. E. J. Bigwood (Editor). Pergamon Press, Elmsford, NY.

Miller, C. F., Guadagni, D. G., and Kon, S. 1973. Vitamin retention in bean products: Cooked, canned and acid. J. Food Sci. 38, 493–495.

Moore, H. W., and Folkers, K. 1968. Vitamin B_{12}. II. Chemistry. In The Vitamins, Vol. 2. W. H. Sebrell, Jr. and R. S. Harris (Editors). Academic Press, New York.

Morrison, A. B., and McLaughlin, J. M. 1972. Availability of amino acids in foods. In International Encyclopedia of Food and Nutrition, Vol. 2. E. J. Bigwood (Editor). Pergamon Press, Elmsford, NY.

Newmark, H. L. 1958. Stable vitamin B_{12} containing solution. U.S. Pat. 2,823,167, Feb. 11.

Newmark, H. L. et al. 1974. Stability of ascorbate in bacon. Food Technol. 28, 28–31, 60.

O'Dell, B. L. 1969. Effect of dietary components upon zinc availability. Am. J. Clin. Nutr. 22, 1315–1322.

Olliver, M. 1967. Ascorbic acid occurrence in food. In The Vitamins, Vol. 1. W. H. Sebrell, Jr. and R. S. Harris (Editors). Academic Press, New York.

Rubin, S. H., and Cort, W. M. 1968. Aspects of vitamin and mineral enrichment. In Protein-rich cereal Foods for World Needs. M. Miller (Editor). American Association of Cereal Chemists, St. Paul, MN.

Schroeder, H. A. 1971. Losses of vitamins and trace minerals resulting from processing and preservation of foods. Am. J. Clin. Nutr. 24, 562–573.

Schudel, P., Mayer, H., and Isler, O. 1972. Tocopherol chemistry. In The Vitamins, Vol. 5. W. H. Sebrell, Jr. and R. S. Harris (Editors). Academic Press, New York.

Schweigert, B. S., and Lushbough, C. H. 1960. Effects of processing on meat products. *In* Nutritional Evaluation of Food Processing. R. S. Harris and H. von Loesecke (Editors). John Wiley, New York.

Shenoy, K. G., and Ramasarma, G. B. 1955. Iron as a stabilizer of vitamin B_{12} activity in liver extracts. Arch. Biochem. Biophys. *55*, 293–295.

Sistrunk, W. A., and Cash, J. N. 1970. Ascorbic acid and color changes in summer squash as influenced by blanch, pH, and other treatments. J. Food Sci. *35*, 645–648.

Societe Civile de Recherches Scientifiques et Industrielles. 1964. Stable aqueous polyvitamin solutions. French Pat. 1,372,408, Aug. 10.

Waddell, J. 1974. Bioavailability of iron sources. Food Prod. Develop. *8*(1), 80–86.

Use of Ionizing Radiation to Preserve Food

Miriam H. Thomas

INTRODUCTION

The chief methods used for food preservation have been canning, salting, pickling, dehydration, and refrigeration. However, during the past 35 years, there has been widespread interest throughout the world in using ionizing radiation for this purpose, and as early as 1921, the use of ionizing radiation was studied to preserve food using X rays to kill *Trichinella spiralis* in meat (Schwartz 1921).

According to Goresline (1981), in the early 1950s no significant support had been given by the U.S. Government to food irradiation research. However, the Atomic Energy Commission (AEC) negotiated and supervised research contracts with the Massachusetts Institute of Technology (MIT), the University of Michigan, Columbia University, the Food Research Institute, the American Meat Institute Foundation, the Stanford Research Institute, the National Canner Association, the Brookhaven National Laboratory, and the Vitro Corporation. These contracts were followed by the U.S. Navy and the Quartermaster Food and Container Institute (QMF&CI) awarding contracts to MIT. Since the Army Quartermaster Corps had the responsibility for subsistence research and development for the Department of Defense, it was tasked to enlarge its program on food irradiation.

Prior to 1959, most of the radiation experiments were performed with spent-fuel rods from nuclear reactors. Indeed, the QMF&CI did not have a cobalt-60 (^{60}Co) source, and therefore, most samples were irradiated at the Argonne National Laboratory, Lemont, Illinois in their spent fuel rod source. Finally, a Quartermaster Radiation Facility was constructed at the Quartermaster Research and Engineering Center, now named U.S. Army Natick Research and Development Center (now the U.S. Army Natick Res., Develop. Eng. Ctr.) located at Natick, Massachusetts. An excellent review of the Army's contribution to the national food irradiation program has been presented by Brynjolfsson (1976).

Numerous studies have shown that the effects of ionizing irradiation on the nutrient content of food are not particularly different from those of other methods of preservation. It has been shown that procedures can be employed during the radiation process to protect the nutritional value of the food; for example, by holding the food at low temperature during irradiation (Thomas and Josephson 1970) and by reducing or excluding free oxygen from the environment (Metlitskii *et al.* 1968; Kharlamov and Shubnyakova 1964; Southern and Rhodes 1967), nutrients can be protected.

The radiation process has many advantages. It can be used to insect deinfest cereals, flour, fresh and dried fruit, and other foods which have not been fumigated chemically. Irradiation can inhibit sprouting of tubers and bulbs and thereby extend their storage life. Since no refrigeration is required, irradiated products can be stored like their thermally processed counterparts. Intensive worldwide studies have shown that this technique is effective, has no detrimental effects on human health, and can be applied safely to the preservation of food.

TYPES OF RADIATION

In food processing, there are three basic types of ionizing radiation: electrons,[1] X rays produced by electrons in an X-ray target, and γ rays from ^{60}Co and ^{137}Cs. All three types cause ionization in food by either the primary electrons or by the secondary electrons resulting from γ- or X-ray interactions in the food. The ionized and activated molecules form unstable secondary products, notably free radicals and peroxides. The focus of this chapter will be on the effects of ionizing radiation on nutrients in the foods themselves, rather than the same constituents irradiated in pure form or in artificial solutions and mixtures, because it is difficult to extrapolate findings from test model systems to explain effects in food where protective mechanisms may be present.

Electrons and γ rays having energies between 100 kV and 10 MeV may affect all food components, in contrast to ultraviolet radiation, which affects only those compounds that absorb energy at the particular wavelength of that radiation.

HAZARDS

In the United States, radiation is defined as a food additive and therefore, it is necessary to provide scientific evidence of the wholesomeness

---

[1] See Glossary following the text for definitions of terms used in this chapter.

of food so treated. A wholesome food has satisfactory nutritional quality and is safe for human consumption from a microbiological and toxicological point of view. Of major concern are carcinogenicity, toxicity, teratogenicity, mutagenicity, hepatic microsomal enzyme function, induced radioactivity, viable pathogens, nutrition, and packaging (Urbain 1978). These considerations are the basis for the elaborate protocols developed for safety evaluation from animal feeding studies. The studies must utilize large numbers of test animals (multigeneration and multispecies) to provide sufficient data for meaningful statistical analyses. Food consumption and food utilization efficiency, growth measurements, reproduction, longevity, gross and microscopic pathology, urology, hematology, and enzyme function are some of the parameters utilized to measure animal health and performance.

Subsequent to the development of elaborate protocols for animal studies, a human feeding study was undertaken with nine men. Their diet consisted of up to 100% irradiated foods for periods of 15 days. The foods, 54 in total, were either frozen or at room temperature after irradiation and were stored. No evidence of toxic effects from eating irradiated foods was observed in any of the men. Digestibilities of the macronutrients and metabolizable energy were similar in the irradiated and control diets. There were no significant differences in urinary excretion of total glucuronides, total ketones, or total organic acids between subjects consuming irradiated versus control diets (Plough *et al.* 1960).

Tests used to determine teratologic and mutagenic effects have been questioned because either the responses in experimental animals are not necessarily the same as in humans (Chauhan 1974), or the results involve extrapolation from comparatively simple organisms to man. Carcinogenic studies are customarily made with rats and mice because they have a tendency toward cancer development. Since it is not possible to conduct comparable studies with humans, there is no choice but to undertake extrapolation.

Irradiation of foods results in radiolytic products. Most radiolytic products detected in irradiated foods can also be found in unirradiated foods, and many have been produced in foods by other processing techniques. Merritt *et al.* (1975) reported that the response of various food components to radiation is quite similar, regardless of the food in which they occur, and knowledge of the food composition permits prediction of the radiolytic products that result when it is irradiated. A Select Committee on Health Aspects of Irradiated Beef (U.S. Army Medical Research and Development Command 1977, 1979) reviewed the possible toxicity to man of the volatile compounds detected in irradiated beef and concluded that, of the 65 compounds identified in irradiated beef, there were no grounds to suspect the conclusion that the radiolytic compounds evaluated would create any hazard to the health of persons consuming reasonable quantities of irradiated beef. The later report (U.S. Army Medical Research and Development Command 1979) by the Committee stated that the possible presence of undetected substances cannot be excluded and, therefore, coupling chemical studies with suitable animal feeding studies would provide complementary approaches to ensure the wholesomeness and safety of irradiated foods.

Microbiological hazards have been eliminated by employing minimum radiation doses sufficient to kill the most radiation-resistant strains of *Clostridium botulinum*. The increased incidence of mutants due to exposure to radiation and the alteration of the outgrowth pattern to favor pathogenic organisms have caused much concern. Idziak (1973) and Ingram (1975) reported that pathogenic organisms of public health significance, subjected to single or multiple irradiations, produced no evidence of a microbiological health hazard associated with food irradiation. In foods containing *C. botulinum* type E (possibly other types as well), the change in the outgrowth pattern by radurization appears to lead to a potential health hazard. However, no comparable hazard has been identified with the radurization of meat (Urbain 1978).

PACKAGING

Since ionizing radiation passes through the packaging material as it travels to the food inside the container, that material must not be affected by the treatment or affect the food being treated. Furthermore, it must be strong enough to withstand damage during commercial production, shipment, and storage (Killoran 1983). A number of food packaging materials have been approved by the Food and Drug Administration (FDA) under the Code of Federal Regulation 21, Food and Drugs: (1) Part 199: Irradiation in the Production, Processing, and Handling of Food, Subpart C, Packaging Materials for Irradiated Foods, Regulation 179.45. Tables 18.1 and 18.2 list polymeric films and multilayered flexible materials approved by the FDA. Additionally, the properties of tinplate enamels, end-sealing compounds, and solder were examined to determine the quantity and type of extractives obtained due to irradiation by comparison with the nonirradiated control. From these results and others, it can be concluded that both rigid and flexible materials used for foods to be irradiated pose no safety hazard (Killoran 1983).

Nutritional considerations, which will be discussed elsewhere in this chapter, can be assessed by chemical analyses. However, to measure all nutritional constituents at the same time, the best approach is through animal feeding studies to measure growth, reproduction, food consumption and efficiency, and the occurrence of gross abnormalities.

Table 18.1. FDA-Approved Polymeric Films: CFR 179.45

Material	Description of approved material	Maximum radiation dose (kGy)[a]
Nitrocellulose, or vinylidene-chloride-coated cellophane	176.1200	10
Wax-coated paperboard	176.170	10
Glassine paper	176.170	10
Polyolefin	175.1520	10
Kraft paper	176.170	5
Polystyrene	176.1630	10
Rubber hydrochloride	175.300	10
Nylon hydrochloride	177.1500	10
Polyethylene	177.1530	60
Polyethylene terephthalate	177.1630	60
Polyiminocaproyl (nylon 6)	177.1500	60
Vinylidene chloride-vinyl chloride	175.320	60
Vinyl chloride-vinyl acetate	179.320	60
Vegetable parchment	179.45	60
Ethylene-vinyl acetate	177.1350	80[b]

Source: Killoran (1983).
[a] Incidental to use of γ radiation.
[b] Incidental to use of γ or electron radiation.

Table 18.2. FDA-Approved Multilayered Flexible Materials: CFR 179.45

Combination	Material	Thickness (μm)
1	Polyethylene terephthalate	13
	Aluminum foil	9
	Polyethylene terephthalate	13
	Polyethylene, 0.960 g/ml	80
2	Polyethylene terephthalate	13
	Aluminum foil	9
	Ethylene-butene-1 copolymer polyisobutylene blend (70–30)	80
3	Polyiminocaproyl	25
	Aluminum foil	9
	Polyiminocaproyl	25
	Ethylene-butene-1 copolymer, 0.950 g/ml	80
4	Polyethylene terephthalate	13
	Aluminum foil	9
	Polypropylene-ethylene vinyl acetate copolymer (94–6)	80
5	Polyiminocaproyl	25
	Aluminum foil	9
	Polyethylene terephthalate	13
	Polypropylene	80

Source: Killoran (1983).

Many of the practical applications of food irradiation require radiation doses lower than 500 krad. In July, 1980, the Food and Agriculture Organization of the United Nations (FAO)/the International Atomic Energy Agency (IAEA)/World Health Organization (WHO) Expert Committee resolved, after evaluating the available data, that no toxicological hazard is caused by irradiating any food up to a dose of 1 Mrad, and therefore, foods so treated need not be tested for toxicity (World Health Organization 1981). Table 18.3 lists the irradiated foods cleared for human consumption to different countries.

CARBOHYDRATES

The use of irradiation to inhibit microbial damage in foodstuffs has numerous advantages compared with heat treatment since structural changes are small. Changes that can occur in carbohydrates result from the influence of air and water and the reactions associated with radiolysis (McManus 1982; Raffi *et al.* 1981; Diehl *et al.* 1978). In dilute aqueous solution, simple sugars, such as glucose, respond to radiation through the indirect effect. Glucose produces glucuronic, gluconic acids, and saccharic acids as well as glyoxal, arabinose, erythrose, formaldehyde, and dehydroxyacetone. Oligosaccharides form monosaccharides and products similar to those obtained with the irradiation of simple sugars. Irradiation of starch and cellulose (polysaccharides) causes degradation into glucose, maltose, dextrins, and the products of irradiation of these substances. Glycogen is also broken into smaller units by radiation.

Postirradiation effects have been reported in pectins, cellulose, and dextrins and continued in storage. These changes are dependent upon the presence of water and temperature also and are explained as connected with long-lived free radicals (Kertesz *et al.* 1956). The constituents of the cell wall of plant tissues become softened, which can result in practical difficulties in the application of radiation to fruit and vegetables. For example, pectin substances lose jelling powers and some browning occurs, which is accentuated in the presence of protein (Kraybill 1982). The browning reaction occurs, but it occurs likewise in heat-processed foods. Although irradiation causes changes in texture and reactions that might give rise to reductones or change sweetness and color, thus affecting the acceptance of food, these changes have not been shown to be of any nutritional consequence.

The high-dose radiolysis of sugars in solution produces many compounds, some of which have been found to be toxic in model systems. On the other hand, in vivo experiments have failed to confirm the toxicity of irradiated carbohydrates. When potatoes were irradiated to either 10 or 100 krad, dried, and incorporated into the diet as 72%

Table 18.3. Irradiated Foods Cleared for Human Consumption in Different Countries[a]

Country	Product	Date
Australia	Frozen shrimp	1978
Belgium	Potatoes**	1980
	Strawberries**	1980
	Onions	1980
	Garlic	1980
	Shallots	1980
	Paprika	1980
	Black pepper	1980
Bulgaria	Potatoes*	1971
	Potatoes*	1972
	Onions*	1972
	Garlic*	1972
	Grain*	1972
	Dry food concentrates*	1972
	Dried fruits*	1972
	Fresh fruits*	1972
Canada	Potatoes	1960
	Onions	1965
	Wheat, flour	1965
	Whole wheat flour	1969
	Poultry****	1973
	Cod/haddock****	1973
Chile	Potatoes* ****	1974
Czechoslovakia	Potatoes*	1976
	Onions*	1976
	Mushrooms*	1976
Denmark	Potatoes	1970
France	Potatoes**	1972
	Onions**	1977
	Garlic**	1977
	Shallots**	1977
Federal Republic of	Deep-frozen meals* ***	1972
Germany	Potatoes*	1974
Hungary	Potatoes****	1969
	Potatoes****	1972
	Potatoes****	1973
	Onions****	1973
	Onions****	1975
	Onions*	1976
	Strawberries****	1973
	Mixed spices*	1974
Israel	Potatoes	1967
	Onions	1968
Italy	Potatoes	1973
	Onions	1973
	Garlic	1973
Japan	Potatoes	1972
Netherlands	Asparagus*	1969
	Cocoa beans*	1969

(continued)

Table 18.3.   *(Continued)*

Country	Product	Date
Netherlands *(continued)*	Strawberries****	1969
	Mushrooms	1969
	Deep frozen meals***	1969
	Potatoes	1970
	Peeled potatoes****	1976
	Shrimps*	1970
	Shrimps****	1976
	Onions*	1971
	Onions	1975
	Poultry, in bags	1971
	Chicken	1976
	Fresh, tinned and liquid foodstuffs***	1972
	Spices*	1971
	Spices**	1974
	Spices**	1975
	Spices**	1978
	Vegetable filling* ****	1974
	Powdered batter mix****	1974
	Endive****	1975
	Fresh vegetables****	1977
	Haddock, whiting coal-fish****	1976
	Cod/plaice****	1976
	Fried frog legs**	1978
	Rice and ground rice products**	1979
	Rye bread	1980
	Spices**	1980
Philippines	Potatoes**	1972
South Africa	Potatoes	1977
	Onions	1978
	Garlic	1978
	Chicken	1978
	Papaya	1978
	Mango	1978
	Strawberries	1978
	Dried banana	1977
	Avocados	1977
Spain	Potatoes	1969
	Onions	1971
Thailand	Onions	1973
USSR	Potatoes	1958
	Potatoes	1973
	Grain	1959
	Fresh fruits and vegetables*	1964
	Raw beef, pork, rabbit products in bags*	1964
	Dried fruits	1966
	Dry food concentrates	1966
	Poultry, in bags*	1966
	Culinary meats in bags*	1967
	Onions*	1967
	Onions	1973

Table 18.3. *(Continued)*

Country	Product	Date
United Kingdom	Foods for patients requiring sterile diet	1969
United States	Wheat and wheat flour	1963
	White potatoes	1964
Uruguay	Potatoes	1970
World Health Organization	Potatoes**	1969
	Potatoes	1976
	Onions	1976
	Papaya	1976
	Strawberries	1976
	Wheat and ground wheat products**	1969
	Wheat and ground wheat products	1976
	Rice	1976
	Chicken	1976
	Cod and redfish	1976
	Foods in general	1980

Source: Goresline (1982).

[a] Key: *, experimental batches; **, temporary acceptance; ***, hospital patients; ****, test marketing; underlined, unlimited clearance.

of the total weight, no differences were found between animals receiving either the irradiated or control product over a 4- or 8-week period (Lang and Bassler 1966A). Saint-Lèbe *et al.* (1973) fed to rats both raw and cooked dry maize starch irradiated with ^{60}Co to either 300 or 600 rad as 62% of the diet for 1 year. With respect to growth or reproduction, no significant differences between groups receiving either irradiated or nonirradiated starch were found. Although enzymatic digestibility was raised with an increase of dose of irradiation in raw potato starch, no difference was obtained in the feed efficiency between rats fed nonirradiated or irradiated starch treated with up to 10 Mrad. Further experiments with rats showed that the absorption ratio of irradiated:nonirradiated starch was increased with irradiation dose and that both feed efficiency and weight gain increased with increasing dose of irradiation.

Nine foods, nonirradiated or irradiated at $15°C$ with 5.58 Mrad from spent fuel rods, were fed to rats (Read *et al.* 1961). In fact, the radiation treatment had no effect on the availability of carbohydrate, fat, or protein, as shown in Table 18.4. There are many substances which protect carbohydrates against radiation degradation (Phillips 1972), and among these are amino acids and proteins (Diehl *et al.* 1978). This demonstrates the potential effect that compounds associated with carbohydrates in a food can exert on the end product. Therefore, extrapolations of findings with pure substances to those of complex systems that exist in foods must be performed with care.

Table 18.4. Availability of Macronutrients (%) in
Irradiated Diet Fed to Rats[a]

	Carbohydrate	Fat	Protein
Control[b]	90.6	93.6	87.7
Irradiated[c]	90.4	94.1	88.5

Source: Raica *et al.* (1972).
[a] Rats fed a nine-component irradiated diet through
   four generations.
[b] Stored frozen.
[c] Stored at room temperature, 5.58 Mrad.

LIPIDS

Many investigators have used low-dose irradiation of less than 1 Mrad,
while others have employed high-dose irradiation of 7 Mrad and above
to preserve food. However, the nature of radiolysis of lipids is basically
the same and the products formed are similar, regardless of the dose or
source of energy (Hammer and Wills 1979; Delincee and Paul 1981;
Takyi and Amuh 1979). With electron-spin resonance (ESR) spectro-
scopy, free radicals are detected in fats after either high or low radiation doses. The concentration of radicals is appreciably lower in fats
irradiated with low than high doses of radiation. Free radicals are
detectable in fats after irradiation at high doses and low temperatures,
which is expected, since radicals are more stable at very low temperatures. The course of radiolysis in fats is significantly influenced by the
phase state and temperature (Nawar 1978).

The irradiation of vegetable and animal fats at dose levels anticipated
for food irradiation results in only minor changes in the usual parameters for measuring fat quality, that is, peroxide value, iodine value,
Kreis test, viscosity, and acid value (Jaddou 1979; Lyaskovskaya and
Piul'Skaya 1975). The major reactions which take place during the
irradiation of lipid material include hydrogen abstraction, addition H^+
and OH^- to double bonds, isomerization, hydrolysis, polymerization,
dehydration, and decarboxylation. Irradiation can also cause cross-
linking, dimerization, and aggregation along with degradation. The
literature reports that these alterations are not unlike those occurring
due to heat and/or oxidative processes (Mitchell 1957; Partman 1962;
Chipault 1962; Nawar 1972). Sensitivity to radiation damage of food
lipids can be controlled by such factors as rate, amount, and temperature of irradiation; absence of oxygen and light during irradiation; and
length and temperature of storage (Coleby 1959). Lipids as a constituent
of food are protected, as evidenced by greater destruction in separated
lipids for the same irradiation does. This protective effect has been
attributed to antioxidants such as cysteine (Read 1960). The presence

of anitoxidants in natural lipids not only can influence the reactions and the physical state of the lipid, but, regulated by temperature, can play an important role during both irradiation and subsequent storage.

Peroxides are known to form to a greater extent in animal than in vegetable fats with similar treatment (Mead *et al.* 1956; Morgan 1958) and could lead to oxidative rancidity (Goldblith 1955; Sedláček 1958). However, in the absence of oxygen, the production of peroxides is prevented (Morgan 1958; Lundberg 1960).

Gel'fand (1970) reported that fewer oxidative products were formed in steaks packaged in polyethylene–foil–cellophane (to exclude light) and irradiated to 0.8 Mrad than similar samples packaged in transparent polyethylene cellophane.[1] During storage, this difference increased. On the other hand, ^{60}Co irradiation of a chicken-based wet pet food product to 4.5 Mrad did not change the relative composition of the total lipid extract or of the triglyceride fraction from the nonirradiated control (Rao and Novak 1973).

Monty (1960), Moore (1961), and Nassett (1957) have reported that irradiated fat is digested and absorbed at a slower rate than nonirradiated fat, but that there is no alteration in its nutritive value to the consumer. It is believed that in those cases where digestion and absorption was delayed, the product fed may have been packaged in material through which oxygen could permeate during the irradiation process, causing the experienced delayed reported above. Studies with dogs, reported by Schreiber and Nassett (1959), indicate that the rate of absorption of lard irradiated to 5.58 Mrad by an electron source was reduced due to delayed emptying of the stomach contents. Since the overall digestibility was unaffected, they concluded that lypolysis and absorption of end products were not seriously disturbed by feeding irradiated lard. Corn oil irradiated to either 2.79 or 5.58 Mrad was fed to rats with no adverse affect on its digestibility (Moore 1961). The availability in rats of fats obtained from major food components that had been irradiated with spent fuel rods to 5.58 Mrad was 95.8% compared to 94.8% for unirradiated control (Read *et al.* 1961). When Lang and Bassler (1966B) compared the digestibility in rats of soybean oil electron irradiation to 100 Mrad in air at room temperature with an unirradiated control, digestibility of the irradiated product was diminished. It should be pointed out that the dose administered was 20–30 times the level required for sterilization of foods and that these authors found that soybean oil irradiated to 2.5 Mrad was not unfavorably affected.

Plough and associates (1957) fed human volunteers pork irradiated to 2.7 Mrad and stored 1 year at room temperature and found the digestibility of the fat (in pork) to be no different from that of unirradiated fat.

---

[1] A broad spectrum of research on packaging irradiated foods has been reported by Killoran (1983).

Extensive studies and reports have been made on the mechanisms involved in the radiolysis of fats (Nawar 1972, 1978; Schaich 1980). However, the observations above lead one to conclude that when lipids are irradiated under conditions anticipated for commercial food processing, which is not expected to exceed 7 Mrad, irradiation does not result in significant loss of nutritional value.

PROTEINS

Many studies have been undertaken on the effects of radiations on isolated amino acids, retention of amino acids in irradiated foods, effects of radiation on the biological value of proteins, and the effects of radiation on the physicochemical properties of proteins irradiated in vitro. The chemistry of irradiated proteins and related compounds has been reviewed by Garrison (1972), Urbain (1977), Simic (1978), and more recently by Simic (1983). As stated earlier for other food constituents, the radiation chemistry of amino acids cannot be extrapolated directly to peptides and proteins, but model studies of amino acids and peptides do yield valuable information.

Very high levels of irradiation have marked effects on protein and amino acids. Radiolytic compounds of protein, when irradiated at 50 Mrad, originate from cleavage of side chains of peptide or end groups (Merritt et al. 1966, Taub et al. 1976). However, levels intended for use in food processing show only minimum adverse effects. Studies by Ley et al. (1969) reported that radappertized protein supplied in a rat diet in the form of soya, meat and bone, and fish meals showed that irradiation at doses up to 7.0 Mrad has no significant effect on digestibility, biological value, and net protein utilization (Table 18.5), or on amino acid composition (Table 18.6).

No significant changes were found in protein, fat, and mineral contents of wheat, gamma irradiated to 20 and 200 krad for insect disinfestation

Table 18.5. Effect of Irradiation on the Protein Quality of Rat Diet

Dose (Mrad)	True digestibility	Biological value	Net protein utilization
0	85.6	80.5	68.9
0.5	83.6	75.8	63.5
1.0	86.5	81.7	70.6
2.5	87.0	78.1	68.0
3.5	84.8	77.3	65.4
7.0	85.3	76.4	65.2

Source: Ley et al. (1969).

Table 18.6. Effect of a Radiation Dose of 7.0 Mrad on the Amino Acid Composition of the Protein in Rat Diet

Amino acid	Diet (g/16 gN)	
	Unirradiated	Irradiated
Asparagine	8.85	8.38
Threonine	3.80	3.73
Serine	4.17	4.16
Glutamic acid	15.70	15.61
Glycine	5.82	5.79
Alanine	5.61	5.54
Valine	4.78	4.68
Isoleucine	3.99	3.99
Leucine	7.44	7.47
Tyrosine	3.28	3.38
Phenylalanine	4.12	4.28
Lysine	5.72	5.82
Histidine	2.29	2.37
Arginine	6.04	6.05
Methionine	2.33	2.11
Cystine	1.34	1.44
Tryptophan	1.16	1.32

Source: Ley *et al.* (1969).

by Vakil *et al.* (1973). Total amino acid profiles and available lysine content of irradiated wheat revealed no change, but there was an 8% increase in free amino acid levels on irradiation up to 1 Mrad. They concluded that the changes in physicochemical properties of the starch and protein in wheat were not nutritionally significant. These findings are in agreement with those of Pape (1973), Doguchi (1969), Nair and Brownell (1965) and Metlitskii *et al.* (1968). Comparable results have been reported by Leonova and Sosedov (1972) for maize and kidney beans, and by Metta and Johnson (1959) for wheat and corn.

The nutritive value of radiation-pasteurized chicken has been studied by De Groot *et al.* (1972). No significant difference was found in the amino acid content of chicken, nonirradiated or irradiated with either 300 or 600 krad, stored at refrigerated temperature for 6 days, and subsequently cooked and homogenized. The protein efficiency ratio of

Table 18.7. Nutritive Value of Protein in Chicken Stored at 5°C for 4–7 Days and Cooked

Dose (krad)	PER
0	2.18
300	2.34
600	2.21

Source: Derived from De Groot *et al.* (1972).

Table 18.8. Amino Acid Content of Raw Beef (g/100 g dry weight) Exposed to Accelerated Electrons or γ Radiation (0.6 Mrad)

Amino acid	Control (not irradiated)	2 MeV		4 MeV		^{60}Co γ radiation 1.17 MeV
		20 krad/sec	200 krad/sec	20 krad/sec	200 krad/sec	0.53 krad/sec
Cystine	0.72	0.71	0.87	0.65	0.62	0.86
Lysine and histidine	15.42	13.46	15.07	14.29	13.79	14.95
Arginine	7.95	7.72	8.09	7.32	7.65	7.23
Aspartic acid	7.04	6.85	6.65	6.41	6.78	7.15
Serine	2.82	2.97	2.60	3.04	2.96	2.79
Glycine	3.37	3.39	3.61	3.91	3.75	3.42
Glutamic acid	11.82	11.75	11.11	12.04	11.72	11.50
Threonine	4.64	4.23	4.52	4.52	4.54	4.67
Alanine	4.64	5.10	4.95	5.12	5.19	4.82
Tyrosine	2.84	2.74	2.89	3.02	2.77	3.03
Methionine	2.48	2.38	2.46	1.91	2.30	2.52
Valine	5.35	5.21	5.08	5.71	5.63	5.15
Phenylalanine	4.10	4.57	4.90	4.69	4.96	4.15
Leucine and isoleucine	9.19	10.04	9.74	9.96	9.93	9.32

Source: Derived from Frumkin et al. (1973).

of these treatments is given in Table 18.7. It was concluded by Frumkin *et al.* (1973) that radiation doses of 0.6 Mrad applied to raw beef and 0.8 Mrad to cooked beef for arresting spoilage do not lower protein nutritional value (Tables 18.8 and 18.9).

No significant effect on the digestibility or biological value of potato protein was found by Jaarma and Henricson (1964), Varela and Urbano (1971), Lang and Bassler (1966B), or Fujimaki *et al.* (1968).

When beef was heated to an F_0 value of 5.8 and the volatile compounds formed were compared to those produced by irradiation treatment of 5.6 Mrads, the two treatments gave equivalent lethality to microorganisms. Further, irradiation caused no more degradation compounds than steam heat sterilization (U.S. Army Medical Research and Development Command 1977).

In summary, the evidence indicates that by carefully controlling conditions of radiation processing and the added stress of storage (Frumkin *et al.* 1973, Brooke *et al.* 1966), there should be no significant impairment in the nutritional quality of the protein constituents of food for consumption by humans.

Table 18.9. Amino Acid Content[a] of Stored, Culinary-Treated (Ready to Eat) Beef Preserved by Exposure to Ionizing Radiation (0.8 Mrad)

			After 6 months' storage	
Amino acid	Control (deep frozen)	After irradiation	Control (deep frozen)	Irradiated
Lysine	8.98	8.95	8.12	8.81
Histidine	2.46	2.76	2.17	2.62
Arginine	5.41	5.20	4.97	5.36
Aspartic acid	7.99	7.44	8.00	7.26
Threonine	3.70	3.82	4.38	3.60
Serine	3.19	3.34	3.67	3.10
Glutamic acid	13.17	11.77	13.31	11.86
Proline	3.30	3.42	3.47	3.27
Glycine	3.57	3.94	3.65	3.72
Alanine	4.89	4.66	5.00	4.56
Valine	2.93	2.77	2.53	2.42
Methionine	2.10	1.88	3.01	1.30
Isoleucine	3.49	3.38	3.74	3.36
Leucine	6.30	6.12	6.87	5.33
Tyrosine	2.73	2.61	2.35	2.53
Phenylalanine	3.11	2.96	2.91	2.88
Tryptophan	1.37	1.47	1.32	1.35

Source: Derived from Frumkin *et al.* (1973).

[a] Expressed as percentage of protein.

VITAMINS

Vitamins, micronutrients in food, are divided into two subdivisions: water- and fat-soluble vitamins. Some vitamins are sensitive to ionizing radiation, although the effect is influenced by the nature and composition of the food.

Water-Soluble Vitamins

As early as 1949, it was reported by Proctor and Goldblith that niacin was the most and ascorbic acid the least resistant of the water-soluble vitamins to irradiation injury. Because of the instability of ascorbic acid, the change in its content in a food is often used to indicate the extent to which essential nutrients are destroyed by processing.

Tests on three varieties of potato radiated at doses up to 60 krad to inhibit sprouting showed that reduced ascorbic acid decreased as the dosage increased (Dallyn and Sawyer 1959). Highlands (1958) reported after 4 months of storage an initial loss in ascorbic acid content that was greater in the irradiated than the unirradiated potatoes. At this point, the loss was arrested, and an apparent conversion of ascorbic acid to the hydrated form took place in both treated and untreated samples until the eighth or ninth month of storage. Synthesis was then followed by another decrease which was much greater for the control than the irradiated samples (Mikaelsen and Roer 1956). Doses from 5 to 15 krad, which are approved for commercial processing of white potatoes to prevent sprouting during storage, result in minimal losses of ascorbic acid. However, McKinney (1971) reported no loss of ascorbic acid in potatoes subjected to radiation treatment.

Onions are also irradiated to inhibit sprouting during storage. The usual dose is between 8 and 10 krad, although doses up to 12 krad had little or no effect on the ascorbic acid content of onions. Frozen green beans, carrots, and corn irradiated at room temperature with 4.8 Mrad from ^{60}Co retained approximately 75% of their original vitamin C content (Thomas and Calloway 1961). On the other hand, Nickerson et al. (1956) report that treatment of asparagus, broccoli, green beans, and spinach with high-voltage cathode rays (1.86 Mrad) results in 28, 14, 8, and 35% retention of ascorbic acid, respectively.

The ascorbic acid content in fruit decreases during irradiation, but the degree of diminution has been known to be dependent upon both the species and the variety of fruit. Orange juice treated with 0.093, 0.279, 0.372, and 0.93 Mrad from high-voltage cathode rays retained 96, 78, 74, and 41%, respectively, of the initial ascorbic acid content, demonstrating that destruction increases with increasing dosage (Proctor and O'Meara 1951). Ascorbic acid retention in oranges, tangerines, tomatoes, and papayas varies from 100 to 72% with radiation doses from 40 to 300 krad as shown in Table 18.10.

Table 18.10. Effect of Radurization on Ascorbic Acid Retention in Fruit

Product	Dose (krad)	Retention (%)
Orange, temple	100	97
	200	72
Tangerines	40	104
	80	94
	160	94
Tomatoes	100	86
	200	86
	300	91
Papayas	125	110

Source: Calculated from Dennison and Ahmed (1971–1972), Wenkam and Moy (1968).

The length of storage and the storage conditions after irradiation treatment also have an effect on the ascorbic acid concentration. In lemons, losses at a 400-krad dose were slight 24 hr after irradiation, but as high as 95% after 40 days of storage at $10°C$ (Frumkin et al. 1973). Formation of mold in strawberries can be retarded using a dose of up to 500 krad without affecting either the flavor or the ascorbic acid content of the berries (Zeeuw 1961). On the other hand, investigations by Wells et al. (1963) indicated that 2 days after irradiation, treated berries were significantly lower in ascorbic acid than were untreated berries. Strawberries receiving 0.8 Mrad had significantly less ascorbic acid than those receiving 0.3 Mrad; however, after 95 days at $2°C$, differences between irradiated and unirradiated berries were slight.

Intermediate in sensitivity to irradiation is vitamin B_{12} and p-aminobenzoic acid. Pyridoxine is also radiosensitive and thiamin under some conditions is more sensitive to damage than is ascorbic acid. The extent of destruction is usually a function of radiation dose and temperature of the medium during irradiation. Thomas and Josephson (1970) have reported that thiamin destruction in food can be minimized by keeping the product frozen during irradiation. These investigators have shown that thiamin, riboflavin, niacin, and pyridoxine in pork and ham are less susceptible to destruction by sterilization at 4.5–5.6 Mrad at $-80°C$ than by the conventional thermal treatment (Table 18.11).

Later studies by Thomas et al. (1975) with ground pork, enzyme inactivated and irradiated by exposure to a ^{60}Co or 10-MeV linear-accelerator (linac) source at 2.0, 4.0, 6.0, or 8.0 Mrad at temperatures from +5 to $-80°C$ showed that thiamin retention is decreased as the irradiation dose is increased, but that retention is increased as the temperature of irradiation is decreased. In this study, the linac, as a source of radiation, was more favorable to thiamin retention in pork.

Table 18.11. Effect of Processing on the Vitamin Content of Canned Pork Loin and Ham

Vitamin	Treatment	Pork		Ham	
		mg/100 g[a,b]	Retention (%)	mg/100 g[a,b]	Retention (%)
Thiamin	Control	3.69 ± 0.22[a,b]		3.82 ± 0.38	
	4.5 Mrad at −80 ± 5°C	3.14 ± 0.25	85	3.25 ± 0.79	85
	Thermally processed	0.76 ± 0.08	20	1.27 ± 0.36	32
Riboflavin	Control	1.02 ± 0.28		1.01 ± 0.18	
	4.5 Mrad at −80 ± 5°C	0.79 ± 0.06	78	1.25 ± 0.09	123
	Thermally processed	0.82 ± 0.02	81	1.10 ± 0.24	109
Niacin	Control	20.3 ± 5.1		31.5 ± 0.81	
	—	15.9 ± 2.6	78	23.8 ± 2.92	76
	—	13.2 ± 1.8	65	14.6 ± 4.49	46
Pyridoxine	Control	0.76 ± 0.05		1.11 ± 0.15	
	—	0.75 ± 0.07	98	1.02 ± 0.12	92
	—	0.63 ± 0.07	84	0.64 ± 0.03	57

Source: Thomas and Josephson (1970).
[a] Mean ± S.D., three samples per treatment.
[b] Moisture, fat, salt-free basis.

Table 18.12.   Effect of Processing on Thiamin in Pork

Treatment	Temperature (°C)	Dose (Mrad)	Retention (%)
Thermal, $F_0 = 6.0$	116		12
	121		9
γ rays (^{137}Cs)	−45	1.5	72
		3.0	50
		4.5	40
		6.0	35
		7.5	27
Electrons	−20	1.2	82
(linac)		2.4	68
		3.6	57
	−45	1.5	83
		3.0	75
		4.5	66
		6.0	58
		7.5	52
		9.0	50

Source: Thomas *et al.* (1981A).

These results were confirmed by Thomas *et al.* (1981A). Additionally, the study addressed the phenomenon that pork irradiated with electrons retains more thiamin than when irradiated with γ rays under the same conditions. Table 18.12 illustrates these results; the fraction of thiamin retained in the sample irradiated in the frozen state is plotted semilogarithmically against dose in Fig. 18.1. Figure 18.2 shows that the loss in the γ ray-irradiated unfrozen sample is well above the others and that the losses in γ ray- and electron-irradiated samples in the frozen state follow a quasi-Arrhenius temperature dependence, the lines for both being practically parallel. Differences in thiamin loss between γ ray and electron beam irradiation shown in Fig. 18.1 and 18.2 are consequences of a dose-rate effect. To illustrate further, ground pork was irradiated at a fixed temperature to a fixed dose using three different dose rates by varying the peak current of the linac. These results are given in Table 18.13 and shown graphically in Fig. 18.3. Thiamin loss after 6 Mrad of irradiation is shown as a function of dose rate, which is proportional to beam current. The dotted line (drawn freehand) is assumed to correspond with the increased loss that would be encountered at dose rates lower than those actually used. The dose-rate effect and related considerations have been discussed previously by Taub *et al.* (1979).

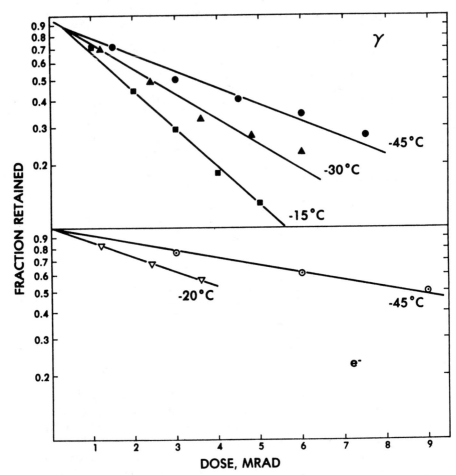

Fig. 18.1. Fraction of thiamin retained as a function of dose. Each point is an average of two samples. Initial temperatures are given; temperatures throughout irradiation rose less than 5°C. All samples had an initial concentration of thiamin of about 0.9 mg/100 g pork.

Table 18.13.   Effect of Dose Rate on Thiamin in Pork

Temperature (°C)	Dose (Mrad)	Current (mA)	Retention (%)
−45	6.0	600	60
−45	6.0	150	63
−45	6.0	24	52

Source: Thomas *et al.* (1981A).

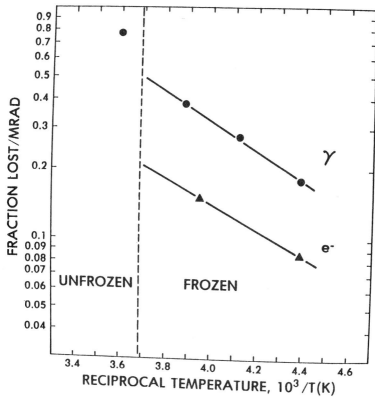

Fig. 18.2.   Fraction of thiamin lost per megarad of absorbed dose as a function of reciprocal temperature.   Vertical dotted line corresponds to the transition point of 271 K (−2°C).

Interestingly enough, these results for irradiated pork under controlled conditions are consistent with results for thiamin loss in beef and chicken irradiated on a production basis for animal feeding studies. Samples of this beef and chicken were used by the Letterman Army Institute for Research to investigate and ultimately demonstrate the absence of any antithiamin properties.   Results of their analyses of the irradiated and thermally processed samples are shown in Table 18.14. It should be pointed out that the electron-irradiated products retained 2–2.5 times as much thiamin as the γ ray-irradiated products.

In a study to further investigate the effects of low and high dose-rate irradiation on thiamin retention, Thomas et al. (1981B) exposed fortified and unfortified ground pork to irradiation at a fixed temperature and dose using electrons and X rays from a linac (pulsed source). The fortified product was employed to investigate the effect of thiamin concentration on its retention during irradiation under various conditions.

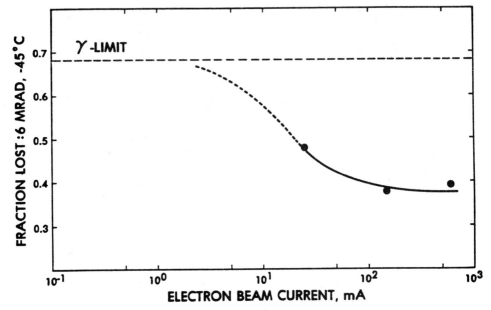

Fig. 18.3. Fraction of thiamin lost at $-45°C$ for a 6-Mrad dose as a function of dose rate. The abscissa is given in milliamperes (mA) of peak electron beam current during the ~5 μsec pulses from the linac. Dose rate is proportional to beam current. The solid line is drawn through the points corresponding to the indicated peak currents. Each point represents the average of two samples. The dashed line represents the results for γ ray irradiation, which corresponds to a low dose-rate limit. The dotted line is drawn hypothetically to connect the lower and upper dose-rate limits.

Table 18.14. Thiamin Retention (%) in Beef and Chicken after Processing

Process	Beef	Chicken
Thermal	21	22
γ Irradiation	23	27
Electron irradiation	44	66

Source: Data adapted from the Letterman Army Institute for Research, McGown *et al.* (1979A,B).

X rays were used so as to attain a wide range of doses per pulse in the product. The results not only verified previous conclusions reported above, but also demonstrated that the effects are independent of thiamin concentration (Tables 18.15, 18.16, 18.17).

On the basis of these observations, it appears that the indirect effect is due to the attack of radicals on thiamin and is responsible for much of the loss. The higher the instantaneous concentration of radicals

Table 18.15.   Thiamin Retention (%) in Ground Pork Irradiation with ^{60}Co at Various Temperatures

Temperature (°C)	Dose (Mrad)	Unfortified	Fortified
−15	1.5	57	57
	3.0	35	36
	4.5	25	21
	6.0	16	17
−45	1.5	79	76
	3.0	63	63
	4.5	53	53
	6.0	46	44
−80	2.0	86	79
	4.0	82	75
	6.0	75	67
	8.0	70	67

Source: Thomas *et al.* (1981B).

Table 18.16.   Thiamin Retention (%) in Ground Pork Irradiated with Electrons at Various Temperatures

Temperature (°C)	Dose (Mrad)	Unfortified	Fortified
−20	1.2	88	85
	2.4	78	71
	3.6	67	65
−45	2.5	88	78
	5.0	72	69
	7.5	65	63
−80	3.0	89	
	6.0	76	
	9.0	68	

Source: Thomas *et al.* (1981B).

Table 18.17.   Comparison of Thiamin Retention (%) in Ground Pork Irradiated at −45°C and 3 Mrad with Either Electrons or X rays

Source	Current (mA)	Duration (μsec)	Unfortified	Fortified
Electrons	300	5.0	82	77
	300	2.5	86	77
	300	0.5	76	70
	30	5.0	70	
X rays	300	5.0	55	54
	300	2.5	39	

Source: Thomas *et al.* (1981B).

following the pulse irradiation, the more likely that radical–radical reactions predominate and the less likely are radical–thiamin reactions. If the thiamin concentration is increased, then more radical–thiamin reactions occur at the expense of radical–radical reactions. Consequently, the loss is greater at low dose rates, but increases at a fixed dose rate at the higher thiamin concentrations. Some of the loss is due to direct absorption of energy by the thiamin. The loss observed at the plateau in the high dose-rate region presumably corresponds to the direct effect; it increases with increased thiamin concentrations.

The change in thiamin retention due to temperature is also consistent with indirect effects. Since the yields and/or diffusion of radicals increase with increasing temperature, the extent to which radical–thiamin reactions would occur should also increase. Irrespective of the mechanism involved, the temperature and dose-rate effects observed have significant implication for the nutritional quality of irradiated pork products. Highest retention of thiamin would be attained by irradiating with high dose rates at or near $-50°C$. The retention for electron irradiation sterilizing doses of 4 Mrad at $-50°C$ would be approximately 60%, which is significantly higher than in conventional thermoprocessing.

Wheat irradiated at either 20 or 200 krad retained approximately 90% of its thiamin, riboflavin, and niacin (Vakil et al. 1973) (Table 18.18). Irradiation of bleached, enriched, hard wheat flour in the range of 30–50 krad had no detrimental effect on the thiamin, riboflavin, niacin, or pyridoxine content. Furthermore, the nutritive quality of bread made from this flour was unaffected (Heiligman et al. 1973).

Much less is known concerning the effects of irradiation upon vitamin B_{12}, pantothenic acid, folacin, biotin, para-aminobenzoic acid, and choline. Most are radiosensitive in aqueous solution but not in food (Bregvadze and Bokeriya 1971; Metlitskii et al. 1968). Sheffner and Spector (1957) reported that considerable reduction in the radiosensitivity of vitamin B_{12} was obtained in raw whole milk. Irradiation of

Table 18.18. Effect of Irradiation on Vitamin Retention (%) of Wheat and Wheat Products

krad	Thiamin	Riboflavin	Niacin	Pyridoxine
20[a]	88	91	88	—
200[a]	88	87	91	—
30–50[b]	100	100	89	100
30–50[c]	100	100	117	100

Source: Calculated from Vakil et al. (1973), Heiligman et al. (1973).
[a] Wheat.
[b] Flour.
[c] Bread.

Table 18.19. Effect of Irradiation on Vitamin Retention (%) of Seafoods

Vitamin	Clams[a]		Haddock[b]	
	Air packed, 450 krad	Vacuum packed, 350 krad	Air packed, 250 krad	Vacuum packed, 150 krad
Thiamin	80	67	37	78
Riboflavin	99	111	105	100
Niacin	84	97	106	100
Pyridoxine	63	93	125	115
Pantothenic acid	115	115	164	178
Vitamin B_{12}	92	91	110	90

Source: Calculated from Brooke *et al.* (1964, 1966).
[a] Stored 30 days at 0°C postirradiation.
[b] Stored 30 days in ice.

ground pork with γ rays from spent fuel rods produced less than 10% destruction of pantothenic acid and no destruction of folacin with doses up to 5.58 Mrad. Moreover, Richardson (1955) found no significant decrease in folacin activity in irradiated diets fed to chicks. On the other hand, Thomas and Calloway (1961) and Thomas and Josephson (1970) determined that 68% of the pantothenic acid was lost in pork after irradiation at ambient temperature at a dose of 4.8 Mrad. A study by Liuzzo *et al.* (1966) reported no appreciable losses for riboflavin, niacin, pantothenic acid, biotin, folacin, or vitamin B_{12} in oysters radurized by 0.2 Mrad. However, losses were extensive for thiamin and pyridoxine. Similar changes took place in air-packed clams irradiated at 450 krad at 0°C or vacuum-packed clams irradiated at 350 krad (Brooke *et al.* 1964) after 30 days of storage in ice. Further studies by Brooke *et al.* (1966) show the same pattern of vitamin retention after irradiation at these doses and storage conditions (Table 18.19).

Fat-Soluble Vitamins

Fewer data are available on the effects of irradiation on fat-soluble vitamins than on water-soluble vitamins. Early reports by Goldblith and Proctor (1949) indicated that carotene was radiosensitive to cathode rays. Other studies by Kung *et al.* (1953) showed that irradiation of whole milk with 440 krad resulted in the destruction of 40% of the carotenoids, 70% of the vitamin A, and 60% of the tocopherols. Further studies with dairy products indicate 31–68% losses of vitamin A. Carotene destruction can be minimized during radiation treatment by the addition of ascorbic acid.

Vitamin A sensitivity is influenced by the media in which it is exposed. For example, it is more stable to margarine than in butter because the vitamin A esters used to supplement margarine are more resistant to irradiation than the natural vitamin A in butter (Sheffner and Spector 1957). Diehl (1979A) reported that vitamin A losses caused by 10 MeV electrons in cream cheese, calf liver sausage, pig liver, whole egg powder, and margarine continued to increase during storage for 4–8 weeks in the presence of air. Vitamin A loss in sausage irradiated with 5 Mrad was 22% on the day after irradiation and 61% after 4 weeks. Irradiation and storage at $0°C$, instead of ambient temperature, reduced these losses considerably. Exclusion of air by vacuum or nitrogen, or irradiation with solid carbon dioxide (approximately –80°C), was even more effective in preventing destruction of vitamin A. After 4 weeks of storage, cream cheese irradiated at 5 Mrad had lost 60% of its original vitamin A when irradiated and stored in air at ambient temperature, 20% in a nitrogen atmosphere, 5% in a vacuum package, and 5% when irradiated on solid carbon dioxide and stored at ambient temperature.

Although vitamin D is obtained by the ultraviolet irradiation of ergosterol, irradiation of ergosterol with γ photons results in only traces of vitamin D. Additionally, biological evidence indicates that the vitamin D activity for chicks is decreased by γ irradiation of the total diet with 2.79 Mrad at ambient temperature (Sheffner and Spector 1957). Knapp and Tappel (1961) reported that vitamin D is apparently unaffected by ionizing radiation, as determined by the absence of change in vitamin D content in salmon oil when irradiated. It is quite possible that the vitamin E in salmon oil could have provided some protection.

Thomas and Calloway (1961) studied five foods of animal origin (chicken, beef, pork, shrimp, and bacon). Nutrient content was determined before and after dehydration, irradiation, and the usual thermal process. The tocopherol content of dehydrated samples was greater than that of their thermally sterilized counterparts. In all instances, the irradiated products were equal or superior to the canned product. The protective effect of low temperature during irradiation on vitamin E levels in foods is not diminished by subsequent storage or heating. Sunflower oil irradiated at $20°C$ with 3 Mrad in the presence of air and subsequently heated for 1 hour at $180°C$ lost 98% of its α-tocopherol content, but only 65% when irradiated at –30°C. Radiation-induced losses of α-tocopherol in sunflower seed oil or in an emulsion of oil–water were independent of the type of radiation or dose rate (Diehl 1979B).

The loss of vitamin E in rolled oats irradiated with 0.1 Mrad was reduced from 56 to 5% by packaging under nitrogen. Vacuum packaging was equally effective during the first 3 months of storage but less so during the following 5 months. No advantage was gained by packaging under carbon dioxide (Diehl 1979C).

Under identical experimental conditions, vitamin K_3 is about twice as stable as vitamin A acetate and about 20 times as stable as vitamin E. Vitamin K_3 is even more stable under aerobic than under anaerobic conditions. Differences in radiation sensitivity among the K vitamins have been reported, but vitamin K_3 seems to possess the lowest stability.

The small amount of vitamin K in beef is destroyed or unavailable after irradiation with Mrad doses. Richardson *et al.* (1956) reported no loss of vitamin K content in alfalfa leaf meal irradiated to a dose of 2.79 Mrad at ambient temperature. In spinach and broccoli irradiated with 2.79–5.58 Mrad, the vitamin K levels were found to be as high as in frozen samples of the same products. No destruction of K_1, K_3, or K_5 in irradiated semisynthetic diets was apparent when they were fed to chicks. Due to the findings reported above and the fact that bacterial synthesis of the vitamin takes place in the intestine, no one receiving irradiated diets of natural foods is likely to develop a hemorrhagic condition because of a vitamin K deficiency in the diet.

CONCLUSIONS

Even though food preserved by ionizing radiation under processing conditions proposed for commercial production is nutritionally comparable to food preserved by conventional means, very few foods have been approved by the United States, and they are not offered commercially on the U.S. civilian market. This procedure is not intended to replace other processing methods, but to offer an alternative, particularly when the end product results in a more desirable product than that resulting from dehydration or canning. The main obstacles have been the costly and time-consuming procedures required to obtain government food and drug clearances. By law, it must be proved that food preserved by irradiation is wholesome. Therefore, officials place far more rigorous safety requirements on foods so treated than on more conventional processes for pasteurization or sterilization of foods. In addition to government approval to produce and market irradiated foods, industry must feel the end justifies the means and that the cost to the consumer will be competitive with the cost of foods produced by alternative processing technologies.

GLOSSARY OF SOME BASIC TERMS AND CONCEPTS

absorbed dose: The amount of energy absorbed per unit mass of irradiated matter. The unit of absorbed dose is the gray (Gy). 1 rad = 100 erg; 1000 rad = 1 kilorad (krad); 1 million rad = 1 Megarad (Mrad).

Becquerel (Bq): The unit of activity being one radioactive disintegration per second of time. 1 Bq = 2.7027×10^{-11} Ci.

β particle: A high-speed electron ejected from an atomic nucleus in certain types of radioactive disintegration. Electrons and β particles are identical in nature.

Curie (Ci): The unit of activity which is being superseded by the becquerel (Bq). 1 Ci = 3.7 $\times$ 10^{10} disintegrations per second = 3.7 $\times$ 10^{10} Bq.

electron: A particle that is negatively charged, a common constituent of all atoms, having a mass (m) = 9 $\times$ 10^{-28} g.

electron volt (eV): The amount of energy gained by an electron when accelerated by a potential of 1 volt. 1 eV = 1.6 $\times$ 10^{12} erg; 1 million eV = 1 MeV.

γ rays: Electromagnetic radiation of very short wavelength, emitted by the nuclei of radioactive substances during decay.

Gray (Gy): The unit of energy absorbed from ionizing radiation by the matter through which the radiation passes. 1 Gy = 100 rad.

ionizing radiation: Radiation, either corpuscular (α/β rays, or neutrons) or electromagnetic (γ rays), which is capable of producing ions in the matter through which it passes.

isotope: Nuclide having the same atomic number and the same chemical element but having a different mass number.

nuclide: Any given atomic species characterized by the number of protons, Z, in the nucleus; the number of neutrons, N, in the nucleus; and, the energy state of the nucleus.

rad: The unit of energy absorbed from ionizing radiation by the matter through which the radiation passes. 1 million rad = 1 Mrad = 10 kGy.

radappertization: Sterilization of food by exposure to ionizing radiation at doses greater than 1 Mrad and considered equivalent to canning.

radicidation: Pasteurization of food by exposure to ionizing radiation at doses lower than 1 Mrad to kill all non-spore-forming pathogens.

radurization: Pasteurization of food by exposure to ionizing radiation at doses lower than 1 Mrad to delay onset of spoilage by reducing the population of organisms.

X rays: Electromagnetic radiation of short wavelength, produced when a beam of fast electrons in a high vacuum bombards a metallic target.

ACKNOWLEDGMENT

I wish to take this occasion to thank Mrs. Sharon Jarboe, whose assistance made this contribution possible.

REFERENCES

Bregvadze, U. D., and Bokeriya, N. M. 1971. Effect of γ-irradiation on amino acid composition in wines. (Russian). Tr. Gruz. Nauch-Issled. Inst. Pishch. Prom. *4*, 90–96.

Brooke, R. O., Ravesi, E. M., Gadbois, D. F., and Steinberg, M. A. 1964. Preservation of fresh unfrozen fishery products by low-level radiation. III. The effects of radiation pasteurization on amino acids and vitamins in clams. Food Technol. *18*, 1060–1064.

Brooke, R. O., Ravesi, E. M., Gadbois, D. F., and Steinberg, M. A. 1966. Preservation of fresh unfrozen fishery products by low-level radiation. V. The effects of radiation pasteurization on amino acids and vitamins in haddock fillets. Food Technol. *20*, 1479–1482.

Brynjolfsson, A. 1976. The national food irradiation program conducted by the Department of the Army. Food Irradiation: The Past 200 . . . The Next 200? Inst. Food Technol. Symp. 36th Annual Meeting, Anaheim, CA, June 6–9.

Chauhan, P. 1974. Assessment of irradiated foods for toxicological safety — Newer methods. *In* Food Irradiation Information, No. *5*, pp. 20–38. Int. Project Field Food Irradiation, Karlsruhe, W. Germany.

Chipault, J. R. 1962. High-energy irradiation. Lipids and their oxidation. *In* Symposium on Foods. H. W. Schultz (Editor). AVI Publishing Co., Westport, CT.

Coleby, B. 1959. Chemical changes produced in lipids by irradiation. Int. J. Appl. Radiat. Isot. *6*, 71.

Dallyn, S., and Sawyer, R. L. 1959. Physiological effects of ionizing radiation on onions and potatoes. Cornell University, Contract No. DA19–129–QM–755, Final Report, January.

De Groot, A. P., van der Mijll Dekker, L. P., Slump, P., Vos, H. J., and Willems, J. J. L. 1972. Composition and Nutritive Value of Radiation-Pasteurized Chicken. Rept. No. R.3787. Central Inst. for Nutr. and Food Res, The Netherlands.

Delincee, H. 1981. Protein aggregation in food models: Effect of gamma-irradiation and lipid oxidation. J. Food Proc. Preserv. *5*, 145–159.

Dennison, R. A., and Ahmed, E. M. 1971–1972. Effects of low-level irradiation on the preservation of fruit: A 7-year summary. Isot. Radiat. Technol. *9*, 194–200.

Diehl, J. F. 1979A. Vitamin A to irradiated foods. (German). Z. Lebensm. Unters. Forsch. *168*, 29–31.

Diehl, J. F. 1979B. Reduction of radiation-induced vitamin losses by irradiation of foodstuffs at low temperatures and by exclusion of atmospheric oxygen. (German). Z. Lebensm. Unters. Forsch. *169*, 276–280.

Diehl, J. F. 1979C. Influence of irradiation conditions and storage on radiation-induced vitamin E losses in foods. (German). Chem. Mikrobiol. Techn. Lebensm. *6*, 65–70.

Diehl, J. F. and Scherz, H. 1975. Estimation of radiolytic products as a basis for evaluating the wholesomeness of irradiated foods. J. Appl. Radiat. Isotopes *26*, 499.

Diehl, J. F., Adam, S., Delincee, H., and Jakubick, V. 1978. Radiolysis of carbohydrates and carbohydrate-containing foodstuffs. J. Agric. Food Chem. *26*(1), 15–20.

Doguchi, M. 1969. Effects of gamma radiation on wheat gluten. Agric. Biol. Chem. *33*, 1769–1774.

Frumkin, M. L., Koval'skaya, L. P., and Gel'fand, S. Y. 1973. Technological Principles in the Radiation Treatment of Food Products. (Russian). Pischevaya Promyschlenmost' Publ., U.S.S.R.

Fujimaki, M., Makoto, T., and Matsumoto, T. 1968. Effect of gamma-irradiation on the amino acids in potatoes. Agric. Biol. Chem. *32*, 1228–1231.

Garrison, W. G. 1972. Radiation-induced reactions of amino acids and peptides. Radiat. Res. Rev. *3*, 305–326.

Gel'fand, S. Y. 1970. Effect of packaging materials on the changes of the intramuscular lipids of culinary irradiated meat products. *In* Proc. Sci. Technol. Conf. Util. Ionizing Radiation Nat. Economy. Issue *3*, 90–95. (Russian). Prioks Book Printing Office, Tula, U.S.S.R.

Goldblith, S. A. 1955. Preservation of foods by ionizing radiation. J. Amer. Diet. Assn. 31, 243.

Goldblith, S. A., and Proctor, B. E. 1949. Effect of high-voltage x-rays and cathode rays on vitamins (riboflavin and carotene). Nucleonics 5, 50–58.

Goresline, H. E. 1982. Historical aspects of the radiation preservation of food. In Preservation of Food by Ionizing Radiation, Vol. 1. E. S. Josephson and M. S. Peterson (Editors). CRC Press, Boca Raton, FL.

Hammer, C. T. and Wills, E. D. 1979. The effect of ionizing radiation on the fatty acid composition of natural fats and on lipid peroxide formation. Int. J. Radiat. Biol. 35, 323.

Heiligman, F., Rice, L. J., Smith, L. W., Jr., Thomas, M. H., Kelley, N. J., and Wierbicki, E. 1973. Irradiation Disinfection of Flour. II. Storage Studies of Irradiated Flour. Presented at 33rd Ann. Meeting. Inst. Food Technol.

Highlands, M. E. 1958. Performing a Study of the Biochemistry of Irradiated Potatoes Under Commercial Conditions. Univ. of Maine, Contract No. DA19–129–QM–857, Final Report, January.

Idziak, E. S. 1973. Radiation sensitivity of microorganisms. Effect of radiation on microorganisms. Int. J. Radiat. Steril. 1, 45–49.

Ingram, M. 1975. Microbiology of Foods Pasteurized by Ionizing Radiation. Tech. Rep. IFIP–R33. Int. Project Field Food Irradiat., Karlsruhe, W. Germany.

Jaarma, M., and Henricson, B. H. 1964. On the wholesomeness of gamma-irradiated potatoes. Acta Vet. Scand. 5, 238.

Jaddou, H. 1979. Effect of irradiation on the flavour of Iraqi dates. In Food Preservation by Irradiation, Int. Congr. Food Sci. Technol. Jaddow, Baghdad, Iraq.

Kennedy, T. S. 1965. Studies on the nutritional value of foods treated with γ-radiation. II. Effects on the protein in some animal feeds, egg and wheat. J. Sci. Food Agric. 16, 433–437.

Kertesz, Z. I., Glegg, R. E., Boyle, F. P., Schulz, E. R., Davidson, M., Fox, G., Lind, L., Connor, M., and Eucare, M. 1956. Effects of Radiations on Structure of Fruit and Vegetables. Final Report, QMF&CIAF, Chicago, IL, 1–6. Contract No. DA–19–129–QM–328.

Kharlamov, V. T., and Shubnyakova, L. P. 1964. Radioactive decomposition of methionine by gamma-radiation. (Russian). Zh. Prikl. Khim. (Leningrad) 37, 1714–1718.

Killoran, J. J. 1983. Packaging irradiated food. In Preservation of Food by Ionizing Radiation, Vol. 2, p. 317. E. S. Josephson and M. S. Peterson (Editors). CRC Press, Boca Raton, FL.

Knapp, F. W., and Tappel, A. L. 1961. Comparison of the radiosensitivities of the fat-soluble vitamins by gamma-irradiation. J. Agric. Food Chem. 9, 430–433.

Kraybill, H. F. 1982. Effect of processing on nutritive value of food: Irradiation. In Handbook of Nutritive Value of Processed Foods, Vol. 1. M. Rechcigl, Jr. (Editor). CRC Press, Boca Raton, FL.

Kung, H., Gaden, E. L., and King, C. G. 1953. Vitamins and enzymes in milk. Effect of gamma-radiation on activity. J. Agric. Food Chem. 1, 142–144.

Lang, K., and Bassler, K. H. 1966A. Nutritional value of irradiated potatoes. In Food Irradiation. Proc. Symp. Karlsruhe, June 6–10. Int. Atomic Energy Agency, Vienna.

Lang, K., and Bassler, K. H. 1966B. Biological effects of irradiated fats. In Food Irradiation, Proc. Symp. Karlsruhe, June 6–10. Int. Atomic Energy Agency, Vienna.

Leonova, T. A., and Sosedov, N. I. 1972. Action of γ-irradiation on the amino acid composition of rice and buckwheat grains. (Russian). Radiobiologiya 12, 629.

Ley, F. J., Bleby, J., Coates, M. E., and Patterson, J. S. 1969. Sterilization of laboratory animal diets using gamma radiation. Lab. Anim. 3, 221–254.

Liuzzo, J. A., Barone, W. B., and Novak, A. F. 1966. Stability of B-Vitamins in Gulf Oysters Preserved by Gamma Radiation. Presented at 50th Meeting Fed. Am. Soc. Exptl. Biol., Atlantic City, April 11–16. Fed. Proc. 25, 722 (Abstr).

Lundberg, W. O., and Chipault, J. R. 1960. Effect of high energy irradiation on the stability of fats. In QMF&CIAF Rep. 3, 1–8, Chicago, IL.

Lyaskovskaya, Yu. N. and Piul'skaya, V. I. 1975. Effect of gamma-irradiation on polyunsaturated fatty acids of cooked pork. (Russian). Vopr. Pitan. 6, 74–75.

McGown, E. L., Lewis, C. M., and Waring, P. P. 1979A. Investigation of possible antithiamin properties in irradiation sterilized beef. Inst. Rep. 71, Div. Nutr. Technol. Letterman Army Institute of Research (LAIR), Presidio of San Francisco, CA.

McGown, E. L., Lewis, C. M., and Waring, P. P. 1979B. Investigation of possible antithiamin properties in irradiation sterilized chicken. Inst. Rep. 72, Div. Nutr. Technol., LAIR, Presidio of San Francisco, CA.

McKinney, F. E. 1971. Wholesomeness of irradiated food, especially potatoes, wheat, and onions. Isot. Radiat. Technol. 9, 188.

McManus, W. R. 1982. Effect of processing on nutrient content of foods: Irradiation. In Handbook of Nutritive Value of Processed Food. M. Rechcigl, Jr. (Editor). CRC Press, Boca Raton, FL.

Mead, J. F., Griffith, W. H., and Barrett, H. L. 1956. Effect of Ionizing Radiations on the Nutritive and Safety Characteristics of Foodstuffs. Final Rep., QMF&CIAF, 1–22.

Merritt, C. P., Jr., Angelini, P., and McAdov, D. J. 1966. Volatile compounds induced by irradiation in basic food substances. Adv. Chem. Ser. 65, 26.

Merritt, C. Jr., Angelini, P., Wierbicki, E., and Shults, G. L. 1975. Chemical changes associated with flavor in irradiated meat. J. Agric. Food Chem. 23, 1037–1041.

Merritt, C., Jr., Angelini, P., and Graham, R. A. 1978. The effect of radiation parameters on the formation of radiolysis products in meat and meat substances. J. Agric. Food Chem. 26, 29–35.

Metlitskii, L. V., Rogachev, V. N., and Krushchev, V. G. 1968. Radiation processing of food products. Status of food irradiation program. In Hearings Before the Subcommittee on Research, Development and Radiation of the Joint Committee on Atomic Energy, Congress of the United States, July 18 and 30. U.S. Govt. Printing Office, Washington, DC.

Metta, V. C., and Johnson, B. C. 1959. Biological value of gamma-irradiated corn protein and wheat gluten. J. Agric. Food Chem. 7, 131–133.

Mikaelsen, K., and Roer, L. 1956. Improved storage ability of potatoes exposed to gamma radiation. Acta Agric. Scand. 6, 145.

Mitchell, J. H. Jr. 1957. Action of ionizing radiations on fats, oils and related compounds. In Radiation Preservation of Food. S. D. Bailey, J. M. Davies, B. H. Morgan, R. Pomerantz, R. G. Hi Siu, and R. G. Rischer (Editors). U.S. Govt. Printing Office, Washington, DC.

Monty, K. J. 1960. Carbonyl compounds as inhibitors of lipid metabolism and their significance in irradiated foods. Fed. Proc. 19, 1034.

Moore, R. O. 1961. The Influence of Irradiated Foods on the Enzyme Systems Concerned With Digestion. Final Report, Department of Army. Contract No. DA49–007–MD–787, Defense Documentation Center, Alexandria, VA.

Morgan, B. H. 1958. Radiation chemistry of foods. In Proc. Second UN Int. Conf. Peaceful Uses of Atomic Energy, Geneva, pp. 423–429.

Nair, K. K., and Brownell, L. E. 1965. The clearance of gamma-irradiated wheat and the international importance of this act. In Radiation Preservation of Foods (Proc. Int. Conf., Boston, 1964). Publ. 1273. National Academy of Sciences, National Research Council, Washington, DC.

Nawar, W. W. 1972. Radiolytic changes in fats. Radiat. Res. Rev. 3, 327–334.

Nawar, W. W. 1978. Reaction mechanisms in the radiolysis of fats: A review. J. Agric. Food Chem. *26*, 21.

Nassett, E. S. 1957. Effect of Ionizing Irradiation of Fat and Protein on Their Digestion in vivo. Final rep. *1–20*, Defense Documentation Center, Alexandria, VA.

Nickerson, J. T. R., Proctor, B. E. and Goldblith, S. A. 1956. Ionizing radiations in the processing of plant and animal products. Food Technol. *10*, 305.

Pape, G. 1973. Some observations regarding irradiated wheat. *In* Radiation Preservation of Food (Proc. Symp. Bombay, 1972). Int. Atomic Energy Agency, Vienna.

Partmann, W. 1962. The effect of ionizing radiation on lipid. *In* Report of the Meeting on the Wholesomeness of Irradiated Foods. Food and Agriculture Organization, Rome.

Phillips, G. O. 1972. Effects of ionizing radiations on carbohydrate systems. Radiat. Res. Rev. *3*, 335–351.

Plough, I. C., Sellars, J. H., McGary, V. E., Nuss, J., Baker, E. M., Harding, R. S., Taylor, R. L., and Weiser, O. L. 1957. An Evaluation in Human Beings of the Acceptability, Digestibility, and Toxicity of Pork Sterilized by Gamma Radiation and Stored at Room Temperature. Rep. *204*. U.S. Army Medical Nutrition Laboratory, Denver.

Plough, I. C., Bierman, E. L., Levy, L. M., and Witt, N. F. 1960. Human feeding studies with irradiated foods. Fed. Proc. *19*, 1052.

Proctor, B. E., and Bhatia, D. S. 1950. Effect of high-voltage cathode rays on amino acids in fish muscle. Food Technol. *4*, 357.

Proctor, B. E., and Bhatia, D. S. 1952. Effect of high-voltage cathode rays on aqueous solutions of tryptophan, tyrosine, phenylalanine, and cystine. Biochem. J. *51*, 535.

Proctor, B. E., and Bhatia, D. S. 1953. Mode of action of high-voltage cathode rays on aqueous solutions of amino acids. Biochem. J. *53*, 1–3.

Proctor, B. E., and Goldblith, S. A. 1949. Effect of soft x-rays on vitamins (niacin, riboflavin, and ascorbic acid). Nucleonics *5*, 56.

Proctor, B. E., and O'Meara, J. P. 1951. Effect of high-voltage cathode rays on ascorbic acid. Ind. Eng. Chem. *43*, 718–721.

Raffi, J. J., Angel, J. L., Thiery, C. J., Frejaville, C. M., and Saint-Lèbe, L. R. 1981. Study of γ-irradiated starches derived from different foodstuffs: A way for extrapolating wholesomeness data. J. Agric. Food Chem. *29*, 1227–1232.

Raica, N., Jr., and Howie, D. L. 1966. Review of the United States Army wholesomeness of irradiated food program (1955–1966). *In* Food Irradiation. Proc. Symp. Karlsruhe, June 6–10. Int. Atomic Energy Agency, Vienna.

Raica, N., Jr., Scott, J., and Nielson, W. 1972. The nutritional quality of irradiated foods. Radiat. Res. Rev. *3*, 447–457.

Rao, M. R. A., and Novak, A. F. 1973. Fatty acids in irradiated chicken product. *In* Radiation Preservation of Food, pp. 73–85. Proc. Symp. Bombay. Int. Atomic Energy Agency, Vienna.

Read, M. S. 1960. The effects of ionizing radiation on the nutritive value of foods. *In* Proc. Int. Conf. on the Pres. of Foods by Ionizing Radiations. pp. 138–152. USARC Techn. Inf. Serv., Washington, DC.

Read, M. S., Kraybill, H. F., Worth, W. S., Thompson, S. W. Jr., Issac, G. J., and Witt, N. J. 1961. Successive generation rat feeding studies with a composite diet of gamma-irradiated foods. Toxicol. Appl. Pharmacol. *3*, 153.

Revetti, L. M. 1973. Preservation of maize (*Zea mays* L.) and kidney beans (*Phaseolus vulgaris* L.) by gamma irradiation. *In* Radiation Preservation of Food. Proc. Symp. Bombay, 1972 (Spanish). Int. Atomic Energy Agency, Vienna.

Richardson, L. R. 1955. A Long Range Investigation of the Nutritional Properties of Irradiated Food. Progress Report *111*, September 1, 1954–July 1, 1955. Texas Agric. Exp. Stn., College Park, TX. Contract DA49–007–MD–582. Defense Documentation Center, Alexandria, VA.

Richardson, L. R., Woodworth, P., and Coleman, S. 1956. Effect of ionizing radiations on vitamin K. Fed. Proc. *15*, 924–926.

Saint-Lèbe, L., Berger, G., Mucchielli, A., and Coquet, B. 1973. Toxicological evaluation of the starch of irradiated maize: An account of work in progress. *In* Radiation Preservation of Food. (French). Proc. Symp. Bombay, 1972. Int. Atomic Energy Agency, Vienna.

Schaich, K. M. 1980. Free radical initiation in proteins and amino acids by ionizing and ultraviolet radiations and lipid oxidation. CRC Crit. Rev. Food Sci. Nutr. *13*, 89–129.

Schreiber, M., and Nassett, E. S. 1959. Digestion of irradiated fat in vivo. J. Appl. Physiol. *14*, 639.

Schwartz, B. 1921. Effect of x-rays on trichinae. J. Agric. Res. *20*, 845.

Sedláček, B. A. J. 1958. Influence of ionising radiation of fats. Nahrung *2*, 547.

Sheffner, A. L. and Spector, H. 1957. Action of ionizing radiations on vitamins, sterols, hormones and other physiologically active compounds. *In* Radiation Preservation of Food. U.S. Army Quartermaster Corps. U.S. Govt. Printing Office, Washington, DC.

Simic, M. G. 1978. Radiation chemistry of amino acids and peptides in aqueous solutions. J. Agric. Food Chem. *26*, 6–14.

Simic, M. G. 1983. Radiation chemistry of water-soluble food components. *In* Preservation of Food by Ionizing Radiation. E. S. Josephson and M. S. Peterson (Editors). CRC Press, Boca Raton, FL.

Southern, E. M., and Rhodes, D. N. 1967. Radiation chemistry of polyamino acids in aqueous solutions. *In* Radiation Preservation of Foods. Am. Chem. Soc. Advan. Chem. Ser. *65*, 58–77.

Takyi, E. E. K., and Amuh, I. K. A. 1979. Wholesomeness of irradiated cocoa beans. The effect of γ-irradiation on the chemical constituents of cocoa beans. J. Agric. Food Chem. *27*, 979.

Taub, I. A., Halliday, J. W., Holmes, L. G., Walker, J. E., and Robbins, F. M. 1976. Chemistry of hydrated muscle proteins irradiated at $-40°C$. Proc. Army Science Conf. III, p. 289. West Point, PA, June.

Taub, I. A., Kaprielian, R. A., Halliday, J. W., Walker, J. E., Angelini, P., and Merritt, C. 1979. Factors affecting radiolytic effects in food. Radiat. Phys. Chem. *14*, 639.

Thomas, M. H., and Calloway, D. H. 1961. Nutritional value of dehydrated foods. J. Amer. Diet. Assoc. *39*, 105.

Thomas, M. H., and Josephson, E. S. 1970. Radiation preservation of foods and its effect on nutrients. Sci. Teacher *37*, 59–63.

Thomas, M. H., McMullen, J. J., Atwood, B. M., Heiligman, F., and Calhoun, W. K. 1975. Unpublished results.

Thomas, M. H., Atwood, B. M., Wierbicki, E., and Taub, I. A. 1981A. Effect of radiation and conventional processing on the thiamin content of pork. J. Food Sci. *46*(3), 824–828.

Thomas, M. H., Atwood, B. M., Ross, E. W., Jr., and Taub, I. A. 1981B. Effects of low and high dose-rate irradiation on thiamin retention. Presented at 41st Ann. Meeting, Inst. Food Technol., Atlanta, GA.

U.S. Army Medical Research and Development Command. 1977. Evaluation of the health aspect of certain compounds found in irradiated beef. DAMD–17–76–C–6055. Life Sciences Research Office, Federation of American Societies for Experimental Biology, Bethesda, MD.

U.S. Army Medical Research and Development Command. 1979. Evaluation of
    the health aspect of certain compounds found in irradiated beef. Supplement *1*
    and *2*. DAMD-17-76-C-6055. Life Sciences Research Office, Federation of
    American Societies for Experimental Biology, Bethesda, MD.

Urbain, W. M. 1977. Radiation chemistry of proteins. *In* Radiation Chemistry of
    Major Food Components, pp. 63-130. P. S. Elias and A. J. Cohen (Editors).
    Elsevier, Amsterdam.

Urbain, W. M. 1978. Food irradiation. *In* Advances in Food Research, Vol 24,
    p. 155. C. O. Chichester, E. M. Mrak, and F. F. Stewart (Editors). Academic
    Press, New York.

Vakil, U. K., *et al.* 1973. Nutritional and wholesomeness studies with irradiated
    foods: India's Program. *In* Radiation Preservation of Food. Proc. Symp. Bom-
    bay, 1972. International Atomic Energy Agency, Vienna.

Varela, G., and Urbano, G. 1971. Effects of irradiation on the nutritive quality
    of proteins in potatoes. (Spanish). Atti Simp. Int. Agro-Chim. *8*, 563-568.

Wells, C. E., Tichenor, D. A., and Martin, D. C. 1963. Ascorbic acid retention and
    color of strawberries as related to low level irradiation and storage time. Food
    Technol. *17*, 77.

Wenkam, N. S., and Moy, A. P. 1968. Nutritional composition of irradiated fruit.
    I. Mango and papaya. Ann. Rep., June 1, 1967-May 31, 1968. Hawaii Univ.
    Coll. Tropical Agr. AEC Report UH-235-P-5-4, 126-135.

World Health Organization 1981. Wholesomeness of irradiated food. Report of a
    Joint FAO/IAEA/WHO Expert Committee. Technical Rep. Series *659*, Geneva.

Zeeuw, D. 1961. Experiments on the preservation of fresh fruit by irradiation.
    Food Irrad. *1*, 5.

19

Stability of Nutrients during Storage of Processed Foods

Seymour G. Gilbert

HISTORICAL BASIS OF STABILIZATION OF FOODS BY PACKAGING

Packaging originated functionally as containerization enabling more effective movement of foods from initial source to ultimate point of consumption. With the addition of the storage function, the stability of the food during the total time period became an important design requirement. This aspect increased in dominance as food storage became an integral part of the development of civilization.

The present century has seen industrially developed nations become totally dependent on packaged foods for the major part of their nutritional needs. Thus, the retention of nutritional quality of such foods is second only to processing in determining the nutritional status of all industrialized nations, with only about one-tenth of its population engaged in primary food production.

SCIENTIFIC BASIS OF NUTRIENT RETENTION IN PACKAGED FOODS

The initial quality of the food when enclosed in the package is the overall determinant, particularly for processed food. Except for ripening of fresh produce and a few fermented foods such as wine and cheese, quality only deteriorates at a rate determined by the interaction of three major factors: (1) initial composition, (2) environmental hazards, and (3) the degree of resistance to those hazards afforded by the package as a barrier to reduce their effective concentration inside the package and, thus, affect a corresponding abatement of the rate of change from initial quality.

In addition, the package may add or subtract chemical entities, which can affect both hedonic and functional food quality by nutritional and toxicological changes.

The principal environmental hazards are oxygen and moisture changes by differential transport, depending on the relative free energy of these molecules within and external to the package wall. Since many biological and chemical oxidations produce carbon dioxide, the rate of accumulation of CO_2 within the package also can affect reactivity of the contents.

Light, particularly in ultraviolet (UV) region, can act as a catalyst or promoter of oxidative change. If the package wall is not hermetic, that is, if significantly large discontinuities such as unsealed or broken wall areas are at least microscopically visible, transport of gas phase components will take place exponentially proportional to the radii of such discontinuities in the package wall. Metals and glass as integral container walls are impervious to gas transport at all temperatures capable of storing food. These materials were the first used and remain important in food preservation for prolonged storage. Their weight, cost, and limitations in design capabilities have led to an accelerating change to organic polymers as alternate packaging materials, even when their barrier properties are inferior.

Since these organic materials have measurable permeation of gas-phase migrants, the need for quantifying adequate barrier properties is a paramount consideration in package design.

Discontinuities of even a few microns in diameter can allow for ingress of microbiological contaminants, particularly of spore-forming molds and bacteria. Thus, the twin problems of seal integrity and mechanical damage resistance are the primary concerns in design of packages for effective long-term storage.

Physical abuse tests include ASTM F2 using Gelbo flex tester, shock, and a protocol proposed by the U.S. Department of Agriculture (USDA) requiring a regimen of drop tests, inclined plane stress, and so forth under conditions simulating damages produced on packages in assembled shipping containers by truck or rail transport.

In the past 30 years (1955–1985), the body of both empirical and scientifically based tests for functional quality of packaging materials and packages has become sufficiently extensive to predict accurately the degree to which the package will provide a functional physical and chemical protection of the product from the diverse hazards of normal environments in the distribution chain.

The major need for effective design of packages for food stability is the reactivity of the food itself. In part, this need is a reflection of the rapid proliferation of food products and processes.

When the principal shelf-stored foods were dried grains and other dehydrated foods, the storage problems were minimal to restrict access to moisture. Canned foods introduced additional problems of metallic corrosion (Mannheim and Passy 1984).

The advent of films and laminations, based on organic material, produced problems of gas and light permeation and increased the need for physical resistance.

Food processing changes and new types of processing further complicated the storage stability problem. The shift from relatively slow 120°C retort sterilization to high-temperature–short-time (HTST) processing changed the inherent reactivity of food products to a chemical system as yet incompletely characterized. To this change has been added the aseptic packaging process, with further complications involving new material properties and modes of sterilization.

Thus, older literature on food packaging and retention of nutrients requires extensive reevaluation in terms of materials and processes as well as of food products themselves.

PACKAGING MATERIALS

Glass

Glass containers or similar ceramics are the oldest package forms still in wide use. They provide the most inert storage and highest protections against external hazards, including light, if needed. The two major detractions are weight and brittleness, which are inversely proportional, so that lightweight, one-way glass containers are the most susceptible to mechanical damage. Despite many attempts to overcome this dilemma, glass containers have declined in relative importance in recent years even though they remain unexcelled where maximum inertness is required, as in packaging of reactive chemicals and drugs.

Metal

The second oldest and still most widely used food containers are fabricated from metals. The relative ease of fabrication, abundance of raw materials, and physical resistance to mechanical stress and heat contributed to the close identification of the "tin can" to the development of food packaging in the past century.

An important part of that development is the adaptation of the tinker's art to automated high-speed machine-age technology that began in the 1800s.

The major contributions of modern technology are the change from the early use of molten tin as a dip coating for steel can bodies to tinless steel constructions. These include various inorganic coatings and alloys, such as chromium oxides and other passivators, and, particularly in recent years, organic coatings ranging from those of natural origin, such as shellac and polymerizable vegetable oils, to epoxies, vinyls, and other relatively inert synthetic resin-based lacquers.

In recent years, major attention has been focused on the contamination of foods with lead from soldered seams. Cemented and welded seams have been developed to avoid the need for lead-based solder. Most recently, the two-piece or unseamed body has achieved commercial production to eliminate the problem.

Despite the wide array of coatings, passivators, and lacquers, can corrosion is still a recurring problem and limitation on shelf stability of ferrous metal-based packages. A recent review of the subject has been made by Mannheim and Passy (1984).

Aluminum has replaced steel and extended the use of metal containers in increasing areas of food packaging. Fabrication of two-piece containers is facilitated by the superior ductility of aluminum. Light weight, greater inertness by coatings, and more feasible recycling have also contributed to the rising use of aluminum which, in common with glass and ferrous containers, offers complete isolation from environmental factors other than heat.

Most recently, nitrogen and carbon dioxide gas-pressurized containers have permitted further reduction in wall thickness so that the barrier function has been retained at considerable cost reduction in fabrication and transport.

Metal Foils

The only important metallic foils or very thin integral sheets are nearly pure aluminum alloys. While a monatomic layer of aluminum atoms is impervious to water and other gases, self-supported foils of aluminum require at least 10 μm thickness, with 25 μm being the minimum for stress resistance. Since mechanical strength can be obtained at less cost by other less impermeable materials, many flexible food packages use laminations of very thin aluminum foils. The unavoidable presence of pinholes in thinner foils required laminations or coatings to avoid pneumatic transfer of gases through such discontinuities, restricting transport of gases to permeation of the negligible exposed area of properly adhered caulking or supporting polymeric layers.

Aluminum containers have also found increasing use as trays and similar shallow containers because of the high ductility of aluminum alloys. The advent of microwave ovens, however, has created an obstacle to the use of such construction for convenience foods of the heat and serve type. The resolution of this problem is still under development, since aluminum offers superior barrier protection compared to the polymer-based trays offered as alternates for packaging convenience foods.

Paper

Despite the increasing availability of synthetic polymers, the natural polymer, cellulose, continues to dominate the food packaging market.

This highly versatile linear polymer offers the greatest amount of mechanical protection per unit cost. Its worldwide availability, from wood and other fibrous plant materials, its highly automated manufacturing process, and its superior recyclability have contributed to its predominate position in packaging.

The paper manufacturing process provides a hydrogen-bonded network of cellulosic fibers which serves as a base for treatments, such as calendering, and for inclusion of fillers and bonding agents, which enhance its mechanical properties.

Physicochemical properties, such as water resistance and permeability to various environmental hazards, can be modified or completely changed by the addition of organic compounds, such as polyolefins, as coatings and laminations. The further use of metals as foils or by metallizing in extremely thin layers can convert such constructions into impervious barriers for use in aseptic packaging or in pouches for dehydrated foods.

Rigid paperboard containers can be made by a variety of techniques. Creasing and folding, often with glued flaps, is very common. Drums now are made of heavy paperboard or laminates with a barrier of adhesively mounted aluminum foil. Spirally wound paper foil cylinders are used as replacements for metal cans to provide a high degree of containment and barrier protection at low cost.

Rather than plastics replacing paper as a packaging material, such synergistic uses have enhanced the scope of packaging in a variety of forms and total usage.

Plastics

Plastics are macromolecules or repeating combinations of atomic groupings (monomers) whose relatively large-sized, primary-bonded backbone structures confer physicochemical properties characteristic of the structure itself, in addition to those determined by the composition of the monomers. Thus, widely diverse properties such as ductility, brittleness, gas barrier, chemical inertness, and thermal properties affecting sealability and heat resistance can be developed.

Inorganic polymers have also been developed into important commercial articles, silicones being the most evident.

Cellophane

Since this linear polymer of glucose is a natural and widely available one, it was the first to become a major factor in the development of packaging. While a close relative, glassine, preceded it as a packaging film, commercialization of cellophane in place of paper by DuPont and Sylvania in the early part of the twentieth century played an integral role in the technical and economic development of the converter industry. The basic technology of web transport, flexographic and rotogravure printing, coating and lamination, extrusion for film casting and coating, overwrap machine development, and heat sealing are among the processes originating in or becoming high-speed industrial processes.·

While cellophane itself contributed greatly to the rise in food packaging since 1940, its share began to decline by 1960 and to nearly disappear in the subsequent two decades as new polymers, such as polypropylene, arose with properties such as transparency, high tensile strength, and heat resistance at lower cost without the problems of moisture sensitivity.

Polyolefins

These polymers are based on the hydrocarbon groups of atoms of differing C:H ratio, with the polymerization of ethylene ($-CH_2-CH_2-$) as the first and still major representative. The linear form, or high-density polyethylene, is the most flexible and sealable. The propylene monomer

$$(-\underset{\underset{H}{|}}{\overset{\overset{CH_3}{|}}{C}}-CH_2-)$$

in stereospecific structures has greater stiffness and heat resistance to provide the properties of a cellophane replacement.

Vinyl Derivatives

Replacement of one or more hydrogens in a hydrocarbon monomer with a more polar atom or atomic group, $-CH_2X$, permits a much wider range of properties to be incorporated in the polymer. Copolymers also can be constructed to further increase the scope of applications. Thus, the substitution of highly polar electron-dense atoms, like chlorine or oxygen, enhance the stiffness, barrier properties, and chemical resistance, while large atomic groups have the opposite effect.

Other useful polymers are the homopolymers (PC), polyethylene, polypropylene (PP), polyvinyl chloride (PVC), polyvinylidine chloride (PVDC), polystyrene (PS), polyethylene terephthalate (PET), polyamides (nylons), polyvinyl alcohol (PVOH). Copolymers are often designated by trade names, such as Saran®, Mylar®, Capran®, Teflon®, Eval®, and Surlyn®.

EFFECTS OF STORAGE CONDITIONS
ON NUTRIENT CONTENT

Kramer (1977) has pointed out that, contrary to popular belief, there is only relatively minor damage to nutrient levels in commercial processing. In most aspects, these losses are related to the total energy input from the integration of the temperature and time of exposure. While processing involves relatively high temperature, times are kept short and both factors closely controlled in good manufacturing processes by instrumental and analytical checks. Low- or moderate-temperature storage is common, with attention needed for the specific requirements of the product, especially when long-term storage is needed. Distribution controls are less stringent, except for very perishable products, with unrefrigerated truck or rail transport being the worst offenders. Thus, the major problems in nutrient losses in packaged foods concern those food nutrients most sensitive to storage temperature.

Kramer (1977) considers that ascorbic acid or vitamin C is the most temperature-sensitive nutrient, particularly when oxygen is available (Table 19.1). The nonacid foods, such as vegetables, are most sensitive. The work of Kristbergsson and Gilbert (1985) has shown a further close relationship between ascorbic acid loss and thermodynamic availability or state of water in foods. Water availability involves a complex relationship between the composition and water content of foods. Contrary to the widely held view that water activity or equilibrium relative humidity is the critical parameter, it is the distribution as well as the average thermodynamic state of the water in the food that governs the chemical reactivity of water-mediated changes in food stability.

Vojnovich and Pfeifer (1970) presented data on the stability of ascorbic acid in cereal products that have been extensively used by other investigators to relate water activity and temperature to the kinetics of ascorbic acid loss (Lee and Labuza 1975; Wanninger 1979).

Table 19.1. Maximum Storage Temperatures ($^{\circ}$C) for 90% Retention of Vitamins in Fruit and Vegetable Juices (12–24 Months)

Canned juice	Ascorbic acid (vitamin C)			Thiamin (vitamin B$_1$)			Carotene (vitamin A precursor)			Niacin		
	12	18	24	12	18	24	12	18	24	12	18	24
Carrot	—	—	—	—	—	—	27+	27+	27+	—	—	—
Grapefruit	18	11	7	—	—	—	—	—	—	—	—	—
Orange	20	14	8	—	—	—	—	—	—	—	—	—
Pineapple	28	25	21	27	27	27	—	—	—	—	—	—
Tomato	24	22	20	23	19	16	27+	27+	27+	x	x	x

Source: Kramer (1977).
x = 10% loss in 24 months, no temperature effect.

Table 19.2. Maximum Storage Temperatures (°C) for Canned Foods to Assure Not More Than 10% Loss of Vitamins C, B$_1$, Carotene, Niacin, or Riboflavin (12–24 months)

Canned product	Ascorbic acid (vitamin C)			Thiamin (vitamin B$_1$)			Carotene (vitamin A precursor)			Niacin			Riboflavin (vitamin B$_2$)		
	12	18	24	12	18	24	12	18	24	12	18	24	12	18	24
Apricots	25	20	16	>0	—	—	21	17	12	—	—	—	—	—	—
Asparagus	23	18	15	8	3	0	22	15	8	b	b	b	14	10	8
Beans, green	16	8	0	14	8	0	—	—	—	b	b	b	14	10	8
Beans, lima	22	16	8	>0	—	—	—	—	—	c	c	c	18	5	0
Carrots	—	—	—	—	—	—	27+	27+	27+	—	—	—	—	—	—
Corn, sweet	22	16	10	18	14	12	14	19	24	d	d	d	21	13	8
Frankfurters and beans	—	—	—	13	9	6	—	—	—	—	—	—	—	—	—
Grapefruit segments	16	8	0	—	—	—	—	—	—	—	—	—	—	—	—
Peaches	18	10	5	25	27	29	21	5	0	c	c	c	—	—	—
Peas	23	19	11	17	13	10	27	14	8	b	b	b	13	10	8
Plums	—	—	—	—	—	—	27+	27+	27+	d	d	d	f	f	f
Pineapple slices	20	12	0	27	27	—	8	6	3	—	—	—	—	—	—
Spinach	20	16	11	17	14	9	a	a	a	c	c	c	17	8	0
Tomatoes	20	16	8	21	16	10	a	a	a	e	e	e	d	d	d

Source: Kramer (1977).

a 10% loss in 17 months, no temperature effect.
b 20% loss in 12 months, 15% in 24 months, no temperature effect.
c No loss.
d 10% loss, no time or temperature effect.
e 8% loss in 12 months, 13% in 24 months, no temperature effect.
f 20% loss, no time or temperature effect.

Our data support the conclusion of Wanninger (1979) that water is a reactant in this study and contradict the speculations that the effects are related to viscosity or dilution effects.

Kramer (1977) notes that while a number of vitamins are heat sensitive, such as vitamin C (Table 19.2), the need for refrigerated storage of heat-sterilized foods goes beyond the potential of these losses, since fortification of the food and/or diet can replace such losses. He considers the most important temperature-dependent loss of nutritional quality that of protein (Table 19.3). These losses in protein availability or nutritional quality are accelerated by access to oxygen and water vapor. Thus, a major function of packaging with effective barriers is the retention of bioavailability of proteins. Here again, the role of water in the denaturation process is obscured by the concept that the mechanism is related to the water activity of the food rather than to the kinetics of activation energy of specific reaction mechanisms involving water molecules as reactants.

The general principles governing changes in quality of foods during storage (shelf life) are well understood for many foods. Three broad classifications of effects can be distinguished: (1) sensory properties involving color, flavor (odor and taste), and texture; (2) nutritional value, such as vitamins and protein availability; and (3) toxicological state, primarily of microbiological origin, but also involving contaminants having both acute and chronic effects. When microbial contamination is present, the effect is particularly important above $0°C$ where the formation of ice changes the physical state of water. Most stored foods are stable if kept frozen below $-18°C$ or where the rates of deterioration are sufficiently low for prolonged storage.

Moreover, since most foods consist of macromolecules such as starch and proteins, the ratio and amount of crystalline:amorphous structures can drastically affect the ability of water to act as a reaction

Table 19.3. Effect of Storage Temperature on Bioavailability of Protein (PER) in Some Protein Concentrates[a]

Product	Initial	PER after 6 months' storage at		
		$22°C$	$0°C$	$-20°C$
TVP[b]	2.27	2.12	2.21	2.25
SCP[c]	2.23	1.79	2.12	2.23
Milk[d]	2.37	1.75	2.35	2.36

[a] Reference casein adjusted to 2.7.
[b] Textured vegetable protein packed in carton with inner liner.
[c] Single-cell protein, produced from alcohol–yeast fermentation, packed in carton with inner liner.
[d] Defatted milk solids packed in 4-ply paper bag with one 2-mil polyethylene ply.

Table 19.4. Maximum Storage Temperatures ($^{\circ}$C) for Limiting Losses of Thiamin and Vitamin A in Dehydrated Eggs

	%	Months in storage			
		1	3	2	12
Thiamin	10	—	33	6	−18
	25	—	37	31	0
	50	—	—	37	31
Vitamin A	10	27	−15	−18	−24
	25	34	−12	−16	−19
	50	—	18	2	−12

Source: Kramer (1977).

catalyst at low and intermediate moisture contents. The water activity of saturated salt solutions often shows only slight change with temperature. Foods, on the other hand, may show strong temperature-dependent shifts in water activity at lower moisture contents, particularly in freeze–thaw cycles.

Storage temperature as the major factor in deterioration must be considered in terms of heat sensitivity. Water is perhaps the most important reactant governing termperature sensitivity.

Much evidence has accumulated since the pioneering concept of Scott (1953) to show that total water is not the critical determinant for reactivity. Fugacity, or the excess free energy of water in the gas phase in equilibrium with food at any one water content, is his determinant.

Reactivity, however, is determined by the energy to transfer water molecules in the food matrix. These energy states vary from strongly chemisorptive bonds of food proteins to weak water–water bonds of "active" water.

Dehydrated foods, when properly packaged to avoid moisture gain and oxygen access, can be quite stable even at higher temperatures for short periods. Table 19.4, from Kramer (1977), illustrates this principle that water molecules are reactants in vitamin C loss by oxidation.

Food technology progress, by the development of processes and products with enhanced nutritional quality as well as by more sales, related hedonic appeal. Packaging is an important factor in the retention of the enhanced quality, with the packaging design an optimization of the desired marketing and intrinsic nutritional attributes. The current rapid proliferation of materials and forms for food packaging requires a corresponding enhanced knowledge of how more effective as well as safe designs can be provided. This review has as its objective the update of the general knowledge of packaging of foods.

REFERENCES

Kramer, A. 1977. Effect of storage on nutritive value of food. J. Food Qual. *1*, 23–55.

Kristbergsson, K., and Seymour, S. G. 1985. Effect of the State of Water in Foods on Ascorbic Acid Degradation. Ph.D. thesis. Rutgers Univ., New Brunswick, NJ.

Lee, S. H., and Labuza, T. P. 1975. Destruction of ascorbic acid as a function of water activity. J. Food Sci. *40*, 370.

Mannheim, C. H., and Passy, N. 1984. Internal corrosion and shelf-life of food cans and methods of evaluation, CRC Crit. Rev. Food Sci. Nutr. *17*, 371–407.

Scott, W. J. 1953. Water relations of *Staphylococcus aureus* at 30°C. Aust. J. Biol. Sci. *6*, 549.

Vojnovich, C., and Pfeifer, V. F. 1970. Stability of ascorbic acid in blends with wheat flour, CSM and infant cereals. Cereal Sci. Today *19*, 317.

Wanninger, L. A., Jr. 1979. Mathematical model predicts stability of ascorbic acid in food products. Food Technol. *33*(6), 42–44.

Part 4

Effects of
Preparation and Service
of Food on Nutrients

20

Effects of Food Preparation Procedures in Nutrient Retention with Emphasis on Foodservice Practices

Paul A. Lachance
Michele C. Fisher

INTRODUCTION

Foodservice is a misnomer. In the classic sense, away-from-home eating provided by public eating establishments and institutions, such as at medical facilities, schools, and colleges, are understood to comprise the foodservice market. However, the food industry has evolved preprepared single-serve food items to meet individual foodservice needs, be it at home or away from home, and has continued to provide preprepared bulk food items for foodservice use. More people than ever before are now dependent upon the nutritive quality of foods preprepared at the manufacturing level. Both the foodservice operator and the consumer obtain their food variety needs to various degrees via the preprepared frozen entrées and other single-serving food items. Meals prepared from "scratch," utilizing fresh (and sometimes frozen) foods and other ingredients (milk, flour, and spices), are available at select restaurants and occasionally at home. However, the life-style of the burgeoning single-member and small-family household has created markets for ready foods from preprepared infant formulas (wherein assuring nutritive value has been extensively researched and applied), to nursery school and other preschool, especially day-care, snacks and meals, to elementary and secondary school U.S. Department of Agriculture (USDA)-prescribed and à la carte meals, vending machine foods, and fast-food snacks and meals, to entrées, such as pizza or stromboli, delivered to the college dormitory room, to the home, or eaten on site.

Any and all food that is preprepared by the food industry, irrespective of whether it is used in the home or in catering or other foodservice establishments, is subject to the question of responsibility for nutritive value, and this includes a responsibility for the effects of preparation on the nutritive quality the consumer can expect to realize. The food industry, for the most part, has reluctantly accepted only the responsibility for nutritive composition value data for the nutrition information panel of retail foods where regulation and competition have forced the issue. The acquisition of these data for labeling purposes does not assure the delivery of responsible nutritive value. The increasing use of partitioned ingredients, especially proteins, carbohydrates, and fats/oils in the manufacture of formulated and fabricated foods, is diluting the dietary value the consumer receives. As the consumer moves from drinking and using fluid milk in the home and in cooking from scratch to dependence on products such as cheese in which the milk has been partitioned in the process of cheese making (whey is removed), the consumer realizes considerably fewer micronutrients than the starting ingredient portends. Tomato sauces used for retail pizza making can be extended up to 25% by starch-based tomato extender, again diluting the nutritive value of the pizza and/or related Italian food preparations. Low-calorie frozen entrées are in demand for weight control, yet the sauces for these foods are not nutrified, and the nutrient delivery of the product is not balanced and does not assure one-fourth or one-third of the recommended dietary allowance of micronutrients implied by label designations such as "entrée," "dinner," or "restaurant classic." The foodservice industry, particularly mass feeding operations providing meals "in flight" and "in school," are passively unaware of the nutritive balance and value of the foods served.

The problem of the dilution of nutrients becomes blatant in the case of doughnuts, cream filled or coated with icings, yet an entire foodservice approach frequented by millions of Americans never questions the nutritive values of these products and combinations sold, not only as between-meal snacks, but as meal substitutes.

The marketing advantage of "natural" has further served to dilute American diets by conveying the image of naturally occurring nutrients likely occurring. In an effort to decrease waste in fruit processing, techniques have emerged to process fruit components into rollups and other novelties. The fruit image justifies purchase for use by children, but the fruit product is devoid of micronutrients because of the partitioning and processing involved. Responsible product development would have included a profile of the equivalent fruit micronutrients. Fruit replacement drinks have a similar problem, but are irresponsibly fortified with one nutrient, ascorbic acid, which the consumer happens to know is associated with fruit, but the product is not fortified with the several other vitamins and minerals delivered by fruit per se.

This chapter provides data on the effect on nutritive values of conventional foodservice practices, utilizing commodity foods. The data are not comprehensive, but sufficient to provide indications of the type and duration of foodservice practice requiring care in operations in order to conserve nutrients. To facilitate the presentation of the facts, the data have been organized into major sections which follow the flow in classical foodservice operations: purchasing and storage prior to use; preparation of animal and plant products; cooking, including reheating, holding hot, chilled, or frozen; and serving.

In all issues of nutrient retention, four physicochemical variables need to be considered. These are the extent and duration (time) of exposure to temperature, oxygen, light, and changes in pH. At the onset, it must be understood that no comprehensive model that integrates all of the variables (dependent as well as independent) over time exists, nor, for that matter, does all the data exist that would be needed to arrive at a model that could be applied in the immediate future. In other words, there are many blind spots and gaps in the data currently available. As we discuss each foodservice operation, we will summarize the current knowledge and attempt to identify the gaps. We will point to some preliminary models, but they are indeed primitive and limited. However, we predict that with computer-assisted modeling, very sophisticated predictive decision-making techniques will become available.

GARDEN FRESH VERSUS MARKET FRESH

Both the consumer and foodservice operator, particularly the restauranteur, desire fresh fruits and vegetables; however, "fresh" (meaning not preserved or processed) is a relative term. Lachance (1978) proposed a differentiation between the designation "garden fresh" and the designation "market fresh." Fresh vegetables and some fruit picked in the garden or purchased freshly picked at a farmer's roadside stand approximate the sensory and nutritive value of garden freshness, whereas fresh produce purchased at a supermarket or even at a wholesale market out of season (or in season, if it has passed through one or more redistributions after picking) is more accurately defined as market fresh. Produce, although fresh, but which originated in fields in California, Florida, or elsewhere, and over a period of days has been expedited to the market, cannot be expected to meet the same sensory and nutritive values as freshly picked produce. The combined supplies of garden- and market-fresh produce assures access to an almost year-round supply. Some examples are self-evident: "new" potatoes versus "old" potatoes; "hothouse" tomatoes versus "native" tomatoes; Florida carrots or corn purchased in New Jersey in April in contrast to native equivalents in late July.

The consumer often fails to appreciate that thermally processed and frozen fruits and vegetables are garden-fresh produce, scheduled for processing within hours of picking in order to capture the garden-fresh attributes. This means that the nutritive values of such processed foods can, and often do, exceed those of market-fresh produce, but not that of the equivalent garden-fresh products. The seasonal nature of certain high-volume produce requires that large volumes be processed into concentrates (e.g., tomato paste) which can be shipped in bulk and processed into other formulated products (e.g., tomato sauce or ketchup) during the off-season. Data relevant to the nutritive composition and the changes in nutritive composition occurring in the transition between garden fresh and market fresh and at the time of use (usually after some further holding) are limited, but sufficient to make the point. Other food categories, such as dairy foods and eggs, could be included in this concept if the precise starting point of freshness can be established and the effects of holding studied. Several studies emanating from the USDA/Rutgers Urban Food Marketing Research Center have attempted to study facets of this problem.

The highest concentration of ascorbic acid in broccoli florets is found at the wholesale level and diminishes at the retail level and with a 3-day consumer holding (Hudson et al. 1985A). Total ascorbic acid in the retail and consumer-stored florets was 17 and 27% less, respectively, than in the florets at the wholesale level. The stems of broccoli retain ascorbic acid better than the florets. The increased surface area of the florets permits a greater susceptibility to water loss and oxidation, a phenomenon reported by Spiers et al. (1951) for turnip greens.

Fresh spinach is a vegetable now available throughout the year. Market-fresh spinach is 4 to 13 days postharvest before it reaches the consumer. Field samples (i.e., garden fresh) of spinach show a substantial variation between varieties, crop year, and so forth. It has been estimated that there is a 30% coefficient of variability for ascorbic acid in fresh foodstuffs. Transportation/storage losses of field-grown spinach was reported by Russell et al. (1983) for periods up to 10 days after harvest to have resulted in as high as 90% loss in ascorbic acid. Russell et al. (1983) state that tabulated (i.e., USDA Food Composition Data) values tend to overestimate actual ascorbic values and that approximately 50% of the field value at picking (i.e., garden-fresh value) is normally lost before consumption (i.e., market-fresh values are lower).

Market-fresh strawberries are available almost year-round. In the New York area, 98% of fresh strawberries come from California and Florida. The strawberry is ranked as 11th in ascorbic acid, 17th in riboflavin, and 36th in thiamin content among 42 fruits and vegetables (Salunkhe 1976). Total ascorbic acid in individual strawberry samples (16–19 replicates in 1981 and 1982) ranged from 28 to 82 mg/100 g fresh weight (FW). Average values for New Jersey berries (49 mg/100 g FW) were less than those of California and Florida berries (65 mg/100 g FW). New Jersey berries lost significant amounts of ascorbic acid during 0, 4, and 7 days of storage, from 62 to 53 to 33 mg/100 g, respectively. No such losses were detected in berries from California and Florida sampled at the wholesale and retail market levels. There is no explanation for such findings. The varieties were different, but the maturity level was judged to be about the same. The same investigation (Hudson et al. 1985B) revealed that the thiamin content in the strawberry samples ranged from 29 to 130 μg/100 g FW, respectively. Although total values were higher (more sunlight) the market-fresh level of nutrients may have already reached a plateau in California varieties.

Some vegetables are very stable in nutrient content during distribution and storage for reasons that are not understood. For example, sweet peppers are available throughout the year and are ranked 4th in ascorbic acid and 16th in riboflavin and thiamin among 42 fruits and vegetables (Salunkhe 1976). Under optimum conditions, fresh peppers can be in the distribution channel and/or stored for 2–3 weeks. The total ascorbic acid, thiamin, and riboflavin content of sweet peppers varies less during this period than does the variation attributable to variety, crop year, and so forth. The consumer cannot assume that standard handbook values apply to a specific horticultural sample (Hudson et al. 1985C).

LOSSES DURING COOKING

Meats and Poultry

Broiling

In the Toepfer et al. (1955) study, steaks broiled on a griddle without added fat retained most of their protein, 96.6%, and fat, 95.8% (Table 20.1). The finding on protein was similar to that in oven roasts. The retention of fat during broiling was higher, no doubt because of the shorter cooking time. According to Noble (1964), Tucker et al. (1946) reported thiamin retention of 77 and 70% respectively, and riboflavin retention of 92% in beef loin steaks broiled to interior temperatures of 58° and 70°C, while Causey et al. (1950A) reported retentions of slightly over 80% for both thiamin and riboflavin in frozen ground beef that had been broiled to 74°C. McIntire et al. (1943) found retentions of 70 and 79% of thiamin and riboflavin, respectively, in broiled sirloin of lamb, and Causey et al. (1950B) in the neighborhood of 85 and 55%, respectively, in frozen ground lamb broiled to 85°C.

Noble (1964) demonstrated that pan- and oven-broiled cuts were not significantly different in percentages of thiamin or riboflavin retained. Comparisons based on averages for individual cuts within each type of meat showed that thiamin retention was significantly higher in broiled

Table 20.1. Summary of Retention (%) of Protein and Fat in Thaw Juices, Drippings, and Cooked Meat from Various Cuts and Forms of Beef

Cut or form of beef	Protein			Fat[a]	
	Thaw juices	Drippings	Cooked beef or recipe	Drippings	Cooked beef or recipe
Beef cuts					
Oven roasts	2.6	1.8	95.6	20.6	79.4
Pot roasts	2.5	7.6	89.9	31.1	68.9
Griddle-broiled steaks	3.0	0.4	96.6	4.2	95.8
Swiss steaks	1.6	14.7	83.7	39.2	60.8
Diced beef, stew	3.1	—	96.9	—	100.0
Ground beef					
Hamburger	2.4	0.4	97.2	18.2	81.8
Meat loaf	1.4	0	98.6	12.6	87.4

Source: Toepfer *et al* (1955).

[a] No fat was reported in thaw juice.

beef loin steaks and 1-serving patties (78%) than in rib steaks and 3-serving patties (average 62%); likewise, in lamb chops and 1-serving lamb patties (average 66%) than in 3-serving lamb patties (55%); and in Canadian-style bacon (79%) than in ham slices (65%). Riboflavin retentions overlapped considerably, with that for broiled rib and loin steaks (90%) not significantly different from that for either 1- or 3-serving patties, and that for Canadian-style bacon (82%) not significantly different from that for ham slices. Riboflavin retention in lamb chops (96%) was significantly higher, however, than in lamb patties (average 75%).

Comparisons based on averages for each of the three types of meat showed that thiamin retentions in beef and pork were not significantly different (average 70%), but were higher than in lamb (62%), while riboflavin retentions in beef (92%) were significantly higher than in pork and lamb, which were not significantly different (average 82%). The data are presented in Table 20.2; although retail cuts were used, it is presented here because of its uniqueness in the field.

In a sophisticated study, Meyer *et al.* (1963) studied the effect of broiling in an oven (5 min/side at a distance of 3 in. from the broiler unit) on the content of niacin, thiamin, and riboflavin of pork gluteus medius (loin) muscle. Pale, soft, watery (PSW) and dark, firm, dry (DFD) muscles were subjectively classified, and the classification objectively substantiated with Hunter color values and expressible juice ratios. PSW pork had about twice as much niacin ($p < .005$) as DFD, both fresh and cooked (see Table 20.3). Fresh DFD muscle had slightly higher riboflavin and thiamin contents and in the cooked form contained a higher thiamin level. PSW muscle showed greater

Table 20.2. Mean Thiamin and Riboflavin in Raw and Broiled Meat and Percentage Retention after Broiling

Cut	Thiamin			Riboflavin		
	Raw meat (mg/100 g)	Cooked meat (mg/100 g)	Retention (%)[a]	Raw meat (mg/100 g)	Cooked meat (mg/100 g)	Retention (%)[a]
Beef						
Ground beef, 3-portion patty	0.066 ± 0.006[b]	0.066 ± 0.006	65	0.120 ± 0.006	0.192 ± 0.010	100
Rib steak	0.072 ± 0.001	0.062 ± 0.001	59	0.136 ± 0.003	0.184 ± 0.006	91
Loin steak	0.062 ± 0.002	0.066 ± 0.002	78	0.146 ± 0.002	0.180 ± 0.005	89
Ground beef, 1-portion patty	0.092 ± 0.013	0.099 ± 0.008	78	0.152 ± 0.011	0.181 ± 0.012	84
Lamb						
Ground lamb, 3-portion patty	0.072 ± 0.007	0.076 ± 0.008	55	0.145 ± 0.019	0.205 ± 0.013	73
1-portion patty	0.087 ± 0.002	0.111 ± 0.006	67	0.147 ± 0.009	0.204 ± 0.008	78
Chops	0.111 ± 0.008	0.104 ± 0.005	66	0.185 ± 0.006	0.257 ± 0.009	96
Pork						
Ham slices	1.775 ± 0.092	1.922 ± 0.167	65	0.157 ± 0.006	0.208 ± 0.013	80
Canadian style bacon	1.550 ± 0.091	1.960 ± 0.195	79	0.208 ± 0.008	0.271 ± 0.016	82

Source: Noble (1964).

[a] Any two means not side-scored by the same line may be considered significantly different at the 5% level.

[b] Mean ± S.E.

Table 20.3. Vitamin Content of Four Pale, Soft, Watery and Four Dark, Firm, Dry Gluteus Medius Muscles

Vitamin[a]		Pale, soft, watery		Loss in Cook-ing[b](%)	Dark, firm, dry		Loss in Cook-ing[b](%)
		Fresh	Cooked		Fresh	Cooked	
Niacin	$\bar{x}$	87.2	74.7	41.2	32.4	35.2	20.7
	$s_{\bar{x}}$	2.9	8.2	6.2	2.2	8.9	7.3
Riboflavin	$\bar{x}$	2.27	3.14	8.5	2.38	2.50	22.8
	$s_{\bar{x}}$	0.06	0.44	7.1	0.06	0.21	3.9
Thiamin	$\bar{x}$	13.0	13.8	29.72	14.2	16.5	16.6
	$s_{\bar{x}}$	0.50	0.40	5.4	1.4	2.1	2.0

Source: Meyer *et al.* (1963).

[a] Expressed as $\mu g/g$ fresh tissue.

[b] Vitamin loss calculated to dry weight: $\dfrac{(\mu g/g \text{ raw} - \mu g/g \text{ cooked} \times \% \text{ cooked weight})}{\mu g/g \text{ raw.}}$

exudate formation, more expressible juice, and consequently, significantly higher cooking weight loss (30–45% versus 25–32.5%). This higher cooking loss contributed to a significantly higher nutrient loss on a fresh-weight basis. When equal amounts of the vitamins were present in the fresh form, the PSW muscle lost a greater quantity of vitamins during cooking, either by destruction or due to "drip." The PSW muscle had a higher niacin level in the cooked form, even though these muscles had a considerably higher cooking loss.

Frying

Kotschevar *et al.* (1955), who cooked liver slices in margarine melted in a pan over a low gas flame, reported a loss in fresh liver of 15% of the thiamin, 6% of the riboflavin, and 13% of the niacin. Amounts of liver cooked in one pan were not given. He found greater cooking losses of thiamin from frozen liver slices, but an increase in riboflavin. Results with niacin were variable, ranging from a cooking loss of 15% to a gain of 30%.

Overfrying hamburgers to a temperature of 98°C has been found to reduce their linoleic acid content by 15% (Jonsson and Karlstrom 1981). This could be explained by the rate of fat oxidation which increases with temperature.

Braising

Toepfer *et al.* (1955) reported (Table 20.4) that retentions in Swiss steaks were very similar to those in pot roasts and showed the effect of addition of water on losses. Swiss steak retained 83.7% of the protein and 60.8% of the fat; pot roasts retained 89.9% of the protein and 68.9% of the fat. On the other hand, over 95% of the protein was retained during methods of cooking in which no water was added.

Table 20.4. Retention of Food Energy, Protein, Fat, and Ash in Boneless Beef after Thawing and Cooking

Type of beef and type of cooking	Weight[a]		Retention[b]			
	Raw frozen (kg)	Drained cooked (kg)	Food energy (cal)	Protein (%)	Fat (%)	Ash (%)
Oven roasts						
Blade roll	1.670	1.148	85.4	90.4	83.4	111.7
Inside of round	7.385	4.568	82.9	91.9	77.4	86.6
Knuckle of round	4.086	2.463	88.1	92.5	83.2	72.3
Loin strip	4.652	3.132	85.0	91.3	82.9	84.2
Sirloin butt	6.162	3.874	81.5	87.1	79.5	94.3
Spencer roll	4.306	2.794	76.7	95.0	72.8	74.2
Tenderloin	2.411	1.574	72.5	95.1	65.8	97.9
Pot roasts						
Clod	7.156	5.132	92.3	95.9	91.1	107.6
Chuck roll	5.086	3.098	79.8	92.5	73.3	76.1
Chuck tender	1.074	0.631	91.6	101.4	82.4	88.1
Outside of round	5.777	3.716	76.8	92.8	69.4	80.4
Rump butt	2.367	1.520	82.8	86.1	81.5	64.2
Griddle-broiled steaks						
Blade roll	1.538	1.060	99.0	87.2	103.8	77.5
Inside of round	7.386	4.710	89.9	81.4	90.9	77.9
Knuckle of round	4.147	2.558	89.1	89.4	87.7	82.2
Loin strip	5.074	3.495	90.8	88.4	91.1	68.9
Spencer roll	4.735	3.381	88.2	85.9	88.6	95.2
Tenderloin	2.825	1.952	85.6	97.9	82.2	69.1
Swiss steaks						
Clod	7.202	5.842	93.7	87.4	89.7	71.0
Chuck roll	4.776	3.064	71.8	80.3	63.7	64.2
Chuck tender	1.144	0.747	92.2	91.4	86.5	52.2
Outside of round	5.474	4.104	87.9	93.4	80.6	45.0
Rump butt	2.188	1.747	90.1	94.3	85.4	79.8

Source: Toepfer *et al.* (1955).
[a] Weight average values. The inside of round represents more than four times that of blade roll.
[b] Calculated from data given in Toepfer *et al.* (1955).

Schlosser *et al.* (1957) reported that braised turkey meat contained as much lysine as did that steamed under 5- or 10-lb pressure. The only meaningful studies of vitamin retentions in braised meats are those of Noble (1965, 1970), who studied several cuts of beef, veal, and pork (Table 20.5).

For the beef cuts, thiamin retention was significantly higher in the round pot roasts and braised steaks (40% of the amount present in the raw samples) than in the braised chuck and short ribs (average of 24%).

Table 20.5. Mean Thiamin and Riboflavin in Raw and Braised Meat and Retention after Braising

	Thiamin			Riboflavin		
Cut	Raw meat (mg/100 g)	Cooked meat (mg/100 g cooked weight)	Retention[a, b] (%)	Raw meat (mg/100 g)	Cooked meat (mg/100 g cooked weight)	Retention[a, b] (%)
Beef						
Short ribs	0.070 ± 0.003	0.040 ± 0.003	25	0.077 ± 0.002	0.106 ± 0.006	58
Chuck	0.076 ± 0.005	0.033 ± 0.004	23	0.204 ± 0.015	0.234 ± 0.015	74
Flank steak	0.056 ± 0.001	0.032 ± 0.005	30	0.082 ± 0.003	0.112 ± 0.010	72
Round (roast)	0.073 ± 0.020	0.062 ± 0.005	40	0.208 ± 0.021	0.250 ± 0.023	73
Round (steak)	0.081 ± 0.003	0.058 ± 0.002	40	0.229 ± 0.009	0.269 ± 0.004	65
Veal						
Chops	0.148 ± 0.008	0.105 ± 0.005	38	0.217 ± 0.012	0.289 ± 0.019	73
Round steak	0.125 ± 0.004	0.119 ± 0.015	48	0.200 ± 0.005	0.303 ± 0.016	76
Pork						
Chops	1.990 ± 0.012	1.600 ± 0.168	44	0.155 ± 0.019	0.178 ± 0.021	64
Spareribs	0.680 ± 0.016	0.355 ± 0.004	26	0.262 ± 0.014	0.372 ± 0.003	72
Tenderloin	2.728 ± 0.202	2.569 ± 0.035	57	0.302 ± 0.015	0.425 ± 0.016	83

Source: Noble (1965).
[a] Any two means not side-scored by the same line may be considered significantly different at the 5% level. The interrupted line beside the riboflavin retention figures is interpreted as follows: the retentions for short ribs and round steaks are not significantly different from each other.
[b] Calculated on the basis of the entire sample, before and after cooking.

It was intermediate in the flank steaks, which retained neither a significantly higher percentage than the round cuts, on the one hand, nor a significantly higher percentage than the chuck and short ribs, on the other. Riboflavin retention showed a pattern different from that of thiamin. It was highest in chuck, flank steaks, and round roasts, which were not significantly different and averaged 73%, and lowest in short ribs and round steaks, which were not significantly different and averaged 62%.

For the veal cuts, thaimin retention in the round steaks (48%) was significantly higher than in chops (38%), but riboflavin retention was not significantly different and averaged 74%.

For the pork cuts, thiamin retention was significantly different among the different cuts, tenderloin retaining the highest (57%), spareribs the lowest (26%), and chops the intermediate percentage (44%). Riboflavin retention was also highest in tenderloin, but lowest in chops and intermediate in spareribs; the retention in spareribs was not significantly different from that in either tenderloin or chops.

Thiamin and riboflavin retentions were very similar from one type of animal to another when all cuts were considered. Thus, the mean thiamin value for all beef cuts (32%) was significantly lower than those for either veal or pork, but the values for the last two and all the riboflavin means were not significantly different (averages of 42 and 72%, respectively).

The cooking liquids from the beef cuts contained approximately 25% thiamin, those from the veal chops and round, 17 and 33% respectively, and those from the pork tenderloin, spareribs, and chops 5, 1, and 13%, respectively, of the thiamin originally present in the raw samples. Liquids from the beef and pork cuts also contained approximately 20% and those from the veal chops and round 17 and 24%, respectively, of the riboflavin originally present.

The thiamin and riboflavin contents and retentions of braised or simmered sweetbreads, beef kidney, lamb heart, and pork heart are given in Table 20.6. For the meats as a group, braising as compared to simmering was found to cause a significantly higher retention of thiamin (46% versus 39%), but not riboflavin (retention of 70% for both cooking methods).

The kind of meat made a significant difference in the average amount of thiamin and riboflavin retained in the combined braised and simmered samples. Thus, sweetbreads retained the largest percentage of thiamin (60% was the average retention in braised and simmered) and beef, veal, and pork heart the lowest (average, 29%). Veal, beef, lamb, and pork hearts, on the other hand, retained the highest percentage of riboflavin (average, 75%) and beef kidney the lowest (55%).

The cooking liquids contained from 12 to 25% (average, 19%) of the thiamin and from 13 to 22% (average, 16%) of the riboflavin originally present in the raw sample.

Table 20.6. Mean (± S.E.) Thiamin and Riboflavin Content of Variety Meats and Retention after Cooking

Meat	Number of purchase lots	Mean raw content (mg/100 g)	Braised content		Simmered content		Retention		Dissolved in cooking liquid	
			Mean, on cooked-weight basis (mg/100 g)	Mean, on raw-weight basis (mg/100 g)	Mean, on cooked-weight basis (mg/100 g)	Mean, on raw-weight basis (mg/100 g)	Braised (%)	Simmered (%)	Braised (%)	Simmered (%)
				Thiamin						
Sweetbreads	9	0.081 ± 0.008	0.087 ± 0.006	0.053	0.063 ± 0.003	0.045	66	55	16	35
Beef kidney	4	0.790 ± 0.053	0.673 ± 0.050	0.355	0.554 ± 0.043	0.290	45	37	25	53
Lamb heart	5	0.983 ± 0.084	0.931 ± 0.066	0.501	0.773 ± 0.084	0.483	51	49	23	31
Pork heart	5	0.999 ± 0.083	0.636 ± 0.046	0.340	0.474 ± 0.031	0.297	34	30	12	23
				Riboflavin						
Sweetbreads	9	0.244 ± 0.021	0.268 ± 0.047	0.149	0.266 ± 0.037	0.168	61	69	13	27
Beef kidney	4	3.677 ± 0.413	4.577 ± 0.730	2.380	3.262 ± 0.600	1.705	65	46	22	37
Lamb heart	5	1.111 ± 0.020	1.621 ± 0.048	0.852	1.294 ± 0.155	0.805	77	72	15	31
Pork heart	5	1.314 ± 0.056	1.899 ± 0.116	0.944	1.504 ± 0.063	0.907	72	69	13	30

Source: Noble (1970).

The loss in weight of the various meats during braising ranged from 42 to 50% (average, 46%) and during simmering from 34 to 47% (average, 40%).

Roasting

In a study of boneless beef cut to Army specifications, Toepfer et al. (1955) showed the effect of several factors on losses of calories, protein, fat, and ash during oven roasting and pot roasting.

Weights of the cuts varied (Table 20.4) and, as a result, probably also cooking time. Protein suffered little loss in oven roasting: 95.6% was retained in the drained roast. Since 2.6% of the protein had been lost to thaw juice and 1.8% to pan drippings, all of the protein was accounted for.

The effect of the addition of water was evident in the smaller retention of protein, 89.9%, in the pot roast and the larger loss to the drippings, 7.6%. The retention of fat was also slightly lower in the drained pot roast.

Cover et al. (1949) reported the effect of high oven temperature on the retention of B vitamins after large-scale roasting of beef and pork. One-muscle roasts were used: longissimus dorsi (eye of rib), semimembranosus (inside of top round), and biceps femoris (outside of bottom round) of both beef and pork. These isolated muscles vary both in shape (Tucker et al. 1952) and weight (Wellington 1954).

Beef roasted at 150°C (302°F) to an internal temperature of 80°C (176°F) retained 61% of the thiamin; that roasted at 205°C (450°F) and cooked to an internal temperature of 98°C (209°F) retained only 47%. Pork roasted at 150°C (302°F) to an internal temperature of 84°C (183°F) retained 64% of the thiamin; that roasted at 205°C (459°F) to an internal temperature of 98°C (209°F) retained 54% (Table 20.7).

The lower temperatures resulted in practically complete retention of the riboflavin, niacin, and pantothenic acid in the drained meat plus the drippings; about 75% of each vitamin was in the drained meat. At the higher temperature, pantothenic acid retention in the meat was 13% less than at the lower temperature, but the retention of the heat-stable vitamins, riboflavin and niacin, was only slightly less. Pan drippings at the higher temperature were unusable.

Statistical analysis showed that beef roasts cooked at 150°C (302°F) to an internal temperature of 80°C retained significantly more thiamin, pantothenic acid, and riboflavin than did those roasted at 204°C (450°F) to a temperature of 98°C. In the pork, however, thiamin was the only vitamin retained in statistically significantly greater quantities at the lower temperature.

Roasting times required by the above muscles at the two temperatures were not reported. However, the destructive effect of increased cooking on thiamin is well known (Farrer 1955).

Table 20.7. Vitamin Retention in Beef and Pork after Large-scale Roasting

Oven temperature, type and internal temperature of meat	Thiamin			Pantothenic acid			Niacin			Riboflavin		
	Meat only (%/pan)	Drip-pings (%/pan)	Total (%/pan)	Meat only (%/pan)	Drip-pings (%/pan)	Total (%/pan)	Meat only (%/pan)	Drip-pings (%/pan)	Total (%/pan)	Meat only (%/pan)	Drip-pings (%/pan)	Total (%/pan)
Low oven temperature (150°C)												
Beef to 80°C[a]	61	6	67	73	20	93	76	16	92	75	16	91
Pork to 84°C	64	17	81	65	25	90	69	26	95	73	19	92
High oven temperature (205°C)												
Beef to 98°C[a]	47	b	—	60	b	—	71	b	b	68	b	—
Pork to 98°C	54	b	—	63	b	—	67	b	b	69	b	—

Source: Cover et al. (1949).
[a] Isolated muscles longissimus dorsi, semimembranosus, biceps femoris of beef and pork, and semitendinosus of beef only.
[b] Drippings from roasts cooked at high oven temperature were charred and unusable.

In 1960, Noble and Gomez clarified the work of Cover *et al.* (1949) by roasting beef to a constant internal temperature. Standing-rib pairs of choice beef were roasted at 149° and 177°C, and rolled and standing-rib pairs were roasted to the same interior temperature at 177°C, to determine if the lower heating period required by the first treatment would affect thiamin retention. The other cuts roasted were top round, rump, tenderloin, and beef loaf, the meat for which came from the chuck arm. All roasts were heated to an interior temperature of 71°C; the loaves were heated to 75°C (Table 20.8).

Longer heating did not affect the thiamin retention in the cooked meat. Roasted beef loaf retained an average of 70% of the amount of thiamin in the raw ingredients. This retention was significantly higher than that of cooked top round and rib roasts, which averaged 54%. It was not significantly different, however, from the retention in rump and tenderloin roasts, both of which showed intermediate values.

Roasted beef loaf and top round retained the lowest proportion, about 80%, of the riboflavin originally present in the raw samples, while rib and rump roasts retained the highest proportion, an average of 87%. Tenderloin roasts were intermediate in riboflavin retention and not significantly different in this respect from any of the other roasts.

The raw meat findings are in agreement with the values for raw meat as reported by others (Watt and Merrill 1963; Schweigert and Payne 1956; Cover *et al.* 1949). The cooked values are in agreement with the values reported by Watt and Merrill (1963), and Leverton and Odell (1958) provided results for roast lamb that are given in Table 20.9. The results were subsequently verified by Noble and Gomez (1958) in a study comparing the electronic cooking of lamb and bacon with conventional roasting.

Mahon *et al.* (1956) roasted approximately 40-lb lots of smoked ham, consisting of 4 hams, at 300°F to an internal temperature of 170°F. The mean cooking times of the 40-lb lots was 4 and 9 min. Before roasting, the lean ham had a mean thiamin content of 0.527 mg/100 g on the moist, fat, salt basis, and 2.14 mg/100 g on the moisture-, fat-, chloride-free basis. After roasting, the mean thiamin content was 0.476 mg/100 g and on the moisture-, fat-, chloride-free basis, it was 1.71 mg/100 g (Leeking *et al.* 1956).

Broasting

This is a foodservice process involving pressure frying which requires specialized equipment. The system, because of pressure, is more rapid than regular deep-fat frying and results in less absorption of fat into the product. There are no known data on nutrient retention advantages and disadvantages.

Table 20.8. Mean Thiamin and Riboflavin in Raw and Roasted Beef and Retention after Roasting

Cut of beef	Mean thiamin[a,b]			Mean riboflavin[a,b]		
	Raw roast (mg/100 g)	Cooked roast (mg/100 g cooked weight)	Retention[c] (%)	Raw roast (mg/100 g)	Cooked roast (mg/100 g cooked weight)	Retention[c] (%)
Top round	0.102 ± 0.01	0.084 ± 0.02	54	0.182 ± 0.01	0.227 ± 0.05	81
Ribs, 6–12	0.058 ± 0.01	0.044 ± 0.01	54	0.126 ± 0.02	0.171 ± 0.04	88
Rump	0.098 ± 0.01	0.084 ± 0.01	61	0.193 ± 0.08	0.236 ± 0.07	86
Tenderloin	0.091 ± 0.02	0.082 ± 0.02	63	0.197 ± 0.03	0.230 ± 0.02	84
Beef loaf prepared from ground chuck arm[d]	0.162 ± 0.02	0.184 ± 0.01	70	0.213 ± 0.02	0.284 ± 0.05	80

Source: Noble and Gomez (1960).

[a] Any two means not side-scored by the same line may be considered significantly different at the 5% level, except for the riboflavin value for top round. This mean is not significantly different from those for tenderloin and beef loaf. Shortest significant ranges at the 5% level of significance are for thiamin, 11 for 5 means, 10 for 2 means; for riboflavin, 6 for 5 means, 5 for 2 means.

[b] Mean ± S.D.

[c] Calculated on entire roast basis.

[d] Mean thiamin and riboflavin content of beef from which loaves were prepared: 0.186 and 0.195 mg/100 g raw weight, respectively.

Table 20.9. Mean Thiamin and Riboflavin in Raw and Roasted Lamb and Retention after Roasting

Cut	Mean thiamin[a]			Mean riboflavin[a]		
	Raw roast (mg/100 g)[b]	Cooked roast (mg/100 g)[c]	Retention (%)[d]	Raw roast (mg/100 g)[b]	Cooked roast (mg/100 g)[c]	Retention (%)[d]
Leg	0.176 ± 0.05	0.194 ± 0.09	64 ± 8	—	—	—
Shoulder	0.088 ± 0.02	0.078 ± 0.02	63 ± 10	0.164 ± 0.07	0.207 ± 0.07	93 ± 11
Rack	0.110 ± 0.06	0.082 ± 0.04	62 ± 6	0.205 ± 0.04	0.219 ± 0.04	85 ± 9
Loin	0.169 ± 0.04	0.138 ± 0.02	66 ± 5	0.333 ± 0.06	0.242 ± 0.05	88 ± 12

Source: Noble and Gomez (1958).
[a] Mean ± S.D.
[b] Raw weight.
[c] Cooked weight.
[d] Calculated on entire roast basis.

521

Pressure Cooking

Only one report was found on nutrient losses in large-scale pressure cooking of foods of animal origin. This was by Schlosser *et al.* (1957) and was on one nutrient, lysine, in older turkeys. These workers found that cooking cut-up, older, fresh-killed tom turkeys by steaming at 5- or 15-lb pressure in a self-contained high-compression steamer or covered with aluminum foil and braised in an oven at 325°F made no appreciable difference in the lysine content of the cooked meat. Percentage retention of lysine during cooking was not obtained. Steaming under pressure required one-fifth the time of braising.

Infrared and Convective Heating

Infrared and convective heating of pork roast, turkey breast, and corned beef were evaluated for nutrient losses by Unklesbay *et al.* (1983A). Few significant differences between the heat-processed samples were found for vitamins and minerals (see Table 20.10). Corned beef that was cooked in a convection oven had a significantly higher content of riboflavin compared to corned beef prepared by infrared heating. Convective heating also produced a higher yield of turkey breast and corned beef. In another study by Unklesbay *et al.* (1983B), convective-heated hamburger patties had signficantly greater product yield compared to infrared heating. In addition, riboflavin and vitamin A levels in hamburgers were significantly greater after infrared heating, as were the total amino acid contents in both hamburgers and cod fillets.

Microwave

In conventional cooking, heat is applied to the outside of food by convection (baking), radiation (broiling), or by conduction (frying) and the heat is then conducted to the interior of the food. Heat generated from within the food by a series of molecular vibrations is the basis for microwave cooking. Advantages of microwave cookery include higher energy efficiencies, greater time savings, convenience, and easy cleanup (Cross and Fung 1982). Its disadvantages include greater cooking losses, inability to brown foods, and less palatability (Korschgen *et al.* 1976).

The use of microwave cookery in foodservice has been on the rise and it is estimated that by the year 2000, microwave ranges will be commonplace in foodservice units (Korschgen *et al.* 1976). Early use of microwave energy in the food industry was primarily for frozen food defrosting. Microwave thawing of precooked frozen meals, an adaption from the "cook-chill" or "ready foods" system, has provided a breakthrough in traditional hospital foodservice which results in higher quality meals with lower food and labor costs (Cross and Fung 1982).

Table 20.10. Selected Vitamin and Mineral Content of Roasts[a,b]

Roast	Nutrient	Raw		Infrared oven		Convection oven	
		Mean	S.E.	Mean	S.E.	Mean	S.E.
Pork loin	Thiamin	26.99a	2.49	9.89b	1.38	15.21b	2.10
	Riboflavin	6.03	0.36	6.73	0.39	5.40	0.67
	Phosphorus	7985.71a	43.80	6375.00b	209.37	6171.42b	227.52
	Sodium	2257.14a	106.58	1900.00b	80.17	1814.28b	124.2b
	Iron	56.57	5.85	53.37	4.53	44.28	5.39
Turkey breast	Thiamin	0.81	0.07	0.55b	0.07	0.51b	0.02
	Riboflavin	4.29	0.27	3.54	0.61	4.20	0.79
	Phosphorus	7862.50a	86.47	6362.50b	114.86	6637.40b	80.04
	Sodium	1850.00a	152.36	1575.00a	83.98	1412.50b	85.43
Corned beef	Thiamin	1.89	0.27	0.53b	0.09	0.79b	0.05
	Riboflavin	9.96	0.77	5.31b	0.44	7.60c	0.18
	Phosphorus	6087.50	367.63	5700.00	197.30	5600.00	165.83
	Sodium	6372.50a	203.32	5160.00b	191.48	5242.50b	317.67
	Iron	93.70a	4.14	78.70b	4.74	71.25b	3.98

Source: Unklesbay et al. (1983A).

[a] μg/g; moisture-free, fat-free basis.
[b] $N = 8$, except for pork loin, where $N = 7$ for convection. Where letters differ in a row, mean values differ significantly ($p < .05$) from each other.

Ziprin and Carlin (1976) evaluated the effect of microwave cookery versus conventional roasting of beef and beef–soy loaves made with either 0, 15% soy flour, or 15% soy concentrate. Cooking losses, fat and moisture contents, and thiamin retention were examined. Microwave-cooked loaves (960 g) reached 74°C in 19 min and had consistently higher cooking losses compared to those cooked conventionally for 78 min. The use of 15% soy reduced cooking losses more in conventional electric than microwave ovens. The addition of soy had no effect on the fat content, although the cooking method significantly affected fat content; 11.5% fat in microwave-cooked loaves versus 9.6% in conventional ovens. Thiamin content was unaffected by soy substitution and cooking method.

Baldwin et al. (1976) cooked beef, pork, and lamb roasts using two 2450 MHz microwave ranges (one operated at 1054 W cooking power, the other at 492 W cooking power) and one conventional gas oven. Meat cooked by microwave (492 W) had lower levels of thiamin, riboflavin, and niacin compared to the two other methods. There was a trend toward less retention of sodium, chloride, phosphorus, and iron in microwave-cooked versus conventionally cooked meats. While total proteins were not significantly different between the two methods, microwave cookery formed less free amino acids compared to the gas oven.

The effect of broiling, grill frying, and microwave cooking on lipid and cholesterol contents of ground beef patties was studied by Janicki and Appledorf (1974). Microwave cooking had the greatest reduction in crude fat. Crude fat values for broiling, grill frying, and broiling and microwave reheating yielded similar values (Table 20.11). This was believed to result from the formation of a brown crust from the browning reaction in the broiled, grill fried, and broiled/reheated beef. The crust did not form in the microwave-heated patties. All cooking methodologies resulted in lowered cholesterol levels compared to the raw patty except for the microwave-cooked patties.

Top round beef roasts cooked in a microwave oven (77.6 min to an internal temperature of 68.3°C) and an electric oven (134.8 min to an internal temperature of 149°C) were evaluated by Voris and Van Duyne (1979) for thiamin content and palatability. Total cooking losses, moisture, fat, and thiamin contents of the cooked meats were not significantly different with respect to cooking method. Microwave-cooked roasts were rated lower in aroma, flavor, and exterior color compared to conventionally cooked roasts, but no difference was found when compared for tenderness, juiciness, or interior color.

Boneless rib eye, top round, and bone-in blade chuck roasts cooked in microwave ovens and in conventional gas ovens were compared for cooking time, yield, and palatability by Fulton and Davis (1983). Cooking time was shorter in microwave ovens, an average of 82 min

Table 20.11. Effect of Cooking Method on Lipid Constituents
in Ground Beef Patties[a]

Cooking method	Crude fat (g)	Cholesterol (mg)
Raw	18.1 ± 3.0a	77 ± 11a
Broiled	10.0 ± 1.0bc	63 ± 12b
Grilled-fried	10.5 ± 1.2b	62 ± 14b
Microwave	8.0 ± 1.0d	70 ± 17ab
Broiled-frozen-microwave	8.9 ± 1.2c	61 ± 11b

Source: Janicki and Appledorf (1974).
[a] Mean ± S.D. for 12 patties per treatment. Values in each column
followed by same letter are not significantly different ($p < .05$).

versus 160 min for conventional ovens. The yield of cooked lean meat
was the same for round and chuck roasts cooked by either type of
oven, while the yield was lower for rib eye roasts cooked in a microwave
versus a conventional oven. Palatability/acceptability rating for tenderness (by a flavor panel and shear-force measurement), softness, and
natural flavor were found to be similar between cooking methods. Rib
eye roasts were found to be browner and less juicy when cooked by
microwaves.

Moore *et al.* (1980) evaluated top round steaks cooked by dry or
moist heat in conventional or microwave ovens with rotary hearths.
Cooking time, volatile cooking losses, total moisture, and sensory
juiciness and tenderness scores were less, while total and drip-cooking
losses were more for steaks cooked by microwaves than be conventional
methods. Cooking time was longer but total and drip-cooking losses
were less for steaks cooked by dry heat than for those cooked by moist
heat.

Pork muscles cooked by microwaves had greater drip loss, volatile
loss, and total cooking loss compared to those cooked in an electric
oven (Bowers *et al.* 1974B). Vitamin B_6 levels in the pork were similar
between cooking methods.

Microwave cookery has been widely used on poultry products.
Chicken breasts cooked by microwaves were found to have significantly
greater retention of vitamin B_6 compared to meat cooked by roasting
in a conventional oven (Wing and Alexander 1972). Prusa *et al.* (1981)
found that moisture, fat, and thiamin levels in hens were not significantly affected by microwave heating compared to those conventionally
baked. Thiamin content was found to be greater in broilers cooked in
a microwave oven compared to an electric oven (see Table 20.12)
(Hall and Lin 1981). No difference in the thiamin content of broilers
cooked in an 800 W versus a 1600 W microwave oven was found.
Cooking chicken at a higher temperature (204°C) in an electric oven for
a shorter time of 45 min significantly increased thiamin retention.

Table 20.12. Thiamin Retention in Broilers Cooked by Microwaves and in Electric Ovens

Sample	Cooking method	Temperature (°C)	Time (min)	Thiamin (% retention)
Light meat	Electric oven	121	120	75.5
Dark meat		121	120	68.1
Light meat		204	45	83.2
Dark meat		204	45	70.0
Light meat	Microwave, 800 W	—	10	85.1
Dark meat		—	10	70.1

Source: Hall and Lin (1981).

Turkey breast muscle heated to an internal temperature of either $75°$ or $85°C$ in microwave and conventional electric ovens were found to have similar vitamin B_6 levels based on a dry weight basis (Bowers *et al.* 1974A). Microwave-cooked samples had higher vitamin B_6 contents on a cooked weight basis, but this was a result of having greater total cooking losses and lowered moisture contents compared to those prepared in the electric ovens.

Soy Products

Soy products have become an economical way of extending meat without substantially lowering the nutritive quality. In addition to these meat extending properties, they also have been recommended to prevent shrinkage in meat products, thus reducing cooking losses. Nielsen and Carlin (1974) found that soy-substituted beef loaves (0, 10, 20, and 30% soy) cooked at $163°C$ to a temperature of $74°C$ had cooking losses of 14.3, 12.5, 9.7, and 7.6%, respectively. As soy substitution was increased there was a similar decrease in total cooking losses seen. Yoon *et al.* (1974) also found that progressive decreases in total cooking losses occurred with increasing soy substitutions. Williams and Zabik (1975) reported total cooking losses of 13.3% and 9.8% for 0 and 30% soy-substituted beef loaves, respectively, that were frozen, thawed, and cooked at $177°$ to $77°C$.

The type of soy products used can have an effect on the functional properties of the resultant soy–meat mixture. According to Ali *et al.* (1982), the substitution of cooked ground soybeans or textured soy protein for 30% of the ground beef in meat loaf mixtures was equally effective in decreasing drip, evaporation, and total cooking losses in freshly cooked; raw, frozen (3.5 and 7 months), and cooked; and cooked, frozen and reheated meat loaves. All beef mixtures and loaves and those with 30% replacements with ground soybeans or textured soy protein contained similar amounts of protein and thiamin. Thiamin retention increased slightly in substituted loaves, but only after 7 months of storage did the textured soy protein loaves have significantly higher thiamin levels than the all-beef loaves. Palatability scores were highest for all-beef loaves and higher for soybean than textured soy-protein loaves.

Hamburger patties containing all beef or beef extended (20% reconstituted soy product, 80% beef) with soy isolate, soy concentrate, or textured soy flour, or beef extended with one of the three soy products fortified with iron (60 mg/100 g soy protein) and zinc (25 mg/100 g soy protein) were evaluated in both the raw and cooked states by Miles *et al.* (1984) for moisture, protein, fat, calcium, phosphorus, magnesium, sodium, iron, copper, zinc, and manganese. They found no significant differences in the retention of protein, fat, total ash, calcium, or copper between the all-beef patties and beef patties extended with any of the soy proteins tested. Moisture retention in the patties decreased as the refinement of the soy added to the patties increased. In general, the higher the mineral content of the raw patty, the higher its nutrient retention.

Cooking and Protein Quality

Siedler (1961) reviewed the effects of standard cooking and processing methods on the nutritional value of meat protein, and, on the basis of the reports of Lushbough *et al.* (1957), Schweigert and Guthneck (1954), and Heller *et al.* (1961), concluded that little of the essential amino acids, tryptophan, methionine, and lysine, are destroyed or lost by heat treatment using standard cooking or processing procedures, and that their biological availability is not impaired. In view of this and the price of protein food of animal origin, it would appear wise to de-emphasize meat as a source of vitamins.

Drippings during Cooking — Protein

Toepfer *et al.* (1955) showed the effect of the addition of water on loss of protein to pan drippings. Beef cooked without added water (oven roasts, griddle-broiled steaks and hamburgers, and meat loaf) lost only from 0.4 to 1.8% of protein to the pan drippings, while that cooked with added water (pot roasts and Swiss steak) lost 7.6 to 14.7% (Table 20.4). All of the beef was apparently cooked at low or moderate temperatures. The authors concluded that trimming of fat did not influence the protein loss to pan drippings.

Drippings during Cooking — Vitamins

Cover *et al.* (1949) showed the damaging effect of high oven temperatures, 205°C, and cooking to a high internal temperature, 98°C; the pan drippings of both pork and beef were so burned that they were not usable. On the other hand, pan drippings of beef roasted at 150°C to an internal temperature of 80°C contained 6% of the thiamin, 20% of the pantothenic acid, and 16% of the niacin and riboflavin; those of pork roasted at the same temperature but to a higher internal temperature (84°C) contained a higher percentage of the vitamins, 17% of the thiamin, 25% of the pantothenic acid, 26% of the niacin, and 19% of the riboflavin (Table 20.7).

Thomas *et al.* (1949) reported appreciable amounts of thiamin (19%), riboflavin (17%), and niacin (20%) in the juice from beef patties cooked in an electronic oven. Causey *et al.* (1950B) found from 1 to 4% of the thiamin and from 3 to 12% of the riboflavin in the cooking drip of frozen beef patties.

Wing and Alexander (1972) recovered 5.4% vitamin B_6 in the drip from roasting chicken breast in conventional ovens for 45 min, as compared to a 1.5% loss when the breasts were cooked in an electronic oven for 1.5 min.

These and other studies show that appreciable vitamin B_6, in addition to moisture and fat, may be lost to pan drippings. Pan drippings are sometimes used in soups and casserole dishes to give flavor, and are an integral part of meat dishes such as Swiss steak and stews. The practice of making gravies from drippings and serving gravies with meals is much less common, and the various dry gravy mixes marketed for their convenience in preparation have not been analyzed for vitamin content. The ingredient listing would indicate no appreciable source of vitamins.

Carving Juice

In the carving of beef, pork, lamb, and veal roasts, and of roasted poultry, appreciable cutting juice may be lost if carving is done while the roasts are very hot. No studies on nutritive loss to carving juices were found.

Foods of Plant Origin

Boiling (Proportion of Water to Solid Material)

Great variations occur in the proportion of water to solid material commonly used; the ratio of water to solids usually varies from 1:2 to 2:1. Krehl and Winters (1950) measured the effect of cooking approximately 1-lb amounts of 12 vegetables to the same state of doneness, in varying amounts of water, on losses of both minerals and vitamins. In the pressure saucepan, 1/2 cup of water was added; in "waterless" cooking none was added. These methods were compared with boiling in water to cover and in 1/2 cup of added water. In all cases the pan was kept covered. Results of ascorbic acid and carotene losses are given in Table 20.13.

These results show clearly that the greatest retention of both vitamins is obtained when vegetables are cooked without water, and that least retention is associated with cooking in the largest amount of water, that is, water to cover. Losses when a pressure saucepan or a small amount of water were used were intermediate. Other studies show that

Table 20.13. Effect of Cooking Vegetables in Varying Amounts of Water on Retention of Ascorbic Acid and Carotene[a]

Vegetable	Pressure-cooked		Water to cover		½ Cup water		Waterless	
	Ascorbic acid	Carotene	Ascorbic acid	Carotene	Ascorbic acid	Carotene	Ascorbic acid	Carotene
Asparagus	67.6	78.5	45.2	64.6	66.4	92.3	69.4	101.5
Beets	93.8	81.4	74.0	72.4	87.3	82.8	81.1	96.2
Broccoli	68.0	88.6	50.6	76.0	68.7	84.3	70.2	97.7
Cabbage	75.5	96.8	44.3	73.3	57.4	89.7	68.4	95.6
Carrots	79.1	88.4	63.1	84.5	75.1	86.3	72.5	98.9
Cauliflower	75.5	89.8	47.3	80.7	54.0	83.7	70.7	97.4
Corn	74.9	88.2	60.2	86 4	65.1	87.3	69.6	93.1
Green beans	76.1	94.4	58.5	85.6	64.0	90.3	74.8	96.3
Peas	73.7	89.7	51.3	83 2	70.0	89.4	78.8	91.2
Potatoes	57.3	86.3	41.0	78.9	48.4	80.5	79.4	85.8
Squash	65.3	92.3	50.5	82.4	66.5	84.2	74.8	91.9
Spinach	61.7	74.8	49.1	80.7	51.7	87.2	70.0	91.3

Source: Krehl and Winters (1950).
[a] Percentage of ascorbic acid and carotene retained.

cooking by steaming above water gives retentions similar to those for cooking in a pressure saucepan or in a small amount of water. Krehl and Winters (1950) also obtained data on the minerals calcium, iron, and phosphorus; and the vitamins thiamin, riboflavin, and niacin. Losses of these nutrients were in the same direction as those of ascorbic acid and carotene so far as they were affected by the amount of water added. Also, the percentage of other nutrients lost was usually more than that for carotene and less than that for ascorbic acid. Thus, retention of ascorbic acid is used as a measure of the relative desirability of a cooking procedure for foods, but it is unfortunate that so much work has been done on vitamin C alone.

In waterless cooking, retentions of vitamin C in the 12 vegetables ranged from about 70% to about 80% (Table 20.13). The results of Gordon and Noble (1964), conducted on 4-serving portions, did not show as good a retention for vitamin C as was found in the more exhaustive Krehl and Winters study; however, the percentage retention of ascorbic acid during cooking in the pressure saucepan was greater than during cooking by either the waterless technique or the boiling water to cover technique for 5 out of 6 vegetables tested. The waterless method was superior to boiling for 5 out of 6 vegetables (Table 20.14). These data and those from other studies demonstrate that it is possible to retain to a high degree the original nutritive value of a vegetable in cooking. On the other hand, an amount of water enough to cover usually resulted in a retention of one-half or less of the original

Table 20.14. Ascorbic Acid in Raw Vegetables and Percentage Retention after Cooking[a]

Vegetable	In raw vegetable		Retention in cooked vegetable[b]			Retention in cooking water		
	Mean (mg/100 g)	Standard error (mg/100 g)	Pressure saucepan	"Waterless" saucepan	Boiling water	Pressure saucepan	"Waterless" saucepan	Boiling water
Broccoli	131.7	13.27	85	51	45	5	3	52
Brussels sprouts	97.6	2.84	78	63	60	4	None	21
Cabbage	49.5	2.65	74	56	41	6	4	38
Cauliflower	60.0	3.03	88	69	53	7	None	23
Rutabagas	30.6	0.84	85	75	46	15	2	33
Turnips	22.5	1.36	69	76	43	16	1	27

Source: Gordon and Noble (1964).

[a] Each percentage is the average of 4 separate cookings.

[b] Within each vegetable, any two means not underscored by the same line are significantly different. Shortest significance range, 5% level of significance equals 8.8 for 18 means, 7.3 for 2 means.

Table 20.15. Percentage Retention of Proximate Components, Minerals, and Vitamins in Selected Legumes[a]

Legume	Protein	Ash	Fat	Potassium	Iron	Zinc	Copper	Thiamin	Riboflavin	Niacin	Vitamin B6	Pantothenic acid
Beans												
Pinto	99	98	100	—	—	—	—	—	—	—	—	—
Great northern	—	90	100	77	98	100	68	73	79	73	67	67
Small white	100	72	90	75	94	91	57	73	83	60	68	79
Broadbeans	93	76	100	70	86	92	77	47	79	64	53	55
Cowpeas	96	—	100	76	92	100	85	65	76	66	59	63
Chickpeas	—	—	—	75	99	100	85	56	78	72	57	46
Lentils	97	86	100	—	—	—	—	85	100	75	83	81

Source: Haytowitz and Matthews (1983).

[a] Based on samples from Virginia Polytechnic Institute and State University and the University of Idaho.

vitamin. In any case, since the lost nutrients are for the most part in the cooking water, utilizing the cooking liquids is definitely worth the effort, but it seems to be a lost art.

Legumes are most often cooked by simmering in an excess of water until tender. Haytowitz and Matthews (1983) have found that factors such as legume size, amount of water used in cooking, cooking time, permeability of legume seed coat to leaching, and type of cookware can all affect nutrient retentions. Table 20.15 lists the retained nutrients found in legumes following simmering. Leaching accounted for most losses of nutrients, such as protein and potassium, and many of the water-soluble vitamins, such as thiamin, niacin, and vitamin B_6.

Augustin et al. (1981) found that cooked *Phaseolus vulgaris* had average retentions of water-soluble vitamins (thiamin, riboflavin, niacin, vitamin B_6, and folacin) between 70 and 75%. Retention of minerals ranged from a low of 38.5% for sodium to total retention of calcium, with phosphorus, potassium, magnesium, zinc, manganese, copper, and iron being retained at levels between 80 and 90% (see Table 20.16).

Pasta

Cooked commercially produced pasta products have been found to have modest losses (less than 20%) of the minerals iron, calcium, phosphorus, zinc, manganese, and magnesium. Significant amounts, up to 60% of potassium, were lost in the cooking water (see Table

Table 20.16. Nutrient Content and Cooking Retention Values of Commercial *Phaseolus vulgaris* Classes[a]

Nutrient	Nutrient content (mg%)		% retention
	Before cooking	After cooking	
Thiamin	0.99 (9.1)	0.72 (7.5)	73.1 (6.4)
Riboflavin	0.20 (27.5)	0.15 (24.5)	75.9 (11.4)
Niacin	1.79 (25.6)	1.22 (29.6)	70.4 (11.6)
Vitamin B_6	0.49 (16.7)	0.35 (24.6)	70.9 (9.1)
Folacin	0.30 (46.6)	0.22 (46.0)	73.0 (12.5)
Phosphorus	0.46 (6.3)	0.43 (6.0)	94.9 (3.5)
Sodium	10.3 (37.4)	3.4 (31.4)	38.5 (23.5)
Potassium	1.54 (6.4)	1.29 (8.4)	81.6 (9.0)
Calcium	0.15 (25.1)	0.15 (24.4)	103.2 (5.9)
Magnesium	0.20 (7.6)	0.17 (9.9)	86.6 (7.1)
Zinc	3.2 (21.7)	3.0 (18.7)	94.0 (10.0)
Manganese	1.4 (19.3)	1.5 (21.6)	102.1 (4.8)
Copper	0.95 (17.1)	0.71 (16.8)	78.9 (9.9)
Iron	5.84 (18.9)	5.84 (21.0)	96.1 (4.3)

Source: Augustin et al. (1981).
[a] Mean value, dry-weight basis; numbers in parentheses are the coefficient of variation in %. P, K, Ca, and Mg values are on a gram % basis.

Table 20.17. Retention of Minerals in Cooked Pasta Products[a]

Mineral	Product	Mean ± S.D. (mg/100 g)		Retention[b] (%)
		Cooked	Uncooked	
Sodium	Spaghetti	1.3 ± 0.4	1.4 ± 0.8	Inconsequential
	Noodles	3.4 ± 1.8	13.2 ± 6.8	
	Macaroni	0.9 ± 0.3	2.2 ± 1.5	
Potassium	Spaghetti	79 ± 18	198 ± 29	39.7 ± 3.9 (37.4)
	Noodles	58 ± 17	219 ± 29	26.3 ± 6.0 (24.8)
	Macaroni	76 ± 16	181 ± 15	42.6 ± 12.6 (40.2)
Iron	Spaghetti	3.98 ± 0.88	3.83 ± 0.72	103.5 ± 7.7 (97.6)
	Noodles	5.44 ± 1.05	4.78 ± 1.24	115.0 ± 10.0 (108.4)
	Macaroni	3.74 ± 0.22	3.54 ± 0.41	106.6 ± 11.2 (100.5)
Copper	Spaghetti	0.298 ± 0.099	0.313 ± 0.038	94.5 ± 18.2 (89.1)
	Noodles	0.326 ± 0.028	0.324 ± 0.019	101.0 ± 10.4 (95.2)
	Macaroni	0.308 ± 0.036	0.281 ± 0.019	109.9 ± 13.6 (103.6)
Phosphorus	Spaghetti	144 ± 40	157 ± 43	91.7 ± 1.1 (86.5)
	Noodles	203 ± 21	207 ± 18	97.6 ± 3.4 (92.0)
	Macaroni	137 ± 14	143 ± 18	96.2 ± 6.4 (90.7)
Zinc	Spaghetti	1.37 ± 0.38	1.32 ± 0.37	104.5 ± 4.8 (98.5)
	Noodles	1.73 ± 0.15	1.61 ± 0.17	108.2 ± 5.7 (102.0)
	Macaroni	1.30 ± 0.09	1.11 ± 0.18	119.1 ± 16.2 (112.3)
Manganese	Spaghetti	0.72 ± 0.24	0.68 ± 0.22	105.1 ± 5.5 (99.1)
	Noodles	0.70 ± 0.12	0.69 ± 0.11	101.5 ± 5.7 (95.7)
	Macaroni	0.67 ± 0.12	0.68 ± 0.16	100.7 ± 10.1 (95.0)
Calcium	Spaghetti	20 ± 2	18 ± 2	108.7 ± 4.2 (102.5)
	Noodles	33 ± 4	30 ± 3	108.9 ± 3.6 (102.7)
	Macaroni	19 ± 4	18 ± 3	102.3 ± 8.9 (96.5)
Magnesium	Spaghetti	41 ± 14	47 ± 13	86.5 ± 5.8 (81.6)
	Noodles	47 ± 11	47 ± 11	101.2 ± 8.7 (95.4)
	Macaroni	38 ± 6	39 ± 6	98.0 ± 12.9 (92.4)

Source: Ranhotra et al. (1982).

[a] On moisture-free basis.

[b] In cooked products; values in parentheses are values corrected for dry-matter losses (average loss, 5.7%) in cooking.

20.17) (Ranhotra et al., 1982). Enriched spaghetti readily lost thiamin, riboflavin, and niacin, having retentions of 39, 30, and 48%, respectively (Dexter et al. 1982; Ranhotra et al. 1983). Losses of thiamin and riboflavin were due to a combined effect of leaching into the cooking water and thermal degradation, while all of the niacin lost during cooking was recovered in the cooking water.

Cooking without Paring or in Large Pieces

As might be expected, there is evidence that solution losses in cooking are affected by the amount of surface, especially cut surface, exposed to the water. The skins of potatoes are such an effective barrier that boiled or steamed whole potatoes show little loss of vitamin C. When peeled, losses may amount to about 13% (Van Duyne et al.

Table 20.18. Vitamin Retention (%) During Boiling, Large-scale Cooking

	Cooking time (min)	Caro-tene	Thiamin	Ribo-flavin	Niacin	Ascorbic acid
Cereals						
Corn (canned)	30		78	95		32
Rice, white	20		46	52	59	
Rice, white, enriched	20		46	62	59	
Vegetables						
General		100	70–75			25–60
			46–100	50–97	36–98	8–100
Student meals		90	90	100	87	60
Earth vegetables						
Carrot		96	50	66	53	27
	30	96			99	
Carrot (dehyd.)	25–45	81–99	52–75	55–89	58	
Carrot (canned)	30		95			38
Carrot	45		48	29	55	77
		96	50	66	53	27
	23		100			
Onion	15		89			
Parsnips	30					30
	15					91
	10		97			
						64
Potato	10		87–92			
	20					69
	15–20		79			
Potato (dehyd. sulfited)	35–45				56–97	56–84
Potato	36		80			
	Done		83	97	83	89
	26					48
	15		89–92			
			70–80	85	75	25–60
	25		96	97	100	98
Pumpkin	15		100			
Swede	45					54
Sweet potato			92	100	100	
		90				100
Squash	10		89			
Turnip	15–20		60			
Taro	35		89			
Fruit vegetables						
Tomatoes (canned)	40	89–110			94–106	88–102
Tomatoes	30	95				
Tomatoes (canned)	30		71–94			99
Herbage vegetables						
Asparagus		97	71	78		81
Asparagus (canned)	30		87	99		93
Beans, snap	45		74			91
Beans (canned)	30		92	100		53
Beans	11		55–85	56–79		44–55
	18–140		59–77	48–83		8–98
			30–59			

Table 20.18. *(Continued)*

	Cooking time (min)	Carotene	Thiamin	Riboflavin	Niacin	Ascorbic acid
Beans (frozen)	25–45		45–85	64–96	68	26–34
Beans	40–85		41–100			
	17–19					62–66
				57–71		25–84
Broccoli	5–6					53–82
Broccoli (frozen)	7–7					80
	8–20		44–61	48–71		46–61
Broccoli	13		80	95		74
	30	100	95	73	88	67
Brussels sprouts	2					77
	5–20					39–62
	15					53
	30–40					44
Cabbage (dehyd.)						67
Cabbage			50	59		50
	120	84–87	33–43	39–50		18–30
	4–8		64–85	66–90		57–74
	20		73			
Cabbage, red	60		18			5
Cabbage	13		46	58		51
	12–20					30
	18					38
	30–40					60
	7					57
Cauliflower	30–40					73
	3					81
	15		52			
	12		87			
Chard, Swiss	10					42
Corn, cob			80	97	87	63
Kale	6		65			50
	25					23
	180–240					3–53
	30		100			
Lima beans (frozen)	14–81		56–82	59–89		52–76
	25–50		37–65	67	78–55	23–73
Lima beans	17					62
Lima beans (canned)	30		88	86–95		45
Okra	20					55–75
Peas	2					70
	9		93	89		63
	9		97	100		86
	30	90	94	93	97	86
						40–80
	8	96	80	69	87	50
	12		91			
Peas (canned)	65		61–66	66	63	35
Peas	8		80	65		45–60
Peas (frozen)	20–27		50–75	62	59	32
Peas	35–135				45	

(continued)

Table 20.18. *(Continued)*

	Cooking time (min)	Carotene	Thiamin	Riboflavin	Niacin	Ascorbic acid
Peas	15–129		66–94	69–98		38–92
	20		70			
Spinach	5			65		23
	30–40					38
	7		78			
	3					70
Spinach (frozen)	23–45		36–78	78		20–35
Spinach	6	97	50	52		24
	5		100			
	10–15	85–88	13–34	19–24	17–42	4–14
	7		50	53		33
Spinach (canned)	30		92–99	95		75–78
Soya sprouts	13–21		63–72			27–38
Turnips						40
Turnip greens						16–53
Legumes						
Legumes					8	
Beans	35–135				45	
	225					84–95

Source: Harris (1960).

1945). "Frenched" green beans (cut in lengthwise strips) retain only 28% of the original vitamin C as compared with 54% retention in those cooked whole and 52% retention in those cut in 1-in. lengths (Noble and Worthington 1948).

Vitamin Retention during Boiling

Harris (1960) prepared a summary of the many studies on the effects of large-scale boiling upon nutrient content. Table 20.18 is an abbreviated version of the original table. More recent studies of the effect of boiling consider ascorbic acid retention only and were not added to the table.

Vitamin Retention during Pressure Cooking and Steam Cooking

Invariably, the loss of nutrients is considerably less during pressure cooking or steam cooking of vegetables as compared to boiling at atmospheric pressures. This is readily evident from Tables 20.19 and 20.20 on vitamin retention during pressure cooking and steaming, respectively. What is startling is that no new studies of any consequence have been published in the open literature since the 1950s.

Meanwhile, the use of steamers has augmented foodservice applications, whereas the routine use of pressure cookers in the home is now nil. Less cooking is being done from fresh foods at both home and institutional levels. More frozen raw foods and precooked frozen

Table 20.19. Vitamin Retention (%) during Pressure Cooking

	Cooking time (min)	Pressure (lb)	Thiamin	Riboflavin	Ascorbic acid
Earth vegetables					
Carrots	10	7	75		49
Potato			96		89
	20	6	95		100
Fruit vegetables					
Chili		10			71–93
Bitter gourds		10			71–93
Herbage vegetables					
Broccoli (frozen)	6	15			72
Broccoli	5–7	5–15	76–95	84–100	77–83
Broccoli (frozen)	5–6	5–15			75–81
Brussels sprouts	0.33	15			97
Cabbage	10	15			60
Cauliflower	0.5	15			92
Lima beans	10				64
Okra (115°C)	2				82
Peas	1	15			88
	9–10	5–15	98	86–92	68–72
Squash	45	6	52		42
Spinach	0.75	15			80
Turnips	30	6	55		100

Source: Harris (1960).

foods are now in use. The foodservice steamer is used as much, if not more, for conditioning convenience foods as it is for cooking in the classical sense. Since nutrient retention is generally better in frozen products and the duration of cooking and the amount of water necessary in steaming is less, all indications are that nutrient retention is probably improved, but there are no systematic studies to confirm or deny such a hypothesis as it applies to the foods, equipment, and practices in use today.

Vitamin Losses into Cooking Water

Even the very unstable vitamin, ascorbic acid, can be found in cooking water. Although only three vitamins have ever been repeatedly studied, it appears probable that other vitamins could also be expected in cooking water. Table 20.21 is a condensation of the information tabulated by Harris (1960). Other investigations show that time of cooking is evidently a critical variable; for example, broccoli boiled for 2, 5 1/2, and 11 min lost 25, 32, and 33%, respectively, of the ascorbic acid content into the cooking water (Barnes *et al.* 1943). These losses can be reduced considerably by limiting the volume of the cooking water. For instance, Barnes *et al.* (1943) observed ascorbic acid retentions of 82, 57, and 53% when broccoli was cooked in 100, 500, and

Table 20.20.   Vitamin Retention (%) during Steam Cooking

	Cooking time (min)	Carotene	Thiamin	Riboflavin	Niacin	Ascorbic acid
Cereals						
Corn			85	100	100	64
Rice	32		95			
Earth vegetables						
Carrots						70–83
	20					86
		93	82	92	84	62
Carrots (dehyd.)	15	91	49–57	63–67	21–57	
Parsnips	25					86
Potato	60		86			
	53		84	72	78	88
	60					46
	50					95
Sweet potato						98
	25–64		70–93	71–100		87–100
Herbage vegetables						
Asparagus						83
Beans, snap						73
	36		81–95	78–93		37–46
Broccoli	16					80
	8–9		56–83	70–86		59–87
Brussels sprouts	7					89–94
	20					60–64
						73
Cabbage	30					52
			89	95		68
	20		88	100		67
	9		85	82		84
Cauliflower	10					71–83
						76
Kale	30–50					40–67
Lima beans						65
Peas	12					68
						74
Peas (frozen)			89	91		53
Spinach			90	85		76
Spinach (frozen)	10					71–73
Spinach	90	98	61	74	72	14
			82	78		30
	5–6		79–81	80–89		50–67
Legumes and oilseeds						
Beans			79	83		28
Soybeans						81

Source: Harris (1960).

Table 20.21. Vitamin Losses (%) into Cooking Water

	Cooking time (min)	Thiamin	Riboflavin	Niacin	Ascorbic acid
Cereals					
Corn		15	12	14	30
Corn (canned)	30	22	27		
Earth vegetables					
Carrots (dehyd.)	25–45	52–93	55–89	42–58	
Carrots (canned)	30	19			12
Potato				2–19	
					48–82
		2–45	2–48		8–38
	25				5
Sweet potato					15–19
				3–4	
Herbage vegetables					
Asparagus (canned)	30	22	22		23
Beans, snap				8–41	
	30				7
Beans (canned)	30	31	30		23
Broccoli				6–13	
	5–8				13–15
	5–13	17–22	11–14		10–12
	9–16	40–46	41–54		16–35
Brussels sprouts					30–64
					49–53
Cabbage	20–120	46–72	53–78		26–33
		6–40	6–41		3–35
	4–8	24–35	20–53		14–38
	8				37
Cauliflower					57–65
				14–18	
Lima beans				5–13	
Lima beans (canned)	30	22	19		16
Okra	20				13
Peas			1	15–33	
		8–62	1–69		4–44
	9				9–14
Spinach	5	14–43	10–39		18–43
		5–26	7–47		7–30
Spinach (canned)	30	26–32	23		21–28

Source: Harris (1960).

1000 cc of water, respectively. McIntosh *et al.* (1942) observed retentions of 84, 63, and 65% ascorbic acid when cauliflower was cooked in 120, 250, and 480 cc of water. When 400 g of cabbage was cooked in 200 and 800 cc water, the ascorbic acid retention was 74 and 47%, respectively (Van Duyne *et al.* 1948). Gilpin *et al.* (1959) reported similar ascorbic acid changes in broccoli. Leaching into the cooking liquid rather than destruction by heat is therefore to be expected.

Table 20.22. Nutrient Losses (%): Steam versus Boiling[a]

Vegetable	Cooking method	Dry matter	Protein	Calcium	Magnesium	Phosphorus	Iron
Asparagus	Boiled	14.0	20.0	16.5	8.8	25.8	34.4
	Steamed	7.9	13.3	15.3	1.4	10.4	20.0
Beans, string	Boiled	24.6	29.1	29.3	31.4	27.6	38.1
	Steamed	14.2	16.6	16.3	21.4	18.8	24.5
Beetgreens	Boiled	29.7	22.2	15.9	41.6	44.9	43.1
	Steamed	15.7	6.9	3.8	14.1	14.0	24.5
Cabbage	Boiled	60.7	61.5	72.3	76.1	59.9	66.6
	Steamed	26.4	31.5	40.2	43.4	22.0	34.6
Cauliflower	Boiled	37.6	44.4	24.6	25.0	49.8	36.2
	Steamed	2.1	7.6	3.1	1.7	19.2	8.3
Celery	Boiled	45.4	52.6	36.1	57.1	48.7	—
	Steamed	22.3	22.3	11.6	32.4	15.7	—
Celery cabbage	Boiled	63.2	67.1	49.7	61.6	66.1	67.6
	Steamed	38.3	33.5	16.3	32.6	30.2	44.1
Spinach	Boiled	33.9	29.0	5.5	59.1	48.8	57.1
	Steamed	8.4	5.6	0.0	17.8	10.2	25.7
Beets	Boiled	30.9	22.0	18.7	30.9	33.6	—
	Steamed	21.5	5.4	1.5	29.4	20.1	—
Carrots	Boiled	20.1	26.4	8.9	22.8	19.0	34.1
	Steamed	5.1	14.5	5.1	5.6	1.1	20.7
Kohlrabi	Boiled	33.6	23.2	27.8	40.4	27.7	51.7
	Steamed	7.6	1.0	1.0	14.3	7.7	21.3
Onions	Boiled	21.3	50.2	15.6	27.8	40.2	36.1
	Steamed	11.0	30.7	7.1	15.7	31.5	15.9
Parsnips	Boiled	21.9	13.3	11.4	46.8	23.7	27.6
	Steamed	4.6	20.0	4.2	8.2	5.7	8.1
Potatoes	Boiled	9.4	—	16.8	18.8	18.3	—
	Steamed	4.0	—	9.6	14.0	11.7	—
Sweet potatoes	Boiled	29.0	71.5	38.3	45.3	44.4	31.5
	Steamed	21.1	15.0	22.1	31.5	24.5	25.1
Rutabagas	Boiled	45.8	48.6	37.1	42.7	57.2	50.0
	Steamed	13.2	15.7	13.4	3.4	24.6	14.3
Average for all	Boiled	39.4	43.0	31.9	44.7	46.4	48.0
vegetables	Steamed	14.0	16.0	10.7	18.6	16.7	21.3

Source: Anonymous (1965).

[a] This chart shows the dramatic savings of nutrients when steam is used in preference to boiling.

Mineral Losses with Boiling and Steaming

McCance *et al.* (1936) investigated the effect of food preparation upon calcium content. Baking, frying, roasting, and steaming had no important effect upon calcium content. During boiling, measurable amounts of calcium are extracted from vegetables. When scarlet runner beans were boiled for 40 min and carrots for 120 min, between 12 and 20% of the calcium passed into the cooking water. At the same time, over 60% of the chlorine and potassium were extracted from the beans. The addition of alkali to the water had no effect.

Krehl and Winters (1950) reported that over 20% of the calcium was extracted from cabbage during boiling, and only 9% during pressure cooking. The average results with 11 vegetables showed nearly 25% of the calcium was leached when the vegetables were covered with water during cooking, and less was lost when less water was added. Table 20.22 provides a comparison of boiling and steaming losses for calcium, magnesium, phosphorus, and iron from several vegetables (Anonymous 1965). Some of the cooking losses can be associated with the dry-matter and protein losses, but in several instances mineral losses, especially for magnesium and iron, are substantial. The very beneficial effects of steaming as compared to boiling on mineral retention are self-evident.

Frying

Okra fried with fat for 15 min retained 55% of its original ascorbic acid content (Walker and Arvidsson 1952). Levy (1937) noted only 20–45% retention of ascorbic acid when potatoes were fried and 55–80% retention when baked. Fenton (1940) and Richardson *et al.* (1937) observed ascorbic acid retentions of 67% in fried and 60% in baked potatoes. Domah *et al.* (1974) studied the effect of frying potatoes at 140°C for 10, 20 or 30 min and at 180°C for 5 min. The results are given in Table 20.23. The retention of total vitamin C was good and, in fact, better than that in boiled potatoes (see Table 20.24). However, ascorbic acid (AA) is oxidized to dehydroascorbic acid (DAA) more rapidly with frying, but the hydrolysis of DAA is slowed by the dehydration of the product during frying and, therefore, DAA accumulates in the fried potato. During boiling, DAA is hydrolyzed to 2,3-diketogluconic acid.

Table 20.23. Influence of Frying on Stability of Ascorbic Acid (AA) and Dehydroascorbic Acid (DAA) in Potatoes[a]

Sample	Dry matter	DAA (mg/100 g dry matter)	AA (mg/100 g dry matter)	Total content of vitamin C (mg/100 g dry matter)
Raw, peeled potatoes before frying	26.20	7.4	44.6	52.0
Fried potatoes				
140° C/10 min	83.01	29.7	20.6	50.3
140° C/20 min	84.00	33.7	7.3	41.0
140° C/30 min	88.00	42.7	0.0	42.7
180° C/5 min	89.10	42.8	0.0	42.8

Source: Domah *et al.* (1974).
[a] Results are average values of eight experiments.

Table 20.24. Influence of Sodium Chloride on Stability of Ascorbic Acid (AA) and Dehydroascorbic Acid (DAA) of Potatoes[a]

Sample	DAA (mg/100 g dry matter)	AA (mg/100 g dry matter)	Total content of vitamin C (mg/100 g dry matter)
Raw, peeled potatoes	7.4	43.1	50.5
Cooked, peeled potatoes in water	9.0	17.1	26.1
Infusion	4.9	5.4	10.3
Cooked, peeled potatoes in 1% NaCl	9.1	13.1	22.2
Infusion	5.7	5.0	10.7
Cooked, peeled potatoes in 5% NaCl	7.1	11.2	18.3
Infusion	7.6	4.1	11.7
Cooked, peeled potatoes in 10% NaCl	5.8	8.9	14.7
Infusion	7.0	6.6	13.6

Source: Domah *et al.* (1974).

[a] Cooking time, 25 min; results are average values of four experiments.

No retention data exist on other foods, in particular fast-foods such as chicken, fish, and onion, which are commonly deep-fried on a large scale.

Vitamin Losses in Baking Vegetables

Baking destroys significant amounts of unstable nutrients in some foods. Spiers *et al.* (1945) reported that baked potatoes retained 76% carotene and 96% ascorbic acid, while parallel samples of boiled potatoes retained 90% carotene and 110% ascorbic acid. Similarly, Pearson and Luecke (1945) compared baked and boiled sweet potatoes, and reported respective retentions of 76 and 92% thiamin, 89 and 103% riboflavin, 86 and 101% niacin, and 77 and 100% pantothenic acid. Kahn and Halliday (1944) compared baked (in skin), pare-baked, pared-cut baked, and French-fried potatoes and observed ascorbic acid retentions of 80, 80, 42 and 77%, respectively. After standing approximately 1 hr, the retentions were 41, 52, 11, and 71%, respectively. Page and Hanning (1963) studied 58 samples of boiled and baked potatoes for vitamin B_6 and niacin retention. The results are given in Table 20.25. Baking losses (9% for B_6 and 4% for niacin) were less than for boiling (20 and 18%, respectively). The difference was essentially found in the cooking liquid.

A study by Pelletier *et al.* (1977) found that the cooking method used on potatoes has a significant effect on the retention of vitamin C (Table 20.26), with boiled potatoes retaining about 80% compared

Table 20.25.   Niacin and Vitamin B_6 Retention (%) in Boiled and Baked Potatoes[a]

Location and cultivar	Number of samples	Retention in boiled potatoes	Loss in cooking liquid	Retention in baked potatoes
		Niacin		
Wisconsin				
'Cobbler'	7	80.7 ± 2.73	17.1 ± 1.47	91.2 ± 6.25
'Triumph'	14	82.4 ± 4.45	15.5 ± 2.32	99.1 ± 4.60
Minnesota, 'Cobbler'	12	82.6 ± 6.76	16.1 ± 6.11	93.6 ± 3.05
Kentucky, 'Cobbler'	9	82.6 ± 3.14	17.6 ± 2.04	91.1 ± 4.66
Indiana, 'Chippewa'	10	79.0 ± 2.36	17.3 ± 1.15	94.1 ± 4.93
Colorado, 'McClure'	3	84.8 ± 5.01	16.8 ± 1.91	105.4 ± 5.36
Idaho, 'Russet Burbank'	3	84.7 ± 2.92	16.2 ± 3.57	90.6 ± 0.85
Overall mean		81.9	16.6	95.8
		Vitamin B_6		
Wisconsin				
'Cobbler'	7	81.0 ± 3.03	15.9 ± 1.32	90.9 ± 9.17
'Triumph'	14	78.5 ± 6.24	14.5 ± 2.14	92.8 ± 9.44
Minnesota, 'Cobbler'	12	81.8 ± 8.03	15.8 ± 5.67	93.2 ± 8.52
Kentucky, 'Cobbler'	9	78.2 ± 10.70	15.2 ± 1.84	88.6 ± 12.10
Indiana, 'Chippewa'	10	79.8 ± 8.10	14.0 ± 1.11	88.8 ± 5.32
Colorado, 'McClure'	3	79.0 ± 4.31	15.4 ± 1.35	91.8 ± 8.06
Idaho, 'Russet Burbank'	3	84.7 ± 8.26	18.4 ± 5.40	91.3 ± 2.85
Overall mean		80.0	15.2	91.2

Source: Page and Hanning (1963).
[a] Mean ± S.D.

to only about 30% being retained in hash browns. During the baking of potatoes, the movement of minerals such as potassium, phosphorus, and iron toward the interior tissues has been demonstrated by Mondy and Ponnampalm (1983). Baking increased the content of potassium (14–23%), phosphorus (2–9%), and iron (2–8%) in the interior pith tissue. Frying decreased significantly the mineral content in both the cortical (outer) and pith (interior) areas, with most of the loss occurring in the cortical area (10–45%).

Baking sweet potatoes causes less amino acid destruction than does canning (Purcell and Walter 1982). The less severe heat treatment of baking, in which the internal temperature of the root probably does not exceed 100°C, results in less lysine destruction, which can be significant during canning.

Microwave

Limited data are available on the effects of microwaves on the nutrients in foods of plant origin.

Microwave heating and boiling caused tissue structural changes in fresh asparagus, as detected using scanning electron microscopy by Harbers and Harbers (1983). Boiling distorted parenchymal tissues,

Table 20.26. Percentages of Weight Changes and Vitamin C Retained in Canadian Potatoes after Different Types of Cooking*

Preparation	% Weight change 4 seasons	Percentage of vitamin C retained				
		Fall 75	Winter 76	Spring 75	Summer 75	4 seasons
Boiled in skin	94 ± 2	82 ± 10	84 ± 11	79 ± 15	79 ± 4	81 ± 10
Boiled, pared before cooking	99 ± 2	(77 ± 7)	71 ± 9	66 ± 6[a]	76 ± 7	73 ± 8
Boiled, mashed + milk	120 ± 2	80 ± 10	74 ± 12	78 ± 11	75 ± 7	77 ± 10
Boiled, mashed + margarine + milk	123 ± 2	(79 ± 11)	74 ± 11	66 ± 10[c]	69 ± 12	72 ± 12
Boiled, browned	72 ± 4	(38 ± 6)	22 ± 10[a]	19 ± 4[a,α]	32 ± 9[a]	28 ± 11
Fried	57 ± 5	(80 ± 12)	66 ± 10[c]	72 ± 12	70 ± 20	72 ± 14
Baked	85 ± 2	(85 ± 9)	77 ± 7	76 ± 10	72 ± 6[b]	78 ± 9
Raw, browned	68 ± 4	(75 ± 9)	56 ± 11[a]	59 ± 10[a]	51 ± 13[c]	60 ± 13
Scalloped + cheese	123 ± 6	77 ± 14[b]	79 ± 11[b,β]	67 ± 8[a,β]	(95 ± 13)	80 ± 15
Scalloped	113 ± 6	66 ± 9	66 ± 12	67 ± 12	74 ± 8	68 ± 10

Source: Pelletier et al. (1977).

* Mean ± S.D. of eight different brands in each season, and mean ± S.D. of 32 samples for four seasons.

[a,b,c] Significantly different from value between parentheses for same type of cooking at $p < .01$, $p < .02$, and $p < .05$, respectively.

[α,β] Significantly different from values with same indice for same type of cooking at $p < .01$ and $p < .02$, respectively.

Table 20.27. Comparison of Microwave versus Conventional Cooking Effects on Vitamin Retention of Vegetables

Food	Cooking method	Temperature (°C)	Time (min)	Nutrient	Retention (%)
Fresh spinach[a]	Conventional	100	7	Ascorbic acid	51
				Folacin	77
	Microwave	—	6.5	Ascorbic acid	47
				Folacin	101
Frozen peas[b]	Conventional	100	8	Ascorbic acid	71
	Microwave	—	5–10	Ascorbic acid	72–100
Frozen Leaf spinach[c]	Conventional	100	10	Folacin	81
	Microwave	—	8	Folacin	85
Frozen peas[c]	Conventional	100	6	Folacin	84
	Microwave	—	7	Folacin	78
Frozen Green beans[c]	Conventional	100	9	Folacin	101
	Microwave	—	8.5	Folacin	103
Frozen Broccoli spears[c]	Conventional	100	5	Folacin	51
	Microwave	—	8	Folacin	53

[a] Klein et al. (1981).
[b] Mabesa and Baldwin (1979).
[c] Klein et al. (1979).

while microwaves produced cracks and distorted adjacent tissues. Neither treatment affected the digestibility of the tissue by rats.

Fresh spinach cooked by microwaves had comparable losses of both ascorbic acid and folacin compared to conventionally prepared (boiled) spinach (Klein et al. 1981). Microwave-cooked frozen peas tended to have greater retention of total ascorbic acid than those cooked via conventional methods (Mabesa and Baldwin 1979). Folacin retention in frozen leaf spinach, green peas, green beans, and broccoli spears was about the same for each vegetable, regardless of cooking method, either microwave or conventional, and ranged from 78 to 105%, except for broccoli (Klein et al. 1979). Low retention of folacin in broccoli was attributed to the presence of heat-labile forms of folacin. Table 20.27 summarizes the results of these studies.

The internal structure of a food may have an effect on nutrient retentions when subjected to microwaves. A comparison between conventional and microwave baking of potatoes was studied by Klein and Mondy (1981). Results of their work are presented in Table 20.28. Overall, they found that constituents and minerals of potatoes depended upon the heat transfer and the particular tissue under investigation. Conventional cooking primarily resulted in the migration of some nutrients from the cortex to the pith, whereas microwave cooking

Table 20.28. Changes in Nutrient Composition of Potatoes Baked by Microwaves and Conventional Means

| Nutrient | Tissue | Retention (%) | |
		Conventional (60 min/400°F)	Microwave (3 min)
Protein	Cortex	87	94
	Pith	87	84
Total amino acids	Cortex	97	102
	Pith	109	96
Free amino acids	Cortex	85	108
	Pith	108	83
Potassium	Cortex	85	101
	Pith	122	113
Phosphorus	Cortex	88	98
	Pith	110	100
Calcium	Cortex	98	102
	Pith	104	117
Magnesium	Cortex	90	104
	Pith	104	99
Manganese	Cortex	89	91
	Pith	104	109
Iron	Cortex	88	98
	Pith	122	90
Copper	Cortex	93	96
	Pith	93	105
Zinc	Cortex	91	100
	Pith	136	100

Source: Klein and Mondy (1981).

resulted mainly in the loss of volatiles from the interior pith tissue. It appears that baking potatoes conventionally is less nutritious with respect to nitrogenous and mineral constituents, especially when the skin and adhering cortical tissue is not consumed.

Sweet potatoes had similar total solid, total sugar, and pectin contents when either baked or microwaved, and these were higher than those for boiled or steamed sweet potatoes (Reddy and Sistrunk 1980). Those prepared by microwaves had higher cellulose and hemicellulose levels compared to ones that were baked, steamed, or boiled. Sweet potatoes that were cooked by microwaves were firm and somewhat coarse in texture, which indicated that the carbohydrates were more firmly bound after cooking. Baked sweet potatoes produced the highest quality cooked product compared to other methods.

The use of microwaves to cook legumes has been shown to affect their nutritive value. Microwave cooking of whole soybeans was found to improve the protein quality, as determined by the protein efficiency ratio (PER) values (Sanchez *et al.* 1981). There was an increased destruction of the trypsin inhibitor as the cooking temperature was increased to 137°C. The high-temperature–short-time of the process did not thermally inactivate lysine, as is common with other conventional processing methods.

Chung *et al.* (1981) studied the nutrient retention in Colossus peas (*Vigna uniguiculata*), an experimental variety of the brown chowder pea, subjected to microwave and conventional cooking. Neither cooking method caused significant changes in the fat, protein, β-carotene, or ascorbic acid content of the peas. Microwave cooking resulted in a significant reduction in several amino acids, but thiamin and riboflavin were significantly increased compared to conventional cooking. Iron and copper were completely retained in peas cooked by either method.

Microwaves have been used in the drying of pasta products (Sale 1976), the production of baked goods, such as doughnuts (Schiffman *et al.* 1971) and the most popular baked product, bread (Tsen 1980). One of the biggest disadvantages of microwave baking of bread is its inability to produce the desirable brown crust. Tsen *et al.* (1977) have found that bread baked by microwaves or steamed had a higher PER and feed conversion rates in rats compared to bread that was baked in a conventional oven. Although lysine and other amino acids varied little among three preparation methods, lysine did become less available nutritionally with conventional baking than with either microwave baking or steaming. It is ironic that the desired dark crust on the bread is a result of the Maillard browning reaction that is known to reduce the nutritional value of bread. The use of microwaves in the production of dark breads, such as wheat or rye, may be more acceptable, since brown crust formation is less important (Tsen 1980).

Reheating

The cook–chill and cook–freeze foodservice systems are often used by hospitals as a means of optimizing the economic and sensory attributes of hot entrées. The reheating method most commonly used is microwave, but other methods, including convection, infrared, and steam, have all been used. Limited data exist on the effect of the heating method on the nutrient quality of foods.

Kahn and Livingston (1970) determined the retention of thiamin in beef stew, chicken á la king, shrimp Newburg, and peas in cream sauce which was freshly prepared, frozen at –23°C, and reheated to 90°C using microwaves, infrared heating, and boiling water immersion. Similar treatments had similar effects on thiamin retention in the various products, with average thiamin retentions for the four products being 93.5% for the microwave reheated products, 90% for the infrared reheated products, and 86% for the immersion-heated products.

Dahl and Matthews (1980) found that microwave reheating of a beef loaf did not significantly lower its thiamin content. There were no statistically significant differences found between reheating method (either conduction, convection, or microwave) of frozen beef loaf or peas in a study by Dahl-Sawyer et al. (1982). Microwave reheating of cooked, frozen turkey was not significantly different in the percentage of retention of thiamin or riboflavin compared to turkey reheated in a conventional gas oven (Bowers and Fryer 1972).

Beef–soy patties that were reheated by hot-air convection, high-pressure steam, or microwave retained at least 80% of their riboflavin, while infrared reheated patties retained only 80% (Ang et al. 1978). The same study evaluated the same reheating procedures on frozen, fried, breaded chicken parts and found that reheated chicken retained 87–93% of its riboflavin with no significant difference among treatments. The thiamin content of oven-baked, frozen chicken that was reheated using conventional or microwave ovens was not significantly different between treatments (Lee et al. 1981).

Bodwell and Womack (1978) found that the protein content of instant mashed potatoes, peas with onions, beans with frankfurters, beef pot roast with gravy, and breaded fish portions was not significantly affected by either microwave, high-pressure steam, infrared, or hot-air convective reheating. The vitamin retention in the same food items and same reheating methods were evaluated by Ang et al. (1975). They found that microwave reheating, which required shorter heating times, resulted in higher retentions of heat-labile nutrients, such as ascorbic acid and thiamin. Infrared reheating had results similar to the microwave reheating. Convective oven reheating, which had the longest heating times, was lower in thiamin in the mashed potatoes and comparable in the other food items to microwave and infrared reheating. High-pressure steam reheating resulted in the lowest levels of thiamin and riboflavin of all the methods evaluated.

Augustin et al. (1980) evaluated the retention of several water-soluble vitamins in baked and rehydrated potatoes during cooking, chilling, and microwave reheating. With baked, chilled, and reheated potatoes, overall retention values ranged from near 100% for thiamin, riboflavin, and niacin to near 70% for ascorbic acid and folic acid. Losses of ascorbic acid and folic acid occurred during the handling steps. Rehydrated cooked, chilled, and reheated potato granules had an overall vitamin retention ranging from over 90% for riboflavin, niacin, and vitamin B_6 to 86% for ascorbic acid and folic acid. Most of the vitamin destruction occurred during the initial preparation of the mashed potatoes from the dehydrated granules and, to a lesser degree, during microwave reheating of the chilled product.

Italian spaghetti prepared in a university cafeteria foodservice was frozen and reheated by microwave and conventional ovens (Khan *et al.* 1982). No significant losses occurred in the thiamin content of the Italian spaghetti after either the microwave or conventional reheating procedures.

Hot Holding

Previous paragraphs of this chapter have provided some data that apply to the effects of hot holding of food; however, a succinct overview is deemed appropriate. Hot holding or warm holding of food involves the use of stationary steam tables or a movable (usually insulated) cart. Holding is considered by some experts (Bengtsson and Dagersbog 1978) to be a major cause of sensory quality deterioration: 30 min should be the maximum hot holding allowed. However, anyone familiar with mass feeding in health care facilities realizes this duration is substantially exceeded.

A cooperative experiment station project studied the effect on three vitamins of reheating and/or holding a standardized formulation for spaghetti and meat sauce (Table 20.29) (Klein *et al.* 1984). The results demonstrate that riboflavin is relatively stable; thiamin loss with reheating was greater than with holding, but not more than 35% loss occurs. Ascorbic acid was substantially lost, exceeding 75% with reheating in contrast to 40–27% retention with holding 90 min to 3 hr, respectively. It appears that reheating after freezing is harsher than hot holding. Ang *et al.* (1975) reported that freshly prepared mashed potatoes retained 66% ascorbic acid after 30 min and 40% after 3 hr of holding.

Table 20.29. Vitamin Retention (%) in Spaghetti with Meat Sauce

State and product	Ascorbic acid	Thiamin	Riboflavin
Michigan			
Freshly prepared (all beef)	100[a]	100[a]	
Frozen, reheat stove	24	100	
Frozen, reheat microwave	21	70	
Freshly prepared (20% soy, 80% beef)	100	100	
Frozen, reheat stove	16	65	
Frozen, reheat microwave	19	95	
Iowa			
Freshly prepared (all beef)	100[b]	100[b]	
Held 90 min at 79°C/174°F	59	77	
Held 3¾ hr at 72°C/162°F	73	78	
Illinois			
Freshly prepared (all beef)		100[a,b]	100[a,b]
Held 90 min at 65°C/149°F		83[a], 87[b]	99[a], 104[b]

Source: Klein *et al.* (1984).
[a] Retention on dry-weight basis.
[b] Retention on wet-weight basis.

Reheating with steam holding for 30 min resulted in 40% retention. Reheating with microwave and holding for 30 min gave a 24% retention. Again, it appears that reheating is harsher than holding per se. For a comprehensive review of the effect of hot holding on nutritive value changes in foodservice systems, the recent review of Snyder and Matthews (1984) is recommended. Of the 44 studies reviewed spanning 40 years of research, holding times and temperatures of holding equipment ranged from 10 to 300 min and 113° to 210°F (45° to 99°C), respectively. Ascorbic acid was the most unstable nutrient studied. Entrée items show better retention of nutrients than do vegetable items. In general, the higher the holding temperature and/or the longer the holding time, the greater the nutrient loss.

SUMMARY

Nutrient retention in foodservice systems is dependent upon many variables. A number of questions need to be asked in order to select and to optimize nutrient retention:

1. Is the food garden fresh or market fresh?
2. If not fresh, is the food formulated or fabricated? Does the ingredient listing reveal known valuable sources of nutrients or added nutrients?
3. What storage and/or transportation conditions did the product undergo, or does the product have a use-by or expiration date?
4. What types and extent of preparation steps were involved, particularly steps that increase the surface area and/or increase exposure to light and air (oxygen)?
5. What type of container (configuration) was used? What was the quantity of food? Was the container covered? Was water minimized?
6. What method of cooking was used? What was the rate of heating?
7. Was the product handled during heating, exposing it to light and air (oxygen)?
8. Was the product chilled or frozen for subsequent reheating? How rapidly? How adequate was the holding facility?
9. Was the product reheated? By what method?
10. How long was the product held hot prior to being served? By what method?

The relatively stable nutrients are protein, minerals, and niacin. The nutrients appearing to decay as the sensory qualities of the product also decay are riboflavin, thiamin, and possibly vitamin B_6. The nutrient most susceptible to light is vitamin A (both the natural and fortificant form). The nutrients appearing to decay faster than the sensory qualities of the food are ascorbic acid, the folacins, and possibly pantothenic acid.

Nearly 100 million customer transactions occur each day in commercial foodservices in the United States. Many individuals, ranging from school children to the aged in various institutions of learning and health care are completely dependent on foodservice meals to ensure nutrient needs. Research on the nutrient delivery profile of school meals (Lachance *et al.* 1972) and of hospital meals (Koehler and Hard 1983) would indicate that selected foods in foodservice should be nutrified or vitamin supplementation routinely provided. Since fast-food meals also share in this deficit, Lachance (1981) has advocated the nutrification of cereal grain products, because these foods invariably are common components of meals. Foodservice provides those foods that are preferred or foods prescribed by some regulation (e.g., Type A lunch of USDA), but experience indicates selected foods are consumed and the remainder become plate waste. It requires basic research to be able to predict nutrient retention changes with various foodservice practices; but applied research is required to deliver nutrient needs *in spite of* various foodservice practices and the varied preferences of the consumer.

REFERENCES

Ali, F. S., Perry, A. K., and Van Duyne, F. O. 1982. Soybeans vs. textured soy protein as mean extenders. J. Am. Diet. Assoc. *81*, 439.

Ang, C., Chang, C., Frey, A., and Livingston, G. 1975. Effects of heating methods on vitamin retention in 6 fresh or frozen prepared food products. J. Food Sci. *40*, 977.

Ang, C., Basillo, L., Cato, B., and Livingston, G. 1978. Riboflavin and thiamine retention in frozen beef–soy patties and frozen fried chicken heated by methods used in food service operations. J. Food Sci. *43*, 1024.

Anonymous 1965. Cooking for Profit. August. p. 15.

Augustin, J., Marousek, G. I., Tholen, L. A., and Bertelli, B. 1980. Vitamin retention in cooked, chilled and reheated potatoes. J. Food Sci. *45*, 814.

Augustin, J., Beck, C., Kalbfleish, G., and Kagel, L. 1981. Variation in the vitamin and mineral content of raw and cooked commercial *Phaseolus vulgaris* classes. Food Technol. *35*, 75.

Baldwin, R., Korschgen, B., Russell, M., and Mabesa, L. 1976. Proximate analysis, free amino acid, vitamin and mineral content of microwave cooked meat. J. Food Sci. *41*, 762.

Barnes, B., Tressler, D. K., and Fenton, F. 1943. Thiamin content of fresh and frozen peas and corn before and after cooking. Food Res. *8*, 420.

Bengtsson, N., and Dugersbog, H. 1978. Fried meat and meat patties — the influence of preparation and processing on quality and yield. *In* How to Serve Foods? K. Paulus (Editor). S. Karger, New York.

Bodwell, C., and Womack, M. 1978. Effects of heating methods on protein nutritional value of 5 fresh or frozen prepared food products. J. Food Sci. *43*, 1543.

Bowers, J., and Fryer, B. A. 1972. Thiamin and riboflavin in cooked and frozen, reheated turkey — Gas vs. microwave ovens. J. Am. Diet. Assoc. 63, 399.

Bowers, J., Fryer, B., and Engler, P. 1974A. Vitamin B_6 in turkey breast muscle cooked in microwave and conventional ovens. Poult. Sci. 53, 844.

Bowers, J., Fryer, B., and Engler, P. 1974B. Vitamin B_6 in pork muscle cooked in microwave and conventional ovens. J. Food Sci. 39, 426.

Causey, K., Hausrath, M. E., Ramstad, P. E., and Fenton, F. 1950A. Effect of thawing and cooking methods on palatability and nutritive value of frozen ground meat. 1. Food Res. 15, 237.

Causey, K., Hausrath, M. E., Ramstad, P. E., and Fenton, F. 1950B. Effect of thawing and cooking methods on palatability and nutritive value of frozen ground meat. 2. Food Res. 15, 249.

Chung, S., Morr, C., and Jen, J. 1981. Effect of microwave and conventional cooking on the nutritive value of Colossus peas (*Vigna uniguiculata*). J. Food Sci. 46, 272.

Cover, S., Dilaver, E. M., Hays, R. M., and Smith, W. H. 1949. Retention of B vitamins after large-scale cooking of meat. II. Roasting by two methods. J. Am. Diet. Assoc. 25, 949.

Cross, G., and Fung, D. 1982. A review of the effects of microwave cooking on foods. J. Environ. Health 44, 188.

Dahl, C. A., and Matthews, M. E. 1980. Cook/chill foodservice system with a microwave oven: Thiamin content in portions of beef loaf after microwave heating. J. Food Sci. 45, 608.

Dahl-Sawyer, C. A., Jen, J. J., and Huang, P. D. 1982. Cook/chill foodservice with conduction, convection, and microwave reheat systems: Nutrient retention in beef loaf, potatoes, and peas. J. Food Sci. 47, 1089.

Dexter, J. E., Matsuo, R. R., and Morgan, B. C. 1982. Effects of processing conditions and cooking times on riboflavin, thiamine, and niacin in enriched spaghetti. Cereal Chem. 9, 328.

Domah, Aabmud A. M. B., Davidek, J., and Velisek, J. 1974. Changes of L-ascorbic acid and L-dehydroascorbic acids during cooking and frying of potatoes. Z. Lebensm. Unters.-Forsch. 154, 272.

Farrer, K. T. H. 1955. Thermal destruction of vitamin B_1 in foods. *In* Advances in Food Research, Vol. 6. M. Mrak and G. F. Stewart (Editors). Academic Press, New York.

Fenton, F. 1940. Vitamin C retention as a criterion of quality and nutritive value in vegetables. J. Am. Diet. Assoc. 16, 524.

Fulton, L., and Davis, C. 1983. Roasting and braising beef roasts in microwave ovens. J. Am. Diet. Assoc. 83, 560.

Gilpin, G. L., Sweeney, J. P., Chapman, V. J., and Eisen, J. N. 1959. Effect of cooking methods on broccoli. J. Am. Diet. Assoc. 22, 8.

Gordon, J., and Noble, I. 1964. "Waterless" vs. boiling water cooking of vegetables. J. Am. Diet. Assoc. 44, 378.

Hall, K. N., and Lin, C. S. 1981. Effect of cooking rates in electric or microwave oven on cooking losses and retention of thiamin in broilers. J. Food Sci. 46, 1292.

Harbers, C. A. Z., and Harbers, L. H. 1983. Asparagus tissue changes by cooking methods and digestion in rats as observed by scanning electron microscopy. Nutr. Rep. Int. 27, 97.

Harris, R. S. 1960. Effects of large-scale preparation on nutrients of foods of plant origin. *In* Nutritional Evaluation of Food Processing. R. S. Harris and H. von Loesecke (Editors). AVI Publishing Co., Westport, CT.

Haytowitz, D. B., and Matthews, R. H. 1983. Effects of cooking on nutrient retention of legumes. Cereal Foods World 28, 362.

Heller, B. S., *et al.* 1961. Utilization of amino acids from foods by the rat. 5. Effects of heat treatment on lysine in meat. J. Nutr. 73, 113.

Hudson, D. E., Fisher, M. C., and Lachance, P. A. 1985A. Ascorbic acid content of broccoli (buds and stems) during marketing. J. Food Qual. 9(1): 31–37.

Hudson, D. E., Mazur, M., and Lachance, P. A. 1985B. Semi-automated fluorometric determination of ascorbic acid, riboflavin and thiamin of strawberries during postharvest handling. HortScience 20(1): 71–72.

Hudson, D. E., Butterfield, J. E. and Lachance, P. A. 1985C. Ascorbic acid, riboflavin and thiamin content of sweet pepper during marketing. HortScience 20(1), 129–130.

Janicki, L., and Appledorf, H. 1974. Effect of broiling, grill frying and microwave cooking on moisture, some lipid components and total fatty acids of ground beef. J. Food Sci. 39, 715.

Jonsson, L., and Karlstrom, B. 1981. Effect of frying and warm holding on protein quality, linoleic acid content and sensory quality of hamburgers. Lebensm. Wissensch. Technol. 14, 127.

Kahn, L. N., and Livingston, G. E. 1970. Effect of heating methods on thiamine retention in fresh and frozen prepared foods. J. Food Sci. 35, 349.

Kahn, R. M., and Halliday, E. G. 1944. Ascorbic acid content of white potatoes as affected by cooking and standing on steam table. J. Am. Diet. Assoc. 20, 220.

Khan, M., Klein, B., and Lee, F. 1982. Thiamin content of freshly prepared and leftover Italian spaghetti served in a university cafeteria foodservice. J. Food Sci. 47, 2093.

Klein, B. P., Lee, H. C., Reynolds, P. A., and Wangles, N. C. 1979. Folacin content of microwave and conventionally cooked frozen vegetables. J. Food Sci. 44, 286.

Klein, B., Luo, C., and Boyd, G. 1981. Folacin and ascorbic acid retention in fresh raw, microwave, and conventionally cooked spinach. J. Food Sci. 46, 640.

Klein, B. P., Matthews, M. E., and Setser, C. S. 1984. Food service systems: Time and temperature effects on food quality. North Central Regional Research Publication 293. University of Illinois Bull. 779. Urbana, IL.

Klein, L. B., and Mondy, N. I. 1981. Comparison of microwave and conventional baking of potatoes in relation to nitrogenous constituents and mineral composition. J. Food Sci. 46, 1874.

Koehler, H. H., and Hard, M. K. 1983. Vitamin content of preprepared foods sampled from a hospital food service line. J. Am. Diet. Assoc. 82, 622.

Korschgen, B., Baldwin, R., and Snider, S. 1976. Quality factors in beef, pork, and lamb cooked by microwaves. J. Am. Diet. Assoc. 69, 635.

Kotschevar, L. H., Mosso, A., and Tugwell, T. 1955. B vitamin retention in frozen meat. J. Am. Diet. Assoc. 31, 589.

Krehl, W. A., and Winters, R. W. 1950. Effect of cooking methods on retention of vitamins and minerals in vegetables. J. Am. Diet. Assoc. 26, 966.

Lachance, P. A. 1978. Nutritional implications of eating more meals away from home. Proc. Kellogg Nutr. Symp., Toronto, pp. 156–181.

Lachance, P. A. 1981. The role of cereal grain products in the U.S. diet. Food Technol. 35, 49.

Lachance, P. A., Moskowitz, R. B., and Winawer, H. H. 1972. Balanced nutrition through food processor practice of nutrification: Model experience in school food service. Food Technol. 26, 30. Cited in Miskimin, D., Bowers, J., and Lachance, P. A. 1974. Nutrification of frozen preplated school lunches is needed. Food Technol. 28, 52.

Lee, F. V., Khan, M. A., and Klein, B. P. 1981. Effect of preparation and service on the thiamin content of oven-baked chicken. J. Food Sci. 46, 156.

Leeking, P., et al. 1956. The quality of smoked hams as affected by adding antibiotic and fat to the diet and phosphate cure. 3. Moisture, fat, chloride, and thiamine content. Food Technol. 10, 274.

Leverton, R. M., and Odell, G. V. 1958. The nutritive value of cooked meat. Oklahoma Agr. Exp. Stn. Misc. Publ. *MP-49*.

Lushbough, C. H., Porter, T., and Schweigert, B. S. 1957. Utilization of amino acids from foods by the rat. 4. Tryptophan. J. Nutr. *62*, 513.

Mabesa, L., and Baldwin, R. 1979. Ascorbic acid in peas cooked by microwaves. J. Food Sci. *44*, 932.

Mahon, P., *et al.* 1956. The quality of smoked ham as affected by adding antibiotic and fat to the diet and phosphate cure. Food Technol. *10*, 265.

McCance, R. A., Widdowson, E. M., and Shackleton, L. 1936. The nutritive value of fruits, vegetables and nuts. Med. Res. Council Spec. Rep. *213*.

McIntire, J. M., Schweigert, B. S., Henderson, L. M., and Elvehjem, C. A. 1943. The retention of vitamins in meat during cooking. J. Nutr. *25*, 143.

McIntosh, J. A., Tressler, D. K., and Fenton, F. 1942. Ascorbic acid content of five quick frozen vegetables. J. Home Econ. *34*, 314.

Meyer, J. A., Briskey, E. J., Hoekstra, W. G., and Weckel, K. G. 1963. Niacin, thiamine and riboflavin in fresh and cooked pale, soft, watery versus dark, firm, dry pork muscle. Food Technol. *17*, 485.

Miles, C. W., Ziyad, J., Bodwell, C. E., and Steele, P. D. 1984. True and apparent retention of nutrients in hamburger patties made from beef or beef extended with three different soy proteins. J. Food Sci. *49*, 1167.

Mondy, N. I., and Ponnampalam, R. 1983. Effect of baking and frying on nutritive value of potatoes: Minerals. J. Food Sci. *48*, 1475.

Moore, L., Harrison, D., and Dayton, A. 1980. Differences among top round steaks cooked by dry or moist heat in a conventional or microwave oven. J. Food Sci. *45*, 777.

Nielsen, L. M., and Carlin, A. F. 1974. Frozen, precooked beef and beef–soy loaves. J. Am. Diet. Assoc. *65*, 35.

Noble, I. 1964. Thiamine and riboflavin retention in broiled meat. J. Am. Diet. Assoc. *45*, 447.

Noble, I. 1965. Thiamine and riboflavin retention in braised meat. J. Am. Diet. Assoc. *47*, 205.

Noble, I. 1970. Thiamin and riboflavin content in cooked variety meats. J. Am. Diet. Assoc. *56*, 225.

Noble, I., and Gomez, L. 1958. Thiamine and riboflavin in roast lamb. J. Am. Diet. Assoc. *34*, 157.

Noble, I., and Gomez, L. 1960. Thiamine and riboflavin in roast beef. J. Am. Diet. Assoc. *36*, 46.

Noble, I., and Worthington, J. 1948. Asorbic acid retention in cooked vegetables. J. Home Econ. *40*, 129.

Page, E., and Hanning, F. M. 1963. Vitamin B_6 and niacin in potatoes. J. Am. Diet. Assoc. *42*, 42.

Pearson, P. B., and Luecke, R. W. 1945. The B vitamin content of raw and cooked sweet potatoes. Food Res. *10*, 325.

Pelletier, O., Nantel, C., Leduc, R., Tremblay, L., and Brassard, R. 1977. Vitamin C in potatoes prepared in various ways. Can. Inst. Food Sci. Technol. *10*, 138.

Prusa, K. J., Chambers, E., Bowers, J. A., Cunningham, F., and Dayton, A. D. 1981. Thiamin content, texture, and sensory evaluation of postmortem papain-injected chicken. J. Food Sci. *46*, 1684.

Purcell, A. E., and Walter, W. M. 1982. Stability of amino acids during cooking and processing of sweet potatoes. J. Agr. Food Chem. *30*, 443.

Ranhotra, G. S., Gelroth, J. A., Novak, F. A., and Bock, M. A. 1982. Retention of selected minerals in cooked pasta products. Nutr. Rep. Int. *26*, 821.

Ranhotra, G. S., Gelroth, J. A., Novak, F. A., and Bock, M. A. 1983. Losses of enrichment vitamins during the cooking of pasta products. Nutr. Rep. Int. *28*, 423.

Reddy, N. N., and Sistrunk, W. A. 1980. Effect of cultivar, size, storage, and cooking method on carbohydrates and some nutrients of sweet potatoes. J. Food Sci. *45*, 682.

Richardson, J. E., Davis, R., and Mayfield, H. L. 1937. Vitamin C content of potatoes prepared for table use by various methods of cooking. Food Res. *2*, 85.

Russell, L. F., Mullin, W. I., and Wood, D. F. 1983. Vitamin C content of fresh spinach. Nutr. Rep. Int. *28*, 1149.

Sale, A. J. H. 1976. A review of microwaves for food processing. J. Food Technol. *11*, 319.

Salunkhe, D. K. 1976. Storage, Processing and Nutritional Quality of Fruits and Vegetables. CRC Press, Cleveland, OH.

Sanchez, A., Register, U., Blankenship, J., and Hunter, C. 1981. Effect of microwave heating of soybeans on protein quality. Arch. Latinam. Nutr. *31*, 44.

Schiffmann, R. F., Roth, H., Stein, E. W., Kaufman, H. B., Hochhauser, A., and Clark, F. 1971. Applications of microwave energy to doughnut production. Food Technol. *25*, 718.

Schlosser, G. E., Seaquist, R., Rea, E. W., and Dawson, E. H. 1957. Food yields and losses in pressure cooking. J. Am. Diet. Assoc. *33*, 1154.

Schweigert, B. S., and Guthneck, B. T. 1954. Utilization of amino acids from foods by the rat. 3. Methionine. J. Nutr. *54*, 333.

Schweigert, B. S., and Payne, B. J. 1956. A summary of nutrient content of meat. Am. Meat Inst. Found. Bull. *30*.

Siedler, A. J. 1961. Effect of standard cooking and processing methods on the nutritional values of meat protein. Am. Meat Inst. Found. Bull. *51*.

Snyder, P. O., and Matthews, M. E. 1984. Effect of hot holding on the nutritional quality of menu items in food service systems: A review. Sch. Food Serv. Res. Rev. *8*, 6.

Spiers, M., *et al.* 1945. The effects of fertilizer treatments, curing storage and cooking on the carotene and ascorbic acid content of sweet potatoes. Southern Coop. Ser. Bull. *3*.

Spiers, M., Miller, J., Tucker, H. P., *et al.* 1951. Variations in size of sample for the determinations of moisture, ascorbic acid and carotene in turnip greens. Southern Coop. Ser. Bull. *10*.

Thomas, M. H., Brenner, S., Eaton, A., and Craig, V. 1949. Effect of electronic cooking on nutritive value of foods. J. Am. Diet. Assoc. *25*, 39.

Toepfer, E. W., Pritchett, C. A., and Hewston, E. M. 1955. Boneless beef: Raw, cooked and stewed. Results of analysis for moisture, protein, fat and ash. U.S. Department of Agriculture Bull. *1137*. USDA, Washington, DC.

Tsen, C. 1980. Microwave energy for bread baking and its effect on the nutritive value of bread — A review. J. Food Prot. *43*, 638.

Tsen, C., Reddy, P., and Gehrke, C. 1977. Effects of conventional baking, microwave baking and steaming on nutritive value of regular and fortified breads. J. Food Sci. *42*, 402.

Tucker, H. Q., Voegeli, M. J., Wellington, G. H., and Bratzler, L. J. 1952. A Cross Sectional Muscle Nomenclature of the Beef Carcass. Michigan State College Press, East Lansing.

Tucker, R. E., Hinman, W. F., and Halliday, E. G. 1946. The retention of thiamine and riboflavin in beef cuts during braising, frying and broiling. J. Am. Diet. Assoc. *22*, 877.

Unklesbay, N., Davis, M. E., and Krause, G. 1983A. Nutrient retention in pork, turkey breast and corned beef roasts after infrared and convective heat processing. J. Food Sci. *48*, 866.

Unklesbay, N., Davis, M. E., and Krause, G. 1983B. Nutrient retention of portioned menu items after infrared and convective heat processing. J. Food Sci. *48*, 869.

Van Duyne, F. O., Chase, J. T., and Simpson, J. I. 1945. Effect of various home practices on ascorbic acid content of potatoes. Food Res. *10*, 72.

Van Duyne, F. O., Chase, J. T., Owens, R. F., and Fanska, J. R. 1948. Effects of certain home practices on riboflavin content of cabbage, peas, snap beans and spinach. Food Res. *13*, 162.

Voris, H. H., and Van Duyne, F. O. 1979. Low wattage microwave cooking of top round roasts: Energy consumption, thiamin content and palatability. J. Food Sci. *44*, 1447.

Walker, A. R. P., and Arvidsson, U. B. 1952. The vitamin C content of braised cabbage cooked under pressure and prepared on a very large scale. S. Afr. J. Med. Sci. *17*, 143.

Watt, B. K., and Merrill, A. L. 1963. Composition of foods: Raw, processed and prepared. *In* Agriculture Handbook 8. USDA, Washington, DC.

Wellington, G. H. 1954. Body composition and carcass changes of young Holstein cattle. Unpublished Ph.D. thesis. Michigan State Univ.

Williams, C. W., and Zabik, M. E. 1975. Quality characteristics of soy-substituted ground beef, pork and turkey meat loaves. J. Food Sci. *40*, 502.

Wing, R. W., and Alexander, J. C. 1972. Effect of microwave heating on vitamin B_6 retention in chicken. J. Am. Diet. Assoc. *61*, 661.

Yoon, S., Perry, A. K., and Van Duyne, F. O. 1974. Textured vegetable protein palatable in meat loaves. Illinois Agric. Exp. Stn. Research Bull. *16*, 10.

Ziprin, Y., and Carlin, A. 1976. Microwave and conventional cooking in relation to quality and nutritive value of beef and beef–soy loaves. J. Food Sci. *41*, 4.

21

Effects of Home Food Preparation Practices on Nutrient Content of Foods

Catherine E. Adams
John W. Erdman, Jr.

In the first edition, Agnes Fay Morgan (1960) stated that "it is impossible to separate most effects of commercial from home processing because the physical and chemical changes involved are identical." Although new commercial technologies are in use today, Dr. Morgan's statement is still largely correct. This chapter will avoid repeating much of the known information on the effects of various commercial practices. These issues are discussed in detail in other chapters, and our topic, as it pertains to food preparation procedures and foodservice in particular, has been reviewed in the previous chapter. This current work updates the equivalent chapter in the last edition (Lachance and Erdman 1975).

CHANGING FOOD HABITS

In recent years, food consumption in the United States has shifted from traditional to nonconventional patterns. Food habits have changed dramatically from the turn of the century when almost all meals were consumed at home and with the family unit. Since that time, our society has become more affluent, more mobile, and more diffuse. Our habits no longer center around a routine of three meals a day at home. Results of nationwide food consumption surveys performed by the U.S. Department of Agriculture (USDA) revealed that in 1965, 17% of our total expenditure for food in the United States was spent on food consumed away from home. In 1977, that percentage had increased to 25%. Furthermore, households with relatively higher incomes spent more money on food purchased away from home than did lower income households (USDA 1980).

Changes in the socioeconomic and demographic composition of the U.S. population have contributed to the observed differences in life-style in recent years. Changes have included more women in the work force, more two-income households, more homemakers who have less time for meal preparation, and easier access to convenience and fast foods. Gone are the days when a pattern of three meals a day was considered the norm. It is estimated that 30–50% of U.S. families have one or more members who regularly skip breakfast (Bauman 1971). Results of the most recent nationwide household food survey also indicated that the types of foods purchased by households has changed. Compared with 1965, households in 1977 spent more money for poultry, fish, meat, fruit, soft drinks, punches, and prepared desserts. The greatest increases appeared for soft drinks, punches, and prepared desserts, poultry, and fish, in that order (USDA 1980). Less money was spent for fats and oils, sugar, syrup, jelly and candy. Decline in purchases of cooking fats and sugars may reflect a concern about these foods in the diet as well as a decline in home preparation of items requiring these food ingredients.

These changing life-styles have caused some groups of individuals to voice concern about the nutritional quality of the "all-American" diet. There is concern that today's diet, which includes processed foods, is less nutritious than when the diet consisted only of home-prepared items. While some commercially processed foods suffer inevitable nutrient losses relative to the fresh product, improper handling, storage, or preparation of foods for meals cooked at home may lead to greater losses of nutrients. Care must be taken at all stages of food preparation, from field to table, in order to optimize nutrient retention. It may be that some market-fresh vegetables have spent 10 days in transport prior to delivery to a store, then 2–3 days on the shelf before purchase. These foods may be stored for further time periods after purchase, prior to their preparation for consumption. The nutrient quality of these products may be less than the same vegetables taken directly from the field to the processing plant, quick-cooled, and frozen, all within hours of harvest. Similarly, poultry may be sold as market fresh 3 days or more after slaughter, but if processed and frozen immediately after killing, may actually have greater nutrient retention than the so-called market-fresh item. Daniels (1974) evaluated this difference between harvest fresh and market fresh related to vitamin C content. He expressed the results in terms of a percentage of the figure quoted in the USDA food consumption tables (± standard deviation): harvest-fresh peas, 121 ± 35; market-fresh peas, 65 ± 26; frozen peas, 98 ± 46; and canned peas, 102 ± 22. Processed peas were similar in ascorbic acid content and retained more vitamin value than did market-fresh peas.

It is also noteworthy to mention the distinction that may exist between "as purchased" and "as prepared" nutrient composition. USDA handbooks contain extensive tables for nutritional value of foods, both raw and prepared, using common cooking methods, for example, broiled or boiled foods. The differences in nutrient retention, using a variety of other preparation methods, is not indicated. The commercial processor has been trained to know the method of food handling and process that maximizes the nutrient retention for each food item prepared. For this reason, processed foods are generally very good sources of nutrients. Carelessness or lack of knowledge on the part of a homemaker may lead to excessive loss of nutritional quality that could easily have been avoided. These problems may be a matter of education and we hope to impress the reader of the need for proper food preparation practices to be more widely communicated. Traditional nutrition education related to food has not focused on cooking practices, but rather on the basic four food groups and servings of each that should be consumed daily.

STORAGE

The effects of packaging and storage on commercially processed foods are discussed in Chapters 3 and 4. Therefore, this chapter will only address the storage and preparation of foods using various home practices.

Nutritional attributes of foods are rarely enhanced by holding or by storage. Nutrients in foods, whether of animal or plant origin, are differentially susceptible to the effects of heat, light, air, metal catalysts, and natural endogenous enzymes. Since food products are frequently held for substantial periods of time in the home and/or improperly handled or prepared, it is conceivable that the primary damage to nutrient levels in foods occurs within the home (Lachance et al. 1973).

Foods of Animal Origin

Freezing

Foods of animal origin, including meats, fish, and poultry, are frequently purchased and stored in a home freezer until used. There are several factors that will influence the nutrient stability of frozen foods. These include (1) the rate of freezing; (2) temperature of the freezer unit; (3) range of temperature fluctuation; (4) length of storage; (5) size of cut; (6) type of meat product; (7) method of thawing; and (8) packaging.

The rate of freezing is contingent upon the temperature of the freezing unit. The temperature of storage must be a compromise between optimal and practical, and is suggested to be at least $-18°C$ (Anonymous 1972). At this temperature, there is a slow deterioration of the food product, but the rate of nutrient loss is generally acceptable (Bender 1978). The temperature of $-18°C$ ($0°F$) is considered a break point for quality retention in frozen foods. The actual freezer temperature, if possible, should be below this point. Unfortunately, home refrigerator freezer compartments rarely keep frozen food below the break point.

Lee *et al.* (1950) found that the rate of freezing had no significant effect on thiamin, riboflavin, niacin, pantothenic acid, or vitamin B_6 value of beef steak. Results from studies investigating the B vitamin content of pork chops are more variable, but in general the stability of B vitamins was not found to be dramatically affected by rate of freezing (Lee *et al.* 1954). Freezing rate did seem to affect the evaporation loss from frozen meat products (Schweigert and Lushbough 1960). Moisture losses were greater for meats frozen more slowly relative to quick-frozen items. However, oxidative changes may occur more rapidly for quick-frozen beef and pork (Lachance and Erdman 1975). When storage temperature was considered, Lachance and Erdman (1975) reported no significant differences for niacin, thiamin, or riboflavin content for pork chops stored at $-26°$ or $-18°C$. Storage temperature did not appear to be a factor for pork chops; however Kramer *et al.* (1976) showed that thiamin and ascorbic acid were better retained in Salisbury steaks stored at $-20°C$ and $-30°C$ than at $-10°C$ (Table 21.1).

Considerable variation in home freezer temperature can occur, and temperature fluctuation can have a detrimental effect on both the nutritional and sensory qualities of meat products. The effect of freezer temperature fluctuation on nutrient retention in Salisbury steaks was studied by Kramer *et al.* (1976). Of the vitamins tested, thiamin and ascorbic acid retention was poor over time. Kramer and his co-workers compared the effects of a constant temperature ($1°C$) and fluctuating temperatures ($5°C$ every 20 min) in beef stored for 3 and 6 months. There was a substantial reduction in vitamin C at 6 months, even at a constant temperature (Table 21.1). However, losses were greater at 3 months for vitamin C in beef stored at fluctuating temperatures than at a constant temperature. Thiamin content of beef seemed primarily influenced by storage temperature and showed greater reduction at 3 and 6 months when temperature of storage varied. Other nutrients including vitamin A, carotene, riboflavin, calcium, and iron appeared to be well maintained in all storage conditions.

Kramer's study (1976) also demonstrated the effect of length of storage on nutrient retention. Table 21.1 shows that ascorbic acid in beef was more diminished by the longer storage period (6 months

Table 21.1. Effect of Constant and Fluctuating Temperatures (°C) upon Ascorbic Acid and Thiamin Contents of Salisbury Steak

Storage conditions	Ascorbic acid[a]		Thiamin[a]	
	Constant	Fluctuating	Constant	Fluctuating
Initial	3.6		3.0	
3 months				
−10	1.8	1.0	2.8	1.8
−20	2.8	2.0	2.9	2.1
−30	2.8	2.5	3.2	2.6
6 months				
−10	1.2	1.1	1.9	1.8
−20	1.6	1.1	2.7	1.7
−30	1.3	1.1	2.7	2.6

Source: Kramer et al. (1976).
[a] mg/100 g.

versus 3 months). However, it should be noted that meat, in general, is not a significant source of vitamin C in the diet and, thus, data revealing thiamin content of meat during storage are more relevant for nutritional status. Morgan et al. (1949) determined the thiamin, riboflavin, and niacin contents of various chicken tissues before and after cooking and after frozen storage for 4, 8, or 12 months. Samples retained thiamin at 75–100% of original levels, except in one lot of small broilers. Loss of riboflavin was generally small for up to 8 months of storage, as was loss of niacin. After 12 months, losses of niacin in leg and heart muscles and riboflavin in nearly all tissues were significant. Fennema (1977) reviewed the loss of B vitamins in a variety of meats during storage. He reported that the greatest losses occur for thiamin and riboflavin, and these losses tend to increase with greater length of storage time. However, the variability between species and particular cuts of meat was dramatic. Ang (1981) reported vitamin B_6 loss from broiler meat stored for various time periods, frozen as an intact half-carcass, as a large portion (200 g) of ground meat, or as a small portion (5 g) of ground meat. The results indicate that vitamin B_6 loss was most dramatic for small portions of meat with the greatest surface area. Percentage of retention for vitamin B_6 was 84% at 3 months, but only 72% at 5 months (−34°C). Larger portions of meat had improved vitamin B_6 retention, but retention again diminished after longer storage periods. Retention was 99% at 4 months (−34°C). for the intact carcass and 95% for the large portion (200 g) of ground meat. At 12 months, the large portion of the ground meat sample had 91% vitamin B_6 retention. Thus, it is clear that larger pieces of meat, with less exposed surface area, are more resistant to nutrient loss in frozen storage.

The amount and type of processing prior to storage may also affect nutrient retention. Breading of meats seems to protect the product during frozen storage (Jul 1969). Breaded meats have very satisfactory storage lifetimes despite elevated freezer storage temperatures (greater than $-15°C$). Products that were frozen following precooking with gravy demonstrated longer high-quality storage life than did prepared foods not in a sauce or gravy. Bengtsson and co-workers (1972) found that beef patties in gravy retained high sensory quality for at least 6 months if stored at $-30°C$ or lower. Thiamin and ascorbic acid were also retained well in products containing gravy.

Fish is another meat product that is often purchased in a frozen form. Fish is more susceptible to nutritional and quality changes during frozen storage, since it has a higher proportion of polyunsaturated fatty acids than do red meats. Species of fish most resistant to storage changes include haddock, cod, flounder, shrimp, crab, halibut, scallops, and perch (storage life of 7–12 months at $-32°C$), while more susceptible species include the higher-fat fish such as mackerel, tuna, catfish, herring, salmon, clams, and chub (storage life of 4–6 months at $-32°C$). Slavin (1963) considered the suitability for frozen storage of a wide variety of fish species. Slavin found that frozen storage stability depended greatly upon the handling of the fish product prior to freezing. Extended periods spent on ice (7 days versus 2 days) considerably reduced shelf life of the frozen product. Chemical reactions, including oxidation and autolysis, as well as dehydration and bacterial action, all reduce the textural and nutritional quality of fish.

In addition to the losses already discussed during freezer storage, nutrient losses occur when a frozen product is thawed in preparation for serving. In meats, the exudation of a bloodlike juice, called the thaw drip, appears upon thawing. This fluid can contain considerable quantities of B vitamins and protein.

The method of thawing is an important consideration, since it affects both the retention of nutrients and sensory quality of the meat. The amount of thaw-drip loss may alter the eating quality of a meat, since meats with excessive moisture loss may be less tender. Frozen ground beef patties thawed in the original wrappings at room temperature or cooked unthawed by four different cooking methods were found to retain 84% of the thiamin, 79% of the riboflavin, and 89% of the lysine of the original meat (Causey et al. 1950A). Similar results were found with ground lamb patties (Causey et al. 1950B). Causey and co-workers (1950C) also evaluated the thawing effect on pork and found no appreciable losses of thiamin, riboflavin, or niacin.

Westerman et al. (1949) evaluated round steaks thawed before cooking in four different ways: (1) in the refrigerator, (2) at $73°C$, (3) at room temperature, and (4) in running tap water. All meats were cooked by braising and compared to similar steaks analyzed in the raw state. Thawing in water reduced the acceptibility of the meat. Retention of thiamin, riboflavin, and niacin were not significantly altered by method of thawing, but pantothenic acid was better retained after thawing in the refrigerator or at room temperature than by the other two methods. When the vitamins in drip were added to those in the cooked meat, it was noted that riboflavin and niacin were fully recovered after thawing but that thiamin and pantothenic acid were partially destroyed during thawing at 73°C, as well as in running water. This is not surprising, since both of these vitamins are more heat labile and more soluble than the others. Loss of pantothenic acid in drip from frozen beef thawed 14–15 hr at 26°C was found by Pearson *et al.* (1951) to be greater (33%) than losses of the other B vitamins. Losses ranged from 8% for folic acid to 14.5% for niacin.

Thaw-drip loss appears to depend on factors including species of meat and exposed surface area. Pearson *et al.* (1959) found weight loss from pork chops to be between 6 and 12%. Thaw-drip losses from frozen fish were reported by the U.S. Department of the Interior (1955) to be even more variable than pork, ranging between 4.5 and 15.2%. Protein loss in the drip from frozen and thawed beef is generally small, ranging from 1.4 to 3.1%; essentially no fat is lost in the drip portion (Toepfer *et al.* 1955). Pieces of meat with greater exposed surface area per volume tend to have higher drip losses. Kotschevar *et al.* (1955) found protein losses from liver slices with a large exposed surface ranged from 8 to 15%.

Since the use of microwave cooking in the home has increased dramatically over recent years (Decareau 1979), considerable interest has been vested in studying the effects of microwave thawing and cooking on the nutritional value of foods. Bezanson *et al.* (1973) compared the protein content of frozen shrimp thawed in water versus microwave defrosting. Microwave thawing proved to be the better method for retaining protein in shrimp.

Since it has been shown that a proportion of the B vitamins and a small amount of protein is lost in the drip fluid, it is logical to suggest the utilization of the drip juice in gravies or soups. However, the microbial growth in thaw juices is often high, and the question becomes less one of nutrition and more one of safety. Thus, utilization of thaw juices is not generally recommended.

Refrigeration

Some foods of animal origin do not hold up well to frozen storage, but may be stored for extended periods of time in the home at refrigerator temperatures.

Deuel and Greenberg (1953) reported 75% retention of vitamin A in margarine held for 2 years at –10°C, 52–60 weeks at 5°C, 17 weeks at 18°C, and 15 weeks at 28°C. Retention of vitamin A in butter was slightly less. Preformed vitamin A and carotene were stable in margarine to the extent of 97–98% during shelf life at 7°C.

Loss of nutrients from milk during refrigerated storage depend upon exposure to light and oxygen and upon the severity of heat treatment. Sunlight and fluorescent lighting pose the greatest potential for nutrient loss from milk. Milk was traditionally marketed in clear glass or plastic containers, since this practice appeared to convey the message for a sanitary product. While it is an accepted tradition, it also allows for rapid destruction of light-sensitive riboflavin and the small amount of vitamin C present. Milk exposed to bright sunlight in a clear container loses as much as 50% of initial riboflavin in 2 hr, or 20% if exposed to subdued or clouded light. Light-sensitive riboflavin is converted to lumichrome and lumiflavin. Both of these chemical forms are catalytic for vitamin C destruction. In addition, milk exposed to sunlight develops a characteristic oxidized flavor, due to a reaction between sulfur-containing amino acids and riboflavin (Aurand et al. 1966; Hedrick and Glass 1975; Singh et al. 1975; Patton 1954; Gregory 1975).

Milk packaged in fiberboard cartons offers some protection from the effects of sunlight and fluorescent lighting, but prolonged storage under fluorescent lights, as in a supermarket dairy case, will lead to development of off-flavor and destruction of riboflavin (Demick 1973). The characteristic light-flavor could be detected after only 20 min in clear glass bottles, after 5 hr in amber glass, and after 1–15 hr in various types of fiberboard containers (Dunkley et al. 1962).

Vitamin B_6 (pyridoxine) in milk is converted to the compound bis-4-pyridoxyl disulfide upon storage (Bender 1978). This complex of pyridoxamine and sulfur is a less biologically active form of vitamin B_6 than the original vitamin. The quantity of vitamin B_6 in milk is diminished by heat treatment but only at extreme temperatures (Srncová and Davidek 1972). High temperatures involved in sterilization and drying destroy vitamin B_6, but these processes are not typical in home preparation.

A study of the changes in vitamin content of shell eggs during cold storage from 3–12 months has shown significant losses in niacin, vitamin B_6, riboflavin, folic acid, and vitamin B_{12}. Table 21.2 is a compilation of these results (Evans et al. 1951A, B, 1952 A, B, 1953, 1954, 1955). Apparently, shell eggs lose no biotin or choline, but up to 47% of vitamin B_6, 6% of the pantothenic acid, 27% of folic acid, 23% of vitamin B_{12}, and 14–18% of riboflavin and niacin after 1 year. A 6% composite loss of all the vitamins occurred after 3 months, 11% after 6–7 months, and 19% after 12 months.

Time and temperature of storage are also critical factors determining shelf life for canned meat products. It is generally thought that the canning process stabilizes a food product indefinitely, but cans improperly stored at either high temperatures (greater than room temperature)

Table 21.2. Loss of Vitamins in Shell Eggs in Cold Storage at $0°C$

Vitamin	Fresh eggs	Stored eggs					
		3 months	Loss (%)	6–7 months	Loss (%)	12 months	Loss (%)
Niacin, mg/g	0.66	0.60	9	0.54	18	—	—
Choline, mg/g	14.9	14.4	0	15.4	0	14.9	0
Vitamin B_6, $\mu g/g$	2.52	2.06	18	1.78	29	1.34	47
Riboflavin, $\mu g/g$	3.49	3.32	5	2.93	16	3.07	14
Pantothenic acid, $\mu g/g$	12.5	11.7	6	11.7	6	11.8	6
Folic acid, ng/g	94	93	0	80	16	74	27
Biotin, ng/g	225	244	0	220	0	228	0
Vitamin B_{12}, ng/g	6.54	6.07	7	6.17	5	5.03	23

Source: Evans *et al.* (1951A,B, 1952A, B, 1953A, 1954, 1955).

or for prolonged periods of time (depending on the particular product) will lose both nutritional value and quality characteristics.

Nutritional loss in canned meats has not been extensively studied, but it appears that thiamin is the most susceptible nutrient to deterioration. Other B vitamins, including riboflavin, niacin, and pantothenate, are relatively stable. Rice and Robinson (1944) were unable to detect losses of riboflavin, niacin, or pantothenate in canned pork or beef stored at $37°C$ for a period of 31 weeks. However, these researchers found that 48% of thiamin was destroyed after 43 weeks of storage at $27°C$ (room temperature). Thomas and Calloway (1961) found similar results, with thiamin suffering the greatest loss due to the effect of extended time or high temperature. Cecil and Woodroof (1962) found that optimal storage temperatures for retention of thiamin are less than $13°C$ for 1 year of storage, less than $5°C$ for 2 years, and less than $0°C$ if storage is 3 years.

Cured or dehydrated meats are also susceptible to thiamin loss. Hoagland *et al.* (1947) studied the effect of storage in hams cured by various methods. Hams stored at $20°C$ had a 21% thiamin loss for artery cured, 26% for dry cured, and 32% for brine cured. Rice and Robinson (1944) found greater losses of thiamin in dehydrated pork and beef after 31 weeks of storage. Thiamin loss was 71% for meats stored at room temperature ($27°C$), and thiamin was completely destroyed at temperatures greater than room temperature. This research team found little effect on riblflavin, niacin, and pantothenic acid in meats stored at room temperatures ($27°C$), but observed a gradual loss of riboflavin and pantothenic acid at a higher storage temperature ($44°C$).

Foods of Plant Origin

Foods of plant origin, including fruits, vegetables, and cereal grains, are important sources of vitamins and minerals in the diet. Storage parameters significantly affect the quality and nutrient retention of these foodstuffs. Furthermore, the picutre is made complex by the variety of products, each with their individual characteristics for optimal retention of vitamin and mineral quantity and quality.

Freezing

Freezing is considered an optimal method of nutrient retention in stored fruits and vegetables from the standpoint of both nutritional and quality characteristics. Kramer (1979) found that temperatures for frozen storage that were required to retain 90% of vitamin C activity corresponded closely with those required to maintain quality characteristics. For this reason, and the fact that fruits and vegetables are the major source of vitamin C in most diets, vitamin C is often used as the indicator of quality retention. Erdman and Klein (1982) have published an extensive review of harvesting, processing, and cooking influences on vitamin C in foods.

Vitamin loss during frozen storage of fruits and vegetables generally occurs due to chemical degradation. The same factors that affect freezer storage stability in meats affect the nutrient stability in fruits and vegetables. However, in meats, the focus is on B vitamin retention. In produce, the emphasis is on preservation of ascorbic acid. Factors including (1) rate of freezing, (2) freezer temperatures, (3) range of temperature fluctuation, (4) length of storage, (5) type of product, and (6) type of package, collectively determine nutrient stability, particularly for the vitamin C content of fruits and vegetables. Other nutrients are considered relatively stable during frozen storage, yet Heinze (1973) reported that vitamin A was rapidly destroyed in certain fruit and vegetable products stored at temperatures above freezing.

The key for preservation of nutrients and quality in frozen fruits and vegetables is rapid freezing (Anonymous 1972). Commercially processed products may have greater vitamin retention than those that are homegrown because of the rapid freezing of the commercial process. Commercial operations emphasize speed in handling, from field to packaged frozen product. It is then the consumer's responsibility to handle frozen food properly, which includes rapid transfer to frozen storage after purchase (Erdman and Erdman 1982). Homegrown foods should be treated with similar speed of processing in preparation for freezing. A delay in freezing permits opportunity for enzymatic and microbial action that can deteriorate appearance, flavor, and nutritional quality (Salunkhe et al. 1973).

Although it is well known that the optimal and traditional temperature for home freezers is $-18°C$ (Anonymous 1972), it is also known that this is frequently not attained. Fennema (1975) points out that freezing compartments of home refrigerators are more likely to be about $-5.5°C$, which invariably leads to greater losses of vitamin C, β-carotene, folic acid, and pantothenic acid when compared to frozen storage at $-18°C$. Other nutrients including niacin, riboflavin, thiamin, vitamin B_6 and minerals are only minimally affected at elevated storage temperatures.

Freezer temperature is a critical concern for retention of product quality. Frozen storage is used to arrest microbial growth and to minimize chemical degradation processes. In short, the lower the temperature, the greater the storage period without significant quality and nutritive loss. Goldblith (1975) found that strawberries stored below $-18°C$ retained total and reduced ascorbic acid well for 12 months or longer. As temperature of storage increased (well within the range of home freezers), there was a conversion of the native forms of vitamin C to partially oxidized dehydroascorbic and the inactive 2,3-diketogulonic acid forms of ascorbic acid. Guadagni and Kelly (1958) showed complete conversion of vitamin C in strawberries to the inactive form in 8 months at $-10°C$ and even more rapidly at $-2°C$ for 2 months. Guadagni (1961) summarized the effect of temperature on quality. As freezer temperature increases every $2.8°C$, the rate of quality loss increases 2- to 2 1/2-fold. Dietrich *et al.* (1962) found a 4-fold reduction in quantity and ascorbic acid content of frozen cauliflower for every $5.6°C$ increase in storage temperature in the range from $-40°$ to $-23°C$.

In some home freezers, location of the product within the freezing unit will affect temperature of storage. The temperature may be elevated for a product that is positioned closer to the freezer door, especially if the unit is less than optimally insulated or the freezer door is opened frequently. Ashby *et al.* (1977) and Moleeratanond (1978) found that when peas, okra, and strawberries were compared, peas were most affected by location within the freezer over a 12-month storage period; yet, only sensory characteristics appear altered. Ascorbic acid content was less affected by location.

Fluctuating temperatures in home freezers impact both sensory and nutritional characteristics, although the effects upon nutritional parameters are more severe for animal than for plant foods. Ashby *et al.* (1977) and Moleeratanond (1978) showed that no nutritional deterioration of plant products occurred when freezing temperatures fluctuated $\pm 5°C$. This is in contrast to the results depicted in Table 21.1 for a meat product.

Length of frozen storage is also a factor in determining quality retention in fruits and vegetables. The International Institute of Refrigeration in Paris (Anonymous 1972) reports that frozen foods may be adequately stored in home freezers at $-18°C$ for up to 3 months. Commercial operations practice cycling of their frozen inventory with

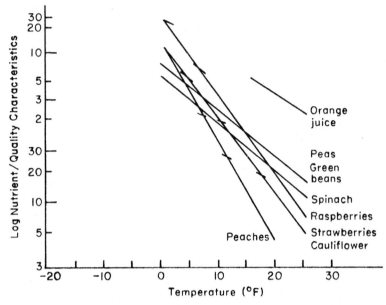

Fig. 21.1. The interrelationship of temperature of storage to the high quality shelf life of various frozen foods (adapted from Kramer, 1979).

first in–first out as their operating procedure. A similar practice should be used in the home so that foods do not get buried in home freezers, to be left for several months, a year, or longer. Foods must be stored at progressively lower storage temperatures if they are to be protected from degradative changes for long periods of time.

Various fruit and vegetable products are affected differently by frozen storage. Citrus juice is considerably more resistant to vitamin C loss than are broccoli, cauliflower, spinach, and peaches (Kramer 1979). Freshly frozen asparagus and broccoli, both initially containing 30 mg% ascorbic acid, may be held in storage for 12–18 months at –18° to –24°C. At the end of that time period, the asparagus may still contain 90% of its ascorbic acid, yet broccoli may only have 75% of the initial 30 mg%. Figure 21.1 illustrates the various rate of nutrient and quality loss from several fruits and vegetables. Products with the greater slope of change indicate those which are more sensitive to low temperature storage.

Finally, the type of package can dramatically alter storage characteristics of frozen fruits and vegetables. The recommendation of the International Institute of Refrigeration (Anonymous 1972) is that food be sealed in a container with a minimum amount of surrounding air or placed in moisture- and vapor-proof wrap that is an effective barrier to air.

Refrigeration

Consumption patterns of fresh and frozen fruits and vegetables in U.S. households today include less fresh fruit and more processed fruit products. However, consumers still purchase more fresh vegetables than processed ones (Gallo and Blaylock 1982). Results of the 1977–1978 nationwide food consumption survey (USDA 1980) indicate that fresh vegetables were consumed by seven out of every eight households, and light green vegetables were most frequently purchased. Of households surveyed, 80% ate potatoes and most were fresh, not processed products. The maximization of nutrients from fresh products is therefore still paramount today.

Factors that affect the nutritional value of fresh foods include storage temperature, humidity, length of storage, and light (Erdman and Erdman 1982). Protection of fresh product and unprocessed grains from the invasion of rodents, insects, and microbes is a major problem and the cause of considerable losses from the food supply, especially for developing countries.

Fresh vegetables, including lettuce, broccoli, and spinach, should be stored in a refrigerated vegetable crisper or sealed in moisture-proof bags in order to maintain their nutritional quality (Anonymous 1971A; Curran and Erdman 1980). Zepplin and Elvehjem (1944) found that broccoli stored at room temperature lost ascorbic acid rapidly, but losses were slowed if the product was refrigerated.

The combination of cold temperature and appropriate humidity for storage should retard wilting. Research has shown that wilted cabbage, cauliflower, kale, collard greens, and turnip greens have diminished ascorbic acid and carotene contents relative to their fresh condition (Ezell and Wilcox 1959; 1962).

Some products are more sensitive than others to ascorbic acid loss in refrigerator storage. Green beans lose their vitamin C more rapidly at $2°C$ than does broccoli (Eheart and Odland 1972). Folic acid was better retained in cold storage than at room temperature for green leafy vegetables and for crucifers (Fager *et al.* 1949; Olson *et al.* 1947). Freshly harvested cabbage did not lose vitamin C value when stored in closed containers at $-0.5°$ to $4°C$ or when heads were kept refrigerated for 1 week (Van Duyne *et al.* 1944). Root vegetables, including potatoes, sweet potatoes, and onions, should be kept cool and moist, but should not be stored in the refrigerator in order to optimize their nutrient retention. Grains, dry legumes, and flours must be kept cool and dry. These products are susceptible to microbial damage, especially at higher moisture levels. If stored properly, these products will not suffer nutrient losses and are stable for extended periods of time (Erdman and Erdman 1982). Storage of dry legumes in dark jars or in the refrigerator minimize destruction of light-sensitive B vitamins (Curran and Erdman 1980).

Fresh fruits are not stable for long periods in the refrigerator and will deteriorate rapidly. The climateric fruits, for example, bananas, peaches, apples, and pears, are rapidly respiring fruits and must be kept cool to retain their ripe, but not spoiled quality. Citrus fruits have more extended storage lives, since they are less rapidly respiring and are non-climateric.

Reheating Stored Vegetables

Charles and Van Duyne (1958) studied the effects of refrigerator storage and of reheating on the ascorbic acid content of cooked vegetables. Cooled broccoli, brussels sprouts, shredded cabbage, sliced cabbage, cauliflower, peas, and snap beans lost significant amounts of ascorbic acid during 1 day of refrigeration, whereas cooked asparagus and spinach lost insignificant amounts. When these vegetables were reheated, they all showed a further significant loss. The ascorbic acid in the cooking liquid was stable during refrigeration and during reheating, indicating that the vitamins in the vegetables were being destroyed. When the refrigerator storage was extended to 3 days, the losses were even greater.

More research is essential on the effects of contemporary food practices on nutrient content. Today, there is a greater reliance on convenience or leftover foods that are stored and reheated in the home. More complete nutritional information is needed regarding these practices.

Growing conditions will affect the nutritional quality of fresh fruits and vegetables (Nagy 1980; Smith and Rasmussen 1961; Smith 1969; Jones et al. 1970; Marsanija 1970; Embleton et al. 1973; Reitz and Koo 1960; Smith and Rasmussen 1960; Embleton and Jones 1966; Jones 1961; Sites and Reitz 1951). Geographic location influences growing conditions. Tomatoes grown in Michigan and New Jersey have 71 and 72%, respectively, of the ascorbic acid found in California-grown fruit (Burge et al. 1975). It is most likely that these results reflect differences in available sunlight and total heat. Klein and Perry (1982) analyzed cabbage, carrots, celery, corn, onions, and tomatoes from six different geographical regions for vitamins C and A. These researchers found considerable and significant variations between locations, seasons, and cultivars. Some reported values of both vitamins C and A were below the level listed in Agriculture Handbook 8 (Watt and Merrill 1963).

Those who grow garden produce at home should be aware that the degree of ripeness affects the nutrient composition of harvested fruits and vegetables. Vitamin C concentration declines during ripening of citrus fruits. However, the volume of juice and size of fruit increases with ripening, so that the total vitamin C content of each fruit actually increases (Nagy 1980). Liu and Luh (1979) evaluated ascorbic acid in tomato paste and found that pastes made from vine-ripe tomatoes had less vitamin C than pastes made from the near-ripe product. Thus, it would appear that ascorbic acid level declines in tomatoes as they ripen; however, reports are conflicting (Watada *et al.* 1976; Betancourt *et al.* 1977).

Canned Storage

Canned fruits and vegetables are not immune from the effects of time and temperature with respect to nutrient retention. Although canned products are considered shelf stable, there are losses of vitamin C caused by oxidation by the very small amount of oxygen present. Chemical degradation from the oxidative reaction causes a darkening of color which occurs more rapidly in concentrated fruit juices than in dilute or single-strength juices. This is due to the higher concentration of sugars, acids, and nitrogenous compounds that are chemically active agents (Bender 1978). Kefford (1973) studied the effect of storage temperature on orange juice either hot-packed or aseptically sealed in glass bottles. Juice stored at the recommended temperature ($10°C$) lost only 1% of vitamin C over a 12-month period. Even at $18°C$, only 5–10% of vitamin C was lost after 1 year. At room temperatures ($24°C$), only 75% of the original vitamin C remained after 1 year.

Considerably more juice products are currently being stored in plastic containers. Despite the fact that oxygen may diffuse through the container walls and degrade ascorbic acid (Adam 1941; Bender 1978), plastic containers appear to protect ascorbic acid from the effects of oxygen more effectively than do waxed cartons. Orange juice stored at $5°C$ in waxed cartons lost 5–7% of vitamin C/week (Rushing and Senn 1964). If the product was stored in large containers with more oxygen, then losses due to oxidation were even greater.

Other canned foods have been studied. Ang (1978) evaluated nutrient loss in canned peas and found that after 2 years of storage at $27°C$, 19% ascorbic acid, 30% thiamin, and 10% carotene were lost. In the same study, orange juice lost 50% of the original ascorbic acid content.

Since it is impractical and costly to use refrigerator space in the home for canned foods, it is advised that canned foods be used within 6 months to 1 year after purchase. Canned foods should, if possible, be stored in a cool ($18°C$ or cooler) and dry location (Curran and Erdman 1980).

More dehydrated foods are being used in the home, principally as a matter of convenience and to alleviate refrigerator storage problems. Stability of the nutrients in dehydrated foods may become a more significant issue as more of such foods are marketed. Vitamin C is the nutrient that is most sensitive to deterioration in most dehydrated fruits and vegetables (Reimer and Karel 1977). Gee (1979) reported values for retention of ascorbic acid, β-carotene, and thiamin in dehydrated cut carrots, spinach, and tomatoes. The products were packaged and stored in air, under vacuum, N_2 or CO_2, for 5–7 months at room temperature. Vitamin content diminished rapidly in air storage. Vitamin C loss progressed regardless of method of storage. Conditions that precluded exposure of β-carotene to air and light maintained high nutrient levels for at least 7 months. Thiamin was relatively stable, regardless of storage environment. In another study using a model system, Gregory and Kirk (1978) found that vitamin B_6 was stable when stored at 37°C and 0.6 a_w (water activity) for 128 days.

Some dried fruits are treated with sulfur dioxide to prevent oxidation and to retain their initial color. Hollingsworth (1970) reported that vitamin A in dried fruit was susceptible to light and heat, but that ascorbic acid was stabilized by sulfur dioxide. Heikal *et al.* (1972) found that sulfur dioxide was not helpful in protecting vitamin C. Bolin and Stafford (1974) determined that vitamin C in sulfured fruit was more stable than in nonsulfured product. As the sulfur dioxide concentration of apricots was increased, vitamin C showed progressively greater stability. Apricot halves dried without sulfuring and stored at 32°C retained only 5% of their initial ascorbic acid after 12 weeks and 88% of their β-carotene. Fruit dried with 0.3% sulfur dioxide retained 26% of it vitamin C content and 95% of the β-carotene. However, sulfur dioxide treatment rapidly diminishes the thiamin content of foods. It is apparent that some degree of processing for apricots, prior to drying, is beneficial for ascorbic acid retention, but that sulfur dioxide treatment of foods that are rich sources of thiamin would be counterproductive.

Food irradiation has received more attention as an effective method of food preservation. Irradiation is used as a means of prolonging shelf storage of foods and may be approved by the Food and Drug Administration (FDA) for several food items in the near future. Currently, the FDA has granted approval for use of irradiation to prevent sprouting in stored potatoes and to kill insects and pathogenic organisms in wheat and wheat flour. A total of 26 commodities have been cleared in one or more of 19 countries having legislation for irradiated foods.

A benefit of using irradiation for produce is that there is a reduction in pathogenic microorganisms, helminths, and insects on the surface and below the surface of a product, without causing some of the detrimental changes that occur during heat processing. Irradiation techniques may even be used on frozen products, thus minimizing the deterioration of nutritional quality. One of the great nutrient benefits is that the processing (irradiation) can be done at reduced temperatures, thus reducing heat destruction of vitamins.

Cereal Products

Cereal products are a staple component of many diets and their nutritional value and storage characteristics are extremely important. Cereal products have the virtue of being quite stable over extended periods of storage. Cereal products are rich sources of B vitamins and

Table 21.3. Shelf Life for Retail Products

Product	Days	Weeks	Months
Bread, white (summer)	2–5		
Bread, white (winter)	3–7		
Bread, white (frozen)	30+		
Cake, angel		2	
Cake, cup		2	
Cake, fruit			24
Donuts	1–4		
Flour, all-purpose			15
Refrigerated dough		9–10	
Evaporated milk			12
Fluid milk	5–7		
Cottage cheese	10–15		
Creamed cheese			3
Ice cream			3
Canned apricots			36
Canned asparagus			24
Canned kidney beans			36
Canned tomatoes			30–36
Catsup			24
Canned fruit cocktail			36
Canned fruit and vegetable juices			24
Frozen lobster			3
Frozen dinners			6
Frozen foods (general)			12
Cereal, ready-to-eat			6–8
Macaroni (dry)			6–8
Spaghetti (dry)			9–12
Dehydrated gravy/sauce mixes			6–12
Sweet or dill pickles			12–15
French/Italian dressings			10–12
Pizza sauce (jar)			36
Lard			3
Vegetable oil (liquid)			4
Margarine			2–6
Canned puddings			24

Source: Anonymous (1971B).

should be stored in a dark, cool place to prevent destruction of thiamin and other B vitamins (Curran and Erdman 1980). Storage stability of unmilled grains depends upon moisture content. Rice and maize stored for 2 years at moisture content below 10% had no loss of thiamin (Bayfield and O'Donnell 1945; Cuendet et al. 1954). White rice stored for 2 1/2 years lost 30% thiamin, 5% riboflavin, and 5% niacin. Brown rice lost somewhat less thiamin (Kik 1955). Another researcher (Caileau et al. 1945) reported more rapid loss of thiamin in brown rice, white rice, and bran. After 6 months of storage at 20°C, the product lost 30% thiamin, and 50–70% after 2 years.

If moisture content was elevated to 17%, thiamin was destroyed more rapidly. Rice lost 30% of thiamin in 5 months compared to a 12% loss at 12% moisture. Cuendet et al. (1954) found no thiamin loss at low moisture levels of 6%.

Jones et al. (1943) determined that provitamin A in unmilled yellow maize was quite stable in cool storage. However, provitamin A was unstable in milled maize (Fraps and Kemmerer, 1937).

Shelf life in prepared baked products ranges between 2 days and 2 weeks. Table 21.3 lists retail shelf life for a variety of cereal products. In addition, shelf life for perishable dairy, canned, and frozen items are also given.

LOSSES DUE TO PREPARATION PROCEDURES

There can be extensive loss of nutrients in the preparatory stages between storage and cooking. However, with the appropriate care, losses can be minimized.

Trimming of Meats

It may be necessary for the consumer to trim fat from meats purchased from a supermarket. Toepfer et al. (1955) evaluated oven roasts in boneless beef that had been trimmed to U.S. Army specifications (external fat maximum of 3/4-in. thickness) or trimmed to leave 1/4-in. external fat. Trimming of the beef resulted in 6% loss in weight with little nutrient loss. The trim contained 82.6–87.5% fat and 2.1–4.5% protein. Phosphorus and magnesium were also in high concentration in the fat portion. Meat trimmings may contain one-third of the phosphorus and magnesium concentration of the lean and marble portions (Leverton and Odell 1959).

Given the caloric cost of consuming visible fat, such as meat trimmings, it is practical to recommend that Americans trim away most visible fat from meats. While a small amount of protein may be lost from the trimmed meat, most Americans can less afford the calories that fat trim would provide.

Preparations of Fruits and Vegetables

To the best of our knowledge, the losses due to trimming, washing, soaking, chopping, and mincing as prepared for consumption in the home are similar in nature and extent to those that occur in large-scale food preparation. In general, it is better to delay the preparation of foods until a few minutes before they are to be cooked and served. Protracted soaking should be avoided. Frozen vegetables should not be thawed or washed before cooking; instead, they should be placed directly into a minimum quantity of rapidly boiling water. In this respect, boil-in-the-bag procedures offer superior conditions because losses into cooking water are completely avoided and nutrients are theoretically held by the butter or cream sauces usually associated with food packaged in this manner.

Salads should be prepared just before they are to be served in order to minimize losses in nutrients, especially ascorbic acid (Curran and Erdman 1980).

Although weight loss due to trimming of fruits and vegetables may be small, nutrient losses can be excessive. Vitamins and trace minerals are often concentrated at the outer layers of vegetables, seeds, root crops, and fruits (Lachance 1975).

EFFECTS OF COOKING

Changes that occur during processing either result in nutrient loss or destruction, or can be beneficial. Although cooking effects are generally discussed with regard to losses, it is important to realize that some nutrients can be made more bioavailable by processing. This is particularly true in the legumes, which contain a variety of substances that inhibit digestive enzymes or bind nutrients, making them unavailable. For example, heat-labile trypsin inhibitors complex with the pancreatic protease trypsin and decrease protein digestion. Solanine in potatoes is a recognized food neurotoxin that is only safe when consumed in small quantities. Solanine is largely destroyed in cooking. Avidin in raw eggs is a substance that binds the essential nutrient biotin, yet avidin is destroyed with heat during the cooking process. Heating generally increases the overall digestibility of foods, therefore increasing nutrient utilization. Overheating reduces sensory and nutritional value. However, the key in home or industrial processing is to optimize the cooking process to provide the best sensory and nutritional characteristics.

Foods of Animal Origin

Animal products are significant sources of protein, vitamins, and minerals in the U.S. diet. Research regarding losses during cooking of meats has concentrated on protein and vitamin retention. Methods that use no water or minimum liquid yield greatest retention of nutrients. Thiamin is the nutrient most susceptible to thermal degradation and leaching from meat; thus, most research uses thiamin retention as the indicator of cooking losses.

Effect of Liquid Used in Cooking

Methods that include no water (e.g., broiling and frying) or minimum water result in greater nutrient retention than do methods that require that meat be submerged in liquid (e.g., stewing or use of a Crock-Pot®). Broiling is considered the mildest cooking method and results in retention of 60–85% of thiamin and 60–100% of riboflavin. Frying results in lower retention of thiamin, 50–89%; and roasting, 40–70%.

Thiamin retention is dramatically dependent on the presence of water. Wilcox and Galloway (1952) reported that 63–68% of thiamin was retained in pan-broiled lamb chops and 49–63% in roasted leg of lamb. Stewed lamb lost approximately 50% of thiamin. Broiled and roasted lamb and veal lost from 30 to 43% of thiamin, while braised or stewed meats lost 60 and 74%, respectively. Causey *et al.* (1950A) found good retention of B vitamins in broiled ground pork patties. The cooking process was responsible for losses of 6–21% of thiamin, 5–39% of riboflavin, and 0–12% of niacin. Broiled lamb patties lost 6–20% thiamin, 40–60% of riboflavin, and 2–15% of lysine (Causey *et al.* 1950B). For both pork and lamb, loss of B vitamins in the drip accounted for less than 10% of the initial value.

Pork is a richer source of thiamin than any other meat and appears to retain more thiamin than do other meats. Beef cooked in a small amount of water loses 40–45% of thiamin. Pork, similarly cooked, loses only 20–30% (Farrer 1955). Other researchers have confirmed this report (Cover *et al.* 1949).

Oven and pan roasting results in nutrient retention similar to broiling (Erdman 1979). Toepfer *et al.* (1955) found good retention of protein (95.6% in meat with 1.8% loss in drip) in boneless roasts when no water was added. Retention of protein dropped to 89.9% in meat, with 7.6% loss in drip when water was added.

Frying liver in a pan with margarine resulted in 85% retention of thiamin, 94% of riboflavin, and 87% of niacin (Kotschevar *et al.* 1955). Farrer (1955) found greater losses of thiamin in fried meats, with losses ranging generally from 40 to 50%.

Other types of cooking require that the meat be placed in varying amounts of water. Braised meats are generally first pan-browned and then cooked with water. The amount of water added is usually 8–10% of the meat weight. The pan is then tightly covered and the meat is cooked. Noble (1970) tested several types of meats for thiamin and riboflavin retention, using both braising and simmering methods of cooking (Table 21.4). The difference between the methods is that simmering includes a greater amount of water (approximately one-half to two times the meat's weight of water added). Braising of meats yielded consistently better thiamin or riboflavin retention than did simmering. Some simmered meats had greater cooked weight due to less fluid loss.

Table 21.4. Mean Thiamin, Riboflavin, and Weight Retention (%) of Variety Meats after Braising or Simmering

Meat type	Thiamin		Riboflavin		Total Weight	
	Braised	Simmered	Braised	Simmered	Braised	Simmered
Calf						
Sweetbreads	66	55	61	69	58	66
Beef kidney	45	37	65	46	53	53
Lamb heart	51	49	77	72	53	62
Pork heart	34	30	72	69	50	60

Source: Noble (1970).

Other B vitamins are also leached in cooking liquid along with thiamin. Niacin in braised or stewed meats is substantially reduced (33–50% lost), but can be recovered in the broth. From 3 to 27% is lost in broiling, frying, and oven roasting. Most of the heat-stable niacin is lost through leaching or dripping, and only an insignificant portion appears to be chemically destroyed. Moss *et al.* (1980) reported retention of niacin in broiled and roasted meats as 79 and 74%, respectively.

One-half or more of pantothenic acid may be found in broth when a large amount of water is used, but only about 40% when a small amount is used. These results are predictable based on this nutrient's known solubility characteristics. Schweigert and Guthneck (1953) evaluated cuts of pork, beef, and lamb and found higher values of pantothenic acid retained in broiled meats than in roasted samples. Meyer *et al.* (1969) compared roasted and braised beef for retention of pantothenic acid. Retention in oven-roasted loin averaged 89%, with a mean of 19% being transferred to the drip. Braised roasts retained only an average of 56% of pantothenic acid in the meat and 44% in the cooking drip. Thus, more than twice as much pantothenic acid was extracted from the meat by braising as by roasting. These results supported earlier work using heel-of-round and chuck beef roasts (Meyer *et al.* 1947). Meyer and co-workers, in both braising studies, found good total retention for pantothenic acid when meat and drip values are added. Cover *et al.* (1947A) found only 78% total retention in beef stew.

Early reports of folic acid retention (Cheldelin *et al.* 1943) showed that the nutrient was seriously affected by cooking. Recent advances in folic acid research have yielded more reliable and consistent data for nutrient retention. Recent assays using new methodology revealed 35% loss of folic acid in braised beef, while broiled beef lost only 14% and roasted beef only 5% of folic acid (Moss *et al.* 1980).

Vitamin B_6 (pyridoxine) is also a water-soluble vitamin and is thus predictably affected by the presence of water in cooking. McIntire *et al.* (1944) reported poor retention of vitamin B$_6$ for all cooking methods. Roasting and broiling produced about 30% retention, braising and stewing resulted in only about 18%. Lushbough *et al.* (1959) used the *Saccharomyces carlsbergenesis* microbiological yeast assay for vitamin B$_6$ in fresh, cooked, and processed meats. The results indicate retention between 67 and 43%. Veal retained vitamin B$_6$ best. Lamb and Boston cut beef had the least retention of this vitamin. More recent data by Meyer *et al.* (1969) show vitamin B$_6$ retention in roasted and braised beef. Retention in the oven-roasted loin averaged 92%, and 16% was recovered in the drip. Retention in the oven-braised round averaged 49%, with 34% transference to the drip. Approximately twice as much pyridoxine was transferred to the drip by braising as by roasting.

It could be noted that mean retention of vitamin B$_6$ in roasted and braised beef in Meyer's investigation was considerably higher than in earlier studies with beef and other meats. More recent work by Moss *et al.* (1980) revealed data for broiling and roasting beef that show only modest retention (50–60%). Results for braised beef more closely correlated with those of McIntire *et al.* in 1944, which showed extremely poor retention rates for pyridoxine.

Limited data have been published regarding choline and biotin retention. McIntire *et al.* (1944) showed choline was stable in cooking of meat. Schweigert *et al.* (1943) found that 77% of biotin was retained in cooked meats.

Effect of Time and Temperature

The relationship of time and temperature influences the nutrient stability of meats during a variety of cooking treatments. Home preparation practices that utilize shorter periods of time (and higher temperatures) may yield greatest B vitamin retention. However, the effect of temperature is not reported to be as great as may be expected given the thermolability of thiamin, riboflavin, and pantothenic acid and other B complex vitamins in nonfood systems. Since many B vitamins exist in foods in coenzyme complexes, they are probably more thermodynamically stable than the free vitamin in solution.

Noble and Gomez (1960) roasted five different cuts of beef at both 149° and 177°C to an internal temperature of 71°C. Beef loaf was heated to an internal temperature of 75°C. The longer cooking period was not more detrimental to thiamin or riboflavin. Beef loaf retained 70% of the thiamin and top round and rib roasts retained, on an average, 54% thiamin. Rump and tenderloin cuts retained intermediate values for thiamin. Riboflavin retention was greatest in rib and rump roasts (87%) and was lowest in roasted beef loaf and top round (80%).

Noble and Gomez (1958) showed similar results in various cuts of lamb. Roasting lamb to internal temperatures of either 82° or 79°C at an oven temperature of 149°C failed to have a significant effect on either thiamin or riboflavin.

Cover *et al.* (1949A) found that high oven temperatures (204°C) resulted in greater destruction of B vitamins than did lower oven temperatures (149°C) when cooking beef and pork roasts. Cover and co-workers evaluated retention of thiamin, pantothenic acid, niacin, and riboflavin in beef and pork cooked on a large scale and on a small scale (Cover *et al.* 1944) and found consistently greater retention when cooking was done at low rather than high temperatures. For rib roasts cooked to rare and well done, retentions were, respectively, 75 and 69% for thiamin, 83 and 77% for riboflavin, 75 and 79% for niacin, and 91 and 75% for pantothenic acid.

Cover *et al.* (1947A) reported that pantothenic acid retention was decreased by 10% in stewed meat that was browned first. The author states that increased temperature may have been a factor affecting increased losses found in pressure-cooked beef. The same effect was not evident in lamb similarly cooked.

Alternatively, Bognar (1978) reported that reduced cooking time at higher temperatures could have been a factor contributing to increased thiamin retention in roasted pork. Thiamin loss was reduced to 40% by using a porous earthenware pot in an electric oven or by microwave cooking. These methods included higher temperature and shorter cooking times than roasting pork in glass containers, plastic film, or aluminum foil in electric ovens or roasting on a grill in a gas oven. These latter methods resulted in a 50% reduction in thiamin.

Hall and Lin (1981) compared thiamin retention in broilers cooked at 204° and 121°C. Poultry cooked at the lower temperature was heated for 85.2 min longer. Contrary to previous studies with red meats, broilers that were cooked for the shorter time at the higher temperature retained more thiamin than when the long-time–low-temperature method was used. The considerable difference in cooking times may have resulted in these differing results.

Protein quality has been assessed in meat as affected by cooking time and temperature. It has been concluded that the biological value of meat protein is little affected by home cooking practices (Mayfield and Hedrick 1949; Thomas and Calloway 1961).

Effect of Size of Cut

Smaller cuts of meat require less cooking time and will have greater nutrient retention [e.g., Bognar (1978) for thiamin]. However, protein quality may be adversely affected by direct and intense heat if cut in slivers. Protein quality was assessed in beef roasted as thin slivers (thickness 0.5 cm) or large beef pieces (Mglinets and Zheleznyak 1980). Both in vitro digestibility and a microbiological method were used to determine protein value. Protein quality of beef slivers diminished 2- to 3-fold by roasting 15–20 min at 250°C. Large meat pieces roasted for 70–80 min to reach an internal temperature of 75°C were minimally affected (only a 10% reduction in the nutritional value). It was determined that cooking affected principally the outer layers of beef, and digestibility of the protein in the outer layers was reduced by approximately one-third. The research team of Mglinets and Zheleznyak concluded that meat should not be overcooked or burnt if the protein nutritional value of the product is to be maintained.

Mineral Retention in Meat

Reports for mineral retention in cooked meats are conflicting. A recent study conducted by the USDA/Meat Board (Moss et al. 1980) indicates that nearly all zinc, copper, and iron is retained in beef cooked in any of three cooking methods. However, Freeland-Graves and Day (1980) report that mineral loss in beef round steak ranged between 25.4 and 92.6%. The large variance depended on the degree of meat shrinkage during cooking. Manganese was the most stable mineral, followed by iron, zinc, and copper. Given the minimal amount of research on mineral retention in cooked meats, more research is needed in order to make a conclusive interpretation of conflicting results.

Microwave (Electronic) Cooking

Microwave ovens have been on the market for over 20 years, and in recent years there has been a dramatic increase in the utilization of microwave cooking. The use of microwaves in cooking has been promoted for its economy in terms of both energy and time savings. The use of high-energy, electromagnetic radiation is an extremely efficient process, since it heats only the food (Wing and Alexander 1972) and not the external environment. Several researchers have shown that meat can be cooked in a microwave oven four to five times faster than in a conventional oven (Bowers et al. 1974; Headley and Jacobson 1960; Marshall 1960; Wooldridge 1974).

Initial reports on vitamin retention indicated that losses were reduced using electronic cooking methods compared to conventional ovens (Thomas et al. 1949). Thomas et al. reported that thiamin loss was less for beef and pork patties cooked in a microwave oven (9–23%) than when grilled (21–45%). Niacin and riboflavin were relatively stable. Yet other researchers have failed to show differences in thiamin, riboflavin, or niacin retention between cooking methods for pork (Kylen et al. 1964; Baldwin et al. 1976), lamb (Noble and Gomez 1962; Baldwin et al. 1976), or beef (Baldwin et al. 1976) and Baldwin reported less thiamin retention in microwave-cooked beef roast. Baldwin and co-workers (1976) found that more thiamin was lost in a 2450 MHz microwave oven operating at 115 V than at 220 V.

Moore et al. (1980) and Kylen et al. (1964) found greater drip loss in microwave-cooked beef top round steak and beef roasts. Moore and co-workers (1980) did not consider vitamin retention in their study, but greater drip losses correlated with less total moisture and lower sensory scores for juiciness and tenderness. Greater drip loss has also been shown in pork (Bowers *et al.* 1974) and poultry (Wing and Alexander 1972).

Janicki and Appledorf (1974) analyzed lipid content in ground beef patties from various fast-food chains. Beef patties were either broiled, grill fried (over 371°C gas flame) or microwave cooked (2450 MHz), or raw patties were broiled, frozen, and reheated in a microwave oven. Microwave-treated patties contained the largest ratio of unsaturated:saturated fatty acids. The authors postulated that the saturated fatty acids are lost to a greater extent in the drip during cooking. The C18:1 and C18:2 fatty acids are more integrally related to the structural components in meat and are present in phospholipids and are, thus, less likely to be lost to drip. The health benefit of a high proportion of polyunsaturated fat in the diet is still controversial, but it may be a factor in the prevention of heart disease.

Bowers and Fryer (1972) investigated thiamin and riboflavin loss from turkey meat cooked in conventional gas and microwave ovens. Frozen turkey pectoralis muscle was either (1) cooked and stored 1 day at refrigerator temperature, (2) cooked, frozen, or (3) cooked, frozen, and then reheated. There was no difference in thiamin content. However, riboflavin was better retained with conventional cooking preparation than with microwave heating if retention was expressed in a moisture-free, fat-free basis.

Hall and Lin (1981) using fresh broiler chickens, found better thiamin retention when cooked in a microwave as compared with an electric oven. Cooking time may be a factor for thiamin retention, since chickens cooked in an electric oven at 204°C for a shorter time retained significantly more thiamin than when cooked at 121°C for a longer time. The difference between cooking times in the electric ovens was 85.2 min. There was no difference for thiamin retention in poultry cooked in microwave ovens at 800 or 1600 W. The difference in cooking times in the case of the microwave cooking was only 4.4 min.

Vitamin B_6 retention in chicken breasts was evaluated by Wing and Alexander (1972). Researchers showed that, contrary to riboflavin, vitamin B_6 was better retained in microwave-cooked chicken breasts (cooked for 1.5 min) than in conventionally cooked chicken (heated for 45 min). Bowers *et al.* (1974), using pork loin to study the effect of cooking method on vitamin B_6 retention, showed a significantly higher retention in conventionally cooked pork based on a moisture-free basis.

In summary, there seems to be good agreement between researchers using various species of meat that greater drip loss occurs from microwave-cooked meats than from conventionally cooked products. Results for nutrient retention are variable, but appear to depend on the particular nutrient, species, and cooking time applied. If drip losses are added to nutrients retained in meat, microwave cooking is usually equivalent or superior to conventional methods. Thiamin may be better retained with microwave cooking in beef, pork, and poultry. Riboflavin and niacin appear relatively stable and are independent of cooking method. Vitamin B_6 is more stable in microwave-cooked poultry but may be lost more rapidly in pork similarly treated if results are expressed on a moisture-free basis.

Other Cooking Methods

There is a paucity of data reporting nutrient retention for home canning of meats. A single study (Cover *et al.* 1949B) reported the effect on thiamin, pantothenic acid, niacin, and riboflavin after a home processing method for canning beef and veal. Meats were packed in No. 2 and No. 3 tin cans and in pint and quart glass jars and processed at 15 psi, 121°C for at least 60 minutes. After 3 months storage, thiamin retention was as low as 45%, while pantothenic acid was highest at 70%. Riboflavin and niacin appeared relatively stable.

Other common methods of home preparation, including long-time–low-temperature methods (e.g., Crock-Pot® type), have not been reported. However, prediction of nutrient retention can be made from other studies. Other reports on cooking methods using a low oven temperature for a longer time period reveal that nutrient retention is lower than when high temperature for a short time is applied. Also, the detrimental effect with large amounts of water used in cooking has already been reviewed in this chapter. It is predictable that such methods, including crockery cooking, may be convenient, but are not recommended for nutrient retention.

Foods of Plant Origin

Traditionally, fruits and vegetables are prepared in the home on the basis of convenience and taste preference rather than on nutrient retention. Particular food preferences are important considerations, since even the most nutritious food is void of nutritional value until it is consumed. If foods are not prepared according to individual likes and dislikes, either small quantities of the product will be eaten, or the disliked food will not be eaten at all. Therefore, the ideal situation in the home is for foods to be served in a form that is preferred, using preparation practices that minimize nutrient losses.

Vitamins have been the most widely studied of the nutrients in fruits and vegetables. First, these foods provide significant sources of vitamins in most U.S. diets and second, vitamins are the nutrients most at risk of being destroyed during common preparation practices. Ascorbic acid, thiamin, and pantothenic acid are the most heat labile, and the water-soluble vitamins are the most susceptible since most cooking methods utilize water. Ascorbic acid is generally used as the indicator nutrient for studying cooking losses in fruits and vegetables, since it is present in significant levels, is sensitive to thermal and oxidative destruction, and also is lost by leaching to water. Thiamin is also used as an index of retention. Vitamin A is generally the indicator vitamin for evaluating fat-soluble nutrient losses.   Pennington (1976) proposed that a selected group of nutrients be evaluated in order to determine the adequacy of a group of foods or an entire diet. Vitamin B_6, pantothenic acid, vitamin A, folacin, magnesium, iron, and calcium were suggested as the best indicator micronutrients. The theory is that if these nutrients are supplied at adequate levels, then the diet is most likely providing sufficient amounts of all other required nutrients. As Lund (1979) points out, to utilize this concept requires that significant increases in knowledge regarding the effect of processing on these seven nutrients must be forthcoming.

In a classic study conducted in 1948, Hewston *et al.* reported the results of a comprehensive study of the effect of home preparation on the vitamin and mineral content of 20 common foods. Ascorbic acid was the most sensitive of all the nutrients studied. Retention was lowest when (1) the volume of cooking water was large, (2) the time of cooking was long, and (3) the size of food particles was small.

Effect of Liquid Used in Blanching and Cooking

The effect of cooking liquid on nutrient retention is a factor in several methods of home preparation.   Methods including boiling, steaming, pressure cooking, home canning, and boil-in-the-bag cooking utilize the cooking liquid in different ways.

The USDA (1971) recommendation for nutrient retention is to cook vegetables until just tender, in only enough water to prevent scorching. Covering saucepans with tight-fitting lids is suggested in order to reduce cooking time and the amount of water required. The USDA recommendation is based on published research demonstrating the leaching of nutrients to the cooking water. Krehl and Winters (1950) studied vitamin and mineral loss from 12 different vegetables cooked in small portions to simulate family-style preparation. Four different cooking methods were compared: (1) boiling in enough water to cover, (2) boiling with 1/2 cup water added, (3) pressure cooking with 1/2 cup water added, and (4) cooking with no water added (only water that remained on vegetables after rinsing was present). Vitamin retention was best for waterless pressure cooking and cooking with 1/2 cup water. Boiling vegetables with water to cover resulted in about a 10% greater loss for thiamin, riboflavin, niacin, ascorbic acid, and carotene relative to the other methods. Retention for calcium, iron, and phosphorus decreased by 15% for boiled vegetables covered in water compared to waterless cooking.   Kamalanathan *et al.* (1974) confirmed that pressure cooking better preserved calcium, phosphorus, ascorbic acid, thiamin, and riboflavin than steaming or boiling. McIntosh *et al.* (1942) found pressure cooking vegetables to be superior for vitamin C retention.   For other studies on ascorbic acid retention, see Noble (1967), Gordon and Noble (1959B), Sweeney *et al.* (1960), Erdman and Klein (1982), and Chapter 12 in this book.

Table 21.5. Effect of Water:Food Ratio on the Retention (%) of Vitamins during Small-scale Boiling of Foods of Plant Origin

	Water:food ratio	Cooking time (min)	Thiamin	Riboflavin	Niacin	Ascorbic acid
Carrots	3.5/2	30			71	
	1/30	30			99	
Potatoes	1/1	30	70	55	74	88
	1/7.5	25	96	97	100	98
Bean, snap	2/1	15–30				48–50
	1/2	15				74
Broccoli (frozen)	1/1	5.5				82
	5/1	5.5				57
Broccoli	1/4	30	56	63	36	47
	1/9	30	95	73	88	67
Cabbage	1/2	7				78
	2/1	7				60
	4.2/1	6–8				60
	5/1	10				68
	5/1	8				46
	4/1	12.5				70
	4/1	5.5				51
	2/1	8.5				50
	2.5/4	15				82
	3/1	15				24
Kohlrabi	1/1	2				45
Peas (300 g/150 cc)	1/2	15				74
Peas (300 g/600 cc)	2/1	15–30				48–50
Peas	4/5	24	54	69	64	68
	1/30	20	94	93	97	86
	1/3	8				71–76
	1/1					54–57
Spinach	2/4	7				47
	2/1	7				36
	1/1	2				63
	2/1	2				25
	2/1	8				24
	1/5	8				62
Soybeans	1/2	12				71
	2/1	12–24				52–45

Adapted from Harris and Levenberg (1960).

Vegetables that were cooked while covered in water may retain better color and be milder in flavor than vegetables that are steamed under pressure or cooked without added water (Gordon and Noble 1964). However, vitamin C is least effectively retained by cooking with excessive water (Harris and Levenberg 1960; Clyde *et al.* 1979). Table 21.5 and Fig. 21.2 present data on the effect of the water:food ratio on percentage of retention of four vitamins using home preparation methods. It seems appropriate, given the research published, to

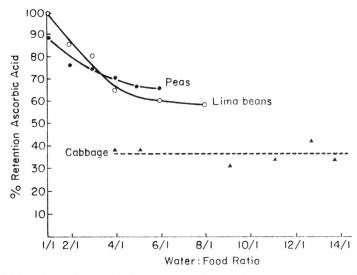

Fig. 21.2. Percentage retention of ascorbic acid during small-scale cooking as a result of increasing water to food ratio. Source: Lachance and Erdman (1975); McIntosh *et al.* (1942); Olliver (1943).

recommend steaming or pressure cooking of vegetables to minimize the effects of cooking on nutrient loss. Microwave cooking of vegetables is discussed later in this chapter.

Blanching and Losses into Cooking Water

Blanching of produce prior to freezing or canning is a home process as well as a commercial one. The objectives of blanching are to inactivate enzymes that would contribute to undesirable color, texture, and flavor changes; to fix color; to reduce microbial levels; to soften the product; and to minimize loss of nutritive value. An issue facing both commercial and home food processors is the question of steam versus water blanching.

Studies indicate that the loss of nutrients from vegetable foods during cooking with water is primarily caused by extraction into the cooking water rather than by destruction. Munsell *et al.* (1949) evaluated the water used in cooking cabbage. The cooking water contained more thiamin, riboflavin, and niacin than did the cabbage. Brush *et al.* (1944) demonstrated that the water phase of canned foods contained considerable amounts of vitamins extracted during canning.

Thus, the objective in blanching and cooking is to minimize both the leaching of nutrients to the cooking water and the oxidative changes that occur in heating. Several studies comparing steam and water blanching are intended for commercial application (see Chapter 12), but the same theories are appropriate for home use. Odland and Eheart (1975) compared blanch methods for broccoli. Steam-blanched product retained significantly more ascorbic acid than did water-blanched broccoli. Steam-blanched broccoli also was found to be firmer, as measured by a shear press, than that which had been water-blanched. Lathrop and Leung (1980) found that vitamin C loss from steam-blanched peas was greater than from water-blanched peas during the first 0.5 min of the blanch process. However, for blanch times longer than 0.5 min vitamin C content of peas decreased more rapidly in water blanching than that in steam blanching. Authors remarked that the substantial vitamin C loss during the first 0.5 min of steam blanching was probably due to the availability of oxygen and the enzyme ascorbic acid oxidase in the peas. Once the enzyme was inactivated, ascorbic acid was quite stable during times of 0.5–5 min in steam blanching, since there was no leaching of the vitamin to the steam environment.

A cooking method more common to commercial processing than to home practice is boil-in-the-bag or retort pouches. Both products have the nutritional advantage of retaining cooking liquids, often in creamed or seasoned sauces that are generally consumed with the product. It is noteworthy that the boil-in-the-bag method of food preservation is increasing in the home, probably more for its convenience than its nutritional profits.

Food processing in retort pouches is increasing. Chen and George (1981) showed that vitamin C stability in green beans packed in metal cans was superior to that in retort pouches. Sensory quality of the retort pouch product was better, and it is likely that retort pouch processing will be designed for greater nutrient retention in the future.

Effect of Time and Temperature

The time–temperature relationship is important in all forms of home food preparation using heat, but the impact varies for the various cooking methods and products. For example, some vegetables require longer heat processing to inactivate enzymes or to render the product tender. Eheart and Gott (1965) found that stir-frying green beans caused poorer retention of ascorbic acid in green beans (57.5%) as compared with broccoli (76.6%); however, the green beans required 5 min of frying while the broccoli was cooked for only 1 min.

Effect of Size and Cut

Some vegetable products are more sensitive to nutrient destruction than are others. Some of this enhanced sensitivity is due to the surface: weight ratio of the food product. Vegetables with larger surface:weight ratios are more easily affected by the amount of cooking water present, the time, and, perhaps, temperatures applied in the cooking process. Slicing and quartering vegetables increases vitamin losses. Quartering of potatoes may reduce cooking time, which may help reduce thermal cooking losses of some vitamins. Thiamin, for example, was better retained in quartered potatoes than in potatoes cooked in the skin since cooking time was reduced by 17 min for the portioned product. However, loss of vitamin C in the cook water was accelerated by exposing more product surface to the cooking medium.

Effect of Cooking Utensils

A variety of cooking vessels are used in home preparation of foods. The type of utensil used is more frequently a factor of cost, availability, or decor rather than nutrient retention; however, the particular cooking utensil used may affect nutrient value. Brown and Fenton (1942) found that boiled parsnips contained more ascorbic acid if cooked in enamel or Pyrex (84 and 81%, respectively) than if prepared in either aluminum or stainless-steel pans (71 and 66%, respectively). Other researchers have seen little effect from glass, stainless steel, aluminum, and enamel; however, copper, brass, and monel could lead to great nutrient losses (Harris and Levenberg 1960; Van der Laan and Van der MijllDekker 1945).

Bicarbonate in Cooking

Sodium bicarbonate and other alkaline salts are occasionally added to the cooking water because the color is preserved better and because the rate of cooking is increased. This practice is destructive to nutrients that are sensitive to alkali, especially thiamin and ascorbic acid. Alkali should not be used in cooking vegetables. It appears that this practice is less common in today's homes than in previous times.

Mineral Retention

Minerals in food products are generally considered stable, with minimal losses during processing. Losses are generally related to the leaching of minerals into the cooking water, although some changes in the oxidative state of minerals can occur during heating. Few studies have been done using home processing techniques, but Schroeder (1971) showed that mineral losses occur in commercially thermal-processed vegetables. The amount of mineral loss depended on the particular product, the packing medium, and the length of storage. Schroeder showed that mineral losses from the food product could be substantial if cooking water was discarded. Canned spinach lost 82% of the manganese, 71% of the cobalt, and 40% of the zinc found in raw spinach. Canned beans lost 60% of their original zinc and canned tomatoes lost 83%. If the cooking medium was considered, then losses were minimized.

Lee et al. (1982) studied mineral and amino acid content in canned green peas. Water blanching has only a minimal effect on mineral losses. Canning losses can be significant (again with discarded water), especially for potassium, and losses were also recorded for magnesium, manganese, zinc, and phosphorus (Chung et al. 1981). There was a dramatic increase in sodium content in canned peas which is a reflection of the salt used in canning. Only a small amount of calcium was absorbed in canned peas from the water and the iron content was unaffected.

The application of heat in cooking may alter the chemical form of the mineral and thus affect the bioavailability of the nutrient. Lee and

Clydesdale (1979) have extensively reviewed the effect of food components and cooking processes on iron availability. Lee and Clydesdale (1981) studied the changes in endogenous and added iron during cooking and processing. Heating caused a decrease in insoluble iron from 96 and 93% to 87 and 85% for spinach samples with and without ascorbic acid added, respectively. An increase in iron solubility with heating suggests a more bioavailable form of iron which is created upon heating. Rosenbloom and Potter (1981) investigated the change in bioavailability of zinc in spinach, beef, and potatoes during processing. These researchers found that most of the endogenous zinc in spinach and potatoes and at least half of the total zinc in beef will be available for intestinal absorption, regardless of processing methods, which included canning, thermal processing, freezing, storage, and boiling. Phytic acid in vegetables may bind minerals and make them unavailable, but Rosenbloom and Potter were unable to show that appreciable amounts of insoluble phytic acid-zinc chelates or other complexes resistant to acid-enzyme digestion were formed as a result of processing treatments. They concluded that processing appeared to have little effect on zinc-macromolecule associations.

In summary, some minerals may be more resistant to leaching than others, and potassium is probably the most sensitive mineral to leaching losses. In light of the limited quantity of research available on mineral retention, particularly in home practices, a greater focus should be placed for research in this area. Also of importance is the need for more studies considering the effects of home preparation practices on mineral availability in prepared foods.

Microwave and Other Cooking Methods

Gordon and Noble (1959A) compared four methods of cooking, including microwave, pressure saucepan, boiling water, or cooking on an electric range, with a small amount of water for cabbage, broccoli, and cauliflower. Researchers found superior retention of ascorbic acid in microwave cooked vegetables (80–90%), followed by pressure saucepan cooking (70–82%). Least effective for vitamin C retention was boiling in a large excess of water (38–73%). Eheart and Gott (1965) showed that microwave cooking resulted in better retention of ascorbic acid in broccoli than did boiling with a large water:food ratio (4:1). However, broccoli that was stir-fried or boiled with a small water:food ratio (1:2) resulted in less destruction of vitamin C. Green beans boiled using a small water:food ratio (1:2) had greater vitamin C value than did microwave-cooked green beans. Ascorbic acid retention in microwave cooking is dependent on the particular food product (Eheart and Gott 1964). Five vegetables were cooked by boiling or microwave, using similar amounts of added water or with no water added. Greater vitamin C retention was observed for frozen spinach cooked in the microwave than by conventional means (66 and 50%, respectively).

Yet, neither peas, potatoes, nor broccoli showed significant differences in vitamin retention between cooking methods.

Although most literature reporting nutrient retention in microwave cooking is for ascorbic acid, other nutrients have been studied. Lanier and Sistrunk (1979) explored the relationship between the method of preparation for consumption and vitamin content in sweet potatoes, including ascorbic acid, niacin, riboflavin, pantothenic acid, and total cartenoids. Other quality attributes were considered by the researchers, who also reported on sensory factors of color, firmness, and mouthfeel. The results indicated that microwave-prepared sweet potatoes retained significantly more pantothenic acid than did potatoes that were baked, boiled, steamed, or canned.   Baked sweet potatoes contained more ascorbic acid than did microwave-cooked or canned potatoes. Except for carotene, canned vegetables consistently showed poor nutrient retention, while microwave and baking methods or preparation were superior for all nutrients.

Augustin *et al.* (1978) also found that white potatoes baked in a microwave had better vitamin retention than did conventionally baked potatoes.   Other factors including peel thickness, moisture content (Augustin *et al.* 1979), and location of the nutrient within the potatoes (Mondy and Mueller 1977) all influence nutrient retention when comparing cooking methods.

A comparison of microwave and conventional cooking on the contents of total and nonprotein nitrogen, amino acids, and minerals of potato tuber cortex and pith was conducted by Klein and Mondy (1981). The study was conducted because of the knowledge that conventional and microwave heating systems operate with different mechanisms of heat transfer.   Conventional baking, which heats by external heat penetrating inwards, caused destruction of nitrogen-containing compounds throughout the potato. Microwave baking, which heats inner portions of food products first, actually caused an increase in nitrogen compounds at the outer cortical layers, but resulted in nutrient damage at the inner pith region. Potassium and iron content decreased in the cortical layer by 15 and 12% by conventional and baking systems, respectively, but was increased in the inner pith area by 22 and 23%. Mineral composition of microwave-cooked potatoes was only minimally affected. The authors propose that minerals migrate from the outer to the inner portions during conventional baking as result of the drying of the outer layer from the high temperature and prolonged exposure to heat.

An early study considering conventional cooking methods showed that baking may be quite destructive for vitamins in sweet potatoes. Pearson and Luecke (1945) found better retention of thiamin, riboflavin, nicotinic acid, and pantothenic acid in boiled whole, unpared sweet potatoes than in baked potatoes. Baked sweet potatoes retained 75% of ascorbic acid, 89% thiamin, 85% niacin, and 77% pantothenic acid. Vitamin B_6 and niacin were significantly leached to cooking water in boiled, halved potatoes. Baking an intact potato preserved these nutrients (Page and Hanning 1963).

There is little published research regarding the effect of baking on products other than potatoes. However, one study evaluated the loss of ascorbic acid from apples during baking. Curran et al. (1937) found that apples baked 60–90 min at 204°C in an open dish retained 40% ascorbic acid. The retention was only 25% during baking in a covered dish and 20% during baking in a pie.

Few vegetables are fried, and there are few reports in the literature on the effects of frying on nutrient content. In 1942, a study was made on the effects of frying for 30 vegetables. Losses of ascorbic acid ranged from 0.7 to 32.7%. Vegetables that were boiled, then fried, lost from 22.2 to 78.8% ascorbic acid. Potatoes fried for 15 min in deep fat retained 72% ascorbic acid, yet potatoes fried in butter or Crisco® were reported to lose no ascorbic acid (Richardson et al. 1937). Other reports reveal that frying may be more detrimental to nutrient retention. Potatoes fried for 20 min retained only 20–45% ascorbic acid (Rudra 1937). Basu and Neogy (1948) evaluated ascorbic acid retention in several fried foods as follows: potato, 60% (12 min); sweet potato, 19% (20 min); jackfruit, 22% (5 min); papaya, 48% (5 min); and peas, 60% (4 min). In a more recent report, Domah et al. (1974) studied the ascorbic acid content of potatoes after frying. They reported that reduced ascorbic acid is rapidly oxidized to the less active dehydroascorbic acid form. Further hydrolysis to the inactive diketo form proceeds more slowly. Frying of potatoes for even 30 min at 140°C resulted in at least 80% retention of the total vitamin value, but this is almost entirely as the dehydro form.

Data on nutrients other than ascorbic acid are fragmentary. Cheldelin et al. (1943) reported a 74% loss of riboflavin in onions after 20 min of frying. Recently, Augustin et al. (1981) evaluated various cuts of fried potatoes for thiamin, niacin, vitamin B_6, ascorbic acid, and folic acid. Authors found that niacin and vitamin B_6 retention was little affected by home frying. Retention of ascorbic acid in large french fries, small french fries, and potato rounds was less than or equivalent to oven-baked samples. There was total thiamin retention in pan-fried hashbrowns, but only 59% retention in pan-fried shoestring french fries. Ascorbic acid retention ranged between 53 and 91%, and was lowest for potatoes prepared as large fries. Folic acid retention was low and ranged from 14 to 75%. Folic acid was lowest for deep-fried potatoes rounds. In general, fried potatoes scored lower in respect to vitamin retention than before cooking samples, but values were not always less than the equivalent product that had been overbaked.

Frying as a means of retaining water-soluble nutrients such as ascorbic acid is often castigated and there currently is no experimental basis for such a view. The effect of high temperatures for even a short time during frying appears to be sufficient to cause significant reduction in heat-labile vitamin content. In addition, the absorption of fat used for frying increases the fat content of foods consumed. Fried foods therefore have a lower nutrient:calorie ratio compared to vegetables cooked in a minimum of water. For this reason, and the availability of alternative cooking methods with good vitamin retention, use of fried vegetables in a low-calorie diet is inappropriate.

Essential fatty acid degradation occurs in oils (safflower, cottonseed, and corn) used for frying (Kilgore and Bailey 1970). Fleishman *et al.* (1963) found that linoleic acid was also degraded in sesame, coconut, olive, peanut, and soy oils. Fleishman and co-workers also showed that frying oils may influence nutrient stability. Poor quality frying oils adversely affect ascorbic acid content in fried foods. Ascorbic acid and essential fatty acid stability may become important in diets rich with fried foods.

With the increased concern for conservation of energy, solar drying has become increasingly appealing for home food preservation. Little research exists regarding the effect of drying on nutritional quality. Labuza (1972) reported that vegetables dried by conventional methods suffered losses of ascorbic acid ranging from 10 to 50%. Gooding (1960) reported that a major factor determining ascorbic acid stability after drying was the final moisture content of the food product. The higher the final percentage of moisture corresponds with a higher percentage of nutrient losses. In a recent study by Maeda and Salunkhe (1981), the researchers used ascorbic acid and total carotene as indicator nutrients for loss during sun drying, both in direct sunshine and in solar driers with and without shade provided. In general, maximum nutrient retention was obtained for four vegetables dried in enclosed driers with shade provided. However, retention for ascorbic acid ranged from only 1.6 to 24.4%, and for total carotene between 4.2 and 57.1%. Vegetables that were selected for study were extremely rich sources of both nutrients in their fresh form, but after drying were only minimal sources of ascorbic acid and total carotene. Therefore, it is clear that sun drying and solar driers are quite harmful to vitamins despite their energy savings.

Cereal Products

Cereal products are a staple food in many diets worldwide. For most western cultures, cereal foods are primarily sources of dietary carbohydrate. However, for some they make a significant contribution to the daily protein intake and, thus, the protein quality is also important. Factors that affect nutrient stability in baked grain products include (1) type of flour, (2) leavening agents and other ingredients, (3) time and temperature of heating, and (4) surface area exposed to heat.

The type of flour used for baked goods is important, since flours differ in their nutritional content. Moran (1959) calculated that 80–95%

of seven B complex vitamins were retained in whole wheat flour (95% extraction). White flour (70% extraction) retained only 15–60% of these vitamins. Four nutrients are added in enriched flour, including thiamin, riboflavin, niacin, and iron. Other nutrients, including fiber, are removed in milling and must be obtained from other dietary sources. Some ingredients added to baked products affect the alkalinity or acidity of the product. Baking powders, sodium aluminum sulfate, and phosphates increase the alkalinity of the product and may cause significant destruction of thiamin. When large amounts of these leavening agents are used, as much as 84% of thiamin is destroyed (Briant and Hutchins 1946; Briant and Klosterman 1950). A pH of 6.0 or lower is desirable for satisfactory stability of thiamin during baking.

The composition of the bread formula also seems important. The retention of thiamin was 87, 84, 83, and 81% when biscuits were made with fresh milk, evaporated milk, dry milk, and water, respectively (Briant and Hutchins 1946).

The presence of reducing sugars to bind amino acids, such as lysine, will diminish the quality of the protein in bread. During baking, lysine and reducing sugars such as glucose form a linkage that can not be broken down by human digestive enzymes. The linkage is cleaved in laboratory analyses of amino acids by acid hydrolysis. The biological availability of lysine may therefore not concur with reports from chemical analysis alone (Sabry 1969). Baked goods are commonly prepared using quantities of dry milk powder. Jansen *et al.* (1964A,B) added 6–14% of nonfat dry milk to breads before baking and found that the nutritive loss of natural and fortified lysine averaged 36%. Presumably, the amino acid loss was due to the large content of the reducing sugar D-lactose in the dried milk. L-Lysine loss is extremely detrimental to the protein quality of wheat products since it is already the most limiting amino acid in wheat.

The presence of yeast in bread doughs can actually increase the B complex vitamin content due to synthesis by the yeast organism (Matz 1975). Also, the action of fermentation causes liberation of minerals, including calcium and iron, from phytic acid complexes (Ranhotra 1972). Zinc may also be made more available. There are yeast phytases and natural wheat phytases that cleave mineral inositol-phosphate complexes and make minerals more bioavailable (Ranhotra *et al.* 1974).

Yeast fermentation also increased the natural folacin in bread dough by about 30% (Keagy *et al.* 1975). However, this increase in folacin was lost during the baking process.

Time and temperature of baking can greatly affect nutrient content of baked goods. The intensity of the baking process will affect thiamin retention. Bread baked to a dark brown retained 9.7% less thiamin compared to bread baked to a pale color (Zaehringer and Personius (1949). This detrimental effect of baking appears largely as thiamin loss from the crust. Direct exposure of the outer crust to heat results in 35% more thiamin destruction than for the crumb portion (Morgan and Frederick 1935). There is evidence of a 20–29.5% loss in bread during baking (Coppock *et al.* 1957; Bottomley and Nobile 1962). Niacin and riboflavin, which are less heat labile, are generally well retained in baking (Harris and Levenberg 1960).

The destruction of lysine during baking is also dependent on time and temperature. The vulnerability of lysine to heat leads to serious impairment in the nutritive quality of the protein because of its relatively exposed ϵ-amino group (Liener 1960). Again, most destruction takes place in the crust, where the browning reaction occurs. Reports of lysine loss due to the heat in baking vary from 12.5 (Tara *et al.* 1972) to 15% (Rosenberg and Rohdenberg 1951; Ericson *et al.* 1961). Tsen *et al.* (1982) evaluated amino acid loss in pizza crust. Lysine was the most significant amino acid that was lost with a range between 7.1% destruction for whole wheat pizza to 19.4% for a commercial pizza crust. Relative to bread baking, pizza crust is generally exposed to higher temperatures (316°–344°C) for a shorter time period (4–10 min). Breads are generally baked at 218°–232°C for 20–25 min. Authors reported that the nutritive loss of lysine in baking was due to a destruction of a portion of lysine in the pizza crust, since the difference between total and available lysine was small.

Tsen and Reddy (1977) demonstrated the physiological effect of a diminished lysine value after toasting of bread. The authors studied weight gain in rats, feed efficiency, and protein efficiency ratio (PER) of breads toasted to varying degrees of brownness. The toasted breads did not differ in their proximate analysis, but the effect on growing rats was significant. Weight gain was especially low with diets consisting of dark-toasted bread. Adjusted PER was 2.50 for the control (casein) diet, 0.90 for untoasted bread crumb and 0.64, 0.45, and 0.32 for light, medium, and dark-toasted bread-based diets, respectively.

In toasting bread, the greater surface area exposed to toasting heat allows a greater proportion of the product to become browned and lysine destruction is greater. For example, thickly sliced bread would be less susceptible to nutritional loss than thinly sliced bread since less surface area is exposed.

Abdel-Rahman (1982) studied the effect of cooking time on the vitamin and mineral content of spaghetti. Pasta was cooked for either 10, 15, or 20 min in 500 ml of water. Mineral losses were small, with the exception of potassium. Potassium was reduced by 6.1, 14.5, and 16% for each of the three cooking times, respectively. The rate of loss for thiamin, riboflavin, niacin, and pantothenic acid was greatest during the initial 10 min of cooking and then diminished as cooking time increased. Authors recommended that for retention of quality and nutritional value, the maximum cooking time for spaghetti be 15 min.

Reheating Prepared Foods

The effect of refrigerator storage on nutritional quality of cooked foods has already been discussed in this chapter. Unfortunately, there is little research that has been reported concerning the nutritional value of reheated convenience foods or leftovers. This void is of particular concern given the prevalence of these practices in the home.

One of the most comprehensive studies is that of Charles and Van Duyne (1958). Vitamin C content of eight vegetables was evaluated (1) when raw, (2) after boiling until done with half their weight in water, (3) after holding for 24 hr refrigerated (4°–9°C), and (4) after 24 hr refrigeration and reheating. After 24 hr refrigerated storage, cooked broccoli, brussels sprouts, shredded cabbage, sliced cabbage, cauliflower, peas, and snap beans lost about 22% ascorbic acid each, whereas asparagus and spinach reportedly lost only about 4% each. Reheating of the cooked and stored vegetables increased ascorbic acid losses to an average of 32%. Extended storage resulted in greater nutrient destruction. The losses that occurred with reheating apparently were from the vegetable itself, since ascorbic acid in the cooking liquids was stable during storage and in reheating.

Wood *et al.* (1946) found significant destruction of vitamin C in cooked, drained, and refrigerator-stored (24 hr) cabbage. Thiamin and riboflavin were considerably more stable than vitamin C. Ang *et al.* (1975) compared ascorbic acid, thiamin, and riboflavin retention in cooked, frozen, and reheated mashed potatoes. Potatoes were reheated by convection, infrared, steam, or microwave oven. Large losses of ascorbic acid were recorded, particularly for the microwave-heated product. Thiamin and riboflavin showed good retention, regardless of the reheating system.

More recently, Augustin *et al.* (1980) studied vitamin retention in baked and rehydrated mashed potatoes. Potatoes were cooked, chilled, and microwave reheated, then analyzed for thiamin, riboflavin, niacin, vitamin B_6, ascorbic acid, and folic acid content. Nutrient losses occurred with each step; however, total retention values after microwave reheating were high for thiamin, riboflavin, niacin, and vitamin B_6. All were retained at 90% or more of their original values. Ascorbic acid and folic acid were more susceptible to destruction, with total retention around 70%. These two vitamin values were significantly reduced relative to the fresh product.

From these results, using only a limited number of different products, it is clear that ascorbic acid and folic acid are susceptible to significant losses in stored and reheated foods. More research should be done since, for some segments of the population, reheated foods may comprise a significant portion of the diet.

Table 21.6.   Major Sources of Nutrient Losses during Preparation and Service

Animal products	Plant products
Thaw drip, especially from chopped or ground meats	Spoilage of unprocessed plant foods
Cooking drip, especially from micro-wave cooking	Excessive trimming, cutting, chopping, slicing, washing, soaking
Nutrient leaching, especially during braising or stewing	Excessive use of water in cooking
Heat losses, especially thiamin, during roasting at high temperatures	Excessive use of heat in cooking
Excessive (more than 3 hr) steam table holding in food-service operations	Discarded cooking water
	Use of alkaline processes in soaking or baking
	Refrigeration of once-cooked plant foods in excess of 1 day
	Reheating of once-cooked plant dishes

Source: Adapted from Erdman (1979).

CONCLUSION

The food habits of the U.S. population are changing toward use of convenient, quick-to-prepare foods. In addition, packaging is gearing towards use of smaller or single-serving containers that require a minimum of preparation. The nutritional value of foods prepared in these manners should be considered in order to ensure the general good health of the population. This chapter has highlighted the techniques of food handling and preparation that best retain nutrients, and has noted that specific nutrients are more susceptible to heat or to water leaching than are others. Although general guidelines for nutrient retention may be practiced in the home, specific practices may vary, depending on the particular product, cut of meat or vegetable, and type of preparation technique. The goal is to optimize the nutritional value of prepared foods, yet to provide desirable sensory characteristics. Foods, no matter how nutritious, do not provide nutrition until they are consumed, and nutritious, but less enjoyable foods may not be consumed.

Major sources of nutrient losses during home preparation and service of foods of animal and plant origin are listed in Table 21.6.

REFERENCES

Abdel-Rahman, A. H. Y. 1982. Effect of cooking time on the quality, minerals and vitamins of spaghetti produced from two Italian durum wheat varieties. J. Food Technol. *17*(3), 349.

Adam, W. B. 1941. Rep. Fruit Veget. Pres. Res. Stn. *14*.

Ang, C. Y. W. 1978. Nutritional considerations in menu and systems design of food service operations. *In* Analysis, Design and Implementation. G. E. Livingston and C. M. Chang (Editors). Academic Press, New York.

Ang, C. Y. W. 1981. Comparison of sample storage methods for vitamin B_6 assay in broiler meats. J. Food Sci. *47*, 336–337.

Ang, C. Y. W., Chang, C. M., Frey, A. E., and Livingston, G. E. 1975. Effects of heating methods on vitamin retention in six fresh or frozen prepared foods. J. Food Sci. *40*, 997.

Anonymous 1971A. Conserving the nutritive values in foods. Home Garden Bull. *90*. U.S. Department of Agriculture, 1963 (revised January 1971), Washington, DC.

Anonymous 1971B. Food Stability Survey. Vol. 2. Dept. of Food Sci., Rutgers Univ. Available from U.S. Govt. Printing Office, Washington, DC.

Anonymous 1971C. Nutritive value of foods. Home and Garden Bull. *72*. U.S. Department of Agriculture, 1963 (revised January, 1971), Washington, DC.

Anonymous 1972. Recommendations for the Processing and Handling of Frozen Foods, 2nd Edition, p. 144. International Institute of Refrigeration, Paris.

Ashby, B. H., Bennett, A. H., Bailey, W. A., Moleeratanond, W., and Kramer, A. 1977. Energy savings during frozen food storage. Paper 77-6527. Presented at Ann. Meeting Am. Soc. Agric. Eng., Chicago.

Augustin, J., Johnson, S. R., Teitzel, C., True, R. H., Hogan, J. M., Toma, R. B., Shaw, R. L., and Deutsch, R. M. 1978. Changes in the nutrient composition of potatoes during home preparation. 2. Vitamins. Am. Potato J. *55*, 653.

Augustin, J., Toma, R. B., True, R. H., Shaw, R. L., Teitzel, C., Johnson, S. R., and Orr, P. 1979. Composition of raw and cooked potato peel and flesh: Proximate and vitamin composition. J. Food Sci. *44*, 805.

Augustin, J., Marousek, G. I., Tholen, L. A., and Bertelli, B. 1980. Vitamin retention in cooked, chilled and reheated potatoes. J. Food Sci. *45*, 814–816.

Augustin, J., Marousek, G. I., Artz, W. E., and Swanson, B. G. 1981. Retention of some water-soluble vitamins during home preparation of commercially frozen potato products. J. Food Sci. *46*, 1697.

Aurand, L. W., Singleton, J. A., and Noble, B. W. 1966. Photo-oxidation reactions in milk. J. Dairy Sci. *49*, 138.

Baldwin, R. E., Korschgen, B. M., Russell, M. S., and Mabesa, L. 1976. Proximate analysis, free amino acid, vitamin and mineral content of microwave cooked meat. J. Food Sci. *41*, 762.

Basu, N. M., and Neogy, R. 1948. Vitamin C content of some ordinary foods before and after cooking. Indian J. Physiol. Appl. Sci. *2*, 15.

Bauman, H. E., and Ruch, D. 1971. Problems of researching and marketing fortified foods and its application on consumption trends. AMA symp. Vitamins and Minerals in Processed Foods, pp. 236–247.

Bayfield, E. G., and O'Donnell, W. W. 1945. Observations on thiamin content of stored wheat. Food Res. *10*, 485–488.

Bender, A. E. 1958. The stability of vitamin C in commercial fruit squash. J. Sci. Food Agric. *11*, 754–760.

Bender, A. E. 1978. Effects of processes. *In* Food Processing and Nutrition. Academic Press, New York.

Bengtsson, N., Liljemark, A., Olsson, P., and Nilsson, B. 1972. An attempt to systematize time–temperature–tolerance (T.T.T.) data as a basis for development of time–temperature indicators. Bull. Inst. Int. Froid, Annexe *2*, 303.

Betancourt, L. A., Stevens, M. A., and Kader, A. A. 1977. Accumulation and loss of sugars and reduced ascorbic acid in attached and detached tomato fruits. J. Am. Soc. Hort. Sci. *102*, (6), 721–723.

Bezanson, A., Learson, R., and Teich, W. 1973. Defrosting shrimp with microwave. Microwave Energy Appl. Newsletter 6,3.

Bognar, A. 1978. Studies on the effect of conventional and novel roasting methods and grilling on the nutritive value of pork. Fleischwirtschaft 58(7), 1176–1182; Food Sci. Technol. Austr. (1979) 11(2), 225.

Bolin, H. R., and Stafford, A. E. 1974. Effect of processing and storage on provitamin A and vitamin C in apricots. J. Food Sci. 39, 1034.

Bottomley, R. A., and Nobile, S. 1962. The thiamin content of flour and white bread in Sydney, New South Wales. J. Sci. Food Agric. 13, 550.

Bowers, J. A., and Fryer, B. A. 1972. Thiamin and riboflavin in cooked and frozen, reheated turkey. J. Am. Diet. Assoc. 60, 399.

Bowers, J. A., Fryer, B. A., and Engler, P. P. 1974. Vitamin B_6 in pork muscle cooked in microwave and conventional ovens. J. Food Sci. 39, 426.

Briant, A. M., and Hutchins, M. R. 1946. Influence of ingredients on thiamin retention and quality in baking powder biscuits. Cereal Chem. 23, 512.

Briant, A. M., and Klosterman, A. M. 1950. Influence of ingredients on thiamin and riboflavin retention and quality of plain muffins. Trans. Am. Assoc. Cereal Chem. 8, 69.

Brown, E. J., and Fenton, F. 1942. Losses of vitamin C during cooking of parsnips. Food Res. 7, 218.

Brush, M. K., Hinman, W. F., and Halliday, G. 1944. The nutritive value of canned foods. 5. Distribution of water-soluble vitamins between solid and liquid portions of canned vegetables and fruits. J. Nutr. 28, 131.

Burge, J., Mickelsen, O., Nicklow, C., and Marsh, G. L. 1975. Vitamin C in tomatoes: Comparison of tomatoes developed for mechanical or hand harvesting. Ecol. Food Nutr. 4, 27–31.

Caileau, R., Kidder, L. E., and Morgan, A. F. 1945. The thiamine content of raw and parboiled rices. Cereal Chem. 22, 50–60.

Causey, K., Hausrath, M. E., Ramsted, P. E., and Fenton, F. 1950A. Effect of thawing and cooking methods on palatability and nutritive value of frozen ground meat. 2. Beef. Food Res. 15, 237.

Causey, K., Hausrath, M. E., Ramsted, P. E., and Fenton, F. 1950B. Effect of thawing and cooking methods on palatability and nutritive value of frozen ground meat. 3. Lamb. Food Res. 15, 249.

Causey, K., Andreausseu, E. G., Hausrath, M. E., Along, C., Ramstad, P. E., and Fenton, F. 1950C. Effect of thawing and cooking methods on palatability and nutritive value of frozen ground meat. 1. Pork. Food Res. 15, 237.

Cecil, S. R., and Woodroof, J. G. 1962. Long-term storage of military rations. Georgia Exp. Stn. Tech. Bull. 25.

Charles, V. R., and Van Duyne, F. O. 1958. Effect of holding and reheating on the ascorbic acid content of cooked vegetables. J. Home Econ. 50, 159.

Cheldelin, V. H., and Williams, R. J. 1943. Studies of the average American diet. 2. Riboflavin, nicotenic acid and pantothenic acid content. J. Nutr. 26, 417.

Cheldelin, V. H., Woods, A. A., and Williams, R. J. 1943. Losses of B vitamins due to cooking of foods. J. Nutr. 26, 477.

Chen, T. S., and George, W. L. 1981. Ascorbic acid retention in retort-pouched green beans. J. Food Sci. 46, 642.

Chung, S. Y., Morr, C. V., and Jen, J. J. 1981. Effect of microwave and conventional cooking on the nutritional value of Colossus peas (Vigna uniguiculata). J. Food Sci. 46, 272.

Clyde, D. D., Bertini, J., Dmochowski, and Koop, H. 1979. The vitamin A and C content of Coriandrum satiuum and the variations in the loss of the latter with various methods of food preparation and preservation. Qual. Plant. Plant Foods Hum. Nutr. 28(4), 317–322.

Coppock, J. B. M., Carpenter, B. R., and Knight, R. A. 1957. Thiamine losses in bread baking. Chem. Ind. (London) 23, 735.

Cover, S., McLaren, B. A., and Pearson, P. B. 1944. Retention of the B vitamins in rare and well-done beef. J. Nutr. 27, 363.

Cover, S., Dilsaver, E. M., and Hays, R. M. 1947A. Retention of the B vitamins in beef and lamb after stewing. 3. Pantothenic acid. J. Am. Diet. Assoc. 23, 693.

Cover, S., Dilsaver, E. M., and Hays, R. M. 1947B. Retention of the B vitamins in beef and lamb after stewing. 6. Similarities and differences among the four vitamins. J. Am. Diet. Assoc. 23, 962–966.

Cover, S., Dilsaver, E. M., Hays, R. M., and Smith, W. H. 1949A. Retention of B vitamins after large-scale cooking of meats. 2. Roasting by two methods. J. Am. Diet. Assoc. 25, 949.

Cover, S., Dilsaver, E. M., Hays, R. M. 1949B. Retention of B vitamins in beef and veal after home canning and storage. Food Res. 14, 104.

Cuendet, L. S., Larson, E., Norris, C. G., and Geddes, W. F. 1954. The influence of moisture content and other factors on the stability of wheat flour at $37.8°C$. Cereal Chem. 31, 362–389.

Curran, J., and Erdman, J. W. 1980. How to prepare tasty meals yet retain nutrients. Profess. Nutr. 12(3), 7.

Curran, K. M., Tressler, D. K., and King, C. G. 1937. Losses of vitamin C during cooking of Northern Spy apples. Food Res. 2, 549.

Daniels, R. W. 1974. Handbook 8 and nutritional labelling. Food Technol. 28, 46.

Decareau, R. V. 1979. Microwaves and nutrition. Profess. Nutr. Summer, 11, 9–10.

Demick, P. S. 1973. Effect of fluorescent light on the flavor and selected nutrients of homogenized milk held in conventional containers. J. Milk Food Technol. 36, 383–387.

Deuel, H. J., Jr., and Greenberg, S. M. 1953. A comparison of the retention of vitamin A in margarines and in butter based on bioassays. Food Res. 18, 497.

Dietrich, W. C., Nutting, M. D. F., Boggs, M. N., and Weinstein, N. E. 1962. Time–temperature tolerance of frozen foods. Quality changes in cauliflower. Food Technol. 16, 123.

Domah, A. A. M. B., Davidek, J., and Velisek, J. 1974. Changes of L-ascorbic and L-dehydroascorbic acids during cooking and frying of potatoes. Z. Lebensm. Unters. Forsch. 154, 272.

Downs, D. E., and Meckel, R. B. 1943. Thiamin losses in toasting bread. Cereal Chem. 20, 352.

Dunkley, W. L., Franklin, J. D., and Pangborn, R. M. 1962. Effect of fluorescent light on flavor, ascorbic acid and riboflavin in milk. Food Technol. 16, 112–118.

Eheart, M. S., and Gott, C. 1964. Conventional and microwave cooking of vegetables. J. Am. Diet. Assoc. 44, 116.

Eheart, M. S., and Gott, C. 1965. Chlorophyll, ascorbic acid and pH changes in green vegetables cooked by stir-fry, microwave and conventional methods and a comparison of chlorophyll methods. Food Technol. 19(5), 185.

Eheart, M. S., and Odland, D. 1972. Storage of fresh broccoli and green beans. J. Am. Diet. Assoc. 60, 402.

Embleton, T. W., and Jones, W. W. 1966. Calif. Citrogr. 51, 269.

Embleton, T. W., Reitz, H. J., and Jones, W. W. 1973. In The Citrus Industry, Vol. 3, p. 122. W. Reuther (Editor). Univ. California Press, Riverside.

Erdman, J. W. 1979. Effect of preparation and service of food on nutrient value. Food Technol. 33(2), 38–48.

Erdman, J. W., and Erdman, E. A. 1982. Effect of home preparation practices on nutritive value of food. In Handbook of Nutritive Value of Processed Food,

Vol. 1. Food for human use, pp. 237–263. M. Rechcigl, Jr. (Editor). CRC Press, Boca Raton, FL.

Erdman, J. W., Jr., and Klein, B. P. 1982. Harvesting, processing, and cooking influences on vitamin C in foods. *In* Ascorbic acid: Chemistry, Metabolism, and Uses, pp. 499–532. P. A. Seib and B. M. Tolbert [Editors]. Amer. Chem. Soc., Washington, DC.

Ericson, L. E., Larsson, S., and Lid, G. 1961. The loss of added lysine and threonine during the baking of wheat bread. Acta Physiol. Scand. *53*, 85.

Evans, R. J., Butts, H. A., and Davidson, J. A. 1951A. The niacin content of fresh and stored shell eggs. Poult. Sci. *30*, 132.

Evans, R. J., Butts, H. A., and Davidson, J. A. 1951B. The vitamin B_6 content of fresh and stored shell eggs. Poult. Sci. *30*, 515.

Evans, R. J., Butts, H. A., and Davidson, J. A. 1952A. The riboflavin content of fresh and stored shell eggs. Poult. Sci. *31*, 269.

Evans, R. J., Butts, H. A., and Davidson, J. A. 1952B. The pantothenic acid content of fresh and stored shell eggs. Poult. Sci. *31*, 777.

Evans, R. J., Davidson, J. A., Bauer, D., and Butts, H. A. 1953. The biotin content of fresh and stored shell eggs. Poult. Sci. *32*, 680.

Evans, R. J., Davidson, J. A., Bauer, D., and Butts, H. A. 1954. Folic acid in fresh and stored shell eggs. J. Agric. Food Chem. *1*, 170.

Evans, R. J., Bandemer, S. L., Bauer, D. H., and Davidson, J. A. 1955. The vitamin B_{12} content of fresh and stored shell eggs. Poult. Sci. *34*, 922.

Ezell, B. D., and Wilcox, M. S. 1959. Loss of vitamin C in fresh vegetables as related to wilting and temperature. J. Agric. Food Chem. *7*, 507.

Ezell, B. D., and Wilcox, M. S. 1962. Loss of carotene in fresh vegetables as related to wilting and temperature. J. Agric. Food Chem. *10*(2), 124–126.

Fager, E. E. C., Olson, O. E., Burris, R. H., and Elvehjem, C. A. 1949. Folic acid in vegetables and certain other plant materials. Food Res. *14*, 1.

Farrer, K. T. H. 1955. The thermal destruction of B_1 in foods. Adv. Food Res. *6*, 257–311.

Fennema, O. 1975. Effects of frozen-preservation on nutrients. *In* Nutritional Evaluation of Food Processing, 2nd Edition, p. 244. R. S. Harris and E. Karmas [Editors] AVI Publishing Co., Westport, CT.

Fennema, O. 1977. Loss of vitamins in fresh and frozen foods. Food Technol. *31*(2), 32–36.

Fleishman, A. I., *et al.* 1963. Studies on cooking fats and oils. J. Am. Diet. Assoc. *42*, 394.

Fraps, G. S., and Kemmerer, A. R. 1937. Texas Agr. Exp. Stn. Bull. *557*.

Freeland-Graves, J. H. and Day, P. J. 1980. Effect of cooking method on trace mineral retention in foods. Presented at the 40th Ann. IFT Meeting, New Orleans, June. Abstr. *282*.

Gallo, A. E., and Blaylock, J. R. 1982. What foods do Americans avoid? Consumer Nutr. Inst. Weekly Rep. *12*(14), 4–5.

Gee, M. 1979. Stability of ascorbic acid, thiamin and β-carotene in some low temperature dried vegetables. Lebensm.-Wiss. Technol. *12*, 147–149.

Goldblith, S. A. 1975. Food processing nutrition and the feeding of man during the next 25 years. Paper presented at Symp. on World Food Supply and Refrigeration. Frigoscandia, Stockholm.

Gooding, E. G. B. 1960. The storage behavior of dehydrated foods. *In* Recent Advances in Food Science, Vol. 2. J. Letch and J. Howthorn (Editors). Butterworth, London.

Gordon, J., and Noble, I. 1959A. Comparison of electronic vs. conventional cooking of vegetables. J. Am. Diet. Assoc. *35*, 241.

Gordon, J., and Noble, I. 1959B. Effect of cooking method on vegetables. J. Am. Diet. Assoc. *35*, 578.

Gordon, J., and Noble. I. 1964. "Waterless" vs. boiling water cooking of vegetables. J. Am. Diet. Assoc. *44*, 378.

Gregory, J. F., and Kirk, J. R. 1978. Assessment of storage effects on vitamin B_6 stability and bioavailability in dehydrated food systems. J. Food Sci. *43*, 1801.

Gregory, M. E., 1975. Water-soluble vitamins in milk and milk products. J. Dairy Res. *42*, 197–216.

Guadagni, D. C. 1961. Integrated time–temperature experience as it relates to frozen food quality. ASHRAE J., April.

Guadagni, D. C., and Kelly, S. H. 1958. Time–temperature tolerance of frozen foods. 14. Ascorbic acid and its oxidation products as a measure of temperature history in frozen strawberries. Food Technol. *12*(12), 645.

Guerrant, N. B., Vavich, M. G., Fardig, O. B., Ellenberger, H. A., Stern, R. M., and Coonen, N. H. 1947. Effect of duration and temperature of blanch on vitamin retention by certain vegetables. Ind. Eng. Chem. Edn. *39*, 1000–1007.

Hall, K. N., and Lin, C. S. 1981. Effect of cooking rates in electric or microwave oven on cooking losses and retention of thiamin in broilers. J. Food Sci. *46*, 1292–1293.

Harris, R. S., and Levenberg, R. K. 1960. Effects of home preparation on nutrient content of foods of plant origin. *In* Nutritional Evaluation of Food Processing, p. 462. R. S. Harris and H. von Loesecke (Editors). John Wiley, New York.

Headley, M. E., and Jacobson, M. 1960. Electronic and conventional cooking of lamb roasts. J. Am. Diet. Assoc. *36*, 337.

Hedrick, T. I., and Glass, L. 1975. Chemical changes in milk during exposure to fluorescent light. J. Milk Food Technol. *38*, 129–131.

Heikel, H. A., El-Sanafiri, N. Y., and Shooman, M. A. 1972. Factors affecting the quality of dried mango sheets. Agric. Res. Rev. *50*(4), 185.

Heinze, P. H. 1973. Effects of storage, temperature and marketing conditions on the composition and nutritional values of fresh fruit and vegetables. Pub. *3786*, p. 29. USDA Eastern Reg. Res. Lab., Beltsville, MD.

Hewston, E. M., Dawson, E. H., Alexander, L. M., and Orent-Keiles, E. 1948. Vitamin and mineral content of certain foods as affected by home preparation. U.S. Department Agric. Misc. Publ. *628*., Washington, DC.

Hoagland, R., Hankins, O. G., Ellis, N. R., Hiner, R. L., and Snider, G. G. 1947. Composition and nutritive value of hams as affected by method of curing. Food Technol. *1*, 540–552.

Hollingsworth, D. F., 1970. Effects of some new production and processing methods in nutritive values. J. Am. Diet. Assoc. *57*, 246.

Horowitz, I., Fabry, E. M., and Gerson, C. D. 1976. Bioavailability of ascorbic acid in orange juice. J. Am. Med. Assoc. *235*, 2624.

Hurdle, A. D. F., Barton, D., and Searles, I. H. 1968. A method of measuring folate in food and its application to a hospital diet. Am. J. Clin. Nutr. *21*(1), 1202.

Janicki, L. J., and Appledorf, H. 1974. Effect of broiling, grill frying and microwave cooking on moisture. Some lipid components and total fatty acids of ground beef. J. Food Sci. *39*, 715.

Jansen, G. R., Ehle, S. R., and Hause, N. L. 1964A. Studies of the nutritive loss of supplemental lysine in baking. 1. Loss in standard white bread containing 4% nonfat dry milk. Food Technol. *18*, 367.

Jansen, G. R., Ehle, S. R., and Hause, N. L. 1964B. Studies of the nutritive loss of supplemental lysine in baking. 2. Loss in water bread and in breads supplemented with moderate amounts of nonfat dry milk. Food Technol. *18*, 372.

Jones, D. B., Fraps, G. S., *et al.* 1943. Bull. Nat. Res. Council, Repr. Circ. Ser. *116*.

Jones, W. W. 1961. *In* The Orange: Its Biochemistry and Physiology, p. 25. W. B. Sinclair (Editor). Univ. California Press, Riverside.

Jones, W. W., Embleton, T. W., Boswell, S. B., Goodall, G. E., and Barnhart, E. L. 1970. J. Am. Soc. Hort. Sci. *95*, 46.

Jul, M. 1969. Quality and stability in frozen meats. *In* Quality and Stability of Frozen Foods, pp. 191–217. W. B. van Arsdel, M. J. Copley, and R. L. Olson (Editors). Wiley Interscience, New York.

Kamalanathan, G., Giri, J., Jaya, T. V., and Priyadarsani. 1974. The effect of boiling, steaming, pressure-cooking and panning on the mineral and vitamin content of three vegetables. Ind. J. Nutr. Diet. *11*, 10.

Keagy, P. M., Stokstad, E. L. R., and Fellers, D. A. 1975. Folacin stability during bread processing and family flour storage. Cereal Chem. *52*, 348.

Kefford, J. F. 1973. Citrus fruits and processed citrus products in human nutrition. World Rev. Nutr. Diet. *18*, 60–120.

Kik, M. C. 1955. Influence of processing on the nutritive value of milled rice. J. Agric. Chem. *3*, 600–603.

Kilgore, L., and Bailey, M. 1970. Degradation of linoleic acid during potato frying. J. Am. Diet. Assoc. *56*, 130.

Klein, L. B., and Mondy, N. I. 1981. Comparison of microwave and conventional baking of potatoes in relation to nitrogenous constituents and mineral composition. J. Food Sci. *46*, 1874.

Klein, B. P., and Perry, A. K. 1982. Ascorbic acid and vitamin A activity in selected vegetables from different geographical areas of the United States. J. Food Sci. *47*, 941–945.

Kotschevar, L. H., Mosso, A., and Tugwell, T. 1955. B vitamin retention in frozen meat. J. Am. Diet. Assoc. *31*, 589.

Kramer, A. 1979. Effects of freezing and frozen storage on nutrient retention of fruits and vegetables. Food Technol. *33*(2), 58–61.

Kramer, A., King, R. L., and Westhoff, D. C. 1976. Effects of frozen storage on prepared foods containing protein concentrate. Food Technol. *30*(1), 56.

Krehl, W. A., and Winters, R. W. 1950. Effect of cooking method on retention of vitamins and minerals in vegetables. J. Am. Diet. Assoc. *26*, 966.

Kylen, A. M., McGrath, B. H., Hallmark, E. L., and Van Duyne, F. O. 1964. Microwave and conventional cooking of meat. J. Am. Diet. Assoc. *45*, 139.

Labuza, T. P. 1972. Nutrient losses during drying and storage of dehydrated foods. CRC Crit. Rev. Food Technol. *3*, 217.

Lachance, P. A. 1975. Effects of food preparation procedures on nutrient retention with emphasis upon food service practices. *In* Nutritional Evaluation of Food Processing. 2nd Edition, p. 463. R. S. Harris and E. Karmas (Editors). AVI Publishing Co., Westport, CT.

Lachance, P. A., and Erdman, J. W., Jr. 1975. Effects of home food preparation on nutrient content of food. *In* Nutritional Evaluation of Food Processing, 2nd Edition, p. 529. R. S. Harris and E. Karmas (Editors). AVI Publishing Company, Westport, CT.

Lachance, P. A., Ranadive, A. S., and Matas, J. 1973. Effects of reheating convenience foods. Food Technol. *27*(1), 36.

Lanier, J. J., and Sistrunk, W. A. 1979. Influence of cooking method on quality attributes and vitamin content of sweet potatoes. J. Food Sci. *44*, 374.

Lathrop, P. J., and Leung, H. K. 1980. Thermal degradation and leaching of vitamin C from green peas during processing. J. Food Sci. *45*, 995.

Lee, F. A. *et al.* 1950. Effect of freezing rate on meat. Appearance, palatability and vitamin content of beef. Food Res. *15*, 8.

Lee, F. A., *et al.* 1954. Effect of freezing rate on pork quality. Appearance, palatability and vitamin content. J. Am. Diet. Assoc. *30*, 351.

Lee, K., and Clydesdale, F. M. 1979. Quantitative determination of the elemental ferrous, ferric, soluble and complexed iron in foods. J. Food Sci. *44*, 549.

Lee, K., and Clydesdale, F. M. 1981. Effect of thermal processing on endogenous and added iron in canned spinach. J. Food Sci. *46*, 1064.

Lee, C. Y., Parsons, G. F., and Downing, D. L. 1982. Effects of processing on amino acid and mineral contents of peas. J. Food Sci. *47*, 1034.

Leverton, R. M., and Odell, G. V. 1959. The nutritive value of cooked meat. Oklahoma Agric. Exp. Stn. Misc. Publ. *MP-49.*

Liener, I. E., 1960. Effect of processing on cereal proteins. *In* Nutritional Evaluation of Food Processing. R. S. Harris and H. von Loescke (Editors). John Wiley, New York. Reprinted in 1971 by AVI Publishing Co., Westport, CT.

Liu, Y. K., and Luh, B. S. 1979. Effect of harvest maturity on free amino acids, pectins, ascorbic acid, total nitrogen and minerals in tomato pastes. J. Food Sci. *44*(2), 425.

Lund, D. B. 1979. Effect of commercial processing on nutrients. Food Technol. *33*, 28.

Lushbough, C. H., Weichman, J. M., and Schweigert, B. S. 1959. The retention of vitamin B_6 in meat during cooking. J. Nutr. *67*, 451.

Maeda, E. E., and Salunkhe, D. K. 1981. Retention of ascorbic acid and total carotene in solar dried vegetables. J. Food Sci. *46*, 1288.

Marsanija, I. I. 1970. Tr. Sukhum. Opytn. Stn. Efiromaslichn. Kul't. *9*, 49. Hort. Abstr. 1971 *41*, 1167.

Marshall, N. 1960. Electronic cookery of top round of beef. J. Home Econ. *52*, 31.

Matz, S. A. 1975. Effects of baking on nutrients. *In* Nutritional Evaluation of Food Processing. 2nd Edition. R. S. Harris and E. Karmas (Editors). AVI Publishing Co., Westport, CT.

Mayfield, H. L., and Hedrick, M. T. 1949. The effect of canning, roasting and corning on the biological value of the proteins of western beef, finished on the grass or grain. J. Nutr. *37*, 487–494.

McIntire, J. M., Schweigert, B. S., and Elvehjem, C. A. 1944. The choline and pyridoxine content of meats. J. Nutr. *28*, 219.

McIntosh, J. A., Tressler, D. K., and Fenton, F. 1942. Ascorbic acid content of five quick-frozen vegetables as affected by composition of cooking utensil and volume of cooking water. J. Home Econ. *34*, 314.

Meyer, B. H., Hinman, W. F., and Halliday, E. G. 1947. Retention of some vitamins of the B complex in beef during cooking. Food Res. *12*, 203.

Meyer, B. H., Mysinger, M. A., and Wodarski, L. A. 1969. Pantothenic acid and vitamin B_6 in beef. J. Am. Diet. Assoc. *54*, 122.

Mglinets, A. I., and Zheleznyak, K. D. 1980. Changes in the nutritional value of proteins during roasting. Vopr. Pitan. *3*, 74–75; Food Sci. Technol. Austr. 1981. *13*(11), 220.

Moleeratanond, W. 1978. Effect of fluctuating storage temperature on energy consumption and quality changes of palletized frozen peas, okra and strawberries. M.S. Thesis, Univ. Maryland, College Park.

Mondy, N. I., and Mueller, T. O. 1977. The effect of cooking methods on the lipid composition of potatoes. Amer. Potato J. *54*, 203.

Moore, L. J., Harrison, D. L., and Dayton, A. D. 1980. Differences among top round steaks cooked by dry or moist heat in a conventional or a microwave oven. J. Food Sci. *45*, 777.

Moran, T. 1959. Nutritional significance of recent work on wheat flour and bread. Nutr. Abstr. Rev. *29*, 1–16.

Morgan, A. F. 1960. Losses of nutrients in foods during home preparation. *In* Nutritional Evaluation of Food Processing. R. S. Harris and H. von Loescke (Editors). John Wiley, New York. Reprinted in 1971 by AVI Publishing Co., Westport, CT.

Morgan, A. F., and Frederick, H. 1935. Vitamin B(B_1) in bread as affected by baking. Cereal Chem. *12*, 390.

Morgan, A. F., *et al.* 1949. Thiamin, riboflavin and niacin content of chicken tissues as affected by cooking and frozen storage. Food Res. *14*, 439.

Moss, M., Ono, K., Cross, R., Holden, J., and Stewart, K. 1980. Nutrient retention in cooked retail cuts of beef, 40th Ann. Meeting, New Orleans.

Moyer, J. C., Robinson, W. B., Stolz, G. H., and Kertesz, Z. I. 1952. Effect of blanching and subsequent holding in some chemical constituents and enzyme activities in peas, snap beans and lima beans. New York Agric. Exp. Stn. Bull. *754*, Geneva, NY.

Munsell, H. E., *et al.* 1949. Effect of large-scale methods of preparation on the vitamin content of food. 3. Cabbage. J. Am. Diet. Assoc. *25*, 420.

Nagy, S. 1980. Vitamin C content of citrus fruit and their products: A review. J. Agric. Food Chem. *28*(1), 8–18.

Noble, I. 1967. Ascorbic acid and color of vegetables. J. Am. Diet. Assoc. *50*, 304.

Noble, I. 1970. Thiamin and riboflavin retention in cooked variety meats. J. Am. Diet. Assoc. *56*, 225.

Noble, I., and Gomez, L. 1958. Thiamin and riboflavin in roast lamb. J. Am. Diet. Assoc. *34*, 157.

Noble, I., and Gomez, L. 1960. Thiamin and riboflavin in roast beef. J. Am. Diet. Assoc. *36*, 46.

Noble, I., and Gomez, L. 1962. Vitamin retention in meat cooked electronically. J. Am. Diet. Assoc. *41*, 217.

Odland, D., and Eheart, M. S. 1975. Ascorbic acid, mineral and quality retention in frozen broccoli blanched in water, steam and ammonia–steam. J. Food Sci. *40*, 1004.

Olliver, M. 1943. Ascorbic acid values of fruits and vegetables for dietary surveys. Chem. Ind. *62*, 146.

Olson, O. E., Burris, R. H., and Elvehjem, C. A. 1947. A preliminary report of the folic acid content of certain foods. J. Am. Diet. Assoc. *23*, 200.

Page, E., and Hanning, F. M. 1963. Vitamin B_6 and niacin in potatoes. J. Am. Diet. Assoc. *42*, 42.

Patton, S. 1954. The mechanism of sunlight-flavor in formation in milk with special reference to methionine and riboflavin. J. Dairy Sci. *37*, 446.

Pearson, A. M., *et al.* 1951. Vitamin loss in drip obtained upon defrosting frozen meat. Food Res. *16*, 85.

Pearson, A. M., West, R. G., and Luecke, R. W. 1959. The vitamin and amino acid content of drip obtained upon defrosting frozen pork. Food Res. *24*, 515.

Pearson, P. B., and Luecke, R. W. 1945. The B-vitamin content of raw and cooked sweet potatoes. Food Res. *10*, 325.

Pennington, J. A. 1976. Dietary Nutrient Guide. AVI Publishing Co., Westport, CT.

Ranhotra, G. S. 1972. Hydrolysis during bread-making of phytic acid in wheat protein concentrate. J. Food Sci. *37*, 12.

Ranhotra, G. S., Loewe, R. J., and Puyat, L. V. 1974. Phytic acid in soy and its hydrolysis during bread-making. J. Food Sci. *39*, 1023.

Reimer, J., and Karel, M. 1977. Shelf-life studies of vitamin C during food storage. Prediction of L-ascorbic acid retention in dehydrated tomato juice. Food Proc. Pres. *1*, 293–312.

Reitz, H. J., and Koo, R. C. J. 1960. Proc. Am. Soc. Hort. Sci. *75*, 244.

Rice, E. E., and Robinson, H. E. 1944. Nutritive value of canned and dehydrated meat and meat products. Am. J. Public Health *34*, 487–492.

Richardson, J. E., Davis, R., and Mayfield, H. L. 1937. Vitamin C content of potatoes prepared for table use by various methods of cooking. Food Res. *2*, 85.

Rosenberg, H. R., and Rohdenburg, E. L. 1951. The fortification of bread with lysine. 1. The loss of lysine during baking. J. Nutr. *45*, 593.

Rosenbloom, N. J., and Potter, N. N. 1981. Effects of processing on zinc levels in spinach, beef and potatoes. J. Food Sci. *46*, 1707.

Rudra, M. N. 1937. Studies in vitamin C. The effects of cooking and storage on the vitamin C contents of foodstuffs. J. Indian Med. Res. *25*, 89.

Rushing, N. B., and Senn, V. J. 1964. Effect of preservatives and storage temperature on shelf life of chilled citrus salads. Food Technol. *16*, 77–79.

Sabry, Z. I. 1969. The nutritional consequences of development of food processing. Can. J. Public Health. *59*, 471.

Salunkhe, D. K., Pao, S. K., and Dull, G. G. 1973. Assessment of nutritive value, quality and stability of cruciferous vegetables during storage and subsequent to processing. CRC Crit. Rev. Food Technol. *4*(1), 1–38.

Schroeder, H. A. 1971. Losses of vitamins and trace minerals resulting from processing and preservation of foods. Am. J. Clin. Nutr. *24*, 562.

Schweigert, B. S., and Guthneck, B. T. 1953. Liberation and measurement of pantothenic acid in animal tissue. J. Nutr. *51*, 283.

Schweigert, B. S., and Lushbough, C. H. 1960. *In* Nutritional Evaluation of Food Processing, pp. 261–277. R. S. Harris and H. von Loescke (Editors). John Wiley, New York.

Schweigert, B. S., Nielson, E., McIntire, J. M., and Elvehjem, C. A. 1943. Biotin content of meat and meat products. J. Nutr. *26*, 65.

Singh, R. P., Heldman, D. R., and Kirk, J. R. 1975. Kinetic analysis of light-induced riboflavin loss in whole milk. J. Food Sci. *40*(1), 164–167.

Sites, J. W., and Reitz, H. J. 1951. Proc. Am. Soc. Hort. Sci. *56*, 103.

Slavin, J. W. 1963. Freezing and cold storage. *In* Industrial Fishing Technology, p. 288. M. E. Stansby and J. A. Dassow (Editors). Reinhold Publishing, New York.

Smith, P. F. 1969. *In* Proceedings First Int. Citrus Symposium, p. 1559. H. D. Chapman (Editor). Univ. California Press, Riverside.

Smith, P. F., and Rasmussen, G. K. 1960. Proc. Florida State Hort. Soc. *73*, 42.

Smith, P. F., and Rasmussen, G. K. 1961. Proc. Florida State Hort. Soc. *74*, 32.

Srncová, W., and Davidek, J. 1972. Reaction of pyridoxal and pyridoxal-5-phosphate with proteins. J. Food Sci. *37*, 310–312.

Sweeney, J. P., Gilpin, G. L., Martin, M. E., and Dawson, E. H. 1960. Palatability and nutritive value of frozen broccoli. J. Am. Diet. Assoc. *36*, 122.

Tara, K. H., Usha, M. S. M., and Bains, G. S. 1972. Effects of lysine on dough and protein quality of whole wheat meal chapatis and leavened bread. J. Agric. Food Chem. *20*(1), 116.

Thomas, M. H., and Calloway, D. H. 1961. Nutritional value of dehydrated foods. J. Am. Diet. Assoc. *39*, 105–116.

Thomas, M. H., Brenner, S., Eaton, A., and Craig, V. 1949. Effect of electronic cooking on nutritive value of foods. J. Am. Diet. Assoc. *45*, 139.

Toepfer, E. W., Pritchett, C. A., and Hewston, E. M. 1955. Boneless beef: Raw, cooked and stewed. Results of analysis for moisture, protein, fat and ash. Bull. *1137*, U.S. Department of Agriculture, Washington, DC.

Tsen, C. C., and Reddy, P. R. K. 1977. Effect of toasting on the nutritive value of bread. J. Food Sci. *42*(5), 1370.

Tsen, C. C., Bates, L. S., Wall, L. L., Sr. and Gehnke, C. W. 1982. Effect of baking on amino acids in pizza crust. J. Food Sci. *47*, 674.

U.S. Department of Agriculture (USDA) 1971. Textured vegetable protein products (B_1) to be used in combination with meat in lunches and suppers served under child feeding program. USDA, FNS Notice *219*.

U.S. Department of Agriculture (USDA) 1980. Nationwide food consumption survey results. Family Econ. Rev. Spring, 4–10.

U.S. Department of the Interior 1955. Compilation of laboratory data: Yields and losses in preparation of foods. U.S. Fish and Wildlife Service Mimeo.

Van der Laan, P. J., and Van der MijllDekker. 1945. Voeding 6, 128.

Van Duyne, F. O., Chase, J. T., and Simpson, J. I. 1944. Effects of various home practices on ascorbic acid content of cabbage. Food Res. 9, 1.

Watada, A. E., Aulenbach, B. B., and Worthington, J. T. 1976. Vitamins A and C in ripe tomatoes as affected by stage of ripeness at harvest and by supplementing ethylene. J. Food Sci. 41, 850.

Watt, B. K., and Merrill, A. L. 1963. Composition of foods. . . Raw, processed and prepared. In Agriculture Handbook 8. U.S. Department of Agriculture, Washington, DC.

Westerman, B. D., Vail, G. E., Tinklin, G. L., and Smith, J. 1949. Food Technol. 3, 184.

Wilcox, E. B., and Galloway, L. S. 1952. The B vitamins in raw and cooked lamb. Food Res. 17, 67.

Wing, R. W., and Alexander, J. C. 1972. Effect of microwave heating on vitamin B_6 retention in chicken. J. Am. Diet. Assoc. 61, 661.

Woolridge, M. D. 1974. Microwave cooking of frozen pork using plastic film. Ph.D. dissertation, Purdue Univ., W. Lafayette, IN.

Wood, M. A., Collings, A. R., Stadola, Burgoin, A. M., and Fenton, F. 1946. Effect of large-scale food preparation on vitamin retention in cabbage. J. Am. Diet. Assoc. 22, 677.

Zaehringer, M. V., and Personius, C. J. 1949. Thiamin retention in bread and rolls baked to different degrees of brownness. Cereal Chem. 26, 384.

Zepplin, M., and Elvehjem, C. A. 1944. Effect of refrigeration on retention of ascorbic acid in vegetables. Food Res. 9, 100–111.

Part 5

Nutrification, Legal Aspects, and Nutrient Analysis

22

Addition of Vitamins, Minerals, and Amino Acids to Foods

Benjamin Borenstein
Howard T. Gordon

In the context of this chapter, fortification is a generic term for the addition to foods of vitamins, minerals, and amino acids for the purpose of nutritional improvement. The emphasis here is on vitamins, since the bulk of the literature is in this area.

The technology of fortification involves the selection of the in-process point for addition of micronutrients, the mode of addition, and the market forms of the micronutrients. These decisions are dependent on a number of interrelated factors, including stability, bioavailability, organoleptic problems, safety, cost, production practicality, and the reliability of the system. An important ancillary capability is analytical methodology for micronutrients at the low concentration found in foods.

STABILITY

Vitamin stability results are so dependent on the process specifics and the specific micronutrient market forms used that extrapolation to other applications should not be made without detailed knowledge of the process and product. The influence of temperature, moisture, pH, and so on can be critical. For example, Beetner *et al.* (1974), in studying stability of added vitamins B_1 and B_2 during extrusion of corn grits, found that a temperature increase in the extruder of 22°C caused a 21% lower vitamin B_1 retention and that increasing moisture of the grits by 1.5% decreased vitamin B_2 retention by 21%. This type of specific processing data is obviously highly desirable in studying forti-fication problems. Similarly, even though the kinetics approach to predicting stability of vitamins in foods was used at least as early as 1948, this type of data is rarely published except in model systems. An excellent article on the thermal destruction of folic acid added to model systems and to low pH foods with kinetics data is available (Mnkeni and Beveridge 1982). Prediction of nutrient losses from a mathematical point of view is reviewed by Karel (1979).

Several reviews of fortification technology and related stability problems are available (Borenstein 1971, 1974). The mechanics of fortification of rice, wheat, and salt with vitamins and amino acids was discussed by Rubin and Cort (1969). The properties and stability of indigenous and added vitamins and amino acids during food processing has been reviewed (Borenstein 1972). A comprehensive survey of food applications of vitamin A is available (Bauernfeind and Cort 1974). Nutrient stability of cereal products fortified with seven vitamins and four minerals was evaluated by Cort et al. (1976).

The more labile vitamins, which can present stability problems in food processing and storage, are vitamins A, D, B_1, C, pantothenic acid, vitamin B_{12}, and folacin. Although serious degradation of these vitamins can be encountered under adverse conditions, measures can be employed to minimize losses. These include protective coating of individual vitamins, addition of antioxidants, control of temperature, moisture, and pH, and protection from air, light, and incompatible metals during processing and storage. By applying appropriate technology and using a suitable manufacturing overage of added vitamins based on a critical evaluation of stability data, it is possible in most food applications to maintain desired label claims for the normal shelf life of food products. Overages above label claim are essential, even in fortification with stable micronutrients, due to analytical, distribution, and sampling errors.

The stability of added micronutrients generally parallels the stability of indigenous food micronutrients., Differences, however, can occur in the case of vitamins B_1, B_6, A, and E.

Vitamin B_6 occurs in food primarily as pyridoxal, pyridoxamine, and pyridoxine. Of these, pyridoxal is the least stable, and vitamin B_6 added in the form of pyridoxine hydrochloride is more stable than native pyridoxal in heat stress processes. Kinetics data for the loss of B_6 vitamers in dehydrated model systems at 37°C is shown in Table 22.1 (Gregory and Kirk 1978).

Similarly, thiamin is more stable than thiamin pyrophosphate, which may account for over 50% of the native vitamin B_1 in specific foods. Vitamin E occurs in nature primarily as α-tocopherol, which is highly reactive compared to α-tocopheryl acetate, the most widely used synthetic analog of vitamin E.

Vitamin A occurs in animal source foods primarily as retinyl palmitate and as provitamin A carotenoids in plant products. β-Carotene is the most important indigenous provitamin A carotenoid, both because of its high provitamin A value and its widespread occurrence in foods. In plant products the provitamin A carotenoids are stable (≥85% retention

Table 22.1. Kinetics Data for the Loss of the B_6 Vitamins from Dehydrated Model Systems during Storage at $37°C$

	k^a (days^{-1})	$t_{1/2}{}^b$ (days)
Pyridoxal	0.0170	41
Pyridoxine		
Days 0–58	NMD^c	—
After 58 days	0.0049	141
Pyridoxamine	0.0200	35

Source: Adapted from Gregory and Kirk (1978).
^{a} First-order rate constant.
^{b} Half-life.
^{c} No measurable degradation.

in most food products and processes. A notable exception is the poor stability of carotenoids in freeze-dried carrots exposed to air during storage.

Vitamin A esters and β-carotene added to foods may oxidize quickly during processing and storage of many products. Therefore, most food applications require coated and/or antioxidant-stabilized market forms of these compounds to obtain adequate stability during product storage. Many market forms for specific vitamin A fortification applications have been commercialized. An important example is a spray-dried, stabilized vitamin A palmitate product specifically developed for flour and bread fortification. Applications of this product were thoroughly investigated by Parrish *et al.* at Kansas State University. Distribution and stability in flour, flour handling, shipping, and storage were satisfactory for commercial needs (Parrish *et al.* 1980A). Excellent stability was reported in white pan bread, corn bread, corn mush, cakes, pancakes, and spaghetti (Parrish *et al.* 1980B). Retention of vitamin A during baking (or other processing) of these products was generally $\geqslant 90\%$ when processed with flours stored less than 6 months. When these products were stored at room temperature for 5–6 days, retention was 72–108%. Vitamin A stability in corn curls fortified via corn flour was unsatisfactory. Corn curls can be satisfactorily fortified by addition of vitamin A and other vitamins postextrusion. Biopotency and bioavailability of the vitamin A in fortified flour after accelerated storage at $40–45°C$ was excellent (Liu and Parrish 1979).

The difficulty of predicting vitamin C stability in food systems is demonstrated in model systems studies by Yu *et al.* (1974), who reported that all amino acids except cysteine reacted with ascorbic acid, resulting in more pronounced color formation than when ascorbic acid was present alone. Cysteine protected ascorbic acid against the formation of the brown pigment. Tryptophan enhanced the browning of ascorbic acid more than the other amino acids. At 72°C, color development caused by ascorbic acid plus tryptophan was further enhanced by the addition of malic acid, citric acid, $FeSO_4$, $CuSO_4$, and Na_2HPO_4, but color formation was reduced by fumaric acid, tartaric acid, succinic acid, calcium salts, bisulfite, tetrasodium pyrophosphate, sodium tripolyphosphate, sodium tetraphosphate, sodium metaphosphate, and sodium polyphosphate.

The comparative stability of vitamin C in beverages reconstituted and stored under home usage conditions was studied by Beston and Henderson (1974) to determine differences in vitamin C stability between orange juice from frozen concentrate, canned orange juice, and formulated beverage powders. Stability curves for 96 hr at 42°F (5.5°C) were very similar for all products.

The effect on ascorbic acid retention in orange juice of the type of container used (glass, polyethylene, polystyrene, or cardboard) was studied by Bissett and Berry (1975), who confirmed the superiority of glass over oxygen-permeable materials. The significance of container packaging materials on vitamin stability is also shown in a kinetics analysis of light-induced riboflavin loss in whole milk (Singh *et al.* 1975). Exposure of enriched macaroni packaged in transparent bags to fluorescent light, 50–250 fc for 7 days, caused riboflavin losses of 30–35% (Furuya and Warthesen 1984).

The stability of added vitamins in canned fruits and vegetables generally parallels the stability pattern of the naturally occurring vitamins in the same products. Processing plus long-term storage of canned and frozen vegetables can be expected to degrade significant amounts (20–50%) of vitamins C, B_1, and B_2 (Guerrant and O'Hara 1953). Although frozen products have a higher initial vitamin C content than canned, storage of 9–12 months tends to equalize the vitamin C levels because of oxidation of ascorbic acid in oxygen-permeable containers even at 0°C. Thus, packaging of frozen foods becomes an important variable in vitamin C stability

Equally important is the difference in vitamin C stability during storage of vegetables processed in tin versus glass (Guerrant and O'Hara 1953). The dissolved stannous ion in canned products is an effective reducing agent and significantly retards ascorbic acid degradation.

The stability of reduced and total ascorbic acid has been studied in a low moisture dehydrated model food system as a function of water activity, moisture content, oxygen content of the container, and temperature (Dennison and Kirk 1978). The kinetics data obtained substantiate prior empirical conclusions that the headspace oxygen dissolves rapidly as the oxygen in the moisture phase of the product is consumed by reaction with ascorbic acid. Headspace oxygen accelerates ascorbic degradation at a water activity as low as 0.1 a_w.

Table 22.2. Stability of Ascorbic Acid in Orange Drink Circulated by a Jet Spray Dispenser

	mg/8 fl oz	Retention (%)
Initial	100	—
8 hr	77	77
24 hr	76	76
48 hr	62	62

Source: DeRitter and Metzner (1978).

Table 22.3. Stability of Ascorbic Acid in Apple Sauce[a]

	mg/3 av. oz		Retention (%)	
	Refrigerated	Freezer	Refrigerated	Freezer
Initial	86	86	—	—
1 week	86	NR	100	—
2 weeks	81	NR	94	—
3 weeks	68[b]	NR	79	—
1 month	75[c]	83	87	97
2 months	NR	75	—	87
3 months	NR	78	—	91

Source: Gordon and Gerenz (1982).
[a] Not run.
[b] Sample gaseous and container ballooned.
[c] Container ballooned and white mold on surface of apple sauce.

A comprehensive review on the problems of incorporating vitamin C in baked goods is available (Seib and Hosney 1974).

In an unpublished study of a vitamin C-fortified orange drink, the beverage was circulated in a commercial jet spray unit continuously for 48 hr. The results are presented in Table 22.2 (DeRitter and Metzner 1978). In another study, single-service 3 oz plastic containers of apple sauce fortified with ascorbic acid showed the stability results reported in Table 22.3 (Gordon and Gerenz 1982).

In evaluating the stability of added nutrients, it is important that factors such as market form, processing/storage conditions, moisture level, product pH, other ingredients, and type of container be considered.

Insistence on detailed information surrounding the product, its production/handling, and its storage is not frivolous. It is needed in order to make a proper judgment on the true stability of a nutrient in a given food product or, inversely, the reasons for nutrient losses in a given product.

For instance, Bookwalter *et al.* (1980) has shown the superior stability of ethyl cellulose-coated ascorbic acid over uncoated ascorbic acid

Table 22.4.   Storage Stability of Ascorbic Acid Added to Prune Juice

| | After 11 months at room temperature | |
Addition Rate (mg/6 fl oz)	Assay (mg/6 fl oz)	Retention (%)
78	13	17
120	30	25
200	64	32

Source: Gordon and Cort (1979).

Table 22.5.   Stability of Ascorbic Acid Added to Cookies via the Dough (mg/cookie)

| | Oatmeal | | Sugar | |
Addition rate	Assay	Retention (%)	Assay	Retention (%)
78	50.4	65	66.7	86
96	80.1	83	72.6	76
114	88	77	87.3	77

Source: Gordon and Borenstein (1982).

in heat-treated CSM (corn–soy–milk formulated dry food). However, without proper attention to all variables, we would not have learned that the most significant factor in the rate of destruction was the moisture level in the product rather than the heat treatment process step.

The level of addition, that is, concentration of vitamin C, is also an important variable, as shown in a prune juice study (Table 22.4) (Gordon and Cort 1979).

Unexpectedly good vitamin C stability results were obtained in baking cookies (Table 22.5) (Gordon and Borenstein 1982).

BIOAVAILABILITY

In almost all cases, commercial synthetic vitamins are chemically and biologically identical to naturally occurring vitamins. In the most important exception, vitamin E, potency is expressed in biological units to account for the differences in biopotency between analogs and optical isomers.

Bioavailability, in the context of this discussion, is the percentage of the ingested dose that is absorbed still in a biologically active form. In the case of vitamin A, for example, the trans isomer could be isomerized to lower biological potency cis isomers in the intestinal tract and then be absorbed. The bioavailability of spray-dried vitamin A palmitate in stored flour was demonstrated by Liu and Parrish (1979).

Vitamins indigenous to food are not absorbed completely. This is due to poor solubility of specific vitamins, destruction of specific vitamins in the gastrointestinal tract, the occurrence of vitamins in bound form in specific foods, and the poor digestibility of specific foods.

For example, foods containing higher glutamate conjugates of folic acid have poorer bioavailability than foods containing the monoconjugate, folic acid, which happens to be the article of commerce. The addition of folic acid to foods, unless it becomes bound in an indigestible form, should result in bioavailability as good as or better than that of indigenous folate in foods.

The concern that an added vitamin may become bound and, hence, less available can be dispelled in those cases where the analytical extraction procedure indicates ready solubility or extractability in water. This important principle has received little attention by nutritionists.

The available data base on absorption of vitamins added to foods demonstrates absorption equivalent to that of indigenous vitamins. The bioavailability of synthetic and natural ascorbic acid provided by orange juice was very similar (Pelletier and Keith 1974). The slight superiority of synthetic L-ascorbic acid in this study was explained by a slightly higher urinary excretion of the vitamin after consuming orange juice.

In the case of β-carotene, absorption is probably superior from fortified foods. The intestinal absorption of provitamin A carotenoids from foods such as carrots is less than 30%, and it was suggested by the Food and Nutrition board (FNB) (1980) that the average absorption of food carotenoids be calculated as one-third of the provitamins ingested compared with retinol, which is assumed to be completely absorbed. Since 1 IU of vitamin A activity is equivalent to 0.3 μg retinol and 0.6 μg β-carotene, the overall utilization (intestinal absorption plus convertibility of β-carotene to retinol) of indigenous β-carotene is calculated as one-sixth that of retinol by the FNB.

On the other hand, crystalline β-carotene dissolved in margarine is absorbed as well as the U.S. Pharmacopeia vitamin A standard and has a provitamin A activity of 1.66 million units/g (Marusich et al. 1957). Therefore, the calculation suggested by the FNB for determining the retinol equivalent of β-carotene in foods is inappropriate for β-carotene added in fortification.

TECHNOLOGY OF ADDITION

Fruit and Vegetable Products

The technological problems in fortification are best demonstrated by considering fruit and vegetable products. This large group of foods is diverse chemically, physically (e.g., corn-on-the-cob, diced carrots, sliced string beans, juices, and purees), and in processing technology (e.g., frozen, canned, dehydrated, blanched, refrigerated, concentrated, or fried). Newer technologies such as asceptic packaging and retort pouches, which decrease the exposure of food products to heat, tend to improve stability of the more labile vitamins.

Each food product in each form poses its own potential technological difficulties. For example, a fortification technique for canned corn kernels with lysine or other water-soluble nutrients would require careful development to ensure that most of the lysine is not in the canning liquid and, thus, discarded by the consumer when used. On the other hand, with cream-style corn there is no problem of distribution of nutrients between particles and a liquid phase likely to be discarded. Fortification of corn products with iron could cause the formation of iron sulfides, which seriously discolor corn products. The addition of insoluble iron salts might circumvent this problem; however, they are not generally favored by nutritionists.

Fortification of particulate canned foods with any and all nutrients is difficult because of the distribution of nutrients between the particles and the canning liquid, and the potential waste and deception of the water-soluble vitamins being discarded by the consumer. In theory, it is easier to fortify frozen than canned vegetables. A spray solution or suspension of nutrients can be applied to frozen food products directly at the packaging line and the losses during frozen storage would be moderate for most of the vitamins. The losses during home preparation will also be moderate as long as the weight ratio of cooking liquid:solids is low and controlled.

Small-particle dehydrated fruits and vegetables (40–200 mesh) are relatively easy to fortify, since all the commercial vitamins, amino acids, and minerals are available in dry market forms in this particle size range. Blended foods containing dehydrated vegetables (e.g., soup mixes with seasonings or salt) are easy to fortify with respect to distribution of the added nutrients. Stability of nutrients in dehydrated foods is greatly dependent on moisture content. Vitamin C can both discolor and degrade at high relative humidity in dehydrated foods. Nitrogen flushing of packaged, dehydrated foods improves vitamin C stability. Stable forms of vitamin A for fortification of dehydrated foods are available. Stability of most of the other vitamins in dehydrated foods is satisfactory.

Vitamin C stability in canned foods is dependent on pH and reactants present. Anthocyanins, iron, and copper accelerate vitamin C degradation. For example, the high levels of both anthocyanins and iron in prune juice cause very rapid degradation of added vitamin C. Vitamin B_2 is unstable in glass packs exposed to light. Vitamins B_1 and B_{12} have poor stability at high pH. Vitamin B_1 added to a high-pH (10.4) tortilla was almost completely destroyed during baking (Gordon

1978). Vitamin B_1 can cause off-flavor in some fruit and vegetable products, but the threshold flavor level is dependent on the specific food. The flavor of vitamin B_1 is due to trace amounts of sulfhydryl compounds caused by degradation and off-odors can be produced by almost immeasurable destruction of vitamin B_1. In the case of vegetables, vitamin B_1 can also catalyze pyruvic acid degradation to acetoin, which produces off-flavors.

Apple sauce has been commercially fortified with vitamin C by metering an ascorbic acid solution directly into the cooker. It is also theoretically possible to meter an ascorbic acid solution into glass or tin containers prior to filling with sauce. The limiting factor in this approach is the rate of diffusion of ascorbic acid throughout the container. It is essential that there be sufficient agitation during the filling, sealing, and cooling operations plus diffusion during the first 2–4 weeks of storage to produce reasonable distribution of vitamin C throughout the container so that each serving of sauce meets the label claim.

Particulate Dry Foods

Dry-mix fortification presents minimal technological problems. For example, the reliability of fortifying flour by continuous metering of a dry, free-flowing premix into flour streams was shown by Fortmann *et al.* (1974), who took flour samples at 15–min intervals while processing a carload (1000 cwt) of bulk flour at a flour mill. The flour was then resampled at the bakery as it was fed from the bakery storage bins into the dough mixers. The vitamin B_1 varied from 2.31 to 2.56 mg/lb and vitamin B_2 from 1.25 to 1.34 mg/lb in 14 samples at the bakery. Reduced iron analyses were equally satisfactory, ranging from 15.3 to 16.4 mg/lb of flour. Stability of micronutrient premixes per se and in flour was reviewed by Cort *et al.* (1976).

Dehydrated Potato Flakes

It is more difficult to fortify large-particle products such as dehydrated potato flakes or breakfast cereal flakes than it is flour, cake mixes, and other fine-particle dry products. Dehydrated potato flakes can be fortified at the mash stage prior to dehydration. However, two problems exist in this procedure, namely vitamins degradation of vitamins A and C and "pinking." Degradation of vitamins A and C is primarily an economic problem, since high overages can be used to make up for process losses. Pinking is an unpredictable problem due to vitamin C. Apparently, ascorbate reacts with potato protein causing a pink Schiff-base compound. Pinking occurs erratically and takes time to appear after dehydration. Oxygen is necessary for this reaction, since nitrogen flush-packaged flakes do not pink until opened and exposed to air.

Flake fortification after dehydration with dry vitamins presents the serious problem of vitamin segregation in the retail package. This problem was solved in a patented process by Pedersen and Sautier (1974). "Vitamin flakes" of approximately the same size and shape as potato flakes are mixed with the potato flakes and are nonsegregating and difficult to detect visually. These vitamin flakes are actually 50–75% fat, mp 110°–165°F, containing water-soluble vitamins and minerals. The stability data on vitamins C, B_1, B_2, and niacin shown in this patent are satisfactory. It is essential in this approach that the vitamin flakes be added uniformly to the potato flakes and that they be organoleptically satisfactory.

Breakfast Cereals

A different approach to the same type of physical distribution problem was used by Duvall and Stone (1974) for the fortification of ready-to-eat cereals. In their process a precooked cereal is coated with a sugar solution, dried, and then coated with dry vitamins while the cereal is hot and tacky. In this patent the preferred procedure is the use of fat-coated vitamins to prevent formation of undesirable flavors and to enhance vitamin adherence to the cereal particles.

Heat-labile vitamins such as B_1, C, and A are usually sprayed onto toasted breakfast cereals as they leave the oven. Emulsions (or water-dispersible solutions) of vitamin A can be sprayed onto breakfast cereals after toasting, but stability during product storage is greatly dependent upon the composition of the spray solution. A high carbohydrate level in the spray solutions is desirable. Added sugars, in effect, coat the vitamin A and act as an oxygen barrier during cereal storage. Losses during process and cereal storage cannot be specified because of the large number of vitamin A market forms available, and cereal product and process variables. Vitamin A overages above label claim would usually be 30–50% for ready-to-eat cereals.

If a product is to be fortified with both vitamins A and D, it is best to add vitamin D at the same stage as vitamin A. The vitamin D market form should be similar in composition and stability to the vitamin A market form so that the vitamin A stability profile can be used to monitor vitamin D. This is desirable because of the poor accuracy of vitamin D assays at food fortification levels. Modern high-performance liquid chromatography has greatly improved analysis of vitamins in food, but vitamin D analysis is still difficult.

Tea

Spraying particulate foods to optimize distribution of added fortificants was recommended by Brooke and Cort (1972) for fortification of tea leaves, as distinct from tea dust, with vitamin A. In this study, oil-in-water emulsions of vitamin A palmitate or acetate, diluted in 50% sucrose solution and sprayed on tea leaves, resulted in 90% retention after 6 months of storage at $37°C$. This is excellent stability for vitamin A, substantiating the fact that coating vitamin A in situ with carbohydrates improves stability. A further stress for vitamin A in this application is the tea-brewing step. Brooke and Cort (1972) reported 100% retention of vitamin A palmitate after cooking tea for 1 hr in boiling water, but only 4% retention using the vitamin A acetate emulsion-spray system. This large differential in stability between the two esters was not explained.

Textured Soy Protein

Textured soy proteins can usually be fortified either before or after granulation, or "texturization," of the soy flour, following the processor's personal preference as to production ease and control. The two major concerns in soy fortification are uniformity of distribution of the added micronutrients and compliance with label claims. Micronutrient requirements for these products issued by the U.S. Department of Agriculture (USDA) (1982) include magnesium, iron, zinc, calcium, phosphorus, vitamins A, B_1, B_2, B_6, B_{12}, niacin, pantothenic acid, and folate. The most stable vitamin in this specification is niacin. Riboflavin and vitamin B_6 are somewhat less stable, and vitamins A, B_1, B_{12}, and calcium pantothenate present the highest potential losses.

A convenient way to monitor fortification and improve physical distribution in soy fortification is to premix all the micronutrients, thus adding 50–100 mg of premixed ingredients to 100 g of soy protein, instead of each ingredient separately. This premix can be added directly to the soy flour before granulation by batch mixing, continuous metering, or with the "dough water," if the production process and equipment lends itself to this approach. The major concern when the premix is added prior to texturizing is stability during processing. The short processing time required to texturize with heat, pressure, and high moisture does not significantly degrade vitamins B_1, B_{12}, and pantothenic acid in the authors' experience.

The nutritional requirements for protein products established by the USDA Food and Nutrition Service are for protein products used as partial replacement of meat, poultry, or seafood in meals served under the National School Lunch Program, Summer Food Service Program for Children, and the Child Care Food Program. While the regulations refer generically to vegetable protein products, only soy protein products have, thus far, found their way into this market.

The nutritional specifications for these products cover protein level, protein efficiency ratio (PER), product hydration and product use

Table 22.6. USDA Micronutrient Requirements for Protein Products

	Per gram protein
Vitamin A	13 0 IU
Thiamin	0.02 mg
Riboflavin	0.01 mg
Niacin	0.3 mg
Pantothenic acid	0.04 mg
Vitamin B_6	0.02 mg
Vitamin B_{12}	0.1 μg
Iron	0.15 mg
Magnesium	1.15 mg
Zinc	0.5 mg
Copper	24.0 μg
Potassium	17.0 mg

Source: USDA (1982).

rate, as well as stipulating the levels of nutrients per gram of protein (USDA 1982) shown in Table 22.6.

The nutrient requirements are designed by USDA to provide nutritional equivalence with raw ground beef containing a maximum of 30% fat and to meet the nutrient profile proposed by the Food and Drug Administration (FDA) in their tentative final regulations for vegetable protein products.

One of the most interesting aspects of these regulations is the adjustment in the zinc level to compensate for the inhibiting effect the phytate found in vegetable protein products has on zinc absorption.

Based on a number of studies and plant trials, fortification of protein products to meet USDA nutrient requirements can successfully be achieved with relative ease by utilizing a vitamin–mineral premix designed with both USDA specifications and the product's processing parameters in mind.

Unfortunately, this may require a manufacturer to use different premixes if different protein products are produced by significantly differing processing procedures, unless the producer is willing to slightly "overfortify" some of his products in order to enjoy the advantage of only needing one premix.

Because of the extremely low vitamin profile of the unfortified protein product, one or two vitamin premixes could probably be used industrywide. The apparent stumbling block to this approach is that there is no industry agreement on the baseline levels of vitamins present.

Some processors may prefer to add the micronutrients to the finished textured protein via a spray of the premix suspended in vegetable oil.

In this approach, uniformity of addition is the most serious problem and requires careful engineering and control of the spray system.

The natural mineral content of soy protein is relatively high, and it is desirable to make a conservative calculation of these levels and adjust the fortification addition levels accordingly. For example, soy protein contains well over the 57 mg magnesium/100 g level proposed by the FDA and there is no reason to add magnesium to comply with this specification.

MINERALS

The technical problems in mineral fortification pertain more to organoleptic deficits and bioavailability than to stability of the compounds per se or to methods of incorporation in foods. Large amounts of calcium and magnesium salts are required to obtain nutritionally significant levels of these minerals, and their compounds; for example, tribasic calcium phosphate, calcium sulfate, and magnesium oxide can produce chalky flavors, opacity, sediment, and color changes in food products. Furthermore, little is known about the bioavailability of these compounds to man (as opposed to laboratory animals). Their poor solubility suggests poor absorption compared to soluble salts such as calcium gluconate, but soluble calcium salts cannot be used in most food applications because of the reactivity and undesirable flavor of calcium ions. The absorption of the more insoluble calcium salts probably decreases as a person ages, at least for those individuals who become hypochloric resulting in higher stomach pH.

The recommendation by the FNB that all cereal grain products be fortified with magnesium, calcium, iron, and zinc led to increased research on their bioavailability as it relates to fortification technology. The American Institute of Baking investigated the bioavailability of various zinc and magnesium compounds and their effect on bread-making characteristics. Zinc absorption by rats from zinc acetate, stearate, chloride, oxide, and sulfate did not differ much from one another. None of the zinc sources tested (2.2 mg zinc/100 g flour) exerted any adverse effect on loaf volume or on general bread quality (Ranhotra et al. 1977). Absorption of zinc from different dietary sources by women was studied by two techniques, which did not agree with each other (Swanson et al. 1983).

The absorption of magnesium from a variety of compounds did not differ significantly from each other (Ranhotra et al. 1976A) but magnesium oxide, hydroxide, and carbonate (44.1 mg magnesium/100 g flour) raised bread pH and adversely affected loaf volume and flavor (Ranhotra et al. 1976B). This was partially corrected by either pH adjustment with acetic acid or adding the magnesium salt to the dough instead of the sponge in the sponge–dough process. The relative bio-availability of magnesium from breads fortified with minerals or soy protein was recently reported (Winterringer and Ranhotra 1983). Magnesium absorption from leafy vegetables was 40–60% in a recent study (Schwartz *et al.* 1984).

Both iron and copper compounds catalyze oxidation of fat, vitamin A, and vitamin C. Fortification with these minerals requires thorough evaluation of possible organoleptic changes and effects on product shelf life.

The iron source may not be the critical absorption factor in specific fortification situations. Schricker and Miller (1982) compared the relative iron availability or eight iron fortification sources and concluded that meal composition had a greater influence than the iron form. For the technologist, this is good news as, generally, the more available ferrous iron forms are the most reactive and may cause a number of technological problems such as catalyzing fat oxidation, destroying vitamin C, and causing product discoloration. These problems are generally avoided when ferric orthophosphate or elemental iron are used. There is also the possibility that ferric iron will be partly con-verted to ferrous during storage in liquid products which, one might argue, provides the best of both worlds.

The bioavailability of iron is an active research area. Gastrointestinal absorption of iron depends on a number of variables, including the oxidation state of the iron (Fe, Fe^{2+}, or Fe^{3+}), whether the iron is bound to organic compounds, the type of binding, the redox poten-tial and pH of the gastrointestinal tract, and the specific anions in the food or foods consumed simultaneously. Rat experiments with ferric chloride indicated that lumen pH may be the most important variable effecting absorption of ferric salts. Within 5 min of adding an acid solution of ferric chloride directly into tied-off intestinal segments in vivo, the lumen pH rose above pH 4, where ferric ion is insoluble, and mucosal iron uptake ceased. Addition of ascorbate to the same solu-tion prevented the cessation of iron uptake despite the pH rise (Hunger-ford and Linder 1983).

In effect, meal components enter an equilibrium pool, which deter-mines the ratio of $Fe^{2+}:Fe^{3+}$ present and the rate of iron absorption. Factors which shift the ratio to Fe^{3+} and increase the formation of ferric hydroxide decrease absorption; reducing agents and ions, which form soluble iron chelates, increase the iron absorption rate. Ascorbic acid is particularly effective as shown in numerous human studies (Hallberg *et al.* 1982). Hallberg and Rossander (1984) reported on several approaches to increase iron absorption from Latin American meals (maize, rice, and black beans). Nonheme iron absorption from the basal meal was 3.6% compared to 8.5% with meat added, 6% with added ferrous sulfate, 9.5–10.5% with ascorbic acid (50–65 mg) added, 5% with added soy flour, and surprisingly, only 1.4% with citric acid added. Insoluble compounds such as iron phytates and oxalates are poorly absorbed. Meal composition greatly effects iron absorption since so many compounds can effect iron solution chemistry. Heme iron is well absorbed, perhaps as high as 35% in deficient subjects.

AMINO ACIDS

As a generalization, the first nutritionally limiting amino acids for humans in cereal grains is lysine. Most studies, however, show that cereal grains also require the addition of the second limiting amino acid (tryptophan or threonine) to approach the protein quality of animal protein.

Although synthetic lysine and methionine (and methionine analogs) are widely used in animal nutrition, primarily in monogastric species, fortification of human foods with amino acids is not widely practiced. L-Lysine monohydrochloride is commercially available and technologically can be added to foods and treated as if it were a moderately stable B vitamin. Lysine reacts with reducing sugars, decreasing its biological value.

Methionine is the first limiting amino acid in legumes and has received particular attention in fortification of soy-based foods. Methionine presents potentially serious odor and flavor problems in fortification projects. This problem can be minimized by the use of N-acetyl-L-methionine (NAM), which is an approved food additive (FDA 21 CFR 172.372) for use as a source of L-methionine "to improve significantly the biological quality of the total protein in a food containing naturally occurring primarily intact vegetable protein . . . ." It may not be used in infant foods or foods containing added nitrates or nitrites. It must be used in sufficient concentration to increase the PER of the protein in the finished ready-to-eat food to the equivalent of casein. NAM is much more stable than methionine in model food systems conducive to Maillard browning, but is less stable under oxidative conditions (Schleske and Warthesen 1982).

All of the amino acids commonly occurring in food proteins are approved by the FDA as special dietary and nutritional additives to improve protein quality, but may be used only under very specific limitations. The researcher should review current regulations before initiating any development work in fortifying with amino acids.

REFERENCES

Bauernfeind, J. C., and Cort, W. M. 1974. Nutrification of foods with added vitamin A. Crit. Rev. Food Technol. *5*, 337–375.

Beetner, G., *et al.* 1974. Degradation of thiamine and riboflavin during extrusion processing. J. Food Sci. *39*, 207–208.

Beston, G. H., and Henderson, G. A. 1974. Vitamin C stability in reconstituted beverage products. Can. Inst. Food Sci. Technol. *7*, 183.

Bissett, O. W., and Berry, R. E. 1975. Ascorbic acid retention in orange juice as related to container type. J. Food Sci. *40*, 178–180.

Bookwalter, G. N. *et al.* 1980. Nutritional stability of corn–soy–milk blends after dry heating to destroy salmonellae. J. Food Sci. *45*, 975–980.

Borenstein, B. 1971. Rationale and technology of food fortification with vitamins, minerals and amino acids. Crit. Rev. Food Technol. *2*, 171–186.

Borenstein, B. 1972. Vitamins and amino acids. *In* Handbook of Food Additives, 2nd Edition. T. E. Furia (Editor). CRC Press, Cleveland, OH.

Borenstein, B. 1974. Enrichment of wheat food products. *In* Wheat Production and Utilization. G. E. Inglett (Editor). AVI Publishing Co., Westport, CT.

Brooke, C. L., and Cort, W. M. 1972. Vitamin A fortification of tea. Food Technol. *26*(6), 50–52, 58.

Cort, W. M., *et al.* 1976. Nutrient stability of fortified cereal products. Food Technol. *30*(4), 52–60, 62.

Dennison, D. B., and Kirk, J. R. 1978. Oxygen effect on the degradation of ascorbic acid in a dehydrated food system. J. Food Sci. *43*, 609–612.

DeRitter, E., and Metzner, A. A. 1978. Unpublished material. Hoffmann-LaRoche Inc., Nutley, NJ.

Duvall, L. F., and Stone, C. D. 1974. The method of vitamin coating of cereal products. U.S. Pat. 3,782,963. Jan. 1.

Food and Drug Administration (FDA) 1982. *N*-Acetyl-L-methionine. 21 CFR, 172.372.

Food and Nutrition Board (FNB) 1980. Recommended Dietary Allowances. 9th Edition. National Academy of Sciences, Washington, DC.

Fortmann, K. L., *et al.* 1974. Uniformity of enrichment in baker's flour applied at the mill. Baker's Dig. *48*(3), 42–47.

Furuya, E. M., and Warthesen, J. J. 1984. Packaging effects on riboflavin content of pasta products in retail markets. Cereal Chem. *61*, 399–402.

Gordon, H. T. 1978. Unpublished material. Hoffman-LaRoche Inc., Nutley, NJ.

Gordon, H. T., and Borenstein, B. 1982. Unpublished material. Hoffman-LaRoche Inc., Nutley, NJ.

Gordon, H. T., and Cort, W. M. 1979. Unpublished material. Hoffman-LaRoche Inc., Nutley, NJ.

Gordon, H. T., and Cort, W. M. 1981. Unpublished material. Hoffman-LaRoche Inc., Nutley, NJ.

Gordon, H. T., and Cort, W. M. 1983. Unpublished material. Hoffman-LaRoche Inc., Nutley, NJ.

Gordon, H. T., and Gerenz, C. 1982. Unpublished material. Hoffman-LaRoche Inc., Nutley, NJ.

Gregory, J. F., and Kirk, J. R. 1978. Assessment of storage effects on vitamin B_6 stability and bioavailability in dehydrated food systems. J. Food Sci. *43*, 1801–1808.

Guerrant, N. B., and O'Hara, M. B. 1953. Vitamin retention in peas and lima beans after blanching, freezing, processing in tin and in glass, after storage and cooking. Food Technol. *7*, 473–477.

Hallberg, L., and Rossander, L. 1984. Improvement of iron nutrition in developing countries: Comparison of adding meat, soy protein, ascorbic acid, citric acid and ferrous sulphate on iron absorption from a simple Latin American-type of meal Am. J. Clin. Nutr. *39*, 577–583.

Hallberg, L., *et al.* 1982. Deleterious effect of prolonged warming of meals on ascorbic acid content and iron absorption. Am. J. Clin. Nutr. *36*, 846–850.

Hungerford, D. M., and Linder, M. C. 1983. Interactions of pH and ascorbate in intestinal iron absorption. J. Nutr. *113*, 2615–2622.

Karel, M. 1979. Prediction of nutrient losses and optimization of processing conditions. *In* Nutritional and Safety Aspects of Food Processing. S. R. Tannenbaum (Editor). Marcel Dekker, New York.

Liu, L. I., and Parrish, D. B. 1979. Biopotency of vitamin A in fortified flour after accelerated storage. J. Agric. Food Chem. *27*, 1134–1136.

Marusich, W., *et al.* 1957. Provitamin A activity and stability of β-carotene in margarine. J. Am. Oil Chem. Soc. *34*, 217–221.

Mnkeni, A. P., and Beveridge, T. 1982. Thermal destruction of pteroylglutamic acid in buffer and model food systems. J. Food Sci. *47*, 2038–2041.

Parrish, D. B. *et al.* 1980A. Distribution of vitamin A in fortified flours and effect of processing, simulated shipping and storage. Cereal Chem. *57*, 284–287.

Parrish, D. B., *et al.* 1980B. Recovery of vitamin A in processed foods made from fortified flours. J. Food Sci. *45*, 1438–1439.

Pedersen, D. C., and Sautier, P. M. 1974. Vitamin enriched potato flakes. U.S. Pat. 3,833,739. Sept. 3.

Pelletier, O., and Keith, M. O. 1974. Bioavailability of synthetic and natural ascorbic acid. J. Am. Diet. Assoc. *64*, 271–275.

Ranhotra, G. S., *et al.* 1976A. Bioavailability of magnesium from wheat flour and various organic and inorganic salts. Cereal Chem. *53* 770–776.

Ranhotra, G. S., *et al.* 1976B. Effect of various magnesium sources on breadmaking characteristics of wheat flour. J. Food Sci. *41*, 952–954.

Ranhotra, G. S., *et al.* 1977. Bioavailability and functionality (breadmaking) of zinc in various organic and inorganic sources. Cereal Chem. *54*, 496–502.

Rubin, S. H., and Cort, W. M. 1969. Aspects of vitamin and mineral enrichments. *In* Protein-Enriched Cereal Foods for World Needs. M. Milner (Editor). Am. Assoc. Cereal Chem., St. Paul, MN.

Schleske, K. L., and Warthesen, J. J. 1982. Detection and stability of *N*-acetylmethionine in model food systems. J. Agric. Food Chem. *30*, 1172–1175.

Schricker, B. R., and Miller, D. D. 1982. In vitro estimation of relative iron availability in breads and meals containing different forms of fortification iron. J. Food Sci. *47*, 723–727.

Schwartz, R., *et al.* 1984. Magnesium absorption in human subjects from leafy vegetables, intrinsically labeled with stable 26Mg. Am. J. Clin. Nutr. *39*, 571–576.

Seib, P. A., and Hoseney, R. C. 1974. The case for stable forms of vitamin C suitable for bread enrichment. Baker's Dig. *48*(5), 46–57.

Singh, R. P., *et al.* 1975. Kinetic analysis of light-induced riboflavin loss in whole milk. J. Food Sci. *40*, 164–167.

Swanson, C. A., *et al.* 1983. Effect of dietary zinc sources and pregnancy in zinc utilization in adult women fed controlled diets. J. Nutr. *113*, 2557–2567.

U.S. Department of Agriculture (USDA) 1982. Vegetable protein products. Federal Register *47*(142), 31882–31886. USDA, Washington, DC.

Winterringer, G. L., and Ranhotra, G. S. 1983. Relative bioavailability of magnesium from mineral- and soy-fortified breads. Cereal Chem. *60*, 14–18.

Yu, M. H., *et al.* 1974. Nonenzymatic browning in synthetic systems containing ascorbic acid, amino acids, organic acids, and inorganic salts. Can. Inst. Food Sci. Technol. J. *7*, 279–282.

23

Protein Complementation of Foods

Ricardo Bressani

INTRODUCTION

The concept of protein quality is one that measures the efficiency with which a food carrier of protein and its components, the essential amino acids and nonessential nitrogen, meet the needs of the individual in his different physiological states. The efficiency of utilization is determined by the amounts of essential amino acids as well as by the proportion in which they are present in the protein, in comparison with the specific needs at the particular physiological state of the individual.

It is not altogether surprising, therefore, to find that most foods, with the exception of those from animal origin, are utilized at a lower efficiency because, in their amino acid pattern, there is one or more amino acid present in a lower amount and, in some instances, out of proportion.

The efficiency of utilization of the amino acids is also affected by the availability of the amino acid, even if it is present in appropriate amounts. The availability may be conditioned by the structure of the protein, by specific effects of processing, or by reactions between specific components in the food and amino acids (Cheftel 1979).

The deficiencies of amino acids in protein foods, either because the content is low or because of a low availability, may be corrected by supplementation with the appropriate amount of the deficient amino acid, as discussed elsewhere in this chapter. Addition of synthetic amino acids, carried out following well-established principles, results in increased protein quality due to the improvement of the essential amino acid pattern in the protein that is supplemented.

The deficiency can also be overcome by supplementation with a protein rich in the deficient amino acid or by protein complementation.

Before going any further, it may be useful to define the terminology used, particularly with respect to "protein supplementation" and "protein complementation." Both terms express the same overall effect, that is, to improve the efficiency of utilization of a poor-quality protein with another protein. As will be shown, protein supplementation represents a section of a complementation response. A complementation response is one in which two protein sources provide an essential amino acid pattern approximating or equal to those found in animal proteins. Some authors use the expression "mutual protein supplementation" to signify complementation.

This chapter attempts to discuss the principles of supplementation and of complementation, the different types of response obtained, and the application of the information for the preparation of better protein quality foods and for other purposes.

PROTEIN QUALITY IMPROVEMENT

It is well known that most proteins, with the possible exception of only a very few, have essential amino acid deficiencies. Likewise, essential amino acid excesses may be responsible to some extent for lower than expected protein quality values, even though this condition is not often appreciated.

As is well documented, amino acid deficiencies can be overcome by the addition of the appropriate amounts of the deficient amino acids, either as crystalline compounds or as proteins, which are rich sources of the deficient amino acids. Addition of synthetic amino acids, when carried out following well-established principles, results in increased protein quality due to the improvement of the essential amino acid pattern, and due only to that, since there are no other variables involved. The problem in this situation is that the addition of the most limiting amino acid may induce the deficiency of the second limiting amino acid, and so on.

On the other hand, addition of the deficient amino acids as protein will result also in an increased protein quality, but the effect is the result of at least two variables, improved essential amino acid pattern and higher protein content. This situation is defined as protein supplementation, which, though it corrects the deficiency of the most limiting amino acid, may also increase the levels beyond the adequate balance of other essential amino acids. In contrast, protein complementation, another alternative to improving protein quality, is the result of a more balanced mixture of amino acids coming from two or more protein sources, which is used with a greater efficiency.

The Protein Supplementation Approach

The method usually utilized to improve protein quality by the protein supplementation approach is to add to a protein with a deficient pattern a quantity of a protein that is a good source of the deficient amino acid. The amount of protein added should increase the level of

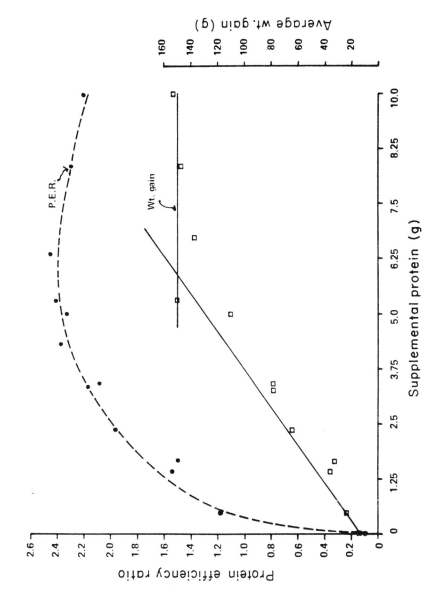

Fig. 23.1.   Protein quality improvement of maize from soy protein supplementation.

the deficient amino acid to a point where it is no longer limiting protein quality. To establish the amount of protein to add to the deficient protein, increasing amounts of the supplemental protein are added, and the biological response is measured, as shown in Fig. 23.1. The biological response may be the usual protein quality indices as well as biochemical changes. As seen in the figure, as the amount of supplementary protein increases, there is an increase in biological response, which reaches a plateau at the high level of supplemental protein (Bressani et al. 1978). The point of optimum quality achieved may be established by calculating two linear regressions, one on the points around the plateau and one using the values in the increasing section of the response. The point of interception of the two regressions represents the optimum amount to add. A second approach is to calculate a quadratic equation and, by developing the first derivative, obtain the optimum level. With the amount of available data on the amino acid content of foods, the level of the deficient amino acid to add is calculated and then converted into protein or amount of supplement, this representing a third possibility. This approach, as well as other mathematical approaches (Hayes et al. 1978; Wadsworth et al. 1979; Traver et al. 1981; Ballesteros et al. 1983), assumes that the biological availability of the limiting amino acid is close to, or is, 100%.

There are many examples in the literature showing the amounts of protein supplements to add to improve the quality of proteins deficient in specific amino acids. The examples found usually involve cereal grains, be they wheat flour, rice, sorghum, or maize, because of their well-known deficiency of lysine (Bressani et al. 1968) and because they are consumed in relatively large amounts by the world population. Table 23.1 gives some results for maize quality improvement (Bressani and Marenco 1963) as well as for rice (Elias et al. 1968) and for whole wheat and wheat flour (Jarquin et al. 1966). One aspect that is apparent is that besides the increase in protein quality, there is also an increase in total protein content. Likewise, the levels needed for maximum improvement are relatively small.

One aspect of interest is that the optimum amounts of supplemental protein reported, for example, for rice, are not the same for all protein supplements. The possible reasons for this observation are that the level of bioavailability of the amino acid to be added as protein is not the same for all proteins; likewise, other amino acids may be, in low or high amounts, introducing imbalances in the supplemented food. This, however, has no practical significance. However, a positive correlation is always found between the amount of the limiting amino acid provided and the protein quality improvement measured (Bressani and Marenco 1963; Jarquin et al. 1966). Similar results have been obtained by many other researchers (Sure 1948; Westerman et al. 1954; Kik 1960; Mouron and Motter 1962).

Table 23.1. Improvement of the Protein Quality of Cereal Grains by Supplementation with Various Protein Sources

Protein supplement	Lime-treated corn		Polished rice		Whole wheat		Wheat flour	
	Optimum amount (%)	PER	Optimum amount (%)	PER	Optimum amount (%)	PER	Optimum amount (%)	PER
Corn	—	1.00	—	—	—	—	—	—
Rice	—	—	—	1.71	—	—	—	—
Whole wheat	—	—	—	—	—	1.62	—	—
Wheat flour	—	—	—	—	—	—	—	0.86
Fish flour	2.5	2.44	6.0	2.70	—	—	—	—
Soy flour	8.0	2.25	8.0	2.88	6.0	1.89	10.0	2.01
Cottonseed flour	8.0	1.83	12.0	2.32	10.0	2.10	12.0	1.96
Torula yeast	2.5	1.97	8.0	3.29	4.0	2.13	6.0	2.31
Casein	4.0	2.21	6.0	3.22	4.0	2.54	6.0	2.62
Egg	3.0	2.24	—	—	—	—	—	—
Skim milk	—	—	12.0	3.16	6.0	1.98	10.0	2.19

Source: Elias et al. (1968).

Since the objective is to supply, as protein, the deficient amino acid in another protein, the supplementation approach is also applicable to proteins deficient in sulfur amino acids. However, the examples are not as numerous as those to be found when lysine is the deficient amino acid. The protein quality of common beans, navy beans, and broad beans can be improved through supplementation with Brazil nuts (Antunes and Markakis 1977) and with sesame (Boloorforooshan and Markakis 1979; Al-Nouri *et al.* 1980); common beans can be improved in protein quality by supplementing them with soybeans (Bressani 1981; Sgarbieri *et al.* 1978). The response is due to the contribution of sulfur amino acids from soybean to common bean protein which contains lower levels of total sulfur amino acids than soybeans.

Finally, although the protein efficiency ratio (PER) has been often used to measure the response, other biological tests give equal results (Bressani and de Villareal, 1963). Likewise, the improvement in protein can also be measured by nitrogen balance in children. For example, nitrogen retention at the same intake of protein increased from 30 to 63 mg/kg/day, when lime-treated corn was supplemented with 8% soybean flour (Viteri *et al.* 1972; Bressani *et al.* 1976).

The protein quality improvement resulting from protein supplementation is mainly due to an increase in the deficient amino acid in the supplemented food, although the resulting protein increase may also contribute to the response. An example on this is shown in Fig. 23.2. In this particular study, lime-treated corn flour was supplemented with

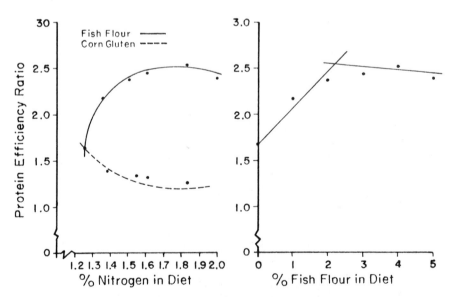

Fig. 23.2. *(Left)* Effect of fish flour and of corn gluten protein in the PER of lime-treated corn. *(Right)* Improvement of the PER of lime-treated corn with fish flour.

Table 23.2. Selected Amino Acid Content (mg/g) in Diets of Lime-treated Corn Supplemented with Fish Flour or Corn Gluten

	Fish flour level of supplementation (%)						FAO/ WHO[a]
	0	1	2	3	4	5	
Lysine	180	218	250	276	298	319	340
Tryptophan	33	35	37	39	40	42	65
Isoleucine	280	286	292	296	298	302	250
PER	1.61	2.16	2.36	2.44	2.51	2.38	—
Weight gain	25	42	74	79	112	109	—
	Corn gluten level of supplementation (%)						
	0	1.4	2.7	4.1	5.4	6.8	
Lysine	180	174	169	165	160	157	340
Tryptophan	33	32	31	30	30	29	65
Isoleucine	280	276	273	270	267	265	250
PER	1.61	1.38	1.34	1.32	1.27	1.22	—
Weight gain	25	27	33	32	33	37	
N in diet (%)	1.26	1.38	1.50	1.62	1.75	1.87	—

[a] Food & Agriculture Organization/World Health Organization standard.

fish flour in one case, and with equivalent amounts of protein derived from corn gluten in the other (Bressani and Marenco 1963). The protein quality response for fish flour, which is rich in lysine, is different from the response to corn gluten, which is deficient in lysine. However, the effect of the increase in protein content due to added corn gluten is seen in the increase in weight gain of the experimental animals. The changes in the content of selected essential amino acids with respect to the level of supplement added is shown in Table 23.2 for the two cases. While there is a continuous increase in all three amino acids for the fish flour case, there is a decrease or no change for the corn gluten case. An additional aspect which must be considered is that the essential amino acid pattern of the food to be supplemented and of the supplemental protein is affected by processing, thus influencing the response observed at a fixed level of supplemental protein. This is observed in the results shown in Table 23.3 in which various corn selections or products were supplemented with a fixed level of different soybean protein sources (Bressani *et al.* 1981). As shown, soybean flour, the least damaged of the soybean products, gave the highest supplemental effect. Likewise, the whole corn flours performed better than the degerminated corn flours.

As already indicated, the levels of supplemental protein are relatively small; however, lower levels result when the protein content of the supplement is higher, since amino acid content on a weight basis is higher, although on a protein basis it is usually the same. The use of

Table 23.3. Supplementary Effect of Different Sources of Soybean Protein on the Protein Quality Improvement of Different Sources of Corn Protein[a]

Supplement (%)	Corn product			
	Degermed	Cuarenteño	Azotea	Opaque-2
None	0.40 ± 0.08^a	1.19 ± 0.06	1.02 ± 0.07	2.02 ± 0.08
Soy flour protein				
2.5	1.41 ± 0.08	2.06 ± 0.06	2.16 ± 0.03	2.28 ± 0.06^a
5.0	1.98 ± 0.05	2.07 ± 0.04	2.36 ± 0.07	2.12 ± 0.08
7.5	2.13 ± 0.06	2.03 ± 0.05	2.37 ± 0.08	2.12 ± 0.08
Text soy protein				
2.5	1.05 ± 0.04	1.77 ± 0.06	1.87 ± 0.08	2.18 ± 0.05^a
5.0	1.90 ± 0.05	1.99 ± 0.03	2.13 ± 0.06	1.99 ± 0.10
7.5	2.04 ± 0.03	2.03 ± 0.08	2.14 ± 0.09	1.95 ± 0.08
Soy protein				
2.5	1.44 ± 0.07	1.98 ± 0.05	1.98 ± 0.05	2.14 ± 0.06^a
5.0	1.97 ± 0.06	1.97 ± 0.04	2.12 ± 0.09	2.10 ± 0.11
7.5	2.14 ± 0.05	1.89 ± 0.06	2.14 ± 0.09	1.98 ± 0.11

Source: Bressani et al. (1981).
[a] Average standard error ±.

more concentrated forms of protein supplements, for example, soy flour (50% protein) versus soy protein isolates (over 90% protein), is recommended because of the lower amounts needed for maximum improvement in protein quality. Such low levels will reduce possible changes in the organoleptic and functional properties of the supplemented food.

The Protein Complementation Approach

Types of Response Observed

The responses shown in Fig. 23.3 were obtained from the results of biological trials using young growing rats (Bressani and Elias 1968; Woodham 1978; de Groot and Van Stratum 1963); however, similar responses can be obtained from other species, including man. The method used to obtain the responses shown consists of mixing two proteins in different proportions in a series of diets. The nitrogen from one of the proteins is progressively replaced by an equal amount from the second one in such a way that all combinations have the same protein content, usually 7–12%. Two of the diets, the extremes, are prepared exclusively from the individual protein sources. These series of diets, properly supplemented with calories, vitamins, and minerals, are then fed to the animal species chosen to measure the biological response.

The response may be measured by any of the techniques used to measure protein quality, such as net protein utilization (NPU) (Bender and Doell 1957), nitrogen balance (NB) (Bressani 1977), or PER

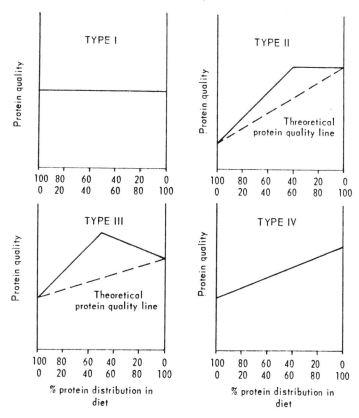

Fig. 23.3.   Types of response lines obtained when mixing two protein sources.

[Association of Official Agricultural Chemists (AOAC) 1972]. The responses are also similar between animal species, such as rats, poultry (Woodham and Clark 1977; Woodham and Deans 1977), and humans (Kofranyi and Jekat 1967). The dotted lines in the graphs in Fig. 23.3. represent the responses to be expected if there were no complementary effects, thus, all values above such lines may be interpreted as the results of complementary effects.

Of the four types of responses shown, the only one representing true complementation is type III, since there is a synergistic effect from the two amino acid patterns mixed. Even though type II may also be a case of protein complementation, there is no synergistic effect on protein quality as for type III. The difference is appreciated by drawing a vertical line from the maximum response to the dotted diagonal line drawn between the extreme points. The height of the vertical line for true complementation (type III) is higher than that from type II. The condition yielding type II are obviously different from those yielding type III.

Type I results when the protein sources mixed have common essential amino acid deficiencies, and to the same extent. The quality of such mixtures is essentially the same throughout.

Type II is usually the result of the combination of two protein foods with a common amino acid deficiency and a similar overall essential amino acid pattern; however, one of the two proteins contains a higher level of the deficient amino acid than the other one. This relatively higher amount of the deficient amino acid in one of the proteins is able to maintain, up to a certain point, the protein quality of the mixture. From the point of view of the protein with lower amounts of the common deficient amino acid, there is some contribution of this amino acid from the other source, which explains the increase in quality, followed by a plateau, as more of this second protein contributes to the total protein of the mixture.

Type II also results from the dilution of the essential amino acid pattern of high-quality proteins, such as egg and lactalbumin (Braham and Bressani 1969; Huang *et al.* 1966, Young and Villarela 1970; Bressani *et al.* 1972). Type III represents true complementation, the response showing a higher value than that observed from each individual component, and higher than expected from amino acid content.

Finally, in type IV responses, the individual quality values of the two proteins are significantly different. One of the two proteins is highly deficient in one amino acid, which is supplied by the other protein usually having a good amino acid balance. The linear response is probably due to either an overall better essential amino acid balance or higher amino acid availability, or both.

Differences between Supplementation and Complementation

Figure 23.4 further clarifies the differences between protein complementation and protein supplementation. The graph on the upper left (A) was obtained by mixing maize and soy protein in different proportions, but keeping protein content of the diet constant.

On the other hand, the graph on the lower left (C) was obtained by adding to a fixed level of maize increasing amounts of soy protein; therefore, protein content of the diet increased. Graph A shows a complementary effect of soy to maize protein, while graph C shows a supplementary response.

The same results are shown on the right side. In this case, however, protein quality is not represented by PER, but is expressed as utilizable protein, a figure which includes protein concentration.

As shown, the shape of graph B is the same as graph A. This is because only protein quality changed, since protein content remained constant. Graph D, however, is now almost linear, which resulted when the protein quality factor was corrected for protein content.

Other differences include the following: lower amounts of protein are used or are added for protein supplementation than for complementation;

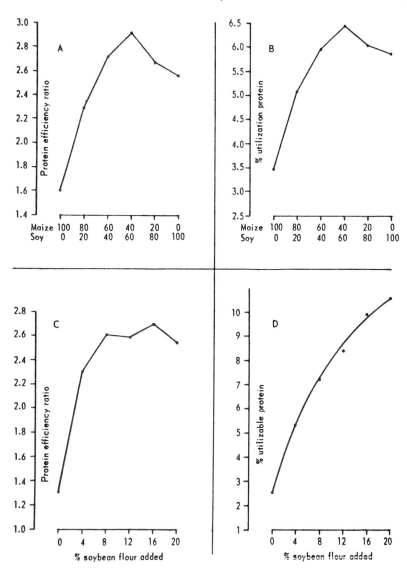

Fig. 23.4.   Protein complementation and protein supplementation.

total protein in a supplemented food is lower than in complemented foods; the essential amino acid pattern in complemented foods has a better balance than in supplemented foods (Bressani and Elias 1968; Woodham 1978).   This last point is presented in Table 23.4, which shows selected amino acid values expressed as mg/g N when corn is supplemented with soybean protein (Bressani and Marenco 1963; Bressani *et al.* 1974).   The 11% soybean supplementation level showed the mixed protein to contain 274, 51, 285, and 184 mg/g N of lysine,

Table 23.4. Selected Amino Acid Content (mg/g N) in Diets of Lime-treated Corn Supplemented with Soybean Flour

	0	1	3	5	7	9	1	FAO/WHO
Lysine	180	194	217	236	251	264	274	340
Tryptophan	33	36	40	43	46	48	51	65
Isoleucine	280	280	281	282	283	284	285	250
T.S.A.[a]	176	177	179	181	182	183	184	220
PER	0.82	1.19	1.54	1.96	2.09	2.37	2.42	—
Weight gain	12	22	36	64	79	113	125	—
$P_1:P_2$	100:0	80:20	70:30	60:40	50:50	40:60	20:80	0:100
Lysine	180	224	245	266	310	352	396	340
Tryptophan	38	48	52	57	67	76	86	65
Isoleucine	280						336	250
T.S.A.	198	197	197	197	196	196	195	220
PER	1.50				2.80			

[a] T.S.A., total sulfur amino acids.

tryptophan, isoleucine, and total sulfur amino acids. On the other hand, the 50:50 protein mixture of soy and corn contained more of the same amino acids and closer to the levels to the Food and Agriculture Organization/World Health Organization (FAO/WHO) reference pattern (FAO/WHO 1973).

MIXTURES OF PROTEINS GIVING MAXIMUM PROTEIN QUALITY

Cereal Grains and Food Legumes

The first example represents the results obtained when mixing normal maize with black beans, as shown in Fig. 23.5. Results for opaque-2 maize (Mertz *et al.* 1964) and black beans are also shown for comparative purposes. The response observed for opaque-2 maize and black beans is different from that resulting from normal maize and black beans (Bressani *et al.* 1962; Bressani and Elias 1969).

As shown, the isonitrogenous replacement of black bean nitrogen by opaque-2 maize nitrogen resulted in a constant increase up to the 50:50 protein distribution level, with no further change when the nitrogen of the diet was provided more and more from opaque-2 maize. On the other hand, the replacement of bean nitrogen by normal maize nitrogen resulted in a maximum response at the 50:50 protein distribution level; however, as more nitrogen was derived from maize, a lower response was measured.

The reason for both curves is to be found in the deficient amino acids in the three protein sources under consideration. Bean protein is

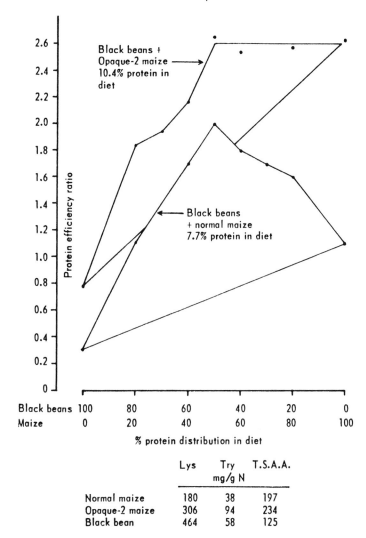

Fig. 23.5. Protein efficiency ratio of combinations of normal or opaque-2 maize and black beans.

deficient in methionine and, to a lower extent, in tryptophan, although it is a relatively good source of lysine (Tobin and Carpenter 1978; Jansen 1973).

Normal maize is deficient in lysine and tryptophan and adequate in methionine. These differences may explain the responses found. On the left side of the maximum point, methionine is more deficient; on the right side, lysine and tryptophan form the bean–normal maize curve. The same is true for the bean–opaque-2 maize, with the exception that to the right of the maximum point lysine and methionine are deficient, to the left, only methionine is deficient.

Table 23.5.   Amino Acid Supplementation of Maize and Beans, and Optimum Protein Quality of Maize–Bean Diets

Protein ratio, maize:black beans	Amino acid added (%)	Average weight gain (g)	PER
100:0	None	29	1.05
	Lysine, tryptophan, isoleucine	74	2.47
50:50	None	51	2.10
	Methionine, tryptophan	59	2.03
	Methionine, lysine	75	2.42
0:100	None	−3	—
	Methionine, tryptophan, leucine	23	1.04

Evidence for this is shown in Table 23.5. The 50:50, bean–normal maize mixture responded to the addition of lysine and total sulfur amino acids, in contrast to the 100% maize diet, which responded to lysine and tryptophan. This last amino acid is not deficient in the 50:50 mixture, since its addition with methionine resulted in no change in PER.

The last two lines show the effect of methionine, tryptophan, and leucine on the 100% bean protein diet. Although three amino acids were added, other results suggest that methionine alone would cause the same, if not higher, increase in protein quality (Bressani *et al.* 1962).

The proteins of soybean flour and of maize, whether normal or opaque-2, have complementary amino acid patterns, as shown in Fig. 23.6. The results show that soybean–normal maize and soybean-opaque-2 maize have complementary patterns when they are mixed in a protein ratio of 60 soy to 40 maize. The difference between the two is in weight gain, but the maximum value for PER was the same (Bressani and Elias 1969; Bressani and Elias 1967).

Examination of the amino acid patterns of both sets show the largest difference to be in lysine, which is found in greater concentrations in the soy–opaque-2 maize combination. Further comparison shows that the concentration of sulfur amino acids and of threonine is very similar in both sets.

In the soyflour–opaque-2 maize system the limiting amino acids are methionine, threonine, and lysine, as shown in Table 23.6. The soybean–opaque-2 maize combination responded to the addition of methionine and to threonine in the presence of the first. However, the soybean–normal maize responded to methionine, threonine, and lysine addition. It should be indicated that most proteins responded to amino acid supplementation when fed at low levels. For example, the normal maize–soybean mixtures, 60:40 at the 10% protein level in the diet responded to methionine and the mixture methionine–threonine and lysine. These amino acids were without effect when the protein

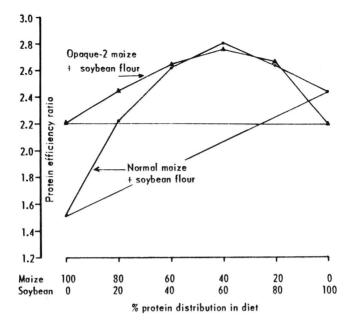

Fig. 23.6. Protein efficiency ratio of combination of normal or opaque-2 maize and soybean flour.

Table 23.6. Effect of Amino Acid Supplementation of Soybean–Opaque-2 Maize and of Soybean–Normal Maize 60:40 Protein Combination

Maize	Amino acid (% added)	PER
Opaque-2	None	2.30
	0.20 DL-Methionine	2.65
	0.20 DL-Methionine + 0.20 DL-threonine	2.95
	0.20 DL-Methionine + 0.20 DL-threonine + 0.20 L-lysine HCl	2.66
Normal	None	2.23
	0.20 DL-Methionine	2.81
	0.20 DL-Methionine + 0.20 DL-threonine	2.85
	0.20 DL-Methionine + 0.20 DL-threonine + 0.20 L-lysine HCl	3.06
Casein	—	2.65

Source: Bressani and Elias (1969).

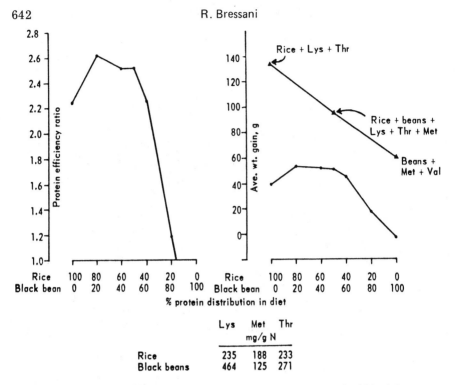

Fig. 23.7.   Protein complementation between rice and cooked black beans.

in the diet was increased to about 18%. The lack of effect of the amino acids is to be expected, because of the well-established effect of protein level on PER (Bressani and Elias 1967, Bressani and Elias 1969).

Results of studies with rice and cooked black beans (Bressani and Valiente 1962; Vargas *et al.* 1982) are given in Fig. 23.7. The study was carried out with diets containing 6.2% protein, because of the low levels of this nutrient in rice. At this low level of dietary protein, rats fed the 100% black bean diet did not gain weight, as shown on the graph at the right.

From the protein quality point of view, the best rice–bean protein combination was 80% from rice and 20% from beans. The increase in protein quality of the 100% rice diet to the 80% rice was due to the lysine and threonine contribution of 20% beans, while rice provided beans with methionine.

This can be seen from the amino acid values of the two proteins studied, also shown in the lower section of the graph. The weight gained by the animals on each diet followed PER, as can be seen on the graph to the right.

The graph also shows the effects on weight gain when some of the diets are supplemented with the limiting amino acids. A significant response was obtained in each case. Of interest is the fact that bean protein supplemented with methionine and valine did not reach the levels obtained with rice supplemented with lysine and threonine.

This was interpreted on the basis of the lower protein digestibility of bean protein. These results also show that even though a mixture of rice and beans has a protein quality higher than each component alone, the individual components, as well as any of the mixtures, may be improved by amino acid supplementation. Similar findings have been reported by other workers, with combinations of cereal grains and food legumes, such as *Vicia faba* and various cereal grains (Bressani 1982); mung bean and rice Asian Vegetable Research Development Center (1976); common beans, maize, and sorghum (Cabezas *et al.* 1982; Sirinit *et al.* 1965); and cowpeas and maize (Sirinit *et al.* 1965). In all these examples the mixture giving maximum protein-quality response is around 70 parts cereal grain and 30 parts food legume, with a few exceptions. Similarly, the amino acid deficiencies at the maximum point have also been reported to be as those indicated above (Sirinit *et al.* 1965; Sarway *et al.* 1975).

Oilseed Proteins and Other Vegetable Sources

Results on combinations of torula yeast with sesame flour are shown in Fig. 28.8. Torula yeast protein has been shown to be a good source of lysine, containing higher levels of this amino acid than sesame flour, as indicated in the figure (Elias and Bressani 1970; Bressani 1968).

With respect to total sulfur amino acids, sesame flour contains (Evans and Bandemer 1967) twice as much as torula yeast. Therefore, when these two proteins combine, they result in mixtures with higher quality than either component.

The increase in protein quality of torula yeast by sesame flour at the optimum level of 60:40 was equivalent to 108%, and the increase in the protein quality of sesame flour by torula yeast at the same point was on the order to 54%. Obviously, these factors are due to the respective contributions of the limiting amino acids by the two proteins to each other. Similar results have been reported for common beans and sesame by Boloorforooshan and Markakis (1979) and by Akpapunam and Markakis (1981). As indicated before, the sulfur amino acid deficiency in common beans is met by the relative abundance of this amino acid in sesame. On the other hand, the relative deficiency of lysine is met by the high amounts present in common beans.

Three legume grains of different protein quality were combined individually with cottonseed flour (Elias and Bressani 1971). The legume grains were *Vigna sinensis* (cowpea) and pigeon pea, deficient in sulfur amino acids and of a high protein digestibility; and *Phaseolus vulgaris* (black bean), deficient in total sulfur amino acids and of a relatively low protein digestibility. However, all are sources of lysine, an amino acid deficient in cottonseed protein.

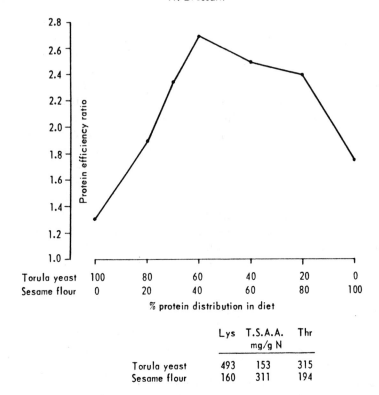

Fig. 23.8.   Protein quality of mixtures of torula yeast and sesame flour

This protein also contains higher levels of tryptophan and slightly higher levels of sulfur amino acids than the legume grain proteins. The protein quality of these mixtures is shown in Fig. 23.9. Optimum mixtures with cowpea and cottonseed took place at the 40:60 protein ratio. The same was also true for pigeon pea and cottonseed, although at a lower level of quality.

Finally, the black bean–cottonseed flour mixture giving optimum values was the 30:70 protein mixture. In all cases, the tendency is to increase levels of legume grain protein to cottonseed flour, suggesting the greater importance of the lysine contribution of the legume grains in contrast to the methionine contribution of cottonseed.

Other Studies

Following the same procedure described, other investigators have also found optimum mixtures between two proteins, using rats as experimental animals (de Groot and Van Stratum 1963; Dutra de Oliveira and De Souza 1972). These results are summarized in Table 23.7. The optimum mixtures correspond closely to those already shown. Of

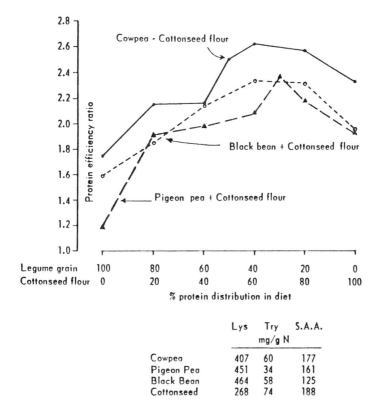

	Lys	Try	S.A.A.
		mg/g N	
Cowpea	407	60	177
Pigeon Pea	451	34	161
Black Bean	464	58	125
Cottonseed	268	74	188

Fig. 23.9. Protein quality of combination of cowpea, pigeon peas, and black beans with cottonseed flour.

Table 23.7. Protein Quality of Optimum Combinations of Food Proteins

Component	Optimum mixture (%)	Protein quality	Reference
Rice:beans	40:60	61 NPU	de Groot and Van Stratum (1963).
Oats:beans	60:40	61 NPU	
Wheat:beans	50:50	62 NPU	
Wheat gluten:beans	60:40	58 NPU	
Brown bread:beans	60:40	63 NPU	
White bread:beans	60:40	63 NPU	
Egg:beans	50:50	81 NPU	
Sesame:peas	40:60	66 NPU	
Maize:milk	50:50	2.8 PER	Dutra de Oliveira and
Opaque-2:milk	66:34	2.74 PER	De Souza (1972).

interest are the normal maize–milk and opaque-2 mixture, suggesting the economy of food proteins through improved quality. This case is similar to the normal or opaque-2 maize and soybean flour described earlier. There are many other studies based on the principles described. Almquist and Grau (1944) described systems between sesame and soybeans, while various composite protein foods based on ground nuts, soybean, and sesame flour were studied by Krishnamurthy *et al.* (1960). Other studies reported include combinations between wheat milling by-products and vegetable protein concentrates (Elias and Bressani 1973) and mixtures of food legumes (Bressani *et al.* 1977A). Other have been reviewed by Bressani and Elias (1968), Bressani (1974), Woodham (1978), and de Groot and Van Stratum (1963).

Human Studies

Studies with human subjects, following the same methodology described for rats, are very few, for obvious reasons. However, the results of Kofranyi and Jekat (1967) are summarized in Table 23.8.

In these studies, the authors indicate that the mixtures of the two foods shown in the middle column gave what they called a "balance minimum" when their intake in grams of protein per kilogram body weight was according to the figures shown in the third column. This value is equal to the minimum protein requirement, as suggested by the authors of the study. They define balance minimum as the lower protein intake giving nitrogen equilibrium. It follows, therefore, that the higher the protein quality or biological value of the protein, the lower will be the balance minimum.

The average balance minimum for whole egg was 0.5 g protein/kg body weight. The values shown in the last column, therefore, have

Table **23.8.** Minimum Requirement of Protein from Optimum Combinations of Food Proteins

Components	Optimum mixture (%)	Minimum protein requirement (g/kg)
Egg:beans	30:70	0.45
Egg:soybean	60:40	0.41
Egg:corn	88:12	0.44
Egg:potato	35:65	0.37
Egg:rice	62:38	0.46
Egg:wheat	72:24	0.43
Milk:wheat	75:25	0.47
Egg	100	0.50

Source: Kofranyi and Jekat (1967).

better protein than egg. This is probably due to a better overall essential amino acid balance in the mixtures than in egg, particularly for the egg–potato mixture studied. The results also show that for cereal grains, less egg protein is needed for cereals of better protein quality, which, in descending order, are rice, wheat, and maize.

These same authors reported an optimum protein quality mixture of 55% bean to 45% maize on a protein basis, a value close to those reported earlier in this paper.

Other results in humans are those reported by Viteri *et al.* (1981), who allowed children to feed freely on cooked maize and cooked beans. The results of their study confirmed the findings in rats (Bressani *et al.* 1962), as well as those of Kofranyi *et al.* (1967).

Although the results presented have been interpreted in terms of the limiting amino acids in the proteins being studied and their mutual complementation, the results obtained in some cases are higher than expected, suggesting that other factors are influencing the results. One such factor is overall amino acid balance (Bressani and Elias 1968; Woodham 1978). It is, however, very difficult to estimate how much of the improvement is due to this factor, since the concomitant correction of the individual amino acid deficiencies is also changing amino acid balance. Even though a higher protein quality is obtained, the mixture is still deficient in some amino acids, as shown.

Figure 28.10 is presented to indicate the changes taking place, which permit some understanding of the results. Line A represents the

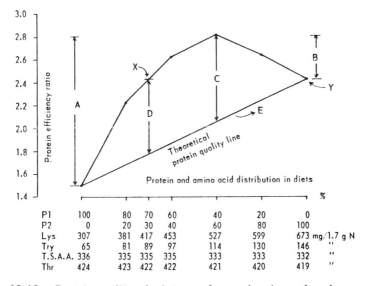

Fig. 23.10. Protein quality of mixtures of normal maize and soybean protein.

increase in quality of protein P^1 due to the addition of protein P^2. Similarly, line B represents the converse.

Line E may be considered as the theoretical protein quality value of the various mixtures; therefore, the actual increase in protein quality is represented by line C for the optimum mixtures and by line D for one of the various other mixtures, in this case the 70:30 mixture. Point X should have an amino acid pattern similar to point Y; it does not, however, except in the limiting amino acids of protein P^2.

From these considerations, it appears that the optimum mixture becomes limiting in those amino acids that do not change between different amounts of the component's proteins. This point was shown previously.

The second point, which would be desirable, is to be able to predict the protein quality of the optimum mixture. The optimum mixture may be calculated from the individual essential amino acid patterns in comparison with a reference pattern to be discussed.

AMINO ACID PATTERNS RESULTING FROM OPTIMUM PROTEIN QUALITY MIXTURES

The essential amino acid pattern of the optimum mixtures discussed in this chapter from animal and human studies was calculated. These values are shown in Table 23.9, where amino acids are expressed as milligrams per gram N.

Table 23.9.   Essential Amino Acid (E.A.A.) Patterns (mg/g N)[a]

| | Rats | | | | |
Amino acid	PER 2.0–2.4	PER 2.6–2.9	Overall average	Required	Human
Lysine	322	342	335	351	378
Tryptophan	63	78	73	58	87
Total sulfur-containing amino acids	176	205	195	234	257
Threonine	234	247	243	195	280
Isoleucine	303	318	313	195	370
Leucine	510	508	508	312	525
Phenylalanine	340	316	324	351	335
Valine	336	337	337	273	412
Arginine	436	424	428	78	362
Histidine	160	163	162	117	143
Total E.A.A.	2883	2938	2919	2164	3151

[a] Calculated from mixture giving maximum protein quality values.

The table also shows the rat requirements and the amino acid patterns calculated from the human studies. The results with rats were divided into two groups, those having a PER value between 2.0 and 2.4 and between 2.6 and 2.9, as well as the overall average. Comparing the amino acid patterns of the optimum mixtures with the pattern required by the young rat, a very high correlation becomes evident, with slightly lower values in lysine and sulfur-containing amino acids in the optimum protein mixtures, which may explain the positive effects upon supplementation with these amino acids.

These mixtures show high values for leucine, arginine, and possibly others, which are probably due to the high levels of these amino acids in the vegetable proteins used. For practical applications it is suggested that the essential pattern from the mixtures be used as a reference pattern.

This reference pattern guarantees a PER value above 2.5, if the pattern under the 2.6–2.9 range is used. The essential amino acid pattern of the mixtures with a PER value above 2.6 is practically the same as that suggested by the FAO/WHO in 1973.

Finally, one interesting aspect of this analysis is the fact that the essential amino acid pattern of the optimum mixtures resulting from human studies is very similar, although, in general, slightly higher than the experimentally derived pattern from the rat studies. This was interpreted to mean that the rat pattern can be used to predict the protein quality of foods to be used in human nutrition. Total essential amino acid content also was similar between rat and human work.

The theoretical protein quality can then be calculated from the individual protein quality values of the two components according to the degree in which they are combined. Mathematical calculations to accomplish this by linear programming have been attempted. Recently, the determination of the combination of specific sets of ingredients, giving optimum quality, has been estimated using computer programs such as a flexible simplex pattern search optimization scheme (Hayes et al. 1978), an indirect approach employing linear programming (Wadsworth et al. 1979), and a computer based graphical method (Traver et al. 1981). Least-cost formulations using linear programming were used by Ballesteros et al. (1984) for the elaboration of products based on cereals and legumes. The data base needed for these programs includes the chemical composition of the ingredients and their amino acid profiles. The methods also introduce a number of constraints, such as protein content, minimum level of fat, total percentage of ingredients equal to 100, cost, chemical score, and others. These methods are valuable in many respects since they decrease the time and cost in product formulation. Their limitation, however, is that of amino acid bioavailability, which is not taken into consideration.

This problem could be improved by correcting amino acid content by a digestibility factor, assuming equal bioavailability for all amino acids. Finally, even with this correction, it would be required to subject such mathematically formulated blends to biological testing in experimental animals or, better, with human subjects for confirmation of the results obtained. None of these studies conducted biological tests and used chemical score as the evaluation method.

APPLICATIONS

General Considerations

Until now in this chapter, the emphasis on supplementation and/or complementation was mainly from the nutritional point of view. However, the successful implementation of the potential of supplementation/complementation to increase and improve the world food supply will depend also on paying the necessary attention to the eating quality of the supplemented or complemented foods, since eating quality is the primary criterion for acceptance.

Although the increase in nutritional quality of protein through supplementation and complementation has been very well demonstrated, the number of cases in actual use is relatively small, mainly because only recently is increased attention being given to the organoleptic and functional properties of the nutritionally improved food, such as flavor, texture, and color. This implies that it will be necessary to establish the role and interaction of the chemical components in the supplement or in the complement being added to the basic food, and how these chemical components are affected by the standard process usually applied to the basic ingredient to make specific foods as we have known them. Therefore, the challenge is to retain the nutritional quality at the same cost with organoleptic and functional properties that will ensure eating quality.

Protein Supplementation

The findings of the studies carried out on protein supplementation have significant nutritional implications if such findings were implemented into practical applications, particularly in developing countries. In these, where the production and availability of animal food proteins is inefficient and low, and where there is a malnutrition problem, the use of the information of protein supplementation implies better quality protein more efficiently utilized, as well as small increases in total protein intake. If such increased quality and quantity of protein were to be supplemented with other nutrients, the overall utilization would, of course, be greater.

The main applications have been in the protein supplementation of cereal grain food products. Among these, wheat flour supplemented with soy flour has yielded bread with higher protein quality (Betschart 1978; Yáñez et al. 1982). The same kind of approach has been used for protein-supplemented tortillas, with soy protein products (Bressani et al. 1978), including whole soybeans (Del Valle et al. 1976), to be manufactured industrially or at the home level. Similar applications have been indicated for arepa flour (Salazar de Buckle et al. 1972; Chávez 1972) and a variety of other types of bread and supplemental proteins. Examples include sweet lupine (El-Dash and Sgarbieri 1980), common beans (Sathe et al. 1981), single-cell protein (Volpe and Zabik 1981), various food legumes (Morad et al. 1980) and cottonseed flour (El-Minyawi and Zabik 1981), fish protein concentrate (Arafah et al. 1980), and germinated and ungerminated faba beans (Finney et al. 1980) for Baladi bread.

A second area of application of supplementation is associated with the preparation of composite flours (Dendy et al. 1975; McWatters 1980; Nielsen et al. 1980; Finney et al. 1982; Jeffers et al. 1979; McConnell et al. 1974; Okaka and Potter 1977) to be used in bakery and pasta products, in increasing demand among the population. Governments are forced to increase their purchase of wheat, since most of these countries do not produce this cereal grain. As a measure to extend the wheat supplies, programs designed to extend wheat flour have been proposed and in some cases implemented. The products used include cassava flour and other cereal grain flours. The inclusion of cassava flour, for instance, reduces the protein level of the product as well as its quality. To bring these back to the original value, or even to improve it, protein sources, mainly soy flour, have been used.

Many of the experimental results available have not been implemented for various reasons. One is that the functional properties or organoleptic characteristics have not been critically considered. A second reason is the lack of nationally produced supplements with the required specifications, as well as economic applications. Finally, there has been reluctance on the part of manufacturers to accept such technologies and lack of interest by governments to support such programs.

Protein Complementation

The results of protein complementation have had a number of applications. One such application is in the formulation of "high protein quality food mixtures" used in nutrition programs in many developing countries, or produced as commercial products. Examples are Incaparina (Bressani and Elias 1968), Maisoy (Bressani 1981), and others (Hayes et al. 1978; Wadsworth et al. 1979; Traver et al. 1981; Terrel et al. 1981; Guerra et al. 1981; Reber et al. 1983; Cheryan et al. 1979). These new products, based on a cereal grain and protein-rich flours from oilseeds or food legumes, have been formulated to contain variable amounts of protein and have been presented either raw or processed. If mixtures of high-protein flours are complemented, for example soy and corn gluten, these may be texturized and used as regular soy-textured products. These mixtures would be high in protein content, thus they could be used to formulate other foods based on starchy food flours, such as cassava, plantain, or banana (Dendy et al. 1975; Bressani et al. 1977B).

A second application of interest is associated with agricultural production and grain storage programs. For example, the combination of corn and beans in a 70:30 weight ratio is nutritionally superior to just corn or beans. Agricultural policies should, therefore, attempt to induce a production of the two staples in a 2.8:1 ratio. Since yield is different for the two, more land should be used for beans. This, of course, does not imply that the land for corn should be reduced, since the cereal grain has more applications, it only indicates that for human use and for purposes of storage the above ratio should be maintained (Bressani 1979).

Other types of agricultural programs could benefit from the significance of findings such as the one above. The system may be very useful in genetic programs to increase the nutritional value of food crops. For example, bean cultivars should be selected for higher methionine content but not at the expense of lysine, the amino acid mainly responsible for the significant increase in the quality of corn and beans. These could be screened biologically on the basis of the optimum protein quality found, which may be more discriminative than feeding the protein source alone (Vargas et al. 1982; Bressani 1982).

An additional application of protein complementation is associated with national food and nutrition programs, which distribute basic staples and other foods among the rural and poor populations. The food distributed should be based on the amounts giving the higher nutritional-quality response. These programs have a number of drawbacks; however, better nutrition is implied if the distributed foods are in th correct weight ratio, and they would be more successful if they were accompanied by nutrition education programs (Araya 1981).

Finally, protein complementation is useful in the preparation of simulated foods of either animal or vegetable origin. For example, common beans and soybeans can be processed in an equal weight ratio to simulate common beans in flavor and texture but with improved chemical composition, such as higher oil content and improved quality. Similar approaches can be used for common beans and cowpeas. The examples for animal-simulated foods are quite extensive and more will be available in the future. The potential of protein supplementation and/or complementation to increase, extend, and improve the world food supply is great, particularly if the problem is considered from the economic, organoleptic, and nutritional point of view.

REFERENCES

Akpapunam, M. A., and Markakis, P. 1981. Protein supplementation of cowpeas with sesame and watermelon seeds. J. Food Sci. *46*, 960–961.

Almquist, H. J., and Grau, C. R. 1944. Mutual supplementary effect of the proteins of soybean and sesame meals. Poult. Sci. *23*, 341–343.

Al-Nouri, F. F., Siddigi, A. M., and Markakis, P. 1980. Protein supplementation of broad beans with sesame. Food Chem. *5*, 309–313.

Antunes, A. J., and Markakis, P. 1977. Protein supplementation of Navy beans with Brazil nuts. J. Agric. Food Chem. *25*, 1097–1099.

Arafah, A., Abassy, M., Morcos, S., and Hussein, L. 1980. Nutritive quality of Balady bread supplemented with fish protein concentrate, green algae, or synthetic amino acids. Cereal Chem. *57*: 35–39.

Araya, H. 1981. Examining the nutritive value of basic foods as a tool for the study of diets in poor countries. Food Nutr. Bull. *3*(2):21–27.

Asian Vegetable Research Development Center (AVRDC) 1976. Mung bean. *In* Progress Report on Mixtures of Mung Bean/Rice and Variability in Methionine Content, pp. 61–67. AVRDC Taiwan.

Association of Official Agricultural Chemists (AOAC). 1965. Official methods of Analysis of the Association of Official Agricultural Chemists. 10th Edition. AOAC, Washington, DC.

Ballesteros, M. N., Yepiz, G. M., Grijalba, M. I., Ramos, E., and Valencia, M. E. 1984. Elaboración, por programación lineal, de nuevos productos a partir de cereales y leguminosas. Arch. Latinoam. Nutr. *34*(1), 130–145.

Bender, A. E., and Doell, B. H. 1957. Biological evaluation of proteins. A new aspect. Brit. J. Nutr. *11*, 140–148.

Betschart, A. A. 1978. Improving protein quality of bread nutritional benefits and realities. Adv. Exp. Med. Biol. *105*.

Boloorforooshan, M., and Markakis, P. 1979. Protein supplementation of Navy beans with sesame. J. Food Sci. *44*, 390–391.

Braham, J. E., and Bressani, R. 1969. Dilution of proteins with non-essential amino acids and inorganic nitrogen. Arch. Latinoam. Nutr. *19*, 421–432.

Bressani, R. 1968. The use of yeast in human foods. *In* Single Cell Protein, pp. 90–121. R. I. Mateles and S. R. Tannenbaum (Editor). MIT Press, Cambridge, MA.

Bressani, R. 1974. Complementary amino acid patterns. *In* Nutrients in Processed Foods. Proteins. P. L. White and D. C. Fletcher, (Editors). Publishing Sciences Group, Acton, MA.

Bressani, R. 1977. Human assays and applications. *In* Evaluation of Proteins for Humans. C. E. Bodwell (Editor). AVI Publishing, Westport, CT.

Bressani, R. 1979. El sistema alimentario cereal-leguminosa de grano. Interciencia *4*(5), 254–259.

Bressani, R. 1981. The role of soybeans in food systems. J. Am. Oil Chem. Soc. *58*, 392–400.

Bressani, R. 1982. Nutritional goals for plant breeders with particular reference to food legumes of the ICARDA Programme. Conference on the Interfaces between Agriculture, Food Science and Human Nutrition in the Middle East. ICARDA/UNU. February 21–25, 1982, Aleppo, Syria.

Bressani, R., and de Villareal, E. M. 1963. Nitrogen balance of dogs fed lime-treated corn supplemented with proteins and amino acids. J. Food Sci. *18*, 611–615.

Bressani, R., and Elias, L. G. 1967. All-vegetable protein mixtures for human feeding. The development of INCAP vegetable mixture 14 based on soybean flour. J. Food Sci. *31*, 626–631.

Bressani, R., and Elias, L. G. 1968. Processed vegetable protein mixtures for human consumption in developing countries. Advan. Food Res. *16*, 1–103.

Bressani, R., and Elias, L. G. 1969. Studies on the use of opaque 2 corn in vegetable protein-rich foods. J. Agric. Food Chem. *17*, 659–662.

Bressani, R., and Marenco, E. 1963. The enrichment of lime-treated corn flour with proteins, lysine and tryptophan and vitamins. J. Agric. Food Chem. *11*, 517–522.

Bressani, R., and Valiente, A. T. 1962. All-vegetable protein mixtures for human feeding. 7. Protein complementation between polished rice and cooked black beans. J. Food Sci. *27*, 401–406.

Bressani, R., Valiente, A. T., and Tejada, C. 1962. All-vegetable protein mixtures for human feeding. 6. The value of combinations of lime-treated corn and cooked black beans. J. Food Sci. *27*, 394–400.

Bressani, R., Elias, L. G., and Braham, J. E. 1968. Suplementación con aminoácidos del maíz y de la tortilla. Arch. Latinoam. Nutr. *18*, 123–134.

Bressani, R., Braham, J. E., Gonzalez, J. M., and Jarquin, R. 1972. Efecto de la sustitución del nitrógeno de la proteína de leche por nitrógeno de urea en terneros no rumiantes. Arch. Latinoam. Nutr. *23*, 389–407.

Bressani, R., Murillo, B., and Elias, L. G. 1974. Whole soybeans as a means of increasing protein and calories in maize-based diets. J. Food Sci. *39*, 577–580.

Bressani, R., Urrutia, J. J., and Elias, L. G. 1976. Nutritive quality improvement of diets based on corn. *In* Proceedings of the Conference on Cereal and Fortification. Report of Second Workshop on Breeding and Fortification, pp. 288–319. Boulder, Colorado, Sept. 12–17, 1976. Agency for International Development, Washington, DC.

Bressani, R., Elias, L. G., Huezo, M. T., and Braham, J. E. 1977A. Estudios sobre la producción de harinas precocidas de frijol y caupi, solos y combinados mediante cocción-deshidratación. Arch. Latinoam. Nutr. *27*, 247–260.

Bressani, R., Elias, L. G., Molina, M. R., and Navarrete, D. A. 1977. Composition and potential use of some tropical fruits. Arch. Latinoam. Nutr. *27*, 475–493.

Bressani, R., Elias, L. G., and Braham, J. E. 1978. Improvement of the protein quality of corn with soybean protein. Adv. Expl. Med. Biol. *105*.

Bressani, R., Hernandez, E., Colon, A., Wolzak, A., and Gomez-Brenes, R. 1981. Efecto suplementatio de tres fuentes de proteína de soya sobre diferentes selecciones o productos de maíz. Arch. Latinoam. Nutr. *31*, 52–62.

Cabezas, M. T., Cuevas, B., Murillo, B., Elías, L. G., and Bressani, R. 1982. Evaluación nutricional de la sustitución de la harina de soya y sorgo por harina de frijol caupí crudo (*Vigna sinensis*). Arch. Latinoam. Nutr. *32*, 559–578.

Chávez, J. F. 1972. Nutritive quality of the protein of arepa flour and its improvement by fortification in Venezuela. *In* Nutritional Improvement of Maize. R. Bressani, J. E. Braham, and M. Béhar (Editors). Proc. Conf., March 6–8, Pub. *L-4*. Inst. of Nutrition of Central America & Panama (INCAP), Guatemala.

Cheftel, J. C. 1979. Nutritional aspects of food processing. 1. Effects of processing on the nutritional value of foods: An overview. *In* Proceedings 5th Int. Cong. Food Sci. and Technol, pp. 170–180. H. Chiba, M. Fujimaki, K. Iwai, H. Mitsuda, and Y. Morita (Editors). Elsevier Scientific Publishing Company, Amsterdam.

Cheryan, M., McCune, T. D., Nelson, A. I., and Ferrier, L. K. 1979. Preparation and properties of soy-fortified cereal weaning foods. Cereal Chem. *56*, 548–551.

De Groot, A. P., and Van Stratum, P. G. C. 1963. Biological evaluation of legume proteins in combination with other plant protein sources. Qual. Plant. Mat. Beg. *10*, 168–184.

Del Valle, F. R., Montemayor, R., and Bourges, H. 1976. Industrial production of soy-enriched tortilla flour by lime cooking of whole raw corn–soybean mixtures. J. Food Sci. *41*, 349–357.

Dendy, D. A. V., Kasasian, R., Bent, A., Clarke, P. A., and James, A. W. 1975. Composite Flour Technology Bibliography. 2nd Ed. Tropical Products Inst., London.

Dutra de Oliveira, J., and De Souza , N. 1972. El valor nutritivo de productos de la molinda del maíz, de la suplementación con aminoácidos y de mezclas de maíz, común y de opaco 2. *In* Mejoramiento Nutricional del Maíz, pp. 209–215. R. Bressani, J. E. Braham, and M. Béhar (Editors). Pub. *L-3*. INCAP, Guatemala.

El-Dash, A. A., and Sgarbieri, V. C. 1980. Sweet lupine-fortified bread: Nutritional value and amino acid content. Cereal Chem. *57*, 9–11.

Elias, L. G., and Bressani, R. 1970. Valor nutritivo de la proteína de la levadura torula y complemento de concentrados proteicos. Arch. Latinoam. Nutr. *20*, 135–149.

Elias, L. G., and Bressani, R. 1971. Amino acid and protein supplementation of defatted cottonseed flour. Arch. Latinoam. Nutr. *21*, 149–167.

Elias, L. G., and Bressani, R. 1973. Valor proteinico de los subproductos de la industria del trigo. Complementación y suplementación del granillo de trigo con concentrados porteinicos. Arch. Latinoam. Nutr. *23*(4), 95–111.

Elias, L. G., Jarquin, R., Bressani, R., and Albertazzi, C. 1968. Suplementación del arroz con concentrados proteicos. Arch. Latinoam. Nutr. *18*, 27–38.

El-Minyawi, M. A., and Zabic, M. E. 1981. Cottonseed flour's functionality in Egyptian Baladi bread. Cereal Chem. *58*, 413–417.

Evans, R. J., and Bandemer, S. L. 1967. Nutritive value of some oilseed proteins. Cereal Chem. *44*, 417.

Finney, P. L., Morad, M. M., and Hubbard, J. D. 1980. Germinated and ungerminated faba bean in conventional U.S. bread made with and without sugar and in Egyptian Baladi breads. Cereal Chem. *57*:267–270.

Finney, P. L., Beguin, D., and Hubbard, J. D. 1982. Effects of germination on bread-baking properties of mung bean (*P. aureus*) and garbanzo bean (*Cicer arietinum*). Cereal Chem. *59*, 520–524.

Food and Agriculture Organization/World Health Organization (FAO/WHO) 1973. Energy and protein requirements. Report of a Joint FAO/WHO ad-hoc Organization. Tech. Rep. Ser. *522*.

Guerra, M. J., Gonzalez, D., Jaffe, W. G., and Calderon, M. 1981. Formulación de una bebida de alto valor nutritivo a base de arroz. Arch. Latinoam. Nutr. *31*, 337–349.

Hayes, R. E., Wadsworth, J. I., and Spadaro, J. J. 1978. Corn- and wheat-based blended food formulations with cottonseed or peanut flour. Cereal Foods World *23*, 548–553.

Huang, P. C., Young, V. R., Cholakos, B., and Scrimshaw, N. S. 1966. Determination of the minimum dietary essential amino acid to total nitrogen ratio for beef protein fed to young men. J. Nutr. *90*, 416–422.

Jansen, G. R. 1973. Amino acid supplementation of common beans and other legumes. *In* Nutritional Aspects of Common Beans and Other Legume Seeds as Animal and Human Foods. W. G. Jaffé (Editor). Proc. Meet. Nov. 6–9. Ribeirao Preto, Brazil.

Jarquin, R., Noriega, P., and Bressani, R. 1966. Enriquecimiento de harinas de trigo, blanca e integral, con suplementos de origen animal y vegetal. Arch. Latinoam. Nutr. *16*, 89–103.

Jeffers, H. C., Noguchi, G., and Rubenthaler, G. L. 1979. Effects of legume fortifiers on the quality of Udon noodles. Cereal Chem. *56*, 573–576.

Kik, M. C. 1960. Rice protein supplementation. Further studies on the nutritional improvement of rice. J. Agric. Food Chem. *8*, 380–382.

Kofranyi, E., and Jekat, F. 1967. Zur Bestimmung der Biologischen Wertigkeit von Nahrungsproteinen. 12. Hoppe Seyler's Z. Physiol. Chem. *348*, 84.

Krishnamurthy, K., Ramakrishan, T. N., Rajagopala, R., Swaminathan, M., and Subrahmanyan, Y. 1960. Studies on the nutritive value of composite protein foods based on ground nut, soybean and sesame flour. Food Sci. (Mysore) *9*, 86–88.

Mertz, E. T., Bates, L. S., and Nelson, O. E. 1964. Mutant gene that changes protein composition and increases lysine content of maize endosperm. Science *145*, 279–280.

McConnell, L. M., Simmonds, D. H., and Bushuk, W. 1974. High-protein bread from wheat–faba composite flours. Cereal Sci. Today *19*, 517.

McWatters, K. H. 1980. Replacement of milk protein with protein from cowpea and field pea flour in baking powder biscuits. Cereal Chem. *57*, 223–226.

Morad, M. M., Leung, H. K., Hsu, D. L., and Finney, P. L. 1980. Effect of germination on physicochemical and bread-baking properties of yellow pea, lentil and faba bean flour and starches. Cereal Chem. *57*, 390–396.

Mouron, J., and Motter, F. 1962. Sweetened condensed vs evaporated milk in improving the protein efficiency of wheat flour. J. Agric. Food Chem. *10*, 512–515.

Nielsen, M. A., Summer, A. K., and Whalley, L. L. 1980. Fortification of pasta with pea flour and air-classified pea protein concentrate. Cereal Chem. *57*, 203–206.

Okaka, J. C., and Potter, N. N. 1977. Functional and storage properties of cowpea powder-wheat flour blends in bread making. J. Food Sci. *42*, 828.

Reber, E. F., Eboh, L., Aladeselu, A., Brown, W. A., and Marshall, D. D. 1983. Development of high-protein low-cost Nigerian foods. J. Food Sci. *48*, 217–219.

Salazar de Buckle, T., Pardo, C. A., De Sandoval, A. M., and Silva, G. 1972. Functional properties of fortified and non-fortified maize flour for use in arepa preparation. *In* Nutritional Improvement of Maize. R. Bressani, J. E. Braham, and M. Béhar (Editors). Proc. Conf., March 6–8, Pub. *L-4*. Inst. of Nutrition of Central America & Panama. Guatemala.

Sarway, G., Sosulski, F. W., and Holt, N. W. 1975. Protein nutritive value of legume–cereal blends. Can Inst. Food Sci. Technol. *8*, 170–174.

Sathe, S. K., Ponte, Jr., J. G., Rangnekar, P. D., and Salunkhe, D. K. 1981. Effects of addition of Great Northern bean flour and protein concentrates on rheological properties of dough and baking quality of bread. Cereal Chem. *58*, 97–100.

Sgarbieri, V. C., Garruti, R., Moraes, M. A. C., and Hartman, L. 1978. Nutritional and sensory evaluation of mixtures of soybean (*Glycine maz* L.) and common bean (*Phaseolus vulgaris* L.), for direct use as human food. J. Food Sci. *43*, 208–210.

Sirinit, K., Soliman, A. G. M., Van Loo, A. T., and King, K. W. 1965. Nutritional value of Haitian cereal–legume blends. J. Nutr. *86*, 415.

Sure, B. 1948. Relative supplementary values of dried food yeasts, soybean flours, peanut meal, dried non-fat milk solids, and dried butter milk to the proteins in milled white corn meal and milled enriched wheat flour. J. Nutr. *36*, 65–73.

Terrel, R. N., Swasdee, R. L., Wan, P. J., and Lusas, E. W. 1981. Cottonseed protein in frankfurters: Effect on pH, cured color and sensory and physical properties. J. Food Sci. *46*, 845–849.

Tobin, G. and Carpenter, K. J. 1978. The nutritional value of the dry bean (*Phaseolus vulgaris*): A literature review. Nutr. Abstr. Rev. *48*, 919–936.

Traver, L. E., Bookwalter, G. N., and Kwolek, W. F. 1981. A computer-based graphical method for evaluating protein quality of food blends relative to cost. Food Technol. *35*, 72–78.

Vargas, E., Bressani, R., Elias, L. G., and Braham, J. E. 1982. Complementación y suplementación de mezclas vegetales a base de arroz y frijol. Arch. Latinoam. Nutr. *32*, 579–600.

Viteri, F. E., Martinez, C., and Bressani, R. 1972. Evaluation of the protein quality of common maize, opaque 2 maize and common maize supplemented with amino acids and other sources of protein. *In* Nutritional Improvement of Maize, p. 191. R. Bressani, J. E. Braham, and M. Béhar (Editors). Conf. Proc. March 6–8, Pub. *L-4*. Inst. of Nutrition of Central America & Panama (INCAP), Guatemala.

Viteri, F. E., Torun, B., Arroyave, G., and Pineda, O. 1981. Use of corn–bean mixtures to satisfy protein and energy requirements of pre-school children. *In* Protein–Energy Requirements of Developing Countries: Evaluation of New Data. B. Torún, V. R. Young, and W. M. Rand (Editors). Food and Nutr. Bull. Suppl. *5*. United Nations University, Tokyo.

Volpe, T. A., and Zabik, M. E. 1981. Single-cell protein substitution in a bread system: Rheological properties and product quality. Cereal Chem. *58*, 441–443.

Wadsworth, J. I., Hayes, R. E., and Apadaro, J. J. 1979. Optimum protein quality food blends. Cereal Foods World *24*, 274–280.

Westerman, B. D., Oliver, B., and May, E. 1954. Improving the nutritive value of flour. 6. A comparison of the use of soy flour and wheat germ. J. Nutr. *54*, 225–236.

Woodham, A. A. 1978. The nutritive value of mixed proteins. Adv. Exp. Med. Biol. *105*.

Woodham, A. A., and Clarke, E. M. W. 1977. Nutritive value of mixed proteins. 2. As determined by net protein utilization and protein efficiency ratio tests. Brit. J. Nutr. *37*, 309–319.

Woodham, A. A., and Deans, P. S. 1977. Nutritive value of mixed proteins. 1. In cereal-based diets for poultry. Brit. J. Nutr. *37*, 289–308.

Yáñez, E., Ballester, D., Aguayo, M., and Wulf, H. 1982. Enriquecimiento de pan con harina de soya. Arch. Latinoam. Nutr. *32*, 417–428.

Young, V. R., and Villareal, A. 1970. Effect in rats of partial replacement of cow's milk protein by supplementary nitrogen. J. Food Sci. *35*, 170–174.

24

Improving the Nutritional Quality of Vegetables through Plant Breeding

H. C. Bittenbender
John F. Kelly

Our understanding of the genetic and environmental factors controlling nutrient levels in vegetables is incomplete. Several factors contribute to this situation. First, the number of vegetable crops greatly exceeds the number of staple grain crops. The number of vitamins and minerals warranting consideration is large compared to the other nutrients; starch, oil, sugar, and protein. The instrumentation and methodology necessary for rapid, precise, and inexpensive analysis are lacking for many nutrients. Strong environmental and genetic interactions control nutrient levels in most vegetables (Mengel 1979). Lastly, there has not been a strong demand by farmers, consumers, or governments to include a thorough understanding of the control of nutritive content of vegetables among major agricultural research priorities. Kelly (1975) estimates that worldwide, less than 10 scientist-years were, at that time, devoted to understanding the basic effects of genetics and environment on nutrients in vegetables.

Several recent reviews indicate that past genetic efforts to improve nutritional content of crops have been primarily to increase the protein content of wheat, maize, beans, and, to a lesser extent, potatoes (Andryushchenko 1981; Baker 1975; Gableman and Peters 1979; Kelly and Rhodes 1975; Meiners and Litzenberger 1973; Silano *et al.* 1982; Tomes 1972; Williams 1979). Most reviews discuss few nutrients, using a few crops as examples, such as β-carotene in carrot or tomato (Baker 1975) or ascorbic acid in potato or tomato (Gableman and Peters 1979), or antinutritive compounds such as protease inhibitors, tannins, and toxins (Kehr 1973; Silano *et al.* 1982).

The current efforts to improve vitamin and protein quantity and quality and to reduce antinutritional factors over a wide range of vegetable crops are discussed.

COMMON BEAN: *Phaseolus vulgaris*

The common bean is the major legume consumed in the New World. It is grown primarily as a grain legume in Central and South America and as a grain and pod legume in the United States and Canada. Compared to the less than 20 legume species frequently consumed by humans, its protein content is about midrange. Methionine, cystine, and tryptophan, the most commonly limiting amino acids, have a wide range of genetic variation (Bressani and Elias 1980). Bean protein digestibility is limited by hemagglutinins, trypsin inhibitors, protease-resistant proteins, and tannins, which reduce protein digestibility by 44–84% (Griffiths 1979; Silano *et al.* 1982).

In the 1960s, interest in protein content of legumes and cereals was enhanced by the public concern about overpopulation and starvation in less developed countries. These problems were frequently interpreted as protein deficiency rather than as a complex socioeconomic problem including protein and calorie malnutrition. Until the mid-1970s, breeding efforts had concentrated on increasing the yield of legumes first and protein content second. Afterward, attention turned to amino acid quality of proteins (Hulse *et al.* 1977; Meiners and Litzenberger 1973). Today, the focus is manipulation of individual proteins and their polypeptides (Barton *et al.* 1983).

Scientists at the University of Wisconsin have been active in developing an understanding of the genetics of and breeding strategies for bean protein. Bliss (1980) lists those factors affecting legumes as protein sources in general, and beans, in particular, as (1) the quantity of protein per seed, (2) the quality of the protein, (3) the biological activity of certain proteins (e.g., trypsin inhibitors and hemagglutinins), (4) inhibition due to protein complexes (e.g., tannins), and (5) poor protein digestibility.

As with most legumes and cereal crops, percentage of protein content is negatively correlated with yield (Silano *et al.* 1982). However, this negative relationship can be avoided by reducing the selection pressure for protein and selecting for protein within a yield potential or simultaneously with yield [Adams 1973; Centro Internacional de Agricultura Tropical (CIAT) 1981, 1983; Parraga *et al.* 1982]. Dickson and Hackler (1973) noted that the maternal genotype, and not the maternal cytoplasm, controls protein content. The backcross and recurrent selection methods are employed with high rates of heritability (56%) and rapid advance from 21.9 to 24.6% protein, dry-weight basis, in two cycles (Poligano 1982; Sullivan 1982).

The major shift from protein content to protein quality, specifically methionine content, was initiated by Kelly (1971) using a *Streptococcus zymogenes* microbiological assay. He demonstrated that a wide range of available methionine, from less than 50 to more than 200% of 'Sanilac,' a standard cultivar, existed among 3600 bean lines. The environmental effect was small compared to the genetic variation. Adams (1973) proposed a three-gene model to explain the range of methionine and protein from Kelly's work involving three proteins of varying methionine content present at high or low levels. Kelly later suggested simultaneous screening for available methionine and cystine using a *Leuconostoc mesenteroides* microbiological assay and the importance of maximum biological value of bean protein rather than amino acid or protein content alone (Kelly and Rhodes 1975; Kelly 1973). Wood *et al.* (1978) reported a high positive association ($r = .86$) between available methionine per gram of protein (AM/P) and protein efficiency ratio (PER) in rats, and higher heritability for AM/P compared to total methionine or methionine per gram of protein. However, the relationship was not consistent (Wood *et al.* 1979).

The successful improvement of maize protein quality through the incorporation of the opaque-2 gene has stimulated interest in specific bean proteins. University of Wisconsin scientists found that variation in a distinct globulin-1 fraction protein (G-1), also called phaseolin, in different cultivars can be used to classify cultivars into three groups (Brown *et al.* 1980). Using gel electrophoresis, 14 phaseolin protein subunit bands have been identified. 'Tendergreen' and 'Sanilac' groups share no common subunits, while the 'Contender' group is intermediate (Brown *et al.* 1981). A series of crosses was made to further clarify the inheritance of the phaseolin subunit and globulin-2–albumin protein subunits using these cultivars. No recombinant electrophoretic phenotypes were noted for phaseolin or globulin-2–albumin groups (Brown *et al.* 1981). With use of a wheat RNA translation system, cultivar subunit banding patterns were shown to be different, according to the structural coding genes for the protein, and not regulator genes alone (Buchbinder *et al.* 1979). In a six-line diallel, the broad-sense heritability of phaseolin was 37–95% (Mutschler and Bliss 1981). They compared the accumulation of phaseolin between high- and low-phaseolin-accumulating lines. Phaseolin accumulation commenced earlier, proceeded at a higher rate, and ceased later in the high-phaseolin lines (Mutschler *et al.* 1980). Recent work with phaseolin indicates that the level is simply inherited, low-phaseolin percentage being controlled by a single dominant gene (Romero-Andreas and Bliss 1982).

Hall *et al.* (1980) suggest that bean globulin is suitable for a major effort to direct genomic sequences, the end product being the alteration of the amino acid composition. This may not increase the yield of high-quality protein, as change in amino acid sequence also affects protein secondary structure and stability, mRNA stability and metabolism, and may induce a metabolic imbalance through high demand on a specific amino acid pool (Barton and Brill 1983).

Mutation breeding to increase protein and methionine content has been used in Soviet and Indian breeding programs with some success (Vardanyan and Vardanyan 1980; Prasad and Prasad 1981).

Improvement of the high-quality albumin proteins is complicated by the association of hemagglutinin (lectin) activity with various globulin-2–albumin protein fractions. Brown *et al.* (1982) separated bean cultivars into eight groups, based on electrophoretic protein/subunit bands, and their agglutinating activity. They list the phaseolin and globulin-2–albumin types and agglutination ratios of more than 107 cultivars. This is in contrast to earlier work suggesting that hemagglutinin activity was under the control of a single gene (Pusztai *et al.* 1979). Cultivars lacking hemagglutinins are available; moreover, the hemagglutinins are heat labile, their activity is destroyed during cooking.

High-yielding cultivars generally have high trypsin inhibitors activity through lack of selection for low levels, but again, cooking denatures the enzyme (Cury *et al.* 1980).

Beans naturally have very low levels (2 mg/100 g dry weight or less) of cyanogenic glycosides (Liener 1973A). Wild types and local cultivars of *P. lunatus*, lima beans have fairly high levels of cyanogenic glycosides (210–300 mg/100 g). Breeding programs in the United States and Europe have developed very low hydrogen cyanide (HCN)-producing cultivars (less than 20 mg/100 g), generally associated with the white seed types. High HCN content in lima beans from an F_2 population ranged from 8 to 240 mg/100 g, indicating dominance for high cyanide and polygenic inheritance (Vanderborght, 1979).

PEA: *Pisum sativum*

The pea is consumed both as fresh and grain legume in the Western countries and as a grain legume throughout the parts of Asia experiencing cool seasons. As with most legumes, yield and protein are negatively correlated. Blixt (1978) studied 20 characters in 2000 lines of the Swedish pea collection. However, among those lines carrying the gene for short internodes, he reported a positive association between yield and protein content (Blixt 1979). Other associated characters may hold promise for selecting for high-protein content. O. P. Singh *et al.* (1980) tried to bridge this negative association with yield by selecting for seed size, which correlates positively with both yield and protein. A Polish study indicates that the inheritance of crude protein content can show dominance for low protein in one cross and additive effects in another. This suggests the need to look more closely at specific proteins (Swiecicki *et al.* 1981).

Bajaj's (1973) classic work with rats measured the PER levels of various cultivars associated with a range of albumin contents. It clearly shows a high positive correlation between PER and albumin content and a low correlation of PER with N or globulin contents. Furthermore, he found that albumin has twice the concentration of sulfur amino acids as globulins. Schroeder (1982), on the other hand, was unable to predict protein fraction ratios (globulin:albumin) using crude seed sulfur content. Gel filtration of albumins from five *Pisum* spp. indicates general similarity with greater differences in the total amount of albumins. Among species, Jakubek and Przybylska (1979) find electrophoretic patterns that reveal qualitative albumin differences.

Legumin, the major globulin protein, has significant variation in amino acid content; methionine varies from 0.28 to 0.72 mol% and cystine from 0.81 to 1.20 mol%, respectively (Casey and Short 1981). A pleiotropic gene, r^a, appears to control the amount of total legumin, starch quality and quantity, and sugar content (Davies 1980). Earlier work by Thompson and Schroeder (1978) suggests five legumin and three vicilin electrophoretic bands, of which all the vicilin bands and two legumin bands were multiple alleles at a single locus. More recently, three legumin genes have been identified, of which two are linked. Vicilin still appears to be controlled by one gene (Matta and Gatehouse 1982).

Inheritance of methionine and tryptophan levels, based on a nine-line diallel, exhibits more nonadditive gene action with heterosis, ranging from 60 to 150% and 30 to 140% of the better parent for tryptophan and methionine, respectively (Gupta *et al.* 1982).

The inheritance of seed-coat tannins is related to flower color. White seed coats from white-flowered lines lack tannins and have no effect on trypsin, α-amylase, or cellulase activities (Griffiths 1981). A five-line diallel using Soviet cultivars indicates that trypsin inhibitors are controlled by one to three genes, showing both additive and dominant effects (Mukhsinov 1981).

Soviet mutation breeding programs, using ionizing radiation and chemomutagens, report 6–15% higher levels of protein compared to initial forms (Masalova 1980; Vasileva 1980).

BROAD BEAN: *Vicia faba*

Interest in the broad bean as a cool-temperature, high-protein grain legume for food and feed has increased (Bond 1979). Significant genetic variation exists, whole-seed protein and starch ranging from 26 to 39% and 35 to 53% (dry weight), respectively (Barratt 1982). The legumin to vicilin ratio for these globulin fraction proteins ranges from 1.75 to 2.3, with legumin accounting for up to 70% of the globulin in fraction (Martensonn 1979). Differences in the protein electrophoretic banding patterns for cultivars differing in cooking quality also suggests variation in these proteins (Stegemann *et al.* 1980). Complete analysis and understanding of the three polypeptide subunits of legumin and the four of vicilin may permit genetic manipulation in the future (Williams 1979).

Major breeding efforts in Europe indicate a variety of selection strategies to improve protein quality and quantity. Some breeders advocate selection for protein content rather than amino acid composition for rapid results (Rakowska 1980). In an effort to avoid the traditional negative association of protein content and seed yield, de Vries (1981) developed a selection index to increase yield and protein simultaneously. The selection index evaluated four yield conponents: plant height, duration of reproductive phase, ratio of podless portion of the plant to overall height, and date of final seed filling. Plants selected were intermediate-sized with many pods.

Those urging protein-quality selection within populations find seed protein content associated positively with total methionine and methionine content of the protein (Pandey et al. 1979). Among genetic populations, only tryptophan and arginine levels are higher in association with higher protein contents (Baudet and Mosse 1980). Sjodin et al. (1981A) recommends selecting for increased sulfur content or legumin fraction within a constant protein level, followed by crosses for higher protein later to maintain high-quality protein.

New sources of genetic variation, such as the wild subspecies V. faba spp. minor, major, equina, and paucijuga, indicate highest protein in paucijuga, but greatest variation in minor (Lafiandra et al. 1979). A mutation program using γ radiation and subsequent selection yielded lines with 35% higher relative protein content (Abo-Hegazi 1979).

Several toxic reactions are associated with broad beans, the most infamous being a hemolytic anemia known as favism. Favism is associated with a human genetic disorder (the inability to produce the enzyme glucose-6-phosphate dehydrogenase) within populations indigenous to the southern Mediterranean region. The heat-stable pyrimidines, vicine and convicine, seem to be associated with favism. However, these substances have been identified in other legumes that do not produce symptoms (Williams 1979). Concentrations of these pyrimidines are highest in pods and seeds, 3–4 weeks after flowering. Favism is associated more with green pod consumption than with consumption of cooked, mature seeds. Of 242 cultivars analyzed for vicine and convicine, concentrations ranged from 0.44 to 0.82% and 0.13 to 0.64% (dry weight) respectively (Pitz et al. 1981).

Other antinutritional substances include hemagglutinins, trypsin inhibitors, and tannins. Sjodin (1977) developed screening methods for hemagglutinins and trypsin inhibitors. Working with populations containing high and low concentrations of these in a rat feeding program, he concluded that hemagglutinins do not affect the biological value of the diet, but high concentrations of either trypsin inhibitors or tannins do give lower biological values (Sjodin et al. 1981B). Tannins not only reduce utilization of seed protein but they inhibit digestive enzymes in vivo (Griffiths 1981). Fortunately, the inheritance of a tannin-free seed coat is well understood. A pleiotropic recessive gene controls white flower color, unpigmented nectaries of the stipules, lack of anthocyanin pigment in the stem, and tannin-free seed coat (Crofts *et al.* 1980). These characters permit early and rapid selection.

COWPEA AND YARDLONG BEAN:
Vigna unguiculata spp. *unguiculata* AND
V. unguiculata ssp. *sesquipedalis*

Cowpea, the black-eyed or crowder pea of the United States, is the dominant grain legume in Africa, and an important pod and grain legume in southern and southeastern Asia. Silano (1982) reports the protein range as 21 to 34% (dry weight). Earlier Bliss (1973) found Nigerian accessions with as high as 36% protein (dry weight).

Globulin is the main seed protein in Philippine cultivars. It ranges from 63 to 67% of total N. Albumin content is less, but its variation is greater. Several lines have been selected for protein quality based on sulfur and albumin content (del Rosario *et al.* 1981A). Crosses made for high-methionine content with the Philippine local cultivar, 'Bush Sitao,' indicate that high methionine is recessive and under maternal control (Dessauer and Hannah 1978). Bliss (1973), also selecting for high methionine, reported a 14% advance over the higher methionine parent and significant location and genotype–location effects on methionine content.

Yardlong bean is consumed as a pod and grain legume in southern and southeastern Asia. Malaysian breeders, using seven diverse lines in a diallel, found that protein content variation was controlled by dominance rather than additive effects and that high protein is recessive (Mak and Yap 1980).

MUNG BEAN AND BLACK GRAM:
Vigna radiata AND *V. mungo*

The mung bean is a grain legume consumed in flour products and as sprouts in southeastern and eastern Asia. Both the mung bean and black gram are important grain legumes in southern Asia. The Asian Vegetable Research and Development Center (AVRDC) has a world mandate for overall mung bean improvement (AVRDC, 1981). Their protein improvement program utilizes the black gram *V. mungo* as a source of high-methionine genes because of limited variation for protein content and quality in mung bean (Tsou *et al.* 1979). An eight-line diallel grown in three locations in India revealed consistent, general combining ability over several environments with dominant genes controlling high protein content (Malhotra *et al.* 1979).

Indian breeders, using an eight-line diallel, found 70% of the black gram F_1 hybrids exhibited heterosis over midparental values for protein and tryptophan. The best parental combinations were identified (Waldia *et al.* 1981). A study of 10 characters in 268 lines revealed that protein content was negatively correlated with seed yield, seeds per pod, pod length, pod clusters per plant, and pods per plant. Pod length appeared to be the simplest selection criteria for protein content (Sandhu *et al.* 1978).

LUPINES: *Lupinus albus, L. angustifolius, L. luteus,* AND *L. mutabilis*

Lupines are a minor grain legume in cool, temperate regions. Hudson (1979) reviewed the breeding program at the University of Reading, England. He reports significant progress in reducing the toxic quinolizidine alkaloids to acceptable levels in the first three of the above listed species. This program has set the stage for development of this crop, which has protein content and quality equal to or better than soybean and is free of protease inhibitors and hemagglutinins.

PIGEON PEA: *Cajanus cajan*

This grain legume is important throughout southern Asia and the Caribbean. The major breeding effort on pigeon pea has been in India, particularly at the International Center for Research in the Semi-Arid Tropics (ICRISAT). The breeding program emphasizes improved yielding ability, disease and insect resistance, and enhanced nutritional value (Remanandan 1981). A range of short- (102 days) and medium- (200 days) duration vegetable-type cultivars have been evaluated in a number of countries. Protein contents ranged from 18 to 23%, sugar from 7 to 15%, and starch from 36 to 54% (dry weight) (Jain *et al.* 1981).

CHICKPEA: *Cicer arietinum*

Commonly consumed in the United States as a salad condiment, the chickpea or garbanzo has been a major grain legume of the drier areas of southern Asia and the Middle East for centuries. The small-seeded "desi" type has higher trypsin and chymotrypsin inhibitor activity, associated with high tannin concentration, than the large-seeded "kabuli" type (Singh and Jambunathan 1981).

Breeding results in India indicate that protein content is positively associated with seed color and size (Govil 1980) and seeds per pod (Rang *et al.* 1980). Sulfur content, although positively associated with methionine, is not associated with tryptophan levels and is negatively associated with protein content (Rang *et al.* 1980). Specific combining abilities for protein content in a 15-parent diallel indicate that protein content is governed by nonadditive gene action and is maternally inherited (Rao 1980; M. P. Singh *et al.* 1980). Electrophoretic banding of nine diverse cultivars with a protein range of 18–29% (dry weight) were found to differ only in minor bands (Tyagi *et al.* 1982).

HYACINTH BEAN: *Dolichos lablab*

Both pods and mature seeds are consumed in India. Path coefficient analysis reveals that protein content is positively associated with yield; which is unusual for a grain or edible legume (Pandey *et al.* 1980). The value of hyacinth bean protein must be determined before any effort is made to enhance protein levels. The author (unpublished data) found very low PER values in selected lines.

WINGED BEAN: *Psophocarpus tetragonolobus*

The winged bean is consumed as a pod legume, leafy vegetable, and root crop in southern and southeastern Asia and has promise as a high protein oilseed adapted to high rainfall and short photoperiod areas [National Academy of Sciences (NAS) 1981]. A comparison of Southeast Asian types with 32–35% protein and 14–15% crude oil (dry weight) shows that the electrophoretic patterns of high methionine and cystine globulin fractions differ among cultivars. This suggests significant genetic variation is available for improvement (del Rosario *et al.* 1981B).

TOMATO: *Lycopersicon esculentum*

Due to the tomato's high consumption per capita throughout the United States and much of the world, its nutritional contribution is significant even without special breeding efforts to improve its nutritional quality (Gableman and Peters 1979). Baker (1975), in an earlier edition, reviewed the nutritional breeding efforts for carotenes by Tomes and for organic acids, flavor factors, and phosphorus content by Stevens.

Tomes' four-gene system, in explaining the various carotene phenotypes, included an R gene controlling carotene precursors, and a T gene directing synthesis from other carotenes to lycopene (red) or β-carotene (orange). A B gene controls the relative proportion of lycopene to β-carotene when R and T are present. A fourth gene, *hp*, proportionally increases the concentration of all pigments (Baker 1975). Tomes (1972), in discussing the history of β-carotene breeding in tomatoes, relates that initial efforts were directed toward increasing disease resistance by crossing *L. esculentum* with a wild, green fruited species, *L. hirsutum*. The discovery of high β-carotene content led to the subsequent development of the 'Caro-Red' cultivar. However, the orange-red cultivar had low consumer acceptability, not because of off-flavor, but because it lacked the traditional red color. Today, U.S. breeding efforts continue with high-lycopene, low-β-carotene tomatoes.

Soviet breeders, also using interspecific crosses, observe a similar β-carotene-enhancing effect in a cross using *Solanum pennellii*. The line selected for advancement had 3.3 mg/100 g β-carotene; others were as high as 17 mg/100 g. They hypothesize that a gene analogous or identical to the *B* gene from *L. hirsutum* in 'Caro-Red' is responsible, as the progeny had carotene content from 10 to 20 times higher than either parent (Vorob'eve and Glushchenko 1981). Another interspecific cross, involving *L. cheesmanii*, revealed dominance and additive effects for high carotene and low lycopene (Daskaloff and Konstaninova 1981).

Efforts to improve ascorbic acid content reveal dominance for high concentration in crosses with *L. cheesmanii* (Daskaloff and Konstantinova 1981). Higher levels are associated with homozygous *hp* (Fedrowitz and Tigchelaar 1979) as well as a high specific combining ability necessary for hybrid development (Singh *et al.* 1980). High ascorbic acid content has been incorporated in a yield and quality breeding program in India via a weighted discriminate function program to select breeding lines (Bhattacharya *et al.* 1979). A soviet mutation breeding program irradiated F_1 pollen to increase phenotypic variation (Zhuchenko *et al.* 1981). The observed reduction of silver nitrate by ascorbic acid in fruits, leaves, and even pollen may serve in the development of a rapid and inexpensive screening method for ascorbic acid (Airapetova and Stepanyas 1981).

CUCUMBER AND BITTER GOURD:
Cucumis sativa AND *Momordica charantia*

Over a 15-year period, Soviet breeders have been developing high-yielding cucumber hybrids with enchanced sugar, dry-matter, and ascorbic acid contents for irrigated areas (Glukhova and Malychenka 1980).

An extensive study of bitter gourd by Ramachandran and Gopalakrishnan (1980) reveals heritability estimates of additive genes for ascorbic acid, phosphorus, and iron. Protein and potassium are under nonadditive gene control. They conclude that selection for high total soluble solids will increase ascorbic acid, vitamin K, and phosphorus while maintaining high protein. Increasing iron in this high-iron vegetable may require a separate program.

CHILI: *Capsicum annum*

Soviet breeders, using chemomutagens, are developing processing cultivars with contents of niacin, pantothenic acid, thiamin, and pyridoxine higher than the standard cultivars (Gukasyan and Gevorkyan 1983).

LETTUCE: *Lactuca sativa*

Soviet breeders are evaluating new breeding lines and have introduced cultivars with high ascorbic acid, sugar, and dry-matter contents (Kochneva 1982; Yudaeva 1982). Under conditions of high nitrate fertility, many vegetables, including lettuce, accumulate nitrates. Subramanya *et al.* (1980), using crosses between high and low nitrate-accumulating cultivars, found that nitrate accumulation is controlled by a few recessive genes.

SPINACH AND INDIAN CHARD: *Spinacia sativa* AND
Beta vulgaris var. *bengalensis*

Maynard and Barker (1979) rejected the hypothesis that the savoyed (wrinkled) leaf trait compared to the smooth leaf is associated with high levels of nitrates in spinach cultivars. They found a stronger relationship existing between high leaf nitrate levels and low leaf dry-matter content. With the use of chemomutagens, a long-standing high dry-matter spinach with four times more iron, one-fourth the oxalic acid, and twice the yield of standard spinach cultivars has been developed in Germany (Handke 1981). 'Pusa Jyoti,' an Indian chard or palak selected from colchicine-treated seeds of 'All Green,' is higher in dry matter and nutritive value than other Indian chards (Choudhury and Rejendran 1980).

CELERY AND PARSLEY: *Apium graveolens*
AND *Petroselinum hortense*

An attempt by Soviet breeders to obtain resistance to parsley *Septoria* leaf spot by crossing parsley with celery produced unexpected changes in nutritional composition. A parsley × celery hybrid released as a new parsley-like cultivar 'Festival 68' is significantly higher yielding and contains more ascorbic acid and β-carotene than the parsley parent. Celery X parsley hybrids have segregated into four distinct types; those commercially useful as leaf celery have more protein, iron, calcium, and twice as much ascorbic acid than the celery parent (Madjarova and Bubarova 1978).

CELOSIA: *Celosia argentea*

In Nigeria, breeding celosia, an important West African, leaf vegetable has resulted in improved iron content in nonpigmented cultivars, which are higher in protein and ascorbic acid than anthocyanin-pigmented types (Omueti 1982).

Brassica spp.

The genus *Brassica* contains many important vegetable crops, *B. oleracea* being one of the most important species. Breeding objectives to improve the nutritional value of these vegetables include increased dry-matter, protein, and vitamin content and reduction of toxins, such as erucic acid and glucosinolates. Glucosinates, single-chained carbon groups with the thiocynate ion (—SCN), have been associated with thyroid problems leading to goiter (Liener 1973B).

Analyses of approximately 1000 cultivars of *B. nigra*, *B. oleracea*, *B. campestris*, *B. carinata*, *B. juncea*, and *B. napus* revealed differences in glucosinolate carbon-side chain lengths. *Brassica nigra* produces glucosinolate side chains 3C or less in length. *B. oleracea* had 3C and 4C side chains and *B. campestris* 3C, 4C, and 5C side chains. Analysis of the amphidiploid species *B. carinata*, *B. juncea*, and *B. napus* suggests that enzyme systems necessary for elongation or hydroxylation of side chains are controlled by additive gene effects (Gland *et al.* 1981).

Red and savoy cabbage (*capitata* group) cultivars contain more goiterogenic precursors than other cultivars (VanEtten *et al.* 1980), as do late-maturing cultivars compared to early-maturing cultivars (Bible *et al.* 1980). VanEtten *et al.* (1976) place cabbage cultivars into four groups based on the relative amounts of 11 different glucosinolates, suggesting the involvement of several genes. Tookey *et al.* (1980) note that seeds proportionally contain 10 times more glucosinolates than leaf tissue. This relationship can be used in a glucosinolate screening program. An enzymatic degradation of glucosinolates to glucose can further facilitate analyses of multiple samples (Kerber and Buchloch 1980).

Brussels sprouts (*gemmifera* group) genotypes have a range of total glucosinolates 100–400 mg/100 g (Heaney *et al.* 1980).

In cauliflower and broccoli (*botrytis* group) cultivars, thiocyanate concentrations decrease at maturity. Large curd and late-maturing types have the highest thiocyanate contents. Ju *et al.* (1980) found a range of thiocyanate concentrations from 0.95 to 1.4 mg/g and 0.77 to 0.95 mg/g (dry weight), in cauliflower and broccoli, respectively.

Kale (*acephala* group) breeding programs in Europe have concentrated on yield and higher protein content (Anonymous 1979). One approach is to redesign the plant to decrease the ratio of petiole and midrib to leaf (Schuphan 1970). In Scotland, selection for dry matter and digestibility plus near-infrared analysis for thiocyanate and other toxic compounds is incorporated into an annual breeding cycle, thus, shortening the biennial generation time (Bradshaw and MacKay 1981).

Soviet workers (Ter-Manuel'Yants 1982) examined various cole crops for vitamin content: cultivars of brussels sprouts and kale had highest ascorbic acid, broccoli and highest in phylloquinone, and cauliflower was highest in niacin and choline.

TURNIP AND RUTABAGA: *Brassica rapa*
AND *B. napus*

Cultivars of the root vegetables rutabaga (Swede) and turnip have glucosinolate concentrations from 0.9 to 10 mg/100 g and 1 to 12 mg/100 g, respectively (Mullin 1978). A turnip lacking goitrin, but not all glucosinolates, has been identified (Chong *et al.* 1982). Chong and co-workers noted that thiocyanate was higher in late-maturing cultivars, reaching a maximum later in the season. In both species, as in cabbage, glucosinolate concentrations in seeds or in etiolated leaves can be used as a screening tool (Jurges and Robbelen 1981).

CHINESE CABBAGE: *Brassica rapa* OR *campestris*
(*chinensis* AND *pekinensis* GROUPS)

The major thrust of the breeding program for Chinese cabbage at AVRDC has been toward higher yields through high dry matter and soluble solids content, which may result in higher carbohydrate, protein, and ascorbic acid levels (AVRDC 1981). Total glucosinolate levels in the cultivars examined range from 23 to 130 mg/100 g in leaves, with a high proportion of 5C glucosinolate side chains. Williams and Daxenbichler (1981) established a qualitative and quantitative baseline for glucosinolates to monitor lines resulting from wide species crosses.

OILSEED RAPE AND MUSTARD: *Brassica napus* AND *B. campestris* OR *rapa*

Rape oil has been used in Asia for centuries. Breeding programs have successfully reduced the toxic erucic acid content. Coupled with the naturally low level of saturated fatty acids, this crop should increase in commercial importance (Williams 1979). A German program, utilizing the world *Brassica* collection, has analyzed glucosinolate content in *B. oleracea, B. campestris,* and *B. napus.* The objective is to produce synthetic *B. napus* from its diploid parents, *B. oleracea* and *B. campestris.* Glucosinolate concentration in defatted natural *B. napus* seed meal ranges from 10 to 250 μmol/g, while in the new synthetic lines it ranges from 66 to 196 μmol/g (Gland 1981). The defatted meal has great value as a protein concentrate. Amino acid content in *B. campestris* is greater in alanine, valine, and aspartic acid than is *B. napus;* and *B. alba* is higher in glycine and aspartic acid than is *B. napus* (Appelquist and Nair 1977).

POTATO: *Solanum tuberosum*

The European Association for Potato Research lists the following breeding areas to improve potato quality: greening, after-cooking blackening, protein and ascorbic acid content, reduction of toxic factors, and flavor and tuber quality for processing (Holden 1981). Soviet breeders emphasize starch content in addition to the above (Osipchuk 1980).

In their review of breeding to improve nutritional quality of vegetables, Gableman and Peters (1979) reason that potato protein should be the focus for major breeding efforts for five reasons: (1) Potato continues to be a major staple food in many parts of the world; (2) potato protein yields per hectare can exceed wheat protein yield by a factor of two; (3) potato protein quality has a biological value comparable to soybean; (4) genetic variability necessary for protein quantity and quality improvement exists; and (5) as recently as the mid-1970s, potato has been a major source of the ascorbic acid, riboflavin, thiamin, and niacin in the U.S. diet [Food and Agriculture Organization (FAO) 1980].

Various breeding strategies have successfully enhanced potato protein content. Soviet breeders use high (2.5–2.9%) protein *S. tuberosum* lines as parents and maintain high starch content. They also have developed chemomutants with 2.65–2.85% protein. The potential protein gain from interspecific hybridization involving *S. andigena, S. demissum, S. stoloniferum,* (Kiryukhin *et al.* 1981), *S. rybinii* with 3.5% protein (Kogut 1981), *S. chacoense,* and *S. phureja* (Demidko

1981) is being considered. In factorial crossing, U.S. breeders using diploid *S. phureja* lines, a species capable of producing unreduced 2*x* gametes, and high-protein 4*x* lines, observed favorable combining abilities for protein. High variability observed in the *S. phureja* progeny may have resulted from lack of photoperiodic adaptation (Veilleux *et al.* 1980, 1981). The International Potato Center in Peru has developed breeding lines with 20% protein (dry weight) compared to average cultivars with 7% protein (dry weight) [Centro Internacional Potato (CIP) 1979].

Several new selection techniques promise advances in breeding for high protein. Gel electrophoresis separates albumins and globulins from species with a range of PERs (Boody and Desborough 1981). The trypsin inhibitor electrophoretic patterns from more than 500 clones of *S. tuberosum* and hybrids with *S. andigena* and *S. demissum* show a distinct association between specific trypsin inhibitor patterns and high protein (Lewosz *et al.* 1981). Thus, specific trypsin inhibitor levels can be used as an aid in selecting high protein lines.

Polish breeders suggest screening for high starch based on positive correlations between dry-matter content of tuber sap and tuber dry matter. They indicate the potential use of refractometrically determined soluble solids which correlate with tuber Kjeldahl nitrogen to screen for high protein (Samotus *et al.* 1980, 1982). Schuphan (1970), in Germany, suggests selection based on tuber morphology, since the bulk of potato protein is found in crystals in the outer cortex; therefore, selection for a thicker outer cortex should increase protein.

At Michigan State University, a protocol to regenerate potato shoots from roots has been developed. Cell lines with twice the free methionine and 1.5 times the total methionine found in unselected cell lines can be isolated and cloned to the callus stage (Hunsperger, 1982). German workers successfully regenerated plants from microspore, protoplast suspension, and shoot tips. Plants were obtained from *S. phureja* and calluses from *S. infundibuliforme*, *S. sparsipilium*, and *S. tarijense* protoplasts (Wenzel *et al.* 1979). Thus, completely new approaches are available for genetic improvement of potato.

Inheritance of various toxic glycoalkaloids (solanine, chaconine, and commaursonine), via simple dominance from its wild parent *S. chacoense*, forced the recall of a new cultivar, 'Lenape' (McCollum and Sinden 1979). The discovery of elevated levels of glycoalkaloids in 'Lenape' precipitated an effort to regulate nutrient and toxin levels in crop varieties previously on the Food and Drug Administration's GRAS (Generally regarded as safe) list (Anonymous 1966, 1970).

An investigation of solamarine glycoalkaloids in more than 100 potato cultivars revealed that, in 'Kennebec' and 10 other cultivars, 42–85% of the total glycoalkaloid concentration is solamarine. The remaining cultivars had much less or lacked solamarines. A selection from *S. demissum*, USDA–96–56, is the male parent of 'Kennebec' and 9 other cultivars, and the source of genes for the synthesis of solamarine and R_1, the gene conferring resistance to late blight (*Phytophthora infestans*). There is no association between solamarine synthesis and late blight resistance from the R_1 (Sinden and Sanford 1981).

Soviet breeders consider glycoalkaloid concentrations of 20 mg/100 g in potatoes as potentially toxic to humans. A chemomutation program has developed new cultivars significantly lower in glycoalkaloids than parent clones (Kolesnikova 1980).

The development of rapid, simple, and inexpensive methods to evaluate glycoalkaloid content has been problematic. A new method of acid extraction of the material has low recovery, though subsequent hydrolysis of the glycoalkaloids and titration is accurate. It should be suitable as a screen for large genetic differences in breeding programs (Coxon *et al.* 1979; MacKenzie and Gregory 1979).

SWEET POTATO: *Ipomoea batatas*

Sweet potato breeding programs in China, Taiwan, the southern United States, and Africa have nutritional objectives. Some U.S. cultivars released in recent years have higher β-carotene levels (17 mg/100 g versus 6 mg/100 g) than do older cultivars. 'Nancy Hall,' an old cultivar, is noted for high (19 mg/100 g) ascorbic acid, although cultivars lacking ascorbic acid are also available.

Sweet potato protein is generally deficient in lysine and total sulfur amino acids. However, protein extracts with PER comparable to casein have been identified in some U.S. breeding lines (Collins and Walter 1982). High protein lines (up to 18% dry weight) are being incorporated into the North Carolina program.

Both the Taiwan and AVRDC programs emphasize protein, β-carotene, and dry-matter content. Selection indices based on multiple characters are expected to enhance root yield by 85% compared to selection for root yield alone (Li 1983).

A selection index based on percentage of soluble solids and root flesh color was 50% more effective than selection for protein content alone (Li 1983). Li (1982) found 70% of the phenotypic variation for protein content was genetically based on F_5 progeny testing over years and locations. Heritability for protein was 57%. Using mass selection with root color as the selection criterion (which correlates with root protein content), and advancing 10% of each generation, he obtained a 7% genetic advance for protein content.

Lin and Chen (1980) report that trypsin inhibitor activity and heat stability range from 20 to 99% among 50 cultivars, and trypsin inhibitor activity correlates positively with water-soluble protein content.

Edible leaves and stem tips make the sweet potato a multipurpose food crop. Some breeding lines high in root protein are high in leaf protein and lysine, containing 13% protein and 4 g lysine/100 g protein, respectively, in the leaves (Zheng, 1980). Villareal *et al.* (1982) noted the need to select for leaf color and flavor to gain consumer acceptance.

At both the International Institute for Tropical Agriculture (IITA) in Nigeria and AVRDC, major selection emphasis for high dry matter and yield resulted in lines with enhanced protein and β-carotene contents (IITA 1981; AVRDC 1981).

CASSAVA: *Manihot esculenta*

A 1978 review of cassava breeding objectives emphasizes high yield and starch content. Higher protein content, and low cyanide (HCN) are less important (dos Satos Filho *et al.* 1980). The CIAT, the international agriculture research center responsible for cassava improvement, has similar objectives (CIAT 1982). A Brazilian program identifies breeding lines both high in starch and low in HCN. Root HCN contents range from 0.06 to 0.32 mg/g and starch, as acid-digestible carbohydrate, from 25 to 39% (de Miranda *et al.* 1982). De Battisti (1982) suggests selecting for high-soluble carbohydrate in leaf tissue, which correlates with high dry matter in the roots. By eliminating the need for roots in preliminary screening, it should be possible to reduce the length of the generation cycle. Furthermore, soluble carbohydrate and HCN contents do not correlate. Thus, selection for high soluble carbohydrate should not affect HCN content.

CARROT: *Daucus carota*

Intensive investigation of the genetics and breeding of carrots in Gableman's laboratory at Wisconsin reveal at least five genes controlling total carotene, α-carotene, and β-carotene in the phloem and xylem of the root. The expression of the carotenoid pigments is recessive to three major genes, X, Y, and Y_2. In the xylem, any dominant allele of the X, Y, or Y_2 genes prevent orange coloration. In the phloem, orange coloration is prevented when Y and Y_2 are present, even if the pigment-enhancing genes IO and O are present. The range of carotene content controlled by these genes is at least 200-fold (Gableman and Peters 1979).

The inheritance of carotene is independent of the inheritance of flavor components, thus, allowing enhancement of flavor without loss of nutritional value (Simon and Peterson 1979). Freeman *et al.* (1980) demonstrated that glucose and fructose concentrations are simply inherited, high sugar being dominant. Differences in sugar contents were explained by high sugar lines having delayed maturity, which results in prolonged photosynthetic activity, compared to low sugar lines (Lester *et al.* 1982).

ASSESSING BREEDING PRIORITIES

The number of vegetable crops for which there are nutrient improvement programs is large. The combination of crops in the average U.S. family diet and the varying amounts of nutrients, protein, vitamins, minerals, plus calorie and fiber content in each crop is difficult to comprehend. How can a breeder decide which nutrient to increase? In the United States the answer to this question is not as crucial as in a country where malnutrition, as a result of insufficient calories, protein, vitamins, and minerals in the diet plus disease and poverty, is a life or death issue.

Two basic breeding strategies can be used: increase the nutrient content of a crop high in a particular nutrient, or increase the nutrient content of a crop low in a particular nutrient but which provides a significant portion of that nutrient in the diet. For example, consider protein supply in the U.S. and Nigerian diets. From Table 24.1 we note that legumes supply 5% of the recommended dietary allowances (RDA) as established by the FAO for protein in the United States. Legumes, chili, green leafy vegetables, and corn-on-the-cob together supply 16% of the RDA for protein in Nigeria. These crops have the highest protein content in the diet. However, in Table 24.2, we note that the consumption of potatoes, beans, corn-on-the-cob, and tomatoes supply three times more protein than all legumes in the U.S. diet. A similar situation exists in Nigeria, where yams, cowpeas, taro, chili, and cassava supply twice as much protein as those crops with high protein content.

Using the Nigerian situation, suppose the decision was made to increase protein in the diet. Breeding to double the protein content of cowpea from 23 to 46%, considering the genetic variation, would most likely be unsuccessful. Alternatively, doubling the protein content of yam (from 2 to 4%) is feasible with known genetic variation. Doubling the protein content of these crops within the present Nigerian food production and consumption situation would provide 9.6 and 14 g/day of protein, from cowpea and yam, respectively. A 200% increase in present cowpea production at the current protein level is necessary to permit consumption equal to 14 g/day of protein. Simply doubling the protein content of yams would require no increase in yield to supply 14 g/day with no increase in yam production.

From the U.S. standpoint, it is interesting to note that potato, lettuce and tomato, not legumes or spinach, are the major noncereal sources of protein, calcium, iron, β-carotene, and ascorbic acid in the American diet. These calculations are based on household supply and

Table 24.1. Percentage of FAO Recommended Dietary Allowances (RDA) Attainable from Vegetables,[a] Roots, Tubers, and Legumes with the Highest Specific Nutrient Concentration Available per Capita

Country	Protein	% FAO RDA	Calcium	% FAO RDA	Iron	% FAO RDA	β-Carotene	% FAO RDA	Ascorbic acid	% FAO RDA
U.S.	Beans Peas Cowpeas Green beans	5	Beans Peas Spinach Cowpeas	2	Beans Peas Spinach Green beans	10	Carrot Spinach Sweet pepper Sweet potato	52	Cauliflower Spinach Cabbage Green beans	43
Brazil	Beans Peas Broadbeans Chickpeas	21	Green leafy vegetables Beans Broadbeans Peas	10	Beans Broadbeans Green leafy vegetables Peas	40	Green leafy vegetables Sweet potato Tomato	39	Green leafy vegetables Cabbage Cassava Sweet potato	160
Nigeria	Cowpeas Chili Green leafy vegetables Corn-on-the-cob	16	Green leafy vegetables Chili Cowpeas Okra	16	Cowpea Chili Green leafy vegetables Taro	17	Chili Green leafy vegetables Sweet potato Tomato	170	Chili Green leafy vegetables Cassava Sweet potato	220
India	Beans Peas Chickpeas Pigeon peas	16	Green leafy vegetables Chickpeas Pigeon peas Chili	10	Beans Peas Chili Pigeon peas Green leafy vegetables	20	Chili Green leafy vegetables Sweet potato	70	Green leafy vegetables Chili Cauliflower Cabbage	50

Source: Food and Agriculture Organization (1980).

[a] All vegetable crops could not be identified by FAO. Therefore, nutrient contribution and content is unknown for a percentage of the diet. For each country the percentage of the daily per capita supply from this category is U.S. 11% of 244 g/day, Brazil 31% of 67 g/day, Nigeria 21% of 67 g/day, and India 64% of 140 g/day. Crops are arranged in descending order of specific nutrient concentration. Note that legumes are dry, vegetables and roots are fresh weight.

Table 24.2. Percentage of FAO Recommended Dietary Allowances (RDA) Attainable from Those Vegetables,[a] Roots, Tubers, and Legumes That Supply the Bulk of Each Nutrient per Capita

Country	Protein	% FAO RDA	Calcium	% FAO RDA	Iron	% FAO RDA	β-Carotene	% FAO RDA	Ascorbic acid	% FAO RDA
U.S.	Potato Beans Corn-on-the-cob Tomato	15	Lettuce Potato Cabbage Tomato Beans	11	Potato Lettuce Tomato Beans	32	Carrot Tomato Spinach Sweet pepper	80	Potato Tomato Cabbage Lettuce	200
Brazil	Beans Cassava Potato Tomato	25	Beans Cassava Green leafy vegetables Sweet potato	17	Beans Cassava Potato Green leafy vegetables	53	Green leafy vegetables Sweet potato Tomato	39	Cassava Tomato Potato Sweet potato	179
Nigeria	Yams Cowpeas Taro Chili Cassava	33	Yams Green leafy vegetables Cassava Cowpeas Chili	38	Yams Cowpeas Green leafy vegetables Cassava Chili	70	Chili Green leafy vegetables Sweet potato Tomato	170	Yams Cassava Chili Green leafy vegetables	290
India	Chickpeas Beans Pigeon peas Other legumes	16	Green leafy vegetables Chickpeas Beans Pigeon peas	10	Beans Green leafy vegetables Chickpeas Pigeon peas	20	Green leafy vegetables Chili Sweet potato	70	Green leafy vegetables Chili Potato Cassava	60

Source: Food and Agriculture Organization (1980).

[a] All vegetable crops could not be identified by FAO. Therefore, nutrient contribution is unknown. For each country the percentage of the daily per capita supply from this category is U.S. 11% of 244 g/day, Brazil 31% of 67 g/day, Nigeria 21% of 88 g/day, and India 64% of 140 g/day. Crops are arranged in descending order of quantity of a nutrient supplied in the national diet.

not on actual consumption and absorption data. Potatoes and fresh cassava provide significant amounts of potential ascorbic acid in the diets of the United States, Brazil, Nigeria, and India. If either is cooked too long, if potatoes are stored too long or if cassava is ground and dried into flour, then the ascorbic acid content is greatly reduced.

Therefore, the choice of which nutrient to enhance in a given crop is not as simple as considering which nutrient is important in the diet of a particular population. Rather, the normal diet and production potential of the farmers and the relative price of the nutrient from various sources should be considered. It may be more feasible for the public to eat the same amount of high protein potatoes or cassava than it is for farmers to produce twice as many beans and for the consumer to buy twice as much.

REFERENCES

Abo-Hegazi, A. M. T. 1979. High protein lines in field beans *Vicia faba:* A breeding programme using gamma rays. 1. Seed yield and heritability of seed protein. 2. Proceedings of a symposium, September 4–8. IAEA, Vienna.

Adams, M. W. 1973. On the quest for quality in the field bean. *In* Nutritional Improvement of Food Legumes by Breeding. Max Milner (Editor). Protein Advisory Group, United Nations, New York.

Airapetova, S. A., and Stepanyas, S. S. 1980. Rapid evaluation of tomato for vitamin C. Plant Breed. Abstr. *51*, 7710.

Andryushchenko, V. K. 1981. Methods of improving the breeding of vegetable crops for chemical composition. Plant Breed. Abstr. *51*, 5261.

Anonymous 1966. Toxicants occurring naturally in foods. Nat. Acad. Sci. Pub. *1354*.

Anonymous 1970. Eligibility of substances for classification as generally recognized as safe in food. Fed. Reg. *35*.

Anonymous 1979. High protein kale. World Crops *31*, 23.

Appelquist, L. A., and Nair, B. M. 1977. Aminoacid composition of some Swedish cultivars of *Brassica* species determined by gas liquid chromatography. Qual. Plant. *27*, 255–263.

Asian Vegetable Research and Development Center (AVRDC) 1981. Progress Report for 1980, p. 110. Shanhua, Taiwan.

Bajaj, S. 1973. Biological value of legume proteins as influenced by genetic variation. *In* Nutritional Improvement of Food Legumes by Breeding. Max Milner (Editor). Protein Advisory Group, United Nations, New York.

Baker, L. R. 1975. Genetic manipulation to improve nutritional quality of vegetables. *In* Nutritional Evaluation of Food Processing. AVI Publishing Co., Westport, CT.

Barratt, D. H. P. 1982. Chemical composition of mature seed from different cultivars and lines of *Vicia faba* L. J. Sci. Food Agric. *33*, 603–608.

Barton, K. A., and Brill, W. J. 1983. Prospects in plant genetic engineering. Science *219*, 671–676.

Baudet, J., and Mosse, J. 1980. Amino acid composition of different cultivars of broad beans *Vicia faba*. Comparison with other legume seeds. *In* World Crops, Vol. 3. E. A. Bond (Editor). Martinus Nijhoff, The Hague.

Bhattacharya, M. K., Nandpuri, K. S., and Singh, S. 1979. Screening of tomato germplasm for quality and yield. Acta Hort. *93*, 301–306.

Bible, B. B., Ju, H. Y., and Chong, C. 1980. Influence of cultivar, season, irrigation and date of planting on thiocyanate ion content in cabbages. J. Amer. Soc. Hort. Sci. *105*, 88–91.

Bliss, F. A. 1973. Cowpeas in Nigeria. *In* Nutritional Improvement of Food Legumes by Breeding. Max Milner (Editor). Protein Advisory Group, United Nations, New York.

Bliss, F. A. 1980. Breeding legumes for nutritional quality. *In* Advances in Legume Science. R. J. Summerfield and A. H. Bunting (Editors). Royal Botanic Gardens, Kew, England.

Blixt, S. 1978. Problems relating to pea-breeding. Agric. Hort. Genet. *36*, 56–87.

Blixt, S. 1979. Natural and induced variability for seed protein in temperate legumes. *In* Seed Protein Improvement in Cereal and Grain Legumes, Vol. 10. Proceedings of a symposium, Sept. 4–8, 1978, IAEA. Vienna, Austria.

Bond, D. A. 1979. *Vicia faba:* Feeding value, processing and viruses. *In* World Crops, Vol. 3. D. A. Bond (Editor). Martinus Nijhoff, The Hague.

Boody, G. and Desborough, S. 1981. Soluble tuber proteins from selected hybrids and their relation to nutritional quality of potato protein. Potato J. *58*, 497–498.

Bradshaw, J. E., and MacKay, G. R. 1981. Kale population improvement and cultivar production. *In* Quantitative Genetics and Breeding Methods. INRA/EUCARPIA Meeting. September 2–4. Versailles, France.

Bressani, R., and Elias, L. G. 1980. Nutritional value of legume crops for humans and animals. *In* Advances in Legume Science. R. J. Summerfield and A. H. Bunting (Editors). Royal Botanical Gardens, Kew, England.

Brown, J. W. S., Ma, Y., Bliss, F. A., and Hall, T. C. 1980. Genetic variation in the subunits of globulin-1 storage protein of French bean. Theor. Appl. Genet. *59*, 83–88.

Brown, J. W. S., Bliss, F. A., and Hall, T. C. 1981. Linkage relationships between genes controlling seed proteins in French bean. Theor. Appl. Genet. *60*, 251–259.

Brown, J. W. S., Osborn, T. C., Bliss, F. A., and Hall, T. C. 1982. Bean lectins 1. Relationships between agglutinating activity and electrophoretic variation in the lectin-containing G2/albumin seed proteins of French bean *Phaseolus vulgaris* L. Theor. Appl. Genet. *62*, 263–271.

Buchbinder, B. U., Ma, Y., and Hall, T. C. 1979. Phenotypic variation of the G1 storage protein of *Phaseolus vulgaris* at the translational level of gene expression. Plant Physiol. *63*, 95–100.

Casey, R., and Short, M. N. 1981. Variation in amino acid composition of legumin from *Pisum*. Phytochemistry *20*, 21–23.

Centro Internacional de Agricultura Tropical (CIAT). 1981. Bean Program Annual Report 1980. Cali, Colombia.

Centro Internacional de Agricultura Tropical (CIAT). 1982. CIAT Report, 1981. Cali, Colombia.

Centro Internacional de Agricultura Tropical (CIAT). 1983. Bean Program Annual Report, 1982. Cali, Columbia.

Centro Internacional Potato (CIP). 1979. Removing the potato from the list of "Luxury vegetables." CIP Circ. 7, 3. Lima, Peru.

Chong, C., Ju, H. Y., and Bible, B. B. 1982. Glucosinolate composition of turnip and rutabaga cultivars. Can. J. Plant Sci. *62*, 533–536.

Choudhury, B., and Rajendran, R. 1980. Pusa Jyoti, a highly nutritive palak. Ind. Hort. *24*, 5–6.

Collins, W. W., and Walter, W. M., Jr. 1982. Potential for increasing nutritional value of sweet potatoes. *In* Sweet Potato Proceedings of the First Int. Symposium. R. L. Villareal and T. D. Griggs (Editors). Asian Vegetable Research and Development Center, Shanhua, Taiwan.

Coxon, D. T., Price, K. R., and Jones, P. G. 1979. A simplified method for the determination of total glycoalkaloids in potato tubers. J. Sci. Food Agric. *30*, 1043–1049.

Crofts, H. J., Evans, L. E., and McVetty, P. B. E. 1980. Inheritance, characterization and selection of tannin-free fababeans (*Vicia faba* L.) Can. J. Plant Sci. *60*, 1135–1140.

Cury, J. A., Crocomo, O. J., Tulmann Neto, A., and Ando, A. 1980. Antitryptic activity of *Phaseolus vulgaris* varieties. Plant Breed. Abstr. *50*, 5839.

Daskaloff, C., and Konstantinova, M. 1981. The inheritance of some quantitative characters determining tomato fruit quality in view of developing high quality lines and cultivars. *In* Genetics and Breeding Tomato. Proceedings of the meeting of the Eucarpia Tomato Working Group, May, Avignon, France.

Davies, D. R. 1980. A gene affecting protein composition of pea seed. Heredity *45*, 138.

de Battisti, C. R., Teles, F. F. F., Coelho, D. T., da Silveira, A. J., and Batista, C. M. 1982. Determination of cyanogenic toxicity and total soluble carbohydrates in cultivars of cassava (*Manihot esculenta* Crantz.) Plant Breed. Abstr. *52*, 8567.

del Rosario, R. R., Lozano, Y. and Noel, M. G. 1981A. The chemical and biochemical composition of legume seeds. 2. Cowpea. Philipp. Agric. *64*, 49–57.

del Rosario, R. R., Lozano, Y., Noel, M. G., and Flores, D. M. 1981B. The chemical and biochemical composition of legume seeds. 3. Winged bean. Philipp. Agric. *64*, 143–153.

Demidko, Y. D. 1981. Use of the species *Solanum chacoense* and *S. phureja* in breeding potato for high protein content. Plant Breed. Abstr. *51*, 501.

de Miranda, L. C. G., Coelho, D. T., Teles, F. F. F., da Silveira, A. J., and Rezende, J. L. M. 1982. Comparison between starch and HCN contents of some cassava (*Manihot esculenta* Crantz) cultivars grown in Minas Gerais. Plant Breed. Abstr. *52*, 8568.

Dessauer, D. W., and Hannah, L. C. 1978. Genetic characterization of two high-methionine cowpea lines. Trop. Grain Legume Bull. *13/14*, 9–11.

de Vries, A. P. 1981. The search for an effective method of selection for seed yield and protein content in faba bean (*Vicia faba*). FABIS Newsletter *19*(3), 20.

Dickson, M. H., and Hackler, L. R. 1973. Protein quantity and quality in high yielding beans. *In* Nutritional Improvement of Food Legumes by Breeding. Max Milner (Editor). Protein Advisory Group, United Nations, New York.

dos Satos Filho, J. M., dos Valle, D. C., and de V. Sampaio, H. S. 1980. Some aspects of cassava breeding. Plant Breed. Abstr. *50*:10530.

Fedrowitz, J. H., and Tigchelaar, E. C. 1979. Diallel analysis for yield and tomato fruit quality utilizing high pigment and crimson parents. HortScience *14*, 458.

Food and Agriculture Organization (FAO). 1980. Food Balance Sheets and Per Caput Food Supplies 1975–1977 Avg. FAO, Rome.

Freeman, R. E., Simon, P. W., and Peterson, C. E. 1980. The inheritance of sugars in carrot (*Daucus carota*). HortScience *15*, 421.

Gableman, W. H., and Peters, S. 1979. Genetical and plant breeding possibilities for improving the quality of vegetables. Acta Hort. *93*, 243–259.

Gland, A. 1981. Content and pattern of glucosinolates in seeds of resynthesized *Brassica napus* and its diploid progenitors, *B. oleracea* and *B. campestris.* Cruciferae Newsletter *5*, 43–46.

Gland, A., Robbelen, G., and Thies, W. 1981. Variation of alkenyl glucosinolates in seeds of brassica species. Z. Pflanzenzuecht. *87*, 96–110.

Glukhova, V. M., and Malychenko, L. P. 1980. Chemical composition of the fruit in cucumber under irrigation in the Volga-Akhtuba flood plain. Plant Breed. Abstr. *50*, 8229.

Govil, J. N. 1980. Plant type in relation to protein yield and disease resistance in chickpea (*Cicer arietinum* L.) Legume Res. *3*, 38–44.

Griffiths, D. W. 1979. The role of field bean polyphenolics in digestive enzyme inhibition. *In* World Crops, Vol. 3. E. A. Bond (Editor). Martinus Nijhoff, The Hague.

Griffiths, D. W. 1981. The polyphenolic content and enzyme inhibitory activity of testas from bean (*Vicia faba*) and pea (*Pisum* spp.) varieties. J. Sci. Food Agric. *32*, 797–804.

Gukasyan, L. A., and Gevorkyan, L. A. 1983. B group vitamins in the fruits of red pepper mutants. Plant Breed. Abstr. *53*, 3506.

Gupta, K. R., Dahita, B. S., Popli, S., Dhillon, S., and Dhindsa, K. S. 1982. Genetics of tryptophan and methionine content in pea. Ind. J. Agric. Sci. *52*, 448–451.

Hall, T. C., Sun, S. M., Buchbinder, B. U., Pyne, J. W., Bliss, F. A., and Kemp, J. D. 1980. Bean seed globul in mRNA; translation, characterization, and its use as a probe towards genetic engineering of crop plants. C. J. Leaver (Editor). NATO Advanced Study Inst. Ser. *29*, 259–272.

Handke, S. 1981. A mutant with a very long lasting vegetative phase in spinach. Mutation Breed. Newsletter *18*, 11–12.

Heaney, R. K., Curl, C. L., Spinks, E. A., and Fennwick, G. R. 1980. Factors influencing the glucosinolate content of brassicas. Cruciferae Newsletter *5*, 47.

Holden, J. H. W. 1981. The contribution of breeding to the improvement of potato quality. *In* Survey Papers of the Eighth Triennial Conference of the European Association for Potato Research. Munich, German Federal Republic.

Hudson, B. J. F. 1979. The nutritional quality of lupinseed. Qual. Plant. *29*, 245–251.

Hulse, J. H., Rachie, K. O., and Billingsley, L. W. 1977. Nutritional standards and methods of evaluation for food legume breeders. Int. Develop. Res. Centre, Ottawa, Canada.

Hunsperger, J. P. 1982. Development of selection strategies for the isolation strategies for the isolation of methionine accumulating cell lines in *Solanum tuberosum* L. Ph.D. disseration. Michigan State Univ., East Lansing.

International Institute of Tropical Agriculture (IITA) 1981. Annual Report for 1980. Ibadan, Nigeria.

Jain, K. C., Sharma, D., Gupta, S. C., Reddy, L. J., and Singh, U. 1981. Breeding for vegetable-type pigeonpeas. *In* Proceedings of the International Workshop on Pigeonpeas, Int. Center for Research in Semi-Arid Tropics, December 15–19, 1980, Vol. 2. Patancheru, India.

Jakubek, M., and Przybylska, J. 1979. Comparative study of seed proteins in the genus *Pisum*. 3. Electrophoretic patterns and amino acid composition of albumia fractions separated by gel filtration. Genet. Polon. *20*, 369–380.

Ju, H. Y., Bible, B. B., and Chong, C. 1980. Variation of thiocynate ion content in cauliflower and broccoli cultivars. J. Am. Soc. Hort. Sci. *105*, 187–192.

Jurges, K., and Robbelen, G. 1981. Possibilities of selection of glucosinolate content in Swedes (*Brassica napus* L. var. *napobrassica* L.) Plant Breed. Abstr. *51*, 4321.

Kehr, August E. 1973. Naturally-occurring toxicants and nutritive value in food crops. HortScience *8*, 4–5.

Kelly, J. F. 1971. Genetic variation in the methionine levels of mature seeds of common bean (*Phaseolus vulgaris* L.). J. Am. Soc. Hort. Sci. *96*, 561–563.

Kelly, J. F. 1973. Increasing protein quantity and quality. *In* Nutritional Improvement of Food Legumes by Breeding. Max Milner (Editor). Protein Advisory Group, United Nations, New York.

Kelly, J. F. 1975. Improving food values of vegetables. HortScience *10*, 568–569.

Kelly, J. F., and Rhodes, B. B. 1975. The potential for improving the nutrient composition of horticultural crops. Food Technol. 27:139–140.

Kerber, E., and Buchloh, G. 1980. Glucosinolate contents of seeds of *Brassica oleracea* L. convar. *capitata* (L.) Alef. var. *capitata alba* var. *capitata rubra*. Plant Breed. Abstr. *50*, 10871.

Kiryukhin, V. P., Kyazeva, V. P., and Chernikova, M. F. 1981. Methods of increasing tuber protein content in potato. Plant Breed. Abstr. *51*, 8979.

Kochneva, V. N. 1982. Evaluation of lettuce varieties in greenhouses in the Polar region. Plant Breed. Abstr. *52*, 7056.

Kogut, I. D. 1981. Content of protein in the tubers of wild potato species in the Poles'e. Plant Breed. Abstr. *51*, 2267.

Kolesnikova, L. G. 1980. Effect of supermutagens of content of glycoalkaloids in potato tubers. Plant Breed. Abstr. *50*, 5240.

Lafiandra, D., Polignano, G. B., and Colaprico, G. 1979. Protein content and amino acid composition of seed in varieties of *Vicia faba* L. Z. Pflanzenzuecht. *83*, 308–314.

Lester, G. E., Baker, L. R., and Kelly, J. F. 1982. Physiology of sugar accumulation in carrot breeding lines and cultivars. J. Am. Soc. Hort. Sci. *107*, 381–387.

Lewosz, J., Reda, S., and Rys, D. 1981. The protease inhibitors as genetic markers of high protein content in potato tubers. *In* Abstracts of Conference Papers of the Eighth Triennial Conference of the European Association for Potato Research. Munich, German Federal Republic.

Li, L. 1982. Breeding for increased protein content in sweet potato. *In* Sweet Potato Proceedings of the First Int. Symposium. R. L. Villareal and T. D. Griggs (Editors). Asian Vegetable Research and Development Center, Shanhua, Taiwan.

Li, L. 1983. Improvement of yield and quality in sweet potatoes. Plant Breed. Abstr. *53*, 601.

Liener, I. E. 1973A. Antitryptic and other antinutritional factors in legumes. *In* Nutritional Improvement of Food Legumes by Breeding. Max Milner (Editor). Protein Advisory Group, United Nations, New York.

Liener, I. E. 1973B. Naturally occurring toxicants of horticultural significance. HortScience *8*, 112–116.

Lin, Y. H., and Chen, H. L. 1980. Level and heat stability of trypsin inhibitor activity among sweet potato (*Ipomoea batatas* L.) varieties. Bot. Bull. Acad. Sin. *21*, 1–13.

MacKenzie, J. D., and Gregory, P. 1979. Evaluation of a comprehensive method for total glycoalkaloid determination. Am. Potato J. *56*, 27–33.

Madjarova, M. J., and Bubarova, M. G. 1978. New forms obtained by hybridization of *Apium graveolens* and *Petroselinum hortense*. Acta Hort. *73*, 65–72.

Malhotra, R. S., Gupta, P. K., and Arora, N. D. 1979. Combining ability and inheritance studies for protein content in mungbean (*Vigna radiata* (1.) Wilczek). Qual. Plant. *28*, 323–331.

Mak, C., and Yap, T. C. 1980. Inheritance of seed protein content and other agronomic characters in yardlong bean (*Vigna sesquipedalis* Fruw.) Theor. Appl. Genet. *56*, 233–239.

Martensonn, P. 1979. Variation in legumin vicilin ratio between and within cultivars of *Vicia faba* 1. var. *minor*. *In* World Crops, Vol. 3. D. A. Bond (Editor). Martius Nihoff, The Hague.

Masalova, V. L. 1980. Chemical mutagenesis in breeding pea for quality. Plant Breed. Abstr. *50*, 7660.

Matta, N. K., and Gatehouse, J. A. 1982. Inheritance and mapping of storage protein genes in *Pisum sativum* L. Heredity *48*, 383–392.

Maynard, D. N., and Barker, A. U. 1979. Regulation of nitrate accumulation in vegetables. Acta Hort. *93*, 153–172.

McCollum, G. D., and Sinden, S. L. 1979. Inheritance study of tuber glycoalkaloids in a wild potato, *Solanum chaeoense* Bitter. Am. Potato J. *56*, 95–113.

Meiners, J. P., and Litzenberger, S. C. 1973. Breeding for nutritional improvement. *In* Nutritional Improvement of Food Legumes by Breeding. Max Milner (Editor). Protein Advisory Group, United Nations, New York.

Mengel, K. 1979. Influence of exogenous factors on the quality and chemical composition of vegetables. Acta Hort. *93*, 133–151.

Mukhsinov, V. K. H. 1981. Inheritance of trypsin inhibitor activity in the seeds of pea (*Pisum sativum* L.). Plant Breed. Abstr. *51*, 4751.

Mullin, W. J. 1978. A survey of the glucosinolate content of rutabaga (*Brassica napobrassica* Mill.) and turnip (*B. rapa* L.). Cruciferae Newsletter *3*, 22.

Mutschler, M. A., and Bliss, F. A. 1981. Inheritance of bean seed globulin content and its relationship in protein content and quality Crop Sci. *21*, 289–294.

Mutschler, M. A., Bliss, F. A., and Hall, T. C. 1980. Variation in the accumulation of seed storage protein among genotypes of *Phaseolus vulgaris* L. Plant Physiol. *65*, 627–630.

National Academy of Sciences (NAS) 1981. The Winger Bean: A High Protein Crop for the Tropics. NAS, Washington, DC.

Omueti, O. 1982. Effects of age on the elemental nutrients of *Celosia* cultivars. Exp. Agric. *18*, 89–92.

Osipchuk, A. A. 1980. Parental pairs for breeding potato for high starch content combined with other characters. Plant Breed. Abstr. *50*, 1357.

Pandey, M. P., Frauen, M., and Paul, C. 1979. Selection of methionine by GLC after CNBr treatment in a germplasm collection and a mutagen-tested population of *Vicia faba* L. 2. Proceedings of a symposium, September 4–8. IAEA, Vienna.

Pandey, R. P., Assawa, B. M., and Assawa, R. K. 1980. Correlation and patho-coefficient analysis in *Dolichos labiab* Linn. Ind. J. Agric. Sci. *50*, 481–484.

Parraga, M. S., Junqueira Netto, A., de S. Bueno, L. C., Pereira, P., and dos S. Penoni, J. 1982. Assessment of total protein content of 200 cultivars of French bean (*Phaseolus vulgaris* L.), with a view to breeding. Plant Breed. Abstr. *52*, 10883.

Pitz, W. J., Sosulski, F. W., and Rowland, G. G. 1981. Effect of genotype and environment on vicine and convicine levels in fababeans (*Vicia faba* minor). J. Sci. Food Agric. *32*, 1–8.

Poligano, G. B. 1982. Breeding for protein percentage and seed weight in *Phaseolus vulgaris* L. J. Agric. Sci. *99*, 191–197.

Prasad, P. R., and Prasad, A. B. 1981. Induced variability in methionine content in *Phaseolus vulgaris* L. Persp. Cytol. Genet. *3*, 679–688.

Pusztai, A., Clarke, E. M. W., King, T. P., and Stewart, J. C. 1979. Nutritional evaluation of kidney beans (*Phaseolus vulgaris*): Chemical composition, lectin content and nutritional value of selected cultivars. J. Sci. Food Agric. *30*, 843–848.

Rakowska, M. 1980. The nutritional value of the protein of broad bean seeds and the prospects of breeding for its improvement. Plant Breed. Abstr. *50*, 20978.

Ramachandran, C., and Gopalakrishnan, P. K. 1980. Variability studies for biochemical traits in bitter gourd. Agric. Res. Kerala *18*, 27–32.

Rang, A., Sandhu, T. S., and Bhullar, B. S. 1980. Protein and amino-acid association with yield and its components in gram. Ind. J. Genet. Plant Breed. *40*, 423–426.

Rao, P. U. 1980. Protein and amino acid content of high yielding varieties of bengal gram (*Cicer arietinum*) and their diallel crosses. Ind. J. Nutr. Diet. *17*, 408–409.

Remanandan, P. 1980. The wild gene pool of *Cajanus* at ICRISAT, present and future. *In* Proceedings of the International Workshop on Pigeonpeas, Vol. 2, December 15–19. Int. Center for Research in Semi-Arid Tropics, Patancheru, India.

Romero-Andreas, J., and Bliss, F. A. 1982. A dominant regulator gene of phaseolin. HortScience *17*, 504.

Samotus, B., Leja, M., Scigalski, A., Dulinski, J., and Siwanowicz, R. 1980. A simplified method of determining protein in potato tubers. Plant Breed. Abstr. 50, 8623.

Samotus, B., Leja, M., Scigalski, A., Dulinski, J., and Siwanowicz, R. 1982. Refractometric method of protein determination in potato tubers. Plant Breed. Abstr. 52, 563.

Sandhu, T. S., Bhullar, B. S., Cheema, H. S., and Brar, J. S. 1978. Grain protein, yield and its components in urdbean. Ind. J. Genet. Plant Breed. 38, 410–415.

Schroeder, H. E. 1982. Quantitative studies of the cotyledonary proteins in the genus *Pisum*. J. Sci. Food Agric. 33, 623–633.

Schuphan, W. 1970. Control of plant proteins: The influence of genetics and ecology of food plants. *In* Proteins as Human Food. R. A. Lawrie (Editor). AVI Publishing Co., Westport, CT.

Silano, V., Bansul, H. C., and Bozzini, A. 1982. Improvement of Nutritional Quality of Food Crops. FAO Plant Prod. Prot. Paper 34. FAO, Rome.

Simon, P. W., and Peterson, C. E. 1979. Genetic and environmental components of carrot culinary and nutritive value. Acta Hort. 93, 271–278.

Sinden, S. L., and Sanford, L. L. 1981. Origin and inheritance of solamarine glycoalkaloids in commercial potato cultivars. Am. Potato J. 58, 305–325.

Singh, B., Kalloo, A., Pandita, M. L. 1980. Combining ability for quality characters in tomato (*Lycopersicon esculentum* Mill.). Haryana Agric. Univ. Res. 10, 179–183.

Singh, M. P., Singh, H. P., and Katiyar, R. P. 1980. Note on genetic architecture of protein content in advanced generation of chickpea. Trop. Grain Legume Bull. 19, 48–50.

Singh, O. P., Singh, R. B., and Singh, F. 1980. Combining ability of yield and some quality traits in peas (*Pisum sativum* L.). Z. Pflanzenzuecht. 84, 133–138.

Singh, U., and Jambunathan, R. 1981. Studies on desi and kabuli chickpea (*Cicer arietinum* L.) cultivars 4. Levels of protease inhibitors, levels of polyphenolic compounds and *in vitro* protein digestibility. J. Food Sci. 46, 1364–1367.

Sjodin, J. 1977. Breeding for quality factors in broad beans. *In* Breeding Methods in Food Legumes. FAO Plant Prod. Paper, 9. FAO, Rome.

Sjodin, J., Martensson, P., and Magyarosi, T. 1981A. Selection for improved protein quality in field bean (*Vicia faba* L.). Z. Pflanzenzuecht. 86, 221–230.

Sjodin, J., Martensson, P., and Magyarosi, T. 1983. Selection for antinutritional substances in field bean (*Vicia faba* L.). Z. Pflanzenzuecht. 86, 231–247.

Stegemann, H., El-Tabey Shehata, A., and Hamza M. 1980. Broad bean proteins (*Vicia faba* L.). Electrophoretic studies on seeds of some German and Egyptian cultivars. Z. Acker Pflanzenbau. 149, 447–453.

Subramanya, R., Vest, G., and Honma, S. 1980. Inheritance of nitrate accumulation in lettuce. HortScience 15, 525–526.

Sullivan, J. G. 1982. Recurrent selection for increased seed yield and percentage seed protein in the common bean (*Phaseolus vulgaris* L.) using a selection index; and isolation and analysis of major genes controlling phaseolin. Ph.D. dissertation. Univ. of Wisconsin, Madison.

Swiecicki, W. K., Kaczmarek, Z., and Surma, M. 1981. Inheritance and heritability of protein content in seeds of selected crosses of pea (*Pisum sativum* L.) Genet. Polon. 22, 189–195.

Ter-Manuel Yants, E. E. 1982. Vitamin content in different *Brassica* species. Plant Breed. Abstr. 52, 8749.

Thompson, J. A., and Schroeder, H. E. 1978. Cotyledonary storage proteins in *Pisum sativum*. 2. Hereditary variation in components of the legumin and vicillin fractions. Aust. J. Plant Physiol. 4, 281–294.

Tomes, Mark L. 1972. Breeding for improved nutritional value. HortScience, 7, 154–156.

Tookey, H. L., Daxenbichler, M. E., VanEtten, C. H., Kwolek, W. F., and Williams, P. H. 1980. Cabbage glucosinolates: Correspondence of patterns in seeds and leafy heads. J. Am. Soc. Hort. Sci. *105*, 714–717.

Tsou, C. S., Hsu, M. S., Tan, S. T., and Park, H. G. 1979. The protein quality of mungbean and its improvement. Acta Hort. *93*, 279–287.

Tyagi, P. S., Singh, B. D., and Jaiswal, H. K. 1982. Studies on the genetics of protein content in chickpeas. Int. Chickpea Newsletter *6*, 6–8.

Vanderborght, T. 1979. Measuring the hydrocyanic acid content of *Phaseolus lunatus* L. Plant Breed. Abstr. *50*, 9760.

VanEtten, C. H., Daxenbichler, M. E., Williams, P. H., and Kowlek, W. F. 1976. Glucosinolates and derived products in cruciferous vegetables. Analysis of the edible part from twenty-two varieties of cabbage. J. Agric. Food Chem. *24*, 452–455.

VanEtten, C. H., Daxenbichler, M. E., Tookey. H. L., Kwolek, W. F., Williams, P. H., and Yoder, O. C. 1980. Glucosinolates: Potential toxicants in cabbage cultivars. J. Am. Soc. Hort. Sci. *105*, 71–714.

Vardanyan, K. H., and Vardanyan, J. H. 1980. Study of biochemical mutants of French bean. Plant Breed. Abstr. *51*, 1573.

Vasileva, M. 1980. The application of induced mutation in obtaining genetic diversification in peas. Plant Breed. Abstr. *50*, 5907.

Veilleux, R. E., Desborough, S., and Lauer, F. I. 1980. Utilization of unreduced gametes in breeding for yield and total tuber protein in potatoes. Am. Pot. J. *57*, 497–498.

Veilleux, R. C., Lauer, F. I., and Desborough, S. L. 1981. Breeding behavior for tuber protein in *Solanum tuberosum* and *tuberosum-phureja* hybrids. Euphytica *30*, 563–577.

Villareal, R. L., Tsou, S. C., Lo, H. F., and Chiu, S. C. 1982. Sweet potato tips as vegetables. *In* Sweet Potato Proceedings of the First Int. Symposium. R. L. Villareal and T. D. Griggs (Editors). Asian Vegetable Research and Development Center, Shanhua, Taiwan.

Vorob'eva, G. A., and Glushchenko, E. Y. 1981. Characteristics of high-carotene hybrids of *Lycopersicon esculentum* Mill. Plant Breed. Abstr. *51*, 8545.

Waldia, R. S., Pupli, S., and Dhindsa, K. S. 1981. Heterosis for protein and tryptophan contents in urdbean (*Vigna mungo* (L.) Hepper). Haryana Agric. Univ. J. Res. *11*, 27–30.

Wenzel, G., Schieder, D., Przewozny, T., Sopory, S. K., and Melchers, G. 1979. Comparison of single cell culture derived *Solanum tuberosum* L. plants and a model for their application in breeding programs. Theor. Appl. Genet. *55*, 49–55.

Williams, P. H., and Daxenbichler, M. E. 1981. Glucosinolates in Chinese cabbage. *In* Chinese Cabbage, Proceedings of the First International Seminar. N. S. Talekar and T. D. Griggs (Editors). Asian Vegetable Research and Development Center, Shanhua, Taiwan.

Williams, W. 1979. Genetic means and cultural methods for improving nutritional value of crops. Qual. Plant. *29*, 197–217.

Wood, D. R., Nowick, E. A., Fabian, H. J., and McClean, P. E. 1978. Genetic variability and heritability of available methionine in seed protein improvement in cereal and grain legumes. Proceedings of a symposium, September 4–8. IAEA, Vienna.

Wood, D. R., McClean, P., and Mattjik, A. 1979. Location and year effects on protein, available methionine and total methionine in dry beans. Agron. Abstr. *82*, 175.

Yudaeva, V. E. 1982. Promising lettuce varieties for field cultivation in Moscow province. Plant Breed. Abstr. *52*, 7055.

Zheng, X. X. (Cheng, H. H.). 1980. Protein and aminoacid composition of tubers, stems and leaves of sweet potato. Plant Breed. Abstr. *50*, 6456.

Zhuchenko, A. A., Andryushchenko, V. K., Safronova, L. I., and Korol, A. B. 1981. Treatment of F_1 gametes as a method of altering the composition of the F_2 population. Plant Breed. Abstr. *51*, 894.

The Role of
the United States Government
in Regulating
the Nutritional Value
of the Food Supply

Victor P. Frattali
John E. Vanderveen
Allan L. Forbes

For the most part, the role that the United States government plays in regulating the nutritional value of the national food supply has been, and continues to be, based on authority contained in various federal laws. In chronological order, according to date of enactment, key examples include the Food and Drugs Act of June 30, 1906, the Federal Meat Inspection Act of March 4, 1907, the Federal Food, Drug, and Cosmetic Act of June 25, 1938, which superseded the Food and Drugs Act of 1906, and the Poultry Products Inspection Act of August 28, 1957. This chapter will be limited almost exclusively to a consideration of the Federal Food, Drug, and Cosmetic Act (FFD&C Act) because it is on the basis of this law that the Food and Drug Administration (FDA), a Public Health Service agency in the Department of Health and Human Services, has promulgated regulations dealing with the nutritional value of the food supply. The Food Safety and Inspection Service of the U.S. Department of Agriculture (USDA) has responsibility under the Federal Meat Inspection Act and the Poultry Products Inspection Act for ensuring that meat and poultry products in the marketplace are wholesome, unadulterated, and properly labeled.

HISTORY

Prior to a discussion of federal regulations pertaining to the nutritional value of foods, a brief review of past and current food laws is in order. The first federal food and drug law banned from interstate commerce any traffic in adulterated or misbranded food or drugs. The statute also made it unlawful to manufacture adulterated or misbranded foods or drugs within any territory of the United States and the District of Columbia. The term food included all articles used by man or animals for food, drink, confectionary, or condiment, whether simple, mixed, or compounded. Several conditions, among others, whereby a food was deemed in violation of the 1906 Act included the following: (1) if any substance was mixed and packed with an article so as to reduce or lower or injuriously affect its quality or strength; (2) if any substance was substituted wholly or in part for the article; (3) if any valuable constituent of the article was wholly or in part abstracted; (4) if the article contained any added poisonous or other deleterious ingredient which might render it injurious to health; and (5) if it consisted in whole or in part of a filthy, decomposed, or putrid animal or vegetable substance, or any portion of an animal unfit for food, or if the food was the product of a diseased animal, or one that had died otherwise than by slaughter. Food was to be considered misbranded if it was an imitation of or if it was for sale under the name of another article. Labeling or branding so as to deceive or mislead the purchaser, purporting to be a foreign product when not so, partial or total replacement of the contents of the package as originally put up, or failure to state certain ingredients on the label all constituted mislabeling. Any packaging or labeling bearing a statement, design, or device which was misleading in any particular rendered a food misbranded. The Secretary of Agriculture, the Secretary of the Treasury, and the Secretary of Commerce and Labor were to promulgate rules and regulations for carrying out the provisions of the Act, including the collection and examination of foods and drugs. The Bureau of Chemistry of the USDA, predecessor of the current FDA, was to examine specimens of food and drugs for adulteration or misbranding. Any product which was adulterated or misbranded within the meaning of the Act was subject to seizure and condemnation.

As with most initial endeavors, it became apparent after some years that the 1906 Act had serious weaknesses in several areas of food and drug regulation. Attempting to strengthen federal authority, Senator Royal S. Copeland of New York introduced new legislation in 1933. Congress, however, was not spurred toward developing any new law until the "Elixir of Sulfanilamide" incident occurred in 1937. The drug, a sulfanilamide, marketed as a solution in diethylene glycol, a deadly poison, eventually caused the deaths of 107 persons. This incident brought out one of the inherent weaknesses of the 1906 Act and provided the impetus for passage of the FFD&C Act of 1938, which is the progenitor of the law currently in effect.

With regard to foods, the 1938 Act provides for the promulgation of a reasonable definition and standard of identity, a reasonable standard of quality, and/or reasonable standards of fill of container. It prohibits traffic in food which is injurious to health, whereas the 1906 Act permitted regulation of injurious food only in the event poison was added. The 1938 Act requires the label of nonstandardized food to bear the common or usual name of the food and, in case it was fabricated from two or more ingredients, the common or usual name of each ingredient. Spices, flavorings, and colorings can be so designated, however, without naming each. The Act requires the label of a food which is purported to be or is represented for special dietary use to bear such information concerning its vitamin, mineral, and other dietary properties as is determined to be necessary in order to inform purchasers as to its value for such use.

Among the general provisions applying to any food, drug, or cosmetic, the 1938 Act deems illegal any commodity whose labeling is false or misleading in any particular. It prohibits traffic in food, drugs, or cosmetics which were prepared or handled under unsanitary conditions. It authorizes factory inspections of establishments producing commodities covered by the Act, subject to certain conditions. It deems illegal any food, drug, or cosmetic whose container is made, formed, or filled so as to be misleading. The FDA is authorized to procure transportation records and other documents necessary to establish federal jurisdiction. The 1938 Act also authorizes the federal courts to restrain violations by injunction.

Although a number of amendments were made to the Act from 1941 to 1980, only two deal directly with the nutrient content of foods, whereas a few others deal indirectly or have the potential for dealing with the nutritional value of foods.

FOOD STANDARDS AMENDMENTS

In 1954, the FFD&C Act was amended to simplify the procedure for establishing standards of identity, quality, and fill of container for foods. Previously, the law required a formal hearing upon any proposal to issue, amend, or repeal regulations regarding several sections of the Act, including definitions and standards for foods. The 1954 amendments eliminated the requirement for a formal hearing when there was no controversy over the facts of the proposed rule. In 1956, legislation was passed to further simplify the rulemaking process for food standards. Taking the changes made in 1954, the 1956 amendment applied this simplified procedure to the regulations on foods for special dietary uses, tolerances for poisonous ingredients, use of emergency permits, and certain other areas requiring rule making.

THE FOOD ADDITIVES AMENDMENT

In 1958, the Committee on Interstate and Foreign Commerce of the House of Representatives reported out the Food Additives Amendment of 1958. The bill contained, among other things, a specific requirement for preclearing certain chemical additives for safety before such substances could be used in foods. The legislation provided that no additive could be intentionally added unless the formula and a description of the proposed conditions for use had been submitted to and approved by the FDA. If the agency approved the petition for use of the additive, it could also establish the maximum amount of the substance, or tolerance, which would be permitted for use in foods.

The 1938 Act already prohibited poisonous or deleterious substances in foods except in certain instances where such substances were allowed in small amounts. However, the lack of a premarket clearance requirement made this provision relatively ineffective. In order to bar the use of a dangerous additive, the FDA had to assume the burden of proof and show that the additive was poisonous or deleterious. This process was extremely time-consuming and, while it continued, the additive remained on the market. The House bill applied the principle of premarket testing to food additives for the first time.

One problem area in the bill related to the question of how to deal with additives already in use on the market. Industry spokesmen originally proposed that additives already in use be exempted from the provisions of the bill, while a number of members of Congress objected on the ground that such an exemption would leave many untested additives still in use. As a result, the bill provided for the following scheme: most new additives not in use before January 1, 1958 would be automatically subject to the preclearance requirements set out in the bill; substances generally recognized as safe (GRAS substances) after years of repeated use were to be exempted from the procedures of the bill; additives approved under the old procedures contained in the FFD&C Act or under the meat and poultry inspection laws were also exempted, although they could be removed from the market if later discovered to be hazardous; and additives previously untested and unapproved already on the market as of January 1, 1958, would be subject to the procedure in the bill. It is important to note that the bill (and the law, after the bill was passed) did not apply the preclearance safety procedures to GRAS substances among experts qualified by training and experience to evaluate such safety considerations. It was noted by agency officials in 1958 that, although GRAS substances would be exempt from the preclearance procedure, such substances could immediately become controlled if evidence appeared to warrant the conclusion that their safety was not generally recognized by experts. The amendment was signed into law by President Eisenhower on September 6, 1958.

VITAMIN AND MINERAL
SUPPLEMENTS AMENDMENT

In 1976, legislation was passed which had the effect of curtailing proposed regulations of the FDA dealing with the sale of vitamins and minerals. For more than 10 years, the FDA had tried to revise the regulations dealing with special dietary foods, including food supplements such as vitamins. A controversy erupted with considerable intensity following the publication of a tentative rule in the *Federal Register* of January 19, 1973 (FDA 1973A). The proposed potency limits, labeling restrictions, and other matters brought on a reaction from the health food industry and thousands of users of vitamin and mineral supplements. There was so much controversy on the proposed FDA action that an estimated 1 million pieces of mail flooded congressional offices. Objectively viewed, there were fundamental issues on both sides. The FDA contended that research over a long period of time revealed that some vitamins consumed in excessive amounts can produce harmful effects; notable examples are vitamins A and D. Furthermore, the FDA contended that false or unproved therapeutic claims were being made for some products. Opponents claimed that the consumer was well able to choose those items required in their diet and no "diet dictation" was necessary. Civil libertarians, both right and left, professed fear of a perceived excess in governmental regulation.

Representative Craig Hosmer introduced legislation by the end of the first session of the 93rd Congress; a simple majority of 218 representatives also introduced legislation to overturn the regulations. A similar bill was introduced by Senator William Proxmire and was cosponsored by 10 other Senators. The amendments, which passed both the House and the Senate, placed certain restrictions on the Secretary of the FDA's parent, Department of Health and Human Services. Accordingly, the Secretary may not establish maximum limits on the potency of any synthetic or natural vitamin or mineral within an applicable supplement, classify any natural or synthetic vitamin or mineral as a drug solely because it exceeds the level of potency which is nutritionally rational and useful, require the presence in dietary supplements of nutritionally essential vitamins and minerals, and prohibit in dietary supplements questionable additional ingredients of no nutritional value A large number of other responsibilities remain unchanged. This amendment, for example, does not preclude the FDA from regulating the potency of a vitamin or mineral preparation based on safety. Contained in this amendment is a current definition of a food for special dietary use. This term means a particular use for which a food purports or is represented to be used, including but not limited to the following: (1) supplying a special

dietary need that exists by reason of a physical, physiological, patho-
logical, or other condition, including but not limited to the condition
of disease, convalescence, pregnancy, lactation, infancy, allergic hyper-
sensitivity to food, underweight, overweight, or the need to control the
intake of sodium; (2) supplying a vitamin, mineral, or other ingredient
for use by man to supplement his diet by increasing the total dietary
intake; (3) supplying a special dietary need by reason of being a food
for use as the sole item of the diet.

It is of interest to note that consumption of supplemental vitamins
and minerals continues to grow in popularity among Americans. In a
recent national survey, 39.9% of adults 16 years of age or older, but
excluding pregnant or lactating women, consume one or more supplements daily (McDonald *et al.* 1983). Of these, 52.4% consume 1
supplement, while 10.9% consume 4 or more, up to a maximum of 14
separate products. Both vitamins and minerals show a wide range of
intake, extending to five to ten times the recommended daily levels
for individual nutrients.

THE INFANT FORMULA ACT

In 1978, a major U.S. manufacturer of soy-based infant formulas
made changes in their formulations to lower sodium content by reducing the levels of sodium chloride. Unfortunately, a concomitant
consequence was a substantial reduction of the chloride content of the
product, far below the minimum level for this essential nutrient recommended in 1976 by the Committee on Nutrition of the American
Academy of Pediatrics. Because food manufacturers, including those
who produce infant formulas, are not required to obtain premarket
clearance from the FDA for new or reformulated products when approved or safe ingredients are used, the FDA was unaware of possible
problems with the chloride-deficient formulas until several incidents
involving a serious illness among infants were brought to the agency's
attention late in July 1979. The illness, hypochloremic metabolic
alkalosis, is characterized in infants by constipation, lethargy, loss of
appetite, and failure to gain weight and thrive. Subsequently, more
than 200 clinically diagnosed cases of hypochloremic metabolic alkalosis
were documented among the estimated 20,000 infants who were fed
either of the two chloride-deficient formulas during the year or so that
the faulty products were on the market. Immediately upon discovery
of the problem, the FDA undertook audit procedures to determine
the effectiveness of the manufacturer's product recall, while informing
the company that their recall was not progressing satisfactorily. The
entire incident, however, became the subject of a TV report in Washington, DC and came under the scrutiny of Representative Albert Gore,
Jr., who was the parent of a child fed one of the deficient formulas.

As a result, Congressional hearings were held, several bills were introduced in the House and Senate, and less than a year later the Infant Formula Act was signed into law in September 1980 as the latest amendment to the FFD&C Act.

The Infant Formula Act ensures the nutritional safety of formulas by establishing specific requirements for nutrient content. Through regulation, the Secretary of the Department of Health and Human Services may revise the list of nutrients specified by law as new clinical knowledge is developed with respect to requirements in infant nutrition. The required level for any nutrient may also be revised, and requirements for quality factors for such nutrients may be established by regulation. Quality control procedures may be established by regulation to assure that an infant formula provides nutrients in accordance with the specifications of the Infant Formula Act. These quality-control procedures include the periodic testing of infant formulas by the manufacturers to determine whether they are in compliance with the Act.

Drawing from recommendations made by the Committee on Nutrition of the American Academy of Pediatrics in 1976, and subsequently reaffirmed in 1980, the Act establishes minimum levels, and maximum levels in a few cases, for protein, fat, essential fatty acids, and 26 vitamins, minerals, and other nutrients. All nutrients are required to be present at these levels per 100 kcal. Possibly because of oversight when the Infant Formula Act was written, nothing is stipulated about a minimum energy density of an infant formula as it is normally prepared in ready-to-feed form. The Committee on Nutrition of the American Academy of Pediatrics did specify an energy level of 670 kcal/liter of formula. The Act specifies that, at the minimum level, the source of protein shall be at least nutritionally equivalent to casein. There is also a specification for a minimum and a maximum value for the ratio of calcium content to phosphorus content. It should be noted that the nutrient specifications in the Act apply to food for normal, full-term infants, which is represented for special dietary use by reason of its simulation of human milk or its suitability as a complete or partial substitute for human milk. Specifically exempted from some of the requirements of the Act, particularly the requirements for nutrient content, is any formula which is represented and labeled for use by an infant who has an inborn error of metabolism or a low birth weight, or who otherwise has an unusual medical problem requiring some extraordinary dietary treatment.

The minimum level for iron content in infant formulas is appreciably below that contained in the current regulation for infant foods (21 CFR 105.65[1]) as well as the 1980 recommended dietary allowance (RDA) established by the Food and Nutrition Board of the National

---

[1] This designation and others elsewhere in the text represent current codification of federal regulations; e.g., Title 21 in the Code of Federal Regulations, Section 105.65.

Research Council. For practically all intents and purposes, the Infant Formula Act supersedes the current regulation on infant foods specifically with regard to formulas. The latter requires, for example, that a formula which contains less than 1 mg iron/100 kcal bear a label statement to the effect that an additional quantity of iron should be supplied from other sources. In their 1976 statement, the Committee on Nutrition of the American Academy of Pediatrics recommended that infant formulas contain an amount of iron equal to the lower end of the range commonly found in human milk, a value of about 0.15 mg iron/100 kcal, and that the iron be in a bioavailable form. This is the level that was incorporated into the Infant Formula Act. Part of the rationale for maintaining the minimum level is to permit some flexibility in the selection of foods and formulas for those infants who might be intolerant to some forms of iron. The Committee also affirmed its recommendation that infants at risk for iron deficiency be given formmulas supplemented with iron at levels between 1 and 2 mg/100 kcal. In 1981, the Committee maintained its position that the minimum level for iron is 0.15 mg/100 kcal, and also indicated that the caution statement for infant formulas containing less than 1 mg/100 kcal is appropriate. This brief review on iron addresses only part of a much larger issue. From a regulatory standpoint, one critical aspect centers on what level of iron is considered to be appropriate to support claims that a product is fortified with iron. A corollary deals with the achievement of some labeling practices for all infant foods. Issues such as these are part of a proposal for revision of 21 CFR 105.65, which was published in the *Federal Register* (FDA 1983A). Using comments received on the proposal, the FDA will seek to develop the best possible regulation.

The list of nutrients in the Infant Formula Act is not necessarily all-inclusive. In their 1980 statement of recommended dietary allowances, the Food and Nutrition Board of the National Research Council established what is termed an "estimated safe and adequate daily dietary intake" for four trace elements that are not listed in the Act, namely, fluoride, chromium, molybdenum, and selenium. In contrast to a recommended allowance, which is a single value, the estimated safe and adequate daily dietary intakes are presented as ranges of intakes because it is felt that the available data do not permit the definition of a single intake for these nutrients. The Secretary of the Department of Health and Human Services can, through regulation, revise the list of nutrients for infant formulas if such an action is considered appropriate.

With regard to regulations stemming from the Infant Formula Act and other sections of the FFD&C Act, the FDA recently has issued final rules regarding quality control procedures for the manufacture of infant formulas (FDA 1982A, 21 CFR Part 106)[2] and enforcement policy for recall of infant formulas from the marketplace (FDA 1982B, 21 CFR Part 7). In addition to the proposed rule for labeling of infant formulas cited above (FDA 1983A), other proposals include those for revision of nutrient requirements (FDA 1984A) and for quality-control, nutrient, and labeling requirements for exempt infant formulas (FDA 1983B).

RELATIONSHIP OF THE FFD&C ACT
TO THE NUTRITIONAL QUALITY OF FOODS

The provisions of the FFD&C Act presented above establish a basis upon which to consider how the nutritional value of the U.S. food supply is regulated. It is generally accepted that the FDA has the responsibility for assuring a safe, wholesome, and nutritious food supply in the United States. However, insofar as such remarks assume that the FDA has ample authority to assure the nutritional quality of the United States' food supply, they are not necessarily justified. The FFD&C Act provides the FDA explicit and extensive authority to undertake regulatory action with respect to toxic substances or filth in food; in contrast, the agency's ability to regulate the nutritional quality of the food supply is much more dependent upon agruments of implicit authority, and the extent of that authority may be much narrower.

Perhaps in former decades this was a matter of small import. In the last few decades, however, significant new developments in food technology have made possible new fabricated food products, which substitute for and resemble traditional foods but which may not provide the same nutritional value as the traditional foods. Fabricated substitutes for meat, cheese, and eggs are already on the market; such products may be purchased directly by consumers for use in place of traditional articles of food (e.g., cholesterol-free egg substitutes or hamburger meat extenders), or they may be used by manufacturers to replace traditional ingredients in food products (e.g., a frozen pizza product may be made with a cheese substitute instead of cheese). All commentators seem to agree that the substitute foods now on the market are only the beginning of an anticipated explosion of new

---

[2] Citations to final rules are provided with reference to original date or publication in the *Federal Register* as well as codification under Title 21 of the Code of Federal Regulations. The latter is the preferred reference for all final rules since the CFR is revised and issued on an annual basis and will, thereby, provide the current version of a rule if any revision to that rule is made after first publication in the *Federal Register*.

developments with respect to synthesized food products, made possible by rapid advances in food technology and encouraged by the economic conditions of the era immediately facing us.

Clearly, it is the responsibility of the FDA's Center for Food Safety and Applied Nutrition (formerly the Bureau of Foods) to apply existing strategies and find new ways to assure that the appearance of new fabricated foods does not lead to significant degradation of the U.S. food supply. Following is a brief review of some of the FDA's possible regulatory options in taking action to ensure the nutritional quality of the food supply under the authority of the FFD&C Act. Included are various approaches the FDA has taken in the past with respect to nutrition regulation and consideration of their possible application to new substitute food products.

Generally, the FDA has six existing nutrition regulation programs which might have significance for new food products. A seventh category dealing with a few miscellaneous issues is also included for completeness.

Standards of Identity

The FFD&C Act authorizes the FDA to establish a "definition and standard of identity" for a food "whenever in the judgement of the Secretary [in practice, the FDA] such action will promote honesty and fair dealing in the interest of consumers." The FDA has used this authority to establish more than 300 definitions and standards covering a wide array of foods and classes of food. In addition to defining the composition of a food, a standard also prescribes mandatory ingredients, lists optional ingredients that may be used, and sets the amounts or relative proportions of each. Important to this chapter is that a number of standards deal with vitamins and essential minerals as mandatory or optional ingredients. It should not be overlooked that such standardized foods have been significant contributors in maintaining the overall high nutritional quality of the U.S. food supply. Although it is not the purpose of this chapter to provide a comprehensive review of those standards that list vitamin or mineral ingredients, a few will be mentioned to serve as representative examples.

A number of standards exist for the class of milk and cream products (21 CFR Part 131). The standard for milk provides for the addition of vitamins A and D as optional ingredients (21 CFR 131.110), whereas the standard for skim milk requires the presence of vitamin A at a level of 2000 IU/qt and allows for the optional addition of vitamin D (21 CFR 131.143). The standard for margarine requires the presence of vitamin A at not less than 15,000 IU/lb and permits the addition of vitamin D as an optional ingredient (21 CFR 166.110). More germane to this discussion are the standards and definitions for cereal grain foods that include bakery products (21 CFR Part 136), cereal flours and related products (21 CFR Part 137), and macaroni and noodle products (21 CFR Part 138). Generally, standards for enriched products contain specifications for thiamin, niacin, riboflavin, iron, calcium, and vitamin D. For example, the standards for enriched flour (21 CFR 137.165) and for enriched corn meals (21 CFR 137.260) require the presence of thiamin, riboflavin, niacin, and iron. The enriched flour standard permits the optional addition of calcium, while the enriched-corn meals standard contains options for calcium and vitamin D. Generally speaking, the effect of a standard for an enriched food is to require that if any vitamin or mineral is added to the food, the food must provide all of the nutrients required by the standard, in the amounts required by the standard. Historically, such enrichment practices have had a profound effect on the nation's nutritional health. It is fairly well established that such enrichment practices around the early 1940s were a major contributing factor, if not the major factor, in the eventual conquest of pellagra, a niacin deficiency disease once prevalent in the southern United States.

Although the FFD&C Act provides the FDA with the authority to standardize an enriched food, the FDA has not attempted to use this authority to prohibit the existence of an unenriched article. For example, although standards of identity for both bread and enriched bread have been established, the FDA has depended upon the marketplace for consumer selection of the enriched article rather than the unenriched product. As noted, standards of identity for enriched products were promulgated soon after enactment of the FFD&C Act and, through the intervening years, the FDA has continued to promulgate and revise such standards. However, more than 30 years passed before the FDA seriously undertook additional types of regulatory programs bearing upon the nutritional quality of the U.S. food supply. In the 1970s, partly in response to increased interest by consumers in the nutritional quality of the foods they eat, partly out of concern to protect the nutritional quality of the U.S. food supply, the FDA instituted several additional regulatory programs with respect to nutrition.

Nutrition Labeling

In 1973, the FDA ushered in a new era of nutrition regulation by publishing a final regulation with respect to nutrition labeling of foods (FDA 1973A, B, 21 CFR 101.9). Generally, this regulation provides that if any vitamin, mineral, or protein is added to a food, or if any nutrition claim or information is included in labeling or in advertising for a food, full nutrition information must be contained on the label in a standardized format. This includes information on the serving size of the food; the caloric content in Calories (kcal) per serving; the protein, carbohydrate, and fat content in grams per serving; and the

Table 25.1. Recommended Fortification Levels Based on a 2,000 kcal/day Standard

Nutrient and unit of measure	U.S. RDA[a]	Amount/100 kcal
Protein, g	65[b]	3.25[c]
	45	2.25[c]
Vitamin A, IU	5000	250
Vitamin C, mg	60	3
Thiamin, mg	1.5	0.075
Riboflavin, mg	1.7	0.085
Niacin, mg	20	1.0
Calcium, g	1	0.05
Iron, mg	18	0.9
Vitamin D, IU	400	20[c]
Vitamin E, IU	30	1.5
Vitamin B_6, mg	2	0.1
Folic acid, mg	0.4	0.02
Vitamin B_{12}, μg	6	0.3
Phosphorus, g	1	0.05
Iodine, μg	150	7.5[c]
Magnesium, mg	400	20
Zinc, mg	15	0.75
Copper, mg	2	0.1
Biotin, mg	0.3	0.015
Pantothenic acid, mg	10	0.5
Potassium, g	—[d]	0.125
Manganese, mg	—[d]	0.2

Source: 21 CFR 104.20.

[a] U.S. RDA for adults and children 4 or more years of age.

[b] If the protein efficiency ratio (PER) of protein is equal to or better than casein, then the U.S. RDA is 45 g.

[c] Optional.

[d] No U.S. RDA has been established for either potassium or manganese.

percentages of the U.S. RDA per serving for protein, vitamin A, vitamin C, thiamin, riboflavin, niacin, calcium, and iron. Optional listing in percent of the U.S. RDA of any one or more of 12 other vitamins and minerals is permitted as part of the format. The U.S. RDAs, which are listed in Table 25.1, were developed by the FDA in response to a need for a single set of standard nutrient requirements applicable to nutrition labeling and other regulations with nutrition components. The U.S. RDA values were derived, through simplification, from RDA values established for various age–sex population groups by the Food and Nutrition Board of the National Academy of Sciences, National Research Council. Accordingly, the designation U.S. RDA was created to distinguish this set of values from any single set of RDA values established by the Food and Nutrition Board.

In addition to the above, fatty acid and cholesterol content may be incorporated in the nutrition labeling format (FDA 1973A, B, 21 CFR

101.25). Recently, the FDA published a rule for the declaration of the sodium content of a food (FDA 1984B, 21 CFR Parts 101 and 105). This rule provides definitions for use of such terms as sodium free, low sodium, and reduced sodium. Although this rule provides for declaration of sodium content in isolation of other label information, it does require that, whenever nutrition labeling information is given for a product, sodium content will be included as part of the required format.

Although nutrition labeling does not impose any requirements with respect to the nutritional quality of a food, the FDA believes that such labeling will cause consumers to become more aware of the nutritional value of the foods they purchase and more likely to consider nutritional value in making purchasing selections. It should be noted that the FFD&C Act does not explicitly require nutrition labeling. It does, however, prohibit labeling which is "misleading in any particular," and provides that in determining whether labeling is misleading, "there shall be taken into account (among other things) not only representations made or suggested by statement, word, design, device, or any combination thereof, but also the extent to which the labeling. . .fails to reveal facts material in the light of such representations. . . ." Furthermore, the FDA has "authority to promulgate regulations for the efficient enforcement of this chapter [the FFD&C Act]." The FDA's nutrition labeling regulations are based on the premise that failure to provide "full" nutrition information, in the manner established by the regulations, would cause labeling to be misleading within the meaning of the FFD&C Act for failure to reveal facts that are material in light of "triggering" nutritional representations. The addition of a nutrient to a food product results in a triggering nutrition claim or information because the presence of the nutrient ingredient must be declared in the labeling in the list of ingredients, as required by the Act.

On a periodic basis since 1978, the FDA has conducted surveys of the U.S. marketplace to determine the extent to which nutrition labeling is being utilized. Results for the 1983 Food Label and Package Survey indicate that 55.2% of sales for packaged, processed foods consisted of products bearing nutrition information panels (Schucker 1984). This percentage is a sales-weighted measure, based upon a sampling of FDA-regulated, packaged, processed foods. Interestingly, only approximately one-third of nutrition labeling is required in order to be in compliance with the regulation; the balance of such labeling is provided on a voluntary basis by food manufacturers.

Common or Usual Names

The FFD&C Act provides that the label of a food must bear "the common or usual name of the food, if any there be." In the interest of efficient enforcement of the Act, the FDA has provided that, in appropriate circumstances, it will establish by regulation the common or usual name for a particular food. Although most common or usual name regulations published prior to the early 1970s have not focused on nutritional factors, the FDA has established a final common or usual name regulation for frozen heat-and-serve dinners, which requires, among other things, that frozen dinner products include at least one component which is "a significant source of protein" (FDA 1973B, 21 CFR 102.26). In addition to protein, the regulation also specifies minimum levels for seven vitamins and iron. Similarly, there has been established a common or usual name regulation for peanut spreads (FDA 1977, 21 CFR 102.23). Accordingly, a spreadable peanut product shall be considered nutritionally equivalent to peanut butter if it meets specified conditions for protein content and biological quality, and if it contains specified levels per 100 grams of product of the following nutrients: niacin, vitamin B_6, folic acid, iron, zinc, magnesium, and copper. The agency has also published a tentative rule to establish a common or usual name for plant protein products (extenders and replacements for meat, seafood, poultry, eggs, or cheese which are produced from edible plant protein sources such as soybeans), which would establish minimum nutritional criteria to be met by certain types of such products (FDA 1978).

Nutritional Quality Guidelines

FDA regulations provide for the establishment of "nutritional quality guidelines" for particular foods (FDA 1973B, 21 CFR Part 104, Subpart A). A nutritional quality guideline prescribes the minimum level or range of nutrient composition (nutritional quality) appropriate for a given class of food. The regulations provide that a food which complies with all of the requirements of an applicable nutritional quality guideline may bear a label statement that "this product provides nutrients in amounts appropriate for the class of food as determined by the U.S. Government." At the present time, the only food for which a nutritional quality guideline has been established is "frozen 'heat and serve' dinners" (FDA 1973B, 21 CFR 104.47).

Imitation Foods Policy

The FFD&C Act provides that a food which is an "imitation" of another shall clearly be labeled as such. The FDA has concluded that the imitation section of the Act should not be interpreted so as to become a trade barrier, which might present a serious obstacle to the development and marketing of new substitute food products with sound nutritional content. Indeed, in light of the connotations of inferiority applicable to the term imitation, it might be misleading to consumers to require that a new substitute food be labeled as an imitation if it is nutritionally equivalent, or superior, to its traditional counterpart.

Pursuant to this policy favoring informative labeling the FDA has promulgated a regulation providing, among other things, that a food which substitutes for and resembles another food must be labeled as an imitation if it is nutritionally inferior to the other food, but that a food which substitutes for and resembles another food need not be labeled as an imitation if it is not nutritionally inferior to the food for which it substitutes and which it resembles, and if it bears an appropriate name which accurately identifies or describes its basic nature [FDA 1973C, 21 CFR 101.3(e)]. Obviously, the FDA intended this regulation on imitation foods to have a carrot effect, to encourage that a new substitute food be formulated so as to be nutritionally equivalent to its traditional counterpart in order to avoid pejorative imitation labeling.

Fortification Policy

In 1980, the FDA issued a policy statement concerning the nutrient fortification of foods that expresses a series of guidelines which manufacturers are urged to follow if they elect to add nutrients to a manufactured or processed food (FDA 1980, 21 CFR 104.20). This policy statement is intended to promote the rational addition of nutrients to foods in order to preserve a balance of nutrients in the diets of U.S. consumers. It is clearly stated that widespread fortification is not to be encouraged, but that the guidelines should be followed to nutritionally improve or restore foods by fortification. These guidelines are intended to cover most types of foods, with the notable exceptions of fresh produce, meat, poultry, and fish products (foods that are adequately nutritious in the absence of fortification), as well as sugars, candies, carbonated beverages, and other snack foods (foods considered inappropriate for fortification). The guidelines do not apply to any food covered by any other federal regulation that requires, permits, or prohibits nutrient additions. Such regulations supersede the guidelines and include, but are not limited to, standards of identity, nutritional quality guidelines, and common or usual name regulations.

The guidelines list three main situations in which fortification of foods is deemed appropriate. First, fortification of food is desirable to correct a dietary insufficiency recognized by the scientific community to exist and known to result in a deficiency disease. In order to identify the dietary insufficiency, adequate information must be available to pinpoint the specific nutritional problem and affected population groups. In addition, a suitable carrier food for the nutrient(s) to be added must be selected. Suitable carrier foods are generally inexpensive staple foods already consumed by the target population. The foods must not react with the added nutrient(s) in a way that would alter the biological value of the nutrient(s).

Fortification of foods is also considered appropriate when nutrients are added to restore levels inherent in a food prior to conventional processing and storage. Only nutrients which are known to have been present in the food in quantities of at least 2% of the U.S. RDA can be restored, and all nutrients contained at that level should be added. Restoration of nutrients lost from poor manufacturing practices or storage and handling procedures is not appropriate.

Nutrients may also be added to foods to balance protein, vitamins, and minerals to the caloric content of the food. The food to be fortified in this situation must contain at least 40 kcal in a normal serving. This quantity is 2% of the 2000 kcal/day standard established in the guidelines. The 2000 kcal/day standard was selected as being representative, generally, of a uniform daily calorie requirement for individuals. The standard is intended to provide a baseline for fortification of new or unique foods in relation to their caloric content, but not to provide a recommended caloric requirement for all individuals. It was reasoned that, when the specific use of new or unique products cannot be predicted, it is not possible to anticipate a specific and limited nutrient content or profile. Therefore, when products cannot be categorized as substitutes or replacements for a particular food and a manufacturer elects to add nutrients to such products, the nutrient additions should conform to a profile reflecting all the foods which the product might substitute for or replace in the diet. Because it is impractical to develop such a profile for each food, the logical alternative selected by the FDA is a profile that would sustain a balance in the average person's overall nutrient intake by relating nutrient content to caloric content. All nutrients identified for addition are required to be added to achieve this nutrient-to-calorie balance. These nutrients are listed in Table 25.1 along with their amounts per 100 kcal in a fortified food. The guidelines also allow nutrient addition to a food intended to replace a traditional food in the diet. Allowance for addition of nutrients to these substitute foods is designed to prevent nutritional inferiority of such foods. The guidelines stress that nutrients added to food should be stable in the carrier food, physiologically available from the food, added at levels unlikely to result in an adverse reaction due to excessive intake, and in compliance with federal regulations governing the safety of food substances.

Miscellaneous Programs

As a possible health measure to deal with endemic goiter, supplementation of the diet by the use of iodized table salt on a voluntary basis became widespread throughout the United States beginning in the 1920s. This practice remains in effect and, in 1972, the FDA issued a policy statement with regard to label declarations for noniodized and iodized salt to dispel consumer confusion over terms used to describe the physical and chemical characteristics of table salt (FDA 1972, 21

CFR 100.155). Accordingly, common retail packages of iodized salt are required to bear the label statement: "This salt supplies iodide, a necessary nutrient." Noniodized salt is required to bear a comparable statement to the effect that the product does not supply iodide.

In 1973, a final rule was issued on the conditions for safe use of amino acids in foods (FDA 1973D, 21 CFR 172.320). This food additive regulation provides for properly controlled additions of amino acids to appropriate protein-containing foods in order to improve protein quality. By the same token, it is intended to prevent uncontrolled uses of amino acids in the fortification of certain foods that may result in risk to the public health from excessive intakes of free amino acids. This regulation permits addition of amino acids as nutrients to those foods considered to be significant sources of dietary protein in order to achieve a substantial improvement in the biological quality of the total naturally occurring protein in a food.

The programs listed above represent the major approaches the FDA has used to regulate nutrient content of foods. These approaches do not, however, assure that the nutritional quality of the U.S. food supply will be maintained. Consider the hypothetical situation of the development of new dairy substitutes (cheese, yogurt, or milk products) that have the appearance and taste of their traditional counterparts but that are twice as shelf stable and cost half as much. Suppose, however, that such products contained insignificant levels of calcium and amounts of sodium that were severalfold those of the traditional products. In view of the importance of the traditional foods, particularly for their calcium content, it is conceivable that the health of a significant segment of the U.S. population might be adversely affected by substantial use of the substitute products. Considering the FDA's existing programs for nutrition regulation, it is worthwhile to examine each of the first six programs listed above to see whether the agency is able to take effective action under any program to prevent the adverse nutritional impact posed by any one or more of the hypothetical products.

A standard of identity or a common or usual name regulation may be promulgated, establishing appropriate nutritional requirements for a class of food products. If a manufacturer should decide, however, not to reformulate his product to comply with the standard or not to have the product bear the common or usual name, he would be free to market the product by calling it an imitation without improving its nutritional characteristics. If a manufacturer adds a vitamin or mineral to a product, or makes a nutrition claim, nutrition labeling will be required for the product. If neither is done, the manufacturer may sell his product without nutrition labeling. The FDA could promulgate a nutritional quality guideline for substitute products, thereby encouraging manufacturers to formulate such products in compliance with the guidelines to permit use of the label statement that the product "provides nutrients in amounts appropriate for this class of food as determined by the U.S. Government." But a manufacturer would remain free to forego use of this stamp of approval and instead sell a less nutritious product. The FDA's imitation regulation, in effect, tells a manufacturer of a substitute product that he may avoid imitation labeling if the product is fortified to be nutritionally equivalent to the traditional commodity and an appropriately informative name is used. A manufacturer is, nevertheless, not required to take this action. Finally, the FDA's fortification policy establishes approved rationales for the addition of nutrients to foods, but does not compel a manufacturer to fortify his product. In sum, the FDA's existing nutrition regulation programs might be used to encourage manufacturers to produce, and consumers to select, a substitute product with a sound nutrition profile, but none of the programs compel a manufacturer to add calcium, to limit sodium, or even to reveal the product's nutrient composition in nutrition labeling if the product is sold as an imitation without making a nutrition claim.

Fortunately, so far, there has not been any reason to conclude that one or more new substitute foods have significantly degraded the nutritional quality of typical U.S. diets. If the opposite were true, that is, if the existing programs already discussed proved ineffective in preventing an adverse impact on the nutritional quality of the food supply, then the FDA would have to attempt some new approach under existing statutory authority to correct such a situation. Clearly, the FDA's existing regulatory programs with respect to nutrition may not be sufficient to assure indefinitely that significant degradation of the nutritional quality of the U.S. food supply will not result from the appearance of new fabricated food products, which substitute for and resemble traditional articles of food. Whether or not the FDA undertakes any new regulatory program will be determined by whether or not a need is perceived to do so. Accordingly, the FDA's Center for Food Safety and Applied Nutrition will continue to keep abreast of new scientific information on human nutrition, clinical survey and other data on the nutritional health of Americans, trends in the marketing of foods, and trends and attitudes of U.S. consumers with regard to food selection, in order to consider the best possible regulatory options to improve the health status of the U.S. populace by improving the nutritional quality of the food supply.

REFERENCES

FDA 1972. Salt and iodized salt: label statements. Fed. Reg. 37(17), 1166–1167, Jan. 26.
FDA 1973A. Food labeling. Fed. Reg. 38(13), 2152–2164, Jan. 19.

FDA 1973B. Food labeling. Fed. Reg. *38*(49), 6950–6975, Mar. 14.

FDA 1973C. Food and food products; definitions, identity, and label statements. Fed. Reg. *38*(148), 20702–20750, Aug. 2.

FDA 1973D. Food additives; amino acids in food for human consumption. Fed. Reg. *38* (143), 20036–20039, July 26.

FDA 1977. Part 102—Common or usual names for nonstandardized foods, peanut spreads. Fed. Reg. *42*(136), 36452–36455, July 15.

FDA 1978. Common or usual names for vegetable protein products and substitutes for meat, seafood, poultry, eggs, or cheeses which contain vegetable protein products as sources of protein. Fed. Reg. *43*(136), 30472–20491, July 14.

FDA 1980. Nutritional quality of foods; addition of nutrients. Fed. Reg. *45*(18), 6314–6324, Jan. 25.

FDA 1982A. Infant formula quality control procedures. Fed. Reg. *47*,(76), 17016–17027, Apr. 20.

FDA 1982B. Enforcement policy; infant formula recalls. Fed. Reg. *47*(84), 18832–18836, Apr. 30.

FDA 1983A. Infant formula, labeling requirements. Fed Reg. *48*(134), 31880–31887, July 12.

FDA 1983B. Exempt infant formula. Fed. Reg. *48* (134), 31875–31880, July 12.

FDA 1984A. Nutrient requirements for infant formulas. Fed. Reg. *49*(71), 14396–14402, Apr. 11.

FDA 1984B. Food labeling; declaration of sodium content of foods and label claims for foods on the basis of sodium content. Fed. Reg. *49*(76), 15510–15535, Apr. 18.

McDonald, J. T., *et al.* 1983. Assessment of vitamin and mineral usage by means of a telephone survey. Fed. Proc. *42*(3), 530.

Schucker, R. E. 1984. Nutrition labeling in the retail processed food supply. Division of Consumer Studies, FDA, Washington, DC.

The Contribution of Consumption of Processed Food to Nutrient Intake Status in the United States

John P. Heybach
Gus. D. Coccodrilli, Jr.
Gilbert A. Leveille

FOOD PROCESSING, NUTRIENT INTAKE, AND HEALTH STATUS

Any analysis of the nutritional contribution of food processing must, of necessity, proceed from a knowledge of health status (Murphy 1982), nutrient needs, and food and nutrient intake patterns in the population. As the health status of the U.S. population has improved, the nutritional considerations underlying food processing practices have begun, and will continue, to shift from emphasis on ameliorating relatively well-defined specific nutrient deficiencies (i.e., goiter and iodine fortification of salt, Quick and Murphy 1982) to recognition of the important but less well-defined role of a nutritious diet in preventing the development of marginal nutrient deficiencies, and promoting and maintaining a general level of health and functional well-being.

However, the relationships between nutrient intake levels, biochemical measures of nutritional status, and health are extremely complex (Anderson *et al.* 1982; Beaton 1971). In the absence of clear nutrient deficiency symptoms these relationships are often not completely understood (Kerr *et al.* 1982; Singer *et al.* 1982). Consideration of these relationships is therefore beyond the scope of this chapter and we will restrict ourselves to nutrient intake considerations.

Rather than undertaking a detailed analysis of the impact of past and present food processing technology, including restoration, enrichment, and fortification, on the nutrient content of the food supply (Friend 1972; Quick and Murphy 1982), we will attempt here to construct some overall estimate of the patterns of consumption and the contribution of processed foods in each of several food categories to total nutrient intake status in the U.S. population.

Table 26.1. Comparison of Nutrient Intakes in Total Diet from NHANES I (1971–74) and NHANES II (1976–80)

	Calcium (mg/1000 kcal)	Iron (mg/1000 kcal)	Vitamin A (IU/1000 kcal)	Vitamin C (mg/1000 kcal)	Thiamin (mg/1000 kcal)	Riboflavin (mg/1000 kcal)	Niacin (mg/1000 kcal)
Males							
NHANES I	425	5.91	2147	38	0.62	0.94	8.42
NHANES II	411	6.53	2385	45	0.66	0.95	10.03
Females							
NHANES I	448	6.11	2738	51	0.66	1.00	8.40
NHANES II	430	6.72	2938	59	0.67	0.97	9.79

Source: DHEW (1979); Carroll *et al.* (1983).

POPULATION NUTRIENT INTAKE STATUS

Despite the fact that on a per capita basis the amount of food energy available for consumption in the United States has increased over the last 80 years (Welsh and Marston 1982) to a 1981 level of 3420 kcal (Prescott 1982), the actual consumption of calories, as measured in national food consumption surveys, is considerably lower and decreasing. The National Health and Nutrition Examination Survey (NHANES II) conducted in 1976–1980 showed a mean energy intake of 2381 and 1578 kcal for males and females, respectively (Carroll *et al.* 1983), reflecting a slight reduction from 2393 and 1618 kcal for males and females, respectively, measured in NHANES I, 1971–1974 (DHEW, 1979).

However, despite continuation of the general trend of reduced caloric intake, the actual intake of some selected nutrients has increased. Table 26.1 shows a comparison, on a per calorie basis, of selected nutrient intakes from the last two NHANES surveys. In general, these figures reflect an increase in the nutrient density of the U.S. diet. Fortunately, this increase in nutrient density tends to compensate for what otherwise could be a reduced nutrient intake due to the reduction in caloric intake. As will be seen below, processed foods play a significant role in providing these nutrients.

Cereal Grain Products

Cereal grains, particularly wheat and corn, are processed into a variety of foods, which as a category account for about 25% of our food energy intake [U.S. Department of Agriculture (USDA) 1980]. Probably the most important cereal grain products, in terms of consumption, are baked bread products, pastas and ready-to-eat breakfast cereals. An analysis of the results of the Nationwide Food Consumption Survey, 1977–1978 show that on a day in Spring, 1977, 79% of the individuals surveyed used bread, rolls or biscuits, 29% used ready-to-eat cereals and 14% used pastas indicating widespread use of these grain products as a basis for their contribution to nutrient intake. The majority of consumption of cereal grains occurs after some level of processing has been applied to the whole grain. Table 26.2 shows the use patterns in the U.S. population of some of these product categories.

Table 26.2. Percentage of Individuals in Different Use Pattern Categories of Some Processed Grain Products

Use patterns	Yeast breads (%)	Pasta (%)	Ready-to-eat cereals (%)
Once in 3 days	93.7	11.4	43.4
Daily	32.0	0.5	12.4

Source: USDA (1982).

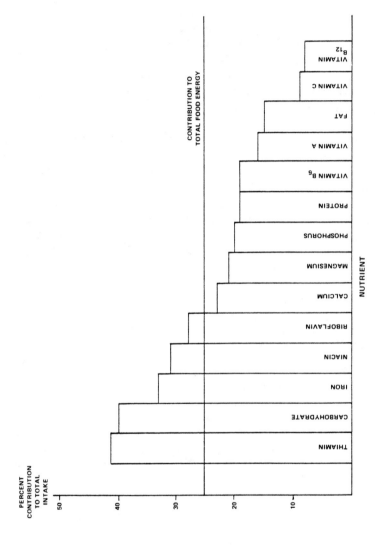

Fig. 26.1. Percentage contribution to total intake of selected nutrients contributed from grain products. Source: Data from Nationwide Food Consumption Survey, 1977–1978; adapted from USDA (1980).

Cereal grain products, due primarily to enrichment and fortification, supply an increasing percentage of total intake of several key nutrients. Figure 26.1 shows the contribution of foods from the grain products category to total daily intake of selected nutrients. The contribution of grain products to total intake of the nutrients shown is significant, but particularly so for thiamin, iron, niacin, and riboflavin. As can be seen, the percentage contribution from grain products of these nutrients exceeds the percentage of total dietary energy intake from grain products. The important contribution of the consumption of grain products to nutrient intake is demonstrated even more convincingly when nutrient intake contributions are compared over time. Figure 26.2 shows the increased contribution to total nutrient intake of cereal grain products between 1965 and 1977 (Pao 1981).

Although it is difficult to precisely assess the actual nutrient contribution of consumption of food in a particular food category, the contribution of a food can be estimated. One approach to this assessment is exemplified by an analysis of the role of ready-to-eat breakfast cereals to nutrient consumption at the breakfast meal (Morgan *et al.* 1981). As can be seen in Table 26.3 users of ready-to-eat cereals have a better nutrient intake profile than nonusers at breakfast, highlighting

Table 26.3. Nutrient Intake at Breakfast of Users and Nonusers of Ready-to-eat Cereals

	Users		Nonusers	
	Amount	RDA (%)	Amount	RDA (%)
Energy (kcal)	409	18	413	18
Protein (g)	13	36	12	33
Carbohydrate (g)	60	—	53	—
Fat (g)	14	—	17	—
Ascorbic acid (mg)	49	96	31	75
Thiamin (mg)	0.50	45	0.28	24
Niacin (mg)	5.2	35	2.2	14
Riboflavin (mg)	0.75	55	0.41	29
Pyridoxine (mg)	0.56	47	0.22	17
Vitamin B_{12} (μg)	1.48	73	0.84	39
Folacin (μg)	100	35	55	18
Vitamin A (IU)	1559	48	817	24
Iron (mg)	3.9	35	2.5	21
Calcium (mg)	310	35	243	17
Phosphorus (mg)	323	37	269	30
Magnesium (mg)	57	23	46	18
Copper (mg)	0.345	—	0.275	—
Zinc (mg)	1.9	17	1.7	15

Source: Morgan *et al.* (1981).

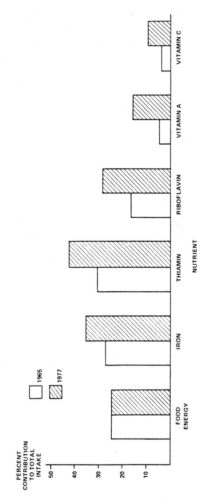

Fig. 26.2. Percentage contribution of consumption of cereal grain products to total intake of selected nutrients. Source: Data from Nationwide Food Consumption Surveys, 1965–1966 (USDA, 1972) and 1977–1978; adapted from Pao (1981).

the important role ready-to-eat cereals play in the diet of 5- to 12-year-old children consuming these products. A similar type of analysis, applied to data from the first National Health and Nutrition Examination Survey (1971–1974), has demonstrated generally superior nutrient intake profiles in users versus nonusers of pasta products for several important nutrients (Khoo *et al.* 1983).

In general, this brief overview indicates some of the areas where the consumption of processed cereal grain products makes an important contribution to total nutrient intake in the diet of the U.S. population.

Processed Milk Products

The vast majority of milk and milk-derived dairy products consumed in the United States undergoes some form of processing and fortification. Milk is pasteurized, homogenized, and widely fortified with vitamins A and D. Figure 26.3 shows that despite a slight reduction in the contribution of milk and milk products in the total intake of food energy between 1965 and 1977, the contribution of milk and milk products to total vitamin A intake has increased, while the contribution of nonfortified nutrients (protein, thiamin, riboflavin, calcium) has remained relatively stable or decreased.

Over the past 15 years, due to changing food preferences and health concerns about intake of calories and saturated fats, the production and consumption of fat-reduced milk products has increased dramatically. Per capita sales of whole milk have dropped from 265 to 150 lb from 1954 to 1980, while sales of low fat milk have increased over the same period from essentially 0 to 75 lb (Prescott 1983). The increasing trend toward consumption of low fat fluid milk probably makes a meaningful and important contribution to increasing the nutrient density of the diet for important nutrients, particularly calcium and magnesium, while reducing fat intake. In addition to fluid milk, there has been a general increase in the consumption of milk-derived processed food products, particularly cheeses and yogurts (Pao 1981; Prescott 1983). Table 26.4 shows the relationship between use patterns of various fluid milk categories as assessed in the Nationwide Food Consumption survey, 1977–1978 (Pao *et al.* 1982).

Fruits and Vegetables

Although generally not involving the addition of nutrients (with the exception of some fortified juices), the processing of vegetables and fruits through canning, drying, and freezing does allow for wider distribution of these important foods both geographically and seasonally. Figure 26.4 shows the contribution of vegetable consumption to nutrient intake as measured in the Nationwide Food Consumption Survey, 1977–1978. Although great variability in nutrient content arises from

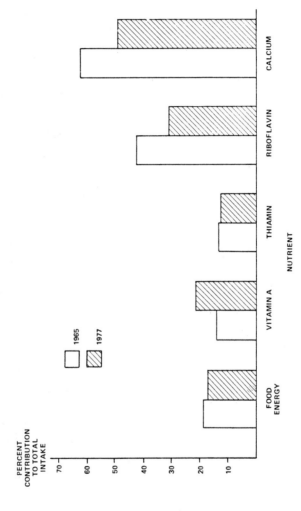

Fig. 26.3. Contribution of consumption of milk and milk products to total intake of selected nutrients in 1965 and 1977. Source: Data from Nationwide Food Consumption Surveys, 1965–1966 (USDA, 1972) and 1977–1978; adapted from Pao (1981).

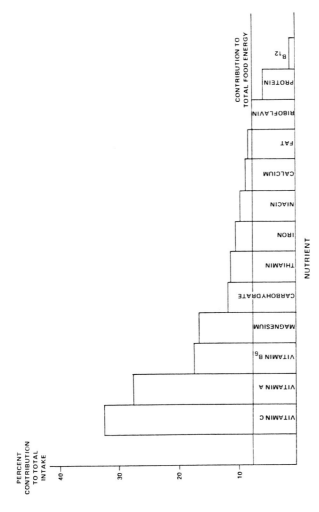

Fig. 26.4. Percentage contribution to total intake of selected nutrients contributed from vegetable products. Source: Data from Nationwide Food Consumption Survey, 1977–1978; adapted from USDA, 1980.

Table 26.4. Percentage of Individuals in Each Use Pattern for Various Fluid Milk Categories

Use patterns	Whole milk (%)	Low fat milk (%)	Skim milk (%)
At least once in 3 days	64.6	17.3	5.6
Daily	37.1	8.6	2.6

Source: Adapted from Pao *et al.* (1982).

Table 26.5. Percentage of of Households Using Fruits and Vegetables in Fresh and Various Processed Categories in a Week

	Fresh (%)	Processed		
		Frozen (%)	Canned (%)	Dried (%)
Vegetables	34.7	34.7	72.3	19.8
Fruits	44.7	38.7	35.0	10.2

Source: USDA (1982).

a wide variety of factors, such as growing region and processing method (Dudek *et al.* 1982), it is becoming clear that processed vegetables compare favorably with fresh vegetables and are in some instances superior to "fresh" vegetables, particularly after time in distribution channels (harvest to consumption) is considered (Dudek *et al.* 1982). A currently active research area involves assessing the relative nutrient content due to the differing methods of processing of canned and frozen vegetables compared to not processed (i.e., supermarket fresh) vegetables. This has been, and will continue to be, an area of intense research activity. Table 26.5 shows the relative household consumption of fresh, canned, and frozen fruits and vegetables (USDA 1982).

Citrus juices, and orange juice in particular, deserve some additional comment with respect to vitamin C due to the fact that consumption of processed juice, including vitamin C-fortified juice, accounts for the majority of juice intake. Frozen juice consumption leads in terms of per capita intake and, with chilled juice, continues to increase, while canned juice intake appears to be decreasing or stabilizing (Prescott 1982). Consumption of citrus and non citrus juices contribute measurably to vitamin C intakes as measured in the Nationwide Food Consumption Survey, 1977–1978 (Pao 1981).

SUMMARY AND CONCLUSIONS

The consumption pattern of a particular food or food category in conjunction with its nutrient content, the nutrient content of associated accompaniment items and ingredients, and the nutrient needs of the population that consumes the food in question determines the contribution of that food to total dietary nutrient intake. It has become clear over the last several years and been made explicit in this brief review, that processed foods are an extremely important contributing source of many important nutrients in the U.S. diet. This contribution is based not only on restoration and enrichment of foods, but also on the wider availability of food nutrients due to preservation and distribution technologies and other less visible processes, such as fat reduction of milk, that lead to increased nutrient density of our diets in the face of continuing reductions in caloric intake.

It is also clear that the processed food industry has contributed and will continue to contribute and respond, through application of current and developing food technologies, to consumer behavioral, nutritional and health challenges in the future.

REFERENCES

Anderson, G. H., Peterson, R. D., and Beaton, G. H. 1982. Estimating nutrient deficiencies in a population from dietary records: The use of probability analyses. Nutr. Res. 2, 409–415.

Beaton, G. H. 1971. The use of nutritional requirements and allowances. In Proc. Western Hemisphere Nutrition Congress III. P. L. White and N. Selvey (Editors). Futura Publishing, Mount Kisco, NY.

Carroll, M. D., Abraham, S., and Dresser, C. M. 1983. Dietary Intake Source Data: United States, 1976–80. Vital and Health Statistics Series 11, 231. DHHS Pub. (PHS) 83–1681. Public Health Service, National Center for Health Statistics, U.S. Govt. Printing Office, Washington, DC.

DHEW 1979. Dietary Intake Source Data: United States, 1971–74. Public Health Service 79–1221. Office of Health Research Statistics and Technology, National Center for Health Statistics, Hyattsville, MD.

Dudek, J. A., Elkins, E. R., Jr., Chin, H. B., and Hagen, R. E. 1982. Investigations to determine nutrient content of selected fruits and vegetables — Raw, processed and prepared. Final Report prepared for Science and Education Administration, Agricultural Research Service, USDA, Hyattsville, MD.

Friend, B. 1972. Enrichment and fortification of foods, 1966–70. National Food Situation, Economic Research Service, USDA, Hyattsville, MD.

Kerr, G. R., Sul Lee, E., Lam, M-K. M., Lorimor, R. J., Randall, E., Forthofer, R. N., Davis, M. A., and Magnetti, S. M. 1982. Relationships between dietary and biochemical measures of nutritional status in HANES I data. Am. J. Clin. Nutr. 35, 294–308.

Khoo, C. S., Rawson, N., and Riley, A. M. 1983. Nutritional health status and dietary patterns of pasta users and non-users. Proc. Western Hemisphere Nutrition Congress, Alert 84, Miami, FL.

Morgan, K. J., Zabik, M. E., and Leveille, G. A. 1981. The role of breakfast in nutrient intake of 5- to 12-year old children. Am. J. Clin. Nutr. *34*, 1418–1429.

Murphy, R. S. 1982. The national health and nutrition examination survey data and food fortification policy. *In* Adding Nutrients to Foods: Where Do We Go From Here? J. L. Vatter (Editor). American Assoc. Cereal Chem., St. Paul, MN.

Pao, E. M. 1981. Changes in American food consumption patterns and their nutritional significance. Nationwide Food Consumption Survey, 1977–78. Food Technol. *35*, 43–53.

Pao, E. M., Fleming, K. H., Guenther, P. M., and Mickle, S. J. 1982. Foods Commonly Eaten by Individuals: Amount Per Day and Per Eating Occassion. Consumer Nutrition Center, Human Nutrition Information Service, Home Economics Research Report *44*. USDA, Hyattsville, MD.

Prescott, R. 1982. Food Consumption, Prices and Expenditure 1960–81. ERS Stat. Bull. *694*. USDA, Washington, DC.

Prescott, R. 1983. Charts on U.S. Food Consumption. ERS Staff Rep. AGES-821124. USDA, Washington, DC.

Quick, J. A., and Murphy, E. W. 1982. The Fortification of Foods: A Review. Agriculture Handbook *598*. USDA, Washington, DC.

Singer, J. D., Granahan, P., and Goodrich, N. N., *et al.* 1982. Diet and iron status, a study of relationships: United States, 1971–1974. Vital and Health Statistics. Ser. 11, *229*. DHHS Publ. (PHS) 83-1679. U.S. Gov't. Printing Office, Washington, DC.

U.S. Department of Agriculture (USDA) 1972. Food and Nutrient Intake of Individuals in the United States, Spring 1965. USDA Household Food Consumption Survey 1965–66. Rep. *11*. Consumer and Food Economics Research Division, Agr. Res. Serv. USDA, U.S. Government Printing Office, Washington, DC.

USDA 1980. Food and Nutrient Intakes of Individuals in One Day in the United States, Spring 1977. USDA Nationwide Food Consumption Survey, 1977–78. Prelim. Rep. *2*. Consumer Nutrition Center, Human Nutrition, Science and Education Administration, USDA, Hyattsville, MD.

USDA 1982. Food Consumption: Households in the United States, Spring 1977. Nationwide Food Consumption Survey 1977–78, Rep. *H-1*. U.S. Gov't. Printing Office, Washington, DC.

Welsh, S. O., and Marston, R. M. 1982. Review of trends in food use in the United States, 1909–1980. J. Am. Diet. Assoc. *81*, 120–125.

27

Methodology for
Nutrient Analysis [1]

Jesse F. Gregory III

The preservation of foods by thermal processing, drying and other osmotic manipulation, and freezing has been nutritionally beneficial by enhancing the distribution and accessibility of many products. However, losses of quality factors such as flavor and texture, along with certain nutrients, are to some degree inevitable.

Efforts to adjust processing conditions to maximize the retention of quality factors, while assuring microbiological safety, require accurate and precise data for mathematical modeling of the physical, chemical, and biological processes involved. Such models must include terms that describe the reaction rate at a reference temperature, the concentration dependence of the reaction rate, the temperature dependence of the reaction rate, and the influence of environmental variables such as pH, ionic strength, or competing reactants. Processing experiments are generally performed with multiple regression or similar design, utilizing various processing or storage times, temperatures, reactant concentrations, and varied environmental factors. In order to accommodate an analytical load involving large numbers of samples and replicates and provide data suitable for accurate modeling, the methods used must be as precise, accurate, simple, and rapid as possible. The determination of the nutrient content of foods for routine quality-control applications in industry, nutritional data gathering, or for regulatory purposes poses similar analytical needs.

Potential nutritional effects of food processing, as discussed in previous chapters, may include enhancement or impairment of protein digestibility and amino acid bioavailability, alteration in the chemical form and bioavailability of certain minerals, degradation or reduction in the biological activity or availability of certain vitamins, and alteration of compounds that affect the biological activity of certain nutrients. This chapter will be limited to a discussion of methodology for vitamins. It is not intended to be a comprehensive review of vitamin

---

[1] Based on "Methods of Vitamin Assay for Nutritional Evaluation of Food Processing," by J. F. Gregory III. Food Technol. 37(1):75–80 (1983). Copyright © by Institute of Food Technologists.

assay procedures, but, rather, a discussion of current technology and research needs pertaining to physicochemical and biological assay methods.

VITAMIN ASSAY METHODS

Selection of a Method

While many of the vitamins can be quantified in fairly pure form using direct spectrophotometric, fluorometric, or electrochemical methods, more specific procedures are required for the analysis of foods and other biological materials. Chemical methods suitable for food analysis ordinarily employ spectrophotometric quantitation, after the formation of specific chromophores or fluorophores, or high efficiency separations such as high-performance liquid chromatography. In addition, certain vitamins have been assayed traditionally by microbiological methods based on the specific nutritional requirements of various microorganisms. Other biologically specific assay methods for certain vitamins involve quantitation of binding to specific binding proteins.

Several analytical approaches are presently available for the determination of many of the vitamins, such that methodology may be selected on the basis of the type of data needed, number of samples, and capabilities of the laboratory. When justified by the sample load, automation of all or part of an assay may be desirable. Accurate assessment of nutritional quality of foods requires that the assay chosen respond equally to all biologically active forms of the vitamin. This is particularly important in modeling studies of vitamins that can undergo interconversion of vitamers differing markedly in stability properties (e.g., vitamin B_6 and folacin). The ability to quantify individual vitamers is another desirable characteristic for assays used in modeling studies. In contrast, knowledge of specific vitamer concentration is less important when gathering data for use in applications such as nutritional labeling and nutrient data banks.

The accuracy of any analytical method must be carefully established for the particular sample to be analyzed. Lack of sufficient confirmation of an analytical method can be responsible for erroneous interpretation of experimental results. Relatively recent examples of erroneous interpretation of data include research concerning the content and distribution of vitamin B_6 (Gregory and Kirk 1977; Gregory and Kirk 1978A) and folacin compounds (Tyerman et al. 1977; Maruyama et al. 1978; Lewis and Rowe 1979) in foods or other biological materials. In each case, an analytical procedure was reexamined and found to be inadequate for accurate quantitation of naturally occurring forms of the vitamins being studied. Stewart (1980) summarized the

Table 27.1. State of Current Methods for the Determination of Vitamins in Foods

	Needing further development	
	Conflicting data	Fragmentary data
Niacin	Folacin	Biotin
Riboflavin	Pantothenic acid	Vitamin K
Thiamin	Vitamin A	
Ascorbic acid	Vitamin B_6	
	Vitamin B_{12}	
	Vitamin D	
	Vitamin E	

Source: Adapted from Stewart (1980).

current status of analytical methodology for vitamins and other nutrients in foods.   As summarized in Table 27.1, it is apparent that there are conflicting reports and inadequate data concerning the suitability of analytical methods for the determination of many vitamins in foods.   While improvements have been made since this evaluation, a great deal of refinement, adaptation, and development of analytical methods is still clearly needed.

Adequate extraction techniques are vital to the success of all vitamin assay, although they are often taken for granted in methods development.   Extraction efficiency, in contrast to recovery, is difficult to determine for many biological materials and should be the subject of further research.   The ability of an extraction procedure to solubilize all of the bound or entrapped analyte is a primary factor affecting accuracy.   Studies with radiolabeled vitamins injected into experimental animals and allowed to equilibrate with tissue vitamin pools prior to analysis are one means of obtaining data concerning extraction efficiency.   Typical experimental data are shown in Table 27.2. Similar studies with plants, such as those employed for pesticide extraction research (Wheeler *et al.* 1978), could be performed using

Table 27.2. Examination of Extraction Efficiency for Liver Folacin Determination in a Rat Injected with ^{14}C-Folic Acid 24 Hr Prior to Sacrifice and Liver Analysis

Liver fraction	^{14}C extracted (% of total hepatic ^{14}C)
Incubated in 1.0 *M* mercaptoethanol at $100°C$ for 5 min, blended, and centrifuged	~90
Two washes of pellet	~10
Remaining insoluble material	0.3

Source: McMartin *et al.* (1981).

labeled vitamins or their precursors. Limitations in this approach center mainly on the identification of unextracted residues, although currently there are few alternatives. It is also important that the extraction conditions do not cause artifactual shifts in the proportions of the various forms of the vitamin being assayed. Thorough studies by Vanderslice et al. (1981A) illustrate the importance of attention to extraction conditions for vitamin B_6 determinations.

Microbiological Assays

Microbiological assays for the B vitamins were developed initially as an extension of early metabolic research. Quantification of bacterial and yeast growth assays has been performed largely by turbidimetric methods or titration of acid produced. Assessment of growth on the basis of metabolic products such as ATP (Harber and Asscher 1979) or $^{14}CO_2$ release from labeled substrates (Chen et al. 1978; Voigt and Eitenmiller 1979; Guilarte et al. 1981) could improve assay precision and shorten incubation times. Further research is needed concerning the application of these alternate methods of quantitation. While being extremely sensitive, microbiological assays are not well suited for studies of food processing or other large-scale analysis because of their length and cumbersome nature, susceptibility to culturing variables, limited sample analysis capacity, the poor precision often encountered, the differences in response to various forms of a vitamin, possible stimulation or growth inhibition by other compounds, and possible nonlinear response (drift) for various volumes of food extract analyzed. Assay response nonlinearity, as illustrated in Table 27.3, introduces serious uncertainity and indicates interference. Potentially

Table 27.3. Examples of Drift in Microbiological Assays for B Vitamins

Vitamin	Sample	Volume of extract added per assay tube (ml)	Apparent vitamin concentration (μg)
B_6[a]	Super Sugar Crisps® cereal	0.05/5 ml	50.2/g
		0.10/5 ml	43.2/g
		0.15/5 ml	40.5/g
B_6[a]	Cocoa Pebbles® cereal	0.05/5 ml	61.5/g
		0.10/5 ml	53.4/g
		0.15/5 ml	46.6/g
Pantothenic acid[b]	Beef puree (1.5 hr, 143°C)	1/10 ml	0.28/ml
		2/10 ml	0.41/ml
		3/10 ml	0.58/ml
		4/10 ml	0.61/ml

[a] Gregory (1980A); *Saccharomyces uvarum* assay.
[b] Hamm and Lund (1978); *Lactobacillus plantarum* assay.

Table 27.4.   Example of Differential Response to B_6 Vitamers in Yeast Growth Assays

Assay organism	B_6 vitamer[a]	Relative activity[b]	
		Mean	Range
Saccharomyces uvarum	PL	0.92	0.78–1.01
	PM	0.76	0.53–0.99
Kloeckera brevis	PL	1.03	0.79–1.17
	PM	0.60	0.36–0.83

Source: Adapted from Gregory (1982).

[a] PL, pyridoxal; PM, pyridoxamine.

[b] Relative activity (pyridoxine = 1.00). Values are for dose–response curves for each vitamer under typical assay conditions. Range = 0–10 ng/5 ml assay tube for each vitamer, triplicate tubes.

interfering factors, including neutralization salts and certain foods additives, have been evaluated by Voigt *et al.* (1979).

Microbiological assays are also subject to error if certain forms of the vitamin yield a lower response than that used as a standard. Conflicting data have been reported in this regard concerning the activity of various folacin monoglutamates in the *Lactobacillus casei* assay (Shane *et al.* 1980; Phillips and Wright 1982). Many researchers have reported unequal response of the three nonphosphorylated B_6 vitamers in yeast growth assays (Table 27.4), although recent studies have suggested that careful control of culturing conditions and selection of an alternate assay organism may minimize these response differences (Guilarte *et al.* 1980). Problems in quantitation arising from unequal response can be alleviated by chromatographic separation and individual microbiological determination of each of the B_6 vitamers against its own standard curve (Toepfer and Polansky 1970); however, this method is unsatisfactory for multiple analysis. Whereas the magnitude of errors introduced by such response variables may be obscured by the imprecision of certain microbiological assays, low response to certain vitamers could be responsible for underestimation in the assay. Problems involving drift and variable response would limit the usefulness of a microbiological assay method regardless of the technique used for growth measurement. These problems encountered in microbiological vitamin assay methods emphasize the need for refinement and development of alternate assay methods. This is particularly true for folacin, pantothenic acid, biotin, and vitamin B_{12}, for which microbiological procedures are currently the principal methods used. Advanced techniques in microbiological genetics currently are being applied to the development of organisms that exhibit highly specific requirements for the specific analyte and that are much less susceptible to the limitations of conventional microbiological assays. Such methodology will be an important addition to the field of nutrient analysis.

Spectrophotometric Assay Methods

Absorption and fluorescence spectrophotometric assay methods have long been available for the determination of ascorbic acid, niacin, thiamin, and riboflavin. The chemical reactions involved in the formation of absorbing or fluorescing species in these methods impart greater sensitivity and specificity than can be obtained by direct spectrophotometric examination of a food extract. Although these procedures are somewhat cumbersome for large-scale multiple analysis, they can be employed realiably and with minimal expense (Thornburg 1977). The documented accuracy and comparative simplicity of these methods made them well suited for automation. A variety of continuous-flow methods has been reported and widely used for the determination of these vitamins (e.g., Kirk 1974A, B; Kirk and Ting 1975; Egberg and Potter 1975; Roy et al. 1976; Egberg et al. 1977B; Jacobson 1977; Pelletier and Madere 1977; Behrens and Madere 1979). Application of automated methods to the determination of water-soluble vitamins has been reviewed by Roy (1979). Research concerning the nutritional effects of food processing, along with routine analysis, has been greatly enhanced by the application of automated methods. Continuous-flow methodology ordinarily improves analysis rate, reduces technician time requirements, improves the precision of reactions in which timing and reagent volume are critical (e.g., alkaline ferricyanide oxidation of thiamin), and improves overall assay precision (Kirk 1974A, B; Egberg and Potter 1975; Snyder and van der Wal 1981).

Automated vitamin assay methods based on the segmented-flow technique of continuous-flow analysis employ a Technicon Autoanalyzer® or similar system, which uses a peristaltic pump to meter precisely samples and reagents through the manifold system (Snyder et al. 1976; Snyder 1980), much as originally devised by Skeggs (1957). Segmented-flow analysis is based on the use of air bubbles to provide segmentation between adjacent portions of the mixed sample–reagent stream to minimize carryover and enhance mixing. Segmented-flow methods are normally operated at sampling rates of 30–60/hr.

An alternate technique for automated analysis is flow-injection analysis, which is a continuous-flow method based on narrow-bore flow manifolds and valve injection of small sample volumes to provide controlled dispersion in the absence of air segmentation (Ruzicka and Hansen 1975; Stewart et al. 1976; Betteridge 1978; Ruzicka and Hansen 1980; Ranger 1981). Flow-injection systems yield fast sampling rates (e.g., 60->200/hr) with baseline resolution between samples, require little stabilization time, usually consume less reagent than comparable segmented-flow methods, and in many respects are more versatile than segmented-flow systems (Ruzicka and Hansen 1980; Ranger 1981). Although the application of flow-injection methodology has been extensive for the analysis of many inorganic and organic materials, and for enzyme activity assays, application of the technique to vitamin analysis has been limited to several preliminary reports concerning ascorbic acid and thiamin (Ruzicka and Hansen 1978; Karlberg and Thelander 1978, 1980; Strohl and Curran 1979). Many of the conventional chemical methods for vitamin assays may not be well suited for flow-injection analysis because of the relatively long reaction times involved and the residence time limitation of most flow-injection systems ($\leqslant 2$ min). Future applications of flow injection analysis appear likely to enhance analytical capabilities for automated vitamin analysis.

High-Performance Liquid Chromatography

Vitamin assay methods based on analytical chromatography have centered mainly on high-performance liquid chromatography (HPLC). Most vitamins are poorly suited for gas chromatography, while HPLC provides a wide range of applicable separation and detection methods. In contrast to the other methods discussed, HPLC offers the potential for limited multivitamin analysis of a single food extract, but few such procedures have yet been developed. For example, procedures have been reported for the simultaneous determination of thiamin and niacin in pasta and cereals (Kamman *et al.* 1980); niacin, riboflavin, and thiamin in rice products (Toma and Tabekhia 1979); pyridoxine, thiamin, and riboflavin in fortified cereals (Wehling and Wetzel 1984); vitamins A and E in fortified cereal products (Widicus and Kirk 1979); and vitamins A, D, and E in animal feeds and premixes (Cohen and Lapointe 1978). Limitations in further development of HPLC methods for multivitamin determinations include (1) the complexity of resolving and quantifying all biologically active forms of many vitamins, (2) the need for multiple detectors to maximize detection sensitivity and specificity, and (3) techniques suitable for sample extract purification, which depend on the chemcial nature of the analytes.

High-performance liquid chromatography methods for the determination of individual vitamins in certain foods have been applied to both fat-soluble and water-soluble vitamins. Comprehensive listings of HPLC applications to vitamin assays have been published in recent reviews (Foltz *et al.* 1983; Yeransian *et al.* 1985). Numerous HPLC procedures have been reported for vitamins A, D, and E and certain metabolites in many foods and other biological materials (e.g., Dennison and Kirk 1977; Egberg *et al.* 1977A; Head and Gibbs 1977; Thompson *et al.* 1977; Cohen and Lapointe 1978; Jones 1978; Thompson 1978; McMurray and Blanchflower 1979; Widicus and Kirk 1979; Howell and Wang 1982). An HPLC method also has been reported for the determination of phylloquinone, a form of vitamin K, in milk and formula products (Haroon *et al.* 1982). These methods improve the specificity and simplify fat-soluble vitamin assays by reducing the need for extensive sample preparation and eliminating the need for correction for the spectral characteristics of potentially interfering compounds (Erdman *et al.* 1973). Separations of various vitamin E compounds have been developed and applied to foods (Manz and Phillip 1981; Cort *et al.* 1983). Procedures such as these are important because they permit individual quantitation of various tocopherols and tocotrienols differing widely in vitamin E activity.

High-performance liquid chromatography methods also have been reported for the determination of ascorbic acid (Pachla and Kissinger 1976; Sood *et al.* 1976; Augustin *et al.* 1981; Dennison *et al.* 1981; Vanderslice and Higgs 1984; Kacem *et al.* 1986), riboflavin (Toma and Tabekhia 1979; Ang and Moseley 1980; Fellman *et al.* 1982), niacin (Toma and Tabekhia 1979; Kamman *et al.* 1980), and thiamin (Toma and Tabekhia 1979; Ishi *et al.* 1979; Ang and Moseley 1980; Kammen *et al.* 1980; Kimura *et al.* 1980; Fellman *et al.* 1982) in biological materials. Although HPLC methods often provide a greater assurance of specificity than other methods, HPLC analysis for these water-soluble vitamins generally offers little advantage over the well-established continuous-flow automated methods in many cases and often decreases analysis rate.

A major advantage of HPLC for B vitamin assay is for vitamins for which there is no widely suitable chemical assay method (e.g., vitamin B_6 and folacin). Numerous methods for the separation and quantitation of B_6 vitamers have been reported and recently reviewed (Gregory and Kirk 1981). Successful application of vitamin B_6 HPLC to the analysis of certain foods and other biological materials has been reported using reverse-phase (Gregory 1980A; Gregory and Feldstein 1985) and ion-exchange methods (Vanderslice *et al.* 1980, 1981A, B, C; Coburn and Mahuren 1983). Numerous HPLC methods also have been reported for the separation of folacin monoglutamates. Initial reports indicated varied success in certain HPLC applications to food folacin analysis (Clifford and Clifford 1977; Reingold and Picciano 1982; Day and Gregory 1981; Gregory *et al.* 1982). Gregory *et al.* (1984) recently modified a reverse-phase HPLC procedure to permit the determination of naturally occurring folacin vitamers in a wide variety of materials. Although these HPLC methods for vitamin B_6 and folacin are rather lengthy, they provide a potentially favorable alternative to microbiological assay methods.

Another promising area for extension of HPLC to vitamins is post-column derivatization using the principles of flow-injection analysis to enhance sensitivity and specificity. Postcolumn derivatization methods have been employed in the HPLC determination of folates (Day and Gregory 1982), various thiamin compounds (Osborne and

Voogt 1978; Ishi *et al.* 1979; Kimura *et al.* 1980), and niacin (Osborne and Voogt 1978).

Ligand Binding Assays

Ligand binding assays represent a potentially important methodology for the simple, rapid, and highly sensitive determination of many water-soluble vitamins. These techniques are based mainly on the interaction of the analyte with either a naturally occurring binding protein or an antibody formed against a protein–analyte conjugate. Quantification is ordinarily based on competition for the binding protein between the vitamin in a food extract or standard solution and a known quantity of a radiolabeled derivative. Competitive binding radioassays also have been applied to the individual quantification of vitamin D compounds in milk following HPLC fractionation (Hollis 1983; van den Berg *et al.* 1986). Competitive binding assays for folacin and vitamin B_{12} have been used widely for clinical analysis, although their use in other applications has not been extensive. The accuracy of initial radioassay methods for vitamin B_{12} has been questioned (Anonymous 1979); however, assays using a sufficiently specific binding protein and rigorous extraction and pretreatment methods assure accuracy (Beck 1979). Vitamin B_{12} radioassays have been applied successfully to foods and a variety of other materials (Beck 1978, 1979). The accuracy of several folacin radioassay methods for plasma analysis has been questioned

Table 27.5. Comparison of Assay Methods for the Determination of Folacin in Selected Foods and Other Biological Materials

Sample	Radioassay (μg/g)	Microbiological (μg/g)	HPLC (μg/g)
Rat liver[a]			
0 hr autolysis	20.4	6.7	—
3 hr autolysis	20.7	19.9	—
5 hr autolysis	18.5	19.5	—
Spinach, frozen, uncooked[b]	4.0	2.5	—
Spinach, fresh, raw[b]	4.2	1.6	—
Spinach, cooked[b]	5.0	1.8	—
Brussels sprouts[c]	1.05	1.05	—
Collard greens[c]	1.08	0.93	—
Meat loaf[c]	20.1	17.9	—
Cabbage, raw[d]	1.34	0.59	2.24
Oat cereal, fortified[d]	7.83	9.30	6.19
Infant formula, fortified[d]	0.06	0.19	0.18

[a] Tigner and Roe (1979).
[b] Klein and Kuo (1981).
[c] Graham *et al.* (1980).
[d] Gregory *et al.* (1982).

(Waxman and Schreiber 1977), although methods for accurate plasma folacin determinations are available (Waxman and Schreiber 1980). The validity of folacin radioassays for analysis of other biological materials is uncertain because of the varying affinity of different folacin vitamers for folacin-binding proteins (Shane et al. 1980). Data supporting the accuracy of folacin radioassays for certain foods and animal tissues (Tigner and Roe 1979; Graham et al. 1980; Gregory et al. 1982) have been reported; however, several studies have shown variable agreement between the results of radioassays and other methods (Reingold et al. 1980; Klein and Kuo 1981; Gregory et al. 1982). Typical data are shown in Table 27.5. A potential source of error in food analysis using ligand binding assays is the possible assay response due to binding of biologically inactive vitamin degradation products. Radioassay methods have been employed in a study of folacin stability, although the assay specificity with respect to degradation products was not examined (Ruddick et al. 1980).

Competitive binding radioassays for biotin have been developed using avidin as the binding protein (Hood 1979; Dakshinamurti and Allan 1979). Similar methods using thiamin- and riboflavin-binding proteins have been reported, but these procedures do not appear to offer an advantage over chemical methods. A radioimmunoassay for pantothenic acid has been reported to be a favorable alternative to microbiological methods (Walsh et al. 1979). Radioimmunoassays also have been reported for folic acid (DaCosta and Rothenberg 1971; Hendel 1981) and the phosphorylated B_6 vitamers (Thanassi and Cidlowski 1980), but these are of limited use because they do not respond to other biologically active B_6 and folacin vitamers.

An innovative concept for ligand binding assays was recently developed for the determination of biotin based on a biotinyl–lysozyme conjugate and the inhibition of lysozyme activity by its complexation with avidin (Gebauer and Rechnitz 1980). The basis of quantification is the degree of avidin binding to free biotin in standards or sample extracts, which, in turn, influences the enzymatic activity of the lysozyme conjugate. This technique presumably could be applied to other vitamins for which specific binding proteins exist (i.e., riboflavin, thiamin, folacin, and vitamin B_{12}), and thus eliminate the need for radiochemicals in their ligand binding assays. Similarly, Viceps-Madore et al. (1983) prepared monoclonal antibodies which, as indicated by initial data, could be used to quantify all of the biologically active vitamin B_6 compounds using an enzyme-linked immunosorbent assay (ELISA) technique. Methods such as this show great promise for rapid, simple and highly sensitive assays for various water-soluble vitamins in the future. With further research and validation, ligand binding methods may become suitable alternatives to microbiological assays.

Enzymatic Assays

Other biologically specific assay methods, which may be applicable to food analysis, are based on the coenzymatic activity of certain vitamins. Enzymatic assays have been reported for certain folacin, vitamin B_6, riboflavin, pantothenic acid, and vitamin B_6 compounds. Their use in the determination of total vitamin activity would be limited by the need to convert other vitamers to a coenzymatically active form. The sensitivity of such assays would be inversely proportional to the Michaelis constant for each coenzyme. An enzymatic assay for biotin using pyruvate apocarboxylase appears to be an attractive alternative to other assay procedures for this vitamin (Haarasilta 1978). Relatively few applications of enzymatic methods have been reported for the nutritional evaluation of foods.

BIOLOGICAL ACTIVITY AND BIOAVAILABILITY

Evaluating Biological Activity

The basic assumption in the use of vitamin assays by any of the previously discussed methods is that the result is an accurate reflection of the biological activity or potency of the specific vitamin in a food sample. Biological activity, in this context, refers to the ability of a compound to function in fulfilling a specific metabolic requirement. This should be distinguished from bioavailability, which is normally used in reference to the extent of absorption and metabolic utilization of a nutrient. In order for an assay to accurately reflect the biological activity of a vitamin in a food, it must respond to all vitamers in proportion to their biological activity.

Several examples of differences between biological activity and vitamin assay response illustrate this point. Many conventional assays for vitamin A compounds are based on direct spectrophotometry or colorimetric assay of chromophores produced with various Lewis acids. The extent of vitamin A isomerization during food processing and storage is presently unclear. Cis-geometric isomers have lower vitamin A activity than the all–trans reference compounds (Ames 1965), although all isomers yield equivalent response in nonspecific vitamin A assays. High-performance liquid chromatographic methods have been developed which permit individual determination of vitamin A isomers for more accurate assessment of biological activity (Egberg et al. 1977A; Mulry et al. 1982, 1983). Similarly, two oxidation products of vitamin E, α-tocopheryl oxide and α-tocopheryl quinone, have been found to exhibit approximately 100 and 35% molar vitamin E activity, respectively, in rat bioassays using plasma pyruvate kinase activity as an index of quantitation (Widicus 1980). Conventional chemical assays for vitamin E would not respond to these derivatives.   A similar situation has been found with respect to ϵ-pyridoxyllysine, a reduced protein-bound complex of vitamin B_6 aldehyde vitamers formed in thermal processing and storage.   This complexed form of vitamin B_6 exhibits partial vitamin B_6 activity for the rat (Gregory 1980B) by virtue of its enzymatic conversion the vitamin B_6 coenzyme form (Gregory 1980C), although it would not be detected by many assay procedures. Conversely, pyridoxine-S'-β-glucoside, a naturally occurring form of vitamin B_6 in fruits and vegetables, exhibits little vitamin B_6 activity in the rat but yields a full response in microbiological assays employing acid hydrolysis (Ink et al. 1986; Gregory and Ink 1987). These examples illustrate the need for characterization of the various forms of a vitamin present in a food, along with the biological activity of its derivatives or degradation products, before biological activity and processing effects can be fully determined.

Animal Bioassay Methods

The determination of biological vitamin activity of foods or purified compounds is performed using animal bioassay procedures.   Such methods are lengthy, less precise than physicochemical procedures, and are expensive to conduct.   In vitro alternatives to bioassay methods obviously would be desirable. However, until the correlation between the results of in vitro (microbiological or physicochemical) and bioassay methods is fully determined for a particular sample, there is no alternative to the use of animal bioassays for the evaluation of biological activity.

As stated previously, the bioavailability of a nutrient in a food refers to the fraction (or percentage) which is absorbed and metabolically utilized by an animal or person. In view of the length, expense, and difficulty of human bioassays, many bioavailability studies are performed using animal models. In this experimental context, bioavailability is defined as the concentration of biologically available forms of a nutrient (as determined by animal bioassay) divided by the total concentration of the nutrient determined chemically or microbiologically. In most cases microbiological assay procedures cannot adequately substitute for animal bioassays for the evaluation of nutrient bioavailability because of the extreme difficulty of devising sample extraction procedures which would adequately model mammalian (or avian) digestion and intestinal absorption processes.

Animal bioassays are performed typically using at least three (preferably four to five) levels of the purified reference compounds and one or more levels of the test compound (or dried food sample) added to a basal diet which is adequate in all nutrients except that being assayed. Ordinarily at least 8–10 animals per group are employed. The sensitivity of many bioassays is increased by a preliminary depletion period in which all animals are fed a diet deficient in the assayed nutrient in order to induce a state of moderate deficiency prior to the repletion phase of the assay. Proper selection of the test animal is important to the success of the bioassay. The inbred laboratory rat is commonly used as a test animal in many vitamin bioassays because of its rapid growth rate, relative ease of handling and genetic uniformity. In cases where the rat is not satisfactory and a nonmammalian species would be acceptable, the chick often is a suitable alternative for vitamin bioassays.

Although early bioassay work was performed almost exclusively using animal growth as the response criterion, assay specificity can only be assured by using biologically specific response criteria. Examples of commonly used response criteria for B vitamins include urinary thiamin: creatinine ratio, liver thiamin pyrophosphate concentration, and erythrocyte transketolase activity for thiamin (Gregory and Kirk 1978C; Trebukhina *et al.* 1981; Brin 1964); erythrocyte glutathione reductase activity for riboflavin (Tillotson and Sauberlich 1971); plasma or liver folacin concentration for folacin (Keagy 1983; Ristow *et al.* 1982; Abad and Gregory 1987); plasma pyridoxal 5'-phosphate or erythrocyte aspartate animotransferase activity for vitamin B_6 (Lumeng *et al.* 1978); urinary methylmalonic acid for vitamin B_{12} (Barness *et al.* 1963); and urinary N-methyl-nicotinamide excretion for niacin (Carter and Carpenter 1982). Another quantitative factor, which is useful in bioassays for riboflavin, thiamin, and vitamin B_6, is the relative increase in the enzymatic activity of erythrocyte glutathione reductase, transketolase, and aspartate aminotransferase, respectively, after in vitro incubation with the appropriate coenzyme (flavin adenine dinucleotide, thiamin pyrophosphate and pyridoxal 5'-phosphate, respectively; Bayoumi and Rosalki 1976). The percentage of stimulation by added coenzyme provides an index of the degree of apoenzyme saturation, which is a sensitive functional measure of the animal's nutritional status for these vitamins. Biologically specific functional criteria, which have been used for quantitation of bioassays for fat-soluble vitamins, include plasma tocopherol, fetal resorption, and degree of myopathy as indicated by the enzymatic activity of plasma pyruvate kinase in vitamin E bioassays (Leth and Sondergaard 1977; Machlin *et al.* 1978; Ames 1979); the extent of rat vaginal epithelial cornification for vitamin A assays (Pugsley *et al.* 1944; Sietsema and DeLuca 1982); the degree of metaphysial calcification in rachitic rats or chicks for vitamin D assays (Anonymous 1970); and plasma prothrombin for vitamin K assays (Knauer *et al.* 1976).

Whereas the measurement of biologically specific criteria such as those listed increases the analytical requirements and expense of animal bioassays, their use is essential to the accuracy of the results.

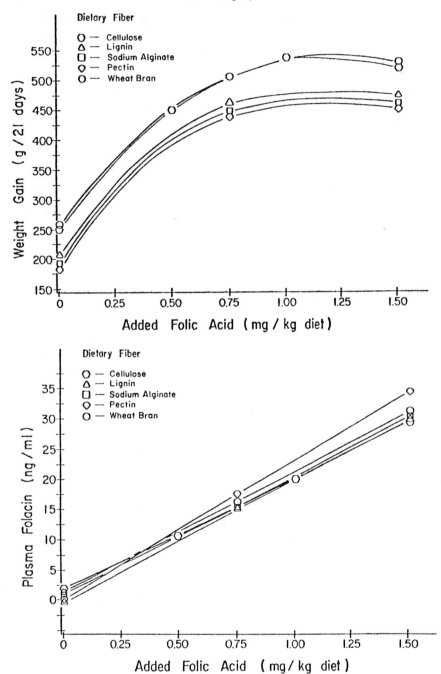

Fig. 27.1. Dose-response curves for folic acid of diets varying in type of dietary fiber. Differences observed in growth were not due to an effect of diet on folacin absorption or metabolism. Source: Ristow *et al.* (1983); courtesy of the American Institute of Nutrition.

Animal growth is a highly sensitive indicator of nutritional status, but growth is subject to dietary influences other than that of the variable being studied. An example is the depressed growth observed in chick bioassays used to determine the effect of dietary fiber on folic acid bioavailability (Ristow *et al.* 1982). In this study diets containing lignin, sodium alginate, and pectin yielded lower chick growth than diets containing wheat bran or cellulose, while the actual folacin status of the chick (as indicated by plasma or liver folacin) was equivalent for each source of dietary fiber (Fig. 27.1).

A limitation of bioassay data, even for studies conducted using specific criteria for quantitation, is that there may be a lack of agreement between results based on different biochemical parameters. For example, many vitamin B_6 bioassays are monitored using several functional indicators of vitamin B_6 status, in addition to growth-based data. As typified by the results of Table 27.6, estimates of the concentration of biologically available vitamin B_6 often differ widely among the criteria used in a single assay. Statistically significant differences between bioassay results based on various biochemical indicators are not uncommon. Although these criteria would ordinarily provide consistency in general experimental conclusions, quantitative evaluation is often difficult. Such differences may be due to subtle influences of diet composition on the metabolism and pharmacokinetics of the vitamins; however, little data are available in this regard. Another problem encountered in the quantitation of certain vitamins by bioassay

Table 27.6. Concentration of Total and Biologically Available Vitamin B_6 in Selected Foods

Assay method[b]	Vitamin B_6 concentration (nmol/g dry weight)[a]		
	Nonfat dry milk[c]	Rice-base cereal[c]	Raw potato[d]
Total vitamin B_6			
Microbiological	40 ± 1	201 ± 7	89 ± 4
HPLC	—	210 ± 5	—
Available vitamin B_6 (rat bioassay)			
Growth	48 ± 2	91 ± 11	37 ± 8
Feed efficiency	42 ± 2	55 ± 9	62 ± 5
Liver PLP	35 ± 10	37 ± 11	—
AspAT activity	53 ± 8	89 ± 11	—
AspAT stimulation	28 ± 3	220 ± 56	—
Plasma PLP	—	—	85 ± 9

[a] Mean ± S.E.
[b] HPLC, high performance liquid chromatography; PLP, pyridoxal 5'-phosphate; AspAT, erythrocyte aspartate aminotransferase.
[c] Adapted from Gregory (1980D).
[d] Adapted from Nguyen and Gregory (1983).

Table 27.7. Differences in Apparent Relative Activity of B_6 Vitamers as a Function of the Bioassay Response Criterion Employed

Response criterion[a]	Relative activity of B_6 vitamer[b, c]	
	Pyridoxal	Pyridoxamine
Rat growth	0.92 ± 0.06	0.86 ± 0.03
Feed efficiency	1.05 ± 0.03	1.12 ± 0.04
AspAT activity	0.47 ± 0.02	0.24 ± 0.02
AspAT stimulation	0.29 ± 0.01	0.17 ± 0.01
Plasma PLP	0.75 ± 0.08	0.99 ± 0.26

[a] AspAT, erythrocyte aspartate aminotransferase; PLP, pyridoxal 5'-phosphate.

[b] Biological activity calculated relative to pyridoxine dose–response curves. A value of 1.0 would indicate full activity of pyridoxal or pyridoxamine, relative to that of pyridoxine. Mean ± S.E., 9 rats per group.

[c] From Nguyen *et al.* (1983).

methods is a differential response to various forms of the vitamin. Research has shown that B_6 vitamers exhibit differing biological responses in rat bioassays, the magnitude of which varies as a function of the response criteria employed (Table 27.7; Nguyen *et al.* 1983). The magnitude of these differences in apparent activity of the B_6 vitamers has been shown to vary as a function of the dose employed (Gregory and Litherland 1986).

A major problem with bioassays for B vitamins using rats or other rodents is the pronounced effect of diet on the extent of vitamin biosynthesis by the intestinal microflora. The contribution of intestinal microorganisms to the B vitamin nutritive of mammals is difficult to quantify. Absorption of microbially synthesized nutrients may occur directly after release from microbial cells, as appears to be the case for biotin (McGregor *et al.* 1947; McCormick 1976) and probably most other B vitamins. In the case of most rodents, the practice of coprophagy provides a recycling of initially unabsorbed vitamins from both microbial synthesis and the diet. The contribution of coprophagy to the nutriture of rodents for B vitamins and vitamin K has been shown in many studies which employed feces-retaining tail-cup devices (Barki *et al.* 1949; Kulwich *et al.* 1953; Barnes and Fiala 1958, 1959; Barnes *et al.* 1959; Gregory and Litherland 1986; Abad and Gregory 1987). Research concerning the effects of dietary antibiotics on vitamin status also indicates a role of the intestinal microflora in vitamin nutriture.

Because of the significant role of the intestinal microflora and the well-documented influence of diet composition variables on the types and numbers of microorganisms present, careful design and evaluation of animal bioassays is required to achieve accurate results. It is often difficult to ascertain whether a response to a test material is due to the assayed nutrient or stimulation of its synthesis by the intestinal microflora. Bioassay results which exceed chemically or microbiologically determined values for the total concentration of the assayed vitamin also are suggestive of microfloral interference. Whenever possible, test materials should be analyzed in a bioassay at several levels of addition to the basal diet (Bliss and White 1967) in order to permit testing for dose dependence of response and to provide increased precision via a slope-ratio method of quantitation. Dose dependence and/or a Y intercept of the dose–response curve for the tested material that is significantly different from that of the standard dose–response curve suggest interfering effects involving the intestinal microflora. A method has been reported recently whereby dose–response curves of standards and test materials exhibiting unequal Y intercepts can still be quantified (Keagy and Oace 1984), although its application has been limited. Efforts to reduce microfloral interference by the prevention of coprophagy have been partially successful in improving bioassay accuracy in our laboratory (Gregory and Litherland 1986; Abad and Gregory 1987). While the prevention of coprophagy improves accuracy in some applications, biases may be induced by changes in intestinal microbial populations (Fitzgerald *et al.* 1964) and interferences can still be encountered via apparent direct absorption of microbially synthesized vitamins (Gregory and Litherland 1986). Use of the chick as an animal model has partially alleviated this problem in certain applications in which a nonmammalian species was acceptable (Ristow *et al.* 1982; Nguyen *et al.* 1981). In studies of the behavior of vitamins during processing in model systems, the use of an unfortified control permitted an evaluation of ingredient effects on the bioassay response (Gregory and Kirk 1978A, B).

In spite of the length, expense, relatively low precision, and the problems previously discussed, animal bioassays provide a great deal of otherwise unobtainable information concerning the nutritional quality of foods. In addition to their application in the determination of the biological activity and bioavailability of nutrients, bioassays also have been used extensively in the study of naturally occurring antinutritional factors (e.g., Balloun and Johnson 1953; Carlson *et al.* 1964; Thompson *et al.* 1968; Klosterman 1981) and are useful in evaluating the accuracy of physicochemical assay methods. Through careful experimental design and evaluation of data, extremely useful data can be obtained with animal bioassay procedures.

SUMMARY

The selection of analytical methods is of critical importance in nutritional evaluation of food processing and for routine monitoring.

Assay methods must be precise and accurate and ideally should be able to accommodate the analysis of large numbers of samples. Much more research is needed concerning the development and application of vitamin assay procedures for research and routine use and for the confirmation of their efficacy.

REFERENCES

Abad, A. R., and Gregory, J. F. 1987. Determination of folate bioavailability with a rat bioassay. J. Nutr. *117*, 866–873.

Ames, S. R. 1965. Bioassay of vitamin A compounds. Fed. Proc. *24*, 917–923.

Ames, S. R. 1979. Biopotencies of several forms of alpha-tocopherol. J. Nutr. *109*, 2198–2204.

Anonymous 1970. Bioassay methods — Vitamin D. *In* Methods of Analysis, 11th Edition. Association of Official Analytical Chemists, Washington, DC.

Anonymous 1979. Pitfalls in the diagnosis of vitamin B_{12} deficiency by radio-dilution assay. Nutr. Rev. *37*, 313–316.

Ang, C. Y. W., and Moseley, F. A. 1980. Determination of thiamin and riboflavin in meat and meat products by high-pressure liquid chromatography. J. Agric. Food Chem. *28*, 483–486.

Augustin, J., Beck, C., and Marousek, G. I. 1981. Quantitative determination of ascorbic acid in potatoes and potato products by high-performance liquid chromatography. J. Food Sci. *46*, 312–316.

Balloun, S. L., and Johnson, E. L. 1953. Anticoagulant properties of defatted soybean meal in chick diets. Arch. Biochem. Biophys. *42*, 355–359.

Barki, V. H., Derse, P. H., Collins, R. A., Hart, E. B., and Elvehjem, C. A. 1949. The influence of coprophagy on the biotin and folic acid requirements of the rat. J. Nutr. *37*, 443–455.

Barnes, R. H., and Fiala, G. 1958. Effects of the prevention of coprophagy in the rat. 2. Vitamin B_{12} requirements. J. Nutr. *65*, 103–114.

Barnes, R. H., and Fiala, G. 1959. Effects of the prevention of coprophagy in the rat. 6. Vitamin K. J. Nutr. *68*, 603–614.

Barnes, R. H., Kwong, E., and Fiala, G. 1959. Effects of the prevention of coprophagy in the rat. 4. Biotin. J. Nutr. *67*, 599–610.

Barness, L. A., Young, D. G., and Nocho, R. 1963. Methylmalonate excretion in Vitamin B_{12} deficiency. Science *140*, 76–77.

Bayoumi, R. A., and Roaslki, S. B. 1976. Evaluation of methods of coenzyme activation of erythrocyte enzymes for detection of deficiency of vitamins B_1, B_2 and B_6. Clin. Chem. *22*, 327–335.

Beck, R. A. 1978. Competitive intrinsic binding assay technique for cobalamins in natural waters. Anal. Chem. *50*, 200–202.

Beck, R. A. 1979. Comparison of two radioassay methods for cyanocobalamin in seafoods. J. Food Sci. *4*, 1077–1079.

Behrens, W. A., and Madere, R. 1979. Improved automated method for determining vitamin C in plasma and tissues. Anal. Biochem. *92*, 510–516.

Betteridge, D. 1978. Flow injection analysis. Anal. Chem. *50*, 832A–846A.

Bliss, C. I., and White, C. 1967. Statistical methods in biological assay of the vitamins. *In* The Vitamins, 2nd ed., Vol. 6. P. Gyorgy and W. N. Pearson (Editors). Academic Press, New York.

Brin, M. 1964. Use of the erythrocyte in functional evaluation of vitamin adequacy. *In* The Red Blood Cell. C. Bishop and D. S. Surgenor (Editors). Academic Press, New York.

Carlson, C. W., Saxena, H. C., Jensen, L. S., and McGinnis, J. 1964. Rachitogenic activity of soybean fractions. J. Nutr. *82*, 507–511.

Carter, E. G. A., and Carpenter, K. J. 1982. The available niacin values of foods for rats and their relation to analytical values. J. Nutr. *112*, 2091–2103.

Chen, M. F., McIntyre, P. A., and Kertcher, J. A. 1978. Measurement of folates in human plasma and erythrocytes by a radiometric microbiologic method. J. Nucl. Med. *19*, 906–912.

Clifford, C. K., and Clifford, A. J. 1977. High pressure liquid chromatographic analysis of food for folates. J. Assoc. Offic. Anal. Chem. *60*, 1248–1251.

Coburn, S. P., and Mahuren, J. D. 1983. A versatile cation-exchange procedure for measuring the seven major forms of vitamin B_6 in biological samples. Anal. Biochem. *129*, 310–317.

Cohen, H., and Lapointe, M. 1978. Methods for the extraction and cleanup of animal feed for the determination of liposoluble vitamins D, A and E by high-pressure liquid chromatography. J. Agric. Food Chem. *26*, 1210–1213.

Cort, W. M., Vincente, T. S., Waysek, E. H., and Williams, B. D. 1983. Vitamin E content of feedstuffs determined by high-performance liquid chromatographic fluorescence. J. Agric. Food Chem. *31*, 1330–1333.

DaCosta, M., and Rothenberg, S. P. 1971. Identification of an immunoreactive folate in serum extracts by radioimmunoassay. Br. J. Haematol. *21*, 121–130.

Dakshinamurti, K., and Allan, L. 1979. Isotope dilution assay for biotin: Use of [^{3}H] biotin. Methods Enzymol. *62*, 284–287.

Day, B. P., and Gregory, J. F. 1981. Determination of folacin derivatives in selected foods by high-performance liquid chromatography. J. Agric. Food Chem. *29*, 374–377.

Dennison, D. B., and Kirk, J. R. 1977. Quantitative analysis of vitamin A in cereal products by high-speed liquid chromatography. J. Food Sci. *42*, 1376–1379.

Dennison, D. B., Brawley, T. G., and Hunter, G. L. K. 1981. Rapid high-performance liquid chromatographic determination of ascorbic acid and combined ascorbic acid–dehydroascrobic acid in beverages. J. Agric. Food Chem. *29*, 927–929.

Egberg, D. C., and Potter, R. H. 1975. Improved automated determination of riboflavine in food products. J. Agric. Food Chem. *23*, 815–820.

Egberg, D. C., Heroff, J. C., and Potter, R. H. 1977A. Determination of all—trans and 13-*cis* vitamin A in food products by high-pressure liquid chromatography. J. Agric. Food Chem. *25*, 1127–1132.

Egberg, D. C., Potter, R. H., and Heroff, J. C. 1977B. Semiautomated method for the fluorometric determination of total vitamin C in food products. J. Assoc. Offic. Anal. Chem. *60*, 126–131.

Erdman, J. W., Hou, S.-H. F., and LaChance, P. A. 1973. Fluorometric determination of vitamin A in foods. J. Food Sci. *38*, 447–449.

Fellman, J. K., Artz, W. E., Tassinari, P. D., Cole, C. L., and Augustin, J. 1982. Simultaneous determination of thiamin and riboflavin in selected foods by high-performance liquid chromatography. J. Food Sci. *47*, 2048–2067.

Fitzgerald, R. J., Gustafsson, B. E., and McDaniel, E. G. 1964. Effects of coprophagy prevention on intestinal microflora in rats. J. Nutr. *84*, 155–160.

Foltz, A. K., Yeransian, J. A., and Sloman, K. G. 1983. Food. Anal. Chem. *55*, 164R–196R.

Gebauer, C. R., and Rechnitz, G. A. 1980. Ion selective electrode estimation of avidon and biotin using a lysozyme label. Anal. Biochem. *103*, 280–284.

Graham, D. C., Roe, D. A., and Ostertag, S. G. 1980. Radiometric determination and chick bioassay of folacin in fortified and unfortified frozen foods. J. Food Sci. *45*, 47–51.

Gregory, J. F. 1980A. Comparison of high-pressure liquid chromatographic and *Saccharomyces uvarum* methods for the determination of vitamin B_6 in fortified breakfast cereals. J. Agric. Food Chem. *28*, 486–489.

Gregory, J. F. 1980B. Effects of ϵ-pyridoxyllysine bound to dietary protein on the vitamin B_6 status of rats. J. Nutr. *110*, 995–1005.

Gregory, J. F. 1980C. Effects of ϵ-pyridoxyllysine and related compounds on liver and brain pyridoxal kinase and liver pyridoxamine (pyridoxine) 5′-phosphate oxidase. J. Biol. Chem. *225*:2355–2359.

Gregory, J. F. 1980D. Bioavailability of vitamin B_6 in nonfat dry milk and a fortified rice breakfast cereal product. J. Food Sci. *45*, 84–86.

Gregory, J. F. 1982. Relative activity of the nonphosphorylated B-6 vitamers for *Saccharomyces uvarum* and *Kloeckera brevis* in vitamin B_6 microbiological assay. J. Nutr. *112*, 1643–1647.

Gregory, J. F., and Feldstein, D. 1985. Determination of vitamin B_6 in foods and other biological materials by paired-ion high-performance liquid chromatography, J. Agric. Food Chem. *33*, 359–363.

Gregory, J. F., and Ink, S. L. 1987. Identification and quantification of pyridoxine-β-glucoside as a major form of vitamin B_6 in plant-derived foods. J. Agric. Food Chem. *35*, 76–82.

Gregory, J. F., and Kirk, J. R. 1977. Improved chromatographic separation and fluorometric determination of vitamin B_6 compounds in foods. J. Food Sci. *42*, 1073–1076.

Gregory, J. F., and Kirk, J. R. 1978A. Assessment of storage effects on vitamin B_6 stability and bioavailability in dehydrated food systems. J. Food Sci. *43*, 1801–1815.

Gregory, J. F., and Kirk, J. R. 1978B. Assessment of roasting effects on vitamin B_6 stability and bioavailability in dehydrated food systems. J. Food Sci. *43*, 1585–1589.

Gregory, J. F., and Kirk, J. R. 1978C. Comparison of chemical and biological methods for determination of thiamin in foods. J. Agric. Food Chem. *26*, 338–341.

Gregory, J. F., and Kirk, J. R. 1981. Determination of vitamin B-6 compounds by semiautomated continuous-flow and chromatographic methods. *In* Methods in Vitamin B-6 Nutrition, p. 149. J. E. Leklem and R. D. Reynolds (Editors). Plenum Press, New York.

Gregory, J. F., and Litherland, S. A. 1986. Efficacy of the rat bioassay for the determination of biologically available vitamin B-6. J. Nutr. *116*, 87–97.

Gregory, J. F., Day, B. P. F., and Ristow, K. A. 1982. Comparison of high performance liquid chromatographic, radiometric, and *Lactobacillus casei* methods for the determination of folacin in selected foods. J. Food Sci. *47*, 1568–1571.

Gregory, J. F., Sartain, D. B., and Day, B. P. F. 1984. Fluorometric determination of folacin in biological materials using high performance liquid chromatography. J. Nutr. *114*, 341–353.

Guilarte, T. R., McIntyre, P. A., and Isan, M.-F. 1980. Growth response of the yeasts *Saccharomyces uvarum* and *Kloeckera brevis* to the free biologically active forms of vitamin B-6. J. Nutr. *110*, 954–958.

Guilarte, R. R., Shane, B., and McIntyre. 1981. Radiometric-microbiologic assay of vitamin B-6: Application to food analysis. J. Nutr. *111*, 1869–1875.

Haarasilta, S. 1978. Enzymatic determination of biotin. Anal. Biochem. *87*, 306–315.

Hamm, D. J., and Lund, D. B. 1978. Kinetic parameters for thermal inactivation of pantothenic acid. J. Food Sci. *43*, 631–633.

Harber, M. J., and Asscher, A. W. 1979. Bioluminescence assay for antibiotics and vitamins. *In* Proceedings of the First International Symposium on Analytical Bio- and Chemi-Luminescence. E. Schram and P. E. Stanley (Editors). State Printing and Publishing, Westlake Village, CA.

Haroon, Y., Shearer, M. J., Rahim, S., Gunn, W. G., McEnery, G., and Barkhan, P. 1982. The content of phylloquinone (vitamin K) in human milk, cows' milk and infant formula foods determined by high-performance liquid chromatography. J. Nutr. *112*, 1105–1117.

Head, M. K., and Gibbs, E. 1977. Determination of vitamin A in food composites by high-speed liquid chromatography. J. Food Sci. *42*, 395–398.

Hendel, J. 1981. Radioimmunoassay for pteroylglutamic acid. Clin. Chem. *27*, 701–703.

Hollis, B. W. 1983. Individual quantitation of vitamin D_2, vitamin D_3, 25-hydroxyvitamin D_2, and 25-hydroxyvitamin D_3 in human milk. Anal. Biochem. *131*, 211–219.

Hood, R. L. 1979. Isotopic dilution assay for biotin: use of [^{14}C] biotin. Methods Enzymol. *62*, 279–283.

Howell, S. K., and Wang, Y.-M. 1982. Quantitation of physiological α-tocopherol, metabolites and related compounds by reversed-phase high-performance liquid chromatography. J. Chromatogr. *227*, 174–180.

Ink, S. L., Gregory, J. F., and Sartain, D. B. 1986. Determination of pyridoxine-β-glucoside bioavailability using intrinsic and extrinsic labeling in the rat. J. Agric. Food Chem. *34*, 857–862.

Ishi, K., Sarai, K., Sanemori, H., and Kawasaki, T. 1979. Concentrations of thiamine and its phosphate esters in rat tissues determined by high-performance liquid chromatography. J. Nutr. Sci. Vitaminol. *25*, 517–523.

Jacobson, B. S. 1977. Hydroxylamine hydrochloride in automated and manual methods for riboflavin determination. J. Assoc. Offic. Anal. Chem. *60*, 147–150.

Jones, G. 1978. Assay of vitamins D_2 and D_3, and 25-hydroxyvitamins D_2 and D_3 in human plasma by high performance liquid chromatography. Clin. Chem. *24*, 287–298.

Kacem, B., Marshall, M. R., Matthews, R. F., and Gregory, J. F. 1986. Simultaneous analysis of ascorbic acid and dehydroascorbic acid by high-performance liquid chromatography with postcolumn derivatization and UV absorbance. J. Agric. Food Chem. *34*, 271–274.

Kamman, J. F., Labuza, T. P., and Warthesen, J. J. 1980. Thiamin and riboflavin analysis by high performance liquid chromatography. J. Food Sci. *45*, 1497–1504.

Karlberg, B., and Thelander, S. 1978. Determination of readily oxidized compounds by flow injection analysts and redox potential detection. Analyst *103*, 1154–1159.

Karlberg, B., and Thelander, S. 1980. Extraction based on the flow-injection principle. 3. Fluorometric determination of vitamin B_1 by the thiochrome method. Anal. Chim. Acta *114*, 129–136.

Keagy, P. 1983. Folic acid-biological analysis. *In* Methods of vitamin assay. 4th Edition. J. Augustin, B. Klein, and B. Venugopal (Editors). John Wiley, New York.

Keagy, P. M., and Oace, S. M. 1984. Bioassay of wheat bran folacin and effect of bran and xylan on intestinal folacin synthesis in rats. J. Nutr. *114*, 1252–1259.

Kimura, M., Fujita, T., Nishida, S., and Itokawa, Y. 1980. Differential fluorimetric determination of picogram levels of thiamine, thiamine monophosphate, diphosphate and triphosphate using high-performance liquid chromatography. J. Chromatogr. *188*, 417–419.

Kirk, J. R. 1974A. Automated method for the analysis of thiamin in milk, with application to other selected foods. J. Assoc. Offic. Anal. Chem. *57*, 1081–1084.

Kirk, J. R.   1974B.   Automated method for the analysis of riboflavin in milk, with application to other selected foods. J. Assoc. Offic. Anal. Chem. *57*, 1085–1088.

Kirk, J. R., and Ting, N.   1975.   Fluorometric assay for total vitamin C using continuous flow analysis. J. Food Sci. *40*, 463–466.

Klein, B. P., and Kuo, C. H. Y.   1981.   Comparison of microbiological and radiometric assays for determining total folacin in spinach. J. Food Sci. *46*, 552–554.

Klosterman, H. J.   1981.   Vitamin B_6 antagonists in natural products. *In* Antinutrients and Natural Toxicants in Foods. R. L. Ory (Editor). Food & Nutrition Press, Westport, CT.

Knauer, T. E., Siegfried, C. M., and Matschiner, J. T.   1976.   Vitamin K requirement and the concentration of vitamin K in rat liver. J. Nutr. *106*, 1747–1756.

Kulwich, R., Struglia, L., and Pearson, P. B.   1953.   The effect of coprophagy on the excretion of B vitamins in the rabbit. J. Nutr. *49*, 639–645.

Lewis, G. P., and Rowe, P. B.   1979.   Oxidative and reductive cleavage of folates. A critical appraisal. Anal. Biochem. *93*, 91–97.

Leth, T., and Sondergaard, H.   1977.   Biological activity of vitamin E compounds and natural materials by the resorption-gestation test, and chemical determination of the vitamin E activity in foods and feeds. J. Nutr. *107*, 2236–2243.

Lumeng, L., Ryan, M. P., and Li, T. K.   1978.   Validation of the diagnostic value of plasma pyridoxal 5'-phosphate measurements in vitamin B_6 nutrition of the rat. J. Nutr. *108*, 545–553.

Machlin, L. J., Gabriel, E., Spiegel, H. E., Horn, L. R., Brin, M., and Nelson, J.   1978.   Plasma activity of pyruvate kinase and glutamic oxalacetic transaminase as indices of myopathy in the vitamin E deficient rat. J. Nutr. *108*, 1963–1968.

Manz, U., and Phillip, E.   1981.   A method for the routine determination of tocopherols and tocotrienols in animal feeds and human foodstuffs with the aid of high performance liquid chromatography. Int. J. Vit. Nutr. Res. *51*, 342–348.

Maruyama, T., Shiota, T., and Krumdieck, C. L.   1978.   The oxidative cleavage of folates. A critical study. Anal. Biochem. *84*, 277–295.

McCormick, D. B.   1976.   Biotin. *In* Present Knowledge in Nutrition. D. M. Hegsted, C. O. Chichester, W. J. Darby, K. W. McNutt, R. M. Stalvey, and E. H. Stotz (Editors). The Nutrition Foundation, New York.

McGregor, M. A., Parsons, R. H., and Peterson, W. H.   1947.   Biotin balance in the albino rat. J. Nutr. *33*, 517–527.

McMartin, K. E., Virayotha, V., and Tephly, T. R.   1981.   High-pressure liquid chromatography separation and determination of rat liver folates. Arch. Biochem. Biophys. *209*, 127–136.

McMurray, C. H., and Blanchflower, W. J.   1979.   Application of a high-performance liquid chromatographic fluorescence method for the rapid determination of α-tocopherol in the plasma of cattle and pigs and its comparison with direct fluorescence and high-performance liquid chromatography-ultraviolet detection methods. J. Chromatogr. *178*, 525–531.

Mulry, M. C., Kirk, J. R., and Schmidt, R. H.   1982.   Quantitation of retinyl palmitate isomers using high performance liquid chromatography. Second Chemical Congress North American Continent and 183rd National Meeting American Chemical Society. Paper AGFD *108*.

Mulry, M. C., Schmidt, R. H., and Kirk, J. R.   1983.   Isomerization of retinyl palmitate during heating of a coconut oil model system. 43rd Annual Meeting Institute of Food Technologists. Paper *84*.

Nguyen, L. B., and Gregory, J. F.   1983.   Effects of food composition in the bioavailability of vitamin B_6 in the rat. J. Nutr. *113*, 1550–1560.

Nguyen, L. B., Gregory, J. G., and Damron, B. L.   1981.   Effects of selected polysaccharides on the bioavailability of pyridoxine in rats and chicks. J. Nutr. *111*, 1403–1410.

Nguyen, L. B., Hiner, M. E., Litherland, S. A., and Gregory, J. F. 1983. Relative biological activity of nonphosphorylated vitamin B_6 compounds in the rat. J. Agric. Food Chem. *31*, 1282–1287.

Osborne, D. R., and Voogt, P. 1978. The Analysis of Nutrients in Foods. Academic Press, New York.

Pachla, L. A., and Kissinger, P. T. 1976. Determination of ascorbic acid in foodstuffs, pharmaceuticals and body fluids by liquid chromatography with electrochemical detection. Anal. Chem. *48*, 365–367.

Pelletier, O., and Madere, R. 1977. Automated determination of thiamine and riboflavin in various foods. J. Assoc. Offic. Anal. Chem. *60*, 140–146.

Phillips, D. R., and Wright, A. J. A. 1982. Studies on the response of *Lactobacillus casei* to different folate monoglutamates. Br. J. Nutr. *47*, 183–189.

Pugsley, L. I., Wills, G., and Crandall, W. A. 1944. The biological assay of vitamin A by means of its influence on the cellular contents of the vagina in rats. J. Nutr. *28*, 365–379.

Ranger, C. B. 1981. Flow-injection analysis. Principles, techniques, applications, design. Anal. Chem. *53*, 20A–32A.

Reingold, R. N., and Picciano, M. F. 1982. Two improved high-performance liquid chromatographic separations of biologically significant forms of folate. J. Chromatogr. *234*, 171–179.

Ristow, K. A., Gregory, J. F., and Damron, B. L. 1982. Effects of dietary fiber on the bioavailability of folic acid monoglutamate. J. Nutr. *112*, 750–758.

Roy, R. B. 1979. Application of the Technicon Auto Analyzer II to the analysis of water-soluble vitamins in foods. *In* Topics in Automatic Chemical Analysis, Vol. 1. J. K. Foreman and P. B. Stockwell (Editors). Ellis Horwood, Ltd., Chichester, U.K.

Roy, R. B., Conetta, A., and Salpeter, J. 1976. Automated fluorometric method for the determination of total vitamin C in food products. J. Assoc. Offic. Anal. Chem. *59*, 1244–1250.

Ruddick, J. E., Vanderstoep, J., and Richards, J. F. 1980. Kinetics of thermal degradation of methyltetrahydrofolic acid. J. Food Sci. *45*, 1019–1022.

Ruzicka, J., and Hansen, E. H. 1975. Flow injection analysis. 1. A new concept of fast continuous flow analysis. Analy. Chim. Acta *78*, 145–157.

Ruzicka, J., and Hansen, E. H. 1978. Flow injection analysis. 10. Theory, techniques, and trends. Anal. Chim. Acta *99*, 37–76.

Ruzicka, J., and Hansen, E. J. 1980. Flow injection analysis. Principles, applications and trends. Anal. Chim. Acta *114*, 19–44.

Shane, B., Tamura, T., and Stokstad, E. L. R. 1980. Folate assay: A comparison of radioassay and microbiological methods. Clin. Chim. Acta *100*, 13–19.

Sietsema, W. K., and DeLuca, H. F. 1982. A new vaginal smear assay for vitamin A in rats. J. Nutr. *112*, 1481–1489.

Skeggs, L. T. 1957. An automatic method for colorimetric analysis. Am. J. Clin. Pathol. *28*, 311–322.

Snyder, L. R. 1980. Continuous-flow analysis: Present and future. Anal. Chim. Acta *144*, 3–18.

Snyder, L. R., and van der Wal, S. J. 1981. Precision of assays based on liquid chromatography with prior solvent extraction of the sample. Anal. Chem. *53*, 877–884.

Snyder, L. R., Levine, J., Stoy, R., and Conetta, A. 1978. Automated chemical analysis: Update on continuous-flow approach. Anal. Chem. *48*, 942A–956A.

Sood, S. P., Sartori, L. E., Wittmer, D. P., and Haney, W. G. 1976. High-pressure liquid chromatographic determination of ascorbic acid in selected foods and multivitamin products. Anal. Chem. *48*, 796–797.

Stewart, K. K. 1980. Nutrient analysis of foods: State of the art for routine analyses. *In* Proceedings, Symposium on State of the Art for Routine Analyses. K. K. Stewart (Editor). Association of Official Analytical Chemists, Washington, DC.

Stewart, K. K., Beecher, G. R., and Hare, P. E. 1976. Rapid analysis of discrete samples: The use of nonsegmented, continuous flow. Anal. Biochem. 70, 167–173.

Strohl, A. N., and Curran, D. J. 1979. Flow injection analysis with reticulated vitreous carbon flow-through electrodes. Anal. Chem. 51, 1045–1049.

Thanassi, J. W., and Cidlowski, J. A. 1980. A radioimmunoassay for phosphorylated forms of vitamin B_6 using a matrix-bound antibody. J. Immunol. Methods 33, 261–266.

Thompson, O. J., Carlson, C. W., Palmer, I. S., and Olson, O. E. 1968. Destruction of rachitogenic activity of isolated soybean protein by autoclaving as demonstrated with turkey poults. J. Nutr. 94, 227–232.

Thompson, J. N., Maxwell, W. B., and L'Abee, M. 1977. High pressure liquid chromatographic determination of vitamin D in fortified milk. J. Assoc. Offic. Anal. Chem. 60, 998–1002.

Thornburg, W. 1977. Devil's advocate—the AOAC manual methods. J. Assoc. Offic. Anal. Chem. 60, 1255–1258.

Tigner, J., and Roe, D. A. 1979. Tissue folacin stores in rats measured by radioassay. Proc. Soc. Exp. Biol. Med. 160, 445–448.

Tillotson, J. A., and Sauberlich, H. E. 1971. Effect of riboflavin depletion and replation on the erythrocyte glutathione reductase in the rat. J. Nutr. 101, 1459–1466.

Toepfer, E. W., and Polansky, M. M. 1970. Microbiological assay of vitamin B_6 and its components. J. Assoc. Offic. Anal. Chem. 53, 546–550.

Toma, R. B., and Tabekhia, M. M. 1979. High-performance liquid chromatographic analysis of B-vitamins in rice and rich products. J. Food Sci. 44, 263–268.

Trebukhina, R. V., Ostrovsky, Y. M., Petushok, V. G., Velichko, M. G., and Tumanov, V. N. 1981. Effect of thiamin deprivation on thiamin metabolism in mice. J. Nutr. 111, 505–513.

Tyerman, M. J., Watson, J. E., Shane, B., Schutz, D. E., and Stokstad, E. L. R. 1977. Identification of glutamate chain lengths of endogenous folylpoly-γ-glutamates in rat tissues. Biochim. Biophys. Acta 497, 234–240.

van den Berg, H., Boshuis, P. G., and Schreurs, W. H. P. 1986. Determination of vitamin D in fortified and nonfortified milk powder and infant formula using a specific radioassay after purification by high-performance liquid chromatography. J. Agric. Food Chem. 34, 264–268.

Vanderslice, J. T., and Higgs, D. J. 1984. High performance liquid chromatography analysis with fluorometric detection of vitamin C in food samples. J. Chromatogr. Sci. 22, 485–489.

Vanderslice, J. T., Maire, C. E., Doherty, R. F., and Beecher, G. R. 1980. Sulfosalicylic acid as an extraction agent for vitamin B_6 in food. J. Agric. Food Chem. 28, 1145–1149.

Vanderslice, J. T., Maire, C. E., and Beecher, G. R. 1981A. Extraction and quantitation of B_6 vitamers from animal tissues and human plasma: A preliminary study. In Methods in Vitamin B_6 Nutrition. J. E. Leklem and R. D. Reynolds (Editors). Plenum Press, New York.

Vanderslice, J. T., Maire, C. E., and Beecher, G. R. 1981B. B_6 vitamer analysis in human plasma by high-performance liquid chromatography: A preliminary report. Am. J. Clin. Nutr. 34, 947–950.

Vanderslice, J. T., Maire, C. E., and Yakupkovic, J. E. 1981C. Vitamin B_6 in ready-to-eat cereals: Analysis by high performance liquid chromatography. J. Food Sci. 46, 943–946.

Viceps–Madore, D., Cidlowski, J. A., Kittler, J. M., and Thanassi, J. W. 1983. Preparation, characterization and use of monoclonal antibodies to vitamin B_6. J. Biol. Chem. 258, 2689–2696.

Voigt, M. N., and Eitenmiller, R. R. 1979. A liquid scintillation technique for microbial vitamin analyses. J. Food Sci. *44*, 1780–1781.

Voigt, M. N., Eitenmiller, R. R., and Ware, G. O. 1979. Vitamin analysis by microbial and protozoan organisms: Response to food preservatives and neutralization salts. J. Food Sci. *44*, 723–734.

Walsh, J. H., Wyse, B. W., and Hansen, R. G. 1979. A comparison of microbiological and radioimmunoassay methods for the determination of pantothenic acid in foods. J. Food Biochem. *3*, 175–189.

Waxman, S., and Schreiber, C. 1977. Measurement of serum folate levels: Current status of the radioassay methodology. *In* Folic Acid: Biochemistry and Physiology in Relation to the Human Nutrition Requirement. National Academy of Sciences, Washington, DC.

Waxman, S., and Schreiber, C. 1980. Determination of folate by use of radioactive folate and binding proteins. Methods Enzymol. *66*, 468–483.

Wehling, R. L., and Wetzel, D. L. 1984. Simultaneous determination of pyridoxine, riboflavin, and thiamin in fortified cereal products by high-performance liquid chromatography. J. Agric. Food Chem. *32*, 1326–1331.

Wheeler, W. B., Thompson, N. P., Andrade, P., and Krause, R. T. 1978. Extraction efficiencies for pesticides in crops. 1. [14C] carbaryl extraction from mustard greens and radishes. J. Agric. Food Chem. *26*, 1333–1337.

Widicus, W. A. 1980. Degradation and biological activity of alpha-tocopherol during storage in a dehydrated model system. Ph.D. dissertation. Univ. of Florida, Gainesville.

Widicus, W. A., and Kirk, J. R. 1979. High pressure liquid chromatographic determination of vitamins A and E in cereal products. J. Assoc. Offic. Anal. Chem. *62*, 637–641.

Yeransian, J. A., Sloman, K. G., and Foltz, A. K. 1985. Food. Anal. Chem. *57*, 278R–315R.

Nutrient Data Banks for Nutrient Evaluation in Foods

Lena Bergström

During the past decades, the use of computers in nutrition and dietetics has increased. In North America, about 70 nutrient analysis systems are listed in the 1984 edition of the Nutrient Data Bank Directory (Hoover 1984), but over 165 developers of nutrient analysis systems were contacted. In Sweden, 16 systems were found in an inventory (Bergström 1985). In the United States, cooperation in this field started in 1976 with the First Annual National Nutrient Data Bank Conference. For coordination of food composition tables and of nutrient data banks, a Nordic project group (NORFOODS) was created in 1982, and in the same year plans for an international (INFOODS) and a European (EUROFOODS) collaboration began to take form. INFOODS (International Network of Food Data Systems) activities began with a planning conference, reported in *Food and Nutrition Bulletin* (1983, Vol. 2). The goal of INFOODS is to improve the amount, quality, and availability of food composition data (Rand 1984). For reaching this goal INFOODS has set up a secretariat and initiated international working committees on various topics such as users and needs, information systems, and data quality and terminology. There are also several regional committees working independently and together with IN-FOODS. EUROFOODS is working on several projects (West 1985), as is NORFOODS (Bergström 1985). For example, both INFOODS and the regional committees are creating food composition tables and nutrient data base systems for user needs.

USERS OF FOOD COMPOSITION DATA

There are many users who need food composition data for various tasks. International, national, and local users are involved as well as individuals. International organizations require food composition data for calculating food supplies, as do epidemiologists for tracing the relationship between diet and disease.

Government agencies at the national level need nutritional information on foods for planning agricultural policies, for evaluating national food supply, and for assessing nutritional status of the population by performing surveys of different kinds. These surveys, such as the National Health and Nutrition Examination Surveys (NHANES) and the Nationwide Food Consumption Survey (NFCS) in the United States, provide objective data from which a government can base decisions regarding nutrition-related public policies. The food industry needs data for optimizing recipes (replacing a component by another with similar nutrient content) for nutrition labeling and for creating new food products.

At the local level, hospitals and other institutions systematically plan menus and special diets. This planning includes production, purchasing, and menu and fiscal controls (Buchanan 1983; Moore and Tuthill 1971). Food composition data can be used in research projects in such disciplines as nutrition and dietetics, medicine, odontology, food science and economics, food technology, home economics, psychology, sociology, ethnology, cultural anthropology, economic history, and economics.

Diet counseling and consumer guidance are examples of uses of food composition data at the individual level. Nowadays, a person who needs to check the intake of special nutrients can do so on a personal computer with a special nutrient analysis program.

NUTRIENT DATA BASE SYSTEMS

A nutrient data base system or a nutrient analysis system consists of three main parts: a computer (hardware), programs (software), and a nutrient data bank.

Computers in nutrition are usually divided into three categories, depending on their size and capability: maxi- (mainframe), mini-, and microcomputers. The boundary lines between the sizes are diffuse, especially between mini and micro, and change in pace with the development of computer technology. This technology is developing so quickly that in selecting a computer for a system, one has to examine carefully all new information. What was true yesterday may be false today. The computer is outside the scope of this chapter, but three references for further study are given: Maloff and Zears (1979), McMurray and Hoover (1984), and Williams and Burnet (1984).

More important than hardware is the selection of software for the system. Presently, there are many tools to help with this task. The most important are unbiased reports and information from colleagues working with analysis systems. An entire issue of the *Journal of Nutrition Education* (1984, 2) is devoted to the use of computers in nutrition education. Software programs with short descriptions are listed on 40 pages. Another journal, the *Journal of Dietetic Software*, deals exclusively with this topic.

The Consumer Nutrition Center of the U.S. Department of Agriculture (USDA) has one of the most well-known nutrient data banks in the world, the National Nutrient Data Bank (NDB).

The NDB is a computer-based management system analyzing nutrient values in food and is designed for storage, summary, and retrieval of food composition data. Sources of the data are scientific literature, unpublished data from government and university laboratories, industry laboratories, and contract research.

Data evaluation and food identification coding are performed through three data bases before data are entered into the system for processing: (1) individual analyses, (2) average values of like items, and (3) representative values. This last data base was used to create the revised USDA Agriculture Handbook No. 8 (USDA 1976–1984) and different data bases which are available for purchase (Butrum and Gebhardt 1976; Rizek *et al.* 1981; Hepburn 1982). These data bases, together with other nutrient data sources, can be found in U.S. systems.

Countries with limited resources cannot use the same procedures in creating food composition tables and nutrient data bases as the USDA. Usually the country's own comprehensive or abbreviated food composition tables are the main nutrient data sources in the different systems. Nutrient data from national laboratories as well as information from food manufacturers and from the literature are included. Many bases also have a recipe file and programs for calculating nutrients in different dishes.

DESIGNS OF A NUTRIENT DATA BASE SYSTEM

If the decision is made to use a nutrient analysis system and not to purchase it or buy services, then it must be developed. Developing computerized systems is expensive, laborious, and time-consuming. Accuracy and knowledge in nutrition, chemistry, biochemistry, physiology, medicine, food technology, cooking, mathematics, statistics, and computer technology are required. Since it is very rare that a single individual has insight into all these disciplines, developing systems is typically a team effort.

Before starting the work, careful planning is needed. First, the purpose of the system has to be decided because selection of foods, nutrients, and programs is related to the purpose(s). Systems can be divided into three main types: comprehensive, for nearly all purposes; abbreviated, for use in schools, slimming courses, and so on; and specialized, for research in a special field.

Selection of Foods

For the comprehensive system, the raw foods, the products purchased in the particular country, and recipes or analyses for dishes generally consumed are needed. In the abbreviated system, only selected core foods and recipes for the most common dishes are included. In a specialized system, the foods included in the comprehensive base are supplemented with special foods.

Selection of Nutrients

In the comprehensive system, as many nutrients as possible need to be included, although many may eventually be missing. These gaps must be flagged. The nutrients included in the national nutrition recommendations will be enough for an abbreviated base, but, of course, only approximations may be used. For a specialized system, analysis of food for special nutrients will have to occur (Bruce and Bergström 1983).

Selection of Programs

The comprehensive system includes input and output programs for recalls, records, dietary histories, food frequencies, menu planning, meal patterns, consumption analyses, nutrition calculations, dietary analyses of different kinds, energy percentages of protein, fat, carbohydrates, and alcohol, percentages of national and special nutrition recommendations, P:S ratios, and statistical parameters. The abbreviated base may only include a simple input program of food items and outputs for nutrition calculation, energy percentages, percentages of nutrition recommendations, and perhaps, P:S ratios. The specialized system programs depend on the topic.

In designing a nutrient analysis system, one should choose a flexible data base management system and programs for easy and continuous revisions. It is extremely important that a system is well documented with manuals, flow charts, and so on.

NUTRITION EVALUATION

Data Quality

The goal for all users of nutrient analysis systems is to work with reliable nutrient data. As analyses of nutrients always are costly (some are extremely expensive), nutrient data base developers and compilers of food composition tables have to "borrow" values from others. However, before doing so, one may need to know the corresponding food name in a particular foreign language. (Sometimes the scientific name can be of some help, INFOODS and the other committees are now working on thesauri.) The food standards and the additions of vitamins and minerals to food, the methods of analyses, and the number of analyses are also required.

Products with or without brand names and cooked dishes are more difficult to identify correctly with only a name; therefore, lists of main ingredients, preferably in grams, and recipes can be helpful. There are natural variations in the composition of plant foods because of weather and soil conditions, fertilizers, harvesting time, storage time, and so forth. In animal food, the race, sex, addition of vitamins and minerals to the feeds, breeding, and seasonal variations (e.g., in fish and milk) are important.

Different processing and preparation methods of foods will also generate variations in nutrient content. Fortification, enrichment, and standards in a foreign food are further sources of incompatibility. Therefore, an accurate description of foods analyzed is a necessity. The analytical methods and procedures used also need to be described (Southgate 1974).

In the United States, the state of development of methods for analyzing nutrients in foods has been reported. The state of methodology for quite a few common nutrients is conflicting, and for other more unusual nutrients, the methodology is missing. The state of knowledge of nutrition composition for different food groups has also been surveyed. The use of quality indices and confidence codes for foods can be helpful for the compilers of food composition data (Stewart 1983).

Guidelines for the production, management, and use of food composition data will improve the quality of data in the future (Greenfield and Southgate 1985).

Foods and Dishes

In the following tables, nutrient contents in selected foods are compared. The values derive from published German, Danish, British, and American food composition tables and the Swedish and Finnish (Helsinki University) nutrient data base systems (Souci *et al.* 1981; Møller 1983; Paul and Southgate 1978; USDA 1976–1984; Kost 1981; Food System 1981). It is assumed that the values in the tables are included in the nutrient data bases of the country concerned, but since computerized systems can be easily updated, the values might not be current. Nevertheless, these values are still good for comparative purposes. In order not to overload the tables, certain information has been omitted. The figures will speak for themselves, but some comments are appropriate.

Dairy products in different countries are usually regulated by different food standards (e.g., fat content). Lowfat milk products are also often fortified with vitamins. If a product is missing in a base, it has to be replaced by a similar one. An example is quark instead of cottage cheese in Table 28.1.

If comparing beef meat with pork, for example, the thiamin content is higher in pork, but the iron content is higher in beef (Table 28.2).

As shown in Table 28.3, in the calculation of food supplies, the edible portion values are important. Refuses must be described carefully. Different energy values depend also on different methods of calculation. Vitamin D in fish is sometimes calculated. The low and high retinol contents in American (and Swedish) tuna and shrimp are probably due to rather old methods of analyses.

Table 28.4 shows that for fats and oils, different kinds of standards may be used for different products. Margarine is usually supplemented with vitamins A and D. Some oils might also be enriched with these vitamins. Fatty acids in margarine depend on the use of oils and fats, which differ from country to country.

Cereal products very often have added vitamins and minerals such as thiamin, riboflavin, niacin, B_6, and iron. Before one borrows a value from another country, the enrichment practices must be known (Table 28.5).

Variation in the edible portion of core vegetables such as cabbage, carrots, and potatoes is important (Table 28.6). The high protein quality in peas and potatoes should be kept in mind.

Fruits are usually eaten for vitamin C content. Processing of fruit products such as orange juice will affect the vitamin C level, as can be seen in Table 28.7. Vitamin C content in apples varies according to variety. Apple with skin has more vitamin C than peeled apples.

Nuts are important contributors of protein and fat to the diet in some parts of the world. With a fat percentage of 50 and above, the fatty acid composition is of interest. In Table 28.8, only the linoleic acid is included. The high potassium levels should be noted.

Although confectionary and sugars are mostly "empty calories," some nutrients other than carbohydrate are found.

For the beverage examples in Table 28.10, it is of interest to note that 10 cups (about 1 dl) of coffee a day for a woman will encompass 50% of the RDA of niacin in England, but only ~20% in the United States. Coffee seems to provide more energy than tea.

Today, computers are commonly used to produce food composition tables. Even if three decimal figures seem to be appropriate in computer calculations, the output should perhaps be rounded off. Too many figures give a wrong impression of accuracy. For nutrition evaluation the calculation of recipes is a source of error. Different food yields, lack of food yields, "guesstimated" yields, and different factors for the calculation of nutrient losses and gains make recipe-calculated values uncertain.

Table 28.1. Nutrients in Dairy Products and Eggs (per 100 g, Edible Portion)

Food	Ref. code[a]	Protein (g)	Fat (g)	Retinol (μg)	Vitamin D (μg)	Vitamin C (mg)	Riboflavin (mg)	Calcium (mg)	Tryptophan (mg)
Cheese									
Emmenthal	D	28.700	29.700	320	1.100	0.500	0.340	1020	430
Firm	DK	26.0	26.9	256	0.27	0.5	0.330	946	360
Cheddar-type	GB	26.0	33.5	310	0.261	0	0.50	800	370
Hard	S	26.9	28.1	218	0.197	0	0.34	744	379
Swiss	USA	28.43	27.45	(RE 253)[b]	0	0	0.365	961	401
Quark 20% fat (dry basis)									
(cottage cheese)	D	12.500	5.100	40	0.085	0.600	0.270	85.000	160
	DK	12.2	5.4	51	0.11	1	0.300	220	170
	GB	13.6	4.0	32	0.023	0	0.19	60	190
	S	12.3	3.9	30	0.027	0	0.14	68	173
	USA	12.49	4.51	(RE 48)		Trace	0.163	60	139
Cream, coffee	D	3.100	10.500	66	0.820	1.000	0.160	101.000	44
	DK	3.2	9.0	86	0.14	0.9	0.17	105	36
	GB	2.4	21.2	145	0.081	1.2	0.12	79	34
	S	3.0	12.0	93	0.084	0.5	0.15	102.5	42
	USA	2.70	19.31	(RE 182)		0.76	0.148	96	38
Milk	D	3.340	3.570	28	0.060	1.700	0.180	120.000	46
	DK	3.4	3.5	33	0.1	1.2	0.178	121	45
	GB	3.3	3.8	26	0.013	1.5	0.19	120	47
	S	3.4	3.0	23	0.021	0.5	0.15	113	48
	USA	3.29	3.34	(RE 31)		0.94	0.162	119	46
Egg, whole, raw	D	12.900	11.200	220	1.780	0.000	0.310	56.000	180
	DK	12.1	11.2	204	1.4	0	0.450	40	170
	GB	12.3	10.9	140	1.75	0	0.47	52	220
	S	12.7	9.4	208	1.75	0	0.30	51	223
	USA	12.14	11.15	(RE 156)		0	0.301	56	194

[a] D, Federal Republic of Germany; DK, Denmark; GB, Great Britain; S, Sweden; USA, United States.
[b] RE = retinol equivalent.

Table 28.2. Nutrients in Meat and Meat Products (per 100 g, Edible Portion)

Food	Ref. code[a]	Protein (g)	Fat (g)	Thiamin (mg)	Riboflavin (mg)	Niacin (mg)	Vitamin B$_6$ (mg)	Vitamin B$_{12}$ (μg)	Iron (mg)
Beef, minced, raw (meat)	D	22.900	14.000	0.584	0.196	5.6	0.45	1.4	2.2
	DK	19.7	14.2	0.06	0.31	4.0	0.27	2	2.7
	GB	18.8	16.2	0.07	0.15	4.1	0.33	1.4	2.7
	S	19.5	14.3	0.08	0.16	4.3			2.7
	USA	17.9	21.2						
Chicken with skin, raw	D	20.600	5.600	0.083	0.16	6.800	0.500	0.500	1.800
	DK	18.6	15.1	0.15	0.18	8.0	0.55	0.33	0.7
	GB	17.6	17.7	0.08	0.14	6.0	0.30	Trace	0.7
	S	18.0	11.0	0.07	0.18	6.5	0.35	0.3	1.2
	USA	18.60	15.06	0.060	0.120	6.801	0.35	0.31	0.90
Pork chop, raw	D	17.600	19.000	0.820	0.200	4.300	0.500		1.800
	DK	15	32	0.57	0.18	2.8	0.26	0.65	0.63
	GB	15.9	29.5	0.57	0.14	4.2	0.29	2	0.8
	S	20.7	14.9	0.91	0.17	5.4	0.54	0.6	2.1
	USA	18.39	21.76	0.988	0.194	4.386	0.44	0.52	0.72
Liver, calf, raw	D	19.200	4.140	0.280	2.610	15.000	0.900	60	7.900
	DK	19.1	1.5	0.18	2.15	15.0	0.90	60	4.5
	GB	20.1	7.3	0.21	3.1	12.4	0.54	100	8.0
	S	18.9	4.5	0.27	2.72	11.4	0.67	60	3.0
	USA	19.2	4.7	0.20	2.72	11.4			8.8
Ham, canned	D	20.200	10.700	0.410	0.160	3.000	0.27	0	2.500
	DK	15.7	5.4	0.52	0.25	3.9	0.22	Trace	0.7
	GB	18.4	5.1	0.52	0.25	3.9	0.22		1.2
	S	24.7	5.3	0.72	0.25	3.9		0.7	2.1
	USA	17.97	7.46	0.879	0.230	4.585	0.46	0.80	0.90

[a] D, Federal Republic of Germany; DK, Denmark; GB, Great Britain; S, Sweden; USA, United States.

Table 28.3. Nutrients in Fish and Fish Products (per 100 g, Edible Portion)

Food	Ref. code[a]	Edible portion (%)	Energy (kJ)	Water (g)	Protein (g)	Fat (g)	Retinol (μg)	Vitamin D (μg)	Calcium (mg)
Cod, raw	D	75	341.75	80.800	17.700	0.400	10.000	1.300	24.000
(fillet)	DK	100	331	80.4	18.1	0.6	0	1	15
(fillet)	GB	89	322	82.1	17.4	0.7	Trace	Trace	16
	S	66	334 7	81.2	18.1	0.6	10	0.72	29
	USA	31	326.35	81.2	17.6	0.3	0		10
Salmon, raw	D	64	906.92	65.500	19.900	13.600	65	16.300	13.000
	DK	65	584	71.0	20.5	6.2	15	30	20
	GB		757	68.0	18.4	12.0	Trace	Trace	27
	S	65	918.4	63.9	20.8	14.5	30	17.4	79
	USA	65	907.93	63.6	22.5	13.4			79
Plaice, raw	D	56	346.60	80.700	17.100	0.800			61.000
	DK	50	391	79.3	17.4	2.5	16	3	45
	GB	42	386	79.5	17.9	2.2	Trace	Trace	51
	S	44	397.5	79.0	17.1	2.7	16	3.24	41
(flatfishes)	USA	33	330.54	81.3	16.7	0.8			12
Tuna, canned, solids and liquid	D	100	1268.88	52.500	23.800	20.900	370		7.000
	DK	100	1222	56.1	23.8	21.5	372	4.5	13
	GB	100	1202	54.6	22.8	22.0		5.8	7
	S	100	1205	52.6	24.2	20.5	27	5.33	6
	USA	100	1205	52.6	24.2	20.5	27		6
Shrimps, raw	D		399.66	78.4	18.6	1.44	Trace		92.000
canned, drained solids	DK	100	469	71.8	24.1	1.2	0	0	115
	GB		398	74.9	20.8	1.2	Trace	Trace	110
	S		485.3	70.4	24.2	1.1	18	0.6	115
	USA	100	485.34	70.4	24.2	1.1	18		115

[a] D, Federal Republic of Germany; DK, Denmark; GB, Great Britain; S, Sweden; USA, United States.

Table 28.4. Nutrients in Fats and Oils (per 100 g, Edible Portion)

Food	Ref. code[a]	Energy (kJ)	Fat (g)	Retinol (μg)	Vitamin E total (mg)	Vitamin E = α-tocopherol (mg)	Fatty acids Saturated (g)	Fatty acids Monounsaturated (g)	Fatty acids Polyunsaturated (g)
Butter	D	3244.24	83.200	590	2.200	1.9	53.3	21.2	3.3
	DK	3146	82.3	782	1.9	2.0	48.97	26.10	2.24
	GB	3041	82.0	750	2.1	2.1	52.48	19.92	2.24
	S	3129	80.0	620					
	USA	3000	81.11	(RE 754)[b]	1.58	1.58	50.5	23.4	3.0
Lard	D	3964.72	99.700	9	2.200	0.4	42.4	41.4	9.0
	DK	3762	99.0	Trace	0.4	Trace	41.82	41.65	8.99
	GB	3663	99.0	0			48.80	37.3	9.20
	S	3770	100			1.2			
	USA	3774	100	0	1.3	1.2	39.2	45.1	11.2
Corn oil	D	3891.12	100.000	0	84.000	14.3	16.4	29.3	49.3
	DK	3796	99.9	0	18	12	16.43	29.32	49.28
	GB	3696	99.9	0		11.2	16.44	29.34	49.32
	S	3698	100			12			
	USA	3698.7	100		83.2	14.3	12.7	24.2	58.7
Margarine	D	3148.99	80.500	530	20.200	5.2	32.7	27.9	16.6
	DK	3089	81.2	720	6.5	8.0	29.79	34.61	13.78
	GB	3000	81.0	900		7.7	35.20	28.0	12.72
	S	3117	80.0	900	10				
	USA	3007.1	80.5	(RE 993)			15.8	35.8	25.4
Mayonnaise	D	3238.23	82.5		7.6	7.6			
	DK	3152	82.4	60		4.9			
	GB	2952	78.9	80					
	S	3289	88.0	50		12.5	14.86	26.42	42.43
	USA	2999.2	79.4	(RE 84)	58.0	20.8	11.8	22.7	41.3

[a] D, Federal Republic of Germany; DK, Denmark; GB, Great Britain; S, Sweden; USA, United States.
[b] RE = retinol equivalent.

Table 28.5. Nutrients in Cereals and Cereal Products (per 100 g, Edible Portion)

Food	Ref. code[a]	Energy (kJ)	Carbohydrate (g)	Thiamin (mg)	Riboflavin (mg)	Niacin (mg)	Vitamin B_6 (mg)	Iron (mg)	Zinc (mg)
Bread, white	D	1083.20	50.100	0.086	0.060	0.850	0.140	0.950	0.20–0.80
	DK	1125	54 5	0.370	0.048	1.0	0.090	3.2	0.6
	GB	991	49.7	0.18	0.03	1.4	0.04	1.7	0.8
	S	1205	53 0	0.27	0.15	3.0	0.25	5.3	0.8
	USA	1213.4	55.4	0.08	0.08	0.8		0.7	
Corn flakes	D	1619.69	82.500	0.02–0.10		1.400	0.070	2.000	0.300
	DK	1649	85.1	0.015	0.060	1.1	0.07	0.6	0.3
	GB	1567	85.1	1.8	1.6	21.0	0.03	0.6	0.3
	S	1598.3	83.8	1.0	1.0	15.0	0.07	6	0.3
	USA	1627	86.1	1.3	1.5	17.6	1.8	6.3	0.28
Oatmeal, raw	D	1696.21	66.400	0.590	0.150	1.000	0.160	4.600	4.400
	DK	1620	65.6	0.51	0.11	0.8	0.20	4.6	4.5
	GB	1698	72.8	0.50	0.10	1.0	0.12	4.1	3.0
	S	1610.8	65.0	0.69	0.13	0.9	0.18	5.3	3.19
	USA	1605	67.0	0.73	0.14	0.78	0.120	4.21	3.07
Pasta, raw	D	1624.85	71.900	0.170	0.073	1.900	0.060	1.600	1.600
	DK	1633	79.6	0.15	0.035	1.0	0.05	1.7	1.2
	GB	1574	79.2	0.14	0.06	2.0	0.06	1.4	1.0
	S	1548	75.0	0.4	0.15	4.0	0.35	6.5	1.0
	USA	1543.9	75.2	0.09	0.06	1.7		1.3	
Rice polished, raw	D	1540.36	78.700	0.060	0.032	1.300	0.150	0.600	0.20–0.80
	DK	1528	82.3	0.070	0.035	1.4	0.150	1.2	1.3
	GB	1536	86.8	0.08	0.03	1.5	0.30	0.5	1.3
	S	1518.8	80.4	0.11	0.03	1.6	0.17	0.8	0.85
	USA	1518.8	80.4	0.07	0.03	1.6		0.8	

[a] D, Federal Republic of Germany; DK, Denmark; GB, Great Britain; S, Sweden; USA, United States.

Table 28.6. Nutrients in Vegetables (per 100 g, Edible Portion)

Food	Ref. code[a]	Edible portion (%)	Energy (kJ)	Protein (g)	Carbohydrate (g)	Calcium (mg)	Magnesium (mg)	Zinc (mg)	Potassium (mg)
Cabbage, white, raw	D	78	103.79	1.370	4.240	46.000	23.000	0.16–1.50	227.000
	DK	80	125	1.1	6.0	55	12	0.15	254
	GB	100	93	1.9	3.8	44	13	0.3	280
	S	80	100.4	1.3	5.4	49	13	0.258	233
	USA	80	99	1.21	5.37	47	15	0.18	246
Carrots, raw	D	81	168.93	0.980	8.710	41.000	18.000	0.390	290.000
	DK	85	169	0.9	8.8	36	12	0.20	303
	GB	96	98	0.7	5.4	48	12	0.4	220
	S	82	175.7	1.1	9.7	37	23	0.337	341
	USA	89	181	1.03	10.14	27	15	0.20	323
Peas, green, raw	D	40	362.05	6.550	12.600	24.000	33.000	2.650	304.000
	DK	40	325	6.3	10.8	30	28	1.0	300
	GB	37	283	5.8	10.6	15	30	0.7	340
	S	38	351.5	6.3	14.4	26	35	0.8	316
	USA	38	339	5.41	14.46	25	33	1.24	244
Potatoes, raw	D	80	361.54	2.050	18.500	9.500	25.000	0.270	443.000
	DK	75	381	2.0	20.2	5	20	0.35	395
	GB	86	372	2.1	20.8	8	24	0.3	570
	S	83	364	1.9	18.3	5.5	22	0.414	407
	USA	75	331	2.07	17.98	7	21	0.39	543
Tomatoes, red, raw	D	96	80.72	0.950	3.280	14.000	20.000	0.240	297.000
	DK	100	99	1.1	4.3	10	6.5	0.11	216
	GB	100	60	0.9	2.8	13	11	0.2	290
	S	98	92	1.1	4.7	13	14	0.183	264
	USA	91	81	0.89	4.34	7	11	0.11	207

[a] D, Federal Republic of Germany; DK, Denmark; GB, Great Britain; S, Sweden; USA, United States.

Table 28.7. Nutrients in Fruits and Fruit Juices (per 100 g, Edible Portion)

Food	Ref. code[a]	Edible portion (%)	Energy (kJ)	Water (g)	Protein (g)	Fat (g)	Carbohydrate (g)	Vitamin C (mg)	Iron (mg)
Apple, raw	D	92	232.06	85.300	0.340	0.400	12.600	12.000	0.480
	DK	90	174	84.4	0.3	0.1	9.7	8	0.12
	GB	77	196	84.3	0.3	Trace	11.9	3	0.3
	S	78	240	84.4	0.2	0.6	14.5	10	0.3
	USA	85	237	84.46	0.15	0.31	14.84	4.0	0.07
Banana, raw	D	67	415.96	73.900	1.150	0.180	23.300	12.000	0.550
	DK	60	404	76	1.1	0.3	22.0	11	0.35
	GB	59	337	70.7	1.1	0.3	19.2	10	0.4
	S	60	360	75.7	1.1	0.2	22.2	13.5	0.7
	USA	65	384	74.26	1.03	0.48	23.43	9.1	0.31
Orange, raw	D	72	225.14	85.700	1.000	0.200	12.000	50.000	0.400
	DK	71	193	86.1	0.2	0.1	10.2	56	0.12
	GB	75	150	86.1	0.8	Trace	8.5	50	0.3
	S	71	210	86.0	1.0	0.2	12.2	55	0.4
	USA	73	197	86.75	0.94	0.12	11.75	53.2	0.10
Orange juice canned product	D	100	202.11	87.700	0.650	0.230	10.900	44.000	0.270
	DK	100	164	86.5	0.7	0.2	8.5	40	0.18
	GB	100	143	88.7	0.4	Trace	8.5	35	0.5
frozen, diluted	S	100	190	88.3	0.7	0.2	10.4	43	0.2
	USA	100	188	88.10	0.68	0.06	10.78	38.9	0.10
Strawberries, raw	D	97	154.30	89.500	0.820	0.400	7.480	64.000	0.960
	DK	97	139	88.9	0.6	0.4	6.7	67	0.35
	GB	97	109	88.9	0.6	Trace	6.2	60	0.7
	S	97	166	90.1	0.8	0.1	8.6	66	0.3
	USA	94	127	91.57	0.61	0.37	7.02	56.7	0.38

[a] D, Federal Republic of Germany; DK, Denmark; GB, Great Britain; S, Sweden; USA, United States.

Table 28.8. Nutrients in Nuts (per 100 g, Edible Portion)

Food	Ref. code[a]	Energy (kJ)	Protein (g)	Fat (g)	Calcium (mg)	Magnesium (mg)	Iron (mg)	Potassium (mg)	Linoleic acid (18:2 g)
Almonds	D	2726.98	18.300	54 100	252.000	170.000	4.130	835.000	9.860
	DK	2691	20.1	53.5	240	265	4.5	725	9.77
	GB	2336	16.9	53.5	250	260	4.2	860	9.77
	S	2502	18.6	54.2	234	270	4.7	773	10.84
	USA	2465	19.95	52.21	266	296	3.66	732	10.495
Coconut meat	D	1674.24	3.920	36.500	20.000	39.000	2.250	379.000	0.660
fresh	DK	2960	5.6	62.0	22	90	3.6	750	1.05
desiccated	GB	2492	5.6	62.0	22	90	3.6	750	1.05
	S	2769.8	7.2	64.9	26	90	3.3	588	0.91
	USA	2762	6.88	64.52	26	90	3.32	543	0.706
Filberts, hazel nuts	D	2900.20	14.100	61.600	226.000	156.000	3.800	636.000	7.360
	DK	2869	12.6	62.4	125	158	2.8	738	6.34
	GB	1570	7.6	36.0	44	56	1.1	350	3.68
	S	2652.7	12.6	62.4	209	184	3.4	704	9.98
	USA	2643	13 04	62.64	188	285	3.27	445	5.833
Peanuts, roasted	D	2723.03	26 400	49.400	65.000	182.000	2.320	777.000	13.800
	DK	2610	26.0	49.8	74	—	2.1	674	13.7
	GB	2364	24.3	49.0	61	180	2.0	680	13.58
	S	2447.6	26.0	49.8	74	175	2.1	674	17.52
	USA	2426	26 78	49.19	86	188	1.92	703	15.593
Walnuts, English	D	2949.59	14 400	62.500	87.000	129.000	2.500	544.000	37.900
	DK	2307	10.6	51.5	80	144	2.1	471	29.5
	GB	2166	10.6	51.5	61	130	2.4	690	29.54
	S	2723.8	14.8	64.0	99	131	3.1	450	39.68
	USA	2686	14.29	61.87	94	169	2.44	502	31.762

[a] D, Federal Republic of Germany; DK, Denmark; GB, Great Britain; S, Sweden; USA, United States.

Table 28.9. Nutrients in Confectionaries and Sugars (per 100 g, Edible Portion)

Food	Ref. code[a]	Energy (kJ)	Carbohydrate (g)	Calcium (mg)	Phosphorus (mg)	Glucose (g)	Fructose (g)	Invert sugar/reducing sugar (g)	Sucrose (g)
Chocolate, dark	D	2308.27	62.200	63.000	287.000	0	0		47.000
	DK	2278	62.9	80	140				55.9
	GB	2197	64.8	38	140				58.7
	S	2351.4	60.6	34	170				
	USA	2209.2	57.9	94	142				—
Honey	D	1274.03	80.800	4 500	18.000	33.900	38.800		2,370
	DK	1380	80.8	5	7.2	33.9	38.8		2.4
	GB	1229	76 4	5	17				
	S	1271.9	82.3	5	6	34.5	40.4		1.9
	USA	1271.9	82.3	5	6				
Marmalade/jam	D	1126.30	67.800	32.000	4.500			43.900	16.00
	DK								
	GB	1114	69.5	35	13				
	S	1014.6	59.0	18	3	16.2	13.5		29.7
	USA	1075.3	70.1	35	9				
Sugar, white	D	1649.37	99.800	0.600	0.300			0.010	99.800
	DK	1698	99.9	0.4	0.1				99.9
	GB	1680	105.0	2	Trace				99.9
	S	1671.5	99.9	5	0				99.9
	USA	1610.8	99.5	0	0				99.5
Sugar, brown	D	1613.02	97.600	55.000	24.000			0.700	96.700
	DK								
	GB								
	S	1573.2	94.0	185	5	0.5	0.5		93.0
	USA	1560.6	96.4	85	19	0.5	0.5		

[a] D, Federal Republic of Germany; DK, Denmark; GB, Great Britain; S, Sweden; USA, United States.

Table 28.10. Nutrients in Beverages (per 100 g, Edible Portion)

Food	Ref. code[a]	Energy (kJ)	Water (g)	Carbohydrate (g)	Alcohol (g)	Niacin (mg)	Calcium (mg)	Iron (mg)
Coffee, beverage	D							
	DK	9		0.3		0.7	2	0
	GB	8	98.1	0.3		0.7	2	Trace
	S	4.2	98.25	0		0.3	2	0.1
	USA	8.4		0.43		0.29	2	0.04
Cola, drink	D	184.10	88.000	11.000		0	4.000	
	DK							
	GB	168	89.8	10.5		0	4	Trace
	S	160		10.0				
	USA	180	88.88	11.03		0	3	0.05
Tea, beverage	D							
	DK	2	99.9	0		0.1	0	0
	GB	2		Trace		0.1	Trace	Trace
	S	8.4	99.4	0.4		0	0	0
	USA	0	99.61	0.2		0.05	0	0.02
Beer, alcohol 3–4 g	D	197	91.100	5.000	3.500	0.880	3.000	
	DK	153		2.6	3.5			
	GB	133		2.0	3.3			
	S	138.1		0.3	2.8			
	USA	171.5	92.37	3.67	3.6	0.35	9	0.02
Wine, red	D	326	88.000		9.500	0.50	4	0.03
	DK	294		0.3	9.5	0.100	7.600	0.590
	GB	284	87.5	0.3	9.5	0.09	8	1
	S	301.2	87.5	0.3	9.9	0.07	7	1.1
	USA	313.8	87.83	2.47	9.27	0.08	8	0.95

[a] D, Federal Republic of Germany; DK, Denmark; GB, Great Britain; S, Sweden; USA, United States.

Table 28.11. Nutrients in Recipes (per 100 g, Edible Portion)

Food	Ref. code[a]	Water loss (%)	Energy (kJ)	Water (g)	Protein (g)	Fat (g)	Carbohydrate (g)	Iron (mg)	Sodium (mg)
Meat loaf	SF	32.5	1212	74.5	14.4	21.6	9.1	1.76	840.5
	GB	25.0	1168	50.3	18.2	18.6	10.7	2.7	614
	S	33 4	1010.9	61.37	14.05	17.21	6.0	2.2	559.5
Pancake, thick, baked	SF	14.6	653	83.6	7.0	4.8	20.7	1.610	388.5
	S	33.4	837.2	58.99	8.62	7.45	23.33	0.9	282.6
Pancake, thin	GB	25.0	1267	47.1	7.4	19.3	26.6	1.1	61
	S	25.0	860.6	59.28	7.11	8.6	23.64	0.7	244.4
Potato salad	SF	0	397	78.8	2.1	4.1	13.0	0.46	99.4
	GB	0	558	76.1	1.3	8.3	14.4	0.4	254
	S	0	639.3	73 27	1.6	9.23	15.07	0.6	94.1

[a] SF, Finland; GB, Great Britain; S, Sweden.

Table 28.12. Recipe Ingredients (Grams)

Meat loaf	GB[a, b]	SF[b]	S[b]
Beef, minced	140		
Pork, minced		648	666
Pork sausage meat	100		
Onion	100	108	25
Breadcrumbs	100	99	32
Eggs	50	130	81
Salt	5	18	12
Potatoes			124
Butter		13	
Margarine			25
Milk			167
Cream		216	
Water			167

	Thick		Thin	
Pancake	SF	S	GB	S
Wheat flour	199	247	100	261
Milk, summer			125	
Milk, winter		987	125	871
Milk, low fat	725			
Eggs	217	239	60	141
Lard			50	
Margarine		25		55
Butter	11			
Salt	8	5		4
Sugar	24			

Potato salad	GB	SF	S
Potatoes, boiled	100	569	573
Salad cream	60		
Water (=vinegar)	40		
Cream, sour		335	95
Mayonnaise			91
Mustard, prepared			30
Capers (=cucumber), pickled			25
Apple			100
Onion		71	82
Salt		2	
Sugar		25	
Parsley			4

[a] Wiles *et al.* (1980).
[b] GB, Great Britain; SF, Finland; S, Sweden.

The best system is, of course, to have all dishes analyzed, but as this usually is impossible due to economic reasons, calculations has to be used. At the USDA, three methods have been used for calculating the nutrient content of a cooked dish: (1) applying a retention factor to each raw ingredient for each nutrient to be determined, (2) using nutrient data for cooked ingredients together with information about yield of cooked ingredients from raw materials, and (3) using retention factors for each nutrient for the whole dish (Marsh 1984). In Tables 28.11 and 28.12, some dishes with calculated nutrient content and ingredients serve as examples.

Discrepancies in Nutrient Evaluation

In comparing different nutrient analysis systems, discrepancies can be related to the nutrient data base, calculating procedures, computer programs, and the user. One reason for these discrepancies are different sources of data in the bases, particularly those data entered additionally to a standard data set. Data must be reliable, valid, and current, and missing, uncertain, or estimated values should be marked. Especially in research, there have to be enough food items in the base so that substitutions of foods to similar items can be avoided. Sufficient choices of household measures and serving sizes should be provided.

Calculation of recipes is not standardized. Different food yields and loss and gain factors are used. Computer programs may not be accurate and must always be checked before being used in standard procedures. Usually the food items are entered with codes. If the user inputs a wrong code or wrong weight of a food item, the consequences are unpredictable. A nutritionist or dietitian has to be familiar with food values so that errors can be detected. Several comparative studies of nutrient analysis systems have been performed (Hoover 1983; Dwyer and West Suitor 1984), and methods for appraisal of nutrient data base system capabilities now exist (Hoover and Perloff 1983).

INFOODS, EUROFOODS, NORFOODS, LATINFOODS, MEDIFOODS, NOAFOODS, and ASIAFOODS, etc., are all working toward the same goals: improving the quantity, quality, and accessibility of food composition data.

REFERENCES

Bergström, L. 1985. Review of food composition tables and nutrient data banks in Europe; Sweden. Activities of norfoods. The Nordic project on food composition tables and nutrient data banks. Am Nutr. Metab. *29* (Suppl. 1), 11–13, 16–24.

Bruce, Å., and Bergström, L. 1983. User requirements for data bases and applications in nutrition research. Food Nutr. Bull. 5(2), 24–29.

Buchanan, P. W. 1983. Quantity Food Preparation. American Dietetic Association, Chicago.

Butrum, R. R., and Gebhardt, S. E. 1977. Nutrient data bank: computer-based management of nutrient values in foods. J. Am. Oil Chem. 53(12), 727A–730A.

Dwyer, J., and West Suitor, C. 1984. Caveat emptor: Assessing needs, evaluating computer options. J. Am. Diet. Assoc. 84(3), 302–312.

Food System. 1981. Department of Nutrition. University of Helsinki. (Nutrient data base.)

Greenfield, H., and Southgate, D. A. T. 1985. Guidelines to the Production, Management, and Use of Food Composition Data Systems. 4th Edition. (In manuscript.)

Hepburn, F. N. 1982. The USDA national nutrient data bank. Am. J. Clin. Nutr. 35(5), 1297–1301.

Hoover, L. W. 1983. Computerized nutrient data bases. 1. Comparison of nutrient analysis systems. J. Am. Diet. Assoc. 82(5), 501–505.

Hoover, L. W. 1984. Nutrient Data Bank Directory. 4th Edition. Presented at the Ninth Annual National Nutrient Data Bank Conference.

Hoover, L. W., and Perloff, B. P. 1983. Computerized nutrient data bases. 2. Development of model for appraisal of nutrient data base system capabilities. J. Am. Diet. Assoc. 82(5), 506–508.

KOST 1981. Swedish National Food Administration. (Nutrient data base.)

Maloff, C., and Zears, R. W. Computers in Nutrition. Artech House, Dedham, MA.

Marsh, A. 1984. Problems associated with recipe analysis. Presented at the Ninth Annual National Nutrient Data Bank Conference.

McMurray, P., and Hoover, L. W. 1984. The educational uses of computers: Hardware, software, and strategies. J. Nutr. Educ. 16(2), 39–42.

Møller, A. 1983. Levnedsmiddeltabeller. Danish National Food Agency, Søborg.

Moore, A. N., and Tuthill, B. H. (Editors). 1971 (3rd printing, 1982). Computer-Assisted Food Management Systems. Univ. of Missouri, Columbia.

Paul, A. A., and Southgate, D. A. T. 1978. McCance and Widdowson's The Composition of Foods, H. M. S. O., London.

Rand, W. M. 1984. The need for an international food system. Presented at ASIAFOODS conference, Sept.

Rizek, R. L., Perloff, B. P., and Posati, L. P. 1981. USDA's nutrient data bank. Food Technol. Austr. 33(3), 112–114.

Souci, S. W., Fachmann, W., and Kraut, H. 1981. Food Composition and Nutrition Tables 1981/82. Wissenschaftliche Verlagsgesellschaft, Stuttgart.

Southgate, D. A. T. 1974. Guide Lines for the Preparation of Tables of Food Composition. Karger, Basel.

Stewart, K. K. 1983. The state of food composition data: An overview with some suggestions. Food Nutr. Bull. 5(2), 54–68.

U.S. Department of Agriculture (USDA) 1976–1984. Agriculture Handbook 8, Vols 1–12. U.S. Government Printing Office, Washington, D.C.

West, C. E. (Editor). 1985. Towards Compatability of nutrient data banks in Europe. Ann. Nutr. Metab. 29 (Suppl. 1).

Wiles, S. J., et al. 1980. The nutrient composition of some cooked dishes eaten in Britain: A supplementary food composition table. J. Hum. Nutr. 34(3), 189–223.

Williams, C. S., and Burnet, L. W. 1984. Future applications of the microcomputer in dietetics. Hum. Nutr. 38A(2), 99–109.

Index